BANKING LAW

Cases and Materials

FIFTH EDITION

edited by

M.H. Ogilvie

Department of Law and Legal Studies
Carleton University

CANADIAN LEGAL STUDIES SERIES

Captus Press

Canadian Legal Studies Series
Banking Law: Cases and Materials, Fifth edition

First Captus Press edition, 1990
Fifth edition, 2015

Captus Press Inc.
Units 14 & 15
1600 Steeles Avenue West
Concord, ON
L4K 4M2   Canada
Telephone: (416) 736–5537
Fax: (416) 736–5793
Email: Info@captus.com
Internet: http://www.captus.com

Library and Archives Canada Cataloguing in Publication

Banking law : cases and materials / edited by M.H. Ogilvie.
— Fifth edition.

(Canadian legal studies series)
Includes bibliographical references.
ISBN 978-1-55322-320-7

1. Banking law — Canada. 2. Banking law — Canada — Cases.
I. Ogilvie, M. H., editor   II. Series: Canadian legal studies series

KE998.5.B346 2015   346.71'082   C2014-907205-8
KF973.B346 2015

Canada ▪▪ *We acknowledge the financial support of the Government of Canada through the Canada Book Fund (CBF) for our publishing activities.*

0 9 8 7 6 5 4 3 2 1
Printed and bound in Canada

Table of Contents

I
Introduction

II
Banks as Corporations

III

"Banking Business"

IV

The Banker and Customer Relationship

V

Account Operations

I

Introduction

1   What Is "Banking"?

Background Reading: M.H. Ogilvie, *Bank and Customer Law in Canada*, 2d Edition (Toronto: Irwin Law, 2013) Chapters 1 and 2.

(a) *Constitution Act, 1867*[†]

V.   PROVINCIAL CONSTITUTIONS

. . . .

LEGISLATIVE POWER

. . . .

4. NOVA SCOTIA AND NEW BRUNSWICK

Constitutions of Legislatures of Nova Scotia and New Brunswick

88. The Constitution of the Legislature of each of the Provinces of Nova Scotia and New Brunswick shall, subject to the Provisions of this Act, continue as it exists at the Union until altered under the Authority of this Act.

5. ONTARIO, QUEBEC, AND NOVA SCOTIA

89. Repealed.

6. THE FOUR PROVINCES

Application to Legislatures of Provisions respecting Money Votes, etc.

90. The following Provisions of this Act respecting the Parliament of Canada, namely, — the Provisions relating to Appropriation and Tax Bills, the Recommendation of Money Votes, the Assent to Bills, the Disallowance of Acts, and the Signification of Pleasure on Bills reserved, — shall extend and apply to the Legislatures of the several Provinces as if those Provisions were here re-enacted and made applicable in Terms to the respective Provinces and the Legislatures thereof, with the Substitution of the Lieutenant Governor of the Province for the Governor General, of the Governor General for the Queen and for a Secretary of State, of One Year for Two Years, and of the Province for Canada.

VI.   DISTRIBUTION OF LEGISLATIVE POWERS

Powers of the Parliament

91. It shall be lawful for the Queen, by and with the Advice and Consent of the Senate and House of Commons, to make Laws for the Peace, Order, and good Government of Canada, in relation to all Matters not coming within the Classes of Subjects by this Act assigned exclusively to the Legislatures of the Provinces; and for greater Certainty, but not so as to restrict the Generality of the foregoing Terms of this Section, it is hereby declared that (notwith-

---

[†] (U.K.), 30 & 31 Vict., c. 3, ss. 88–92.

standing anything in this Act) the exclusive Legislative Authority of the Parliament of Canada extends to all Matters coming within the Classes of Subjects next hereinafter enumerated; that is to say,

1. Repealed.
1A. The Public Debt and Property.
2. The Regulation of Trade and Commerce.
2A. Unemployment insurance.
3. The raising of Money by any Mode or System of Taxation.
4. The borrowing of Money on the Public Credit.
5. Postal Service.
6. The Census and Statistics.
7. Militia, Military and Naval Service, and Defence.
8. The fixing of and providing for the Salaries and Allowances of Civil and other Officers of the Government of Canada.
9. Beacons, Buoys, Lighthouses, and Sable Island.
10. Navigation and Shipping.
11. Quarantine and the Establishment and Maintenance of Marine Hospitals.
12. Sea Coast and Inland Fisheries.
13. Ferries between a Province and any British or Foreign Country or between Two Provinces.
14. Currency and Coinage.
15. Banking, Incorporation of Banks, and the Issue of Paper Money.
16. Savings Banks.
17. Weights and Measures.
18. Bills of Exchange and Promissory Notes.
19. Interest.
20. Legal Tender.
21. Bankruptcy and Insolvency.
22. Patents of Invention and Discovery.
23. Copyrights.
24. Indians, and Lands reserved for the Indians.
25. Naturalization and Aliens.
26. Marriage and Divorce.
27. The Criminal Law, except the Constitution of Courts of Criminal Jurisdiction, but including the Procedure in Criminal Matters.
28. The Establishment, Maintenance, and Management of Penitentiaries.
29. Such Classes of Subjects as are expressly excepted in the Enumeration of the Classes of Subjects by this Act assigned exclusively to the Legislatures of the Provinces.

And any Matter coming within any of the Classes of Subjects enumerated in this Section shall not be deemed to come within the Class of Matters of a local or private Nature comprised in the Enumeration of the Classes of Subjects by this Act assigned exclusively to the Legislatures of the Provinces.

Exclusive Powers of Provincial Legislatures

92. In each Province the Legislature may exclusively make Laws in relation to Matters coming within the Classes of Subjects next hereinafter enumerated; that is to say,

1. Repealed.
2. Direct Taxation within the Province in order to the raising of a Revenue for Provincial Purposes.
3. The borrowing of Money on the sole Credit of the Province.
4. The Establishment and Tenure of Provincial Offices and the Appointment and Payment of Provincial Officers.
5. The Management and Sale of the Public Lands belonging to the Province and of the Timber and Wood thereon.
6. The Establishment, Maintenance, and Management of Public and Reformatory Prisons in and for the Province.
7. The Establishment, Maintenance, and Management of Hospitals, Asylums, Charities, and Eleemosynary Institutions in and for the Province, other than Marine Hospitals.
8. Municipal Institutions in the Province.
9. Shop, Saloon, Tavern, Auctioneer, and other Licences in order to the raising of a Revenue for Provincial, Local, or Municipal Purposes.
10. Local Works and Undertakings other than such as are of the following Classes:
    (a) Lines of Steam or other Ships, Railways, Canals, Telegraphs, and other Works and Undertakings connecting the Province with any other or others of the Provinces, or extending beyond the Limits of the Province;
    (b) of Steam Ships between the Province and any British or Foreign Country;
    (c) Such Works as, although wholly situate within the Province, are before or after their Execution declared by the Parliament of Canada to be for the general Advantage of Canada or for the Advantage of Two or more of the Provinces.
11. The Incorporation of Companies with Provincial Objects.
12. The Solemnization of Marriage in the Province.
13. Property and Civil Rights in the Province.

14. The Administration of Justice in the Province, including the Constitution, Maintenance, and Organization of Provincial Courts, both of Civil and of Criminal Jurisdiction, and including Procedure in Civil Matters in those Courts.

15. The Imposition of Punishment by Fine, Penalty, or Imprisonment for enforcing any Law of the Province made in relation to any Matter coming within any of the Classes of Subjects enumerated in this Section.

16. Generally all Matters of a merely local or private Nature in the Province.

(b) *United Dominions Trust Ltd. v. Kirkwood*†

[LORD DENNING M.R.:]

THE CHARACTERISTICS OF BANKING

Seeing that there is no statutory definition of banking, one must do the best one can to find out the usual characteristics which go to make up the business of banking. In the eighteenth century before cheques came into common use, the principal characteristics were that the banker accepted the money of others on the terms that the persons who deposited it could have it back again from the banker when they asked for it, sometimes on demand, at other times on notice, according to the stipulation made at the time of deposit; and meanwhile the banker was at liberty to make use of the money by lending it out at interest or investing it on mortgage or otherwise. Thus, Dr. Johnson in 1755 in his dictionary defined a "bank" as a "place where money is laid up to be called for occasionally" and a "banker" as "one that traffics in money, one that keeps or manages a bank". Those characteristics continued for a long time to dominate thought on the subject. Thus, in 1914 Isaacs J., in the High Court of Australia said that

> the essential characteristics of the business of banking may be described as the collection of money by receiving deposits on loan, repayable when and as expressly or impliedly agreed upon, and the utilisation of the money so collected by lending it again in such sums as are required,

see *State Savings Bank of Victoria Comrs. v. Permewan Wright & Co., Ltd.*[1] You notice that those characteristics do not mention the use of cheques, or the keeping of current accounts. Accordingly, you find in the courts cases in which a company was held to carry on the business of banking even though it issued no cheques and kept no current accounts but only issued deposit receipts, repayable on notice (see *Re Shields Estate, Bank of Ireland (Governor & Co.) Petitioners*[2]); or only kept deposit accounts from which the depositors could withdraw their money on demand or on notice, this being on production of a passbook, not by cheque — see *Re Bottomgate Industrial Co-operative Society*[3]; *State Savings Bank of Victoria Comrs. v. Permewan.*[4] If that were still the law, it would mean that the building societies were all bankers.

The march of time has taken us far beyond those cases of fifty years ago. Money is now paid and received by cheque to such an extent that no person can be considered a banker unless he handles cheques as freely as cash. A customer nowadays who wishes to pay money into his bank takes with him his cash and the cheques, crossed and uncrossed, payable to him. Whereas in the old days it was a characteristic of a banker that he should receive *money* for deposit, it is nowadays a characteristic that he should receive *cheques for collection* on behalf of his customer. How otherwise is the customer to pay his money into the bank? It is the only practicable means, particularly in the case of crossed cheques. Next, when a customer wishes to withdraw the money which he has deposited or to pay his

---

† [1966] 1 All E.R. 968 (C.A.). [Notes omitted.]

creditors with it, he does it in most cases by drawing a cheque on the bank. Occasionally he does it by a draft on the bank or a written order. Whereas in the old days he might withdraw it on production of a passbook and no cheque, it is nowadays a characteristic of a bank that the customer should be able to withdraw it by cheque, draft or order. This view has gradually gained acceptance; see *Re District Savings Bank, Ltd., Ex p. Coe,*[5] by Turner L.J., *Re Shields Estates,*[6] by Lord Ashbourne.

In 1924 Atkin L.J., gave a modern picture of a characteristic banking account in *Joachimson v. Swiss Bank Corpn.*:[7]

> The bank undertakes to receive money and to collect bills for its customer's account. The proceeds so received are not to be held in trust for the customer, but the bank borrows the proceeds and undertakes to repay them. The promise to repay is to repay at the branch of the bank where the account is kept, and during banking hours. It includes a promise to repay any part of the amount due against the written order of the customer addressed to the bank at the branch ... bankers never do make a payment to a customer in respect of a current account except upon demand.

This was followed in 1948 by the *Bank of Chettinad, Ltd. of Colombo v. Income Tax Comr., Colombo,*[8] where the Privy Council accepted the Ceylon description of a "banking company" as

a company which carries on as its principal business the accepting of deposits of money on current account or otherwise, subject to withdrawal by cheque, draft or order.

And now the *Shorter Oxford Dictionary* gives the meaning of a "bank" in modern use as:

> An establishment for the custody of money received from, or on behalf of, its customers. Its essential duty is to pay their drafts on it: its profits arise from the use of money left unemployed by them.

There are, therefore, two characteristics usually found in bankers today: (i) they accept money from, and collect cheques for, their customers and place them to their credit; (ii) they honour cheques or orders drawn on them by their customers when presented for payment and debit their customers accordingly. These two characteristics carry with them also a third, namely, (iii) they keep current accounts, or something of that nature, in their books in which the credits and debits are entered.

Those three characteristics are much the same as those stated in *Paget's Law of Banking*, 6th ed. (1961), p. 8:

> No-one and nobody, corporate or otherwise, can be a 'banker' who does not (i) take current accounts; (ii) pay cheques drawn on himself; (iii) collect cheques for his customers.

(c)   *Tennant v. Union Bank of Canada*†

[LORD WATSON:]

Christie, Kerr & Co., saw-millers and lumberers at Bradford, in the Province of Ontario, became insolvent in April, 1889. The Union Bank of Canada, respondents in this appeal, subsequently took possession of and removed a quantity of lumber which was stored in the yard of the firm at Bradford. This action was brought against the respondents in December, 1889, for damages in respect of their alleged conversion of the lumber, by Mickle, Dyment

& Son, personal creditors of the insolvent firm, in the name of James Tennant, as assignee or trustee of the firm's estate, by whom they were duly authorized to sue, in his name, for their own exclusive use and benefit.

Christie, Kerr & Co., to whom it may be convenient to refer as the firm, had a timber concession in the county of Simcoe, where, according to the course of their business, the pine wood was felled and cut into logs, which were marked with the letters "C.K.," the initials of the firm. The logs were

---

† [1894] A.C. 31 (P.C.). [Notes omitted.]

then conveyed, chiefly by water, to their mill at Bradford, where they were sawn and stored for sale.

In order to obtain funds for carrying on their trade during the season of 1888, the firm, in October 1887, entered into a written agreement with Peter Christie, son of Alexander Christie, its senior partner, who agreed to advance the money necessary upon receiving a lien by way of security upon all the timber cut or manufactured by the firm. On the other hand, the firm undertook to do everything that was necessary in order to make such lien effectual, and for that purpose to execute any documents which might be required.

In pursuance of that agreement promissory notes were granted by Peter Christie, which the Federal Bank of Canada discounted under an arrangement by which they were to receive warehouse receipts covering all the timber belonging to the firm. Peter Christie assigned to the bank all right and benefit which he had under the agreement of October, 1887. The course of dealing with the bank was, that the firm granted warehouse receipts to themselves, which they indorsed to Peter Christie, by whom they were indorsed to the bank.

The Federal Bank went into liquidation in June, 1888, at which date their advances amounted to about $50,000. In order to meet the claim of the liquidator, Alexander Christie applied for accommodation to the respondents, who agreed to give it upon terms which were arranged between him and Mr. Buchanan, their manager. The agreement was verbal; and its terms, which are of considerable importance in this case, appear from the following statements made by Alexander Christie in the course of his evidence, which are substantially corroborated by Mr. Buchanan, and are nowhere contradicted: "That we and Peter Christie should give his notes, that Christie, Kerr & Co. and A.R. Christie should indorse them, and that there should be a warehouse receipt covering all the logs that they had, and the lumber that was to be manufactured from them." "The intention was to give the security of the logs and of the lumber as it was manufactured." "We were to give them a receipt at once upon the whole of the logs, and as the logs progressed we made a continuation to where they were." "Warehouse receipts were to be furnished until the debt was paid."

There was not, as in the case of the Federal Bank, any assignment to the respondents of Peter Christie's rights under the agreement of October, 1887. It is clear, from the account which he gives of the transaction, that Alexander Christie dealt with the respondents as the representative of his firm, and also as representing his son Peter, from

whom he held a power of attorney. Peter Christie took no part, personally, in any of the transactions, either with the Federal Bank or with the respondents. From first to last, so far as his interests were concerned, all arrangements were made and all documents connected with them, whether promissory notes or warehouse receipts, were executed and subscribed by his father, on his behalf.

Upon the faith of the agreement the respondents made advances to the amount of $52,600 upon promissory notes of Peter Christie, indorsed to them by his attorney and also by the firm. On the 20th of June, 1888, they received a warehouse receipt for 70,000 pine saw logs, marked "C.K.," which were described as then stored in the Lakes St. Jean and Couchiching, en route to Bradford mill. These logs represented the whole pine timber which had been cut for transportation to Bradford during the season of 1888; and as they arrived at their destination, and were sawn up, fresh receipts were given to the respondents, containing a description of the timber in its manufactured state. Portions of the lumber were from time to time sold by the firm, with the consent of the respondents, and the proceeds applied in reduction of their advances.

The last of the series of receipts deposited as security with the respondents is dated the 1st of January, 1889, by which time all the logs covered by the first receipt of the 20th of June, 1888, had reached Bradford, and had been converted into lumber. It includes the whole of the timber forming the original subject of the security which then remained unsold and in the possession or custody of the firm. Though not in precisely the same form as the rest, it may be taken as a specimen, because it was not contended that the differences of form were material. It runs thus:

> The undersigned acknowledges to have received from Christie Kerr and Company, owners of the goods, wares and merchandise herein mentioned, and to have now stored in the premises known as the Bradford sawmill yard, adjoining the village of Bradford, in the county of Simcoe, the following goods, wares and merchandise, viz.: — Five millions eight hundred and fifty-three thousand nine hundred and twenty-four feet of lumber, one hundred and ninety-three thousand of shingles, all marked 'C.K.,' and manufactured during season 1888 out of saw logs cut in the townships of Oakley and Hindon, and transported to Bradford mill and cut there, which goods, wares and merchandise are to be delivered pursuant to the order of the said Peter Christie to be indorsed hereon, and are to be kept in store till delivered pursuant to such order.

This is intended as a warehouse receipt within the meaning of the statute of Canada, entitled 'An Act relating to Banks and Banking,' and the amendments thereto, and within the meaning of all other Acts and laws under which a bank of Canada may acquire a warehouse receipt as a security.

This receipt was, like its predecessors, signed by the firm, and by them indorsed to Peter Christie, and was then indorsed on his behalf by Alexander Christie, and delivered to the respondents.

It is not matter of dispute that the timber of which the respondents took possession, after the insolvency of the firm, was included, either as saw logs or as lumber, in all the receipts which they received as security. But it does not appear to their Lordships that these receipts could be regarded as negotiable instruments carrying the property of the timber if their effect depended upon the provisions of the *Mercantile Code* which is contained in the Revised Statutes of Ontario, 1887.

The Mercantile Amendment Act (c. 122 of the Revised Statutes) deals with warehouse receipts and other mercantile documents which are effectual to transmit the property of goods without actual delivery. That statute not only recognises the negotiability of warehouse receipts by custodiers who are not the owners of the goods; it extends the privilege to receipts by one who is both owner and custodier, but that only in cases where the grantor of the receipt is, from the nature of his trade or calling, a custodier for others as well as himself and therefore in a position to give receipts to third parties. The receipts in question do not comply with the requirements of the Act, because it is neither averred nor proved, that the firm, in the course of their business, had the custody of any goods except their own.

It may also be noticed that c. 125 of the *Revised Statutes* enacts that when goods are transferred by way of conveyance or mortgage, possession being retained by the transferor, the deed of conveyance or mortgage, if not duly registered, shall be absolutely null and void as against creditors of the grantor or mortgagor.

In these circumstances, certain provisions of the *Bank Act*, which was passed by the legislature of the Dominion (46 Vict. c. 120) and is specially referred to in the receipts held by the respondents, become important. Although now repealed, the Act was in force during the whole period of these transactions; and, if competently enacted, its provisions must, in so far as they are applicable, govern the rights of parties in this litigation.

Sect. 45 provides that the bank shall not, either directly or indirectly, lend money or make advances upon the security or pledge of any goods, wares, or merchandise except as authorized by the Act.

Sect. 53, sub-sect. 2, authorizes the bank to acquire and hold any warehouse receipt or bill of lading as collateral security for the payment of any debt incurred in its favour in the course of its banking business. The document so acquired vests in the bank "all the right and title of the previous holder or owner thereof, or of the person from whom such goods wares or merchandise were received or acquired by the bank, if the warehouse receipt or bill of lading is made directly in favour of the bank, instead of to the previous holder or owner of such goods wares or merchandise." Sub-sect. 3 of the same clause provides that if the previous holder of such warehouse receipt or bill of lading is the agent of the owner, the bank shall be vested with all the right and title of the owner, subject to his right to have the goods re-transferred to him upon payment of the debt for which they are held in security by the bank.

Sect. 54, which deals specially with the case of the custodier and owner of the goods being one and the same person enacts that:

> If any person who grants a warehouse receipt or a bill of lading is engaged in the calling, as his ostensible business, of keeper of a yard, cove, wharf or harbour, or of warehouseman, miller, saw-miller, maltster, manufacturer of timber, wharfinger, master of a vessel, or other carrier by land or by water, or by both, curer or packer of meat, tanner, dealer in wool or purchaser of agricultural produce, and is at the same time the owner of the goods, wares and merchandise mentioned in such warehouse receipt or bill of lading, every such warehouse receipt or bill of lading, and the right and title of the bank thereto and to the goods, wares and merchandize mentioned therein, shall be as valid and effectual as if such owner, and the person making such warehouse receipt or bill of lading, were different persons.

These enactments go beyond the provisions of sect. 16 of the *Mercantile Amendment Act*. They omit the limitation of the provincial statute, which requires, in order to validate a warehouse receipt by a custodier who is also owner, that the trade or calling in which he is ostensibly engaged must be one which admits of his granting receipts on behalf of other owners whose goods are in his possession.

The Chancellor of Ontario dismissed the suit with costs; and the Court of Appeal affirmed his decision. Upon the evidence before them, all the learned judges, with one exception, came to the conclusion that the transaction was substantially one between the firm and the respondents, and that Peter Christie's position was really that of an intermediary; and consequently that the respondents had a right, against the firm, to demand and receive warehouse receipts for the timber in security for their advances. Burton J.A., was of opinion that the respondents must be held to have dealt with Peter Christie alone; that the receipts in his hands were not valid either according to provincial law or under the provisions of the *Bank Act*, and that his indorsation could not pass any interest in the timber to the respondents.

In the view which he took of the real character of the transaction, the Chancellor held that the receipts were effectual, mainly on the ground that Peter Christie, in indorsing them, ought to be regarded as the agent of the firm within the meaning of sect. 53, sub-sect. 3, of the Bank Act. Hagarty C.J., and Maclennan J., who with Osler J., constituted the majority of the Appeal Court, held that the receipts, having been given directly to the respondents by the firm, under an obligation to that effect, were made effectual by the provisions of the *Bank Act*. They also held that, assuming the receipts not to be within the protection of the *Bank Act*, Peter Christie had, as between himself and the firm, an equitable lien on the timber which passed to the respondents; and also that they had the same rights against the trustee of the insolvent firm as they had against the firm itself. Osler J., whilst agreeing that the respondents dealt directly with the firm, examined the case on the contrary hypothesis, and held that, even in that view, the receipts were validated by the *Bank Act*, and carried the property of the timber to the respondents.

In the Courts below, the appellant pleaded that the provisions of the *Bank Act* with respect to warehouse receipts, in so far as they differ from the provisions of the *Mercantile Amendment Act*, were *ultra vires* of the Dominion Legislature. The plea was not discussed, because it was admittedly at variance with the decision of the Supreme Court of Canada in *Merchants' Bank of Canada v. Smith*,[1] which was a precedent binding on provincial tribunals. The case was therefore disposed of by the Chancellor and the Appeal Court upon the footing that the provisions of the *Bank Act* were not open to challenge.

At the first hearing of this appeal, the whole points arising in the case were fully and ably argued by counsel, with the exception of the plea taken by the appellant against the validity of the *Dominion Act*. Further discussion at the time was prevented by the *Labrador Case*, which had been specially set down for the consideration of a full Board.

Their Lordships, having considered the argument which had been addressed to them, came to the conclusion that the majority of the learned judges were right in holding that, notwithstanding the form of the documents by which it was carried out, the arrangement made in June, 1888, by Alexander Christie and Mr. Buchanan was one between the respondents and the firm, as well as between them and Peter Christie.

It does not admit of doubt that the advances obtained from the bank were intended to be for the use and benefit of the firm. Although the promissory notes were signed by his father as representing Peter Christie, it is clear that they were signed for the accommodation of the firm, and that, in any question between him and the firm, Peter Christie was a mere surety. In a question with the respondents he was, no doubt, the primary debtor; but the firm, as indorsers of the promissory notes, were also under a direct liability to the respondents, for which security might be given. And it is a material circumstance that the evidence of Alexander Christie, which has already been cited, is only consistent with the view that the firm undertook to give the respondents the security of the timber. The whole course of dealing between the parties is also consistent with that view. The advances appear to have been paid over to the firm, and the warehouse receipts for the timber to have been delivered by the firm to the respondents; and it does not appear that either the money or the receipts ever passed or were intended to pass into the possession of Peter Christie.

Their Lordships also came to the same conclusion with the majority of the learned judges, that, assuming the provisions of the *Bank Act* to be *intra vires*, the receipts in question were such as the firm could give and the respondents could lawfully receive. The obvious effect of sect. 54 is that, for the purposes of the *Bank Act*, a warehouse receipt by an owner of goods who carries on, as the firm did, the trade of a saw-miller, is to be as effectual as if it had been granted by his bailee, although his business may be confined to the manufacture of his own timber. That enactment plainly implies that such a receipt is to be valid, not only in the hands of the bank, but in the hands of a borrower who gives it to the bank in security of a loan. Their Lordships do not think that the provisions of sect. 53, sub-sect. 2, which are somewhat obscure, can be held to cut down the plain enactments of sect. 54, especially in a case where the grantor of the receipt himself delivers it to the bank as a security for his own debt.

It seems clear that the firm, so long as they were solvent, could not have refused to make delivery of all the timber in their possession to the respondents, although the legal ownership was still with the firm. But on that assumption, and assuming also that their trustee had no higher right than the insolvents, the question remains whether a creditor having an assignment from the trustee could plead the nullity enacted by c. 125 of the Revised Statutes. Their Lordships, before dealing with these questions, thought it expedient to determine for themselves whether the provisions of the *Bank Act*, to which the appellant takes exception, were competently enacted.

The appellant's plea against the legislative power of the Dominion Parliament was accordingly made the subject of further argument; and, the point being one of general importance, their Lordships had the advantage of being assisted, in the hearing and consideration of it, by the Lord Chancellor and Lord Macnaghten. The question turns upon the construction of two clauses in the *British North America Act*, 1867. Sect. 91 gives the Parliament of Canada power to make laws in relation to all matters not coming within the classes of subjects by the Act exclusively assigned to the legislatures of the provinces, and also exclusive legislative authority in relation to certain enumerated subjects, the fifteenth of which is "Banking, Incorporation of Banks, and the Issue of Paper Money." Sect. 92 assigns to each provincial legislature the exclusive right to make laws in relation to the classes of subjects therein enumerated; and the thirteenth of the enumerated classes is "Property and Civil Rights in the Province."

Statutory regulations with respect to the form and legal effect, in Ontario, of warehouse receipts and other negotiable documents, which pass the property of goods without delivery, unquestionably relate to property and civil rights in that province; and the objection taken by the appellant to the provisions of the *Bank Act* would be unanswerable if it could be shewn that, by the Act of 1867, the Parliament of Canada is absolutely debarred from trenching to any extent upon the matters assigned to the provincial legislature by sect. 92. But sect. 91 expressly declares that, "notwithstanding anything in this Act," the exclusive legislative authority of the Parliament of Canada shall extend to all matters coming within the enumerated classes; which plainly indicates that the legislation of that Parliament, so long as it strictly relates to these matters, is to be of paramount authority. To refuse effect to the declaration would render nugatory some of the legislative powers specially assigned to the Canadian Parliament. For example, among the enumerated classes of subjects in sect. 91, are "Patents of Invention and Discovery," and "Copyrights." It would be practically impossible for the Dominion Parliament to legislate upon either of these subjects without affecting the property and civil rights of individuals in the provinces.

This is not the first occasion on which the legislative limits laid down by sects. 91 and 92 have been considered by this Board. In *Cushing v. Dupuy*[2] their Lordships had before them the very same question of statutory construction which has been raised in this appeal. An Act relating to bankruptcy, passed by the Parliament of Canada, was objected to as being *ultra vires*, in so far as it interfered with property and civil rights in the province; but, inasmuch as "bankruptcy and insolvency" form one of the classes of matters enumerated in sect. 91, their Lordships upheld the validity of the statute. In delivering the judgment of the Board, Sir Montague Smith pointed out that it would be impossible to advance a step in the construction of a scheme for the administration of insolvent estates without interfering with and modifying some of the ordinary rights of property.

The law being so far settled by precedent, it only remains for consideration whether warehouse receipts, taken in security by a bank in the course of the business of banking, are matters coming within the class of subjects described in sect. 91, sub-sect. 15, as "Banking, Incorporation of Banks, and Issue of Paper Money." If they are, the provisions made by the *Bank Act* with respect to such receipts are *intra vires*. Upon that point their Lordships do not entertain any doubt. The legislative authority conferred by these words is not confined to the mere constitution of corporate bodies with the privilege of carrying on the business of bankers. It extends to the issue of paper currency, which necessarily means the creation of a species of personal property carrying with it rights and privileges which the law of the province does not, and cannot, attach to it. It also comprehends "banking," an expression which is wide enough to embrace every transaction coming within the legitimate business of a banker.

The appellant's counsel hardly ventured to dispute that the lending of money on the security of goods, or of documents representing the property of goods, was a proper banking transaction. Their chief contention was that, whilst the legislature of Canada had power to deprive its own creature, the bank, of privileges enjoyed by other lenders under the provincial law, it had no power to confer upon the bank any privilege as a lender which the provincial law does not recognise. It might enact that a security, valid in the case of another lender, should be invalid in the hands of the bank, but could not enact that a security should be available to the bank which would not have been effectual in the hands of another lender. It was said in support of the argument, that the first of these things did, and the second did not, constitute an interference with property and civil rights in the province. It is not easy to follow the distinction thus suggested. There must be two parties to a transaction of loan; and, if a security, valid according to provincial law, was made invalid in the hands of the lender by a Dominion statute, the civil rights of the borrower would be affected, because he could not avail himself of his property in his dealings with a bank.

But the argument, even if well founded, can afford no test of the legislative powers of the Parliament of Canada. These depend upon sect. 91, and the power to legislate conferred by that clause may be fully exercised, although with the effect of modifying civil rights in the province. And it appears to their Lordships that the plenary authority given to the Parliament of Canada by sect. 91, sub-sect. 15, to legislate in relation to banking transactions is sufficient to sustain the provisions of the *Bank Act* which the appellant impugns.

On these grounds, their Lordships have come to the conclusion that the judgments appealed from ought to be affirmed, and they will humbly advise Her Majesty to that effect. The appellant must bear the costs of this appeal.

(d) *Re Bergethaler Waisenamt*†

[RICHARDS J.A. (McPherson C.J.M. and Williams C.J.K.B. (ad hoc) concurring):]

The Bergethaler Waisenamt was incorporated by a special Act of the Legislature, 1907 (Man.), c. 50. The English translation of the name is "Bureau for Orphans of Bergethaler Community".

The powers given to the corporation were to act as administrator or executor, guardian of any minor, or committee for any lunatic or person of unsound mind, and to hold real and personal property upon trust. The special Act provided further that the *Manitoba Trustee Act* [R.S.M. 1902, c. 170] should apply to the corporation and that the corporation should have the power to invest such moneys as may come into its hands upon such securities as are authorized by said Act.

The Act further provided that the corporation should not be entitled to do business until authorized by an Order in Council. The Order in Council was not passed until October 1919. But in the meantime the corporation engaged in business and acted as executor, administrator and trustee, as well as

borrowing or receiving moneys on deposit and lending money. There was no express authority to receive money on deposit or to borrow money.

In the year 1920 by c. 160, and again in 1922 by c. 72, the Manitoba Legislature passed special Acts validating all acts of the corporation purporting to be done in pursuance of the powers given it, and in particular the receipt of money on deposit and the lending of money on securities. In 1922 the corporation was authorized to receive money on deposit, to lend money on real and personal securities and to borrow money on its own assets.

In February 1930, the corporation required ready money and borrowed $42,000 from the Monarch Life Ass'ce Co. on the security of the best mortgages, lands and agreements of sale which it owned or controlled. Shortly afterwards the corporation, being unable to meet its current liabilities, made an assignment in bankruptcy and was ordered to be wound up.

By orders made in the winding-up proceedings, dated March 4, 1931 and May 28, 1931, a list of creditors was admitted with the amounts owing to

---

† [1949] 1 D.L.R. 769 (Man. C.A.).

them respectively. All were treated as ordinary creditors without qualification or priority, except claims for wages and claims of the Crown which were given preference. No appeal was taken against the orders.

The mortgage to the Monarch Life Ass'ce Co. fell into arrears and in 1934 the Assurance Company commenced foreclosure proceedings. The Assurance Company and the Liquidator then negotiated an agreement dated September 25, 1935, whereby the titles to all the mortgaged assets were to be conveyed to the Assurance Company which agreed to sell the assets to a nominee of the Liquidator on easy terms. A company called Waisenamt Limited was incorporated to be the purchaser and the Monarch Life Ass'ce Co. entered into an agreement of sale to it. All the shares of the new company were held by the Liquidator. The agreements were approved and ratified by Court orders made in 1935 and 1936 which were not appealed. Eventually the debt owing to the Monarch Life Ass'ce Co. was paid, mainly out of collections from the assets, and the remaining assets were conveyed to Waisenamt Ltd. The assets having been realized, the Liquidator caused Waisenamt Ltd. to be wound up and, being desirous of paying the moneys in his hands to the creditors of the Bergethaler Waisenamt Limited, applied to the Master and obtained an order dated June 28, 1946, directing a dividend to be paid to the creditors on the list fixed by the orders made in 1931.

One David D. Fehr appealed from the order of the Master and claimed to rank as a creditor in priority to the creditors on the above-mentioned list on the ground that the corporation had received his monies as trustee. This claim was dismissed by Dysart J., now J.A., because the terms of Fehr's agreement with the corporation provided that the moneys received by the corporation were on the basis of debtor and creditor: see *Re Bergethaler Waisenamt, Re Fehr*, [1947] 2 D.L.R. 234, 54 Man. R. 484.

David D. Fehr and one Margaret Buhr, however, also claimed priority on behalf of themselves and others whose claims arose out of the administration of estates by the Bergethaler Waisenamt, over claims of the creditors who had deposited money with that corporation. The ground of the claim was that the transactions which gave rise to depositors' claims were actually banking business, and were *ultra vires* of the corporation, it having been created by the Legislature of the Province of Manitoba, which was not competent to authorize it to conduct a banking business, as "Banking" is one of the subjects allotted exclusively to the Parliament of Canada by s. 91 of the *B.N.A. Act*. This case, also, was tried before Dysart J. and is reported in [1948] 1 D.L.R. 761.

Evidence was taken as to the business carried on by the corporation and the learned Judge found that it had carried on a banking business for about 23 years, from the time of its incorporation until the assignment in bankruptcy, and held that the claims of the deposit creditors were based upon banking transactions which the corporation had no right to engage in because they were not authorized by the Parliament of Canada which had the exclusive legislative authority over "Banking" and "Incorporation of Banks", and were invalid as against those whose claims arose from the legitimate estate business of the corporation; and that the deposit creditors were entitled to be paid only after the estate claimants had been paid in full.

The learned Judge relied on the well-known case of *Sinclair v. Brougham*, [1914] A.C. 398. In that case it was established beyond question that the Birkbeck Permanent Benefit Bldg. Soc. carried on for many years a very extensive banking business contrary to the provisions of the *Building Societies Act*, 1836, under which it was formed. The society was popularly known as the Birkbeck Bank and used that title in connection with its banking business.

The learned trial Judge referred to the amendments to the Bergethaler Waisenamt Charter made by the Manitoba Legislature in 1920 and 1922, as purporting to ratify and confirm previous banking transactions, and to authorize the continuance of them and other such transactions into the future, and he said that such ratification was wholly ineffectual to legalize the corporation's banking business. I think the amending validating Acts do not bear any such meaning. In any event the Legislature had the right, I think, without doubt, under its authority over property and civil rights, to enact legislation affecting the respective interests of persons and parties in Manitoba as between themselves, regardless of how such interests came into being or whether they were valid or invalid because of acts of the corporation which might or might not have been *ultra vires*. Such legislation does not mean or purport to mean the validation of banking business.

The right of a provincial Legislature to incorporate a loan, trust or financial corporation without authority to do a banking business is not questioned. That is all the Legislature purported to do here. The conduct of a banking business was not contemplated.

In *Reference re Alberta Bill of Rights Act, A.-G. Alta v. A.-G. Can.*, [1947], 4 D.L.R. 1, A.C. 503, Viscount Simon, in discussing operations which fall within the connotation of "Banking" as that word is used in s. 91 of the *B.N.A. Act*, made a statement which is very pertinent to any consideration of what is banking business. He is reported, at p. 9 D.L.R., p. 516 A.C., as saying: "The question is not what was the extent and kind of business actually carried on by banks in Canada in 1867, but what is the meaning of the term itself in the Act." He pointed out, too, that actually the business of banking has developed since Confederation.

Expert opinion was not given in evidence in this case as to what is banking business, but it is common knowledge that during the period of the corporation's operations banking did include the following:

1. Receiving money on deposit from its customers.
2. Paying a customer's cheques or drafts on it to the amount on deposit by such customers, and holding Dominion Government and Bank notes and coin for such purpose.
3. Paying interest by agreement on deposits.
4. Discounting commercial paper for its customers.
5. Dealing in exchange and in gold and silver coin and bullion.
6. Collecting notes and drafts deposited.
7. Arranging credits for itself with banks in other towns, cities and countries.
8. Selling its drafts or cheques on other banks and banking correspondents.
9. Issuing letters of credit.
10. Lending money to its customers:
    (a) on the customers' notes;
    (b) by way of overdraft;
    (c) on bonds, shares and other securities.

The business of a Canadian chartered bank is wider still because of the statutory rights and powers given to a bank under the provisions of the *Bank Act*.

The evidence of A.D. Friesen, joint manager of Bergethaler Waisenamt from 1915 until it went into bankruptcy, shows that the corporation did not carry on any of the above-listed functions except to borrow money on deposit and to pay interest thereon, and in turn to lend money to others who, as a rule, were not its deposit customers. In particular it did not pay cheques or orders on it by its customers (depositors) or pay the customers in cash across its counter. The customers called in person and, on their oral requests, were given the cheques of the corporation on the Canadian Bank of Commerce which did all the banking business effected. It did not discount or lend on commercial paper but only on direct indebtedness. It collected as executor or administrator a few notes for estates but, otherwise, did not make a practice of making collections for customers. It did

not deal in exchange or in gold or silver bullion. It had no Canadian or foreign banking correspondents. Any remittances to other countries or cities were sent, without charge, as secretary or agent for the remitter of the money and any banking business in connection therewith was done by the Canadian Bank of Commerce which sold and made charges for the drafts. The total amount remitted in this manner for the year 1927 was only $1,467.30. The evidence does not show what, if any, was remitted in other years. It did not issue letters of credit. It did not make a practice of lending by way of overdraft.

The learned Judge quoted a number of authorities defining or referring to the meaning of the business of banking. None, however, gave a complete list of the usual functions of a bank. Many of them do, however, state that the bank is bound to honour any cheques or orders for the payment of money which the customer may send to it to the extent of the sum deposited. In other words, as stated in the Oxford Dictionary, the banks' "essential duty is the payment of the orders given on it by its customers".

In *Pott v. Clegg* (1847), 16 M.&W. 321 at p. 328, 153 E.R. 1212, Sir Frederick Pollock C.B. said that the majority of the Court were of the opinion:

> That money in the hands of a banker is merely money lent, with the superadded obligation that it is to be paid when called for by the draft of the customer.

Foley v. Hill (1848), 2 H.L.C. 28, 9 E.R. 1002, is a leading case on the relation existing between banker and customer. The headnote states:

> The relation between a Banker and Customer, who pays money into the Bank, is the ordinary relation of debtor and creditor, with a superadded obligation arising out of the custom of bankers to honour the customer's drafts.

Lord Brougham said at p. 43:

> I am now speaking of the common position of a banker, which consists of the common case of receiving money from his customer on condition of paying it back when asked for, or when drawn upon.

And Lord Campbell is reported at p. 45 as saying:

> It has been said, that the banker is liable to do something more than merely to repay the money. He is bound to honour cheques, and perhaps to accept bills of exchange, if drawn upon him, he having assets in his hands.

Joachimson v. Swiss Bank Corp., [1921] 3 K.B. 110, is an important case. It decided that when money is standing to the credit of a customer on current account with a banker, in the absence of a special agreement, a demand by the customer is a necessary ingredient in the cause of action against the banker for money lent. The relation of banker and customer is discussed at length in this case by the Court of Appeal. Bankes L.J. at p. 118 refers to the headnote in *Foley v. Hill, supra*, and states that it correctly summarized the opinions expressed by the Law Lords but the decision cannot be treated as an exhaustive definition of all the obligations arising out of the relation between banker and customer. And Atkin L.J. is reported at p. 127 as saying, in reference to that relation, that, while the plaintiff claimed it was simple contract of loan:

> It is admitted that there is added, or super-added, an obligation of the bank to honour the customers' drafts to any amount not exceeding the credit balance at any material time.

And:

> I think that there is only one contract made between the bank and its customer. The terms of that contract involve obligations on both sides and require careful statement. They appear upon consideration to include the following provisions. The bank undertakes to receive money and to collect bills for its customer's account. The proceeds so received are not to be held in trust for the customer, but the bank borrows the proceeds and undertakes to repay them. The promise to repay is to repay at the branch of the bank where the account is kept, and during banking hours. It includes a promise to repay any part of the amount due against the written order of the customer addressed to the bank at the branch.

In *A.-G. Can. v. A.-G. Que., Bk. of Montreal v. A.-G. Que.*, [1947], 1 D.L.R. 81 at p. 87, A.C. 33 at p. 44, Lord Porter, who delivered the judgment of the Judicial Committee of the Privy Council, is reported as saying:

> The relation between banker and customer who pays money into the bank is stated in words which have ever since been accepted in *Foley v. Hill* (1848), 2 H.L.C. 28, 9 E.R. 1002, as 'the ordinary relation of debtor and creditor, with a superadded obligation arising out of the custom of bankers to honour the customer's drafts'.

In 1 Hals., 2nd ed., s. 1299, p. 793, after stating that Acts of 1844 and 1857 restricted banking associations to not more than six persons and then to not more than ten, in note (f) it is said:

> It is not clear whether the restriction applies only to combinations formed for the exclusive purpose of banking, or whether it would include combinations carrying on banking business *as part* of their undertaking, *or what precisely constitutes banking business*. See *Re District Savings Bank, Ltd., Ex parte Coe* (1861), 3 De G.F.&J. 335; 3 Digest 134, 97, where a society formed to receive deposits and conduct emigration operations was held not a banking company within the Joint Stock Companies Acts and 21 & 22 Vict. c. 91 (1858).... Probably the real test is the receiving money *to be withdrawn by cheque*.

The business carried on by most banks includes the totality of the functions I have enumerated, but, of course, a banking business can be carried on without performing all of them and most corporations and individuals engaged in a financial business of any kind are required to carry on or perform some of them, and it does not follow from the fact that banks perform them that every exercise of one or more of the functions is a form of banking.

The common business and callings of life, the ordinary trades and pursuits which are innocent of themselves and have been followed for a long time, are free to all, subject to any restrictions or prohibitions of law.

Here many important functions, including the important or essential duty or obligation to pay the customers' orders, were lacking.

The acts of the corporation were, in my opinion, no more than those of a loan or trust company, or a combined loan and trust company and did not amount to carrying on a banking business.

The answer to the question whether the corporation was engaged in "banking" decides this case I think. The learned Judge based his decision on that point alone and it does not appear to be necessary to consider or discuss further, in the event of the Court holding the corporation was engaged in banking, whether the acts of the corporation were *ultra vires* or whether *Sinclair v. Brougham*, [1914] A.C. 398, as interpreted by the Court of Appeal in *Re Diplock*, [1948] 1 Ch. 465, applies. Mr. Sutton, however, argued also that the moneys of estates received by the corporation, having been mixed by it with its own funds, the *cestuis que trust* were entitled to a charge on the assets of the corporation and to rank on the estate of the corporation in priority to general creditors. He relied on statements in *Re Hallett, Knatchbull v. Hallett* (1880), 13 Ch. D. 696; in *Sinclair v. Brougham*, and *Re Diplock* cases; in *Br. Can. Securities v. Martin* (1917), 27 Man. R. 423, and in many others. These judgments do not support his claim. Whatever may be the case where trust moneys or property acquired by its moneys can be traced, that is not the situation here. There were no moneys in the corporation's bank account or in its hands when it was ordered to be wound up and there is no evidence on which any property could be identified as having been acquired with trust moneys.

A similar claim was put forward in *Western Trust Co. & Wah Sing v. Wah Sing* (1920), 56 D.L.R. 584, 14 S.L.R. 41. The Court of Appeal for Saskatchewan held that to be entitled, to priority a claimant must show that the property in the trust moneys never passed but was at all times in himself, and that it was sufficiently earmarked to be identified as part of the assets of the insolvent estate, and, if the identity of the trust fund is lost, the claimant is imply a creditor and must rank with the others.

There has been no appeal from the orders settling the list of creditors made in 1931 and, while the Court orders made in 1935 and 1936, expressly preserved the rights to preference between creditors, no claim for preference was made until 1946 after the Liquidator had obtained the order for payment of a dividend. I think that after so many years the Court should not be acute to defeat the rights of the ordinary creditors who did business with the corporation in good faith.

The appeal should be allowed.

There has been some suggestion by Mr. Sutton that one individual creditor could trace his own money into a particular asset but has not made any application to prove his claim. Subject to such an application the Liquidator should distribute the assets amongst all the creditors without priority as soon as possible. I think February 1, 1949 should be fixed as the final date before which claims for particular assets must be made.

The parties may speak to the matter of costs. It was not mentioned during the argument before us.

[COYNE J.A.:]

I concur. It is unnecessary to consider in detail other grounds on which the judgment of the Court might be supported since those stated by Richards J.A. are sufficient for the decision. But the following brief reference to some other points and to some further authorities may be useful.

> "Subject, however, to these exclusive privileges (of the Bank of England) ... *the trade of banking* has from its first introduction, been always free, both in London and in the country": *Stephen's Commentaries of the Laws of England*, 16th ed., vol. 3, p. 185.

> "All British subjects have equal rights of trading within the dominions and dependencies of the Crown, unless *prohibited* by Act of Parliament": 6 Hals., 1st ed., p. 488, s. 764.

> "What the Act of Incorporation has done is to create a legal and artificial person with capacity to carry on certain kinds of business": *Colonial Bldg. & Inv. Ass'n v. A.-G. Que.* (1883), 9 App. Cas. 157 at p. 166. "Creating a corporation can hardly be said to be making a law": *Re Junction R. Co. & Peterborough* (1880), 45 U.C.Q.B. 302 at p. 317, *per* Cameron J.; unaffected by appeal in 6 O.A.R. 339, and 8 S.C.R. 76. "The Provincial Legislatures have ... exclusive power to make laws in relation to the incorporation of companies with provincial objects; but *the body politic created* by any such act of incorporation becomes, *like a natural body, subject to the laws* of the land": *Shoolbred v. Clarke* (1890), 17 S.C.R. 265 at p. 274, *per* Patterson J.

Banking is not a technical or legal term but a loose popular one, comprehending activities carried on by those who, likewise popularly, are called bankers. Of these activities some are often and some are usually carried on by bankers. Some are essential to the conception. But very few are exclusive activities of bankers. Chequing privileges accorded depositors, and general dealing in credit, are characteristic of and perhaps essential to banking. But even that does not make them exclusive rights of bankers, even in the absence of prohibition by statute against others carrying them on.

The presence of many positive features which are essential to banking do not make a business embracing these features, or a combination of some of them, a banking business: Paget, *Law of Banking*, 3rd ed., pp. 4 and 6, and Grant, *Law of Banking*, 7th ed., p. 1.

In distinguishing banking from other business, "probably the real test is the receiving money to be withdrawn by cheque": quoted by Richards J.A. from *Halsbury's Laws of England*.

A banker "undertakes *by the very carrying on* of his business that *he will honour any cheque drawn upon an account*, provided that that account is in credit to the amount of the draft": Hart, *Law of Banking*, 4th ed., vol. 1, p. 24.

Moreover, "he must hold himself out as a banker and the public take him as such", assuming "openly, avowedly and notoriously the character of a banker", "held out to the world openly" as such: *Stafford v. Henry* (1850), 12 Ir. Eq. R. 400 (Exch.), see pp. 404, 407 foot, 408, 410 middle, cited in *Davies v. Kennedy* (1869), Ir. R. 3 Eq. 668, Christian

L.J. at pp. 693, 708; *sub. nom. Copland v. Davies* (1872), L.R. 5 H.L. 358 at p. 388, where Lord Chelmsford refers to "the high authority of the Lord Justice"; Paget, p. 4.

I refer also to Falconbridge on *Banking and Bills of Exchange*, 5th ed., p. 156, regarding what is a bank.

Grant of legislative power does not disturb general rights. The Parliament of Canada, it is true, has legislated in respect of the so-called "chartered" banks. But it has placed no restriction on what other persons, natural or artificial, may do in respect of any business such as Bergethaler carried on, except that such others may not advertise themselves as banks or bankers and are subject to a fine if they do: *The Bank Act*, R.S.C. 1906, c. 29, s. 156; continued in the revisions of 1913, c. 9, and 1923, c. 32; and into R.S.C. 1927, c. 12, s. 166. "Express enactments shuts the door to further implication. 'Expressio unius est exclusio alterius'": Lord Dunedin in *Whiteman v. Sadler*, [1910] A.C. 514 at p. 527, and the Privy Council in *Blackburn v. Flavelle* (1881), 6 App. Cas. 628 at p. 634. In free translation: "Express mention of one implies exception or rejection of any others." Besides, it may be argued, the provision in the *Bank Act* relating to deposits recognized provincial jurisdiction to authorize receipt of deposits by others than chartered banks: (1923, c. 32, s. 156(3); R.S.C. 1927, c. 12, s. 166(3)). This provision was omitted in 1934.

In Canada, others than bankers may lawfully carry on legitimate banking business in many of its activities, including all those of this company, provided such others do not advertise as prohibited in s. 166 (old s. 156) of the *Bank Act*.

The Bergethaler's incorporation statute of 1907, s. 10, conferred all the powers and imposed the duties and liabilities under the *Manitoba Trustee Act*, which, by s. 35, prohibited receiving of moneys on deposit at interest but permitted the receiving of money for investment and the payment of interest thereon. The *Loan and Trust Corporations Act*, 1924 (Man.), c. 41, which, from that time on, applied to all companies doing a trust or loan company business on or after that date — including this corporation — made them trustees of moneys deposited, with a guarantee by them of repayment and an obligation to set aside and earmark securities in value equal to the full aggregate amount of such deposit moneys. All the securities and assets of the company at the time of winding-up were much less in value than the aggregate sum of such moneys received from such depositors.

To turn to another aspect: there is no evidence in respect of Bergethaler Waisenamt on which any property could be identified as acquired with moneys belonging to any of those composing the class which Mr. Sutton represents (with one exception or perhaps two). Even if they could be so identified, there is no evidence to show that they would have priority over depositor creditors in view of considerations set out above, as well as in the judgment of Richards J.A.

There is a further consideration:

> What happened over the long period of administration of this insolvent estate might well constitute estoppel, or at any rate, evidence of *laches*, acquiescence or delay sufficient to disentitle the others from asserting, after 17 years, priority rights over the depositors, even if such rights had existed those many years ago. But such rights have not been asserted or acted on at all during that period, and all the claimants, depositors and others, have stood on a par during that protracted period. Some have died; beneficiaries have succeeded; and undoubtedly transactions have been made and actions taken by depositors and others, and their successors, on the strength of that position. The Court should not disregard these circumstances and considerations in dealing now with claimants of such priority rights.

[ADAMSON J.A.:]

I agree with my brother Richards. The Provinces have jurisdiction in respect of "The Incorporation of Companies with Provincial Objects", and in respect of "Property and Civil Rights". Borrowing money and receiving it on deposit is primarily a matter of "Property and Civil Rights". Taking money or goods on deposit for investment or safekeeping is essentially trust business rather than banking. This has been recognized as being so by Parliament in the incorporation of numerous trust companies by private Act: for example see ss. 8 and 15, 6 Edw. VII, c. 180. The fact that Parliament has exclusive jurisdiction over "Banking, Incorporation of Banks, and the Issue of Paper Money", and the fact that banks invariably take deposits, does not make it *ultra vires* of the Province to grant power to a company to take deposits. Where it a fact that every activity incidental to the subjects over which parliament has jurisdiction was *ultra vires* of the Provinces, very little, if anything, would be left upon which the Provinces could legislate. The wide difference between taking deposits in "checking accounts" as the banks do and simply taking deposits as this company did is an important point in considering whether a banking business was or was not carried on. The bare fact of taking deposits does not constitute "banking" and the Province has jurisdiction to grant such a power to a company of its creation.

Appeal allowed.

(e) *Canadian Pioneer Management Ltd. v. Labour Relations Board of Saskatchewan*†

[BEETZ J. (Estey and McIntyre JJ. concurring):]

The two points in issue are whether under the *Trade Union Act*, 1972 (Sask.), c. 137 [now R.S.S. 1978, c. T-17], the Labour Relations Board of Saskatchewan (the "Board") has jurisdiction to certify the respondent union to represent the employees of (1) Pioneer Life Assurance Company ("Pioneer Life") and (2) Pioneer Trust Company ("Pioneer Trust"), and to hear charges of unfair labour practices against Pioneer Life and Pioneer Trust.

The jurisdiction of the Board was challenged from the start on the ground that the labour relations of Pioneer Life and Pioneer Trust were regulated by the *Canada Labour Code*, R.S.C. 1970, c. L-1, or otherwise came within the exclusive competence of Parliament. The Board held that it had jurisdiction and certified the respondent union to represent employees of the appellants in the City of Regina.

The appellants applied to the Court of Queen's Bench of Saskatchewan for an order of *certiorari* to quash the Board's certification order and for an order of prohibition to prevent the Board from proceeding to hear nine complaints of unfair labour practices [87 D.L.R. (3d) 625, [1978] 5 W.W.R. 157]. Halvorson J., dismissed both applications and his judgment was affirmed by the unanimous judgment of Culliton C.J.S., Woods and Brownridge JJ.A., of the Saskatchewan Court of Appeal [93 D.L.R. (3d) 472, [1979] 1 W.W.R. 271]. Hence the present appeal, by leave of this Court.

In this Court, all the intervenors except the Attorney-General of Canada supported the judgments of the Courts below. The Attorney-General of Canada took the position that the Courts below were right with respect to the jurisdiction of the Board over Pioneer Life but wrong with respect to the jurisdiction of the Board over Pioneer Trust.

I. PIONEER LIFE

Pioneer Life was incorporated under the laws of the Province of Saskatchewan but later registered under the *Canadian and British Insurance Companies Act*, R.S.C. 1970, c. I-15, and is thus deemed to have been incorporated thereunder. Together with Pioneer Trust, it is a wholly-owned subsidiary of Canadian Pioneer Management Ltd., which was incorporated pursuant to Part I of the *Canada Corporations Act*, R.S.C. 1970, c. C-32, and continued under s. 181 [am. 1978-79, c. 9, s. 57] of the *Canada Business Corporations Act*, 1974-75-76 (Can.), c. 33. Canadian Pioneer Management Ltd. provides certain management services to its two subsidiaries.

The appellants have approximately 90 employees in the City of Regina including eight whose employment was terminated before the application for certification was filed. Approximately 35 persons are employed by Canadian Pioneer Management Ltd., but some of these have responsibilities in the two subsidiary companies. The Board found that "the industrial relations of the three corporate entities are inseparable" but the whole case was argued quite apart from the possible impact of this finding on the two points in issue.

Pioneer Life carries on the business of life insurance and has offices in Alberta, Saskatchewan and Manitoba. Under the *Canadian and British Insurance*

---

† (1980), 107 D.L.R. (3d) 1 (S.C.C.).

Companies Act, it is subject to federal controls with respect to licensing, statements and returns, contracts, operations, investments, reserves for unmatured obligations under policies, distribution of profits, securities to be held in Canada, etc. Pursuant to the *Department of Insurance Act*, R.S.C. 1970, c. I-17, the Superintendent of Insurance administers the *Canadian and British Insurance Companies Act*.

It was submitted on behalf of the appellants that while each Province has jurisdiction over the business of insurance within the Province, Parliament does have jurisdiction to regulate federally incorporated insurance companies which carry on business in several Provinces. Thus, it could not be said that the business of life insurance carried on in more than one Province by a federally incorporated company was a matter of exclusive provincial concern and this shared jurisdiction brought the business of Pioneer Life within the statutory definition of a federal work, undertaking or business in s. 2(i) of the *Canada Labour Code*:

> (i) a work, undertaking or business outside the exclusive legislative authority of provincial legislatures;

After having heard counsel for the appellants, the Court did not call on counsel for the respondents or the intervenors to respond on this point. Given the long list of judicial decisions starting with *Citizens Ins. Co. of Canada v. Parsons* (1881), 7 App. Cas. 96, and culminating in *Canadian Indemnity Co. et al. v. A.-G. B.C.* (1976), 73 D.L.R. (3d) 111, 30 C.P.R. (2d) 1, [1977] 2 S.C.R. 504, [1976] 5 W.W.R. 748, the Court could not be persuaded, despite Mr. Rendeck's able and indeed valiant argument, that the business of insurance does not come within exclusive provincial control.

II.   PIONEER TRUST

1.   The Facts

As was noted above, Pioneer Trust is a wholly-owned subsidiary of Canadian Pioneer Management Ltd. It was incorporated pursuant to the *Trust Companies Act*, R.S.C. 1970, c. T-16, and carries on its business and has offices in Alberta, Saskatchewan and Manitoba.

According to the statement of facts contained in appellants' factum, which has been accepted by the Attorney-General for Saskatchewan and which corresponds substantially to the findings of the Board, and according also to a brochure outlining the services provided by Pioneer Trust, which has been produced as an exhibit and the accuracy of which does not appear to have been challenged, the business or operations of Pioneer Trust can be described in terms of the services which it provides to its customers. These include the following:

1. "chequing" accounts (while cheques drawn on Pioneer Trust are not cheques within the meaning of s. 165(1) of the *Bills of Exchange Act*, R.S.C. 1970, c. B-5, since they are not drawn on a bank, they appear to play the same role as true cheques: they do pass through the clearing system of the banks. Pioneer Trust utilizes the clearing facilities of the Bank of Montreal);
2. savings accounts;
3. loans on the security of mortgages;
4. personal loans against the collateral and lending by way of overdraft;
5. loans under federal Government guarantees pursuant to such statutes as the *Canada Students Loans Act*, R.S.C. 1970, c. S-17, the *Farm Improvement Loans Act*, R.S.C. 1970, c. F-3, the *Fisheries Improvement Loans Act*, R.S.C. 1970, F-22, and the *National Housing Act*, R.S.C. 1970, N-10;
6. commercial loans with securities, other than accounts receivable and inventory, and commercial lending without security;
7. exchange services;
8. money orders;
9. travellers' cheques;
10. strong boxes renting;
11. securities safe-keeping;
12. term deposits, guaranteed investment certificates in amounts of $1,000 or more for terms of from one to five years, guaranteed income averaging certificates and guaranteed deposit receipts;
13. registered retirement savings plans, retirement accumulation savings plans, registered home ownership savings plans and deferred profit sharing plans;
14. estate administration services.

Of the services outlined above, two are not carried on by chartered banks: the issuance of income averaging certificates and estate administration services. But it was contended that Pioneer Trust does very little fiduciary work. On the other hand, and according to the testimony of Mr. Price, vice-president and general manager of Pioneer Trust, the only banking function not open to Pioneer Trust is the provision of commercial loans on the security of accounts receivable and inventory, although Pioneer

Trust is involved in commercial lending with other securities and on an unsecured basis. Mr. Price testified that 99% of the actual business conducted by the company is identical to the business carried on by chartered banks. The brochure outlining the services offered by Pioneer Trust carries the slogan: "You can Bank on Pioneer".

Just as banks, and like all federally incorporated trusts, Pioneer Trust is a member of the Canada Deposit Insurance Corporation, pursuant to s. 9(b) of the *Canada Deposit Insurance Corporation Act*, R.S.C. 1970, c. C-3. It is inspected by the Superintendent of Insurance. It must file with the Government of Canada annual statements, quarterly liquidity statements and semi-annual statements of changes in investments and loans. Pioneer Trust is subject to minimal provincial regulation: it submits an annual summary of capital and shares to the Registrar of Companies in Regina and annual statements to the provincial jurisdictions in which it operates but is not subject to inspection by any of the provincial jurisdictions.

2. Submissions Made on Behalf of Appellants and the Attorney-General for Canada

It was submitted on behalf of Pioneer Trust that while, *prima facie*, the Provinces have jurisdiction to legislate with respect to labour relations, Parliament has exclusive jurisdiction over the labour relations of federal works, undertakings and businesses. It was further submitted that in order to determine whether the business of Pioneer Trust was a federal business, it was necessary to consider its normal operations without regard to exceptional or casual factors: *Letter Carriers' Union of Canada v. Canadian Union of Postal Workers et al.* (1973), 40 D.L.R. (3d) 105, [1975] 1 S.C.R. 178, [1974] 1 W.W.R. 452. Ninety-nine per cent of the business of Pioneer Trust was identical to that carried by a chartered bank and was therefore in the nature of a banking business although the company was not chartered as a bank under the *Bank Act*, R.S.C. 1970, c. B-1. "Banking" within the meaning of s. 91(15) of the *British North America Act*, 1867, includes not only the business carried on by chartered banks but also banking carried on by other financial institutions. *The Trust Companies Act* went beyond mere incorporation. The day-to-day operations of Pioneer Trust were regulated pursuant to the provisions of this Act, under the power of Parliament to make laws in relation to banking. It was because of such regulation and

because of the banking nature of its operation that Pioneer Trust ought to be considered as a federal business for the purposes of the *Canada Labour Code*. Provincially incorporated trusts doing the same type of business were not federally regulated as was Pioneer Trust and the Provinces could continue to incorporate and regulate them as long as federal law permitted. But Pioneer Trust, being in the business of banking and being subject to federal regulations was a federal business within the meaning of s. 2 of the *Canada Labour Code*:

> 2. In this Act
>
> "federal work, undertaking or business" means any work, undertaking or business that is within the legislative authority of the Parliament of Canada, including without restricting the generality of the foregoing:
>
> ...
>
> (g) a bank;
>
> ...
>
> (i) a work, undertaking or business outside the exclusive legislative authority of provincial legislatures;

It was conceded that Pioneer Trust is not a "bank": s. 28 of the *Interpretation Act*, R.S.C. 1970, c. I-23, provides:

> 28. In every enactment
>
> ...
>
> "bank or chartered bank" means a bank to which the *Bank Act* applies;

and s. 4 of the *Bank Act* provides:

> 4. This Act applies to each bank named in Schedule A and does not apply to any other bank.

Pioneer Trust is not named in Sched. A [am. 1972, c. 24, s. 6; 1974-75-76, c. 114, s. 5; c. 16, s. 5; 1976-77, c. 28, s. 4] of the *Bank Act* and therefore, by virtue of the *Interpretation Act*, is not a bank within the meaning of s. 2(g) of the *Canada Labour Code*.

But it was contended that Pioneer Trust is a federal business within the meaning of s. 2(i) of the *Canada Labour Code* quoted above.

Counsel for the Attorney-General of Canada agreed with counsel for Pioneer Trust that, although Pioneer Trust is not a bank, banking is its business. The test was not what Pioneer Trust could do under its corporate powers, but what it actually did. At this point, however, the two counsel parted company. Counsel for the Attorney-General of Canada dismissed any suggestion that there was room for shared or concurrent jurisdiction in the field of banking. Banking came under exclusive federal authority. Once it was held, as it should be, that Pioneer Trust was a banking undertaking, the regulation of its labour relations came under the exclusive authority of Parliament, whether or not the *Canada Labour Code* applied to it: Reference re *Industrial Relations and Disputes Investigation Act*, etc. (the *Stevedoring* case), [1955] 3 D.L.R. 721, [1955] S.C.R. 529. It was contended that Pioneer Trust was a federal work, undertaking or business within the meaning of s. 2(i) of the *Canada Labour Code*, but even if it was not, the *Trade Union Act* was inapplicable and the Board was without jurisdiction. The entire scope of Parliament's jurisdiction over banking and the incorporation of banks was not encompassed in the *Bank Act*. The fact that the banking undertaking of *Pioneer Trust* was not regulated by federal legislation under all its aspects did not render provincial legislation applicable to this exclusively federal undertaking: *Union Colliery Co. of B.C. v. Bryden*, [1899] A.C. 580; *Commission du Salaire Minimum v. Bell Telephone Co. of Canada* (1966), 59 D.L.R. (2d) 145 at pp. 148–9, 150–51, [1966] S.C.R. 767 at pp. 772, 774.

If those submissions express the law, the consequences are quite far-reaching.

Thus, should the submissions made on behalf of Pioneer Trust be accepted, a trust company with the same type of business as Pioneer Trust would be subject either to provincial or federal legislation with respect to its labour relations, depending on whether it is provincially incorporated or incorporated under the *Trust Companies Act*. This goes against settled authority according to which the origin of incorporation has no bearing on jurisdiction over labour relations: *C.P.R. Co. v. A.-G. B.C.*, [1950] 1 D.L.R. 721; [1950] A.C. 122, [1950] 1 W.W.R. 220 *sub nom. Reference re Application of Hours of Work Act, etc.* (the *Empress Hotel* case); *Canada Labour Relations Board v. C.N.R.* (1974), 45 D.L.R. (3d) 1, [1975] 1 S.C.R. 786, [1974] 4 W.W.R. 661 (the *Jasper Park Lodge* case); *Morgan et al. v. A.-G. P.E.I. et al.* (1975), 55 D.L.R. (3d) 527 at pp. 538–9, [1976] 2 S.C.R. 349 at p. 364, 7 Nfld. & P.E.I.R. 537, *per* Laskin C.J.C.; the *Canadian Indemnity* case, *supra, per* Martland J., at p. 122 D.L.R. p. 519 S.C.R. Furthermore, trust companies incorporated pursuant to the Trust Companies Act and, for that matter, provincially incorporated trust companies would come under either federal or provincial jurisdiction with respect to their labour relations, depending on how little they elect to do fiduciary work and how much they render

other types of services resembling those rendered by Pioneer Trust.

The contentions advanced on behalf of the Attorney-General for Canada are even more far-reaching: if acceded to and pushed to their logical consequences, they might mean that provincially incorporated trust companies and perhaps even credit unions and "caisses populaires" with the same type of business as Pioneer Trust were unlawfully incorporated and have been operating invalidly.

The issue turns on the elusive concept of banking.

3. Difficulty of Defining Banking

In *The Law of Banking and the Canadian Bank Act*, 2nd ed. (1968, Toronto), the author, Ian F.G. Baxter, wrote at p. 5:

> ... it would be a bold man who would undertake to state categorically which business activities legally appertain and which do not appertain to the business of banking.

Chorley, in his book on the *Law of Banking*, 4th ed., p. 23, has even gone as far as to say that "to construct a definition which would embrace the whole of it is manifestly impossible".

The reasons why banking is so difficult to define are manifold. First,

> Banking is not a technical or legal term but a loose popular one, comprehending activities carried on by those who, likewise popularly, are called bankers.

Coyne J.A., in *Re Bergethaler Waisenamt (No. 2)*, [1949] 1 D.L.R. 769 at p. 778, [1949] 1 W.W.R. 323 at p. 334, 57 Man. R. 66.

"Banking" on the other hand, while not a legal term, evokes economic notions which are notoriously not amenable to the discipline of the law. Furthermore, the meaning of the word has evolved considerably over the centuries. Finally, because of the expansion of credit and the development of competition between banks and other types of institutions sometimes called near banks, such as trust companies, the latter have entered certain fields of activities previously carried on by banks while banks have begun operations which were not traditionally considered to appertain to the business of banking, leading to considerable overlapping of functions.

Still, many attempts have been made in judicial decisions as well as in doctrinal works, to define the notion of banking or at least to reduce the uncertainties. In some of the attempts, the problem was approached from the point of view of the substance of the matter and, in others, from the point of view of form.

4. Nature of the Relationship Between the Institution and Its Customers

One approach related to substance has focused on the nature of the relationship between the institution and its customers. The relation between a banker and a customer who pays money into the bank is not a fiduciary one. It is the ordinary relation of debtor and creditor, with a superadded obligation arising out of the custom of bankers to honour the customer's cheques. Possession of or property in the deposit remains with the bank the obligation of which is a debt under a contract of *mutuum*, not *commodatum*: *Foley v. Hill* (1848), 2 H.L. Cas. 28, 9 E.R. 1002; *Joachimson v. Swiss Bank Corp.*, [1921] 3 K.B. 110 at p. 127; *A.-G. Can. v. A.-G. Que.; Bank of Montreal v. A.-G. Que. et al.*, [1947] 1 D.L.R. 81 at p. 87, [1947] A.C. 33 at p. 44, [1946] 3 W.W.R. 659 (the *Bank Deposits* case). By contrast, s. 63 [am. R.S.C. 1970, c. 47 (1st Supp.), s. 22] of the *Trust Companies Act* which relates to the powers of a trust company emphasizes their fiduciary nature by the use of the words "in trust", "entrusted", "trustee" or some other similar expression in practically each of its subsections; and it would appear that a trust company has no power to receive money on deposit in such a way that it is the simple debtor of the depositor: Daniel J. Baum, "The Near-Banks: Trust Companies of Canada", XLV *Tulane L. Rev.* 546 (1970-71), at pp. 558 and 568. It has been contended that this legal distinction is of little or no practical effect and that in fact the relationship between a trust company and a depositor "is indistinguishable from the debtor-creditor relationship between a bank and its customer": Peter W. Hogg, *Constitutional Law of Canada* (1977), p. 367, note 97. I cannot subscribe to the view that the distinction entails no practical differences. It was on this very basis that in the *Bank Deposits* case, at pp. 87–9 D.L.R., pp. 44–6 A.C., the Judicial Committee distinguished a judgment of this Court relating to unclaimed trust property which vested in the Province under provincial legislation: *Provincial Treasurer of Manitoba v. Minister of Finance for Canada; A.-G. Man. v. Minister of Finance for Canada*, [1943] 3 D.L.R. 673, [1943] S.C.R. 370, 24 C.B.R. 320. Furthermore, s. 66 of the *Trust Companies Act* prescribes that trust funds are to be kept distinct from those of the company and

ss. 64 [am. R.S.C. 1970, c. 47 (1st Supp.), s. 24] and 68 [am. R.S.C. 1970, c. 47 (1st Supp.), s. 25; 1976-77, c. 28, s. 45] provide that trust money is not to be invested in a manner which is identical to the investment of its own funds by the company, whereas money deposited with a bank becomes the property of the bank which may invest it as it pleases, as long as it does so in accordance with the provisions of the *Bank Act*.

In connection with the fiduciary character of Pioneer Trust, I find rather misleading the assertion that, on the one hand, it does very little fiduciary work but, on the other, that it is in the banking business because, like banks, it is involved in activities which include the operation of certain plans such as registered home ownership savings plans and registered retirement plans. Under s. 146.2(1)(d) [enacted 1974-75-76, c. 26, s. 100] of the *Income Tax Act*, 1970-71-72 (Can.), c. 63, and amendments, only a Canadian trust company is empowered to issue a registered home ownership savings plan. If it authorizes a bank, credit union or mutual fund to act as its agent in the sale of shares in the plan, it continues to be the issuer and trustee of the plan and, as such, it remains responsible for the application, the registration of the plan, the issue of receipts for contributions to the plan and the filing of tax and information returns. So this is not at all an instance of a trust company doing any banking business but, on the contrary, of a bank acting as the agent of a trustee. Similarly, under s. 146(1)(j) [rep. & sub. 1977-78, c. 32, s. 34(6)] of the *Income Tax Act*, registered retirement savings plans cannot be issued by banks but only by certain insurance companies, by Canadian trust companies and certain other approved companies. This type of operation has nothing to do with banking and is not connected with banks unless banks act as mere agents of trust companies, insurance companies and other approved companies.

In the same vein, I do not think that Pioneer Trust can accurately argue that it is doing a banking operation when, like banks, it provides its customers with travellers' cheques. The evidence reveals that Pioneer Trust sells to its customers travellers' cheques of the American Express Company. While the case does not disclose what type of agreement governs the legal relationship between Pioneer Trust and the American Express Company, the usual or normal practice would appear to be that the issuer of the cheques delivers blank cheques to its selling agent, whether a bank, a trust company or a travel agency, who agrees to hold them as trustee of the issuer and to sell them on his behalf. "The trust receipt invariably stipulates that the proceeds of such sales are to be held by the agent as a specific trust fund in favour of the issuing banker": E.P. Ellinger, "Travellers' cheques and the Law", 19 University of Toronto L. Jo. 132 (1969) at p. 150. Since the operation of selling travellers' cheques on behalf of and in trust for the issuer involves a trust agreement, it cannot appertain more to the business of a bank than to that of a trust company.

Furthermore, I find it somewhat strange that the safe-keeping of securities and the renting of safety deposit boxes be represented, at the present day, as banking operations. Of course in earlier days, as today, banks provided the means for the safe-keeping of valuables, because dealing in coins, bullion, money and other valuables, they had to be provided with vaults and strong-boxes which could also be of service to customers of the banks for purposes other than banking. But the renting of safety deposit boxes merely puts the bank in the position of a bailee in accordance with the terms of an ordinary civil contract which can be concluded by anyone, including a bank or a trust company, who happens to be provided with the secured facilities. And the safe-keeping of securities appertains much more, in my view, to the business of a trust company than to that of a bank. It is a power which is specifically bestowed upon trust companies by s. 63(h) of the *Trust Companies Act*. Indeed, it is by nature a fiduciary service even when it happens to be rendered by a bank. I fail to see how it is transformed into a banking service when it is rendered by a trust company. (See the opinion of Adamson J.A., as he then was, in the *Bergethaler Waisenamt* case, *supra*, at p. 781 D.L.R., p. 337 W.W.R.)

As for the submission, made on behalf of Pioneer Trust, that the *Trust Companies Act* goes beyond incorporation and rises to the level of regulation, I do not think it should be entertained. This aspect of the matter has been alluded to but not argued in any detail by any of the parties or the intervenors. The *Trust Companies Act* does not apply to trust institutions in general but only to federally incorporated trust companies. It is most doubtful that Parliament could regulate the fiduciary activities of trust institutions, whether federally or provincially incorporated. That is why the provisions of the *Trust Companies Act* must not be construed as going beyond what they can constitutionally do and what, on their face, they purport to do: to allow for the incorporation of trust companies and impose limitations on their corporate capacity as conditions of their incorporation. The authority so to legislate is not derived from the power of Parliament over

banking but from its power to make laws for the incorporation of companies with objects other than provincial, this being taken to include objects within provincial authority in more than one Province: *Colonial Building & Investment Ass'n v. A.-G. Que.* (1883), 9 App. Cas. 157.

In short, under the *Trust Companies Act*, all the transactions of Pioneer Trust, or most of them, appear to be fiduciary by operation of law, whether or not they are so by nature. Furthermore, several of them, described by Pioneer Trust as banking operations, are fiduciary by nature as well as by operation of law and are not banking transactions although some of them, not all, may lawfully be carried on by chartered banks. These factors may not by themselves be determinative of the issue. But they are relevant and indicative that the business of Pioneer Trust is not that of banking.

5. The Functional Test

Another approach to the problem of defining banking, also related to the substance of the matter, consists in the consideration of the functions of banking, from an economic or legal point of view.

(a) The Economic Point of View

According to a view widely held in the nineteenth century, banks were considered as the main channel for the transfer of savings; the function of banking was one of financial intermediation in which the public had an interest with respect to solvency and allocation of financial resources. But under this particular economic view, the list of financial intermediaries would include, as well as chartered banks, some other very different types of institutions such as life insurance companies, finance companies, mortgage companies, trust companies, etc. (See Patrick N. McDonald, "The B.N.A. Act and the Near Banks: A Case Study in Federalism", 10 *Alta. L. Rev.* 155 (1972) at p. 158 and ff. This article is, to the best of my knowledge, the most exhaustive study published on the question.)

Judges, however, have not always shrunk from the functional economic approach. They had little choice in *Reference re Alberta Legislation*, [1938] 2 D.L.R. 81, [1938] S.C.R. 100 (the Alberta Statutes Reference), since they had to deal with the legislative implementation of a specific economic doctrine; the Court found *ultra vires* a provincial legislative scheme the essence of which was to set up a new form of credit and currency within Alberta. Three bills had been referred to the Court: Bill No. 1, "An Act Respecting the Taxation of Banks"; Bill No. 8,

"An Act to Amend and Consolidate the Credit of Alberta Regulation Act"; and Bill No. 9, "An Act to ensure the Publication of Accurate News and Information". The three bills were found unconstitutional together with a statute which had not been explicitly referred to the Court but which contained, expressed in legislative terms, the core of the social credit system, the *Alberta Social Credit Act*, 1937 (Alta.). c. 10. Bill No. 9 does not concern us here. Bill No. 1 attempted to tax the banks out of existence and was found *ultra vires* as directed to the frustration of the banking system established by the *Bank Act*. (This part of the judgment was upheld by the Judicial Committee in *A.-G. Alta. v. A.-G. Can.*, [1938] 4 D.L.R. 433, [1939] A.C. 117, [1938] 3 W.W.R. 337 (the *Alberta Bank Taxation* case). The Judicial Committee did not pronounce on the other issues which had become academic.) The main trust of the *Alberta Social Credit Act* was described as follows by Duff C.J.C., at p. 89 D.L.R., p. 113 S.C.R.:

> ... it is clear ... that the substitution generally in internal commerce of Alberta credit for bank credit and legal tender as the circulating medium is of the very essence of the plan.

The Act provided for the distribution of Alberta credit by the Provincial Treasurer by means of treasury credit certificates. It also provided for the creation of a credit house with branches that could accept deposits, convert currency and negotiable instruments on demand into Alberta credit, etc. The practicability of the scheme would have depended upon the general acceptance by the people of Alberta, of Alberta credit as a medium of payment. The Act was found *ultra vires* by five of the six members of the Court, as relating to "Banking and the Incorporation of Banks", and also, by three of those five, as dealing with "Currency" and the "Regulation of Trade and Commerce". By comparison to what he said with respect to Bill No. 8, Duff C.J.C., did not deal at great length with the functions of banking; the *Alberta Social Credit Act* was in relation to banking because it purported to set up a parallel system of banks for the issuance and circulation of a parallel system of credit. While the reasons of Duff C.J.C., may not be capable of being interpreted as meaning that the *Alberta Social Credit Act* would not have been found *ultra vires* had it not interfered with chartered banks, Duff C.J.C., did say, in the passage quoted above, that the *substitution* of one system for the other was the *very essence* of the plan. And if one couples the *Alberta Social Credit Act* with Bill No. 1, the taxing bill, which would have prevented the continued operation of chartered banks, one can

entertain no doubt, looking at the scheme as a whole, that the parallel system was intended to prevail over the established one, and to that extent, to interfere with it.

But it is mostly in relation to Bill No. 8, "An Act to Amend and Consolidate the Credit of Alberta Regulation Act", that Duff C.J.C., and Kerwin J., as he then was, dealt in detail with the function of banking, and sought to get hold of its quintessence in terms involving economic concepts. At pp. 99–100 D.L.R., pp. 124–5 S.C.R., after saying, "A banker is a dealer in credit", Duff C.J.C., focused upon the monetary function of banks and dwelt upon the particular way in which bankers, as opposed to money-lenders, create credit and deal in credit by way of book-keeping entries. He quoted with approval the following passage from M. Walter Leaf's volume on banking:

> ... when the creation of credit is discussed there is general agreement that by credit is meant banker's credit, that is to say, the right to draw cheques on a bank. The exercise of this right involves either the withdrawal from the bank of legal tender, in the shape of bank notes or silver and bronze coin, or the transfer of such a right to some other person in the books of the same or another bank.

At p. 128 D.L.R., pp. 155–6 S.C.R., Kerwin J., quoted a paragraph of the *Encyclopaedia Britannica*, 14th ed., containing the following passage:

> Banks create credit. It is a mistake to suppose that bank credit is created to any important extent by the payment of money into the banks. Money is always being paid in by tradesmen and others who receive it in the course of business, and drawn out again by employers to pay wages and by depositors in general for use as pocket money. But the change of money into credit money and of credit money back into money does not alter the total amount of the means of payment in the hands of the community. When a bank lends, by granting an advance or discounting a bill, the effect is different. Two debts are created; the trader who borrows becomes indebted to the bank at a future date, and the bank becomes immediately indebted to the trader. The bank's debt is a means of payment; it is credit money. It is clear addition to the amount of the means of payment in the community. The bank does not lend money. The borrower can, if he pleases, take out the whole amount of the loan in money. He is in that respect in the same position as any other depositor. But like other depositors he is likely in practice to use credit for all major payments and

only to draw out money as and when needed for minor payments.

Kerwin J., then continued at pp. 128–9 D.L.R. p. 156 S.C.R.:

> It is not necessary to refer to the various schools of economists with their divergent views as to the extent to which banks create credit or as to the wisdom or otherwise of a state empowering such institutions to do so. It suffices that by current common understanding a business transaction whereby credit is created, issued, lent, provided or dealt in by means of bookkeeping entries is considered to be part of the business of banking as it has been practised and developed. It is well known that in addition to creating credit banks also issue, lend, provide and deal in credit by means of bookkeeping entries.

The type of provincial legislation found *ultra vires* in the *Alberta Statutes Reference* would still be invalidated today, but whether the same reasons would all be relied upon is a matter of doubt, for economic theory has evolved. Be that as it may, there were other reasons of a more classical type from a legal point of view why Bill No. 8, "An Act to Amend and Consolidate the Credit of Alberta Regulation Act", was found *ultra vires*: it was a licensing statute; it depended upon machinery created by the *Alberta Social Credit Act* which was found *ultra vires*, and it was ancillary to the latter. By themselves, these reasons which were also invoked by Duff C.J.C., at pp. 97–8 D.L.R., pp. 122–3 S.C.R., sufficed to dispose of Bill No. 8 and I do not think that the other reasons are decisive of the case at bar. (It should be noted, however, that these other reasons commended themselves to Porter J.A., whose partly dissenting opinion to the effect that the *Treasury Branches Act*, R.S.A. 155, c. 344, was unconstitutional, was adopted by two members of this Court in *Breckenridge Speedway Ltd. v. The Queen* (1969), 9 D.L.R. (3d) 142, [1970] S.C.R. 175, 70 W.W.R. 481; the seven other members of the Court refrained from expressing any view on the question, and I do the same.)

(b) The Legal Point of View

Attempts to define banking in functional terms but from a strictly legal angle have been studied by C.C. Johnston, in "Judicial Comment on the Concept of 'Banking Business'", 2 *Osgoode Hall L.J.* 347 (1962). Typical of such attempts is the description of banking given by Richards J.A., for the majority of the Manitoba Court of Appeal in the *Bergethaler*

Waisenamt case, *supra*, at pp. 773–4 D.L.R., pp. 328–9 W.W.R.:

> Expert opinion was not given in evidence in this case as to what is banking business, but it is common knowledge that during the period of the corporation's operations banking did include the following:
> 1. Receiving money on deposit from its customers.
> 2. Paying a customer's cheques or drafts on it to the amount on deposit by such customer, and holding Dominion Government and Bank notes and coin for such purpose.
> 3. Paying interest by agreement on deposits.
> 4. Discounting commercial paper for its customers.
> 5. Dealing in exchange and in gold and silver coin and bullion.
> 6. Collecting notes and drafts deposited.
> 7. Arranging credits for itself with banks in other towns, cities and countries.
> 8. Selling its drafts or cheques on other banks and banking correspondents.
> 9. Issuing letters of credit.
> 10. Lending money to its customers:
>   (a) on the customers' notes;
>   (b) by way of overdraft;
>   (c) on bonds, shares and other securities.
>
> The business of a Canadian Chartered bank is wider still because of the statutory rights and powers given to a bank under the provisions of the *Bank Act*.

But Richards J.A., added the following comment at p. 776 D.L.R., p. 332 W.W.R.:

> The business carried on by most banks includes the totality of the functions I have enumerated, but, of course, a banking business can be carried on without performing all of them and most corporations and individuals engaged in a financial business of any kind are required to carry on or perform some of them, and it does not follow from the fact that banks perform them that every exercise of one or more of the functions is a form of banking.

I agree with this comment.

Take long term borrowing, by way of term deposits or otherwise. It was held by the English Court of Appeal in *United Dominions Trust Ltd. v. Kirkwood*, [1966] 1 All E.R. 968, that the acceptance of money against deposit receipts, usually in sums ranging between £5,000 and £1,000,000 for definite periods of three; six or nine months, was not an aspect of the business of banking. Under this standard, Pioneer Trust's borrowing by way of guaranteed investment certificates is not a banking activity although it is widely practised by chartered banks and other types of institutions. I should think it is an activity that may be appropriate for savings banks but it could not be said that, on that account, they should have a monopoly thereon.

The hard core of banking is usually what lawyers will try to circumscribe. The issuance of banknotes intended for circulation would probably have been considered as part of that core in earlier days when the issuance of banknotes had not become the monopoly of the central bank: it is significant in this regard that in s. 91(15) of the Constitution, legislative jurisdiction over the issue of paper money is linked with jurisdiction over banking and the incorporation of banks. At the present day in England, the features which, according to most, are characteristic of the business of bankers have been described as follows by Lord Denning, M.R., in the *United Dominion Trust* case, at p. 975:

> ... (i) they accept money from, and collect cheques for, their customers and place them to their credit; (ii) they honour cheques or orders drawn on them by their customers when presented for payment and debit their customers accordingly. These two characteristics carry with them also a third, namely, (iii) they keep current accounts, or something of that nature, in their books in which the credits and debits are entered.
>
> Those three characteristics are much the same as those stated in *Paget's Law of Banking* (6th Edn.) (1961), p. 8:
>
>> No-one and nobody, corporate or otherwise, can be a 'banker' who does not (i) take current accounts; (ii) pay cheques drawn on himself; (iii) collect cheques for his customers.

It will be noticed that this statement links up with the banking concept of Duff C.J.C., and Kerwin J., in the *Alberta Statutes Reference* stripped from its economic aspect relating to credit. (See also *Re District Savings Bank Ltd., Ex p. Coe* (1861), 3 De G.F.&J. 335, 45 E.R. 907 at p. 909; *Re Bottomgate Industrial Co-op. Society* (1891), 65 L.T. 712; *Bank of Chettinad Ltd. of Colombo v. Income Tax Com'r of Colombo*, [1948] A.C. 378. In *Re Dominion Trust Co.*, [1918] 3 W.W.R. 1023, 26 B.C.R. 339, and *La Caisse Populaire Notre Dame Ltée v. Moyen* (1967), 61 D.L.R. (2d) 118, 59 W.W.R. 129, single Judges took the view that a provincial trust company and a provincial credit union could validly provide chequing facilities to their depositors.)

Assuming that no corporation can be said to be in the banking business unless it provides its deposi-tors with chequing privileges, it does not follow that these activities are exclusive to the business of banking. I agree, in this respect with what Coyne J.A., said in the *Bergethaler Waisenamt* case, *supra*, at pp. 778–9 D.L.R., p. 334 W.W.R., that:

> Chequing privileges accorded depositors ... are characteristic of, and perhaps essential to, banking. But even that does not make them exclusive rights of bankers, even in the absence of prohibition by statute against others carrying them on.

On the whole, I do not think that it is possible, at least for the purpose of this case, to define banking in purely functional terms.

6. The Formal and Institutional Tests

In the United Kingdom, the peculiar status of bankers, their importance at the centre of the financial community, the expectation of the public that it can grant them implicit and utmost confidence have led, given the uncertainty of substantive tests, to various methods to identify or recognize banks and banking by way of formal and institutional means.

Two of these means which are closely connected with each other, have been elaborated in the cases. The first is the holding out of one-self as a banker. The second is one's reputation as a banker. The holding out is evidently aimed at the acquisition of the reputation.

A banker "'must hold himself out as a banker and the public take him as such', assuming 'openly, avowedly and notoriously the character of a banker'": *Stafford v. Henry* (1850), 12 Ir. Eq. 400, quoted by Coyne J.A., in the *Bergethaler Waisenamt* case, at p. 779 D.L.R., p. 335 W.W.R.

In *Re Shields*, [1901] 1 I.R. 172, FitzGibbon L.J., wrote at p. 197:

> In all his dealings with the public, Shields held his firm out as "Bankers." He so described himself for the purpose of inducing custom and giving dignity to his operations. It may be conceded that people who are not bankers, cannot make themselves so by adopting the name.... But the name was assumed by Shields, and the Bank of Ireland accepted it as a truthful designation.... From beginning to end they treated him as a banker. That being so, it is only a question of fact, and one upon which the presumption is in the affirmative, whether there is reasonable evidence to warrant the conclusion that Shields was what he professed to be, and what the Bank of Ireland took him to be — namely a "Banker".

In the *United Dominions Trust* case, Lord Denning, M.R., held that the United Dominions Trust, although it had not succeeded in proving that its business, as distinct from its reputation, was effectively a banking business, had discharged the onus of proving that it was a banker because it had established that for a long period of years it had been accepted as having the status of a banker by the banking community and government departments. Harman L.J., dissented from that view on the ground that reputation alone was not enough and that there had to be some performance behind it. Diplock L.J., as he then was, agreed in the result with Lord Denning, with some hesitation, because he could not infer that the witnesses who had established the reputation of United Dominions Trust as a banker had been mistaken as to the substantive factors to be taken into consideration.

In Canada, Parliament has recognized the importance of the holding out test and, in order to prevent individuals or institutions which are not banks from acquiring the reputation of being in the banking business, has enacted s. 157(1) of the *Bank Act*:

> **157.**(1) Every person who, in any language, uses the word "bank", "banker" or "banking", either alone or in combination with other words, or any word or words of import equivalent thereto, to indicate or describe his business in Canada or any part of his business in Canada without being authorized so to do by this or any other Act, is guilty of an offence against this Act.

Pioneer Trust is not authorized by the *Bank Act* nor any other Act to use the forbidden words to describe its business or any part thereof including its chequing account service. If Parliament, which is the competent authority in the matter, wishes to prevent members of the public from mistaking any part of the business of Pioneer Trust and other trust companies for a banking business, it seems to me that it is because Parliament considers that it is *not* a banking business. I am also of the view that the opinion of Parliament should be considered as decisive in this case.

I am confirmed in this view by the legislative technique used by Parliament in the *Bank Act* to define a chartered bank (which consists in a list of specific institutions designated by name), together with the definition of a bank for the purposes of every enactment in s. 28 of the *Interpretation Act*, quoted above, and s. 20(3) of the same Act which provides:

> **20.**(3) No corporation shall be deemed to be authorized to carry on the business of banking unless such power is expressly conferred upon it by the enactment establishing the corporation.

This last provision practically suffices by itself to dispose of the issue. Pioneer Trust was established under the *Trust Companies Act*, no provision of which expressly authorizes it to carry on the business of banking. If any part of Pioneer Trust's business is banking business, then it is unauthorized and ought not to be taken into consideration to remove Pioneer Trust from the jurisdiction of the Board and bring it under the jurisdiction of the Canada Labour Relations Board as a federal business. If on the other hand Pioneer Trust's business is authorized business, it must be because it is deemed not to be banking business.

Nobody, let alone Pioneer Trust, has suggested that its business is unauthorized. The only part of its business which, in this respect, appears to raise a problem is the taking of deposits, coupled with chequing privileges.

Pioneer Trust is given the following powers by s. 63(a), (e) and (k) of the *Trust Companies Act*:

> **63.** The company may
> (a) receive money in trust for the purposes herein specified, and invest and accumulate it at such lawful rates of interest as may be obtained therefor;
>
> ...
>
> (e) guarantee repayment of the principal or payment of the interest or both of any moneys entrusted to the company for investment, on such terms and conditions as are agreed upon;
>
> ...
>
> (k) receive money on deposit in trust and allow interest thereon from the time of deposit at such rate as may be agreed upon and advance moneys to protect any estate, trust or property entrusted to it as aforesaid, and charge lawful interest upon any such advances, but nothing herein shall be held either to restrict or to extend the powers of the company as trustee or agent under the terms of any trust or agency that may be conferred upon it;

The powers given by s. 63(a) are of the traditional fiduciary type whereas those given by s. 63(e) and (k) are not of that type: they contemplate the guarantee of repayment by the company of moneys entrusted to it for investment and the allowing of interest on deposits in trust at such rate as may be agreed upon. The latter type of powers facilitates the development between a trust company and its depositor of a legal relationship which bears some resemblance with that between a bank and its depositor. To that extent, Professor Hogg's remark, quoted above, is justified. But the point is that these powers, which must be deemed not to be banking powers, are specifically given to Pioneer Trust by Parliament.

I fail to see what is to prevent Pioneer Trust from concluding with the depositor an agreement under which the money so deposited shall be repayable on demand or short notice (see s. 67 of the *Trust Companies Act*) to the depositor or to some third party if, by way of an appropriate instrument, the trust company is requested so to do by the depositor. I also fail to see what is to prevent a trust company from undertaking to collect negotiable instruments on behalf of its depositor and place them to his credit. There is nothing against public policy in such undertakings, and, so far as I know, no statutory prohibition in the *Bank Act*, the *Bills of Exchange Act* or any other Act. It would take a provision much more specific than s. 20(3) of the *Interpretation Act* to render such agreements unlawful.

I accept the submission made on behalf of the Attorney-General for New Brunswick that, to resolve the issue, we should adopt an institutional approach. Such an approach, it is true, emphasizes formal tests. But, in the case at bar, these tests are bolstered by the consideration of the substantive factors referred to above. I agree with the contention which I quote from the factum of the Attorney-General for New Brunswick that:

> "Banking" involves a set of interrelated financial activities carried out by an institution that operates under the nomenclature and terms of incorporation which clearly identify it as having the distinctive institutional character of a bank.

There are several reasons for adopting such an approach.

First, it is the approach taken by Parliament, and federal legislation may properly be considered as an aid to constitutional interpretation: *Citizens Ins. Co. of Canada v. Parsons, supra*, at p. 116.

Second, it is an approach which was also taken by the Courts: in most instances where provincial legislation was found *ultra vires* on the ground that it impinged upon exclusive federal authority over banking, there has also been an attempt to regulate or to interfere with the business of established banks: the *Alberta Bank Taxation* case, *supra*; the *Bank Deposits* case; *supra*; *Reference re Alberta Bill of Rights Act, A.-G. Alta. v. A.-G. Can. et al.*, [1947] 4 D.L.R. 1, [1947] A.C. 503, [1947] 2 W.W.R. 401 (the *Alberta Bill of Rights* case).

Third, it is an approach which is particularly appropriate in a case where what has to be decided is whether a given institution falls within the concept of banking as a business, and not whether a legislative enactment is constitutionally depending on its relationship to banking within the meaning of s. 91(15) of the Constitution. The characterization of legislation and the characterization of a business are not identical processes. Legislation, for instance, may be divisible whereas a business as a going concern is indivisible and must stand or fall as a whole on one side of the constitutional line or the other. The concept of banking as a business and the meaning of the word "banking" in s. 91(15) are not necessarily co-extensive; the meaning of "banking" in the section might very well be wider than the concept of banking as a business. Some of the reasons for such distinction have been explained by Latham C.J., in *Commonwealth of Australia v. Bank of New South Wales* (1948), 76 C.L.R. 1 (the *Australian Banking* case) at p. 195:

> I agree with the argument of the plaintiffs that the acquisition of a share in a bank by any person (whether a bank or not) is not itself a banking operation, and similarly that the purchase by any person, whether a bank or not, of assets from a bank is not itself a banking operation and that the taking over of the business of another bank probably would not be described as a banking "transaction". But a law which controls such matters is a law dealing with the business of banking, because such matters affect the conduct and control of the business and are things which may be done from time to time in the course of the business of banking, although they are not banking transactions between a banker and a customer. It is easy to give examples of laws which are laws having a most immediate relation to banking and which are therefore laws with respect to banking, though they do not deal with banker-customer relations as such. Among such laws would be a law requiring a bank to have a certain minimum capital or to maintain a percentage of uncalled capital, or a law prescribing the persons who may be allowed to hold bank shares, e.g. excluding bankrupts, or a law preventing banks in certain circumstances from disposing of their assets, or a law prescribing permissible forms of investment by banks. A law dealing with the management and staffing of banks would be a law relating to essential elements in the business of banking though not dealing with any transactions between any bank and any customer.

Judicial opinions on the constitutional meaning of the word "banking" in Australia should carry some weight in Canada because s. 51(xiii) of the *Commonwealth of Australia Constitution, 1900* (63 & 64 Vict.), c. 12 (U.K.), is, except for a reference to state banking, identical to s. 91(15) of the Canadian Constitution and, as was noted by some Australian Judges, seems to have been inspired by the latter. It reads:

> (xiii) Banking, other than State banking; also State banking extending beyond the limits of the State concerned, the incorporation of banks, and the issue of paper money;

Latham C.J., was dissenting in part in the *Australian Banking* case but, more than his views on the nature of banking, one of the main reasons for his partial dissent would appear to have been his interpretation of another provision of the Australian Constitution, s. 92, relating to the freedom of trade, commerce and intercourse among the States, of which there is no exact counterpart in the Canadian Constitution. The majority view on one of the issues raised in the *Australian Banking* case was upheld in an opinion of the Judicial Committee: [1950] A.C. 235.

One of the earliest pronouncements on the meaning of banking in Canadian constitutional law is to be found in *Tennant v. Union Bank of Canada*, [1894] A.C. 31, where Lord Watson wrote, at p. 46, that "banking" is "an expression which is wide enough to embrace every transaction coming within the legitimate business of a banker".

This statement was again referred to in more recent times: the *Bank Deposits* case, *supra*, at p. 85 D.L.R., p. 42 A.C., and the *Alberta Bill of Rights* case, *supra*, at p. 10 D.L.R., at p. 517 A.C.

Appellants have relied upon that expression of opinion but I do not think it helps them. It cannot be read literally for it would then mean, for instance, that the borrowing of money or the lending of money, with or without security, which come within the legitimate business of a great many other types of institutions as well as of individuals, would, in every respect, fall under the exclusive legislative competence of Parliament. Such a result was never intended. But Lord Watson was then speaking of the federal legislative authority with respect to institutions which had been chartered as banks and his statement makes sense if understood in institutional terms. Take the business of money-lending on the security of mortgages. This operation was not previously open to banks and, because of the problem of liquidity, would have frightened nineteenth century bankers. That it became open to banks did not mean that it was transformed into a banking operation so that all the institutions such as loan companies, trust companies like Pioneer Trust and individuals who were heavily engaged in this type of transactions

found themselves suddenly plunged into the banking business. It could not be contended either that the provincial Legislatures had lost their jurisdiction over the law of mortgages, mortgage companies and their employees. It would be more accurate to say that it was the banks which were beginning a non-banking type of activity, but it is a well established principle that federal undertakings may be empowered by Parliament to engage in business under provincial jurisdiction: the *Empress Hotel* case, *supra*; the *Jasper Park Lodge* case, *supra*.

The same comments and qualifications might apply to other loans made by banks.

7. The Objection of the Exclusiveness Rule

Only one serious objection to the institutional approach can be raised and it has been raised by Counsel for the Attorney-General of Canada. It is based on the exclusiveness of federal legislative powers relating to banking and the incorporation of banks. It was contended that provincial legislative jurisdiction and the extent and applicability of provincial legislation cannot depend on the abstinence of Parliament from legislating to the full limit of its exclusive powers. The *Union Colliery and Commission du Salaire Minimum* cases, both *supra*, were relied upon.

I do not think this objection is valid in this case.

Legislative jurisdiction involves certain powers of definition which are not unlimited but which, depending on the particular manner in which they are exercised, may affect other jurisdictional fields.

For instance, Parliament has exclusive legislative jurisdiction over the establishment, maintenance, and management of penitentiaries under s. 91(28) of the Constitution, and each Province has exclusive legislative jurisdiction over the establishment, maintenance and management of public and reformatory prisons in and for the Province, under s. 92(6). At present the line of demarcation between the two appears to depend in part upon federal legislation such as s. 659 [am. 1974-75-76, c. 93, s. 79; 1976-77, c. 53, s. 13] of the *Criminal Code*.

Another example is provided by the legal status of the Eskimo inhabitants of Quebec. They are not Indians under the *Indian Act*, R.S.C. 1970, c. I-6; s. 4(1), but they are Indians within the contemplation of s. 91(24) of the Constitution: *Re Eskimos*, [1939] 2 D.L.R. 417, [1939] S.C.R. 104 *sub nom. Reference as to whether "Indians" in s. 91(24) of the B.N.A. Act includes Eskimo inhabitants of Quebec.* Should Parliament bring them under the *Indian Act*, provincial laws relating to descent of property and to testamentary matters would cease to apply to them and be replaced by the provisions of the *Indian Act* relating thereto.

Parliament having chosen to exercise its jurisdiction over banking and the incorporation of banks from an institutional aspect rather than in functional terms, as was perhaps unavoidable, did not necessarily exhaust its exclusive jurisdiction; but it left institutions which it did not characterize as being in the banking business to the operation of provincial labour laws.

8. Conclusion

To summarize and conclude:

The relationship of Pioneer Trust with its customers is of a fiduciary nature and several of its operations appertain to the business of a trust company. A great many of its other operations are not characteristic of the banking business although they are also carried on by chartered banks. The one operation carried on by Pioneer Trust which may be characteristic of the banking business, the chequing account service, is not exclusive to the business of banking. And finally, Parliament, which is the competent constitutional authority in matters of banks and banking, considers that Pioneer Trust is not a bank and that its business is not the banking business. Hence, Pioneer Trust is not in the business of banking.

The appeal should be dismissed with costs. There should be no order as to cost for or against the intervenors.

Appeal dismissed.

(f) *Bank of Montreal v. Hall*[†]

[La FOREST J.:]

The principal issue in this appeal is whether a security interest created pursuant to ss. 178 and 179 of the *Bank Act*, R.S.C. 1985, c. B-1, may constitutionally be subjected to the procedures for enforcement of security interests prescribed by the Saskatchewan *Limitation of Civil Rights Act*, R.S.S. 1978, c. L-16. It also raises the constitutional validity of the relevant provisions of both the federal and provincial Acts.

FACTS

The respondent, Arthur Hall, a farmer in Saskatchewan, contracted loans from the appellant Bank of Montreal in the early 1980s. As collateral, Mr. Hall granted two mortgages on his real property in favour of the bank. The loans were also secured by a security interest in a piece of farm machinery, a 1980 Versatile swather, pursuant to s. 88 of the *Bank Act*, R.S.C. 1970, c. B-1, subsequently s. 178 of the *Banks and Banking Law Revision Act, 1980*, S.C. 1980-81-82-83, c. 40, now s. 178 of the *Bank Act*, R.S.C. 1985, c. B-1.

Mr. Hall defaulted on his loan, and in August 1984, the bank, pursuant to the provisions of the *Bank Act*, seized the swather and commenced an action to enforce its real property mortgage loan agreement. By way of defence to the foreclosure proceedings, Mr. Hall alleged that the bank had not served the notice of intention to seize required under the provisions of the *Limitation of Civil Rights Act* and accordingly sought to have the foreclosure proceedings dismissed. He also brought an action for cancellation of the security agreement and to recover all moneys paid thereon as provided by this Act. The Bank of Montreal countered by alleging that it was not subject to the Act in respect of proceedings taken under the *Bank Act*.

In November, 1985, the parties, by notice of motion filed before the Court of Queen's Bench for Saskatchewan, applied for a determination of the question whether the plaintiff, as a chartered bank, was required to comply with the *Limitation of Civil Rights Act* in enforcing a security interest under the *Bank Act*.

. . . .

---

† (1990), 65 D.L.R. (4th) 361 (S.C.C.).

JUDICIAL HISTORY

. . . .

The Appeal to This Court

Leave to appeal to this court was then sought and granted, and the following constitutional questions were stated:

1. Are ss. 19 to 36 of *The Limitation of Civil Rights Act*, R.S.S. 1978, c. L-16, *ultra vires* the Legislature of Saskatchewan in whole or in part?
2. Are ss. 178 and 179 of the *Banks and Banking Law Revision Act*, S.C. 1980-81-82-83, c. 40, *ultra vires* the Parliament of Canada in whole or in part?
3. Do ss. 178 and 179 of the *Banks and Banking Laws Revision Act*, S.C. 1980-81-82-83, c. 40, conflict with ss. 19 to 36 of *The Limitation of Civil Rights Act*, R.S.S. 1978, c. L-16, so as to render inoperative ss. 19 to 36 in respect of security taken pursuant to s. 178 by a chartered bank?

The Attorneys-General of Canada, New Brunswick and Saskatchewan intervened. Those of Ontario, Quebec, Manitoba and British Columbia also intervened but later withdrew. As well, the National Farmers Union applied for and was granted leave to intervene.

Sections 19 to 36 of the *Limitation of Civil Rights Act*

Apart from the possible conflict with federal legislation (a matter I shall deal with later), no argument was made in the courts below or in this court challenging the constitutionality of ss. 19 to 36 of the *Limitation of Civil Rights Act* and, in my view, no such challenge could be seriously mounted. It is not necessary to reproduce these provisions here. Suffice it to say that they confer on a debtor the right to seek court supervision of the realization of a secured debt, and thus may have the effect of suspending the right of a secured creditor to realize on its security. They allow a debtor an opportunity to redeem or reinstate a security agreement. In particular, s. 21 requires a secured creditor to give notice to the debtor of its intention to take possession of secured property, and if it fails to do so, the security agreement (by s. 27) is terminated and the debtor is released from all liability under the agreement and is entitled to recover any moneys already paid. I have

no difficulty holding, questions of paramountcy apart, that such legislation may fairly be said to come within property and civil rights in the province, and thus *intra vires* the provincial legislature: see *Abitibi Power & Paper Co. v. Montreal Trust Co.*, [1943] 4 D.L.R. 1, [1943] A.C. 536, [1943] 3 W.W.R. 33 (P.C.), and *Canada Trust Co. v. Hanson*, [1950] 1 D.L.R. 375, [1949] O.W.N. 803, 30 C.B.R. 126 (C.A.); affirmed [1951], D.L.R. 402, [1951] S.C.R. 366, 31 C.B.R. 155.

Sections 178 and 179 of the *Banks and Banking Law Revision Act, 1980*

The analysis of the question whether ss. 178 and 179 of the *Bank Act* are in any way *ultra vires* the Parliament of Canada begins with an examination of the federal banking power itself, s. 91(15) of the *Constitution Act, 1867*, which reads as follows:

> **91.** ... the exclusive Legislative Authority of the Parliament of Canada extends to all Matters coming within the Classes of Subjects next herein-after enumerated; that is to say, —
>
> ...
>
> 15. Banking, Incorporation of Banks, and the Issue of Paper Money.

The *locus classicus* as to the meaning of this provision is, of course, the pronouncement of Lord Watson in *Tennant v. Union Bank of Canada*, [1894] A.C. 31, where the Privy Council was called upon to consider "whether warehouse receipts, taken in security by a bank in the course of the business of banking" are matters falling within the provision. In the course of his judgment, Lord Watson, at p. 46, gave a broad interpretation of the federal banking power in the following passage:

> The legislative authority conferred by these words is not confined to the mere constitution of corporate bodies with the privilege of carrying on the business of bankers. It extends to the issue of paper currency, which necessarily means the creation of a species of personal property carrying with it rights and privileges which the law of the province does not, and cannot, attach to it. It also comprehends "banking," an expression which is wide enough to embrace every transaction coming within the legitimate business of a banker.

Lord Watson's pronouncement echoes the view taken by this court in *Merchants' Bank of Canada v. Smith*, [1884] 8 S.C.R. 512, where, at p. 541, Henry J. held that everything necessarily connected with banking fell within the powers of Parliament even though they might interfere, in some respects, with property and civil rights.

Given the broad sweep of his definition of banking, it was hardly necessary for Lord Watson to venture an exhaustive enumeration of the actual practices that fell within the ambit of the "legitimate business of a banker". But in remarks with immediate relevance to this case, he, again at p. 46, did make it clear that he took for granted that the business of banking would necessarily embrace the "lending of money on the security of goods, or of documents representing the property of goods".

The respondent did not directly challenge this proposition, but sought to qualify it somewhat. He conceded, rightly in my view, that the federal banking power extends to allowing Parliament to define a security interest and to permit borrowing on the strength of that interest. He submitted, however, that Parliament could not, pursuant to this power, legislate with respect to the requirements relating to the realization and enforcement of that interest. Such provisions, he argued, would trench on the exclusive jurisdiction of the provinces respecting property and civil rights.

Consideration of this proposition logically begins with a general outline of the nature of the ss. 178 and 179 security interest itself. In essence, as is apparent from s. 178(1)(a) to (j), the security interest in question here is designed to allow the banks to "lend money and make advances" to certain classes of borrowers on the security of certain specified goods, comprehensively defined in paras. (a) to (j), and including loans and advances "to any farmer for the purchase of agricultural implements, on the security of such agricultural implements".

By s. 178(2), a bank may take security in property owned by the borrower at the time of the loan transaction, and any property acquired during the pendency of the security agreement. The rights and powers of the bank with respect to the secured property are set out in s. 178(2)(c). By the terms of s. 178(2)(c), these rights and powers are stated to be "the same rights and powers as if the bank had acquired a warehouse receipt or bill of lading in which such property was described". These powers are defined, in turn, in s. 186 of the Act where it is specified that any warehouse receipt or bill acquired by a bank as security for the payment of a debt, vests in the bank all the right and title to goods, wares and merchandise covered by the holder or owner thereof.

The nature of the rights and powers vested in the bank by the delivery of the document giving the security interest has been the object of some debate.

Argument has centred on whether the security interest should be likened to a pledge or bailment, or whether it is more in the nature of a chattel mortgage. I find the most precise description of this interest to be that given by Professor Moull in his article "Security Under Sections 177 and 178 of the Bank Act" (1986), 65 Can. Bar Rev. 242, at p. 251. Professor Moull, correctly, in my view, stresses that the effect of the interest is to vest title to the property in question in the bank when the security interest is taken out. He states, at p. 251:

> The result, then, is that a bank taking security under section 178 effectively acquires legal title to the borrower's interest in the present and after-acquired property assigned to it by the borrower. The bank's interest attaches to the assigned property when the security is given or the property is acquired by the borrower and remains attached until released by the bank, despite changes in the attributes or composition of the assigned property. The borrower retains an equitable right of redemption, of course, but the bank effectively acquires legal title to whatever rights the borrower holds in the assigned property from time to time.

Section 179(4) sets out the general powers of the bank in the event of non-payment of the loan or advance secured by the property assigned to it by s. 178. In a word, this section authorizes the bank to sell all or any part of that property and provides that the proceeds of that sale shall be applied against the debt in question. These provisions complement the bank's right under s. 178(3) to take possession of secured property on default.

. . . .

THE CASES

The above considerations establish, to my satisfaction, that the s. 178 security interest, which originated as a policy response to structural deficiencies in the lending regimes of the nascent Canadian economy, has, since its inception, played a primordial role in facilitating access to capital by several groups that play a key role in the national economy. One's instinctive reaction is that the federal banking power should extend to allowing Parliament to provide, on a nation-wide basis, for just such an innovative form of financing. An examination of the judicial response to the creation of the s. 178 security confirms this view. The courts have consistently taken the position that the creation of the s. 178 security interest, and the definition of the rights and obligations of the bank and its borrowers pursuant to that interest, fall squarely within the limits of the federal banking power and is, accordingly, constitutionally valid. I turn to the decisions of this court that bear on the matter.

The historical considerations I have touched on earlier have clearly left their mark on the following excerpts from the reasons of Mignault J. in *Landry Pulpwood Co. v. Banque Canadienne Nationale*, [1928] 1 D.L.R. 493, [1927] S.C.R. 605. In *Landry*, this court addressed the question whether the appellant could acquire ownership of a quantity of pulpwood "purchased" after the owner of the same had pledged it to the bank as security for a s. 88 loan, the predecessor to ss. 178 and 179. Mignault J., at p. 499, commented on the purpose behind the section:

> As I read s. 88, a bank, for its advances, may acquire a lien on the products of the forest (as defined) or on goods, wares and merchandise (also as defined) to be manufactured, or in process of manufacture, although the finished product will come into existence only after the process of manufacture is completed.
>
> The present case affords an apt illustration of the object Parliament undoubtedly had in view when it enacted section 88, *this object being to come to the assistance both of the manufacturer of goods, and the bank which lends him money for the purposes of his business.* Thus the owner of a timber license proposes to go into the forest, to cut down the trees and transform them into what is commercially known as pulpwood. Before the pulpwood is produced in its commercial form, considerable expense is necessary to cut the trees, peel off the bark and saw them into the required lengths. The manufacturer of pulpwood therefore requires financial assistance from the outset, and unless he can give the bank that assists him a lien on the finished product, although not then in existence, his business cannot be carried on. [Emphasis added.]

Noting that by s. 88(7) of the *Bank Act* the security conferred on the bank the same rights and powers in respect of the products as if it had acquired them by virtue of a warehouse receipt, Mignault J. concluded, at p. 500:

> There is no doubt, however, that we must look solely to the Bank Act to determine the effect of a lien acquired by a bank by virtue of s. 88.

In *Royal Bank of Canada v. Workmen's Compensation Board of Nova Scotia*, [1936] 4 D.L.R. 9, [1936] S.C.R. 560, this court again had occasion to deal with the provision. The issue there was far removed from that of the instant case, namely the question whether property assigned to a bank under

a s. 88 security was meant to be exempt from provincial taxes exacted pursuant to s. 92(2) of the *British North America Act, 1867*, now the *Constitution Act, 1867*. It is important to note, however, that in rejecting that proposition this court, in express terms, affirmed that the creation of a s. 88 security was *intra vires* the jurisdiction of Parliament. Crocket J. held at p. 12:

> While we have no doubt that the provisions of s. 88 the Bank Act are provisions which strictly relate to banking, and are therefore within the competency of the Dominion of Parliament under s. 91(15), we are of opinion that in enacting them Parliament did not intend to remove any property, which might be assigned to a bank by way of security thereunder, from the operation of any statute enacted by the Legislature of the Province, in which the property is situated, in the legitimate exercise of its power in relation to direct taxation for provincial purposes under s. 92(2).

In *Royal Bank of Canada v. Workmen's Compensation Board of Nova Scotia*, as in *Landry Pulpwood Co. v. Banque Canadienne Nationale*, this court again took pains to underline that the s. 88 security interest, in and of itself, conferred on the bank the same rights and powers in respect of the goods pledged as if it had acquired them by virtue of a warehouse receipt. At p. 15, Davis J. had this to say:

> Section 88 set up by the Bank Act enables manufacturers, who desire to obtain large loans from their bankers in order to carry on their industrial activities, to give to the bank a special and convenient form of security for the bank's protection in the large banking transactions necessary in the carrying on of industry throughout the country. Until the moneys are repaid, the bank is the legal owner of the goods but sale before default is prohibited and provision is made for the manufacturer regaining title upon repayment. To say that Parliament did not use language to expressly provide that the bank shall have a first lien on the goods is beside the mark. The bank acquires ownership in the goods by the statute.

In *Re Canadian Western Millwork Ltd.; Flintoft v. Royal Bank of Canada* (1964), 47 D.L.R. (2d) 141, [1964] S.C.R. 631, 49 W.W.R. 30, this court reiterated the point. The dispute in *Flintoft v. Royal Bank of Canada* centred on the claims of a trustee in bankruptcy to the unregistered book debts of a borrower who had sold goods covered by a security under s. 88 of the *Bank Act*. The court gave short shrift to the submission that a lack of timely registration of the book debts on the part of the bank would entitle the trustee to collect them for adminis-tration under the *Bankruptcy Act*. Judson J., noting that ss. 88(2) and 86(2) of the *Bank Act* denied the property rights of the bank in the pledged goods so as to give a bank the same rights and powers as if it had acquired a warehouse receipt or bill of lading in which the property was described, went on to com-ment, at p. 144:

> Section 88 is a unique form of security. I know of no other jurisdiction where it exists. It permits certain classes of persons not of a custodier character, in this case a manufacturer, to give security on their own goods with the conse-quences above defined. Notwithstanding this, with the consent of the bank, the one who gives the security sells in the ordinary course of business and gives a good title to purchasers from him. But this does not mean that he owns the book debts when he has sold the goods. To me the fallacy in the dissenting reasons is the assump-tion that there is ownership of the book debts in the bank's customer once the goods have been sold and that the bank can only recover these book debts if it is the assignee of them.

An apt summary of the conclusions that flow from the above authorities is to be found in the remarks of Muldoon J. in *Canadian Imperial Bank of Commerce v. R.* (1984), 52 C.B.R. (N.S.) 145 (F.C.T.D.). Muldoon J., citing the decision of this court in *Flintoft v. Royal Bank of Canada* as a con-clusive starting point for a determination of the "effect and force of the s. 178 security", stated at p. 159 of his judgment:

> In the interpretation of the Bank Act security enunciated by the Supreme Court of Canada and latterly by Grant D.J., one can appreciate the great commercial utility and overriding impor-tance which is inherent in Parliament's creation of that security. *The bank obtains and may assert its right to the goods and their proceeds against the world, except as only Parliament itself may reduce or modify those rights.* [Emphasis added.]

The case law thus fully supports the conclusion that Parliament, in the exercise of its power over banking, can both create the ss. 178 and 179 security interest *qua* interest, and define the rights and obli-gations of the bank and its borrowers pursuant to that interest. The reiteration in these cases of the point that the rights, duties and obligations of credi-tor and debtor are to be determined solely be refer-ence to the *Bank Act* cannot be reconciled with the respondent's position that there has yet to be a pro-nouncement on the constitutional validity of the enforcement provisions of the *Bank Act* security

interest. In truth, however, what I think the respon-dent really sought was a re-evaluation of the issues, and I shall now turn specifically to the arguments advanced by him.

As I noted earlier, the basis of the respondent's challenge to the constitutionality of ss. 178 and 179 is founded on the proposition that the federal bank-ing power cannot extend to allowing Parliament to define the procedures for realization and enforce-ment of a federal security interest. The submission that such legislation trenches on the provinces' juris-diction in property and civil rights invites closer scru-tiny of the decision of the Privy Council in *Tennant v. Union Bank of Canada*, upon which I touched briefly earlier.

The issue in *Tennant v. Union Bank of Canada* turned on a conflict between provisions of the *Bank Act* and provincial legislation, the Ontario *Mercantile Amendment Act*, R.S.O. 1887, c. 122. In provisions that will be immediately familiar from the above dis-cussion, the federal legislation essentially authorized a bank to acquire, and hold as security for loans, warehouse receipts which persons engaged in certain defined occupations might give in respect of their own goods. By the terms of the Act, any such receipt vested in the bank the right and title of the owner of the goods. The Ontario Act, which also dealt with warehouse receipts, incorporated a limita-tion not found in the federal Act. It provided that a warehouse receipt would only be effective to give right and title if the issuer was actually engaged in the business of a warehouseman. The Privy Council was called on to decide whether the federal legisla-tion was *ultra vires* inasmuch as it allowed for right and title to be conveyed in circumstances not recog-nized by provincial law.

The Privy Council rejected this proposition, Lord Watson, at p. 47, holding that the federal banking power extended to allowing Parliament to confer upon a bank privileges which had "the effect of modifying civil rights in the province". In rejecting the notion that the federal banking power could not be exercised so as to have the effect of modifying civil rights in the provinces, the Privy Council, we saw, followed the lead given by this court in *Mer-chants' Bank of Canada v. Smith, supra*. The princi-ples that emerged in *Merchants' Bank of Canada v. Smith* and *Tennant v. Union Bank of Canada* have never been placed in doubt, and, indeed, have been consistently repeated. I would point to the decisions of the Privy Council in *A.-G. Can. v. A.-G. Que.*, [1947] 1 D.L.R. 81, [1947] A.C. 33, [1946] 3 W.W.R. 659, and *Reference re Alberta Bill of Rights; A.-G. Alta. v. A.-G. Can.*, [1947] 4 D.L.R. 1, [1947] A.C.

503, [1947] 2 W.W.R. 401, as well as the decision of this court in *Reference re Alberta Legislation*, [1938] 2 D.L.R. 81, [1938] S.C.R. 100.

This unbroken line of authority is, of course, predicated on the basic premise that no practical effect could be given to the division of powers in the *Constitution Act, 1867* if Parliament were "absolutely debarred from trenching to any extent upon the matters assigned to the provincial legislature by sect. 92", to borrow the phrasing of Lord Watson in *Tennant v. Union Bank of Canada, supra*, at p. 45. Thus it is clear that there can be no hermetic division between banking as a generic activity and the domain covered by property and civil rights. A spillover effect in the operation of banking legislation on the general law of the provinces is inevitable. Viscount Simon makes this very point in his judgment in *A.-G. Alta. v. A.-G. Can., supra*, at pp. 9–10. The fact that a given aspect of federal banking legislation cannot operate without having an impact on property and civil rights in the provinces cannot ground a conclusion that that legislation is *ultra vires* as interfering with provincial law where the matter concerned constitutes an integral element of federal legislative competence: see *Montcalm Construction Inc. v. Minimum Wage Com'n* (1978), 93 D.L.R. (3d) 641 at pp. 652–53, (1979) 1 S.C.R. 754, 79 C.L.L.C. ¶14, 190, *per* Beetz J.

Turning to the particular facts of this case, there is no difficulty in defining the interference or modification of provincial law that flows from the operation of the federal legislation. Sections 178 and 179 of the *Bank Act* provide for a procedure for the realization and enforcement of a security interest that is distinct from, and in conflict with, the applicable provincial legislation. Thus, as was the case in *Tennant v. Union Bank of Canada*, federal law confers a "right and privilege" which is not recognized by provincial law. This raises the question whether this derogation from the general law of the province is intra vires Parliament. By application of the principles I have just touched on, the answer must turn on whether the legislative provisions in which Parliament has defined the manner in which a chartered bank may seize and realize on secured property can be considered legislation that Parliament may legitimately enact in the exercise of its banking power or, whether, on the contrary, it must be viewed as legislation which, in pith and substance, has taken on the true identity of valid provincial legislation.

The answer to this question takes one back to the policy reasons behind the creation of the ss. 178 and 179 security interest. As we saw earlier, the creation of this security interest was predicated on the pressing need to provide, on a nationwide basis, for a uniform security mechanism so as to facilitate access to capital by producers of primary resources and manufacturers. Such a security interest, precisely because it freed borrower and lender from the obligation to defer to a variety of provincial lending regimes, facilitated the ability of banks to realize on their collateral. This in turn translated into important benefits for the borrower: lending became less complicated and more affordable.

It follows that the definition of the precise manner in which a bank is permitted to realize on its s. 178 security interest cannot be viewed as a mere appendage or gloss upon the overall scheme of the Act. Rather, the provisions by which the bank, on assignment of the security interest, effectively acquires legal title to the secured property must be viewed as the very linchpin of the security interest that Parliament, in its wisdom, has created. Far from being incidental, these provisions are integral to, and inseparable from, the legislative scheme. To sunder from the *Bank Act* the legislative provisions defining realization, and, as a consequence, to purport to oblige the banks to contend with all the idiosyncrasies and variables of the various provincial schemes for realization and enforcement would, in my respectful view, be tantamount to defeating the specific purpose of Parliament in creating the *Bank Act* security interest.

In summary, I conclude that the definition of the exact manner in which a bank may realize on property secured pursuant to the s. 178 security interest is integral to the exercise by Parliament of the federal jurisdiction in the field of banking. The issue, in the final analysis, is really the same as that addressed by the Privy Council in *Tennant v. Union Bank of Canada*, and I think the same result must follow.

This conclusion is in no way undermined by the decision of this court in *Royal Bank of Canada v. Workmen's Compensation Board of Nova Scotia, supra*. I do not share the view of the majority in the Court of Appeal that that decision in any way cuts down the ambit of the Privy Council's decision in *Tennant v. Union Bank of Canada*. As reflected in the excerpt I have cited above, *Royal Bank of Canada v. Workmen's Compensation Board of Nova Scotia* simply settled that, in applying a provincial tax on property, a bank, as a property owner in respect of property assigned to it by operation of the *Bank Act* security, must be treated like any other property owner. That has nothing to do with the issue here. There is no logical nexus between the conclusion that a bank is to be treated as an ordinary taxpayer in respect of property to which it holds title by virtue of the operation of a federally defined security interest, and the conclusion that legislation defining that security interest is *ultra vires* to the extent that it interferes with or modifies provincial law. Davis J., in the following excerpt (at pp. 16–17), puts it beyond dispute that Parliament enjoys sole jurisdiction to define such a security interest:

> ... I have reached the conclusion that the goods in question, though owned by the bank subject to all the statutory rights and duties attached to the security, were property in the Province of Nova Scotia "used in or in connection with or produced in or by the industry with respect to which the employer (was) assessed though not owned by the employer" and became subject to the lien of the provincial statute the same as the goods of other owners.... *It is a provincial measure of general application for the benefit of workmen employed in industry in the Province and is not aimed at any impairment of bank securities though its operation may incidentally in certain cases have that effect.* [Emphasis added.]

Nor do I see how the respondent can place any reliance on the decision of this court in *Canadian Pioneer Management Ltd. v. Labour Relations Board of Saskatchewan* (1980), 107 D.L.R. (3d) 1, [1980] 1 S.C.R. 433, [1980] 3 W.W.R. 214. To begin with, that decision did not specifically address, nor was there need to address, the question whether a particular activity authorized by Parliament could be carried on by the banks as a legitimate exercise of the federal banking power. As I read *Canadian Pioneer Management Ltd. v. Labour Relations Board of Saskatchewan*, all it decided, for present purposes, was that the definition of what constitutes a bank is not to be gleaned merely from an examination of the particular activities carried on by an institution engaged in the provision of financial services, but rather depends on an institutional test, i.e., on the definition of a bank as fixed by Parliament. This is clear from the judgment of Laskin C.J.C., especially at pp. 5–6, and the comments of Beetz J., at p. 24 *et seq*.

It is true that Beetz J. at p. 26 went on to observe that the pronouncement of Lord Watson in *Tennant v. Union Bank of Canada, supra*, to the effect that "banking" was "wide enough to embrace every transaction within the legitimate business of a banker" could not be read literally. As he explained:

> It cannot be read literally for it would then mean, for instance, that the borrowing of money or the lending of money, with or without security, which come within the legitimate business of a great many other types of institutions as well

as of individuals, would, in every respect, fall under the exclusive legislative competence of Parliament. Such a result was never intended. *But Lord Watson was then speaking of the federal legislative authority with respect to institutions which had been chartered as banks and his statement makes sense if understood in institutional terms.* [Emphasis added.]

It is important to bear in mind that Beetz J.'s remarks were made with an eye to the transformation of the financial services industry that has taken place in this country: see also Laskin C.J.C., at p. 5. If at one time the lending of money in Canada was primarily the preserve of the chartered banks, this is, of course, no longer true. Myriad institutions now lend money on security and engage in the enforcement and realization of their loans, among them trust companies,. credit unions, finance companies, caisses populaires and department stores. The decision in *Canadian Pioneer Management Ltd. v. Labour Relations Board of Saskatchewan* addresses this reality and recognizes that it would be unrealistic to hold that federal jurisdiction extends to every entity engaged in transactions that might literally be described as coming within the "legitimate business of a banker". It is solely in this sense that the respondent is correct in its submission that not every transaction coming within the legitimate business of a banker is within the jurisdiction of Parliament.

This finding, however, cannot serve as a basis for the conclusion that a given aspect of the business of banking carried on by "institutions chartered as banks" no longer falls within the confines of the federal banking power. Such a result could only flow from a case in which the constitutionality of a given legislative provision bearing on banking had been specifically put in issue. The following remarks of Beetz J., in which he qualifies the limits to the application of this "institutional approach" to the definition of banking, make this abundantly clear, at p. 25:

> ... it is an approach which is particularly appropriate in a case where what has to be decided is whether a given institution falls within the concept of banking as a business, *and not whether a legislative enactment is constitutionally depending on its relationship to banking within the meaning of s. 91(15) of the Constitution. The characterization of legislation and the characterization of a business are not identical processes.* Legislation for instance, may be divisible whereas a business as a going concern is indivisible and must stand or fall as a whole on one side of the constitutional line or the other. The concept of banking as a business and the meaning of the word "banking"

in s. 91(15) are not necessarily co-extensive; the meaning of "banking" in the section might very well be wider than the concept of banking as a business. [Emphasis added.]

In short, *Canadian Pioneer Management Ltd. v. Labour Relations Board of Saskatchewan* simply has no bearing on the question of the constitutionality of the security interest created by ss. 178 and 179, and can, therefore, in no way be taken as being in contradiction with *Tennant v. Union Bank of Canada* and the other authorities canvassed earlier.

I would thus answer the second question in the negative. Based on the unbroken line of authority stretching back to the decision in *Tennant v. Union Bank of Canada*, I take it to be beyond dispute that the federal banking power empowers Parliament to create an innovative form of financing and to define, in a comprehensive and exclusive manner, the rights and obligations of borrower and lender pursuant to that interest.

THE QUESTION OF PARAMOUNTCY

Do ss. 178 and 179 of the *Bank Act* conflict with ss. 19 to 36 of the *Limitation of Civil Rights Act* so as to render inoperative ss. 19 to 36 in respect of security taken pursuant to s. 178 by a chartered bank?

The decision of this court in *Multiple Access Ltd. v. McCutcheon, supra*, has delimited the circumstances that will justify application of the doctrine of paramountcy, whereby otherwise validity enacted provincial legislation will be held to be inoperative to the extent that it conflicts with federal legislation. In a widely quoted passage, Dickson J., as he then was, espoused the view that the doctrine of paramountcy would only need to be invoked in instances where it is impossible to comply with both legislative enactments. He stated, at pp. 23–24:

In principle, there would seem to be no good reason to speak of paramountcy and preclusion except where there is actual conflict in operation as where one enactment says "yes" and the other says "no"; "the same citizens are being told to do inconsistent things"; compliance with one is defiance of the other.

Multiple Access Ltd. v. McCutcheon was a case involving duplicative federal and provincial legislation. This court rejected the view that such enactments could not operate concurrently simply because resort to the one would preclude resort to the other. On the contrary, Dickson J., borrowing the

phrase coined by Professor Lederman in his seminal article "The Concurrent Operation of Federal and Provincial Laws in Canada" (1963), 9 *McGill L.J.* 185, expressed the view that in a federal system such legislation was expressive of the "ultimate in harmony". In the following excerpt Dickson J. provides a cogent and succinct rationale for this view, at p. 23:

... the cases where overlapping provincial legislation has not been rendered inoperative cannot be validly distinguished on the basis that in each of them there were elements of difference between the provincial and the federal legislation; *there is no true repugnancy in the case of merely duplicative provisions since it does not matter which statute is applied; the legislative purpose of Parliament will be fulfilled regardless of which statute is invoked by a remedy-seeker; application of the provincial law does not displace the legislative purpose of Parliament.* [Emphasis added.]

On the basis of these principles, the question before me is thus reducible to asking whether there is an "actual conflict in operation" between the *Bank Act* and the *Limitation of Civil Rights Act* in the sense that the legislative purpose of Parliament stands to be displaced in the event that the appellant bank is required to defer to the provincial legislation in order to realize on its security. This calls for an examination of the provincial legislation.

As is apparent from s. 20, the purpose of ss. 21 to 35 of the *Limitation of Civil Rights Act* is to prescribe, in a comprehensive manner, the procedure which a secured creditor must follow in Saskatchewan in order to take possession of his security. Failure to follow the prescribed procedure results in the imposition of a sweeping penalty provision; s. 27 provides, in these circumstances, for the determination of the security agreement and the release of the debtor from all liability. I shall assume for the purposes of this appeal that the Court of Appeal correctly interpreted the provision as applying to federally created securities.

The most salient feature of the procedure set out is ss. 21 to 35 of the Act, as I understand it, is that it is designed to ensure that a judge determine the terms and conditions under which a creditor may repossess and seize articles. Section 33 makes this clear. It is a judge who is to decide if, when, and under what circumstances the pledged article is to be returned to the secured party.

The contrast with the comprehensive regime provided for in ss. 178 and 178 of the *Bank Act* could not be more striking. The essence of that regime, it hardly needs repeating, is to assign to the bank, on the taking out of the security, right and title to the goods in question, and to confer, on default of the debtor, an *immediate* right to seize and sell those goods, subject only to the conditions and requirements set out in the *Bank Act.*

On a comparison of the two enactments, can it be said that there is an "actual conflict in operation" between them, giving that phrase the meaning above described? I am led inescapably to the conclusion that there is. The *Bank Act* provides that a lender may, on the default of his borrower, seize his security, whereas the *Limitation of Civil Rights Act* forbids a creditor from immediately repossessing the secured article on pain of determination of the security interest. There could be no clearer instance of a case where compliance with the federal statute necessarily entails defiance of its provincial counterpart. The necessary corollary to this conclusion is that to require the bank to defer to the provincial legislation is to displace the legislative intent of Parliament. As the dissenting judge, Wakeling J., put it in the Court of Appeal, at p. 528:

> The provincial legislation obviously intends that the unqualified right of seizure granted to the bank is to be restricted. It does so by saying a bank may exercise the right of seizure given by s. 178(3) but only by leave of a judge, who will apply criteria formulated by the province as to when and under what circumstances seizure can take place.

I do not think it is open to a provincial legislature to qualify in this way a right given and defined in a federal statute: see *A.-G. Alta. v. Atlas Lumber Co.,* [1941] 1 D.L.R. 625 at pp. 629–30, [1941] S.C.R. 87, *per* Duff C.J.C.

I am not, with respect, dissuaded from this conclusion by the reasoning of the majority in the Court of Appeal to the effect that requiring a bank to defer to the provisions of the *Limitation of Civil Rights Act* would, in any given instance, have, in all likelihood, the sole effect of delaying the bank's ability to take possession of its security. As Sherstobitoff J.A. put it, at pp. 535–36:

> The *Limitation of Civil Rights Act* simply requires that a creditor give notice to a debtor before seizure of property so as to enable the debtor to make application to the court. The application and resulting order may have the effect of delaying the taking of possession by the creditor. It does not affect the amount of the indebtedness or liability for payment of same except in cases of non-compliance with the terms of the Act so as to bring s. 27 into play.

> Put simply, it requires the bank to follow certain procedures before realizing upon its security, and nothing more.

The reasoning of the majority on this point cannot be determinative of the question of paramountcy. Such a view, with respect, rests on a misinterpretation of what was said in *Multiple Access Ltd. v. McCutcheon.* For, as we have seen, dual compliance will be impossible when application of the provincial statute can fairly be said to frustrate Parliament's legislative purpose. In this instance, as I have already noted, Parliament's legislative purpose in defining the unique security interest created by ss. 178 and 179 of the *Bank Act* was manifestly that of creating a security interest susceptible of uniform enforcement by the banks nationwide, that is to say a lending regime *sui generis* in which, to borrow the phrase of Muldoon J. in *Canadian Imperial Bank of Commerce v. R., supra,* at p. 159, the "bank obtains and may assert its right to the goods and their proceeds against the world, *except as only Parliament itself may reduce or modify those rights*" [Emphasis added]. This, of course, is merely another way of saying that Parliament, in its wisdom, wished to guard against creating a lending regime whereby the rights of the banks would be made to depend solely on provincial legislation governing the realization and enforcement of security interests.

I can only conclude that it was Parliament's manifest legislative purpose that the sole realization scheme applicable to the s. 178 security interest be that contained in the *Bank Act* itself. Again, as I pointed out earlier, I am firmly of the view that the security interest and realization procedure must, in essence, be viewed as a single whole in that both components of the legislation are fully integral to Parliament's legislative purpose in creating this form of financing. In other words, a s. 178 security interest would no longer be cognizable as such the moment provincial legislation might operate to superadd conditions governing realization over and above those found within the confines of the *Bank Act.* To allow this would be to set at naught the very purpose behind the creation of the s. 178 security interest.

Accordingly, the determination that there is no repugnancy cannot be made to rest on the sole consideration that, at the end of the day, the bank might very well be able to realize on its security if it defers to the provisions of the provincial legislation. A showing that conflict can be avoided if a provincial Act is followed to the exclusion of a federal Act can hardly be determinative of the question whether the provincial and federal acts are in conflict, and, hence, repugnant. That conclusion, in my view, would simply beg the question. The focus of the inquiry, rather, must be on the broader question whether operation of the provincial Act is compatible with the federal legislative purpose. Absent this compatibility, dual compliance is impossible. Such is the case here. The two statutes differ to such a degree in the approach taken to the problem of realization that the provincial cannot substitute for the federal.

I have dealt with this case on the basis of paramountcy to meet the arguments put forward by counsel. But the issue can, I think, be answered more directly. At the end of the day, I agree with counsel for the Attorney-General of Canada that this is simply a case where Parliament, under its power to regulate banking, has enacted a complete code that at once defines and provides for the realization of a security interest. There is no room left for the operation of the provincial legislation and that legislation should, accordingly, be construed as inapplicable to the extent that it trenches on valid federal banking legislation.

In response to the third question, then, I would hold that ss. 19 to 36 of the *Limitation of Civil Rights Act*, if interpreted to include a s. 178 security, conflict with ss. 178 and 179 of the *Bank Act* so as to render ss. 19 to 36 inoperative in respect of the security taken pursuant to s. 178 by a chartered bank. To put it another way, ss. 19 to 36 of the *Limitation of Civil Rights Act* are inapplicable to security taken pursuant to ss. 178 and 179 of the *Bank Act*.

DISPOSITION

I would allow the appeal and set aside the judgment of the Court of Appeal, and reply to the legal question put to the chambers judge in the same manner as he did, with costs throughout.

I would reply to the constitutional questions as follows:

1. Are ss. 19 to 36 of *The Limitation of Civil Rights Act*, R.S.S. 1978, c. L-16, *ultra vires* the Legislature of Saskatchewan in whole or in part?

   No.

2. Are ss. 178 and 179 of the *Banks and Banking Law Revision Act*, S.C. 1980-81-82-83, c. 40, *ultra vires* the Parliament of Canada in whole or in part?

   No.

3. Do ss. 178 and 179 of the *Banks and Banking Law Revision Act*, S.C. 1980-81-82-83, c. 40, conflict with ss. 19 to 36 of *The Limitation of Civil Rights Act*, R.S.S. 1978, c. L-16, so as to render inoperative ss. 19 to 36 in respect of security taken pursuant to s. 178 by a chartered bank?

   Sections 19 to 36 of the *Limitation of Civil Rights Act* are inapplicable to a security taken pursuant to ss. 178 and 179 of the *Bank Act*.

Appeal allowed.

(g) *Canadian Western Bank v. Alberta*†

[BINNIE and LeBEL JJ. (McLachlin C.J. and Fish, Abella and Charron JJ. concurring):]

I.   INTRODUCTION

The framers of the *Constitution Act, 1867* must have thought that the content of the federal power over "Banking, Incorporation of Banks, and the Issue of Paper Money" (s. 91(15)) was tolerably clear. Banking, according to one early authority, is more or less what "com[es] within the legitimate business of a banker" (*Tennant v. Union Bank of Canada*, [1894] A.C. 31 (P.C.), at p. 46). Bankers today are not limited in their activities to the activities their predecessors pursued in the nineteenth century. In recent years, they have persuaded Parliament to open the

† 2007 SCC 22.

door to lines of business formerly closed to them, such as the promotion (though not underwriting) of certain lines of insurance. Indeed, more generally, there has been a blurring of the traditional "four pillars" of the Canadian financial services industry, which formerly were neatly divided into banks, trust companies, insurance companies, and security dealers, the first under federal regulation and the last three regulated by the provinces.

The question that arises on this appeal is the extent to which banks, as federally regulated financial institutions, must comply with provincial laws regulating the promotion and sale of insurance. Specifically, we are required to consider whether and to what extent the market conduct rules enacted for consumer protection in Alberta's *Insurance Act*, R.S.A. 2000, c. I-3, govern the promotion of credit-related insurance by banks as now permitted under the *Bank Act*, S.C. 1991, c. 46, as amended.

The appellant banks say that the provincial insurance regulations strike at the core of what banking is all about, namely enhancing the security of loan portfolios. As the appellants' counsel puts it, "the primary character of this insurance, tied as it is to the provision of loans by banks of their own loans, is security collateral for bank loans" (transcript, at p. 23) and such promotion therefore "lies at the core of what the bank does, lend money and take security" (transcript, at p. 11). Further, "the lending of money and the promotion of security are intimately tied together and together go to the core of banking" (transcript, at p. 13). The regulations cannot, the appellants say, be allowed to affect such a vital part of their banking undertaking. Alternatively, the appellants argue, the provincial regulations are in operational conflict with the *Bank Act* and its regulations, and the application of the provincial law would frustrate Parliament's purpose.

We agree with the conclusion of the courts in Alberta that the appellants' claim to interjurisdictional immunity should be rejected. The fact that Parliament allows a bank to enter into a provincially regulated line of business such as insurance cannot, by federal statute, unilaterally broaden the scope of the exclusive legislative power granted by the *Constitution Act, 1867*. When promoting insurance, the banks are participating in the business of insurance and only secondarily furthering the security of their loan portfolios, as the evidentiary record clearly established. This means, it is true, that banks will have to comply with both federal and provincial laws, but when federally regulated entities take part in provincially regulated activities there will inevitably result a measure of jurisdictional over-

lap. Nevertheless, the paramountcy doctrine is not engaged. Absent conflict with a valid federal law, valid provincial legislation will apply. Here there is no operational conflict. Compliance by the banks with provincial insurance laws will complement, not frustrate, the federal purpose. On both branches of the appellants' argument, the appeal should be dismissed.

II. FACTS

Revisions to the *Bank Act* in 1991 permitted banks to engage in the promotion of certain types of insurance, an activity from which, historically, they had been excluded. The Canadian Bankers Association chronicled this evolution in a consumer information booklet *Your Guide to Financial Services: An overview of Canadian financial products and services* (1999), as follows:

> Up until the mid-20th century, the bank's main function was to act as society's "financial intermediary," pooling the funds of savers through deposit-taking and making them available to borrowers. While their core services are still deposits and loans, banks have expanded to offer hundreds of different products and services to a diverse clientele. Offerings include basic savings and chequing accounts, RRSPs, money orders, foreign exchange, letters of credit, mortgages, financial planning, insurance products such as creditor life insurance and investment products. [Emphasis added; p. 5.]

Specifically, the *Bank Act* and its *Insurance Business (Banks and Bank Holding Companies) Regulations*, SOR/92-330 ("*IBRs*"), now authorize banks to promote at their branches eight kinds of insurance ("authorized insurance") as follows:

(a) *credit or charge card-related insurance*: this insurance covers damage to goods acquired with a credit card, including rented vehicles.

(b) *creditors' disability insurance*: the insurer will pay all or part of a bank loan if a borrower becomes disabled. The beneficiary of the policy is the bank. The amount of the insurance usually corresponds to the amount of the payments that fall due during the period of disability.

(c) *creditors' life insurance*: this is a group insurance policy which pays off the loan when the borrower dies. The beneficiary is the bank, and the amount of the insurance is the amount of the loan outstanding from time to time, subject to any limits in the policy.

(d) *creditors' loss of employment insurance*: the insurer pays all or part of the debt owed to the bank if the borrower becomes unemployed. The beneficiary is the bank, and the amount of the insurance would generally be the amount of payments falling due while the borrower is unemployed.

(e) *creditors' vehicle inventory insurance*: the insurer covers damage to vehicles held as inventory by customers of the bank (usually dealerships) where the vehicles have been financed by the bank and pledged as collateral for repayment of the bank loan.

(f) *export credit insurance*: the insurer protects an exporter against non-payment by the purchaser of the goods. Where the bank has provided financing to the exporter's business, the insurance will generally be assigned to the bank as collateral for the loan.

(g) *mortgage insurance*: this insures the bank against default by one of its mortgagors. The beneficiary of the policy is the bank, the amount payable under the policy is the balance outstanding on the mortgage (usually the net after proceeds of foreclosure), and the insured risk is default by the mortgagor.

(h) *travel insurance*: the insurer will pay losses arising from the cancellation of trips, the loss of personal property while on a trip, the loss of baggage, as well as medical expenses incurred on a trip.

The evidence showed that a large percentage of the banks' customers purchase credit-related insurance. Therefore, even though the purchase is optional, the fact is that promotion of insurance as collateral may to some extent increase the security of the banks' overall loan portfolio. The trial judge considered this effect to be small. He found that banks generally insist on adequate collateral *before* the loan is made, and the decision to grant credit is not afterwards reconsidered if the borrower declines the offer of optional insurance. From the bank's perspective, its position is already fully protected. The availability of yet more collateral in the form of after-acquired insurance may therefore simply pile Mount Pelion on Olympus.

The trial judge noted that of these eight types of insurance "products" only mortgage insurance and export credit insurance actually insure against the risk of default in the payment of a loan. In contrast, credit-card related insurance and travel insurance, including personal accident insurance, have no significant connection to the amount of a loan owed to a bank and are payable irrespective of any default. While he recognized that insurance against the risk of a customer's disability or of loss of life or of employment enhances the safety of the bank's loan portfolio, the risk insured against is not default on the payment of the loan but the insured's disability or loss of life or of employment. The insurance, which is entirely optional for the borrower, is promoted on the basis of providing the borrower (not the bank) with peace of mind. The insurer will generally be required to pay the proceeds of the insurance directly to the bank in the event the risk materializes, even if the loan remains in good standing and there is no question about the insured's ability to pay. As the trial judge noted, "[r]emoving the necessity for the bank to pursue widows and orphans can undoubtedly improve the bank-customer relationship, although it is difficult to determine how big a factor this would be ((2003), 21 Alta. L.R. (4th) 22, 2003 ABQB 795, at para. 41).

The trial judge added that the way in which banks promote insurance varies somewhat from product to product. Credit card and travel insurance coverage are generally sold as a feature of credit cards. Mortgage insurance is promoted in concert with the granting of mortgages (although it is mandatory under s. 418 of the *Bank Act* in the case of a high-ratio mortgage worth more than 75 percent of the value of the mortgaged residence). The insurance relating to a calamity in the life of a debtor (disability, unemployment and death) is sometimes promoted at the time the loan is taken out but is also promoted quite independently by direct mail or through telemarketers. If the borrower answers certain health questions in the negative, the insurance is automatically approved through a group policy.

In 2000, Alberta enacted changes to its *Insurance Act* purporting to make federally chartered banks subject to the provincial licensing scheme governing the promotion of insurance products. Under s. 454, a bank wanting to promote insurance must obtain a "restricted insurance agent's certificate of authority". The banks thereby became subject to market standards regulation including, for example, s. 486 that requires training procedures to be in place, s. 500 that targets misrepresentations about the levels of premiums and ss. 480 and 764 that provide sanctions for non-compliance and improper market conduct. In addition, the statute empowers the provincial Minister of Finance to make regulations respecting the ethical, operational and trade practices of agents. It is consumer protection legislation.

Upon the coming into force of the *Insurance Act*, the appellant banks sought a declaration that their promotion of insurance is "banking" under s. 91(15) of the *Constitution Act, 1867* and that the *Insurance Act* and its associated regulations are constitutionally inapplicable and/or inoperative to the banks' promotion of insurance.

III. JUDICIAL HISTORY

A. *Court of Queen's Bench of Alberta* (2003), 21 Alta. L.R. (4th) 22, 2003 ABQB 795

Slatter J. noted that, except for mortgages for an amount in excess of 75 percent of the home value, the purchase of insurance by a bank customer is optional. Being optional, it is obviously not considered by the bank as vital and essential to its undertaking. The trial judge concluded, on the evidence, that in the majority of cases where the loan is paid by insurance, the borrower would in any event have been able to retire the loan without the insurance. The trial judge found as fact that "[t]he overall effect on portfolio strength is small and is not the main reason why the banks promote insurance" (para. 48). Instead, he concluded:

> On this record it is clear that the primary reason the banks want to promote authorized types of insurance is because they make a profit from it. The sale of insurance is simply another product line, no more and no less. [para. 53]

Slatter J. held that the *Insurance Act* was not rendered inapplicable to the banks under the doctrine of interjurisdictional immunity. He reviewed the evidence in detail. The insurance is not part of the credit-making decision and, on the evidence, has almost nothing at all to do with the granting of loans. He ruled:

> On this record it is not possible to say that the promotion of insurance is an "unassailable part" of the credit [granting] process or banking. It is collateral or "subsidiary" to both; a new product and profit centre unrelated to core banking. The promotion of insurance is analogous to mortgage lending and the sale of registered retirement savings plans which, while carried on by banks, are not a part of "banking" for constitutional purposes. This conclusion is particularly compelling for those types of insurance that have no relation to loan balances, but it applies to all insurance. [para. 173]

As to the doctrine of federal paramountcy, Slatter J. held that "the provincial regulatory scheme does not frustrate Parliament's intentions in empowering the banks to promote insurance; the provincial regulations complement the new powers of the banks. There is no operational conflict. The doctrine of paramountcy is not engaged on this record" (para. 204).

B. *Court of Appeal of Alberta (McFadyen, Hunt and Berger JJ.A.)* (2005), 39 Alta. L.R. (4th) 1, 2005 ABCA 12

Hunt J.A., writing for herself and McFadyen J.A., agreed with the trial judge's conclusion that the impugned provisions of the *Insurance Act* apply to banks. Only the "basic, minimum and unassailable core" of a matter under federal jurisdiction is immune from provincial regulations. The banks' insurance products are (except in the case of certain mortgage loans) not mandatory, can be cancelled independently by the consumer, are often not promoted until after the loan arrangement has been finalized, are not triggered by default on the loan and are often terminated by default on loan payments. They agreed with the trial judge that "the insurance is mostly optional and outside the Banks' control. Borrowers' insurance-related decisions do not affect the Banks' credit-granting decisions" (para. 81).

Hunt and McFadyen JJ.A. also rejected the application of federal paramountcy. There was no conflict between the provincial and federal laws. The insurance provisions contained in the *Bank Act* and *IBR*s are permissive rather than exhaustive. Nothing in the federal enactments or the legislative history suggests a parliamentary intent to authorize banks to promote insurance without complying with otherwise valid provincial laws. There is no operational incompatibility.

In concurring reasons, Berger J.A. emphasized that overlap of federal and provincial legislation is to be expected and accommodated, and that courts should exercise restraint in applying interjurisdictional immunity and paramountcy. The provincial *Insurance Act* does not restrict the banks' lending operations, nor does it restrict the ability of the banks to take any type of security at any time they choose. The banks remain free to promote insurance, and compliance with the impugned provincial legislation does not result in a sterilization or frustration of the parliamentary purpose.

IV. RELEVANT STATUTES AND REGULATIONS

See Appendix.

V. CONSTITUTIONAL QUESTIONS

On September 19, 2005, the Chief Justice stated the following constitutional questions:

1. Are Alberta's *Insurance Act*, R.S.A. 2000, c. I-3, and the regulations made thereunder, in whole or in part, constitutionally inapplicable to the promotion by banks of an "authorized type of insurance" or "personal accident insurance" as defined in the *Insurance Business (Banks and Bank Holding Companies) Regulations*, SOR/92-330, by reason of the doctrine of interjurisdictional immunity?

2. Are Alberta's *Insurance Act*, R.S.A. 2000, c. I-3, and the regulations made thereunder, in whole or in part, constitutionally inoperative in relation to the promotion by banks of an "authorized type of insurance" or "personal accident insurance" as defined in the *Insurance Business (Banks and Bank Holding Companies) Regulations*, SOR/92-330, by reason of the doctrine of federal legislative paramountcy?

1. Est-ce que la loi de l'Alberta intitulée *Insurance Act*, R.S.A. 2000, ch. I-3, et les règlements pris en vertu de cette loi, sont pour tout ou partie constitutionnellement inapplicables, par l'effet de la doctrine de l'exclusivité des compétences, à la promotion par les banques d'«assurance autorisée» et d'«assurance accidents corporels» au sens du *Règlement sur le commerce de l'assurance (banques et société de portefeuille bancaires)*, DORS/92-330?

2. Est-ce que la loi de l'Alberta intitulée *Insurance Act*, R.S.A. 2000, ch. I-3, et les règlements pris en vertu de cette loi, sont pour tout ou partie constitutionnellement inopérants, par l'effet de la doctrine de la prépondérance des lois fédérales, à l'égard de la promotion par les banques d'«assurance autorisée» et d'«assurance accidents corporels» au sens du *Règlement sur le commerce de l'assurance (banques et société de portefeuille bancaires)*, DORS/92-330?

VI. ANALYSIS

A. The Issues

In the present appeal, we are not confronted with a dispute between the federal government and Alberta. Rather, the appellant banks are independently making the claim to carry on their insurance activities in Alberta free of the insurance regulations imposed on all other promoters and vendors of insurance products in the province. The banks assert that as federal undertakings they are "immune" from provincial insurance regulation aimed generally at fair market practices and consumer protection in the province. At the same time, the appellants acknowledge that for 125 years the regulation of insurance has been held generally to be a matter of "Property and Civil Rights in the Province" within provincial jurisdiction under s. 92(13) of the *Constitution Act, 1867*; see *Citizens Insurance Co. of Canada v. Parsons* (1881), 7 App. Cas. 96 (P.C.); *Canadian Indemnity Co. v. Attorney-General of British Columbia*, [1977] 2 S.C.R. 504; and *Canadian Pioneer Management Ltd. v. Labour Relations Board of Saskatchewan*, [1980] 1 S.C.R. 433. The appellants' argument is that when banks promote credit-related insurance, they are carrying on the business of banking, not the business of insurance. As the Attorney General of Canada put it in oral argument, the issue is "whether the authorized creditor insurance products are themselves so vital and essential to lending that they join lending at the core of banking" (transcript, at p. 34). On that issue, as stated, the Alberta courts flatly rejected the banks' position. We agree.

B. Principle of Federalism

The disposition of this case requires the consideration and application of important constitutional doctrines governing the operation of Canadian federalism. Despite the doubts sometimes expressed about the nature of Canadian federalism, it is beyond question that federalism has been a "fundamental guiding principle" of our constitutional order since the time of Confederation, as our Court emphasized in the *Reference re Secession of Quebec*, [1998] 2 S.C.R. 217, at para. 55.

As the Court noted in that decision, federalism was the legal response of the framers of the Constitution to the political and cultural realities that existed at Confederation. It thus represented a legal recognition of the diversity of the original members. The division of powers, one of the basic components of federalism, was designed to uphold this diversity within a single nation. Broad powers were conferred on provincial legislatures, while at the same time Canada's unity was ensured by reserving to Parliament powers better exercised in relation to the country as a whole. Each head of power was assigned to the level of government best placed to exercise the power. The fundamental objectives of federalism were, and still are, to reconcile unity with diversity, promote democratic participation by reserving meaningful powers to the local or regional level and to foster co-operation among governments and legislatures for the common good.

To attain these objectives, a certain degree of predictability with regard to the division of powers between Parliament and the provincial legislatures is essential. For this reason, the powers of each of these levels of government were enumerated in ss. 91 and 92 of the *Constitution Act, 1867* or provided for elsewhere in that Act. As is true of any other part of our Constitution — this "living tree" as it is described in the famous image from *Edwards v. Attorney-General for Canada*, [1930] A.C. 114 (P.C.), at p. 136 — the interpretation of these powers and of how they interrelate must evolve and must be tailored to the changing political and cultural realities of Canadian society. It is also important to note that the fundamental principles of our constitutional order, which include federalism, continue to guide the definition and application of the powers as well as their interplay. Thus, the very functioning of Canada's federal system must continually be reassessed in light of the fundamental values it was designed to serve.

As the final arbiters of the division of powers, the courts have developed certain constitutional doctrines, which, like the interpretations of the powers to which they apply, are based on the guiding principles of our constitutional order. The constitutional doctrines permit an appropriate balance to be struck in the recognition and management of the inevitable overlaps in rules made at the two levels of legislative power, while recognizing the need to preserve sufficient predictability in the operation of the division of powers. The doctrines must also be designed to reconcile the legitimate diversity of regional experimentation with the need for national unity. Finally, they must include a recognition that the task of maintaining the balance of powers in practice falls primarily to governments, and constitutional doctrine must facilitate, not undermine what this Court has called "co-operative federalism" (*Reference re Employment Insurance Act (Can.), ss. 22 and 23*, [2005] 2 S.C.R. 669, 2005 SCC 56, at para. 10; *Husky Oil Operations Ltd. v. Canada Minister of National Revenue*, [1995] 3 S.C.R. 453, at para. 162). We will now turn to the issue of how, in our view, the main constitutional doctrines and the interplay between them should be construed so as to facilitate the achievement of the objectives of Canada's federal structure.

C. Constitutional Doctrines and How They Interrelate

(1) "Pith and Substance" Doctrine

It is now well established that the resolution of a case involving the constitutionality of legislation in relation to the division of powers must always begin with an analysis of the "pith and substance" of the impugned legislation (*Reference re Anti-Inflation Act*, [1976] 2 S.C.R. 373, at p. 450; *Reference re Firearms Act (Can.)*, [2000] 1 S.C.R. 783, 2000 SCC 31, at para. 16; *Kitkatla Band v. British Columbia (Minister of Small Business, Tourism and Culture)*, [2002] 2 S.C.R. 146, 2002 SCC 31, at para. 52). The analysis may concern the legislation as a whole or only certain of its provisions.

This initial analysis consists of an inquiry into the true nature of the law in question for the purpose of identifying the "matter" to which it essentially relates. As Rand J. put it in *Saumur v. City of Quebec*, [1953] 2 S.C.R. 299, at p. 333:

> [t]he courts must be able from its language and its relevant circumstances, to attribute an enactment to a matter *in relation to which* the legislature acting has been empowered to make laws. That principle inheres in the nature of federalism.... [Emphasis in original.]

If the pith and substance of the impugned legislation can be related to a matter that falls within the jurisdiction of the legislature that enacted it, the courts will declare it *intra vires*. If, however, the legislation can more properly be said to relate to a matter that is outside the jurisdiction of that legislature, it will be held to be invalid owing to this violation of the division of powers.

To determine the pith and substance, two aspects of the law must be examined: the purpose of the enacting body and the legal effect of the law (*Firearms Reference*, at para. 16). To assess the purpose, the courts may consider both intrinsic evidence, such as the legislation's preamble or purpose clauses, and extrinsic evidence, such as Hansard or minutes of parliamentary debates. In so doing, they must nevertheless seek to ascertain the *true* purpose of the legislation, as opposed to its mere stated or apparent purpose (*Attorney-General for Ontario v. Reciprocal Insurers*, [1924] A.C. 328 (P.C.), at p. 337). Equally, the courts may take into account the effects of the legislation. For example, in *Attorney-General for Alberta v. Attorney-General for Canada*, [1939] A.C. 117 ("*Alberta Banks*"), the Privy Council held a provincial statute levying a tax on banks to be invalid on the basis that its effects on banks were so great that its true purpose could not be (as the province argued) the raising of money by levying a tax (in which case it would have been *intra vires*), but was rather the regulation of banking (which rendered it *ultra vires*, and thus invalid).

The fundamental corollary to this approach to constitutional analysis is that legislation whose pith and substance falls within the jurisdiction of the legislature that enacted it may, at least to a certain extent, affect matters beyond the legislature's jurisdiction without necessarily being unconstitutional. At this stage of the analysis of constitutionality, the "dominant purpose" of the legislation is still decisive. Its secondary objectives and effects have no impact on its constitutionality: "merely incidental effects will not disturb the constitutionality of an otherwise *intra vires* law" (*Global Securities Corp. v. British Columbia (Securities Commission)*, [2000] 1 S.C.R. 494, 2000 SCC 21, at para. 23). By "incidental" is meant effects that may be of significant practical importance but are collateral and secondary to the mandate of the enacting legislature: see: *British Columbia v. Imperial Tobacco Canada Ltd.*,[2005] 2 S.C.R. 473, 2005 SCC 49, at para. 28. Such incidental intrusions into matters subject to the other level of government's authority are proper and to be expected: *General Motors of Canada Ltd. v. City National Leasing*, [1989] 1 S.C.R. 641, at p. 670. In *Bank of Toronto v. Lambe* (1887), 12 App. Cas. 575, by way of further example, and in contrast to the *Alberta Banks* case already mentioned, the Privy Council upheld the validity of legislation levying a tax on banks, holding that the pith and substance of the legislation was indeed to generate revenue for the province, and its essential purpose was therefore in relation to direct taxation, not banks or banking. See P. W. Hogg, *Constitutional Law of Canada* (looseleaf ed.), vol. 1, at para. 15.5(a).

The "pith and substance" doctrine is founded on the recognition that it is in practice impossible for a legislature to exercise its jurisdiction over a matter effectively without incidentally affecting matters within the jurisdiction of another level of government. For example, as Brun and Tremblay point out, it would be impossible for Parliament to make effective laws in relation to copyright without affecting property and civil rights, or for provincial legislatures to make effective laws in relation to civil law matters without incidentally affecting the status of foreign nationals (H. Brun and G. Tremblay, *Droit constitutionnel* (4th ed. 2002), at p. 451).

Also, some matters are by their very nature impossible to categorize under a single head of power: they may have both provincial and federal aspects. Thus the fact that a matter may for one purpose and in one aspect fall within federal jurisdiction does not mean that it cannot, for another purpose and in another aspect, fall within provincial competence: *Hodge v. The Queen* (1883), 9 App. Cas. 117 (P.C.), at p. 130; *Bell Canada v. Quebec (Commission de la santé et de la securité du travail)*, [1988] 1 S.C.R. 749 ("*Bell Canada (1988)*"), at

p. 765. The double aspect doctrine, as it is known, which applies in the course of a pith and substance analysis, ensures that the policies of the elected legislators of both levels of government are respected. A classic example is that of dangerous driving: Parliament may make laws in relation to the "public order" aspect, and provincial legislatures in relation to its "Property and Civil Rights in the Province" aspect (*O'Grady v. Sparling*, [1960] S.C.R. 804). The double aspect doctrine recognizes that both Parliament and the provincial legislatures can adopt valid legislation on a single subject depending on the perspective from which the legislation is considered, that is, depending on the various "aspects" of the "matter" in question.

When problems resulting from incidental effects arise, it may often be possible to resolve them by a firm application of the pith and substance analysis. The scale of the alleged incidental effects may indeed put a law in a different light so as to place it in another constitutional head of power. The usual interpretation techniques of constitutional interpretation, such as reading down, may then play a useful role in determining on a case-by-case basis what falls exclusively to a given level of government. In this manner, the courts incrementally define the scope of the relevant heads of power. The flexible nature of the pith and substance analysis makes it perfectly suited to the modern views of federalism in our constitutional jurisprudence.

That being said, it must also be acknowledged that, in certain circumstances, the powers of one level of government must be protected against intrusions, even incidental ones, by the other level. For this purpose, the courts have developed two doctrines. The first, the doctrine of interjurisdictional immunity, recognizes that our Constitution is based on an allocation of exclusive powers to both levels of government, not concurrent powers, although these powers are bound to interact in the realities of the life of our Constitution. The second, the doctrine of federal paramountcy, recognizes that where laws of the federal and provincial levels come into conflict, there must be a rule to resolve the impasse. Under our system, the federal law prevails. We will now discuss these doctrines, beginning with interjurisdictional immunity.

(2) The Doctrine of Interjurisdictional Immunity and its Sources

Interjurisdictional immunity is a doctrine of limited application, but its existence is supported both textually and by the principles of federalism.

The leading modern formulation of the doctrine of interjurisdictional immunity is found in the judgment of this Court in *Bell Canada (1988)* where Beetz J. wrote that "classes of subject" in ss. 91 and 92 must be assured a "basic, minimum and unassailable content" (p. 839) immune from the application of legislation enacted by the other level of government. Immunity from such intrusion, Beetz J. observed in the context of a federal undertaking, is

> an integral and vital part of [Parliament's] primary legislative authority over federal undertakings. If this power is exclusive, it is because the Constitution, which could have been different but is not, expressly specifies this to be the case; and it is because this power is exclusive that it preempts that of the legislatures both as to their legislation of general and specific application, in so far as such laws affect a vital part of a federal undertaking. [p. 840]

The doctrine is rooted in references to "exclusivity" throughout ss. 91 and 92 of the *Constitution Act, 1867*. The opening paragraph of s. 91 refers to the "exclusive [l]egislative [a]uthority of the Parliament of Canada" in relation to matters coming within the listed "classes of subjects" including "Banking, Incorporation of Banks, and the Issue of Paper Money" (s. 91(15)). If that authority is truly exclusive, the reasoning goes, it cannot be invaded by provincial legislation even if the federal power remains unexercised. "The abstinence of the Dominion Parliament from legislating to the full limit of its powers, could not have the effect of transferring to any provincial legislature the legislative power which had been assigned to the Dominion by s. 91 of the [*Constitution Act, 1867*]": *Union Colliery Co. of British Columbia Ltd. v. Bryden*, [1899] A.C. 580 (P.C.), at p. 588. Equally, s. 92 (headed "Exclusive Powers of Provincial Legislatures") is introduced by the words "In each Province the Legislature may exclusively make Laws in relation to Matters coming within the Classes of Subjects next herein-after enumerated", including "Property and Civil Rights in the Province" (s. 92(13)) and "Generally all Matters of a merely local or private Nature in the Province" (s. 92(16)). The notion of exclusivity and the reciprocal notion of non-encroachment by one level of legislature on the field of exclusive competence of the other gave rise to Lord Atkin's famous "watertight compartments" metaphor, where he wrote of Canadian federalism that "[w]hile the ship of state now sails on larger ventures and into foreign waters she still retains the watertight compartments which are an essential part of her original structure" (*Attorney-*

General for Canada v. Attorney-General for Ontario*, [1937] A.C. 326 (P.C.), at p. 354). Its modern application expresses a continuing concern about risk of erosion of provincial as well as federal competences (*Bell Canada (1988)*, at p. 766). At the same time, the doctrine of interjurisdictional immunity seeks to avoid, when possible, situations of concurrency of powers (Laskin C.J., in *Natural Parents v. Superintendent of Child Welfare*, [1976] 2 S.C.R. 751, at p. 764).

(3) *The Dominant Tide of Constitutional Interpretation Does Not Favour Interjurisdictional Immunity*

Despite the efforts to find a proper role for the doctrine, the application of interjurisdictional immunity has given rise to concerns by reason of its potential impact on Canadian constitutional arrangements. In theory, the doctrine is reciprocal: it applies both to protect provincial heads of power and provincially regulated undertakings from federal encroachment, and to protect federal heads of power and federally regulated undertakings from provincial encroachment. However, it would appear that the jurisprudential application of the doctrine has produced somewhat "asymmetrical" results. Its application to federal laws in order to avoid encroachment on provincial legislative authority has often consisted of "reading down" the federal enactment or federal power without too much doctrinal discussion, e.g., *Attorney General of Canada v. Law Society of British Columbia*, [1982] 2 S.C.R. 307, *Dominion Stores Ltd. v. The Queen*, [1980] 1 S.C.R. 844, and *Labatt Breweries of Canada Ltd. v. Attorney General of Canada*, [1980] 1 S.C.R. 914. In general, though, the doctrine has been invoked in favour of federal immunity at the expense of provincial legislation: Hogg, at p. 15-34.

A view of federalism that puts greater emphasis on the legitimate interplay between federal and provincial powers was championed by the late Chief Justice Dickson, who described the doctrine of interjurisdictional immunity as "not ... particularly compelling" (*OPSEU v. Ontario (Attorney General)*, [1987] 2 S.C.R. 2, at p. 17):

> The history of Canadian constitutional law has been to allow for a fair amount of interplay and indeed overlap between federal and provincial powers. It is true that doctrines like interjurisdictional and Crown immunity and concepts like "watertight compartments" qualify the extent of that interplay. But it must be recognized that these doctrines and concepts have not been the dominant tide of constitutional

doctrines; rather they have been an undertow against the strong pull of pith and substance, the aspect doctrine and, in recent years, a very restrained approach to concurrency and paramountcy issues. [p. 18]

This statement was reproduced in Dickson C.J.'s judgment (for a unanimous bench that included Beetz J.) in *General Motors*, at p. 669.

The "dominant tide" finds its principled underpinning in the concern that a court should favour, where possible, the ordinary operation of statutes enacted by *both* levels of government. In the absence of conflicting enactments of the other level of government, the Court should avoid blocking the application of measures which are taken to be enacted in furtherance of the public interest. Professor Paul Weiler wrote over 30 years ago that

> the court should refuse to try to protect alleged, but as yet unoccupied, enclaves of governmental power against the intrusions of another representative legislature which has ventured into the area. Instead, the court should try to restrict itself to the lesser but still important role of interpreting statutes of different jurisdictions in the same area, in order to avoid conflict, and applying a doctrine of paramountcy in the few situations which are left. (Paul C. Weiler, "The Supreme Court and the Law of Canadian Federalism" (1973), 23 *U.T.L.J.* 307, at p. 308.)

In our view, the sweeping immunity argued for by the banks in this appeal is not acceptable in the Canadian federal structure. The argument exposes the dangers of allowing the doctrine of interjurisdictional immunity to exceed its proper (and very restricted) limit and to frustrate the application of the pith and substance analysis and of the double aspect doctrine. The latter have the ability to resolve most problems relating to the validity of the exercise of legislative powers under the heads of power applicable to the activities in question.

It is not without interest that the present doctrine of interjurisdictional immunity, which is the result of a long process of constitutional evolution, was originally developed in a very special context, namely to protect federally incorporated companies from provincial legislation affecting the essence of the powers conferred on them as a result of their incorporation (*John Deere Plow Co. v. Wharton*, [1915] A.C. 330 (P.C.); *Great West Saddlery Co. v. The King*, [1921] 2 A.C. 91 (P.C.)). Since the creation of corporations by letters patent issued by the Crown constituted an exercise of the Crown's prerogative to create corporations, it would have seemed

natural to the Privy Council to extend the Crown's immunity to the entities it incorporated. Thus, to apply a province's general statutes to these corporations could be conceived as interfering with the exercise of the prerogative of incorporation.

The doctrine of interjurisdictional immunity was subsequently applied to protect "essential" parts of federal "undertakings" (*Attorney-General for Ontario v. Winner*, [1954] 4 D.L.R. 657 (P.C.); see also *Toronto Corporation v. Bell Telephone Co. of Canada*, [1905] A.C. 52 (P.C.) ("*Toronto Corporation*")). Still later, the courts resorted to interjurisdictional immunity to shield Aboriginal peoples and their lands from provincial legislation of general application affecting certain aspects of their special status (*Natural Parents*; *Derrickson v. Derrickson*, [1986] 1 S.C.R. 285).

Thus, broadly speaking, the doctrine of interjurisdictional immunity was used to protect that which makes certain works or undertakings things (e.g., Aboriginal lands) or persons (e.g., Aboriginal peoples and corporations created by the federal Crown) specifically of federal jurisdiction. As Gonthier J. observed in *Commission de transport de la Communauté urbaine de Québec v. Canada (National Battlefields Commission)*, [1990] 2 S.C.R. 838:

> The immunity pertaining to federal status applies to <u>things or persons falling within federal jurisdiction</u>, some specifically federal aspects of which would be affected by provincial legislation. This is so because these specifically federal aspects are an integral part of federal jurisdiction <u>over such things or persons</u> and this jurisdiction is meant to be exclusive. [Emphasis added; p. 853.]

Of course, what is of specific federal interest may well be the federally regulated activity itself rather than the identity of the participants. In *Natural Parents*, at p. 760, Laskin C.J. observed:

> It cannot be said therefore that because a provincial statute is general in its operation, in the sense that its terms are not expressly restricted to matters within provincial competence, it may embrace <u>matters</u> within exclusive federal competence.... This is because to construe the provincial legislation to embrace such activities would have it encroaching on an exclusive federal legislative area. (Cited with approval by Beetz J. in *Bell Canada (1988)*, at p. 834)

In *Ordon Estate v. Grail*, [1998] 3 S.C.R. 437, in the course of considering federal jurisdiction over maritime law, the Court acknowledged that the doctrine could potentially apply to all "activities" within Parliament's jurisdiction. See also *McKay v. The Queen*, [1965] S.C.R. 798, where the issue was the applicability of a municipal sign law to a federal activity, namely a federal election; *OPSEU*, Beetz J., at p. 30; and *Scowby v. Glendinning*, [1986] 2 S.C.R. 226, La Forest J., at p. 257.

While the text and logic of our federal structure justifies the application of interjurisdictional immunity to certain federal "activities"; nevertheless, a broad application of the doctrine to "activities" creates practical problems of application much greater than in the case of works or undertakings, things or persons, whose limits are more readily defined. A broad application also appears inconsistent, as stated, with the flexible federalism that the constitutional doctrines of pith and substance, double aspect and federal paramountcy are designed to promote. See F. Gélinas, "La doctrine des immunités interjuridictionnelles dans le partage des compétences : éléments de systématisation", in *Mélanges Jean Beetz* (1995), 471, and Hogg, at para. 15.8(c). It is these doctrines that have proved to be most consistent with contemporary views of Canadian federalism, which recognize that overlapping powers are unavoidable. Canadian federalism is not simply a matter of legalisms. The Constitution, though a legal document, serves as a framework for life and for political action within a federal state, in which the courts have rightly observed the importance of co-operation among government actors to ensure that federalism operates flexibly.

Excessive reliance on the doctrine of interjurisdictional immunity would create serious uncertainty. It is based on the attribution to every legislative head of power of a "core" of indeterminate scope — difficult to define, except over time by means of judicial interpretations triggered serendipitously on a case-by-case basis. The requirement to develop an abstract definition of a "core" is not compatible, generally speaking, with the tradition of Canadian constitutional interpretation, which favours an incremental approach. While it is true that the enumerations of ss. 91 and 92 contain a number of powers that are precise and not really open to discussion, other powers are far less precise, such as those relating to the criminal law, trade and commerce and matters of a local or private nature in a province. Since the time of Confederation, courts have refrained from trying to define the possible scope of such powers in advance and for all time: *Citizen's Insurance*, at p. 109; *John Deere Plow*, at p. 339. For example, while the courts have not eviscerated the federal trade and commerce power, they have, in interpreting it, sought to avoid draining of their content the provincial pow-

ers over civil law and matters of a local or private nature. A generalized application of interjurisdictional immunity related to "trade and commerce" would have led to an altogether different and more rigid and centralized form of federalism. It was by proceeding with caution on a case-by-case basis that the courts were gradually able to define the content of the heads of power of Parliament and the legislatures, without denying the unavoidable interplay between them, always having regard to the evolution of the problems for which the division of legislative powers must now provide solutions.

Moreover, as stated, interjurisdictional immunity means that despite the absence of law enacted at one level of government, the laws enacted by the other level cannot have even incidental effects on the so-called "core" of jurisdiction. This increases the risk of creating "legal vacuums", as this Court recognized in *Law Society of British Columbia v. Mangat*, [2001] 3 S.C.R. 113, 2001 SCC 67, at para. 52. Generally speaking, such "vacuums" are not desirable.

Further, a broad use of the doctrine of interjurisdictional immunity runs the risk of creating an unintentional centralizing tendency in constitutional interpretation. As stated, this doctrine has in the past most often protected federal heads of power from incidental intrusion by provincial legislatures. The "asymmetrical" application of interjurisdictional immunity is incompatible with the flexibility and co-ordination required by contemporary Canadian federalism. Commentators have noted that an extensive application of this doctrine to protect federal heads of power and undertakings is both unnecessary and "undesirable in a federation where so many laws for the protection of workers, consumers and the environment (for example) are enacted and enforced at the provincial level" (Hogg, at p. 15-30; see also Weiler, at p. 312; J. Leclair, "The Supreme Court of Canada's Understanding of Federalism: Efficiency at the Expense of Diversity" (2003), 28 *Queen's L.J.* 411). The asymmetrical effect of interjurisdictional immunity can also be seen as undermining the principles of subsidiarity, i.e. that decisions "are often best [made] at a level of government that is not only effective, but also closest to the citizens affected" (*114957 Canada Ltée (Spraytech, Société d'arrosage) v. Hudson (Town)*, [2001] 2 S.C.R. 241, 2001 SCC 40, at para. 3).

Finally, the doctrine would seem as a general rule to be superfluous in that Parliament can always, if it sees fit to do so, make its legislation sufficiently precise to leave those subject to it with no doubt as to the residual or incidental application of provincial legislation. As we shall see, sufficient confirmation of this can be found in the history and operation of the doctrine of federal paramountcy.

For all these reasons, although the doctrine of interjurisdictional immunity has a proper part to play in appropriate circumstances, we intend now to make it clear that the Court does not favour an intensive reliance on the doctrine, nor should we accept the invitation of the appellants to turn it into a doctrine of first recourse in a division of powers dispute.

D. A More Restricted Approach to Interjurisdictional Immunity

(1) Impairment Versus Affects

Even in situations where the doctrine of interjurisdictional immunity is properly available, we must consider the level of the intrusion on the "core" of the power of the other level of government which would trigger its application. In *Bell Canada (1988)*, Beetz J. wrote, at pp. 859–60:

> In order for the inapplicability of provincial legislation rule to be given effect, it is sufficient that the provincial statute which purports to apply to the federal undertaking affects a vital or essential part of that undertaking without necessarily going as far as impairing or paralyzing it. [Emphasis added.]

Our colleague Bastarache J. agrees with the substitution in *Bell Canada (1988)* of "affects" for "impairs". He writes:

> ... the meaning of the word "affects" should be interpreted as a kind of middle ground between the perhaps overly vague or broad standard of "touches on" and the older and overly restrictive standard of "sterilizes" or "impairs". Without requiring complete paralysis of the core of the federal power or the operations of the undertaking, the impact of the application of the by-law must be sufficiently severe and serious to trigger immunity. (*British Columbia (Attorney General) v. Lafarge Canada Inc.*, 2007 SCC 23, at para. 48)

With great respect, we cannot agree. We believe that the law as it stood prior to *Bell Canada (1988)* better reflected our federal scheme. In our opinion, it is not enough for the provincial legislation simply to "affect" that which makes a federal subject or object of rights specifically of federal jurisdiction. The difference between "affects" and "impairs" is that the former does not imply any adverse consequence whereas the latter does. The shift in *Bell Canada (1988)* from "impairs" to "affects" is not consistent with the view subsequently adopted in *Mangat* that "[t]he existence of a double aspect to

the subject matter ... favours the application of the paramountcy doctrine rather than the doctrine of interjurisdictional immunity" (para. 52). Nor is the shift consistent with the earlier application by Beetz J. himself of the "impairment" test in *Dick v. The Queen*, [1985] 2 S.C.R. 309, at pp. 323–24. It is when the adverse impact of a law adopted by one level of government increases in severity from "affecting" to "impairing" (without necessarily "sterilizing" or "paralyzing") that the "core" competence of the other level of government (or the vital or essential part of an undertaking it duly constitutes) is placed in jeopardy, and not before.

In *Irwin Toy Ltd. v. Quebec (Attorney General)*, [1989] 1 S.C.R. 927, Dickson C.J. and Lamer and Wilson JJ. observed in passing that a distinction could be drawn between the *direct* application of provincial law (where the operative verb is "affects") and the *indirect* application (where the operative verb may still be "impairs") (p. 957). This further exercise in line drawing signalled a measure of dissatisfaction with the "affects" test without doing anything about it. At this point, we should complete the reassessment begun in *Irwin Toy* and hold that, in the absence of impairment, interjurisdictional immunity does not apply.

(2) Identification of the "Basic, Minimum and Unassailable" Content of a Legislative Power

One of the important contributions of *Bell Canada (1988)* was to limit the scope of the doctrine to the "basic, minimum and unassailable content" (p. 839) sometimes referred to as the "core" of the legislative power in question. (By "minimum", we understand that Beetz J. meant the minimum content necessary to make the power effective for the purpose for which it was conferred.) This is necessary, according to Beetz J., to give effect to what he called "the principle of federalism underlying the Canadian Constitution" (p. 766). Thus, the success of the appellants' argument in this appeal depended in part on locating the promotion of "peace of mind" insurance at the core of banking. For the reasons already discussed, and particularized below, we do not believe that this aspect of the appellants' argument can be sustained.

(3) The Vital or Essential Part of an Undertaking

In the exercise of their legislative powers, federal and provincial legislators bring into existence "undertakings". The appellant banks are "federal undertakings" constituted pursuant to the s. 91(15) banking power. In *Bell Canada (1988)*, Beetz J. spoke of interjurisdictional immunity in relation to "essential and vital elements" of such undertakings (pp. 839, 859–60). In our view, some text writers and certainly the appellants have been inclined to give too wide a scope to what should be considered "vital or essential" to a federal undertaking. We believe that Beetz J. chose his words carefully and intended to use "vital" in its ordinary grammatical sense of "[e]ssential to the existence of something; absolutely indispensable or necessary; extremely important, crucial" (*Shorter Oxford English Dictionary* (5th ed. 2002), vol. 2, at p. 3548). The word "essential" has a similar meaning, e.g. "[a]bsolutely indispensable or necessary" (vol. 1, at p. 860). The words "vital" and "essential" were not randomly chosen. The expression "vital part" was used as a limitation on the scope of interjurisdictional immunity by Abbott J. in *Reference re Industrial Relations and Disputes Investigation Act*, [1955] S.C.R. 529, at p. 592, and by Martland J. in *Commission du salaire minimum v. Bell Telephone Co. of Canada*, [1966] S.C.R. 767 ("*Bell Canada (1966)*"), at p. 774. Martland J. also referred to an "essential part of the operation of such an undertaking", at p. 777. What is "vital" or "essential" is, by definition, not co-extensive with every element of an undertaking incorporated federally or subject to federal regulation. In the case of federal undertakings, Beetz J. referred to a "general rule" that there is *no* interjurisdictional immunity, provided that "the application of [the] provincial laws does not bear up on those [federal] subjects in what makes them specifically of federal jurisdiction" (*Bell Canada (1988)*, at p. 762 (emphasis added)). In the present appeal, for example, the appellants' argument inflates out of all proportion what could reasonably be considered "vital or essential" to their banking undertaking. The promotion of "peace of mind" insurance can hardly be considered "absolutely indispensable or necessary" to banking activities unless such words are to be emptied of their ordinary meaning.

In this respect, following the sage common law adage that it is wise to look at what the courts do as distinguished from what they say, a useful approach to understanding the limited scope of the doctrine of interjurisdictional immunity in respect of undertakings is to see how it has been applied to the facts. A comparison between *Bell Canada (1988)* and the present case is instructive. In *Bell Canada (1988)*, the Court concluded that the application of a provincial *Act respecting occupational health and safety* could not apply to a federal telephone undertaking

because such application would "enter directly and massively into the field of working conditions and labour relations ... and ... management and operation" of the federal utility (p. 798). Amongst other things, the provincial Act would impose "a system of partial co-management of the undertaking by the workers and the employer" (p. 810), thereby regulating the federal undertaking in a manner not sanctioned by Parliament. To the same effect is *Canadian National Railway Co. v. Courtois*, [1998] 1 S.C.R. 868, released concurrently with *Bell Canada (1988)*, where the same provincial Act was declared inapplicable to a federally regulated railway (p. 890). In the third case of the 1988 trilogy, *Alltrans Express Ltd. v. British Columbia (Workers' Compensation Board)*, [1988] 1 S.C.R. 897, the Court held that the preventative (as distinguished from compensatory) aspects of the B.C. provincial *Workers' Compensation Act* could not apply to an interprovincial and international trucking undertaking because to do so would intrude on the management of the federally regulated undertaking, including the "B.C. Board's power to order an employer to close down all or part of the place of employment to prevent injuries" (p. 911). These cases may usefully be contrasted with *Canadian Pacific Railway Co. v. Corporation of the Parish of Notre Dame de Bonsecours*, [1899] A.C. 367 (P.C.), where it was held *not* to be vital or essential for the federal government to regulate the clearance of trash and debris from the ditch on the south side of the railway undertaking's roadbed. (See also *Ontario v. Canadian Pacific Ltd.*, [1995] 2 S.C.R. 1028.) Yet it seems that clearing debris from the roadbed is at least as essential to the operations of a rail service as is selling optional "peace of mind" insurance to bank borrowers.

Nor do the other authorities relied on by the appellants, in our view, justify their expansive view of the elements that are vital and essential to their banking operations. It is simply not credible, in our view, to suggest that the promotion of "peace of mind" insurance is "absolutely indispensable or necessary" to enable the banks to carry out their undertakings in what makes them specifically of federal jurisdiction.

E. The Interjurisdictional Immunity Case Law Relied on by the Appellants

(1) The Federal Transportation Cases

The appellants rely on *Greater Toronto Airports Authority v. Mississauga (City)* (2000), 50 O.R. (3d)

641 (C.A.), leave to appeal to S.C.C. refused, [2001] 1 S.C.R. ix, in which it was held that a neighbouring municipality could not impose its land-use development controls (and charges) on the planned expansion of terminal facilities at Toronto's Pearson Airport. Of course interprovincial and international carriers have a vital and essential interest in being able to land at an airport or having access to a safe harbour. Aircraft cannot remain aloft indefinitely awaiting planning permission from other levels of government. This activity does not lend itself to overlapping regulation. See *Johannesson v. Rural Municipality of West St. Paul*, [1952] S.C.R. 292, *Re Orangeville Airport Ltd. and Town of Caledon* (1976), 66 D.L.R. (3d) 610 (Ont. C.A.), and *Venchiarutti v. Longhurst* (1992), 8 O.R. (3d) 422 (C.A.). Equally, a provincial law that purported to regulate the access of its residents to banks would likely meet the same constitutional objections as provincial laws that purported to regulate the collection and discharge of international or interprovincial cargo and passengers. In *Winner*, the Judicial Committee held that a provincial law which required a particular licence to be obtained before a bus company operating an interprovincial and international bus service could "embu[s] or debu[s]" passengers would "destroy the efficacy" of the federal undertaking (pp. 668 and 675). For a province to regulate that part of the undertaking would be to usurp the regulatory function of the federal government. Access to passengers and cargo, in other words, was absolutely indispensable and necessary to the carriers' viability: see to the same effect *Registrar of Motor Vehicles v. Canadian American Transfer Ltd.*, [1972] S.C.R. 811, and *R. v. Toronto Magistrates, Ex Parte Tank Truck Transport Ltd.*, [1960] O.R. 497 (H.C.J.).

On the other hand, courts have consistently held that there is no vital or essential federal interest that would justify holding transportation undertakings immune from the rules of the road or legislation dealing with safety in the transportation industry. See, e.g., *R. v. Greening* (1992), 43 M.V.R. (2d) 53 (Ont. Ct. (Prov. Div.)); *National Battlefields Commission*, at p. 860; *R. v. TNT Canada Inc.* (1986), 37 D.L.R. (4th) 297 (Ont. C.A.), at p. 303. These cases, in our view, are more closely analogous to the facts here.

In *Construction Montcalm Inc. v. Minimum Wage Commission*, [1979] 1 S.C.R. 754, the Court held that it was not vital or essential to the federal interest to regulate the wages and working conditions of employees of an independent contractor (not itself a federal undertaking) constructing an airport building. In *Air Canada v. Ontario (Liquor Control Board)*, [1997] 2 S.C.R. 581, provincial liquor laws were held applicable to airlines because the sale of liquor was a benefit but not essential to the airline undertaking. The same could be said of the relationship between the promotion of insurance and the banking business.

(2) The Federal Communication Undertakings

Reference has already been made to the appellants' reliance on *Bell Canada (1966)* and *Bell Canada (1988)*. One of the first cases to find a valid provincial law inapplicable to a federal undertaking was *Toronto Corporation*. The province purported to authorize the municipality to regulate the construction of Bell's conduits, poles and cables, but the court held that "no provincial legislature ... is competent to interfere with [Bell's] operations, as authorized by ... Parliament" (p. 57). Reference should be made to *Re Public Utilities Commission and Victoria Cablevision Ltd.* (1965), 51 D.L.R. (2d) 716 (B.C.C.A.), to the same effect. The federal interest extends not only to the management of the undertaking but also to ensuring that the undertaking can fulfill its fundamental mandate "in what makes them specifically of federal jurisdiction" (*Bell Canada (1988)*, at p. 762). Unimpeded access to conduits and poles was, in other words, absolutely indispensable and necessary to allow Bell to fulfill its federal mandate.

These cases do not assist the appellants. Alberta's insurance law does not deny banks access to insurance as collateral. Just because banks require collateral does not mean they must have an essential role as an insurance agent or promoter. Banks can simply indicate their requirements to the prospective borrower, and let the borrower find its own insurance. Of course, profits from the promotion of insurance support the bottom line of banks just as advertising dollars support broadcasters, yet the Court found a provincial law regulating advertising applicable to a company seeking to advertise on a federal broadcast undertaking in *Attorney-General of Quebec v. Kellogg's Co. of Canada*, [1978] 2 S.C.R. 211.

(3) The Maritime Law Cases

The appellants rely on *Ordon Estate*, citing the proposition that maritime negligence law is considered part of the unassailable core of Parliament's exclusive jurisdiction over navigation and shipping and this was in part

> because of the intrinsically multi-jurisdictional nature of maritime matters, particularly claims against vessels or those responsible for their operation. This concern for uniformity is one

reason, among others, why the application of provincial statutes of general application to a maritime negligence claim cannot be permitted. [para. 93]

We would have thought that in the case of insurance, the concern for uniformity favours the provincial law so that all promoters of insurance within the province are subject to uniform standards of marketing behaviour and fair practices.

(4) The Indian Cases

The appellants relied on certain observations about interjurisdictional immunity in *Paul v. British Columbia (Forest Appeals Commission)*, [2003] 2 S.C.R. 585, 2003 SCC 55, but of course the actual holding in that case was that notwithstanding exclusive federal jurisdiction over "Indians, and Lands reserved for the Indians", a provincial Forest Appeals Commission could properly consider questions relating to aboriginal rights arising in the execution of its valid provincial mandate respecting forestry resources. In *Kitkatla Band*, our Court held that a provincial law relating to the preservation of heritage objects applied because its application did not affect aboriginal rights or title. These cases further demonstrate that the Court has taken a strict view of the "basic, minimum and unassailable content" of the federal power in relation to "Indians" who are, in limited respects, federal "persons", and to that extent these cases undermine rather than advance the banks' argument.

In some cases, it is true, the Court has found a vital or essential federal interest to justify federal exclusivity because of the special position of aboriginal peoples in Canadian society or, as Gonthier J. put it in the *National Battlefields Commission* case mentioned earlier, "the fundamental federal responsibility for a thing or person" (p. 853). Thus, in *Natural Parents*, Laskin C.J. held the provincial *Adoption Act* to be inapplicable to Indian children on a reserve because to compel the surrender of Indian children to non-Indian parents "would be to touch 'Indianness', to strike at a relationship integral to a matter outside of provincial competence" (pp. 760–61). Similarly, in *Derrickson*, the Court held that the provisions of the British Columbia *Family Relations Act* dealing with the division of family property were not applicable to lands reserved for Indians because "[t]he right to possession of lands on an Indian reserve is manifestly of the very essence of the federal exclusive legislative power under s. 91(24) of the *Constitution Act, 1867*" (p. 296). In *Paul v. Paul*, [1986] 1 S.C.R. 306, our Court held that provincial family law could not govern disposition of the matrimonial home on a reserve. In these cases, what was at issue was relationships within Indian families and reserve communities, matters that could be considered absolutely indispensable and essential to their cultural survival. On the other hand, in *Four B Manufacturing Ltd. v. United Garment Workers of America*, [1980] 1 S.C.R. 1031, this Court held that a non-Indian business on a reserve that was partly owned and operated by Indians (but not the band) was subject to provincial labour regulation. The Court could not discern a need for federal exclusivity in a matter so remote from its special responsibilities for aboriginal peoples. In other words, in their federal aspect ("Indianness"), Indian people are governed by federal law exclusively, but in their activities as citizens of a province, they remain subject to provincial laws of general application. As it is with Indians, so it must be with chartered banks.

(5) The Management of Federal Institutions

The cases relied upon by the appellants dealing with the management of federal undertakings, including the 1988 trilogy, belong in fact to a broader line of cases dealing with federal institutions, where management has been considered an absolutely indispensable and necessary element of federal jurisdiction. These include the post office: *Reference re Minimum Wage Act of Saskatchewan*, [1948] S.C.R. 248 (province cannot fix wages of postal employees); *Letter Carriers' Union of Canada v. Canadian Union of Postal Workers*, [1975] 1 S.C.R. 178 (province cannot regulate labour relations in the post office); and the RCMP: *Attorney General of Quebec v. Attorney General of Canada*, [1979] 1 S.C.R. 218 (circumscribing a provincial public enquiry because "no provincial authority may intrude into its management" (p. 242)), and *Attorney General of Alberta v. Putnam*, [1981] 2 S.C.R. 267 (holding inapplicable a provincial police complaints procedure). Yet RCMP officers are obliged to observe, for example, provincial highway traffic laws. Such laws do not affect the core of "what they do and what they are" that is specifically of federal interest.

Viewed in this larger context, it seems evident that the 1988 trilogy, focussed as it is on management, cannot be read as broadly as the appellant banks urge. The optional sale of borrowers' "peace of mind" insurance is not connected to a "basic, minimum and unassailable element" of the federal banking power or a "vital" part of the *banking* undertaking of the appellant banks.

(6) The Regulation of Federal Companies and Undertakings

The respondent, for its part, relied on *Canadian Indemnity*. In that case, British Columbia had introduced a universal compulsory automobile insurance plan to be administered by the Insurance Corporation of British Columbia to the exclusion of the appellants who were insurance companies incorporated federally or abroad. The Court held that "[t]he fact that a federally-incorporated company has, by federal legislation, derived existence as a legal person, with designated powers, does not mean that it is thereby exempted from the operation of such provincial regulation" (p. 519). In the present case, of course, the exclusive federal power is in relation to "banking" as well as "the incorporation of banks".

As to what constitutes "banking", however, the Court has taken the view that it does *not* include "every transaction coming within the legitimate business of a banker" because taken literally such a definition

> would then mean for instance that the borrowing of money or the lending of money, with or without security, which come[s] within the legitimate business of a great many other types of institutions as well as of individuals, would, in every respect, fall under the exclusive legislative competence of Parliament. Such a result was never intended. (*Canadian Pioneer Management*, at p. 468, *per* Beetz J.)

This observation takes on particular relevance here. Section 409(2) of the *Bank Act* provides that "[f]or greater certainty, the business of banking includes (*a*) providing <u>any</u> financial service". The appellants cannot plausibly argue that banks are immune from provincial laws of general application in relation to "any" financial service, as this would not only render inapplicable elements of the *Insurance Act* but potentially render inapplicable provincial laws relating to mortgages, securities and many other "services" as well.

Of greater relevance to the present appeal is the line of cases that have applied provincial environmental law to federal entities engaged in activities regulated federally. In *Ontario v. Canadian Pacific*, the federally regulated railway was held to be subject to the Ontario *Environmental Protection Act* with respect to smoke it caused by burning dead grass along its right-of-way, despite the fact that the fires were set by the railway company to comply with the federal *Railway Act*. The Ontario Court of Appeal held that the principle of interjurisdictional immunity did not apply (see (1993), 13 O.R. (3d) 389), and an appeal to this Court was unanimously dismissed with brief reasons. In *TNT Canada*, an interprovincial trucking company was held bound by provincial regulations governing the carriage of PCB waste. As Mackinnon A.C.J.O. observed, at p. 303:

> In the same way that the province can regulate speed limits and the mechanical conditions of vehicles on the roads of the province for the protection and safety of other highway users, it can set conditions for the carriage of particular toxic substances within the province, provided that the conditions do not interfere in any substantial way with the carrier's general or particular carriage of goods, and are not in conflict either directly or indirectly with federal legislation in the field.

(7) Conclusion

In our view, the above review of the case law cited by the appellants and other parties and interveners shows that not only *should* the doctrine of interjurisdictional immunity be applied with restraint, but with rare exceptions it *has* been so applied. Although the doctrine is in principle applicable to all federal and provincial heads of legislative authority, the case law demonstrates that its natural area of operation is in relation to those heads of legislative authority that confer on Parliament power over enumerated federal things, people, works or undertakings. In most cases, a pith and substance analysis and the application of the doctrine of paramountcy have resolved difficulties in a satisfactory manner.

We turn, then, to the second branch of the appellants' argument, namely that they are relieved of compliance with provincial insurance regulations by the doctrine of federal paramountcy.

F. Doctrine of Federal Paramountcy

According to the doctrine of federal paramountcy, when the operational effects of provincial legislation are incompatible with federal legislation, the federal legislation must prevail and the provincial legislation is rendered inoperative to the extent of the incompatibility. The doctrine applies not only to cases in which the provincial legislature has legislated pursuant to its ancillary power to trench on an area of federal jurisdiction, but also to situations in which the provincial legislature acts within its primary powers, and Parliament pursuant to its ancillary powers. This doctrine is much better suited to contemporary Canadian federalism than is the doctrine of interjurisdictional immunity, as this Court has expressly acknowledged in the "double aspect" cases (*Mangat*, at para. 52).

Of course, the main difficulty consists in determining the degree of incompatibility needed to trigger the application of the doctrine of federal paramountcy. The answer the courts give to this question has become one of capital importance for the development of Canadian federalism. To interpret incompatibility broadly has the effect of expanding the powers of the central government, whereas a narrower interpretation tends to give provincial governments more latitude.

In developing its approach, this Court, despite the problems occasionally caused by certain relevant aspects of its case law, has shown a prudent measure of restraint in proposing strict tests: *General Motors*, at p. 669. In *Multiple Access Ltd. v. McCutcheon*, [1982] 2 S.C.R. 161, the Court defined the fundamental test for determining whether there is sufficient incompatibility to trigger the application of the doctrine of federal paramountcy. Dickson J. stated:

> In principle, there would seem to be no good reasons to speak of paramountcy and preclusion except where there is actual conflict in operation as where one enactment says "yes" and the other says "no"; "the same citizens are being told to do inconsistent things"; compliance with one is defiance of the other. [p. 191]

Thus, according to this test, the mere existence of a duplication of norms at the federal and provincial levels does not in itself constitute a degree of incompatibility capable of triggering the application of the doctrine. Moreover, a provincial law may in principle add requirements that supplement the requirements of federal legislation (*114957 Canada Ltée (Spraytech, Société d'arrosage*). In both cases, the laws can apply concurrently, and citizens can comply with either of them without violating the other.

Nevertheless, there will be cases in which imposing an obligation to comply with provincial legislation would in effect frustrate the purpose of a federal law even though it did not entail a direct violation of the federal law's provisions. The Court recognized this in *Bank of Montreal v. Hall*, [1990] 1 S.C.R. 121, in noting that Parliament's "intent" must also be taken into account in the analysis of incompatibility. The Court thus acknowledged that the impossibility of complying with two enactments is not the sole sign of incompatibility. The fact that a provincial law is incompatible with the purpose of a federal law will also be sufficient to trigger the application

of the doctrine of federal paramountcy. This point was recently reaffirmed in *Mangat* and in *Rothmans, Benson & Hedges Inc. v. Saskatchewan*, [2005] 1 S.C.R. 188, 2005 SCC 13.

That being said, care must be taken not to give too broad a scope to *Hall*, *Mangat* and *Rothmans*. The Court has never given any indication that it intended, in those cases, to reverse its previous decisions and adopt the "occupied field" test it had clearly rejected in *O'Grady* in 1960. The fact that Parliament has legislated in respect of a matter does not lead to the presumption that in so doing it intended to rule out any possible provincial action in respect of that subject. As this Court recently stated, "to impute to Parliament such an intention to 'occup[y] the field' in the absence of very clear statutory language to that effect would be to stray from the path of judicial restraint in questions of paramountcy that this Court has taken since at least *O'Grady*" (*Rothmans*, at para. 21).

An incompatible federal legislative intent must be established by the party relying on it, and the courts must never lose sight of the fundamental rule of constitutional interpretation that, "[w]hen a federal statute can be properly interpreted so as not to interfere with a provincial statute, such an interpretation is to be applied in preference to another applicable construction which would bring about a conflict between the two statutes" (*Attorney General of Canada v. Law Society of British Columbia*, at p. 356). To sum up, the onus is on the party relying on the doctrine of federal paramountcy to demonstrate that the federal and provincial laws are in fact incompatible by establishing either that it is impossible to comply with both laws or that to apply the provincial law would frustrate the purpose of the federal law.

G. Order of Application of the Constitutional Doctrines

The above review of constitutional doctrines inevitably raises questions about the logical order in which they should be applied. It would be difficult to avoid beginning with the "pith and substance" analysis, which serves to determine whether the legislation in question is in fact *valid*. The other two doctrines serve merely to determine whether a valid law is *applicable* or *operative* in specific circumstances.

Although our colleague Bastarache J. takes a different view on this point, we do not think it appropriate to *always* begin by considering the doctrine of interjurisdictional immunity. To do so could mire the Court in a rather abstract discussion of "cores" and "vital and essential" parts to little practical effect. As we have already noted, interjurisdictional immunity is of limited application and should in general be reserved for situations already covered by precedent. This means, in practice, that it will be largely reserved for those heads of power that deal with federal things, persons or undertakings, or where in the past its application has been considered absolutely indispensable or necessary to enable Parliament or a provincial legislature to achieve the purpose for which exclusive legislative jurisdiction was conferred, as discerned from the constitutional division of powers as a whole, or what is absolutely indispensable or necessary to enable an undertaking to carry out its mandate in what makes it specifically of federal (or provincial) jurisdiction. If a case can be resolved by the application of a pith and substance analysis, and federal paramountcy where necessary, it would be preferable to take that approach, as this Court did in *Mangat*.

In the result, while in theory a consideration of interjurisdictional immunity is apt for consideration after the pith and substance analysis, in practice the absence of prior case law favouring its application to the subject matter at hand will generally justify a court proceeding directly to the consideration of federal paramountcy.

H.   Application to the Facts of This Case

While the particular factual elements of this case have already been canvassed for the purpose of the legal analysis, we will address them in greater depth out of respect for the detailed arguments of the parties.

(1) The Pith and Substance of the Alberta Insurance Act Relates to Property and Civil Rights in the Province

The Alberta *Insurance Act* is a valid law. As the banks acknowledge, the business of insurance in general falls within the authority of the provinces as a matter of property and civil rights. See, e.g., *Parsons* and *Canadian Pioneer Management*. As noted earlier, a federally incorporated company remains subject to provincial regulation in respect of its insurance business: *Canadian Indemnity*. The banks say however that the promotion of their eight lines of "authorized" insurance products is integral to their lending practices, and thus to banking, which is a federally regulated activity.

Nevertheless, banks, as such, are not exempt from provincial law. In *Bank of Toronto v. Lambe*, as mentioned earlier, it was held that the bank was sub-

ject to a provincial tax aimed at banks. In *Gregory Co. v. Imperial Bank of Canada*, [1960] C.S. 204, it was held by the Quebec Superior Court that a bank is subject to provincial securities laws. Accordingly, the mere fact that the banks now participate in the promotion of insurance does not change the essential nature of the insurance activity, which remains a matter generally falling within provincial jurisdiction.

In this respect, the banks' argument is also that while insurance is generally a provincial matter, when used as collateral for bank loans, credit-related insurance is "integrated" into banking in the same way that negligence law was held to be "integral" to shipping and navigation in *Ordon Estate*. This integration contention fails on the facts, as discussed here.

(2) The onus lies on the proponent of interjurisdictional immunity on the facts of a particular case to demonstrate that credit-related insurance is part of the basic, minimum and unassailable content of the banking power.

The purpose of allocating "Banking, Incorporation of Banks and the Issue of Paper Money" to Parliament under s. 91(15) of the *Constitution Act, 1867* was to create an orderly and uniform financial system, subject to exclusive federal jurisdiction and control in contrast to a regionalized banking system which in "[t]he years preceding the Canadian Confederation were characterized in the United States by 'a chaotic era of wild-cat state banking'" (P. N. McDonald, "The B.N.A. Act and the Near Banks: A Case Study In Federalism" (1972), 10 *Alta. L. Rev.* 155, at p. 156; B. Laskin, *Canadian Constitutional Law: Cases, Text and Notes on Distribution of Legislative Power* (3rd ed. 1969), at p. 603).

At least in part, the importance of national control was because of "the peculiar status of bankers [as financial intermediaries], their importance at the centre of the financial community [and] the expectation of the public that it can grant them implicit and utmost confidence" (*Canadian Pioneer Management*, at p. 461). In 1914, the High Court of Australia said:

> The essential characteristics of the business of banking ... may be described as the collection of money by receiving deposits upon on loan, repayable when and as expressly or impliedly agreed upon, and the utilization of the money so collected by lending it again in such sums as are required.... (*Commissioners of the State Savings Bank of Victoria v. Permewan Wright & Co.* (1914), 19 C.L.R. 457, at p. 471)

It is unnecessary, for present purposes, to delve deeply into the notoriously difficult task of defining banking. It includes the incorporation of banks. It certainly includes, as the banks argue, the securing of loans by appropriate collateral. At issue is the difference between *requiring* collateral (a banking activity) and promoting the acquisition of a certain type of product (e.g. insurance) that could then be *used* as collateral. The respondent, for its part, complains that the appellants' argument would render the "basic, minimum and unassailable" content of the banking power more or less co-extensive with what bankers are authorized to do. There is no doubt that banking is crucial to the economy and that even the basic, minimum and unassailable content of the exclusive power conferred on Parliament in this regard must not be given a cramped interpretation. Banks are institutions of great importance. The federal authorities monitor all aspects of their activities to ensure that they remain safely solvent and that they do not abuse their privileged position as takers of deposits and granters of credit. Courts have recognized that in its regulation of banks, Parliament may well trench on matters that would otherwise lie within provincial jurisdiction such as property and civil rights in the province, including insurance. As early as 1894, it was held that the federal banking power allowed Parliament to confer upon a bank privileges which had "the effect of modifying civil rights in the province" (*Tennant*, at p. 47). (See also *Attorney-General for Alberta v. Attorney-General for Canada*, [1947] A.C. 503 (P.C.), and *Bank of Montreal v. Hall*, at pp. 132–33.) Such considerations, however, should not lead to confusion between the scope of the federal power and its basic, minimum and unassailable content.

(3) Credit-related insurance is not a vital or essential element of the banking undertaking

The appellants rely on *Turgeon v. Dominion Bank*, [1930] S.C.R. 67, for the proposition that when a bank takes insurance as security for a loan, it is engaged in the business of banking. But that too is not the issue. The question is whether the bank in *promoting* optional insurance is engaged in an activity vital or essential to banking. The answer, as found by the courts in Alberta, is no. We agree with that conclusion.

The appellants rely on the decision in their favour by the British Columbia Court of Appeal in *Bank of Nova Scotia v. British Columbia (Superintendent of Financial Institutions)* (2003), 11 B.C.L.R.

(4th) 206 ("*Optima*" case), leave to appeal to S.C.C. refused, [2003] 3 S.C.R. viii. That case dealt with the sale by a telemarketer of Scotia Visa Balance Insurance. The question was whether the telemarketers could be required by provincial law to obtain a provincial licence. The B.C. Court of Appeal held:

> A provincial licensing regime which allows the province to say who gets a licence and under what conditions, and which could prevent the bank from obtaining security in a certain way, would affect a vital part of a federal enterprise.... [I]t is sufficient to say that the taking of security generally is a core aspect of the banking power. [Emphasis added; paras. 90–91.]

In this appeal, as well, the appellants centred their argument on the provincial licensing requirement. However if, as we conclude, the promotion of insurance is not vital or essential to the banking activity, there is no reason why the banks *should* be shielded from the consequences of non-compliance with the provincial *Insurance Act*. If a bank were to misrepresent the amount of a policy premium, or wrongfully disclose confidential information to third parties, or engage in other market practices considered by the Alberta Legislature to be unfair, there is no reason why it should escape the regulatory discipline to which all other promoters of insurance in the province are subject. Of course, if the Minister should single out banks for discriminatory treatment, the banks would have recourse to judicial review in the ordinary way. (We note parenthetically, as much stress was laid by the appellants on the refusal by this Court of leave to appeal the *Optima* case, that refusal of leave should not be taken to indicate agreement with the judgment sought to be appealed, from any more than the grant of leave can be taken to indicate disagreement. In the leave process, the Court does not hear or adjudicate a case on the merits. The notation "leave to appeal to S.C.C. refused" is inserted in law reports for editorial convenience.)

The appellants also then rely on this Court's holding in *Bank of Montreal v. Hall* in which it was held

> ... beyond dispute that the federal banking power empowers Parliament to create an innovative form of financing and to define, in a comprehensive and exclusive manner, the rights and obligations of borrower and lender pursuant to that interest. [p. 150]

However, it must be repeated that just because Parliament *can* create innovative forms for financing does not mean that s. 91(15) grants Parliament *exclusive* authority to regulate their promotion. If provincial legislation were held to be inapplicable to all forms of security held as collateral by banks, then the application of provincial legislation such as the *Personal Property Security Act*, R.S.A. 2000, c. P-7 ("*PPSA*"), would also be in jeopardy. The appellants claim that the *Insurance Act* differs from the *PPSA* because the *Insurance Act* may lead to a prohibition of the activity (promoting insurance), whereas the *PPSA* deals only with *how* the creditor realizes on a security. However, the *Insurance Act* does not prohibit the promotion of insurance any more than the *PPSA* prohibits realization on a security provision. In both cases, compliance with provincial rules is a pre-condition to obtaining the benefit of the statute. The rigid demarcation sought by the banks between federal and provincial regulations would not only risk a legal vacuum, but deny to lawmakers at both levels of government the flexibility to carry out their respective responsibilities.

Other circumstances of this case, some of them previously noted, also support the rejection of the appellants' position by the courts in Alberta.

First, while s. 416(1) of the *Bank Act* allows bank corporations to engage in some insurance activities, it recognizes insurance as a business separate from banking. Section 416(1) reads: "A bank shall not undertake <u>the business of insurance</u> except to the extent permitted by this Act or the regulations." Parliament itself appears not to consider the promotion of insurance to be "the business of banking". While Parliament cannot unilaterally define the scope of its powers, the fact is that Parliament has always treated insurance and banking as distinct and continues to do so.

Second, on the facts, the insurance promoted by the banks is not mandatory, can be cancelled at any time by the customer and is often not promoted until after the loan agreement has been finalized. The banks themselves therefore do not consider the insurance to be vital to their credit granting since apart from high-ratio s. 418 mortgages, the loan agreement is not, in practice, made contingent on obtaining insurance, as found by the trial judge. This is to be contrasted with *mandatory* mortgage insurance. As Berger J.A. observed:

> [M]andatory loan insurance is not promoted by the bank, is not optional, generates no fee for the bank, is a part of the credit granting decision, and cannot be cancelled without defaulting on the loan. The authorized types of insurance are to the opposite effect on all these points. [para. 129]

Third, the insurance at issue is only loosely connected to the eventual payment of the debt. The triggering event for the "personal calamity" insurance is not default on the loan but rather an event in the life of the insurer. As the trial judge rightly noted, no prudent banker would extend credit if repayment was only guaranteed by a catastrophic event in the debtor's life. Further, some of the life insurance coverage is terminated by default on the loan payments, which makes the insurance worthless to the banks when it is most needed to ensure repayment of the loan.

Fourth, the banks operate their insurance business as a separate profit centre completely distinct from their banking operations. Promotion of insurance may be a significant source of profit for banks and may enhance their competitive edge, but commercial convenience does not transform the promotion of insurance into a core banking activity.

Fifth, the appellants contend that the promotion of insurance helps reduce their overall portfolio risk. However, the evidence shows that loans are secured in other ways and then insurance is offered so that the bank need not resort to that security. The banks' evidence of the number of customers who carry insurance (or the value of the loans insured) is not helpful because most of those loans are secured by other means. Section 416 of the *Bank Act* does not lay out a manner in which the banks may realize on collateral (as in *Hall*) but merely allows the banks to promote an insurance product which they do for profit.

The banks' final argument is that the promotion of insurance is vital to banking because it provides a means of realizing on a debt without having to enforce security in times of customer distress. However, as pointed out by the trial judge, this is a matter of customer relations and retention, which is no more or less important to the business of banking than it is to any other.

As the constitutional questions stated in this case are expressly limited to "authorized type of insurance" and "personal accident insurance", this opinion is not to be taken to deal with constitutional issues that may arise in relation to mandatory mortgage insurance.

(4) Federal Paramountcy Does Not Apply on the Facts of this Case

The banks' alternative argument is that if the provincial law is applicable to the promotion of insurance by banks, it is nevertheless rendered inoperative by virtue of the doctrine of paramountcy. They argue that the federal *Bank Act* authorizes the banks to promote insurance, subject to enumerated restrictions, and that these enactments are comprehensive and paramount over those of the province. In our view, neither operational incompatibility nor the frustration of a federal purpose have been made out.

(A) NO OPERATIONAL INCOMPATIBILITY

Since 2000, the banks have been promoting insurance in Alberta while complying with both the federal *Bank Act* and the provincial *Insurance Act*. All of the appellants presently hold the provincial restricted certificates of authority and are actively promoting insurance in Alberta. It cannot be said, in the words of Dickson J., that one enactment says "yes" and the other says "no"; or that compliance with one is defiance of the other: *Multiple Access*, at p. 191.

The appellants say there is conflict between s. 416(2) of the *Bank Act*, which *prohibits* banks from acting as "agents", and the provincial *Insurance Act* which *requires* the banks to hold a "restricted insurance agent's certificate" (s. 454(1)). However, it is apparent that the term "agent" is not used in the same sense in the two enactments. The term "agent" in the *Bank Act* is undefined and bears the common law meaning of a person who can legally bind his or her principal. This the banks cannot do. They cannot bind an insurance underwriter. They merely "promote" insurance. By contrast, the term "insurance agent" is a defined term in the provincial *Insurance Act* and includes a person "who, for compensation, ... solicits insurance on behalf of an insurer, insured or potential insured" (s. 1). Accordingly, the banks may properly act as an insurance agent within the meaning of the provincial *Insurance Act* by promoting (soliciting) insurance and transmitting applications without binding the insurer or potential insured within the prohibition of the *Bank Act*. This is not a case where the provincial law prohibits what the federal law permits.

(B) NO FRUSTRATION OF FEDERAL PURPOSE

A classic example of a provincial law that frustrates a federal purpose is *Mangat*. In that case, the provincial prohibition against non-lawyers appearing before a tribunal for a fee would, if applied, frustrate Parliament's intention to enable non-lawyers to appear before immigration proceedings so as to promote hearings that are informal, accessible and expeditious.

The banks argue that the *Bank Act* and its *IBR*s are similar to the legislation in *Mangat* and should be taken to express Parliament's intent that its regu-

lations are exhaustive. However, this is not borne out by the record.

Here, as in *Rothmans*, the federal legislation is permissive. Section 416(1) provides that "[a] bank shall not undertake the business of insurance except to the extent permitted by this Act or the regulations". This formulation bears some similarity to the law under consideration in *Spraytech* which held the federal law controlling pesticides to be "permissive, rather than exhaustive" (para. 35). Parliament did not intend to fully regulate pesticide use, nor was its purpose to authorize their use. The federal pesticide legislation itself envisioned the existence of complementary municipal by-laws; see paras. 40 and 42. Similarly, the federal legislation at issue in this case, while permitting the banks to promote authorized insurance, contains references that assume the relevant provincial law to be applicable. Section 7(2) of the *IBR*s reads:

> 7. ...
>   (2) Notwithstanding subsection (1) and section 6, a bank may exclude from a promotion referred to in paragraph (1)(*e*) or 6(*b*) persons
>   (*a*) in respect of whom the promotion would contravene an Act of Parliament <u>or of the legislature of a province</u> ...

The relevant legislative history may be used to shed light on Parliament's object and purpose in passing the 1991 amendment. As stated by McIntyre J. in *Reference re Upper Churchill Water Rights Reversion Act*, [1984] 1 S.C.R. 297, in constitutional cases, "extrinsic evidence may be considered to ascertain not only the operation and effect of the impugned legislation but its true object and purpose as well" (p. 318).

Here the relevant legislative record begins with the 1985 Department of Finance Green Paper, *The Regulation of Canadian Financial Institutions: Proposals for Discussion* (at pp. 84–85). While the sale of insurance by banks was not discussed in detail, the Green Paper did endorse the concept of a level playing field for all participants selling a particular product. The Senate Standing Committee responding to the Green Paper agreed, and also recommended a level playing field such that no institution would obtain a competitive advantage as a result of being subject to a different regulatory regime than its competitors (*Towards a More Competitive Financial Environment* (1986), Sixteenth Report of the Standing Committee, at p. 64).

Because of the extent of the reforms eventually enacted in 1991, it was agreed that a review of the changes would occur in five years. The review of the Task Force on the Future of the Canadian Financial Services Sector, *Change Challenge Opportunity* (1998) ("MacKay Task Force") postdates the enactment of the 1991 amendments. For that reason, it is not entitled to much weight, but it does represent a considered after-the-fact statement by some Parliamentarians of their legislative purpose. To that extent, it provides some after-the-fact confirmation of the respondent's position. The MacKay Task Force discussed the role of provincial regulation and stated

> ... that employees of deposit-taking institutions engaged in the sale of insurance should comply with applicable provincial requirements with respect to the education and licensing of insurance salespersons, so long as such requirements are non-discriminatory. [Emphasis added.] (Mackay Task Force, Background Paper No. 2, *Organizational Flexibility for Financial Institutions: A Framework to Enhance Competition* (1998), at p. 93)

A statement in the final report of the Mackay Task Force specifically addressed licences such as the Alberta's restricted insurance agent's certificate of authority:

> 19) Employees of deposit-taking institutions who are engaged in the sale of insurance should comply with applicable provincial requirements with respect to the education and licensing of insurance salespersons, so long as such requirements are non-discriminatory. (MacKay Task Force, Report, Recommendation 19, p. 197)

The House of Commons Standing Committee on Finance considered the MacKay Task Force Report and agreed with this proposition: "Those selling insurance products must be licensed and meet all of the qualifications that are required of others selling similar products" (*The Future Starts Now: A Study on the Financial Services Sector in Canada* (1998), p. 130).

We do not place much weight on the post-enactment activities in Parliament. The intention of the 1991 amendments is clear on their face. The appellants argue that Parliament intended to create a unified national "banking" scheme for the promotion of insurance, but there is nothing in the record to support such a conclusion. Parliamentarians were concerned as early as 1985 to maintain a level playing field among all financial service providers participating in the same business. To hold the banks immune from provincial market conduct regulation would give them a privileged position in the marketplace. Every indication is that Parliament wished to avoid this result.

These reasons focus, as did those of Hunt J.A., on the banks' arguments on paramountcy related to the provincial requirement of licences and the alleged conflict in the definition of agent. Other more specific conflicts were argued before the trial judge, and rejected by him. Those objections were not carried forward in the Court of Appeal or this Court. Should an issue arise in future with respect to a conflict not dealt with here or in the reasons of the courts below, it would, of course, be open to the banks to pursue a paramountcy argument on the basis of the facts as they may then appear.

VII. CONCLUSION

For these reasons, we would dismiss the appeal with costs and answer the constitutional questions as follows:

1. Are Alberta's *Insurance Act*, R.S.A. 2000, c. I-3, and the regulations made thereunder, in whole or in part, constitutionally inapplicable to the promotion by banks of an "authorized type of insurance" or "personal accident insurance" as defined in the *Insurance Business (Banks and Bank Holding Companies) Regulations*, SOR/92-330, by reason of the doctrine of interjurisdictional immunity?

   Answer: No.

2. Are Alberta's *Insurance Act*, R.S.A. 2000, c. I-3, and the regulations made thereunder, in whole or in part, constitutionally inoperative in relation to the promotion by banks of an "authorized type of insurance" or "personal accident insurance" as defined in the *Insurance Business (Banks and Bank Holding Companies) Regulations*, SOR/92-330, by reason of the doctrine of federal legislative paramountcy?

   Answer: No.

NOTE

In a recent trilogy of cases, the Supreme Court of Canada applied *Canadian Western Bank v. Alberta* to find that provinces are permitted to regulate the calculation of interest charges in relation to credit cards. The doctrines of interjurisdictional immunity and of paramountcy were found to be inapplicable. See: *Bank of Montreal v. Marcotte*, 2014 SCC 55

(CanLII); *Amex Bank of Canada v. Adams*, 2014 SCC 56 (CanLII); and *Marcotte v. Fédération des caisses Desjardins du Québec*, 2014 SCC 57 (CanLII).

II

Banks as Corporations

2 Regulation

For a description of the Canadian and international frameworks within which Canadian banks operate, see M.H. Ogilvie, *Bank and Customer Law in Canada*, 2d Edition (Toronto: Irwin Law, 2013) Chapters 2 and 3.

3 Incorporation

Background Reading: M.H. Ogilvie, *Bank and Customer Law in Canada*, 2d Edition (Toronto: Irwin Law, 2013) Chapter 4.

(a) *Bank Act*†

PART I
INTERPRETATION AND APPLICATION

. . . .

APPLICATION

Application of Act

13. This Act is the charter of and applies to each bank.

Schedule I and Schedule II banks

14.(1) Subject to this Act,
  (a) there shall be set out in Schedule I
    (i) the name of every bank named in Schedules I and II as those Schedules read immediately before the day section 184 of the *Financial Consumer Agency of Canada Act* comes into force that was not a subsidiary of a foreign bank,
    (ii) the name of every bank incorporated or formed under this Act that is not a subsidiary of a foreign bank, and
    (iii) the province in which the head office of the bank is situated; and

  (b) there shall be set out in Schedule II

    (i) the name of every bank named in Schedule II as that Schedule read immediately before the day section 184 of the *Financial Consumer Agency of Canada Act* comes into force that was a subsidiary of a foreign bank,
    (ii) the name of every bank incorporated or formed under this Act that is a subsidiary of a foreign bank, and
    (iii) the province in which the head office of the bank is situated.

Amending the schedules

  (2) Where
  (a) a bank is incorporated,
  (b) a body corporate is continued as a bank,
  (c) one or more bodies corporate are amalgamated as a bank,
  (d) the name of a bank is changed,
  (e) the head office of a bank is changed,
  (f) a bank becomes, or ceases to be, a subsidiary of a foreign bank,
  (g) a bank is dissolved, or
  (h) a bank is continued, or amalgamated and continued, as a body corporate to which another Act of Parliament applies,
Schedules I and II shall be amended accordingly.

---

† S.C. 1991, c. 46, as am. by S.C. 2014, c. 20, ss. 13–44, 983.

Notice of amendments

(3) If in any year either Schedule I or II is amended, the Superintendent shall, within sixty days after the end of the year, cause a notice to be published in the *Canada Gazette* showing Schedule I or II in its complete amended form as at the end of the year.

Schedule III authorized foreign banks

14.1(1) There shall be set out in Schedule III

(a) the name of every authorized foreign bank and, where applicable, any other name under which it is permitted to carry on business in Canada;

(b) the province in which the principal office of the authorized foreign bank is situated; and

(c) whether the authorized foreign bank is subject to the restrictions and requirements referred to in subsection 524(2).

Amending Schedule III

(2) Schedule III shall be amended accordingly where

(a) an order made under subsection 524(1) is revoked;

(b) any of the information referred to in paragraph (1)(a) or (b) changes; or

(c) the restrictions and requirements referred to in subsection 524(2) to which an authorized foreign bank is subject are added or removed.

Notice of amendments

(3) Where in any year Schedule III is amended, the Superintendent shall, within sixty days after the end of the year, cause a notice to be published in the *Canada Gazette* showing Schedule III in its complete amended form as at the end of the year.

Exemption of foreign banks

14.2 The Governor in Council may make regulations exempting any class of foreign banks from the application of any provision of this Act.

PART II
STATUS AND POWERS

Corporate powers

15.(1) A bank has the capacity of a natural person and, subject to this Act, the rights, powers and privileges of a natural person.

Powers restricted

(2) A bank shall not carry on any business or exercise any power that it is restricted by this Act from carrying on or exercising, or exercise any of its powers in a manner contrary to this Act.

Business in Canada

(3) A bank may carry on business throughout Canada.

Powers outside Canada

(4) Subject to this Act, a bank has the capacity to carry on its business, conduct its affairs and exercise its powers in any jurisdiction outside Canada to the extent and in the manner that the laws of that jurisdiction permit.

No invalidity

16. No act of a bank or authorized foreign bank, including any transfer of property to or by a bank or authorized foreign bank, is invalid by reason only that the act or transfer is contrary to

(a) in the case of a bank, the bank's incorporating instrument or this Act; or

(b) in the case of an authorized foreign bank, this Act.

By-law not necessary

17. It is not necessary for a bank to pass a by-law in order to confer any particular power on the bank or its directors.

No personal liability

18.(1) The shareholders of a bank are not, as shareholders, liable for any liability, act or default of the bank except as otherwise provided by this Act.

No personal liability — federal credit unions

(2) The members of a federal credit union are not, as members, liable for any liability, act or default of the federal credit union except as otherwise provided by this Act.

No constructive notice

19. No person is affected by or is deemed to have notice or knowledge of the contents of a document concerning a bank or authorized foreign bank by reason only that the document has been filed with the Superintendent or the Minister or is available for inspection at a branch of the bank or authorized foreign bank.

Authority of directors and officers

20.(1) No bank and no guarantor of an obligation of a bank may assert against a person dealing with the bank or against a person who has acquired rights from the bank that

(a) the bank's incorporating instrument or any by-laws of the bank have not been complied with;

(b) the persons named as directors of the bank in the most recent return sent to the Superintendent under section 632 are not the directors of the bank;

(c) the place named in the incorporating instrument or by-laws of the bank is not the place where the head office of the bank is situated;

(d) a person held out by the bank as a director, officer or representative of the bank has not been duly appointed or has no authority to exercise the powers and perform the duties that are customary in the business of the bank or usual for a director, officer or representative; or

(e) a document issued by any director, officer or representative of the bank with actual or usual authority to issue the document is not valid or not genuine.

Exception — knowledge

(2) Subsection (1) does not apply in respect of a person who has or ought to have knowledge of a situation described in that subsection by virtue of their relationship to the bank.

Sunset provision

21.(1) Subject to subsections (2) and (4), banks shall not carry on business, and authorized foreign banks shall not carry on business in Canada, after the day that is the fifth anniversary of the day on which this section comes into force.

Extension

(2) The Governor in Council may, by order, extend by up to six months the time during which banks may continue to carry on business and authorized foreign banks may continue to carry on business in Canada. No more than one order may be made under this subsection.

Order not a regulation

(3) The order is not a regulation for the purposes of the *Statutory Instruments Act*. However, it shall be published in Part II of the *Canada Gazette*.

Exception

(4) If Parliament dissolves on the fifth anniversary of the day on which this section comes into force, on any day within the six-month period before that anniversary or on any day within an extension under subsection (2), banks may continue to carry on business, and authorized foreign banks may continue to carry on business in Canada, until the end of 180 days after the first day of the first session of the next Parliament.

PART III
INCORPORATION AND CONTINUANCE
FORMALITIES OF INCORPORATION

Incorporation of bank

22.(1) On the application of one or more persons made in accordance with this Act, the Minister may, subject to this Part, issue letters patent incorporating a bank, other than a federal credit union.

Incorporation of federal credit union

(2) On the application of five or more persons, a majority of whom are natural persons, made in accordance with this Act, the Minister may, subject to this Part, issue letters patent incorporating a federal credit union.

Restrictions on incorporation

23. Letters patent incorporating a bank may not be issued if the application therefor is made by or on behalf of

(a) Her Majesty in right of Canada or in right of a province, an agency of Her Majesty in either of those rights, or an entity controlled by Her Majesty in either of those rights;

(b) the government of a foreign country or any political subdivision thereof;

(c) an agency of the government of a foreign country or any political subdivision thereof; or

(d) an entity that is controlled by the government of a foreign country or any political subdivision thereof, other than an entity that is a foreign bank, a foreign institution or a subsidiary of a foreign bank or foreign institution.

Subsidiary of foreign bank

24. If a proposed bank would be a subsidiary of a foreign bank, within the meaning of paragraphs (a) to (f) of the definition "foreign bank" in section 2, and the application for letters patent to incorporate the bank is made by a non-WTO Member foreign bank, letters patent to incorporate the bank may not be issued unless the Minister is satisfied that treatment as favourable for banks to which this Act applies exists or will be provided in the jurisdiction in which the foreign bank principally carries on business, either directly or through a subsidiary.

Application for incorporation

25.(1) An application for letters patent to incorporate a bank setting out the names of the first directors of the bank shall be filed with the Superintendent, together with such other information, material and evidence as the Superintendent may require.

Publishing notice of intent

(2) Before filing an application referred to in subsection (1), the applicant or one of the applicants, as the case may be, shall, at least once a week for a period of four consecutive weeks, publish, in a form satisfactory to the Superintendent, a notice of intention to make the application in the *Canada Gazette* and in a newspaper in general circulation at or near the place where the head office of the bank is to be situated.

Objections to incorporation

26.(1) Any person who objects to the proposed incorporation of a bank may, within thirty days after the date of the last publication under subsection 25(2) in respect of the proposed bank, submit the objection in writing to the Superintendent.

Minister to be informed

(2) On receipt of an objection under subsection (1), the Superintendent shall inform the Minister of the objection.

Inquiry into objection and report

(3) On receipt of an objection under subsection (1), and if the application for the issuance of the letters patent to which the objection relates has been received, the Superintendent shall, if satisfied that it is necessary and in the public interest to do so, hold or cause to be held a public inquiry into the objection as it relates to the application and, on completion of the inquiry, the Superintendent shall report the findings of the inquiry to the Minister.

Report to be made available

(4) Within thirty days after receiving a report under subsection (3), the Minister shall make the report available to the public.

Rules governing proceedings

(5) Subject to the approval of the Governor in Council, the Superintendent may make rules governing the proceedings at public inquiries held under this section.

Matters for consideration

27. Before issuing letters patent to incorporate a bank, the Minister shall take into account all matters that the Minister considers relevant to the application, including

(a) the nature and sufficiency of the financial resources of the applicant or applicants as a source of continuing financial support for the bank;

(b) the soundness and feasibility of the plans of the applicant or applicants for the future conduct and development of the business of the bank;

(c) the business record and experience of the applicant or applicants;

(d) the character and integrity of the applicant or applicants or, if the applicant or any of the applicants is a body corporate, its reputation for being operated in a manner that is consistent with the standards of good character and integrity;

(e) whether the bank will be operated responsibly by persons with the competence and experience suitable for involvement in the operation of a financial institution;

(f) the impact of any integration of the businesses and operations of the applicant or applicants with those of the bank on the conduct of those businesses and operations;

(g) the opinion of the Superintendent regarding the extent to which the proposed corporate structure of the applicant or applicants and their affiliates may affect the supervision and regulation of the bank, having regard to

(i) the nature and extent of the proposed financial services activities to be carried out by the bank and its affiliates, and

(ii) the nature and degree of supervision and regulation applying to the proposed financial services activities to be carried out by the affiliates of the bank;

(h) if the bank will be a federal credit union, that it will be organized and carry on business on a cooperative basis in accordance with section 12.1; and

(i) the best interests of the financial system in Canada including, if the bank will be a federal credit union, the best interests of the cooperative financial system in Canada.

Contents of letters patent

28.(1) There shall be set out in the letters patent incorporating a bank
 (a) the name of the bank;
 (a.1) in the case of a bank that is to be a federal credit union, a statement that it is a federal credit union;
 (b) the province in which the head office of the bank is to be situated; and
 (c) the date that the bank came, or is to come, into existence.

Provisions in letters patent

(2) The Minister may set out in the letters patent incorporating a bank any provision not contrary to this Act that the Minister considers advisable in order to take into account the particular circumstances of the proposed bank.

Terms and conditions

(3) The Minister may impose such terms and conditions in respect of the issuance of letters patent incorporating a bank as the Minister considers necessary or appropriate.

Letters patent of incorporation on application of certain companies

29.(1) If the Minister issues letters patent, under section 22, incorporating a bank on the application of a company to which the *Trust and Loan Companies Act* or the *Insurance Companies Act* applies and the paid-in capital of the bank immediately following its incorporation will be not less than five million dollars or any greater amount that the Minister may specify under subsection 46(1), there may, on the request of the company and with the approval of the Minister, be included in the letters patent a provision deeming shares of the bank to be issued, on a share for share basis, to all shareholders of the company in exchange for all the issued and outstanding shares of the company.

Effect of provision

(2) Shares of a bank deemed to be issued pursuant to subsection (1) are subject to the same designation, rights, privileges and restrictions or conditions and, subject to any agreement to the contrary, to the same charges, encumbrances and other restrictions as the shares of the company for which they are exchanged and the shares of the company, on the issuance of the letters patent, become the property of the bank free and clear of any charge, encumbrance or other restriction.

Idem

(3) An exchange of shares of a company referred to in subsection (1) pursuant to a provision included in the letters patent incorporating a bank does not deprive a person who was a holder of shares of the company immediately prior to the exchange of any right or privilege with respect to the shares or relieve the person of any liability in respect thereof, but any such right or privilege shall be exercised in accordance with this Act.

Transfer and voting of bank shares

(4) Notwithstanding subsection (3), no share of a bank that is deemed to be issued pursuant to a provision included in the letters patent incorporating a bank may subsequently be transferred or voted contrary to this Act, but any shareholder of a bank who acquired shares of the bank by means of an exchange of shares of a company referred to in subsection (1) pursuant to that provision may, for a period of ten years from the date of issuance of the letters patent, exercise the voting rights attached to the shares without regard to any provisions of this Act, other than subsection (7), that would otherwise prohibit the shareholder from voting the shares.

Shareholder approval

(5) No provision described in subsection (1) may be included in letters patent issued pursuant to section 22 unless the application therefor is accompanied by evidence that the request for such a provision was approved by a vote of at least two thirds of those shareholders of the applicant company entitled to vote thereon, present or represented by proxy and voting at a shareholders' meeting called to consider the application.

Exchange of share certificates

(6) Where, pursuant to a provision included in the letters patent incorporating a bank, a share exchange is deemed to have taken place, the bank shall, within ninety days after the issuance of the letters patent, make provision for the issue of share certificates representing shares of the bank and for the exchange of those certificates for share certificates representing the shares of the company that were outstanding on the day the letters patent were issued.

Shares of bank may continue to be held

(7) Notwithstanding any other provision of this Act, where letters patent incorporating a bank include a provision described in subsection (1) and, on the date of issuance of the letters patent, another bank and any entities controlled by that other bank held, in the aggregate, more than ten per cent of any class of shares of the applicant company, that other bank may have a significant interest in any class of shares of the bank deemed to be issued pursuant to subsection (1) in exchange for the shares of the company for a period of two years from the date of issuance of the letters patent.

Extension of period

(8) On application of a bank authorized by subsection (7) to hold, directly or through a subsidiary, shares of another bank, the Minister may, by order, extend the period referred to in subsection (7), but the aggregate of such extensions from time to time granted to a bank and of the period referred to in subsection (7) may not, in any case, exceed ten years.

(9) [Repealed, 2001, c. 9, s. 48]

Notice of issue of letters patent

30. The Superintendent shall cause to be published in the *Canada Gazette* a notice of the issuance of letters patent incorporating a bank.

First directors

31. The first directors of a bank are the directors named in the application for letters patent to incorporate the bank.

First members of federal credit union

31.1 The incorporators of a federal credit union are deemed to be its first members.

Effect of letters patent

32. A bank comes into existence on the date provided therefor in its letters patent.

CONTINUANCE

Federal corporations

33.(1) A body corporate incorporated under the *Canada Business Corporations Act* or any other Act of Parliament, including a bank holding company, may apply to the Minister for letters patent continuing the body corporate as a bank under this Act.

Other corporations

(2) A body corporate incorporated otherwise than by or under an Act of Parliament may, if so authorized by the laws of the jurisdiction where it is incorporated, apply to the Minister for letters patent continuing the body corporate as a bank under this Act.

Continuance for the purpose of amalgamation

(3) A local cooperative credit society may, if so authorized by the laws of the jurisdiction in which it is incorporated, apply to the Minister for letters patent continuing it as a federal credit union if it proposes to be continued under this Act for the purpose of amalgamating with another federal credit union in compliance with this Act.

Application for continuance

34.(1) If a body corporate applies for letters patent under section 33, sections 23 to 27 apply in respect of the application, with any modifications that the circumstances require.

Special resolution approval

(2) If a body corporate applies for letters patent under section 33, the application must be duly authorized by a special resolution.

Copy of special resolution

(3) A copy of the special resolution referred to in subsection (2) shall be filed with the application.

Power to issue letters patent

35.(1) On the application of a body corporate under section 33, the Minister may, subject to this Part, issue letters patent continuing the body corporate as a bank under this Act.

Issue of letters patent

(2) Where letters patent are issued to a body corporate under subsection (1), section 28 applies in respect of the issue of letters patent, with such modifications as the circumstances require.

Power to issue letters patent

35.1(1) On the application of a local cooperative credit society under subsection 33(2), the Minister may, subject to this Part, issue letters patent continuing the local cooperative credit society as a federal credit union only if the Minister is of the opinion that the local cooperative credit society has complied with the regulations respecting notice and disclosure requirements.

Power to issue letters patent

(2) On the application of a local cooperative credit society under subsection 33(3), the Minister may, subject to this Part, issue letters patent continuing the local cooperative credit society as a federal credit union only if the Minister is of the opinion that

(a) the local cooperative credit society has complied with the regulations respecting notice and disclosure requirements; and

(b) the federal credit union that results from the amalgamation will satisfy the requirements for incorporation as a federal credit union.

Regulations

(3) The Governor in Council may make regulations respecting notice and disclosure requirements for the purpose of subsections (1) and (2).

Effect of letters patent

36. On the day set out in the letters patent continuing a body corporate as a bank,

(a) the body corporate becomes a bank as if it had been incorporated under this Act; and

(b) the letters patent are deemed to be the incorporating instrument of the continued bank.

Copy of letters patent

37.(1) Where a body corporate is continued as a bank under this Part, the Superintendent shall forthwith send a copy of the letters patent to the appropriate official or public body in the jurisdiction in which the body corporate was authorized to apply to be continued under this Act.

Notice of issuance of letters patent

(2) The Superintendent shall cause to be published in the *Canada Gazette* a notice of the issuance of letters patent continuing a body corporate as a bank under this Act.

Effects of continuance

38.(1) Where a body corporate is continued as a bank under this Part,

(a) the property of the body corporate continues to be the property of the bank;

(b) the bank continues to be liable for the obligations of the body corporate;

(c) an existing cause of action or claim by or against the body corporate or any liability of the body corporate to prosecution is unaffected;

(d) a civil, criminal or administrative action or proceeding pending by or against the body corporate may continue to be prosecuted by or against the bank;

(e) a conviction against, or any ruling, order or judgment in favour of or against the body corporate may be enforced by or against the bank;

(f) a person who, on the day the body corporate becomes a bank, was the holder of a security issued by the body corporate is not deprived of any right or privilege available to the person at that time in respect of the security or relieved of any liability in respect thereof, but any such right or privilege may be exercised only in accordance with this Act; and

(g) the by-laws of the body corporate, except those that are in conflict with this Act, continue as the by-laws of the bank.

Membership shares

(2) In addition, if the body corporate is continued as a federal credit union,

(a) in the case of a body corporate with common shares,

(i) its common shares are deemed to be membership shares to which are attached the rights, privileges and restrictions set out in this Act,

(ii) the holders of those common shares are deemed to be the members of the federal credit union, and

(iii) any agreement made before continuance under which the holders of any common shares of the body corporate have agreed to vote those shares in a manner provided in the agreement is of no effect; and

(b) in the case of a body corporate that has members,

(i) the membership shares, however designated, of the body corporate are deemed to be membership shares of the federal credit union to which are attached the rights, privileges and restrictions set out in this Act,

(ii) the members of the body corporate are deemed to be the members of the federal credit union, and

(iii) any agreement made before continuance under which the members of the body corporate have agreed to vote in a manner provided in the agreement is of no effect.

Transitional

39.(1) Notwithstanding any other provision of this Act or the regulations, the Minister may, on the recommendation of the Superintendent, by order, grant to a bank in respect of which letters patent were issued under subsection 35(1) permission to

(a) engage in a business activity specified in the order that a bank is not otherwise permitted by this Act to engage in and that the body corporate continued as the bank was engaging in at the time the application for the letters patent was made;

(b) continue to have issued and outstanding debt obligations the issue of which is not authorized by this Act if the debt obligations were outstanding at the time the application for the letters patent was made;

(c) [Repealed, 1994, c. 47, s. 14]

(d) hold assets that a bank is not otherwise permitted by this Act to hold if the assets were held by the body corporate continued as the bank at the time the application for the letters patent was made;

(e) acquire and hold assets that a bank is not otherwise permitted by this Act to acquire or hold if the body corporate continued as the bank was obliged, at the time the application for the letters patent was made, to acquire those assets; and

(f) maintain outside Canada any records or registers required by this Act to be maintained in Canada.

Duration

(2) The permission granted under subsection (1) shall be expressed to be granted for a period specified in the order not exceeding

(a) with respect to any activity described in paragraph (1)(a), 30 days after the date of issue of the letters patent or

　(i) if the activity is conducted under an agreement existing on the date of issue of the letters patent, the expiry of the agreement, or

　(ii) if the bank is a federal credit union and an undertaking to cease engaging in the activity has been given under subsection

973.02(1), the cessation date set out in the undertaking in respect of the activity;

(b) with respect to any matter described in paragraph (1)(b), ten years; and

(c) with respect to any matter described in any of paragraphs (1)(d) to (f), two years.

Renewal

(3) Subject to subsection (4), the Minister may, on the recommendation of the Superintendent, by order, renew a permission granted by order under subsection (1) with respect to any matter described in paragraphs (1)(b) to (e) for such further period or periods as the Minister considers necessary.

Limitation

(4) The Minister shall not grant to a bank any permission

(a) with respect to matters described in paragraph (1)(b), that purports to be effective more than ten years after the date of the approval for the bank to commence and carry on business, unless the Minister is satisfied on the basis of evidence on oath provided by an officer of the bank that the bank will not be able at law to redeem at the end of the ten years the outstanding debt obligations to which the permission relates; and

(b) with respect to matters described in paragraphs (1)(d) and (e), that purports to be effective more than ten years after the date of the approval for the bank to commence and carry on business.

DISCONTINUANCE

Transferring to other federal Acts — banks

39.1(1) A bank that is not a federal credit union may

(a) apply, with the approval in writing of the Minister, under the *Canada Business Corporations Act* for a certificate of continuance as a corporation under that Act;

(b) apply, with the approval in writing of the Minister, under the *Canada Cooperatives Act* for a certificate of continuance, or a certificate of continuance and a certificate of amalgamation, as a cooperative under that Act;

(c) apply, under the *Cooperative Credit Associations Act*, for letters patent continuing the bank as an association under that Act, or amalgamating and continuing the bank as an association under that Act;

(d) apply, under the *Insurance Companies Act*, for letters patent continuing the bank as a company (other than a mutual company) or an insurance holding company under that Act, or amalgamating and continuing the bank as a company (other than a mutual company) or an insurance holding company under that Act; or

(e) apply, under the *Trust and Loan Companies Act*, for letters patent continuing the bank as a company under that Act, or amalgamating and continuing the bank as a company under that Act.

Conditions for approval

(2) The approval referred to in paragraph (1)(a) or (b) may be given only if the Minister is satisfied that

(a) the bank has published, once a week for four consecutive weeks in the *Canada Gazette* and in a newspaper in general circulation at or near the place where the head office of the bank is situated, a notice of its intention to apply for the approval;

(b) the application has been authorized by a special resolution; and

(c) the bank does not hold deposits, other than deposits that are made by a person who controls the bank or by a person who has a significant interest in a class of shares of the bank and that are not insured by the Canada Deposit Insurance Corporation.

Withdrawing application

(3) If a special resolution authorizing the application for the certificate or letters patent so states, the directors of the bank may, without further approval of the shareholders, withdraw the application before it is acted on.

Restriction on other transfers

(4) A bank may not apply to be continued, or to be amalgamated and continued, as the case may be, as a body corporate other than one referred to in subsection (1).

Transferring to other federal Acts — federal credit union

39.2(1) A federal credit union may

(a) apply, with the approval in writing of the Minister, under the *Canada Cooperatives Act* for a certificate of continuance, or a certificate

of continuance and a certificate of amalgamation, as a cooperative under that Act; or

(b) apply under the *Cooperative Credit Associations Act* for letters patent continuing the federal credit union as an association under that Act or amalgamating and continuing the federal credit union as an association under that Act.

Conditions for approval

(2) The approval referred to in paragraph (1)(a) may be given only if the Minister is satisfied that

(a) the federal credit union has published, once a week for four consecutive weeks in the *Canada Gazette* and in a newspaper in general circulation at or near the place where its head office is situated, a notice of its intention to apply for the approval;

(b) the application has been authorized by a special resolution of the members and, if the federal credit union has issued shares, by a separate special resolution of the shareholders of each class of shares; and

(c) the federal credit union does not hold deposits.

All shares have right to vote

(3) For the purpose of paragraph (2)(b), each share carries the right to vote in respect of the special resolution, whether or not it otherwise carries the right to vote in respect of any other matter.

Restriction on other transfers

(4) A federal credit union may not apply to be continued, or to be amalgamated and continued, as the case may be, as a body corporate other than one referred to in subsection (1).

Act ceases to apply

39.3 If a bank applies for a certificate or letters patent referred to in section 39.1 or 39.2 in accordance with that section and the certificate is given or the letters patent are issued, this Act ceases to apply to the bank as of the day on which the certificate or the letters patent take effect.

CORPORATE NAME

Prohibited names

40. A bank may not be incorporated under this Act with a name

(a) that is prohibited by an Act of Parliament;

(b) that is, in the opinion of the Superintendent, deceptively misdescriptive;

(c) that is the same as or, in the opinion of the Superintendent, substantially the same as or confusingly similar to, any existing

    (i) trade-mark or trade name, or

    (ii) corporate name of a body corporate,

except where the trade-mark or trade name is being changed or the body corporate is being dissolved or is changing its corporate name and consent to the use of the trade-mark, trade name or corporate name is signified to the Superintendent in such manner as the Superintendent may require;

(d) that is the same as or, in the opinion of the Superintendent, substantially the same as or confusingly similar to, the known name under or by which any entity carries on business or is identified;

(e) that is reserved under section 43 for another bank or an authorized foreign bank or a proposed bank or a proposed authorized foreign bank or under section 697 for a bank holding company or a proposed bank holding company;

(f) that includes the phrase "credit union" or "coopérative de crédit", or any abbreviation, combination or derivative of those phrases, unless it is to be a federal credit union and its name also includes the word "bank", "banque", "federal" or "fédérale" in conjunction with those phrases; or

(g) that includes the words "cooperative" or "coopérative", or any abbreviation, combination or derivative of those words, unless it is to be a federal credit union and its name also includes the word "bank", "banque", "federal" or "fédérale" in conjunction with those words.

Name of federal credit union

40.1 Despite any other Act, but subject to paragraphs 40(f) and (g), a bank may be incorporated or formed under this Act with the words "credit union" "coopérative de crédit", "cooperative" or "coopérative", or any abbreviation, combination or derivative of those words, in its name, but only if it will be a federal credit union.

Affiliated bank

41. Despite section 40, a bank that is affiliated with another entity may, with the consent of that entity, be incorporated with, or change its name to, substantially the same name as that of the affiliated entity.

French or English form of name

42.(1) The name of a bank may be set out in its letters patent in an English form, a French form, an English form and a French form or in a combined English and French form, and the bank may use and be legally designated by any such form.

Alternate name

(2) A bank may identify itself outside Canada by its name in any language and the bank may use and be legally designated by any such form of its name outside Canada.

Other name

(3) Subject to subsection (4) and section 255, a bank may carry on business under or identify itself by a name other than its corporate name.

Directions

(4) If a bank is carrying on business under or identifying itself by a name other than its corporate name, the Superintendent may, by order, direct the bank not to use that other name if the Superintendent is of the opinion that that other name is a name referred to in any of paragraphs 40(a) to (g).

Reserved name

43. The Superintendent may, on request, reserve for ninety days a name for a proposed bank or proposed authorized foreign bank or for a bank or authorized foreign bank that intends to change its name.

Directing change of name

44.(1) If through inadvertence or otherwise a bank

(a) comes into existence or is continued with a name, or

(b) on an application to change its name, is granted a name

that is prohibited by section 40, the Superintendent may, by order, direct the bank to change its name and the bank shall comply with that direction.

Revoking name

(2) If a bank has been directed under subsection (1) to change its name and has not, within sixty days after the service of the direction, changed its name to a name that is not prohibited by this Act,

the Superintendent may revoke the name of the bank and assign to it a name and, until changed in accordance with section 215 or 217, the name of the bank is thereafter the name so assigned.

. . . .

PART XVII
SANCTIONS

. . . .

Use of name

983.(1) Except to the extent permitted by the regulations, every person who uses the name of a bank or of a bank holding company in a prospectus, offering memorandum, takeover bid circular, advertisement for a transaction related to securities or in any other document in connection with a transaction related to securities is guilty of an offence.

Unauthorized name

(2) Subject to the regulations and subsections (4) to (5.1), (6) and (12), every entity, other than a bank, that acquires, adopts or retains a name that includes the word "bank", "banker" or "banking", either alone or in combination with other words, to indicate or describe a business in Canada or any part of a business in Canada, without being authorized to do so by this Act or any other Act of Parliament, is guilty of an offence.

Unauthorized name — "credit union" and "bank"

(2.01) Subject to the regulations and subsections (4) to (5.1) and (12), every entity, other than a federal credit union, that acquires, adopts or retains a name that includes both the phrase "credit union" and the word bank", either alone or in combination with other words, to indicate or describe a business in Canada or any part of a business in Canada, without being authorized to do so by this Act or any other Act of Parliament, is guilty of an offence.

Unauthorized name — "credit union" and "federal"

(2.02) Subject to the regulations and subsections (4) to (5.1) and (12), every entity, other than a federal credit union, that acquires, adopts or retains a name that includes both the phrase "credit union" and the word "federal", either alone or in combination with other words, to indicate or describe a business in Canada or any part of a business in Canada, without being authorized to do so by this Act or any other Act of Parliament, is guilty of an offence.

Unauthorized name — "cooperative" and "bank"

(2.03) Subject to the regulations and subsections (4) to (5.1) and (12), every entity, other than a federal credit union, that acquires, adopts or retains a name that includes both of the words "cooperative" and "bank", either alone or in combination with other words, to indicate or describe a business in Canada or any part of a business in Canada, without being authorized to do so by this Act or any other Act of Parliament, is guilty of an offence.

Unauthorized name — "cooperative" and "federal"

(2.04) Subject to the regulations and subsections (4) to (5.1) and (12), every entity, other than a federal credit union, that acquires, adopts or retains a name that includes both of the words "cooperative" and "federal", either alone or in combination with other words, to indicate or describe a business in Canada or any part of a business in Canada, without being authorized to do so by this Act or any other Act of Parliament, is guilty of an offence.

Unauthorized use of word "bank", "banker" or "banking"

(2.1) Subject to the regulations and subsections (4) to (5.1), (6) and (12), every person, other than a bank, who uses the word "bank", "banker" or "banking" to indicate or describe a business in Canada or any part of a business in Canada, without being authorized to do so by this Act or any other Act of Parliament, is guilty of an offence.

Unauthorized use of name or identifying mark of bank or foreign bank

(2.2) Subject to the regulations and subsections (4), (5), (5.2), (5.3) and (10) to (12), every person who uses the name or any identifying mark of a bank or a foreign bank to indicate or describe a business in Canada or any part of a business in Canada, without being authorized to do so by this Act or any other Act of Parliament, is guilty of an offence.

Unauthorized statements regarding association with a bank, etc.

(2.3) Subject to the regulations and subsections (4), (5.2) and (12), every person is guilty of an offence who, without being authorized to do so by this Act or any other Act of Parliament, makes any statement that a business is connected, associated or affiliated with a bank or a foreign bank.

Unauthorized use of name or identifying mark of a bank holding company

(3) Subject to the regulations and subsections (7) to (9.1) and (12), every entity that acquires, adopts or retains the name of a bank holding company and every person who uses the name or any identifying mark of a bank holding company to indicate or describe a business in Canada or any part of a business in Canada, without being authorized to do so by this Act or any other Act of Parliament, is guilty of an offence.

Permitted use

(4) No person commits an offence under any of subsections (2) to (2.3) if the activity referred to in that subsection is done

(a) in a description of the corporate relationship between a bank and an entity controlled by the bank;

(b) subject to the regulations, in a description of a corporate relationship between a bank and an entity affiliated with the bank;

(b.1) in a description of the corporate relationship between a bank holding company and an entity controlled by the bank holding company;

(b.2) and (b.3) [Repealed, 2007, c. 6, s. 129]

(c) in an advertisement in Canada by or on behalf of a foreign bank in respect of its facilities outside Canada;

(d) in the identification of representative offices of a foreign bank in Canada;

(e) in relation to the business in Canada of an authorized foreign bank;

(f) in a description of the corporate relationship between a bank or a bank holding company and a foreign bank that controls the bank or the bank holding company;

(f.1) in a description of the corporate relationship between a bank or a bank holding company and an entity that is associated with a foreign bank and that controls the bank or the bank holding company;

(g) subject to the regulations, in a description of the corporate relationship between a non-bank affiliate of a foreign bank, within the meaning of subsection 507(1), and a foreign bank that controls the non-bank affiliate, if the non-bank affiliate is not a bank holding company or an entity that is controlled by a bank holding company;

(h) subject to the regulations, in a description of the corporate relationship between a non-bank affiliate of a foreign bank, within the meaning of subsection 507(1), and an entity that is associated with a foreign bank that controls the non-bank affiliate, if

(i) the non-bank affiliate is not a bank holding company or an entity that is controlled by a bank holding company, and

(ii) the entity is not a bank, a bank holding company, a foreign bank or an entity controlled by a bank or a bank holding company;

(i) in the identification of a body corporate that was a non-bank affiliate of a foreign bank within the meaning of subsection 303(1) of the *Bank Act*, being chapter B-1 of the Revised Statutes of Canada, 1985, at any time before June 1, 1981;

(j) in the identification of a Canadian financial institution that

(i) was controlled by a bank that was a subsidiary of a foreign bank before June 15, 1997 but that has ceased to be so controlled,

(ii) is controlled by a foreign bank that, before June 15, 1997, controlled the subsidiary, and

(iii) used, before June 15, 1997, the word "bank", "banker" or "banking" to identify itself; or

(k) in the identification of a bank holding company.

Permitted use

(4.1) No person commits an offence under any of subsections (2.01) to (2.04) if the activity referred to in that subsection is done

(a) in relation to a prescribed use;

(b) under prescribed circumstances; or

(c) in accordance with a prescribed approval and any terms and conditions that the Minister may impose.

Permitted use

(5) No subsidiary of a bank commits an offence by reason only that it uses the name of the bank of which it is a subsidiary in its corporate name or a name under which it carries on business or by reason only that it uses any identifying mark of that bank in carrying on its business.

Permitted use

(5.1) No person commits an offence under subsections (2) to (2.1) if the activity referred to in that subsection is in relation to a business that is not engaged in financial activities, unless the business is carried out by a prescribed entity.

Permitted use

(5.2) No bank commits an offence under subsection (2.2) or (2.3) if it is affiliated with the bank or the foreign bank.

Permitted use

(5.3) Subject to the regulations, no entity affiliated with a bank commits an offence by reason only that the entity uses the name of the bank in the entity's corporate name or in a name under which the entity carries on business or by reason only that it uses any identifying mark of the bank in carrying on its business, if the entity does not use any of the words "bank", "banker" or "banking" or the phrase "federal credit union" in its corporate name, in a name under which it carries on business or in any of its identifying marks.

Permitted use

(6) No financial institution that was controlled by a bank on June 25, 1999 and that had a name that included the word "bank", "banker" or "banking" on that day commits an offence by reason only that it uses that word in its corporate name or in a name under which it carries on business if the financial institution is a subsidiary of a bank holding company that controls the bank.

(6.1) [Repealed, 2007, c. 6, s. 129]

Permitted use

(7) No subsidiary of a bank holding company commits an offence by reason only that it uses the name of the bank holding company in the subsidiary's corporate name or in a name under which it carries on business, or by reason only that it uses any identifying mark of the bank holding company in carrying on its business, so long as, if the subsidiary is not a bank or a subsidiary of a bank, it does not use the word "bank", "banker" or "banking" in its corporate name, in a name under which it carries on business or in any of its identifying marks.

(7.1) [Repealed, 2007, c. 6, s. 129]

Permitted use

(8) Subject to the regulations, no entity affiliated with a bank holding company commits an offence by reason only that the entity uses the name of the bank holding company in the entity's corpo-

rate name or in a name under which the entity carries on business or by reason only that it uses any identifying mark of the bank holding company in carrying on its business, if the entity does not use the word "bank", "banker" or "banking" in its corporate name, in a name under which it carries on business or in any of its identifying marks.

(8.1) [Repealed, 2007, c. 6, s. 129]

Permitted use

(9) No subsidiary of a bank holding company commits an offence by reason only that it uses the name of the bank holding company in a description of its corporate relationship to the bank holding company.

Permitted use

(9.1) Subject to the regulations, no entity affiliated with a bank holding company commits an offence by reason only that the entity uses the name of the bank holding company in a description of the entity's corporate relationship with the bank holding company.

Permitted use

(10) Subject to the regulations, no Canadian entity that is an entity associated with a foreign bank commits an offence by reason only that it uses the name of the foreign bank in its corporate name or in a name under which it carries on business, or by reason only that it uses any identifying mark of the foreign bank in carrying on its business, if

(a) it does not use the word "bank", "banker" or "banking" in its corporate name, in a name under which it carries on business or in any of its identifying marks; and

(b) the foreign bank has consented to the use.

(10.1) [Repealed, 2007, c. 6, s. 129]

Permitted use

(11) Subject to the regulations, no foreign bank that carries on a business or activity referred to in section 510.1, 522.05, 522.18 or 522.19, and no entity incorporated or formed by or under the laws of a country other than Canada that carries on a business or activity referred to in any of those provisions and that is an entity associated with a foreign bank, commits an offence by reason only that it uses its name or any of its identifying marks if it does not use the word "bank", "banker" or "banking".

Permitted use — consent

(12) No person commits an offence under any of subsections (2) to (3) if the activity referred to in that subsection has been approved by the Superintendent and is in accordance with any terms and conditions that the Superintendent may impose and, if the activity involves the use of the name or any identifying mark of a bank, a bank holding company or a foreign bank, the bank, bank holding company or foreign bank has consented to the use.

Words "bank", "banker" or "banking"

(13) For the purposes of this section, the word "bank", "banker" or "banking" includes

(a) any of those words in any language; and

(b) any word or words, in any language, that are equivalent to any of those words.

Phrase "credit union"

(13.1) For the purposes of this section, the phrase "credit union" includes

(a) that phrase in any language; and

(b) any word or words, in any language, that are equivalent to any of the words in that phrase.

Words "cooperative" and "federal"

(13.2) For the purposes of this section, the words "cooperative" and "federal" include

(a) any of those words in any language; and

(b) any word or words, in any language, that are equivalent to any of those words.

Entity's name

(14) For the purposes of this section, other than subsection (1), an entity's name includes

(a) a name that is substantially similar to the entity's name; and

(b) the entity's name in any language.

Identifying marks

(15) For the purposes of this section, an identifying mark of an entity includes

(a) any logogram, insignia or logo of the entity;

(b) the initials or any acronym of the entity; and

(c) any mark that is substantially similar to any identifying mark of the entity.

Definition of "foreign bank"

(16) In this section, "foreign bank" means a foreign bank to which Part XII applies.

Entity associated with a foreign bank

(17) For the purposes of this section, an entity is associated with a foreign bank if the entity is or is deemed to be associated with the foreign bank within the meaning of section 507 and is an entity to which Part XII applies.

Regulations

(18) The Governor in Council may make regulations for the purposes of subsections (1) to (3), paragraphs (4)(b), (g) and (h) and subsections (5.3), (8) and (9.1) to (11).

For a description of the corporate governance structure of Canadian banks, see M.H. Ogilvie, *Bank and Customer Law in Canada*, 2d Edition (Toronto: Irwin Law, 2013) Chapter 4.

(a)   *Cappuccitti v. Bank of Montreal*†

[O'DRISCOLL J.:]

I.   TYPE OF APPLICATIONS

The applicant seeks an order under s. 65(8) of the *Bank Act*, R.S.C. 1985, c. B-1; the respondent Bank of Montreal (the "Bank") seeks an order under s. 65(9) of the *Bank Act*.

     The applicant's motion fails, and the Bank's motion succeeds.

II.   BACKGROUND

1. Rocco Cappuccitti and his brother, Gordon Cappuccitti, are equal shareholders in Ontario Potato Distributing, Inc. ("O.P.D.I."), a company incorporated under the laws of Ontario. O.P.D.I. is the holder of all of the shares of O.P.D.I.-U.S. Inc. ("O.P.D.I.-U.S."), a company incorporated under the laws of the state of Georgia. The applicant has testified in the Georgia lawsuit that he and his brother are "the essence" of O.P.D.I.-U.S.

2. On January 15, 1988, O.P.D.I.-U.S. commenced an action for "lender liability" against the Bank in the State of Georgia; the claim is for breach of trust, breach of contract, conversion, etc. The Bank has counterclaimed for 5.7 million (U.S.), plus interest pursuant to a loan granted by the Bank.

     On January 18, 1988 the Ontario corporation (O.P.D.I.) commenced a similar action in Ontario (25513/88) for a declaration that the securities held by the Bank are of no force and effect together with a claim for exemplary damages, etc. In the Ontario action, the Bank has counterclaimed against the applicant, his brother, and their wives based upon personal guarantees of the debt.

3. On June 10, 1988, in the Georgia action, the applicant said:

> And, I advised him then, I said, 'if you push me, there is going to be a lawsuit' ... I told him there the Bank better be careful on how they're treating me ... if this Bank keeps on like this, I says, 'you guys aren't so pure yourself, your Bank'. I said, 'you're on the verge of bankruptcy as far as I can see. Now there is going to be a shareholders — I am going to get a few shareholders together and I am going to start a shareholders action...you're not only going to have lawsuits as a client, you are going to have it as a shareholder.' I said, 'now you better remember that'.

† (1989), 46 B.L.R. 255 at 256–61 (Ont. H.C.J.).

4. The applicant owns 100 common shares of the Bank with a present market value of approximately $3,400.

5. On July 25, 1989, the applicant signed a shareholder's proposal and caused the same to be delivered to the Bank:

> Shareholder's Proposal pursuant to Section 65 of the Bank Act, R.S.C., 1985, Chap. B-1, as amended.

> The undersigned, being a shareholder of Bank of Montreal, hereby submits to the Bank notice of the following matter which he proposes to raise at the next Annual Meeting of Shareholders to be held in or about January, 1990 (hereinafter referred to as the 'Proposal'):

> *PROPOSAL*

> I am concerned that certain policies have been adopted by the Bank that are financially prejudicing the interests of its shareholders. I am therefore requesting that the Board of Directors undertake an immediate investigation of the following matters:

> 1. The Bank does not keep a central ledger to record the history of a customer's loan account. The Bank files all documents not by customer name but only chronologically. Consequently the Bank is unable to provide a breakdown of payments made by a customer on its loans and needs to rely on a customer's own records to establish the debt owing. Will the Bank be able to properly account for loans of billions of dollars to third world countries?
> 2. The Bank refuses to release financial information already on file with the Government when so requested under the Access to Information Act.
> 3. The Bank does not disclose the full interest rates, including reserve charges, on loans to its customers.
> 4. Senior officers such as Bernard Barth and Peter Wilkins do not fully inform themselves as to the status of customers' accounts before making costly decisions;
> 5. The Bank is making use of confidential information, the effect of which is to prefer one customer over another.

> The undersigned hereby requests that the above statement in support of this shareholder's proposal be included in the management proxy circular or attached thereto pursuant to section 65(3) of the Bank Act.

> DATED at Toronto, this 25th day of July, 1989.

> ROCCO CAPPUCCITTI
> 1947 Pagehurst Court
> Mississauga, Ontario

6. On August 1, 1988, the Bank's general counsel advised the applicant that the Bank would not include the proposal in the Bank's management proxy circular because the points raised were matters in issue in the litigation and the proposal did not qualify under s. 65 of the *Bank Act.*

7. By letter of August 9, 1989, applicant's counsel offered to delete item 3 of the proposal. On August 24, 1989, the Bank's general counsel stated that the proposal was "inappropriate in its entirety" and repeated the Bank's position.

8. On August 28, 1989, the applicant submitted another proposal in which items 4 and 5 were deleted from the original proposal.

9. By letter dated September 6, 1989, the Bank reiterated its position with regard to the amended proposal.

10. The applicant launched this motion on October 3, 1989; the Bank launched its counter-motion on November 7, 1989.

III.   THE RELEVANT SECTION OF THE BANK ACT

65.(1) A shareholder entitled to vote at an annual meeting of shareholders may

(a) submit to the bank notice of any matter that he proposes to raise at the meeting (in this section referred to as a 'proposal'); and

(b) discuss at the meeting any matter in respect of which he would have been entitled to submit a proposal.

(2) A bank that solicits proxies shall set out any proposal submitted for consideration at a meeting of shareholders in the management proxy circular required by section 163 or attach the proposal thereto.

(3) If so requested by a shareholder by whom a proposal is submitted, the bank shall include in the management proxy circular or attach thereto a statement by the shareholder of not more than two hundred words in support of the proposal, and the name and address of the shareholder.

...

(5) A bank is not required to comply with subsections (2) and (3) if

...

(b) it clearly appears that the proposal is submitted by the shareholder primarily for the purpose of enforcing a personal claim or redressing a personal grievance against the bank or its directors, officers or security holders, or primarily for the purpose of promoting general economic, political, racial, religious, social or similar causes;

...

(e) the rights conferred by this section are being abused to secure publicity.

...

(8) On the application of a shareholder claiming to be aggrieved by a bank's refusal under subsection (7), a court may restrain the holding of the meeting to which the proposal is sought to be presented and make any further order it thinks fit.

(9) The bank or any person claiming to be aggrieved by a proposal may apply to a court for an order permitting the bank to omit the proposal from the management proxy circular, and the court, if it is satisfied that subsection (5) applies, may make such order as it thinks fit.

IV.   CONCLUSIONS

1. It is true that the applicant is a named litigant only as a defendant on the Bank's counter-claims. However, it would be nonsense to suggest that the proposal is anything but a personal grievance. It cannot be forgotten that whether or not the corporate veils are lifted, the applicant is a personal guarantor.

2. It is apparent that items 4 and 5 of the original proposal were designed to attempt to embarrass the Bank and hold up to ridicule the individuals named. The proposal was tainted ab initio.

3. In my view, the proposal in any of its forms, is designed to provide the applicant with leverage in his Georgia and Ontario lawsuits.

4. Counsel for the applicant submits that the Bank has no choice but to include the proposal because of the wording of s. 65(2) of the *Bank Act*. In my view, my duty under s. 65(5)(b) of the *Bank Act* is to distinguish between "substance" and "form".

5. It is not necessary for me to catalogue all the moves made by the applicant regarding the Bank and the Information Commissioner of Canada, nor is it necessary to compare all the allegations made by the applicant in the Georgia and Ontario actions with the proposals to conclude that the proposals are not what they appear to be. Once you scratch the surface, it is apparent that the applicant's proposals have vindictiveness written all over them.

6. In my view:
    (a) it is clear to me that any and all proposals submitted by the applicant are primarily for the purpose of enforcing personal claims or redressing personal grievances against the Bank; *and*
    (b) the applicant is abusing the shareholder's rights under s. 65 in order to secure publicity.

7. It follows that because of my findings in either paragraph 6(a) or 6(b), supra, the Bank "is not required" to include the applicant's proposal in the 124,000 management proxy circular to be mailed out by the Bank for the Annual General Meeting scheduled for January 15, 1990.

V.   RESULT

1. The applicant's application under s. 65(8) of the *Bank Act* is dismissed.
2. The respondent bank's application under s. 65(9) of the *Bank Act* is allowed.

VI.   COSTS

The applicant is to pay forthwith to the Bank its assessed costs of the applications (limited to one set of costs), but to include the disbursements of each application.

Application dismissed;
Cross-application dismissed.

(b) *Verdun v. Toronto-Dominion Bank*†

[IACOBUCCI J. (Sopinka, Gonthier, Cory and Major JJ. concurring):]

At the hearing on April 29, 1996, this appeal was dismissed with reasons to follow. This appeal requires us to determine whether the appellant, a beneficial shareholder of the respondent bank, is entitled to have his shareholder's proposals included in the respondent's management proxy circular.

I.   FACTUAL BACKGROUND

The appellant, John Robert Verdun, is the beneficial owner of 200 common voting shares of the respondent, Toronto-Dominion Bank. These shares are held through a registered retirement savings plan ("R.R.S.P."), and the registered owner is the R.R.S.P. trustee, Montreal Trust. The appellant is also the beneficial co-owner (with his wife) of 2,100 common voting shares of the respondent, and the registered owner of these shares is RBC Dominion Securities.

On October 25, 1994, the appellant submitted to the respondent 10 proposals (later increased to 11), with accompanying statements, for inclusion in a management proxy circular. This circular was to be sent to shareholders of the respondent in connection with the annual shareholders' meeting scheduled for January 25, 1995. The proposals related to the structure, composition, and operation of the respondent's board of directors, and to procedures at the annual shareholders' meetings.

On November 4, 1994, solicitors for the respondent wrote to the appellant, advising him that the respondent would not include the proposals in the circular because the appellant was not a registered shareholder, i.e., the appellant did not satisfy the requirements of s. 143(1) of the *Bank Act*, S.C. 1991, c. 46, as the respondent understood those requirements. In the alternative, the respondent declined to include the proposals because, in the respondent's opinion, the proposals came within the terms of both s. 143(5)(*b*) of the *Bank Act*, in that they were submitted to enforce a personal claim or grievance, namely the appellant's desire, expressed in an earlier letter, to be nominated for election to the respondent's Board, and s. 143(5)(*e*) of the *Bank Act*, in

that they were submitted to secure publicity for the appellant.

In this regard, it may be noted that the appellant had a history of somewhat strained relations with the respondent. The appellant, who is the owner, editor and publisher of several small newspapers, had published articles which criticized the respondent in rather vivid language. The appellant had also participated in shareholders' meetings and corresponded with the respondent in a manner that could be described as aggressive in nature and tone. Of course, these matters are irrelevant to s. 143(1); they are relevant only to s. 143(5).

II.   ISSUES

This appeal raises two issues. First, is a beneficial shareholder a "shareholder entitled to vote", within the meaning of s. 143(1) of the *Bank Act*? This is a threshold question. Under s. 143(1), only a "shareholder entitled to vote" may submit a shareholder's proposal for inclusion in a management proxy circular. Second, do the appellant's proposals run afoul of s. 143(5)(*b*) or s. 143(5)(*e*) of the *Bank Act*? Under s. 143(5)(*b*) and (*e*), the bank is not required to include a proposal in the circular if it is clear that the proposal was submitted primarily to enforce a personal claim or redress a personal grievance, or to promote general political, social or other listed causes; or if the rights associated with the submission of the proposal are being abused to secure publicity.

The second question is reached only if the answer to the first question is in the affirmative. Because I answer the first questions in the negative, I do not reach the second question. Therefore, I refrain from commenting upon the analysis of the learned trial judge with respect to s. 143(5).

· · · ·

IV.   JUDGMENTS APPEALED FROM

Ontario Court (General Division)

The appellant brought an application for an order to restrain the respondent from holding its annual meeting until the respondent included the

---

† (1996), 139 D.L.R. (4th) 415 at 418–26 (S.C.C.).

appellant's proposals in its management proxy circular. In an endorsement, Kent J. dismissed the application, relying upon s. 143(5) of the *Bank Act*. He did not consider s. 143(1) of the Act. Kent J. was not persuaded that appellant's proposals were an attempt to redress a personal grievance (s. 143(5)(*b*) of the Act), but he was persuaded that the appellant's proposals were submitted to secure publicity (s. 143(5)(*e*) of the Act). Accordingly, the respondent was entitled to refuse to include the appellant's proposals in the management proxy circular. Kent J. made no order as to costs.

Ontario Court of Appeal (*per* Grange J.A., Labrosse and Abella JJ.A. concurring)

The appellant appealed, and the respondent cross-appealed. The respondent asked that the application be dismissed on the additional ground that the appellant did not satisfy the requirements of s. 143(1) because he was not a registered shareholder. In an endorsement, the Ontario Court of Appeal held that the appellant was not a "shareholder entitled to vote at an annual meeting" within the meaning of s. 143(1), and therefore he was not entitled to submit a proposal. It was unnecessary to consider s. 143(5). The appeal was dismissed and the cross-appeal was allowed. The Court of Appeal awarded to the respondent the costs of one appeal, including the costs of an order to expedite (which had been made on the appellant's motion).

V. ANALYSIS

We are asked to determine a straightforward question of statutory interpretation; namely, whether a beneficial shareholder is a "shareholder entitled to vote" within the meaning of s. 143(1) of the *Bank Act*.

Both parties made use of several methods of statutory interpretation. These methods included the "plain meaning" approach, a contextual or structural approach (including the use of the *expressio unius est exclusio alterius* principle), and a purposive approach drawing upon understandings of possible legislative intent, particularly in light of the origins of comparable legislation in Canada and the development of securities regulation rules in the United States. Also included was a policy-oriented approach which invited us to consider the desirability of interpreting s. 143(1) in a manner that would recognize the evolution of extensive beneficial holdings, and the movement towards granting to beneficial share-

holders many of the rights traditionally enjoyed by registered shareholders, with respect to promoting active shareholder participation in corporate governance.

While the parties' use of these various interpretive techniques is adept, a full discussion of these techniques is unnecessary to the resolution of this appeal. This is so because the language and context of the provisions in question make their meaning clear.

To state the obvious, the first step in a question of statutory interpretation is always an examination of the language of the statute itself. As Elmer A. Driedger wrote in his text, *Construction of Statutes*, 2nd ed. (Toronto: Butterworths, 1983), at p. 87:

> Today there is only one principle or approach, namely, the words of an Act are to be read in their entire context and in their grammatical and ordinary sense harmoniously with the scheme of the Act, the object of the Act, and the intention of Parliament.... Lord Atkinson in *Victoria (City) v. Bishop of Vancouver Island* [[1921] 2 A.C. 384, at p. 387] put it this way:
>
> > "In the construction of statutes their words must be interpreted in their ordinary grammatical sense, unless there be something in the context, or in the object of the statute in which they occur, or in the circumstances with reference to which they are used, to show that they were used in a special sense different from their ordinary grammatical sense."

This principle has been cited by our Court on numerous occasions: see, for example, *Friesen v. Canada*, [1995] 3 S.C.R. 103, 127 D.L.R. (4th) 193 (S.C.C.), *Stubart Investments Ltd. v. The Queen*, [1984] 1 S.C.R. 536, 10 D.L.R. (4th) 1 (S.C.C.), and *Québec (Communauté urbaine) v. Corp. Notre-Dame de Bon-Secours*, [1994] 3 S.C.R. 3 (S.C.C.). When I apply this principle to this case, I conclude that the appellant's arguments must fail, as I will now discuss.

For convenience, I will again reproduce s. 143(1) and (2):

143(1) A shareholder entitled to vote at an annual meeting of shareholders of a bank may
(*a*) submit to the bank notice of any matter that the shareholder proposes to raise at the meeting; and
(*b*) discuss at the meeting any matter in respect of which the shareholder would have been entitled to submit a proposal.

(2) A bank that solicits proxies shall, in the management proxy circular required by subsec-

tion 261(1), set out any proposal of a shareholder submitted for consideration at a meeting of shareholders or attach the proposal to the management proxy circular. [Emphasis added.]

In order to submit a proposal, a person must be "a shareholder entitled to vote at an annual meeting of shareholders of a bank". This phrase is not defined expressly in the *Bank Act* nor in provisions which are very similar to s. 143(1). These similar provisions are found in a number of federal and provincial statutes, including the *Canada Business Corporations Act, R.S.C.* 1985, c. C-44 ("*CBCA*"). A previous formulation (in force prior to February 1, 1977) of Rule 14a-8 under §14(a) of the American *Securities Exchange Act of 1934*, 48 Stat. 881 (now 15 U.S.C. §§78a *et seq.* (1994)), is also comparable, but the differences in statutory context, and the fact that in the present appeal there is no need to look outside the four corners of the *Bank Act*, have persuaded me not to address it.

The appellant urges us to interpret the term "shareholder" and the phrase "a shareholder entitled to vote" as including both registered and beneficial shareholders. To this end, he draws our attention to a number of sections of the *Bank Act* which he argues are supportive of this view. For instance, he points out that s. 2 of the Act defines the term "complainant" as "a registered holder *or a beneficial owner*" (emphasis added). He notes that s. 7(1) of the Act defines "shareholder" as a person who, "according to the securities register of the body corporate ... is the owner of one or more shares of the body corporate *or is entitled to be entered in the securities register or like record of the body corporate as the owner of the share or shares*" (emphasis added). Section 7(2) of the Act defines a "holder of a share" by reference "to the fact that the person is registered *or is entitled to be registered in the securities register or like record of the body corporate as the holder of that share ...*" (emphasis added). The appellant also submits that by virtue of s. 263 of the *Bank Act*, which requires registrants to vote beneficial-owned shares in accordance with the beneficial owner's instructions, and the Canadian Securities Administrators' National Policy Statement No. 41, which reinforces the right of beneficial shareholders to direct the voting of their shares, a beneficial shareholder is, effectively, a shareholder entitled to vote.

The respondent offers a number of replies to these points. The respondent submits that ss. 2 and 7 of the Act actually militate against the appellant's position. Section 2 provides an express definition of the term "beneficial ownership" (it includes "ownership through one or more trustees, legal representatives, agents or other intermediaries"). This indicates that Parliament turned its mind to beneficial owners, and selected a term to designate them. The fact that both the "registered holder" and the "beneficial owner" are included in the definition of "complainant" in s. 2 demonstrates that when Parliament wished to refer to beneficial owners, it did so by using the designated term. The fact that s. 7 uses the terms "person ... entitled to be entered" and "person ... entitled to be registered" rather than the term "beneficial owner" indicates that the former terms do not embrace beneficial shareholders. Respondent suggests that the former terms may refer to registration entitlements flowing from the death of a registered owner (s. 96 of the Act) or the transference of the shares (s. 126 of the Act). With respect to National Policy Statement No. 41, the respondent submits that the Policy imposes obligations as between the beneficial shareholder and the registrant (the intermediary) precisely because the *Bank Act* and other legislation do not grant the relevant rights as between the beneficial owner and the company.

But the respondent's most compelling argument is based on s. 93(1) of the Act. Again, for convenience, I will reproduce the section:

> 93(1) *A Bank* or a trustee within the meaning of section 294 *may*, subject to subsections 137(2) to (5) and sections 138 to 141 and 145, *treat the registered owner of a security as the person exclusively entitled to vote*, to receive notices, to receive any interest, dividend or other payment in respect of the security and to exercise all of the rights and powers of an owner of the security. [Emphasis added.]

Subsections (2) to (5) of s. 137 relate to the fixing of record dates, ss. 138 to 140 establish notice requirements for meetings, s. 141 addresses special business, and s. 145 relates to the list of shareholders who are entitled to receive notice of a meeting. None of these provisions has direct application to the facts of this appeal.

As we have seen, s. 143(1) provides that only a "shareholder entitled to vote" is entitled to submit a shareholder's proposal. Section 93(1) provides that a bank is entitled to treat the *registered owner* as the person *exclusively* entitled to vote. In the face of the express language and clear meaning of s. 93(1), the appellant's arguments about the interpretation of the word "shareholder", and the significance of the beneficial shareholder's right to vote by means of proxy, are, with respect, unpersuasive. The appellant's valiant endeavour to construct purposive and policy-based arguments to support his position must also fail. The statute is clear on its face. The respondent may treat the registered owner as the person exclusively "entitled to vote"; the appellant is not the registered owner, and therefore is not "entitled to vote"; only a shareholder "entitled to vote" can submit a shareholder's proposal; the appellant is not "entitled to vote" and therefore cannot submit a shareholder's proposal.

To return to the Driedger rule on statutory construction referred to above, there is nothing in the context of the provisions in question to contradict their plain meaning.

I note that the Ontario Court of Appeal came to the same conclusion in *Re Greenpeace Foundation of Canada and Inco Ltd.*, March 21, 1984 (summarized at 25 A.C.W.S. (2d) 149 (Ont. C.A.)), affirming [1984] O.J. No. 274 (QL) (Ont. H.C.J.) [summarized 24 A.C.W.S. (2d) 176], a case which in involved the *CBCA* counterparts to s. 143(1) and s. 93(1) of the *Bank Act* (ss. 137(1) (formerly s. 131(1)) and s. 51(1)(formerly s. 47(1)) of the *CBCA*).

This is not to say that the appellant's position is without merit from a policy perspective. While the respondent argues persuasively that requiring a bank to go beyond its share registry to verify the status of beneficial holders may cause administrative difficulties, the appellant counters that the Securities Exchange Commission of the United States has been able to manage these difficulties and is apparently of the opinion that the benefits of allowing beneficial shareholders to submit shareholder proposals outweigh the costs. It is evident that s. 143(1) of the *Bank Act* and its counterparts on federal and provincial levels represent a legislative commitment to the promotion of shareholder participation in corporate governance. It is perhaps equally evident that, as the Joint Regulatory Task Force on Shareholder Communication (reporting to the Canadian Securities Administrators) observed in its July 1987 report (at p. 5), "[t]here is no going back to the system of widespread registration in the name of individual security holders, nor should there be from the point of view of market efficiency."

It may well be that Parliament will see fit to amend s. 143(1) of the *Bank Act* and its counterparts. The respondent drew our attention to a paper entitled *Canadian Business Corporations Act Discussion Paper: Proposals for Technical Amendments* (Ottawa: Industry Canada, September, 1995), which recommended that 137 *CBCA*, a counterpart to s. 143(1) of the *Bank Act*, be amended to expressly permit a beneficial owner of shares to submit a shareholder proposal. The authors of the discussion paper observe (at pp. 56–57) that

> [a]n amendment to permit beneficial shareholders to submit shareholder proposals under s. 137 would both reflect the current market reality of share holdings and fit into a broader effort to improve communication among the corporation and the owners of its shares.

But however desirable or undesirable such changes might be, they are in the domain of the legislature, not the courts.

I would also observe that, at present, shareholders in the appellant's position are not entirely without recourse. The beneficial holder may ask the registered holder to submit the beneficial holder's proposal. Or the beneficial holder may arrange to have one or more shares registered in his or her name. As a registered holder, the shareholder would be entitled to submit proposals in his or her own right. To the extent that these options may be considered unwieldy or otherwise problematic, it is open to Parliament to revisit them.

VI.   DISPOSITION

As noted at the outset, this appeal was dismissed at the hearing. Both parties made oral submissions on the question of costs. Upon hearing these submissions, the Court concluded that, inasmuch as we dismissed the appeal, the order for costs in the courts below would not be disturbed and there would be no order as to costs in this Court.

Appeal dismissed.

III

"Banking Business"

5   "Banking Business"

Background Reading: M.H. Ogilvie, *Bank and Customer Law in Canada*, 2d Edition (Toronto: Irwin Law, 2013) Chapter 5.

(a)   *Bank Act*[†]

PART VIII
BUSINESS AND POWERS

GENERAL BUSINESS

Main business

409.(1) Subject to this Act, a bank shall not engage in or carry on any business other than the business of banking and such business generally as appertains thereto.

Idem

(2) For greater certainty, the business of banking includes
(a) providing any financial service;
(b) acting as a financial agent;
(c) providing investment counselling services and portfolio management services; and
(d) issuing payment, credit or charge cards and, in cooperation with others including other financial institutions, operating a payment, credit or charge card plan.

Additional activities

410.(1) In addition, a bank may
(a) hold, manage and otherwise deal with real property;

(b) provide prescribed bank-related data processing services;
(c) outside Canada or, with the prior written approval of the Minister, in Canada, engage in any of the following activities, namely,
(i) collecting, manipulating and transmitting
(A) information that is primarily financial or economic in nature,
(B) information that relates to the business of a permitted entity, as defined in subsection 464(1), or
(C) any other information that the Minister may, by order, specify,
(ii) providing advisory or other services in the design, development or implementation of information management systems,
(iii) designing, developing or marketing computer software, and
(iv) designing, developing, manufacturing or selling, as an ancillary activity to any activity referred to in any of subparagraphs (i) to (iii) that the bank is engaging in, computer equipment integral to the provision of information services related to the business of financial institutions or to the provision of financial services;

[†]   S.C. 1991, c. 46, as am. by S.C. 2014, c. 20, ss. 409–463.

(c.1) with the prior written approval of the Minister, develop, design, hold, manage, manufacture, sell or otherwise deal with data transmission systems, information sites, communication devices or information platforms or portals that are used

    (i) to provide information that is primarily financial or economic in nature,

    (ii) to provide information that relates to the business of a permitted entity, as defined in subsection 464(1), or

    (iii) for a prescribed purpose or in prescribed circumstances;

(c.2) engage, under prescribed terms and conditions, if any are prescribed, in specialized business management or advisory services;

(d) promote merchandise and services to the holders of any payment, credit or charge card issued by the bank;

(e) engage in the sale of

    (i) tickets, including lottery tickets, on a non-profit public service basis in connection with special, temporary and infrequent non-commercial celebrations or projects that are of local, municipal, provincial or national interest,

    (ii) urban transit tickets, and

    (iii) tickets in respect of a lottery sponsored by the federal government or a provincial or municipal government or an agency of any such government or governments;

(f) act as a custodian of property; and

(g) act as receiver, liquidator or sequestrator.

Restriction

(2) Except as authorized by or under this Act, a bank shall not deal in goods, wares or merchandise or engage in any trade or other business.

Regulations

(3) The Governor in Council may make regulations

(a) respecting what a bank may or may not do with respect to the carrying on of the activities referred to in paragraphs (1)(c) to (c.2);

(b) imposing terms and conditions in respect of

    (i) the provision of financial services referred to in paragraph 409(2)(a) that are financial planning services,

    (ii) the provision of services referred to in paragraph 409(2)(c), and

    (iii) the carrying on of the activities referred to in any of paragraphs (1)(c) to (c.2); and

(c) respecting the circumstances in which banks may be exempted from the requirement to obtain the approval of the Minister before carrying on a particular activity referred to in paragraph (1)(c) or (c.1).

Networking

411.(1) Subject to section 416, a bank may

(a) act as agent for any person in respect of the provision of any service that is provided by a financial institution, a permitted entity as defined in subsection 464(1) or a prescribed entity and may enter into an arrangement with any person in respect of the provision of that service; or

(b) refer any person to any such financial institution or entity.

Regulations

(2) The Governor in Council may make regulations respecting the disclosure of

(a) the name of the principal for whom a bank is acting as agent pursuant to subsection (1); and

(b) whether any commission is being earned by a bank when acting as agent pursuant to subsection (1).

Restriction on fiduciary activities

412. No bank shall act in Canada as

(a) an executor, administrator or official guardian or a guardian, tutor, curator, judicial adviser or committee of a mentally incompetent person; or

(b) a trustee for a trust.

Restriction on deposit taking

413.(1) A bank shall not accept deposits in Canada unless

(a) it is a member institution, as defined in section 2 of the *Canada Deposit Insurance Corporation Act*;

(b) it has been authorized under subsection 26.03(1) of that Act to accept deposits without being a member institution, as defined in section 2 of that Act; or

(c) the order approving the commencement and carrying on of business by the bank authorizes it to accept deposits solely in accordance with subsection (3).

(2) [Repealed, 2001, c. 9, s. 102]

Deposits that fall below $150,000

(3) A bank referred to in paragraph (1)(b) or (c) shall ensure that, on each day that is at least 30 days after the bank receives the authorization referred to in that paragraph,

$$A/B \leq 0.01$$

where

A is the sum of all amounts each of which is the sum of all the deposits held by the bank at the end of a day in the preceding 30 days each of which deposits is less than $150,000 and payable in Canada; and

B is the sum of all amounts each of which is the sum of all deposits held by the bank at the end of a day in those preceding 30 days and payable in Canada.

Exchange rate

(4) For the purpose of subsection (3), the rate of exchange that shall be applied on any day in determining the amount in Canadian dollars of a deposit in a currency of a country other than Canada shall be determined in accordance with rules prescribed under subsection 26.03(2) of the *Canada Deposit Insurance Corporation Act*.

Definition of "deposit"

(5) For the purpose of subsection (3), "deposit" has the meaning that would be given to it by the schedule to the *Canada Deposit Insurance Corporation Act* for the purposes of deposit insurance if that schedule were read without reference to subsections 2(2), (5) and (6) of that schedule, but does not include prescribed deposits.

Regulations

(6) The Governor in Council may make regulations

(a) prescribing the deposits referred to in subsection (5); and

(b) prescribing terms and conditions with respect to the acceptance of those deposits.

Notice before opening account or providing prescribed product

413.1(1) Before a bank referred to in paragraph 413(1)(b) or (c) opens a deposit account in Canada or provides in Canada a prescribed product that relates to a deposit, the bank shall, at the prescribed time and place and in the prescribed form and manner, give the person requesting the opening of the account or the provision of the product

(a) a notice in writing that deposits to the deposit account, or that the deposit that relates to the prescribed product, as the case may be, will not be insured by the Canada Deposit Insurance Corporation or, if the request is made by telephone, a verbal notice to that effect; and

(b) any other information that may be prescribed.

Other notice

(2) A bank referred to in paragraph 413(1)(b) or (c) shall, in accordance with the regulations,

(a) post notices at all of its branches, and at prescribed points of service, in Canada where deposits are accepted, and on all of its websites at which deposits are accepted in Canada, to inform the public that deposits with the bank are not insured by the Canada Deposit Insurance Corporation; and

(b) include in its advertisements notices to inform the public that deposits with the bank are not insured by the Canada Deposit Insurance Corporation.

Regulations

(3) The Governor in Council may make regulations

(a) prescribing the time and place at which and the form and manner in which notices referred to in subsection (1) are to be given and the other information to be contained in the notices; and

(b) respecting notices for the purpose of subsection (2).

Deposits less than $150,000

413.2(1) Subject to the regulations, a bank referred to in paragraph 413(1)(b) or (c) may not, in respect of its business in Canada, act as agent for any person in the taking of a deposit that is less than $150,000 and payable in Canada.

Meaning of "deposit"

(2) In this section, "deposit" has the meaning assigned to that term by subsection 413(5).

Regulations

(3) The Governor in Council may make regulations respecting the circumstances in which, and the conditions under which, a bank referred to in subsection (1) may act as agent for any person in the taking of a deposit that is less than $150,000 and payable in Canada.

Shared premises

413.3(1) Subject to the regulations, no bank referred to in paragraph 413(1)(b) or (c) shall carry on business in Canada on premises that are shared with those of a member institution, within the meaning of section 2 of the *Canada Deposit Insurance Corporation Act*, that is affiliated with the bank.

Limitation

(2) Subsection (1) only applies in respect of premises or any portion of premises on which both the bank and the member institution carry on business with the public and to which the public has access.

Adjacent premises

(3) Subject to the regulations, no bank referred to in paragraph 413(1)(b) or (c) shall carry on business in Canada on premises that are adjacent to a branch or office of a member institution, within the meaning of section 2 of the *Canada Deposit Insurance Corporation Act*, that is affiliated with the bank, unless the bank clearly indicates to its customers that its business and the premises on which it is carried on are separate and distinct from the business and premises of the affiliated member institution.

Regulations

(4) The Governor in Council may make regulations

(a) respecting the circumstances in which, and the conditions under which, a bank referred to in paragraph 413(1)(b) or (c) may carry on business in Canada on premises that are shared with those of a member institution referred to in subsection (1); and

(b) respecting the circumstances in which, and the conditions under which, a bank referred to in paragraph 413(1)(b) or (c) may carry on business in Canada on premises that are adjacent to a branch or office of a member institution referred to in subsection (3).

Restriction on guarantees

414.(1) A bank shall not guarantee on behalf of any person the payment or repayment of any sum of money unless

(a) the sum of money is a fixed sum of money with or without interest thereon; and

(b) the person on whose behalf the bank has undertaken to guarantee the payment or repayment has an unqualified obligation to reimburse the bank for the full amount of the payment or repayment to be guaranteed.

Exception

(2) Paragraph (1)(a) does not apply where the person on whose behalf the bank has undertaken to guarantee the payment or repayment is a subsidiary of the bank.

Regulations

(3) The Governor in Council may make regulations imposing terms and conditions in respect of guarantees permitted by this section.

Restriction on securities activities

415. A bank shall not deal in Canada in securities to the extent prohibited or restricted by such regulations as the Governor in Council may make for the purposes of this section.

Prohibition

415.1(1) It is prohibited for a bank to issue a debt obligation in relation to which the amounts of principal and interest owing are guaranteed to be paid from loans or other assets held by an entity that is created and organized for the principal purpose of holding those loans or other assets and with the intention of legally isolating those loans or other assets from the bank, unless

(a) the debt obligation is a covered bond as defined in section 21.5 of the *National Housing Act*;

(b) the bank is a registered issuer as defined in section 21.5 of that Act other than one whose right to issue covered bonds has been suspended; and

(c) the debt obligation is issued under a registered program as defined in section 21.5 of that Act.

Exception

(2) The Governor in Council may make regulations exempting any type of debt obligation from the application of subsection (1).

Derivatives — regulations

415.2(1) The Governor in Council may make regulations respecting a bank's activities in relation to derivatives.

Definition of "derivative"

(2) In this section, "derivative" means an option, swap, futures contract, forward contract or other

financial or commodity contract or instrument whose market price, value, delivery obligations, payment obligations or settlement obligations are derived from, referenced to or based on an underlying interest, including a price, rate, index, value, variable, event, probability or thing.

Benchmarks — regulations

415.3(1) The Governor in Council may make regulations respecting a bank's activities in relation to benchmarks.

Definition of "benchmark"

(2) In this section, "benchmark" means a price, estimate, rate, index or value that is
(a) determined from time to time by reference to an assessment of one or more underlying interests;
(b) made available to the public, either free of charge or on payment; and
(c) used for reference for any purpose, including
  (i) determining the interest payable, or other sums that are due, under loan agreements or other financial contracts or instruments,
  (ii) determining the value of financial instruments or the price at which they may be bought or sold, and
  (iii) measuring the performance of financial instruments.

Restriction on insurance business

416.(1) A bank shall not undertake the business of insurance except to the extent permitted by this Act or the regulations.

Restriction on acting as agent

(2) A bank shall not act in Canada as agent for any person in the placing of insurance and shall not lease or provide space in any branch in Canada of the bank to any person engaged in the placing of insurance.

Regulations

(3) The Governor in Council may make regulations respecting the matters referred to in subsection (1) and regulations respecting relations between banks and
(a) entities that undertake the business of insurance; or
(b) insurance agents or insurance brokers.

Saving

(4) Nothing in this section precludes a bank from
(a) requiring insurance to be placed by a borrower for the security of the bank; or
(b) obtaining group insurance for its employees or the employees of any bodies corporate in which it has a substantial investment pursuant to section 468.

(5) [Repealed, 1997, c. 15, s. 45]

Definition of "business of insurance"

(6) In this section, "business of insurance" includes
(a) the issuance of any annuity if the liability in respect of the annuity is contingent on the death of a person; and
(b) the issuance of any debt obligation, any of whose terms and conditions are established on the basis of mortality considerations, under which the issuer is obliged to make periodic payments.

Restriction on leasing

417. A bank shall not engage in Canada in any personal property leasing activity in which a financial leasing entity, as defined in subsection 464(1), is not permitted to engage.

Restriction on residential mortgages

418.(1) A bank shall not make a loan in Canada on the security of residential property in Canada for the purpose of purchasing, renovating or improving that property, or refinance such a loan, if the amount of the loan, together with the amount then outstanding of any mortgage having an equal or prior claim against the property, would exceed 80 per cent of the value of the property at the time of the loan.

Exception

(2) Subsection (1) does not apply in respect of
(a) a loan made or guaranteed under the *National Housing Act* or any other Act of Parliament by or pursuant to which a different limit on the value of property on the security of which the bank may make a loan is established;
(b) a loan if repayment of the amount of the loan that exceeds the maximum amount set out in subsection (1) is guaranteed or insured by a government agency or a private insurer approved by the Superintendent;

(c) the acquisition by the bank from an entity of securities issued or guaranteed by the entity that are secured on any residential property, whether in favour of a trustee or otherwise, or the making of a loan by the bank to the entity against the issue of such securities; or

(d) a loan secured by a mortgage where
  (i) the mortgage is taken back by the bank on a property disposed of by the bank, including where the disposition is by way of a realization of a security interest, and
  (ii) the mortgage secures payment of an amount payable to the bank for the property.

Restriction on charges to borrowers

418.1(1) Subject to any regulations made under subsection (2), a bank that has obtained insurance or a guarantee against default on a loan made in Canada on the security of residential property shall not charge a borrower an amount for the insurance or guarantee that exceeds the actual cost to the bank of the insurance or guarantee.

Regulations

(2) The Governor in Council may make regulations
  (a) respecting the determination of the actual cost to a bank for the purposes of subsection (1);
  (b) respecting the circumstances in which a bank is exempt from the application of subsection (1);
  (c) respecting, in relation to insurance or a guarantee against default on a loan made by a bank in Canada on the security of residential property,
    (i) the arrangements into which the bank and any affiliates that it controls, and the representatives and the employees of each, may or may not enter, and
    (ii) the payments or benefits that the bank and any affiliates that it controls, and the representatives and the employees of each, may or may not accept from an insurer or the insurer's affiliates; and
  (d) respecting any other matters necessary to carry out the purposes of subsection (1).

Regulations — disclosure

(3) The Governor in Council may make regulations respecting the disclosure by a bank of information relating to insurance or a guarantee against default on a loan made by the bank in Canada on the security of residential property, including regulations respecting

(a) the information that must be disclosed, including information relating to
  (i) the person who benefits from the insurance or guarantee,
  (ii) the arrangements between
    (A) the bank or any affiliates that it controls, or the representatives or the employees of each, and
    (B) the insurer or the insurer's affiliates, and
  (iii) the payments and benefits that the bank and any affiliates that it controls, and the representatives and the employees of each, accept from an insurer or the insurer's affiliates;

(b) the time and place at which, the form and manner in which and the persons to whom information is to be disclosed; and

(c) the circumstances under which a bank is not required to disclose information.

Policies re security interests

419.(1) The directors of a bank shall establish and the bank shall adhere to policies regarding the creation of security interests in property of the bank to secure obligations of the bank and the acquisition by the bank of beneficial interests in property that is subject to security interests.

Order to amend policies

(2) The Superintendent may, by order, direct a bank to amend its policies as specified in the order.

Compliance

(3) A bank shall comply with an order made under subsection (2) within the time specified in the order.

Regulations and guidelines

419.1 The Governor in Council may make regulations and the Superintendent may make guidelines respecting the creation by a bank of security interests in its property to secure obligations of the bank and the acquisition by the bank of beneficial interests in property that is subject to security interests.

Exception

419.2 Sections 419 and 419.1 do not apply in respect of a security interest created by a bank to secure an obligation of the bank to the Bank of Canada or the Canada Deposit Insurance Corporation.

Restriction on receivers

420. A bank shall not grant to a person the right to appoint a receiver or a receiver and manager of the property or business of the bank.

Restriction on partnerships

421.(1) Except with the approval of the Superintendent, a bank may not be a general partner in a limited partnership or a partner in a general partnership.

Meaning of "general partnership"

(2) For the purposes of subsection (1), "general partnership" means any partnership other than a limited partnership.

422.(1) [Repealed, 2001, c. 9, s. 109]
(2) [Repealed, 1993, c. 44, s. 27]

Definition of "non-WTO Member bank subsidiary"

422.1 In section 422.2, "non-WTO Member bank subsidiary" means a bank that is a subsidiary of a foreign bank and that is not controlled by a WTO Member resident.

Limitation on branches in Canada of non-WTO Member bank subsidiaries

422.2 No non-WTO Member bank subsidiary shall have any branch in Canada, other than its head office and one branch, without the approval of the Minister.

422.3 to 424. [Repealed, 1994, c. 47, s. 25]

SPECIAL SECURITY

Definitions

425.(1) For the purposes of sections 426 to 436,

"agricultural equipment" means implements, apparatus, appliances and machinery of any kind usually affixed to real property, for use on a farm, but does not include a farm electric system;

"agricultural implements" means tools, implements, apparatus, appliances and machines of any kind not usually affixed to real property, for use on or in connection with a farm, and vehicles for use in the business of farming and, without restricting the generality of the foregoing, includes plows, harrows, drills, seeders, cultivators, mowing machines, reapers, binders, threshing machines, combines, leaf tobacco tying machines, tractors, movable granaries, trucks for carrying products of agriculture, equipment for bee-keeping, cream separators, churns, washing machines, spraying apparatus, portable irrigation apparatus, incubators, milking machines, refrigerators and heating and cooking appliances for farming operations or use in the farm home of a kind not usually affixed to real property;

"aquacultural electric system" means all machinery, apparatus and appliances for the generation or distribution of electricity in an aquaculture operation, whether or not affixed to real property;

"aquacultural equipment" means implements, apparatus, appliances and machinery of any kind usually affixed to real property for use in an aquaculture operation, but does not include an aquacultural electric system;

"aquacultural implements" means tools, implements, apparatus, appliances and machines of any kind not usually affixed to real property, for use in an aquaculture operation, and includes net pen systems, vehicles and boats for use in aquaculture;

"aquacultural stock growing or produced in the aquaculture operation" means all products of the aquaculture operation;

"aquaculture" means the cultivation of aquatic plants and animals;

"aquaculture operation" means any premises or site where aquaculture is carried out;

"aquaculturist" includes the owner, occupier, landlord and tenant of an aquaculture operation;

"aquatic broodstock" means any aquatic plants and animals used to produce aquatic seedstock;

"aquatic plants and animals" means plants and animals that, at most stages of their development or life cycles, live in an aquatic environment;

"aquatic seedstock" means aquatic plants and animals that at any stage of their development are purchased or collected by an aquaculturist for cultivation;

"bill of lading" includes all receipts for goods, wares and merchandise accompanied by an undertaking
(a) to move the goods, wares and merchandise from the place where they were received to some other place, by any means whatever, or
(b) to deliver to a place other than the place where the goods, wares and merchandise were received a like quantity of goods, wares and merchandise of the same or a similar grade or kind;

"crops growing or produced on the farm" means all products of the farm;

"farm" means land in Canada used for the purpose of farming, which term includes livestock raising, dairying, bee-keeping, fruit growing, the growing of trees and all tillage of the soil;

"farm electric system" means all machinery, apparatus and appliances for the generation or distribution of electricity on a farm whether or not affixed to real property;

"farmer" includes the owner, occupier, landlord and tenant of a farm;

"fish" includes shellfish, crustaceans and marine animals;

"fisherman" means a person whose business consists in whole or in part of fishing;

"fishing" means fishing for or catching fish by any method;

"fishing equipment and supplies" means equipment, apparatus, appliances and supplies for use in the operation of a fishing vessel and not forming part thereof, or for use in fishing, and, without restricting the generality of the foregoing, includes detachable engines and machinery, lines, hooks, trawls, nets, anchors, traps, bait, salt, fuel and stores;

"fishing vessel" means any ship or boat or any other description of vessel for use in fishing and equipment, apparatus and appliances for use in the operation thereof and forming part thereof, or any share or part interest therein;

"forest" means land in Canada covered with timber stands or that, formerly so covered, is not put to any use inconsistent with forestry, and includes a sugar bush;

"forestry" means the conservation, cultivation, improvement, harvesting and rational utilization of timber stands and the resources contained therein and obtainable therefrom, and includes the operation of a sugar bush;

"forestry equipment" means implements, apparatus, appliances and machinery of any kind usually affixed to real property, for use in a forest;

"forestry implements" means tools, implements, apparatus, appliances and machines of any kind not usually affixed to real property, for use in forestry, and includes vehicles for use in forestry;

"forestry producer" means a person whose business consists in whole or in part of forestry and includes a producer of maple products;

"goods, wares and merchandise" includes products of agriculture, products of aquaculture, products of the forest, products of the quarry and mine, prod-ucts of the sea, lakes and rivers, and all other articles of commerce;

"grain" includes wheat, oats, barley, rye, corn, buckwheat, flax, beans and all kinds of seeds;

"hydrocarbons" means solid, liquid and gaseous hydrocarbons and any natural gas whether consisting of a single element or of two or more elements in chemical combination or uncombined and, without restricting the generality of the foregoing, includes oil-bearing shale, tar sands, crude oil, petroleum, helium and hydrogen sulphide;

"livestock" includes

   (a) horses and other equines,

   (b) cattle, sheep, goats and other ruminants, and

   (c) swine, poultry, bees and fur-bearing animals;

"manufacturer" means any person who manufactures or produces by hand, art, process or mechanical means any goods, wares and merchandise and, without restricting the generality of the foregoing, includes a manufacturer of logs, timber or lumber, maltster, distiller, brewer, refiner and producer of petroleum, tanner, curer, packer, canner, bottler and a person who packs, freezes or dehydrates any goods, wares and merchandise;

"minerals" includes base and precious metals, coal, salt and every other substance that is an article of commerce obtained from the earth by any method of extraction, but does not include hydrocarbons or any animal or vegetable substance other than coal;

"products of agriculture" includes

   (a) grain, hay, roots, vegetables, fruits, other crops and all other direct products of the soil, and

   (b) honey, livestock (whether alive or dead), dairy products, eggs and all other indirect products of the soil;

"products of aquaculture" includes all cultivated aquatic plants and animals;

"products of the forest" includes

   (a) logs, pulpwood, piling, spars, railway ties, poles, pit props and all other timber,

   (b) boards, laths, shingles, deals, staves and all other lumber, bark, wood chips and sawdust and Christmas trees,

   (c) skins and furs of wild animals, and

   (d) maple products;

"products of the quarry and mine" includes stone, clay, sand, gravel, metals, ores, coal, salt, precious stones, metalliferous and non-metallic minerals and hydrocarbons, whether obtained by excavation, drilling or otherwise;

"products of the sea, lakes and rivers" includes fish of all kinds, marine and freshwater organic and inorganic life and any substances extracted or derived from any water, but does not include products of aquaculture;

"unperfected", in relation to a security interest, means that the security interest has not been registered in a public register maintained under the law under which the security interest is created, or has not been perfected or published by any other means recognized by that law, where the registration or other means of perfection or publication would have made the security interest effective against third parties or would have determined priorities in rank in respect of rights in, on or in respect of the property that is subject to the security interest;

"warehouse receipt" includes

(a) any receipt given by any person for goods, wares and merchandise in the person's actual, visible and continued possession as bailee thereof in good faith and not as the owner thereof,

(b) receipts given by any person who is the owner or keeper of a harbour, cove, pond, wharf, yard, warehouse, shed, storehouse or other place for the storage of goods, wares and merchandise, for goods, wares and merchandise delivered to the person as bailee, and actually in the place or in one or more of the places owned or kept by the person, whether or not that person is engaged in other business,

(c) receipts given by any person in charge of logs or timber in transit from timber limits or other lands to the place of destination of the logs or timber,

(d) Lake Shippers' Clearance Association receipts and transfer certificates, British Columbia Grain Shippers' Clearance Association receipts and transfer certificates, and all documents recognized by the *Canada Grain Act* as elevator receipts, and

(e) receipts given by any person for any hydrocarbons received by the person as bailee, whether the person's obligation to restore requires delivery of the same hydrocarbons or may be satisfied by delivery of a like quantity of hydrocarbons of the same or a similar grade or kind.

Interpretation — products and by-products

(2) For the purposes of sections 426 to 436, each thing included in the following terms as defined in subsection (1), namely,

(a) "aquacultural stock growing or produced in the aquaculture operation",

(b) "crops growing or produced on the farm",

(c) "livestock",

(d) "products of agriculture",

(e) "products of aquaculture",

(f) "products of the forest",

(g) "products of the quarry and mine", and

(h) "products of the sea, lakes and rivers",

comprises that thing in any form or state and any part thereof and any product or by-product thereof or derived therefrom.

Loans on hydrocarbons and minerals

426.(1) A bank may lend money and make advances on the security of any or all of the following, namely,

(a) hydrocarbons or minerals in, under or on the ground, in place or in storage,

(b) the rights, licences or permits of any person to obtain and remove any such hydrocarbons or minerals and to enter on, occupy and use lands from or on which any of such hydrocarbons or minerals are or may be extracted, mined or produced,

(c) the estate or interest of any person in or to any such hydrocarbons or minerals, rights, licences, permits and lands whether the estate or interest is entire or partial, and

(d) the equipment and casing used or to be used in extracting, mining or producing or seeking to extract, mine or produce, and storing any such, hydrocarbons or minerals,

or of any rights or interests in or to any of the foregoing whether the security be taken from the borrower or from a guarantor of the liability of the borrower or from any other person.

Security

(2) Security under this section may be given by signature and delivery to the bank, by or on behalf of the person giving the security, of an instrument in the prescribed form or in a form to the like effect, and shall affect the property described in the instrument giving the security

(a) of which the person giving the security is the owner at the time of the delivery of the instrument, or

(b) of which that person becomes the owner at any time thereafter before the release of the security by the bank, whether or not the property is in existence at the time of the delivery,

all of which property is for the purposes of this Act property covered by the security.

Rights under security

(3) Any security given under this section vests in the bank, in addition to and without limitation of any other rights or powers vested in or conferred on it, full power, right and authority, through its officers, employees or agents, in the event of

(a) non-payment of any loan or advance as security for the payment of which the bank has taken the security, or

(b) failure to care for, maintain, protect or preserve the property covered by the security,

to do all or any of the following, namely, take possession of, seize, care for, maintain, use, operate and, subject to the provisions of any other Act and any regulations made under any other Act governing the ownership and disposition of the property that is the subject of the security, sell the property covered by the security or part thereof as it sees fit.

Liability to account for surplus

(4) Where a bank exercises any right conferred on it by subsection (3) in relation to property given to it as security, the bank shall provide to the person entitled thereto any surplus proceeds resulting from the exercise of the right that remain after payment of all loans and advances, together with interest and expenses, in relation to which the property was given as security.

Effect of sale

(5) A sale pursuant to subsection (3) of any property given to a bank as security vests in the purchaser all the right and title in and to such property that the person giving the security had when the security was given and that that person thereafter acquired.

Sale to be by public auction

(6) Unless a person by whom property was given to a bank as security has agreed otherwise, a sale pursuant to subsection (3) shall be made by public auction after

(a) notice of the time and place of the sale has been sent by registered mail to the recorded address of the person by whom the property was given as security at least ten days prior to the sale; and

(b) publication of an advertisement of the sale, at least two days prior to the sale, in at least two newspapers published in or nearest to the place where the sale is to be made.

Priority of bank's rights

(7) Subject to subsections (8), (9) and (10), all the rights and powers of a bank in respect of the property covered by security given under this section have priority over all rights subsequently acquired in, on or in respect of the property and also over the claim of any mechanics' lien holder, of any unpaid vendor of equipment or casing or of any person who had a security interest in that property that was unperfected at the time the bank acquired its security in the property.

Exception

(7.1) The priority referred to in subsection (7) does not extend over the claim of any unpaid vendor who had a lien on the equipment or casing, or of any person who has a security interest in the property that was unperfected at the time the bank acquired its security in the property, if the bank acquired its security with knowledge of that unpaid vendor's lien or that other person's security interest.

Idem

(8) The rights and powers of a bank in respect of the property covered by security given under this section do not have priority over an interest or a right acquired in, on or in respect of the property unless, prior to

(a) the registration of such interest or right, or

(b) the registration or filing of the deed or other instrument evidencing such interest or right, or of a caution, caveat or memorial in respect thereof,

there has been registered or filed in the proper land registry or land titles office or office in which are recorded the rights, licences or permits referred to in this section,

(c) an original of the instrument giving the security,

(d) a copy of the instrument giving the security, certified by an officer or employee of the bank to be a true copy, or

(e) a caution, caveat or memorial in respect of the rights of the bank.

Procedure for registering

(9) Every registrar or officer in charge of the proper land registry or land titles or other office to whom a document mentioned in paragraph (8)(c), (d) or (e) is tendered shall register or file the document according to the ordinary procedure for registering or filing within that office documents that evidence liens or charges against, or cautions, caveats or memorials in respect of claims to, interests in or

rights in respect of any such property and subject to payment of the like fees.

Exception

(10) Subsections (8) and (9) do not apply if the law of the appropriate province does not permit the registration or filing of the tendered document or if any law enacted by or under the authority of Parliament, governing the ownership and disposal of the property that is the subject of security given under this section, does not provide by specific reference to this section for the registration or filing of the tendered document.

Further security

(11) When making a loan or an advance on the security provided for by this section, a bank may take, on any property covered by the security, any further security it sees fit.

Substitution of security

(12) Notwithstanding anything in this Act, where the bank holds any security covering hydrocarbons or minerals, it may take in lieu of that security, to the extent of the quantity covered by the security taken, any security covering or entitling it to the delivery of the same hydrocarbons or minerals or hydrocarbons or minerals of the same or a similar grade or kind.

Loans to certain borrowers and security

427.(1) A bank may lend money and make advances
  (a) to any wholesale or retail purchaser or shipper of, or dealer in, products of agriculture, products of aquaculture, products of the forest, products of the quarry and mine, products of the sea, lakes and rivers or goods, wares and merchandise, manufactured or otherwise, on the security of such products or goods, wares and merchandise and of goods, wares and merchandise used in or procured for the packing of such products or goods, wares and merchandise,
  (b) to any person engaged in business as a manufacturer, on the security of goods, wares and merchandise manufactured or produced by that person or procured for such manufacture or production and of goods, wares and merchandise used in or procured for the packing of goods, wares and merchandise so manufactured or produced,
  (c) to any aquaculturist, on the security of aquacultural stock growing or produced in the aquaculture operation or on the security of aquacultural equipment or aquacultural implements,
  (d) to any farmer, on the security of crops growing or produced on the farm or on the security of agricultural equipment or agricultural implements,
  (e) to any aquaculturist
    (i) for the purchase of aquatic broodstock or aquatic seedstock, on the security of the aquatic broodstock or aquatic seedstock and any aquatic stock to be grown therefrom,
    (ii) for the purchase of pesticide, on the security of the pesticide and any aquatic stock to be grown from the site on which the pesticide is to be used, and
    (iii) for the purchase of feed, veterinary drugs, biologicals or vaccines, on the security of the feed, veterinary drugs, biologicals or vaccines and any aquatic stock to be grown in the aquaculture operation on which the feed, veterinary drugs, biologicals or vaccines are to be used,
  (f) to any farmer
    (i) for the purchase of seed grain or seed potatoes, on the security of the seed grain or seed potatoes and any crop to be grown therefrom, and
    (ii) for the purchase of fertilizer or pesticide, on the security of the fertilizer or pesticide and any crop to be grown from land on which, in the same season, the fertilizer or pesticide is to be used,
  (g) to any aquaculturist on the security of aquatic plants and animals, but security taken under this paragraph is not effective in respect of any aquatic plants and animals that, at the time the security is taken, by any statutory law that is then in force, are exempt from seizure under writs of execution and the aquaculturist is prevented from giving as security for money lent to the aquaculturist,
  (h) to any farmer or to any person engaged in livestock raising, on the security of feed or livestock, but security taken under this paragraph is not effective in respect of any livestock that, at the time the security is taken, by any statutory law that is then in force, is exempt from seizure under writs of execution and the farmer or other person engaged in livestock raising is prevented from giving as security for money lent to the farmer or other person,
  (i) to any aquaculturist for the purchase of aquacultural implements, on the security of those aquacultural implements,

(j) to any farmer for the purchase of agricultural implements, on the security of those agricultural implements,

(k) to any aquaculturist for the purchase or installation of aquacultural equipment or an aquacultural electric system, on the security of that aquacultural equipment or aquacultural electric system,

(l) to any farmer for the purchase or installation of agricultural equipment or a farm electric system, on the security of that agricultural equipment or farm electric system,

(m) to any aquaculturist for

   (i) the repair or overhaul of an aquacultural implement, aquacultural equipment or an aquaculture electric system,

   (ii) the alteration or improvement of an aquacultural electric system,

   (iii) the erection or construction of fencing or works for drainage in an aquaculture operation for the holding, rearing or protection of aquatic plants and animals or for the supply of water to such plants and animals or the disposal of effluent from them,

   (iv) the construction, repair or alteration of or making of additions to any building or structure in an aquaculture operation, and

   (v) any works for the improvement or development of an aquaculture operation for which a loan, as defined in the *Canada Small Business Financing Act*, or a business improvement loan, as defined in the *Small Business Loans Act*, may be made,

on the security of aquacultural equipment or aquacultural implements, but security taken under this paragraph is not effective in respect of aquacultural equipment or aquacultural implements that, at the time the security is taken, by any statutory law that is then in force, are exempt from seizure under writs of execution and the aquaculturist is prevented from giving as security for money lent to the aquaculturist,

(n) to any farmer for

   (i) the repair or overhaul of an agricultural implement, agricultural equipment or a farm electric system,

   (ii) the alteration or improvement of a farm electric system,

   (iii) the erection or construction of fencing or works for drainage on a farm,

   (iv) the construction, repair or alteration of or making of additions to any building or structure on a farm,

   (v) [Repealed, 2009, c. 15, s. 13]

   (vi) any purpose for which a loan as defined in the *Canadian Agricultural Loans Act* may be made,

on the security of agricultural equipment or agricultural implements, but security taken under this paragraph is not effective in respect of agricultural equipment or agricultural implements that, at the time the security is taken, by any statutory law that is then in force, are exempt from seizure under writs of execution and the farmer is prevented from giving as security for money lent to the farmer,

(o) to any fisherman, on the security of fishing vessels, fishing equipment and supplies or products of the sea, lakes and rivers, but security taken under this paragraph is not effective in respect of any such property that, at the time the security is taken, by any statutory law that is then in force, is exempt from seizure under writs of execution and the fisherman is prevented from giving as security for money lent to the fisherman, and

(p) to any forestry producer, on the security of fertilizer, pesticide, forestry equipment, forestry implements or products of the forest, but security taken under this paragraph is not effective in respect of any such property that, at the time the security is taken, by any statutory law that is then in force, is exempt from seizure under writs of execution and the forestry producer is prevented from giving as security for money lent to the forestry producer,

and the security may be given by signature and delivery to the bank, by or on behalf of the person giving the security, of a document in the prescribed form or in a form to the like effect.

Rights and powers vested by delivery of document

(2) Delivery of a document giving security on property to a bank under the authority of this section vests in the bank in respect of the property therein described

(a) of which the person giving security is the owner at the time of the delivery of the document, or

(b) of which that person becomes the owner at any time thereafter before the release of the security by the bank, whether or not the property is in existence at the time of the delivery, the following rights and powers, namely,

    (c) if the property is property on which security is given under paragraph (1)(a), (b), (g), (h), (i), (j) or (o), under paragraph (1)(c) or (m) consisting of aquacultural implements, under paragraph (1)(d) or (n) consisting of agricultural implements or under paragraph (1)(p) consisting of forestry implements, the same rights and powers as if the bank had acquired a warehouse receipt or bill of lading in which that property was described, or

    (d) if the property

        (i) is property on which security is given under paragraph (1)(c) consisting of aquacultural stock growing or produced in the aquaculture operation or aquacultural equipment,

        (ii) is property on which security is given under paragraph (1)(d) consisting of crops or agricultural equipment,

        (iii) is property on which security is given under any of paragraphs (1)(e), (f), (k) and (l),

        (iv) is property on which security is given under paragraph (1)(m) consisting of aquacultural equipment,

        (v) is property on which security is given under paragraph (1)(n) consisting of agricultural equipment, or

        (vi) is property on which security is given under paragraph (1)(p) consisting of forestry equipment,

a first and preferential lien and claim thereon for the sum secured and interest thereon, and as regards a crop as well before as after the severance from the soil, harvesting or threshing thereof, and, in addition thereto, the same rights and powers in respect of the property as if the bank had acquired a warehouse receipt or bill of lading in which the property was described, and all rights and powers of the bank subsist notwithstanding that the property is affixed to real property and notwithstanding that the person giving the security is not the owner of that real property,

and all such property in respect of which such rights and powers are vested in the bank under this section is for the purposes of this Act property covered by the security.

Power of the bank to take possession, etc.

    (3) Where security on any property is given to a bank under any of paragraphs (1)(c) to (p), the bank, in addition to and without limitation of any other rights or powers vested in or conferred on it, has full power, right and authority, through its officers, employees or agents, in the case of

    (a) non-payment of any of the loans or advances for which the security was given,

    (b) failure to care for or harvest any crop or to care for any livestock covered by the security,

    (c) failure to care for or harvest any aquatic stock growing or produced in the aquaculture operation or to care for any aquatic plants and animals covered by the security,

    (d) failure to care for any property on which security is given under any of paragraphs (1)(i) to (p),

    (e) any attempt, without the consent of the bank, to dispose of any property covered by the security, or

    (f) seizure of any property covered by the security,

to take possession of or seize the property covered by the security, and in the case of aquacultural stock growing or produced in the aquaculture operation or a crop growing or produced on the farm to care for it and, where applicable, harvest it or thresh the grain therefrom, and in the case of livestock or aquatic plants and animals to care for them, and has the right and authority to enter on any land, premises or site whenever necessary for any such purpose and to detach and remove such property, exclusive of wiring, conduits or piping incorporated in a building, from any real property to which it is affixed.

Notice of intention

    (4) The following provisions apply where security on property is given to a bank under this section:

    (a) the rights and powers of the bank in respect of property covered by the security are void as against creditors of the person giving the security and as against subsequent purchasers or mortgagees in good faith of the property covered by the security unless a notice of intention signed by or on behalf of the person giving the security was registered in the appropriate agency not more than three years immediately before the security was given;

    (b) registration of a notice of intention may be cancelled by registration in the appropriate agency in which the notice of intention was registered of a certificate of release signed on behalf of the bank named in the notice of intention stating that every security to which the notice of intention relates has been released or that no security was given to the bank, as the case may be;

(c) every person, on payment of the fee prescribed pursuant to subsection (6), is entitled to have access through the agent to any system of registration, notice of intention or certificate of release kept by or in the custody of the agent;

(d) any person desiring to ascertain whether a notice of intention given by a person is registered in an agency may inquire by sending a prepaid telegram or written communication addressed to the agent, and it is the duty of the agent, in the case of a written inquiry, only if it is accompanied by the payment of the fee prescribed pursuant to subsection (6), to make the necessary examination of the information contained in the system of registration and of the relevant documents, if any, and to reply to the inquirer stating the name of the bank mentioned in any such notice of intention, which reply shall be sent by mail unless a telegraphic reply is requested, in which case it shall be sent at the expense of the inquirer; and

(e) evidence of registration in an agency of a notice of intention or a certificate of release and of the place, date, time and serial number, if any, of its registration may be given by the production of a copy of the notice of intention or certificate of release duly certified by the agent to be a true copy thereof without proof of the signature or of the official character of the agent.

Definitions

(5) In subsections (4) and (6),

"agency" means, in a province, the office of the Bank of Canada or its authorized representative but does not include its Ottawa office, and in Yukon, the Northwest Territories and Nunavut means the office of the clerk of the court of each of those territories respectively;

"agent" means the officer in charge of an agency, and includes any person acting for that officer;

"appropriate agency" means

(a) the agency for the province in which is located the place of business of the person by whom or on whose behalf a notice of intention is signed,

(b) if that person has more than one place of business in Canada and the places of business are not in the same province, the agency for the province in which is located the principal place of business of that person, or

(c) if that person has no place of business, the agency for the province in which the person resides,

and in respect of any notice of intention registered before the day this Part comes into force, means the office in which registration was required to be made by the law in force at the time of such registration;

"notice of intention" means a notice of intention in the prescribed form or in a form to the like effect, and includes a notice of intention registered before the day this Part comes into force, in the form and registered in the manner required by the law in force at the time of the registration of the notice of intention;

"principal place of business" means

(a) in the case of a body corporate incorporated by or under an Act of Parliament or the legislature of a province, the place where, according to the body corporate's charter, memorandum of association or by-laws, the head office of the body corporate in Canada is situated, and

(b) in the case of any other body corporate, the place at which a civil process in the province in which the loans or advances will be made can be served on the body corporate;

"system of registration" means all registers and other records required by subsection (4) to be prepared and maintained and any such system may be in a bound or loose-leaf form or in a photographic film form, or may be entered or recorded by any system of mechanical or electronic data processing or any other information storage device that is capable of reproducing any required information in intelligible written form within a reasonable time.

Regulations

(6) The Governor in Council may, for the purposes of this section, make regulations

(a) respecting the practice and procedure for the operation of a system of registration, including registration of notices of intention, the cancellation of such registrations and access to the system of registration;

(b) requiring the payment of fees relating to the system of registration and prescribing the amounts thereof; and

(c) respecting any other matter necessary for the maintenance and operation of a system of registration.

Priority of wages and money owing for perishable agricultural products

(7) Despite subsection (2) and despite the fact that a notice of intention by a person giving security on property under this section has been registered

under this section, if, under the *Bankruptcy and Insolvency Act*, a bankruptcy order is made against, or an assignment is made by, that person,

(a) claims for wages, salaries or other remuneration owing in respect of the period of three months immediately preceding the making of the order or assignment, to employees of the person employed in connection with the business or farm in respect of which the property covered by the security was held or acquired by the person, and

(b) claims of a grower or producer of products of agriculture for money owing by a manufacturer to the grower or producer for such products that were grown or produced by the grower or producer on land owned or leased by the grower or producer and that were delivered to the manufacturer during the period of six months immediately preceding the making of the order or assignment to the extent of the lesser of

(i) the total amount of the claims of the grower or producer therefor, and

(ii) the prescribed amount

have priority over the rights of the bank in a security given to the bank under this section, in the order in which they are mentioned in this subsection, and if the bank takes possession or in any way disposes of the property covered by the security, the bank is liable for those claims to the extent of the net amount realized on the disposition of the property, after deducting the cost of realization, and the bank is subrogated in and to all the rights of the claimants to the extent of the amounts paid to them by the bank.

(8) [Repealed, 1997, c. 15, s. 47]

Priority of bank's rights

428.(1) All the rights and powers of a bank in respect of the property mentioned in or covered by a warehouse receipt or bill of lading acquired and held by the bank, and the rights and powers of the bank in respect of the property covered by security given to the bank under section 427 that are the same as if the bank had acquired a warehouse receipt or bill of lading in which that property was described, have, subject to subsection 427(4) and subsections (3) to (6) of this section, priority over all rights subsequently acquired in, on or in respect of that property, and also over the claim of any unpaid vendor or of any person who has a security interest in that property that was unperfected at the time the bank acquired its security in the property.

Affixation to real property

(1.1) If security is given to the bank under paragraph 427(1)(c) or (m) consisting of aquacultural equipment, under paragraph 427(1)(d) or (n) consisting of agricultural equipment, under paragraph 427(1)(k) consisting of aquacultural equipment or an aquacultural electric system, under paragraph 427(1)(l) consisting of agricultural equipment or a farm electric system or under paragraph 427(1)(p) consisting of forestry equipment, the priority referred to in subsection (1) exists even if the property is or becomes affixed to real property.

Exception

(2) The priority referred to in subsection (1) does not extend over the claim of any unpaid vendor who had a lien on the property, or of any person who has a security interest in the property that was unperfected at the time the bank acquired its warehouse receipt, bill of lading or security, if the bank acquired it with knowledge of that unpaid vendor's lien or that other person's security interest.

Bank required to register against land in certain cases

(3) Where security has been given to a bank under paragraph 427(1)(c) or (m) consisting of aquacultural equipment, under paragraph 427(1)(d) or (n) consisting of agricultural equipment, under paragraph 427(1)(k) consisting of aquacultural equipment or an aquacultural electric system, under paragraph 427(1)(l) consisting of agricultural equipment or a farm electric system or under paragraph 427(1)(p) consisting of forestry equipment that is or has become affixed to real property, the rights and powers of the bank do not have priority over any interest or right acquired in, on or in respect of the real property after that property has become affixed thereto unless, prior to

(a) the registration of the interest or right, or

(b) the registration or filing of the deed or other instrument evidencing the interest or right, or of a caution, caveat or memorial in respect thereof,

there has been registered or filed in the proper land registry or land titles office,

(c) an original of the document giving the security,

(d) a copy of the document giving the security, certified by an officer or employee of the bank to be a true copy, or

(e) a caution, caveat or memorial in respect of the rights of the bank.

Procedure for registering

(4) Every registrar or officer in charge of the proper land registry or land titles office to whom a document mentioned in paragraph (3)(c), (d) or (e) is tendered shall register or file the document according to the ordinary procedure for registering or filing within that office documents that evidence liens or charges against, or cautions, caveats or memorials in respect of claims to, or interests or rights in respect of, real property and subject to payment of the like fees, but subsection (3) and this subsection do not apply if the provincial law does not permit such registration or filing of the tendered document.

Security on fishing vessels

(5) If security has been given to a bank under paragraph 427(1)(o) on a fishing vessel that is recorded or registered under the *Canada Shipping Act, 2001*, the rights and powers of the bank do not have priority over any rights that are subsequently acquired in the vessel and are recorded or registered under that Act unless a copy of the document giving the security, certified by an officer of the bank to be a true copy, has been recorded or registered under that Act in respect of the vessel before the recording or registration under that Act of those rights.

Effect of registration of security

(6) A copy of the document giving the security described in subsection (5), certified by an officer of the bank, may be recorded or registered under the *Canada Shipping Act, 2001* as if it were a mortgage given under that Act and, on the recording or registration of the document, the bank, in addition to and without limitation of any other rights or powers vested in or conferred on it, has all the rights and powers in respect of the vessel that it would have if the security were a mortgage recorded or registered under that Act.

Sale of goods on non-payment of debt

(7) In the event of non-payment of any debt, liability, loan or advance, as security for the payment of which a bank has acquired and holds a warehouse receipt or bill of lading or has taken any security under section 427, the bank may sell all or any part of the property mentioned therein or covered thereby and apply the proceeds against that debt, liability, loan or advance, with interest and expenses, returning the surplus, if any, to the person by whom the security was given.

Idem

(8) The power of sale referred to in subsection (7) shall, unless the person by whom the security mentioned in that subsection was given has agreed to the sale of the property otherwise than as herein provided or unless the property is perishable and to comply with the following provisions might result in a substantial reduction in the value of the property, be exercised subject to the following provisions, namely,

(a) every sale of such property other than livestock shall be by public auction after

   (i) notice of the time and place of the sale has been sent by registered mail to the recorded address of the person by whom the security was given, at least ten days prior to the sale in the case of any such property other than products of the forest, and at least thirty days prior to the sale in the case of any such property consisting of products of the forest, and

   (ii) publication of an advertisement of the sale, at least two days prior to the sale, in at least two newspapers published in or nearest to the place where the sale is to be made stating the time and place thereof; and

(b) every sale of livestock shall be made by public auction not less than five days after

   (i) publication of an advertisement of the time and place of the sale in a newspaper, published in or nearest to the place where the sale is to be made, and

   (ii) posting of a notice in writing of the time and place of the sale, in or at the post office nearest to the place where the sale is to be made,

and the proceeds of such a sale of livestock, after deducting all expenses incurred by the bank and all expenses of seizure and sale, shall first be applied to satisfy privileges, liens or pledges having priority over the security given to the bank and for which claims have been filed with the person making the sale, and the balance shall be applied in payment of the debt, liability, loan or advance, with interest and the surplus, if any, returned to the person by whom the security was given.

Right and title of purchaser

(9) Any sale of property by a bank under subsections (7) and (8) vests in the purchaser all the right and title in and to the property that the person

from whom security was taken under section 435 had when the security was given or that the person from whom security was taken under section 427 had when the security was given and that the person acquired thereafter.

Duty to act honestly and in good faith

(10) In connection with any sale of property by a bank pursuant to subsections (7) and (8) or pursuant to any agreement between the bank and the person by whom the security was given, the bank shall act honestly and in good faith and shall deal with the property in a timely and appropriate manner having regard to the nature of the property and the interests of the person by whom the security was given and, in the case of a sale pursuant to an agreement, shall give the person by whom the security was given reasonable notice of the sale except where the property is perishable and to do so might result in a substantial reduction in the value of the property.

Duty to act expeditiously in respect of seized property

(11) Subject to section 427 and this section and any agreement between the bank and the person by whom the property was given as security, where, pursuant to subsection 427(3), a bank takes possession of or seizes property given as security to the bank, the bank shall, as soon as is reasonably practical having regard to the nature of the property, sell the property or so much thereof as will enable it to satisfy the debt, liability, loan or advance, with interest and expenses, in relation to which the property was given as security.

Goods manufactured from articles pledged

(12) Where goods, wares and merchandise are manufactured or produced from goods, wares and merchandise, or any of them, mentioned in or covered by any warehouse receipt or bill of lading acquired and held by a bank or any security given to a bank under section 427, the bank has the same rights and powers in respect of the goods, wares and merchandise so manufactured or produced, as well during the process of manufacture or production as after the completion thereof, and for the same purposes and on the same conditions as it had with respect to the original goods, wares and merchandise.

Subrogation of security

(13) Where payment or satisfaction of any debt, liability, loan or advance in respect of which a bank has taken security under section 426, 427 or 435 is guaranteed by a third person and the debt, liability, loan or advance is paid or satisfied by the guarantor, the guarantor is subrogated in and to all of the powers, rights and authority of the bank under the security that the bank holds in respect thereof under sections 426, 427 and 435 and this section.

Bank may assign its rights

(14) A bank may assign to any person all or any of its rights and powers in respect of any property on which security has been given to it under paragraph 427(1)(i), (j), (k), (l), (m), (n), (o) or (p), whereupon that person has all or any of the assigned rights and powers of the bank under that security.

Conditions under which bank may take security

429.(1) A bank shall not acquire or hold any warehouse receipt or bill of lading, or any security under section 427, to secure the payment of any debt, liability, loan or advance unless the debt, liability, loan or advance is contracted or made

(a) at the time of the acquisition thereof by the bank, or

(b) on the written promise or agreement that a warehouse receipt or bill of lading or security under section 427 would be given to the bank, in which case the debt, liability, loan or advance may be contracted or made before or at the time of or after that acquisition,

and such debt, liability, loan or advance may be renewed, or the time for the payment thereof extended, without affecting any security so acquired or held.

Exchange of one security for another

(2) A bank may

(a) on the shipment of any property for which it holds a warehouse receipt or any security under section 427, surrender the receipt or security and receive a bill of lading in exchange therefor;

(b) on the receipt of any property for which it holds a bill of lading, or any security under section 427, surrender the bill of lading or security, store the property and take a warehouse receipt therefor, or ship the property, or part of it, and take another bill of lading therefor;

(c) surrender any bill of lading or warehouse receipt held by it and receive in exchange therefor any security that may be taken under this Act;

(d) when it holds any security under section 427 on grain in any elevator, take a bill of lading covering the same grain or grain of the same grade or kind shipped from that elevator, in lieu of that security, to the extent of the quantity shipped; and

(e) when it holds any security whatever covering grain, take in lieu of that security, to the extent of the quantity covered by the security taken, a bill of lading or warehouse receipt for, or any document entitling it under the *Canada Grain Act* to the delivery of, the same grain or grain of the same grade or kind.

Loans to receiver, liquidator, etc.

430. A bank may lend money and make advances to a receiver, to a receiver and manager, to a liquidator appointed under any winding-up Act, or to a custodian, an interim receiver or a trustee under the *Bankruptcy and Insolvency Act*, if the receiver, receiver and manager, liquidator, custodian, interim receiver or trustee has been duly authorized or empowered to borrow, and, in making the loan or advance, and thereafter, the bank may take security, with or without personal liability, from the receiver, receiver and manager, liquidator, custodian, interim receiver or trustee to such an amount and on such property as may be directed or authorized by any court of competent jurisdiction.

Securities may be sold

431. Securities acquired and held by a bank as security may, in case of default in the payment of the loan, advance or debt or in the discharge of the liability for the securing of which they were so acquired and held, be dealt with, sold and conveyed, in like manner as and subject to the restrictions under which a private individual might in like circumstances deal with, sell and convey the same, and the right to deal with and dispose of securities as provided in this section may be waived or varied by any agreement between the bank and the person by whom the security was given.

Rights in respect of personal property

432. The rights, powers and privileges that a bank is by this Act declared to have, or to have had, in respect of real property on which it has taken security, shall be held and possessed by it in respect of any personal property on which it has taken security.

Purchase of realty

433. A bank may purchase any real property offered for sale

(a) under execution, or in insolvency, or under the order or decree of a court, or at a sale for taxes, as belonging to any debtor to the bank,

(b) by a mortgagee or other encumbrancer, having priority over a mortgage or other encumbrance held by the bank, or

(c) by the bank under a power of sale given to it for that purpose, notice of the sale by auction to the highest bidder having been first given by advertisement for four weeks in a newspaper published in the county or electoral district in which the property is situated,

in cases in which, under similar circumstances, an individual could so purchase, without any restriction as to the value of the property that it may so purchase, and may acquire title thereto as any individual, purchasing at a sheriff's sale or sale for taxes or under a power of sale, in like circumstances could do, and may take, have, hold and dispose of the property so purchased.

Bank may acquire absolute title

434.(1) A bank may acquire and hold an absolute title in or to real property affected by a mortgage or hypothec securing a loan or an advance made by the bank or a debt or liability to the bank, either by the obtaining of a release of the equity of redemption in the mortgaged property, or by procuring a foreclosure, or by other means whereby, as between individuals, an equity of redemption can, by law, be barred, or a transfer of title to real property can, by law, be effected, and may purchase and acquire any prior mortgage or charge on such property.

No act or law to prevent

(2) Nothing in any charter, Act or law shall be construed as ever having been intended to prevent or as preventing a bank from acquiring and holding an absolute title to and in any mortgaged or hypothecated real property, whatever the value thereof, or from exercising or acting on any power of sale contained in any mortgage given to or held by the bank, authorizing or enabling it to sell or convey any property so mortgaged.

Warehouse receipts and bills of lading

435.(1) A bank may acquire and hold any warehouse receipt or bill of lading as security for the payment of any debt incurred in its favour, or as security for any liability incurred by it for any person, in the course of its banking business.

Effect of taking

(2) Any warehouse receipt or bill of lading acquired by a bank under subsection (1) vests in the bank, from the date of the acquisition thereof,

(a) all the right and title to the warehouse receipt or bill of lading and to the goods, wares and merchandise covered thereby of the previous holder or owner thereof; and

(b) all the right and title to the goods, wares and merchandise mentioned therein of the person from whom the goods, wares and merchandise were received or acquired by the bank, if the warehouse receipt or bill of lading is made directly in favour of the bank, instead of to the previous holder or owner of the goods, wares and merchandise.

When previous holder is agent

436.(1) Where the previous holder of a warehouse receipt or bill of lading referred to in section 435 is a person

(a) entrusted with the possession of the goods, wares and merchandise mentioned therein, by or by the authority of the owner thereof,

(b) to whom the goods, wares and merchandise are, by or by the authority of the owner thereof, consigned, or

(c) who, by or by the authority of the owner of the goods, wares and merchandise, is possessed of any bill of lading, receipt, order or other document covering the same, such as is used in the course of business as proof of the possession or control of goods, wares and merchandise, or as authorizing or purporting to authorize, either by endorsement or by delivery, the possessor of such a document to transfer or receive the goods, wares and merchandise thereby represented,

a bank is, on the acquisition of that warehouse receipt or bill of lading, vested with all the right and title of the owner of the goods, wares and merchandise, subject to the right of the owner to have the same re-transferred to the owner if the debt or liability, as security for which the warehouse receipt or bill of lading is held by the bank, is paid.

Possessor

(2) For the purposes of this section, a person shall be deemed to be the possessor of goods, wares

and merchandise, or a bill of lading, receipt, order or other document,

(a) who is in actual possession thereof; or

(b) for whom, or subject to whose control the goods, wares and merchandise are, or bill of lading, receipt, order or other document is, held by any other person.

Regulations — aircraft objects

436.1(1) The Governor in Council may make regulations respecting the application of sections 426 to 436 to aircraft objects, including regulations

(a) removing classes of aircraft objects from the application of those sections or reinstating their application to those classes of aircraft objects; and

(b) eliminating rights and powers acquired under those sections in relation to aircraft objects.

Definition of "aircraft objects"

In subsection (1), "aircraft objects" has the same meaning as in subsection 2(1) of the *International Interests in Mobile Equipment (aircraft equipment) Act.*

DEPOSIT ACCEPTANCE

Deposit acceptance

437.(1) A bank may, without the intervention of any other person,

(a) accept a deposit from any person whether or not the person is qualified by law to enter into contracts; and

(b) pay all or part of the principal of the deposit and all or part of the interest thereon to or to the order of that person.

Exception

(2) Paragraph (1)(b) does not apply if, before payment, the money deposited in the bank pursuant to paragraph (1)(a) is claimed by some other person

(a) in any action or proceeding to which the bank is a party and in respect of which service of a writ or other process originating that action or proceeding has been made on the bank, or

(b) in any other action or proceeding pursuant to which an injunction or order made by the court requiring the bank not to make payment of that money or make payment thereof to some person other than the depositor has been served on the bank,

and, in the case of any such claim so made, the money so deposited may be paid to the depositor with the consent of the claimant or to the claimant with the consent of the depositor.

Execution of trust

(3) A bank is not bound to see to the execution of any trust to which any deposit made under the authority of this Act is subject.

Payment when bank has notice of trust

(4) Subsection (3) applies regardless of whether the trust is express or arises by the operation of law, and it applies even when the bank has notice of the trust if it acts on the order of or under the authority of the holder or holders of the account into which the deposit is made.

UNCLAIMED BALANCES

Unclaimed balances

438.(1) Where

(a) a deposit has been made in Canada that is payable in Canada in Canadian currency and in respect of which no transaction has taken place and no statement of account has been requested or acknowledged by the creditor during a period of ten years

    (i) in the case of a deposit made for a fixed period, from the day on which the fixed period terminated, and

    (ii) in the case of any other deposit, from the day on which the last transaction took place or a statement of account was last requested or acknowledged by the creditor, whichever is later, or

(b) a cheque, draft or bill of exchange (including any such instrument drawn by one branch of a bank on another branch of the bank but not including such an instrument issued in payment of a dividend on the capital of a bank) payable in Canada in Canadian currency has been issued, certified or accepted by a bank in Canada and no payment has been made in respect thereof for a period of ten years after the date of issue, certification, acceptance or maturity, whichever is later,

the bank shall pay to the Bank of Canada not later than December 31 in each year an amount equal to the principal amount of the deposit or instrument, plus interest, if any, calculated in accordance with the terms of the deposit or instrument, and payment accordingly discharges the bank from all liability in respect of the deposit or instrument.

Provision of information

(2) A bank shall, on making a payment under subsection (1), provide the Bank of Canada, for each deposit or instrument in respect of which the payment is made, with the following information current as of the day the payment is made, in so far as it is known to the bank:

(a) in the case of a deposit,

    (i) the name of the depositor in whose name the deposit is held,

    (ii) the recorded address of the depositor,

    (iii) the outstanding amount of the deposit, and

    (iv) the branch of the bank at which the last transaction took place in respect of the deposit, and the date of that last transaction; and

(b) in the case of an instrument,

    (i) the name of the person to whom or at whose request the instrument was issued, certified or accepted,

    (ii) the recorded address of that person,

    (iii) the name of the payee of the instrument,

    (iv) the amount and date of the instrument,

    (v) the name of the place where the instrument was payable, and

    (vi) the branch of the bank at which the instrument was issued, certified or accepted.

Copies of signature cards and signing authorities

(2.1) A bank shall, on written request by the Bank of Canada, provide the Bank of Canada with copies of signature cards and signing authorities relating to any deposit or instrument in respect of which it has made a payment under subsection (1). If it does not have any with respect to a deposit or instrument to which the request relates, it shall so inform the Bank of Canada.

Payment to claimant

(3) Subject to section 22 of the *Bank of Canada Act*, where payment has been made to the Bank of Canada under subsection (1) in respect of any deposit or instrument, and if payment is demanded or the instrument is presented at the Bank of Canada by the person who, but for that section, would be entitled to receive payment of the deposit or instrument, the Bank of Canada is liable to pay, at its agency in the province in which the deposit or instrument was payable, an amount equal to the amount so paid to it together with interest, if interest was payable under the terms of the deposit or instrument,

(a) for a period not exceeding ten years from the day on which the payment was received by the Bank of Canada until the date of payment to the claimant; and

(b) at such rate and computed in such manner as the Minister determines.

Enforcing liability

(4) The liability of the Bank of Canada under subsection (3) may be enforced by action against the Bank of Canada in the court in the province in which the deposit or instrument was payable.

Application of subsection (1)

(5) Subsection (1) applies only in respect of
(a) deposits made, and cheques, drafts and bills of exchange issued, certified or accepted, in the ten year period immediately preceding the day on which this section comes into force; and
(b) deposits made, and cheques, drafts and bills of exchange issued, certified or accepted, on or after the day on which this section comes into force.

Notice of unpaid amount

439.(1) A bank shall mail to each person, in so far as is known to the bank,
(a) to whom a deposit referred to in paragraph 438(1)(a) is payable, or
(b) to whom or at whose request an instrument referred to in paragraph 438(1)(b) was issued, certified or accepted,
at the person's recorded address, a notice stating that the deposit or instrument remains unpaid.

When notice to be sent

(2) The notice must be sent during the month of January next following the end of the first two-year period, during the month of January next following the end of the first five-year period and also during the month of January next following the end of the first nine-year period
(a) in the case of a deposit made for a fixed period, after the fixed period has terminated;
(b) in the case of any other deposit, in respect of which no transaction has taken place and no statement of account has been requested or acknowledged by the creditor; and
(c) in the case of a cheque, draft or bill of exchange, in respect of which the instrument has remained unpaid.

Notification of transfer to the Bank of Canada

(3) The notice to be sent during the month of January next following the end of the first nine-year period determined under paragraphs (2)(a) to (c), as the case may be, must also
(a) [Not in force]
(b) include the mailing address and websites where information can be obtained on how to claim the unpaid deposit or instrument.

ACCOUNTS

Definitions

439.1 The following definitions apply in this section and in sections 445 to 448.2, 458.1, 459.2 and 459.4.

"low-fee retail deposit account" means a retail deposit account that has the prescribed characteristics.

"member bank" means a bank that is a member institution as defined in section 2 of the *Canada Deposit Insurance Corporation Act*.

"personal deposit account" means a deposit account in the name of one or more natural persons that is kept by that person or those persons for a purpose other than that of carrying on business.

"retail deposit account" means a personal deposit account that is opened with a deposit of less than $150,000 or any greater amount that may be prescribed.

Account charges

440. A bank shall not, directly or indirectly, charge or receive any sum for the keeping of an account unless the charge is made by express agreement between the bank and a customer or by order of a court.

Disclosure on opening account

441.(1) A bank shall not open or maintain an interest-bearing deposit account in Canada in the name of any natural person unless the bank discloses, in accordance with the regulations, to the person who requests the bank to open the account, the rate of interest applicable to the account and how the amount of interest to be paid is to be calculated.

Exception

(2) Subsection (1) does not apply in respect of an interest-bearing deposit account that is opened with a deposit in excess of $150,000 or any greater amount that may be prescribed.

Disclosure in advertisements

442. No person shall authorize the publication, issue or appearance of any advertisement in Canada that indicates the rate of interest offered by a bank on an interest-bearing deposit or a debt obligation unless the advertisement discloses, in accordance with the regulations, how the amount of interest is to be calculated.

Disclosure regulations

443. The Governor in Council may make regulations respecting

(a) the time and place at which and the form and manner in which disclosure is to be made by a bank of

   (i) interest rates applicable to debts of the bank and deposits with the bank, and

   (ii) the manner in which the amount of interest paid is to be calculated; and

(b) such other matters or things as may be necessary to carry out the requirements of sections 441 and 442.

444. [Repealed, 2001, c. 9, s. 115]

Disclosure required on opening a deposit account

445.(1) Subject to subsections (2) to (4), a bank shall not open a deposit account in the name of a customer unless, at or before the time the account is opened, the bank provides in writing to the individual who requests the opening of the account

(a) a copy of the account agreement with the bank;

(b) information about all charges applicable to the account;

(c) information about how the customer will be notified of any increase in those charges and of any new charges applicable to the account;

(d) information about the bank's procedures relating to complaints about the application of any charge applicable to the account; and

(e) such other information as may be prescribed.

Exception

(2) If a deposit account is not a personal deposit account and the amount of a charge applicable to the account cannot be established at or before the time the account is opened, the bank shall, as soon as is practicable after the amount is established, provide the customer in whose name the account is kept with a notice in writing of the amount of the charge.

Exception

(3) If a bank has a deposit account in the name of a customer and the customer by telephone requests the opening of another deposit account in the name of the customer and the bank has not complied with subsection (1) in respect of the opening of that other account, the bank shall not open the account unless it provides the customer orally with any information prescribed at or before the time the account is opened.

Disclosure in writing

(4) If a bank opens an account under subsection (3), it shall, not later than seven business days after the account is opened, provide to the customer in writing the agreement and information referred to in subsection (1).

Right to close account

(5) A customer may, within 14 business days after a deposit account is opened under subsection (3), close the account without charge and in such case is entitled to a refund of any charges related to the operation of the account, other than interest charges, incurred while the account was open.

Regulations

(6) For the purposes of subsection (4), the Governor in Council may make regulations prescribing circumstances in which, and the time when, the agreement and information will be deemed to have been provided to the customer.

Disclosure of charges

446. A bank shall disclose to its customers and to the public, at the prescribed time and place and in the prescribed form and manner, the charges applicable to deposit accounts with the bank and the usual amount, if any, charged by the bank for services normally provided by the bank to its customers and to the public.

No increase or new charges without disclosure

447.(1) A bank shall not increase any charge applicable to a personal deposit account with the bank or introduce any new charge applicable to a personal deposit account with the bank unless the bank discloses the charge at the prescribed time and place and in the prescribed form and manner to the customer in whose name the account is kept.

Mandatory disclosure

(2) With respect to prescribed services in relation to deposit accounts, other than personal deposit accounts, a bank shall not increase any charge for any such service in relation to a deposit account with the bank or introduce any new charge for any such service in relation to a deposit account with the bank unless the bank discloses the charge at the prescribed time and place and in the prescribed form and manner to the customer in whose name the account is kept.

Application

448. Sections 445 to 447 apply only in respect of charges applicable to deposit accounts with the bank in Canada and services provided by the bank in Canada.

Retail deposit accounts

448.1(1) Subject to regulations made under subsection (3), a member bank shall, at any prescribed point of service in Canada or any branch in Canada at which it opens retail deposit accounts through a natural person, open a retail deposit account for an individual who meets the prescribed conditions at his or her request made there in person.

No minimum deposit or balance requirements

(2) A member bank shall not require that, in the case of an account opened under subsection (1), the individual make an initial minimum deposit or maintain a minimum balance.

Regulations

(3) The Governor in Council may make regulations
(a) for the purposes of subsection (1), defining "point of service" and prescribing points of service;
(b) respecting circumstances in which subsection (1) does not apply; and
(c) prescribing conditions to be met by an individual for the purposes of subsection (1).

Low-fee retail deposit accounts — regulations

448.2 The Governor in Council may make regulations
(a) requiring a member bank, at any prescribed point of service in Canada or any branch referred to in subsection 448.1(1), to open a low-fee retail deposit account for an individual who meets the prescribed conditions at his or her request made there in person;

(b) for the purposes of paragraph (a), defining "point of service" and prescribing points of service;
(c) prescribing the characteristics, including the name, of a low-fee retail deposit account;
(d) respecting circumstances in which a regulation made under paragraph (a) does not apply; and
(e) prescribing conditions to be met by an individual for the purposes of paragraph (a).

REGISTERED PRODUCTS

Disclosure required concerning registered products

448.3(1) Subject to subsection (2), a bank shall not open an account that is or forms part of a registered product in the name of a customer, or enter into an agreement with a customer for a prescribed product or service that is or forms part of a registered product, unless the bank provides, in the prescribed manner, to the individual requesting the account or the prescribed product or service
(a) information about all charges applicable to the registered product;
(b) information about how the customer will be notified of any increase in those charges and of any new charges applicable to the registered product;
(c) information about the bank's procedures relating to complaints about the application of any charge applicable to the registered product; and
(d) any other information that may be prescribed.

Regulations

(2) The Governor in Council may make regulations specifying the circumstances under which a bank need not provide the information.

Definition of "registered product"

(3) In this section, "registered product" means a product that is defined to be a registered product by the regulations.

BORROWING COSTS

Definition of "cost of borrowing"

449. For the purposes of this section and sections 449.1 to 456, "cost of borrowing" means, in respect of a loan made by a bank,
(a) the interest or discount applicable to the loan;
(b) any amount charged in connection with the loan that is payable by the borrower to the bank; and

106

(c) any charge prescribed to be included in the cost of borrowing.

For those purposes, however, "cost of borrowing" does not include any charge prescribed to be excluded from the cost of borrowing.

Rebate of borrowing costs

449.1(1) Where a bank makes a loan in respect of which the disclosure requirements of section 450 apply, and the loan is not secured by a mortgage on real property and is required to be repaid either on a fixed future date or by instalments, the bank shall, if there is a prepayment of the loan, rebate to the borrower a portion of the charges included in the cost of borrowing in respect of the loan.

Exception

(2) The charges to be rebated do not include the interest or discount applicable to the loan.

Regulations

(3) The Governor in Council may make regulations governing the rebate of charges under subsection (1). The rebate shall be made in accordance with those regulations.

Disclosing borrowing costs

450.(1) A bank shall not make a loan to a natural person that is repayable in Canada unless the cost of borrowing, as calculated and expressed in accordance with section 451, and other prescribed information have been disclosed by the bank to the borrower at the prescribed time and place and in the prescribed form and manner.

Non-application

(2) Subsection (1) does not apply in respect of a loan that is of a prescribed class of loans.

Calculating borrowing costs

451. The cost of borrowing shall be calculated, in the prescribed manner, on the basis that all obligations of the borrower are duly fulfilled and shall be expressed as a rate per annum and, in prescribed circumstances, as an amount in dollars and cents.

Additional disclosure

452.(1) Where a bank makes a loan in respect of which the disclosure requirements of section 450 are applicable and the loan is required to be repaid either on a fixed future date or by instalments, the bank shall disclose to the borrower, in accordance with the regulations,

(a) whether the borrower has the right to repay the amount borrowed before the maturity of the loan and, if applicable,

   (i) any terms and conditions relating to that right, including the particulars of the circumstances in which the borrower may exercise that right, and

   (ii) whether, in the event that the borrower exercises the right, any portion of the cost of borrowing is to be rebated, the manner in which any such rebate is to be calculated or, if a charge or penalty will be imposed on the borrower, the manner in which the charge or penalty is to be calculated;

(b) in the event that an amount borrowed is not repaid at maturity or, if applicable, an instalment is not paid on the day the instalment is due to be paid, particulars of the charges or penalties to be paid by the borrower because of the failure to repay or pay in accordance with the contract governing the loan;

(c) at the prescribed time and place and in the prescribed form and manner, any prescribed changes respecting the cost of borrowing or the loan agreement;

(d) particulars of any other rights and obligations of the borrower; and

(e) any other prescribed information, at the prescribed time and place and in the prescribed form and manner.

Disclosure in credit card applications

(1.1) A bank shall, in accordance with the regulations, at the prescribed time and place and in the prescribed form and manner, provide prescribed information in any application forms or related documents that it prepares for the issuance of credit, payment or charge cards and provide prescribed information to any person applying to it for a credit, payment or charge card.

Disclosure re credit cards

(2) Where a bank issues or has issued a credit, payment or charge card to a natural person, the bank shall, in addition to disclosing the costs of borrowing in respect of any loan obtained through the use of the card, disclose to the person, in accordance with the regulations,

(a) any charges or penalties described in paragraph (1)(b);

(b) particulars of the person's rights and obligations;

(c) any charges for which the person becomes responsible by accepting or using the card;

(d) at the prescribed time and place and in the prescribed form and manner, any prescribed changes respecting the cost of borrowing or the loan agreement; and

(e) any other prescribed information, at the prescribed time and place and in the prescribed form and manner.

Additional disclosure re other loans

(3) Where a bank enters into or has entered into an arrangement, including a line of credit, for the making of a loan in respect of which the disclosure requirements of section 450 apply and the loan is not a loan in respect of which subsection (1) or (2) applies, the bank shall, in addition to disclosing the costs of borrowing, disclose to the person to whom the loan is made, in accordance with the regulations,

(a) any charges or penalties described in paragraph (1)(b);

(b) particulars of the person's rights and obligations;

(c) any charges for which the person is responsible under the arrangement;

(d) at the prescribed time and place and in the prescribed form and manner, any prescribed changes respecting the cost of borrowing under the arrangement; and

(e) any other prescribed information, at the prescribed time and place and in the prescribed form and manner.

Renewal statement

452.1 If a bank makes a loan in respect of which the disclosure requirements of section 450 apply and the loan is secured by a mortgage on real property, the bank shall disclose to the borrower, at the prescribed time and place and in the prescribed form and manner, any information that is prescribed respecting the renewal of the loan.

Disclosure in advertising

453. No person shall authorize the publication, issue or appearance of any advertisement in Canada relating to arrangements referred to in subsection 452(3), loans, credit cards, payment cards or charge cards, offered to natural persons by a bank, and purporting to disclose prescribed information about the cost of borrowing or about any other matter unless the advertisement discloses prescribed information at the prescribed time and place and in the prescribed form and manner.

Regulations re borrowing costs

454. The Governor in Council may make regulations

(a) respecting the time and place at which, and the form and manner in which, a bank is to disclose to a borrower

  (i) the cost of borrowing,

  (ii) any rebate of the cost of borrowing, and

  (iii) any other information relating to a loan, arrangement, credit card, payment card or charge card referred to in section 452;

(b) respecting the contents of any statement disclosing the cost of borrowing and other information required to be disclosed by a bank to a borrower;

(c) respecting the manner of calculating the cost of borrowing;

(d) respecting the circumstances under which the cost of borrowing is to be expressed as an amount in dollars and cents;

(e) specifying any class of loans that are not to be subject to section 449.1 or subsection 450(1) or 452(1) or (3) or section 452.1 or 453 or the regulations or any specified provisions of the regulations;

(f) respecting the time and place at which, and the form and manner in which, any rights, obligations, charges or penalties referred to in sections 449.1 to 453 are to be disclosed;

(g) prohibiting the imposition of any charge or penalty referred to in section 452 or providing that the charge or penalty, if imposed, will not exceed a prescribed amount;

(h) respecting the nature or amount of any charge or penalty referred to in paragraph 452(1)(b), (2)(a) or (3)(a) and the costs of the bank that may be included or excluded in the determination of the charge or penalty;

(i) respecting the method of calculating the amount of rebate of the cost of borrowing, or the portion of the cost of borrowing referred to in subparagraph 452(1)(a)(ii);

(j) respecting advertisements made by a bank regarding arrangements referred to in subsection 452(3), loans, credit cards, payment cards or charge cards;

(k) respecting the renewal of loans; and

(l) respecting such other matters or things as are necessary to carry out the purposes of sections 449.1 to 453.

COMPLAINTS

Procedures for dealing with complaints

455.(1) A bank shall
  (a) establish procedures for dealing with complaints made by persons having requested or received products or services in Canada from a bank;
  (b) designate an officer or employee of the bank to be responsible for implementing those procedures; and
  (c) designate one or more officers or employees of the bank to receive and deal with those complaints.

Procedures to be filed with Commissioner

(2) A bank shall file with the Commissioner a copy of its procedures established under paragraph (1)(a).

How procedures to be made available

(3) A bank shall make its procedures established under paragraph (1)(a) available
  (a) in the form of a brochure, at its branches where products or services are offered in Canada;
  (b) on its websites through which products or services are offered in Canada; and
  (c) in written format to be sent to any person who requests them.

Information on contacting Agency

(4) A bank shall also make prescribed information on how to contact the Agency available whenever it makes its procedures established under paragraph (1)(a) available under subsection (3).

Approval of external complaints body

455.01(1) Subject to section 455.1, the Minister may, on the Commissioner's recommendation and for the purposes of this section, approve a body corporate incorporated under the *Canada Not-for-profit Corporations Act* or under the *Canada Business Corporations Act* whose purpose, in the Minister's view, under its letters patent is dealing with complaints, made by persons having requested or received products or services from its member financial institutions, that have not been resolved to the satisfaction of those persons under procedures established by those financial institutions under paragraph 455(1)(a).

Obligation to be member

(2) A bank must be a member of one body corporate that is approved under subsection (1).

Regulations

(3) The Governor in Council may make regulations respecting the requirements for the approval of a body corporate under subsection (1) and the requirements for a body corporate approved under that subsection for maintaining that approval.

Not an agent

(4) A body corporate approved under subsection (1) is not an agent of Her Majesty.

Approval to be published

(5) An approval given under subsection (1) must be published in the *Canada Gazette*.

Information, etc.

(6) A body corporate that is seeking an approval under subsection (1) must apply to the Commissioner, and the application must provide, in the form and manner required by the Commissioner, any information, material and evidence that he or she may require.

Designation of complaints body

455.1(1) The Minister may, for the purposes of this section, designate a body corporate incorporated under the *Canada Not-for-profit Corporations Act* whose purpose, in the view of the Minister, is dealing with complaints, made by persons having requested or received products or services from its member financial institutions, that have not been resolved to the satisfaction of those persons under procedures established by those financial institutions under paragraph 455(1)(a).

Effect of designation

(1.1) If the Minister makes a designation under subsection (1), any approval given under subsection 455.01(1) is revoked.

Effect of revocation

(1.2) If the Minister makes a designation under subsection (1), the body corporate designated under that subsection must deal with any complaint that was made to a body corporate approved under subsection 455.01(1) and that has not been resolved.

Obligation to be member

(2) A bank shall be a member of any body corporate that is designated under subsection (1).

Directors

(3) The Minister may, in accordance with the letters patent and by-laws of the body corporate designated under subsection (1), appoint the majority of its directors.

Regulations

(3.1) The Governor in Council may make regulations respecting the requirements to be met by the body corporate designated under subsection (1).

Not an agent

(4) A body corporate designated under subsection (1) is not an agent of Her Majesty.

Designation to be published

(5) A designation under subsection (1) shall be published in the *Canada Gazette*.

Information on contacting Agency

456.(1) A bank shall, in accordance with the regulations, at the prescribed time and place and in the prescribed form and manner, provide a person requesting or receiving a product or service from it with prescribed information on how to contact the Agency if the person has a complaint about a deposit account, an arrangement referred to in subsection 452(3), a payment, credit or charge card, the disclosure of or manner of calculating the cost of borrowing in respect of a loan or about any other obligation of the bank under a consumer provision.

Report

(2) The Commissioner shall prepare a report, to be included in the report referred to in section 34 of the *Financial Consumer Agency of Canada Act*, respecting

(a) procedures for dealing with complaints established by banks pursuant to paragraph 455(1)(a); and

(b) the number and nature of complaints that have been brought to the attention of the Agency by persons who have requested or received a product or service from a bank.

MISCELLANEOUS

Charges for prescribed products or services

457. A bank shall not, directly or indirectly, charge or receive any sum for the provision of any prescribed products or services unless the charge is made by express agreement between it and a customer or by order of a court.

Prepayment protected

458.(1) A bank shall not make a loan to a natural person that is repayable in Canada, the terms of which prohibit prepayment of the money advanced or any instalment thereon before its due date.

Minimum balance

(2) Except by express agreement between the bank and the borrower, the making in Canada of a loan or advance by a bank to a borrower shall not be subject to a condition that the borrower maintain a minimum credit balance with the bank.

Non-application of subsection (1)

(3) Subsection (1) does not apply in respect of a loan

(a) that is secured by a mortgage on real property; or

(b) that is made for business purposes and the principal amount of which is more than $100,000 or such other amount as may be prescribed.

Government cheques

(4) A bank shall not make a charge

(a) for cashing a cheque or other instrument drawn on the Receiver General or on the Receiver General's account in the Bank of Canada, in any bank or other deposit-taking Canadian financial institution incorporated by or under an Act of Parliament or in any authorized foreign bank that is not subject to the restrictions and requirements referred to in subsection 524(2), in respect of its business in Canada;

(b) for cashing any other instrument issued as authority for the payment of money out of the Consolidated Revenue Fund; or

(c) in respect of any cheque or other instrument that is

(i) drawn in favour of the Receiver General, the Government of Canada or any department thereof or any public officer acting in the capacity of a public officer, and

(ii) tendered for deposit to the credit of the Receiver General.

Deposits of Government of Canada

(5) Nothing in subsection (4) precludes any arrangement between the Government of Canada and a bank concerning

(a) compensation for services performed by the bank for the Government of Canada; or

(b) interest to be paid on any or all deposits of the Government of Canada with the bank.

Cashing of government cheques

458.1(1) Subject to regulations made under subsection (2), a member bank shall, at any branch in Canada at which it, through a natural person, opens retail deposit accounts and disburses cash to customers, cash a cheque or other instrument for any individual, if

(a) the cheque or other instrument is drawn on the Receiver General or on the Receiver General's account in the Bank of Canada, or in any bank or other deposit-taking Canadian financial institution incorporated by or under an Act of Parliament, or is any other instrument issued as authority for the payment of money out of the Consolidated Revenue Fund;

(b) the individual makes the request to cash it in person and meets the prescribed conditions; and

(c) the amount of the cheque or other instrument is not more than the prescribed amount.

Regulations

(2) The Governor in Council may make regulations

(a) respecting circumstances in which subsection (1) does not apply;

(b) for the purposes of subsection (1), prescribing the maximum amount of a cheque or other instrument; and

(c) prescribing conditions to be met by an individual referred to in subsection (1); and

(d) [Repealed, 2012, c. 5, s. 46]

Regulations respecting the holding of funds

458.2 The Governor in Council may make regulations respecting the maximum period during which a bank may hold funds in respect of specified classes of cheques or other instruments that are deposited into an account at a branch or prescribed point of service in Canada before permitting the customer in whose name the account is kept to access the funds.

Regulations — activities

458.3 The Governor in Council may make regulations respecting any matters involving a bank's dealings, or its employees', representatives', agents' or other intermediaries' dealings, with customers or the public, including

(a) what a bank may or may not do in carrying out any of the activities in which it is permitted to engage, or in providing any of the services that it may provide, under section 409 and any ancillary, related or incidental activities or services; and

(b) the time and place at which and the form and manner in which any of those activities are to be carried out or any of those services are to be provided.

Regulations re customer information

459. The Governor in Council may make regulations

(a) requiring a bank to establish procedures regarding the collection, retention, use and disclosure of any information about its customers or any class of customers;

(b) requiring a bank to establish procedures for dealing with complaints made by a customer about the collection, retention, use or disclosure of information about the customer;

(c) respecting the disclosure by a bank of information relating to the procedures referred to in paragraphs (a) and (b);

(d) requiring a bank to designate the officers and employees of the bank who are responsible for

(i) implementing the procedures referred to in paragraph (b), and

(ii) receiving and dealing with complaints made by a customer of the bank about the collection, retention, use or disclosure of information about the customer;

(e) requiring a bank to report information relating to

(i) complaints made by customers of the bank about the collection, retention, use or disclosure of information, and

(ii) the actions taken by the bank to deal with the complaints; and

(f) defining "information", "collection" and "retention" for the purposes of paragraphs (a) to (e) and the regulations made under those paragraphs.

Restriction on tied selling

459.1(1) A bank shall not impose undue pressure on, or coerce, a person to obtain a product or service from a particular person, including the bank and any of its affiliates, as a condition for obtaining another product or service from the bank.

Favourable bank product or service tied to other sale

(2) For greater certainty, a bank may offer a product or service to a person on more favourable terms or conditions than the bank would otherwise offer, where the more favourable terms and conditions are offered on the condition that the person obtain another product or service from any particular person.

Favourable other sale tied to bank product or service

(3) For greater certainty, an affiliate of a bank may offer a product or service to a person on more favourable terms or conditions than the affiliate would otherwise offer, where the more favourable terms and conditions are offered on the condition that the person obtain another product or service from the bank.

Bank approval

(4) A bank may require that a product or service obtained by a borrower from a particular person as security for a loan from the bank meet with the bank's approval. That approval shall not be unreasonably withheld.

Disclosure

(4.1) A bank shall, in accordance with the regulations, disclose the prohibition on coercive tied selling set out in subsection (1) in a statement in plain language that is clear and concise, displayed and available to customers and the public at all of its branches where products or services are offered in Canada, on all of its websites through which products or services are offered in Canada and at all prescribed points of service in Canada.

Regulations

(4.2) The Governor in Council may make regulations for the purposes of subsection (4.1)
- (a) respecting the time and place at which, and the form and manner in which, the prohibition on coercive tied selling set out in subsection (1) is to be disclosed, displayed and made available;
- (b) defining "point of service"; and
- (c) prescribing points of service.

Regulations

(5) The Governor in Council may make regulations

- (a) specifying types of conduct or transactions that shall be considered undue pressure or coercion for the purpose of subsection (1); and
- (b) specifying types of conduct or transactions that shall be considered not to be undue pressure or coercion for the purpose of subsection (1).

Notice of branch closure

459.2(1) Subject to regulations made under subsection (5), a member bank with a branch in Canada at which it, through a natural person, opens retail deposit accounts and disburses cash to customers, shall give notice in accordance with those regulations before closing that branch or having it cease to carry on either of those activities.

Pre-closure meeting

(2) After notice is given but before the branch is closed or ceases to carry on the activities, the Commissioner shall, in prescribed situations, require the bank to convene and hold a meeting between representatives of the bank, representatives of the Agency and interested parties in the vicinity of the branch in order to exchange views about the closing or cessation of activities, including, but not limited to, alternative service delivery by the bank and measures to help the branch's customers adjust to the closing or cessation of activities.

Meeting details

(3) The Commissioner may establish rules for convening a meeting referred to in subsection (2) and for its conduct.

Not statutory instruments

(4) The *Statutory Instruments Act* does not apply in respect of rules established under subsection (3).

Regulations

(5) The Governor in Council may make regulations prescribing
- (a) the manner and time, which may vary according to circumstances specified in the regulations, in which notice shall be given under subsection (1), to whom it shall be given and the information to be included;
- (b) circumstances in which a member bank is not required to give notice under subsection (1), circumstances in which the Commissioner may exempt a member bank from the requirement to give notice under that subsection, and circumstances in which the Commissioner may

vary the manner and time in which notice is required to be given under any regulation made under paragraph (a); and

(c) circumstances in which a meeting may be convened under subsection (2).

Public accountability statements

459.3(1) A bank with equity of one billion dollars or more shall, in accordance with regulations made under subsection (4), annually publish a statement describing the contribution of the bank and its prescribed affiliates to the Canadian economy and society.

Filing

(2) A bank shall, at the prescribed time and place and in the prescribed form and manner, file a copy of the statement with the Commissioner.

Provision of statement to public

(3) A bank shall, at the prescribed time and place and in the prescribed form and manner, disclose the statement to its customers and to the public.

Regulations

(4) The Governor in Council may make regulations prescribing

(a) the name, contents and form of the statement referred to in subsection (1) and the time within which, the place at which and the manner in which it must be prepared;

(b) affiliates of a bank referred to in subsection (1);

(c) the time and place at which and the form and manner in which a statement must be filed under subsection (2); and

(d) the time and place at which and the form and manner in which a statement mentioned in subsection (3) is to be disclosed, respectively, to a bank's customers and to the public.

Regulations re disclosure

459.4 The Governor in Council may, subject to any other provisions of this Act relating to the disclosure of information, make regulations respecting the disclosure of information by banks or any prescribed class of banks, including regulations respecting

(a) the information that must be disclosed, including information relating to

(i) any product or service or prescribed class of products or services offered by them,

(ii) any of their policies, procedures or practices relating to the offer by them of any

product or service or prescribed class of products or services,

(iii) anything they are required to do or to refrain from doing under a consumer provision, and

(iv) any other matter that may affect their dealings, or their employees', representatives', agents' or other intermediaries' dealings, with customers or the public;

(b) the time and place at which, the form and manner in which and the persons to whom information is to be disclosed; and

(c) the content and form of any advertisement by banks or any prescribed class of banks relating to any matter referred to in paragraph (a).

Affiliates

459.5 A bank shall not enter into any arrangement or otherwise cooperate with any of its representatives, agents or other intermediaries, with any of its affiliates that is controlled by a bank or a bank holding company and that is a finance entity as defined in subsection 464(1) or other prescribed entity or with any of the representatives, agents or other intermediaries of such an affiliate, to sell or further the sale of a product or service of the bank or the affiliate unless

(a) the affiliate or the representative, agent or other intermediary of the bank or the affiliate, as the case may be, complies, with respect to the product or service, with the consumer provisions that apply to banks — other than section 455.1 — as if they were a bank, to the extent that those provisions are applicable to their activities; and

(b) the persons who request or receive the product or service have access to the bank's procedures for dealing with complaints established under this Act.

Transmission in case of death

460.(1) Where the transmission of a debt owing by a bank by reason of a deposit, of property held by a bank as security or for safe-keeping or of rights with respect to a safety deposit box and property deposited therein takes place because of the death of a person, the delivery to the bank of

(a) an affidavit or declaration in writing in form satisfactory to the bank signed by or on behalf of a person claiming by virtue of the transmission stating the nature and effect of the transmission, and

(b) one of the following documents, namely,

   (i) when the claim is based on a will or other testamentary instrument or on a grant of probate thereof or on such a grant and letters testamentary or other document of like import or on a grant of letters of administration or other document of like import, purporting to be issued by any court or authority in Canada or elsewhere, an authenticated copy or certificate thereof under the seal of the court or authority without proof of the authenticity of the seal or other proof, or

   (ii) when the claim is based on a notarial will, an authenticated copy thereof,

is sufficient justification and authority for giving effect to the transmission in accordance with the claim.

Idem

(2) Nothing in subsection (1) shall be construed to prevent a bank from refusing to give effect to a transmission until there has been delivered to the bank such documentary or other evidence of or in connection with the transmission as it may deem requisite.

Branch of account with respect to deposits

461.(1) For the purposes of this Act, the branch of account with respect to a deposit account is

(a) the branch the address or name of which appears on the specimen signature card or other signing authority signed by a depositor with respect to the deposit account or that is designated by agreement between the bank and the depositor at the time of opening of the deposit account; or

(b) if no branch has been identified or agreed on as provided in paragraph (a), the branch that is designated as the branch of account with respect thereto by the bank by notice in writing to the depositor.

Where debt payable

(2) The amount of any debt owing by a bank by reason of a deposit in a deposit account in the bank is payable to the person entitled thereto only at the branch of account and the person entitled thereto is not entitled to demand payment or to be paid at any other branch of the bank.

Idem

(3) Notwithstanding subsection (2), a bank may permit either occasionally or as a regular practice, the person to whom the bank is indebted by reason of a deposit in a deposit account in the bank to withdraw moneys owing by reason of that deposit at a branch of the bank other than the branch of account or to draw cheques or other orders for the payment of such moneys at a branch other than the branch of account.

Situs of indebtedness

(4) The indebtedness of a bank by reason of a deposit in a deposit account in the bank shall be deemed for all purposes to be situated at the place where the branch of account is situated.

Effect of writ, etc.

462.(1) Subject to subsections (3) and (4), the following documents are binding on property belonging to a person and in the possession of a bank, or on money owing to a person by reason of a deposit account in a bank, only if the document or a notice of it is served at the branch of the bank that has possession of the property or that is the branch of account in respect of the deposit account, as the case may be:

(a) a writ or process originating a legal proceeding or issued in or pursuant to a legal proceeding;

(b) an order or injunction made by a court;

(c) an instrument purporting to assign, perfect or otherwise dispose of an interest in the property or the deposit account; or

(d) an enforcement notice in respect of a support order or support provision.

Notices

(2) Any notification sent to a bank with respect to a customer of the bank, other than a document referred to in subsection (1) or (3), constitutes notice to the bank and fixes the bank with knowledge of its contents only if sent to and received at the branch of the bank that is the branch of account of an account held in the name of that customer.

Notices: Minister of National Revenue

(2.1) Despite subsections (1) and (2), a notice, demand, order or other document issued with respect to a customer of a bank constitutes notice to the bank and fixes the bank with knowledge of its contents and, where applicable, is binding on property belonging to the customer and in the possession of the bank or on money owing to the customer by reason of an account in the bank, if it is sent to the branch of the bank referred to in subsection (1) or (2), an office of the bank referred to in paragraph

(3)(a) or any other office agreed to by the bank and the Minister of National Revenue and it relates to

(a) the administration of an Act of Parliament by the Minister of National Revenue; or

(b) the administration of an Act of the legislature of a province or legislation made by an aboriginal government, where the Minister or the Minister of National Revenue has entered into a tax collection agreement under an Act of Parliament with the government of the province or the aboriginal government.

Exception

(3) Subsections (1) and (2) do not apply in respect of an enforcement notice in respect of a support order or support provision if

(a) the enforcement notice, accompanied by a written statement containing the information required by the regulations, is served at an office of a bank designated in accordance with the regulations in respect of a province; and

(b) the order or provision can be enforced under the laws of that province.

Time of application

(4) Subsection (3) does not apply in respect of an enforcement notice in respect of a support order or support provision until the second business day following the day of service referred to in that subsection.

Regulations

(5) The Governor in Council may make regulations

(a) respecting the designation by a bank, for the purpose of subsection (3), of a place in any province for the service of enforcement notices in respect of support orders and support provisions;

(b) prescribing the manner in which a bank shall publicize the locations of designated offices of the bank; and

(c) respecting the information that must accompany enforcement notices in respect of support orders and support provisions.

Definitions

(6) The following definitions apply in this section.

"designated office" means a place designated in accordance with regulations made for the purpose of subsection (3).

"enforcement notice", in respect of a support order or support provision, means a garnishee summons or other instrument issued under the laws of a province for the enforcement of the support order or support provision.

"support order" means an order or judgment or interim order or judgment for family financial support.

"support provision" means a provision of an agreement relating to the payment of maintenance or family financial support.

Deemed loan

463. For the purposes of sections 425 to 436, where a bank accepts a bill of exchange drawn on it and not payable on demand or pays or makes money available for the payment of such a bill of exchange, or issues a guarantee, or otherwise makes a promise to effect a payment, the bank is deemed to lend money or make an advance.

(b)   *Central Computer Services Ltd. v. Toronto-Dominion Bank*†

[MONNIN J.A.:]

This is an appeal from a decision of Hamilton J., who granted plaintiffs an injunction to restrain the defendant bank from continuing certain business practices which the learned trial judge found *ultra vires* of the bank [[1979] 1 W.W.R. 728].

I am little concerned with the matter of procedure or *locus standi* which was raised by the bench at the hearing. The parties are before us and the

---

† [1980] W.W.R. 206 (Man. C.A.).

bank has been enjoined from doing what it and some others of the Canadian chartered banks have been doing during recent years. It is important for this bank and for the chartered banks that they know where they stand. I am concerned with the application of the facts disclosed to the provisions of s. 75 of the *Bank Act*, R.S.C. 1970, c. B-1. It is regrettable that Parliament has not been able to review the Act pursuant to its decennial policy of revision. Had this occurred, this litigation might not have arisen. Section 75 is quoted in full in the reasons of my brother O'Sullivan, and I need not repeat it here.

The learned trial judge held that the business of banking is the performance of the activities cited in s. 75(1)(a) to (d). He spoke thus [p. 731]:

> The business of banking then is the performance of the activities recited in s. 75(1). The catch-all s. 75(1)(e) must then be read with the preceding paragraphs, which generally define the 'business of banking'. When s. 75(1)(e) says a bank may 'carry on such business generally as appertains to the business of banking', in my opinion that means only that a bank may engage in activities that pertain to the powers defined in s. 75(1)(a) to (d). Section 75(2)(b) makes it clear that a bank may not engage in any other business (or activity).

I do not think that this is a correct statement of the law. Parliament never intended to establish a fixed or restricted definition of banking by enumerating paras. (a) to (d) of s. 75. Banking must have a much broader meaning. English and Canadian authorities have yet to define the terms of bank and banker. All the textbook writers on banking confirm this statement that there is no exact definition of a banker or bank. In fact and in practice, banking is what banks do for the carrying-on of their business; what they do can vary from decade to decade and from century to century. The computer is a mechanical device of recent origin. Looking at the banking practices of the early century in England or Canada gives me no assistance in this case. By s. 75 a bank is limited to the business of banking and that which appertains to banking.

Toronto Dominion Bank offers six types of computerized services. Only two form the basis of the plaintiffs' complaint, namely, the computer payroll service and the "compucount". The bank submits that both activities are part of today's banking business and, alternatively, that they both pertain to the general business of banking.

Banking business must be allowed to develop in accordance with technological advances of today. The computer has revolutionized many an aspect of business and will do so for many years to come. One need only think of the facilities of making reservations with railways or air companies to think of the large benefits of the computer. In the days of Messrs. Falconbridge and McLaren and other early writers on the subject of banking, a drive-in cashier or drive-in teller would have seemed revolutionary, yet this is one of the daily accepted banking services. It is useless to quote the law merchant or what Lord Mansfield said or did in his day, as what he did or said has no relevance whatsoever to modern banking business. What I must look at is the facts of the case as explained by the witnesses who testified and the current practices of reputable bankers in the field or what other banks are doing under the heading of business pertaining to banking.

It is nowadays very simple for a bank, with the assistance of a computer, to obtain information which formerly its clients had in their own ledgers where the entry had been made manually by employees and servants. Today, all these entries can be computerized and made readily available to the bank and to its clients. Is that not part of the day-to-day banking business? Whatever method can be used to provide more accurate and speedier information is obviously to the benefit of both the banker and the client. I find it difficult, if not impossible, to say that this does not pertain to the business of banking. Why should I, as a judge, sitting in judgment, refuse leave to a bank to give this information out to its customers? If Parliament had desired to do so, it could impose such a restriction in clear and unambiguous language. It has not done so; on the contrary, it has spelled out that the bank can "engage in and carry out such business generally as appertains to the business of banking". Parliament has not done so and it is not in my domain to legislate.

I am satisfied that what the bank did in this case was to engage in and carry on such business as now generally appertains to the business of banking. That is within its statutory power and it cannot be faulted for so doing.

The injunction ought not to have been granted. I would allow the appeal and set aside the injunction with costs here and below. I dismiss the cross-appeal without costs.

. . . .

[O'SULLIVAN J.A.:]

I agree substantially with the reasons of my brother Monnin and come to the same conclusion, but add some additional observations.

. . . .

Procedure and status apart, the appeal turns on the application to the facts of the case of the provisions of s. 75 of the *Bank Act*, R.S.C. 1970, c. B-1, which reads:

75.(1) The bank may
(a) open branches;
(b) acquire, deal in, discount and lend money and make advances upon the security of, and take as security for any loan or advance made by the bank or any debt or liability to the bank, bills of exchange, promissory notes and other negotiable instruments, coin, gold and silver bullion and securities;
(c) subject to subsection (3), lend money and make advances upon the security of and take as security for any loan or advance made by the bank or any debt or liability to the bank, any real or personal, immovable or movable property, except shares of the capital stock of the bank on which the bank has a privileged lien under subsection 83(1), but no such security is effective in respect of any personal or movable property that at the time the security is taken is, by any statutory law that was in force on the first of July 1923, exempt from seizure under writs of execution;
(d) lend money and make advances without security, and
(e) engage in and carry on such business generally as appertains to the business of banking.

(2) Except as authorized by or under this Act, the bank shall not, directly or indirectly,
(a) issue or re-issue notes of the bank payable to bearer on demand and intended for circulation;
(b) deal in goods, wares and merchandise or engage in any trade or business;
(c) acquire, deal in or lend money or make advances upon the security of shares of the capital stock of the bank or any other bank;
(d) lend money or make advances to or on the guarantee of the general manager or any officer or employee subordinate to the general manager
   (i) without the consent of the directors, if the principal amount outstanding of loans and advances made to and guaranteed by him, together with the proposed loan or advance, exceeds five thousand dollars, or
   (ii) if the principal amount outstanding of loans and advances made to and guaranteed by him, together with the proposed loan or advance, exceeds twenty-five thousand dollars;
(e) lend money or make advances in a principal amount exceeding five per cent of its paid-up capital to a director of the bank or to any firm or corporation of which a director or the general manager of the bank is a member or shareholder without the consent of two-thirds of the directors present at a regular meeting of the board or a meeting of the board specially called for the purpose;
(f) except with the consent of the Minister, contribute to any guarantee or pension fund if any part of the fund has, at any time after the 30th day of April 1967, been invested in shares of the capital stock of a bank; or
(g) at any time after the 31st day of December 1967 or after such later day, not being a day later than the 31st day of December 1972, as may be prescribed from time to time by the Governor in Council, have outstanding total liabilities (including paid-up capital, rest account and undivided profits) exceeding twenty times its authorized capital stock if more than twenty-five per cent of its issued shares are held by any one resident or non-resident shareholder and his associates as described in section 56.

. . . .

In construing this section, the learned trial judge held that "the business of banking is the performance of the activities recited in s. 75(1) (a) to (d)". He went on to say [p. 731]:

The catch-all s. 75(1)(e) must then be read with the preceding paragraphs, which generally define the 'business of banking'. When s. 75(1)(e) says a bank 'may carry on such business generally as appertains to the business of banking', in my opinion that means only that a bank may engage in activities that pertain to the powers defined in s. 75(1) (a) to (d).

Counsel for the defendant submits that the learned trial judge erred in law. I agree. I do not think that Parliament intended to set out a restricted definition of "banking" by enumerating paras. (a) to (d) in s. 75(1). I am inclined to the view that "banking" in the Bank Act has the same broad meaning it has in s. 91 of the B.N.A. Act, 1867.

In *United Dom. Trust Ltd. v. Kirkwood*, [1966] 2 Q.B. 431, [1966] 1 All E.R. 968 (C.A.), Lord Denning M.R. said at p. 979: "Like many other beings, a banker is easier to recognise than to define." I agree. I do not think it would be helpful in this case for us to attempt to set out a comprehensive definition of what banking is. We know from s. 75 of the

Bank Act that a bank is limited to the business of banking and to business which appertains to banking. What is required in the case before us is to decide whether or not the impugned activities of the particular bank sued do or do not fall within what is prohibited under s. 75.

There are two forms of activity of the defendant complained of by the plaintiffs. One is the bank's computer payroll service; the other is the bank's "Compucount" service. The learned trial judge held the former ultra vires insofar as it is offered to persons who do not have funds on deposit from which payroll payments are made. He held that the latter is altogether *ultra vires*.

The defendant submits that both activities are part of the banking business; alternatively, they are both businesses which pertain to banking. The plaintiffs defend the injunction in the terms given, but also cross-appeal on the ground that the injunction against computer payroll services should be extended to cover all persons, whether they have funds on deposit from which the payroll payments are made or otherwise.

It is common ground that the activities complained of are new to banks in Canada. They have arisen largely because of the advent of the computer. The computer allows banks to do economically what was uneconomical under manual systems. Counsel for the bank argues that the business of banking is not static; it must be allowed to develop in accordance with changing conditions. I agree fully. It is appropriate to note the view of Salmon J. in *Woods v. Martins Bank Ltd.*, [1959] 1 Q.B. 55, [1958] 3 All E.R. 166, in a case where a bank tried to get out of responsibility for financial advice on the ground that the giving of financial advice is not part of the business of banking and hence is ultra vires of a bank. The bank relied on a 1918 case [*Banbury v. Bank of Montreal*, [1918] A.C. 626, 44 D.L.R. 234 (H.L.)], which had held that the Bank of Montreal could not engage in the business of giving financial advice. Salmon J., at p. 70, said:

> In my judgment, the limits of a banker's business cannot be laid down as a matter of law. The nature of such a business must in each case be a matter of fact and, accordingly, cannot be treated as if it were a matter of pure law. What may have been true of the Bank of Montreal in 1918 is not necessarily true of Martins Bank in 1958.

I am not sure I would go as far as Salmon J. in treating the matter as purely one of fact. But I agree with his approach that the answer to the question

"Is this banking business or business that pertains to banking?" must be looked at in the light of all the facts, including the current practices of reputable bankers here and abroad and the custom and understanding of the business community, embracing what was in former times called the law merchant. Unfortunately, the quality of the evidence in these respects is not as good as I would have hoped and it is difficult for us to take judicial notice of the law merchant when we have no special juries, as Lord Mansfield had.

That the business of banking is susceptible of development and even of evolution is apparent from the changes that have taken place in the usual manner of dealing with trade accounts receivable. These trade accounts are among the most "bankable" of assets. In the 19th century it was usual for merchants to obtain cash or immediately available credit on the strength of their time sales by obtaining bills of exchange from trade customers payable at a fixed date in future and by then negotiating them at the bank, which would discount the bills. The bank, as holder in due course, had a direct claim against the merchant's customers in the event the merchant should fail and, at the same time, had recourse against the merchant by virtue of his endorsement of the bill. A discount clerk kept track of the paper and, where "the paper was short", the bank would call for additional bills or other credit arrangements. With the development of legislative protection of trade receivables by assignment, giving the bank priority over most other creditors, the importance of receiving actual bills of exchange fell off and the practice developed of banks extending credit on the strength of aged lists of accounts receivable from trade customers. The process of development was gradual; well into the 20th century, as appears from the testimony of Mr. S.T. Paton, the clerk in charge of keeping track of receivables was still called the "discount clerk" even though credit extended was no longer by way of discount of bills and, where it was deemed that the amount of current receivables was deficient, it was still common to say that "the paper was short".

One of the problems with the system of bills of exchange was the mountain of paper involved. Prior to the advent of computer technology, it would have been difficult and costly for the bank to maintain an up-to-date compilation of accounts receivable and to note when and to what extent each was paid. The banks did have a practice of noting a merchant's large deposits and checking them off against its list of the merchant's accounts receivable, but the process was ad hoc and time-consuming. Now, with the advent of the computer, it appears to be economic and relatively simple for the bank to keep on magnetic tape a record of all of a merchant's accounts receivable by name and due date and to note on the same tape when payments are received on such accounts. The result in practice is that it is simple for a bank to maintain through its computer exactly the same information which, under manual systems, merchants have had to record in their accounts receivable ledges. The usefulness of such a record to the bank is indisputable. It enables the bank to have a reliable and up-to-date picture of a merchant's accounts receivable, aged. Where a bank develops such a record for its own purposes of judging the credit-worthiness of its borrower, it would be absurd, in my opinion, for a court to say it must not allow the borrower to have access to such record. The provision of such information to a merchant customer of the bank would surely be a common-sense extension of the banking business, or at least of a business which appertains to banking. The fact that the merchant would no longer have to pay a clerk's time to keep up an accounts receivable ledger is, in my opinion, no sound argument against allowing banks to offer to their customers access to information which the banks keep, in any event, for their own purposes.

As a result of the computer, it appears that a more radical and even more useful development is possible with respect to accounts payable. Under the manual system, in the ordinary course, banks would not accept orders to pay accounts other than by way of individual dated cheques (or bankers' acceptances). When a merchant was satisfied that a supplier's invoice represented purchases taken into inventory, the merchant had to devise a system of recording the invoices as accounts payable. He did not want to pay them by immediate orders to pay because he wanted to take advantage of credit terms, offered by suppliers or usual in his trade. He issued a cheque only on the expiration of the period of credit. He had to keep close watch on his accounts payable to ensure he was not paying them before the end of the period of credit; many suppliers obliged by marking on their statements the number of days particular invoices were overdue. In practice, he paid from suppliers' statements and then debited the accounts payable ledger.

Now, with computers, it appears that banks find it economic to accept orders to pay, not only in the form of individual dated cheques or acceptances, but also in the form of approved invoices. Once the merchant is satisfied the invoice represents purchases taken into inventory, he can send the invoice to the

bank with an authorization to pay in future. The bank does not have to keep the invoice; it records the information on magnetic tape and can return the invoice to the merchant so it is available for returns. The computer enables the bank to honour the merchant's order to pay on the date when the invoice should be paid without requiring the merchant to give the bank an individual cheque or other individual order to pay. This is an obvious convenience to merchants and to trade in general. But if the bank's computer has a record of all payable invoices, it has a record of all the merchant's accounts payable and, if the bank makes payment on such invoices as they become due, it also has a record of all the debits to accounts payable. It becomes a relatively simple process for the bank to allow the merchant to have access to the information already on the bank's computer tape. But the information there is precisely the same as the information in the merchant's accounts payable ledger. In my opinion, it would be absurd to say that a bank may not give access to such information on the ground that it will enable the merchant to do without the services of a clerk who used to keep track of accounts payable. The provision of such information is a logical and normal and common-sense extension of a new banking practice made possible by computer technology.

It is not difficult to see that the use of computer technology will enable banks to keep records of other ledger accounts with obvious advantage to the banks and to the banks' customers. It would be absurd, in my opinion, to hold that a bank may maintain all this information, but cannot give it out to the bank's customers.

It is argued by the plaintiffs that the computer revolution in banking endangers the profession and practice of accountancy. I see no such danger. The bank's information will normally be limited to transactions that involve bank receipts or payments. It will still be necessary for a merchant to have an accountant to go over his records to make year-end adjustments and to give accounting advice. The people who may be thrown out of work are bookkeepers, not accountants, and also those persons like the plaintiffs, who offer computer services of their own.

Like my brother Monnin, I am satisfied that what the bank did in this case was to engage in and carry on such business as now generally appertains to the business of banking. That is within its statutory power and it cannot be faulted for so doing.

I may add that I do not understand why so much stress was laid in argument by the defendant on the independent character of the compucount service. If it were truly independent, it could not be part of business pertaining to banking. Such business must be ancillary to banking, not independent of it.

I agree that the appeal should be allowed and the injunction set aside with costs here and below and that the cross-appeal be dismissed without costs.

Appeal allowed.

Branch Banking

Background Reading: M.H. Ogilvie, *Bank and Customer Law in Canada*, 2d Edition (Toronto: Irwin Law, 2013) Chapter 5, pages 155–157.

(a) *Prince v. Oriental Bank Corporation*†

[SIR MONTAGUE E. SMITH:]

In this case their Lordships are of opinion that the judgment of the Court below ought to be affirmed.

The action is brought to recover money alleged to have been received by the Defendants for the use of the Plaintiffs. It is essential to the maintenance of such an action that the money sought to be recovered should have been actually received by the Defendants, or that something should have occurred which is equivalent to a receipt of money, or that representations should have been made to the Plaintiffs under circumstances which would estop the Defendants from denying the receipt of the money. In the present case their Lordships think that neither of those positions is established by the evidence.

The facts lie in a small compass. The Defendants' bank, which appears to be an English corporation, has branches at *Sydney, Murrumburrah, and Young, in New South Wales*, the branch at *Sydney* being apparently the head branch. The Appellants, Messrs. *Prince & Co.* held a promissory note made by Messrs. *Hopkins & Gate*, who are described as storekeepers at *Young*, for the sum of £426 9s. The note is dated on the 1st of December, 1874, and fell due on Saturday, the 3rd of April, 1875. *Hopkins & Gate* had an account with the Respondents' branch bank at *Young*, but had no account at the *Murrum-*

burrah or *Sydney* branches. The note was made payable, not at *Young*, but at the *Murrumburrah* branch, and this was done at the request of the Respondents' manager of the *Young* branch in order that the Respondents might get some commission upon the collection of the note. This was the state of facts at the time that the note was coming due. Upon the time for payment of the note approaching, the Appellants lodged it with the *Bank of New South Wales*, who were their own bankers, for the purpose of collection. That bank thereupon became the agent of the Plaintiffs to collect the amount. The *Bank of New South Wales* then handed over the note to the Defendants' bank at *Sydney* to collect for them, that is, for the purpose of sending it on to *Murrumburrah*, where it was made payable.

What occurred at the *Murrumburrah* branch is stated in the Respondents' case, and it may be assumed to be correctly stated, inasmuch as the statement was adopted by the learned counsel for the Appellants. It is this: "The note was transmitted in due course by the Respondents to their *Murrumburrah* branch, at which it was made payable, and it was there stamped as having been paid on the 3rd of April, the day on which it fell due, and on the same day the Respondents' manager at *Murrumburrah* sent to their manager in *Sydney* a transfer draft

† (1878), 3 App. Cas. 325 (P.C.). [Notes omitted.]

in favour of the *Bank of New South Wales* for £758 3s. 8d., being for four separate items, one of which was *Hopkins & Gate's* note for £426 9s." Documents were put in at the trial to shew what occurred at the *Murrumburrah* branch. Exhibit B., headed "Application for a draft," is a memorandum which contains this entry, "Wanted a draft on *Sydney* at D. in favour of *Bank of New South Wales* for the sum of £758 3s. 8d." That sum is made up of this note of *Hopkins & Gate* for £426 9s., and of three other notes or bills, making the amount of £758 3s. 8d. This memorandum appears to have been made in the ordinary course of business by a clerk for the purpose of having the draft made out by another clerk. It appears, though the instrument itself does not appear in the record, that a draft, or what is called a draft, was made out and sent to the *Sydney* branch in a letter (Exhibit G.), dated the 3rd of April, which contains this passage, "I enclose the following transfer drafts with particulars thereon 25/168. Manager at *Melbourne*, £101 18s. 5d. — 176. *Bank of New South Wales*, £758 3s. 8d."

The statement in the Respondents' case then goes on: "In the Respondents' books at *Murrumburrah* there was an account current between the *Young* agency and the *Murrumburrah* agency, and in that account, under date the 3rd of April, the *Young* agency, where *Hopkins & Gate* banked, is debited with their note for £426 9s. and other items, and under the same date credit is given for the above-mentioned draft for £758 3s. 8d. At about 2 P.M. on Sunday, the 4th of April, *Hopkins & Gate's* store at *Young* was entirely destroyed by fire. On Monday, the 5th of April, the *Murrumburrah* manager wrote to the Respondents' *Sydney* manager, requesting him to cancel the transfer draft in favour of the *Bank of New South Wales*, and returning the promissory note dishonoured, and on the receipt of the latter the Respondents' *Sydney* manager returned the note to the *Bank of New South Wales*, and on the 7th of April that bank gave the Plaintiffs notice of the dishonour of the note."

The notice of dishonour is set out. It is an ordinary notice of dishonour, making no reference to what had occurred between the branches of the bank or to the memoranda made upon the bill. It nowhere appears that notice was given by the Respondents to Messrs. *Hopkins & Gate* that their account was charged, and there was no evidence that it ever was in fact charged with the amount of the note, and no intimation was given by the Respondents to the Appellants or to the *Bank of New South Wales* that it had been paid.

The note itself was put in at the trial. It is an ordinary promissory note made payable at the *Oriental Bank, Murrumburrah*, and upon its production it appeared that the names of the makers, *Hopkins & Gate*, had been struck through, or, to use the ordinary term, cancelled. There was also on it a memorandum, "Paid 3/4/75." But a memorandum in pencil also appeared upon the note, "cancelled in error by *J.O. Atchison*."

These being the facts, it is clear beyond dispute that the makers of this note, Messrs. *Hopkins & Gate*, had not paid any money in respect of it into the bank. There is no evidence of the state of their account at *Young*, and it certainly cannot be taken as against the Defendants that that account was in funds. The Plaintiffs, although they called Mr. *Hopkins*, did not attempt to prove that the *Young* branch was in funds, or that *Hopkins & Gate* had any agreement with the Defendants' bank for the payment of this note.

It is contended on behalf of the Plaintiffs that what passed between the *Murrumburrah* and the *Sydney* branches of the bank, and the remittance by the officer at *Murrumburrah* to the officer at *Sydney* of the transfer note, was equivalent to a payment of money to the *Sydney* branch. But even so, the whole case of the Appellants must rest upon the foundation that these branches are to be treated for this purpose as if they were separate and independent banks. If they had been separate and distinct banks, it may be that the remittance by the *Murrumburrah* Bank to the bank at *Sydney* of this draft to be put to the credit of the *New South Wales Bank*, would, if so accepted, have been equivalent to a receipt on the part of the *Sydney Bank* of money from the *Murrumburrah Bank* to be held for the *New South Wales Bank*. But the difficulty of the Plaintiffs' case is that these banks are not separate and distinct banks, but branches of one and the same banking corporation or establishment. They are, indeed, separate agencies, but agencies of one principal, that principal being the corporation of the *Oriental Bank*. How, then, are the Defendants liable? They have not received the money, nor anything equivalent to money, from any source outside their own establishment. Supposing the *Murrumburrah* branch had sent money from their till to the branch at *Sydney*, whose money would it have been? Surely, the money of the *Oriental Bank*. It would have gone from the till at *Murrumburrah* to the till at *Sydney*, but would remain, notwithstanding the transfer, the bank's own money. Then, if so, the remittance of the draft and the entries, which at most are only equivalent to a transfer of money, and might be so as between distinct banks, cannot have greater effect than an actual transfer of money. They are entries and transactions only by and between the respective officers of the same bank.

If these transactions had been communicated to the *New South Wales Bank* or to the Plaintiffs, it may be that the *Oriental Bank* would have been estopped from saying that they did not hold the money to the account of the Plaintiffs or of the *New South Wales Bank*. But no such communication was made; and before anything was known beyond the walls of the bank itself, the order given by the officer at *Murrumburrah* to the *Sydney Bank* to credit the *New South Wales Bank* was cancelled and withdrawn, and the memorandum "cancelled in error" was made upon the note. The first thing that the Plaintiffs or the *New South Wales Bank* hear or know, is that the note is dishonoured. If any damage has arisen in consequence of negligence or delay on the part of the bank in getting payment of this note, an action may lie for such omission or negligence, in which the true amount of damages would be assessed, but their Lordships have nothing to do with any question of that kind. The single question they have now to determine is whether money has been received by the Defendants to the use of the Plaintiffs, or whether they have in any way held out to the Plaintiffs that there was money in their hands belonging to the Plaintiffs.

The mere fact of cancelling the signature of the makers, and writing "paid" on the note, corrected, as it was, before the note was sent back, by the memorandum "cancelled in error," cannot be effectual to charge the bank with the receipt of the money: see *Warwick v. Rogers*;[1] nor, unless the branches are to be regarded as distinct banks, can the uncommunicated entries in the books of the bank have such an effect: see *Simson v. Ingham*.[2]

The case really turns upon the position or *status* of these branch banks.

In principle and in fact they are agencies of one principal banking corporation or firm, and the few decisions which have taken place with respect to them are consistent with this view. In the case of *Clode v. Bayley*[3] it was held that for the purpose of estimating the time at which notice of dishonour should be given, the different branches were for that purpose to be regarded as distinct. In considering whether notice of dishonour was given in time it was thought reasonable that the bill should be sent successively to the branch banks through which it had come to the principal bank, before giving the notice. It was pointed out by Lord *Abinger* that it was not possible for the bank in *London* to know from whom

the bill came; therefore it was necessary, in the ordinary course of the transaction of business, that it should be sent to the branches before notice of dishonour could properly be given.

In the case of *Woodland v. Fear*[4] it was held that a joint stock bank was bound to pay the cheques of a customer at that branch only at which he kept his account, and had not violated its engagement with the customer by refusing to pay his cheque at another branch. The reason of this decision is obvious. It would be difficult for a bank to carry on its business by means of various branches if a customer who kept his account at one branch might draw cheques upon another branch, however distant from that at which he kept his account, and demand that they should be cashed there. The latter branch could not possibly know the state of his account. The case decides no more than this, that the bank came under no engagement or promise to their customer to honour his cheques at any branch except that at which he kept his account.

The only other case is one that affords strong support to the view which their Lordships are disposed to take: *Garnett v. McKewan*.[5] There the Plaintiff had accounts at two branches of the *London and County Bank*. His account at branch A. was in funds; his account at branch B. was over-drawn. He drew a cheque upon his account at branch A. where he had funds, and the bank refused to pay it because his account at branch B. was over-drawn, and the Court held it was justified in so doing. The principle of that decision affirms the identity of the bank and its several branches; though separate agencies, the latter were still agencies of one principal bank, with which alone the Plaintiffs contracted. Acting upon this principle, the Court held that the money of the Plaintiff lodged at one branch, and being still there to the credit of his account, was to be treated as part of the customer's entire account with the bank, and that the whole account was to be looked at to see on which side as between him and the bank the balance stood. Mr. Baron *Bramwell* said: "The question is one of mixed law and fact. It is admitted that in some cases the bank could not debit the customer with a debt due to them; for example, a debt due to the bank as carrying on a different business as that of brewers. Nor again, would they have any right to blend two accounts kept by one person with them in different characters as a personal and a trust account." — No, nor would any bank, whether it had branches or not. "But here there was nothing except the fact that there were two branch establishments." That fact, in the opinion of the learned Judge, established no difference between the case of a bank having branches and an ordinary bank.

Another question of some importance has been argued — whether, assuming that the bank had received the money from the makers of the note, the Plaintiffs could sue the bank for it, or whether their right of action would not be against the *New South Wales Bank*, whom they employed to collect the note. The question thus barely stated does not really arise, because it is not pretended that the bank did receive money specifically for the purpose of taking up the note. If the makers of the note had paid the money to the bank with an express direction that it should be appropriated to the payment of this note, then the point would have arisen which was decided in *De Bernales v. Fuller*. That case, which is reported in a note in the 14th East, 590, appears to be in some degree an exceptional one, and turned upon the precise circumstances existing in it. At first sight it seems opposed to the general rule that a principal cannot sue a sub-agent for want of privity existing between them. The case has been referred to in several later decisions. It has never been overruled, and it has been put on a ground on which it may stand by Mr. Justice *Maule*, in *Warwick v. Rogers*.[6] He says: — "In *De Bernales v. Fuller*,[7] where money was paid into a banking-house for the purpose of taking up a particular bill which was lying there for payment, it was held to be money had and received to the use of the then owner and holder of the bill, and that it could not be applied by the bankers to the general account of the acceptor who paid in the money, though the banker's clerk had said at the time the money was paid in that he would not give up the bill till he had seen his master. But that decision turned upon the fact that the money having been expressly paid into the Defendants' house for the specific purpose declared at the time of taking up that particular bill, and that purpose not having been directly repudiated till afterwards, it must be taken to have been received at the time for the use of the holder of the bill." It would seem, therefore, that the case may be supported on the ground that money had been paid in specifically for the payment of the particular bill, and had been accepted by the bankers for that purpose, and that they made themselves, by so accepting the money, agents to hold it for the Plaintiffs.

The general rule, however, was affirmed by two learned Lords in the House of Lords, in the case of *Mackersy v. Ramsays*.[8] There two bills payable in *India* had been deposited by Mr. *Mackersy* with Messrs. *Ramsays*, who were bankers at *Edinburgh*, to collect for him. They sent the bills to their English correspondents, *Coutts & Co.*, and *Coutts & Co.* remitted them to their own correspondents, one to Messrs. *Palmer*, and the other to Messrs. *Alexander & Co.*, in *India*, to collect. Both bills were paid in *India*, one to Messrs. *Palmer*, and the other to Messrs. *Alexander*, but both these houses failed, and did not remit to *Coutts*. The House of Lords decided that Mr. *Mackersy* was entitled to recover the amount of the bills from Messrs. *Ramsays*, his own bankers in *Edinburgh*, as his principal agents, inasmuch as they were liable to him as soon as their sub-agents received the money; deciding, in fact, that the receipt of the sub-agents was, as between Mr. *Mackersy* and Messrs. *Ramsays*, the receipt of Messrs. *Ramsays*. In the course of giving judgment, Lord *Cottenham* said: "From the time the bills were sent to the Pursuers the Appellant did not interfere. It was not intended that he should do so, nor indeed could he have done so, as none of the intended agents acted under his authority; he therefore had no control over them. All that *Mackersy* undertook to do by the bills has been accomplished." Lord *Campbell* said: "*Mackersy* could not have interfered with the money either in the hands of *Alexander & Co.* or of *Coutts & Co.* There was no privity between him and either of those houses; but payment to *Alexander & Co.* was payment to *Coutts & Co.*, and payment to *Coutts & Co.* was payment to *Ramsays & Co.*

In the view which Lord *Campbell* entertained, no action could have been brought by Mr. *Mackersy* against either *Coutts & Co.* or *Palmer & Co.*, or *Alexander & Co.*, there being no privity between him and them which would have entitled him to sustain it.

There is a further difficulty in the way of the Plaintiffs suing the Defendants directly, and passing over his immediate agents, the *New South Wales Bank*. All that the Defendants apparently undertook to do was to place the amount of the bills when collected to the account of the *New South Wales Bank*, subject, it may be, to the accounts between the two banks.

In their Lordships' view, however, it is not necessary to determine the case upon the questions last referred to, because they are of opinion that neither the Plaintiffs nor the *New South Wales Bank* are entitled, for the reasons they have already given, to sue the *Oriental Bank* for money had and received to their use.

Their Lordships will humbly advise Her Majesty to affirm the judgment of the Supreme Court, with the costs of this appeal.

(b) *Garnett v. McKewan*†

[KELLY, C.B.:]

I am clearly of opinion that there should be no rule. The question substantially raised by the pleadings is whether any money of the plaintiff's was in the hands of the London and County Bank, which they were bound to pay upon whether they were indebted to that amount to the plaintiff. Now, in fact, they were not so indebted. If, therefore, they are liable in this action, it must be by virtue of some special contract or well recognized course of dealing.

It appears that the plaintiff was desirous of keeping an account with the London and County Bank, and it suited his convenience — and was for their profit no doubt — that he should deposit cash in their hands both at Leighton Buzzard and Buckingham, where they had establishments. And if the plaintiff had had a balance in his favour at both places he could of course have drawn at either to the extent of the balance there. But the fact was, that whilst he had a balance in his favour at Leighton Buzzard it was almost exactly equalled by a balance against him at Buckingham. The defendant's bank, therefore, had scarcely a shilling of his money, and I cannot see why they were bound to honour his cheque at Leighton Buzzard just because there was a balance at that branch in his favour. It is contended that the branches are quite distinct, and the defendant's bank have no more right to set off at the Leighton Buzzard branch a debt due to them as bankers at Buckingham than they would have to debit a debt due to them in some other capacity — as brewers, for example — against the plaintiff's account. It must be remembered, however, that the plaintiff might have ordered a transfer of his assets from the one branch to the other, and the defendants' bank, on the other hand, must have a corresponding right. In general it might be proper or considerate to give a notice to that effect, but there is no legal obligation on the bankers to do so, arising either from express contract or the course of dealing between the parties. The customer must be taken to know the state of each account, and if the balance on the whole is against him or does not equal the cheques he draws, he has no right to expect those cheques to be cashed. We all know what the actual practice of bankers is where there are branches. In such cases the managers of each branch are in the habit of communicating with each other, and honour cheques of the customer according to the state of his general account. But there is certainly no usage according to which the customer is entitled to expect his cheques to be honoured at one branch where he happens to have a balance to his credit, when at the same time that balance is counterbalanced by a debit against him at another branch.

With respect to the cases cited, they are distinguishable. In *Hill v. Smith*[1] the customer sent money to the bank for the specific purpose of meeting a particular bill, and that money no doubt the bankers, having accepted it for that purpose, could not set off against the general account. In the other case cited, *Cumming v. Shand*,[2] a special contract was established, and the defendant was on that account held not to be entitled to refuse to honour the plaintiff's cheques. Here there was no special contract and no usage proved, and in the absence of either, the mere fact of there being two branch establishments is not enough to entitle the plaintiff to recover. The rule must therefore be refused.

[MARTIN, B.:]

I am of the same opinion. The question is really one rather of fact than of law. The relation between banker and customer is that of debtor and creditor with a superadded obligation on the part of the banker to honour the customer's cheques so long as there are any assets of his in the banker's hands. So it was expressed in the judgment of the Court in *Pott v. Clegg*.[3] But the mere existence of an apparent balance, if there is no real balance, is not enough to render the bank liable to pay a cheque at the branch where the apparent balance is. There was no evidence that in this case the bankers undertook to cash cheques at one branch when the whole accounts shewed that the customer had no sufficient balance. No special contract, nor any usage or course of dealing to that effect was proved.

---

† (1872), L.R. 8 Exch. 10. [Notes omitted.]

[PIGOTT, B.:]

I also think the rule should be refused. Where there are branch banks the same relation between banker and customer exists, in the absence of any special contract, as in the case where there is one establishment only. There is no duty on the part of the bank to keep the accounts separate. No one would say that a banker might set off against his customer's account a debt due to him from his customer in another capacity, a private debt, for example, or a debt due to him as carrying on some distinct business. Nor has a banker any right to confound two accounts lodged with him by one person in two different capacities. He would have no right to blend a personal and a trust account. But here there is nothing to prevent the banker from taking into account the state of the plaintiff's balance as a whole; and upon such account being taken, it appeared that the plaintiff had no sufficient assets to meet the cheques presented. The banker was therefore justified in dishonouring them.

[BRAMWELL, B.:]

I thought the defendant entitled to the verdict at the trial, and I still think so; though my opinion is not a very confident one. My doubt arises thus: The money is paid to the customer's account at a particular place, and except at that place he cannot call upon the bank to pay, although he may happen to have a balance at another branch establishment. Is not the obligation correlative? The bank is not liable to be called on to pay at one branch just because there is a balance at another. Why, then, may the bank without notice debit the customer's account at one branch with his deficiency at another? The question is one of mixed law and fact. It is admitted that in some cases the bank could not debit the customer with a debt due to them; for example, a debt due to the bank as carrying on a different business, as that of brewers. Nor, again, would they have any right to blend two accounts kept by one person with them in different characters, as a personal and a trust account. But here there was nothing except the fact that there were two branch establishments. Nothing was said as to their being separate, and nothing should be implied. If indeed it was understood and agreed that the branches should be kept separate, then the plaintiff is right, but not otherwise. And with regard to the correlative rights of the parties, it must be remembered that if a customer might draw anywhere where he had a balance, no matter what the real debit against him might be, there would be a real hardship on bankers and a difficulty in their conducting business. But to limit his drawing to the amount of his total actual balance is no hardship on him, for he always knows, or can know if he likes, the state of his account as a whole. In practice, bankers do constantly allow overdrawing at a particular branch, because they know they may debit the customer with his balance at some other branch. It may be convenient and proper for them to give the customer notice of their intention to do so, but there is no legal obligation upon them to give such notice.

I think, therefore, that the customer has no claim, for he is indebted to the bank on his whole account in such an amount as to reduce his assets to almost nothing. There is no duty, in my opinion, apart from usage or contract, on the part of the banker to honour cheques at one branch because the customer has a credit there, if at another branch there is a countervailing debit. I agree, therefore, that the rule must be refused.

Rule refused.

(c) *Irwin v. Bank of Montreal*†

One *I.*, who died in 1870 in Ireland, had deposited money at the branch of defendants' bank in Cobourg in 1869. Letters of administration were granted on 25th April, 1872, by the Probate Court of the District Registry at Ballina in Ireland, to *J.G.*, at whose house *I.* died, who represented himself to be his cousin german and only next

---

† (1876), 38 U.C.Q.B. 375.

of kin. An exemplification thereof was recorded in the Superior Court of Montreal, and on this the bank, in September, 1872, paid over the amount to *G.*'s attorney in Montreal, who handed to them the receipt which he had obtained from *G.* It appeared however that *G.* had obtained the administration by fraud, not being *I.*'s next of kin. In August, 1872, administration was granted by the Court of Probate in Ireland to the plaintiff, *I.*'s brother, and in May, 1872, the plaintiff notified defendant's manager at Cobourg not to pay over any money except to himself.

The evidence shewed that the Probate Court at Ballina had power to grant the administration, and by the C.S.L.C. ch. 91, the administrator of any one dying abroad is recognized and has the same power in Lower Canada as in the country where he was appointed or resides.

Held,

1. That the Ballina administration, though obtained by fraud, was valid until revoked by some express judicial act, and was not revoked by the mere issue of the Dublin grant.
2. That by the Lower Canada law *J.G.* was entitled under that grant to receive payment in Montreal.
3. That although the money was payable at Cobourg, defendants paid it rightfully at their head office at Montreal.
4. That defendants were bound to pay it on demand made under the Ballina grant, notwithstanding the notice served on them.
5. That it was a payment made in Montreal in good faith to the ostensible creditor, under article 1144 and 1145 of the *L.C. Code Civile*.

Remarks upon the necessity for some amendment of the law, in order to prevent the obtaining letters of administration by fraud and without giving security.

[WILSON J.:]

The third question is, whether the money was payable at Montreal or at Cobourg?

In *Willis v. The Bank of England*, 4 A.&E. 21, 38, an Act is referred to which expressly made bank post bills issued by branch banks payable *there* as well as at the principal office in London.

In *Mayhew v. Eames*, 3. B.&C. 601, a notice given at the principal office is a notice to all the agencies of the person. See also *Willis v. Bank of England*, 4 A.&E. at p. 39.

In *Re Brown v. London & N.W.R.W. Co.*, 4 B.&S. 326, a company dwells at its principal place of business, and therefore it cannot be sued at a place where a very considerable part of its business was done.

Each branch of a bank is to be considered as a separate holder for the purpose of giving notice of dishonour: *Clode v. Bayley*, 12 M.&W. 51.

A person who had bound himself not to set up, embark in, or carry on business in certain places, was held to have broken his agreement by soliciting orders in those places and fulfilling them from his store of goods outside of these limits. It was carrying on business within the prohibited places: *Re Turner v. Evans*, 2 E.&B. 512.

In *Woodland v. Fear*, 7 E.&B. 519, a joint stock banking company carried on business at various places, amongst others at G. and B. Each branch kept separate accounts, had separate customers, and in all respects transacted business like separate banks. Defendant held a cheque drawn by a customer of the bank at G. on that branch, and he got it cashed at B. branch. The cheque was without laches forwarded by the B. branch to the G. branch. When it was cashed at B. the balance of the customer in G. branch exceeded the amount of the cheque, but when it arrived at G. that balance had been paid away and the cheque was dishonoured. The company sued the defendant for money had and received, by reason of the failure of consideration: — Held, the bank was entitled to recover, as the B. branch could not under the circumstances be considered as honouring the cheque nor as purchasing it, but as taking it from the defendant on his credit, as they might have done a cheque drawn on any other bank; the circumstance that the banks at G. and B. were branches of the same company being for the purpose immaterial. Lord Campbell said at p. 521:

> The cheque was not drawn on the bank generally, but on the banking company at Glastonbury, and that, coupled with the fact that the drawer kept his account and his balance only there, shews that the Bridgewater establishment was not bound to honour his cheque (even supposing he had assets at Glastonbury) as a banker under the same circumstances is bound to honour the check of his customer. To hold that the customer of one branch, keeping his cash and his account there, has a right to have his cheques paid at all or any of the branches, is

to suppose a state of circumstances so inconsistent with any safe dealing on the part of the banker that it cannot be presumed without direct evidence of such an agreement.

The statutes affecting the defendants' bank are their *Charter Act*, 19-20 Vic. ch. 76, and the *General Bank Act*, 34 Vic. ch. 5.

The chief seat or place of business of the defendants' bank is in the city of Montreal: 19-20 Vic. ch. 76, sec. 3. And they may open and establish branches or agencies at other places in the Dominion: 34 Vic. ch. 5, sec. 4.

The bank may charge commission for discounting at one agency a bill drawn on another: 19-20 Vic. ch. 76, sec. 22.

The bank notes are to be made payable on demand in specie at the place where they are made: Section 24; and 34 Vic. ch. 5, sec. 55.

I come to the conclusion that the money was payable at Cobourg. I am not altogether prepared to say it was not payable in Montreal if a demand according to the terms of the deposit receipt (which I have not seen) were made at Montreal, and a sufficient time allowed to the head office to make the necessary enquiry at the branch office to ascertain if the money could be safely paid, and upon paying the proper charges occasioned by such communication and probably also the discount: *Co.* Litt. 210b, note (1). A person having money at his credit at a branch bank could require the head office by order, bill, or otherwise, to transfer that credit to his account at the head office. The bank although having many places of business is yet the one body — the only debtor to a depositor. A customer having money in different branches has but the one debtor.

Garnett v. McKewan, L.R. 8 Ex. 10, shews that a customer having a credit in his favour at one branch, and having overdrawn his account at another, may have the sum at his credit transferred by the bank to the branch where he is a debtor, to balance it, and that the bank may do so without notice to him.

I feel there are some difficulties in dealing with deposits at one agency by the head office or by another agency.

In this case, on the death of William Irwin, where did the bank, his debtor, reside for the purpose of granting administration? Was it at Cobourg, or was it in Montreal?

Perhaps it may be said it was at either place, according to the election of the applicant for administration, for a person — and the defendants, I presume, in such a case may be treated in the like manner — may have more residences than one: *Walcot v. Botfield*, Kay 534, 18 Jur. 570; *Maltass v. Maltass*, 1 Rob. Eccl. R. 67. Although, for the purpose of the administration of his personal estate, a person cannot have two domicils: *Forbes v. Forbes*, Kay 341, 18 Jur. 642; *Crookenden v. Fuller*, 5 Jur. N.S. 1222.

The case of *Re Brown v. London & N.W.R.W. Co.*, 4 B.&S. 326, shews the bank may be said to dwell at its principal place of business. That must more especially be its place of abode or residence, although it may for many purposes have more residences than one.

I think, if the money were at the Cobourg branch, administration might have been taken out there; but that does not shew if administration could by the law of the Province of Quebec be taken out there, that an administration granted there would not also be sufficient.

If an ordinary debtor had two residences, one here and another in Quebec, where would administration, in order to reach the debt — and assuming administration could be taken out in Quebec — be properly grantable? In my opinion, at either of his residences.

Here practically administration was taken out in Quebec, for their law permits the administration granted in another country to be as operative in Quebec as it was in the country in which it was issued. I come, therefore, to the conclusion that, for the purpose of this administration, the debtor did, at the death of Wm. Irwin, reside in Montreal; and as the defendants chose to consider the money as payable there, and they did pay it there, that the money became payable there, and was rightly paid under the Ballina grant of administration, and it was not necessary to have an Ontario administration.

(d) Clare and Co. v. Dresdner Bank†

Action tried before Rowlatt J. without a Jury.

The plaintiffs claimed the sum of £261 as money had and received by the defendants to their use, being the amount standing to the credit of the plaintiffs' banking account, on August 4, 1914, at the Berlin branch of the defendant bank.

The Dresdner Bank was a foreign corporation, incorporated under the laws of Germany, having its head office in Dresden. It had a branch in Berlin and also a branch in London.

The plaintiffs had an account at the Berlin branch, and on August 4, 1914, there was a sum equivalent to £261 standing to the credit of that account. On December 1 the plaintiffs wrote to the London branch asking for payment of this amount, which was refused. No demand for payment or for remittance of the amount to London was made by the plaintiffs to the head office or the Berlin branch. On December 3 the writ in this action was issued; it was served at the office of the bank in London, and an application at chambers by the defendants to set aside the service was dismissed.

[ROWLATT J.:]

I think that this action fails. [The learned judge stated the facts, and proceeded:] Mr. Hogg contends that the relation of banker and customer is simply that of debtor and creditor, with a superadded obligation to honour cheques. That of course is right. Then he says that before suing the debtor it is not necessary to make any demand of payment, and cites the cases decided upon the *Statutes of Limitation*. It seems to me, however, that locality is an essential part of the debt owing by a banker to his customer, and that his obligation to pay is limited to the place where the account is kept. As a rule, no doubt, a debtor has to seek out his creditor and pay him; but in the case of a bank with several branches that cannot be the true relation of the parties. Money has a different value in different parts of the world even although it may be expressed in the same currency, and I cannot conceive it possible that a man who has, we will say, £1,000 sterling to his credit at a bank in New Zealand on coming to London would have the legal right to demand payment of £1,000 at an office of the same bank in London without being liable to pay anything in consideration of that convenience or even to give time for the bank in London to ascertain whether he was in fact a customer of and had a credit balance at the branch in New Zealand. Everybody knows that in certain states of the exchange people in some parts of the world, having debts to pay in another part of the world, find their account in actually shipping bullion, paying the freight and the insurance involved in that operation; and if a man who has money to his credit at a bank at one end of the world can demand it at another end of the world without paying anything for that advantage, that would put upon his debtor the expense which might be involved in having the money at the one place instead of the other.

I come to the conclusion, therefore, that, although the question seems never to have been raised before, probably because such a thing has never been dreamt of, there is no obligation on a bank to pay in one country a debt due to a customer on current account in another country.

Under these circumstances how am I to apply that here? There was a case of *Leader & Co. v. Direction der Disconto-Gesellschaft* (31 Times L.R. 83.), tried before Scrutton J., against a German bank having a branch in London, where the plaintiffs, who had an account at the Berlin branch, succeeded. In that case, however, there had been a request to the bank abroad, where the account was kept, to remit the money to London. It is well known that a banker will send a remittance to another country, making the proper charges, at the request of his customer having an account, and when the bank, in that case, refused to send the remittance at the customer's expense from the place where the account was kept there was a refusal to perform their obligation and a cause of action accrued which might be enforced wherever the bank could be found.

Now in this case there has not been any demand upon the head office or the Berlin branch and no dishonouring by the bank in Berlin of the obligation to pay or remit. I can deal only with the facts before me, which are simply that the Lon-

---

† [1915] 2 K.B. 576 (K.B.D.).

don office had been asked, not to fetch the money from the other side, if I may use the expression, but to honour an obligation to pay in London money deposited at their branch in Berlin. I do not think that is in accordance with law or business, and therefore I give judgment for the defendants.

Judgment for defendants.

(e) *Royal Bank of Canada v. Boyce; Royal Bank of Canada v. Wildman†*

[COSTELLO CO. CT. J.:]

These actions were tried together on May 17, 1966, pursuant to order to that effect obtained in March. For a matter involving $600, some other interesting points of law are raised and the facts are such as one would expect to find in a script written for a law school moot Court.

I will attempt to set out the facts in chronological order, as near as possible, and I will refer to the parties by name for simplicity. In April, 1965, Wildman decided to sell his 1955 Oldsmobile, advertised it, and in response to the advertisement, Boyce telephoned. On April 7th, Wildman drove to Boyce's residence with the car, Boyce checked it over, tried all the power equipment, drove it around in the city for three or four miles and agreed to buy it for $600. Boyce went into the house and obtained a Royal Bank of Canada cheque form, inserted Wildman's name as payee, dated it April 8th. The cheque form was on the Royal Bank, Thamesford Branch. He crossed out the word "Thamesford" and inserted below it the word "Waterloo". The cheque was signed, delivered to Wildman who handed over the keys to the car, left the car with Boyce and departed.

Before leaving, Wildman agreed to install a window and piece of grille the following Saturday. There was mention that Boyce would bring the cash around to Wildman in the morning if he did not cash the cheque. Boyce said the reason he gave the cheque was that, in the event something happened to him while he was testing the car he wanted Wildman to have a claim against his estate.

The next morning, about 9:40, Boyce drove the car to Wildman's place of employment, the Dominion Tire Retail Store on Belmont Ave., saw Wildman and said he did not want the car because it would not go faster than 95 m.p.h. and had had body work done on it. He put the keys down and he left in another car. Before he left, Wildman told him it was his (Boyce's) car.

Immediately, Wildman, in still another car, drove to the Royal Bank of Canada, King and University Street Branch, Waterloo. I accept his statement that he had been told this was the branch in which Boyce had his account. He passed the Royal Bank's only other branch in Waterloo on the way to the University Avenue Branch. To impute an improper motive to him in doing this would be ridiculous although, as it now unfolds, the branch he passed by was the one where Boyce kept his account. It must be remembered that Boyce, who is a former Royal Bank employee, when he crossed out "Thamesford" and inserted "Waterloo", did not specify which of the Banks' two Waterloo branches was to be the drawee. I am satisfied beyond any shadow of doubt that Wildman, when he presented Boyce's cheque at the University Avenue Branch of the bank understood that he was presenting it to the bank which Boyce had designated as the drawee bank.

Wildman entered the University Branch where he had no account and was not known. He presented Boyce's cheque to a teller. She handed it to him asking him to sign the back. He signed his name on the back of the cheque, handed it to the teller who gave him $600 in cash with no more ado. He was not even asked for identification nor did the teller make any check of any kind; I am referring particularly to a check to see if the drawer had an

---

† (1966), 57 D.L.R. (2d) 683 (Ont. Co. Ct.).

account or had sufficient funds. The teller did not refer the cheque to the accountant or the manager.

With the $600 in his pocket, Wildman returned to his place of employment and either then or very shortly after took the keys and ownership certificate by Boyce's residence and left them with Boyce's landlord. The car remained on the Dominion Tire store lot on Belmont Blvd. in Kitchener. There was some conversation between Boyce and Wildman that evening in which Boyce learned that Wildman had the cash for the cheque. The next morning Boyce again returned the keys and the ownership certificate to Wildman, again throwing them down beside him and leaving. Boyce and Wildman have each maintained throughout from the morning of April 8th that the car is the property of the other party. If there was a sale, Wildman never agreed to take the car back or more technically never agreed to rescission. Boyce maintains he cancelled the deal because the car was not mechanically fit and of sound body.

On April 8th, before banking hours and before seeing Wildman, Boyce put a "Stop Payment" order on the cheque by notifying the King and Erb Street Branch of the Royal Bank and it was duly noted by that branch. The "Stop Payment" order was put in before the cheque was cashed. Boyce said he did not ask Wildman for his cheque on the morning of April 8th because he knew the stop payment order was in. He was unable to affirm that he told Wildman of the stop payment order. He does not deny telling Wildman the account was in the University Avenue Branch and agrees Wildman could have assumed it was in that branch because Boyce worked at the University of Waterloo which is in that area.

Routinely, the cheque was cleared from the King and University Branch to the King and Erb Street Branch of the Royal Bank. On April 9th the manager of the University Avenue Branch became aware of what had happened and became aware of the stop payment order. The cheque was returned to the University Avenue Branch.

Kearney, the manager of the University Avenue Branch, testified that he spoke to both Wildman and Boyce advising them he was looking to them for payment. They both claimed the other one was the owner of the car and neither accepted responsibility for the $600. Kearney at this point went to the Dominion Tire Store lot with a tow-truck and had the car towed to his bank, parked it in the bank parking lot where it has remained to this day. Wildman offered to try to sell it again but Kearney, on instructions from his superiors in Toronto, according to his own evidence, refused to let Wildman take the car from the lot unless he paid

the Bank $600. Wildman, who lives in Bridgeport quite a number of miles from King and University Ave., refused to run back and forth with prospective purchasers, refused to pay the $600 and had the good sense to refuse Kearney's last ditch effort of attempting to have Wildman sign a note for $600 repayable in instalments. Boyce maintained the position that he had stopped payment properly and had no further obligation to anyone.

The bank also claims for the towing and for insurance if placed on the car. What right it had to tow away and retain the car and what insurable interest it had to insure have not been shown.

Dealing with the sale of the car from Wildman to Boyce, it is clear that this was a completed transaction never rescinded. The cheque is evidence both of the amount of the sale and of the consensus between the parties. Boyce took possession of the car, drove it some twenty miles at high speeds. To ask to rescind the sale of a ten-year-old car because it would not go over 95 m.p.h. and because it had had body work on it is at best humorous. The car was not misrepresented by Wildman and the only expert evidence adduced proved the car to be in good condition. Boyce's other complaint the next day was that he had paid too much for it. The time to decide that of course is before the deal is made and the maxim *caveat emptor* applies. Were the action a simple one by Wildman against Boyce for the $600, he would undoubtedly succeed. In an action on the cheque he would be a holder for value.

In argument on the claim by the bank against Boyce, the bank's counsel argued that a stop payment order is ineffective unless it is given to every branch of a bank and that it is not sufficient to lodge the stop payment order only with the branch where the account is.

I thought this to be an astounding proposition but two cases were cited in support of it. *London, Provincial, and South Western Bank Ltd. v. Buszard* (1918), 35 T.L.R. 142, followed in *Garrioch v. Canadian Bank of Commerce*, [1919] 3 W.W.R. 185. These are judgments at trial of the King's Bench Division in England and the Supreme Court of British Columbia respectively.

In the *Buszard* case, the defendant customer had issued a cheque, payment of which he stopped by an order to the bank branch on which the cheque was drawn. Another branch of the bank cashed the cheque and, the payee having gone to Monte Carlo, the bank sued the drawer. Lawrence J., followed *Clode v. Bayley* (1843), 12 M.&W. 51, 152 E.R. 1107, stating that that case decided the point at issue. I quote from the note of the judgment:

The bank was the holder of the cheque for value, and the fact that the branch at Oxford-street had notice not to pay the cheque did not affect the bank, which was entitled to judgment. It appeared from *Clode v. Bayley (supra)* that there was a right to a separate notice of dishonour as between the different branches of a bank. There was no evidence before the Court in the present case of the actual time when the notice not to pay the cheque was given, but it appeared that on February 8 Mr. Trott was absolutely without notice, and he paid the money in good faith. There would be judgment for the amount claimed, with costs.

In the *Garrioch* case, Scott J., followed the above case in these words at p. 186:

> In *London Provincial & South-Western Bank, Ltd. v. Buzzard*, 35 T.L.R. 142, the defendant drew a cheque upon one of the plaintiff's branches and afterwards gave that branch notice that he had stopped payment thereof. The cheque was presented at another of defendant's branches and was there paid, the manager of that branch not having had notice that payment had been stopped. It was held that the plaintiff was entitled to recover the amount of the cheque.
>
> Following that case I give judgment for the defendant upon his counterclaim for $1,210, with costs.

The case of *Clode v. Bayley* which these two cases claim to follow is not at all an authority for the proposition advanced. It was a case in which a bill of exchange was endorsed to a bank branch, sent to another branch of the same bank and endorsed to the head office in London. In London it was presented for payment and dishonoured. It was returned with notice of dishonour to the bank head office then to each of the two branches, the last of which in the chain gave notice of dishonour to the original endorser, the defendant. What was at issue was whether the defendant should have received notice of dishonour directly from the head office or whether each of the two intervening branches were also entitled to notice of dishonour. If they were not, then the extra days which intervened between the dishonouring and the notice of it to the defendant would make the notice too late.

It seems that the trial Judge in the *Buzzard* case confused or equated notice of dishonour with notice of countermand of payment and was duly followed by the trial Judge in the *Garrioch* case. While countermand of payment may, in effect, be the dishonouring, the procedure for notice of dishonour cannot commence until the bill is presented. Then if dishon-

oured it goes back on a chain, each link of which can be ascertained by examining the face or back of the bill. The procedure on notice of dishonour is statutory; there is no procedure for notice of countermand of payment, certainly none that notice be given to every bank branch. In the Canadian branch bank system, this would be absurdly difficult. These two judgments appear to be both wrong and contrary to reasonable business practice. On strict application of the *stare decisis* rule these judgments from another jurisdiction are not binding on me, so, for the aforementioned reasons, I refuse to follow them.

I find then that Boyce by giving a countermand of payment order to the branch in which his account was, did all that was required and he has no obligation to any other branch, the King and University Waterloo Branch in particular, nor was that branch or any other branch entitled to separate notice from Boyce of his countermand of payment or stop payment order.

The bank claims to be a holder in due course. The defendant Wildman claims that the bank, or the University Avenue Branch of it, in accepting the cheque and paying it was the drawee in effect stopping the chain which stretches only from drawer to payee to drawee. The defence contends that there was never a holder in due course of this cheque and that the University Avenue Branch is the Royal Bank of Canada and is the drawee. The defence contends that the endorsing and forwarding of the cheque to the other branch in Waterloo was a nullity and the fact that the drawer did have an account in the other branch is a mere coincidence meriting no consideration in the determination of whether or not this cheque was paid by the University Avenue Branch or by the plaintiff as drawee.

It is clear that if the bank at its University Avenue Branch was drawee, it cannot be a holder in due course, so the first question is whether or not it was drawee.

This cheque was addressed to the Royal Bank of Canada, Waterloo, without specifying the particular branch. Section 88 of the *Bill of Exchange Act*, R.S.C. 1952, c. 15, provides:

> **88.** A bill is presented at the proper place
> (a) where a place of payment is specified in the bill or acceptance, and the bill is there presented;
> (b) where no place of payment is specified, but the address of the drawee or acceptor is given in the bill, and the bill is there presented;
> (c) where no place of payment is specified, and no address given, and the bill is presented at

the drawee's or acceptor's place of business, if known, and if not, at his ordinary residence, if known....

A case very much in point is *Dominion Bank v. Jacobs et ad.*, [1951] O.W.N. 421, [1951] 3 D.L.R. 233 (H.C.J.).

In that case a bank had cashed a cheque on which McDowell was payee and Jacobs the drawer. It was cashed in error for the reason given that there was a "J. Jacobs" account in the branch but it was the wrong J. Jacobs, although the signatures were similar.

LeBel J., at p. 422 O.W.N., pp. 234–35 D.L.R., said:

Thus it is clear that the action as framed against the defendant McDowell is for the recovery of money paid to him in error or by mistake.

The general rule is that where money is paid under a mistake on the part of the payer, as to a material fact, it may be recovered in an action for money had and received, but the rule is subject to exceptions, one of which in my opinion is the type of action now pleaded against McDowell. The subject is dealt with in 23 Halsbury, 2nd ed., pp. 162 *et seq.* Section 238, at p. 164, reads:

The mistake must not only be as to some fact affecting the liability to pay, but it must also be a mistake between the party paying and the party receiving the money. If the fact about which the mistake exists has nothing to do with the payee, the rule does not apply.

I agree with that passage and with the authorities cited to support it....

Counsel for Wildman also cited Baxter, *Law of Banking and Canadian Bank Act* (1956), p. 283.

The payer may be estopped from recovering if the recipient took the money in good faith and subsequently altered his position so that he would suffer detriment by thereafter having to repay. If the recipient acts *bona fide* to his own detriment, on the faith of an untrue (though innocent) representation by the payer (express or implied) that the payment is regular, the payer cannot insist on repayment.

In my view the argument put forth by Mr. Morscher, counsel for Wildman, is valid and is supported by the authorities. Wildman is the innocent party or victim throughout both in his dealings with Boyce and with the bank. There was no suggestion of fraud, he did not know of the stop payment order, he thought he was presenting the cheque to the bank which held Wildman's account and the fact

about which the mistake was made had nothing to do with him. Indeed, I do not have any evidence of what the mistake was which makes Wildman's case stronger than that of McDowell in the *Dominion Bank v. Jacobs* case. According to s. 88 of the *Bills of Exchange Act*, presentment for payment was properly made at the proper place and was certainly in time.

It appears then that the bank cannot be a holder in due course and its actions fail against both defendants. Each defendant is entitled to a separate set of costs, they were separately represented very much in opposite interest, and the defences were different.

It was suggested that the bank was entitled to equitable relief. The point was briefly dealt with in the *Dominion Bank v. Jacobs* case but in this case the arrogant seizure and retention of the car would, in my view, be grounds to refuse to consider equitable relief for the plaintiff. If equitable relief was to be considered anywhere in the action it would be in favour of the defendants, particularly the defendant Wildman.

In view of the dismissal of the two actions, it is not necessary to determine the third party issue formally. I have made a finding in respect of the issues raised for two reasons. It was necessary to give the background for having negatived any fraud, misrepresentation or other impropriety on the part of Wildman and, secondly, it might be required by any appellate Court that may have to deal with these actions.

Since it is unnecessary to deal formally with the third party issue, it will have to be dismissed. The issue was properly and necessarily brought, it was contested in pleadings, discoveries, and at trial. Had the bank not become entangled in the affair, it was an issue that would probably have had to be fought between Boyce and Wildman. Accordingly, I hold that Wildman should have his costs of the third party issue against Boyce. He should not have full costs as of a separate action but only those costs that were incurred as a result of the third party issue being joined in the trial together of the two actions. As a guide to the Taxing Officer, I think the applicable law should be that of taxation of costs of counterclaims. These costs of the third party issue cannot be properly charged to the unsuccessful plaintiff and there will be no order that Boyce may add them to his costs against the unsuccessful plaintiff.

Actions dismissed.

(f) *Bank of Nova Scotia v. Gould*†

[TROTTER CO. CT. J. (orally):]

This is an action by the Bank of Nova Scotia for the sum of $700 against Kenneth G. Gould carrying on business under the firm name and style K.G. Gould Properties. I permitted an amendment so that the words "Yonge and College Branch", would be deleted from the style of cause and that the style of cause would read "The Bank of Nova Scotia versus the Defendant as previously named."

The cause of this action arises as a result of the branch at the Yonge and College Bank of Nova Scotia receiving a cheque dated December 20, 1973, made by Kenneth G. Gould to a person B.B. Wilson.

It would appear from the evidence that I have heard that both the bank and Mr. Gould have been the innocent parties, been the victims of a man named B.B. Wilson who, one might suspect took advantage of both the parties and the cause arises between two innocent parties. Exhibit 1 is a cheque dated December 20, 1973, for $700 made to B.B. Wilson by Mr. Gould. Although the cheque was dated December 20th, there is a great possibility that it was actually written on December 21st.

Mr. Gould gave evidence that he made the cheque and gave it to Mr. Wilson in Mr. Gould's office. Mr. Wilson left hurriedly with the cheque on that Friday afternoon and before closing time that same day which closing time is five o'clock. Mr. Gould telephoned the branch bank, that is, the Barrie, Ontario branch of the Bank of Nova Scotia saying to stop payment.

Mr. Gould admitted that when he gave Wilson the cheque he was apprehensive. Now, first I might clearly point out this was a negotiable instrument at the time the cheque was handed to Mr. Wilson and I find as a fact that it was a cheque and at that time it did not have the words "STOP PAYMENT" on it but it was a cheque on a standard Bank of Nova Scotia cheque form very common to a business community, very common to the general public.

It would appear from the evidence of Mr. Glen Dunbrack that Wilson took the cheque to the Yonge and College branch of the Bank of Nova Scotia and the very same Friday, December 20th, and opened an account and withdrew the money and I find as a fact that Wilson did get the money. I am satisfied with Mr. Dunbrack's evidence that the cheque was, and his term was "negotiated", and I hold this as a fact that Wilson did get the money and of course as a result of that happening I am faced with the problem now before me.

Now, it has been argued by Mr. Uukkivi that Mr. Dunbrack, in effect, was in essence negligent and that he had got information from Mr. Wilson but not enough, that this was a large cheque; Mr. Dunbrack admitted the $700. He should not let Wilson have had the money unless he had more information about Mr. Wilson.

I find as a fact that Dunbrack was not negligent and he certainly acted in good faith. It is true that some time before five o'clock, and I accept Mr. Gould's word on that, that some time before five o'clock he did telephone the Barrie branch and said: "Stop payment", but I also hold as a fact that Mr. Dunbrack had no knowledge of that. He did not act in any way that would be negligent treatment or in bad faith and I do not think that branch in Barrie in any way acted in bad faith. This happened in a relatively short period of time and one must look at that matter on whether or not the bank, and this embraces the various branches, each acted in good faith. Now, the fact that one branch has knowledge, for example, the Barrie branch has knowledge payment was stopped does not mean that the other, any other branch of the same bank has knowledge because those branches, I believe it is quite clear, are distinct although these are branches of the same commercial operation.

Now, Mr. Gould admitted that he was apprehensive and in fact what he did was let loose a wild bull. That cheque dated December 20, 1973, was a negotiable instrument taken to the Yonge and College branch. I believe it is also referred to as the Yonge and Wellesley branch, and the cheque was honoured in good faith. I hold as a fact that that branch was a holder in due course and they acted in proper and reasonable manner and I do not believe, quite frankly, they were negligent. I do not believe Mr. Dunbrack was negligent. I think in all the circumstances he acted in a reasonable manner. I am

---

† (1977), 17 O.R. (2d) 96 (Co. Ct.).

well aware that Mr. Gould is an innocent party but then he was the one who started the whole unhappy story being an apprehensive man who handed over a negotiable instrument to somebody of whom he was apprehensive and he was evidently justified in being apprehensive of him.

Of course Mr. Hill's evidence, which clearly gives the set-up of the Bank of Nova Scotia carrying out its clearing of cheques is evidence I accept and I accept his evidence of it as really an expert in banking field. He said a cheque is negotiable at any branch anywhere in Canada so that if this man Wilson suddenly happened to be somewhere in Canada with that cheque for $700, it is still a negotiable instrument and in Canada it would be a most reasonable thing to accept so I think that Dunbrack acted in a reasonable manner and the bank was a holder in due course.

I accept the law as given by Mr. Giles. I do not think there is any dispute with the law, that is why I do not intend to dwell on the wealth of explanation too long about the good faith. Even though there are the two branches of the same bank they are in essence separate agencies and the knowledge of the one is not the knowledge of the other. It would be impossible under present-day conditions unless the branches are side by side. It is acceptable in that case. In the normal course of business it would be virtually impossible to expect one branch to know what the other is doing unless there are exceptional circumstances; such exceptional circumstances do not exist in this case and I have to hold Mr. Gould author of his own misfortune, and I therefore give judgment for the plaintiff, the Bank of Nova Scotia, in the amount of first of all $700. I think that the claim for interest is 12% and I accept the evidence of Mr. Gould that this was the rate of interest at the time that this unhappy transaction transpired and so that I will give 12% as claimed in the statement of claim. I also give 5% from the date of the issue of the writ of summons until the date of judgment. I have not figured out these amounts but unless counsel have reason it seems I can so endorse the back of the record. I will endorse the record and I will read it back so there is no question of what I have said: It says here "the Writ was issued September 23, 1974. You're asking for 12% from the 27th of December 1974, you mean '73?"

By MR. GILES: "73, yes, Your Honour."

THE COURT: I think that is an obvious error in the statement of claim. Now, I have endorsed the records as follows: "Judgment for the Plaintiff for $700.00 plus interest on $700.00 at 12% from December 27, 1973 to September 23, 1974 and interest on $700.00 at 5% from September 23, 1974 to this day, May 18, 1977. Costs after taxation thereof."

Judgment for plaintiff.

(g) *Royal Bank of Canada v. Hein Real Estate Corp.*†

[MORROW J.A.:]

Under a guaranteed listing with the respondent real estate company the third parties, Ralph N. Smith and Josephina M. Smith, had some $23,000 coming to them in respect of their home at Langdon, Alberta. In order to finance the purchase of livestock and machinery they contacted the Forest Lawn branch, Calgary, of the Royal Bank of Canada. By way of security this branch took an absolute assignment of the total proceeds of the above sale. This assignment, dated 10th April 1974, was signed by both Smiths, was addressed to the respondent company, and was acknowledged by the respondent in writing by letter bearing the same date. It is to be noted that the body of the absolute assignment calls for the money to be sent to the Royal Bank of Canada, 3601 — 17 Ave., S.E., Calgary, which is the Forest Lawn branch. It further contains a clause to the effect that: "This order of instructions may only be cancelled with the written permission of the Manager of the above-mentioned bank." Some $7,699.54 was owing to this branch, and action was commenced for payment, based on the assignment.

---

† [1977] 3 W.W.R. 298 (Alta. C.A.).

The present appeal is the result of a dismissal of the above action, which dismissal was based on the view the learned trial judge took of two subsequent assignments taken.

It seems that the Smiths moved to Redwater, Alberta, and on 5th June 1974 the Redwater branch of the Royal Bank of Canada took an order signed by Mr. Smith only, and addressed to the respondent, directing that $2,000 from the proceeds of the sale of the Langdon home, above, be paid "to the Royal Bank of Canada, Redwater". The Redwater branch forwarded this order to the respondent by covering letter of the same date. In the covering letter the $2,000 was described as representing "a small interim financing loan at this office". Later, on 9th July 1974, Mr. Smith signed an order directing $4,000 to be paid from the sale proceeds, also to the Royal Bank of Canada, Redwater, Alberta. The covering letter to the respondent contains the phrase: "We enclose a new letter of direction", and also states: "This letter cancels and supersedes that of June 5, 1974."

It is common ground that, although there may have been some knowledge in the Forest Lawn bank that the Smiths were moving to Redwater, there is no evidence that either bank branch knew of the actions in respect of the financing and the taking of assignments or orders by the other. On 24th July 1974 the respondent paid off the $4,000 to the Redwater branch pursuant to the third order or assignment.

The learned trial judge, after finding that the first assignment was validly given, went on to find that the respondent considered the second and third assignments to be in substitution for the first one, that both branches were of the same bank, and that the parties knew the Smiths were moving to Redwater. He then went on to state, and I quote:

> Even though the Forest Lawn branch of the plaintiff bank may not have known of the subsequent dealings of the customer at Redwater, I believe that the Redwater branch must have known of the dealings with the third party at the Forest Lawn branch. I would therefore find that the wording of the assignments that were made by the plaintiff on 5th June 1974 and 10th July 1974 and sent by the Redwater branch on behalf of the plaintiff company to the defendant in fact supersedes and cancels the assignment that was given by the defendant, or at least acknowledged by the defendant to the plaintiff branch at Forest Lawn.

The appellant's action was accordingly dismissed with costs.

At the same time the respondent counterclaimed for some $2,020 as against the appellant and as against the Smiths, representing expenditures made in improving the property. The respondent also issued a third-party notice claiming indemnity from Ralph N. Smith and Josephina Smith in the event that the appellant should succeed in its claim. A demand of notice was filed on behalf of Mr. and Mrs. Smith. The Smiths made no appearance on the present appeal.

While counsel for both sides put forward several submissions, the success or failure of this appeal revolves around two main issues:

1. Whether there was any or sufficient evidence upon which the learned trial judge could find that the Redwater branch of the bank must have known of the previous dealings with the other branch and so either misled the respondent or the effect was to estop the Forest Lawn branch from suing;
2. Were the second and third assignments valid or not?

Before examining these propositions I propose quoting the material portion of the reasons for judgment:

> The question, therefore, is whether or not the plaintiff can be estopped from denying that these subsequent assignments in fact cancel the first one.
>
> There is no doubt that it is the same bank. The plaintiff has hundreds of banks throughout the country, and it is probably quite difficult to keep track of business transactions between the different branches, but in this particular case all parties were aware of the fact that the third parties were moving from Calgary to Redwater, Alberta.
>
> Even though the Forest Lawn branch of the plaintiff bank may not have known of the subsequent dealings of the customer at Redwater, I believe that the Redwater branch must have known of the dealings with the third party at the Forest Lawn branch. I would therefore find that the wording of the assignments that were made by the plaintiff on 5th June 1974 and 10th July 1974 and sent by the Redwater branch on behalf of the plaintiff company to the defendant in fact supersedes and cancels the assignment that was given by the defendant, or at least acknowledged by the defendant to the plaintiff branch at Forest Lawn.

The learned trial judge in expressing the belief that the Redwater branch "must have known of the dealings with the third party" had to have reached this conclusion from the testimony of the president of the respondent company, who testified on behalf of the respondent, and perhaps by inference from the documents themselves. There was no evidence called with respect to the Redwater branch of the bank other than the introduction of the two assignments obtained by that bank. The introduction of these documents was on the objection of counsel for the bank but in the view I take of the matter no further comment in that respect is required.

Examining the president's evidence in the most favourable light insofar as the respondent is concerned, it would appear that he thought that the Redwater branch assignment represented the money contemplated originally by the general assignment taken by the Forest Lawn branch. As this witness said on examination in chief: "I was under the impression that Mr. Smith had assigned the proceeds in Calgary to move to Redwater and obtain money there and close his account in Calgary." This witness had known from the beginning that the Smiths were moving to Redwater. This witness also explains that when the sale funds became available he paid the third assignment of $4,000 and then forwarded the balance of the proceeds to his solicitor for distribution. When asked why he did not honour the first assignment his answer was that he thought that he had by the $4,000 payment. It is clear that there were sufficient funds in the company's hands from the sale to have honoured both assignments.

The manager of the Forest Lawn branch in his testimony explained that if a person's account is transferred to another branch such an assignment as the first one here would go along, as well as all other securities, with the account. This evidence was of course predicated upon the first branch becoming aware of the transfer of account to the other branch. This is not the present situation.

A great many decisions were referred to on the question of what the legal position was with respect to branch banks. It is clear from reading these that while branches may be considered as agencies of the principal banking operation they remain separate entities insofar as chequing purposes and related business are concerned. This is only good sense. The above general proposition is examined in such cases as: *Metropolitan Investigation & Security (Can.) Ltd. v. C.F.I. Operating Co.*, [1972] 5 W.W.R. 621, 31 D.L.R. (3d) 190, reversed [1975] 2 S.C.R. 546, 50 D.L.R. (3d) 76 (sub nom. *Bank of Montreal v. Metropolitan Investigation & Security (Can.) Ltd.*); *Prince v. Oriental Bank Corpn.* (1878), 3 App. Cas. 325; *Royal*

Bank of Can. v. Boyce; Royal Bank of Can. v. Wildman, [1966] 2 O.R. 607, 57 D.L.R. (2d) 683; and *Bank of Montreal v. Dominion Bank* (1921), 60 D.L.R. 403 (Ont.).

In the present situation, therefore, while the action taken by the respondent may have been taken in good faith and under a misapprehension of its legal position, in the absence of any representation or action by either or both branches of the appellant bank which could be construed or otherwise taken by the respondent as in effect saying that the general assignment held by one branch was no longer effective or that the subsequent assignments have clearly replaced the other, the respondent cannot be relieved from its responsibility to recognize both sets of assignments. At no time did the Forest Lawn branch ever intimate in any way that its general assignment was to be ignored or that it had been replaced by the assignments from the other branch. And similarly the Redwater branch in presenting it assignments made no representation nor did it by any of its actions do or suggest anything to the respondent which could be properly read by the latter as an indication that the orders being put forward were in any way to be considered as substituted for the Forest Lawn branch's security.

It is with regret that I feel I must interfere with the learned trial judge's assessment of the facts and legal position here.

When the second series of assignments is to be examined, that is, the ones forwarded from the Redwater branch, it is to be noted that they are only signed by Ralph N. Smith, whereas the moneys intended to be affected were the joint property of both Smiths. It can be said therefore, if Mrs. Smith chose to complain, that they were of doubtful validity and should not have been paid by the respondent. In paying the Redwater bank on these assignments it could be said that the respondent was paying under a mistake of law. It is not for me to examine the situation here in any more detail than to say that such payment can have no direct bearing on the present appeal. The respondent will have to consider his position here independent of the present case. Counsel for the respondent has requested that his client receive credit for this payment. Because of the position I have taken I cannot agree. There is no basis whatsoever for requiring this to be done.

In the result I would allow the appeal with costs here and below. The respondent's claim under the third-party notice is preserved, and application may be made to the learned trial judge in this regard.

IV

The Banker and Customer Relationship

Background Reading: M.H. Ogilvie, *Bank and Customer Law in Canada*, 2d Edition (Toronto: Irwin Law, 2013) Chapter 6, pages 183–202.

(a) *Foley v. Hill*†

Appeal against an order of Lord Lyndhurst L.C., reported 1 Ph. 399, reversing a decree of the Vice-Chancellor of England (Knight-Bruce V.-C.) and dismissing the appellant's bill.

In and previously to the year 1829, the appellant and Sir Edward Scott, owners of collieries in Staffordshire, kept a joint account at the respondents' bank at Stourbridge, in Worcestershire. In April, 1829, a sum of £6,117 10s. was transferred from that account to a separate account then opened for the appellant, and the respondents, in a letter enclosing a receipt for the sum so transferred, agreed to allow £8 per cent interest on it. From 1829 to the end of 1834, when the joint account was closed, the appellant's share of the profits of the collieries was from time to time paid by cheques drawn by the colliery agents against the joint account. These cheques were, as the respondents alleged, paid in cash or by bills drawn by them on their London bankers in favour of the appellant, and none of them was entered in his separate account. The only items found in that account were the £6,117 10s. on the credit side, and two sums of £1,700 and £2,000 on the debit side, both being payments made to on or behalf of the appellant in 1830. There were also entries, in a separate column, of interest calculated on the sum or balance in the bank, up to Dec. 25, 1831, and not afterwards.

In January, 1838, the appellant filed his bill against the respondents, praying that an account might be taken of the sum of £6,117 10s. and all other sums received by the respondents for the appellant on his private account since April, 1829, with interest on the same at the rate of £3 per cent, per annum; and also an account of all sums properly paid by them for or to use of the appellant on his account since that day, and that they might be decreed to pay the appellant what, upon taking such accounts, should be found due to him. A schedule annexed to the defendant's answer set forth the separate account of the appellant from the bank book, containing the items and entries before mentioned. The vice-chancellor, on the hearing of the cause, decreed for an account as prayed, being of opinion that the respondents were bound in duty to keep the account clear; that they were to be charged according to their duty, the neglect of which could be no excuse, and that the agreement to allow the interest was in effect the same, in answer to the Statute of Limitations, as if the interest had been regularly entered or paid. Lord Lyndhurst, taking a different view of the case, upon appeal, held, first, that the Statute of Limitations was a sufficient defence; and, secondly, that the account, consisting of only a few simple items, was not a proper subject for a bill in

---

† [1843–60] All E.R. Rep. 16 (H.L.).

equity, but a case for an action at law for money had and received, and his Lordship reversed the decree, and dismissed the bill.

Stuart and G.L. Russell for the appellant. — The judgment appealed from proceeded partly on the ground that the Statute of Limitations is a bar to the appellant's demand, and partly on the ground that the account prayed for is a simple account of debtor and creditor, and, therefore, not a fit subject for a suit in equity. The question is: What is the nature of the relation between a banker and those who deposit money with him, and who are called his customers? If it could be shown that a banker is in the position of a trustee for those who employ him, that he is clothed with a fiduciary character in relation to them, and that there is a personal trust and confidence in him, then the Statute of Limitations would be inapplicable, and the second defense also must be held to fail. The respondents were not in the relation of mere debtors to the appellant for money deposited, which, in ordinary cases, is considered to be a loan, and, therefore, a debt: *Carr v. Carr*; *Devaynes v. Noble, Sleech's Case* (1 Mer. at p. 568); *Sims v. Bond*; *Pott v. Clegg*. Pollack C.B., in *Pott v. Clegg*, doubted whether in all cases there was not an implied contract between a banker and his customer as to the money deposited which distinguishes it from an ordinary case of loan, but he yielded to the opinion of the other judges that it was a simple loan and debt. It may be admitted that bankers are debtors, but they are debtors with superadded obligations, as, for instance, to repay the money deposited by honouring the depositor's cheques: *Marzetti v. Williams*. In the present case there was an additional obligation by the special contract to pay interest on the deposit. It was the duty of the respondents to keep the accounts with the appellant clear and intelligible, to calculate the interest of the balances in their hands from time to time, to make proper entries of it in the account, and the preserve all vouchers and other evidence of their transactions with him. These duties and transactions constitute a relation more complex than that of mere debtor and creditor, and an account to them is a fit subject for a bill of equity, because the account here sought is of moneys received by the respondents, the receipt of which is within their own knowledge, and the entries and record of which they were bound to keep.

Bethell, Kenyon Parker and Craig for the respondents, were not called on to argue.

[LORD COTTENHAM L.C.:]

The bill in this case — as is usual in cases of this description where bills state matters of account, and

where there is concurrent jurisdiction at law and equity — alleges that the account is complicated and consists of a great variety of items, so that it could not be properly taken at law. If that allegation had been made out, it would have prevented the necessity of considering any other part of the case. But that allegation has entirely failed of proof, for it appears that the account consisted of only one payment of £6,117 10s. to a private account of the customer, and that against that sum two cheques were drawn and paid. That is the whole account in dispute as raised by these pleadings. Therefore, there is certainly no such account as would induce a court of equity to maintain jurisdiction as if the question had turned entirely upon an account so complicated, as so long, as to make it inconvenient to have it taken at law. It has been attempted to support this bill upon other grounds, and one ground is that the relative situation of the appellant and the respondents would give a court of equity jurisdiction, independently of the length or the complexity of the accounts. Although it is not disputed that the transactions between the parties gave the legal right, it is said a court of equity, nevertheless, has concurrent jurisdiction, and that is attempted to be supported upon the supposed fiduciary character existing between the banker and his customer.

No case has been produced in which that character has been given to the relation of banker and customer, but it has been attempted to be supported by reference to other cases supposed to be analogous. These are cases where bill have been filed as between principal and agent, or between principal and factor. As between principal and factor, there is no question whatever that that description of case which alone has been referred to in the argument in support of the jurisdiction has always been held to be within the jurisdiction of a court of equity, because the party partakes of the character of a trustee. Partaking of the character of a trustee, the factor — as the trustee for the particular matter in which he is employed as factor — sells the principal's goods, and accounts to him for the money. The goods, however, remain the goods of the owner or principal until the sale takes place, and the moment the money is received the money becomes the property of the principal. So it is with regard to an agent dealing with any property. He obtains no interest himself in the subject-matter beyond his renumeration; he is dealing throughout for another, and though he is not a trustee according to the strict technical meaning of the word, he is quasi a trustee for that particular transaction for which he is engaged. Therefore, in these cases the courts of equity have assumed jurisdiction.

But the analogy entirely fails, as it appears to me, when you come to consider the relative situation of a banker and his customer, and for that purpose it is quite sufficient to refer to the authorities, which have been quoted, and to the nature of the connection between the parties. Money, when paid into a bank, cases altogether to be the money of the customer; it is then the money of that banker, who is bound to return an equivalent by paying a similar sum to that deposited with him when he is asked for it. The money paid into the banker's is money known by the customer to be placed there for the purpose of being under the control of the banker. It is then the banker's money; he is known to deal with it as his own; he makes what profit of it he can, which profits he retains to himself, paying back only the principal and a small rate of interest, according to the custom of bankers in some places, or the principal and a small rate of interest, according to the custom of bankers in other places. The money placed in the custody of a banker is to all intents and purposes the money of the banker, to do with as he pleases. He is guilty of no breach of trust in employing it; he is not answerable to the customer if he puts it in jeopardy, if he engages in a hazardous speculation; he is not bound to keep it or deal with it as the property of the customer, but he is, of course, answerable for the amount, because he has contracted, having received that money, to repay to the customer, when demanded, a sum equivalent to that paid into his hands. That has been the subject of discussion in various cases, and that has been established to be the relative situations of banker and customer, the banker is not an agent or factor, but he is a debtor. Then the analogy between that case and those that have been referred to entirely fails, and the ground upon which those cases have, by analogy to the doctrine of trusteeship, had been held to be the subject of the jurisdiction of a court of equity, had no application here, as it appears to me.

[His Lordship dealt with the question whether under the law existing in 1848 the case came within the jurisdiction of a court of equity, and he added:]

There is nothing in the relative situations of banker and customer which gives, per se, the right to sue in equity. That is proved, I apprehend, by the consideration of the question whether, if there had been no money drawn out at all and simply a sum of money had been deposited with the banker — I will not say deposited, but paid to the banker — on account of the customer, the customer could file a bill to get that money back again. The learned counsel judiciously avoided giving an answer to that question. But that tries the principle, because, if it is merely a sum of money paid to a factor or an agent the party has a right to recall it. He has a right to deal with the factor or agent in his fiduciary character. But the banker does not hold that fiduciary character, and, therefore, there is no such original jurisdiction; and if there be no original jurisdiction growing out of the relative situations of the parties to see if the account is of such a nature that it cannot be taken at law.... The principle upon which my opinion is formed is that there is nothing to bring the demand within the precincts of a court of equity. Upon that ground I think the decree was right in dismissing the bill.

[LORD BROUGHAM:]

My noble and learned friend, Lord Lyndhurst, who from his right of precedence here, would naturally have addressed your Lordships before me — I, nevertheless, take leave, before he addresses your Lordships, to state my entire agreement in the reasons stated by the noble and learned friend, the Lord Chancellor, and in the opinion at which he has arrived through those reasons in favour of the decree of the court below.

There is clearly no such account — whatever may be set forth by the bill — upon the facts of the present case which calls upon a court of equity, upon that head of jurisdiction, to give relief.... The account being excluded by the facts of this case, which show that there is no reason for this statement of account, there being but one sum paid in, and two sums of money drawn out, there is no reason for giving relief in equity. The question then comes to be, whether the appellant has succeeded on one or the other of the two grounds, the first of which is, holding the banker to be in a quasi fiduciary position towards his customer and proceeding against him as if he were a trustee; and the other is whether the stipulation for interest by the banker makes any difference in the case? The latter question may be disposed of in a few words. It does not follow that because a banker contracts to pay any strictly legal demand, therefore that puts the case on a different footing. I should be very sorry if that should be so, because I am sure the Court of Chancery might have then a bill from every tradesman for payment of his account, for goods sold and delivered, and wherever there was a stipulation to pay after a certain time, as in many cases there is, in such a case a bill might be filed. But we know pretty well it is the ABC of the practice of a court of equity that no such bill can be filed.

I come, then, to the only other ground, which was the main contention. As to the banker, in his position with respect to his customers that of a trustee with respect to his *cestui que trust*? Is it that of a principal with respect to an agent, or that of a principal with respect to a factor? I see no ground for contending that there is any identity in those two points. I am now speaking of the common position of a banker — the common case of his receiving money from his customer on condition of paying it back when asked for or when drawn upon, or of receiving money from other parties to the credit of the customer upon like conditions to be drawn out by the customer, or, in common parlance, the money being repaid when asked for, because the banker who receives the money has the use of it as his own, and in the using of it his trade consists, but for which no banker could exist, especially a banker who pays interest. Even a banker who does not pay interest could not possibly carry on his trade if he were to hold the money and to pay it back as a mere depositary of the principal. But he receives it, to the knowledge of his customer for the express purpose of using it as his own, which, if he were a trustee, he could not do without a breach of trust. It is a totally different thing if we take into consideration certain acts which are often performed by a banker and put him in a totally different capacity. He may, in addition to his position of banker, make himself an agent or trustee towards an cestui que trust. For example, suppose I deposit exchequer bills with a banker and he undertakes to receive the interest upon them, or to negotiate or sell them, and to credit my account with the proceeds of the sale, I do not stay to ask whether, in that case, he might not be in the position of a trustee, and might not partly sustain a fiduciary character, but he does that incidentally to his trade of a banker. His trade of a banker is totally independent of that, to it the other is an accidental addition. The trade of a banker is to receive money and use it as if it were his own, he becoming debtor to the person who has lent or deposited with him the money to use as his own, for which money he is accountable as a debtor.

That being the trade of a banker, and that being that nature of the relation in which he stands to his customer, I cannot, without breaking down the bounds between equity and law, confound the situation of a banker with that of a trustee, and conclude that the banker is a debtor with a fiduciary character. I, therefore, entirely agree with my noble and learned friend, thinking that the view taken of this case in the court below was a correct one, and, therefore, I move that this appeal be dismissed, and the decree appealed from be affirmed, with costs.

[LORD CAMPBELL:]

I cannot help thinking that when this case was before Knight-Bruce V.-C. the decree he pronounced must have proceeded upon some incorrect statements of the facts, and that he had thought that several actions would have been necessary. When you come to examine the facts, it is quite clear that this a purely legal demand, the relation between banker and customer, as far as the pecuniary dealings are concerned, being that of debtor and creditor. It has been said that the banker is liable to do something more than merely to repay the money. He is bound to honour cheques, and perhaps to accept bill of exchange, if drawn upon him, he having assets in his hands, but these are purely matters of legal contract, and, it seems to me, that there is nothing of a fiduciary character at all in the relation subsisting between them. I think the noble and learned Lord, Lord Lyndhurst, was perfectly right in reversing the decree of the vice-chancellor, and that we shall do right in dismissing this appeal.

[LORD LYNDHURST:]

I entirely concur in the view that has been taken by my noble and learned friends, with respect to jurisdiction in matter of account. I am of opinion, therefore, with my noble and learned friends, that this judgment must be affirmed.

Appeal dismissed.

143

(b) *Joachimson v. Swiss Bank Corp.*[†]

[BANKES L.J.:]

The material facts of this case are as follows: Before and until August 1, 1914, three persons had carried on business in Manchester in partnership under the firm name of N. Joachimson. On that date one of the partners died, and as a result the partnership was automatically dissolved. The plaintiff in the present action was one of the three partners. He is a naturalized Englishman, at all material times residing and carrying on business in England. The third partner on the outbreak of war became an alien enemy. The partnership banked with the branch of the appellant bank in London. On August 1, 1914, the amount standing to the credit of the partnership current account was something over £2,300. On June 5, 1919, the plaintiff commenced the present action in the name of N. Joachimson (Manchester), claiming payment of the sum standing to the credit of the account of the partnership. The action has had a chequered career during the preliminary stages, but eventually it has taken the form of an action by the plaintiff in the name of N. Joachimson, "a firm name," claiming for the purpose of winding up the affairs of the partnership to recover the amount standing to the credit of the partnership on August 1, 1914, and asserting that the cause of action on which the plaintiff relied was one which accrued on August 1, 1914, "for money lent by the plaintiffs to the defendants for the use of the plaintiffs." To the action as thus constituted several objections were taken. With regard to the form of the action it was said that the facts did not bring it within Order XLVIIIA. r. 1, so as to allow of the action being brought in the firm name. With regard to the substance of the action it was said that on August 1, 1914, there was no accrued cause of action for the amount standing to the credit of the partnership on that date, because no demand had been made upon the defendant bank for payment on or before that date. It was also said that even if there was a cause of action on August 1, 1914, it was not a continuing cause of action at the date of the writ. There was also a set-off and counterclaim. All these points were dealt with by Roche J. in the Court below. Having regard to the view I take on the question whether there was an accrued cause of action on August 1, 1914, it is not necessary to refer to any of the other points, and I express no opinion and give no decision upon them.

The question whether there was an accrued cause of action on August 1, 1914, depends upon whether a demand upon a banker is necessary before he comes under an obligation to pay his customer the amount standing to the customer's credit on his current account. This sounds as though it was an important question. In a sense no doubt it is, but it is very rarely that the question will in practice arise. In most of the cases in which the question is likely to arise, even if a demand is necessary to complete the cause of action, a writ is a sufficient demand. It is only therefore in the unlikely case of a banker pleading the Statute of Limitations, or in a case like the present where the facts are very special, that the question becomes important. In the present case the writ was not issued till June 5, 1919. To succeed in the action, the plaintiffs had to prove a cause of action existing long before that date — namely, on August 1, 1914. Roche J., while recognizing that at first sight the conclusion as a matter of business seemed startling, gave judgment in favour of the plaintiffs, holding that the point had been decided in *Foley v. Hill* and *Pott v. Clegg*. There is no doubt that the general opinion of these decisions, as accepted in some reported cases and as expressed in the text-books, is in accordance with the view taken of them by Roche J. As illustrations I refer to *In re Tidd*, where counsel for the plaintiff admitted that in the case of money paid into a bank on current account the law is that the amount held by the bank is a simple debt in respect of which time runs under the Statute of Limitations without demand, and he cited as authority for the proposition *Pott v. Clegg* and *Foley v. Hill* in the House of Lords. North J. apparently accepted the proposition without any discussion of these cases. In Halsbury's Laws of England, vol. xix., tit. Limitation of Actions, s. 72, the same cases are cited as an authority for the proposition that "in the case of money on current account, time runs from the payment in."

It is necessary, therefore, to consider very carefully what those cases really did decide. Before pro-

---

[†] [1921] 3 K.B. 110 (C.A.). [Notes omitted.]

ceeding to do this, it is helpful to bear in mind what the general law is with reference to payments to be made "on demand." In *Walton v. Mascall* Parke B. states the law thus:

> Now it is clear that a request for the payment of a debt is quite immaterial, unless the parties to the contract have stipulated that it shall be made; if they have not, the law requires no notice or request; but the debtor is bound to find out the creditor and pay him the debt when due.

And again in *Norton v. Ellam* the same learned judge says:

> It is the same as the case of money lent payable upon request, with interest, where no demand is necessary before bringing the action. There is no obligation in law to give any notice at all; if you choose to make it part of the contract that notice shall be given, you may do so. The debt which constitutes the cause of action arises instantly on the loan.

In every case, therefore, where the question arises the test must be whether the parties have, or have not, agreed that an actual demand shall be a condition precedent to the existence of a present enforceable debt. In the ordinary case of banker and customer their relations depend either entirely or mainly upon an implied contract. The questions for decision in the present case must therefore be:

1. whether the cases to which reference was made in the Court below did decide that the relation of banker and customer is such as to negative any implied condition that the making of an actual demand is a condition precedent to the bringing of an action to recover the money lent to the banker by the customer on current account; and
2. whether, if they did not so decide, such a condition should be implied.

Pott v. Clegg is a decision of the Court of Exchequer in 1847, and appears to have turned out entirely upon the form of the pleading. The argument of the Attorney-General in showing cause against the rule was rested as a separate point upon the fact that in the pleadings the balance due from the bank to the customer was treated as an ordinary debt for money lent. In support of the rule counsel argued that as between banker and customer a special relation existed, and further that a demand was necessary as a condition precedent to the accrual of a cause of action; but both Rolfe B. and Parke B. in

the course of the argument pointed out that the latter point was not open on the pleadings. The judgment of the Court was delivered by Pollock C.B., who, after saying that the majority of the Court were of the opinion that money deposited in a banker's hands is equivalent to money lent, went on to say that, even assuming that

> there are peculiar circumstances in a banking account which distinguish it from any other, yet none of those circumstances appear on these pleadings, so as to justify us in considering this case differently form what we should if it were an ordinary case of money lent.

The Chief Baron then goes on to express his own doubt whether

> there is not a special contract between the banker and his customer as to the money deposited, which distinguishes it from the ordinary case of a loan for money.

This decision does not, in my opinion, go further than recognizing that the relation of banker and customer is that of borrower and lender. It certainly does not establish the proposition that, though that is the relation, it may not be in part governed by special implied terms. *Foley v. Hill* was decided, in the first instance, by Lord Lyndhurst L.C. The main question in the action was whether an account between banker and customer, where the former pleaded the Statute of Limitations, was the proper subject for a bill in equity. The Lord Chancellor, in giving judgment, refers to cases in which it had been decided that the relation of banker and customer was that of borrower and lender, and then proceeds:

> Here there was a loan by Foley to the defendants, to be repaid with interest at 3 per cent; that was the simple transaction between them, and if this were a case at law, a plea of the statute would be a sufficient answer, unless there were some special circumstances to take the case out of the statute.

In the House of Lords the point mainly debated was again the question whether the plaintiff's claim was a fit subject for a bill in equity. In this connection the Law Lords expressed their opinions as to the ordinary relation between banker and customer, and those opinions are correctly summarized in the headnote as follows:

> The relation between banker and customer, who pays money into the bank, is the ordinary relation of debtor and creditor, with a superadded obligation arising out of the custom of bankers to honour the customer's drafts; and that rela-

145

tion is not altered by an agreement by the banker to allow the interest on the balances in the bank.

The point which is raised in the present appeal was not mentioned or discussed, either in the Court below or in the House of Lords, and in my opinion the decision cannot be treated as an exhaustive definition of all the obligations arising out of the relation between banker and customer, or as ruling out the possibility of an implied term of that relation, requiring an express demand of repayment as a condition precedent to the right to sue the banker for the amount standing to the credit of the customer's current account. The recent decision of the House of Lords in *London Joint Stock Bank v. Macmillan*, approving *Young v. Grote*, affords one striking instance of an obligation implied in the relation of a banker and customer to which no reference was made in *Foley v. Hill*. Lord Haldane points out that:

> Ever since this House in 1848 decided *Foley v. Hill* it has been quite clear that the relation between a banker and the customer whose balance he keeps is under ordinary circumstances one simply of debtor and creditor. But in other judgments, and notably by a later decision of this House, *Scholfield v. Earl of Londesborough*, it was made equally clear that along with this relation and consistently with it there may subsist a second one.... But the customer of the bank is under a yet more specific duty. The banker contracts to act as his mandatory and is bound to honour his cheques without any delay to the extent of the balance standing to his credit. The customer contracts reciprocally that in drawing his cheques on the banker he will draw them in such a form as will enable the banker to fulfil his obligation, and therefore in a form that is clear and free from ambiguity.

Having regard to the peculiarity of that relation there must be, I consider, quite a number of implied superadded obligations beyond the one specifically mentioned in *Foley v. Hill* and *Pott v. Clegg*. Unless this were so, the banker, like any ordinary debtor, must seek out his creditor and repay him his loan immediately it becomes due — that is to say directly after the customer has paid the money into his account — and the customer, like any ordinary creditor, can demand repayment of the loan by his debtor at any time and any place. It is only necessary in the present case to consider the one question whether there is, arising out of the relation of banker and customer, the implied obligation on the part of the customer to make an actual demand for the amount standing to his credit on current account as a condi-

tion precedent to a right to sue for that amount. I cannot find that the point has ever been discussed in any reported case. For the reasons I have already give, I consider that the point has never been decided, and that it is open to this Court to decide it.

Too much reliance must not be placed upon the language of learned judges who had not the precise point before them, but it is certainly worth noticing that in *Foley v. Hill* in the House of Lords, the Lord Chancellor says this:

> He (the banker) is of course answerable for the amount, because he had contracted, having received that money, to repay to the principal, when demanded, a sum equivalent to that paid into his hands.

Lord Brougham says:

> I am now speaking of the common position of a banker, which consists of the common case of receiving money from his customer on condition of paying it back when asked for, or when drawn upon.

In *Walker v. Bradford Old Bank* A.L. Smith J., in speaking of the relation of banker and customer in connection with an assignment of moneys standing to a customer's credit at the bank, says:

> I am of opinion that before and at the date of the assignment, and as long as the relation of customer and banker continued between the assignor and the bank, the ordinary relation of debtor and creditor existed between them (with the superadded obligation on the bank's part to honour the assignor's cheques, which is immaterial to the point under consideration), and that consequently there existed a contract on the bank's part to pay over on demand to the assignor all moneys then or thereafter standing to his credit.

In *Schroeder v. Central Bank of London* Brett J., in dealing with the suggestion that a cheque on a banker was an assignment of the moneys standing to the customer's credit at the bank, says:

> This is not a case of drawer going himself and demanding all the money in his banker's hands, and I am myself inclined to think that it might be put in this way: that there was no debt on which an action against the defendants could be founded until a sum was demanded, and that when the cheque was drawn there was no debt which could be assigned.

These dicta all favour the contention of the present appellants, and they are supported by the very strong body expert opinion which was given in evidence in the Court below as to the practice of bankers. Applying Lord Esher's test, as laid down in *Hamlyn v. Wood*, to the question whether the term contended for by the appellants must be implied in the contract between banker and customer, I have no hesitation in saying that it must. It seems to me impossible to imagine the relation between banker and customer, as it exists to-day, without the stipulation that, if the customer seeks to withdraw his loan, he must make application to the banker for it. It has been suggested that a decision to this effect would run counter to a line of authorities which have recognized and allowed garnishee proceedings in reference to amounts standing to a customer's credit on his current account, upon the ground that such amounts were debts capable of being attached. I do not agree with this suggestion. the effect of the service of a garnishee order *nisi* is, according to Lord Watson in *Rogers v. Whiteley*, to make the garnishee "custodier for the Court of the whole funds attached." The service of such an order is, in my opinion, a sufficient demand by operation of law, to satisfy any right a banker may have as between himself and his customer to a demand before payment of moneys standing to the credit of a current account can be enforced. As no demand for payment in the present case was made on or before August 1, 1914, it follows, in my opinion, that the plaintiffs had no accrued cause of action on that date, and the claim fails on that ground.

The appeal will be allowed with costs. The judgment must be set aside, and judgment entered for the defendants on the claim with costs. No order on the counterclaim, except that it be discontinued without costs.

[ATKIN L.J.:]

This case raises the question whether the customer of a bank may sue the banker for the balance standing to the credit of his current account without making a previous demand upon the banker for payment. It is unnecessary to recapitulate the circumstances which raise this issue in this case. It is sufficient to state that upon the hearing of a summons for particulars on March 16, 1920, the defendants undertook to limit their causes of action to those arising on or before August 1, 1914, and that at that date no demand for the balance had been made to the bank.

The question seems to turn upon the terms of the contract made between banker and customer in ordinary course of business when a current account is opened by the bank. It is said on the one hand that it is simple contract of loan; it is admitted that there is added, or superadded, an obligation of the bank to honour the customer's drafts to any amount not exceeding the credit balance at any material time; but it is contended that this added obligation does not affect the main contract. The bank has borrowed the money and is under the ordinary obligation of a borrower to repay. The lender can sue for his debt whenever he pleases. I am unable to accept this contention. I think that there is only one contract made between the bank and its customer. The terms of that contract involve obligations on both sides and require careful statement. They appear upon consideration to include the following provisions. The bank undertakes to receive money and to collect bills for its customer's account. The proceeds so received are not to be held in trust for the customer, but the bank borrows the proceeds and undertakes to repay them. The promise to repay is to repay at the branch of the bank where the account is kept, and during banking hours. It includes a promise to repay any part of the amount due against the written order of the customer addressed to the bank at the branch, and as such written orders may be outstanding in the ordinary course of business for two or three days, it is a term of the contract that the bank will not cease to do business with the customer except upon reasonable notice. The customer on his part undertakes to exercise reasonable care in executing his written orders so as not to mislead the bank or to facilitate forgery. I think it is necessarily a term of such contract that the bank is not liable to pay the customer the full amount of his balance until he demands payment from the bank at the branch at which the current account is kept. Whether he must demand it in writing it is not necessary now to determine. The result I have mentioned seems to follow from the ordinary relations of banker and customer, but if it were necessary to fall back upon the course of business and the custom of bankers, I think that it was clearly established by undisputed evidence in this case that bankers never do make a payment to a customer in respect of a current account except upon demand. The contention of the plaintiffs appears to me to ignore the fact that the contract between banker and customer contains special terms, and cannot in its entirety be expressed in the phrasing of an ordinary indebitatus count. A simple promise to pay upon an executed consideration creates a debt, and the creditor may sue without notice. "It is clear that a request for the payment of a debt is quite immaterial, unless the parties to the contract have stipulated that it shall be made; if they have not, the law requires no notice or request; but the debtor is bound to find out the creditor and pay him the debt when due": per Parke B. in *Walton v. Mascall*. The question is in every case whether the parties have stipulated that a request shall be made. In the case of a note made payable on demand it is clear that the words "payable on demand" do not make a demand a term of the contract: see *Norton v. Ellam*, a decision that on a note payable with interest on demand the Statute of Limitations ran from the date of the note. Parke B. says:

> It is the same as the case of money lent payable upon request, with interest, where no demand is necessary before bringing the action. There is no obligation in law to give any notice at all; if you choose to make it part of the contract that notice shall be given, you may do so. The debt which constitutes the cause of action arises instantly on the loan.

On the other hand a note payable on demand at a particular place does contain a stipulation in the contract that demand shall be made *mode et forma*, and no action will lie without such a demand: see now *Bills of Exchange Act, 1882*, s. 87, sub-s. 1. It has been said that a demand can only be necessary where the contract is a collateral promise to pay, meaning thereby a promise such as that of a surety. This is too narrow a view, and I am inclined to think has received countenance from a misreading of the words of Alderson B. in *Norton v. Ellam*, where he adds to the judgment of Parke B.: "It must be so unless there is something to show that a demand is to be a collateral matter"; which I think means is stipulated for as qualifying the promise to pay. The use of the word "collateral" and its true explanation can be seen in the case of *Birks v. Trippet*. There the principal case was an action in assumpsit, which declared that the plaintiff and defendant had submitted differences to arbitration, and that the defendant had promised the plaintiff that if the defendant did not perform the award he would pay £40 if he should be thereunto requested. Saunders, of counsel for the defendant, took objection to the declaration "that the plaintiff (in his declaration) had not laid any request of the penalty of £40," and he argued that there was a difference between a mere duty and a collateral sum:

> For where a mere duty is promised to be paid upon request, as if in consideration of all moneys lent to the defendant, he promised to pay them again on request, no actual request is nec-

essary, but the bringing of the action is a sufficient request. But otherwise it is on a promise to pay a collateral sum on request, for there an actual request ought to be made before action brought. And so was the opinion of the whole Court. And thereupon judgment was given for the defendant.

And Serjeant Williams, in his note, cites a number of cases and then says:

> For the request is parcel of the contract, and must be proved; and no action arises until a request be made.

The question appears to me to be in every case, did the parties in fact intend to make the demand a term of the contract? If they did, effect will be given to their contract, whether it be a direct promise to pay or a collateral promise, though in seeking to ascertain their intention the nature of the contract may be material. In the case of such a contract as this, if I have correctly stated the manifold terms of it, it appears to me that the parties must have intended that the money handed to the banker is only payable after a demand. The nature of the contract negatives the duty of the debtor to find out his creditor and pay him his debt. If such a duty existed and were performed, the creditor might be ruined by reason of outstanding cheques being dishonoured. Moreover, payment can only be due, as it appears to me, at the branch where the account is kept, and where the precise liabilities are known. And if this is so, I apprehend that demand at the place where alone the money is payable must be necessary. A decision to the contrary would subvert banking business. I am glad to think that, so far as I can ascertain, the decisions in the American Courts are uniformly to the same effect as our present judgment.

The practical bearing of this decision is on the question of the Statute of Limitations. Since the case of *Pott v. Clegg* in 1847 it has been laid down in text-books that, in the case of a current account, the statute runs from the time of the money being deposited with the banker. But if that case is looked at, it is plain that it was decided upon the pleadings, the sum in question being claimed to be set off for money lent by the defendant's testator to the plaintiff's predecessor in title. It is stated that the majority of the Court were of opinion that money in the hands of the banker is merely money lent, with the superadded obligation that it is to be paid when called for by the draft of the customer. The Lord Chief Baron was of opinion that it was a question for the jury whether there is not a special contract between the banker and his customer as to the money deposited, which distinguishes it from the ordinary case of a loan for money. The Lord Chief Baron delivered the judgment of the Court, and it is plain from his language that he could not have done so had not the decision been confined to the pleading point. The only other direct authority is the decision of Lord Lyndhurst L.C. in *Foley v. Hill.* The suit was for an account, and I am not certain that in dealing with the Statute of Limitations Lord Lyndhurst was not dealing with those words in the statute that deal with actions of account. The right to such an action may well accrue before a debt becomes payable. But on the assumption that the Lord Chancellor decided that the statute had run against a claim in debt or assumpsit, yet inasmuch as that decision was taken to the House of Lords and affirmed there by all the Lords present, including Lord Lyndhurst himself, upon one only of the grounds relied upon in the judgment below, the point as to the Statute of Limitations being expressly reserved, I do not think that we are bound to treat the whole of Lord Lyndhurst's judgment as binding upon us. It may be noted that the decision of the Court of Exchequer in *Pott v. Clegg* had been given between the dates of the decision of Lord Lyndhurst in *Foley v. Hill* and the hearing in the House of Lords. The decision in the latter case in the House of Lords is confined to the point that the banker is debtor to his customer and not trustee. I do not think it safe to rely upon the language used by the Lord Chancellor and Lord Brougham on the subject of demand and request, though the words used tend to support the contention of the present appellants.

The result of this decision will be that future bankers may have to face legal claims for balances on accounts that have remained dormant for more than six years. But seeing that bankers have not been in the habit as a matter of business of setting up the Statute of Limitations against their customers or their legal representatives, I do not suppose that such a change in what was supposed to be the law will have much practical effect. It was suggested in argument that the effect of our decision will be to alter the facilities given to an execution creditor to attach his debtor's bank account in garnishee proceedings. This appears to be a mistake. The provisions of Order XLV, apply to debts owing or accruing from the garnishee, and this expression includes debts to which the judgment debtor is entitled though they are not presently payable: see the decision of the Court of Appeal in *O'Driscoll v. Manchester Insurance Committee.* The service of the order *nisi* binds the debt in the hands of the garnishee — that is, creates a charge in favour of the judgment creditor. If the bank disputes that the amount is payable, there is simple power to provide for a demand being made before an order for payment is made. Possibly the order *nisi* in itself operates as such a demand.

Finally it is perhaps unnecessary to say that the necessity for a demand may be got rid of by special contract or by waiver. A repudiation by a bank of the customer's right to be paid any particular sum would no doubt be a waiver of any demand in respect of such sum.

For these reasons, I am of opinion that the appeal should be allowed, and that judgment should be entered for the defendants on the claim with costs.

Appeal allowed.

(c)   *Burnett v. Westminster Bank Ltd.*†

[MOCATTA J.:]

The problems that have arisen in this action are due to the use of computers by the defendant bank and the issue by the bank to its customers of cheque forms bearing magnetic ink characters (MICR) capable of being read by the computer or associated machines.

The primary facts in the case are not in dispute and are either contained in the pleadings or in the

---

† [1965] 3 All E.R. 81 (Q.B.D.). [Notes omitted.]

agreed statement of facts, or were agreed in argument before me between counsel. The plaintiff, who is a bookmaker, had for some considerable time before January, 1935, been a customer of the defendants on current accounts at the defendants' Borough and Bromley branches. On Friday, Jan. 22, 1965, he, together with two others, was gaming on the terms that they would equally share their winnings or losses. In fact they lost £3,000. The plaintiff's two partners in gaming could not then pay. The plaintiff accordingly paid the winner £700 in cash and gave him a crossed cheque made out to cash for the balance of £2,300. The printed heading at the top of the cheque showed it to be drawn on the Borough branch of the defendants, but for some reason the plaintiff wished the cheque to be drawn on his account at the Bromley branch. He accordingly in ink deleted "Borough" and substituted "Bromley"; he also altered in ink the printed address of the Borough branch, which had read, "34 Borough High Street, London, S.E.1", so that it read "High Street, S.E.1". To have been correct he should have also deleted "S.E.1". He initialled his alterations on both sides of the printed heading. The next morning, having been let down by his partners in gaming, he decided to stop the cheque. He accordingly telephoned the defendants' Bromley branch, told them the correct number and date of the cheque and its amount and also that it was a Borough cheque altered to Bromley and instructed the Bromley branch not to pay the cheque. He confirmed these instructions by letter to the Bromley branch dated Jan. 25. Nevertheless the cheque having been put through the clearing house by Coutts, found its way to the defendants' Borough branch and was there paid on or about Jan. 27, and the plaintiff's account at that branch was debited with £2,300.

In this action the plaintiff claimed that the defendants, in so debiting his account at the Borough branch, acted without his authority. He accordingly claimed £2,300 in a variety of alternative ways, but it was agreed between counsel that if the plaintiff was entitled to succeed the correct, or at any rate the most convenient, remedy was a declaration that the plaintiff was entitled to have his Borough current account with the defendants credited with £2,300. Somewhat paradoxically the plaintiff indicated through his counsel that he would be prepared to return £300 to the defendants, since he had always recognised his personal liability for £1,000 out of the £3,000 lost at gaming. It was added that should he recover any part of the £2,000 from his gaming partners he would pay this over to the defendants. These

matters clearly cannot affect the legal issues in this action.

The defendants denied that they had acted without the plaintiff's authority in paying the cheque and debiting the plaintiff's account at the Borough branch. They pleaded that it was an express term of the relationship of banker and customer prevailing between them and the plaintiff at the time, that cheque forms issued by the Borough branch would be applied to the account for which they had been prepared and that the plaintiff would not use or permit their use on any other account. These terms were derived from the notice printed on the front cover of the cheque book, first issued to the plaintiff in or about January, 1964, by the Borough branch and containing the cheque in question, and the use by the plaintiff of the cheque book without objection. The front cover of the cheque book, which was orange in colour, read as follows: "Westminster Bank, Ltd. Borough Branch, 34 Borough High Street, London, S.E.1." There then followed a small print of the arms of the defendants below which were printed, in clear and easily legible black type: "J. Burnett. The cheques and credit slips in this book will be applied to the account for which they have been prepared. Customers must not, therefore, permit their use on any other account." Relying on these two sentences, particularly the first, as having contractual effect, the defendants pleaded and argued that notwithstanding the pen and ink alterations on the cheque substituting Bromley for Borough, the cheque must be read as a mandate to the Borough branch with which they had complied. The defendants further pleaded in the alternative that by altering the cheque as he did the plaintiff was in breach of contract. There was, however, no counterclaim and this part of the defence was not relied on in argument.

I gave the plaintiff leave, at his expense, to put in a reply in which he raised the point (inter alia) that there was no consideration given by the defendants for the agreement, if any, relied on by the defendants as having been constituted by the use by the plaintiff of one or more cheques out of the cheque book bearing on its cover the two sentences which I have set out.

It is necessary that I should now explain the relevance of the use of computers made by the defendants and the employment by them of MICR characters on the cheques supplied by them to the plaintiff. In the agreed statement of facts reference was made to the operation of computers in banking, as set out in an article in the "New Scientist" dated Apr. 1, 1965. That article was agreed in so far as it contained statements of historical or present fact and, as regards the future, it was agreed to represent probable lines of development. I need only summarise the facts, so far as I understand them, in relation to this case.

The defendants maintain a central computer to which their Borough branch is connected. Originally computers were used in banks in this country to keep the accounts of groups of branch banks. Information had to be fed into the computers so that it might be stored by them on magnetic tapes. This was initially done by punched cards or paper tape. A major advance came about through a technique called magnetic ink character recognition (MICR), which made available to the banks machines capable of reading characters printed on cheques in "magnetisable" ink. These machines could both automatically sort the cheques as between branches and accounts and read details of the cheque serial number, account number, etc., into the computer at speeds of up to sixteen hundred cheques a minute. Accordingly it became possible to use cheques themselves as direct input to the computer and eliminate much of the punched-card or paper-tape input. In 1961 the banks in Britain agreed on a common code of magnetic information to be recorded on cheques. The first bank to use the direct cheque input for the posting of current accounts was the Westminster Bank, which opened the first MICR centre in Europe in 1962. The use of computers and MICR cheques clearly results in considerable economies in operating the banking system. The article from which I have quoted contemplates an increasingly all-embracing use of computers and MICR cheques so that ultimately normal writing or typing on cheques may be almost if not completely eliminated and there will be a greatly reduced handling of cheques within the banking system. There is, however, still a long way to go before that stage is reached. Nevertheless the Westminster Bank in general and its Borough branch in particular seem to have gone much farther by January, 1964, than many other banks.

The cheque in question in this action, like the twenty-nine other cheque forms in the book of cheques from which it was taken, bore from left to right along its bottom edge three groups of MICR figures. The first was the number of the cheque, the second contained figures indicating the Westminster Bank and the Borough branch thereof, whilst the third group of figures indicated the plaintiff's account at that branch. After the cheque had found its way to the London clearing house via Coutts it was sorted to the defendants by hand. It

then went to the defendants' central computer where it was read by an employee and a fourth group of MICR figures was put on it corresponding with £2,300, the amount for which the cheque was drawn. Simultaneously and automatically all four MICR groups of figures were fed into the magnetic tape in the central computer and stored by it for application to the plaintiff's account at the Borough branch. The computer was, of course, quite unable to read the pen and ink alterations to the Bromley branch. The computer apparently stores the information during a period of suspense before actually applying it to the particular account by way of debit or credit. During that period of suspense the cheque was physically sent to the Borough branch where it was checked for date and signature and as to whether the account was sufficiently in credit to meet the cheque. In an appropriate case the branch manager would decide whether to allow an overdraft. If the computer is not stopped, after the expiry of the period of suspense the account in question is automatically debited or credited as the case may be. In the present case the period of suspense passed and the plaintiff's Borough account was debited.

It will be seen from the above that the whole system is as yet by no means automatic and from the explanation given by counsel for the defendants I conclude that the defendants' employees at the Borough branch could, on their examination of the cheque for date, signature and amount, have taken appropriate steps pursuant to the pen and ink alterations to the Bromley branch, to have prevented the cheque being debited to the Borough branch. They did not so do and counsel for the defendants argued that they were under no obligation so to do, since on the defendants' case the plaintiff, by accepting the notice on the front of the cheque book, agreed that any cheque from that book, however altered in pen and ink, could only constitute a mandate to the defendants to apply the cheque to the plaintiff's account at the Borough branch.

As to the plaintiff's own knowledge it was agreed that he had seen that the front cover of the cheque book bore printed words in fact constituting the notice relied on by the defendants, but it was further agreed that the case had to be decided on the basis that he had not read them. It was agreed that he had not orally or in writing objected to the notice. It appears from the detailed instructions he gave by telephone and letter to the Bromley branch that he could read the MICR figures at the bottom of the cheque, which is not altogether easy at first acquaintance, and knew which group contained the cheque number, since he correctly gave the number to the Bromley branch. It was also agreed that the cheque book containing the cheque in question was the first of its kind issued to him by the Borough branch. No facts were proved as to the cheques issued to him by the Bromley branch, and I therefore think it fair to assume that in January, 1965, when the plaintiff altered the branch on this particular cheque, they were in the same form as those which had been issued to him by the Borough branch before January, 1964.

It is of some importance that I should explain the difference between the cheque books and cheques previously issued to the plaintiff by the Borough and (I am assuming) the Bromley branches and this particular cheque book (which I will call the new book) and its cheques which was issued to the plaintiff in or about January, 1964. The previous cheque books were of more or less the same orange colour but were somewhat thinner and over an inch longer. Each cheque in the previous books was attached to a counterfoil and there were no credit or paying-in slips in the books. In the new book the cheques were of the same size, but had no individual counterfoils. Instead of counterfoils there were three pages ruled in lines and columns on both sides immediately inside the front cover and before the first cheque on which the customer could enter, if he wished, the number, date, amount and payee of each cheque and other details. At the end of the new book were four paying-in or credit slips and two pages with provision for the cashier's stamp to be attached as a receipt for sums paid in. The credit slips had MICR figures along their bottom edges indicating the Westminster Bank, the branch and the account. The old cheques differed from the new in that they only bore the first two groups of MICR figures, that is the cheque number, and bank and branch.

For the purpose of the legal arguments raised perhaps the most important differences are to be found on the front covers. The old cheque books merely had the defendants' name at the top, with no branch name or account name. The front cover went on, in italics, "attention is particularly drawn to the following". There then followed below on the front of the cover four clearly printed paragraphs, occupying the rest of the space, of an admonitory or advisory character indicating, *inter alia*, that cheques should be drawn on the forms supplied by the bank, how they should be filled in, etc. Five further paragraphs followed overleaf, advertising various services of the bank. It was not argued that any of these nine paragraphs was of contractual effect.

The front of the new cheque book was as I earlier described. Its two sentences were said to be of contractual effect once the customer used a cheque from the book. The nine paragraphs from the face and overleaf of the front cover of the old books are now to be found in two columns on the overleaf of the front cover of the new book.

Since there was no disagreement between counsel on the general principles applicable to the legal relationship between banker and customer so far as relevant to this case, I can state in summary form a number of points of importance by way of background in approaching the problem to be decided. First, in the ordinary case of banker and customer their relations depend either entirely or mainly on an implied contract. Secondly, the banker undertakes to repay money received by him on behalf of his customer against the written order of the customer. That promise is to repay at the branch of the bank where the account is kept and similarly when the customer has accounts at more than one branch. Thirdly, unless otherwise agreed, the customer's written order need not be on any particular form, though no doubt in the vast majority of cases the customer today uses cheque forms supplied by his banker. Nevertheless other forms are used, such as "house" cheques, forms prepared by charities to further their appeals on, on rare occasions, a customer may write his mandate to his banker on some handy piece of paper or on some even more informal material. In addition cheque forms issued by one branch or one bank may be altered so as to constitute mandates to another branch or another bank. Fourthly, the customer undertakes to exercise reasonable care in executing his written orders so as not to mislead the banker by ambiguities or to facilitate forgery. Fifthly, the banker must not pay if the customer has countermanded his mandate in time, but notice to stop payment given to one branch of a bank does not per se constitute notice to any other branch of the same bank. As regards these last two points the altered cheque there, if the magnetised ink be ignored, was in no sense ambiguous, whilst the Bromley branch received the plaintiff's instructions not to pay a matter of days before the cheque found its way via the clearing house to the defendants. The Borough branch had no knowledge of the plaintiff's instructions to the Bromley branch not to pay the cheque.

It was not argued for the defendants that the introduction by them of the new cheques, bearing magnetised ink characters to the extent present on the plaintiff's cheque here, in any way altered the position between themselves and their customers in regard to the above points, save only as to one limit on the use of the new cheques. Thus, provided they received unambiguous mandates from their customers, the defendants would continue to deal with these as before even if written, for example, on the cheque forms of other banks or on no forms at all. It was, however, added that if this happened at all frequently in the case of mandates addressed to branches which had gone over to the new system, the customers in question would be likely to be charged heavily and might be asked to take their accounts elsewhere. In the case of these new cheques issued to the plaintiff, however, the defendants argued that by agreement the position had been altered to this extent that if the plaintiff used such a cheque, he could not by anything he wrote on its face validly instruct them to pay out of any account or branch other than those referred to in print on the front of the cover of the cheque book and repeated in print on each cheque contained in it.

It is plain form what I have said that the defendants could not unilaterally so restrict the plaintiff's rights and the contrary was not contended. The restriction could only be made effective by agreement between the plaintiff and the defendants. In some cases, no doubt, express agreement on a similar restriction may be reached between banker and customer, such as, for example, by exchange of letters or the signature on some form by the customer. The defendants were not here in a position to rely on any such express written agreement evidence by any document signed by the plaintiff. They argued, however, that the plaintiff had, by his conduct in using a cheque or cheques taken from the new cheque book containing on the front of its cover the two sentences which I have set out, agreed to the restriction in question.

I was referred by both counsel to the well-known case of *Parker v. South Eastern Ry. Co., Gabell v. Same,*[1] and it was suggested, particularly by counsel for the defendants, that the three general rules therein laid down in relation to ticket cases, were applicable here. Counsel for the defendants based himself on the rules as stated in *Anson's Law of Contract* (22nd ed.) at pp. 143 and 144:

1. If the person receiving the ticket did not see or know that there was any writing on the ticket, then he is not bound by the conditions.
2. If he knew there was writing, and knew or believed that the writing contained conditions, then he is bound by the conditions, even though he did not read them and did not know what they were.

3. If he knew that there was writing on the ticket, but did not know or believe that the writing contained conditions, nevertheless he will be bound if the party delivering the ticket has done all that can reasonably be considered necessary to give notice of the term to persons of the class to which he belongs.

On the facts here counsel submitted that as the plaintiff had seen that the front cover of the new cheque book bore printed words, it did not matter that he had not read them and did not know or believe that they contained conditions affecting the use he was entitled to make of the cheques in the book, provided that the defendants had done all that could reasonably be considered necessary to give him notice of the conditions. Counsel for the defendants submitted that the two sentences on the new cheque book cover constituted in the circumstances such reasonable notice. They were easily legible, the new cheque book both in its cover and contents was noticeably different from the old one previously issued and it was next to impossible for the defendants by writing letters or issuing forms for signature to secure that the customers read the letters or signed the forms. The defendants had therefore given the plaintiff reasonable notice. He also relied on *Underwood (A.L.), Ltd. v. Bank of Liverpool and Martins, Same v. Barclays Bank,* per Scrutton and Atkin L.JJ.,[2] and the recent case of *Westminster Bank, Ltd. v. Zang,*[3] as showing how readily the courts will conclude that the legal relationship between customer and banker had been varied by the filing in by the customer of a paying-in slip containing a sentence as to the banker's rights. I do not think that these two cases are of much assistance here, since the customer in both filled in the slips containing the terms relied on by the banks. There were no terms on the cheque form used by the plaintiff.

I do not consider that the ticket cases afford exact parallels with the circumstances here, since those cases relate to printed documents being handed contemporaneously with the making of the relevant contract. Here the plaintiff and defendants had been in contractual relationship, since the plaintiff first opened his account with the defendants at their Borough branch. If two sentences on the face of the cheque book are to have contractual effect that must be by way of variation of the already existing contract between the parties. The effect of this distinction, however, is in my judgment merely to emphasise the importance of the notice to be given by the defendants to their customer before they can be in a position to plead successfully that he has accepted the proposed variation by using a cheque from the new book.

Despite counsel for the defendants' able argument I am unable to treat the two sentences on the cheque book cover as adequate notice. Whilst it is true that the new cheque book differed materially from previous ones in format, the differences were not very marked. Cheque book covers had never previously been used for the purpose of containing contractual terms and I think that they fell into the category of documents which the recipients could reasonably assume contained no conditions; see, for example, per Mellish L.J., in *Parker v. South Eastern Ry. Co.*[4] and *Chapelton v. Barry Urban District Council*.[5] The position might have been different had the new cheque book been the first issued to the plaintiff on his opening the account. But in the case of a customer like the plaintiff who has had an account for some time under the system prevailing down to the issue of the new cheque book, I am of the opinion that the mere presence of the two sentences on the new cheque book cover is inadequate to affect the pre-existing contractual relationship. In such circumstances I do not consider that the defendants could establish that they had given adequate notice to their customer to bind him to the new restricted use of the cheques unless they could show that he had read the sentences in question, or had signed some document indicating his agreement to

their effect. I would be prepared to accept as the equivalent of the latter the signature of the customer on a cheque provided that the cheque form itself bore words limiting its use to the bank, branch and amount shown in print on it. The present cheque bore no such words.

Since I have reached the conclusion that on the facts here the defendants did not bring themselves within the third of the rules which I have cited from ANSON, the defence in this action must fail. It is not necessary for me, therefore, to express reasoned views on three further points taken for the plaintiff by his counsel, namely (i) that the two sentences were not sufficiently explicit in their language to have affected the contractual relationship even had it been proved the plaintiff had read them; (ii) that there was no consideration for the alleged variation of the contractual relationship, and (iii) that, even if the plaintiff must be taken as being contractually bound by the two sentences, the altered cheque constituted no mandate from the plaintiff to the defendants to debit his account at the Borough branch. I can, however, briefly say that, as at present advised, I do not think that any of these points would have availed the plaintiff had the defendants succeeded on the point as to notice.

I accordingly declare that the plaintiff is entitled to have his Borough account with the defendants credited by them with £2,300.

Judgment for the plaintiff.

(d) *Armstrong Baum Plumbing & Heating v. Toronto Dominion Bank*†

[WILKINS J.:]

The plaintiff is a partnership composed of three corporations: Armstrong Baum Ltd., Plumbright Services Inc. and 526543 Ontario Limited. Seymour Baum is the principal of Armstrong Baum Plumbing and Heating Limited. Henry Kay is the principal of Plumbright Services Inc. and Peter Cooling is the principal of 526543 Ontario Limited.

Mr. Kay testified for the plaintiff. He was the general manager of the plaintiff and, in that capacity, it was his responsibility to undertake various dealings with the partnership's bankers, Toronto-Dominion Bank (the "bank").

Mr. Kay was an experienced businessman who had obtained a Grade XII education and then started as a plumber's apprentice with the old company, Armstrong Baum Plumbing & Heating Lim-

---

† (1994), 15 B.L.R. (2d) 84 (Ont. Gen. Div.); affirmed (1997) 32 B.L.R. (2d) 230 (Ont. C.A.).

ited. After two years, he had moved into the front office to become the day-to-day manager with the "old company" and, in that capacity, he had daily dealings with the Yorkdale branch of the bank.

In 1982, the plaintiff was formed and Mr. Kay became the general manager. He has remained in that capacity to the present time.

In his managerial capacity, Mr. Kay opened the current account utilized by the plaintiff in its day-to-day banking activities. He undertook this process in 1982. At that time, various documents were created, including a borrowing by-law, a banking resolution, a signature card and an operation of account agreement ("OAA").

This account was given the number designation of 335206 (the "1982 current account").

The 1982 current account was the current account on which all of the cheques of the business of the plaintiff were drawn and into which the deposits from the paid receivables were deposited. The bank provided a monthly statement and the plaintiff received copies of its business cheques and/or vouchers with those statements.

In March of 1986, a new account was opened by the principals of the corporate partners. This new account was designated as the trust account and the bank ascribed to this account the identification number 3306887 (the "1986 trust account"). Two OAAs were executed during the process of opening this account.

Both of these 1986 OAAs were identical in form to the 1982 OAA. The form was prepared by the bank as a standard printed form and was designated 13616 (3–79). It was Mr. Kay's evidence, which I accept, that he had read these agreements and that he was familiar with their contents in a general way.

At the time the problems arose in 1991, the plaintiff, the three corporations making up the plaintiff, and the principals of the corporations were operating over 12 different accounts with the bank.

The business carried on by the plaintiff was quite active. Prior to 1991, it employed 30 to 60 people, performed approximately 10,000 jobs per annum and earned gross income in the range of $4,000,000. Each job would involve invoicing. Cheques in the number of 50 to 60 per week would have to be handled. All of the banking procedures were being conducted through the 1982 current account and all of the dealings with the bank involving documents for loans, lines of credit or other significant dealings with the bank were done by Mr. Kay.

It was Mr. Kay's evidence that at the time of the execution of the 1986 OAAs, he was familiar with these documents and generally aware of their contents. He knew that those OAAs applied to all accounts operated by the customer at any of the branches or offices of the bank, and he knew that there was a 30-day limitation for the reporting of discrepancies in the statements he received. He was also aware of clause 5(b) which set out:

> Nothing herein contained shall preclude the customer from later objecting to any unauthorized or forged endorsement of the payee provided notice in writing is given to the Bank forthwith after the customer has acquired knowledge thereof.

Up to 1991, the relationships between the plaintiff and the bank appear to have been very satisfactory. During this time, the wives of Mr. Baum and Mr. Kay kept the books, wrote the cheques and dealt with any discrepancies that might have arisen in the accounts.

At some point in July of 1991, the plaintiff desired to open a new account. It was Mr. Kay's evidence that this was to be a specific account for specific purposes and that this was made clear to the bank. This was to be a confidential account and, to this end, the mailing address for this account was changed to 40 Carmichael Avenue, which was his home address. On July 22, 1991, he attended at the bank and executed the documents which appear at Tabs 15 and 19 of Exhibit I in the book of exhibits. These are respectively an authorization for a form of credit investigation by the bank and a form ordering cheques on this new account. These were signed in the presence of Lois Paddon, a representative of the bank, and it was to Ms Paddon that Mr. Kay explained the special and confidential purpose of this new account. For some unexplained reason, no OAA was requested at that time. The bank ascribed number 332967 to this account (the "1991 confidential account").

Tab 18 is the first statement for this new account and it shows a balance forward date of July 22 and a deposit of July 31 as being the first entries for the 1991 confidential account. These documents show that the account was opened and operating effective July 22, 1991.

Shortly after July 28, 1991, Ms Esposito returned from vacation and, in a manner that Mr. Kay cannot specifically recall, informed him that it was necessary to execute a new agreement for the new account. This document which Mr. Kay was requested to execute was on a different form and was entitled "Operation of Current Account Agreement" ("OCAA").

It would be apparent to anyone familiar with the earlier form of OAA that the new OCAA was different. Mr. Kay has no clear recollection of the circumstances of how he was notified that the bank required him to execute this new OCAA. He recalled that Ms Esposito may have waved him over to her counter or someone might have notified him by telephone. It was his belief that he had gone to the bank that day not for the purpose of executing this document but rather to perform other banking business and that the request to execute this document arose secondarily to his other purpose in attending at the branch.

It was his evidence that Ms Esposito advised him that he had to sign a new form to open this special purpose account and that she showed him the form and advised him that it was similar to the other OAA that he had already executed, except that it was shorter.

At the time this document was presented to Mr. Kay for execution, the new account number of 332967, that of the 1991 confidential account, had already been placed on the upper right-hand corner of the document.

It was Mr. Kay's evidence that the general purport of Ms Esposito's comments was that this document was similar to the earlier OAAs and by this he understood her to mean they were the same. At the time of execution, it was his intention to sign an agreement that was the same or similar to the form 13616 (3-79). In response to his questions about what the document was and why he had to sign it, he was left with the clear understanding that although this new form was shorter, it was the same as the earlier document in function and effect. He testified that he relied upon her comments to reach this conclusion and, on that basis, he did not read the document prior to execution. Ms Esposito was present and aware that the document had not been read.

It was Mr. Kay's evidence that there was no discussion of the contents of this document nor was he ever advised that any of the terms of that document were different from the earlier OAAs he had executed in 1982 and in 1986. He said he relied upon the comment made by Ms Esposito to the effect that the document he was about to sign was ostensibly the same as the one he had signed earlier.

It was Mr. Kay's recollection that he and Ms Esposito talked about cheques and whether or not they could be obtained quickly in order that the 1991 confidential account could be put to use, and that he executed the OCAA in front of Ms Esposito and that she then signed the document in front of him. After execution of the document, Mr. Kay testified he was not given any copy of that OCAA, notwithstanding that the document at Tab 16 contains an acknowledgement of receipt of a duly completed copy.

Questions 136 to 138 inclusive of the examination on discovery were put to Mr. Kay. He testified that he knew the form was different but he believed they were similar in function and he was prepared to accept the new form based upon Ms Esposito's comment that they were similar. It was clear from the way Mr. Kay responded to these questions that he felt his words were being misinterpreted.

Upon a close reading of those questions and both watching and hearing Mr. Kay's responses, I am satisfied he was answering truthfully and that his answer to Question 138 on discovery related to a state of mind after all the facts were known in the litigation, and not at the time of the execution of the OCAA.

During July of 1991, Mrs. Baum apparently indicated her intention to retire as one of their bookkeepers. The plaintiff then made inquiry of its chartered accounts as to whether they could help them locate a competent replacement to do the plaintiff's bookkeeping. The accountants conducted a search and eventually put forward a number of candidates. After an interview, it was decided to hire one Phillip N. Lang to fill the vacancy and, on August 19, 1991, Mr. Lang commenced his employment as the bookkeeper for the plaintiff.

Needless to say, the new bookkeeper was a rogue who shortly set about to embezzle the plaintiff's funds and, unknown to the plaintiff, the new bookkeeper forged Mr. Kay's signature to a cheque, drawn on the 1982 current account, dated September 3, 1991 in the amount of $19,689.37. The rogue followed up on September 10, 1991 by forging Mr. Kay's signature to a cheque drawn on the same account in the amount of $35,025.28. Both cheques were cleared by the bank and the funds withdrawn from that account.

The rogue further forged the signature of Seymour Baum to a cheque dated September 13, 1991 in the amount of $45,987.46, drawn again on the 1982 current account. This cheque was cleared by the bank and the funds were withdrawn from the account.

The rogue forged the signature of Seymour Baum to another cheque dated September 17, 1991 in the amount of $29,541.11, drawn on the same account. This cheque was cleared by the bank and the funds were withdrawn from the account.

On the Friday prior to September 23, Mr. Kay returned from a vacation in Scotland to ascertain that Mr. Lang had been absent from work for some days without excuse and, upon conducting investigations, ascertained that cheques were missing. Upon contacting the bank, the first of the forged cheques was brought to his notice by the bank. Shortly thereafter, the bank notified him of the three additional forged cheques.

At that time, Mr. Kay gave the bank oral notification of the fraud and the forgeries and this notice was followed up shortly thereafter by written notice from the plaintiff to the bank on September 23, 1991 and by further written notice to the bank by Mr. Sclisizzi, solicitor for the plaintiff.

There was no issue that the signatures of the drawers of the cheques were forged and that, in the absence of contractual documentation to the contrary, the provisions of the *Bills of Exchange Act*, R.S.C. 1985, c. B-4, s. 48(1) and (3) would apply.

In 1982, when the plaintiff entered into its banking arrangements for the opening of the 1982 current account, and at the time the plaintiff entered into its banking arrangements for the opening of the 1986 trust account, the signing officers were the same and the OAA was identical on each occasion. The form entered into for both of those accounts was form 13616 (3-79) and the operative clauses applicable to this case were 5(a) and 5(b) which were worded as follows:

5.(a) Upon receipt from the Bank from time to time of statements of the customer's account, together with instruments and vouchers for amounts charged to the said account as appearing in the said statements, the customer will forthwith examine the said instruments, vouchers, and statements and immediately notify the bank in writing of any errors in or objections to the said instruments, vouchers and statements, and, if the customer has not so notified the bank of any such errors or objections at the expiration of thirty days from the date of delivery of said instruments, vouchers and statements to the customer, or at the expiration of thirty days from the date of mailing thereof if the customer has instructed the bank to mail the instruments, vouchers and statements, the customer agrees that the balance shown in the said statement shall be accepted as correct, all the said instruments and vouchers acknowledged as authentic and the Bank released from all claims by the customer in respect of any and every item in the said statements and to accept the Bank's records as conclusive proof of the correctness and authenticity of all such statements and the

items so recorded therein and of the date of the aforesaid delivery or mailing.

(b) Nothing herein contained shall preclude the customer from later objecting to any unauthorized or forged endorsement of the payee provided notice in writing is given to the Bank forthwith after the customer has acquired knowledge thereof.

Both agreements also contained a final paragraph which stated as follows:

This agreement shall apply to all accounts operated by the customer at any of the branches or offices of this Bank, except where the Bank is notified in writing to the contrary.

It was Mr. Kay's evidence that at some point in 1982 and/or in 1986, he had read this particular form and that he was familiar with clauses 5(a) and (b), which he called the "thirty-day clause," and he was familiar with the final paragraph touching upon the effect of the execution of that agreement upon all other accounts which the plaintiff had with the bank when executed on behalf of the plaintiff.

Up to the summer of 1991, the plaintiff's bookkeeping, cheque preparation, cheque storage, bank account reconciliation, day-to-day dealings with the bank on such things as deposits and withdrawals, as well as any complaints that might arise about discrepancies on the bank statements, were handled by either Mrs. Kay or Mrs. Baum. Effective August 19, 1991, Mr. Lang occupied the position of bookkeeper and took over all of those various functions on behalf of the plaintiff.

From August 19, 1991 until Mr. Lang's disappearance shortly after September 17, 1991, no changes were made in the day-to-day operating procedures of the plaintiff and Mr. Lang was expected to carry on in the same manner as Mrs. Kay and Mrs. Baum in all dealings and matters of interest to, and involving, the defendant bank.

It would have been more than apparent to the bank that the plaintiff had changed bookkeepers. Documents in Exhibit I make it clear that Mr. Lang carried on the plaintiff's relationships with the bank and, to some extent, the bank must have become familiar with him and his signature and must have known of the authority that he had acting in the capacity of the plaintiff's bookkeeper.

On or about July 22, 1991, Mr. Kay attended at the bank for purposes of opening the 1991 confidential account. In the course of doing this, he had dealt with Ms Paddon. It was also to Ms Paddon that Mr. Lang directed the transfer notices from the 1986 trust account to the 1982 current account which assisted in facilitating the embezzlement of the plaintiff's money.

There was some evidence that while Mr. Kay was on vacation in Scotland, a female person from the bank had telephoned to speak with him about these transfers apparently because they were unusual. Nothing was ever done by the bank to follow up on this and Mr. Kay, Mr. Baum and Mr. Cooling were not advised.

Ms Esposito testified on behalf of the bank. It was her evidence that she had been on vacation until some time shortly after July 28. When she returned from vacation, the plaintiff's bank folder was on her desk. She indicated that she reviewed the documentation and ascertained that an OCAA had not been executed.

On either July 28 or shortly thereafter, Ms Esposito recalls seeing Mr. Kay in a line-up in front of one of the tellers and going over to speak to him for the purpose of requesting that he attend at the side counter in order to complete the documentation for the 1991 confidential account.

The recollections of Ms Esposito and Mr. Kay are sufficiently similar that it seems most probable that this is exactly what took place.

After completing his business with the teller, Mr. Kay attended at the side counter and Ms Esposito advised him that she wished him to execute an OCAA and gave him form 13616 (4-91). On the upper right-hand corner of that form was written account number 332967, that of the 1991 confidential account.

Ms Esposito specifically denies that Mr. Kay asked her any particular details about the document or what it was. The document was a printed form and it appears at Tab 16 of Exhibit 1. Parts of the form are in bold type but the majority of the wording is in relatively small type. The print is clear and legible but the document is compact and would require some time to be read in full. It is common ground that Mr. Kay did not read the document nor was he requested to read the document by Ms Esposito.

It is apparent from looking at Tab 16 of Exhibit 1 that the form looks different from the earlier forms. Mr. Kay stated that he knew that it was not identical to the earlier forms but that it was similar and that he understood that it was to serve the same function. On the basis of his understanding of the comments made by Ms Esposito, he believed that the content was the same but the form had been shortened.

Although Ms Esposito has no memory of Mr. Kay asking about the form, she asserted that he had

not asked if the form was similar to the earlier forms he had executed. Ms Esposito testified that she might have told Mr. Kay that this was a new OCAA form and that it had been revised. She also recalls informing Mr. Kay that the new document had been compressed, simplified and that it was more organized.

In particular, Ms Esposito emphasized that she did not give any other additional information to Mr. Kay because he did not ask specific questions about the form. From the nature of her testimony and the emphasis that she placed upon not answering questions that were not asked, I have to conclude that Mr. Kay specifically asked some questions about the identity and nature of the form together with the purpose for it being executed. Otherwise, Ms Esposito would not have given him the information which she in fact recalls giving.

Although the witness indicated that she had not told Mr. Kay that the new OCAA was similar to the old OAA, counsel for the defendant admitted that this conversation took place at that time.

It is common ground between the parties that although this document was executed in rather informal circumstances and with conversational discussions, there would have been ample opportunity for Mr. Kay to have made the circumstances somewhat more formal by reading the document or, alternatively, taking it away with him to either read at his leisure or to be reviewed by his solicitors.

Having regard to the concession by counsel for the bank and to the nature of the information that Ms Esposito admits giving to Mr. Kay, and having closely observed the demeanour of both Mr. Kay and Ms Esposito when they were questioned in cross-examination, I find myself compelled to accept the evidence of Mr. Kay as to what transpired that day in the bank.

At the time, Ms Esposito was a current accounts officer of the bank. She was in a position of responsibility and authority for the opening of current accounts and the obtaining of the appropriate documentation. It was her evidence that she was aware that the printed forms prepared by the bank had been changed. She knew that the changes were significant. She knew that they constituted changes to the customer's obligations and the bank's liability. At the time of the execution of the document, she knew that Mr. Kay had not read the document and, from the nature of the information exchanged between them, it would have been clear to her that Mr. Kay did not know the contents of the document as revised.

Mr. Kay's evidence was to the effect that he had read the 1982 and 1986 OAAs. He testified that the documents were, as far as he could recall, the same and, during the course of the trial, a copy of the 1982 OAA was subsequently located, demonstrating Mr. Kay's recollections to be correct. Mr. Kay testified that he knew that there was a limitation clause in respect of the liability of the bank which he described as the "thirty-day clause." He knew that the earlier OAAs had a clause in them which made them applicable to all of the accounts of the plaintiff. In the conversation between Mr. Kay and Ms Esposito, there appears to have been nothing said by either party to suggest that similar limitation clauses and the clause affecting the applicability of the agreement to other accounts would not also be present in this new OCAA.

Ms Esposito testified that when she approached Mr. Kay in the line-up at the bank, it was her intent to get this new document signed and substitute this new document for the old document. At this time, she did not let him know that it was her intent to replace the old agreement with the new agreement, notwithstanding that that is what she had in mind.

It was also Ms Esposito's evidence that after the new form was created, it became a project of the bank to get all of their customers to execute the new form. It is clear on her evidence that the intent was to enable the bank to substitute this new form of agreement for the outstanding old forms executed by Mr. Kay and probably many other customers. The significance of this evidence is driven home by the findings of the Supreme Court of Canada in *Canadian Pacific Hotels Ltd. v. Bank of Montreal* (1987), 40 D.L.R. (4th) 385, 77 N.R. 161, 41 C.C.L.T. 1 (S.C.C.), which cleared the way for the bank to impose contractual limitations on s. 48 of the *Bills of Exchange Act*. The specific amendments contained in clause 5(b) of the new OCAA presented to Mr. Kay seemed clearly to have arisen from that. The wording of clauses 5(a) and 5(b) in the new OCAA (13616 (4-91)) are found at Tab 16 and are as follows:

5(a) RECONCILIATION CONFIRMATION OF BALANCE. Upon receipt from you from time to time of statements of my account, together with instruments, debit memos and vouchers for amounts charged to the account as appearing in the statements, I will forthwith carefully examine the statements, Instruments, debit memos and vouchers and immediately notify you in writing of any errors in or objections to the balance of my account, statements, Instruments, debit memos and vouchers, and of any participation by you in an apparent breach of a fiduciary obliga-

tion owed to me occurring during the period of time for which the relevant statement was issued. If I have not so notified you at the expiration of thirty days from the date of the relevant statement I agree that:

- the balance shown in the relevant statement shall be conclusively deemed to be and accepted as correct except for any amount credited by you in error to the account;
- the Instruments, debit memos and vouchers shall be acknowledged as authentic;
- you shall be released from all claims by me in respect of any and every item in the statements and from any claim by me based on your participation in such apparent breach of fiduciary obligation; and
- I accept your records as conclusive proof of the correctness and authenticity of all statements and the items so recorded therein except for any amount credited by you in error to the account.

I will give you notice in writing of any unauthorized or forged endorsement on any instrument immediately after I have acquired knowledge of it.

(b) PREPARATION OF INSTRUMENTS & INTERNAL SUPERVISION. I hereby agree to have in place systems, procedures and controls, effective to prevent and detect thefts of Instruments or losses due to forgeries or frauds involving Instruments, including without limiting the generality of the foregoing those:

(i)   ensuring that all Instruments are numbered sequentially;

(ii) ensuring that all Instruments are secured in the same manner as large sums of cash;

(iii) ensuring that all instruments, cheque imprinters and facsimile signature devices are kept in a secured locked receptacle, vault, safe, etc. and that designated individual(s) are responsible for them at all times;

(iv) conducting periodic audits of Instruments; and

(v)   ensuring that the individual responsible for doing the bank statement reconciliation shall not be the individual who is responsible for security of Instruments or their preparation.

I will diligently supervise and monitor the conduct and work of all employees and agents having any role in the preparation of my Instruments and in my bank statement reconciliation or other banking function.

I further agree that you shall have no responsibility or liability whatsoever for any loss due to a forged or unauthorized signature unless I prove each of the following: (i) that the forged or unauthorized signature was made by a person who was at no time my employee or agent; (ii) that the loss was unavoidable despite my having had in place the systems, procedures and controls to supervise and monitor my employees and agents; and (iii) that the loss was unavoidable despite my having taken all feasible steps to prevent the forgery or unauthorized signature and the loss arising therefrom.

The new bank form had been issued in March of 1991. Although Ms Esposito could recall some occasions when customers had made changes to the bank's printed form, she could not recall any occasion in which clause 5(b) had been so amended. Given the knowledge and the intent of Ms Esposito at the time of meeting with Mr. Kay, I conclude that when she approached him, she wanted him to execute the bank's printed form without amendment not just for the purpose of executing the form relating to the 1991 confidential account but also specifically to have it replace the old OAA in place at that time.

Clause 12 of the agreement was also significantly amended to read as follows:

> Interpretation. If II(c) above is not completed, any instrument must be signed by all of us. If II(d) above is not completed, the account shall not have a right of survivorship. The singular shall be construed as meaning the plural and vice versa where the context so requires. This agreement shall be binding on my heirs, executors, administrators, successors and permitted assigns and shall govern all accounts operated by me at any of your branches or offices or at the branches or offices of any wholly owned subsidiary of yours, except when I have notified you in writing to the contrary. Headings are included for convenience of reference only. They do not form part of the agreement. "I", "me", "my", "our", "us", and "person" refer to each individual, partnership, company, corporation or other legal entity signing this agreement below. You may amend this agreement by sending a notice to me (or any one of us) in the same manner as a statement of account or by posting a notice in all TD Bank branches.

The old OAA provided that the execution of that particular agreement "shall apply to all accounts operated by the customer at any of the branches or offices of this Bank, except where the Bank is notified in writing to the contrary." The new OCAA provided that the new agreement "shall govern all accounts operated by me at any of your branches or offices or at the branches or offices of any wholly owned subsidiary of yours, except when I have notified you in writing to the contrary." Not only does

the new agreement purport to become paramount — "shall govern," whereas the old agreement simply states that it "shall apply" — but this new agreement goes on to provide that it governs all accounts "at the branches or offices of any wholly owned subsidiary of yours" in addition to the branches and offices of the bank itself. Ms Esposito's evidence was that she did not know the names of the wholly owned subsidiaries of the bank and that no list of wholly owned subsidiaries of the bank was ever provided to her, nor was there any evidence presented as to who might be the wholly owned subsidiaries of the bank or how any customer could ever find out that information.

Possibly even more Draconian in its effect was the clause added in this new agreement that "[y]ou may amend this agreement by sending a notice to me (or any one of us) in the same manner as a statement of account or by posting a notice in all TD Bank branches." On the clear meaning of these words, paragraph 12 was intended to give to the bank a unilateral power to amend the contract by mailed notice or, alternatively, by posting a notice in all the bank branches. No comparable term appears in the earlier OAAs.

Paragraph 12 is a pot-pourri. The sentence purporting to bind all other accounts is neatly tucked away between items of conventional interpretation such that a true appreciation of the meaning of those phrases would require a careful and prudent reading of the paragraph. Given the circumstances in which the document was created and the fact that it was a project of the bank to have every customer execute one of these new OCAAs, it seems likely that the structure and design of this clause was no accident.

A significant feature of clause 12 is the power of amendment. In respect of the customer, the agreement may be excluded from effect on all other accounts provided the customer gives notice in writing. In respect of the bank, the agreement purports to grant a power of unilateral amendment of any term either by notice sent in the terms provided for the sending of statements of account or by a most curious procedure whereby the bank may post notices of amendment in all of its branches. This latter form of unilateral amendment might well be satisfactory for the notification to the public of general amendments to banking forms but, in this particular document, paragraph 12 purports to permit the bank to amend "this agreement." On a plain reading of the words, the bank appears to have reserved to itself the power to amend this specific contract with this specific customer in this unusual fashion.

The original old company had been doing business with the bank since 1967. The corporations and individuals involved in this litigation had been doing business with this bank since 1982 and Mr. Kay had dealings with Ms Esposito over about a three-year time span. It is clear from the comments made by the manager and the manager administration in Tab 39 of Exhibit I that the plaintiff was a good customer of the bank and it is clear from the evidence of Mr. Kay that the plaintiff, the corporations and the individuals had had many satisfactory dealings with the bank over the years.

Taking an overview of the entirety of the relationship between the plaintiff and the bank leading up to and including the execution of the new OCAA and, in particular, having regard to the manner in which Mr. Kay was examined in chief and cross-examined on the subject of his having relied upon the statements made by Ms Esposito, I am fully satisfied as to the truthfulness of that evidence. It is clear that Mr. Kay had read the 1982 and the 1986 OAAs. Given the nature of the agreement and the fact that it was a printed form in relatively small print, I would suspect many people might not ever read the form. The fact that Mr. Kay clearly had read both of the earlier forms suggests to me that he would have read the new OCAA, either then and there at the bank or at some later time, had something not happened to satisfy him that this was not necessary. Although the forgeries complained of in this case happened soon after the execution of this new OCAA, I think it is important to point out that clause 12 of the new agreement provides that the customer has the power to notify the bank in writing that the new agreement shall not govern all of the customer's accounts at the branches and offices of the bank and at the branches or offices of any wholly owned subsidiary. It was Mr. Kay's evidence that shortly after the execution of this document, he went on vacation to Scotland and that he did not return until the Friday prior to September 23, upon which day the fraud was uncovered. This suggests there was little opportunity for him to peruse the form at his leisure but, had he read the form at the time of execution or at any time thereafter, it would have been open to him to send a written notice, creating an exception for the plaintiff's other accounts. This was not done. He did not read the form. In fact, he was not even provided a copy to take away with him and read at his leisure. His first notice that the form was in some way different than the forms he had earlier executed arose only after the fraud had taken place and when the bank refused to honour payment for the forged cheques.

The general principle applicable to a contract of this sort is well set out by Lord Justice Scrutton in *L'Estrange v. F. Graucob Ltd.*, [1934] 2 K.B. 394 (C.A.), at p. 403:

> When a document containing contractual terms is signed, then, in the absence of fraud, or, I will add, misrepresentation, the party signing it is bound, and it is wholly immaterial whether he has read the document or not.

This principle was well-established in *Parker v. South Eastern Railway; Gabell v. South Eastern Railway* (1877), 2 C.P.D. 416 (C.A.), where Lord Justice Mellish laid down, at p. 421:

> In an ordinary case, where an action is brought on a written agreement which is signed by the defendant, the agreement is proved by proving his signature, and, in the absence of fraud, it is wholly immaterial that he has not read the agreement and does not know its contents.

Mr. Justice Dubin, speaking on behalf of the majority of the Ontario Court of Appeal in *Tilden Rent-A-Car Co. v. Clendenning* (1978), 4 B.L.R. 50, 18 O.R. (2d) 601, 83 D.L.R. (3d) 400 (C.A.), at p. 404 (D.L.R.) cited S.M. Waddams, *The Law of Contracts*, where the learned author stated, at p. 191 of his text:

> From the 19th century until recent times an extraordinary status has been accorded to the signed document that will be seen in retrospect, it is suggested, to have been excessive.

In the *Tilden Rent-A-Car* case, the court was dealing with a car rental contract executed at an airport under circumstances where the inference could be drawn that it was never intended for the customer to read the contract. Included in the contract, and for which consideration was specifically paid, were clauses that purported to afford insurance on the vehicle whereas other clauses purported to fasten liability for damage to the vehicle upon the customer in a manner the court found completely inconsistent with the express terms for insurance.

Counsel for the bank argued forcefully that this decision should be regarded as an anomaly and that the decision arose only out of the specific facts of that case where the plaintiff had created a standard form printed contract which was presented to the customer with the intent that it not be read and that, as maker of the document, the plaintiff had inserted clearly conflicting clauses which acted, in effect, to substantially deny the defendant the very thing he believed he had contracted to purchase.

I was referred to the cases of *Trigg v. MI Movers International Transport Services Ltd.* (1991), 2 B.L.R. (2d) 246, 4 O.R. (3d) 562, 84 D.L.R. (4th) 504, 50 O.A.C. 321 (C.A.), leave to appeal to S.C.C. refused (1992), 88 D.L.R. (4th) vii (note), 138 N.R. 410 (note) (S.C.C.), and *Hoffman v. Sportsman Yachts Inc.* (1992), 89 D.L.R. (4th) 600 (Ont. C.A.). In both of these cases the court struck down contracts under circumstances where the signer had not read the agreement and the contract contained limitation or exemption clauses which were onerous and which, if given effect, would have materially altered the bargain which the signer believed had been entered into. In both of these cases, the circumstances surrounding the execution of the document involved conduct of a representative of the maker which actively contributed to the signer's misunderstanding or ignorance of the terms of the limitation/exemption clauses. In the *Hoffman* decision, Galligan J.A., at p. 602, stated:

> Were it not for very important findings of fact made by the trial judge, the purchaser's failure to read cl. 9 would not entitle her to be freed from the burden of it.

The trial judge in the *Hoffman* case [reported at (1990), 47 B.L.R. 101 (Ont. Dist. Ct.), additional reasons at (August 17, 1990), Doc. York 335051/88 (Ont. Dist. Ct.)] had accepted the evidence of Mrs. Hoffman that the salesman of the vendor had actively misrepresented to her the contents of the clauses on the back of the form and that she had relied upon the salesman's misrepresentation. In the *Trigg* decision [(June 2, 1998), Doc. Toronto 18942/84, Ewaschuk J. (Ont. H.C.)], the trial judge found that the sales representative specifically informed Trigg that the defendant would only be liable for damage arising from its proven negligence, but otherwise its liability, such as for "act of God," was limited to $0.10 per pound per item. In fact, the limitation clause in question limited the carrier's liability to $0.10 per pound whether or not the damage resulted from negligence. Acting upon this, Trigg did not purchase marine insurance and, as such, when his Rolls-Royce and Ferrari were damaged to the extent of 20,000 Irish pounds, he was left at a considerable disadvantage.

In both cases, the Court of Appeal found that the signers of the contracts were not bound by the limitation clauses contained in those standard form contracts, notwithstanding that the contracts had been signed.

Mr. Justice Dubin in *Tilden Rent-A-Car*, at p. 404 (D.L.R.), wrote:

Consensus ad idem is as much a part of the law of written contract as it is of oral contracts. The signature to a contract is only one way of manifesting assent to contractual terms. [Emphasis in original.]

He went on at p. 404 to comment on the *L'Estrange* case as follows:

> The justification for the rule in *L'Estrange v. F. Graucob, Ltd.*, appears to have been founded upon the objective theory of contracts, by which means parties are bound to a contract in writing by measuring their conduct by outward appearance rather than what the parties inwardly meant to decide. This, in turn, stems from the classic statement of Blackburn, J., in *Smith v. Hughes* (1871), L.R. 6 Q.B. 597 at p. 607:
>
> > "I apprehend that if one of the parties intends to make a contract on one set of terms, and the other intends to make a contract on another set of terms, or, as it is sometimes expressed, if the parties are not ad idem, there is no contract, unless the circumstances are such as to preclude one of the parties from denying that he has agreed to the terms of the other. The rule of law is that stated in *Freeman v. Cooke* (1848), 2 Ex. 654 [at p. 663, 18 L.J. (Ex.) at p. 119], 154 E.R. 652. *If, whatever a man's real intention may be, he so conducts himself that a reasonable man would believe that he was assenting to the terms proposed by the other party, and that other party upon that belief enters into the contract with him, the man thus conducting himself would be equally bound as if he had intended to agree to the other party's terms.*" [Emphasis added by Dubin J.A. (as he then was).]

At pp. 406–407 (D.L.R.) in *Tilden Rent-A-Car*, Mr. Justice Dubin noted:

> An analysis of the Canadian cases, however, indicates that the approach in this country has not been so rigid. In the case of *Colonial Investment Co. of Winnipeg, Man. v. Borland*, [1911] 1 W.W.R. 171 at p. 189, 19 W.L.R. 588, 5 Alta. L.R. at p. 72 [affirmed 6 D.L.R. 21, 2 W.W.R. 960, 22 W.L.R. 145, 5 Alta. L.R. 71], Beck, J., set forth the following propositions:
>
> > "*Consensus ad idem* is essential to the creation of a contract, whether oral, in writing or under seal, subject to this, that as between the immediate parties (and merely voluntary assigns) apparent — as distinguished from real — consent will on the ground of estoppel effect a

binding obligation unless the party denying the obligation proves:

1) That the other party knew at the time of the making of the alleged contract that the mind of the denying party did not accompany the expression of his consent; or
2) Such facts and circumstances as show that it was not reasonable and natural for the other party to suppose that the denying party was giving his real consent and he did not in fact give it;"

In commenting on the *Colonial Investment Co. of Winnipeg v. Borland* case, Spencer, in the article above cited, observes at p. 121:

"It is instructive to compare a Canadian approach to the problem of confusing documents which are signed but not fully understood."

And at p. 122 the author concludes his article with the following analysis:

"Policy considerations, but of different kinds, no doubt lay behind both the Canadian and the English approaches to this problem. The Canadian court was impressed by the abuses which would result — and, in England, *have* resulted — from enabling companies to hold ignorant signatories to the letter of sweeping exemption clauses contained in contracts in standard form. The English courts, however, were much more impressed with the danger of furnishing an easy line of defence by which liars could evade contractual liabilities freely assumed. It would be very dangerous to allow a man over the age of legal infancy to escape from the legal effect of a document he has, after reading it, signed, in the absence of any express misrepresentation by the other party of that legal effect. Forty years later, most lawyers would admit that the English courts made a bad choice between two evils." [Emphasis in original.]

Mr. Justice Dubin went on at p. 407 (D.L.R.):

I see no real distinction in contracts such as these, where the signature by itself does not truly represent an acquiescence of unusual and onerous terms which are inconsistent with the true object of the contract, and the ticket cases.

In his decision, he went on to cite *Canadian Bank of Commerce v. Foreman*, [1927] 2 D.L.R. 530 (C.A.), and *Jaques v. Lloyd D. George & Partners Ltd.*, [1968] 1 W.L.R. 625 (C.A.). He also quoted [at p. 408, D.L.R.] the comments by Professor Waddams

on the *Jaques* decision and on the case of *O'Connor Real Estate Ltd. v. Flynn* (1969), 3 D.L.R. (3d) 345 (N.S. Co. Ct.), affirmed (1970), 1 N.S.R. (2d) 949, 11 D.L.R. (3d) 559 (C.A.), at pp. 590–591 of 49 Can. Bar Rev., where the author wrote:

These cases suggest that there is a special onus on the supplier to point out any terms in a printed form which differ from what the consumer might reasonably expect. If he fails to do so, he will be guilty of a 'misrepresentation by omission', and the court will strike down clauses which 'differ from the ordinary understanding of mankind' or (and sometimes this is the same thing) clauses which are 'unreasonable or oppressive'. If this principle is accepted, the rule about written documents might be restated as follows: the signer is bound by the terms of the document if, and only if, the other party believes on reasonable grounds that those terms truly express the signer's intention. This principle retains the role of signed documents as a means of protecting reasonable expectations; what it does not allow is that a party should rely on a printed document to contradict what he knows, or ought to know, is the understanding of the other party. Again this principle seems to be particularly applicable in situations involving the distribution of goods and services to consumers, though it is by no means confined to such situations."

Mr. Justice Dubin, in commenting further, stated at p. 408 (D.L.R.):

In modern commercial practice, many standard form printed documents are signed without being read or understood. In many cases the parties seeking to rely on the terms of the contract know or ought to know that the signature of a party to the contract does not represent the true intention of the signer, and that the party signing is unaware of the stringent and onerous provisions which the standard form contains. Under such circumstances, I am of the opinion that the party seeking to rely on such terms should not be able to do so in the absence of first having taken reasonable measures to draw such terms to the attention of the other party, and, in the absence of such reasonable measures, it is not necessary for the party denying knowledge of such terms to prove either fraud, misrepresentation or *non est factum*. [Emphasis in original.]

In modern banking, many of the repetitious transactions have been hardened into standard form documentation created by the bank for convenience, ease and speed in allowing the transactions to be completed. There are many complex transactions between a customer and a bank which, of necessity, might well suggest that the customer could negotiate the terms of the transaction and, if confronted with pre-printed standard forms, that the customer might well be placed on guard to read the documentation in order to be satisfied that the bargain has been properly expressed. There are, however, many routine and daily transactions in which the customer has little contemplation that any negotiation can take place and, when confronted by the standard printed forms presented by the bank, they have no knowledge that on some limited occasions, the bank might be prepared to accede to a change in wording. In what I might call a "common or garden" transaction such as opening a current account, few customers would know that there might be room for some negotiation on terms and, when confronted by the bank's pre-prepared printed forms for what must, to most customers, appear to be a simple and straightforward matter, they would simply execute the documents without taking the fairly lengthy amount of time necessary to read the relatively small print on the two-sided sheet.

In the case at bar, the bank had active knowledge that Mr. Kay did not read the new OCAA prior to its execution. By making the general inquiry as to the nature and purpose of the document, Mr. Kay placed upon the bank the responsibility to answer accurately or not to answer at all. By her response, Ms Esposito not only failed to answer accurately, but she answered in a manner which effectively disguised the nature of the changes in the new OCAA and concealed the purpose for those changes as well as the true intent of the bank in wishing to have all of its current account customers execute the new form.

Unlike the car rental agreements, or ticket cases, or cases of similar circumstance, I do not think that one can conclude that dealings with a bank should fall into that group of cases where it is expected that terms and conditions will not be read. However, it is my view that once the customer, and in particular a customer of longstanding relationship, makes an honest enquiry touching upon the content and purpose of a pre-prepared bank form, there is a responsibility upon the bank to either decline to comment or give advice hence signalling to the customer to satisfy itself or give an accurate and forthright explanation of the form and, if there are terms of the proposed agreement which are of a limiting or exempting nature, or terms which are unusual or onerous, or which might place new or unexpected obligations upon the customer, that the customer's attention should be drawn to those clauses. The decision to read the document or not to read the document remains with the customer, but the bank must not actively engage in a course of conduct that could reasonably be construed as encouraging the customer not to read the form or, as happened at the case at bar, to render a partial and inaccurate answer which was effectively misleading in a circumstance where it was known that the form was not read.

In the result, I find that the conduct of Ms Esposito was such as to discourage the reading of the form in question. The new OCAA was not similar to the old OAA entered into by the plaintiff. The terms and provisions of clause 5(b) had been so radically altered as to virtually reverse the effect of the comparable clause in the earlier agreement. In addition, the amendments to 5(b) imposed upon this plaintiff a requirement of a complete revamping of its internal office and bookkeeping procedures in order to comply with the bank's new requirements.

Similarly, the provisions of clause 12 were a radical departure from the comparable provisions in the old OAA. Perhaps the most offensive of those changes was the purported unilateral power of amendment afforded the bank, and in particular the unique power of amending a private agreement by a public notice.

It is my conclusion that in all the circumstances of this case, the bank contributed directly to the failure of a consensus ad idem by its representative embarking upon a partial and inaccurate description of the document to be executed. The plaintiff could not reasonably have been expected to be aware of and assent to clauses 5(b) and 12 of the standard form contract and, as such, the bank may not rely upon those terms and provisions and is not entitled to any benefit which might have accrued to it therefrom.

I find that the terms and provisions of the OAA entered into by the parties on October 27, 1982 (which may be found as the 7th page in Tab 71 of Exhibit 1) constitutes the agreement as between the plaintiff and the defendant and that each is bound by the terms and provisions of that agreement as it may apply to the facts of this case. This document was specifically executed by the plaintiff to apply to the 1982 current account. This agreement, as a result of my conclusion, has not been altered or amended and at the time of the acceptance by the bank of the forged cheques presented by Mr. Lang, the affairs of the parties were governed by that agreement and none other.

In the case of *Don Bodkin Leasing Ltd. v. Toronto Dominion Bank* (1993), 14 O.R. (3d) 571 (Gen. Div.), the plaintiff had executed an operation of account agreement containing the same provisions as clauses 5(a) and 5(b) of the October 27, 1982 OAA executed by the plaintiff in this action.

In the *Don Bodkin Leasing* case, the plaintiff was a customer of the Toronto-Dominion Bank and was also the victim of a fraud carried out by its own accountant. Among other acts of fraud, some were the drawing of forged cheques on the plaintiff's own bank account, which cheques were honoured by the defendant bank.

Mr. Justice Ewaschuk, at p. 578, held:

> A bank has two principle duties to its customers:
>
> (1) the duty to honour cheques that are properly drawn on the customer's account if the customer has a credit balance exceeding the amount of the drawn cheque; and
>
> (2) a duty to exercise a reasonable standard of care, *i.e.*, to act as a prudent banker would act in the circumstances.
>
> Where the two duties conflict, the latter is the higher duty: *Corporate Bank & Trust Co. (Official Liquidators) v. Toronto-Dominion Bank*, [1987] O.J. No. 418 (H.C.J.). [Emphasis in original.]

He went on to consider the effect of s. 49(1) and s. 49(3) of the *Bills of Exchange Act* and set out the law, at p. 579, as follows:

> A bank may honour cheques which are signed by an authorized signing officer as reflected, in the case of a corporate customer, in its banking resolution. In order to process cheques, the bank requires specimen signatures of the authorized signing officers named in the banking resolution supplied to the bank.
>
> If a bank accepts and pays out customers' funds on a forged or unauthorized signature, the bank is liable to the customer for the funds improperly paid out. In fact, the forged or unauthorized signature renders the cheque inoperative: see s. 49(1) of the *Bills of Exchange Act*, [now] R.S.C. 1985, c. B-4, as interpreted by *Arrow Transfer Co. v. Royal Bank of Canada*, [1972] S.C.R. 845, 27 D.L.R. (3d) 81. Furthermore, the customer may recover damages from the bank for the improper payment of the forged cheque if the customer notifies the bank in writing of the improper payment within one year after the customer has acquired notice of the forgery: see s. 49(3) of the *Bills of Exchange Act*.
>
> The above common law and statutory rules are subject to displacement by contract.

At p. 580, Ewaschuk J. went on to consider the force and effect of what is clause 5(b) of the OAA. Upon citing the provisions of 5(a) and 5(b) as recited above, he went on to state [at pp. 580–581]:

> In this case, the verification clause stipulates that the bank will be *"released from all claims* by the Customer in respect of"errors in the monthly statement. I am satisfied that this clause is broad enough to release the bank from a claim in negligence even though express reference would be required to release it from a claim for breach of trust: see *Claibourne Industries Ltd. v. National Bank of Canada* (1986), 55 O.R. (2d) 289 at p. 310, 28 D.L.R. (4th) 695 (H.C.J.). [Emphasis in original.]

The learned judge went on to deal with forgeries and wrote as follows, at pp. 581–582:

> It is now accepted that a customer owes no common law duty to a bank to implement internal controls which will disclose a fraud committed by the customer's employee in respect of a transaction for which a debit is made to the customer's account and entered on the monthly statement: see *Canadian Pacific Hotels Ltd. v. Bank of Montreal*, [1987] 1 S.C.R. 711, 41 C.C.L.T. 1. A customer only owes its bank two common law duties: (1) the duty to use reasonable care in drawing a cheque so as to avoid facilitating fraud or forgery of the cheque; and (2) the duty to inform the bank of any forgery of a cheque purportedly drawn on the account within one year of the customer gaining actual knowledge of the forgery, or otherwise within a reasonable time of the customer discovering the forgery: see *Greenwood v. Martins Bank Ltd.*, [1933] A.C. 51, [1932] All E.R. Rep. 318 (H.L.); and s. 49(3) of the *Bills of Exchange Act*.
>
> It is also accepted that the bank may expressly impose a contractual duty on the customer to implement internal controls so that errors on the monthly statement will be detected within a reasonable time: see *Canadian Pacific Hotel, supra*, at p. 777. The question then arises as to whether the verification clause applicable here imposed such duty on Bodkin Leasing.

In the case at bar, there is no question of the forgery. Each of the four cheques payable to Commodity Services Group was admitted to be a forgery and there is no issue that they were presented at the bank and honoured by the bank. Notice of the forgery by telephone and by writing was promptly given by the plaintiff in full compliance with clauses 5(a) and 5(b) of their contractual agreement.

Under the circumstances, all of the terms and provisions of the OAA were met by the plaintiff and the bank was in breach of its duties to its customer by accepting and paying out the customer's funds on a forged and unauthorized signature. The bank was in possession of the banking resolution of the plaintiff and the authorizing by-law together with samples of the signatures of the signing officers and a fully-executed OAA signed by each of Henry Kay, Seymour Baum, and Peter Cooling.

The cheque dated September 3, 1991 in the amount of $19,689.37 is to be found at Tab 24 of Exhibit 1. The signature of the drawer is admittedly forged. A photostat of the back of the cheque demonstrates that there is no endorsement per se and that someone has written "for deposit only 25.04413."

The second cheque dated September 10, 1991 in the amount of $35,025.28 is drawn with a forged signature of the drawer and a photostatic copy of the back of the cheque again demonstrates no actual endorsement but the words "for deposit only acct. 25.04413" appears. This cheque is to be found at Tab 27 of Exhibit 1.

The third cheque dated September 13, 1991 is to be found at Tab 31 of Exhibit 1. The forged signature of the drawer is in the name of Seymour Baum and the amount of the cheque is $45,987.46. Again, a copy of the back of that cheque shows no endorsement but the notation appears "deposit only to account 25.04413."

The fourth cheque appears at Tab 37 of Exhibit 1. The forged signature of the drawer is in the name of Seymour Baum. This cheque is dated September 17, 1991 and is in the amount of $29,541.11. A photostat of the back of the cheque demonstrates no endorsement, but it is noted "for deposit only acct. 25-04413."

It is common ground of the parties that Commodities Services Group is a fictitious payee. The total amount paid to the credit of this fictitious payee was $130,243.22.

None of the four cheques was endorsed and nothing appears on the back of any of those cheques that allows identification of an endorsee. The cheques were all payable to order, and, in effect, the bank accepted four unendorsed cheques from an unnamed payee or endorsee. In the *Don Bodkin Leasing* case, Mr. Justice Ewaschuk found this to be negligence and relied upon the decision in *Booth Fisheries Canadian Co. v. Banque provinciale du Canada* (1972), 7 N.B.R. (2d) 138 (Q.B.).

I find that the bank was both negligent and in breach of its duty to its customer in accepting the four cheques with the forged signatures of the drawer and unendorsed by the named payee or its representative.

Mr. Lang was subsequently convicted under his true name of Kenneth James Shockley. A restitution order was made by the court of conviction which was identified to me by Mr. Kay as being Item 3 in the amount of $130,243.22 on the fourth page of Tab 69 of Exhibit 1, and the notation of the plea of guilty is to be found on the fifth page of that same tab. The conclusion which I find, on the balance of probabilities, to be correct, is that the forger, Mr. Shockley, masquerading as Mr. Lang, created the four forged cheques and deposited them in account 25-04413 of the Canadian Imperial Bank of Commerce, Lawrence and Keele branch, unendorsed, for deposit only, which cheques were subsequently cleared and accepted by the bank. It was the evidence of Mr. Kay that the plaintiff had been unable to pursue the funds as they had been removed by Mr. Shockley and, although a restitution order was given, no money was ever paid or recovered.

The bank, as drawee, has clearly accepted as an endorsement on the back of each cheque "for deposit only acct. 25-04413." The payee to order on the cheque was fictitious and so the deposit endorsement on the back must also have been fictitious and fraudulent and, in accepting the forged signatures of the drawers and in accepting the fictitious note of endorsement for deposit of the fictitious payee, the defendant has, by its breach of duty and by its negligence, facilitated the fraudulent scheme of Mr. Shockley.

I therefore find that the defendant is liable to the plaintiff on each of the four cheques and the plaintiff shall have judgment against the defendant in the amount of $130,243.22.

Judgment in this matter having been reserved, I may be spoken to on the issues of prejudgment interest and costs.

Action allowed.

[The decision was appealed but dismissed. Following is the judgment given by the Ontario Court of Appeal on June 6, 1997, delivered by OSBORNE J.A.:]

In our view the trial judge's finding that the Bank misrepresented the terms of the 1991 agreement by describing them as "similar" to the 1986 document was fully supported by the evidence be found to the credible. The two documents are in fact significantly different in so far as the respective liabilities of the Bank and the respondent were concerned.

This finding was determinative of the Bank's liability. The appeal must be dismissed with costs.

Appeal dismissed.

(e) *Royal Bank v. Holoboff*†

[MASON J.:]

INTRODUCTION

This is an appeal from a decision of the Provincial Court of Alberta. At issue in the case is the liability of an infant in contract or in tort arising out of a fraudulent use by a third party of the infant's bank card with the full knowledge and complicity of the infant. There is also an issue of unjust enrichment with respect to recoverable damages and what principles are to be applied in assessing the recovery.

NATURE OF ACTION

This is a claim by the Appellant Royal Bank of Canada ("the Bank") for the sum of $4,931.83 plus interest, from the Respondent, Colin Holoboff. The Bank voluntarily reduced the claim to $4,000.00 pursuant to a Notice of Abandonment executed by the Bank to grant jurisdiction to the Provincial Court for the trial of the proceedings. The Notice of Abandonment was executed pursuant to Section 36(1)(a) of the *Provincial Court Act*, R.S.A. 1980 c. P-20.

FACTS

On July 2nd, 1990, Colin Holoboff opened a Bonus Savings Account at the Deer Valley Branch of the Bank. He was a minor at the time. At all times material to these proceedings, he was still a minor. Shortly following the time he opened it, he received from the Bank a bank client card and executed a Personal Security Code Entry Identification Agreement and selected a personal identification number (commonly referred to as "a PIN number"). He also executed an account signature card agreement and acknowledged receipt of the Personal Deposit Account Agreement and Operating Conditions. The account had no overdraft privileges and there were no loan agreements between Mr. Holoboff and the Bank.

The terms of agreement of the client as set out in the Personal Security Code Entry Identification Agreement are, in material part, as follows:

1. **APPLICATION**: This agreement will apply to each Transaction executed by the use of a Card together with my code.
2. **CODE PRIVACY**: I shall keep my Code confidential at all times.
3. **OTHER RESPONSIBILITIES**: I shall be solely responsible for the security, care and safe preservation of each Card and my Code at all times. I shall restrict the use of any such Card together with such Code to my sole personal use.

...

7. **DEPOSITS**: All cash, cheques and other negotiable instruments ('instruments') placed in your banking machines for deposit or credit to an Account pursuant to a Transaction shall be at my sole risk until the time when such instruments, having first been removed therefrom and then counted and verified by you, are accepted and entered by you as a deposit or credit or are otherwise dealt with by you.

...

11. **LIABILITY**: I shall be liable for all indebtedness and all other obligations arising from or created in connection with each Transaction executed by the use of a Card together with my Code. Where such use is an unauthorized use resulting from the loss or theft of a Card, I shall remain liable to you for all such indebtedness and obligations incurred immediately prior to the time notification by me of such loss or theft has been received and acknowledged by you.

...

13. **OTHER AGREEMENTS**: The terms and conditions of my Royal Bank Client Cardholder Agreement with you and the agreements, rules, regulations and conditions governing the operation of each Account shall remain in full force and effect and shall apply to each Transaction except as expressly modified by the terms of this Agreement.

Further, in the same Agreement of the Bank, the following relevant definitions are provided in Clause 15:

Account — means a deposit account or a credit, charge of payment card account I have with you ... in my name, whether now maintained, opened

---

† (1998), 39 B.L.R. (2d) 193 (Alta. Q.B.).

today or opened in the future by me in respect to which a Transaction may be executed by the use of a Card together with my Code at a banking machine or banking terminal in the Network.

Card — means a Royal Bank Client Card ... you have issued to me or may in the future issue to me which together with my Code may be used to execute a Transaction at either or both a banking machine and banking terminal (as the case may be) in the Network including any and all renewals of such Card.

Network — means the network banking machines and banking terminals operated by the Royal Bank or operated by others and offered through the bank from time to time for purpose of permitting the execution of a Transaction.

Transaction — means a withdrawal or cash advance from an Account, a deposit or credit to an Account, payment from an Account or a transfer between Accounts executed by the use of a Card together with my Code at a bank machine or banking terminal in the Network.

The following facts were found by the learned trial judge and are not in dispute:

The Defendant, who was 17 years old at the time of this Court hearing, gave evidence that in 1995 he was approached by a student ("Student") at his high school. The Student offered to buy his Client Card together with his PIN number for the sum of $100. The Defendant initially turned down the offer, but when that Student persisted and increased the offer to $500, the Defendant accepted the offer. The Defendant was advised by the Student should he be contacted by the Bank in respect of his Client Card, he should report the Client Card lost or Stolen. In any event, the Defendant was instructed by the Student not to report his Client Card lost or stolen before November 14, 1995. The Student advised the Defendant that as he was under the age of majority the Bank would have no recourse against him.

The Defendant confirmed that he gave the Student his Client Card together with his PIN number on Friday November 11, 1995. He was paid $500 by the Student on Tuesday, November 15, 1995.

An officer of the Bank gave evidence to show the history of the Defendant's Account transactions from November 11 to 14, 1995 inclusive, including:

(1) A deposit in the sum of $5,000.00 on the tenth day of November, 1995, and
(2) Cash withdrawals in the sum of $400.00 each occurring on November 11, 12, 13, and 14, 1995, and

(3) A statement showing various point of sale purchases made using the Defendant's Card and dated the 14th November, 1995

The total for (2) and (3) above is the sum of $4,931.83, which is the amount being claimed by the Bank.

The deposit in (1) above was discovered to be an empty envelope deposit by the Bank upon reconciling all transactions in the automatic teller machine (ATM) on the first business day after that November long weekend in 1995. An empty envelope deposit is a deposit made in an envelope at an ATM indicating that funds are enclosed when in fact the envelope is empty. Immediate efforts were made by officers of the Bank to contact the Defendant and the Client Card was 'hot carded'. The Defendant's Client Card had not been reported lost or stolen to the Bank by the Defendant prior to him being contacted on the 14th of November 1995. At the time he claimed that his Client Card had been lost or stolen. Upon the police becoming involved, the Defendant admitted to the police that he had in fact sold his Client Card and in addition had provided his PIN number, and he provided the name of the Student to the police. He advised this Court he had been dealt with by Youth Court, was found guilty of fraud, and is meeting parole requirements by way of prescribed alternative measures.

The Bank's officer alleged that it has been the victim of a series of similar frauds. It asserts that a client card is reported lost or stolen when in fact what, in the Bank's opinion has actually happened, is that the cardholder sold his/her client card and gave the PIN number to the purchaser. Upon being contacted by the Bank regarding outstanding charges to the account, the cardholder alleges that the card was either lost or stolen. If further investigation determines that the cardholder in fact cooperated in the arrangement by agreeing to sell his/her client card and provide his/her PIN number to a fraudulent third party, the cardholder then claims that the Bank is barred from recovery by the fact of the cardholder's infancy and lack of capacity.

THE PROVINCIAL COURT RULING

The learned trial judge determined that while the *Age of Majority Act*, RSA 1980 c. A-4, s. 2 provides that individuals in Alberta do not have contractual capacity before the age of 18, Section 437 of the *Bank Act*, SC 1991, does permit minors to contract with banks. Section 437(1) provides:

Deposit Acceptance

Deposit Acceptance — Exception — Execution of trust

437.(1) A bank may, without the intervention of any other person,

(a) accept a deposit from any person whether or not the person is qualified by law to enter into contracts; and

(b) pay all or part of the principal of the deposit and all or part of the interest thereon to or to the order of that person.

The learned trial judge went on to find that the phoney deposit made by the third party and subsequent withdrawal of funds by the fraudulent use of the Client Card and Security Code directly as a result of the actions of Mr. Holoboff and the third party should be characterized as an overdraft or loan and not damages arising from the breach of Mr. Holoboff's contractual obligations in his Agreement with the Bank. Further, the learned trial judge rejected the proposition of a tort issue based on wrongful conversion on the grounds that such relief by the law of contracts was unavailable.

The learned trial judge also held that the breach of the privacy provisions of the Personal Security Code and Entry Identification Agreement did not make Mr. Holoboff liable for all indebtedness and obligations arising from or in connection with the transactions executed with his Client Card, including the full amount sought by the Appellant Bank. Finally, with respect to damages, the learned trial judge determined that the only restitutionary remedy available for the fraud perpetrated on the Bank by Mr. Holoboff was limited to the sum received by Mr. Holoboff for the selling of his Client Card and Security Access Code (PIN number).

APPELLANT'S POSITION

The grounds of appeal submitted by the Bank can generally be divided into two main issues; the first being breach of contract and the second being conspiracy to commit fraud, In summary, the Bank's submissions regarding the first issue are that the learned trial judge erroneously characterized the transaction in this case as a loan by way of overdraft which constituted the contract in issue. The Bank submits that the agreement between the appellant and respondent made no provisions for an overdraft and there was no evidence that the respondent considered the withdrawals to be a loan or overdraft. The Bank contends that the more appropriate characterization of the withdrawals in this case is as damages that flow from the breach attributable to the respondent releasing his pin number contrary to the provisions of the agreement set out above.

Regarding the second issue, the appellant asserts that the learned trial judge erred because she held that it could not convert an action in contract into an action in tort in an attempt to get around the rule relevant to an infant's liability in contract. The appellant submits that the fraudulent use of the respondent's debit card by a third party with his assistance is not contemplated by the terms of the agreement. These circumstances place this case within the ambit of the law as applied by Judge O'Neil in *Royal Bank v. Robinson* (1997), 55 Alta. L.R. (3d) 127 (Alta. Prov. Ct.).

RESPONDENT'S POSITION

The respondent's position is grounded in the common law that has traditionally afforded protection to minors. That is that the respondent can avoid a contract that is not for necessaries even if the contract is for the benefit of the minor.

While the respondent accepts that s. 437(1) of the *Bank Act* permits contracts for deposits between a Bank and an individual "not qualified by law", which presumably includes a minor, he says that the activity must be restricted to acceptance and payment of deposits. In furtherance of this point, the respondent argues that the agreement between the parties in this case allows more than this narrow area of permitted activity because the agreement states that the respondent is "liable for all indebtedness and all other obligations arising from or created in connection with each Transaction executed by the use of a Card together with my Code." The agreement defines a Transaction as a "withdrawal or cash advance from an Account, a deposit or credit to an Account, payment from an Account or a transfer between Accounts executed by the use of a Card together with my Code at a bank machine or banking terminal in the Network." The respondent submits since that the appellant is not permitted under the *Bank Act* to contract with a minor outside this narrow area, the contract in question is void or voidable.

The thrust of the respondent's submission regarding the claim in tort is that the appellant may only claim an action in tort if the alleged wrong is independent of the contract. The underlying rationale is that the contract was instrumental in allowing the respondent to commit this tort; without the card and pin number which were obtained through execution of the contract, the tort would not have been possible.

DISCUSSION

The respective positions advanced by the parties concerning the role of contract in this case are interesting, however, a common sense approach indicates that the overriding concern is the alleged tortious conduct of the respondent. The contractual analysis, favourable to the respondent, is predicated upon the Learned Trial Judge's characterization of the transaction as a loan. At page 6 of her reasons, she said "[t]he supposed deposit of money and withdrawal of funds by an ATM such as was accomplished by the defendant or persons authorized by him in this particular case would fall into the category of an overdraft which is tantamount to a loan." Other than this brief conclusion, there is no apparent reasoning supporting the finding that this transaction is an overdraft or loan. While the definition of transaction contained in the agreement between the parties is very broad, it does not transform the fraud that took place into a loan. An "overdraft", according to M.H. Ogilvie in *Canadian Banking Law*, (Carswell: Toronto, 1991) at 464, is described as follows:

> An account in overdraft is legally characterized as a loan which is granted to the customer. It is the usual practice for a bank to authorize a customer to draw on the bank's funds via a deposit account up to a stipulated ceiling. An overdraft is for a stipulated sum for a stipulated period of time and at a stipulated rate of interest.
>
> ...
>
> An overdraft is a privilege granted by a banker to a customer, and may be granted by contract or by a course of dealing which has permitted overdrafts. A course of dealing may be established where a customer draws a cheque without having a sufficient balance, and the bank honours the cheque and creates a debit balance in the account. Such conduct is regarded as a request for an overdraft. Repetition of such conduct creates a course of dealing and the bank cannot terminate it without reasonable notice of a change of practice.

The agreement in question does not allow the respondent to draw on the bank's funds. Additionally, the essential ingredients of stipulated sum, time period and interest rate are missing. Similarly, the transaction cannot reasonably be considered to be an overdraft by a course of conduct. There is no history between the parties necessary to form the basis of a course of dealing. Furthermore, it is critical when granting an overdraft that the bank know the customer does not have sufficient funds available and is consciously allowing the customer to use its funds. Obviously, this element is missing because the appel-

lant had no knowledge that the respondent lacked sufficient funds until after the empty envelope was opened. Therefore, the contract under consideration is not a loan contract but rather an agreement to make deposits and withdraw funds on deposit. This is within the reach of s. 437 of the *Bank Act*.

Consequently, this does not mean that the appellant's argument based in contract would not be successful, but, in light of my findings regarding the tort issue, it is unnecessary to consider these arguments.

The learned trial judge refrained from considering the tort issues because she held that since the taking of funds was "within the purview of the [appellant's] contractual arrangement with the [respondent], and based on similar cases, the Bank, in this case cannot recover damages: *Dickson Brothers U-Drive Ltd. v. Woo* (1957), 23 W.W.R. 485 (B.C. C.A.)." In doing so, the learned trial judge erred in law; the cases she based this decision on clearly contemplate recovery of damages in tort where the conduct of the tortfeasor is outside what is normally contemplated by the contract. The appellant relied on *Robinson, supra* not only for the legal principles espoused in it but also because the fact pattern is remarkably similar to the case at bar where an infant had given his card and pin number to another infant who made a phoney deposit and subsequent withdrawals. In *Robinson, supra*, the defendant was to share in the spoils of the other infant's tortious conduct. In that case Judge O'Neil made the following comments:

> It is unnecessary to analyze the scheme described by the defendant further to conclude that it contains the essential elements of both fraud and conspiracy.
>
> To the tort argument an infant defendant may argue that the plaintiff cannot convert an action based on contract into an action in tort for the purpose of getting around the rule relative to infant's liability in contract. If the defendant is entitled to make any argument based on contract in view of his participation in defrauding the plaintiff, which in my opinion he is not, this argument would be met in any case by the reasoning cited by the British Columbia Court of Appeal in *Dickson Bros. Garage and U Drive Limited v. Woo Jai Jing* (1957), 23 W.W.R. 485.
>
> In *Leslie Ltd. v. Sheill* [1914] 3 K.B. 607 at 620, 83 LJKB 1145, Kennedy L. J. adopted the following distinction between the two lines of cases drawn by Sir Frederick Pollock in his work on Contracts, 8th ed., p. 78:

He [i.e., the infant] cannot be sued for a wrong when the cause of action is in substance *ex contractu*, or is so directly connected with the contract that the action would be an indirect way of enforcing the contract — which, as in the analogous case of married women, the law does not allow. But if an infant's wrongful act, though concerned with the subject-matter of a contract, and such that but for the contact there would have been no opportunity of committing it, is nevertheless independent of the contract in the sense of not being an act of the kind contemplated by it, then the infant is liable.

Lord Greene, MR, applied the sage test in *Ballett v. Mingay* [1943] K.B. 281, 112 LJKB 193, to distinguish *Jennings v. Rundle, supra*, and *Burnard v. Haggis supra*. There an infant was sued in detinue for failing to retain goods which had been loaned to him on terms which did not permit him to part with possession of them. Contrary to the terms of the bailment he did so.

In holding the infant liable Lord Greene said, p. 145:

On that basis, there is a remedy against the infant in tort because the circumstances in which the goods passed from his possession and ultimately disappeared were circumstances outside the purview of the contract of bailment altogether or, at any rate, were not shown by him to be within it.

The client card and PIN are incidental to the bank account. They provided the means of perpetrating the fraud and it would not have been possible to perpetrate it without them but the use of the card and PIN in the manner in which they were used was not what was contemplated by any of terms I have assumed the contract would have contained. The plaintiff's claim is for breach of contract. It has not made out that case. The facts support liability in tort. I am therefore amending the Civil Claim to include a claim based on conspiracy to defraud the plaintiff. The plaintiff is entitled to judgment against the defendant for damages in the sum of $4,000 plus interest on that amount from December 23, 1995 and its court costs of $25.

In the case at bar, no speculation as to the terms the contract would have contained is necessary. The terms relevant to this discussion are found in paragraphs 2 and 3 of the agreement as reproduced above. Paragraph 2 mandates that the respondent keep his pin number confidential at all times and paragraph 3 requires the respondent to restrict the use of his card to his personal use only. The respondent's actions of selling his card and revealing his pin number for profit were clearly outside the contemplation of the agreement. I find the interpretation of the case law by Judge O'Neil to be an accurate reflection of the true state of the law in this area and as a result, find that the appellant's tort claim is well founded in law.

The learned Trial Judge found that the respondent was advised by the other student that he would be immune from action by the bank by virtue of his infancy. Other facts as found by the trial judge demonstrate that either the respondent had actual knowledge of the fraud to be perpetrated against the appellant or was wilfully blind to the consequences of his actions. Either way, the conspiracy element is made out. Again reference is made to the comments of Judge O'Neil in *Robinson, supra* where he sets out the meaning of conspiracy in this context:

A definition of conspiracy is contained in the judgment of the Appellate Division of the Alberta Supreme Court in *McKinnon v. F. W. Woolworth and Johnston and Matt Jordison and Commercial Fidelity Audit Agency* (1969), 66 W.W.R. 205 in which Johnson J.A. states at p. 213

The passages I have quoted from the Crofter case, supra leave no doubt that the tort of conspiracy is broader than textbook writers and commentators have suggested and is broad enough to give a cause of action where there has been an agreement to commit an unlawful act or do an otherwise lawful act in an unlawful manner provided that damage results to the person against whom the conspiracy is formed.

DISPOSITION

There is no room for doubt in the present context that the elements necessary to establish the tort of conspiracy to commit fraud have been established by the appellant. Accordingly, I reverse the decision of the Learned Provincial Court Judge and enter judgment in favour of the appellant and against the respondent for $4,000. plus interest and costs.

Appeal allowed.

(f) *Arab Bank Ltd. v. Barclays Bank*†

[LORD REID:]

My Lords, before May 15, 1948, Jerusalem was part of the territory governed under the British mandate for Palestine. The respondents, who are a British bank, had a branch office at Allenby Square in Jerusalem, and the appellants, a bank whose head office is now situated in the territory of the Hashemite Kingdom of Jordan, were then carrying on business at the Morcos building within the Old City. Under an agreement of 1939 the appellants had a current account with the respondents at their Allenby Square branch, and on May 14, 1948, there was a credit balance on that account in favour of the appellants of £P582,931.

The British mandate came to an end at midnight, May 14–15, 1948. The new State of Israel was then set up and immediately war broke out between that State and the Arab States, including the Hashemite Kingdom. Allenby Square was in territory occupied by Israeli forces but the appellants' place of business was in territory occupied by forces of the Hashemite Kingdom.

It is admitted that on all questions relevant to the decision of this case there is no difference between the law of England, the law of Palestine, and the law of Israel which superseded the law of Palestine in the territory occupied by the Israeli forces. So it is necessary to determine what under English law is the effect of the outbreak of war on a current account kept by a bank in this country for a customer resident in enemy territory.

The general principle is not in dispute. With certain exceptions the outbreak of war prevents the further performance of contracts between persons in this country and persons in enemy territory. It is not merely that an enemy cannot sue during the war, and that trading and intercourse with the enemy during the war are illegal. Many kinds of contractual rights are totally abrogated by the outbreak of war and do not revive on its termination. On the other hand, there are other kinds of contractual rights which are not abrogated; they cannot be enforced during the war, but war merely suspends the right to enforce them and they remain and can be enforced after the war.

There is indeed no such general proposition as that a state of war avoids all contracts between subjects and enemies. Accrued rights are not affected though the right of suing in respect thereof is suspended. Further there are certain contracts, particularly those which are really the concomitants of rights of property, which even so far as executory are not abrogated.

Ertel Bieber & Co. v. Rio Tinto Co. Ld.,[1] *per* Lord Dunedin.

The first question in this case is whether the appellants' right to obtain payment of the sum at their credit on their current account was totally abrogated by the outbreak of war or whether that right was merely suspended. For a reason which will appear later, the appellants say that their right was totally abrogated, but the respondents say that it was merely suspended: the appellants say that their right was not an "accrued right"; the respondents say that it was. In the case of *Ertel Bieber & Co.*[2] it was not necessary to consider precisely the scope of the exception of accrued rights from abrogation: it appears to be an extension of the principle that rights of property are not destroyed or confiscated on the outbreak of war. A right to payment of money due under a contract is not strictly speaking a right of property — the creditor has no property in the debtor's money before it is paid to him — but if before the outbreak of war the creditor had an immediate and unqualified right to sue the debtor for money due under a contract then it is not disputed that such a right is suspended but is not abrogated. The creditor in such a case has not only an accrued right but an accrued right of action. But the appellants' right in this case fell short of that, and I must now consider first what was the appellants' right immediately before the outbreak of war.

In *Joachimson v. Swiss Bank Corporation*[3] the firm N. Joachimson had a current account with the defendant bank. On August 1, 1914, the firm was dissolved by the death of one of the partners and on that date a balance of £2,321 was standing to the credit of the firm. Later one of the partners raised an action in the firm name to recover that sum, but

---

† [1954] A.C. 495 (H.L.). [Notes omitted.]

for some reason he gave an undertaking that the only causes of action relied on arose on or before August 1, 1914. His action failed because, although the customer's account was then in credit, the customer had then no cause of action against the bank. The case decides, in my judgment rightly, that a customer must make a demand for payment at the branch where his current account is kept before he has a cause of action against the bank. Generally it is the duty of a debtor to seek out his creditor and tender the amount of his debt, but there is nothing to prevent parties from agreeing, if they wish, that that shall not be the duty of the debtor, and it was held that a contract of current account necessarily implies an agreement that that shall not be the bank's duty; otherwise the whole object of the contract would be frustrated. The balance at the customer's credit is only payable at the branch where the current account is kept and so the customer must go there or send his instructions there before he can get his money.

At one stage of this case the appellants maintained that they had made a demand for payment before the outbreak of war, but they do not now maintain that and therefore the position is that at the outbreak of war they had no cause of action against the respondents. But in my judgment that does not mean that there was no debt owing to them by the respondents. The sum at their credit was immediately payable to them. It is true that it was only payable in a particular place and that to get the money they had to go there and ask for it, but the case is in my opinion quite different from a case where one party still has to perform some service or fulfil some obligation under the contract in order to earn the money. In such a case further performance of such contractual obligation being prevented by frustration that party can never do what is necessary to earn the money and so can never acquire a right to have it paid to him; nothing was owing to him when the war broke out, so there is no "accrued right" to suspend.

But the sum at the credit of a customer on current account has always been regarded as a debt due by the bank to the customer. In *Rogers v. Whiteley*[4] the respondent was a banker, a judgment debtor had a credit on current account with him and a garnishee order attached "all debts owing or accruing due" from him to the judgment debtor. There was no suggestion that the word "debts" in Ord. 45, r. 1, is used in any special sense, and Lord Halsbury L.C. said[5] that the order attached "all debts, that is to say all money which Mr. Whiteley could be called upon

to pay away." In *Plunkett v. Barclays Bank Ld.*[6] du Parcq J. (as he then was) said:

I find it impossible to say that money paid into a client account kept with a bank in the name of a solicitor is not a debt owing from the banker to the solicitor. It cannot be denied that the relation of debtor and creditor subsists between the bank and the solicitor. The solicitor may at any time draw a cheque upon the account and the bank must honour it.

In *Swiss Bank Corporation v. Bochmische Industrial Bank*[7] Scrutton L.J. said:

Does this debt of £9,000 arise in this country? It is a sum held by a banker, who is resident in this country, for his customer and not payable until it is demanded in this country. In my view that is a debt arising in this country and situate in this country.

And Atkin L.J.[8] (as he then was) referred to that debt as "property." In *Richardson v. Richardson*[9] Hill J. cited several cases where judges of great authority have referred to sums due on current account as "debts" or "property."

It was argued that although that may have been the view generally held before *Joachimson's* case,[10] that decision shows that all that the customer of a bank really has is a right to create a debt by performing a condition of the contract of current account, i.e., making a demand for payment. But eminent judges who do not use inaccurate language have since that case continued habitually to refer to sums due on current account as debts although no demand for payment has been made. Indeed, I think that in *Joachimson's* case[11] Atkin L.J. recognized that there is a debt before any demand for payment is made, for he said:

It was suggested in argument that the effect of our decision will be to alter the facilities given to an execution creditor to attach his debtor's bank account in garnishee proceedings. This appears to be a mistake. The provisions of Order 45 apply to debts owing or accruing from the garnishee, and this expression includes debts to which the judgment debtor is entitled though they are not presently payable.

There is no suggestion of any anomaly in treating a sum at credit on current account as a debt for the purpose of garnishee proceedings and I do not see the point of the last part of the passage I have just quoted unless Atkin L.J. regarded such a sum as in fact a debt to which the judgment debtor is entitled but which is not presently payable. It is clear that the existence of a debt does not depend on there being a present right to sue for it. *Debitum in presenti, solvendum in futuro* is a familiar concept and a demand for payment is in my view merely that which makes the debt *solvendum*.

In *Schering Ld. v. Stockholms Enskilda Bank Aktiebolag*[12] a debt was payable by instalments and when war broke out some of the instalments were not yet payable. The right to payment of those instalments was held not to have been abrogated in spite of certain specialities in the case. The view of the majority of the House with regard to the contract was that "all that remained was the payment of the price, and the only provisions remaining operative related to the payment of the debt due in respect of the price, and the relative safeguards for its payment" (*per* Lord Thankerton[13]). The preservation of debts from abrogation is to some extent anomalous and I agree with what Lord Goddard said:[14]

> Now one of the reasons why a suspensory clause to operate in the event of war in a contract for the sale of goods to an enemy will not save the performance of the contract from abrogation as illegal is that to ensure to an enemy a supply of goods or raw material after the war is or may be to enhance his resources during the war. If this consideration were taken to its full logical extent it might be said to apply to debts, as it would certainly be of some benefit to an enemy to have an English debt remaining due to him even though it is not payable till the end of the war. He might be able to raise money from neutrals upon an assignment of his rights which could be enforced at the conclusion of the war. But this doctrine never has been applied to debts arising out of previous contracts, and I am not prepared now for the first time to apply it and to hold that accrued causes of action are destroyed and not suspended because otherwise an enemy might obtain a discount or some other benefit by reason of the continued existence of the obligation.

But I think that Lord Goddard went too far in referring to "accrued causes of action": in *Schering's* case[15] there can have been no accrued cause of action at the outbreak of war because the instalments in question had not then become payable.

Accordingly, I am of opinion that on May 15, 1948, there was a debt of £P582,931 due by the respondents to the appellants and that it was a debt situated in Jerusalem where alone it was payable. Further performance of the contract of current account was prevented by the outbreak of war so that no further banking services could be performed by the respondents for the appellants, but the debt fell within the class of accrued rights and was not abrogated. The respondents have paid the amount of the debt to the Custodian of Absentee Property in Israel, and if this was a debt situated in Israel after May 15 they were bound to make that payment and the appellants cannot recover anything in this action. To succeed, the appellants would have somehow to establish that any debt owing to them was not after May 15 situated in Israel, because it is only in that case that the respondents would have been wrong in making payment to the custodian in Israel.

The appellants' main contention is that their rights under the contract were wholly abrogated, because they follow that up by maintaining that in place of those rights there sprang up a new right to the same sum which was not situated in Israel, and they base this contention on the authority of *Fibrosa Spolka Akcyjna v. Fairbairn Lawson Combe Barbour Ld.*[16] But if their original right to the money was not abrogated the possibility of there being this new right does not arise and I shall say nothing about it.

Alternatively, on the footing that their original rights were not totally abrogated, they contend that the original debt was only situated in Jerusalem because of the terms of the contract, and once those terms have been abrogated the debt ceased to be situated there and became due as an ordinary debt in England where the respondents have their principal place of business. That would be a startling result. In times when transfer of money from one country to another is restricted it may be of great importance to a debtor that his debt should only be payable at the place stipulated. What survived the outbreak of war was the original debt, and the original debt was a debt payable at the respondents' branch in Jerusalem on demand there. The right to demand and to sue for that debt was suspended, but I do not see how that suspension could alter the nature of the debt. For the reasons which I have stated I agreed that this appeal should be dismissed.

(g) *B-Filer Inc. v. TD Canada Trust*†

[ROMAINE J:]

INTRODUCTION

[1] This was an application for a mandatory interlocutory injunction. The Plaintiffs brought the motion to compel the Defendant The Toronto Dominion Bank ("TD") (incorrectly referred to as TD Canada Trust in the style of cause) to continue to provide banking services to the B-Filer Inc., carrying on business as GPAY ("GPAY"). The application was dismissed and the request for an injunction was denied. These are my reasons.

HISTORY

[2] This motion was the fourth time that GPAY had attempted to require a bank to provide accounts and other services to GPAY or related companies. On June 7, 2005 an action was commenced in the Alberta Court of Queen's Bench against the Bank of Nova Scotia ("Scotiabank") after Scotiabank delivered notice of termination of its banking services, seeking an injunction. Lefsrud, J. dismissed the application in its entirety (*B-FILER Inc. v. Bank of Nova Scotia*, 2005 ABQB 704 (hereinafter referred to as "B-FILER")).

[3] At the same time as the *B-FILER* action, GPAY and NPAY (another related company, not a party to this proceeding) commenced proceedings against Scotiabank pursuant to section 75 of the *Competition Act*, R.S.C. 1985, c. C-34 for refusal to deal. An application for an injunction made to a judge of the Federal Court of Canada sitting as Chair of the Competition Tribunal was dismissed.

[4] In addition, NPAY and GPAY pursued proceedings that culminated in a four-week hearing before the Competition Tribunal seeking to have the Tribunal require Scotiabank to provide accounts and other services. The application was dismissed with costs payable to Scotiabank.

FACTS

[5] Raymond Grace incorporated B-Filer Inc. in 1997. In 1999, Mr. Grace registered GPAY as a business name for B-Filer Inc. Mr. Grace later incorporated NPAY Inc., which is not a party to this proceeding.

[6] Mr. Grace is an experienced business person. Before becoming president and controlling shareholder of GPAY and NPAY, Mr. Grace worked for Scotiabank and for Equifax.

[7] In June, 1999, Mr. Grace opened an account at TD's downtown Edmonton branch in the name of GPAY. He described GPAY as a "Financial Services" business when opening the account. Mr. Grace states that when he opened the GPAY account, his intention was to operate a business that facilitated customers' payments to collection agencies. Mr. Grace signed a Business Services Master Agreement, a Business Banking Agreement and a TD Business Access Agreement. In 1999, GPAY also applied for and was granted status as a "bill payee" on TD's system.

[8] Included in the Business Services Master Agreement is a clause that provides as follows:

> Either of us may cancel this Master, any Service or the license to use the Service Materials by giving the other 30 days' written notice ... If this Master is cancelled, all Services are automatically cancelled ...

[9] Mr. Grace executed another Master Agreement with respect to the GPAY account on December 7, 2001. The cancellation/termination provisions are identical to the provisions contained in the agreement of June 25, 1999. Mr. Grace has acknowledged his signature on these documents. Mr. Grace opened two new TD accounts on December 29, 2006 in the names of NPAY Financial Services Inc. and GPAY Holdings Inc., executing agreements which include the same provisions with respect to termination.

[10] In December, 2002, Use My Bank Services ("UMB") and NPAY Inc. entered into a joint ven-

---

† 2008 ABQB 749 at paras. 1–55.

ture agreement. The business of the joint venture is to transfer money from the bank account of Canadian customers to GPAY's accounts and other accounts controlled by Mr. Grace and then ultimately to online casino management companies or other "payment processing gateways" outside of Canada through the use of the internet. The joint venture did this in three ways:

a) through the bill payment system initially, using GPAY's status as a bill payee;

b) when GPAY lost bill payment status at TD and CIBC in late 2003 and at Scotiabank in September, 2005, through e-mail money transfers; and

c) through account-to-account transfers between a banking customer's account and GPAY's account located at the same financial institution.

[11] Regardless of the method of transfer, the joint venture is unable to transfer funds without the banking customer disclosing his bank card number and secret online banking password. The TD cardholder agreement with its customers precludes customers from disclosing their online banking password to others.

[12] GPAY has a management contract with NPAY to perform NPAY's obligations under the joint venture. This includes receiving and handling all payments from customers and remitting the payments to the merchant clients.

[13] The GPAY account was virtually dormant through the end of 2006, but activity in the account increased dramatically in 2007 when UMB reprogrammed its computers to transfer money from TD customers' accounts by way of account-to-account transfers into the GPAY account. TD began to monitor account activity and learned the following:

a) that in order to use GPAY's services, customers were required to provide GPAY with their access card number and internet password in violation of their cardholder agreement with TD;

b) that GPAY was receiving many thousands of third party personal payee transfers into its accounts, conducting business through a service intended for the personal use of customers; and

c) that GPAY collects money on behalf of on-line gambling companies, which are a restricted business category for banking due-diligence policies and requirements.

[14] TD has a policy that precludes it from providing accounts to businesses that accept payments for online gambling. By letter dated May 16, 2007, it exercised its right under contract to terminate its accounts with GPAY, NPAY Financial and GPAY Holdings. Through agreement between the parties, TD continued service to the date of hearing on a without prejudice basis, but, as a condition of an adjournment request by GPAY near the time of the first hearing date, the TD accounts were frozen in September of 2007.

ANALYSIS

[15] The tripartite test that must be satisfied for an injunction to be granted is set out in *RJR Macdonald Inc. v. Canada, (A.G.)*, [1994] 1 S.C.R. 311 at para. 43:

> First, a preliminary assessment must be made of the merits of the case to ensure that there is a serious question to be tried. Secondly, it must be determined whether the applicant would suffer irreparable harm if the application were refused. Finally, an assessment must be made as to which of the parties would suffer greater harm from the granting or refusal of the remedy pending a decision on the merits.

[16] As the Supreme Court noted in *RJR* at paras 50–51, the merits of the case are not to be determined in a hearing for an injunction. This is to be left for trial, except in exceptional circumstances.

The Nature of the Injunction Requested

[17] The first step in the *RJR* analysis is the preliminary assessment of the merits of the case. The nature of this assessment varies depending upon the type of injunction being sought. Lefsrud, J. at paras. 21–22 of *B-FILER* found that the law in Alberta requires that where a mandatory injunction is being sought, the plaintiff must show under the first branch of the *RJR* test that there is a "strong *prima facie* case" rather than only a "serious issue to tried."

[18] In *B-FILER*, the plaintiffs asked the court to require Scotiabank to continue a banking relationship with them. At para. 24 of his judgment, Lefsrud J. wrote:

> I am satisfied that by asking this Court to require Scotiabank to maintain a banking relationship with them, the Plaintiffs are seeking a mandatory injunction ... As a result, the threshold for the first element of the test is high. Instead of simply proving that there is a triable issue, the Plaintiffs must show a strong *prima facie* case.

[19] As in *B-FILER*, GPAY now asks this Court to compel the TD to continue a banking relationship with the company, despite receipt of a notice to terminate. In other words, the application is for interim specific performance of TD's obligations under the Business Services Master Agreement. It is thus an application for a mandatory injunction, and GPAY must show a strong *prima facie* case for this injunction to be granted.

Whether There is a Strong *Prima Facie Case*

[20] While this Court need not determine the entire matter between the parties, it must determine whether GPAY has a strong *prima facie* case. GPAY submits first that cancellation clauses such as found in the agreements signed by Mr. Grace are unconscionable and should not be enforced. It submits that the clauses were not brought to Mr. Grace's attention and therefore that they should not be binding.

[21] GPAY notes that financial institutions usually adopt standard forms of agreement because they are in the business of opening accounts on a regular basis. GPAY correctly points out that courts have typically addressed any imbalance created by onerous or unusual clauses in standard form agreements by requiring a party relying on such a clause to bring its existence sufficiently to the notice of the other party at the time the contract is made. The issues are therefore whether the termination clause is onerous or unusual and whether Mr. Grace was aware of it at the time he entered into the banking agreement.

[22] GPAY further submits that the agreement contains implied terms, including that the bank would continue to provide services to GPAY provided that GPAY fulfilled its obligations under the agreement, and that the bank would provide reasonable notice of changes in service having regard to the nature of GPAY's business. GPAY argues that the breach of these implied terms amounts to unfair competition and unlawful interference with its economic interests. GPAY further submits that allowing the bank to breach the agreement by terminating services would amount to unlawful interference with contracts between GPAY and third parties.

[23] I cannot accept GPAY's assertion that the agreement signed by Mr. Grace is unenforceable because the termination provision is onerous or unreasonable. Mr. Grace is a sophisticated business person and has conceded on cross-examination that he either knew, or could have guessed, that such a term was con-

tained within the contract. There is no evidence that he was rushed, pressured or unduly influenced in signing the agreements. There is no evidence that any of the narrow and limited circumstances that must be found to set aside a contractual provision for unconscionability are present in this case: *Cope v. Hill*, [2007] A.J. No. 83 (C.A.) at para. 16, leave to appeal to S.C.C. refused, [2007] S.C.C.A. No. 138. GPAY concedes that termination clauses are common in commercial contracts such as this one.

[24] In para. 4 of *Budget Rent a Car of Edmonton Ltd. v. University of Toronto*, 165 A.R. 236, the Alberta Court of Appeal noted that the experience of a person signing a contract was a relevant factor, as well as the fact in that case that the physical arrangement of the portions of the contract in question was not ... in any way difficult to read, surprising or tricky.

[25] The same is true in this case. There is also no reason to imply terms as suggested by GPAY that would effectively limit the clear terms of the termination clause. Since there was no breach of the contract by TD, there can be no unfair competition or unlawful interference with GPAY's economic interests. I find GPAY has not established a strong *prima facie* case on these arguments.

[26] GPAY also submits that there is no breach of the cardholder agreement when a banking customer provides his confidential online banking password to UMB on the basis that UMB is the "agent" of the customer. This is a skewed and forced interpretation of the language of the cardholder agreement. In any event, I agree with the Competition Tribunal that, whether or not cardholders breach the terms of the cardholders agreement when authorizing UMB to access their online accounts, this practice poses a significant risk to the security of the electronic banking system.

[27] I cannot find that the first branch of the *RJR* analysis requiring a strong *prima facie* case has been satisfied. Even if I were to find that the cancellation clause was onerous, and I do not, Mr. Grace is an experienced business person who by his own admission would have known of termination clauses similar to the ones contained in the contract. TD was contractually entitled to terminate without giving reasons, and it did so with proper notice. Had reasons been necessary, TD has established a number of valid concerns in the evidence before me.

[28] As all three branches of the tripartite test must be met before an injunction to be granted, the fail-

ure of GPAY to satisfy the first requirement is sufficient to dispose of the application. However, I will consider the remaining branches of the *RJR* test.

Irreparable Harm

[29] The second branch of the *RJR* test requires proof of irreparable harm. Irreparable harm is defined at para 59 as follows:

> "Irreparable" refers to the nature of the harm suffered rather than its magnitude. It is harm which either cannot be quantified in monetary terms or which cannot be cured, usually because one party cannot collect damages from the other. Examples of the former include instances where one party will be put out of business by the court's decision (*R.L. Crain Inc. v. Hendry* (1988), 48 D.L.R. (4th) 228 (Sask. Q.B.)); where one party will suffer permanent market loss or irrevocable damage to its business reputation (*American Cyanamid, supra*); or where a permanent loss of natural resources will be the result when a challenged activity is not enjoined (*MacMillan Bloedel Ltd. v. Mullin*, [1985] 3 W.W.R. 577 (B.C.C.A.)).

[30] GPAY must show that allowing TD to terminate banking services would cause it irreparable harm. GPAY correctly notes that there can be many types of irreparable harm. These can include harm to reputation, harm to a person's career, harm that would put a party out of business or cause permanent market loss or loss of goodwill, irrevocable damage to a business or loss of a person's livelihood or claims where the quantification of damages is known, but unlikely to be recovered.

[31] Even if GPAY were able to establish that there would be harm caused by TD's withdrawal of services, Mr. Grace was able to quantify the losses that would be incurred by this withdrawal. Mr. Grace stated in an affidavit that he projected five year losses at $161,200,000. While he later claimed that he was not sure where the number came from, he agreed that a model could be developed with a business valuator to estimate net losses into the future were TD to discontinue service.

[32] TD submits, and I agree, that GPAY has failed to demonstrate that any irreparable harm has been caused to GPAY by TD terminating the GPAY account. TD notes that Mr. Grace has admitted that if GPAY can no longer process payments for the joint venture, UMB would simply resort to other companies with biller status at a bank. Even if GPAY stops generating revenue from the joint ven-

ture, this will have little or no financial impact on it since it earns nothing from the joint venture arising from the funds transfer business and NPAY, which may be impacted, is not a party to this action.

[33] TD notes that GPAY grew its business without using these accounts. The only reason the accounts are being used now is because other banks have shut-off services over security and reputational concerns. TD submits that this type of harm is self-inflicted and cannot be used as evidence of irreparable harm that could justify a mandatory injunction. I agree. The argument that GPAY would go out of business if a mandatory injunction is not granted since other banks have successfully been able to terminate GPAY as a customer and that this is irreparable harm that should support GPAY's application implies that GPAY has a right to banking services no matter the nature of its banking practices and the concerns and risks they may cause a bank, and that the last bank standing in a series of [litigations] must provide these services. This is clearly not sustainable.

[34] As the *RJR* test for 'irreparable' harm requires the harm to defy quantification or be unable to be cured, I find that a risk of irreparable harm has not been established in this case. While quantifiable damages that could not be recovered might constitute irreparable harm, there was no serious argument on this issue.

Balance of Convenience

[35] The last part of the *RJR* analysis is the balance of convenience test. There are a variety of factors to be considered. In *RJR* at para. 63, the Supreme Court of Canada cites Lord Diplock in *American Cyanamid* as follows:

> [i]t would be unwise to attempt even to list all the various matters which may need to be taken into consideration in deciding where the balance lies, let alone to suggest the relative weight to be attached to them. These will vary from case to case.

[36] GPAY submits that in the balance of convenience test, the court must determine which of the parties will suffer the greater harm by either the granting [or] the refusal of the injunction. Lefsrud, J. in *B-FILER* notes at para 41 that the balance of convenience test "... requires a consideration of the respective positions of the parties as well as the public interest." In *Mead Johnson Canada v. Ross Pediatrics*, 31 O.R. (3d) 237 (Ont. Gen. Div.), Brennan J. wrote with respect to the balance of convenience test that:

[w]here a serious issue is raised between the parties and irreparable harm will be suffered by one of them if an injunction is not granted, substantial inconvenience to one or the other is virtually inevitable.

[37] It is important to consider the business impact that the withdrawal of banking services is likely to have on GPAY. This consideration, however, must be balanced against TD's obligations to comply with applicable legislation. The interest of the public in compliance with applicable legislation and the safety of financial services is also an important consideration. I will first discuss GPAY's interests and then consider those of the bank and the public.

[38] GPAY argues that its loss of good will and market share should almost certainly justify granting the injunction on the basis of balance of convenience. It submits that a failure to grant the injunction will result in permanent market loss impacting the viability of its business and its goodwill. GPAY also describes the inconvenience it will suffer should the injunction not be granted.

[39] GPAY submits that a failure to grant the injunction means that it will no longer be able to receive payments from TD customers who have shown they want the GPAY service by contacting TD to confirm that they want GPAY as a payee in an account-to-account transfer. It submits that TD's termination of GPAY's banking services makes the business appear less legitimate, and the [loss] of access to TD customers lessens its chance to establish a critical mass of customers and gain the network effects and first mover advantage required for a successful business. GPAY argues that this removes the opportunity for GPAY to leverage its business through acquiring a greater number of customers and could allow a 'second mover' to take the opportunity that GPAY now has.

[40] I have previously addressed the issue of irreparable harm, and have found that GPAY's damages have been quantified by Mr. Grace himself. Even if Mr. Grace's own estimate is incorrect, he has conceded that, if the company had losses, they could be quantified by a business valuator. I am left weighing, then, the possibility of a quantifiable financial loss against the inconvenience that would be suffered by the bank if this injunction were granted.

[41] From the bank's perspective, there are serious risks in continuing to provide services to GPAY. While GPAY argues that it has adequate security in place and that the banking agreements do not pro-

hibit an agency relationship whereby confidential information is revealed to the agent, the bank has adduced persuasive evidence that there are still security risks to this type of operation. The bank also points out that granting the injunction would put it in the position of having to offer banking services to a customer whose entire manner of business violates numerous bank policies, creates difficult duties for the bank under money laundering and terrorist financing legislation and precludes it from complying with its own diligence duties.

[42] In *B-FILER*, Lefsrud J. noted at para. 42 that:

> In my opinion, the balance of convenience favours Scotiabank, particularly in light of the real and potential problems associated with the Plaintiff's business. I am satisfied that the way in which the Plaintiff's business operates raises justifiable concerns for Scotiabank. These concerns include disclosure of customer banking information, violation of internal Scotiabank policies, possible reporting obligations and dedication of undue time and resources to fraud investigations.

[43] GPAY submits that its banking practices have changed since the time of the hearing before Lefsrud, J., and that the regulatory risk to the TD is different and less extensive than it was when it used the Scotiabank services. It submits that, since February of 2007 GPAY only uses account-to-account transfers and that those transfers do not breach Rule E2 of the Canadian Payments Association. GPAY at the hearing also suggested that it would voluntarily reduce its client base to three merchants.

[44] TD submits that GPAY's last-minute attempt to change its practices to improve its position in litigation is a repeat of what occurred before the Competition Tribunal, that GPAY was not compliant with many of the rules it now purports to adopt when notice of termination was given, and that it is now trying to negotiate its way through the application. The termination provision does not require that the bank give reasons for termination, but TD adduced compelling evidence that the manner in which the joint venture uses confidential customer information creates periods of significant vulnerability to fraud. It submits through uncontradicted expert evidence that GPAY's business is very attractive to money launderers, as it affords anonymity, and requiring the bank to continue to provide services puts a significant burden on the bank and would require extensive and difficult record-sourcing and keeping. TD concedes that Rule E2 does not apply to account-to-account transfers, but it provides uncontradicted expert opin-

ion that a myriad of other risks still arise from GPAY's business banking practices, and that TD faces significant regulatory, legal and reputational risks as long as it continues to provide banking services to GPAY.

[45] While in most cases, the 'balance of convenience' requires the court to weigh only the interests of the plaintiff and the defendant, this application raises issues of public interest. As noted at para. 68 of *RJR*:

> ... private applicants are normally presumed to be pursing their own interests rather than those of the public at large. In considering the balance of convenience and the public interest, it does not assist an applicant to claim that a given government authority does not represent the public interest. Rather, the applicant must convince the court of the public interest benefits which will flow from the granting of the relief sought.

[46] *RJR* admittedly addressed a very different matter, namely an applicant's opposition to restrictive government legislation on tobacco marketing. However, the point is no less relevant. I accept the bank's evidence that there is a strong public interest against granting the injunction.

[47] There is a significant public interest in preventing money laundering and terrorist financing. The opening line of Terence D. Hall and Alison Manzer's book, *A Guide to Canadian Money Laundering [Legislation]*, 2007 Edition, (Lexis Nexis Canada, 2006) reads:

> In recent years, governments and law enforcement agencies around the world have become increasingly concerned about money laundering and the use of the financial system by criminal.
> The G-7 countries established the Financial Action Task Force on Money Laundering (FATF) in 1989 as a result of proposals based on the idea that stopping the ability to benefit from the profits of crime would reduce criminal activity.

[48] Canada has implemented legislation to help combat money laundering. This legislation has evolved to address the financing of terrorism. The legislation includes several laws of general application. Of particular relevance to this discussion is the *Proceeds of Crime (Money Laundering) and Terrorist Financing Act*, S.C. 2000, c. 17 ("PCMLTF"). Hall and Manzer summarize the objectives of the PCMLTF at p. 2 of their book. Its goals are to implement measures to detect and deter money laundering and activities meant to finance terrorist activities; to respond to the threat posed by organized

crime by providing information to law enforcement to help deprive criminals of the proceeds of their crimes and to help fulfill Canada's international commitments to assist in fighting transnational crime including money laundering and terrorist activities. These goals, of course, require the cooperation of the banking system.

[49] In an affidavit sworn by Christopher Mathers, who provides advice and assistance on money laundering compliance and organized criminal activities to various national and international public and private organizations, and who provided an opinion to the bank with respect to the money laundering risks posed by the plaintiff's business, Mr. Mathers states that financial institutions typically rely on each other, and it is accepted between financial institutions that appropriate due diligence and "know-your-customer" procedure are adhered to. Mr. Mathers explains that when a bank allows its customers to complete transactions over the internet, the bank allows customers to transfer funds only to payees that the bank can say are *bona fide*. For the payee to be accepted as *bona fide*, it must submit to a client acceptance procedure consistent with the know-your-customer requirements in the PCMLTF.

[50] Mr. Mathers states that GPAY's business model places TD in an untenable position in relation to the PCMLTF, as the business model used allows customers to transfer funds to unknown persons, corporations and entities that have not been vetted by the bank. This means the bank may unknowingly allow transactions that are in violation of the PCMLTF.

[51] Mr. Mathers notes, and I accept his uncontradicted evidence, that if TD were required to accept GPAY as a customer, there would be a significant burden placed on TD to conduct appropriate due diligence inquiries to comply with the PCMLTF.

[52] I am not suggesting that GPAY or Mr. Grace are involved in money laundering or terrorist financing. However, TD and all other Canadian banks are required to comply with legislation designed to prevent such activities. There is a significant public interest in compliance with legislation that has been enacted to address these issues. For this reason, I find that the public interest weighs very heavily in favour of TD's position. There is little public interest in ensuring the uninterrupted flow of online gambling payments to offshore casinos.

[53] Finally, I agree with Lefsrud, J. in *B-FILER* where he noted at para 43 that he was ... particularly hesitant to endorse a position that would force

Scotiabank to continue a private contractual relationship against its will.

[54] I note that the plaintiffs have not tendered any kind of meaningful undertaking as to damages, although they undertook to post a bond if they were successful in obtaining the injunction.

CONCLUSION ON INJUNCTION APPLICATION

[55] For the above reasons, I found that GPAY was unable to satisfy the tripartite test for an injunction and dismissed its application.

(h) *Re Farrow's Bank, Ltd.*†

SUMMONS

On Thursday, December 16, 1920, Voyce having received a crossed order cheque for £1,493 drawn on the London Joint City and Midland Bank, West Bromwich branch, indorsed and paid it into his account at Farrow's Bank, Birmingham branch, which having forthwith credited him with the amount in their ledger remitted the cheque to Barclays Bank as their clearing agents.

On Friday, December 17, Barclays Bank presented the cheque at the clearing house to the London Joint City and Midland Bank, who remitted it to their West Bromwich branch. Barclays Bank at the same time credited Farrow's head office on the clearance sheet, subject to recourse.

On Saturday, December 18, the West Bromwich branch of the drawer's bank debited the drawer, credited their head office and advised them that the cheque was cleared.

On Monday, December 20, the London Joint City and Midland Bank having received the letter of advice settled with Barclays Bank through the clearing house at 12.30 P.M. and Barclays Bank thereupon advised their principals, Farrow's head office, that the cheque was cleared.

In the meantime — namely, at 8.30 A.M. — Farrow's Bank had suspended payment, a notice to that effect being posted on the doors of the head office, and instructions to suspend being wired to all the branches at 12.15 P.M. For the purposes of the liquidation the determination to suspend was treated as made on Sunday, December 19, and all cash remittances received on the Monday were returned.

On Monday, December 20, at 2.20 P.M., a petition to wind up Farrow's Bank was presented, and on Tuesday, December 21, the Official Receiver was appointed provisional liquidator pending the hearing. The winding-up order was made on January 11, 1921, and the Official Receiver continued as liquidator.

In these circumstances the question arose whether the proceeds of the cheque belonged to Farrow's Bank as part of their general assets, so that Voyce had merely a right of proof; or whether they were mere collecting agents, so that having suspended payment before the cheque was cleared they remained in that position, and the proceeds belonged entirely to Voyce.

On March 17, 1922, the liquidator issued this summons to determine the point, which arose in many similar instances.

The chief cashier deposed that according to the practice of Farrow's Bank this country cheque though immediately credited could not as a rule have been drawn upon until the third weekday after it was paid in — i.e., in the present case Monday, December 20, at 10 A.M. — though in the case of an overdraft it would at once have reduced the amount on which interest was payable.

Voyce deposed that he paid in the cheque in order that in the ordinary course of banking practice it might be collected and credited to his account and that there was no arrangement that cheques paid in should become the property of the bank, or that he should have immediate credit therefor.

At the time of payment in [*sic*] Voyce had already a substantial credit balance, but certain cheques drawn by him between December 15 and

---

† [1923] 1 Ch. 41 (C.A.). [Notes omitted.]

December 18 both inclusive would more than have exhausted that credit, and would have impinged on the £1,493. These cheques however were all returned unpaid.

The passbook contained the following notices as to "Terms of Business for Current Accounts."

> Para. 1: "Current accounts are opened on the terms usually adopted by Bankers."
>
> Para. 4: "The Bank will not be responsible for any Cheques, Bills, Notes, Coupons, or Securities forwarded by post for collection or acceptance, nor for any delay which may arise. *Proceeds of remittances will only be available after receipt of the same by the Bank.*"

The paying-in slip contained the note:

> Customers are respectfully informed that the Bank reserves to itself the right, at its discretion, to defer payment of cheques drawn against uncleared effects which may have been credited to the account.

The summons came on for hearing before Astbury J. on July 11, 1922.

[ASTBURY J. (after stating the facts):]

There are two questions to be determined on this summons. The first is whether the bank took this cheque on December 16 as holders for value, or according to the more usual practice of bankers as agents for collection. The second question is: If they took the cheque as agents for collection did they so collect the money as to convert the relationship between themselves and Voyce from that of agent and principal into that of debtor and creditor?

On the first point, the question in what character the bank received the cheque on December 16 is a pure question of fact: *M'Lean v. Clydesdale Banking Co.*[1] In that case it was held on the evidence that the bank took the cheque as holders for value. Lord Blackburn said:[2]

> Now in the present case did the bank get the cheque in that way as a mere agent, and nothing else, or did they get it in order that they might have the property in it transferred to them and that they might become holders of it? The condescendence makes this averment: 'The said draft or cheque was indorsed by the said W.B. Cotton, and was by him delivered to the pursuers on or about the 14th day of January, 1882, on their paying to him the said sum of £265 2s. 6d., or placing the same to the credit of his account which was then overdrawn to an amount

in excess of the said sum, and thereby extinguishing the said account to that extent.'

In other words the decision was based on the fact that at the time when the cheque was paid to the bank the person paying in the cheque and the bank both intended that the bank should immediately become holders for value.

The liquidator relies upon *Gordon's Case*.[3] But it seems to me that the expressions relied upon in the judgments must be read, and only can be read, with reference to the facts of that case. The most relevant fact for the present purpose was that as between the customer and the bank there was an arrangement, or course of practice, under which the bank allowed the customer to draw against the amounts of cheques paid in and credited before they were cleared. With these facts before him Lord Macnaghten said:[4]

> It is well settled that if a banker before collection credits a customer with the face value of a cheque paid into his account the banker becomes holder for value of the cheque. It is impossible, I think, to say that a banker is merely receiving payment for his customer and a mere agent for collection when he receives payment of a cheque of which he is the holder for value.

Of course, in a case where the facts were as I have stated that result necessarily follows. Lord Lindley said:[5]

> It must never be forgotten that the moment a bank places money to its customer's credit the customer is entitled to draw upon it, unless something occurs to deprive him of that right.

There, again, the same remark applies.

It is no longer arguable, if ever it was, that the mere crediting by a bank of a cheque paid into a customer's account independently of any knowledge of the customer, or arrangement as between him and the bank, converts the bank into a holder for value as distinct from a recipient for the customer within the meaning of s. 82 of the *Bills of Exchange Act*, 1882. This is now laid down by the *Bills of Exchange (Crossed Cheques) Act*, 1906. But even before that Act it was held in certainly more than one case that the mere crediting of a cheque to the customer's account behind his back and without his knowledge does not prevent the bank being an agent for collection in the ordinary way.

In the *Akrokerri Case*[6] Bigham J. said:

> The expression 'for a customer' has been often discussed, and its meaning has now been made fairly plain by judicial interpretation. Money is received for a customer in those cases only

where the banker acts as a mere agent to collect. Thus it is that if the banker as between himself and his customer becomes the holder of the cheque for value before he collects it he does not receive the payment for his customer; he receives it for himself. The question, then, resolves itself into this — Did the defendants receive the payments as mere collecting agents for Nobbs? It is argued that they did not, because they gave Nobbs credit for the value of the cheques in their ledger before they sent them to Williams Deacon & Co. for collection, and so, it is said, made themselves holders of the cheques for value. But, in my opinion, the entries in the bank's ledgers did not make the bank holders for value. The entries neither conferred any right on Nobbs to draw the money out of the bank, nor did they fix the bank with any liability to pay the money to him. It might have been different if the entries had been made in the passbook, for that book belongs to the customer, and the entries made in it by the bank are statements on which the customer is entitled to act. Suppose, after the ledger entries were made, but before the cheques were sent to Williams Deacon & Co., Nobbs had asked the defendant bank to return him the cheques, could bank have refused to comply with his request? Could they have said, 'No; the cheques are ours, for by entries in our ledger of which you know nothing we have given you credit for the amounts, and so have made ourselves holders for value'? I think not Nobbs, having regard to the terms on which the business was carried on, would have been entitled to say that he had never assented to any transfer of the cheques, and that therefore they were still his. In truth, notwithstanding the ledger entries, no credit was given to Nobbs; nor was it intended that he should have credit; and, if Nobbs had demanded the money, the defendants would have been entitled to refuse to pay it to him. I think, therefore, that the defendants, in forwarding the cheques to Williams Deacon & Co., and so obtaining the money, were acting as mere agents to collect and were receiving the payment for their customer within the meaning of the section of the Act.

In the present case there was no entry made at any relevant date in Voyce's passbook and the only entries made were made in the Birmingham branch of Farrow's Bank in their ledgers or books on December 16.

But the case does not really rest there, because in addition to the evidence that I have read, there is the following notice printed in the customer's passbook:

Current accounts are opened on the terms usually adopted by bankers. The bank will not be responsible for any cheques, bills, notes, coupons, or securities forwarded by post for collection or acceptance, nor for any delay which may arise. Proceeds of remittances will only be available after receipt of the same by the bank.

On the paying-in slip there is this note:

Customers are respectfully informed that the bank reserves to itself the right at its discretion to defer payment of cheques drawn against uncleared effects which may have been credited to the account.

If the bank had become holders for value of the cheque they could do no such thing.

On the first point, therefore, and on the facts I hold that the bank in the present case became agents for collection in respect of the cheque in question and not holders of the cheque for value.

This being so, the second point arises, whether the money in respect of this cheque was received by Farrow's Bank in time for it to become their property as on a debtor and creditor account as distinct from the previous relationship of agent and principal which existed for the reasons I have mentioned.

In *In re Agra and Masterman's Bank*[7] the headnote states:

Where a firm paid a cheque into a branch bank in India to their current account after the stoppage of the parent bank in England, but before the branch had notice of that stoppage, and afterwards, on the same day, the branch received notice of the stoppage of the bank in England, and stopped itself: Held, that an application by the firm to be repaid the amount of the cheque in full must be refused; but this order was without prejudice to a renewal of the application, if the applicants should find that their cheque had not been cashed until after the branch had received notice of the stoppage of the bank in England.

Wood V.-C. said it was clear that after a bank had ceased all functions it could not receive anything in specie for a special purpose if the special purpose had become impossible, and after deciding the case as he did on the facts then before him the learned judge said:

The order would be to refuse this application, but without prejudice to the applicants renewing it if they should find that the cheque was not cashed until after notice of the stoppage of the bank in England had been received by the branch at Calcutta.

That amounts to saying that if after the bank had stopped payment it had then purported to treat cash subsequently received by it as its own and not as the cash of the customer, the decision would have to be reconsidered.

Now in the present case it is common ground that the time at which this cheque was cleared in fact and the moneys made available for Barclays Bank as agent for Farrow's Bank was 12.30 on Monday, December 20. Farrow's Bank, however, had stopped payment, if not on Saturday or Sunday certainly in the early hours of Monday morning, and long before 12.30 in the day. That being so it seems to me that after ceasing to act as a going concern and stating their intention no longer to act as a going concern they had no longer any authority from Voyce to take what was in fact his money received after the stoppage and convert it into money forming part of their assets, in respect of which they would be entitled to assume the position of debtors instead of agents. On that short ground I am of opinion that these moneys never were in fact collected by Farrow's Bank at a time when they were entitled to claim them as part of their assets.

The result is that there must be a declaration on this summons that the liquidator must pay out of the assets the full amount of the cheque in question.

G.R.A.

[THE APPEAL]

The liquidator appealed. The appeal was heard on October 19, 1922.

On the appeal the only question argued was whether, assuming Farrow's Bank received the cheque as agents for collection, the relation between the bank and Voyce had become that of debtors and creditor before the stoppage of the bank. The arguments on this point were the same as those used in the Court below.

[LORD STERNDALE M.R. (Warrington L.J. and Younger L.J. concurring):]

This is an appeal from a judgment of Astbury J. on a question arising in the liquidation of Farrow's Bank in these circumstances. I will take the facts as stated in the affidavit of Mr. Drysdale. "On December 16, 1920, Mr. H.J. Voyce paid into the Birmingham branch of the Bank a cheque for £1,493 15s. 2d. payable to him or his order and drawn on the London Joint City and Midland Bank, West Bromwich. On the same day the Birmingham branch remitted this cheque with others amounting altogether to £2,310 19s. 2d. to Barclays Bank, Fenchurch Street, for clearance," the meaning of that being that Farrow's Bank are not one of the clearing banks, but employ as their clearing agents Barclays Bank. "On December 17, 1920, Barclays Bank received these cheques for clearance and gave credit for £2,310 19s 2d. to the head office of Farrow's Bank on the clearance sheet for that day. Such credit was given subject to recourse in the event of the non-payment of the cheques." There is nothing to show any communication between Barclays Bank and Farrow's Bank with regard to that, but I shall assume that Farrow's Bank would know that Barclays Bank would give them credit in that way for all cheques received upon the clearance sheet. "On the same day Barclays Bank passed these cheques through the Clearing House and the said cheque for £1,493 15s. 2d. was taken up by the London Joint City and Midland Bank who posted it to their West Bromwich branch the same day. On December 18, 1920 (which was a Saturday), the West Bromwich branch received the cheque and after ascertaining that the drawer had funds to meet the cheque debited the drawer's account and credited their head office with the amount and on the same day they sent an advice to their head office that the cheque was cleared." That, of course, cannot be quite an accurate statement, the cheque was not cleared until it had been cleared at the clearing house; what is meant is that the cheque was good and would be met. "On December 20, 1920 (being the day on which the petition in this matter was filed), the London office of the London Joint City and Midland Bank received the advice from their branch and settled with Barclays Bank through the clearing house and on the same day Barclays Bank advised the head office of Farrow's Bank that the said cheques comprising the total of £2,310 19s. 2d. were cleared." What takes place at the clearing house is set out in the affidavit of Mr. Sykes, the secretary of the Institute of Bankers, and all that it is necessary to read with regard to this matter I think is para. 4: "At the Clearing House a cheque is said to be cleared when the final settlement between the banks is made by a transfer in the books of the Bank of England. This takes place as follows:" then he deals with the town clearing, which I need not trouble about. Then: "In the case of cheques drawn on banks in the country cheque clearing on the second day after the cheque reaches the Clearing House.... In all the above cases the settlement is made at the end of the day immediately after the last hour for receiving 'returns.' ...

In the case of the country cheque clearing, the final agreement of the balance to be paid is made at 12.30 o'clock of the day on which the payment is to be made by transfer at the Bank of England (Saturdays 11 o'clock)."

The question is when did Farrow's Bank receive this money? If they received it before they suspended payment, they then held the money simply in the relation of debtors to their customer; if they did not receive it till after the suspension, they had then given up all their functions as a bank, and they had no right to receive the money and retain it, and the customer would be entitled to recover it. There was a question raised whether Farrow's Bank received the cheque as holders or simply as agents for collection. The learned judge below has decided that they held it only as agents for collection, and no appeal is brought before us against that decision. I should mention that in spite of their so holding it they had in their books credited the customer with the amount of the cheque on the day that it was received, but there is on the paying-in slip a note that although the bank do that they reserve to themselves the right not to allow any drawing against the cheque and not to allow it to be treated as cash until it is cleared.

I shall first deal with the matter as if Farrow's Bank were themselves a clearing bank and had themselves done all that Barclays Bank did for them. In that case it seems to me that the money is not received by them and their capacity does not therefore change from that of agents to a principal to debtors to a creditor until the transfers have been made at the Bank of England, as stated by Mr. Sykes. All that was done upon the Saturday by the West Bromwich branch of the London Joint City and Midland Bank in accepting a cheque as one that they would honour and so informing their head office was done merely for the purpose of enabling the clerk of the head office of the London Joint City and Midland Bank, when the final balance came to be settled between that bank and the bank which had brought the cheque to the clearing house, to deal with the cheque as one that came through the clearing house. In the hypothetical case of Farrow's Bank being a clearing bank the payment was not in fact, in my opinion, made until the transfer at the Bank of England, which placed that money at the disposal of Farrow's Bank. Therefore, it seems to me to be quite clear that the learned judge was right, if Farrow's Bank had been a clearing bank and this matter had been carried through by them without an agent.

But then there is another point which is raised and that is this, that although Barclays Bank, who were a clearing bank and who brought this cheque to the clearing house, may not have received the money until Monday, December 20, Farrow's Bank, their principals, had received the money before that date, that is on the 18th, or perhaps earlier when Barclays Bank credited them with recourse in their, Barclays', books or in the clearance sheet. If the meaning of that credit is that on the credit being given Farrow's Bank were entitled to draw against that amount so credited by Barclays Bank or to deal with it for any purpose at that time, then I think there would be a very great deal to be said for that argument. The argument is put in this way: it is said that this was an absolute credit except that there was a right in Barclays Bank of recovery if the cheque was dishonoured, that as the cheque was not dishonoured it was an absolute credit, and, therefore, it was a payment to Farrow's Bank on that day. I think in order to establish such a point as that we should require a very great deal more evidence as to the dealings between Farrow's Bank and Barclays Bank with regard to this matter than we have before us at present. It is said that we must treat what was done as stated by Mr. Drysdale — namely, that Barclays Bank gave credit to Farrow's Bank and that such credit was given subject to recourse in the event of the non-payment of the cheques, as being the same thing as Barclays Bank handing the amount in cash to Farrow's Bank, so that the latter could do what they liked with it, Barclays Bank simply reserving to themselves the right to get the amount back again in case of the non-payment of the cheques. I do not think there is anything like sufficient material here for us to say that a point like that is established. It seems to me that on the materials we have there is no ground for saying that the credit given by Barclays Bank to Farrow's Bank with regard to that cheque was anything more than the credit given by Farrow's Bank to their customer Mr. Voyce, and that there is nothing to show that the agents intended to pay the principals before they, the agents, were themselves paid. I do not say whether or not on further or better materials such a point could be established, but there certainly is nothing before us to establish it. I think, therefore, that the decision of the learned judge was right and that the appeal must be dismissed.

Appeal dismissed.

8 The Fiduciary and Tortious Relationships

Background Reading: M.H. Ogilvie, *Bank and Customer Law in Canada*, 2d Edition (Toronto: Irwin Law, 2013) Chapter 6, pages 202–226.

(I) Fiduciary Obligation

(a) *Woods v. Martins Bank Ltd.*†

[SALMON J.:]

The plaintiff's father died in August, 1948. Approximately one year before he died he gave the plaintiff about £26,000 in cash, the bulk of which was invested by the plaintiff, under his father's guidance, in building societies. At about the same time the father established a fund of between £20,000 and £30,000 to provide an income for the plaintiff's step-mother for her life. When the plaintiff's father died death duties became payable on both sums to which I have referred. The plaintiff voluntarily contributed a large sum of money to his step-mother's fund so that she would not suffer any serious diminution in income by reason of the payment of death duties. Thereafter, the plaintiff had about £17,000 of free money, and, subject to his step-mother's life interest, he was entitled to a further sum of more than £20,000. The plaintiff had not long since left the services, and after a short time as a salesman in a retail store he had entered under his father's auspices a small motor business near the parental home. This was Connaught Motors Ltd. One Darling, in whom the plaintiff's father had had confidence, was

the principal director. The plaintiff's investment in this company was £200. The name of this company was subsequently altered to True Shapes Ltd. when it changed its business to sheet metal working, and it will be necessary for me to refer to it again presently. At this time the plaintiff was a young man about 30 years old with no real business experience or knowledge of affairs. In my judgment, the plaintiff is a pleasant and honest young man but rather stupid and extremely gullible. These attributes can have been no less pronounced or obvious eight years ago than they are today. He was, in fact, the very prototype of the lamb waiting to be shorn. And he did not have long to wait.

In about the month of April, 1950, he met one Brock who was the moving spirit in a company called Brocks Refrigeration Ltd. This was a company which had then been in existence only a few months and whose business was to sell, instal and service refrigerators manufactured by J.&E. Hall Ltd. Between May, 1950, and October, 1951, the plaintiff sank £14,800 in this company, every penny of which he has lost. The plaintiff claims that he invested this money as a result of the advice given to him by the

---

† [1959] 1 Q.B. 55 (Leeds Assizes). [Notes omitted.]

defendant bank through the defendant Johnson who was the manager of the defendant bank's Quayside branch at Newcastle-upon-Tyne. The plaintiff claims that this advice was given negligently or fraudulently.

The writ in this action was not issued until April, 1956. It is therefore apparent that the claim is a stale claim. The plaintiff gives as his principal reason for the delay in issuing the writ that he and his company True Shapes Ltd. became heavily involved with the bank and that he postponed bringing this claim until he was no longer in the hands of the bank. However this may be, it is obvious that such a stale claim must be scrutinized very closely. It would be easy for a young man who had improvidently lost a large amount of money, many years later to persuade himself that he had received bad advice from his bank manager, and that it was as a result of this advice that his money had been lost. If the defendant Johnson had been able categorically to deny the plaintiff's story, if he had said that the plaintiff never came to him for advice, and that he never did and never could have advised the plaintiff that Brocks Refrigeration Ltd. was in a sound financial position, or that it was wise for the plaintiff to make the investments in that company that he in fact made, then, in spite of the fact that the plaintiff impressed me as a most candid witness I might have found it difficult to accept his evidence. It seems to me strange that anyone with the slightest knowledge of financial matters could have considered the finances of Brocks Refrigeration Ltd. as sound in 1950 or 1951, or that the investments which the plaintiff made in that company were other than ludicrously imprudent. But the defendant Johnson admits in effect that the plaintiff did come to him for advice, and does not strongly challenge the fact that he may well have advised the plaintiff that the investments the plaintiff proposed making were wise and prudent investments. At any rate, the defendant Johnson admits that he certainly told the plaintiff that if he, the defendant Johnson, had been able to make the same investments with his own moneys he would have done so. I am quite satisfied that the plaintiff received the advice from the defendant Johnson that the plaintiff says he received. I am bound to say that until I saw the defendant Johnson in the witness-box it seemed to me incredible that any bank manager could be sufficiently ingenuous or ignorant honestly to have believed in such advice. Having seen the defendant Johnson in the witness-box, however, I think that he did, in his muddle-headed way, honestly believe in the advice which he gave the plaintiff.

During the course of this judgment I shall have to refer to the memoranda passing between the defendant Johnson and the defendant bank's district head office. Most regrettably, these documents were not disclosed in the defendants' affidavit of documents although they are of the greatest materiality. It should at all times have been obvious to the defendants and their solicitors that such memoranda existed. Indeed, they are expressly referred to in some of the documents which were disclosed. I am certain that these documents were not purposely suppressed. Nevertheless, the defendants were grossly negligent in omitting these documents from their affidavit of documents. It was not until the trial was well advanced that these documents were produced on my direction. They were then found within a very short space of time, and it was conceded that there was no excuse for their non-disclosure. No doubt the defendants' solicitors explained to their clients that they must disclose all relevant documents which were or had been in their possession. The solicitors' duty, however, does not stop there. It cannot be too clearly understood that solicitors owe a duty to the court, as officers of the court, carefully to go through the documents disclosed by their clients to make sure, as far as possible, that no relevant documents have been omitted from their clients affidavit. In this case I am regretfully driven to the conclusion that this duty was not performed by the defendants' solicitors.

I find the following facts: In April, 1950, True Shapes Ltd. were interested in the project of manufacturing a product known as the Bolden Steriliser. The plaintiff and Darling were directors of this company. Its accountant and secretary was one Gordon Barr. At Barr's suggestion a meeting took place in the office between, amongst others, the plaintiff, Darling, Brock and the defendant Johnson in order to consider the proposal of Brocks Refrigeration Ltd. becoming the distributors of the Bolden Steriliser. It appears that this proposal was carried at the meeting. In point of fact Brocks Refrigeration Ltd. has never sold a single Bolden Steriliser, for no commercial Bolden Steriliser has ever been produced by True Shapes Ltd. At the meeting to which I have referred the defendant Johnson was introduced to the plaintiff as Brock's bank manager and financial adviser. Between the date of that meeting and May 9, 1950, the plaintiff met the defendant Johnson on three or four occasions. At this time the defendant Johnson had learned from Darling that the plaintiff was a man of considerable means. The defendant Johnson then set out to acquire and succeeded in acquiring for the defendant bank the custom of the plaintiff, True Shapes Ltd., and an associated company named Bolden Sterilisers Ltd. The defendant Johnson, as manager of the Quayside branch of the defendant bank, perfectly properly considered it part of his duty to attract such customers as he could for his employers. The defendant Johnson impressed upon the plaintiff that the Quayside branch of the defendant bank was a commercial branch and that he, as the manager of that branch, was at the very hub of financial business in the city of Newcastle-upon-Tyne and in a position to offer the plaintiff of the rival bank at which the plaintiff and True Shapes Ltd. were then customers.

By the beginning of May, 1950, the plaintiff was convinced of the defendant Johnson's financial experience and acumen and had complete confidence in the defendant Johnson's supposed knowledge and skill in financial affairs. The plaintiff asked the defendant Johnson if he would be his financial adviser, to which the defendant Johnson replied that the defendant bank would be only too pleased to take care of the plaintiff's financial affairs. Thereafter the defendant Johnsons told the plaintiff that he might be able to get some preference shares for the plaintiff in Brocks Refrigeration Ltd. At this time, and indeed at all times, Brock was urgently in need of money for his company. Brock, who had then known the plaintiff only for a few weeks or months, was quite cunning enough to realize that the proposition to invest money in his company was more likely to attract the plaintiff if it came to him from a bank manager in whom he had confidence rather than from Brock, who would necessarily be an interested party. I have no doubt that the plaintiff asked the defendant Johnson whether Brocks Refrigeration Ltd. was financially sound and whether it would be wise for him, the plaintiff, to invest £5,000 in that company's preference shares. Brock and his company were, to the plaintiff's knowledge, customers of the defendants' Quayside branch. Accordingly the plaintiff rightly supposed that the defendant Johnson, in whose ability he reposed great confidence, had special knowledge of Brocks Refrigeration Ltd.'s financial affairs. It is to be observed that the defendant Johnson, as bank manager to the company, would be doing them a service by helping to introduce further capital, and he would also thereby be helping to reduce the company's overdraft, which, even as early as May 9, 1950, the district head office was suggesting, in the memoranda to which I have referred, ought to be reduced. He was in an invidious position in suggesting the investment to the plaintiff and in a still more invidious position when he was asked by the plaintiff for his advice. The defendant Johnson

did, however, advise the plaintiff that Brocks Refrigeration Ltd. was financially sound and, if he were able to do so with his own money or if he were in the plaintiff's place, he would invest £5,000 in the company's 6 per cent. cumulative preference shares. This advice meant that the proposed investment was a wise and sound one for the plaintiff to make.

The plaintiff then had a conversation with one Sowerby, the manager of the Gosforth branch of Barclays Bank Ltd., with whom the plaintiff had banked for some time and from whom he had then almost been weaned by the defendant Johnson. As a result Sowerby accompanied the plaintiff to another interview with the defendant Johnson, and the defendant Johnson repeated before Sowerby the advice which he had previously given to the plaintiff. Sowerby has not been called as a witness by either side. I draw no inference from his absence from the witness-box except that it would have been difficult for him to give evidence against a former customer and equally difficult for him to give evidence against a rival bank. It seems to me that there were no ground upon which the defendant Johnson could reasonably have advised that Brocks Refrigeration Ltd. was in a sound or strong financial position. No audited accounts existed. Such figures as the defendant Johnson had did not support the view that the company's finances were sound or strong. Their liquid assets were not sufficient to meet their current liabilities, even leaving out of account their not inconsiderable overdraft. Still less, in my view, could the investment by the plaintiff of £5,000 in preference shares in that company be reasonably recommended as a wise investment. The daunting risks of investing in a company of mushroom growth such as this, and, moreover, a company which was so clearly overtrading, should have been palpable even to the veriest tyro in financial affairs. The plaintiff had never in his life before his occasion bought a share. His inexperience and ignorance and dire need of advice should have been obvious, as I believe they were, to the defendant Johnson. I have no doubt that, but for the defendant Johnson's advice, the plaintiff would not have made the investment in Brocks Refrigeration Ltd. which he in fact made in May of 1950.

On May 9, 1950, the defendant Johnson dictated a letter for the plaintiff to sign. It is addressed to the defendant bank and it is in these terms:

> I hand you herewith Alliance Building Society passbook registered No. A. 18370 showing investments for £5,000 together with my letter of authority to that society requesting them to pay to you the proceeds of that investment against

your discharge. On receipt of such proceeds please pay the sum of £5,000 to the above mentioned company against their acknowledgment and undertaking to issue to me 5,000 6 per cent. preference shares of £1 each and retain to my order the balance of the proceeds.

The balance referred to in this letter amounted to between £40 and £50 and this sum was put to the plaintiff's credit in a suspense account opened for him by the defendant bank. In my view the defendant bank accepted the instructions contained in this letter as the plaintiff's bankers, and at any rate from that date the relationship of banker and customer existed between them. It is true that the express advice was in the first place given before the 9th May, but is was implicitly repeated on that day. On June 1, 1950, the defendant bank opened a current account for the plaintiff, and it is conceded that from this date the relationship of banker and customer existed between them.

At the beginning of October, 1950, the defendant Johnson told the plaintiff that he could acquire a further 2,500 preference shares in Brocks Refrigeration Ltd. He then told the plaintiff that this company was very strong financially and advised the plaintiff that it would be wise for him to subscribe for the shares. At this stage he knew that the plaintiff's disposable capital was about £17,000, £5,000 of which was already invested in the company's preference shares. The defendant Johnson had then no more reason than he had had in May for advising that the company was strong financially or that the investment was a wise one for the plaintiff to make. The plaintiff, relying on the defendant Johnson's advice, decided to make the investment and the defendant Johnson made out the cheque for £2,500 for the plaintiff to sign. The plaintiff signed it. The communications between the defendant Johnson and the district head office make it plain that prior to this transaction the company's overdraft had been allowed by the defendant Johnson considerably to exceed the permitted limit, and the district head office had been pressing the defendant Johnson to procure a reduction of the overdraft. The defendant Johnson in effect assured the district head office that the overdraft position would be eased by the additional capital, which he stated was £2,750. These facts were not disclosed by the defendant Johnson to the plaintiff.

In November, 1950, as appears from the defendants' internal memoranda, the defendant bank's district head office was again urging the defendant Johnson to procure a reduction of the company's overdraft. The defendant Johnson assured the district

head office that this would be accomplished by the company unloading unwanted stock to the value of £3,000 upon factors. To the defendant Johnson's knowledge, as he admitted, the company tried unsuccessfully during November to unload £3,000-worth of stock upon factors and upon J.&E. Hall Ltd.

At the beginning of December, 1950, a meeting took place between the plaintiff, Brock and the defendant Johnson. The defendant Johnson told the plaintiff that the company had a quantity of stock valued at £5,000 to unload and that, in order to obtain liquid cash for expansion, the company was prepared to sell this stock to the plaintiff for £3,000 provided that the plaintiff would leave the stock with the company on the terms that the company would repurchase it from the plaintiff in nine months' time for £3,300. The plaintiff asked the defendant Johnson for his advice about this proposal, and, indeed, the defendant Johnson admits that he knew the plaintiff was looking to him for advice. The defendant Johnson recommended the plaintiff that it would be quite safe and wise for him to enter into this transaction. I think he did tell the plaintiff that the stock should be segregated. He did not tell the plaintiff that the real reason for the company requiring the £3,000 was to reduce the overdraft, nor did he tell him that the company had been trying unsuccessfully to sell the stock to factors and to J.&E. Hall Ltd. Relying on the defendant Johnson's advice, the plaintiff did enter into this transaction and certain documents came into existence which I must read. On December 16, 1950, the plaintiff wrote to the Rock Building Society in the following terms:

I shall be grateful to you if you will pay to Messrs. Martins Bank Ltd., Quayside Branch, Newcastle-upon-Tyne, for credit of my account with them the sum of £3,000 out of my above-mentioned funds with you and I hereby authorize you to accept the bank's receipt as your full and sufficient discharge. Please return the passbook to the bank with your remittance. If you can expedite this I shall be obliged.

On December 16, he wrote to the bank:

I hand you herewith my Rock Building Society preference share passbook together with an authority addressed to that society to pay the sum of £3,000 to you for the credit of my account with you. Kindly expedite the matter and retain the passbook when returned to you.

Then there was a letter from Brocks Refrigeration Ltd. to the plaintiff in these terms:

We hereby acknowledge your cheque for £3,000 in payment of miscellaneous stock as per attached schedule. In accordance with the arrangement with you we agree to hold this said stock to your order in a separate part of our stores and we hereby further agree that there will be no storage charge and undertake to keep such stock fully insured without cost to you. It is a condition of the arrangement that you on your part will not dispose of any or all of such stock for a period of nine calendar months from the date hereof except to this company, Brocks Refrigeration Ltd., and it is agreed between us that all such sales will be on the basis of 10 per cent. added to the price at which we have sold the stock to you as per the attached schedule. We Brocks Refrigeration Ltd. hereby undertake to repurchase from you piecemeal or in bulk on the terms stated herein the whole of the stock within the said period of nine calendar months from the date hereof. We enclose a duplicate of this letter which please sign over the six-penny stamp at the foot thereof and return it to us.

This was done. A list of the stock was drawn up and the summary at the end of the list is in the defendant Johnson's own handwriting. Although the transaction was in form a sale by the plaintiff to the company, in reality it was clearly a loan by the plaintiff on the security of the stock. The documents constitute an unregistered bill of sale, and accordingly afforded the plaintiff no security at all. It would be difficult to imagine a more imprudent transaction from the point of view of the plaintiff, though from the point of view of the company, who were also the defendant bank's customers, and from the point of view of the defendant bank itself the transaction had certain attractions. The defendant Johnson had no reasonable grounds for advising the plaintiff, as he did, that it was safe or wise for the plaintiff to enter into this transaction.

The plaintiff had now, as a result of the defendant Johnson's advice, sunk £10,500 of his disposable capital of about £17,000 in Brocks Refrigeration Ltd. If the company foundered (and there was a grave risk of its doing so, as should have been obvious to the defendant Johnson) the plaintiff would lose his money. If the company made a huge success, as the defendant Johnson no doubt hoped that it would, the equity shareholders would reap the benefit, but it would profit the plaintiff nothing. Any investment in Brocks Refrigeration Ltd. would have been unwise. An investment which gave the investor a share in the equity commensurate with the capital he was investing, though unwise, would at any rate

have been a gamble, if an extremely hazardous one. The investment of £7,500 in preference shares and £3,000 in a loan had nothing to commend it. There is nothing to show that 6 per cent. was an unusually high yield in 1950 on preference shares in sound private companies. There is some evidence that at this time 3-3/4 to 4 per cent. was the average yield on preference shares in "blue chip" companies. One would expect such a difference of yield between a first class public company where the investor can at any time realize his investment and a private company where he cannot. There are two requirements for any preference share: (i) that the money invested shall be safe; and (ii) that the stipulated interest shall be paid. Any ordinarily prudent and competent bank manager, especially the bank manager of a commercial branch, should know that before advising the investment of money in the preference shares of any company, let alone a private company, he should be able to see from the balance-sheet figures that the financial position of the company is strong enough to ensure that the investor's capital is safe and from the trading history of the company that the interest would be paid. I cannot imagine that any ordinarily prudent and competent bank manager, on the facts and figures which the defendant Johnson had before him, could have advised the plaintiff to make any investments in preference shares of this company, whatever the supposed yield had been, still less that he would have advised a customer to enter into the £3,000 loan transaction.

In April, 1951, the company issued a debenture charging all its assets to the defendant bank. A little while before October 17, 1951, the plaintiff went to see the defendant Johnson to seek his advice, as the defendant Johnson admits, about a proposal that had been made to him by Brock. He told the defendant Johnson that Brock had suggested that the plaintiff should invest a further £4,000 in the company's preference shares and should also acquire 300 ordinary shares of a nominal value of £1 each at par, with a seat on the board. The plaintiff explained that he had been told by Brock that the company needed additional capital for further development in the Yorkshire area. The defendant Johnson appeared to know all about the proposal. He confirmed that the company needed the extra capital of £4,000 for further development, and said that J.&E. Hall Ltd. had asked the company to extend their business in the Yorkshire area. He advised the plaintiff that it would be a very wise move on his part to take up the shares. Relying on this advice, the plaintiff decided to take up the shares, and made out cheques for £4,000 and £300, which he left with the defendant

Johnson. At this time the permitted limit of the company's overdraft was £18,000 on the strength of the debenture, the company's assets having been assessed by the defendant bank at £25,000. The company had been allowed by the defendant Johnson to exceed this limit, and in fact had an overdraft of about £20,500. The district head office had been pressing the defendant Johnson, with some acerbity, to secure a reduction of the overdraft to within the permitted limit. The internal memorandum of October 17, 1951, shows that the defendant Johnson told the district head office that the company intended to consolidate and that "their present intense efforts will result in a considerable reduction in the level of their requirements which after the receipt of the £4,000" — from the plaintiff — "will be well within the limit of £18,000 arranged with the bank." No mention of the company's overdraft was made by the defendant Johnson to the plaintiff. The defendant Johnson's statement to the plaintiff that the £4,000 was required for further development in the Yorkshire area was clearly untrue. Nevertheless, having seen the defendant Johnson, I am not satisfied that he realized that it was untrue. In his muddle-headed way he may well have thought that, as the permitted limit of the overdraft had been exceeded to finance development, the £4,000 subscribed to help reduce the overdraft could properly be described as required for further development. The defendant Johnson did not disclose to the plaintiff that a debenture had been issued to the bank, nor did he say a word to the plaintiff about the company's alarming trading position for the year ending October 31, 1951. It is true that the balance sheet and the trading and profit and loss account for the year 1951 were not then in the defendant Johnson's possession but he had been supplied with quarterly figures. During that year the company lost, according to its accounts, over £21,000. In October, 1951, the defendant Johnson had at any rate the balance sheet and trading and profit and loss account of the company for the year ending October 31, 1950. These showed that the liquid assets were not sufficient to meet current liabilities and that the average monthly expenditure exceeded the average monthly revenue. Indeed, it should have been apparent to any bank manager in the defendant Johnson's position in October, 1951, that the company was precariously balanced on the very knife-edge of insolvency and that disaster appeared to be only round the corner. Yet the defendant Johnson, with no conceivable justification, advised the plaintiff that it would be wise for him to invest a further £4,000 in the company's preference shares thus subscribing, with the £3,000 loan, more

than half the total money invested in this company in order to obtain £300 worth of ordinary shares, that is to say about one-sixteenth of the equity, and a seat on the board, for all the good that that might then do him.

Shortly before this transaction, as the defendant Johnson well knew the plaintiff's disposable capital had become exhausted. He had sunk £10,500 in Brocks Refrigeration Ltd. and a considerable sum in True Shapes Ltd., and the balance he had spent on himself. The defendant Johnson advised the plaintiff that he might get his hands on the fund set up by his father to provide his step-mother with an income by buying his step-mother a life annuity equal to her then income. This could apparently be done for about £5,000, leaving the plaintiff with the balance of the fund for his own enjoyment or to be invested in accordance with the defendant Johnson's advice. It was out of the moneys received from this fund that the £4,000 for preference shares was found in October, 1951. So urgent was the necessity on October 17, 1951, to reduce the company's overdraft or to obtain some further security against it that, until such time as the plaintiff was able to realize £4,000 worth of securities from his step-mother's fund, he was asked by the defendant Johnson to give, and he did give, a guarantee to the defendant bank of £4,000 in favour of Brocks Refrigeration Ltd. The plaintiff had only the haziest notion of what was happening in relation to this guarantee and relied entirely upon the defendant Johnson.

One day towards the end of October, 1951, the plaintiff, whose company, True Shapes Ltd., Was then considerably in debt to the defendant bank, remarked to the defendant Johnson in relation to Brocks Refrigeration Ltd. that it was nice to be associated with a company whose account with the bank was in credit. The defendant Johnson told him that this company, far from being in credit, had an overdraft of £22,000. The plaintiff says that he was stunned. I believe him.

In February, 1952, there was an interview between the plaintiff and the defendant Johnson and Brock. A small private company called F. Adamson Ltd., in which Brock was interested and which was a customer of the defendant bank, required a guarantee of £1,000 on its bank overdraft. Brock, who, I am told and can well believe, had a magnetic personality and considerable powers of persuasion, in effect assured the plaintiff that the signing of the guarantee would be a mere formality and that there was no risk of the plaintiff being called upon to pay. The defendant Johnson confirmed this and advised the plaintiff that F. Adamson Ltd. was sound financially, and that its overdraft would undoubtedly be discharged by moneys outstanding that would be coming in during the next 12 months. The defendant Johnson advised the plaintiff that there was no real risk of his being called upon to pay under the guarantee. The defendant Johnson had no reasonable ground for giving this advice. I am satisfied that the plaintiff signed this guarantee relying upon the advice he received from the defendant Johnson. Ultimately the plaintiff was called upon to pay and did pay £990 3s. under this guarantee.

The plaintiff claims in this action the sum of £14,800 which he lost in Brocks Refrigeration Ltd., and the sum of £990 3s. which he was called upon to pay under his guarantee for F. Adamson Ltd. as damages for negligence, alternatively as damages for fraud, against the defendant bank and the defendant Johnson. I have already indicated that the claim in fraud fails, since I am not persuaded that the defendant did not honestly believe in the advice which he gave to the plaintiff. As to the claim in negligence, the defendants take the point that the defendant Johnson did not advise the plaintiff as he alleges. I am against the defendants on this point. It is clear from what I have already said that, in my judgment, the plaintiff did receive the advice from the defendant Johnson that the plaintiff says that he received.

The defendants' next point is that it was no part of their business as bankers to advise upon such financial transactions as the plaintiff entered into with Brocks Refrigeration Ltd. or in relation to F. Adamson Ltd., and that, accordingly, they were under no duty to advise the plaintiff carefully or competently in these matters. They say that, however careless or incompetent the advice the defendant Johnson gave the plaintiff may have been, since the defendants were under no duty to the plaintiff they are not responsible for any loss that may have been caused by that advice. They rely on the well-known case of *Le Lievre v. Gould*,[1] *Low v. Bouverie*[2] and, in particular, on *Banbury v. Bank of Montreal*.[3] This latter case seems to me to turn on its own special facts, and particularly on the fact that the plaintiff there admitted that the bank manager "had no general authority to advise" — in other words, that it was not within the scope of the "bank's business to advise on investments at large," *per* Lord Parker of Waddington.[4]

In my judgment, the limits of a banker's business cannot be laid down as a matter of law. The nature of such a business must in each case be a matter of fact and, accordingly, cannot be treated as if it were a matter of pure law. What may have

been true of the Bank of Montreal in 1918 is not necessarily true of Martins Bank in 1958.

In considering what is and what is not within the scope of the defendant bank's business I cannot do better than look at their own publications. I look first at their advertisement. That is in these terms:

> Although Martins is a bank with over 600 branches and world-wide connexions, our system of decentralization keeps us in touch with the customer's closest problems. We have six district head offices with boards of directors and general managers, so that the very best advice is available through our managers virtually on your doorstep;

and the advertisement is headed "We share your problems." Then I consider their booklet. The material parts read as follows:

> If you want help or advice about investments our managers will gladly obtain for you advice from the best available sources in such matters.

I observe that the "best available source" in this case was the bank itself, who were the bankers for Brocks Refrigeration Ltd. and thus knew everything that there was to know, or were in a position to know all that there was to know, about that company's financial standing. The next passage I read is as follows:

> In all these matters strict secrecy is observed and your affairs will not be divulged to any other person, relative or otherwise, without your knowledge or permission. You may consult your bank manager freely and seek his advice on all matters affecting your financial welfare. All these advantages are yours as the possessor of a bank account, current or deposit, and in these difficult days, when financial problems of one kind or another always seem to be cropping up, it is a great comfort to know that you have an impartial friend whose help you may seek without obligation.

I hardly think that it would be reasonable to construe those words as meaning "without obligation to the bank." The words "you may consult your bank manager freely and seek his advice on all matters affecting your financial welfare," seem to me to be in the widest possible terms. Then at the end of the booklet there is this paragraph:

> We have not gone into great detail, but if there is anything about which you would like more information please call in at the branch most convenient to you. We shall be delighted to make your acquaintance and to help you with your finances in every possible way, and we very much hope that you will have been sufficiently

attracted by the impressions you have formed after reading this booklet to have made up your mind to join the great band of satisfied customers who bank at Martins.

It is true that these publications saw the light of day only recently, but the defendant Johnson, who has a lifelong experience with the defendant bank and who was the only witness called on their behalf, said in evidence that the matters they speak to were as true in 1950 as they are today. I find that it was and is within the scope of the defendant bank's business to advise on all financial matters and that, as they did advise him, they owed a duty to the plaintiff to advise him with reasonable care and skill in each of the transactions to which I have referred. It is at any rate remarkable that the defendant bank, who seem to be keen competitors with other banks to obtain custom and who, in order to do so, apparently spend large sums of money in advertising that one of the advantages that they offer is expert advice in all financial matters without obligation, are taking the point in this court that they are under no duty to use any care or skill in giving such advice.

The defendant bank relies upon a book of secret instructions circulated to their branch managers. So secret is this book of instructions that the bank objected to producing it and produced only a photostat copy of the page containing instructions relating to stock exchange transactions. They read as follows:

> As the giving of advice to customers about stocks and shares other than concerning procedure is fraught with danger, managers must not directly advise the purchase or sale of any investment;

and a little lower down it says:

> The order should be recorded in the stocks and shares bought and sold register and passed in writing to the broker.

Then later it says:

> Each branch should transact stock exchange business through the broker or brokers allotted to it by head office or district office, unless in any particular case a broker is specifically named by the customer.

These instructions, which are headed "Stock Exchange Transactions," appear to relate only to stock exchange transactions and do not affect the kind of transactions with which this case is concerned. In any event these instructions do no, in my judgment, alter the true scope of the bank's business any more than any secret instructions issued by a firm of solicitors to their managing clerks forbidding them to advise on any particular legal topic save through counsel would cut down the scope of the firm's business vis-à-vis its clients.

The next point taken by the defendants is that the plaintiff was not a customer of the defendant bank at the date of the first transaction in May, 1950, in that no current account had then been opened by the plaintiff and that, therefore, they owed the plaintiff no duty of any kind, at any rate in respect of this transaction of May, 1950. I have already stated that, in my judgment, the plaintiff was a customer of the defendant bank on May 9, 1950. Nevertheless, even if he did not become a customer until later, the defendants would still, in my judgment, have been under a duty to exercise ordinary care and skill in advising him in relation to the £5,000 transaction. I have found that it is part of the defendants' business to advise customers and potential customers on financial matters of all kinds. In May of 1950 the plaintiff paid business not social calls on the defendant Johnson in his office. The plaintiff made it plain that he was consulting the defendant Johnson as manager of the defendant bank's Quayside branch. The plaintiff was a potential customer and one whose custom the defendant Johnson was anxious to acquire and soon did acquire. The plaintiff had asked the defendant Johnson if he would become his financial adviser, to which the defendant Johnson had replied that the defendant bank would be glad to take charge of his financial affairs. In my judgment, a fiduciary relationship existed between the plaintiff and the defendants. No doubt the defendant Johnson could have refused to advise the plaintiff, but, as he chose to advise him, the law in these circumstances imposes an obligation on him to advise with reasonable care and skill. This seems to me to be an even stronger case from the point of view of the plaintiff than cases of gratuitous deposit, such as *Giblin v. McMullen*,[5] or gratuitous services, such as *Whitehead v. Greetham*,[6] where it has been held that an obligation to use due care and skill may arise.

The defendants then take the point that the defendant Johnson was not negligent in the advice which he gave the plaintiff. Clearly the defendant Johnson was not negligent merely because his advice turned out to be wrong. Nor could he be negligent because he failed to exercise some extraordinary skill or care. His only obligation was to advise with the ordinary care and skill which the ordinary bank manager in his position might reasonably be expected to possess. It seems to me to be plain that in the circumstances of this case he ought never to have advised the plaintiff at all — certainly not without making a full disclosure to the plaintiff of the conflicting interests between the plaintiff and the defendant bank and the plaintiff and the defendant bank's other customers concerned. No one but an extremely foolish man or a knave could have given the plaintiff the advice given him by the defendant Johnson. As I have already indicated, I do not think that he is a knave. On the other hand, for the reasons stated earlier in this judgment, it is quite plain that none of the advice which he gave the plaintiff comes within measurable distance of being reasonably careful or skilful.

The last point taken by the defendants is that the plaintiff's loss was not occasioned by any negligence on the part of the defendants. It is argued that, even had the defendant Johnson advised the plaintiff against making any investment in Brocks Refrigeration Ltd. and against giving the guarantee, the plaintiff would still have acted as he did. The plaintiff did not strike me as being an over-confident young man or one who would not take advice. I think he had just enough sense to realize that he was no match for Mr. Brock, and I am certain that he relied entirely on the defendant Johnson's advice to protect him in his financial dealings with Mr. Brock. I hold that, but for the defendant Johnson's advice, the plaintiff would never have made any of the investments which he did make in Brock's Refrigeration Ltd., nor have given the guarantee in favour of F. Adamson Ltd. The fact that the plaintiff was the kind of young man who might have lost his money in other unwise transactions or soon spent it, perhaps more enjoyably, on extravagant living is beside the point. He has made out his case in negligence against both defendants and has established that he has lost £15,790 by reason of that negligence. There must, accordingly, be judgment for the plaintiff against both defendants for that sum, with costs.

Judgment for the plaintiff against both defendants.

(b) *Lloyds Bank Ltd. v. Bundy*†

[LORD DENNING M.R.:]

Broadchalke is one of the most pleasing villages in England. Old Herbert Bundy was a farmer there. His home was at Yew Tree Farm. It went back for 300 years. His family had been there for generations. It was his only asset. But he did a very foolish thing. He mortgaged it to the bank. Up to the very hilt. Not to borrow money for himself, but for the sake of his son. Now the bank have come down on him. They have foreclosed. They want to get him out of Yew Tree Farm and to sell it. They have brought this action against him for possession. Going out means ruin for him. He was granted legal aid. His lawyers put in a defence. They said that when he executed the charge to the bank he did not know what he was doing; or at any rate the circumstances were such that he ought not to be bound by it. At the trial his plight was plain. The judge was sorry for him. He said he was a 'poor old gentlemen'. He was so obviously incapacitated that the judge admitted his proof in evidence. He had a heart attack in the witness box. Yet the judge felt he could do nothing for him. There is nothing, he said, 'which takes this out of the vast range of commercial transactions'. he ordered Herbert Bundy to give up possession of Yew Tree Farm to the bank.

Now there is an appeal to this court. The ground is that the circumstances were so exceptional that Herbert Bundy should not be held bound.

1.   THE EVENTS BEFORE DECEMBER 1969

Herbert Bundy had only one son, Michael Bundy. He had great faith in him. They were both customers of Lloyds Bank at the Salisbury branch. They had been customers for many years. The son formed a company called MJB Plant Hire Ltd. It hired out

† [1974] 3 All E.R. 757 (C.A.). [Notes omitted.]

earth-moving machinery and so forth. The company banked at Lloyds too at the same branch.

In 1961 the son's company was in difficulties. The father on 19th September 1966 guaranteed the company's overdraft for £1,500 and charged Yew Tree Farm to the bank to secure the £1,500. Afterwards the son's company got further into difficulties. The overdraft ran into thousands. In May 1967 the assistant bank manager, Mr. Bennett, told the son the bank must have further security. The son said his father would give it. So Mr. Bennett and the son went together to see the father. Mr. Bennett produced the papers. He suggested that the father should sign a further guarantee for £5,000 and to execute a further charge for £6,000. The father said that he would help his son as far as he possibly could. Mr. Bennett did not ask the father to sign the papers there and then. He left them with the father so that he could consider them overnight and take advice on them. The father showed them to his solicitor, Mr. Trethowan, who lived in the same village. The solicitor told the father the £5,000 was the utmost that he could sink in his son's affairs. The house was worth about £10,000 and this was half his assets. On that advice the father on 27th May 1969 did execute the further guarantee and the charge, and Mr. Bennett witnessed it. So at the end of May 1967 the father had charged the house to secure £7,500.

2. THE EVENTS OF DECEMBER 1969

During the next six months the affairs of the son and his company went from bad to worse. The bank had granted the son's company an overdraft up to a limit of £10,000, but this was not enough to meet the outgoings. The son's company drew cheques which the bank returned unpaid. The bank were anxious. By this time Mr. Bennett had left to go to another branch. He was succeeded by a new assistant manager, Mr. Head. In November 1969 Mr. Head saw the son and told him that the account was unsatisfactory and that he considered that the company might have to cease operations. The son suggested that the difficulty was only temporary and that his father would be prepared to provide further money if necessary.

On 17th December 1969 there came the occasion which, in the judge's words, was important and disastrous for the father. The son took Mr. Head to see his father. Mr. Head had never met the father before. This was his first visit. He went prepared. He took with him a form of guarantee and form a charge filled in with the father's name ready for sig-

nature. There was a family gathering. The father and mother were there. The son and the son's wife. Mr. Head said that the bank had given serious thought whether they could continue to support the son's company. But that the bank were prepared to do so in this way. (i) The bank would continue to allow the company to draw money on overdraft up to the existing level of £10,000, but the bank would require the company to pay ten per cent of its incomings into a separate account. So that ten per cent would not go to reduce the overdraft. Mr. Head said that this would have the effect 'of reducing the level of borrowing'. In other words, the bank was cutting down the overdraft. (ii) The bank would require the father to give a guarantee of the company's account in a sum of £11,000 and to give the bank a further charge on the house of £3,500, so as to bring the total charge to £11,000. The house was only worth about £10,000, so this charge for £11,000 would sweep up all that the father had.

On hearing the proposal, the father said that Michael was his only son and that he was 100 per cent behind him. Mr. Head produced the forms that had already been filled in. The father signed them and Mr. Head witnessed them there and then. On this occasion, Mr. Head, unlike Mr. Bennett, did not leave the forms with the father; nor did the father have any independent advice.

It is important to notice the state of mind of Mr. Head and of the father. Mr. Head said in evidence:

> [The father] asked me what in my opinion the Company was doing wrong and the Company's position. I told him. I did not explain the Company's accounts very fully as I had only just taken over.... [The son] said the Company had a number of bad debts. I wasn't entirely satisfied with this. I thought the trouble was more deep-seated.... I thought there was no conflict of interest. I would think the [father] relied on me implicitly to advise him about the transaction as Bank Manager.... I knew he had no other assets except Yew Tree Cottage.

The father said in evidence:

> Always thought Mr. Head was genuine. I have always trusted him.... No discussion how business was doing that I can remember. I simply sat back and did what they said.

The solicitor, Mr. Trethowan, said of the father:

> [The father] is straightforward. Agrees with any-one.... Doubt if he understood all that Mr. Head explained to him.

So the father signed the papers. Mr. Head witnessed them and took them away. The father had charged the whole of his remaining asset, leaving himself with nothing. The son and his company gained a respite. But only for a short time. Five months later, in May 1970, a receiving order was made against the son. Thereupon the bank stopped all overdraft facilities for the company. It ceased to trade. The father's solicitor, Mr. Trethowan, at once went to see Mr. Head. He said he was concerned that the father had signed the guarantee.

In due course the bank insisted on the sale of the house. In December 1971 they agreed to sell it for £7,500 with vacant possession. The family were very disappointed with this figure. It was, they said, worth much more. Estate agents were called to say so. But the judge held that it was a valid sale and that the bank can take all the proceeds. The sale has not been completed, because the father is still in possession. The bank have brought these proceedings to evict the father.

3.   THE GENERAL RULE

Now let me say at once that in the vast majority of cases a customer who signs a bank guarantee or a charge cannot get out of it. No bargain will be upset which is the result of the ordinary interplay of forces. There are many hard cases which are caught by this rule. Take the case of a poor man who is homeless. He agrees to pay a high rent to a landlord just to get a roof over his head. The common law will not interfere. It is left to Parliament. Next take the case of a borrower in urgent need of money. He borrows it from the bank at high interest and it is guaranteed by a friend. The guarantor gives his bond and gets nothing in return. The common law will not interfere. Parliament has intervened to prevent moneylenders charging excessive interest. But it has never interfered with banks.

Yet there are exceptions to this general rule. There are cases in our books in which the courts will set aside a contract, or a transfer of property, when the parties have not met on equal terms, when the one is so strong in bargaining power and the other so weak that, as a matter of common fairness, it is not right that the strong should be allowed to push the weak to the wall. Hitherto those exceptional cases have been treated each as a separate category in itself. But I think the time has come when we should seek to find a principle to unite them. I put on one side contracts or transactions which are voidable for fraud or misrepresentation or mistake. All those are governed by settled principles.

I go only to those where there has been inequality of bargaining power, such as to merit the intervention of the court.

4.   THE CATEGORIES

The first category is that of 'duress of goods'. A typical case is when a man is in a strong bargaining position by being in possession of the goods of another by virtue of a legal right, such as, by way of pawn or pledge or taken in distress. The owner is in a weak position because he is in urgent need of the goods. The stronger demands of the weaker more than is justly due, and he pays it in order to get the goods. Such a transaction is voidable. He can recover the excess: see *Astley v. Reynolds*[1] and *Green v. Duckett*.[2] To which may be added the cases of '*colore officii*', where a man is in a strong bargaining position by virtue of his official position or public profession. He relies on it so as to gain from the weaker — who is urgently in need — more than is justly due: see *Pigot's Case*[3] cited by Lord Kenyon C.J.;[4] *Parker v. Bristol and Exeter Railway Co.*[5] and *Steele v. Williams*.[6] In such cases the stronger may make his claim in good faith honestly believing that he is entitled to make his demand. He may not be guilty of any fraud or misrepresentation. The inequality of bargaining power — the strength of the one versus the urgent need of the other — renders the transaction voidable and the money paid to be recovered back: see *Maskell v. Horner*.[7]

The second category is that of the 'unconscionable transaction'. A man is so placed as to be in need of special care and protection and yet his weakness is exploited by another far stronger than himself so as to get his property at a gross undervalue. The typical case is that of the 'expectant heir'. But it applies to all cases where a man comes into property, or is expected to come into it, and then being in urgent need another gives him ready cash for it, greatly below its true worth, and so gets the property transferred to him: see *Evans v. Llewellin*.[8] Even though there be no evidence of fraud or misrepresentation, nevertheless the transaction will be set aside: see *Fry v. Lane*[9] where Kay J. said:

> The result of the decisions is that where a purchase is made from a poor and ignorant man at a considerable undervalue, the vendor having no independent advice, a Court of Equity will set aside the transaction.

This second category is said to extend to all cases where an unfair advantage has been gained by an unconscientious use of power by a stronger party

196

against a weaker: see the cases cited in Halsbury's Laws of England[10] and in Canada, *Morrison v. Coast Finance Ltd.*[11] and *Knupp v. Bell.*[12]

The third category is that of 'undue influence' usually so called. These are divided into two classes as stated by Cotton L.J. in *Allcard v. Skinner.*[13] The first are these where the stronger has been guilty of some fraud or wrongful act — expressly so as to gain some gift or advantage from the weaker. The second are those where the stronger has not been guilty of any wrongful act, but has, through the relationship which existed between him and the weaker, gained some gift or advantage for himself. Sometimes the relationship is such as to raise a presumption of undue influence, such as parent over child, solicitor over client, doctor over patient, spiritual adviser over follower. At other times a relationship of confidence must be proved to exist. But to all of them the general principle obtains which was stated by Lord Chelmsford L.C. in *Tate v. Williamson*:[14]

> Wherever the persons stand in such a relation that, while it continues, confidence is necessarily reposed by one, and the influence which naturally grows out of that confidence is possessed by the other, and this confidence is abused, or the influence is exerted to obtain an advantage at the expense of the confiding party, the person so availing himself of his position will not be permitted to retain the advantage, although the transaction could not have been impeached if no such confidential relation had existed.

Such a case was *Tufton v. Sperni.*[15]

The fourth category is that of 'undue pressure'. The most apposite of that is *Williams v. Bayley*[16] where a son forged his father's name to a promissory note, and, by means of it, raised money from the bank of which they were both customers. The bank said to the father, in effect: 'Take your choice — give us security for your son's debt. If you do take that on yourself, then it will all go smoothly; if you do not, we shall be bound to exercise pressure.' Thereupon the father charged his property to the bank with payment of the note. The House of Lords held that the charge was invalid because of undue pressure exerted by the bank. Lord Westbury said:[17]

> A contract to give security for the debt of another, which is a contract without consideration, is, above all things, a contract that should be based upon the free and voluntary agency of the individual who enters into it.

Other instances of undue pressure are where one party stipulates for an unfair advantage to which the other has no option but to submit. As where

an employer — the stronger party — had employed a builder — the weaker party — to do work for him. When the builder asked for payment of sums properly due (so as to pay his workmen) the employer refused to pay unless he was given some added advantage. Stuart V.-C. said:

> Where an agreement, hard and inequitable in itself, has been exacted under circumstances of pressure on the part of the person who exacts it this Court will set it aside:

see *Ormes v. Beadel*;[18] *D & C Builders Ltd. v. Rees.*[19]

The fifth category is that of salvage agreements. When a vessel is in danger of sinking and seeks help, the rescuer is in a strong bargaining position. The vessel in distress is in urgent need. The parties cannot be truly said to be on equal terms. The Court of Admiralty have always recognised that fact. The fundamental rule is:

> If the parties have made an agreement, the Court will enforce it, unless it be manifestly unfair and unjust; but if it be manifestly unfair and unjust, the Court will disregard it and decree what is fair and just.

See *Akerblom v. Price*[20] per Brett L.J. applied in a striking case, *The Port Caledonia and The Anna*,[21] when the rescuer refused to help with a rope unless he was paid £1,000.

5. THE GENERAL PRINCIPLES

Gathering all together, I would suggest that through all these instances there runs a single thread. They rest on 'inequality of bargaining power'. By virtue of it, the English law gives relief to one who, without independent advice, enters into a contract on terms which are very unfair or transfers property for a consideration which is grossly inadequate, when his bargaining power is grievously impaired by reason of his own needs or desires, or by his own ignorance or infirmity, coupled with undue influences or pressures brought to bear on him by or for the benefit of the other. When I use the word 'undue' I do not mean to suggest that the principle depends on proof of any wrongdoing. The one who stipulates for an unfair advantage may be moved solely by his own self-interest, unconscious of the distress he is bringing to the other. I have also avoided any reference to the will of the one being 'dominated' or 'overcome' by the other. One who is in extreme need may knowingly consent to a most improvident bargain, solely to relive the straits in which he finds himself. Again, I do not mean to suggest that every transaction is saved by independent advice. But the absence of it may be fatal. With these explanations, I hope this principle will be found to reconcile the cases. Applying it to the present case, I would notice these points.

1. The consideration moving from the bank was grossly inadequate. The son's company was in serious difficulty. The overdraft was at its limit of £10,000. The bank considered that their existing security was insufficient. In order to get further security, they asked the father to charge the house — his sole asset — to the uttermost. It was worth £10,000. The charge was for £11,000. That was for the benefit of the bank. But not at all for the benefit of the father, or indeed for the company. The bank did not promise to continue the overdraft or to increase it. On the contrary, they required the overdraft to be reduced. All that the company gained was a short respite from impending doom.
2. The relationship between the bank and the father was one of trust and confidence. The bank knew that the father relied on them implicitly to advise him about the transaction. The father trusted the bank. This gave the bank much influence on the father. Yet the bank failed in that trust. They allowed the father to charge the house to his ruin.
3. The relationship between the father and the son was one where the father's natural affection had much influence on him.
4. He would naturally desire to accede to his son's request. He trusted his son. There was a conflict of interest between the bank and the father. Yet the bank did not realise it. Nor did they suggest that the father should get independent advice. If the father had gone to his solicitor — or to any man of business — there is no doubt that any one of them would say: 'You must not enter into this transaction. You are giving up your house, your sole remaining asset, for no benefit to you. The company is in such a parlous state that you must not do it.'

These considerations seem to me to bring this case within the principles I have stated. But, in case that principle is wrong, I would also say that the case falls within the category of undue influence of the second class stated by Cotton L.J. in *Allcard v. Skinner*.[22] I have no doubt that the assistant bank manager acted in the utmost good faith and was straightforward and genuine. Indeed the father said

so. But beyond doubt he was acting in the interests of the bank — to get further security for a bad debt. There was such a relationship of trust and confidence between them that the bank ought not to have swept up his sole remaining asset into their hands — for nothing — without his having independent advice. I would therefore allow this appeal.

[CAIRNS L.J.:]

I have had some doubt whether it was established in this case that there was such a special relationship between the defendant and the bank as to give rise to a duty on the part of the bank, through Mr. Head, to advise the defendant about the desirability of his obtaining independent advice. In the end, however, for the reasons given by Sir Eric Sachs in the judgment which he is about to deliver and which I have had the opportunity of reading, I have reached the conclusion that in the very unusual circumstances of this case there was such a duty. Because it was not fulfilled, the guarantee can be avoided on the ground of undue influence. I therefore agree that the appeal should be allowed, the judgment for the plaintiff set aside and judgment entered for the defendant.

[SIR ERIC SACHS:]

At trial in the county court a number of complex defences were raised, ranging from *non est factum*, through undue influence and absence of consideration to negligence in, and improper exercise of, the bank's duty when contracting for the sale of the relevant property. It is thus at the outset appropriate to record that in this court no challenge has been offered to any of the conclusions of the learned county court judge on law or on fact save as regards one aspect of one of the defences — appropriately pleaded as undue influence. As regards that defence, however, it is clear that he vitally misapprehended the law and the points to be considered and that moreover he apparently fell into error — as his own notes disclose — on an important fact touching that issue. In the result this court is thus faced with a task that is very far from being easy.

The first and most troublesome issue which here falls for consideration is whether on the particular and somewhat unusual facts of the case the bank was, when obtaining his signatures on 17th December 1969, in a relationship with the defendant that entailed a duty on their part of what can for convenience be called fiduciary care. (The phrase 'fiduciary care' is used to avoid the confusion with the common law duty of care — a different field of our jurisprudence.)

As was pointed out in *Tufton v. Sperni*,[23] the relationships which result in such a duty must not be circumscribed by reference to defined limits; it is necessary to —

> refute the suggestion that, to create the relationship of confidence, the person owing a duty must be found clothed in the recognizable garb of a guardian, trustee, solicitor, priest, doctor, manager, or the like.

Everything depends on the particular facts, and such a relationship has been held to exist in unusual circumstances as between purchaser and vendor, as between great uncle and adult nephew, and in other widely differing sets of circumstances. Moreover, it is neither feasible nor desirable to attempt closely to define the relationship, or its characteristics, or the demarcation line showing the exact transition point where a relationship that does not entail that duty passes into one that does (cf. Ungoed-Thomas J. in *Re Craig*[24]).

On the other hand, whilst disclaiming any intention of seeking to catalogue the elements of such a special relationship, it is perhaps of a little assistance to note some of those which have in the past frequently been found to exist where the court had been led to decide that this relationship existed as between adults of sound mind. Such cases tend to arise where someone relies on the guidance or advice of another, where the other is aware of that reliance and where the person on whom reliance is placed obtains, or may well obtain, a benefit from the transaction or has some other interest in it being concluded. In addition, there must, of course, be shown to exist a vital element which in this judgment will for convenience be referred to as confidentiality. It is this element which is so impossible to define and which is a matter for the judgment of the court on the facts of any particular case.

Confidentially, a relatively little used word, is being here adopted, albeit with some hesitation, to avoid the possible confusion that can arise through referring to 'confidence'. Reliance on advice can in many circumstances be said to import that type of confidence which only results in a common law duty to take care — a duty which may co-exist with but is not coterminous with that of fiduciary care. 'Confidentiality' is intended to convey that extra quality in the relevant confidence that is implicit in the phrase 'confidential relationship' (cf. per Lord Chelmsford L.C. in *Tate v. Williamson*,[25] Lindley L.J. in *Allcard v.*

Skinner[26] and Wright J. in *Morley v. Loughnan*[27]) and may perhaps have something in common with 'confiding' and also 'confidant', when, for instance, referring to someone's 'man of affairs'. It imports some quality beyond that inherent in the confidence that can well exist between trustworthy persons who in business affairs deal with each other at arm's length. It is one of the features of this element that once it exists, influence naturally grows out of it (cf. Evershed M.R. in *Tufton v. Sperni*,[28] following Lord Chelmsford L.C. in *Tate v. Williamson*[29]).

It was inevitably conceded on behalf of the bank that the relevant relationship can arise as between banker and customer. Equally, it was inevitably conceded on behalf of the defendant that in the normal course of transactions by which a customer guarantees a third party's obligations, the relationship does not arise. The onus of proof lies on the customer who alleges that in any individual case the line has been crossed and the relationship has arisen.

Before proceeding to examine the position further, it is as well to dispose of some points on which confusion is apt to arise. Of these the first is one which plainly led to misapprehension on the part of the learned county court judge. Undue influence is a phrase which is commonly regarded — even in the eyes of a number of lawyers — as relating solely to occasions when the will of one person has become so dominated by that of another that, to use the learned county court judge's words, 'the person acts as the mere puppet of the dominator'. Such occasions, of course, fall within what Cotton L.J. in *Allcard v. Skinner*[30] described as the first class of cases to which the doctrine on undue influence applies. There is, however, a second class of such cases. This is referred to by Cotton L.J. as follows:[31]

> In the second class of cases the Court interferes, not on the ground that any wrongful act has in fact been committed by the donee, but on the ground of public policy, and to prevent the relations which existed between the parties and the influence arising therefrom being abused.

It is thus to be emphasised that as regards the second class the exercise of the court's jurisdiction to set aside the relevant transaction does *not* depend on proof of one party being 'able to dominate the other as though a puppet' (to use the words again adopted by the learned county court judge when testing whether the defence was established) nor any wrongful intention on the part of the person who gains a benefit from it, but on the concept that once the special relationship has been shown to exist, no benefit can be retained from the transaction unless it has been positively established that the duty of fiduciary care has been entirely fulfilled. To this second class, however, the learned judge never averted and plainly never directed his mind.

It is also to be noted that what constitutes fulfilment of that duty (the second issue in the case now under consideration) depends again on the facts before the court. It may in the particular circumstances entail that the person in whom confidence has been reposed should insist on independent advice being obtained or ensuring in one way or another that the person being asked to execute a document is not insufficiently informed of some factor which could affect his judgment. The duty has been well stated as being one to ensure that the person liable to be influenced has formed 'an independent *and informed* judgment', or to use the phraseology of Lord Evershed M.R. in *Zamet v. Hyman*,[32] 'after full, free *and informed* thought'. (The italics in each case are mine.) As to the difficulties in which a person may be placed and as to what he should do when there is a conflict of interest between him and the person asked to execute a document, see *Bank of Montreal v. Stuart*.[33]

Stress was placed in argument for the bank on the effect of the word 'abused' as it appears in the above cited passage in the judgment of Cotton L.J.[1] and in other judgments and textbooks. As regards the second class of undue influence, however, that word in the context means no more than that once the existence of a special relationship has been established, then any possible use of the relevant influence is, irrespective of the intentions of the persons possessing it, regarded in relation to the transaction under consideration as an abuse — unless and until the duty of fiduciary care has been shown to be fulfilled or the transaction is shown to be truly for the benefit of the person influenced. This approach is a matter of public policy.

One further point on which potential confusion emerged in the course of the helpful addresses of counsel stemmed from submissions to the effect that Mr. Head, the assistant bank manager, should be cleared of all blame in the matter. When one has to deal with claims of breach of either common law or fiduciary care, it is not unusual to find that counsel for a big corporation tends to try and focus the attention of the court on the responsibility of the employee who deals with the particular matter rather than on that of the corporation as an entity. What we are concerned with in the present case is whether the element of confidentiality has been established as against the bank; Mr. Head's part in the affair is but one link in a chain of events. Moreover, when it

comes to a question of the relevant knowledge which will have to be discussed later in this judgment, it is the knowledge of the bank and not merely the personal knowledge of Mr. Head that has to be examined.

Having discussed the nature of the issues to which the learned county court judge should have directed his mind, it is now convenient to turn to the evidence relating to the first of them — whether the special relationship has here been shown to exist at the material time.

Counsel for the bank stressed the paucity of the evidence given by the defendant as to any reliance placed by him on the bank's advice — and, *a fortiori*, as to its quality. In cases of the type under consideration the paucity, or sometimes absence, of such evidence may well occur; moreover such evidence, if adduced, can be suspect. In the present case it is manifest that at the date of the trial the defendant's recollection of what happened was so minimal as to be unreliable, though not the slightest attack was made on his honesty. Indeed, his condition at trial was such that his sketchy proof was admitted into evidence. The learned judge's reference to him as 'poor old Mr. Bundy' and to his 'obvious incapacity' are in point on this aspect of the matter. It is not surprising in such a case for the result to depend on the success of the cross-examination of some witness called for the party against whom the special relationship is pleaded.

Prime reliance was accordingly placed by counsel for the defendant on answers given by Mr. Head when under cross-examination by junior counsel for the defendant. In the forefront came an answer which, unfortunately, was misapprehended by the learned judge, who thus came to make a vitally erroneous entry in his notebook. That answer is amended, after trial and judgment, in the notes before us, with the assent of the judge, is agreed to have been: 'I would think the defendant relied on me implicitly to advise him about the transaction as Bank Manager.' It is to be observed that in the judge's original note there is to be found the following, which was erased when the above quoted answer was substituted: 'Q. Defendant relied on you to advise *Company* as to the position in the transaction? A. No.' (The italicising of the word 'Company' is mine — to emphasise the distinction between the answer as noted and the answer now agreed to have been given.)

In the face of that vital answer, counsel for the bank found it necessary to submit that the words 'as bank manager' were intended to confine the reliance to the explaining of the legal effect of the document and the sums involved as opposed to more general advice as a confidant. I reject that submission. Taking Mr. Head's evidence as a whole, it seems plain that the defendant was, for instance, worried about, considered material, and asked questions about the company's affairs and the state of its accounts; and was thus seeking and being given advice on the viability of the company as a factor to be taken into account. (The vital bearing of this factor on the wisdom of the transaction is discussed later in this judgment.) Moreover, the answer to the judge followed immediately after: 'Q. Conflict of interest? A. No, it didn't occur to me at that time, I always thought there was no conflict of interest.' That question and answer (which was in itself immediately preceded by questions on the company's viability) do more than merely indicate a failure on the part of Mr. Head to understand the position; they indicate that at that stage of the cross-examination the questions being addressed to Mr. Head related to the wider issue of the wisdom of the transaction.

Moreover what happened on 17th December 1969 has to be assessed in the light of the general background of the existence of the long-standing relations between the Bundy family and the bank. It not infrequently occurs in provincial and country branches of great banks that a relationship is built up over the years, and in due course the senior officials may become trusted counsellors of customers of whose affairs they have an intimate knowledge. Confidential trust is place in them because of a combination of status, goodwill and knowledge. Mr. Head was the last of a relevant chain of those who over the years had earned or inherited, such trust whilst becoming familiar with the finance and business of the Bundys and the relevant company; he had taken over the accounts from Mr. Bennett (a former assistant manager at Salisbury) of whom the defendant said: 'I always trusted him.'

The fact that the defendant may later have referred to Mr. Head as being 'straight' is not inconsistent with this view — see also the statement of Mr. Trethowan, that: 'Defendant is straightforward. Agrees with anyone.' Indeed more than one passage in the defendant's evidence is consistent with Mr. Head's vital answer as to the implicit reliance placed on his advice.

It is, of course, plain that when Mr. Head was asking the defendant to sign the documents, the bank would derive benefit from the signature, that there was a conflict of interest as between the bank and the defendant, that the bank gave him advice, that he relied on that advice, and that the bank knew of the reliance. The further question is whether on the evidence concerning the matters already recited there was also established that element of confidentiality which has been discussed. In my judgment it is thus established. Moreover reinforcement for that view can be derived from some of the material which it is more convenient to examine in greater detail when considering what the resulting duty of fiduciary care entailed.

What was required to be done on the bank's behalf once the existence of that duty is shown to have been established? The situation of the defendant in his sitting-room at Yew Tree Farm can be stated as follows. He was faced by three persons anxious for him to sign. There was his son Michael, the overdraft of whose company had been, as is shown by the correspondence, escalating rapidly; whose influence over his father was observed by the judge — and can hardly not have been realised by the bank; and whose ability to overcome the difficulties of his company was plainly doubtful, indeed its troubles were known to Mr. Head to be 'deep-seated'. There was Mr. Head, on behalf of the bank, coming with the documents designed to protect the bank's interest already substantially made out and in his pocket. There was Michael's wife asking Mr. Head to help her husband.

The documents which the defendant was being asked to sign could result, if the company's troubles continued, in the defendant's sole asset being sold, the proceeds all going to the bank, and his being left penniless in his old age. That he could thus be rendered penniless was known to the bank — and in particular to Mr. Head. That the company might come to a bad end quite soon with these results was not exactly difficult to deduce (less than four months later, on 3rd April 1970, the bank were insisting that Yew Tree Farm be sold).

The situation was thus one which to any reasonably sensible person, who gave it but a moment's thought, cried aloud the defendant's need for careful independent advice. Over and above the need any man has for counsel when asked to risk his last penny on even an apparently reasonable project, was the need here for informed advice as to whether there was any real chance of the company's affairs becoming viable if the documents were signed. If not, there arose questions such as, what is the use of taking the risk of becoming penniless without benefiting anyone but the bank; is it not better both for you and your son that you, at any rate, should still have some money when the crash comes; and should not the bank at least bind itself to hold its hand for some given period? The answer to such questions could only be given in the light of a worthwhile appraisement of the company's affairs—without which the defendant could not come to an *informed judgment* as to the wisdom of what he was doing.

No such advice to get an independent opinion was given; on the contrary, Mr. Head chose to give his own views on the company's affairs and to take this course, though he had at trial to admit: 'I did not explain the company's affairs very fully I had only just taken over.' (Another answer that escaped entry in the learned judge's original notes.)

On the above recited facts, the breach of the duty to take fiduciary care is manifest. It is not necessary for the defendant to rely on another factor tending to show such a breach. The bank knew full well that the defendant had a well-known solicitor of standing. Mr. Trethowan, who usually advised him on important matters, including the previous charge signed in May 1969, only seven months earlier. Indeed, on that occasion the bank seems very properly to have taken steps which either ensured that Mr. Trethowan's advice was obtained or at least assumed it was being obtained. It is no answer that Mr. Head, relatively a newcomer to the Bundy accounts at the Salisbury branch, may not personally have known these matters; it is the bank's knowledge that is material. Incidentally, Mr. Head discussed the relevant accounts with his manager.

The existence of the duty and its breach having thus been established, there remains the submission urged by counsel for the bank that whatever independent advice had been obtained, the defendant would have been so obstinately determined to help his son that the documents would anyway have been signed. The point fails for more than one reason, of which it is sufficient to mention two. First, on a question of fact it ignores the point that the independent advice might well have been to the effect that it would benefit the son better in the event of an almost inevitable crash if his father had some money left after it occurred—advice which could have affected the mind of the defendant. Secondly, once the relevant duty is established, it is contrary to public policy that benefit of the transaction be retained by the person under the duty unless he positively shows that the duty of fiduciary care has been fulfilled: there is normally no room for debate on the issue as to what would have happened had the care been taken.

It follows that the county court judgment cannot stand. The learned judge having failed to direct his mind to a crucial issue and to important evidence supporting the defendant's case thereon, at the very least the latter is entitled to an order for a new trial.

That would produce as an outcome of this appeal a prolongation of uncertainties affecting others beside the defendant, who still resides at Yew Tree Farm, and could hardly be called desirable even if one left out of account the latter's health and financial position. In my judgment, however, a breach by the bank of their duty to take fiduciary care has, on the evidence, as a whole been so affirmatively established that this court can and should make an order setting aside the guarantee and the charge of 17th December 1969.

I would add that Mr. Head was, of course, not guilty of any intentional wrongful act. In essence what happened was that having gone to Yew Tree Farm 'in the interests of the bank' (as counsel for the bank stressed more than once), he failed to apprehend that there was a conflict of interest as between the bank and the defendant, that he was in an impossible position when seeking to deal with questions of the type that he was being asked, and that he should have insisted on the obvious need for independent advice. In addition, it was unfortunate that he was—through some absence of relevant information from Mr. Bennett (who had previously dealt with the relevant accounts)—not aware of the way Mr. Trethowan had come to advise the defendant as regards the May 1969 guarantee and charge. Though I have not founded any part of this judgment on that facet of the case, I am yet inclined to view the bank's failure to suggest that Mr. Trethowan be consulted when they were pursuing their quest for the defendant's signature in such a potentially disastrous situation, as open to criticism and as something that might of itself have led to an adverse decision against the bank in this particular case.

The conclusion that the defendant has established that as between himself and the bank the relevant transaction fell within the second category of undue influence cases referred to by Cotton L.J. in *Allcard v. Skinner*[34] is one reached on the single issue pursued on behalf of the defendant in this court. On that issue we have had the benefit of cogent and helpful submissions on matter plainly raised in the pleadings. As regards the wider areas covered in masterly survey in the judgment of Lord Denning M.R., but not raised *arguendo*, I do not venture to express an opinion—though having some sympathy with the views that the courts should be able to give relief of a party who has been subject to undue pressure as defined in the concluding passage of his judgment on that point.

There remains to mention that counsel for the bank, whilst conceding that the relevant special relationship could arise as between banker and customer, urged in somewhat doom-laden terms that a decision taken against the bank on the facts of this particular case would seriously affect banking practice. With all respect to that submission, it seems necessary to point out that nothing in this judgment affects the duties of a bank in the normal case where it is obtaining a guarantee, and in accordance with standard practice explains to the person about to sign its legal effect and the sums involved. When, however, a bank, as in this case, goes further and advises on more general matters germane to the wisdom of the transaction, that indicates that it may — not necessarily must — be crossing the line into the area of confidentiality so that the court may then have to examine all the facts, including, of course, the history leading up to the transaction, to ascertain whether or not that line has, as here, been crossed. It would indeed be rather odd if a bank which vis-à-vis a customer attained a special relationship in some ways akin to that of a 'man of affairs' — something which can be a matter of pride and enhance his local reputation — should not where a conflict of interest has arisen as between itself and the person advised be under the resulting duty now under discussion. Once, as was inevitably conceded, it is possible for a bank to be under that duty, it is, as in the present case, simply a question for 'meticulous examination' of the particular facts to see whether that duty has arisen. On the special facts here it did arise and it has been broken.

The appeal should be allowed.

Appeal allowed; judgment below set aside. Judgment for defendant on claim and counterclaim. Legal charge and guarantee dated 17th December 1969 set aside; documents to be delivered up for cancellation. Leave to appeal to the House of Lords refused.

(c) *Standard Investments Ltd. v. C.I.B.C.*†

[GOODMAN J.A.:]

This is an appeal by the plaintiffs from a judgment of Griffiths J. dismissing without costs the plaintiffs' action against the defendant for damages for an alleged breach of fiduciary duties owed them by it and for an alleged breach of its duties as a pledgee of certain property of the plaintiffs. There is also a cross-appeal by the defendant from the trial judge's refusal to award costs to the defendant and from the trial judge's finding that there was initially a fiduciary relationship between the plaintiffs and the defendants.

The events which formed the basis of the action took place during the period November, 1971, to July 17, 1979. The learned trial judge has set forth in his reasons at great length and in meticulous detail the evidence dealing with those events and his findings of fact based on the evidence. Except as hereinafter noted I accept those findings.

For the sake of convenience and a better understanding of the reasons which follow I consider it advisable to repeat the relevant findings of fact. In so doing I will for the most part resort to the words used by the learned trial judge rather than attempt to paraphrase his findings. The trial judgment has been reported in 45 O.R. (2d) 16, 5 D.L.R. (4th) 452, 24 B.L.R. 1.

FACTS

The plaintiff, Mr. Reuben Cohen, is a lawyer who resides and practises law in the City of Moncton, New Brunswick. The plaintiff, Mr. Leonard Ellen, is a businessman who resides in the City of Montreal, Quebec, where he operates a family lumber business. Since 1970 Ellen has also been a licensed stockbroker and investment dealer. Since the early 1950s they have been equal partners in a number of business ventures.

The plaintiff, Standard Investments Limited ("Standard Investments") is a real estate and investment company in which each has an equal interest and which was operated by them as a real estate and

---

† (1985), 22 D.L.R. (4th) 410 (Ont. C.A.); leave to appeal to S.C.C. dismissed February 3, 1986, (1986) 53 O.R. (2d) 663 (note).

investment firm. The plaintiff, Brentwood Realty Ltd. ("Brentwood"), is a real estate and investment company beneficially owned by Cohen and members of his family.

The defendant, Canadian Imperial Bank of Commerce ("CIBC"), is a chartered bank carrying on business throughout Canada.

In the 1950s and 1960s Ellen and Cohen proceeded to purchase shares of maritime provinces trust companies in order to obtain control of them. In 1957 they had acquired a majority interest in Central Trust Company of Canada which had branch offices in New Brunswick and Nova Scotia. By 1967 they had acquired control of Nova Scotia Savings and Loan Company which carried on business in Nova Scotia and Prince Edward Island. By the late 1960s they had acquired a majority interest in the Eastern Canada Savings and Loan Company. In 1974 the first two named trust companies were amalgamated and in 1976 the last named trust company was amalgamated with the prior amalgamated companies under the name Central and Eastern Trust Company.

Standard Investments owned a building in Moncton in which Cohen carried on his law practice. The defendant for many years leased space in the building and operated a branch there. The branch manager was a person with whom Cohen had a close relationship, they having been schoolmates in earlier years. This manager operated the branch from 1968 to 1982.

At the time the manager commenced to manage the branch, Ellen's lumber business banked with the Toronto-Dominion Bank. For personal investment borrowings Ellen and Cohen went to either the Royal Bank of Canada or the Bank of Montreal. The maritime provinces trust companies controlled by Cohen and Ellen banked with the Royal Bank.

The defendant's branch bank manager solicited business from Cohen for the Moncton branch. As a result, Cohen transferred the business of Brentwood to the Moncton branch about 1964. From 1969 to 1973, Cohen had a personal line of credit and later opened a trust account for his law firm at this branch. Between July, 1969 and April, 1973, Brentwood borrowed from the bank amounts ranging from $200,000 to $750,000. The loans were secured by pledges to the bank of Eastern Canada Savings and Loan Company shares and Nova Scotia Savings and Loan shares together with Cohen's personal guarantee.

In applying for credit for Brentwood on September 27, 1971, the branch manager recommended to the regional general manager:

In view of the high value placed on Cohen's business and his goodwill and the fact he has been responsible in directing good lending and deposit business to this branch, we strongly recommend the credit for your favourable consideration.

In the early 1970s Cohen and Ellen contemplated expanding their trust company operations outside of the maritime provinces into the rest of Canada. In order to do so they decided to endeavour to acquire a controlling interest in Crown Trust Company (Crown Trust) which was a major trust company with head office at Toronto, doing business throughout Canada but with little business in the maritime provinces. For various reasons Ellen and Cohen were of the opinion it would make a perfect "fit" if merged with their other trust companies.

The defendant was the banker for Crown Trust. Crown Trust's 750,000 issued shares were widely distributed. Cohen and Ellen began to buy Crown Trust shares through Standard Investments in June, 1971, and by the end of that year had acquired approximately 52,000 shares. These shares yielded a 6% return on investment and Cohen was of the opinion they were a good investment for this reason. He testified that he and Ellen did not wish to embark upon a programme of major purchases until they had achieved the amalgamation of the maritime provinces trust companies.

Ellen and Cohen decided that in order to succeed in their efforts to obtain control of Crown Trust they would require the assistance, advice and financial support of the defendant. They reasoned that they would require the goodwill of the defendant and financing of 12 to 15 million dollars to purchase all of the 750,000 Crown Trust issued shares at a price they considered would average $20 per share. They also considered that their success in acquiring control would depend on obtaining an introduction to and the support of one John A. McDougald.

Cohen and Ellen considered that the acquisition of a 25% block of Crown Trust shares owned by the estate of the late John McMartin was extremely important in their pursuit of control. Crown Trust together with two elderly beneficiaries were the executors of that estate. The beneficiaries appeared to rely heavily on the advice of McDougald. At this time McDougald was a director of the defendant. Prior to 1970 he had been a director of Crown Trust but he gave up the directorship in 1970 when the *Bank Act*, R.S.C. 1970, c. B-1, s. 18(6), prohibited persons from serving as a director of both a bank and trust company. He at that time set up the

"Toronto Advisory Board" of Crown Trust and as chairman of that board continued to exert control and to be a dominant force in the affairs of Crown Trust.

In early 1972, in order to strengthen their relationship with the defendant and to facilitate their plan to acquire control of Crown Trust, Ellen and Cohen transferred the banking business of Standard Investments to the Moncton Main St. branch of the defendant. It obtained a $500,000 line of credit initially. This was increased in later years and by 1979 its borrowings were between two and three million dollars. Brentwood's borrowings increased from $750,000 in January, 1972 to 2.5 million in July, 1979. Standard Investments and Brentwood used the borrowed funds to buy shares in the maritime provinces trust companies and Crown Trust. Standard Investment loans were secured by pledges of the maritime provinces trust companies' stock and Crown Trust stock acquired from time to time and by full personal guarantees of Ellen and Cohen. The same procedure was followed by Brentwood except the personal guarantee was that of Cohen alone.

The trial judge found at p. 21 O.R., p. 457 D.L.R.: "There is no doubt that the banking business of the two companies, particularly that of Standard Investments, were important acquisitions by the Bank." In February, 1974, the Moncton branch manager in a report memorandum to the regional manager reiterated her comment contained in the September 27, 1971 credit application that Cohen in the past had directed good business to the branch and added that further collateral benefits were expected to accrue from the cultivation of the account and the connection was considered to be an important one to the branch. The memorandum stated: "Both men are influential in their fields of endeavour and Mr. Cohen carries considerable influence in New Brunswick...." Neither Cohen nor Ellen discussed their aspirations to expand their maritime provinces trust company interests nationally through Crown Trust with the branch manager nor was specific mention ever made in the written credit applications of the intention of Cohen or Ellen or their investment companies to acquire a controlling interest in Crown Trust.

In late 1971, Cohen had a discussion with Mr. J.L. Seaborn, vice-president in charge of the maritime operations of the defendant, in which he disclosed details of his interest in the maritime provinces trust companies and of his plan to acquire control of another company. Seaborn (deceased at the time of trial) in a memorandum to file (ex. 10) dated November 9, 1971 (erroneously referred to in

the reasons for judgment as dated December 8, 1971) commented:

> We were not furnished with any details of the transactions or companies involved, but Cohen wishes to discuss an acquisition proposal with our President to ascertain his reaction to the feasibility, and if the proposition appears to be acceptable, with credit of $12/$15 million involved, to request his assistance in effecting the necessary introductions to a member of the Bank's board for further discussion.

That memorandum was sent on by Seaborn to the defendant's head office with a further memorandum dated December 8, 1971, which read in part as follows:

> In furtherance of the request he made in the attached, we contacted Cohen by telephone to tell him the writer would be in Toronto next week and he asked us to speak with Mr. Wadsworth. He is not prepared at this stage to furnish names to the writer, but has asked us to arrange that he may call Mr. Wadsworth and discuss the matter, which he indicates is some sort of working arrangement with another Company. He understood one of our directors makes the major decisions in the Company concerned and if Mr. Wadsworth feels after a conversation with Mr. Cohen that the matter might be pursued, Mr. Cohen would ask Mr. Wadsworth to make the necessary introductions. Mr. Cohen proposes he would come to Toronto in January for that purpose at a time to be arranged.
>
> In view of Cohen's substantial holdings therein, we attach herewith the latest interim report of Central Trust Company, and the Annual Report of Nova Scotia Trust Company.

At this time the president and chief executive officer of the defendant was Mr. Page Wadsworth. The director of the defendant referred to in the memorandum was McDougald. The trial judge found as a fact, contrary to the evidence given by Cohen, that Cohen did not reveal to Seaborn the name of the trust company in which he and Ellen wished to acquire a controlling interest.

Arrangements were made for Cohen and Ellen to meet Wadsworth in Toronto on April 6, 1972. Prior to the meeting Seaborn wrote a confidential letter to Wadsworth, dated March 13, 1972. That letter read in part:

> We record having furnished you with a memorandum on Cohen under date of December 8 and while his call has been delayed, *the purpose is unchanged as he wishes your advice and assistance in arrangements which would result in the*

operations of Central Trust Company becoming national instead of only Maritime. He hopes Mr. Leonard Ellen of Montreal will also be available to meet with you and you will see they have worked in concert in their Trust Company investments for some years. [Emphasis added.]

And later in that letter Mr. Seaborn said:

Since our previous advices also approval has been given to our acquiring the account of Standard Investments Limited — the part of the Cohen, Ellen connection — from the Bank of Montreal in the amount of two million dollars, mainly to carry the Company's stock investments. As a matter of interest, Cohen tells us Maurice A. Masse, Executive Vice-President of Bank of Montreal, flew to Moncton and met with him in an unsuccessful attempt to retain the business.

Before the meeting of April 6, 1972, certain significant decisions had been made by senior officers of the defendant as evidenced by a confidential memorandum dated January 5, 1972, issued by Mr. T.L. Avison, who in 1972 was the vice-president in charge of the investment division of the defendant (later to become chief general manager), to Mr. S.F. McCall, a senior officer of that division. In the normal course McCall would report to Avison and Avison would in turn reported to Mr. Russell E. Harrison, at that time chief general manager (who by 1978 had become chairman and chief executive officer of the defendant). The memorandum of January 6, 1972, was as follows:

Yesterday morning I received a phone call from the Chairman. He advised that he and our Director, Mr. J.A. McDougald had had several discussions about the common stock of the subject company. He said that the Chairman of the subject company had mentioned to him that he suspected a group was active in acquiring the common stock, hopefully with the intention of obtaining control eventually of Crown Trust.

In order to prevent any other group from being in a position, possibly, to acquire control he indicated to Mr. McDougald that the Bank would purchase sufficient stock to increase its holdings to just under 10% of the total outstanding common stock issued. At the present time there are 750,000 shares issued. The Bank at the present time hold 15,000 shares, so that purchases not to exceed 59,900 could be made without any contravention of *The Bank Act.*

The Chairman also advised that these shares would be acquired on behalf of the Bank through Dominion Securities Corporation and that Mr. D.H. Ward personally would handle the transactions.

In a subsequent conversation with Mr. Ward he told me that he had been speaking with Mr. McDougald who was aware of the action being taken by the Bank.

Would you be good enough to keep a record in your files of the daily accumulative totals until we reach the amount set or until such time as Mr. Ward's instructions are changed. The Chairman indicated in his initial phone call that while he was anxious to acquire this block of stock, for the reasons given above, he was not anxious to conduct the operation in such a way that we would acquire stock regardless of cost. Mr. Ward is aware of this and will use his best judgment in conducting the market operation to avoid any undue upward pressure on its price.

The subject company referred to in the memorandum was Crown Trust Company and the chairman referred to in the first paragraph thereof, was Neil J. McKinnon, the chairman of the defendant at that time and until December, 1973, when he was replaced by Wadsworth.

The defendant had originally held 15,000 shares of Crown Trust stock. Following the memorandum it increased its shareholding gradually until it held 74,900 shares by November 15, 1972. This was the maximum number which it could legally hold and represented approximately 10% of the issued shares of Crown Trust. In purchasing the shares, the defendant followed the unusual procedure of arranging for the purchase of the stock through a senior officer of the security company to maintain a confidentiality about its stock purchasing activities. In reporting on the purchases the officer referred to the "X" account.

By memorandum of April 6, 1973 (exactly one year after the first meeting between Wadsworth and Cohen and Ellen), Avison reported to Mr. O.L. Robertson, then second-in-command of the defendant's investment division (a copy being forwarded to Harrison, the chief general manager), as follows:

The Bank holds 74,900 common shares of the subject company at a total book cost of $1,358,759, an average book cost of $18.14 per share. The current market is approximately $22-1/2. This holding in the Bank's portfolio represents 9.987% of the outstanding common shares of the Crown Trust Company.

You will recall that at the request of the Chairman we purchased through Mr. D.H. Ward of Dominion Securities Corporation Limited, in accordance with his instructions, 59,900 shares of Crown Trust. This amount of shares plus the 15,000 shares which the Bank previously held brings our total up to the figure mentioned above.

You will also recall that the reason given for the purchase of this stock was that it had been indicated to the Bank, through the Chairman, that there seemed to be an attempt, possibly by the Central Trust in Moncton, New Brunswick, to acquire control of the subject company. To avoid this proportion of the shares being purchased by those attempting to acquire control, through Mr. Ward of D.S. we were asked to, and purchased, the above shares as noted.

The Chairman advised me on Tuesday afternoon that it was possible that some buyer, not necessarily the New Brunswick trust company referred to above, but probably on its behalf, might suggest the sale of the Bank's stock as a block transaction at levels substantially over the quoted market. He asked that no sales of stock be made without reference and I assured him, because you or I would be aware of such an offering that no action would be taken without reference to the Chief General Manager. The impression which I received from the Chairman's comments was that we were holding this stock, quite apart from its intrinsic value as an investment, for reasons of policy and therefore no sales should be contemplated solely on a basis of market or price consideration. [Emphasis added.]

The trial judge found that the purchase of the Crown Trust stock by the defendant was to thwart, if possible, any attempt by Cohen and Ellen or their companies and in particular their maritime provinces trust companies, to acquire a controlling interest in Crown Trust. He found the entry of the defendant into the market to purchase shares to prevent others from acquiring a controlling interest in a customer of the bank an unusual and unprecedented step. Harrison testified at trial that in his 40 years of banking experience he had never known of a similar policy decision by the defendant. Although the purchases of the Crown Trust stock by the defendant commenced shortly after the meeting between Cohen and Seaborn and before the meeting between Wadsworth, Cohen and Ellen and continued for a period of approximately seven months after that meeting, the trial judge was not prepared to find that there was a breach of confidence on the part of Seaborn or Wadsworth by indicating to anyone the interest of Ellen and Cohen in Crown Trust which resulted in the purchase of Crown Trust stock by the defendant to thwart their objective. It was his view that such a finding would be speculative having regard to the fact that prior purchases of Crown Trust stock by the plaintiffs may have been enough to arouse suspicions of their intention.

Notwithstanding the fact that it seems highly suspicious that McKinnon and McDougald were spurred into action shortly after Seaborn's report of December 8, 1971, and during the negotiations for

the meeting between Wadsworth, Ellen and Cohen, I am of the view that the trial judge was entitled to make the finding which he did based on the evidence available and I am not prepared to interfere with such finding nor would I be justified in so doing even if so inclined.

The Meeting with Page Wadsworth on April 6, 1972

The trial judge found that Wadsworth had no information prior to the meeting that Crown Trust would be the main subject of discussion. His only information was that contained in the memorandum of December 8, 1971, and a confidential letter sent by Seaborn to Wadsworth dated March 13, 1972. The relevant parts of that letter have been quoted above.

The letter made it clear that Cohen would be seeking advice and assistance with respect to an acquisition or merger. The memoranda of Seaborn dated November 9, 1971, and December 8, 1971 (not the letter as stated in the trial judge's reasons for judgment), which had been forwarded to Wadsworth indicated that if the proposition appeared feasible then credit financing from the defendant in the order of 12 to 15 million dollars would be required and they would need an introduction to a member of the defendant's board of directors.

The trial judge made the following important findings with respect to what transpired at the meeting. He found that Cohen and Ellen "bared their souls" to Wadsworth and disclosed their plans for eventual amalgamation of the maritime provinces trust companies and of the possible merger of these companies on a national scale with Crown Trust. They told him they would like an introduction to McDougald to discuss with him either an acquisition of or a possible merger with Crown Trust. Ellen and Cohen knew the defendant owned some shares in Crown Trust but did not know the exact extent of such holdings. He concluded that there was probably no specific reference made to the defendant's shareholdings although Ellen and Cohen made it clear to Wadsworth they were interested in acquiring all Crown Trust stock. He found the subject-matter of financing the proposed acquisition of control requiring 12 to 15 million dollars in funds was probably given a passing reference at the meeting but no formal application for credit was made at that time. Wadsworth agreed with Cohen and Ellen that their proposal for merger with Crown Trust was sound and feasible in principle. He concurred that the best person for them to see at that stage for working something out with Crown Trust was McDougald and he undertook to arrange the introduction and said he would do everything he could to help them along in their venture. There was no note of discouragement.

The trial judge also found that Wadsworth had not been informed at the time of the April 6, 1972 meeting of the defendant's policy to purchase Crown Trust stock to thwart the efforts of the maritime provinces trust companies to gain control of Crown Trust nor had he been informed of McDougald's firm position that there should be no merger of Crown Trust with these companies or any other trust company. Although it seems strange indeed that the defendant's president was unaware of such an unusual and important decision and action on the part of his bank, the evidence given at trial indicated that there was during this period in 1972 a breakdown in the normal communication between its chairman, McKinnon and its president, Wadsworth, resulting from a lack of harmony between them. The defendant's decision to enter into the market to purchase shares in Crown Trust to thwart the efforts of the plaintiffs to acquire control of Crown Trust preceded this critical meeting. In my opinion Ellen and Cohen were entitled to assume that Wadsworth, as president of the defendant bank, would be fully informed with respect to any position or decision which the defendant may have taken or made with respect to an attempt by anyone to gain control of Crown Trust. It is unreasonable to expect that they would envisage that a lack of harmony between the president and chairman would result in ignorance on the part of the president with respect to an important and unprecedented policy decision made on behalf of the bank nor should they suffer any loss or damage which may have resulted from such lack of harmony if there has been a breach of duty towards them on the part of the defendant. The trial judge found that Ellen and Cohen left the meeting feeling very "encouraged".

The trial judge has set forth at pp. 27–29 O.R., pp. 463–65 D.L.R., a part of the cross-examination of Wadsworth at the trial. The question and the answers thereto given by Wadsworth make it clear that if he had known at the time of the meeting of the policy decision previously made by the bank, he would have considered that the defendant had a conflict of interest and have advised Ellen and Cohen that he could not discuss the matter of the acquisition of Crown Trust with them. He also stated he would have told them that no purpose could be served in getting them an appointment with McDougald but if they insisted on obtaining an

appointment he might have arranged it "because we were interested in developing our connections with both these gentlemen". [Emphasis added.]

Ellen and Cohen testified that, if Wadsworth had discouraged them, had told them that the defendant was not prepared to assist them or that they would not likely be successful in their quest to obtain control of Crown Trust, they would have discontinued their plans immediately and would probably have disposed of their shareholdings in Crown Trust. The trial judge referred to this evidence at p. 29 O.R., p. 465 D.L.R. He did not state whether he accepted this evidence but there is no evidence to the contrary.

There were at least three other meetings between 1972 and 1976 at which control of Crown Trust was discussed by Wadsworth and Cohen and on one of these occasions in 1973 Ellen was present. Ellen and Cohen gave evidence to the effect that Wadsworth never in any way discouraged them during these years and they were not told that McDougald opposed their plans. Wadsworth gave evidence to the effect that he made it clear to Cohen at these meetings that he and Ellen might not be successful and that "he could go no further" consistent with his duty to breach the confidentiality of the information received by him from McDougald. Wadsworth stated that he told Cohen in particular he would not be successful.

Wadsworth had become chairman of the defendant in December, 1973. Thereafter he had more occasion to talk to McDougald on a regular basis. He testified that in August, 1974, he had a discussion with McDougald regarding Crown Trust and the interests of Cohen and Ellen in which McDougald advised him that he did not favour the proposed merger of Crown Trust with Eastern Canada Savings and Loan and that he had several frank discussions with Cohen and had explained his position. Wadsworth dictated a memorandum of that discussion for his own file dated August 20, 1974. It is set forth at p. 30 O.R., p. 466 D.L.R. of the report. The closing sentence reads: "In the light of the above we should in no way encourage Cohen or Ellen that a deal with Crown Trust is possible."

In dealing with the foregoing evidence and in endeavouring to resolve the minor but important conflicts in the evidence of Wadsworth as opposed to that of Cohen and Ellen, the trial judge said at p. 31 O.R., p. 467 D.L.R.:

> I accept Mr. Wadsworth's evidence that he did not encourage Messrs. Cohen or Ellen to believe that their efforts to acquire control of Crown Trust would inevitably be successful.

He also said that:

> It is common ground that he told them that their success would depend entirely on their ability to obtain the support of Mr. McDougald in their endeavours.

I accept those findings as being findings of fact supported by the evidence. He then concluded:

> In my view, Mr. Wadsworth went as far as he could without revealing information given to him in confidence by Mr. McDougald, to hint or intimate to Mr. Cohen or to Mr. Ellen that their efforts would not necessarily be successful.

I take this to be a conclusion of law of which more will be said later.

Negotiations by the Plaintiffs with Mr. J.A.M. McDougald

The trial judge dealt with this matter at pp. 33–34 O.R., pp. 469–70 D.L.R. In summary the evidence of Ellen and Cohen was that as a result of the letter of introduction which they received from Wadsworth, they first met McDougald in early 1973 and told him of their aspirations and intentions and their desire to acquire the 25% block of shares held by the McMartin estate. They testified that they met with McDougald a number of times over the next five years until his death in March of 1978, and that they were never discouraged by Mr. McDougald and believed they would eventually be successful in obtaining the shares. The trial judge said:

> I find it difficult to justify the optimism now expressed by Messrs. Cohen and Ellen that they would eventually have succeeded in their efforts through Mr. McDougald.

He reached that conclusion in part upon the contents of Wadsworth's file memorandum of August 20, 1974, referred to above, to the effect that McDougald did not favour a merger between Crown Trust and the maritime trust companies and that McDougald had apparently had several frank discussions with Cohen and explained his position. The memorandum reads as follows:

Confidential

August 20, 1974

Crown Trust Company

I have had a discussion with Mr. McDougald regarding the above-named company. Approximately 25% of the common shares are owned by the McMartin estate, which estate will be wound up following the deaths of the two remaining beneficiaries, both in their seventies. The type of the Crown Trust operation and some of its special clients, such as Prudential, is such that it operates best as a small, closely held and controlled company with a continuity of control. There have been approaches from Reuben Cohen in conjunction with Leonard Ellen for a possible merger with Eastern Canada Savings & Loan. McDougald did not favour this, as he felt it would be only a stepping stone to the further sale by Cohen and Ellen. McDougald advised that Cohen & Ellen control about 10% of the outstanding common, and this is confirmed by our records which show that 70,000 shares are pledged in the account of Standard Investments Ltd. and 10,600 shares in the account of Brentwood Realty. Mr. McDougald apparently has had several frank discussions with Cohen and explained his position. Cohen has said that they would probably sell, but McDougald has some doubts as to this as most of their shares were acquired well above the present market.

Some years ago there was discussion as to the possible merger with National Trust, but it was felt best to hold this off and that from this Bank's point of view our interests were best served with a 10% interest in each (we now hold 74,900 shares of Crown Trust out of an outstanding 750,000 shares).

Mr. McDougald just wished to acquaint me with the background, as there is nothing to be done at the moment. However, when the shares of the McMartin estate are to be sold the situation will have to be faced, and at that time a merger with National might be in the best interests of all concerned.

In the light of the above we should in no way encourage Cohen or Ellen that a deal with Crown Trust is possible.

JPRW

The trial judge, on the basis of that evidence said at p. 34 O.R., p. 470 D.L.R.:

> In 1974, at least, it would appear that Mr. McDougald had told Mr. Cohen that he was opposed to any merger or acquisition by them of the McMartin estate shares.

In my opinion the evidence does not form a proper basis for this conclusion. The memorandum to file is most unusual to begin with and of a self-serving nature in so far as the defendant is concerned. More important, however, is the fact that it is at best only hearsay evidence with respect to what McDougald may have told Ellen and Cohen. The memorandum was properly admissible to refresh Wadsworth's memory as to the state of mind of McDougald at the time and as to McDougald's assertion to him as to what he had told Ellen and Cohen. It is also evidence of the knowledge that Wadsworth had of McDougald's intention with respect to the McMartin estate's block of stock and the attempt by Ellen and Cohen to merge with or gain control of Crown Trust. It was not admissible evidence to prove that McDougald had told Mr. Cohen that he was opposed to any merger or acquisition by them of the McMartin shares and there is no other evidence to prove that he did so. As previously stated the trial judge found that Wadsworth's evidence did no more than support a conclusion that he did not encourage Cohen and Ellen to believe that their efforts to acquire Crown Trust would inevitably be successful. Having regard to these findings and the evidence of Ellen and Cohen with respect to the close relationship they felt they had formed with McDougald and the enthusiasm with which they continued to pursue their goals (as stated by the trial judge) the only logical inference to be drawn is that it was not obvious to Ellen and Cohen that they were not making any headway or that they would not eventually succeed in their efforts through Mr. McDougald.

The Meeting with R.D. Fullerton in April of 1978

In April, 1978, Cohen met with R.D. Fullerton, at that time president of the defendant bank, and asked if Fullerton could arrange to help him obtain the shares of Crown Trust held by the bank. Fullerton replied that the shares were not for sale. The trial judge held the plaintiffs were justified in assuming that little purpose would be served by making a formal offer thereafter to purchase these shares. I agree with that conclusion. It should be pointed out that by this time Ellen and Cohen and their companies had acquired 32% of the issued shares of Crown Trust.

Subsequent Transactions Relating to the Disposition of the Defendant's Shares of Crown Trust and Acquisition of Control of Crown Trust

The trial judge has in his reasons for judgment dealt with these matters in great detail. It is sufficient for present purposes to summarize the relevant facts as follows:

In 1978, one Conrad Black was a director and a substantial customer of the defendant. In July, 1978, he purchased through one of his companies 186,350 shares in Crown Trust from the McMartin estate. He

also purchased additional shares through other companies which he controlled so that by 1978 the Black interests had acquired 327,400 shares representing 44% of the total shares issued. To finance these purchases he obtained from the defendant a line of credit of five million dollars in July, 1978, for which he pledged 111,450 shares of Crown Trust as security.

Upon hearing of the sale of the McMartin estate shares to Black, Ellen and Cohen arranged to meet Black, and Cohen advised Black they were interested in acquiring all issued stock including the stock held by the defendant. Black advised him in substance that the defendant would sell its shares as he, Black, directed. Further meetings took place as a result of which, on or about January 3, 1979, a tentative but non-binding agreement was reached for the purchase by Ellen and Cohen of the shares held by the Black interests. Mr. Black in the meantime carried on negotiations with one I.H. Asper, president of Canwest Capital Corporation of Winnipeg, who wished to acquire a controlling interest in Crown Trust. Such acquisition, to use the words of the trial judge, at p. 37 O.R., p. 473 D.L.R., "would inevitably involve acquisition of the 10 per cent holdings of the Bank as well".

The trial judge found that Asper was negotiating the purchase from Black at a price of $44 per share and that Black communicated that information to Ellen who indicated that $41.50 per share would be the highest price he and his associates would pay.

In 1978, Russell E. Harrison was chairman and chief executive officer of the defendant. He was a personal friend of Black who, as I have already noted, was at that time a director and major client of the defendant. In late 1978 or early 1979 he was told by Black that Black proposed to sell his group's shares to Canwest. Harrison told Black to keep the bank in mind during such negotiations and they agreed one would not sell their shares without the other. Harrison recognized that the defendant's 10% holding was a "pivotal" block for a party seeking control and the trial judge found that Black and Harrison reached an understanding that their respective shares would be sold together at the highest price possible.

Harrison conceded on cross-examination that it was important for him to know whether Ellen and Cohen as customers of the bank would match the offer of $44 per share because he was concerned that they be left in a minority position with the inevitable reduction in the market value of the shares. He relied on Black's statement to him that Cohen and Ellen were not even prepared to pay $41.50 per share (in fact Cohen and Ellen were prepared to go as high as $41.50 per share). He also conceded that it was part of the defendant's ethics not to leave a customer in a minority position without giving him an opportunity to purchase the majority shareholding as well but it was his evidence that Cohen and Ellen had never communicated to the defendant that they wished to buy the defendant's shares. In this respect he was in error as they had told Fullerton in April, 1978, of their desire to purchase the defendant's shares. Cohen testified that they would have paid $44 for the defendant's shares.

In July, 1979, the Black group and the defendant sold their shares to Canwest at $44 per share. Cohen and Ellen were not given the opportunity to meet the Canwest offer of $44 per share. As a result of this sale the market value of the Crown Trust shares pledged as security for the loans to the corporate plaintiffs fell by more than 50%. In August, 1982, however, the plaintiffs were able to sell their shares in Crown Trust at $34.50 per share although the stock was trading on the market at that time at between $15 to $17 per share.

LIABILITY

Breach of Fiduciary Relationship

On the facts found by the trial judge as set forth above he reached the conclusion set forth at pp. 47–48 O.R., pp. 484–85 D.L.R.:

> I have no hesitation in holding that in 1972 a fiduciary relationship between the plaintiff and the Bank was created. All of the essential elements were present. Messrs. Cohen and Ellen reposed a trust and confidence in the Bank. On April 6, 1972, they came to the Bank and confidentially outlined their plan for acquisition and control of Crown Trust to Mr. Wadsworth, the president of the Bank. The Bank undertook to advise them generally on the soundness of their plan and, more importantly for their purposes, to effect an introduction to Mr. McDougald. The Bank then had not only a confidence reposed in it but it undertook to act on behalf of the plaintiffs in this limited way.
>
> I find, however, there was no breach of duty by the Bank as fiduciary to the plaintiffs in 1972....
>
> The conduct of the Bank in deciding as a matter of policy to assist one customer to prevent a take-over by purchasing stock ... was not illegal....
>
> In my view, the Bank could not disclose without breaching its duty of confidentiality to Mr. McDougald and to Crown Trust that it was

purchasing shares in Crown Trust at the request of that customer. In any event, one must consider whether it would have made any material difference to Messrs. Cohen and Ellen if it had been disclosed to them that the Bank was purchasing Crown Trust stock with a view to eventually acquiring a 10% interest.

> Both gentlemen suspected that the Bank had a significant shareholding in Crown Trust and I am not persuaded that the disclosure that the Bank had gone into the market to purchase up to 10% of the shareholdings of Crown Trust would have discouraged Messrs. Cohen and Ellen in their quest to purchase a controlling interest in Crown Trust ... it must be recognized again that Mr. Wadsworth was under some legal restraint not to breach the confidentiality of that information [McDougald's opposition to the plan for acquisition and merger] obtained from Mr. McDougald as a controlling officer of a customer of the Bank, Crown Trust ... and in any event, Mr. Wadsworth did his best to convey the message to Messrs. Cohen and Ellen consistent with his duty of confidentiality, that they would not likely succeed.

and further at p. 49 O.R., p. 485 D.L.R.:

> The primary obligation of the Bank at this time was to introduce Messrs. Cohen and Ellen to Mr. McDougald. In effecting such introduction to Mr. McDougald, Mr. Wadsworth could reasonably anticipate, it seems to me, that Messrs. Cohen and Ellen would be told directly by Mr. McDougald of his position in the matter.... As I found earlier, it seems probable that Messrs. Cohen and Ellen must have been told and have realized at the outset of their relationship with Mr. McDougald that he opposed their plans and they could only hope to persuade him to change his mind.
>
> In short, I find no breach of fiduciary relationship by the Bank in failing to disclose the position taken by Mr. McDougald in 1972. I am satisfied there was sufficient disclosure by Mr. Wadsworth consistent with his duty to Mr. McDougald and that in any event, full disclosure by Mr. McDougald of his position was probably made well before August 20, 1974.

The trial judge then turned his attention to the period from January to July of 1979. It was his view that from April, 1972 onward, the relationship between the plaintiffs and the defendant was that of debtor and creditor. He commented that:

> ... the Bank was aware of the plaintiffs' continuing efforts to acquire a controlling interest in Crown Trust but this information was no longer confidential to the Bank.... I am hard pressed to

find in the circumstances of this case that after 1972 and particularly in 1979, that there was any particular trust reposed in the Bank by the plaintiffs, or, more importantly, that the Bank, as a repository of that trust, had undertaken in any way to act for the plaintiffs.

At p. 50 O.R., p. 486 D.L.R., he said:

> The Bank did not receive any confidential information from the plaintiffs in the circumstances of this case of which the Bank could be said to have taken unfair advantage. Assuming the Bank was a fiduciary of confidential information, there is nothing to suggest that the Bank had undertaken to act in any way on behalf of the plaintiffs, other then to lend them money for general and investment purposes. The Bank did not undertake to act on behalf of the plaintiffs in any way so as to impose a fiduciary obligation on the Bank to protect the interests of the plaintiffs and to avoid any situations where the Bank's personal interest would be in conflict.

At p. 51 O.R., p. 487 D.L.R., the trial judge stated in conclusion:

> In this case, the plaintiffs have founded their action principally on the basis that the Bank was at the relevant time a fiduciary. I have concluded that in 1979 that relationship did not exist and accordingly, the plaintiffs' action must fail.

Before considering the findings made by the trial judge it is necessary to consider the law which is applicable in a case of this kind.

To begin with there is the problem which arises from the fact that the defendant is a corporation. The president and chairman of that corporation at the relevant times are not defendants in this action. Their knowledge and intentions are important only in so far as such knowledge and intention may be by law attributed to the corporate defendant. In *H.L. Bolton (Engineering) Co. Ltd. v. T.J. Graham & Sons Ltd.*, [1957] 1 Q.B. 159, Denning L.J. in delivering the unanimous judgment of the court said at p. 172:

> So the judge has found that this company, through its managers, intend to occupy the premises for their own purposes. Mr. Albery contests this finding, and he has referred us to cases decided in the last century; but I must say that the law on this matter and the approach to it have developed very considerably since then. A company may in many ways be likened to a human body. It has a brain and nerve centre which controls what it does. It also has hands which hold the tools and act in accordance with

directions from the centre. Some of the people in the company are mere servants and agents who are nothing more than hands to do the work and cannot be said to represent the mind or will. Others are directors and managers who represent the directing mind and will of the company, and control what it does. The state of mind of these managers is the state of mind of the company and is treated by the law as such.

And further at p. 173:

> So here, the intention of the company can be derived from the intention of its officers and agents. Whether their intention is the company's intention depends on the nature of the matter under consideration, the relative position of the officer or agent and the other relevant facts and circumstances of the case. Approaching the matter in that way, I think that, although there was no board meeting, nevertheless, having regard to the standing of these directors in control of the business of the company, having regard to the other facts and circumstances which we know, whereby plans had been prepared and much work done, the judge was entitled to infer that the intention of the company was to occupy the holding for their own purposes.

In *Lennard's Carrying Co. Ltd. v. Ascotie Petroleum Co. Ltd.*, [1915] A.C. 705, the question was whether damage had occurred without the "actual fault or privity" of the owner of a ship. Viscount Haldane said at pp. 713–14:

> For if Mr. Lennard was the directing mind of the company, then his action must, unless a corporation is not to be liable to all, have been an action which was the action of the company itself within the meaning of s. 502.... It must be upon the true construction of that section in such a case as the present one that the fault or privity is the fault or privity of somebody who is not merely a servant or agent for whom the company is liable upon the footing respondeat superior, but somebody for whom the company is liable because his action is the very action of the company itself.

Lennard's case and the *Bolton* case were considered by the House of Lords in *Tesco Supermarket Ltd. v. Nattrass*, [1972] A.C. 153. In considering the passage quoted above from the judgment of Denning L.J., Lord Reid said at p. 171:

> There have been attempts to apply Lord Denning's words to all servants of a company whose work is brain work, or who exercise some managerial discretion under the direction of superior officers of the company. I do not think that

Lord Denning intended to refer to them. He only referred to those who "represent the directing mind and will of the company, and control what it does".

I think that is right....

At p. 173 he said:

In *Magna Plant v. Mitchell* (unreported) April 27, 1966, the fault was that of a depot engineer and again the company was held not criminally responsible. I think these decisions were right. In the *Magna Plant* case Lord Parker C.J. said:

...knowledge of a servant cannot be imputed to the company unless he is a servant for whose actions the company are criminally responsible, and as the cases show, that only arises in the case of a company where one is considering the acts of responsible officers forming the brain, or in the case of an individual, a person to whom delegation in the true sense of the delegation of management has been passed.

I agree with what he said with regard to a company.

The Tesco case dealt with the matter of corporate criminal liability. This subject-matter has most recently been dealt with by the Supreme Court of Canada in *Canadian Dredge & Dock Co. Ltd. et al. v. The Queen* (1985), 19 D.L.R. (4th) 314, 19 C.C.C. (3d) 1, 45 C.R. (3d) 289. Estey J. in delivering the unanimous judgment of the court said at p. 335 D.L.R., p. 21 C.C.C.:

Criminal responsibility in our courts thus far has been achieved in the *mens rea* offences by the attribution of the corporation of the acts of its employees and agents on the more limited basis of the doctrine of the directing mind or identification.

At p. 351 D.L.R., p. 38 C.C.C., he said:

Where the criminal act is totally in fraud of the corporate employer and where the act is intended to and does result in benefit exclusively to the employee-manager, the employee-directing mind, from the outset of the design and execution of the criminal plan, ceases to be a directing mind of the corporation and consequently his acts could not be attributed to the corporation under the identification doctrine. This might be true as well on the American approach through *respondeat superior*. Whether this is so or not, in my view, the identification doctrine only operates where the Crown demonstrates that the action taken by the directing mind (a) was within the field of operation assigned to him; (b) was not

totally in fraud of the corporation, and (c) was by design or result partly for the benefit of the company.

In my view the identification doctrine is equally applicable in a civil action where the plaintiff seeks to establish liability on the part of a defendant corporation on the basis of an alleged breach of fiduciary duty (without reliance on the principle of *respondeat superior*). It is my further view that in such a case the onus on the plaintiff can be no higher than that placed on the Crown in a case of alleged corporate criminal responsibility.

In the present case the claim against the defendant corporation is based primarily upon the actions taken by Wadsworth (the president) and McKinnon (the chairman). The defendant carried on business across Canada through hundreds of branch banks with thousands of employees. Its organization was divided into regions with regional officers including regional vice-presidents. Its head office was in the City of Toronto. Wadsworth and McKinnon were at the very apex of the corporate organization. It cannot be doubted that it was within the field of operations of both of them to attract, obtain, increase and retain the business of existing or potential valuable customers. It cannot be doubted that McDougald was a director of the defendant and a controlling influence of Crown Trust and that McDougald and Crown Trust were both valued customers of the defendant. It is also beyond doubt that Ellen and Cohen and the investment and trust companies which they controlled, although customers of the defendant in a relatively minor way, prior to their April meeting with Wadsworth, represented great potential future business for the bank if their goodwill could be obtained and used for the purpose of obtaining their business. The evidence makes it quite clear that Wadsworth was at relevant times aware of this. It is my opinion that Wadsworth and McKinnon and their successors in officer were clearly directing minds of the defendant with respect to its activities relating to the endeavour of Ellen and Cohen to obtain control of Crown Trust and Crown Trust's endeavour to resist their efforts. The actions taken by these officers were within the field of operations assigned to them and were by design *and* result for the benefit of the defendant. There is no evidence to suggest that their actions were in fraud of the defendant.

The defendant and trial judge placed considerable importance on the fact that Wadsworth at the time of his meeting with Ellen and Cohen on April 6, 1972, when he agreed with them that their proposed merger with Crown Trust was sound and feasible in principle and said he would do everything he could to help them along in their venture, had no knowledge of the fact that McKinnon, at the instigation of McDougald, had made a decision to buy shares of Crown Trust to assist in thwarting the intention and purpose of those attempting to acquire control. The trial judge found, and there can be no doubt in this regard, that at this time Wadsworth was acting in good faith and his conduct was beyond reproach. By that date, however, McKinnon had made a decision to have the defendant secretly purchase Crown Trust shares for the express purpose of thwarting the plans of those seeking to acquire control of that company. It is my opinion that as matter of law a corporation may have more than one directing mind operating within the same field of operations but I am of the further view that where such a state of affairs exists, a corporation cannot be found in law to have a split personality so that it can rely on the lack of knowledge on the part of one of its directing minds of the acts, intention and knowledge of the other directing mind operating in the same sphere to protect it from liability for the actions of the first directing mind or the combined activities of both directing minds. At least, in civil cases, where the element of *mens rea* is not applicable, when there are two or more directing minds operating within the same field assigned to both of them, the knowledge, intention and acts of each become together the total knowledge, intentions and acts of the corporation which they represent.

By April 6, 1972, the defendant had made a decision to thwart the plans of anyone seeking control of Crown Trust and thereafter continued to accomplish its purpose, which it then knew would thwart the plans of Ellen and Cohen, by acquiring the maximum number of shares of Crown Trust which it could lawfully hold. This was fully accomplished by November 15, 1972, a fact which was fully known to the defendant's senior officers in its investment division by no later than April 6, 1973. They were made aware of the defendant's decision to purchase the stock as early as January 5, 1972. At the April 6, 1972 meeting and later in December, 1972, by a letter of introduction of Ellen and Cohen to McDougald, Wadsworth gave encouragement to Ellen and Cohen to carry out their plan. Applying the principles which I have stated above, the only logical conclusion is that the defendant corporation (as distinct from individual officers) was encouraging one of its customers to proceed with a course of action to achieve a purpose which it had already decided to thwart. There is no evidence to suggest that the defendant at any time deviated from its intention to thwart the plans of Ellen and Cohen up

to the date of the sale of its Crown Trust shares on or about July 17, 1979. The evidence is clear from the memorandum of Avison dated April 6, 1973, and the memorandum of Wadsworth dated August 20, 1974, that the shares were being retained by the defendant for the very purpose for which they had been acquired. By their sale on July 17, 1979, the defendant effectively removed any possibility of the plaintiffs obtaining control of Crown Trust, thereby accomplishing its original purpose.

The question still remains to be answered, however, whether the plaintiff by its action committed a breach of any duty which it may have owed to its customers, the plaintiffs. It was the submission of the plaintiffs that a fiduciary relationship existed between them and the defendant at least from the time of their meeting on April 6, 1972, with Wadsworth until July 17, 1979.

The trial judge has dealt carefully and in my view accurately with the general principles of law relating to fiduciaries and particularly as they apply to the relationship of banker and customer. The plaintiffs allege that they have sustained damages as a result of a breach of duty on the part of the defendant which flowed from a fiduciary relationship which existed between the plaintiffs and the defendant. It is clear that where a fiduciary relationship is found to exist, a court of equity will impose special liabilities and duties upon the persons who stand in a fiduciary relationship to each other. The law is set forth in 16 Hals., 4th ed., p. 981, para. 1456, quoted by the trial judge at p. 44 O.R., p. 481 D.L.R.:

> **1456.** *Conflict of duty and interest.* A court of equity imposes special liabilities and duties upon persons who stand in a fiduciary relationship to others, and it is a principle of equity that no person having duties of a fiduciary nature to discharge should be allowed to place himself in a situation where he has, or can have, a personal interest conflicting, or which may possibly conflict, with the interest of those whom he is bound to protect. The principle extends not only to the relationship between trustee and beneficiary, but to all kinds of fiduciary relationships where a real conflict of duty and interest occurs; it is not dependent on fraud or absence of good faith.

As pointed out by the trial judge at p. 45 O.R., p. 481 D.L.R.:

> The relationship of banker and customer does not *per se* give rise to a fiduciary relationship ... in the absence of special circumstances the general relationship between the bank and its customer or depositor, is simply that of debtor and

creditor: see *Foley v. Hill* (1848), 2 H.L.C. 28, 9 E.R. 1002 ... *Thermo King Corp. v. Provincial Bank of Canada et al.* (1981), 34 O.R. (2d) 369 at p. 373, 130 D.L.R. (3d) 256 at p. 260 (C.A.).

The law is clear, however, that in certain circumstances a fiduciary relationship may be created between a bank and its customer. There are numerous cases where banks have been held to be in a fiduciary position with customers and found liable in damages for breach of duties resulting from such relationship: *Lloyds Bank Ltd. v. Bundy*, [1975] Q.B. 326; *Woods v. Martins Bank Ltd. et al.*, [1959] 1 Q.B. 55; *McBean v. Bank of Nova Scotia et al.* (1981), 15 B.L.R. 296; affirmed 17 A.C.W.S. (2d) 154; *McKenzie v. Bank of Montreal* (1975), 7 O.R. (2d) 521, 55 D.L.R. (3d) 641; affirmed 12 O.R. (2d) 719, 70 D.L.R. (3d) 113; *Guertin v. Royal Bank of Canada* (1983), 43 O.R. (2d) 363, 1 D.L.R. (4th) 640n; *Hayward v. Bank of Nova Scotia et al.* (1984), 45 O.R. (2d) 542, 7 D.L.R. (4th) 135, 6 C.P.R. (3d) at p. 34; affirmed 51 O.R. (2d) 193, 19 D.L.R. (4th) 758, C.P.R. *loc. cit.*, p. 33.

The trial judge at pp. 46–47 O.R., pp. 482–83 D.L.R., has quoted at length from the reasons of Sir Eric Sachs in the case of *Lloyds Bank Ltd. v. Bundy*, *supra*, a leading case with respect to the fiduciary concept as it may apply to the relationship existing between a bank and its customer. The contents are of sufficient importance to justify repetition in part. Sachs J. said at pp. 340–41:

> The first and most troublesome issue which here falls for consideration is as to whether on the particular and somewhat unusual facts of the case, the bank was, when obtaining his signatures on December 17, 1969, in a relationship with Mr. Bundy that entailed a duty on their part of what can for convenience be called fiduciary care.
>
> ...
>
> Everything depends on the particular facts, and such a relationship has been held to exist in unusual circumstances as between purchaser and vendor, as between great uncle and adult nephew, and in other widely differing sets of circumstances. Moreover, it is neither feasible nor desirable to attempt closely to define the relationship, or its characteristics, or the demarcation line showing the exact transition point where a relationship that does not entail that duty passes into one that does (cf. Ungoed-Thomas J. in *In re Craig*, decd. [1971] Ch. 95, 104).
>
> ...
>
> Such cases tend to arise where someone relies on the guidance or advice of another, where the other is aware of that reliance and where the person upon whom reliance is placed obtains, or may well obtain, a benefit from the transaction or has some other interest in it being concluded. In addition, there must, of course be shown to exist a vital element which in this judgment will for convenience be referred to as confidentiality.
>
> ...
>
> "Confidentiality" is intended to convey that extra quality in the relevant confidence that is implicit in the phrase "confidential relationship".... It imports some quality beyond that inherent in the confidence that can well exist between trustworthy persons who in business affairs deal with each other at arm's length. It is one of the features of this element that once it exists, influence naturally grows out of it....
>
> It was inevitably conceded on behalf of the bank that the relevant relationship can arise as between banker and customer. Equally, it was inevitably conceded on behalf of Mr. Bundy that in the normal course of transactions by which a customer guarantees a third party's obligations, the relationship does not arise. The onus of proof lies on the customer who alleges that in any individual case the line has been crossed and the relationship has arisen.

In the *Woods* case, *supra*, the manager of a bank agreed to be the financial adviser of the plaintiff and induced him to invest money in a company which was a customer of the bank and said by the manager to be financially sound. He advised the plaintiff that the investment was a wise one. There were no grounds on which the manager could reasonably have advised that the company was in a sound financial position or that an investment in its shares could be reasonably recommended as a wise one. The bank at all material times was pressing the company to reduce its considerable overdraft. On these facts, Salmon J. found at p. 72:

> In my judgment, a fiduciary relationship existed between the plaintiff and the defendants. No doubt the defendant Johnson could have refused to advise the plaintiff, but, as he chose to advise him, the law in these circumstances imposes an obligation on him to advise with reasonable care and skill.

and further at p. 73:

> It seems to me to be plain that in the circumstances of this case he ought never to have advised the plaintiff at all — certainly not without making a full disclosure to the plaintiff of the conflicting interests between the plaintiff and the defendant bank and the plaintiff and the defendant bank's other customers concerned.

This Court has arrived at the same conclusion in the *McBean* and *Hayward* cases cited above which involved facts somewhat similar to those in *Woods*.

The first issue to be decided is whether a fiduciary relationship existed between the plaintiffs and the defendant at any time between April 6, 1972, and July, 1979. The question to be answered is the one posed by Sachs J. in *Bundy* — have the plaintiffs satisfied the onus of proving that the relationships between the plaintiffs as customers and the defendant as banker crossed the line of that of a mere debtor-creditor relationship to that of a fiduciary relationship?

The trial judge found a fiduciary relationship was created between the plaintiffs and the defendant in 1972. His reasons for so finding have been set forth above. The appellant supports this finding. The respondent cross-appeals from this finding only as a matter of principle. In view of the fact that the trial judge found that there had been no breach of duty flowing from the relationship a reversal of this finding would have no practical effect in so far as the defendant is concerned.

In my view the trial judge was correct in finding that a fiduciary relationship was created between the plaintiffs and the defendant at the time of the meeting between Ellen and Cohen and Wadsworth. The following facts are clear from the evidence and the trial judge's findings thereon:

1. Prior to 1972 — Cohen and his family company Brentwood were customers of the defendant. Ellen and Standard Investments were not.
2. Ellen and Cohen in the early 1970s decided to endeavour to acquire a controlling interest in Crown Trust.
3. They decided that they would need the assistance, advice and financial support of the defendant to acquire such controlling interest.
4. In early 1972, to strengthen their relationship with the defendant, they transferred the Standard Investments' account to the Moncton branch of the defendant.
5. The defendant was aware of the excellent business which could be made available to it through the maritime provinces trust companies controlled by Ellen and Cohen. Wadsworth was pleased with the connection made with Cohen and Ellen who had transferred a two million dollar loan account from the Bank of Montreal prior to Wadsworth's meeting with Ellen and Cohen.
6. Prior to the meeting, Wadsworth knew that Ellen and Cohen were coming to see him to obtain his advice as president of the defendant as to the feasibility of a proposed merger or acquisition of control of a trust company, arrangements for financing the plan and an introduction to a director of the defendant who was influential in the affair of the trust company.
7. At the time of the meeting the name of Crown Trust was revealed by Ellen and Cohen as the company involved and the name of McDougald as the director.
8. At all relevant times Ellen and Cohen knew that the defendant was the banker for Crown Trust and that McDougald effectively controlled Crown Trust. There can be no doubt that Wadsworth had the same knowledge and was aware that it was for that reason that Ellen and Cohen were seeking the advice and assistance of the defendant.
9. On April 6, 1972, Ellen and Cohen confidentially "bared their souls" to Wadsworth and disclosed their plans for eventual amalgamation of the maritime provinces trust companies and of a possible merger of these companies on a national scale with Crown Trust. They made it clear to Wadsworth they were interested in acquiring all of the shares of Crown Trust.
10. Wadsworth undertook to arrange an introduction to McDougald and said he would do everything he could to help them along in their venture. There was no note of discouragement.

On those facts there can be no doubt that Ellen and Cohen were relying on the advice, assistance and guidance of the defendant, that the defendant through Wadsworth was aware of the reliance, that the defendant had already obtained a benefit by way of increased business with companies controlled by Ellen and Cohen and that future increases in business could reasonably be anticipated from the acquisition of the goodwill of Ellen and Cohen and their ever-increasing activity in the trust company field of endeavour and their anticipated need for financial assistance from the bank to support such proposed increased activities. These circumstances together with the revelation on the part of Ellen and Cohen of their past and proposed activities in the trust company field characterized by the trial judge as the baring of their souls, in my opinion, created a "confidential relationship" within the meaning of those words as expressed by Sachs J. The circumstances of this case were more than adequate to create a fiduciary relationship between the defendant and the plaintiffs.

The next issue to be decided is whether the defendant breached any duty flowing from that fiduciary relationship. At the very minimum there was a duty on the defendant to advise the plaintiffs with reasonable care and skill. More important, having regard to the circumstances of this case, if the defendant chose to advise and assist the plaintiff, as it did, there was a duty on the defendant to disclose to the plaintiffs the conflict of interest between the defendant and the plaintiffs and the conflict of interest between the plaintiffs and McDougald and Crown Trust. It may be that the defendant was under a legal obligation not to disclose the intention or actions of McDougald and Crown Trust. That, however, does not excuse the defendant for its behaviour towards the plaintiffs. If for any valid reason the defendant could not disclose the nature of the conflicts of interest or for any reason was unwilling to do so, it should have told the plaintiffs that it was unable to advise and assist them by reason of existing conflicts of interest. If the defendant did not wish to disclose the fact that conflicts of interest existed, it should have simply refused to give advice and assistance to the plaintiffs to effect their purpose.

The trial judge expressly found that there was no breach of duty arising out of the fiduciary relationship by the bank failing to disclose the position taken by McDougald in 1972. He stated there was sufficient disclosure by Wadsworth consistent with his duty to McDougald. With respect, I am unable to find any evidence that he made any disclosure to Ellen and Cohen of McDougald's position prior to their meeting with McDougald. Nor is there any evidence, apart from the memorandum of August 20, 1974, upon which I have previously indicated no reliance can be placed, to support the trial judge's finding that it was probable that Cohen and Ellen must have been told at the outset of their relationship with McDougald that he opposed their plans.

Although the trial judge did not expressly so state, he must also have reached the conclusion that the failure to the bank to advise Ellen and Cohen that it was in the process of acquiring 10% of Crown Trust's shares to thwart any attempt of a take-over by any person did not amount to a breach of duty owed by it to them. The trial judge stressed the fact that it was legal for the bank to assist a corporate customer by purchasing shares of that customer in order to thwart an acquisition of control of it by some other person. That matter is really not the issue. The point is that by so doing the bank had a conflict of interest with other customers who were relying on it for advice as to the feasibility of those other customers acquiring control.

The trial judge found as a fact that the defendant undertook to advise Ellen and Cohen generally on the soundness of their plan and to effect an introduction to McDougald. In my opinion he erred in finding that it had discharged its duty by merely effecting such introduction. He emphasized that the defendant was under some legal restraint not to breach the confidentiality of information obtained from McDougald as a controlling officer of Crown Trust, a customer of the bank. The fact remains, however, that the defendant was purchasing shares in Crown Trust in the year 1972 for its own account. In my view the defendant was not entitled to rely on the principle of confidentiality with respect to another customer, when the defendant was taking action by purchase of shares for its own account and benefit, in a direct conflict with the interests of other customers who were relying on it for advice and assistance. The defendant, by not revealing its conflict of interest, stood to benefit by acquiring and retaining the business of Ellen and Cohen, while at the same time retaining the business of McDougald. It also stood to profit, as it eventually did, by the purchase and later sale of shares of Crown Trust. That situation existed from April 6, 1972, at the latest, onwards.

If the defendant felt it could not lawfully reveal the information which it possessed because of its duty of confidentiality to its customers, information which no doubt would have discouraged the plaintiffs, it was under an obligation to tell the plaintiffs that it had a position adverse to their plans or that it had a conflict of interest. If the defendant did not wish to disclose that it had a conflict of interest, it should simply have refused to give them any advice or assistance in furtherance of their objective. For reasons I have given previously, the defendant must be deemed to have the knowledge of which both Wadsworth and McKinnon were possessed on April 6, 1972. It is not material that Wadsworth personally did not know that the defendant was in the process of purchasing 10% of the shares of Crown Trust. I conclude, accordingly, that the defendant was in breach of its duty to the plaintiffs as a fiduciary on April 6, 1972, and thereafter.

It is convenient to discuss at this point the timing of the fiduciary relationship with which the trial judge finally concerned himself. He said at p. 47 O.R., p. 483 D.L.R.:

Applying the concepts of the fiduciary relationship, can it be said that the Bank stood in the relation of fiduciary to the plaintiffs during the two relevant periods, namely, April, 1972, when Messrs. Cohen and Ellen met with and sought the advice and assistance of Mr. Wadsworth, president of the Bank, and secondly, January to July, 1979. The latter was the period of negotiation and sale of Crown Trust stock to Canwest.

In my view it was essential that the trial judge consider whether a fiduciary relationship existed at any time between April 6, 1972, and July 17, 1979, and if so, whether any breach of its duty as a fiduciary occurred during that period of time in which the relationship existed as a result of which the plaintiffs sustained damages.

Under the heading *"Liability"* the trial judge set out his findings of fact in eight numbered paragraphs at pp. 42–43 O.R., pp. 478–79 D.L.R. These findings are supported by the evidence except that, as previously noted, there is no admissible evidence that McDougald up to his death probably made it reasonably clear to Cohen and Ellen that he was opposed. For the purposes of the present discussion the important findings of the fact are contained in paragraphs numbered 4 and 5 where he found that the defendant was aware of the continuing activities of Cohen and Ellen in the years 1972 to 1979 and was aware of their continued efforts to acquire a majority interest in Crown Trust. He also found that the corporate plaintiffs were regarded as valuable customers of the defendant during this period and that the defendants loaned moneys to these companies to enable them to purchase shares. There is a further finding of fact that in 1979 the defendant through its then president Mr. Harrison agreed with the Black group to jointly sell its share in Crown Trust to Canwest. Harrison was aware of the fact that the sale of the Black shares to Canwest could only be effected if the defendant's shares were included and also of the fact that the sale would adversely affect the plaintiffs as minority shareholders.

I have already indicated that there was a breach of duty as fiduciary on April 6, 1972. In my opinion that breach became more flagrant with the passage of time. Wadsworth had become chairman of the defendant in December, 1973. There can be no doubt that at that time he knew or ought to have known of the defendant's holdings of Crown Trust shares and the purpose thereof. In August, 1974, McDougald made his position clear to Wadsworth.

By 1979, the McMartin estate had disposed of the McMartin shareholdings to Black who was a director of the defendant and one of its customers. By this time Harrison, who had knowledge of the plans of the bank to acquire 10% of the Crown Trust shares in 1972, had become chairman of the defendant and sold the defendant's shares to Canwest for the bank's own benefit and to the detriment of the plaintiffs of which he was aware. During the entire period of time between April 6, 1972, and July 16, 1979, the defendant had a clear and serious conflict of interest with the plaintiffs who were its customers. During that same period of time the defendant's customers McDougald and Black had conflicts of interest with the plaintiffs of which the defendant was aware and those customers were themselves directors of the defendant. There were a number of meetings, although of an informal nature, when Ellen and Cohen discussed with Wadsworth the feasibility of their plan. He did no more than advise them that they would not likely succeed and on one occasion that they might not be successful. He and no other officer of the defendant at any time advised them that the defendant at all times during the relevant period of time had a conflict of interest. Nevertheless the defendant during the entire period of time continued to finance, in part at least, the acquisition of shares of Crown Trust by the corporate plaintiffs. I have no hesitation in concluding that the defendant was in a continuing breach of its fiduciary duty to the plaintiffs during the entire period between April 6, 1972, and July 16, 1979.

The trial judge in reaching his conclusion that the relationship between the plaintiffs and defendants had become only one of debtor and creditor after April, 1972, appears to have relied heavily on the fact that the plaintiffs' intention had become public knowledge by 1975 (erroneously stated in his reasons as 1979). He appears to have concluded that the fact that information initially given to the defendant in confidence had become public knowledge in some way destroyed the fiduciary relationship. As pointed out by the trial judge that aspect of confidentiality, *viz.*, that a bank will not disclose confidential information received from its customer to others without the customer's consent, is a legal obligation imposed by law which arises independently of the establishment of a fiduciary relationship. It is an implied term of the contract between a bank and its customer that it will not do so: *Tournier v. National Provincial & Union Bank of England*, [1924] 1 K.B. 461.

A release by a customer of the bank's obligation in this regard does not discharge the bank from any other duties which flow from a fiduciary relationship which has been found to exist between the bank and its customer. In the present case the defendant had said through Wadsworth at the meeting of April 6, 1972, that it would do everything it could to help Ellen and Cohen along in their venture. They had come to the defendant for its assistance and advice. The defendant supplied its assistance financially. There is no evidence that it ever communicated to Ellen or Cohen that it was resiling from its position of assisting and advising and was terminating the fiduciary relationship into which it had entered. In fact, however, it had at all times maintained a position in direct opposition to one of assisting Ellen and Cohen and the corporate plaintiffs. I must, accordingly, respectfully disagree with the trial judge's finding that no fiduciary relationship existed between the plaintiffs and defendants after April 6, 1972.

There is one other aspect of the trial judge's reasons which warrants comment. As previously noted he said at p. 48 O.R., p. 484 D.L.R.:

> In any event, one must consider whether it would have made any material difference to Messrs. Cohen and Ellen if it had been disclosed to them that the Bank was purchasing Crown Trust stock with a view to eventually acquiring a 10% interest.
>
> ...
>
> ... and I am not persuaded that the disclosure that the Bank had gone into the market to purchase up to 10% of the shareholdings of Crown Trust would have discouraged Messrs. Cohen and Ellen in their quest to purchase a controlling interest in Crown Trust.

In my opinion the trial judge has asked himself the wrong question or at best an incomplete question. The important question is whether it would have made any material difference to Messrs. Cohen and Ellen if it had been disclosed to them that the bank was purchasing Crown Trust stock with a view to eventually acquiring a 10% interest *for the purpose of thwarting any attempt by Ellen and Cohen to acquire control of Crown Trust*. On the basis of the only available evidence, and that is the evidence of Ellen and Cohen, it would seem most probable that it would have dissuaded them from making the attempt.

In the final analysis, however, this distinction is of little importance. The breach of duty on the part of the defendants consisted in its failure to declare its conflict of interest at any time, its subsequent giving of assistance and advice, and its later sale of its share (the acquisition of which and the purpose of such acquisition it had never revealed to the plaintiffs) for its own benefit and to the detriment of the plaintiffs. On and after April 6, 1972, the defendant had a duty to disclose any conflict of interest and to deal fairly with the plaintiffs. This it did not do.

It practised secrecy and non-disclosure while pursuing its own interests in retaining some of the plaintiffs and obtaining others of the plaintiffs as customers of the bank and in the sale of its Crown Trust shares for its own benefit and the benefit of another customer.

LIMITATIONS DEFENCE

On February 5, 1980, Anderson J. upon motion made on behalf of the defendant ordered that certain paragraphs in the statement of claim advancing a cause of action by the plaintiff as shareholders of Crown Trust against the defendant for breach of a fiduciary allegedly owed by the defendant as a shareholder of Crown Trust be struck out on grounds that the allegations therein failed to disclose a reasonable cause of action and might prejudice the fair trial of the action against the defendant as banker. The order permitted the plaintiffs to amend the statement of claim with respect to the cause of action alleged against the defendant as banker. No appeal was taken from this order. An amended statement of claim was duly delivered.

On November 9, 1983, at the conclusion of the plaintiffs' argument at trial and upon motion made by the plaintiffs, the trial judge ordered that the amended statement of claim be further amended. *Inter alia*, it permitted the plaintiffs to allege formally that the 1972 share purchases by the bank were made to "thwart the plaintiffs' purposes", an allegation which had not been formally made prior at that time. The trial judge permitted the amendment on the ground that the defendant was not prejudiced thereby as he was of the view that every living witness to the events had been called. The defendant did not ask for an adjournment to call other witnesses. As I understand the submissions of the defendant it does not take issue with respect to the propriety of the order made by the trial judge in so far as it might affect any finding of liability but rather in so far as it may have resulted in the denial of costs to the defendant. The defendant submitted it could have called witnesses to refute the inferences that the purchases had been made surreptitiously in the circumstances of the case (as opposed to confidentially), or that they were in the circumstances unusual in the experience of the financial community. Even if the defendant did intent to take issue with the propriety of the order, in my opinion, the order was a proper one. The defendant did not request an adjournment to which it was entitled, if it felt it would be prejudiced by the order, and it cannot be said that the trial judge exercised his discretion improperly in permitting the amendment.

The trial judge's order did provide, however, that to the extent that the amendments set up any new cause of action, such new cause of action should be deemed to be brought on the date of the order and the defendant should be entitled to the benefit of any defence based upon any statute of limitation as though the writ in respect of any new cause of action had been issued on that date, *viz.*, November 9, 1983.

The defendant then delivered a fresh amended statement of defence in which it pleaded in para. 10A:

> As to any claim herein founded upon an alleged breach of fiduciary duty by the Bank prior to the 9th day of November, 1977 the Bank pleads and relies on ss. 43 and 45 of the *Limitations Act*, R.S.O. 1980, c. 240.

Section 43 reads as follows:

> **43.**(1) In this section, "trustee" includes an executor, an administrator, a trustee whose trust arises by construction or implication of law as well as an express trustee, and a joint trustee.
>
> (2) In an action against a trustee or a person claiming through him, except where the claim is founded upon a fraud or fraudulent breach of trust to which the trustee was party or privy, or is to recover trust property or the proceeds thereof, still retained by the trustee, or previously received by the trustee and converted to his use, the following paragraphs apply:
>
> 1. All rights and privileges conferred by any statute of limitations shall be enjoyed in the like manner and to the like extent as they would have been enjoyed in such action if the trustee or person claiming through him had not been a trustee or person claiming through a trustee.
> 2. If the action is brought to recover money or other property and is one to which no existing statute of limitations applies, the trustee or person claiming through him is entitled to the benefit of, and is at liberty to plead, the lapse of time as a bar to such action in the like manner and to the like extent as if the claim had been against him in an action of debt for money had and received; but so nevertheless that the statute shall run against a married woman entitled in possession for her separate use, whether with or without restraint upon anticipation, but shall not begin to run against any beneficiary unless and until the interest of such beneficiary becomes an interest in possession.

> (3) No beneficiary, as against whom there would be a good defence by virtue of this section, shall derive any greater or other benefit from a judgment or order obtained by another beneficiary than he could have obtained if he had brought the action and this section had been pleaded.

The relevant part of s. 45 reads as follows:

> **45.**(1) The following actions shall be commenced within and not after the times respectively hereinafter mentioned,
>
> ...
>
> (g) an action for trespass to goods or land, simple contract or debt grounded upon any lending or contract without specialty, debt for arrears of rent, detinue, replevin or upon the case other than for slander,
>
> within six years after the cause of action arose....

Section 42 of the Act which together with ss. 43 and 44 appear in Part II of the Act under the heading "Trusts and Trustees" reads as follows:

> **42.** This Part supplies to a trust created by an instrument or an Act of the Legislature heretofore or hereafter executed or passed.

I have serious doubts as to whether the defendant in the present case can be characterized as a trustee with respect to the plaintiffs. It cannot be disputed that a person who holds property in trust for another is a trustee and that a fiduciary relationship exists between such persons. Fiduciary obligations flow from the trust relationship. As previously indicated, however, a person can, by offering to give advice in a particular matter to another, create in himself fiduciary obligations stemming from the confidential nature of the relationship created: see Shepherd, *Law of Fiduciaries* (1981), at p. 28. One of such obligations would be the duty to act in good faith. Where, however, the circumstances are such that a fiduciary relationship does exist, in my opinion it does not necessarily follow that a relationship of trustee and *cestui que trust* has been created. It is not necessary, however, in the present case to decide that matter.

Assuming, without deciding, that the fiduciary relationship found to exist creates the defendant a trustee within the meaning of s. 43(2) the defendant is faced with another difficulty. Since the trust was not created by an instrument or an Act of the Legislature, it may be that the limitation benefits of Part II are not applicable by virtue of the provisions of s. 42: see *Ankcorn v. Stewart* (1920), 47 O.L.R. 478, 54 D.L.R. 74.

In the view I take of this matter, it is not necessary to determine whether the provisions of ss. 43 and 45 are applicable. Assuming, without deciding, that they are applicable, the obligation on the plaintiffs was to commence their action within six years after the cause of action arose. It has been said (Shepherd, *Law of Fiduciaries*, at p. 339) that:

> ... a conflict of interest can only exist when a fiduciary is faced with a choice between his beneficiary's interests and his personal interests. While the choice is pending, there is a conflict; once the choice is made (whether for or against the beneficiary) the conflict is resolved and ceases to exist. The mainstream of the law of fiduciaries is ... generally unconcerned with the existence of a conflict of interest, instead concentrating on proscribing the actual choice against the interests of the beneficiaries.

In the present case there was a continuing breach of duty on the part of the defendant in failing to disclose its conflict of interest up to the date of the sale of its shares in Crown Trust on July 16, 1979. It was that act on that date, however, which caused the damage sustained by the plaintiffs. Prior to that time the defendant was still in a position to refrain from using the shares to thwart the plans of the plaintiffs and the plaintiffs were still in a position to accomplish their purpose. Thereafter they could not. In my view their cause of action for recovery of damages arose on that date. The date of issue of the writ herein, *viz.*, December 14, 1979, and the date of the trial judge's amending order, *viz.*, November 9, 1983, both fall within the six-year limitation period and accordingly the provisions of the *Limitations Act* do not provide any impediment to the plaintiffs' claims.

DAMAGES

The trial judge, having found no liability on the part of the defendant, decided that it was not necessary for him to assess damages as the plaintiffs had submitted three alternative bases for the assessment of damages none of which involved disputed facts which required specific findings on his part for the assistance of an appellate court. He set out at p. 41 O.R., pp. 477–78 D.L.R., the three alternative bases for assessing damages submitted by the plaintiffs.

In my opinion the proper basis for assessing damages must follow logically from the basis upon which a finding of liability against the defendant has been made. That finding is that if the defendant had not committed a breach of its fiduciary duty on

April 6, 1972, and thereafter by failing to make the plaintiffs aware of its conflict of interest, they would have disposed of their shares of Crown Trust held by them on that date and would not have purchased the additional shares acquired by them thereafter in the years 1972 to 1979 both inclusive. The appropriate measure of damages is then the difference between (a) the purchase price of those shares plus loss of interest which would have been earned in safe investments of those funds of the plaintiffs which were not funds borrowed to acquire the shares plus interest paid by the plaintiffs on funds which were borrowed by them to acquire the shares and (b) the amount of dividends received by them during the period of their ownership after April 7, 1972, plus the proceeds derived from the sale of their shares. This is the approach which appears to have been suggested in the first basis set forth by the trial judge.

There may be some difficulty in determining the appropriate allowance for a return on a safe investment. In my view, for the purposes of assessing damages in this case, it would be appropriate to use the rate of interest payable from time to time on Government of Canada treasury bills. It should be possible for the parties to make the necessary mathematical computations to compute the damages on this basis. In the event that they are unable to do so, a reference is directed to the master for that purpose.

The plaintiffs shall be entitled to interest on the damages from the date upon which they disposed of their Crown Trust shares until the date of the completion of the trial. If the parties cannot agree upon the rate of interest, the court may be spoken to.

It is desirable that I give brief reasons for rejecting the second and third bases for assessing damages outlined by the trial judge. In so far as the second basis is concerned, it ignores the fact that the basis for the finding of liability against the defendant is that if the defendant had not breached its fiduciary duty, the plaintiffs would not have retained and acquired the Crown Trust shares which they had at the time of the sale to Canwest. It would be illogical to award to them damages for loss of profit on the resale of shares, which, absent the breach of duty on the part of the defendant, they would not have owned at the relevant time. The proper award is for the loss which resulted from the breach of duty found.

In so far as the third basis is concerned, it appears to proceed on the basis that the plaintiffs are entitled to receive the difference between the cost of all of the shares acquired by them during the period of 1971 to 1979 plus the interest which such funds would have earned if invested in safe securities during the appropriate time period and the amount which they realized from the disposition of the shares. This method excludes the interest charges which the plaintiffs would have to pay on funds borrowed to acquire the shares and which notionally they would have had to pay if the borrowed funds had been borrowed for investment in safe securities rather than for the acquisition of Crown Trust shares. It is reasonable to assume that the interest costs for such borrowings would have been higher than the rate of return on an investment in safe securities. The approach is accordingly inappropriate. It should be noted, however, that the trial judge has apparently taken the loss figure of

$10,488,927 from ex. 5 which shows the total alleged loss of interest at $10,408,927 (there appears to be a discrepancy caused by a clerical error). Exhibit 5 refers to all of the shares acquired by the plaintiffs during the nine-year period, not just the 58,000 shares mentioned by the trial judge in his reasons.

In the result I would allow the appeal, set aside the judgment below and direct that judgment go in favour of the plaintiffs for the amount to be agreed upon between the parties or if they cannot agree, for the amount found owing to the plaintiffs on a reference, if such is required, together with interest and costs of the action and this appeal. The cross-appeal is dismissed with costs.

Appeal allowed.

(d) *Vita Health Co. (1985) Ltd. v. Toronto Dominion Bank*†

[TWADDLE J.A.:]

At issue in this appeal [from (1993), 11 B.L.R. (2d) 3 (Q.B.)] are the duties of a chartered bank when it provides a credit report to one customer about another.

THE FACTS

Throughout the relevant period, the plaintiff was a customer of the defendant bank at a branch in Winnipeg. Either it or a predecessor corporation had had that relationship with the bank since 1948.

One of the bank's services utilized by the plaintiff was that of credit verification. This service involves an inquiry by the bank about another company's credit worthiness. The inquiry is made of that other company's banker and results in information being supplied as to the existence of an operating line of credit, a general description of its extent (e.g. "high six figures"), a general description of the extent to which the line of credit is utilized, advice as to whether cheques are being returned unpaid due to insufficient funds and a general expression of the opinion of the other company's banker as to its

customer's credit worthiness (e.g. "responsible for its obligations").

At one time, an employee of the defendant bank advised the plaintiff (or a predecessor corporation) that it (the bank) could provide better information, on which more reliance could be placed, where the company being inquired about was also its customer. Although the employee told the plaintiff that the bank may have to withhold information about another customer on account of confidentiality, he also told the plaintiff that a failure to provide a full report in such circumstances would amount to a negative report. He did not explain, however, how the plaintiff would know that a report was incomplete.

One of the plaintiff's customers was a company which I will refer to as GNC. The plaintiff's accounts receivable from GNC varied in amount as new shipments were made and old accounts were paid. The outstanding balance was usually substantial, reaching a high in excess of $500,000 in January, 1989.

The plaintiff's accounts receivable from all sources created a cash flow problem for it. It consequently had a line of credit with the defendant bank to enable it to carry on its business. This line of

† (1994), 22 B.L.R. (2d) 194 (Man. C.A.), leave to appeal to S.C.C. refused May 18, 1995, (1995) 122 D.L.R. (4th) vii (note).

credit was secured by an assignment of its accounts receivable. The defendant bank was therefore aware in general terms of the existence and amount of accounts owing to the plaintiff by GNC.

The plaintiff became anxious about its accounts receivable from GNC towards the end of 1988. It did three things to allay its fears. It requested that all accounts which had been outstanding for more than 90 days be paid by January 31, 1989; it met with GNC representatives to discuss payment of the accounts still owing; and, in March, 1989, it asked the defendant bank to do a credit verification.

GNC was also a customer of the defendant bank doing business with it at a Montreal branch. It had an operating line of credit of $3,600,000. At the time of the plaintiff's credit inquiry in March, 1989, this line of credit had not only been more than fully utilized, but it was also under threat of reduction by the bank. The bank suggests that there was in fact no over-utilization of the line of credit as each time the limit was exceeded express authorization was obtained. Nonetheless, the regular line of credit was exceeded several times and, as internal documents show, the bank itself was concerned.

In response to its credit inquiry in March 1989, the plaintiff was advised that:

(a) the operating line of credit was in the low seven figures;
(b) cheques were not being returned N.S.F.;
(c) the plaintiff should push GNC hard for payment; and
(d) the account was being operated in a satisfactory manner.

According to the bank's evidence, the plaintiff was also told that GNC's line of credit was fully utilized. The trial judge found, however, that this was not so. She found the plaintiff to have been told that GNC's line of credit was not fully utilized.

Save for the information about GNC's utilization of its line of credit, the statements of fact contained in the bank's credit report were, strictly speaking, accurate and the opinion as to the manner in which the account was being operated was that expressed by the Montreal branch to the branch in Winnipeg.

Whilst the Montreal branch of the defendant bank had passed on to the Winnipeg branch all of the information it would ordinarily have made available to another bank, it disclosed neither its own concerns about GNC's ability to pay its debts nor the steps which it had taken to protect the bank's own interest. Nothing was said about the bank's requirement that new equity funding be injected into GNC, funding which had not materialized by the date of the credit report; nothing was said about the bank's unfulfilled requirement that GNC reduce its utilization of credit by $300,000; nothing was said about the other conditions which either had been imposed by the bank on the continued availability of GNC's line of credit or which were under active consideration by the bank; and nothing was said about the fact that on occasions special authority had been required for the payment of cheques, authority which took GNC's line of credit beyond its regular limit.

After receiving the bank's response to its credit inquiry, the plaintiff continued to ship product to GNC on credit. The decision to do so was not reached, however, without concerns and precautions. The plaintiff was concerned that the bank would not lend money to it on the security of any GNC account receivable more than 90 days old. It therefore attempted to get commitments from GNC to satisfy all accounts older than 90 days by the end of April 1989.

Subsequent to March 1989, GNC's financial position did not improve. On occasions, cheques were presented for payment when there were sufficient funds in GNC's account or line of credit with which to honour them. The bank gave GNC the option of stopping payment on those cheques thereby avoiding the necessity of the bank returning the cheques unpaid due to insufficient funds being available to pay them.

The bank's concern about GNC's ability to repay the amounts lent to it continued. By June, 1989, the bank was so concerned that it asked GNC not to issue trade cheques (those in payment of goods received) in order that GNC's indebtedness to the bank might be reduced to an amount within the authorized line of credit. At the time of that request, or shortly thereafter, the bank was aware that GNC's receivables and inventory did not support the line of credit, there being a shortfall of some $500,000.

The bank's response to the plaintiff's further credit inquiry in June, 1989, was stated by the trial judge in these terms [pp. 9–10]:

> ... G.N.C. was experiencing temporary cash flow problems and that it was reorganizing its management. [The bank] advised that there were no NSF cheques, that the line of credit was being operated satisfactorily and that G.N.C. was within its operating line of credit. [The bank] indicated that [it] considered the account satisfactory and that it should not be a risk.

The bank still did not disclose its own concern or any of the facts which had given rise to it.

After receiving the June report, the plaintiff continued shipping product to GNC on credit terms. It also made new arrangement with GNC for the retirement of outstanding accounts.

A third credit verification was requested in August, 1989. The plaintiff was told that GNC's credit line was fully utilized; that it was experiencing tight cash flow problems, but that this was being looked after and was due to "the time of year"; and that it was for the plaintiff to decide whether further business with GNC should be conducted.

Realizing that GNC's kind of business was slow in the summer months, the plaintiff continued to ship product to GNC on credit. The plaintiff nonetheless attempted to arrange for the outstanding accounts to be paid on a more timely basis.

On September 18, 1989, pursuant to its security agreement with GNC, the bank appointed an agent to take possession of and liquidate the secured assets of GNC. These included GNC's inventory. On the same date, GNC made a proposal under the *Bankruptcy Act* which eventually led to GNC's bankruptcy.

The balance then owing to the plaintiff for product supplied was $420,368. It was agreed by the parties that 5% of that amount represented profit to the plaintiff over and above the cost of the product and the expense of shipping it. The entire account was due for product supplied after receipt by the plaintiff of the March, 1989, credit report. All earlier accounts had been paid in full.

There was no surplus in the bankruptcy for the payment of any amount to unsecured creditors.

THE PLEADINGS

The plaintiff alleged a fiduciary relationship to have existed between it and the bank giving rise to a duty "not to withhold information regarding GNC's financial situation" and a further duty "not to prefer the rights of GNC and/or of itself over those of the plaintiff." It further alleged that, in breach of those duties, the bank failed to provide the plaintiff with accurate and complete information regarding GNC and thereby preferred the interests of GNC and the bank over those of the plaintiff.

By reason of those breaches, the plaintiff claimed entitlement to $420,368 as damages, this amount being equal to the credit extended to GNC by the plaintiff in alleged reliance upon the credit reports provided by the bank.

In the alternative, the plaintiff alleged negligent misrepresentation in the making of the August, 1989, credit report. The claim for the alleged negligence

was for $129,043, the invoiced price of the product supplied to GNC after receipt of the August report.

The bank denied the existence of a fiduciary relationship. It nonetheless acknowledged a duty not to misrepresent GNC's financial situation to the plaintiff. The bank further denied breach of any duty owed by it.

The bank denied the plaintiff's reliance on the credit reports and said that the plaintiff was itself negligent in extending further credit to GNC in light of the bank's credit reports. The bank therefore relied on the provisions of *The Tortfeasors and Contributory Negligence Act*.

THE JUDGMENT APPEALED FROM

The trial judge found the relationship between the parties to be fiduciary. The only duty which she found arising from that relationship, however, was a duty of care.

In finding the bank to have "breached its obligation to exercise a reasonable duty of care to the plaintiff", the trial judge found the bank to have done so "in the provision of information requested from credit verifications during the period March to August 1989."

In the alternative, the trial judge found the bank responsible for negligent misstatements. Although she found such misstatements to have been made in response to each of the three credit inquiries, she did not state what the misstatement was in March.

No explanation was given by the trial judge as to how she could hold the bank responsible for negligent misstatements made in March and June when the only allegation of negligent misstatement by the plaintiff was with respect to the August credit verification.

The trial judge found the plaintiff to have relied on the credit reports in deciding to continue shipping products to GNC on credit.

She did not comment on the alleged contributory negligence of the plaintiff.

On the issue of damages, the trial judge found that the plaintiff was entitled to recover the invoiced price of all product shipped to GNC after the receipt of the first credit report in March, 1989. She rejected the bank's submission that, if the plaintiff had stopped shipping product, the accounts outstanding in mid-March, 1989, would not have been paid as too speculative. She also rejected the bank's submission that the profit factor in the invoiced price of the product should be excluded from the damage computation.

In the result, judgment for $420,368 plus pre-judgment interest was entered for the plaintiff.

THE GROUNDS OF APPEAL

The bank appeals on the ground of error on the part of the trial judge in the following respects:

1. in finding there to be fiduciary relationship between the bank and the plaintiff;
2. in finding any of the credit reports to contain misstatements;
3. in finding any misstatement to have been negligently made;
4. in finding that the plaintiff relied on the credit reports, or alternatively, in finding that the plaintiff was entitled to do so;
5. in finding the plaintiff to have suffered detriment as a result of relying on what the bank told it;
6. in not deducting from the damages awarded the profit factor in the invoiced price.

PRELIMINARY OBSERVATIONS

In *International Corona Resources Ltd. v. LAC Minerals Ltd.*, [1989] 2 S.C.R. 574, Sopinka J. said (at p. 595):

> The consequences attendant on a finding of fiduciary relationship and its breach have resulted in judicial reluctance to do so except where the application of this "blunt tool of equity" is really necessary.

It follows from this dicta, and the fact that the trial judge was able to decide the case on the basis of negligent misrepresentation, that the first issue to be resolved in this appeal is whether it is necessary for us even to address the existence of a fiduciary duty.

There are a number of factors which must be taken into account in determining this issue:

(i) the fact that the only claim for negligent misrepresentation which was pleaded was that arising from the August report;

(ii) the fact that the plaintiff's true complaint, at least as far as the March report is concerned, is not so much that the bank misrepresented a material fact, but rather that the bank failed to disclose relevant information known to it; and

(iii) the fact that the plaintiff's entitlement to damages may be reduced on account of contributory negligence if liability is founded on negligent misstatement, but would not be so reduced if

liability is founded on breach of a fiduciary duty: see s. 4 of *The Tortfeasors and Contributory Negligence Act*, R.S.M. 1987, c. T90, which provides for apportionment only in an action founded upon the defendant's negligence.

Having regard to these factors, and to the fact that the trial judge found a fiduciary relationship to exist, I think it is at least desirable that we consider whether a fiduciary relationship existed and, if so, whether the bank was in breach of any duty arising out of it.

FIDUCIARY RELATIONSHIP

The relationship between a bank and its customer is not ordinarily a fiduciary one. That there are exceptions to this rule is quite clear from the decisions in *Lloyds Bank Ltd. v. Bundy*, [1975] Q.B. 326 (C.A.), and *Standard Investments Ltd. v. Canadian Imperial Bank of Commerce* (1985), 22 D.L.R. (4th) 410 (Ont. C.A.).

Identifying the circumstances which convert the ordinary commercial relationship of a bank and its customer into a fiduciary one is no easy task. Indeed, in *Lloyds Bank Ltd. v. Bundy*, supra, Sir Eric Sachs warned against attempts to define the relationship too closely. He said (at p. 341):

> ... it is neither feasible nor desirable to attempt closely to define the relationship, or its characteristics, or the demarcation line showing the exact transition point where a relationship that does not entail that duty passes into one that does....

This caution is also reflected in the judgments delivered in *International Corona Resources Ltd. v. LAC Minerals Ltd.*, supra. Sopinka J. said (at pp. 596–97): "...equity has refused to tie its hands by defining with precision when a fiduciary relationship will arise..."; and La Forest J. said (at pp. 643–44):

> There are few legal concepts more frequently invoked but less conceptually certain than that of the fiduciary relationship. In specific circumstances and in specific relationships, courts have no difficulty in imposing fiduciary obligations, but at a more fundamental level, the principle on which that obligation is based is unclear. Indeed, the term "fiduciary" has been described as "one of the most ill-defined, if not altogether misleading terms in our law": see Finn, *Fiduciary Obligations*, at p. 1.

Despite the difficulty of defining the relationship, judges have tried from time to time to offer comments which will assist others in recognizing a fiduciary relationship when it exists and in rejecting other relationships as fiduciary. These comments are usually made in the context of the case with which the judge is dealing and are not always helpful when totally different facts are involved. It is for this reason that I look for guidance not to the comments of the Supreme Court judges, in *LAC Minerals*, supra, a totally different kind of case than that before us now, but to those of Sir Eric Sachs in *Lloyds Bank Ltd. v. Bundy*, supra, a case dealing with the relationship between a bank and a customer. Sir Eric Sachs' comments were also quoted with approval in *Standard Investments Ltd. v. Canadian Imperial Bank of Commerce*, supra, at pp. 432 and 433.

Sir Eric Sachs' comments began this way (at p. 341):

> ... whilst disclaiming any intention of seeking to catalogue the elements of such a special relationship, it is perhaps of a little assistance to note some of those which have in the past frequently been found to exist where the court has been led to decide that this relationship existed as between adults of sound mind. Such cases tend to arise where someone relies on the guidance or advice of another, where the other is aware of that reliance and where the person upon whom reliance is placed obtains, or may well obtain, a benefit from the transaction or has some other interest in it being concluded. In addition, there must, of course, be shown to exist a vital element which in this judgment will for convenience bee referred to as confidentiality. It is this element which is so impossible to define and which is a matter for the judgment of the court on the facts of any particular case.

The element of confidentiality was considered further by Sir Eric Sachs in the following passage (also at p. 341):

> Reliance on advice can in many circumstances be said to import that type of confidence which only results in a common law duty to take care — a duty which may co-exist with but is not coterminous with that of fiduciary care. "Confidentiality" is intended to convey that extra quality in the relevant confidence that is implicit in the phrase, "confidential relationship" ... and may perhaps have something in common with "confiding" and also "confidant", when, for instance, referring to someone's "man of affairs". It imports some quality beyond that inherent in the confidence that can well exist between trustworthy persons who in business affairs deal with each other at arm's length. It is one of the features of this element that once it exists, influence naturally grows out of it.

Whilst Sir Eric Sachs stressed the confidence which one person places in another as the element essential to a fiduciary relationship, Sopinka J. stressed the resulting dependency or vulnerability as the essential element: see *LAC Minerals*, supra, at p. 599. This difference is, however, only a matter of emphasis. There cannot be a sufficient dependency without confidence reposed by one in the other any more than there can be a sufficient degree of confidentiality without resulting dependency.

Thus the client's confidence in his or her solicitor gives rise to a dependency which is at the heart of the fiduciary relationship between a solicitor and the solicitor's client. This confidence and resulting dependency is also found in all of the other relationships habitually found to be fiduciary in nature. These include guardian and ward, trustee and cestui que trust, priest and penitent and doctor and patient.

When the stronger party is not clothed — to use the language of Sir Eric Sachs — in the recognizable garb of a fiduciary, but is nonetheless one whose advice is knowingly relied upon by the other, the court must examine the relationship and determine whether, by reason of the benefit or other interest derived from the transaction by the stronger party and the confidence and resulting dependency of the other, the relationship is in fact one of a fiduciary nature.

In the case at bar, the trial judge found the plaintiff to have relied on the bank's advice as to the credit worthiness of GNC and the defendant bank to have been aware of this reliance. Quite apart from the bank's service charge for providing the credit check, the bank had a clear interest in the decision made by the plaintiff as to whether it would continue to extend credit to GNC. The withdrawal of credit terms might have resulted in an end to the supply of goods and a consequential reduction in the inventory of GNC which was pledged as security to the bank for GNC's indebtedness to it.

I have no doubt that, in the particular circumstances of this case, a state of confidentiality and a resulting dependency existed. If it did not arise from the advice given by the bank that it could provide better information, on which more reliance could be placed, where the company being inquired about was also a customer of the bank — as it may well have done — it most certainly arose from the assurance that, if the bank was forced to withhold information on account of confidentiality, its failure to provide a full report would amount to a negative one. As a result of this assurance, the plaintiff was surely induced to place undue confidence in the bank's report and was vulnerable to any shortage of pertinent information.

226

For these reasons, I am of the view that the trial judge was perfectly correct in finding a fiduciary relationship to have existed between the bank and the plaintiff.

THE FIDUCIARY DUTY

The plaintiff asserted in its pleadings that the bank was under a duty not to withhold information from it regarding GNC's financial situation. In light of the bank's warning that its obligation of confidentiality to GNC might prevent it from disclosing some facts to the plaintiff, I think the duty as pleaded is too highly stated. I think, however, that the fiduciary duty undertaken by the bank required it to do one of three things: (i) to disclose unfavourable information; (ii) to warn the plaintiff that there were facts affecting GNC's credit worthiness which it could not disclose; or (iii) to make no report, allowing the plaintiff to draw the inevitable conclusion.

The duty to warn the plaintiff in one of those three ways arises from the fiduciary nature of the relationship. Having been invited to place full confidence in the bank's service, the plaintiff was entitled to believe when it received a credit report that nothing material had been withheld.

THE BREACH

In March, 1989, the bank was threatening to reduce GNC's line of credit. Although express authorization had been obtained on each occasion, the line of credit had been exceeded on more than one occasion. The bank itself was concerned about GNC's ability to repay its indebtedness to the bank.

These facts, if disclosed to an ongoing creditor, might well cause that creditor to reconsider the terms on which it was doing business with GNC. Pursuant to the bank's fiduciary obligation to the plaintiff, it was obliged to disclose those facts to the plaintiff, advise the plaintiff that there was information unfavourable to GNC's credit worthiness which it could not disclose, or make no report at all. Its failure to do any one of these things was, in my opinion, a breach of the bank's fiduciary duty.

The breach continued, or was repeated, when the bank failed in response to further credit inquiries made in June and August, 1989, to give the plaintiff the unfavourable information it then had, to alert the plaintiff to the existence of unfavourable information which it could not disclose, or to make no report. The new information, already outlined, contained even stronger indications of GNC's financial problems than those existing in March 1989.

DAMAGES

From the time of the March credit report on, the plaintiff supplied product to GNC on credit in reliance on its belief that the bank would, one way or another, alert it to any change in the risk. The bank failed to take any of the courses open to it. It neither blew the whistle nor rang the bell.

The trial judge found that the plaintiff, if properly advised or warned, would not have continued to supply product on credit. In light of this finding, I am of the view that the plaintiff is entitled to recover the value of the product for which it was not paid and which was supplied to GNC on credit subsequent to the credit report provided in March, 1989. This value includes the shipping expense.

The trial judge held that the value of the goods might properly include a profit factor — which the parties had agreed represented 5% of the invoiced price. I for my part do not agree with the trial judge's ruling on this point.

Damages are intended to place a party in the position the party would have been in if there had been no breach of duty. This is a fundamental principle which requires no authority to support it. If the plaintiff as a result of a warning from the bank had refrained from supplying further product to GNC, it would have retained the product at its pre-sale value. It is this value, together with shipping expenses, which represents its loss. Any additional amount representing profit on the sale to GNC would, if recovered, place the plaintiff in a better position than it would have been in if the bank had warned it. The plaintiff is not entitled to be so placed.

In support of its claim for profit, the plaintiff relies on the decision of the Supreme Court of Canada in *V.K. Mason Construction Ltd. v. Bank of Nova Scotia*, [1985] 1 S.C.R. 271. That was a case in which a general contractor was induced to enter into a fixed price construction contract as a result of a negligent misrepresentation. The Court held that the contractor was entitled to a profit element in its damages because, if it had not entered into that particular contract, it would have found other work that would have earned a profit.

The reasoning in *V.K. Mason* has, in my opinion, no application here. It is confined to cases where the plaintiff has lost the opportunity to make a profit by reason of its contractual commitment. In the present case, there is no evidence that the plaintiff lost the opportunity to sell similar product to others. Nor can such a loss be assumed. A company in the business of selling goods does not lose the opportunity to sell to others because it has sold goods to a particular party unless it is shown that the sale to the particular party so depleted its supply of the goods in question that it was unable to effect other sales. That has not been shown here.

As to the bank's contention that, if the plaintiff had stopped shipping product in March, 1989, the accounts then outstanding would not have been paid, I share the trial judge's view that such a conclusion is speculative. It is entirely possible that GNC would have retired its past indebtedness — as it in fact did — notwithstanding that further credit was refused. It may have done this either in the ordinary course of business or to secure a further supply of product on a cash on delivery basis.

CONCLUSION

In the result, I would reduce the damage award by the profit factor of 5% making the total damages $399,349.60. Otherwise I would confirm the judgment at trial.

Although partially successful, the defendant bank failed to persuade us that the judgment appealed from was substantially in error. I would consequently order the defendant bank to pay the plaintiff's appeal costs.

Order accordingly.

(II) Undue Influence

(e) *National Westminster Bank plc v. Morgan*†

[LORD SCARMAN (Lord Keith, Lord Roskill, Lord Bridge, and Lord Brandon concurring):]

My Lords, the appellant, the National Westminster Bank plc (the bank), seeks against Mrs. Janet Morgan (the wife), the respondent in the appeal, an order for the possession of a dwelling house in Taunton. The house is the wife's family home. She acquired it jointly with her husband, and since his death on 9 December 1982 has been the sole owner. The bank relies on a charge by way of legal mortgage given by her and her husband to secure a loan granted to them by the bank. The manner in which the wife came to give this charge is at the heart of the case. The only defence to the bank's action with which your Lordships are concerned is the wife's plea that she was induced to execute the charge by the exercise of undue influence on the part of the bank. The bank, she says, procured the charge by bringing to bear undue influence on her at an inter-view at home which Mr. Barrow, the bank manager, sought and obtained in early February 1978.

The action was heard in the Bridgwater County Court in November 1982. The assistant recorder, Mr. C.S. Rawlins, delivered a careful judgment in which after a full review of the facts he rejected the defence of undue influence and made the possession order sought by the bank. He also rejected the wife's counterclaim for equitable relief.

The wife appealed. The Court of Appeal reversed the judge, dismissed the bank's claim, and granted the wife relief in the shape of a declaration that the legal charge was not a good and subsisting charge (see [1983] 3 All E.R. 85).

The bank appeals with the leave of the House. Two issues are said to arise: the first, the substantive issue, is whether the wife has established a case of undue influence; the second, said to be procedural, is whether, if she has, she ought properly to be granted equitable relief, and the nature of any such relief. The two issues are, in truth, no more than

---

† [1985] 1 All E.R. 821 (H.L.).

different aspects of one fundamental question: has the wife established a case for equitable relief? For there is no longer any suggestion that she has a remedy at law. Unless the transaction can be set aside on the ground of undue influence, it is inimpeachable [sic]. The House is not concerned with the claim for damages for negligence raised by the wife in her counterclaim but not pursued by her in the Court of Appeal; nor has any case of misrepresentation been advanced.

In the appeal the bank invites the House to review the decision of the Court of Appeal in *Lloyds Bank Ltd. v. Bundy* [1974] 3 All E.R. 757, [1975] Q.B. 326. The case, it would appear, has been widely misunderstood, though not, I hasten to add, by the judges of our courts. The majority of the court in that case addressed themselves to its very special facts and held that the customer's banking transaction (a legal charge on the home, as in this case) was procured by undue influence exercised by the bank manager; but Lord Denning M.R. preferred to base his judgment on inequality of bargaining power. Because this difference of approach may have led to some confusion, I have no doubt that the House should accede to the bank's invitation. Whether the bank is correct in its submission that the majority decision was wrong in law is, however, another matter, to which I shall return later in my speech.

THE FACTS OF THE CASE

There is no dispute as to the primary facts; they were agreed by counsel in the county court. Mr. and Mrs. Morgan, the husband and the wife, bought the house on 17 September 1974 with the assistance of two loans secured by a first and a second mortgage. The first was a charge by way of legal mortgage to the Abbey National Building Society to secure a loan of £12,800; the second was a legal charge to an investment company to secure a loan of £4,200. The total of £17,000 thus borrowed almost certainly approximated at the time to the value of the property; and the consequence of the two loans was to saddle the property with a burden of debt, the servicing of which was to cause the husband great difficulty. The mortgage repayments soon fell into arrears.

The husband was in business as an earth-moving contractor, a business which he conducted first through a company, Highbell Ltd., and later through a company named D.A. Morgan Contracts Ltd. The business was undercapitalised and subject to alarming fluctuations of fortune. Highbell ceased to trade in July 1975.

Between 1975 and 1977 the husband banked at the Basingstoke branch of the National Westminster Bank, though he and his family were living in Taunton. He was frequently in overdraft on his personal account, so that Basingstoke asked the North Street, Taunton branch to try to collect what was due. On at least six occasions Mr. Barrow, the North Street manager, visited the Morgan house in an attempt to collect the debt. Certainly on one occasion he had a discussion with the wife when she told him that the house was on the market and that the debt would be repaid. The trial judge found as a fact that during this period the wife's relationship with the bank was a business one, that the family was in financial difficulty, and that husband and wife were concerned about their inability to maintain the mortgage repayments.

In June 1977 the husband put a proposal to Basingstoke: it was to borrow from the bank sufficient to pay off the second mortgage, and to set up a new company (D.A. Morgan Contracts Ltd.) which he declared to have a rosy future.

The bank agreed subject to a legal charge to be given by both owners of the property, i.e. by the wife as well as the husband. The bank suggested, very wisely and fairly, that the wife should take legal advice, which she did and for which the bank paid. The advice was the amount to be secured should be limited to £6,000; and the bank accepted the limit.

A few days later (end of June 1977) the bank discovered that a possession order in respect of the house had been made by a court in favour of the second mortgage. The trial judge found that the wife knew of this order when she executed the legal charge in favour of the bank.

The bank now had second thoughts. In the result it did not make the loan to the husband, who was rescued by the generosity of his father who paid off the second mortgagee. The charge to secure £6,000 stood, however; and it continued as a support for the husband's borrowing, subject to the limit demanded and obtained by the wife. During these unhappy events husband and wife were, the judge found, desperately anxious not to lose their home.

In October 1977 a crisis arose on the first mortgage. The Abbey National warned the bank that they were starting proceedings for possession in default of payment of mortgage instalments. On 19 October 1977 the husband transferred his personal account (in overdraft £588) to North Street. The Abbey National began their proceedings, alleging a debt of over £13,000. On 12 December 1977 the wife transferred her account to North Street. From this date onward the husband and the wife's banking transactions were with Mr. Barrow, the North Street manager.

A bank rescue operation was decided on by the husband and the wife, if they could arrange it. On 30 January 1978 the husband asked the bank 'to refinance' the Abbey National Loan. By this time the society had obtained a possession order. The husband told the bank that all he needed was a bridging loan of £14,500 for some five weeks. If the bank would pay off the society, he would arrange for the bank's repayment by his company, which it would appear was currently in a prosperous phase and had, it was then believed, good prospects.

The bank accepted the proposal on the recommendation of Mr. Barrow. He was informed of the approval by his area office by letter of 31 January 1978 in these terms:

> D.A.A. Morgan and another: In reply to your letter of 30 January 1978 the following limit has been granted; £14,500 on current account to 7.3.78 on the short term bridging basis submitted, subject to completion of a new unlimited legal mortgage on NWB 1016 over Crossmorr Meadow to replace the existing limited second mortgage.

The 'existing limited second mortgage' was the 1977 legal charge limit to £6,000. In place of it Mr. Barrow was being instructed to obtain an *unlimited* mortgage to secure a *loan limited* to £14,500. There was considerable discussion by counsel as to the true meaning of this approval. But it is really quite simple: the debt to be secured was the loan of a sum which Abbey National required to be paid if they were to call off their proceedings for possession and to discharge their mortgage; the security for the loan limited to £14,500 was to be a mortgage without express limit. The document of approval sent by the area office and quoted above limited the mortgage to the Abbey National debt and did not authorise Mr. Barrow to use the security to support any other lending transaction.

On 1 February 1978 the husband and the wife signed an authority to the bank to pay off the Abbey National and to charge the husband's personal account. The bank, however, required the mortgage to secure the loan to be in joint names (the property being in joint ownership). Between 3 and 6 February a joint account was opened. The details of the transaction were these. In the first week of February the debit of £14,207.22 was transferred from the husband's personal account to the joint account, being the sum which the bank had paid to the Abbey

National, and the husband and the wife signed the legal charge, which is the transaction which the wife seeks in these proceedings to have declared null and void on the ground that it was procured by the bank's exercise of undue influence on her. The charge bears the date 8 March 1978; no point arises on the discrepancy between this date and the date early in February when it was signed, the delay being attributable to the fact that the bank did not receive from the Abbey National the deeds of the property until the end of February.

There can be no doubt as to the terms of the charge: it was a charge to secure 'all present or future actual or contingent liabilities' of the husband to the bank. The wife had, therefore, signed a charge the terms of which were without limit and covered *all* the liabilities of the husband to the bank. It was, however, plainly the intention of the bank, as it was also its instruction to Mr. Barrow, to treat the security as limited to the bridging finance (capital and interest) needed by the joint owners of the house to pay off the Abbey National and to obtain a period of time (about five weeks) in which to repay the bank. The bank had at no time sought to use the security for any other purpose.

I now come to the heart of the case. It is not suggested, nor could it be, that prior to the interview at which the wife signed the charge the relationship between the bank and its two customers, the husband and the wife, had been other than the normal business one of banker and customer. It was business for profit so far as the bank was concerned; it was a rescue operation to save their house so far as the two customers were concerned.

But it is said on behalf of the wife that the relationship between the bank and herself assumed a very different character when in early February Mr. Barrow called at the house to obtain her signature to the charge; the husband had already signed.

The trial judge set the scene for the critical interview by these findings of fact: husband and wife were looking for a rescue operation by the bank to save the home for themselves and their children; they were seeking from the bank only a breathing space of some five weeks; and the wife knew that there was no other way of saving the house.

Mr. Barrow's visit to the house lasted 15 to 20 minutes. His conversation with the wife lasted only five minutes. The wife's concern was lest the document which she was being asked to sign might enable the husband to borrow from the bank for business purposes. She wanted the charge confined to paying off the Abbey National and to the provision of bridging finance for about five weeks. She told Mr. Barrow that she had no confidence in her husband's business ability and did not want the mortgage to cover his business liabilities. Mr. Barrow advised her that the cover was so limited. She expressed her gratitude to the bank for saving their home. The judge found that the bank was not seeking any advantage other than to provide on normal commercial terms but at extremely short notice the bridging finance necessary to secure their home. He rejected the suggestion that the wife had any misgivings on the basis that she would prefer the house to be sold. He accepted that it was never the intention of Mr. Barrow that the charge should be used to secure any other liability of the husband.

The atmosphere in the home during Mr. Barrow's visit was plainly tense. The husband was in and out of the room, 'hovering around'. The wife made it clear to Mr. Barrow that she did not want him there. Mr. Barrow did manage to discuss the more delicate matters when he was out of the room.

Such was the interview in which it is said Mr. Barrow crossed the line which divides a normal business relationship from one of undue influence. I am bound to say that the facts appear to me to be a far cry from a relationship of undue influence or from a transaction in which an unfair advantage was obtained by one party over the other. The trial judge clearly so thought, for he stated his reasons for rejecting the wife's case with admirable brevity. He made abundantly clear his view that the relationship between Mr. Barrow and the wife never went beyond that of a banker and customer, that the wife had made up her own mind that she was ready to give the charge, and that the one piece of advice (as to the legal effect of the charge) which Mr. Barrow did give, though erroneous as to the terms of the charge, correctly represented his intention and that of the bank. The judge dealt with three points. First, he ruled on the submission by the bank that the transaction of loan secured on the property was not one of manifest disadvantage to the wife since it provided what to her was desperately important, namely the rescue of the house from the Abbey National. He was pressed, of course, with the contrast between the unlimited terms of the legal charge and the assurance (to which at all times the bank adhered) by Mr. Barrow that the charge was limited to paying off the Abbey National and the bridging finance. He considered the balance to be between the 'enormous' advantage of preserving the home from the Abbey National and the 'essentially theoretical' disadvantage of the terms of the written charge, and accepted the submission that the transaction was not manifestly disadvantageous to the wife.

Second, he rejected the submission made on behalf of the wife that Mr. Barrow put pressure on her. In his view the pressure on her was the knowledge that Abbey National were on the point of obtaining possession with a view to the sale of her home. It was, however, suggested that Mr. Barrow had made a mistake in the advice which he gave her as to the nature of the charge. Mr. Barrow's mistake was not as to the bank's intentions but as to the wording of the charge. He accurately stated the bank's intention and events have proved him right. I would add in passing that no case of misrepresentation by Mr. Barrow was sought to be developed at the trial and the case of negligence is not pursued.

The judge recognised that Mr. Barrow did not advise her to take legal advice; but he held that the circumstances did not call for any such advice and that she was not harried into signing. She was signing to save her house and to obtain short-term bridging finance. 'The decision,' the judge said, 'was her own.'

Third, he rejected the submission that there was a confidential relationship between the wife and the bank such as to give rise to a presumption of undue influence. Had the relationship been such as to give rise to the presumption, he would have held, as counsel for the bank conceded, that no evidence had been called to rebut it. He concluded that the wife had failed to make out her case of undue influence.

The Court of Appeal disagreed. The two Lords Justices who constituted the court (Dunn and Slade L.JJ.) (surely it should have been a court of three) put an interpretation on the facts very different from that of the judge; they also differed from him on the law.

As to the facts, I am far from being persuaded that the trial judge fell into error when he concluded that the relationship between the bank and the wife never went beyond the normal business relationship of banker and customer. Both Dunn and Slade L.JJ. saw the relationship between the bank and the wife as one of confidence in which she was relying on the bank manager's advice. Each recognised the personal honesty, integrity, and good faith of Mr. Barrow. Each took the view that the confidentiality of the relationship was such as to impose on him a 'fiduciary duty of care'. It was his duty, in their view, to ensure that the wife had the opportunity to make an independent and informed decision; but he failed to give her any such opportunity. They, therefore, concluded that it was a case for the presumption of undue influence.

My Lords, I believe that Dunn and Slade L.JJ. were led into a misinterpretation of the facts by their use, as is all too frequent in this branch of the law, of words and phrases such as 'confidence', 'confidentiality', 'fiduciary duty'. There are plenty of confidential relationships which do not give rise to the presumption of undue influence (a notable example is that of husband and wife: see *Bank of Montreal v. Stuart* [1911] A.C. 120); and there are plenty of non-confidential relationships in which one person relies on the advice of another, e.g., many contracts for the sale of goods. Nor am I persuaded that the charge, limited as it was by Mr. Barrow's declaration to securing the loan to pay off the Abbey National debt and interest during the bridging period, was disadvantageous to the wife. It meant for her the rescue of her home on the terms sought by her: a short-term loan at a commercial rate of interest. The Court of Appeal has not, therefore, persuaded me that the judge's understanding of the facts was incorrect.

But, further, the view of the law expressed by the Court of Appeal was, as I shall endeavour to show, mistaken. Dunn L.J., while accepting that in all the reported cases to which the court was referred the transactions were disadvantageous to the person influenced, took the view that in cases where public policy requires the court to apply the presumption of undue influence there is no need to prove a disadvantageous transaction (see [1983] 3 All E.R. 85 at 90). Slade L.J. also clearly held that it was not necessary to prove a disadvantageous transaction where the relationship of influence was proved to exist. Basing himself on the judgment of Cotton L.J. in *Allcard v. Skinner* (1887) 36 Ch. D. 145 at 171, [1886–90] All E.R. Rep 90 at 93, he said ([1983] 3 All E.R. 85 at 92):

> Where a transaction has been entered into between two parties who stand in the relevant relationship to one another, it is still possible that the relationship and influence arising therefrom has been abused, even though the transaction is, on the face of it, one which, in commercial terms, provides reasonably equal benefits for both parties.

I can find no support for this view of the law other than the passage in Cotton L.J.'s judgment in *Allcard v. Skinner* to which Slade L.J. referred. The passage is as follows:

> The question is — Does the case fall within the principles laid down by the decisions of the Court of Chancery in setting aside voluntary gifts executed by parties who at the time were under such influence as, in the opinion of the Court, enabled the donor afterwards to set the gift aside? These decisions may be divided into two classes — First, where the Court has been satis-fied that the gift was the result of influence expressly used by the donee for the purpose; second, where the relations between the donor and donee have at or shortly before the execution of the gift been such as to raise a presumption that the donee had influence over the donor. In such a case the Court sets aside the voluntary gift, unless it is proved that in fact the gift was the spontaneous act of the donor acting under circumstances which enabled him to exercise an independent will and which justifies the Court in holding that the gift was the result of a free exercise of the donor's will. The first class of cases may be considered as depending on the principle that no one shall be allowed to retain any benefit arising from his own fraud or wrongful act. In the second class of cases the Court interferes, not on the ground that any wrongful act has in fact been committed by the donee, but on the ground of public policy, and to prevent the relations which existed between the parties and the influence arising therefrom being abused.

The transactions in question in *Allcard v. Skinner* were gifts; it is not to be supposed that Cotton L.J. was excluding the applicability of his observations to other transactions in which disadvantage or sacrifice is accepted by the party influence. It is significant for the proper understanding of his judgment that gifts are transactions in which the donor by parting with his property accepts a disadvantage or a sacrifice, and that in *Allcard v. Skinner* the donor parted with almost all her property. I do not, therefore, understand Cotton L.J., when he accepted that Miss Allcard's case fell into the class where undue influence was to be presumed, to have treated as irrelevant the fact that her transaction was manifestly disadvantageous to her merely because he was concerned in the passage quoted to stress the importance of the relationship. If, however, as Slade L.J. clearly thought, Cotton L.J. in the last sentence quoted should be understood as laying down that the transaction need not be one of disadvantage and that the presumption of undue influence can arise in respect of a transaction which provides 'reasonably equally benefits for both parties', I have with great respect to say that in my opinion Cotton L.J. would have erred in law; principle and authority are against any such proposition.

Like Dunn L.J., I know of no reported authority where the transaction set aside was not to the manifest disadvantage of the person influenced. It would not always be a gift: it can be a 'hard and inequitable' agreement (see *Ormes v. Beadel* (1860) 2 Giff. 166 at 174, 66 E.R. 70 at 74); or a transaction 'immoderate and irrational' (see *Bank of Montreal v.*

Stuart [1911] A.C. 120 at 137) or 'unconscionable' in that it was a sale at an undervalue (see *Poosathurai v. Kannappa Chettiar* (1919) L.R. 47 Ind. App. 1 at 3–4). Whatever the legal character of the transaction, the authorities show that it must constitute a disadvantage sufficiently serious to require evidence to rebut the presumption that in the circumstances of the relationship between the parties it was procured by the exercise of undue influence. In my judgment, therefore, the Court of Appeal erred in law in holding that the presumption of undue influence can arise from the evidence of the relationship of the parties without also evidence that the transaction itself was wrongful in that it constituted an advantage taken of the person subjected to the influence which, failing proof to the contrary, was explicable only on the basis that undue influence had been exercised to procure it.

The principle justifying the court in setting aside a transaction for undue influence can now be seen to have been established by Lindley L.J. in *Allcard v. Skinner*. It is not a vague 'public policy' but specifically the victimisation of one party by the other. It was stated by Lindley L.J. in a famous passage (36 Ch. D. 145 at 182–83, [1886–90] All E.R. Rep. 90 at 99):

> The principle must be examined. What then is the principle? Is it that it is right and expedient to save persons from the consequences of their own folly? or is it that it is right and expedient to save them from being victimised by other people? In my opinion the doctrine of undue influence is founded on the second of these two principles. Courts of Equity have never set aside gifts on the ground of the folly, imprudence, or want of foresight on the part of donors. The Courts have always repudiated any such jurisdiction. *Huguenin v. Baseley* ((1807) 14 Ves. 273, [1803–13] All E.R. Rep. 1) is itself a clear authority to this effect. It would obviously be to encourage folly, recklessness, extravagance and vice if persons could get back property which they foolishly made away with, whether by giving it to charitable institutions or by bestowing it on less worthy objects. On the other hand, to protect people from being forced, tricked or misled in any way by others into parting with their property is one of the most legitimate objects of all laws; and the equitable doctrine of undue influence has grown out of and been developed by the necessity of grappling with insidious forms of spiritual tyranny and with the infinite varieties of fraud.

When Lindley L.J. came to state the circumstances which give rise to the presumption, he put it thus

(36 Ch. D. 145 at 183, [1886–90] All E.R. Rep. 90 at 99–100):

> As no Court has ever attempted to define fraud so no Court has ever attempted to define undue influence, which includes one of its many varieties. The undue influence which Courts of equity endeavour to defeat is the undue influence of one person over another; not the influence of enthusiasm on the enthusiast who is carried away by it, unless indeed such enthusiasm is itself the result of external undue influence. But the influence of one mind over another is very subtle, and of all influences religious influence is the most dangerous and the most powerful, and to counteract it Courts of Equity have gone very far. They have not shrunk from setting aside gifts made to persons in a position to exercise undue influence over the donors, although there has been no proof of the actual exercise of such influence; and the Courts have done this on the avowed ground of the necessity of going this length in order to protect persons from the exercise of such influence under circumstances which render proof of it impossible. The Courts have required proof of its non-exercise, and, failing that proof, have set aside gifts otherwise unimpeachable.

And in a later passage he returned to the critical importance of the nature of the transaction (36 Ch. D. 145 at 185, [1886–90] All E.R. 90 at 100–1):

> Where a gift is made to a person standing in a confidential relation to the donor, the Court will not set aside the gift if of a small amount simply on the ground that the donor had no independent advice. In such a case, some proof of the exercise of the influence of the donee must be given. The mere existence of such influence is not enough in such a case; see the observations of Lord Justice *Turner* in *Rhodes v. Bate* ((1866) L.R. 1 Ch. App. 252 at 258, [1861–73] All E.R. Rep. 805 at 809). But if the gift is so large as not to be reasonably accounted for on the ground of friendship, relationship, charity, or other ordinary motives on which ordinary men act, the burden is upon the donee to support the gift.

Subsequent authority supports the view of the law as expressed by Lindley L.J. in *Allcard v. Skinner*. The need to show that the transaction is wrongful in the sense explained by Lindley L.J. before the court will set aside a transaction whether relying on evidence or the presumption of the exercise of undue influence has been asserted in two Privy Council cases. In *Bank of Montreal v. Stuart* [1911] A.C. 120 at 137 Lord Macnaghten, delivering the judgment of the Board, said:

It may well be argued that when there is evidence of overpowering influence and the transaction brought about is immoderate and irrational, as it was in the present case, proof of undue influence is complete. However that may be, it seems to their Lordships that in this case there is enough, according to the recognized doctrine of Courts of Equity, to entitle Mrs. Stuart to relief. Unfair advantage of Mrs. Stuart's confidence in her husband was taken by Mr. Stuart, and also it must be added by Mr. Bruce.

In *Poosathurai v. Kannappa Chettiar* (1919) L.R. 47 Ind. App. 1 at 3 Lord Shaw, after indicating that there was no difference on the subject of undue influence between the *Indian Contract Act* 1872 and English law quoted the Indian Statutory provision, s. 16(3):

> Where a person who is in a position to dominate the will of another enters into a contract with him, and the transaction appears on the face of it, or on the evidence, to be unconscionable, the burden of proving that such contract was not induced by undue influence shall lie upon the person in the position to dominate the will of the other.

He then proceeded to state the principle in a passage of critical importance, which, since, so far as I am aware, the case is not reported elsewhere, I think it helpful to quote in full (at 4):

> It must be established that the person in a position of domination has used that position to obtain unfair advantage for himself, and so to cause injury to the person relying upon his authority or aid. Where the relation of influence, as above set forth, has been established, and the second thing is also made clear, namely, that the bargain is with the "influencer," and in itself unconscionable, then the person in a position to use his dominating power has the burden thrown upon him, and it is a heavy burden, of establishing affirmatively that no domination was practised so as to bring about the transaction, but that the grantor of the deed was scrupulously kept separately advised in the independence of a free agent. These general propositions are mentioned because, if laid alongside of the facts of the present case, then it appears that one vital element — perhaps not sufficiently relied on in the Court below, and yet essential to the plaintiff's case — is wanting. It is not proved as a fact in the present case that the bargain of sale come to was unconscionable in itself or constituted an advantage unfair to the plaintiff; it is, in short, not established as a matter of fact that the sale was for undervalue.

The wrongfulness of the transaction must, therefore, be shown: it must be one in which an unfair advantage has been taken of another. The doctrine is not limited to transactions of gift. A commercial relationship can become a relationship in which one party assumes a role of dominating influence over the other. In *Poosathurai's* case the Board recognised that a sale at an undervalue could be a transaction which a court could set aside as unconscionable if it was shown or could be presumed to have been procured by the exercise of undue influence. Similarly, a relationship of banker and customer may become one in which the banker acquires a dominating influence. If he does and a manifestly disadvantageous transaction is proved, there would then be room for the court to presume that it resulted from the exercise of undue influence.

This brings me to *Lloyds Bank Ltd. v. Bundy* [1974] 3 All E.R. 757, [1975] Q.B. 326. It was, as one would expect, conceded by counsel for the wife that the relationship between banker and customer is not one which ordinarily gives rise to a presumption of undue influence; and that in the ordinary course of banking business a banker can explain the nature of the proposed transaction without laying himself open to a charge of undue influence. This proposition has never been in doubt, though some, it would appear, have thought that the Court of Appeal held otherwise in *Lloyds Bank Ltd. v. Bundy*. If any such view has gained currency, let it be destroyed now once and for all time (see [1974] 3 All E.R. 757 at 763, 766, 767, [1975] Q.B. 326 at 336, 340, 341–42 *per* Lord Denning M.R., Cairns L.J. and Sir Eric Sachs). Your Lordships are, of course, not concerned with the interpretation put on the facts in that case by the Court of Appeal; the present case is not a rehearing of that case. The question which the House does have to answer is: did the court in *Lloyds Bank Ltd. v. Bundy* accurately state the law?

Lord Denning M.R. believed that the doctrine of undue influence could be subsumed under a general principle that English courts will grant relief where there has been 'inequality of bargaining power' (see [1974] 3 All E.R. 757 at 765, [1975] Q.B. 326 at 339). He deliberately avoided reference to the will of one party being dominated or overcome by another. The majority of the court did not follow him; they based their decision on the orthodox view of the doctrine as expounded in *Allcard v. Skinner* (1887) 36 Ch. D. 145, [1886–90] All E.R. Rep. 90. This opinion of Lord Denning M.R., therefore, was not the ground of the court's decision, which has to be found in the view of the majority, for whom Sir Eric Sachs delivered the leading judgment.

Nor has counsel for the wife sought to rely on Lord Denning M.R.'s general principle; and, in my view, he was right not to do so. The doctrine of undue influence has been sufficiently developed not to need the support of a principle which by its formulation in the language of the law of contract is not appropriate to cover transactions of gift where there is no bargain. The fact of an unequal bargain will, of course, be a relevant feature in some cases of undue influence. But it can never become an appropriate basis of principle of an equitable doctrine which is concerned with transactions 'not to be reasonably accounted for on the ground of friendship, relationship, charity, or other ordinary motives on which ordinary men act ...' (see *Allcard v. Skinner* 36 Ch. D. 145 at 185, [1886–90] All E.R. Rep. 90 at 100–1 *per* Lindley L.J.). And even in the field of contract I question whether there is any need in the modern law to erect a general principle of relief against inequality of bargaining power. Parliament has undertaken the task (and it is essentially a legislative task) of enacting such restrictions on freedom of contract as are in its judgment necessary to relieve against the mischief: for example, the hire-purchase and consumer protection legislation, of which the *Supply of Goods (Implied Terms) Act* 1973, the *Consumer Credit Act* 1974, the *Consumer Safety Act* 1978, the *Supply of Goods and Services Act* 1982 and the *Insurance Companies Act* 1982 are examples. I doubt whether the courts should assume the burden of formulating further restrictions.

I turn, therefore, to consider the *ratio decidendi* of Sir Eric Sachs's judgment.

In so far as Sir Eric appears to have accepted the 'public policy' principle formulated by Cotton L.J. in *Allcard v. Skinner*, I think for the reasons which I have already developed that he fell into error if he is to be understood as also saying that it matters not whether the transaction itself was wrongful in the sense explained by Lindley L.J. in *Allcard v. Skinner*, by Lord Macnaghten in *Bank of Montreal v. Stuart* and by Lord Shaw in the *Poosathurai* case. But in the last paragraph of his judgment where Sir Eric turned to consider the nature of the relationship necessary to give rise to the presumption of undue influence in the context of a banking transaction, he got it absolutely right. He said ([1974] 3 All E.R. 757 at 772, [1975] Q.B. 326 at 347):

> There remains to mention that counsel for the bank, whilst conceding that the relevant special relationship could arise as between banker and customer, urged in somewhat doom-laden terms that a decision taken against the bank on the facts of this particular case would seriously affect banking practice. With all respect to that submission, it seems necessary to point out that nothing in this judgment affects the duties of a bank in the normal case where it obtains a guarantee, and in accordance with standard practice explains to the person about to sign its legal effect and the sums involved. When, however, a bank, as in the present case, goes further and advises on more general matters germane to the wisdom of the transaction, that indicates that it may — not necessarily must — be crossing the line into the area of confidentiality so that the court may then have to examine all the facts including, of course, the history leading up to the transaction, to ascertain whether or not that line has, as here, been crossed. It would indeed be rather odd if a bank which vis-à-vis a customer attained a special relationship in some ways akin to that of a "man of affairs" — something which can be a matter of pride and enhance its local reputation — should not, where a conflict of interest has arisen as between itself and the person advised be under the resulting duty now under discussion. Once, as was inevitably conceded, it is possible for a bank to be under that duty, it is, as in the present case, simply a question for "meticulous examination" of the particular facts to see whether that duty has arisen. On the special facts here it did arise and it has been broken.

This is good sense and good law, though I would prefer to avoid the term 'confidentiality' as a description of the relationship which has to be proved. In truth, as Sir Eric recognised, the relationships which may develop a dominating influence of one over another are infinitely various. There is no substitute in this branch of the law for a 'meticulous examination of the facts'.

A meticulous examination of the facts of the present case reveals that Mr. Barrow never 'crossed the line'. Nor was the transaction unfair to the wife. The bank was, therefore, under no duty to ensure that she had independent advice. It was an ordinary banking transaction whereby the wife sought to save her home; and she obtained an honest and trustful explanation of the bank's intention which, notwithstanding the terms of the mortgage deed which in the circumstances the trial judge was right to dismiss as 'essentially theoretical', was correct; for no one has suggested that Mr. Barrow or the bank sought to make the wife liable, or to make her home the security, for any debt of her husband other than the loan and interest necessary to save the house from being taken away from them in discharge of their indebtedness to the building society.

For these reasons, I would allow the appeal. In doing so, I would wish to give a warning. There is no precisely defined law setting limits to the equitable jurisdiction of a court to relieve against undue influence. This is the world of doctrine, not of neat and tidy rules. The courts of equity have developed a body of learning enabling relief to be granted where the law has to treat the transaction as unimpeachable unless it can be held to have been procured by undue influence. It is the unimpeachability at law of a disadvantageous transaction which is the starting point from which the court advances to consider whether the transaction is the product merely of one's own folly or of the undue influence exercised by another. A court in the exercise of this equitable jurisdiction is a court of conscience. Definition is a poor instrument when used to determine whether a transaction is or is not unconscionable: this is a question which depends on the particular facts of the case.

I propose, therefore, that the House order as follows: (1) that the appeal be allowed; (2) that possession of the house be given within 28 days of the date of judgment in this House; (3) that no order be made as to costs in the Court of Appeal or in this House save for a legal aid taxation of the wife's costs.

Appeal allowed.

(f) *Royal Bank of Scotland v. Etridge (No. 2)*†

[LORD NICHOLLS OF BIRKENHEAD:]

Before your Lordships' House are appeals in eight cases. Each case arises out of a transaction in which a wife charged her interest in her home in favour of a bank as security for her husband's indebtedness or the indebtedness of a company through which he carried on business. The wife later asserted she signed the charge under the undue influence of her husband. In *Barclays Bank Plc v O'Brien* [1994] 1 AC 180 your Lordships enunciated the principles applicable in this type of case. Since then, many cases have come before the courts, testing the implications of the *O'Brien* decision in a variety of different factual situations. Seven of the present appeals are of this character. In each case the bank sought to enforce the charge signed by the wife. The bank claimed an order for possession of the matrimonial home. The wife raised a defence that the bank was on notice that her concurrence in the transaction had been procured by her husband's undue influence. The eighth appeal concerns a claim by a wife for damages from a solicitor who advised her before she entered into a guarantee obligation of this character.

UNDUE INFLUENCE

The issues raised by these appeals make it necessary to go back to first principles. Undue influence is one of the grounds of relief developed by the courts of equity as a court of conscience. The objective is to ensure that the influence of one person over another is not abused. In everyday life people constantly seek to influence the decisions of others. They seek to persuade those with whom they are dealing to enter into transactions, whether great or small. The law has set limits to the means properly employable for this purpose. To this end the common law developed a principle of duress. Originally this was narrow in its scope, restricted to the more blatant forms of physical coercion, such as personal violence.

Here, as elsewhere in the law, equity supplemented the common law. Equity extended the reach of the law to other unacceptable forms of persuasion. The law will investigate the manner in which the intention to enter into the transaction was secured: 'how the intention was produced', in the oft repeated words of Lord Eldon LC, from as long ago as 1807 (*Huguenin v Baseley* 14 Ves 273, 300). If the intention was produced by an unacceptable means,

---

† [2001] 4 All E.R. 449 (H.L.) at 457–76, 509–10.

the law will not permit the transaction to stand. The means used is regarded as an exercise of improper or 'undue' influence, and hence unacceptable, whenever the consent thus procured ought not fairly to be treated as the expression of a person's free will. It is impossible to be more precise or definitive. The circumstances in which one person acquires influence over another, and the manner in which influence may be exercised, vary too widely to permit of any more specific criterion.

Equity identified broadly two forms of unacceptable conduct. The first comprises overt acts of improper pressure or coercion such as unlawful threats. Today there is much overlap with the principle of duress as this principle has subsequently developed. The second form arises out of a relationship between two persons where one has acquired over another a measure of influence, or ascendancy, of which the ascendant person then takes unfair advantage. An example from the 19th century, when much of this law developed, is a case where an impoverished father prevailed upon his inexperienced children to charge their reversionary interests under their parents' marriage settlement with payment of his mortgage debts: see *Bainbrigge v Browne* (1881) 18 Ch D 188.

In cases of this latter nature the influence one person has over another provides scope for misuse without any specific overt acts of persuasion. The relationship between two individuals may be such that, without more, one of them is disposed to agree a course of action proposed by the other. Typically this occurs when one person places trust in another to look after his affairs and interests, and the latter betrays this trust by preferring his own interests. He abuses the influence he has acquired. In *Allcard v Skinner* (1887) 36 Ch D 145, a case well known to every law student, Lindley LJ, at p 181, described this class of cases as those in which it was the duty of one party to advise the other or to manage his property for him. In *Zamet v Hyman* [1961] 1 WLR 1442, 1444–1445 Lord Evershed MR referred to relationships where one party owed the other an obligation of candour and protection.

The law has long recognised the need to prevent abuse of influence in these 'relationship' cases despite the absence of evidence of overt acts of persuasive conduct. The types of relationship, such as parent and child, in which this principle falls to be applied cannot be listed exhaustively. Relationships are infinitely various. Sir Guenter Treitel QC has rightly noted that the question is whether one party has reposed sufficient trust and confidence in the other, rather than whether the relationship between

the parties belongs to a particular type: see *Treitel, The Law of Contract*, 10th ed (1999), pp. 380–381. For example, the relation of banker and customer will not normally meet this criterion, but exceptionally it may: see *National Westminster Bank Plc v Morgan* [1985] AC 686, 707–709.

Even this test is not comprehensive. The principle is not confined to cases of abuse of trust and confidence. It also includes, for instance, cases where a vulnerable person has been exploited. Indeed, there is no single touchstone for determining whether the principle is applicable. Several expressions have been used in an endeavour to encapsulate the essence: trust and confidence, reliance, dependence or vulnerability on the one hand and ascendancy, domination or control on the other. None of these descriptions is perfect. None is all embracing. Each has its proper place.

In *CIBC Mortgages Plc v Pitt* [1994] 1 AC 200 your Lordships' House decided that in cases of undue influence disadvantage is not a necessary ingredient of the cause of action. It is not essential that the transaction should be disadvantageous to the pressurised or influenced person, either in financial terms or in any other way. However, in the nature of things, questions of undue influence will not usually arise, and the exercise of undue influence is unlikely to occur, where the transaction is innocuous. The issue is likely to arise only when, in some respect, the transaction was disadvantageous either from the outset or as matters turned out.

BURDEN OF PROOF AND PRESUMPTIONS

Whether a transaction was brought about by the exercise of undue influence is a question of fact. Here, as elsewhere, the general principle is that he who asserts a wrong has been committed must prove it. The burden of proving an allegation of undue influence rests upon the person who claims to have been wronged. This is the general rule. The evidence required to discharge the burden of proof depends on the nature of the alleged undue influence, the personality of the parties, their relationship, the extent to which the transaction cannot readily be accounted for by the ordinary motives of ordinary persons in that relationship, and all the circumstances of the case.

Proof that the complainant placed trust and confidence in the other party in relation to the management of the complainant's financial affairs, coupled with a transaction which calls for explanation, will normally be sufficient, failing satisfactory evidence to the contrary, to discharge the burden of proof. On proof of these two matters the stage is set for the court to infer that, in the absence of a satisfactory explanation, the transaction can only have been procured by undue influence. In other words, proof of these two facts is prima facie evidence that the defendant abused the influence he acquired in the parties' relationship. He preferred his own interests. He did not behave fairly to the other. So the evidential burden then shifts to him. It is for him to produce evidence to counter the inference which otherwise should be drawn.

The case of *Bainbrigge v Browne*, 18 Ch D 188, already mentioned, provides a good illustration of this commonplace type of forensic exercise. Fry J held, at p. 196, that there was no direct evidence upon which he could rely as proving undue pressure by the father. But there existed circumstances 'from which the court will infer pressure and undue influence.' None of the children were entirely emancipated from their father's control. None seemed conversant with business. These circumstances were such as to cast the burden of proof upon the father. He had made no attempt to discharge that burden. He did not appear in court at all. So the children's claim succeeded. Again, more recently, in *National Westminster Bank Plc v Morgan* [1985] AC 686, 707, Lord Scarman noted that a relationship of banker and customer may become one in which a banker acquires a dominating influence. If he does, and a manifestly disadvantageous transaction is proved, 'there would then be room' for a court to presume that it resulted from the exercise of undue influence.

Generations of equity lawyers have conventionally described this situation as one in which a presumption of undue influence arises. This use of the term 'presumption' is descriptive of a shift in the evidential onus on a question of fact. When a plaintiff succeeds by this route he does so because he has succeeded in establishing a case of undue influence. The court has drawn appropriate inferences of fact upon a balanced consideration of the whole of the evidence at the end of a trial in which the burden of proof rested upon the plaintiff. The use, in the course of the trial, of the forensic tool of a shift in the evidential burden of proof should not be permitted to obscure the overall position. These cases are the equitable counterpart of common law cases where the principle of res ipsa loquitur is invoked. There is a rebuttable evidential presumption of undue influence.

The availability of this forensic tool in cases founded on abuse of influence arising from the parties' relationship has led to this type of case sometimes being labelled 'presumed undue influence'. This is by way of contrast with cases involving actual pressure or the like, which are labelled 'actual undue influence': see *Bank of Credit and Commerce International SA v Aboody* [1990] I QB 923, 953, and *Royal Bank of Scotland Plc v Etridge (No 2)* [1998] 4 All ER 705, 711–712, paras. 5–7. This usage can be a little confusing. In many cases where a plaintiff has claimed that the defendant abused the influence he acquired in a relationship of trust and confidence the plaintiff has succeeded by recourse to the rebuttable evidential presumption. But this need not be so. Such a plaintiff may succeed even where this presumption is not available to him; for instance, where the impugned transaction was not one which called for an explanation.

The evidential presumption discussed above is to be distinguished sharply from a different form of presumption which arises in some cases. The law has adopted a sternly protective attitude towards certain types of relationship in which one party acquires influence over another who is vulnerable and dependent and where, moreover, substantial gifts by the influenced or vulnerable person are not normally to be expected. Examples of relationships within this special class are parent and child, guardian and ward, trustee and beneficiary, solicitor and client, and medical adviser and patient. In these cases the law presumes, irrebuttably, that one party had influence over the other. The complainant need not prove he actually reposed trust and confidence in the other party. It is sufficient for him to prove the existence of the type of relationship.

It is now well established that husband and wife is not one of the relationships to which this latter principle applies. In *Yerkey v Jones* (1939) 63 CLR 649, 675 Dixon J explained the reason. The Court of Chancery was not blind to the opportunities of obtaining and unfairly using influence over a wife which a husband often possesses. But there is nothing unusual or strange in a wife, from motives of affection or for other reasons, conferring substantial financial benefits on her husband. Although there is no presumption, the court will nevertheless note, as a matter of fact, the opportunities for abuse which flow from a wife's confidence in her husband. The court will take this into account with all the other evidence in the case. Where there is evidence that a husband has taken unfair advantage of his influence over his wife, or her confidence in him, 'it is not difficult for the wife to establish her title to relief': see *In re Lloyds Bank Ltd, Bomze v Bomze* [1931] 1 Ch 289, at p. 302, per Maugham J.

INDEPENDENT ADVICE

Proof that the complainant received advice from a third party before entering into the impugned transaction is one of the matters a court takes into account when weighing all the evidence. The weight, or importance, to be attached to such advice depends on all the circumstances. In the normal course, advice from a solicitor or other outside adviser can be expected to bring home to a complainant a proper understanding of what he or she is about to do. But a person may understand fully the implications of a proposed transaction, for instance, a substantial gift, and yet still be acting under the undue influence of another. Proof of outside advice does not, of itself, necessarily show that the subsequent completion of the transaction was free from the exercise of undue influence. Whether it will be proper to infer that outside advice had an emancipating effect, so that the transaction was not brought about by the exercise of undue influence, is a question of fact to be decided having regard to all the evidence in the case.

MANIFEST DISADVANTAGE

As already noted, there are two prerequisites to the evidential shift in the burden of proof from the complainant to the other party. First, that the complainant reposed trust and confidence in the other party, or the other party acquired ascendancy over the complainant. Second, that the transaction is not readily explicable by the relationship of the parties.

Lindley LJ summarised this second prerequisite in the leading authority of *Allcard v Skinner*, 36 Ch D 145, where the donor parted with almost all her property. Lindley LJ pointed out that where a gift of a small amount is made to a person standing in a confidential relationship to the donor, some proof of the exercise of the influence of the donee must be given. The mere existence of the influence is not enough. He continued, at p. 185:

> But if the gift is so large as not to be reasonably accounted for on the ground of friendship, relationship, charity, or other ordinary motives on which ordinary men act, the burden is upon the donee to support the gift.

In *Bank of Montreal v Stuart* [1911] AC 120, 137 Lord Macnaghten used the phrase 'immoderate and irrational' to describe this concept.

The need for this second prerequisite has recently been questioned: see Nourse LJ in *Barclays Bank Plc v Coleman* [2001] QB, 20, 30–32, one of the cases under appeal before your Lordships' House. Mr Sher QC invited your Lordships to depart from the decision of the House on this point in *National Westminster Bank Plc v Morgan* [1985] AC 686.

My Lords, this is not an invitation I would accept. The second prerequisite, as expressed by Lindley LJ, is good sense. It is a necessary limitation upon the width of the first prerequisite. It would be absurd for the law to presume that every gift by a child to a parent, or every transaction between a client and his solicitor or between a patient and his doctor, was brought about by undue influence unless the contrary is affirmatively proved. Such a presumption would be too far-reaching. The law would out of touch with everyday life if the presumption were to apply to every Christmas or birthday gift by a child to a parent, or to an agreement whereby a client or patient agrees to be responsible for the reasonable fees of his legal or medical adviser. The law would be rightly open to ridicule, for transactions such as these are unexceptionable. They do not suggest that something may be amiss. So something more is needed before the law reverses the burden of proof, something which calls for an explanation. When that something more is present, the greater the disadvantage to the vulnerable person, the more cogent must be the explanation before the presumption will be regarded as rebutted.

This was the approach adopted by Lord Scarman in *National Westminster Bank Plc v Morgan* [1985] AC 686, 703–707. He cited Lindley LJ's observations in *Allcard v Skinner*, 36 Ch D 145, 185, which I have set out above. He noted that whatever the legal character of the transaction, it must constitute a disadvantage sufficiently serious to require evidence to rebut the presumption that in the circumstances of the parties' relationship, it was procured by the exercise of undue influence. Lord Scarman concluded, at p. 704:

> The Court of Appeal erred in law in holding that the presumption of undue influence can arise from the evidence of the relationship of the parties without also evidence that the transaction itself was wrongful in that it constituted *an advantage taken of the person subjected to the influence which, failing proof to the contrary, was explicable only on the basis that undue influence had been exercised to procure it.* (Emphasis added)

Lord Scarman attached the label 'manifest disadvantage' to this second ingredient necessary to raise the presumption. This label has been causing difficulty. It may be apt enough when applied to straightforward transactions such as a substantial gift or a sale at an undervalue. But experience has now shown that this expression can give rise to misunderstanding. The label is being understood and applied in a way which does not accord with the meaning intended by Lord Scarman, its originator.

The problem has arisen in the context of wives guaranteeing payment of their husband's business debts. In recent years judge after judge has grappled with the baffling question whether a wife's guarantee of her husband's bank overdraft, together with a charge on her share of the matrimonial home, was a transaction manifestly to her disadvantage.

In a narrow sense, such a transaction plainly ('manifestly') is disadvantageous to the wife. She undertakes a serious financial obligation, and in return she personally receives nothing. But that would be to take an unrealistically blinkered view of such a transaction. Unlike the relationship of solicitor and client or medical adviser and patient, in the case of husband and wife there are inherent reasons why such a transaction may well be for her benefit. Ordinarily, the fortunes of husband and wife are bound up together. If the husband's business is the source of the family income, the wife has a lively interest in doing what she can to support the business. A wife's affection and self-interest run hand-in-hand in inclining her to join with her husband in charging the matrimonial home, usually a jointly-owned asset, to obtain the financial facilities needed by the business. The finance may be needed to start a new business, or expand a promising business, or rescue an ailing business.

Which, then, is the correct approach to adopt in deciding whether a transaction is disadvantageous to the wife: the narrow approach, or the wider approach? The answer is neither. The answer lies in discarding a label which gives rise to this sort of ambiguity. The better approach is to adhere more directly to the test outlined by Lindley LJ in *Allcard v Skinner*, 36 Ch D 145, and adopted by Lord Scarman in *National Westminster Bank Plc v Morgan* [1985] AC 686, in the passages I have cited.

I return to husband and wife cases. I do not think that, *in the ordinary course*, a guarantee of the character I have mentioned is to be regarded as a transaction which, failing proof to the contrary, is explicable only on the basis that it has been procured by the exercise of undue influence by the husband. Wives frequently enter into such transactions. There are good and sufficient reasons why they are willing to do so, despite the risks involved for them and their families. They may be enthusiastic. They may not. They may be less optimistic than their husbands about the prospects of the husbands' busi-

nesses. They may be anxious, perhaps exceedingly so. But this is a far cry from saying that such transactions as a class are to be regarded as prima facie evidence of the exercise of undue influence by husbands.

I have emphasised the phrase 'in the ordinary course'. There will be cases where a wife's signature of a guarantee or a charge of her share in the matrimonial home does call for explanation. Nothing I have said above is directed at such a case.

A CAUTIONARY NOTE

I add a cautionary note, prompted by some of the first instance judgments in the cases currently being considered by the House. It concerns the general approach to be adopted by a court when considering whether a wife's guarantee of her husband's bank overdraft was procured by her husband's undue influence. Undue influence has a connotation of impropriety. In the eye of the law, undue influence means that influence has been misused. Statements or conduct by a husband which do not pass beyond the bounds of what may be expected of a reasonable husband in the circumstances should not, without more, be castigated as undue influence. Similarly, when a husband is forecasting the future of his business, and expressing his hopes or fears, a degree of hyperbole may be only natural. Courts should not too readily treat such exaggerations as misstatements.

Inaccurate explanations of a proposed transaction are a different matter. So are cases where a husband, in whom a wife has reposed trust and confidence for the management of their financial affairs, prefers his interests to hers and makes a choice for both of them on that footing. Such a husband abuses the influence he has. He fails to discharge the obligation of candour and fairness he owes a wife who is looking to him to make the major financial decisions.

THE COMPLAINANT AND THIRD PARTIES: SURETYSHIP TRANSACTIONS

The problem considered in *O'Brien's* case and raised by the present appeals is of comparatively recent origin. It arises out of the substantial growth in home ownership over the last 30 or 40 years and, as part of that development, the great increase in the number of homes owned jointly by husbands and wives. More than two-thirds of householders in the United Kingdom now own their own homes.

For most home-owning couples, their homes are their most valuable asset. They must surely be free, if they so wish, to use this asset as a means of raising money, whether for the purpose of the husband's business or for any other purpose. Their home is their property. The law should not restrict them in the use they may make of it. Bank finance is in fact by far the most important source of external capital for small businesses with fewer than ten employees. These businesses comprise about 95 per cent of all businesses in the country, responsible for nearly one-third of all employment. Finance raised by second mortgages on the principal's home is a significant source of capital for the start-up of small businesses.

If the freedom of home-owners to make economic use of their homes is not to be frustrated, a bank must be able to have confidence that a wife's signature of the necessary guarantee and charge will be as binding upon her as is the signature of anyone else on documents which he or she may sign. Otherwise banks will not be willing to lend money on the security of a jointly owned house or flat.

At the same time, the high degree of trust and confidence and emotional interdependence which normally characterises a marriage relationship provides scope for abuse. One party may take advantage of the other's vulnerability. Unhappily, such abuse does occur. Further, it is all too easy for a husband, anxious or even desperate for bank finance, to misstate the position in some particular or to mislead the wife, wittingly or unwittingly, in some other way. The law would be seriously defective if it did not recognise these realities.

In *O'Brien's* case this House decided where the balance should be held between these competing interests. On the one side, there is the need to protect a wife against a husband's undue influence. On the other side, there is the need for the bank to be able to have reasonable confidence in the strength of its security. Otherwise it would not provide the required money. The problem lies in finding the course best designed to protect wives in a minority of cases without unreasonably hampering the giving and taking of security. The House produced a practical solution. The House decided what are the steps a bank should take to ensure it is not affected by any claim the wife may have that her signature of the documents was procured by the undue influence or other wrong of her husband. Like every compromise, the outcome falls short of achieving in full the objectives of either of the two competing interests. In particular, the steps required of banks will not guarantee that, in future, wives will not be subjected to undue influence or misled when standing as sureties. Short of prohibiting this type of suretyship transaction altogether, there is no way of achieving that result, desirable although it is. What passes between a husband and wife in this regard in the privacy of their own home is not capable of regulation or investigation as a prelude to the wife entering into a suretyship transaction.

The jurisprudential route by which the House reached its conclusion in *O'Brien's* case has attracted criticism from some commentators. It has been said to involve artificiality and thereby create uncertainty in the law. I must first consider this criticism. In the ordinary course a bank which takes a guarantee security from the wife of its customer will be altogether ignorant of any undue influence the customer may have exercised in order to secure the wife's concurrence. In *O'Brien* Lord Browne-Wilkinson prayed in aid the doctrine of constructive notice. In circumstances he identified, a creditor is put on inquiry. When that is so, the creditor 'will have constructive notice of the wife's rights' unless the creditor takes reasonable steps to satisfy himself that the wife's agreement to stand surety has been properly obtained: see [1994] 1 AC 180, 196.

Lord Browne-Wilkinson would be the first to recognise this is not a conventional use of the equitable concept of constructive notice. The traditional use of this concept concerns the circumstances in which a transferee of property who acquires a legal estate from a transferor with a defective title may nonetheless obtain a good title, that is, a better title than the transferor had. That is not the present case. The bank acquires its charge from the wife, and there is nothing wrong with her title to her share of the matrimonial home. The transferor wife is seeking to resile from the very transaction she entered into with the bank, on the ground that her apparent consent was procured by the undue influence or other misconduct, such as misrepresentation, of a third party (her husband). She is seeking to set aside her contract of guarantee and, with it, the charge she gave to the bank.

The traditional view of equity in this tripartite situation seems to be that a person in the position of the wife will only be relieved of her bargain if the other party to the transaction (the bank, in the present instance) was privy to the conduct which led to the wife's entry into the transaction. Knowledge is required: see *Cobbett v Brock* (1855) 20 Beav 524, 528, 531, per Sir John Romilly MR, *Kempson v Ashbee* (1874) LR 10 Ch App 15, 21, per James LJ, and *Bainbrigge v Browne*, 18 Ch D 188, 197, per Fry J. The law imposes no obligation on one party to a transaction to check whether the other party's concurrence was obtained by undue influence. But *O'Brien* has introduced into the law the concept that, in certain circumstances, a party to a contract may lose the benefit of his contract, entered into in good faith, if he *ought* to have known that the other's concurrence had been procured by the misconduct of a third party.

There is a further respect in which *O'Brien* departed from conventional concepts. Traditionally, a person is *deemed* to have notice (that is, he has 'constructive' notice) of a prior right when he does not actually know of it but would have learned of it had he made the requisite inquiries. A purchaser will be treated as having constructive notice of all that a reasonably prudent purchaser would have discovered. In the present type of case, the steps a bank is required to take, lest it have constructive notice that the wife's concurrence was procured improperly by her husband, do not consist of making inquiries. Rather, *O'Brien* envisages that the steps taken by the bank will reduce, or even eliminate, the risk of the wife entering into the transaction under any misapprehension or as a result of undue influence by her husband. The steps are not concerned to discover whether the wife has been wronged by her husband in this way. The steps are concerned to minimise the risk that such a wrong may be committed.

These novelties do not point to the conclusion that the decision of this House in *O'Brien* is leading the law astray. Lord Browne-Wilkinson acknowledged he might be extending the law: see [1994] 1 AC 180, 197. Some development was sorely needed. The law had to find a way of giving wives a reasonable measure of protection, without adding unreasonably to the expense involved in entering into guarantee transactions of the type under consideration. The protection had to extend also to any misrepresentations made by a husband to his wife. In a situation where there is a substantial risk the husband may exercise his influence improperly regarding the provision of security for his business debts, there is an increased risk that explanations of the transaction given by him to his wife may be misleadingly incomplete or even inaccurate.

The route selected in *O'Brien* ought not to have an unsettling effect on established principles of contract. *O'Brien* concerned suretyship transactions. These are tripartite transactions. They involve the debtor as well as the creditor and the guarantor. The guarantor enters into the transaction at the request of the debtor. The guarantor assumes obligations. On the face of the transaction the guarantor usually receives no benefit in return, unless the guarantee is being given on a commercial basis. Leaving aside cases where the relationship between the surety and the debtor is commercial, a guarantee transaction is one-sided so far as the guarantor is concerned. The creditor knows this. Thus the decision in *O'Brien* is directed at a class of contracts which has special features of its own. That said, I must at a later stage in this speech return to the question of the wider implications of the *O'Brien* decision.

THE THRESHOLD: WHEN THE BANK IS PUT ON INQUIRY

In *O'Brien* the House considered the circumstances in which a bank, or other creditor, is 'put on inquiry.' Strictly this is a misnomer. As already noted, a bank is not required to make inquiries. But it will be convenient to use the terminology which has now become accepted in this context. The House set a low level for the threshold which must be crossed before a bank is put on inquiry. For practical reasons the level is set much lower than is required to satisfy a court that, failing contrary evidence, the court may infer that the transaction was procured by undue influence. Lord Browne-Wilkinson said ([1994] 1 AC 180, 196):

> Therefore in my judgment a creditor in put on inquiry when a wife offers to stand surety for her husband's debts by the combination of two factors: (a) the transaction is on its face not to the financial advantage of the wife; and (b) there is a substantial risk in transactions of that kind that, in procuring the wife to act as surety, the husband has committed a legal or equitable wrong that entitles the wife to set aside the transaction.

In my view, this passage, read in context, is to be taken to mean, quite simply, that a bank is put on inquiry whenever a wife offers to stand surety for her husband's debts.

The Court of Appeal, comprising Stuart-Smith, Millett and Morritt LJJ, interpreted this passage more restrictively. The threshold, the court said, is somewhat higher. Where condition (a) is satisfied, the bank is put on inquiry if, but only if, the bank is aware that the parties are cohabiting or that the particular surety places implicit trust and confidence in the principal debtor in relation to her financial affairs: see *Royal Bank of Scotland Plc v Etridge (No 2)* [1998] 4 All ER 705, 719.

I respectfully disagree. I do not read (a) and (b) as factual conditions which must be proved in each case before a bank is put on inquiry. I do not understand Lord Browne-Wilkinson to have been saying that, in husband and wife cases, whether the bank is put on inquiry depends on its state of knowledge of the parties' marriage, or of the degree of trust and confidence the particular wife places in her husband in relation to her financial affairs. That would leave banks in a state of considerable uncertainty in a situation where it is important they should know clearly where they stand. The test should be simple and clear and easy to apply in a wide range of circumstances. I read (a) and (b) as Lord Browne-Wilkinson's broad explanation of the reason why a creditor is put on inquiry when a wife offers to stand surety for her husband's debts. These are the two factors which, taken together, constitute the underlying rationale.

The position is likewise if the husband stands surety for his wife's debts. Similarly, in the case of unmarried couples, whether heterosexual or homosexual, where the bank is aware of the relationship: see Lord Browne-Wilkinson in *O'Brien's* case, at p. 198. Cohabitation is not essential. The Court of Appeal rightly so decided in *Massey v Midland Bank Plc* [1995] 1 All ER 929: see Steyn LJ, at p. 933.

As to the type of transactions where a bank is put on inquiry, the case where a wife becomes surety for her husband's debts is, in this context, a straightforward case. The bank is put on inquiry. On the other side of the line is the case where money is being advanced, or has been advanced, to husband and wife jointly. In such a case the bank is not put on inquiry, unless the bank is aware the loan is being made for the husband's purposes, as distinct from their joint purposes. That was decided in *CIBC Mortgages Plc v Pitt* [1994] 1 AC 200.

Less clear cut is the case where the wife becomes surety for the debts of a company whose shares are held by her and her husband. Her shareholding may be nominal, or she may have a minority shareholding or an equal shareholding with her husband. In my view the bank is put on inquiry in such cases, even when the wife is a director or secretary of the company. Such cases cannot be equated with joint loans. The shareholding interests, and the identity of the directors, are not a reliable guide to the identity of the persons who actually have the conduct of the company's business.

THE STEPS A BANK SHOULD TAKE

The principal area of controversy on these appeals concerns the steps a bank should take when it

has been put on inquiry. In *O'Brien* Lord Browne-Wilkinson, at [1994] 1 AC 180, 196–197, said that a bank can reasonably be expected to take steps to bring home to the wife the risk she is running by standing as surety and to advise her to take independent advice. That test is applicable to *past* transactions. All the cases now before your Lordships' House fall into this category. For the *future* a bank satisfies these requirements if it insists that the wife attend a private meeting with a representative of the bank at which she is told of the extent of her liability as surety, warned of the risk she is running and urged to take independent legal advice. In exceptional cases the bank, to be safe, has to insist that the wife is separately advised.

The practice of the banks involved in the present cases, and it seems reasonable to assume this is the practice of banks generally, is not to have a private meeting with the wife. Nor do the banks themselves take any other steps to bring home to the wife the risk she is running. This has continued to be the practice since the decision in *O'Brien's* case. Banks consider they would stand to lose more than they would gain by holding a private meeting with the wife. They are, apparently, unwilling to assume the responsibility of advising the wife at such a meeting. Instead, the banking practice remains, as before, that in general the bank requires a wife to seek legal advice. The bank seeks written confirmation from a solicitor that he has explained the nature and effect of the documents to the wife.

Many of the difficulties which have arisen in the present cases stem from serious deficiencies, or alleged deficiencies, in the quality of the legal advice given to the wives. I say 'alleged', because three of the appeals before your Lordships' House have not proceeded beyond the interlocutory stage. The banks successfully applied for summary judgment. In these cases the wife's allegations, made in affidavit form, have not been tested by cross-examination. On behalf of the wives it has been submitted that under the current practice the legal advice is often perfunctory in the extreme and, further, that everyone, including the banks, knows this. Independent legal advice is a fiction. The system is a charade. In practice it provides little or no protection for a wife who is under a misapprehension about the risks involved or who is being coerced into signing. She may not even know the present state of her husband's indebtedness.

My Lords, it is plainly neither desirable nor practicable that banks should be required to attempt to discover for themselves whether a wife's consent is being procured by the exercise of undue influence of her husband. This is not a step the banks should be expected to take. Nor, further, is it desirable or practicable that banks should be expected to insist on confirmation from a solicitor that the solicitor has satisfied himself that the wife's consent has not been procured by undue influence. As already noted, the circumstances in which banks are put on inquiry are extremely wide. They embrace every case where a wife is entering into a suretyship transaction in respect of her husband's debts. Many, if not most, wives would be understandably outraged by having to respond to the sort of questioning which would be appropriate before a responsible solicitor could give such a confirmation. In any event, solicitors are not equipped to carry out such an exercise in any really worthwhile way, and they will usually lack the necessary materials. Moreover, the legal costs involved, which would inevitably fall on the husband who is seeking financial assistance from the bank, would be substantial. To require such an intrusive, inconclusive and expensive exercise in every case would be an altogether disproportionate response to the need to protect those cases, presumably a small minority, where a wife is being wronged.

The furthest a bank can be expected to go is to take reasonable steps to satisfy itself that the wife has had brought home to her, in a meaningful way, the practical implications of the proposed transaction. This does not wholly eliminate the risk of undue influence or misrepresentation. But it does mean that a wife enters into a transaction with her eyes open so far as the basic elements of the transaction are concerned.

This is the point at which, in the *O'Brien* case, the House decided that the balance between the competing interests should be held. A bank may itself provide the necessary information directly to the wife. Indeed, it is best equipped to do so. But banks are not following that course. Ought they to be obliged to do so in every case? I do not think Lord Browne-Wilkinson so stated in *O'Brien*. I do not understand him to have said that a personal meeting was the only way a bank could discharge its obligation to bring home to the wife the risks she is running. It seems to me that, provided a suitable alternative is available, banks ought not to be compelled to take this course. Their reasons for not wishing to hold a personal meeting are understandable. Commonly, when a bank seeks to enforce a security provided by a customer, it is met with a defence based on assurances alleged to have been given orally by a branch manager at an earlier stage: that the bank would continue to support the business, that the bank would not call in its loan, and

so forth. Lengthy litigation ensues. Sometimes the allegations prove to be well founded, sometimes not. Banks are concerned to avoid the prospect of similar litigation which would arise in guarantee cases if they were to adopt a practice of holding a meeting with a wife at which the bank's representative would explain the proposed guarantee transaction. It is not unreasonable for the banks to prefer that this task should be undertaken by an independent legal adviser.

I shall return later to the steps a bank should take when it follows this course. Suffice to say, these steps, together with advice from a solicitor acting for the wife, ought to provide the substance of the protection which *O'Brien* intended a wife should have. Ordinarily it will be reasonable that a bank should be able to rely upon confirmation from a solicitor, acting for the wife, that he has advised the wife appropriately.

The position will be otherwise if the bank knows that the solicitor has not duly advised the wife or, I would add, if the bank knows facts from which it ought to have realised that the wife has not received the appropriate advice. In such circumstances the bank will proceed at its own risk.

THE CONTENT OF THE LEGAL ADVICE

In *Royal Bank of Scotland Plc v Etridge (No 2)* [1998] 4 All ER 705, 715, para 19, the Court of Appeal set out its views of the duties of a solicitor in this context:

> A solicitor who is instructed to advise a person who may be subject to the undue influence of another must bear in mind that it is not sufficient that she understands the nature and effect of the transaction if she is so affected by the influence of the other that she cannot make an independent decision of her own. It is not sufficient to explain the documentation and ensure she understands the nature of the transaction and wishes to carry it out: see *Powell v Powell* [1900] 1 Ch 243, 247, approved in *Wright v Carter* [1903] 1 Ch 27. His duty is to satisfy himself that his client is free from improper influence, and the first step must be to ascertain whether it is one into which she could sensibly be advised to enter if free from such influence. If he is not so satisfied, it is his duty to advise her not to enter into it, and to refuse to act further for her in the implementation of the transaction if she persists. In this event, while the contents of his advice must remain confidential, he should inform the other parties (including the

bank) that he has seen his client and given her certain advice, and that as a result he has declined to act for her any further. He must in any event advise her that she is under no obligation to enter into the transaction at all and, if she still wishes to do so, that she is not bound to accept the terms of any document which has been put before her: see *Credit Lyonnais Bank Nederland NV v Burch* [1997] 1 All ER 144.

I am unable to accept this as an accurate formulation of a solicitor's duties in cases such as those now under consideration. In some respects it goes much too far. The observations of Farwell J in *Powell v Powell* [1900] 1 Ch 243, 247, should not be pressed unduly widely. *Powell v Powell* was a case where strong moral pressure was applied by a stepmother to a girl who was only just twenty-one. She was regarded as not really capable of dealing irrevocably with her parent or guardian in the matter of a substantial settlement. Farwell J's observations cannot be regarded as of general application in all cases where a solicitor is giving advice to a person who may have been subject to undue influence.

More pertinently, in *In re Coomber, Coomber v Coomber* [1911] 1 Ch 723, 730, Fletcher Moulton LJ summarised the general rules applicable to cases of persons who are competent to form an opinion of their own:

> All that is necessary is that some independent person, free from any taint of the relationship, or of the consideration of interest which would affect the act, should put clearly before the person what are the nature and the consequences of the act. It is for adult persons of competent mind to decide whether they will do an act, and I do not think that independent and competent advice means independent and competent approval. It simply means that the advice shall be removed entirely from the suspected atmosphere; and that from the clear language of an independent mind, they should know precisely what they are doing.

Thus, in the present type of case it is not for the solicitor to veto the transaction by declining to confirm to the bank that he has explained the documents to the wife and the risks she is taking upon herself. If the solicitor considers the transaction is not in the wife's best interests, he will give reasoned advice to the wife to that effect. But at the end of the day the decision on whether to proceed is the decision of the client, not the solicitor. A wife is not to be precluded from entering into a financially unwise transaction if, for her own reasons, she wishes to do so.

That is the general rule. There may, of course, be exceptional circumstances where it is glaringly obvious that the wife is being grievously wronged. In such a case the solicitor should decline to act further. In *Wright v Carter* [1903] 1 Ch 27, 57–58, Stirling LJ approved Farwell J's observations in *Powell v Powell* [1900] 1 Ch 243, 247. But he did so by reference to the extreme example of a poor man divesting himself of all his property in favour of his solicitor.

In *Royal Bank of Scotland Plc v Etridge (No 2)* [1998] 4 All ER 705, 722, para 49, the Court of Appeal said that if the transaction is 'one into which no competent solicitor could properly advise the wife to enter', the availability of legal advice is insufficient to avoid the bank being fixed with constructive notice. It follows from the views expressed above that I am unable to agree with the Court of Appeal on this point.

I turn to consider the scope of the responsibilities of a solicitor who is advising the wife. In identifying what are the solicitor's responsibilities the starting point must always be the solicitor's retainer. What has he been retained to do? As a general proposition, the scope of a solicitor's duties is dictated by the terms, whether express or implied, of his retainer. In the type of case now under consideration the relevant retainer stems from the bank's concern to receive confirmation from the solicitor that, in short, the solicitor has brought home to the wife the risks involved in the proposed transaction. As a first step the solicitor will need to explain to the wife the purpose for which he has become involved at all. He should explain that, should it ever become necessary, the bank will rely upon his involvement to counter any suggestion that the wife was overborne by her husband or that she did not properly understand the implications of the transaction. The solicitor will need to obtain confirmation from the wife that she wishes him to act for her in the matter and to advise her on the legal and practical implications of the proposed transaction.

When an instruction to this effect is forthcoming, the content of the advice required from a solicitor before giving the confirmation sought by the bank will, inevitably, depend upon the circumstances of the case. Typically, the advice a solicitor can be expected to give should cover the following matters as the core minimum.

(1) He will need to explain the nature of the documents and the practical consequences these will have for the wife if she signs them. She could lose her home if her husband's business does not prosper. Her home may be her only substantial asset, as well as the family's home. She could be made bankrupt.

(2) He will need to point out the seriousness of the risks involved. The wife should be told the purpose of the proposed new facility, the amount and principal terms of the new facility, and that the bank might increase the amount of the facility, or change its terms, or grant a new facility, without reference to her. She should be told the amount of her liability under her guarantee. The solicitor should discuss the wife's financial means, including her understanding of the value of the property being charged. The solicitor should discuss whether the wife or her husband has any other assets out of which repayment could be made if the husband's business should fail. These matters are relevant to the seriousness of the risks involved.

(3) The solicitor will need to state clearly that the wife has a choice. The decision is hers and hers alone. Explanation of the choice facing the wife will call for some discussion of the present financial position, including the amount of the husband's present indebtedness, and the amount of his current overdraft facility.

(4) The solicitor should check whether the wife wishes to proceed. She should be asked whether she is content that the solicitor should write to the bank confirming he has explained to her the nature of the documents and the practical implications they may have for her, or whether, for instance, she would prefer him to negotiate with the bank on the terms of the transaction. Matters for negotiation could include the sequence in which the various securities will be called upon or a specific or lower limit to her liabilities. The solicitor should not give any confirmation to the bank without the wife's authority.

The solicitor's discussion with the wife should take place at a face-to-face meeting, in the absence of the husband. It goes without saying that the solicitor's explanations should be couched in suitably non-technical language. It also goes without saying that the solicitor's task is an important one. It is not a formality.

The solicitor should obtain from the bank any information he needs. If the bank fails for any reason to provide information requested by the solicitor, the solicitor should decline to provide the confirmation sought by the bank.

As already noted, the advice which a solicitor can be expected to give must depend on the particular facts of the case. But I have set out this 'core minimum' in some detail, because the quality of the legal advice is the most disturbing feature of some of the present appeals. The perfunctory nature of the advice may well be largely due to a failure by some solicitors to understand what is required in these cases.

INDEPENDENT ADVICE

I turn next to the much-vexed question whether the solicitor advising the wife must act for the wife alone. Or, at the very least, the solicitor must not act for the husband or the bank in the current transaction save in a wholly ministerial capacity, such as carrying out conveyancing formalities or supervising the execution of documents and witnessing signatures. Commonly, in practice, the solicitor advising the wife will be the solicitor acting also for her husband either in the particular transaction or generally.

The first point to note is that this question cannot be answered by reference to reported decisions. The steps a bank must take once it is put on inquiry, if it is to avoid having constructive notice of the wife's rights, are not the subject of exposition in earlier authority. This is a novel situation, created by the *O'Brien* decision.

Next, a simple and clear rule is needed, preferably of well-nigh universal application. In some cases a bank deals directly with a husband and wife and has to take the initiative in requiring the wife to obtain legal advice. In other cases, a bank may deal throughout with solicitors already acting for the husband and wife. The case of *Bank of Baroda v Rayarel* [1995] 2 FLR 376 is an example of the latter type of case. It would not be satisfactory to attempt to draw a distinction along these lines. Any such distinction would lack a principled base. Inevitably, in practice, the distinction would disintegrate in confusion.

Thirdly, here again, a balancing exercise is called for. Some features point in one direction, others in the opposite direction. Factors favouring the need for the solicitor to act for the wife alone include the following. Sometimes a wife may be inhibited in discussion with a solicitor who is also acting for the husband or whose main client is the husband. This occurred in *Banco Exterior Internacional v Mann* [1995] 1 All ER 936: see the finding of the judge, at p. 941F-G. Sometimes a solicitor whose main client is the husband may not, in practice, give the same single-minded attention to the wife's position as would a solicitor acting solely for the wife. Her interests may rank lower in the solicitor's scale of priorities, perhaps unconsciously, than the interests of the husband. Instances of incompetent advice, or worse, which have come before the court might perhaps be less likely to recur if a solicitor were instructed to act for the wife alone and gave advice solely to her. As a matter of general understanding, independent advice would suggest that the solicitor should not be acting in the same transaction for the person who, if there is any undue influence, is the source of that influence.

The contrary view is that the solicitor may also act for the husband or the bank, provided the solicitor is satisfied that this is in the wife's best interests and satisfied also that this will not give rise to any conflicts of duty or interest. The principal factors favouring this approach are as follows. A requirement that a wife should receive advice from a solicitor acting solely for her will frequently add significantly to the legal costs. Sometimes a wife will be happier to be advised by a family solicitor known to her than by a complete stranger. Sometimes a solicitor who knows both husband and wife and their histories will be better placed to advise than a solicitor who is a complete stranger.

In my view, overall the latter factors are more weighty than the former. The advantages attendant upon the employment of a solicitor acting solely for the wife do not justify the additional expense this would involve for the husband. When accepting instructions to advise the wife the solicitor assumes responsibilities directly to her, both at law and professionally. These duties, and this is central to the reasoning on this point, are owed to the wife alone. In advising the wife the solicitor is acting for the wife alone. He is concerned only with her interests. I emphasise, therefore, that in every case the solicitor must consider carefully whether there is any conflict of duty or interest and, more widely, whether it would be in the best interests of the wife for him to accept instructions from her. If he decides to accept instructions, his assumption of legal and professional responsibilities to her ought, in the ordinary course of things, to provide sufficient assurance that he will give the requisite advice fully, carefully and conscientiously. Especially so, now that the nature of the advice called for has been clarified.

If at any stage the solicitor becomes concerned that there is a real risk that other interests or duties may inhibit his advice to the wife he must cease to act for her.

AGENCY

No system ever works perfectly. There will always be cases where things go wrong, sometimes seriously wrong. The next question concerns the position when a solicitor has accepted instructions to advise a wife but he fails to do so properly. He fails to give her the advice needed to bring home to her the practical implications of her standing as surety. What then? The wife has a remedy in damages against the negligent solicitor. But what is the position of the bank who proceeded in the belief that the wife had been given the necessary advice?

Mr Sher contended that, depending on the facts, the solicitor should be regarded as the agent of the bank. Commonly, what happens is that the bank asks the solicitor acting for the husband to undertake the conveyancing formalities on behalf of the bank. The bank also asks the solicitor to undertake the further task of explaining the nature and effect of the documents to the wife, and then confirming to the bank that he has done so. In carrying out these requested tasks, it was submitted, the solicitor is acting for the bank. The bank requires the solicitor to advise the wife, not for her benefit, but for the benefit and protection of the bank. Any deficiencies in the advice given to the wife should be attributed to the bank. In this regard, it was submitted, the solicitor's knowledge is to be imputed to the bank. A certificate furnished by the solicitor to the bank should not prejudice the position of the wife when, as happened in several cases, the contents of the certificate are untrue. If the solicitor has not given the wife any advice, her rights should not be diminished by the solicitor telling the bank that she has been fully advised.

I cannot accept this analysis. Confirmation from the solicitor that he has advised the wife is one of the bank's preconditions for completion of the transaction. But it is central to this arrangement that in advising the wife the solicitor is acting for the wife and no one else. The bank does not have, and is intended not to have, any knowledge of or control over the advice the solicitor gives the wife. The solicitor is not accountable to the bank for the advice he gives to the wife. To impute to the bank knowledge of what passed between the solicitor and the wife would contradict this essential feature of the arrangement. The mere fact that, for its own purposes, the bank asked the solicitor to advise the wife does not make the solicitor the bank's agent in giving that advice.

In the ordinary case, therefore, deficiencies in the advice given are a matter between the wife and her solicitor. The bank is entitled to proceed on the assumption that a solicitor advising the wife has done his job properly. I have already mentioned what is the bank's position if it knows this is not so, or if it knows facts from which it ought to have realised this is not so.

OBTAINING THE SOLICITOR'S CONFIRMATION

I now return to the steps a bank should take when it has been put on inquiry and for its protection is looking to the fact that the wife has been advised independently by a solicitor.

(1) One of the unsatisfactory features in some of the cases is the late stage at which the wife first became involved in the transaction. In practice she had no opportunity to express a view on the identity of the solicitor who advised her. She did not even know that the purpose for which the solicitor was giving her advice was to enable him to send, on her behalf, the protective confirmation sought by the bank. Usually the solicitor acted for both husband and wife.

Since the bank is looking for its protection to legal advice given to the wife by a solicitor who, in this respect, is acting solely for her, I consider the bank should take steps to check *directly with the wife* the name of the solicitor she wishes to act for her. To this end, in future the bank should communicate directly with the wife, informing her that for its own protection it will require written confirmation from a solicitor, acting for her, to the effect that the solicitor has fully explained to her the nature of the documents and the practical implications they will have for her. She should be told that the purpose of this requirement is that thereafter she should not be able to dispute she is legally bound by the documents once she has signed them. She should be asked to nominate a solicitor whom she is willing to instruct to advise her, separately from her husband, and act for her in giving the necessary confirmation to the bank. She should be told that, if she wishes, the solicitor may be the same solicitor as is acting for her husband in the transaction. If a solicitor is already acting for the husband and the wife, she should be asked whether she would prefer that a different solicitor should act for her regarding the bank's requirement for confirmation from a solicitor.

The bank should not proceed with the transaction until it has received an appropriate response directly from the wife.

(2) Representatives of the bank are likely to have a much better picture of the husband's financial affairs than the solicitor. If the bank is not willing to undertake the task of explanation itself, the bank must provide the solicitor with the financial information he needs for this purpose. Accordingly it should become routine practice for banks, if relying on confirmation from a solicitor for their protection, to send to the solicitor the necessary financial information. What is required must depend on the facts of the case. Ordinarily this will include information on the purpose for which the proposed new facility has been requested, the current amount of the husband's indebtedness, the amount of his current overdraft facility, and the amount and terms of any new facility. If the bank's request for security arose from a written application by the husband for a facility, a copy of the application should be sent to the solicitor. The bank will, of course, need first to obtain the consent of its customer to this circulation of confidential information. If this consent is not forthcoming the transaction will not be able to proceed.

(3) Exceptionally there may be a case where the bank believes or suspects that the wife has been misled by her husband or is not entering into the transaction of her own free will. If such a case occurs the bank must inform the wife's solicitors of the facts giving rise to its belief or suspicion.

(4) The bank should in every case obtain from the wife's solicitor a written confirmation to the effect mentioned above.

These steps will be applicable to future transactions. In respect of past transactions, the bank will ordinarily be regarded as having discharged its obligations if a solicitor who was acting for the wife in the transaction gave the bank confirmation to the effect that he had brought home to the wife the risks she was running by standing as surety.

THE CREDITOR'S DISCLOSURE OBLIGATION

It is a well-established principle that, stated shortly, a creditor is obliged to disclose to a guarantor any unusual feature of the contract between the creditor and the debtor which makes it materially different in a potentially disadvantageous respect from what the guarantor might naturally expect. The precise ambit of this disclosure obligation remains unclear. A useful summary of the authorities appears in *O'Donovan and Phillips on the Modern Contract of Guarantee*, 3rd ed (1996), at pp. 122–130. It is not necessary to pursue these difficult matters in this case. It is sufficient for me to say that, contrary to submissions made, the need to provide protection for wives who are standing as sureties does not point to a need to re-visit the scope of this disclosure principle. Wives require a different form of protection. They need a full and clear explanation of the risks involved. Typically, the risks will be risks any surety would expect. The protection needed by wives differs from, and goes beyond, the disclosure of information. The *O'Brien* principle is intended to provide this protection.

A WIDER PRINCIPLE

Before turning to the particular cases I must make a general comment on the *O'Brien* principle. As noted by Professor Peter Birks QC, the decision in *O'Brien* has to be seen as the progenitor of a wider principle: see 'The Burden on the Bank', in Restitution and Banking Law (ed Rose, 1998), at p. 195. This calls for explanation. In the *O'Brien* case the House was concerned with formulating a fair and practical solution to problems occurring when a creditor obtains a security from a guarantor whose sexual relationship with the debtor gives rise to a heightened risk of undue influence. But the law does not regard sexual relationships as standing in some special category of their own so far as undue influence is concerned. Sexual relationships are no more than one type of relationship in which an individual may acquire influence over another individual. The *O'Brien* decision cannot sensibly be regarded as confined to sexual relationships, although these are likely to be its main field of application at present. What is appropriate for sexual relationships ought, in principle, to be appropriate also for other relationships where trust and confidence are likely to exist.

The courts have already recognised this. Further application, or development, of the *O'Brien* principle has already taken place. In *Credit Lyonnais Bank Nederland NV v Burch* [1997] 1 All ER 144 the same principle was applied where the relationship was employer and employee. Miss Burch was a junior employee in a company. She was neither a shareholder nor a director. She provided security to the bank for the company's overdraft. She entered into a guarantee of unlimited amount, and gave the bank a second charge over her flat. Nourse LJ, at p. 146, said the relationship 'may broadly be said to fall under [*O'Brien*]'. The Court of Appeal held that the bank was put on inquiry. It knew the facts from which the existence of a relationship of trust and confidence between Miss Burch and Mr Pelosi, the owner of the company, could be inferred.

The crucially important question raised by this wider application of the *O'Brien* principle concerns the circumstances which will put a bank on inquiry. A bank is put on inquiry whenever a wife stands as surety for her husband's debts. It is sufficient that the bank knows of the husband–wife relationship. That bare fact is enough. The bank must then take reasonable steps to bring home to the wife the risks involved. What, then, of other relationships where there is an increased risk of undue influence, such as parent and child? Is it enough that the bank knows of the relationship? For reasons already discussed in relation to husbands and wives, a bank cannot be expected to probe the emotional relationship between two individuals, whoever they may be. Nor is it desirable that a bank should attempt this. Take the case where a father puts forward his daughter as a surety for his business overdraft. A bank should not be called upon to evaluate highly personal matters such as the degree of trust and confidence existing between the father and his daughter, with the bank put on inquiry in one case and not in another. As with wives, so with daughters, whether a bank is put on inquiry should not depend on the degree of trust and confidence the particular daughter places in her father in relation to financial matters. Moreover, as with wives, so with other relationships, the test of what puts a bank on inquiry should be simple, clear and easy to apply in widely varying circumstances. This suggests that, in the case of a father and daughter, knowledge by the bank of the relationship of father and daughter should suffice to put the bank on inquiry. When the bank knows of the relationship, it must then take reasonable steps to ensure the daughter knows what she is letting herself into.

The relationship of parent and child is one of the relationships where the law irrebuttably presumes the existence of trust and confidence. Rightly, this has already been rejected as the boundary of the *O'Brien* principle. *O'Brien* was a husband–wife case. The responsibilities of creditors were enunciated in a case where the law makes no presumption of the existence of trust and confidence.

But the law cannot stop at this point, with banks on inquiry only in cases where the debtor and guarantor have a sexual relationship or the relationship is one where the law presumes the existence of trust and confidence. That would be an arbitrary boundary, and the law has already moved beyond this, in the decision in *Burch*. As noted earlier, the reality of life is that relationships in which undue influence can be exercised are infinitely various. They cannot be exhaustively defined. Nor is it possible to produce a comprehensive list of relationships where there is a substantial risk of the exercise of undue influence, all others being excluded from the ambit of the *O'Brien* principle. Human affairs do not lend themselves to categorisations of this sort. The older generation of a family may exercise undue influence over a younger member, as in parent–child cases such as *Bainbrigge v Browne*, 18 Ch D 188 and *Powell v Powell* [1900] 1 Ch 243. Sometimes it is the other way round, as with a nephew and his elderly aunt in *Inche Noriah v Shaik Allie Bin Omar* [1929] AC 127. An employer may take advantage of his employee, as in *Credit Lyonnais Bank Nederland NV v Burch* [1997] 1 All ER 144. But it may be the other way round, with an employee taking advantage of her employer, as happened with the secretary-companion and her elderly employer in *In re Craig, Decd* [1971] Ch 95. The list could go on.

These considerations point forcibly to the conclusion that there is no rational cut-off point, with certain types of relationship being susceptible to the *O'Brien* principle and others not. Further, if a bank is not to be required to evaluate the extent to which its customer has influence over a proposed guarantor, the only practical way forward is to regard banks as 'put on inquiry' in every case where the relationship between the surety and the debtor is non-commercial. The creditor must always take reasonable steps to bring home to the individual guarantor the risks he is running by standing as surety. As a measure of protection, this is valuable. But, in all conscience, it is a modest burden for banks and other lenders. It is no more than is reasonably to be expected of a creditor who is taking a guarantee from an individual. If the bank or other creditor does not take these steps, it is deemed to have notice of any claim the guarantor may have that the transaction was procured by undue influence or misrepresentation on the part of the debtor.

Different considerations apply where the relationship between the debtor and guarantor is commercial, as where a guarantor is being paid a fee, or a company is guaranteeing the debts of another company in the same group. Those engaged in business can be regarded as capable of looking after themselves and understanding the risks involved in the giving of guarantees.

By the decisions of this House in *O'Brien* and the Court of Appeal in *Credit Lyonnais Bank Nederland NV v Burch* [1997] 1 All ER 144, English law has taken its first strides in the development of some such general principle. It is a workable principle. It is also simple, coherent and eminently desirable. I venture to think this is the way the law is moving, and should continue to move. Equity, it is said, is not past the age of child-bearing. In the present context the equitable concept of being 'put on inquiry' is the parent of a principle of general application, a principle which imposes no more than a modest obligation on banks and other creditors. The existence of this obligation in all non-commercial cases does not go beyond the reasonable requirements of the present times. In future, banks and other creditors should regulate their affairs accordingly.

THE PARTICULAR CASES

I have had the advantage of reading in draft a copy of the speech of my noble and learned friend Lord Scott of Foscote. He has summarised the facts in the eight appeals. My views on the particular cases are as follows.

(1) *Midland Bank Plc v Wallace*

I would allow this appeal. The bank was put on inquiry, because this was a case of a wife standing as surety for her husband's debts. As the evidence stands at present, Mr Samson's participation in the transaction does not assist the bank. He was not Mrs Wallace's solicitor. Deficiencies in the advice given by a solicitor do not normally concern the bank. That is the position where the solicitor is acting for the wife, or where the solicitor has been held out by the wife to the bank as her solicitor. But where the solicitor was not acting for the wife, the bank is in the same position as any person who deals with another in the belief that the latter is acting on behalf of a third party principal when in truth he is not. Leaving aside questions of ostensible authority or the like, the alleged principal is not bound or affected by the acts of such a stranger. The remedy of the bank lies against the (unauthorised) 'agent'. If the bank has suffered provable loss, it has a claim for damages for breach of implied warranty of authority. This action should go to trial.

(2) *Barclays Bank Plc v Harris*

This is another interlocutory appeal, against an order striking out Mrs Harris' defence. It is common ground that for striking out purposes Mrs Harris has an arguable case on undue influence. The bank was put on inquiry, because Mrs Harris was standing as surety for the debts of the company, S T Harris (Powder Coatings Consultant) Ltd. I consider Mrs Harris has an arguable case that Wragge & Co never acted for her. In this respect the case is similar to *Wallace*. This case should go to trial.

(3) *UCB Home Loans Corporation Ltd v Moore*

This is another interlocutory appeal. For the reasons given by my noble and learned friend Lord Hobhouse of Woodborough, I would allow this appeal.

(4) *Royal Bank of Scotland v Etridge,* (5) *National Westminster Bank Plc v Gill,* (6) *Barclays Bank Plc v Coleman,* (7) *Bank of Scotland v Bennett,* and (8) *Kenyon-Brown v Desmond Banks & Co.*

I agree with Lord Scott that, for the reasons he gives, the appeals of Mrs Bennett and Desmond Banks & Co should be allowed. The appeals of Mrs Etridge, Mrs Gill and Mrs Coleman should be dismissed.

. . . .

[LORD SCOTT OF FOSCOTE:]

. . . .

SUMMARY

My Lords I think, given the regrettable length of this opinion, I should try and summarise my views about the principles that apply and the practice that should be followed in surety wife cases.

1. The issue as between the surety wife and the lender bank is whether the bank may rely on the apparent consent of the wife to the suretyship transaction.

2. If the bank knows that the surety wife's consent to the transaction has been procured by undue influence or misrepresentation, or if it has shut its eyes to the likelihood that that was so, it may not rely on her apparent consent.

3. If the wife's consent has in fact been procured by undue influence or misrepresentation, the bank may not rely on her apparent consent unless it has good reason to believe that she understands the nature and effect of the transaction.

4. Unless the case has some special feature, the bank's knowledge that a solicitor is acting for the wife and has advised her about the nature and effect of the transaction will provide a good reason for the purposes of 3 above. That will also be so if the bank has a reasonable belief that a solicitor is acting for her and has so advised her. Written confirmation by a solicitor acting for the wife that he has so advised her will entitle the bank to hold that reasonable belief.

5. So, too, a sufficient explanation of the nature and effect of the transaction given by a senior bank official would constitute good reason for the purposes of 3 above.

6. If there are any facts known to the bank which increase the inherent risk that the wife's consent to the transaction may have been procured by the husband's undue influence or misrepresentation, it may be necessary for the bank to be satisfied that the wife has received advice about the transaction from a solicitor independent of the husband before the bank can reasonably rely on the wife's apparent consent.

7. If the bank has not taken reasonable steps to satisfy itself that the wife understands the nature and effect of the transaction, the wife will, subject to such matters as delay, acquiescence, change of position etc., be able to set aside the transaction if her consent was in fact procured by undue influence or misrepresentation.

8. Subject to special instructions or special circumstances, the duty of a solicitor instructed to act for a wife proposing to stand as surety, or to give security, for her husband's debts is to try and make sure that she understands the nature and effect of the transaction.

9. In all surety wife cases the bank should disclose to the surety wife, or to the solicitor acting for her, the amount of the existing indebtedness

251

of the principal debtor to the bank and the amount of the proposed new loan or drawing facility.

10. Subject to 9 above, a creditor has no greater duty of disclosure to a surety wife than to any other intending surety.

I am in full agreement with the analysis of the applicable principles of law and with the conclusions

expressed in the opinion of my noble and learned friend Lord Nicholls of Birkenhead. I believe the analysis I have sought to give in this opinion and my conclusions are consistent with them.

[Appeal Allowed: Harris, Wallace, Moore, and Desmond Banks & Co.
Appeal Dismissed: Etridge, Gill, and Coleman.]

(g) *Bank of Montreal v. Duguid*†

[OSBORNE A.C.J.O. (McMurtry C.J.O. concurring):]

OVERVIEW

I have had the advantage of reading the reasons of Feldman J.A., who would dismiss the Bank's appeal but not for the reasons of the trial judge. I agree with Feldman J.A. that the Bank, in these circumstances, was not required to tell its customers (specifically, Mrs. Duguid, a co-signer) of its views on the quality of the investment. I also agree that the Bank's failure to follow its internal policies (specifically, advising Mrs. Duguid to get independent legal or financial advice) is not a basis upon which to dismiss the Bank's action on the note. I cannot, however, agree with my colleague's conclusions on the issue of presumed undue influence.

Mrs. Duguid alleges that the guarantee was procured by the undue influence of her husband; however, she does not seek any relief as against her husband, who is now bankrupt. Rather, she now seeks to set aside the transaction as against a third party, the Bank. The question then is in what circumstances a party can set aside a transaction on the ground of undue influence as against a third party to the alleged wrongdoing.

In my view, the relationship between Mr. and Mrs. Duguid in respect of their financial affairs was not a relationship that would trigger a presumption of undue influence when Mrs. Duguid, at her husband's request, co-signed a promissory note (prepared by the Bank). In any case, having regard to

the trial evidence, it seems to me that if a presumption of undue influence was established, the presumption was rebutted. Thus, I think that the Bank's appeal should be allowed.

ANALYSIS

As a general proposition, a party may set aside a transaction where that party was induced to enter into the transaction by another's undue influence. Thus, where a husband induces his wife to enter into a transaction by means of undue influence, the wife will be entitled to set aside the transaction as against her husband.

As Feldman J.A. has noted, the House of Lords reviewed the doctrine of undue influence in *Barclays Bank plc v. O'Brien*, [1993] 4 All E.R. 417. The facts of O'Brien are somewhat similar to the facts of this case. Mr. O'Brien was a shareholder in a company with an unsecured overdraft. He sought an increase to the company's overdraft limit to be secured by a second charge over the matrimonial home owned jointly by him and his wife. The Bank agreed to grant the increase and prepared the necessary documents, which Mr. O'Brien signed. The following day, Mr. O'Brien brought his wife to the Bank so that she could sign. No one explained the transaction or the documents to her or suggested that she receive independent legal advice. Mrs. O'Brien simply signed the documents. Eventu-

---

† (2000), 185 D.L.R. (4th) 458 at 460–471 (Ont. C.A.); leave to appeal to S.C.C. granted, (2000) 51 O.R. (3d) xvii, but case discontinued 2 August 2001, [2000] S.C.C.A. No. 298.

ally the company failed, and the Bank sought to realize on its security.

Mrs. O'Brien defended the Bank's action on the ground that she had been induced to sign the agreement by her husband's undue influence. The trial judge found that there was no undue influence, and ruled in favour of the Bank. The Court of Appeal granted the wife's appeal, finding that married women providing security for their husbands' debts constituted a specially protected class, requiring the Bank to ensure that the wife received independent legal advice. The House of Lords dismissed the Bank's appeal. While undue influence was not an issue directly before the House of Lords, Lord Browne-Wilkinson reviewed the law regarding undue influence, and noted that there were two different categories of undue influence — actual and presumed. He set out the following classification:

> Class 1: actual undue influence. In these cases it is necessary for the claimant to prove affirmatively that the wrongdoer exerted undue influence on the complainant to enter into the particular transaction which is impugned.
>
> Class 2: presumed undue influence. In these cases the complainant only has to show, in the first instance, that there was a relationship of trust and confidence of such a nature that it is fair to presume that the wrongdoer abused that relationship in procuring the complainant to enter into the impugned transaction. ... [O]nce a confidential relationship has been proved, the burden shifts to the wrongdoer to prove that the complainant entered into the impugned transaction freely, for example by showing that the complainant had independent advice. Such a confidential relationship may be established in two ways, viz:
>
> Class 2A: Certain relationships (for example solicitor and client, medical advisor and patient) as a matter of law raise the presumption that undue influence has been exercised.
>
> Class 2B: Even if there is no relationship falling within class 2A, if the complainant proves the de facto existence of a relationship under which the complainant generally reposed trust and confidence in the wrongdoer, the existence of such a relationship raises the presumption of undue influence. In a class 2B case therefore, ... the complainant will succeed in setting aside the impugned transaction merely by proof that the complainant reposed trust and confidence in the wrongdoer ... .

Lord Browne-Wilkinson then considered whether the specific relationship of husband and wife, without more, gave rise to a class 2A presumption of undue influence. He found that it did not. However, noting the continued existence of relationships where the wife is still subjected to, and yields to, influence by her husband, he concluded at p. 424 that:

> ... in any particular case a wife may well be able to demonstrate that de facto she did leave decisions on financial affairs to her husband thereby bringing herself within class 2B ... Thus, in those cases which still occur where the wife relies in all financial matters on her husband and simply does what he suggests, a presumption of undue influence within class 2B can be established solely from proof of such trust and influence without proof of actual undue influence.

In my view, it is clear from O'Brien that a wife seeking to set aside a transaction on account of undue influence may raise a class 2B presumption of undue influence by demonstrating that her relationship with her husband was one in which she relied on her husband so that it would be reasonable to presume that the transaction in question was procured by the undue influence of her husband. In O'Brien, Lord Browne-Wilkinson rejected at p. 428 a "special equity" theory based on the fact of marriage (or cohabitation) that would allow wives to set aside a transaction where they acted as surety for their husbands' debts:

> ... Should wives (and perhaps others) be accorded special rights in relation to surety transactions by the recognition of a special equity applicable only to such persons engaged in such transactions? Or should they enjoy only the same protection as they would enjoy in relation to their other dealings? In my judgment, the special equity theory should be rejected. ... [T]o require the creditor to prove knowledge and understanding by the wife in all cases is to reintroduce by the back door either a presumption of undue influence of class 2A (which has been decisively rejected) or the Romilly heresy (which has long been treated as bad law). [Emphasis added.]

Lord Browne-Wilkinson concluded that it was "not necessary to have recourse to a special equity theory for the proper protection of the legitimate interests of wives," since the combination of the class 2B presumption and the doctrine of constructive notice provided ample protection for such interests.

A similar approach was employed by the Supreme Court of Canada in *Geffen v. Goodman Estate*, 1991 CanLII 69 (S.C.C.), [1991] 2 S.C.R. 353, a case decided before Pitt and O'Brien. In *Geffen*, the testatrix left $1000 to each of her three sons, with the residue to her daughter for life and remainder to her grandchildren. The daughter had a history of mental illness. The brothers were concerned that their sister might make an unwise disposition of the house because of her condition, and this concern was shared by the daughter. Thus, she and her brothers met with a solicitor to discuss their concerns. After the daughter met the solicitor on her own on several occasions, she decided to settle the house in a trust for herself for life, with the remainder to her children and her nephews and nieces. After the daughter died, her executor brought an application to set the trust aside for undue influence. The trial judge held that there had been no undue influence, or in the alternative, that any presumption of undue influence had been rebutted by the independent legal advice. On appeal, the majority of the Alberta Court of Appeal held that the presumption of undue influence had not been rebutted. On further appeal, the Supreme Court of Canada allowed the appeal and upheld the trust. Wilson J., dissenting but writing for the majority on this point, set out the proper approach at p. 378:

> What then must a plaintiff establish in order to trigger a presumption of undue influence? In my view, the inquiry should begin with an examination of the relationship between the parties. The first question to be addressed in all cases is whether the potential for domination inheres in the nature of the relationship itself....
>
> Having established the requisite type of relationship to support the presumption, the next phase of inquiry involves an examination of the nature of the transaction.

It is clear that the approach set out by Wilson J. is substantially the same as the approach set out in O'Brien: where a claimant relies upon a presumption of undue influence, the court must look to the nature of the relationship and determine whether the potential for domination exists as a matter of fact or whether it may be presumed.

The principles of undue influence outlined in O'Brien were affirmed by the Supreme Court of Canada in *Gold v. Rosenberg*, 1997 CanLII 333 (S.C.C.), [1997] 3 S.C.R. 767. *Gold v. Rosenberg* did not concern undue influence or the presumption of undue influence; nor did the Supreme Court of Canada consider Lord Browne-Wilkinson's statement on that issue. In *Gold v. Rosenberg*, a testator left his estate to his son, Rosenberg, and grandson, Gold, as executors and equal beneficiaries. The assets of the estate were held by two companies. Both Rosenberg and Gold were directors of the companies; however, only Rosenberg was involved in the estate's business.

Rosenberg arranged a bank loan to a business of his own, secured by a guarantee from one of the estate companies, and supported by a mortgage over the estate company's assets. Gold signed a directors' resolution authorizing the guarantee, and the law firm acting for both parties gave an opinion that the guarantee was valid. Subsequently, Gold brought an action against Rosenberg, the bank, and the law firm, alleging that he had been misled. The trial judge held the bank and law firm liable, finding that the bank had knowingly assisted in a breach of trust. An appeal by the bank was allowed by this court, and a further appeal to the Supreme Court of Canada was dismissed. Sopinka J. referred to O'Brien when he considered the bank's duty to enquire. He said, at pp. 799–801:

> In certain circumstances, a third party in the position of the bank will not have discharged its duty to inquire unless the guarantor has been advised to obtain independent legal advice. In certain cases, the law imposes on a creditor a duty to inquire when the transaction is clearly detrimental to the person offering security and the relationship between that person and the principal debtor is particularly close. In such circumstances, the law presumes undue influence on the part of the principal debtor. The clearest type of relationship giving rise to this presumption is that of husband and wife. Iacobucci J. cites *Barclays Bank plc v. O'Brien*, [1993] 4 All E.R. 417 (H.L.), in which the House of Lords extended this presumption to include cohabitees. Lord Browne-Wilkinson held that when a creditor is approached by cohabitees, one the principal debtor and the other the surety, and the proposed transaction is clearly to the disadvantage of the surety, it will be under a duty to inquire. A creditor can discharge this duty by explaining to the surety in a meeting not attended by the principal debtor the amount of her potential liability and the risks involved and advising her to take independent advice: *Barclays, supra*, at pp. 431–32.
>
> ...
>
> When setting out the strict requirements of a separate meeting with the surety, however, Lord Browne-Wilkinson spoke of "the emotional pressure of cohabitation" (p. 431). Elsewhere, he spoke of how "the sexual and emotional ties between the [married] parties provide a ready weapon for undue influence" (p. 424). When a bank is presented with such a relationship, it should recognize the risk of undue influence (assuming that the transaction is on its face detrimental to the party offering security). But by the same logic, a relationship that is more distant will raise less suspicion of undue influ-

ence, even if the transaction is apparently unfavourable to the guarantor. Consequently, less may be required to satisfy an honest and reasonable person that the surety or guarantor is aware of the legal implications of the proposed transaction.

While Sopinka J.'s statement that the law presumes undue influence "when the transaction is clearly detrimental to the person offering security and the relationship between that person and the principal debtor is particularly close" might seem to establish a different test from the one set out in *Geffen* and *O'Brien*, it should be viewed in its context. Furthermore, had Sopinka J. intended to depart from, or change, the law pertaining to undue influence as set out in *Geffen*, *supra*, it seems to me that he would have stated his intention to do so.

The issues in *Gold v. Rosenberg* were whether the Bank had notice of Rosenberg's wrongdoing such that Gold could set aside the transaction, and the Bank's duty to inquire. As I have noted, *Gold v. Rosenberg* was not a case where the presence of undue influence was an issue. In *Gold*, Sopinka J. referred to *O'Brien* for the proposition that, in certain circumstances, a third party will owe a duty to inquire whether a guarantor had received independent legal advice. It should be noted that in the end Sopinka J. concluded that the respondent bank did not owe Gold a duty to advise him to obtain legal advice. In reaching this conclusion, he noted that Gold had "three years of university education in which he had taken courses in business, economics and accounting," and had some business experience. Whether the Bank owed a duty to inquire in this case is one of the issues that arises in this appeal, and it is to this issue that I now turn.

The duty to inquire about the prospect of undue influence in the context of the circumstances in which a third party will be subject to a complainant's equity to set aside a transaction procured by undue influence was central to the House of Lords' decision in *CIBC Mortgages plc v. Pitt*, [1993] 4 All E.R. 433, a companion decision to *O'Brien*. In *Pitt*, the Bank agreed to grant a loan to Mr. Pitt on the security of the matrimonial home. Both Mr. and Mrs. Pitt signed the loan agreement; however, Mrs. Pitt did not read the documents before signing or receive any independent legal advice, nor did any Bank employee suggest that she do so. When Mr. Pitt was unable to keep up the mortgage payments, the Bank sought possession of the house. Mrs. Pitt defended the application on the grounds that she had been induced to sign the agreement by misrepresentation and undue influence on the part of her husband.

The trial judge allowed the Bank's application, and Mrs. Pitt's appeal was dismissed. On further appeal, the House of Lords found that there was actual undue influence; however, the Bank was not affected by it as there was nothing to put the Bank on inquiry. In determining what would put the Bank on inquiry, Lord Browne-Wilkinson found that a complainant will be able to set aside a transaction where he or she can establish either (a) that the wrongdoer acted as a third party's agent in procuring the transaction, or (b) that the third party had actual or constructive notice of the wrongdoing.

As noted by Feldman J.A., the cases in which the wrongdoer will be found to have acted as the third party's agent will arise rarely. It is not argued in this case that the Bank had actual notice of the alleged undue influence. Therefore, it is necessary to consider when a third party, such as the Bank, will have constructive notice of a party's equity to set aside a transaction.

The House of Lords considered this question in *O'Brien*. Lord Browne-Wilkinson stated at p. 429 that:

> ... a creditor is put on inquiry when a wife offers to stand surety for her husband's debt by the combination of two factors: (a) the transaction is on its face not to the financial advantage of the wife; and (b) there is a substantial risk in transactions of that kind that, in procuring the wife to act as surety, the husband has committed a legal or equitable wrong that entitles the wife to set aside the transaction.

In such circumstances, the creditor will be put on inquiry and will be taken to have constructive notice of the complainant's rights unless the creditor has taken reasonable steps to satisfy himself that the complainant's agreement was properly obtained.

Lord Browne-Wilkinson's statement regarding constructive notice was accepted by the Supreme Court of Canada in *Gold v. Rosenberg*. In the course of his majority reasons, Sopinka J. commented generally on the duty owed by the Bank to Gold. He cited *O'Brien* at p. 800 for the proposition that "when a creditor is approached by cohabitees, one the principal debtor and the other the surety, and the proposed transaction is clearly to the disadvantage of the surety, it will be under a duty to inquire." In such circumstances, a creditor is required to explain to the surety in the absence of the principal debtor the amount of the sureties and the risks involved, and to advise the surety to obtain independent advice. However, a transaction is not automatically vitiated merely by the failure of a creditor to satisfy these requirements. The surety must establish her legal entitlement to set aside the transaction. If she is successful, the creditor's failure to satisfy its duty to inquire will prevent the creditor from avoiding the rights of the surety.

The case law, then, establishes that a wife may set aside a transaction where she can establish that the transaction was actually procured by undue influence (class 1 — actual undue influence) or where she can raise a presumption of undue influence by demonstrating that de facto she left decisions on financial affairs to her husband (class 2B — presumed undue influence). A third party, such as a bank, will be bound by the wife's equity to set aside the transaction where it has constructive notice of the wrongdoing, that is of undue influence or the real prospect of undue influence. Constructive notice may be established by a close relationship between the parties — such as husband and wife — coupled with a manifestly disadvantageous transaction. However, it must be noted that the mere fact of a close relationship does not give rise to a presumption of undue influence. Rather, a spouse must establish in each case that the relationship was on in which he or she "generally reposed trust and confidence in the wrongdoer".[1]

Applying these principles to this case, it is clear that the Bank is fixed with constructive notice of any wrongdoing between the parties. The existence of a marital relationship is marked by the characteristics of trust and confidence, which create an increased risk of undue influence. Further, as found by the trial judge, the transaction was to the material disadvantage of Mrs. Duguid. Accordingly, the Bank was subject to a duty to inquire. The Bank's failure to discharge the duty to inquire (to determine if there was undue influence) by advising Mrs. Duguid to obtain independent legal advice precludes the Bank from setting aside the finding of constructive notice of the potential for undue influence.

However, the transaction is not vitiated by the mere fact that the Bank had constructive notice of Mrs. Duguid's rights, if any, and failed to take reasonable steps to ensure that her consent was voluntary and informed. Rather, these facts only mean that Mrs. Duguid may set aside the transaction as against the Bank if, and only if, the transaction was procured by undue influence. Since there is no evidence of actual undue influence, the issue is whether there is a basis in the evidence to presume undue influence.

I am unable to agree with my colleague's conclusion that the transaction was procured by undue influence. Feldman J.A. states in her reasons, correctly in my view, that "this is not a situation where the wife put her trust and confidence in the husband for financial matters in the classic sense ...". Feldman J.A. presumes undue influence on the basis that Mrs. Duguid's concerns about her relationship with her husband provided "a ready weapon" for undue influence. I see a number of problems with this approach. First, Mrs. Duguid must establish that she did in fact repose trust and confidence in her husband. This burden may be met by showing that she left decisions on financial affairs to him. In my opinion, there is little or no evidence that Mrs. Duguid reposed trust and confidence in her husband. Indeed, as I have said, in respect of her financial affairs Feldman J.A. finds that this was not a situation where the "classic" requirements for presuming undue influence were made out.

In my opinion, there is ample evidence that Mrs. Duguid did not repose trust and confidence in her husband in the manner required for a presumption of undue influence. In the circumstances, I will limit my references to the evidence to highlight that part of it that is, in my view, of significance on the presumed undue influence issue.

This was a tax-driven real estate investment by Mr. Duguid, a school principal and another school principal. Mrs. Duguid, was a real estate agent. A short time before she signed the promissory note, the Bank took the position that the income and net worth of Mr. Duguid and his associate were not sufficient. As a result of the Bank's position, Mr. Duguid asked Mrs. Duguid to send an income and net worth statement to the Bank and she did so. Thus, the Bank's request that Mrs. Duguid sign the note did not come out of the blue. Finally, this was not the first time that Mr. Duguid and his associate had made an investment of this type. Mrs. Duguid knew that. These and other features of the evidence support the conclusion that she did not repose trust and confidence in her husband when it came to her, or their, financial affairs.

Moreover, it is clear from the authorities to which I have referred that the mere fact that a close relationship may give rise to "ready weapons for undue influence" is not sufficient to establish the presumption. If that was not the case, every close relationship would give rise to a presumption of undue influence. This would have the very result that Lord Browne-Wilkinson cautioned against in *O'Brien* — it would reintroduce a class 2A presumption of undue influence for every husband and wife relationship (or any other close relationship, for that matter).

There is nothing to suggest that Mr. and Mrs. Duguid had a relationship that would give rise to a finding of presumed undue influence. At trial, Mrs. Duguid testified that she signed the documents because she was not in a stage of her marriage where she would question anything. However, this statement must be viewed in the context of the remainder of her testimony. She testified that she was not aware that her marriage was in a precarious state, and that while she and her husband were "in a valley at that point in time," she did not think that the marriage would end.

Given that there was no actual undue influence and no basis upon which to presume undue influence, Mrs. Duguid has no equity to set aside the transaction as against the Bank. However, assuming that undue influence can be presumed, the inquiry must continue. The presumption of undue influence may be rebutted. As Wilson J. stated at p. 379 in *Geffen*, "[o]nce the plaintiff has established that the circumstances are such as to trigger the application of the presumption ... the onus moves to the defendant to rebut it." Typically, proof that the complainant received, or was advised to receive, independent legal advice will rebut the presumption: *Pitt, supra*; *O'Brien, supra*; *Geffen, supra*.

In my view, evidence that the surety obtained, or was advised to obtain, independent legal advice is not the only way to rebut the presumption of undue influence. While *Cheshire, Fifoot* and *Furmston's Law of Contract* (13th ed.) notes the significance of independent legal advice, the authors state at p. 329 that "the Privy Council has emphasized that if evidence is given of circumstances sufficient to show that the contract was the act of a free and independent mind, the transaction will be valid even though no external advice was given." Such circumstances might include commercial knowledge, experience, general sophistication or independence. See M.H. Ogilvie, "No Special Tenderness for Sexually Contracted Debt? Undue Influence and the Lending Banker" (1996) Can. Bus. L.J. 365 at 388.

The proposition that a presumption of undue influence may be rebutted was accepted in *Laird v. Mulholland*, [1998] O.J. No. 855 (Gen. Div.), where Lax J. considered the nature of proof required to rebut the presumption that a transaction was procured by undue influence. *Laird v. Mulholland* concerned a gift made by the deceased to her attorney. All parties conceded that the presumption of undue influence applied to the gift. The question was whether the presumption could be rebutted. The deceased did not obtain independent legal advice, and the respondents argued that such advice is necessary to rebut the presumption. Lax J. rejected this argument, stating at para. 37:

> I do not understand the Supreme Court of Canada in [*Geffen v.*] *Goodman Estate* to have laid down such an inflexible requirement. ... Obviously, legal advice is desirable in all instances where there is any possibility of influence. In many cases, it will go some distance to rebutting the presumption. However, each case turns on its own facts and the Court must examine the evidence it has to decide if the presumption has been rebutted.

In the end, Lax J. found that the presumption was rebutted notwithstanding the absence of independent legal advice. I agree with Lax J.'s conclusion on this issue.

Even if undue influence may be presumed, in my view, the presumption is rebutted in the circumstances of this case. Those features of the evidence that demonstrate that Mr. and Mrs. Duguid's relationship was not one giving rise to a presumption of undue influence also serve to rebut any presumption that might arise. To repeat, Mrs. Duguid was a real estate agent. As such, it is likely that she knew about the risks involved in her husband's investment, and almost certain that she would have understood the significance of co-signing his promissory note. In addition, I think that it is significant that Mrs. Duguid did not plead, or contend at trial, that her husband procured her signature by exercising actual undue influence. Nor did she defend the Bank's action on the basis of presumed undue influence. Furthermore, in oral argument of this appeal, Mrs. Duguid did not rely on undue influence, actual or presumed. Undue influence, as a live issue, only arose when the court sought written submissions on that issue.

DISPOSITION

For these reasons, I would allow the appeal, set aside the judgment of Day J. and in its place grant judgment in favour of the Bank. In light of the Bank's conduct as referred to by my colleague, I would not grant costs, here or below.

Note

1. These principles were recently applied by Crane J. in *Canadian Imperial Bank of Commerce v. Finlan*, [1999] O.J. No. 54 (Gen. Div.). Finland concerned an action under guarantee by a bank against a husband and wife.

(h) *CIBC Mortgage Corp. v. Rowatt*†

[FELDMAN J.A.:]

The appellant gave the respondent a mortgage on her home as security for her husband's business loans from the Canadian Imperial Bank of Commerce (the "bank"). She eventually discontinued payments on the mortgage and defended this action for enforcement of the mortgage on the basis that the mortgage was obtained by misrepresentation, that she did not understand the documents or the transaction and that she was not provided with full information regarding her husband's indebtedness and the bank's intended use of the funds. The trial judge gave judgment to the respondent enforcing the mortgage, but found that the bank had enforced a guaranty which it had agreed would be replaced by the mortgage. I would uphold the decision of the trial judge to enforce the mortgage, but would give the appellant credit for the amount she paid the bank in the settlement of the earlier action on the guaranty.

FACTS FOUND BY THE TRIAL JUDGE

In 1988 the appellant's husband, a lawyer, was taking advantage of the inflationary local real estate market by investing in second, third and fourth mortgages. He did this using funds borrowed from the bank. He first obtained a $35,000 line of credit, and then a $100,000 demand loan. In May, 1988 the appellant signed a guaranty and collateral mortgage over the matrimonial home which had been transferred into her name some years before in order to protect it from her husband's creditors. The guaranty and mortgage secured $135,000 of the husband's bank indebtedness. The appellant had independent legal advice when she signed these documents. The trial judge found that the appellant knew that the purpose of the guaranty and collateral mortgage was to help secure money borrowed from the bank by her husband for the purpose of his then lucrative mortgage investment business. The trial judge also found that the appellant was prepared to support her husband's business endeavors.

In September, 1988 Mr. Rowatt explained to the appellant that the bank wanted to replace the original guaranty and collateral mortgage with a new con-

ventional mortgage with regular payments, which new mortgage would be for the highest amount that the value of the property could support. He also told her that the new mortgage would support continuing availability of more investment funds from the bank. She agreed to this and was not concerned about the handling of the funds as between her husband and the bank. The mortgage was entered into with the respondent in the amount of $203,000, which amount represented the husband's indebtedness to the bank at that time. The bank used the funds to pay down its debt but made an additional $200,000 and more available to the husband for his mortgage investment business. The real estate market eventually collapsed, and Mr. Rowatt went bankrupt in 1990, owing the bank significant funds.

Contrary to Mr. Rowatt's representation to his wife regarding the mortgage transaction, the bank sued Mrs. Rowatt on the $135,000 guaranty which was supposed to have been replaced by the $203,000 conventional mortgage. Mrs. Rowatt was represented in the action by experienced and knowledgeable counsel. A substantial part of Mrs. Rowatt's defence was that the new mortgage had replaced the guaranty and that she was making payments on the new mortgage. The parties settled the guaranty action. Mrs. Rowatt assigned to the bank some rights she had in a claim belonging to her husband in Quebec. The value of the settlement is unclear in the record, but was between $12,000 and $50,000.

The mortgage was not dealt with in the settlement. The appellant later renewed the mortgage in the amount of approximately $130,000, part having been paid down by Mr. Rowatt. Soon after renewing the mortgage, after speaking to another lawyer in mid-November, 1992, the appellant stopped making payments on the mortgage.

The trial judge dealt with the fact that two bank employees were investing with Mr. Rowatt at the time of the second mortgage and had their investments paid out to them once the new funding arrangements were in place. The trial judge rejected the suggestion of conflict of interest or that the involvement of these two employees influenced anyone's conduct in the matter. He noted that "no one

---

† (2002), 220 D.L.R. (4th) 139 at 141–48 (Ont. C.A.); leave to appeal refused, (2002) 64 O.R. (3d) xvii (S.C.C.).

really says otherwise" and that not much time was spent on this point in argument.

The trial judge made specific findings regarding the credibility of both the appellant and her husband, and rejected their evidence of lack of information and understanding of the loan arrangements with the bank. He also found that Mr. Rowatt exercised no undue influence over the appellant and that Mrs. Rowatt did not need to be pressured or persuaded to join the expanding business venture, nor did Mr. Rowatt make any misrepresentation to her. He concluded his reasons at p. 6:

> I am satisfied that Mrs. Rowatt equably and clearly understood the situation when she independently and with a free mind decided to provide the new mortgage, which at the time I am sure seemed like a sensible idea.

ISSUES

The appellant raises four issues on the appeal:

(1) The bank manager's negligence

The appellant submits that it was the bank manager who caused the bank's losses in this case by the way he lent money to Mr. Rowatt for the purpose of investing in mortgages with insufficient equity. In that regard, the trial judge refused to admit into evidence certain internal bank documents which the appellant says would have supported this submission.

I would not give effect to this ground of appeal. The trial judge heard the evidence of Mr. and Mrs. Rowatt. He rejected much of it. The respondent called no evidence. The trial judge also reviewed the documents which he had ruled were admissible and relevant. He considered the legal and factual submissions of counsel for both parties including, presumably, this argument. Although it was not specifically addressed in the reasons, the trial judge obviously concluded that the appellant was responsible to the bank for its losses and not absolved as a result of any negligence in the handling of its own affairs by the bank.

(2) Undue influence

The appellant submits that the circumstances in this case gave rise to a presumption of undue influence of which the bank had notice. Because the bank took no steps to ensure that the appellant fully understood and freely entered into the mortgage transaction, the mortgage was not enforceable by the bank.[1] The appellant relies on the cases of *Barclays*

Bank plc v. O'Brien, [1993] 4 All E.R. 417 (H.L.); *Bank of Montreal v. Duguid* 2000 CanLII 5710 (ON C.A.), (2000), 47 O.R. (3d) 737 (C.A.) and the important new decision on the issue by the House of Lords in *Royal Bank of Scotland v. Etridge (No. 2)*, [2001] 4 All E.R. 449.

The doctrine of undue influence and the presumption of undue influence were most recently discussed by the Supreme Court of Canada in *Geffen v. Goodman Estate*, 1991 CanLII 69 (S.C.C.), [1991] 2 S.C.R. 353, in the context of both gifts and commercial transactions, and again in *Gold v. Rosenberg*, 1997 CanLII 333 (S.C.C.), [1997] 3 S.C.R. 767, where the court referred with approval to the decision of the House of Lords in *Barclays Bank*, recognizing the presumption of undue influence by a spouse or co-habitee when a guarantee is being given to a bank.

In the *Etridge* case, the House of Lords revisited its landmark decision in *Barclays Bank* where the court first articulated the obligation of a bank, which takes a pledge of assets or guarantee from one spouse or personal partner to secure the debts of the other, to take reasonable steps to ensure that there is no misrepresentation or undue influence, whether actual or presumed, motivating the spouse or partner giving the pledge or guarantee. After five years of experience with the process set out by the court, several cases arose for clarification of the requirements, and were heard together in the *Etridge* case.

One of the issues that required clarification in the *Etridge* case was the use and meaning of the term "presumed undue influence" or the "presumption of undue influence," referred to as "class 2B" as explained in the *Barclays Bank* case in the context of a spousal or like relationship.

In the *Etridge* case, the court clarified that the presumption of undue influence in a spousal, or like relationship, arising from the emotional interdependency of the parties has two effects in this context.

The first is to put a bank on notice and inquiry when a spouse or personal partner is guaranteeing the debts of the other partner. In order to protect itself from a claim that the guaranty was procured by undue influence by the benefitting spouse, the bank must take reasonable steps to try to ensure that the proposed guarantor understands the transaction and is entering into it freely, by suggesting that the guarantor seek and obtain independent legal advice and a full explanation of the transaction.

In *Barclays Bank*, Lord Browne-Wilkinson described the circumstances when a bank will be put on notice in this way at p. 429:

As I have said above in dealing with undue influence, this tenderness of the law towards married women is due to the fact that, even today, many wives repose confidence and trust in their husbands in relation to their financial affairs. This tenderness of the law is reflected by the fact that voluntary dispositions by the wife in favour of her husband are more likely to be set aside than other dispositions by her: a wife is more likely to establish presumed undue influence of class 2B by her husband than by others because, in practice, many wives do repose in their husbands trust and confidence in relation to their financial affairs. Moreover the informality of business dealings between spouses raises a substantial risk that the husband has not accurately stated to the wife the nature of the liability she is undertaking, i.e. he has misrepresented the position, albeit negligently.

> *Therefore, in my judgment a creditor is put on inquiry when a wife offers to stand surety for her husband's debts by the combination of two factors: (a) the transaction is on its face not to the financial advantage of the wife; and (b) there is a substantial risk in transactions of that kind that, in procuring the wife to act as surety, the husband has committed a legal or equitable wrong that entitles the wife to set aside the transaction* [emphasis added].

Following *Barclays Bank*, some courts were requiring proof that the bank had knowledge of the state of the relationship between the particular couple and whether the wife reposed trust and confidence in the husband before requiring the bank to have taken the reasonable steps. In *Etridge*, the court explained that the emphasized portion of the above quotation was Lord Browne-Wilkinson's way of describing why the relationship itself puts the bank on notice. In *Etridge*, the court clarified that "whenever a wife offers to stand surety for her husband's debts" the bank is put on inquiry (pp. 465–66).

The court then went on to discuss in detail the reasonable steps a bank must take in order to protect itself from a later claim by the guarantor/spouse that the guaranty is vitiated by undue influence or misrepresentation. The purpose of those steps is not for the bank to determine if the wife has been wronged by the husband, but "[t]he steps are concerned to minimize the risk that such a wrong may be committed" (p. 465). The consequence of not taking reasonable steps to ensure understanding and free will by the guarantor, is that the bank "is deemed to have notice of any claim the guarantor may have that the transaction was procured by undue influence or misrepresentation on the part of the debtor" (p. 476). If the bank does take these reasonable steps, it is protected from such a claim.

The second effect of the presumption of undue influence arises where the bank has not taken the reasonable steps and the guarantor later seeks to avoid liability on the pledge or guaranty by claiming that it was obtained by undue influence, and relies on a presumption of undue influence based on the relationship of the parties together with the disadvantageous nature of the transaction for the guarantor. In that circumstance, the presumption will not be determinative, but will be one of the evidentiary matters the trial judge considers when deciding whether or not the guaranty or pledge was entered into based on undue influence or misrepresentation by the spouse or partner. Lord Scott explained the confusion over this concept, and its correct application in the following passage at pp. 513–514:

> The presumption of undue influence, whether in a category 2A case,[2] or in a category 2B case, is a rebuttable evidential presumption. It is a presumption which arises if the nature of the relationship between two parties coupled with the nature of the transaction between them is such as justifies, in the absence of any other evidence, an inference that the transaction was procured by the undue influence of one party over the other. This evidential presumption shifts the onus to the dominant party and requires the dominant party, if he is to avoid a finding of undue influence, to adduce some sufficient additional evidence to rebut the presumption. In a case where there has been a full trial, however, the judge must decide on the totality of the evidence before the court whether or not the allegation of undue influence has been proved. In an appropriate case the presumption may carry the complainant home. But it makes no sense to find, on the one hand, that there was no undue influence but, on the other hand, that the presumption applies. If the presumption does, after all the evidence has been heard, still apply, then a finding of undue influence is justified. If, on the other hand, the judge, having heard the evidence, concludes that there was no undue influence, the presumption stands rebutted. A finding of actual undue influence and a finding that there is a presumption of undue influence are not alternatives to one another. The presumption is, I repeat, an evidential presumption. If it applies, and the evidence is not sufficient to rebut it, an allegation of undue influence succeeds.
>
> As to manifest disadvantage, the expression is no more than shorthand for the proposition that the nature and ingredients of the impugned transaction are essential factors in deciding whether the evidential presumption has arisen

and in determining the strength of that presumption. It is not a divining rod by means of which the presence of undue influence in the procuring of a transaction can be identified. It is merely a description of a transaction which cannot be explained by reference to the ordinary motives by which people are accustomed to act.

Applying these principles to this case, based on a consideration of all the evidence, the trial judge made clear and unequivocal findings that the appellant was not subjected to undue influence by her husband, that she entered in to the mortgage freely and that there was no misrepresentation. Any presumption of undue influence in this case was rebutted on the evidence. Consequently, I would not give effect to this ground of appeal.

(3) Unconscionability

The appellant submits that the court should refuse to enforce the mortgage because there was an inequality of bargaining power when the bank, as the stronger party, took undue advantage of the appellant who was in a vulnerable position, to impose an unfair bargain. She relied on the following circumstances:

(a) The misrepresentation by the bank that the guarantee would be discharged.
(b) The investment by the bank manager and loan officer in Mr. Rowatt's business, which may have impaired their judgment in approving the loans to him.
(c) The payment of one of the loan officer's investments after the mortgage funds were advanced.
(d) The negligence of the bank manager in putting forth the loan applications without disclosure to his superiors.
(e) The settlement of the guarantee action with the appellant by accepting a valuable chose in action from the appellant and not paying her costs, when the guarantee sued on was to have been discharged at the time of the mortgage.

Although the trial judge did not refer specifically to the concept of unconscionability, his findings with respect to the dealings between the parties, and the full understanding of the appellant as well as of her husband of what was going on, make it clear that he was satisfied that there was no overbearance or unconscionable conduct by the bank in the all the circumstances of this case, which would vitiate the mortgage transaction. There is no basis to interfere with his findings.

(4) Misrepresentation

The appellant submits that the mortgage was obtained by the misrepresentation that the guaranty of the $135,000 line of credit (together with the collateral mortgage) would be discharged in exchange for the appellant entering into the conventional mortgage for $203,000. The trial judge found as a fact that Mr. Rowatt told Mrs. Rowatt that the new conventional mortgage would replace the existing guarantee and collateral mortgage. Further to that finding, the trial judge stated at p. 4:

> I add now that it is my view that the Rowatts had a right to be angry and upset about the guaranty action, since there is no doubt on the evidence I have that the bank agreed to have the new mortgage replace not just the collateral mortgage but the guaranty as well.

Having made that clear finding, however, the trial judge accorded no legal significance to it or to the fact that the bank accepted a settlement of the guaranty action wherein value was given by Mrs. Rowatt and significant legal expenses were incurred by her. It appears from the Agreed Statement of Facts filed as exhibit 1 that in this action the bank continued to dispute that the guaranty was to be discharged in exchange for the new mortgage, thereby requiring the finding of the trial judge.

The issue on the appeal is, what is the legal significance of this finding of the trial judge? In my view, this is not a misrepresentation in the classic sense. The trial judge found not that the bank misrepresented the terms of the new mortgage transaction, but rather, for reasons unexplained, it breached its agreement by seeking to enforce the guaranty. The appellant suffered damages as a result of that breach, being the amount she paid to settle the guaranty action and the legal costs she incurred defending the action.

Based on the finding of the trial judge in this action, the appellant could sue the bank to recover the damages she suffered. However, in this action, the bank[3] now seeks to enforce the mortgage it obtained to replace that guaranty. As one of her grounds of appeal, the appellant has requested a set-off of the amount of damages she suffered. In my view, this is a case where the doctrine of equitable set-off applies. The claims are "so clearly connected" that "it would be manifestly unjust to allow the plaintiff to enforce payment without taking into consideration" the appellant's claim for damages. See *Holt v. Telford*, 1987 CanLII 18 (S.C.C.), [1987] 2 S.C.R. 193 at 212.

RESULT

The appeal against enforcement of the mortgage is dismissed. However, the appeal is allowed to the extent that the amount of damages suffered by the appellant as a result of the bank's breach of its agreement to discharge the guaranty, being the amount realized by the bank from the chose in action which was transferred to settle the guaranty action, together with the legal costs incurred by the appellant in that action, shall be set off against the amount owing on the mortgage. If the parties cannot agree on those amounts, they may refer the matter to the Master.

As success on the appeal was divided, there shall be no order as to costs.

Appeal allowed in part.

Notes

1. The respondent and the CIBC are described as related corporations in the respondent's pleadings. Although the CIBC and the respondent are separate legal entities, the trial judge did not differentiate between them and effectively treated them as one entity throughout his judgment.
2. Category 2A is the classical group of relationships which automatically give rise to a presumption of undue influence (not including husband/wife) such as priest/penitent, doctor/patient, lawyer/client.
3. See note 1.

(i) *Bank of Montreal v. Courtney*†

[OLAND J.A.:]

INTRODUCTION

The Bank of Montreal claimed against Holly Courtney based on several promissory notes signed by her and by her husband, Raymond Courtney. Mrs. Courtney appeals the decision and order of McDougall, J. which found in favour of the Bank. Her appeal raises issues which concern undue influence in the context of a marital relationship and a lender's duty of inquiry to a borrower who is in such a relationship.

BACKGROUND

Holly Courtney married Raymond Courtney in 1996. Three years later, he sold his 50% interest in MicroNet Information Systems Limited to Knowledge House Inc. The purchase and sale was by way of a pure share swap; that is, Mr. Courtney received no cash for his shares. Mrs. Courtney had never been involved with MicroNet and learned of its sale and the share swap after it had happened.

Knowledge House created a limited partnership to raise funds for research and development. Raymond Courtney, who had become a director and a senior vice-president of that company after the sale of MicroNet, agreed to purchase a limited partnership unit. Each unit cost $150,000. His understanding was that he would potentially save $75,000 in income tax.

Mr. Courtney needed to borrow $120,000 to purchase the limited partnership unit. It was through his broker, Eric Richards of the Financial Concept Group, that the Bank of Montreal agreed to lend him the money.

Holly Courtney and Raymond Courtney met with Gary Cooper, a loans officer with that Bank, on October 17, 1999. They signed a promissory note for $120,000 as co-borrowers. No independent legal advice was provided. The monies were used to buy a unit, in Mr. Courtney's name, of the Knowledge House limited partnership. He ultimately redeemed it for Knowledge House shares.

The Courtneys borrowed from the Bank on two further occasions: (a) a second loan of $300,000 on January 27, 2000; and (b) a third loan of $500,000 on March 28, 2000. On both those occasions Gary Cooper, who had processed those loans, was unavailable to meet. Another loans officer, Barbara Covey, dealt with the Courtneys when they attended at the Bank. Holly Courtney signed promissory notes as principal borrower while her husband signed as guarantor, for each of those second and third loans. No independent legal advice was provided.

---

† (2005), 261 D.L.R. (4th) 665 at 666–78 (N.S.C.A.).

The second loan was used to buy additional shares of Knowledge House which were placed in separate accounts in the names of Mr. and Mrs. Courtney with the Financial Concept Group. $300,000 of the $500,000 third loan was used to pay out the second loan. The remaining monies were used to purchase shares in a company known as ITI and more shares in Knowledge House, in the name of Raymond Courtney only. For each of the second and third loans, the Bank took as security a hypothecation of his shares in Knowledge House.

Each of Mr. and Mrs. Courtney gave evidence as to their discussions surrounding the first loan from the Bank. He testified in part:

> A. I told her that I couldn't get the loan without having her signature on it, she seemed not really to understand why it couldn't be done without — with — why it had to be done with her signature, and I basically berated her into signing it. We had several arguments, I hollered at her, I told her she had to do it, I gave her all kinds of rationale about the company and that I had, you know, millions of dollars of stock, so big deal. I pressured her to sign it, is what I did.
>
> Q. Did you give her any details about the particulars of [inaudible]?
>
> A. I made reference to the tax vehicle, that I would likely receive some benefit from that as well. As part of my pitch to her to tell — to ask her — to get her signature or to obtain her signature for that, I told her that I had promised my partners that I would do this and that I had to do it and it was the nth hour ...

Asked what her husband had told her he needed in relation to the first loan, Holly Courtney testified:

> I think he told me I had to sign on it, I had to guarantee it in some way, and I again said, "Why me?", because I didn't work, I had no means of repaying it, and he assured me that the stock would secure the loan.

According to Mrs. Courtney, the couple had "many, many conversations" which were "very heated." At some point she agreed to sign. Asked why she eventually acquiesced, Holly Courtney responded:

> Because the fighting was escalating to the point that I really didn't think that the marriage would continue if we continued to fight like that and I — Ray told me and pointed out to me on numerous occasions that he had many years of business experience, many more than me at high levels, and that he knew what he was doing.

She also testified that:

> It was very important to Ray, he told me he couldn't get it done without my signature, I felt that if I didn't do it that I would be responsible for him looking bad in the eyes of his co-workers, we were arguing about it constantly, in the end I just felt that I had to trust his judgment. I'd had no reason not to up to that point.

As with the first loan, Mr. Courtney talked to his wife about the second loan only after he had everything all set up and ready to go. When he told her she was needed to sign on it, he described her response as follows:

> She freaked. She got very mad that I would propose this to her, just essentially tell her she had to sign for me again, and I continued to tell her what a great company Knowledge House was and I talked about Charles Keating coming in and buying significant amounts of stock and investing $6 million dollars and I talked about the prognosis of the company and, you know, it's a sound thing to do and it's the right thing to do. I told her I had given the commitment to help the company and to support the company in my best efforts and that's what I wanted to do.

According to Mr. Courtney, these arguments continued over a number of days and he "continued to harass" his wife to sign. In regard to the second and third loans, Mrs. Courtney's evidence was that her husband had told her that there was no risk because the loan was secured with stock.

Each of Gary Cooper and Barbara Covey, the loans officers, had worked in lending for over 25 years. Neither had met Holly Courtney before she came with her husband to sign the promissory notes. Neither recalled her expressing any reluctance or concerns about signing them. Each formed the opinion from the meetings with them that both Courtneys understood the nature and effect of the security documents and were signing willingly. Each decided that independent legal advice was not required.

The value of Knowledge House shares was increasing at the time of each of the three loans. When Mr. Cooper sought authorization for the third, a senior employee of the Bank expressed concern about the risk, considering the high concentration of Knowledge House stock in Raymond Courtney's portfolio as well as its very short history trading at high prices. This concern was not communicated to Mr. Courtney or to Holly Courtney.

After completing a year of university and obtaining her legal secretarial diploma, Holly Courtney had worked outside the home for some 15 years. Ten years as secretary to the president of Halifax-Dartmouth Industries ended in the summer of 1995. She worked as secretary to the president of Nautel Industries until the spring of 1997. Thereafter Mrs. Courtney was not employed outside the home. That was her status at the time the three Bank loans were obtained between October 1999 and March 2000.

In 2001 the stock price of Knowledge House shares collapsed and the shares became worthless. Raymond Courtney subsequently made a proposal under the *Bankruptcy and Insolvency Act*, R.S. 1985, c. B-3, as amended.

DECISION OF THE TRIAL JUDGE

The Bank brought an action against the Courtneys to enforce repayment of their loans with the Bank. Among other things, Holly Courtney's defence alleged duress and undue influence, that the transactions were sufficiently divergent from ordinary standards of commercial morality to justify recision of the loan agreements, and that they were unenforceable in that she received no consideration.

Following a three day trial, the trial judge gave judgment for the Bank. His decision is reported at 2004NSSC182. It noted at ¶ 12 that Holly Courtney never asked any questions or raised any concerns with anyone at the Bank about the pressure allegedly exercised upon her by her husband or about the documents she was asked to sign. His decision concluded:

> ¶ 26 In the final analysis, I do not find that there has been undue influence exerted upon Mrs. Courtney. Furthermore, I do not find that there was anything that should have put the BoM on notice to make inquiries before allowing Mrs. Courtney to sign the loan documents. The loans were for the purpose of investing and not to secure the existing indebtedness of Mr. Courtney's business or to prop up a faltering business. Mrs. Courtney stood to benefit from these investments. She received consideration. By co-signing the first loan the requirement for providing additional security was waived. Although the second and third loans required further security, the Courtneys were given a lower interest rate. Mrs. Courtney, along with her husband, benefited from this.

> ¶ 27 It might have been more prudent for the BoM to recommend independent legal advice for Mrs. Courtney but, in the circumstances of this case, I do not think it was mandatory.

ISSUES

The issues raised on appeal can be divided into two categories: those which pertain to undue influence, and those which pertain to a duty of inquiry on the Bank. Under the first category fall the following:

(a) Did the learned trial judge commit palpable and overriding error:
    (i) in finding that Holly Courtney stood to benefit from the loans advanced by the Bank?
    (ii) in ignoring or misunderstanding evidence of undue influence exerted by Raymond Courtney over his wife?

(b) Did he err in law in failing to apply or consider the presumption of undue influence insofar as the relationship between Mr. and Mrs. Courtney was concerned?

The issues which pertain to a duty of inquiry on the Bank are as follows:

(a) Did the trial judge err in finding that:
    (i) the Bank owed no duty to advise Holly Courtney of dangers associated with the transactions and no obligation to explain her liability in relation to the loans?
    (ii) the Bank had met its obligations to her where it failed to advise her to seek independent legal advice prior to entering into the transactions?
    (iii) the Bank was not required to make reasonable inquiries to ensure no undue influence existed where the loans in question were made for the sole purpose of Raymond Courtney and not Holly Courtney, and also given the potential for influence within the husband and wife relationship?

(b) Did the trial judge err in failing to find that the Bank had constructive notice of undue influence exerted by Raymond Courtney over his wife?

STANDARD OF REVIEW

In *Flynn v. Halifax (Regional Municipality)*, 2005 NSCA 81 (CanLII), 2005 NSCA 81, this court stated:

> 13 An appeal is not a re-trial. The powers of an appellate court are strictly limited. A trial judge's factual findings and inferences from facts are insulated from review unless demonstrating palpable and overriding error. On questions of law the trial judge must be correct. A question of

mixed fact and law involves the application of a legal standard to a set of facts and is subject to a standard of palpable and overriding error unless it is clear that the trial judge made some extricable error in principle with respect to the characterization of the standard or its application, in which case the error may amount to an error of law and, therefore, be subject to a standard of correctness (*Housen v. Nikolaisen* 2002 SCC 33 (CanLII), [2002] 2 S.C.R. 235).

It accepted the description of palpable errors and overriding errors as set out in *Waxman v. Waxman*, 2004 CanLII 39040 (ON C.A.), (2004), 186 O.A.C. 201 (Ont. C.A.).

ANALYSIS

Undue Influence

The trial judge's decision disposed of the issue of undue influence as follows:

¶ 15 Mr. Courtney opted to proceed, with Mrs. Courtney's agreement, to negotiate the first loan in both names. Although I accept that Mrs. Courtney was reluctant at least at first to act as a co-borrower, I do not accept that she was the victim of undue influence by her husband. There might have been some tension between them but it was not enough to constitute undue influence. I find that she knew what she was doing and she did it willingly without undue influence from her husband.

¶ 16 I also do not accept that Mr. Courtney was acting as an agent of the BoM in convincing Mrs. Courtney to co-sign the loan documents. The BoM provided Mr. Courtney with an option. There were certain advantages to having the loan signed by both parties. By proceeding as they did, both Mr. and Mrs. Courtney benefited from these advantages. Even though the limited partnership was put in Mr. Courtney's name only, Mrs. Courtney also stood to benefit if it helped to reduce her husband's income tax liability. This would increase the couple's after-tax household income. What is more, the loan was not intended to secure existing business indebtedness of Mr. Courtney nor to bail out a failing business. It was an investment. The value of KHI shares was increasing at the time. Mrs. Courtney stood to benefit from these investments along with her husband.

...

¶ 18 Like the first loan, the funds from the second loan were used for investment purposes. And since Mr. and Mrs. Courtney did not have a marriage contract that would preclude her from making a claim to a share of these investments in the event of a separation or divorce she stood to potentially benefit. Likewise if they remained together as husband and wife then they would both potentially benefit from the investment.

In my view, none of the grounds of appeal pertaining to undue influence have merit.

The trial judge's finding that Mrs. Courtney stood to benefit from the loans with the Bank was supported by the evidence. Holly Courtney did not sign notes in support of her husband's own business. Rather, the Knowledge House limited partnership unit and the Knowledge House and ITI shares were purchased as investments. It was expected or at least hoped that they would increase in value. There was no marriage or other contract between these spouses which would disentitle the wife from an interest in them. Some of the Knowledge House shares were placed in an account in Mrs. Courtney's own name. A reduction in her husband's income tax liability, which Mr. Courtney testified he expected, would increase their household income. The trial judge did not make any palpable or overriding error in finding that Mrs. Courtney stood to benefit from the loans.

Nor, in my view, did he make any such error by ignoring or misunderstanding the evidence of undue influence allegedly exerted by Mr. Courtney on Mrs. Courtney. Holly Courtney's submissions relied heavily on the uncontradicted evidence of her reluctance to sign and Mr. Courtney's persuasion, and made much of her reliance on her husband's judgment. The evidence did establish that there had been strong disagreement between the Courtneys. However, here the spouse alleging undue influence was not herself unfamiliar with loans and financial terms.

While, at the time she signed for the loans Mrs. Courtney was not employed outside the home, she had had considerable work experience over 15 years until 1997. Moreover, Holly Courtney has a good educational background and an appreciation of financial and business matters. She testified she was critical of her husband when he received no cash as part of the MicroNet sale as she felt MicroNet was an amazingly profitable company. She knew she was signing loan documents and understood the obligation to repay the amount borrowed plus interest. She was sophisticated enough to understand the concept of liquidity in terms of business dealings and stocks. On one occasion Mrs. Courtney had advised Raymond Courtney to reconsider purchasing shares of a certain company as she was concerned about their liquidity, and he accepted her advice.

According to the evidence, it was Mr. Courtney who attended to the couple's financial affairs. He did the trading on his wife's account at Financial Concept Group. However, nothing prevented Mrs. Courtney opening statements from that firm, from speaking with or contacting Eric Richards, or from directing her own account. She chose to refer his messages and correspondence to her husband.

The trial judge found that never during the three loan transactions did Holly Courtney ask any questions or express any concerns whatsoever to anyone at the Bank. Nothing about her behaviour or demeanour during three meetings gave the Bank's loan officers any cause for unease about her understanding of the loan documents or as to her willingness to sign them.

The trial judge found that based on her education and experience, Holly Courtney was well aware of her legal obligations regarding these loans and that whatever influence was exerted upon her husband, it was not sufficient to constitute undue influence. I see no palpable or overriding error in his refusal, based on the evidence before him, to accept that Mrs. Courtney was the victim of undue influence by her husband.

I also reject the argument that the trial judge erred in law by failing to address the presumption of undue influence. Mrs. Courtney submits that instead of asking whether there was sufficient evidence to support the presumption, he went into another debate entirely, namely whether there had been evidence of undue influence.

In *Geffen v. Goodman Estate*, 1991 CanLII 69 (S.C.C.), [1991] 2 S.C.R. 353, [1991] S.C.J. No. 53 (QL version), Wilson, J. (Cory, J. concurring) addressed what a plaintiff had to establish in order to trigger a presumption of undue influence:

> 43. ... In my view, the inquiry should begin with an examination of the relationship between the parties. The first question to be addressed in all cases is whether the potential for domination inheres in the nature of the relationship itself....

> 44. Having established the requisite type of relationship to support the presumption, the next phase of the inquiry involves an examination of the nature of the transaction. When dealing with commercial transactions, I believe that the plaintiff should be obliged to show, in addition to the required relationship between the parties, that the contract worked unfairness either in the sense that he or she was unduly disadvantaged by it or that the defendant was unduly benefited by it....

Once this two-part test is satisfied and the presumption raised, then the onus moves to the defendant to rebut it.

In *Barclay's Bank plc v. O'Brien*, [1994] 1 A.C. 180, [1993] 4 All E.R. 417 (H.L.), at § 16 and 17 Lord Browne-Wilkinson first noted two classes of undue influence (actual and presumed). Then at § 18 and 19, he further divided presumed influence into two parts: Class 2A which encompasses those relationships which, as a matter of law, raise the presumption of undue influence; and Class 2B where the existence of a relationship under which the complainant generally reposed trust and confidence in the wrongdoer, raises that presumption. He continued at § 21:

> Although there is no class 2A presumption of undue influence as between husband and wife, it should be emphasized that in any particular case a wife may well be able to demonstrate that de facto she did leave decisions on financial affairs to her husband thereby bringing herself within class 2B ie that the relationship between husband and wife in the particular case was such that the wife reposed confidence and trust in her husband in relation to their financial affairs and therefore undue influence is to be presumed. Thus, in those cases which still occur where the wife relies in all financial matters on her husband and simply does what he suggests, a presumption of undue influence within class 2B can be established solely from the proof of such trust and confidence without proof of actual undue influence.

The categorization of undue influence set out in *O'Brien* was accepted by the Supreme Court of Canada in *Gold v. Rosenberg*, 1997 CanLII 333 (S.C.C.), [1997] 3 S.C.R. 767, [1997] S.C.J. No. 93 (QL version) at § 60 and § 78–79.

In his decision the trial judge did not make explicit reference to the presumption of undue influence, how that presumption might be triggered, or if the evidence before him raised that presumption. While it would have been preferable had he done so, I am satisfied from my review of the trial judge's decision that he directed his mind to the requirements that give rise to that presumption, and the evidence in support of the presumption and of its rebuttal. This is apparent from his review of the facts pertaining to the relationship between Mr. and Mrs. Courtney in regard to financial matters and in particular these loans, and his description of the "tension" between husband and wife regarding. The trial judge was clearly focussed on the potential for domination within this marital relationship and the extent to which Mrs. Courtney reposed trust and confidence in her husband in relation to their financial affairs. He also considered the nature of these transactions. In finding that Mrs. Courtney stood to benefit, he implicitly decided that the loan arrangement did not work an unfairness. Moreover, his familiarity with *O'Brien, supra* is reflected in his reference to that decision. Finally, he considered those factors which might rebut the presumption. In these circumstances I am unable to agree that the trial judge erred by failing to consider the presumption of undue influence.

Duty of Inquiry

In § 25 of his decision, the trial judge noted that Mrs. Courtney had urged him to apply *Royal Bank of Scotland plc v. Etridge* (No. 2) (HL (E)), [2002] 2 A.C. 773 and then continued:

> ... This House of Lords decision makes it clear that their earlier decision in *Barclays Bank plc v. O'Brien*, [1993] 1 All E.R. 417; [1993] 3 W.L.R. 786; [1994] 1 A.C. 180 (U.K.H.C.) is still good law. There are also a number of Supreme Court of Canada decisions that consider the *O'Brien* authority and which were decided prior to *Etridge*. *Etridge* does not overturn the decision in *O'Brien*; rather, it only serves to better explain it. I am not persuaded that the law has changed substantially if at all. Even if it had, I am not bound by a decision of the House of Lords.

In the following paragraph, he concluded: "I do not find that there was anything that should have put the BoM on notice to make inquiries before allowing Mrs. Courtney to sign the loan documents" and stated at § 27:

> It might have been more prudent for the BoM to recommend independent legal advice for Mrs. Courtney but, in the circumstances of this case, I do not think it was mandatory.

The grounds of appeal allege that the trial judge erred in law in finding that the Bank had met its obligations to Holly Courtney although it had not advised her to seek independent legal advice, or of the risk involved with these transactions. I am not persuaded that he so erred.

I address as a preliminary matter, the argument that the Bank breached its own policy regarding the provision of independent legal advice. That submission is without foundation. The Bank's operating procedure regarding such advice reads in part:

> Introduction
>
> Where a loan transaction involves a third party, lack of consideration (benefit) could prejudice the validity of the guarantee or covenant. A court may dismiss a claim for recovery by the Bank from a third party who co-signed, endorsed, guaranteed or pledged security on behalf of a primary debtor if the court feels that the third party was subjected to pressure from:
> • the primary debtor,
> • the Bank, or
> • any other person.
> Accordingly, determine, under the Lending process, whether the Bank should insist on the third party obtaining independent legal advice (ILA) as to the legal effect and consequences of providing support.
>
> Independent legal advice ILA
>
> ... ILA is often obtained when the third party is an individual and:
> • is the spouse of the primary debtor
>
> Also applies ... for the benefit of a business owned or controlled by the other spouse or of which the other spouse is a principal officer.

A careful reading of this document indicates that, in every case, it is for the loans officer to determine whether such advice should be obtained; the operating procedure does not make it mandatory. These loans were not for the benefit of a business which was a customer of the Bank and in which Mr. Courtney had an ownership interest. Moreover Holly Courtney was not a third party. She co-signed the first loan and it was she, not Raymond Courtney, who was the primary debtor on the second and third.

I turn then to the argument regarding independent legal advice. The absence of such advice does not automatically preclude recovery under a security document. In *Gold v. Rosenberg, supra* Sopinka, J. for the majority stated at p. 803:

> Whether or not someone requires independent legal advice will depend on two principal concerns: whether they understand what is proposed to them and whether they are free to decide according to their own will. The first is a function of information and intellect, while the second will depend, among other things, on whether there is undue influence....

Holly Courtney argues that her interaction with the Bank was limited and that she did not have the information and intellect to fully understand the nature of the loan transactions and her financial exposure. According to her submissions, independent legal advice would have afforded her the opportunity to understand her rights and obligations regarding the loans, and to properly understand the risk she was undertaking.

Earlier in this decision, I determined that the trial judge had not made a palpable and overriding error in finding that Mrs. Courtney fully understood the obligation she was entering into and was doing so freely and voluntarily. As a consequence, independent legal advice would not have made a difference — she would have been told what she already knew and appreciated. The absence of such advice in such circumstances cannot be the basis of impeaching the loan transactions.

Mrs. Courtney then submits that the Bank was fully aware of the risks and dangers associated with the loans. She points to the internal memorandum which urged caution in regard to the third loan because of the high ratio of Knowledge House stock in Mr. Courtney's stock portfolio, and says that the Bank should have drawn its concerns to her attention. She urges as well that where the loans were negotiated by her husband, the Bank should have been "put on inquiry" and that it should have arranged a private meeting with her to advise her of the risks and to assure itself that she understood her obligations.

Her argument relies on *Etridge (No 2), supra.* There the House of Lords held that whenever a wife stands as surety for her husband's debts, the bank is put on inquiry and it should insist upon the wife attending a private meeting where she is advised of the risks of the transaction and her potential liability and should also be urged to seek out independent legal advice. According to that decision, if these steps are taken, the bank is protected from a claim of undue influence.

Etridge (No 2) has been referred to in several Canadian decisions. See, for example, *Faris v. Eftimovski*, [2004] O.J. No. 3407 (S.C.J.) and *Bank of Montreal v. Collum*, [2004] B.C.J. No. 1314

(C.A.), application for leave to appeal dismissed [2004] S.C.C.A. No. 412, where it was referred to as *Barclays Bank plc v. Coleman*, [2001] 4 All E.R. 449. However, here the wife did not serve as surety for her husband's debts and no Canadian case has followed *Etridge (No 2)* and stipulated that a bank must take such steps to avoid a claim of undue influence was identified. I am not satisfied that in deciding not to follow that decision the trial judge erred such that this court should interfere.

Finally, Mrs. Courtney argued that the trial judge had erred in failing to find that the Bank had constructive notice of undue influence exerted by Mr. Courtney over her. I am not persuaded that he so erred. There was nothing about Mrs. Courtney's conduct with respect to these loan transactions that alerted the Bank's loans officers to the possibility of undue influence. At their meetings, she gave no indication that she was not acting freely and voluntarily. She did not call them to express any concern. She admitted that she knew the legal effect of the documents she signed. In light of the evidence it cannot be seriously suggested that because Ms. Courtney was no longer in the workforce or that she was married to Mr. Courtney in whose name most of the investments purchased with the money they borrowed were registered, fixes the Bank with constructive notice of his undue influence over her.

I would dismiss the appeal and would award the Bank costs of $4,000. plus disbursements as agreed or taxed.

Appeal dismissed.

(III) Unconscionability

(j)   *Canadian Imperial Bank of Commerce v. Ohlson*†

[CONRAD J.A.:]

The appellant, Mrs. Ohlson, was 82 years old when she attended at the premises of the respondent,

Canadian Imperial Bank of Commerce ("the Bank") for the purpose of assisting her son with the purchase of lands in California. The Bank structured the transaction as a loan and had her sign a promissory

---

† (1997), 154 D.L.R. (4th) 33 (Alta. C.A.).

note and equitable mortgage, notwithstanding that the funds for the purchase had been advanced to the son the day before her first attendance at the Bank. The appellant alleges that the transaction was unconscionable. She says that it was, in substance, a guarantee and required a certificate of independent legal advice, which advice would have disclosed that at the time she signed the documents, her son had already received the required funds. There was no evidence that she knew that the funds for the California land deal had already been advanced when she signed the documents. By the time of trial the appellant had Alzheimer's disease and was unable to testify. The son, a co-defendant, did not testify.

The trial judge found that the transaction was not unconscionable within the meaning of the *Unconscionable Transactions Act*, R.S.A. 1980, c. U-2 ("*UTA*"), or at all. He found that the appellant understood the nature of the transaction, in part, by drawing an adverse inference against the appellant for failing to compel her son to testify. He awarded judgment of $69,872.70 against the appellant and, in default of payment, ordered that the respondent was entitled to apply for sale, foreclosure or possession of her home.

Issues

The main issue is whether the trial judge erred in failing to find that this transaction was unconscionable and unenforceable without independent advice. A secondary issue is whether the trial judge erred in drawing an adverse inference against Mrs. Ohlson for the failure of her son to testify in circumstances where her son had been sued in the alternative in this action.

Conclusion

I conclude that the appeal must be allowed. First, I am of the view that it was an error to draw the adverse inference against Mrs. Ohlson. Secondly, it was unconscionable on these facts for the Bank to prepare the documents in the form of a loan and thereby deprive Mrs. Ohlson of independent advice. In my view, the trial judge failed to appreciate that the transaction was in substance a guarantee. At the time the document was signed the funds had already been advanced to the son for the loan. The bank officer knew that the loan required security, and thus it was the Bank that required the signature of Mrs. Ohlson at the time she signed, and not her son. Independent advice would have disclosed those facts. There is no evidence that Mrs. Ohlson was ever told

that the funds had already been distributed and such an inference does not arise from the evidence. Moreover, the Bank knew at all times that the loan proceeds were always solely for the son. In my view, it was unconscionable to proceed without independent advice in the circumstances of this case and the Bank cannot take advantage of the promissory note and equitable mortgage signed by Mrs. Ohlson. Finally, while not argued on the basis of consideration, on the findings of fact in this case there was no consideration for the alleged loan.

Background

John Ohlson, the appellant's son and a regular client of the Bank, sought to borrow funds from the Bank to finance a real estate transaction in California. The Bank was not prepared to make a further advance to Mr. Ohlson without security, and he agreed to have his mother provide security. On October 3, 1991, he delivered to the Bank the certificate of title to his mother's home. On that date his mother was neither a customer of the Bank, nor had she ever had any direct dealings with it. As funds were required immediately, the bank advanced $50,000.00 to Mr. Ohlson, notwithstanding that the appellant had never attended at the bank nor signed any documents. The moneys were placed into John Ohlson's account directly on October 3, 1991.

On October 4, 1991, the Bank met with Mrs. Ohlson for the first time. During this meeting, which lasted approximately one hour, she was requested to and did sign a promissory note for $50,000, and a Memorandum of Charging Lands, dated October 4th. The Bank did not obtain a loan application from Mrs. Ohlson, nor did it inquire as to her ability to repay the loan. The source of repayment was always understood by everyone to be from funds derived from the success of the real estate transaction. The Bank was aware at the time that the appellant's only asset was her home and it had no reason to believe that, short of selling her home, she had any means of paying a loan of the magnitude involved in this case.

Notwithstanding that the funds had already been advanced, the Bank structured the transaction as though it were a loan to Mrs. Ohlson and not as a guarantee. The promissory note which she signed was undated. The charge was not registered when executed. Rather, the Bank obtained a consent from the appellant which would allow it to register the charge in the event of default. This transaction had none of the earmarks of a loan to Mrs. Ohlson.

The appellant did not receive independent legal advice, nor was it recommended by the Bank that she seek such advice.

Following execution of the documents, Mrs. Ohlson did not sign a direction authorizing the Bank to apply any money from her "alleged loan" for the benefit of anyone else. The Bank did not open an account in her name to which it deposited the funds, the funds having already been advanced to her son the previous day. It is clear that the Bank only saw Mrs. Ohlson on one occasion, namely October 4, 1991. There is no evidence that Mrs. Ohlson was told that the funds had already been advanced. Rather, the Bank's position at trial was to the contrary, in that it tried to establish that she had signed the documents before the funds were released.

On October 8th, the Bank made a book entry crediting Mr. Ohlson's account which reduced his overdraft by $50,000. The date of October 8th was entered on the promissory note. The charge was not registered but the Bank held a consent which the appellant had signed allowing it to register the charge in the event of default.

When the son defaulted, the Bank commenced an action against Mrs. Ohlson for judgment on the promissory note. In the alternative, it sought judgment against Mr. Ohlson for fraudulently inducing the Bank to enter the transaction on the basis that his mother would provide proper security.

By the time of trial, Mrs. Ohlson had been diagnosed with Alzheimer's disease. Initially, in 1995, her son, Mr. John Ohlson, had been appointed as Trustee of the estate of the appellant. Recognizing the conflict of interest between Mr. Ohlson and his mother arising from the alternative claims by the Bank, the Public Trustee of Alberta was appointed Guardian *ad litem* for purposes of this action on November 10, 1995. Mrs. Ohlson was not competent to testify at trial. The Bank objected to the Trustee's application to read in answers from her earlier examination-for-discovery, and the trial judge denied the application. Mr. Ohlson did not testify and, as a result, the trial judge drew an adverse inference against the appellant as to her understanding of the transaction.

TRIAL JUDGMENT

The trial judge found that the purpose of the transaction was to provide funds for the son to purchase the lands in California. Moreover, he found that it was a loan solely for that purpose and it was not intended as a guarantee of past indebtedness. He examined the transaction to determine whether the

cost of the loan was excessive and whether the transaction was harsh and unconscionable. Since both elements are required under the *UTA*, proof of only one is not sufficient. He concluded that the cost of the loan was not excessive and therefore no statutory relief under s. 2 of the *UTA* was available. The trial judge then went on to consider the equitable principles relating to unconscionable transactions, and concluded that the transaction was not unconscionable at all. Judgment was awarded against Mrs. Ohlson and the Bank was granted the right to enforce the security in the event of default [reported 180 A.R. 248].

Appellant's Position

No issue is taken with the finding that the cost was not excessive and therefore the *UTA* does not apply. Certainly had it been a proper loan the costs would not be excessive. However, it is argued that this transaction was, in substance, a guarantee and since Mrs. Ohlson did not receive independent legal advice the obligation is unenforceable. Further, the appellant submits that the trial judge erred in failing to find that the transaction was unconscionable at equity. Finally, she also submits that the trial judge was wrong in law to draw an adverse inference against her for her son's failure to testify.

Respondent's Position

The Bank takes the position that the trial judge made no reversible error in arriving at his decision. It argues that the facts support his view of the dealings as one transaction. Moreover, it argues that the pleadings were inadequate in that Mrs. Ohlson failed to plead the transaction was unconscionable in equity. In addition, it submits that there is no evidence to substantiate the impact of independent advice had that advice been received.

ANALYSIS

Adequacy of Pleadings

I am satisfied that the pleadings are adequate to cover the issues dealt with by the trial judge. While the appellant did not specifically plead unconscionability in the equitable sense, this lawsuit is based on the conduct of the Bank in structuring this loan in such a manner as to deprive the appellant of the independent advice she would have received had the transaction been structured as a guarantee. There are no surprises here. While the trial judge noted the absence of argument on the specific issue of equitable unconscionability, he nonetheless went on to discuss the components of harshness and unconscionability. In doing so he relied on the principles emerging from the cases dealing with unconscionable conduct generally. Although the trial judge "leave[s] for another day the issue of whether the *UTA* replaces equitable unconscionability, or whether the two can coexist" (A.B. 166) [p. 256 A.R.], he concedes that there is authority to support their coexistence. Specifically, he refers to *Calgary (City) v. Northern Construction Co.*, [1986] 2 W.W.R. 426 (Alta. C.A.) at pp. 441–3; and the *Ontario Law Reform Commission Report on Amendment of the Law of Contract* (Toronto: Ministry of the Attorney General, 1987). He stated further at A.B. p. 166 [p. 256 A.R.]:

> In any event, I believe that the second pre-requisite for invoking s. 2 of the *UTA* is not dissimilar from equitable unconscionability and cases decided on inequity can be used to interpret the word "unconscionability" as it is used in the *UTA*.

It follows that the trial judge reviewed and made his findings with respect to the component requirement for unconscionable transactions generally. In my view, notwithstanding that the argument focused on the *UTA*, the appropriateness of depriving this litigant of independent advice is the very essence of the pleading. The pleadings are broad enough to encompass the question of whether this transaction should be set aside as being unconscionable in equity.

Unconscionability

While it is difficult to articulate a clear definition of unconscionability, generally a transaction must be both disadvantageous and harsh.

The test for unconscionability has been stated in various ways. In *National Westminster Bank plc v. Morgan*, [1985] 1 All E.R. 821 (H.L.), at 831 Lord Scarman captures its amorphous nature. Although speaking of the twin doctrine of undue influence his comments apply readily in the present context:

> There is no precisely defined law setting limits to the equitable jurisdiction of a court to relieve against undue influence. This is the world of doctrine, not of neat and tidy rules. The courts of equity have developed a body of learning enabling relief to be granted where the law has to treat the transaction as unimpeachable unless it can be held to have been procured by undue influence. It is the unimpeachability at law of a disadvantageous transaction which is the starting point from which the court advances to consider whether the transaction is the product merely of one's own folly or of the undue influence exercised by another. A court in the exercise of this equitable jurisdiction is a court of conscience. Definition is a poor instrument when used to determine whether a transaction is or is not unconscionable: this is a question which depends on the particular facts of the case.

Unconscionability, like undue influence and duress, aims to temper the ideal of freedom to contract with the need to prevent abuse and to protect the weak. It is a doctrine permitting the application of judicial discretion to excuse an obligant from performing a contract. The doctrine of unconscionability is identified in the leading Canadian case of *Morrison v. Coast Finance Ltd.* (1965), 54 W.W.R. 257, 55 D.L.R. (2d) 710 (B.C.C.A.), at p. 259 as follows:

> The equitable principles relating to undue influence and relief against unconscionable bargains are closely related, but the doctrines are separate and distinct. The finding here against undue influence does not conclude the question whether the appellant is entitled to relief against an unconscionable transaction. A plea of undue influence attacks the sufficiency of consent; a plea that a bargain is unconscionable invokes relief against an unfair advantage gained by an unconscientious use of power by a stronger party against a weaker. On such a claim the material ingredients are proof of inequality in the position of the parties arising out of the ignorance, need or distress of the weaker, which left him in the power of the stronger, and proof of substantial unfairness of the bargain obtained by the stronger. On proof of those circumstances, it creates a presumption of fraud which the stronger must repel by proving that the bargain was fair, just and reasonable: *Aylesford (Earl) v. Morris* (1873) 8 Ch App 484, 42 LJ Ch 546, *per* Lord Selborne at p. 491, or perhaps by showing that no advantage was taken: See *Harrison v. Guest* (1855) 6 De GM & G 424, at 438, affirmed (1860) 8 HL Cas 481, at 492, 493, 11 ER 517.

This case is significant in relation to *National Westminster* in that it treats undue influence and unconscionability as separate doctrines. The case law and comments by writers on the subject indicate that a general principle of unconscionability exists but precise formulation of this principle remains elusive. This is because of its flexible nature and the variety of situations to which it has been applied. As S.M. Waddams, *The Law of Contracts*, 3rd ed. (Toronto: Canada Law Book Inc., 1993) points out at p. 367, flexibility is desirable to allow stances. Further, Waddams reveals that "[a]nother compelling reason for adopting a general principle of unconscionability is the need to fill the gaps between existing islands of intervention. The clause that is ... just outside the provisions of the statutory power to relieve will fall under the general power" (p. 361).

G.H.L. Fridman, *The Law of Contract in Canada*, 3rd ed. (Scarborough, Ont.: Carswell, 1994) sets out the necessary ingredients of equitable fraud which underline unconscionability at p. 325:

> It is not fraud in the classical, common-law sense, involving misrepresentations of the truth. Nor is there any improper applications of pressure amounting to duress or its equitable analogue of undue influence. Nonetheless, the conduct of one party in obtaining the assent of the other to a particular contract was of such a character that a court might well consider that to uphold the ensuing contract would be to perpetrate an injustice and produce an unfair result.

In *Harry v. Kreutziger* (1978), 9 B.C.L.R. 166, 95 D.L.R. (3d) 231 (C.A.), Lambert J.A. stated at p. 177:

> In my opinion, questions as to whether use of power was unconscionable, an advantage was unfair or very unfair, a consideration was grossly inadequate, or bargaining power was grievously impaired, to select words from both statements of principle, the *Morrison* case and the *Bundy* case, are really aspects of one single question. *That single question is whether the transaction, seen as a whole, is sufficiently divergent from community standards of commercial morality that it should be rescinded.* [Emphasis added.]

Lambert J.A. also stated that it is appropriate to seek guidance as to community standards of commercial reality from legislation that embodies those standards in law. I quote from Lambert J.A., not for the purpose of adopting this as the test, but as an example of one approach taken to aid in the identification of an unconscionable transaction.

In *Calgary (City) v. Northern Construction Co.*, [1986] 2 W.W.R. 426 (Alta. C.A.), Kerans J.A., albeit in *obiter*, adopted the test set out in *McKenzie v. Bank of Montreal* (1976), 70 D.L.R. (3d) 113, 12 O.R. (2d) 719 (C.A.), and *Kreutziger* and recognized that equitable unconscionability may have been available to relieve the contractor if the contract was unconscionable. Since he decided that the contract was not unconscionable, he declined to apply the doctrine. However, he stated at pp. 442–3:

> Equity will intervene to refuse to enforce unconscionable contracts; but this is a rule quite sepa-

rate from the rules respecting the formation of contracts.

> ...

> Inequality of bargaining power as a touchstone for intervention is accepted by most Canadian courts: See *McKenzie v. Bank of Montreal* (1976), 12 O.R. (2d) 719, also *Harry v. Kreutziger* (1978), 9 B.C.L.R. 166, where McIntyre J.A. (as he then was) affirmed the old test:

>> "Where a claim is made that a bargain is unconscionable, it must be shown for success that there was inequality in the position of the parties due to the ignorance, need or distress of the weaker, which would leave him in the power of the stronger, coupled with proof of substantial unfairness in the bargain. When this has been shown a presumption of fraud is raised and the stronger must show, in order to preserve his bargain, that it was fair and reasonable."

I hold the view that flexibility, rather than precision, is required when determining whether a claim for intervention has been demonstrated, and I do not by my comment purport to adopt a single determinative test.

Having discussed the nature of the doctrine, I am faced with the issue of whether the equitable remedy can coexist with the *UTA*.

Coexistence of the Equitable Remedy and the UTA

While *Northern*, *supra*, sets out the general principle, it did not have to decide whether equitable unconscionability could exist in the face of a statutory regime because in that case no statute was applicable. In this case that issue is squarely before us.

There appears to be ample justification for concluding that equitable unconscionability can coexist with the *UTA*. First, in a significant number of cases the lending contracts were declared unconscionable in equity in the face of the provincial and English counterparts of the Alberta *Act* (for example, *Lloyds Bank Ltd. v. Bundy*, [1974] 3 All E.R. 757 (C.A. — Lord Denning M.R.); *Bertolo v. Bank of Montreal* (1986), 57 O.R. (2d) 577, 33 D.L.R. (4th) 610 (C.A.); *Bomek v. Bomek and Dauphin Plains Credit Union* (1983), 20 Man. R. (2d) 150, 146 D.L.R. (3d) 139 (C.A.)). In this jurisdiction *Canadian Imperial Bank of Commerce v. 3L Trucking Ltd.* (1995), 176 A.R. 245 (Q.B.) Moreau J. examined unconscionability, not with reference to the *UTA*, but using equitable principles in a situation that is factually similar to this case.

Secondly, the *UTA* is aimed at only one kind of unconscionability, that is, usurious lending practices. Under the *UTA*, a party wishing to avoid the obligation must prove the excessive cost of the loan and the harsh and unconscionable nature of the transaction. Thus, it was aimed at a specific type of transaction and does not cover all the situations where harshness can result from inequality of bargaining power. This narrow focus of the *UTA* leaves the type of gap that Waddams referred to above, requiring the intervention of equity to provide the remedy.

Thirdly, and related to the second reason, the statute and equity are not in conflict but run parallel to each other. The statute cannot be viewed as a comprehensive codification of the existing law and the equitable remedy is flexible and broad enough to deal with comparable wrongs. Both are aimed at preventing abuse of inequality of position.

Finally, s. 4 of the *UTA* provides that nothing "derogates from the existing powers or jurisdiction of any court". Thus, I see no impediment to the equitable remedy coexisting with the statutory regime.

Application to the Present Case

The trial judge found that there was a weakness and inequality of bargaining power. That finding is not challenged. Mrs. Ohlson was unsophisticated in the ways of the business world as compared with the Bank. She was elderly and the Bank was fully aware that the benefit of the loan was solely to be that of the son. The Bank was in charge of preparing the documents. Moreover it had full knowledge of the transactions and was aware the funds had already been advanced to the son by the time she signed the documents.

The respondent admits that no independent legal advice was given, nor even recommended. The serious issue is whether the weakness here resulted in an unfair advantage for the stronger party. At A.B. p. 183 the trial judge states [p. 263 A.R.]:

> It comes down, in the end to considerations not dissimilar in result to that in *Beaton*, namely that Counsel for Mrs. Ohlson has failed to satisfy the onus that the Bank unfairly exploited Mrs. Ohlson's weaknesses and inequality for its own advantage — that is, while some of the *indicia* of exploitation are present, I *find that there was no advantage unfairly gained by the Bank*. Furthermore, some aspects that might also have been weaknesses were not present. [Emphasis added.]

The trial judge cites the following examples as indication of the second component of exploitation (A.B. pp. 175-6) [p. 260 A.R.]:

a. excessive cost to the loan;

b. additional security extracted for existing loan, as opposed to a fresh advance (e.g. *Bomek* — to "shore up" existing security (at 153); *TD Bank; Bundy*);

c. the usual application and related documentation taken from the third party is performed in a "cursory"or perfunctory manner (e.g. *Bomek*), is misleading (e.g. *Bomek*), or is non-existent;

d. the advances of the funds are made in an irregular way (e.g. *Bomek*);

e. the disclosure of the nature of the transaction and its risks is inadequate; or

f. the defendant does not receive fair value for the consideration it advances (e.g. *3L Trucking II*, relying on Waters, at 48) — although, as intimated above, a genuine desire to assist a relative, without personal monetary gain, is often considered to be proper "consideration" (e.g. *TD Bank*).

He then goes on to conclude that such an exploitation did not occur. Unfortunately, what he seems to overlook is that by the time Mrs. Ohlson signed the document she was, in fact, providing security for Mr. Ohlson's loan as opposed to obtaining a fresh advance for herself. She was not a primary borrower.

To understand the unfairness involved, it is necessary to understand the fact findings made by the trial judge. He found that the transaction was a loan and that the purpose of the loan was to provide funds to Mr. Ohlson for the purchase of property in California. The trial judge, referring to the evidence of the bank officer stated at A.B. p. 161 [p. 254]:

> He said that the loan was made by the Bank to Mrs. Ohlson, but was advanced directly to Mr. Ohlson, notwithstanding that there was no formal authorization by her of that procedure, because the purpose of the loan was to provide funds to Mr. Ohlson. He said that, had the transfer been processed in the normal procedure, as Mrs. Ohlson was not a customer of the Bank, it would have been necessary for her to open an account and for the Bank to deposit the funds in that account, and from there, to transfer them to Mr. Ohlson's account. He said that it was in order to avoid these formal administrative procedures that the transfer was made directly.

The trial judge also found that the transaction was to be a very short-term transaction and that the proceeds were to come from the California transaction shortly after October 8, 1991.

A specific fact finding was made by the judge that the security given by Mrs. Ohlson was not to support any previous indebtedness. At A.B. p. 184 he states [p. 264 A.R.]:

> 4. *[T]he security Mrs. Ohlson provided was not to support any previous indebtedness owed by Mr. Ohlson to the Bank and it did not further or fully secure the position of the Bank vis-à-vis Mr. Ohlson.* In this regard, I find that the difference between October 3rd (when the overdraft was provided to Mr. Ohlson), October 4th (when Mrs. Ohlson executed the Equitable Mortgage and the Promissory Note), and October 8th (when the funds were advanced), were merely to accommodate the timing of the transaction and that the transaction was not undertaken for the purpose of providing additional security for securing the Bank on previous advances, unconnected with the transaction itself; [Emphasis added.]

Lastly, the trial judge found that Mrs. Ohlson did not attend the Bank until October 4th, the day after the money had been forwarded to Mr. Ohlson for the California transaction.

Having regard to these fact findings, I am of the view that the trial judge erred in his assessment of the transaction. First, if this transaction was a loan to Mrs. Ohlson, there is no consideration for the loan as the funds had already been advanced by the time Mrs. Ohlson had any contact with the Bank. Past consideration is not consideration. This case is quite distinguishable from a case where a primary debtor phones and asks for an advance, receives the advance and then signs a promissory note. In those cases the agreement is in place. On these facts there was no suggestion of a finding that Mrs. Ohlson requested a loan earlier, nor was it suggested her son was her agent for the purpose of doing so.

Secondly, and more importantly, the finding that the security provided did not further or fully secure the unsecured position of the Bank *vis-à-vis* Mr. Ohlson is not supportable when one recognizes that the loan was already advanced. What the trial judge refers to as an advance on October 4th was merely a book entry reducing the overdraft of Mr. Ohlson. The cash for the purchase of the property (which the trial judge found to be the purpose of the loan) was advanced on October 3rd, and the alleged "loan" to the appellant indeed secured the prior advance and so furthered the Bank's position.

When Mrs. Ohlson attended the Bank she did so for the purpose of supporting her son to obtain funds for the California property, and not for past indebtedness. The objective for the loan no longer existed and she was no longer a primary borrower for that purpose.

I recognize that the trial judge seemed to accept that Mrs. Ohlson understood the transaction. However, that does not alter the effect of the timing of this transaction. In any event, her understanding is less than clear. That understanding must be garnered from the evidence and the inferences which that evidence is capable of supporting. Mrs. Ohlson could not testify. The trial judge refused admission into evidence of any portion of her examination-for-discovery. The transcript is replete with ambiguous statements that Mrs. Ohlson understood what she was doing. The memory of Mr. Murray, the Bank's officer, was poor. Moreover, while he thought she understood the transaction he never testified to exactly what it was he thought she understood. He stated:

> The nature of the discussion was we were — we were looking at Mr. Ohlson's current indebtedness to the bank. The ramifications of — of why we were unable to lend directly to Mr. Ohlson would have been presented to — to her at that point in time, which she was already aware of, and it was — it *was the case that she approached the bank to assist her son to secure this financing, this additional $50,000 financing* [A.B. p. 114]. [Emphasis added.]

The $50,000 financing refers to the funds for the California transaction. This evidence alone indicates that it was represented to Mrs. Ohlson that she needed to sign the documentation for her son to receive the funds. That, of course, was not true. To lead her to believe the money was still needed by her son is, in these circumstances, unconscionable.

An analysis of the direct examination of the Bank's employee is telling. The following exchange occurs at A.B. p. 118:

> Q Did you consider it necessary at that time to obtain a formal guarantee from Mrs. Ohlson?
> A No.
> Q And why was that, sir?
> A Because this was a new advance, the — the obligation for Mrs. Ohlson was strictly for this new advance. She was fully cognizant of what was happening with respect to this — this $50,000 advance.

and then again at p. 119:

> Q Okay. Perhaps I can take you back a moment, sir.
> A Sure.

Q On October the 3rd when Mr. Ohlson was permitted to withdraw $60,000 from his checking account —

A Hmm-umm.

Q — did you have in your possession at that time the documents executed by Mrs. Ohlson?

A I — I don't remember specifically, *but I certainly would have speculated that I did.*

Q It's fair to say you wouldn't have allowed that overdraft to take place without those documents in hand?

A *I — I would suggest that's the case, yes.* [Emphasis added.]

This line of questioning demonstrates that the respondent sought to establish that Mrs. Ohlson had signed the documents before the actual advance to Mr. Ohlson. But that is not what the trial judge found. Moreover, while Mr. Murray testified that it was his impression that the appellant understood the transaction, his testimony suggests he thought she likely signed before the advance. How then could his testimony support an inference that she knew the funds were advanced?

Finally, the trial judge could not infer that Mrs. Ohlson was fully aware of all the facts. In my view, he erred in drawing an adverse inference against Mrs. Ohlson because her son did not testify, yet he appears to have done so. He stated (A.B. p. 183) [pp. 263–4 A.R.]:

> [T]he fact that there is no evidence before the Court that Mrs. Ohlson did not understand the nature of the transaction — indeed, the uncontradicted evidence of Mr. Murray was that she did understand the transaction, and while it is clear that Mrs. Ohlson could not testify, the Court cannot take her incapacity to testify as evidence that she did not understand the transaction at the time. Mr. Ohlson was present, and the *failure of Counsel for Mrs. Ohlson to call him to provide evidence that she did not understand the loan supports the inference that she did understand the transaction.* [Emphasis added.]

Mrs. Ohlson's interests and those of her son were in direct conflict in this lawsuit. Mrs. Ohlson is sued in the alternative. The trial judge recognizes this conflict in his judgment. In the end result judgment against Mrs. Ohlson resulted in a dismissal of the Bank's claim against Mr. Ohlson. In such a situation, it is unfair to draw an adverse inference against Mrs. Ohlson.

Nothing supports a conclusion that when Mrs. Ohlson signed the documents she was aware that the money had already been sent.

The evidence is quite to the contrary. Had she known, she may well have concluded, and rightly so, that her son did not need her help. Certainly, had she sought independent legal advice from a lawyer aware of those facts, logic dictates she would have been advised she did not need to sign to obtain the funds, and that the risk was great. This transaction was a short-term loan to the son, based solely on the success of the California deal. There was nothing to gain and everything to lose. Whether she would have accepted that advice is unknown, but it is advice she is entitled to receive.

Thus, in my view, the trial judge erred in failing to find that the Bank gained an unfair advantage from structuring this transaction as a loan rather than a guarantee. The Bank did gain an unfair advantage from its stronger position. The Bank had all the relevant information at the time Mrs. Ohlson attended at the Bank, and was the only party who was at risk relating to the funds for this real estate transaction. The purpose of the transaction had already been met as the funds had been released to the son. The loans officer, who knew that the loan could not be advanced without proper security, had nonetheless proceeded to advance the funds on the faith of the son's word that his mother would sign. It was the Bank's officer who needed this security in place. In my view the Bank cannot rely on its promissory note.

When one properly analyzes the facts in this case it becomes apparent that this transaction was, in substance, a guarantee. The real borrower was the son. The source of repayment was to come from the California transaction. The money was already disbursed. The respondent did not complete a loan application, nor did the Bank officer inquire into her ability to repay the loan. No bank account was opened in Mrs. Ohlson's name and the proceeds were deposited directly into Mr. Ohlson's account. Mrs. Ohlson had no knowledge of the loan particulars or repayment requirements or source. She was there to help out her son, who in reality was the primary debtor. To say otherwise is to allow form to triumph over substance.

The significant advantage gained by the Bank is that it went from being in a position of an unsecured creditor to being a secured creditor without any consideration on its part. What is unfair is that the Bank was able to accomplish this end by structuring a transaction that was in substance a guarantee as though it were a loan. The necessity of independent advice is avoided as a promissory note is excluded from the requirements under the *Guarantees Acknowledgment Act*, R.S.A. 1980, c. G-12. Moreover, the Bank knew the facts and no doubt the son knew the facts. But the evidence does not support a conclusion that Mrs. Ohlson knew the crucial facts.

Looking to (without adopting) the standard set out by Lambert J.A. in *Harry v. Kreutziger, supra*, namely that of seeking guidance as to community standards of commercial morality from legislation that embodies those standards in law, it would be appropriate to look at the *Guarantees Acknowledgment Act* for guidance as to what the community standard requires in order for a lender to meet this standard. A guarantee in the normal case requires independent advice. Thus, where the substance of a transaction is a guarantee, one should examine the transaction carefully to see if it is the kind of transaction which the *Act* is intended to protect. On the facts of this case, I am satisfied that the financial institution having this elderly mother sign a promissory note and equitable mortgage where the transaction is in reality a guarantee of past indebtedness, and thereby vastly improving its position, is unconscionable.

The relationship of elderly parent/adult child is frequently one of dependency and therefore one which can be subject to abuse or pressure. It is a relationship which bears some of the earmarks of a husband/wife relationship. The person who is not gaining from the financial transaction may be subject to pressure arising from the relationship. Dependent relationships are not uncommon to financial institutions and indeed Mr. Murray acknowledged that the Bank has a practice of sending a spouse for independent advice when signing for the other spouse's loan. A financial institution would do well to adopt a similar practice in an elderly parent/adult child transaction where the elderly parent is risking the asset for the sole benefit of the child. Independent advice is required for a guarantee. While the *Guarantees Acknowledgment Act* excludes promissory notes from the definition of "guarantee", that does not authorize a bank to structure as a loan a transaction which is, in substance, a guarantee and thereby avoid the protection the law requires. This, of course, would not apply to third party holders of the note.

Finally, I do not accept that the appellant need call evidence of whether she would have signed the document regardless of the advice received. If the transaction is unconscionable, it is unenforceable.

I would allow the appeal, set aside the judgment and declare the equitable mortgage of no force and effect and direct the return of the title to Mrs. Ohlson.

Appeal allowed.

(IV) Misrepresentation

(k)   *Hedley Byrne & Co. v. Heller & Partners Ltd.*[†]

The plaintiffs, a firm of advertising agents, booked advertising time on television channels and space in newspapers, on behalf of a customer, Easipower Ltd., on terms that they became personally liable. Becoming doubtful of the financial position of Easipower Ltd. they asked their bankers, the National Provincial Bank Ltd. to obtain a report from the defendants, merchant bankers with whom Easipower Ltd. had an account. This was done, in the first place, by telephone conversation in the course of which the defendants said that they believed Easipower "to be respectably constituted and considered good for its normal business engagements" and that "we believe that the company would not undertake any commitments they were unable to fulfil". Three months later, a further inquiry was made by letter as to whether Easipower were "trustworthy ... to the extent of £100,000 per annum

---

[†] [1964] A.C. 465 (H.L.).

advertising contract". The defendants replied in a letter [read]: "Confidential. For your private use and without responsibility on the part of this bank or its officials." The letter continued: "... Respectably constituted company, considered good for its ordinary business engagements. Your figures are larger than we are accustomed to see." The plaintiffs relied on these statements and as a result they lost sums, calculated as £1,766l 18s. 6d., when Easipower went into liquidation. In their statement of claim an allegation of fraud was originally made, but this was abandoned. McNair J. held that the defendants were negligent but that they owed no duty of care to the plaintiffs. The Court of Appeal likewise held that there was no duty of care and it was therefore unnecessary to consider whether the finding of negligence was correct. The House of Lords affirmed the judgment on different grounds.

[LORD REID (after considering the distinction between words and deeds, quoted p. 70, *ante*, and considering earlier authorities including a statement by Lord Haldane in *Robinson v. Bank of Scotland*, 1916 S.C. (H.L.) 154, at p. 157):]

... He speaks of other special relationships and I can see no logical stopping place short of all those relationships where it is plain that the party seeking information or advice was trusting the other to exercise such a degree of care as the circumstances required, where it was reasonable for him to do that, and where the other gave the information or advice when he knew or ought to have known that the inquirer was relying on him. I say "ought to have known" because in questions of negligence we now apply the objective standard of what the reasonable man would have done.

A reasonable man, knowing that he was being trusted or that his skill and judgment were being relied on, would, I think, have three courses open to him. He could keep silent or decline to give the information or advice sought: or he could give an answer with a clear qualification that he accepted no responsibility for it or that it was given without that reflection or inquiry which a careful answer would require: or he could simply answer without any such qualification. If he chooses to adopt the last course he must, I think, be held to have accepted some responsibility for his answer being given carefully, or to have accepted a relationship with the inquirer which require him to exercise such care as the circumstances require....

What the appellants complain of is not negligence in the ordinary sense of carelessness, but rather misjudgment in that Mr. Heller, while honestly seeking to give a fair assessment, in fact made a statement which gave a false and misleading impression of his customer's credit. It appears that bankers now commonly give references with regard to their customers as part of their business. I do not know how far their customers generally permit them to disclose their affairs, but even with permission it cannot always be easy for a banker to reconcile his duty to his customer with his desire to give a fairly balanced reply to an inquiry; and inquirers can hardly expect a full and objective statement of opinion or accurate factual information such as skilled men would be expected to give in reply to other kinds of inquiry. So it seems to me to be unusually difficult to determine just what duty, beyond a duty to be honest, a banker would be held to have undertaken if he gave a reply without an adequate disclaimer of responsibility or other warning....

Here, however, the appellants' bank, who were their agents in making the enquiry, began by saying that "they wanted to know in confidence and without responsibility on our part", i.e. on the part of the respondents. So I cannot see how the appellants can now be entitled to disregard that and maintain that the respondents did incur a responsibility to them.

The appellants founded on a number of cases in contract where very clear words were required to exclude the duty of care which would otherwise have flowed from the contract. To that argument there are, I think, two answers. In the case of a contract it is necessary to exclude liability for negligence, but in this case the question is whether an undertaking to assume a duty to take care can be inferred; and that is a very different matter. Secondly, even in cases of contract general words may be sufficient if there was no other kind of liability to be excluded except liability for negligence: the general rule is that a party is not exempted from liability for negligence "unless adequate words are used" — per Scrutton L.J. in *Rutter v. Palmer*. It being admitted that there was here a duty to give an honest reply, I do not see what further liability there could be to exclude except liability for negligence: there being no contract there was no question of warranty.

I am therefore of opinion that it is clear that the respondents never undertook any duty to exercise care in giving their replies. The appellants cannot succeed unless there was such a duty and therefore in my judgment this appeal must be dismissed.

(I)   *V.K. Mason Construction Ltd. v. Bank of Nova Scotia*†

[WILSON J.:]

The court is confronted in this case with appeals in two lawsuits which have been consolidated. The first lawsuit involved an action on the alternative footing of contract and tort brought by V.K. Mason Construction Ltd. ("Mason"), against the Bank of Nova Scotia ("the Bank"). The second action involved a claim by Mason under the *Mechanics' Lien Act*, R.S.O. 1970, c. 267, as amended, against Courtot Investments Ltd. ("Courtot") and the Bank. The claim against Courtot was settled but the claim against the Bank is before us.

The principal source of dispute in the case is on the facts. There is relatively little disagreement over the applicable legal principles and counsel's presentations were substantially directed to the application of those principles to the facts as they saw them. Fortunately, the court has the advantage of a very thorough and competent judgment by the trial judge, Mr. Justice O'Leary [10 B.L.R. 77]. Despite this the parties, and particularly the Bank in the contract/tort action, spent considerable time referring us to the record in an attempt to undermine his findings of fact. I am satisfied, as was the Ontario Court of Appeal, that these findings are amply supported by the evidence and I therefore approach the case on the basis of the facts as found by the learned trial judge.

1.   THE FACTS

Both actions arose out of the financing and construction of an office and retail shopping complex in Toronto known as the "Courtot Centre". The owner and developer of the complex was Courtot, the general contractor in charge of construction was Mason and the Bank provided bridge financing for the construction, taking as part of its security a mortgage contained in a demand debenture on the property.

Courtot was a valued client of the Bank but was inexperienced in the field of property development. It was also shortsighted in its planning for financial contingencies and failed to obtain adequate funding to cope with rising interest rates and costly

architectural changes implemented subsequent to the project's getting underway. As a consequence the litigation between Mason and the Bank took place in the aftermath of the commercial failure of the Courtot Centre project and the inability of Courtot to raise sufficient financing to meet its indebtedness to its general contractor.

The story commences in March, 1972, when Mason submitted a tender for construction of the project containing the following stipulation:

> Our tender and any contract entered into following acceptance of our tender are conditional upon production to us prior to execution of any construction contract, satisfactory evidence of the ability of the Owner to meet the payments as they become due under such contract.

By July 17, 1972, Mason was prepared to sign a fixed price construction contract with Courtot provided it was satisfied of Courtot's ability to meet the payments. Mason had begun construction before a contract was signed but Mr. Justice O'Leary expressly found at trial that it would not have signed the contract had it' not been for assurances from the Bank. The reason for his conclusion on this point was that Mason's investment in the project up to the time of the signing of the contract was small enough that it would have been able, if it had abandoned the project, to recover its investment from Courtot on a *quantum meruit* basis under the *Mechanics' Lien Act* or otherwise.

Courtot meanwhile had been trying to arrange financing for the project from the Bank. In October, 1971, the Bank rejected his application for bridge financing and in January, 1972, it turned down a further application for a loan of $865,500 to cover pre-construction costs. In February, 1972, however, the latter decision was reversed and by July 6, 1972, the branch manager, Mr. Hway, was prepared to recommend a loan of $9,000,000 to provide bridge financing. By August the Bank decided to loan Courtot $8,850,000 U.S., one of the bases for that decision being the fact that Courtot had been able to arrange a fixed price construction contract with Mason for $6,100,000. The Bank's commitment to Courtot, expressed in the form of a letter approv-

---

† (1985), 16 D.L.R. (4th) 598 at 599–610 (S.C.C.).

ing the loan in principle, was conveyed to Mason but this was not sufficient to convince Mason of Courtot's ability to meet the payments.

The events of August 30th through September 12th are crucial to the case and are covered in detail by Mr. Justice O'Leary. Mason through its solicitor sought assurances from the Bank that Courtot had sufficient financing. There was an exchange of telephone conversations and, although the oral evidence is unclear about the outcome of these conversations, the documentary evidence indicates that as of September 7, 1972, Mason was still not satisfied that Courtot was able to pay the contract price. Mr. Justice O'Leary found that, if Mason had continued to be unsatisfied about Courtot's ability to pay, it would not have continued with the project. He further found that the Bank knew or ought to have known this and that it was apparent that further assurances would be necessary.

Mr. Hway, the branch manager, on September 8, 1972, drafted a letter to Mason giving those assurances. He did not send it immediately but discussed the wording of the letter with the Bank's solicitor on September 11th or 12th. The solicitor did not recommend any changes and on September 12, 1972, the letter was delivered to Mason. It read as follows:

> We wish to advise that we have accorded Courtot Investments Limited interim financing sufficient to cover the construction of the subject complex. We shall therefore provide funds for your progress billings as they occur against architects' certificates (Bregman & Hamann) of work completed subject to the usual search for liens by our solicitor.

Acting upon the strength of this assurance, Mason signed the construction contract with Courtot on September 14, 1972. Construction went ahead and Mason performed its part of the bargain, substantially completing construction in August, 1974. The completion of construction had originally been scheduled for December 31, 1973, but changes in the specifications by Courtot had both added to the cost of construction (which resulted in an agreed increase in the contract price) and delayed the completion date. Mr. Justice O'Leary expressly exonerated Mason from any responsibility for the construction delays.

By April 19, 1974, it had become apparent both to Courtot and to the Bank that the amount of the Bank's loan to Courtot would not cover the cost of construction. The Bank did not, however, offer to extend Courtot more money or agree to Courtot's

request for an extension of the due date of the loan. By July 31, 1974, Courtot had called down $8,413,000 U.S. of the $8,850,000 U.S. which the Bank had agreed to lend it. Rather than call for the rest of the money in order to provide at least part payment to Mason, Courtot tried to find excuses in order to delay paying Mason and then engaged in vexatious litigation against Mason for this purpose. The Bank at no point informed Mason that Courtot had insufficient funds to cover the cost of construction.

By August 30, 1974, Mason had substantially completed construction and had not been paid on architects' certificates dating back as far as July 10, 1974. Mason took out mechanics' liens on the property for $1,057,941.98 in work for which it had not been paid. In August, 1975, the Bank demanded payment from Courtot on its loans and exercised its power of sale of the Courtot Centre as mortgagee under the demand debenture. On February 9, 1976, the complex was sold for $11,000,000.

In December, 1977, Mason settled its mechanics' lien action against Courtot and Courtot acceded to the entry of judgment in favour of Mason in the amount of $1,427,487.17. The Bank asserted its priority as mortgagee over the proceeds of the sale and, after it had been paid, there were insufficient funds to pay Mason in full. In the mechanics' lien action, therefore, Mason asserted that by virtue of s. 4 of the *Interest Act*, R.S.C. 1970, c. I-18, the Bank was limited to interest at the rate of 5%. The learned trial judge agreed with this submission and the result was that, by reducing the amount of the Bank's claim, Mason would be enabled to have its claim satisfied out of the proceeds of the sale. Mason had also argued that the Bank was estopped from asserting its priority as mortgagee but, in light of his ruling on the *Interest Act* point, the learned trial judge did not find it necessary to make a ruling on this issue.

Returning to the contract and tort action, Mr. Justice O'Leary found on the facts as stated above that there was a contract between Mason and the Bank and that the Bank had breached that contract. He awarded damages in the amount of $1,057,941.98. The trial judge also found that the Bank was liable to Mason on the alternative basis of negligent misrepresentation. Specifically, he found that the representation in the Bank's letter of September 8, 1972, was false in that the Bank had not committed itself to provide sufficient funds to Courtot to complete the project but only a specified sum of money toward the financing of the project. Furthermore, Mr. Justice O'Leary found that, even at the date the statement was made, the amount of the Bank's loan to Courtot was significantly less than the projected cost of the project, a fact known to the Bank. The learned trial judge awarded damages of $897,941.98 for negligent misrepresentation, this sum being calculated by removing Mason's projected profit of $160,000 from the value of the contract damages.

The Bank's appeal in both actions was heard by Houlden, Goodman and Cory JJ.A. At the conclusion of argument Houlden, J.A. gave an oral judgment for the court [39 O.R. (2d) 630, 19 B.L.R. 136]. With respect to the contract/tort action, he dismissed the Bank's appeal with respect to the breach of contract claim and did not find it necessary to comment on the negligent misrepresentation issue. With respect to the mechanics' lien case, he allowed the Bank's appeal, holding that s. 4 of the *Interest Act* was inapplicable in this case because the Bank's loan was a mortgage on real estate and therefore expressly excluded from the operation of the section. He further held that the Bank was not estopped from asserting its priority as mortgagee over Mason under the *Mechanics' Lien Act*.

2. THE ISSUES

The issues in the two actions may be conveniently dealt with under four main headings, namely: (1) contract; (2) negligent misrepresentation; (3) s. 4 of the *Interest Act*; and (4) estoppel.

It might, however, be useful at the outset to put the case in perspective. This is not a simple situation in which a bank makes a representation about the creditworthiness of one of its clients to a third party. This is a case in which the Bank made a representation to a third party for the specific purpose of inducing the third party to enter into a contract with one of the Bank's own clients, thereby enabling that client to enter into a substantial loan transaction with the Bank. I do not think it is realistic to portray the Bank manager, Mr. Hway, as an inexperienced person who had no motive or intention to mislead anyone. It is quite clear that Mr. Hway wished to check the letter with the Bank's solicitor precisely because he realized that the Bank was inducing Mason to enter into a contract and he wanted to avoid the prospect of the Bank's incurring a liability to Mason.

Mr. Hway, like Courtot, no doubt thought that the transaction would be a profitable one. Had Courtot been able to arrange permanent mortgage financing or find a buyer for the building there would have been no problem about the shortfall in the Bank's bridge financing. Unfortunately for all concerned, the market for commercial properties in that part of Toronto was soft at the time Courtot was looking for commercial tenants for the centre. Also, Courtot was caught by having a floating interest loan at a time when interest rates were rising, thereby significantly increasing the amount of interest which it owed to the Bank. Furthermore, having taken out a loan in U.S. funds Courtot was hurt by currency fluctuations which resulted from the strength of the Canadian dollar as compared to the American dollar. Finally, Mr. Courtot was, as already mentioned, an inexperienced developer and he had not allowed himself sufficient flexibility by taking contingencies of this kind into account in arranging his financing. As a result the project, from Courtot's perspective at least, was a failure and the contest among the creditors was on.

(1) Contract

Mr. Sopinka, counsel for the Bank, put forward three main lines of argument against the existence of a contract in this case, namely; (1) absence of an intention on the part of the Bank and Mason to create legal relations between themselves; (2) absence of offer and acceptance; and (3) absence of consideration. He submitted, moreover, that even if there was a contract between Mason and the Bank there was no breach of it by the Bank.

It seems to me that if there were a contract in existence between these two parties it must be characterized, in terms of traditional contract analysis, as a unilateral contract. The Bank's letter to Mason would, on this analysis, be construed as an offer that, if Mason would sign a fixed price contract with Courtot, the Bank would supply Courtot with sufficient interim financing to complete the project. Mason was entitled to accept this offer either by communication or by performance, *i.e.*, by signing the contract with Courtot: see *Carlill v. Carbolic Smoke Ball Co.*, [1893] 1 Q.B. 256 (C.A.). The consideration which passed to the Bank would be that Mason had obligated itself to Courtot to enter into a fixed price contract, thereby giving the Bank the assurance that the project was sufficiently sound that it could lend money to Courtot.

The problem with this analysis is that it requires a great deal to be implied into the course of conduct of the parties. By implying a contract into this course of conduct one is left unsure of the exact nature of the Bank's obligations. Was the Bank obliged to advance money to Courtot so that Mason would be paid even if Courtot did not demand the money? The trial judge held, in effect, that it was, but I find it difficult to say that sophisticated business people, taking into account the course of conduct leading up to the Bank's statement, would construe the September 8, 1972 letter as imposing that kind of obligation. It is, of course, always a matter of judgment whether the requisite certainty of intention exists as a foundation for implying a contract out of a combination of documents and a course of conduct. I tend to view this as a case which falls on the far side of the line in the sense that I do not believe that reasonable business people would have construed the Bank's letter as an absolute and unqualified guarantee, which is what the courts below have effectively held.

Negligent misrepresentation is, in my view, the appropriate basis of liability in this case. The disadvantage in implying a contract in a commercial context like this is that much of the value of commercial contracts lies in their ability to produce certainty. Parties are enabled to regulate their relationship by means of their understanding of what each others actions are intended to imply. I think this is one reason why the common law imposes an objective rather than a subjective test for the creation of an agreement. The objective test is important because it prevents parties from avoiding obligations which a reasonable person would assume they had undertaken, simply on the ground that there is no document embodying the precise nature of the obligation. On the other hand, if too broad a view is taken of what a reasonable person assumes will give rise to an agreement or obligation, the certainty which is one of the principle virtues of contract may be undermined. Obviously, there are circumstances in which a Bank's conduct could give rise to contractual liability as a guarantor, but I do not believe that this case falls into that category. I conclude therefore that there was no contractual relationship between the Bank and Mason.

(2) Negligent misrepresentation

It seems to me that a negligent misrepresentation analysis properly focuses attention on the gravamen of the cause of action in this case, namely, the fact that the Bank's representation to Mason was false. The parties are in agreement that the applicable law is to be found in the decision of the House of Lords in *Hedley Byrne & Co. Ltd. v. Heller & Partners Ltd.*, [1964] A.C. 465, [1963] 2 All E.R. 575, [1963] 1 Lloyds Rep. 485 (H.L.). Mr. Sopinka sums up the requirements for liability as follows: (a) there must be an untrue statement; (b) it must have been

made negligently; (c) there must be a special relationship giving rise to a duty of care; and (d) there must be reliance which is foreseeable. His submission to the court comprised a reconstruction of the facts to show that none of these prerequisites was present. His problem is that Mr. Justice O'Leary made very clear findings of fact against the Bank on all four requirements.

The main difficulty I have with Mr. Sopinka's approach to the facts is that he attempts to isolate them from their context when it is the context that gives them meaning. For example, with respect to the falsity of the September 8, 1972 letter, Mr. Sopinka attempts to show that, on the basis of Courtot's estimates of total project costs minus soft costs, the Bank was justified in representing that it was loaning Courtot sufficient money to complete the project. This seems to me to completely overlook the fact that what Mason was seeking was an assurance that Courtot would have sufficient funds at a time when Mason already knew the basic terms of the Bank's loan to Courtot. In other words, the September 8, 1972 letter would, as the Bank knew, be construed as an assurance of something over and above the terms of the loan, yet the Bank went ahead and gave that assurance relying solely on the terms of the loan and Courtot's cost estimates. Mr. Hway may have felt at the time that he was justified in his hope that the soft costs would not materialize before permanent financing had been secured, but he was not justified in assuring Mason that there would be sufficient funds without informing them that his assurance was based on the assumption that soft costs would not be incurred.

The same general comment can be made with respect to Mr. Sopinka's submissions on negligence, particularly in relation to special relationship and reliance. The Bank had a special relationship with Mason because it was inducing Mason to sign a contract with Courtot in reliance on the Bank's assurance of adequate financing. The statement was negligent because it was made without revealing that the Bank was giving an assurance based solely on a loan arrangement which Mason had already said was insufficient assurance to it of the existence of adequate financing.

Not only was the Bank's misrepresentation made negligently but it is clear from the finding of fact of Mr. Justice O'Leary that Mason relied on it and that such reliance was foreseeable by the Bank. I believe therefore that all the requirements for negligent misrepresentation are met in this case.

One of the interesting legal issues with respect to negligent misrepresentation is the issue of damages. Mason cross-appealed on this issue. The Bank concedes that in principle the proper aim of a damage award is to restore the plaintiff to the position in which he would have been if the negligent misrepresentation had never been made: see *McGregor on Damages*, 14th ed. (1980), p. 996. The Bank argues that Mason would have lost money in any event even if the misrepresentation had not been made because it would have lost money in severing its relationship with Courtot. The problem with this submission is that the trial judge made an express finding to the contrary. What we have to assume, I believe, is that but for the misrepresentation Mason would have ceased work for Courtot, recovered its expenses for work already done and found another construction project to work on.

The learned trial judge awarded damages for misrepresentation on the basis that they were equal to contract damages minus Mason's anticipated profit. Counsel for Mason submits that the trial judge was wrong in subtracting the anticipated profit because damages in contract and tort are the same. He also submitted that interest should have been awarded on the damages at 12% from the completion of the project on October 7, 1974. While I tend to the view that there is a conceptual difference between damages in contract and in tort, I believe that in many instances the same quantum will be arrived at, albeit by somewhat different routes.

I agree with the submission of counsel for Mason that the trial judge was wrong in subtracting profit. I believe that in principle one is entitled to assume that Mason would have found a profitable means of employing itself had it not been induced to work on the Courtot project by the Bank's misrepresentation. This, in my view, is a reasonably foreseeable head of damage: see *Patrick L. Roberts Ltd. v. Sollinger Industries Ltd. and Ontario Development Corp.* (1978), 84 D.L.R. (3d) 113, 19 O.R. (2d) 44, 3 B.L.R. 174 (Ont. C.A.). In equating Mason's lost profit with the profit estimated on the Courtot project we are simply saying that this is a reasonable estimate of what Mason would have been likely to have made of it had it decided to abandon the Courtot project and find other work. That is to say, the lost profit on *this* contract represents the lost opportunity for profit on the Courtot project it might be disentitled to an award of the entire amount of that profit in tort damages, but this would be so only because it was not reasonably foreseeable that it would have made a similarly exceptional profit on some other contract.

On the basis of the same reasoning it seems to me that Mason ought to be entitled to prejudgment

interest as of the date of completion of the project. In other words, to put Mason in the position it would have been in [the absence of] the misrepresentation we must assume that it would have in hand at the time it completed the project that amount of outlay and anticipated profit which it lost in completing the project. It seems to me to be only reasonable to assume that it would have been able to put that money to profitable use. Interest is the court's way of compensating Mason for the loss of the opportunity to invest that money.

I note that in connection with the issue of negligent misrepresentation the learned trial judge found that the Bank had a duty to warn Mason in April, 1974, that Courtot did not have enough money to complete the project. This, in my view, is a separate (although related) head of liability. However, because the original negligent misrepresentation encompasses a greater liability than the duty to warn, I do not consider it necessary to deal with this aspect of the case.

(3) Section 4 of the Interest Act

I do not believe there is any merit in Mason's appeal on this issue. As Mr. Robinette points out, it would be elevating form over substance to characterize the transaction between the Bank and Courtot as something other than a mortgage on real estate simply because the Bank took other security in addition to the mortgage contained in the demand debenture. Throughout its pleadings and argument Mason concedes that the Bank is a mortgagee but it is attempting to suggest that the meaning of a "mortgage on real estate" in s. 4 of the *Interest Act* is somehow different from its meaning in any other context. I cannot accept this.

Furthermore, I believe that the Bank's interpretation of s. 4 is much more in accord with the legislative purpose of the *Interest Act*. Section 4 is consumer protection law in the sense that, with respect to loans other than real estate mortgages, consumers are entitled to know the annual rate of interest they are paying. A sophisticated commercial borrower like Courtot, who in this case was borrowing at a floating rate of interest, is in scant need of protection by being informed of his rate of interest at the annual, rather than the 360-day, rate. More to the point, as Mr. Robinette points out, since the section allows a borrower to escape from what would otherwise be a valid arm's length financial transaction, it is unfair to adopt a construction which does not take account of the legitimate interests of the lender. I do not think that either the letter or the policy of the law supports the interpretation urged on the court by Mason and I would affirm the Court of Appeal's decision on this issue.

(4) Estoppel

This issue was not pursued in great depth by the parties. I believe, however, that this is not a case for the application of promissory estoppel simply on the ground that the Bank never represented that it would not rely on its priority as mortgage; see *Re Tudale Explorations Ltd. and Bruce* (1978), 88 D.L.R. (3d) 584, 20 O.R. (2d) 593 (Ont. H.C.). Accordingly I do not see how Mason could make out a case of detrimental reliance with respect to its mechanics' lien.

While the case of *Elmvale Lumber Co. Ltd. v. Laurin* (1977), 77 D.L.R. (3d) 711, 16 O.R. (2d) 241 (Ont. S.C.), seems to support Mason, the weight of appellate authority appears to be in the other direction. This may represent less of an anomaly than one might think since I suspect that someone in Mason's position will often be able to recoup its losses in damages for negligent will be more comprehensive than an estoppel with respect to a mechanics' lien. The reason for this is that in a mechanics' lien action the mechanic can only call on his share of the proceeds of the sale of claimants. Postponement of the mortgagee's priority on the lien gives him a better chance of being paid in full but it is no assurance. In a negligent misrepresentation action, however, the mechanic can call on the full assets of the mortgagee (including the proceeds of the exercise of the mortgagee's priority on the sale of the property) and he does not have to compete with other lien claimants unless, of course, they also have a cause of action for negligent misrepresentation. Accordingly I think the Court of Appeal was correct on this issue.

3. CONCLUSIONS

(1) The Bank is not liable to Mason in contract but is liable in negligent misrepresentation.

(2) Although damages for negligent misrepresentation would normally be assessed in terms of actual loss, including lost opportunity, rather than loss of anticipated profit, in this case the commercial context in which the parties operated dictates that Mason's loss should be calculated in the same way in tort as it would be in contract. Mason is accordingly entitled to damages in the sum of $1,138,151.63, being the entire balance outstanding under its contract with Courtot, plus interest on this amount at the rate of 9% from February 9, 1976, as ordered by the Court of Appeal.

(3) The Bank's claim to interest is not limited by s. 4 of the *Interest Act* since the Bank's loan constitutes a mortgage on real estate.

(4) The Bank is not estopped from asserting its priority over Mason's lien since it made no representation that it would not assert such priority.

4. DISPOSITION

In accordance with the foregoing reasons I would dismiss the appeal of the Bank in the contract/tort action. I would allow the cross-appeal of Mason and vary the judgment of the Court of Appeal to award Mason prejudgement interest at the rate of 9% per annum from October 7, 1974 to March 21, 1980. I would award no costs of the appeal or cross-appeal.

I would dismiss the appeal in the mechanics' lien action with costs.

Appeals and cross-appeal dismissed.

(m) *Sugar v. Peat Marwick Ltd.*†

[SOUTHEY J.:]

The plaintiffs sue to recover an investment of about $250,000 in a business that failed. Their invest-ment was in Dimension Furniture Ltd. ("Newco"), a corporation which purchased the assets of Dimension Furniture Design Canada Ltd. ("Oldco") in September, 1983, from the defendant Peat Marwick

---

† (1988), 66 O.R. (2d) 766 (Ont. H.C.) at 767–83.

Limited ("Peats") as receiver and manager and trustee in bankruptcy of Oldco. The defendant bank had appointed Peats as receiver and manager and was the petitioning creditor in the bankruptcy. Newco continued the furniture manufacturing business of Oldco for about 18 months, but without success. Newco went into bankruptcy in June 1985, again on a petition of the bank. The plaintiffs lost all the money they had invested in Newco.

The plaintiffs claim that the bank had knowledge at the time of the sale to Newco of a substantial falsification of the books and records of Oldco pertaining to the accounts receivable of the company. It is common ground that the bank gave no warning of any such falsification to Stanley Sugar ("Sugar"). Sugar is the husband of the plaintiff, Sandra Sugar, and he had acted on behalf of his wife in investigating Oldco and in negotiating the purchase of its assets. Newco was a company incorporated for the purpose of purchasing the assets of Oldco and continuing its business. Sandra Sugar invested money in Newco. The corporate plaintiff, 582087 Ontario Limited, was incorporated after the purchase. It is wholly owned by Sandra Sugar and assumed her investment in Newco. The plaintiffs claim that they would not have invested in Newco, if the bank had disclosed to Sugar its knowledge of the falsifications.

The falsifications resulted in a gross overstatement of the accounts receivable of Oldco in statements and reports prepared by or for Jacqueline and Thomas Klein, the principal shareholders and operators of Oldco. These statements were subsequently used by Peats in its reports and statements at the time of the sale of assets.

THE ISSUES

Among the grounds on which the plaintiffs' claim is based is the allegation that the conduct of the bank and Peats amounted to a fraudulent or negligent misrepresentation as to the state of the accounts receivable. Alternatively, even if there was no misrepresentation, the plaintiffs claim that the bank was guilty of breach of a fiduciary duty owed by it to the plaintiffs as valued customers. It is further submitted that the bank is liable simply because it remained silent at the time of the purchase without disclosing facts which would have led the Sugars to refrain from becoming involved in the purchase.

The issues are complicated by the fact that the Kleins, who were responsible for the falsifications, continued in the business until August, 1984, as owners of 50% of the shares of Newco and managers of its operations. In addition, and perhaps of greater

significance, Sugar admittedly became aware of the falsifications in January, 1984, yet continued to cause the plaintiffs to increase their investment in Newco, and the bank to increase its loans to Newco, without making the claims now asserted in this action. These claims were not made until this action was commenced in May, 1985.

Sugar did not inform the bank of his discovery of the falsifications until a meeting on October 18, 1984. It was at that meeting, according to Sugar, that a statement was made by Peter De Guerre, an employee of the bank, which revealed to Sugar for the first time that the bank had been aware all along of the falsifications. Only then, Sugar says, did Sugar become aware of the actionable conduct of the bank. The claim made at that time was for an adjustment of the purchase price. That was a contractual claim and could be asserted only by Newco. Newco is now bankrupt, and the claims in the action are on behalf of the investors in Newco, and are founded primarily in tort or breach of fiduciary duty.

The bank denies having knowledge of the falsifications at the time of the purchase. The bank also denies that any representation as to the validity of the accounts receivable of Oldco was made by Peats or the bank, or was relied upon by Sugar, or that there was any special relationship between the bank and the Sugars which gave rise to a fiduciary duty by the bank to the plaintiffs. The bank further relies on an "As is, Where is" clause in the agreement of purchase and sale, which confirmed that Peats gave no warranty or condition with respect to the assets sold. Finally, the bank asserts that the Sugars' delay in informing the bank of the falsifications gives rise to an estoppel.

WHAT KNOWLEDGE AND BELIEF AS TO THE FALSIFICATIONS DID THE BANK HAVE AT THE TIME OF THE PURCHASE BY NEWCO?

The bank became concerned in August, 1983, about the safety of its loan to Oldco, which then exceeded $600,000. An important part of the bank's security was the accounts receivable of Oldco, which had been reported by the Kleins as having a face value of $592,119. On August 18, 1983, De Guerre and Klaus Spies, another inspector in the special loans department of the bank, attended at the premises of Oldco. They examined the files of the company relating to accounts receivable and discovered, from spot checks made within a period of several hours, that there was a substantial number of cases in which the price of goods ordered had been entered in the accounts receivable, when the goods had not yet been manufactured, let alone delivered. These entries reflected situations in which the customers could not have been under any legal obligation to pay for the goods, so that the accounts receivable had not yet come into existence. The practice was described as "pre-billing". Its effect was to overstate the amount of the accounts receivable, and De Guerre considered it to be fraudulent.

Because he had made only a cursory examination, De Guerre could not have known with any certainty the extent of the falsifications due to pre-billing. The evidence is conflicting as to what he suspected or believed the extent to be. Sugar's evidence is that De Guerre said at the meeting on October 18, 1984, that he could find valid accounts receivable in August, 1983, of only $150,000 or so. De Guerre's evidence was that Sugar's recollection and notes of what he said at the meeting were inaccurate, and that what he, De Guerre, had said was that the bank inspectors thought the accounts receivable were overstated by $100,000 to $150,000. As accounts receivable of almost $600,000 had been reported to the bank by the Kleins, this would have left valid accounts receivable of $450,000 to $500,000.

The evidence of Spies, the other bank inspector who accompanied De Guerre on the visit to Oldco on August 18, 1983, confirmed that they had found a number of instances of pre-billing. In a memorandum written in April, 1985, he said they had estimated that receivables were overstated by about $150,000. On the other hand, he acknowledged that he had made no effort to correct a report dated August 25, 1983, written by the acting manager of the Alness & Supertest branch at which the Oldco account was located, that some $200,000 of the listed receivables were suspected to be merely orders in hand, and that the real value of the receivables "on a stress collection basis" was estimated at some $150,000. Spies accepted that this report was probably based on information received from him. I assume that the valuation of the accounts receivable on a "stress collection basis" would be considerably lower than that at which they would be included in a sale of the assets of the company as a going concern.

I find as a fact on the foregoing evidence that Spies and De Guerre believed, as a result of their investigations at Oldco on August 18, 1983, that the accounts receivable reports and records of Oldco had been falsely inflated by as much as $200,000.

It is undisputed that Sugar was given no warning by the bank of any suspected falsification in the accounts receivable records of Oldco before he

arranged for the purchase of the assets of Oldco. The purchase by Newco, which involved the investment of funds by Sandra Sugar, avoided for the time being a loss to the bank in the bankruptcy of Oldco, which Spies estimated might have been as much as $200,000.

The difficult legal issue in the case is whether the silence of the bank regarding its knowledge and belief as to the falsifications constituted in the circumstances a misrepresentation to Sugar, on which he relied, respecting the validity of the accounts receivable entries. The determination of this question requires an examination of the roles played by Sugar and Peats.

SUGAR'S CONDUCT AND CAPABILITIES AND HIS RELIANCE ON PEATS

Sugar was a chartered accountant and a sophisticated businessman. He had been considering a purchase of another company in August, 1983, when his brother Harvey, who was engaged in a branch of the furniture business, suggested he get in touch with the Kleins. The Kleins told Sugar that they had a very viable business, but they needed someone to act as financial controller and to provide them with additional working capital of $200,000 or more. One of the bank's documents contained the statement that Sugar and his brother Harvey had reportedly had previous success in restoring the health of ailing businesses.

Sugar was provided with the financial statements of Oldco for the past few years, and he prepared an analysis of them. He said he did not go behind the statements and look at the company's books. His analysis showed a company that was recovering from a disastrous loss, and appeared to have "turned the corner". He decided against investing in Oldco in August, however, because its debt load was too great. The investigations of Oldco by Sugar and the discussions with the Kleins in August, 1983, took place over 10 to 12 days.

Sugar was approached again by the Kleins in mid-September. They told him their relationship with the bank was deteriorating, and that the bank had threatened to call their loan and appoint a receiver. Sugar told them he would be interested in making a deal to purchase the assets, if a receiver was appointed. Peats was appointed receiver and manager on September 14th, and on September 15th, Sugar, accompanied by his lawyer and a business advisor, met with the Kleins to discuss the purchase of the assets of Oldco. The meeting took place at the Toronto General Hospital where Mrs. Klein was receiving treatment. The discussions contemplated the formation of a new company, in which the Kleins would have a 50% interest, after repayment of the investment to be made by the Sugars. The Kleins would continue to direct the sales and manufacturing aspects of the business. The Kleins told Sugar that they thought a price of $450,000 would be required for acquisition of the assets.

On September 20th, Sugar met with Joseph Atkins, the officer of Peats in charge of the receivership of Oldco, at the offices of the bank's solicitors, Strathy, Archibald and Seagram. Sugar and Atkins reached a firm agreement as to the basis of a purchase of the assets of Oldco. The total price would be $450,000, of which $65,000 would be paid in cash on closing, with the balance to be financed by loans from the bank. The portion of the purchase price allocated to accounts receivable was $330,000, with that amount to be adjusted up or down on closing in accordance with any variation in the book value of the accounts receivable from a total of $400,000. Atkins insisted that there be no delay in concluding an agreement. He said that he must have an agreement in writing by the end of the week, Friday, September 23rd, or he would close the business and liquidate the assets on Monday, September 26th.

A written agreement was prepared by Andrew Brands of the Strathy firm for the sale of the assets by Peats as receiver and manager and trustee in bankruptcy of Oldco to Newco, a company to be incorporated. The agreement was made as of September 23, 1983, and was signed on that day on behalf of Newco by Jacqueline Klein, as president, and Sugar as general manager. Jacqueline Klein and Thomas Klein consented in writing to the terms of the agreement. The purchase was completed in escrow on September 26, 1983. The bank entered into a loan agreement with Newco on that date, to which the Kleins and Stanley, Harvey and Sandra Sugar consented. The Kleins executed a formal acknowledgment under seal acknowledging that Newco was purchasing the accounts receivable of Oldco based on the representations and warranties of the Kleins, that the collectable portion of such accounts receivable would be not less than $300,000, and that the Sugars were loaning money to and investing money in the capital of Newco based on such representations and warranties. The Kleins agreed to indemnify Newco for any amount by which the collectable portion of the accounts receivable was less than $300,000 or, alternatively, to indemnify Stanley and Sandra Sugar for 50% of such deficiency.

It was emphasized in the evidence that there was no suggestion, prior to closing, of any problem with the accounts receivable, or of any pre-billing or fraud. Sugar spent several days at the Oldco premises prior to closing, but said he was unable to examine the accounts receivable ledger because it was in the possession of the receiver and manager or of Mrs. Klein in the hospital. All witnesses agreed that the books and records were in bad shape. The ledgers were written up only to July 31st. The bookkeeper was on holidays. Sugar telephoned some of the Oldco customers to determine the outstanding balances of their accounts, but many would give him no information.

Sugar received from John Rivière of Peats a series of typewritten documents marked exs. A to F, prepared by Peats as part of their assessment of the affairs of Oldco done by Peats for the bank. Exhibit A showed accounts receivable (unaudited) at July 31, 1983, in an estimated amount of $592,000. The accounts receivable values at August 19, 1983, were estimated in ex. B at $505,000 for book value and $300,000 for realizable value. In the cash flow projections for the period ending February 28, 1984, cash receipts from accounts receivable were shown at $475,000, which allows a loss of $30,000 for doubtful accounts. Sugar testified that he relied on these documents as showing what Peats had learned about Oldco. I accept that evidence as meaning that he relied on the statements as showing what Peats had found in the books and records of Oldco.

Sugar also received from Peats on September 23rd, the day the agreement was signed, two untyped lists of the outstanding balances for all customers to September 14, 1983. These were prepared by the Kleins or employees of Oldco. They showed total balances ranging from $400,000 to $410,000. I am satisfied that Sugar relied on these statements as well as accurately reflecting the books and records of Oldco.

All of the statements provided to Sugar by Peats were based on the accounting records of Oldco which De Guerre and Spies knew had been falsified.

The accounts receivable were adjusted at closing to $405,955 in a statement prepared by Peats for the purpose of determining the adjusted purchase price. The escrow was lifted on September 28th, notwithstanding a disagreement as to the manner of adjusting the accounts receivable. By letter of that date, Sugar's solicitors proposed that the matter by settled in one of two ways:

(i) adjustments be made from an opening book value of accounts receivable of

$402,883.00 which is the assumption that the Purchaser made at the time of entering into the agreement of purchase and sale; or

(ii) an accurate determination be made of the accounts receivable by way of circulating such accounts receivable, verifying accounts receivable with the Purchaser accepting all risks of collectability being the rationale for the discrepancy between the $400,000.00 book value and the $330,000.00 allocation to accounts receivable.

The letter concluded with these prophetic words:

If neither of the above alternatives are acceptable to the Vendor we once again stress to you difficulties will arise when the adjustments are to be finalized.

It is clear that Atkins was pressing Sugar to proceed with extraordinary haste to make the purchase, and that Sugar did so against the specific advice of his accountant that he carefully check the accounts receivable. Sugar was keen to complete the deal and get on with the business of Newco. Any break in the continuity of operations would probably have caused costly problems with customers, suppliers and employees. Any delay in the sale would have resulted in a rapid decline in the value of the assets. It was in the interests of both sides to avoid delay.

THE ROLE OF PEATS

There were no significant direct communications between the bank and Sugar prior to the purchase. Sugar was dealing with Peats, and their solicitors (who were the bank's solicitors) and with the Kleins. The role of Peats' employees requires careful consideration, not only because they were the persons communicating with Sugar, but also because they made reports to the bank, which both De Guerre and Spies say they relied upon as satisfying their concerns about the accounts receivable, and provide the reason why they gave no warning to Sugar of the falsifications.

Peats had been instructed on the day after the visit by De Guerre and Spies to make a viability study of Oldco. The representatives of Peats were told that the bank's inspectors had been unable to find some of the supporting documentation for the accounts receivable and Peats was asked, while its representatives were there, to check for missing documents, with particular attention being paid to two large accounts, De Boers and the Art Shoppe. On the basis of a random check one afternoon of De Boers and Art Shoppe files, and those of 10 to 20 other customers by Rivière, it was reported by Peats to the bank that there were no documents missing in connection with the accounts receivable. The significance of this report is greatly reduced by the fact that no one at the bank had told any employee of Peats that the bank had found the falsification of records by pre-billing. Peats was told only that documents appeared to be missing. All Rivière did was to check that the normal supporting documents were present. If he had been told of the discovery by De Guerre and Spies of the falsification records, he would no doubt have scrutinized the dates in the documents.

I cannot believe, in these circumstances, that the report by Rivière of Peats that there were no documents missing could have led De Guerre and Spies to believe that they had been mistaken in thinking that they had discovered fraudulent entries, or otherwise affects the legal significance of their failure to warn Sugar of the falsifications.

DID THE BANK MAKE A MISREPRESENTATION?

The result of my findings is this: that the bank stood by and let the Sugars invest in Newco without warning them of the bank's discovery that the books of Oldco had been falsified. Statements containing the false total of accounts receivable were furnished by Peats to Sugar, and were relied on [by] him in proceeding with the investment. There is no evidence that Peats knew them to be false. If Peats had known them to be false, the use of those statements would have constituted a fraudulent misrepresentation by Peats.

Peats was initially appointed by the bank to make investigations of Oldco, and then to monitor its affairs. Later, it was appointed by the bank as receiver and manager of the undertaking, property and assets of Oldco under the security held by the bank. Peats was being paid by the bank, and the bank's solicitors acted for Peats in connection with the sale of assets. There is evidence that Peats acted on the instructions of the bank, and no evidence of Peats receiving instructions from any other creditor. Although Peats was not an agent of the bank in its capacity as trustee in bankruptcy, I am satisfied that one of the capacities in which Peats was acting in dealing with Sugar was as agent of the bank. De Guerre and Spies must have known that Peats was providing Sugar with the statements which the bank knew was false. In the circumstances, in my judgment, the bank was guilty of fraud.

The relevant law is stated as follows in *Chitty on Contracts*, 25th ed. (1983), vol. I, p. 228:

> Again, if one agent makes a statement honestly believing it to be true, but another agent or the principal himself knows that it is not true, knows that the statement will be or has been made, and deliberately abstains from intervening, the principal will be liable. In these circumstances the party with the guilty knowledge can himself be treated as being guilty of fraud.

SUGAR'S KNOWLEDGE AND LACK OF CARE

I accept the evidence of Sugar that he was unaware of the falsification of the accounts receivable records at the time the purchase of assets was completed, and that he did not find out about it until late December, 1983.

On the other hand, it is clear that Sugar was being advised to check the accounts receivable before completing the transaction. According to L.S. Rosen, a chartered accountant called to give evidence on behalf of the plaintiffs, it would have been an obvious thing to do in the circumstances. But Sugar did not do it. As Mr. Crane pointed out, Sugar deliberately took a chance on the validity of the accounts receivable. He may have been negligent in so doing, but it is no defence to the claim for fraud against the bank that he might have discovered the falsity by the exercise of reasonable care (*Chitty on Contracts*, p. 223).

THE MATERIALITY OF THE INDUCEMENT

The evidence as to the extent of the falsifications is conflicting. Sugar calculated them to be $289,464, leaving a balance of genuine accounts receivable at closing of only $116,491. These figures are quite inconsistent with a letter written by Sugar's solicitor, dated December 16, 1983, informing the bank's solicitors that:

> ... it appears that the accurate calculation of the accounts receivable that were acquired by Dimension Furniture Ltd. ... was $333,313.00. As of November 30, 1983, $189,944.00 of the said amount was collected and the balance is still outstanding.

It would appear from that letter that the falsifications would not have totalled more than about $200,000. The expert witnesses who testified on this subject — L.S. Rosen for the plaintiffs and Michael Beber for the defendants — gave totals in the range of $200,000 to $290,000.

It is unnecessary to determine the extent of the falsifications, provided it was such that Sugar, if he had known of it, would not have caused his family to invest in Newco. I am satisfied from the evidence that the falsification totalled at least $150,000, and that Sugar would not have proceeded with the investment if he had known of them. As was explained by L.S. Rosen, if Sugar had known the true state of the accounts receivable, it would have appeared to him not that Oldco had "turned the corner", but that Oldco remained a very sick company that would not have been a reasonable investment.

SUGAR'S DELAY IN REPORTING THE FRAUD TO THE BANK

After the purchase of Newco was completed, and Sugar had taken over control of the accounting of the business, he instructed that a new list of accounts receivable be prepared in which each invoice number was listed. When this was completed in late October or early November, 1983, it showed a total at September 30, 1983, of $349,072, which was more than $50,000 less than the figure used at the closing on September 28, 1983. This total was further reduced later by Mrs. Klein to $335,935. Sugar accepted Mrs. Klein's explanation that the books had not been kept up to date, and that the figure used on closing was simply inaccurate. Sugar informed the bank of the discrepancy in the accounts receivable total, and arranged for the bank to change the margin requirements for the Newco loan, because the accounts receivable were less than what they were believed to have been at the time of closing.

Sugar's evidence is that he did not discover the existence of the falsification of the accounts receivable until the latter part of December, 1983, when the Kleins were away on vacation. Sugar did some "digging" at that time, and found from a partial analysis that there was pre-billing to the extent of $100,000 to $150,000. He did not confront the Kleins with his discovery immediately upon their return, because he needed their help in operating the enterprise which he was struggling to keep alive. He finally confronted them with the pre-billing at a meeting on January 30, 1984, in the presence of lawyers for both Sugar and the Kleins, and Mrs. Klein's father, who had invested in the business. There was no denial by the Kleins of the falsification of accounts receivable records. Mrs. Klein's father left the meeting in tears.

Despite the discovery of what is now regarded as massive fraud, Sugar felt it was necessary for him to live with the Kleins, because he had no one to take over the production and sales aspects of the business. Instead of demanding their withdrawal from Newco, he told them they must somehow get the money back into the business. He gave them two to three months to come up with a viable solution. Sugar thought that Mrs. Klein might be able to "pull a rabbit out of a hat".

The contributions of the Kleins to the business went from bad to worse in the following months, and, by May, Sugar was negotiating with them to withdraw from the business. These negotiations finally resulted in an agreement made as of August 3, 1984, between the Kleins, Sugar, Newco and Harvey Sugar, a brother of Stanley, who had invested money in Newco. The agreement contained the immediate resignation of the Kleins as officers, directors, and employees of Newco, and a non-competition agreement by the Kleins. The Kleins agreed to pay $50,000 to Harvey Sugar, whereupon they would be released from their indemnity agreement regarding the accounts receivable. They also agreed not to withdraw their guarantee of the indebtedness of Newco to the bank until they paid the $50,000 to Harvey Sugar.

The Kleins ceased to be involved in the operation of Newco after August 3, 1984, and a person knowledgeable about the furniture manufacturing business was brought in as general manager. The Kleins never paid to Harvey Sugar any part of the $50,000 provided for in the agreement of August 3, 1984, so that the release of the Kleins from the claims under the indemnification agreement respecting accounts receivable was never effective. No money was ever recovered from the Kleins under that agreement, because they became bankrupt.

During all this time, however, the bank had not been informed of the discovery by Sugar of extensive pre-billing. Sugar said he did not do so, because this would have revealed to the bank that the financial condition of Newco was much worse than had been indicated by the statements produced at the time of closing, and might have resulted in the bank's calling the loan to Newco and putting Newco out of business. What Sugar did not know until the meeting on October 18, 1984, was that the bank had been aware of the pre-billing since De Guerre and Spies visited Oldco on August 18, 1983.

The bank called the Newco loan on November 5, 1984, shortly after Sugar told it of the falsifica-tions. The bank instructed Ernst and Whinney Inc. to conduct an investigation of Newco's financial position, including a review of the accounts receivable purchased by Newco from Peats, to determine, if possible, whether certain accounts receivable were inaccurately stated, as alleged by Sugar. Meanwhile, the bank's solicitors continued to deny all allegations made against the bank.

The Ernst and Whinney report, dated December 17, 1984, concluded from a "cursory review" that the receivables as of June 30, 1983, might have been overstated, and suggested that further evidence might be obtained. Mr. W.C. Simpson, superintendent, special loans department of the bank interpreted this somewhat curious report as saying that there had been fraud perpetrated by the principals of Oldco relating to the receivables, and that Sugar's claims were basically correct.

The bank did not follow up the suggestion of Ernst & Whinney to obtain further evidence, because, according to the evidence of Mr. Cameron of the special loans department, it would serve no good purpose to do so. He said that knowledge as to the exact amount of the discrepancy did not matter, if there was a problem.

The bank did not respond to Sugar's claim for an adjustment in the price paid for the assets of Oldco, but did increase its advances to Newco by $250,000. As a condition of this increase, the Sugars were required to invest an additional $30,000 in Newco. This brought their total investment to $245,000, which is the principal amount claimed in this action.

The action was commenced by statement of claim dated May 23, 1985. The bank responded with a demand for payment, dated June 12, 1985. Ernst & Whinney were appointed as receiver and manager of the undertaking of Newco on June 26, 1985. A petition for a receiving order was filed on June 25, 1985.

The essential element in the claim against the bank for damages for fraudulent misrepresentation is the bank's knowledge, through De Guerre and Spies, of the fraudulent conduct of the Kleins. I accept the evidence of Sugar that he was unaware of the bank's knowledge of the fraud by the Kleins until October 18, 1984. It was, of course, unnecessary for Sugar then to confront the bank with his discovery of its complicity in the fraud, because he had learned of the bank's knowledge from De Guerre, an employee of the bank. I accept the evidence of Sugar that De Guerre was incredulous that Sugar had not known all along of the fraudulent conduct of the Kleins in inflating the accounts receivable, as had been discovered by De Guerre and Spies in short order on August 18, 1983.

In my opinion, the delay of the Sugars after October 18, 1984, in commencing this action does not give rise to any bar to the action by way of estoppel or otherwise. The claim made initially by the Sugars was for an adjustment in the purchase price paid by Newco for the assets of Oldco. The bank made no response to this claim, but co-operated by extending further credit to Newco in hopes that the ill-starred venture could be nursed back to success. Nor does the delay cast doubt on the factual basis of Sugar's claim that he relied on a representation by the bank as to the validity of the accounts receivable. Until Sugar became aware of the bank's knowledge of the inflation of the accounts receivable by the Kleins, Sugar had no reason to suppose that the misrepresentation by the bank was other than innocent.

Different considerations apply in respect of Sugar's knowledge of the fraud by the Kleins. Sugar was aware of pre-billing by the Kleins in January, 1984, but did not inform the bank of the pre-billing until October, 1984. It may be that the bank and the Kleins were joint tortfeasors. In that event, if the Sugars had released the Kleins from liability under the agreement of August 3, 1984, the bank might also have been released. No release of the Kleins occurred, however, because the Kleins never paid to Harvey Sugar any part of the sum of $50,000 specified in the agreement of August 3, 1984.

BREACHES BY NEWCO OF ITS LOAN AGREEMENT

Mr. Crane submitted that the bank had a good defence to the plaintiffs' claim, because of breaches by Newco of its loan agreement with the bank. This agreement is contained in a letter dated September 26, 1983, and was one of the related agreements made at the time the assets of Oldco were purchased. Mr. Crane referred specifically to cls. 6(e) (warranty that statements furnished to the bank should be accurate and complete), 7.1(g) (notice of adverse changes), and 7.2 (covenant against corporate reorganization).

The loan agreement was one of the related transactions which the Sugars were induced by the fraudulent misrepresentation of the bank to enter into, and which caused the loss and damages which the plaintiffs seek to recover. If the bank caused damage to the plaintiffs by fraudulently inducing the Sugars to cause this agreement to be made as part

of the venture, it would be a travesty if the bank could rely on a provision of the agreement as providing a defence to the claim against the bank for fraud. If the fraud had not occurred, there would have been no loan agreement and no provisions to rely on.

In any event, I am not satisfied that any breaches of the covenants in question (or, at least those to which the Sugars were privy) had any material effect on the financial condition of Newco, or the extent of the loan to it from the bank.

"AS IS, WHERE IS" CLAUSE

The "As is, Where is" clause would probably have provided a complete answer to a claim in contract by Newco against Peats. It might also have been relevant to a claim for negligent misrepresentation against Peats or the bank, because it could be taken as a disclaimer of responsibility. But, the "As is, Where is" clause had no application, in my opinion, to a claim in fraud by the Sugars against the bank. It is a provision in the agreement of purchase and sale which would not have been entered into if the fraudulent misrepresentation had not been made. Its only possible relevance to that claim might be to make more doubly certain the loss by the Sugars at being induced to make the investment, if it prevented any claim under the agreement of purchase and sale.

LIABILITY FOR FRAUD

In my judgment, the bank is liable to the plaintiffs, or one of them, for damages for fraudulent misrepresentation. Before considering the amount of those damages, I shall deal with the claim advanced by the plaintiffs at trial that the bank was guilty of a breach of fiduciary duty to the plaintiffs.

CLAIM OF BREACH OF FIDUCIARY RELATIONSHIP

The allegation of breach of fiduciary duty was made by amendment to the statement of claim at trial. The amendment was as follows:

15.(a) The plaintiffs allege that the Defendant C.I.B.C. was in a special relationship with the Plaintiffs as valued customers of the C.I.B.C. As a result, the Plaintiffs allege that the Defendant C.I.B.C. owed them a fiduciary duty which the Defendant C.I.B.C. breached by its failure to reveal to the Plaintiffs its knowledge of the discrepancy in the accounts receivable as aforesaid.

Spies stated in a report dated September 30, 1983, that "the Sugar family are valued customers of our St. Clair & Dufferin Branch". Oldco and Newco dealt at another branch of the bank, namely, Alness & Supertest. There was no other evidence as to the nature of the dealings between the Sugar family and the bank at the St. Clair & Dufferin branch. The mere fact that the Sugars were customers of the bank is not enough to establish a fiduciary relationship.

Sugar accepted at trial the description of himself as a knowledgeable trouble-shooter. He was an experienced businessman. He was introduced to the Oldco situation by his brother, Harvey, not by the bank. There is no evidence that either the bank or Peats offered any advice to Sugar regarding the soundness of an investment in Oldco or Newco. Sugar had his own legal and accounting advisors and was not relying on the bank for advice as to what he should do. Although he was required by Atkins to act quickly to enter into and complete the agreement for the purchase of the assets of Oldco, the health of the business as a going concern required prompt action. There was no evidence of anything that would suggest duress or undue influence in law.

Mr. Youd relied on *Lloyd's Bank Ltd. v. Bundy*, [1975] 1 Q.B. 326; *Woods v. Martin's Bank Ltd.*, [1959] 1 Q.B. 55, and *Standard Investments Ltd. v. C.I.B.C.* (1985), 52 O.R. (2d) 473, 22 D.L.R. (4th) 410, 30 B.L.R. 193 (C.A.). In my judgment, none of these decisions is applicable to the case at bar, because of the facts I have mentioned in the preceding paragraph. The plaintiffs dealt with the bank through Sugar. In my opinion, there was no fiduciary relationship between the plaintiffs and the bank in connection with the sale of assets to Newco.

THE CLAIM AGAINST PEATS

As stated above, the evidence is that the bank did not inform Peats of the discovery of pre-billing by De Guerre and Spies. The employees of Peats did not themselves discover the falsification of records by the Kleins. There is no factual basis for a claim of fraud against Peats.

Nor can there be a valid claim for negligent misrepresentation as against Peats. The employees of Peats did a viability study of Oldco, during the course of which they prepared statements of the assets of Oldco based on existing accounting records. They did not purport to verify those records. The only entries for which Peats was responsible were those which adjusted the Oldco records for transactions occurring after Peats had arrived at the Oldco premises. There was no evidence of any errors in those adjusting entries. There was no evidence that Peats did not accurately represent to Sugar and the bank the contents of the accounting records prepared by Oldco. There was, therefore, no misrepresentation by Peats.

Furthermore, the "As is, Where is" clause in the agreement of sale from Peats to Newco constitutes a valid disclaimer of responsibility by Peats for the accuracy of any statements as to the assets being sold.

Peats was a proper defendant to the action under rule 5.02(2) of the Rules of Civil Procedure, because of doubt as to the person from whom the plaintiff was entitled to relief. Peats was defended by the same solicitors and counsel as the bank, and the presence of Peats as a party defendant did not add to the length or expense of the trial. The action is dismissed as against Peats, but without costs.

DAMAGES

The proper measure of damages for fraudulent misrepresentation is that which will put the innocent party in the position he would have been in if the representation had not been made: see *Doyle v. Olby (Ironmongers) Ltd.*, [1969] 2 Q.B. 158. In this case, if the fraudulent representation had not been made, the plaintiffs would not have invested money in Newco. In my opinion, they are entitled to recover the full amount of that investment up to the time at which they became aware of the bank's knowledge of the falsification.

The evidence is that Sandra Sugar had invested $175,000 in Newco prior to April 30, 1984. On April 30, 1984, the investment by Sandra Sugar in Newco was assumed by her wholly owned company, the corporate plaintiff. Although the evidence was presented in a very confusing way, I understand the facts to be that the indebtedness of Newco to Sandra Sugar was satisfied by payment of $175,000 to 582087 Ontario Limited, but that an equal amount was repaid on the same day from the corporate plaintiff to Newco. The Sugars were aware at the time of these transactions of the falsifications by the Kleins, but not of the complicity of the bank in the fraud. No new money was invested. In my judgment, the effect of the transaction was to place the numbered company in a position where it was entitled to recover from the bank the damages for fraud that were initially sustained by Sandra Sugar.

Further payments of $40,000 were made by the corporate plaintiff to or on behalf of Newco during August and September, 1984. These sums were invested in a futile effort to keep Newco afloat. They were the result of the initial investment caused by the fraudulent misrepresentation, and were made without knowledge of the facts giving rise to a claim for fraud against the bank. I find that the corporate plaintiff is entitled to recover these additional investments of $40,000.

The final investment by the corporate plaintiff was of the sum of $30,000 on February 4, 1985. At the time of this investment, the Sugars were fully aware of the bank's knowledge of the fraudulent conduct of the Kleins. The investment was made, as noted above, as a condition of the further extension of credit by the bank to Newco. In my opinion, the corporate plaintiff cannot recover this last investment of $30,000 that was made with full knowledge of the fraudulent misrepresentation for which the bank was responsible.

For the foregoing reasons, there will be judgment for 582087 Ontario Limited against the bank for $215,000, together with interest at 12% per annum from May 23, 1985, the date of the statement of claim. Counsel may speak to me on the question of costs. This should be done before the end of term.

Judgment for plaintiffs.

(n) *Rancan Fertilizer Systems Inc. v. Bank of Montreal*†

[KROFT J.A.:]

When the events giving rise to this action took place, the plaintiff (Rancan) had been a commercial customer of the defendant Bank of Montreal (the Bank) since at least the early 1980s. Gary Tyhy was the president, controlling shareholder and until the time relevant hereto, the sole signing officer. He was no novice in transacting routine banking business or in completing bank documents.

For a number of years before May 29, 1995, the relationship between Rancan and the Bank was governed by a standard form of "Certificate and Agreement." From time to time, renewals were signed at the request of the Bank, the last of which was dated February 28, 1995. The document consisted primarily of the standard banking resolution dealing with the manner in which the account would be operated. There is no dispute that pursuant to that document, the Bank bore the risk of forgery pursuant to the provisions of sec. 48 of the *Bills of Exchange Act*.

Shortly before May 29, 1995, Mr. Tyhy advised the Bank that because of his frequent absences from Winnipeg he wished to add his wife and son as signing officers. When he attended the Bank on that date, an employee, not the person with whom he usually dealt, presented a new agreement and told him that it would be necessary to sign it together with new signature cards in order to change the authorized signing officers.

Mr. Tyhy's unchallenged evidence on this point, at trial, was as follows:

Q Okay. Let's just back up, because I think His Lordship might want to hear this in some more detail. You've gone to the office. You've asked for Randy, and Randy isn't there; right?

A That's correct.

Q Now, someone who you believe was Norma —

A I believe that was Norma.

Q — brings the document to you?

A That's correct.

Q Do you recall where you were when the document was brought to you?

A I was in Randy's office.

Q All right. And describe, then, how, or, or what happened?

A At that time, I was given a document to, to sign, which, which I did.

Q All right, but, but before that, sir, did you — you were given the document. Was anything said to you about the document?

---

† (1999), 45 B.L.R. (2d) 91 at 92–93 (Man. C.A.).

A No. Just that this was the document to change the signing authority of, of your account that you requested.

Q Those are words that were spoken?

A That's right.

The front page of the form clearly set forth the change which he had requested. He affixed his signature to the document without asking questions, without reading it and without seeking advice. He also signed the signature cards.

What Mr. Tyhy did not know and had not been told was that subsequent to February 28, 1995, the day on which he had last executed documents confirming his banking arrangements, the Bank had significantly altered its standard form of agreement. Inside, on the second page of the document, a completely new paragraph (6.8) had been added to the standard form under the heading "Verification of Account." It provided:

> The Corporation agrees to maintain procedures and controls to detect and prevent thefts of Instruments or losses due to fraud or forgery involving Instruments.
>
> The Corporation further agrees that the Bank shall have no responsibility or liability whatsoever for any loss due to a forged or unauthorized signature unless: (i) the forged or unauthorized signature was made by a person who was at not [sic] time the Corporation's agent or employee; (ii) the loss was unavoidable despite the Corporation having taken all feasible steps to prevent loss arising from forgery or unauthorized signatures; (iii) the loss was unavoidable despite the Corporation having in place the procedures and controls to supervise and monitor the agents and employees of the Corporation; and (iv) the loss was caused solely by the Bank's negligence, fault or wilful misconduct.
>
> The Corporation will diligently supervise and monitor the conduct and work of all agents and employees having any role in the preparation of the Corporation's Instruments and in the Corporation's bank statement reconciliation or other banking functions.

Quite obviously this provision, if accepted by Tyhy, would have materially changed the relationship between Rancan and the Bank. It has the effect of reversing the responsibility of the parties in the event of fraudulent transactions or forgeries by third parties. By virtue of the introduction of para. 6.8, the Bank was relieved of the liability imposed by the *Bills of Exchange Act*.

In the fall of 1995, after the transaction above described, it was discovered that a recently hired employee had forged a number of cheques and other documents which, in the final analysis, resulted in a loss to Rancan of $70,900.50. Under the agreement executed on February 28, 1995, there is no doubt that the Bank had the obligation to pay that sum to the plaintiff. Just as clearly, if para. 6.8 of the revised form is a part of the contract, responsibility lies with Rancan itself. Therein lies the dispute between the parties.

Counsel were advised early in the proceedings that any argument about the parol evidence rule would be unnecessary. There is no dispute as to the meaning of the new para. 6.8. The only question is whether it forms part of the agreement between the parties.

Following the trial Smith J., relying substantially on his findings of fact, concluded that Rancan could not be bound by the new provision of which it had no knowledge. It is from that decision that the Bank now appeals.

Cases dealing with the relationship between banks and their customers are always important and frequently raise difficult issues of law. Here the Bank, in its factum, addressed the concept of *non est factum*, addressed the question of whether or not the parties were *consensus ad idem* and how, if at all, this case fits in with the so-called "ticket cases," and looked at other aspects of the nature of the relationship between a bank and its customers. Its arguments were based upon legal texts and many judicial precedents. Although we heard interesting submissions from both counsel, they were not, in the final analysis, of much importance. This case was decided almost entirely upon the trial judge's findings of fact and there is no justification for appellate intervention in that regard. Neither can I find any need to embark upon more than a fairly superficial analysis of the law.

This is not a judgment which is likely to be of great precedential significance. Based upon the findings of the trial judge, which appear to be well supported, this case was and ought to have been resolved on the basis of simple and well-established legal principles.

Smith J. summarized his findings of fact as follows (at paras. 25–26):

> I find as facts based on the evidence before me that:
> 1. under the circumstances of this particular case the certificate and agreement dated February 28, 1995 ... is relevant to the proper consideration of the case,

2. Mr. Tyhy asked only to have the document prepared necessary to change the signing officers,
3. Mr. Tyhy signed the document ... on May 29, 1995 believing it to be one of the documents that was necessary for him to change the number of signing officers and nothing more,
4. Mr. Tyhy only read the first page which dealt with the changing of signing officers when he signed the document,
5. Mr. Tyhy trusted the Bank and relied on them when they presented the documents,
6. that the Bank had specific knowledge that the plaintiff only wished to add two signing officers and nothing else,
7. that clause 6.8 is a very substantial change in the banking relationship relating to forgeries.

I have considered all the cases referred to me, and although they were instructive, the circumstances in this particular case are most unique. The Bank specifically knew and was advised of the sole purpose for which the plaintiff wished the change in its account. That is the only change that should have been made unless any changes, particularly substantial changes as in this case, were specifically brought to the attention of the plaintiff. I say this notwithstanding there is some case law, which indicates that a bank does not have to come forward or say anything on documents in certain circumstances. The terms of the agreement ... and particularly clause 6.8 deal with a major passing on of the risk of liability for forgery and is, in my opinion, a major change in their relationship. This was a very major shift of responsibility between the bank and its customer from the earlier agreements and forms executed. The customer executed the documents only for the purpose of changing and adding two additional signing officers for cheques on its account.

It is not necessary to find that there was breach of trust, intentional misrepresentation or negligence on the part of the Bank. However, it cannot be ignored that the Bank, at the time material hereto, had never suggested or requested that there be an alteration to its operating arrangement with the customer. Rather, in response to Rancan's simple request to add two more signing officers and upon advising Mr. Tyhy that the documents presented were designed to effect that change, the Bank invited Tyhy to sign a purported agreement which fundamentally changed their long-standing relationship as it related to default and forgeries.

It takes no massaging of facts or stretching of principles to reach the conclusion that the fact scenario before us fits comfortably within the ambit of *Tilden Rent-A-Car Co. v. Clendenning* (1978), 18 O.R. (2d) 601 (C.A.); and of *Armstrong Baum Plumbing & Heating v. Toronto Dominion Bank* (1994), 15 B.L.R. (2d) 84 (Ont. Gen. Div.), the reasons for which were endorsed by the Ontario Court of Appeal ((1997), 32 B.L.R. (2d) 230).

Very simply put, and with no suggestion of impropriety, the Bank misrepresented the terms of the document which it presented to Mr. Tyhy on May 29, 1995. From the face of the agreement and the signature cards, he had every reason to believe that he was continuing his existing relationship but approving two additional signing officers. Although the new document upon which the Bank purports to rely is significantly different from the one signed previously insofar as the respective responsibilities of the Bank and Rancan in the event of forgery, it cannot be relied upon.

The appeal is dismissed with costs.

V

Account Operations

9   Clearing and Settlement

For a description of the clearing and settlement systems in Canada, see M.H. Ogilvie, *Bank and Customer Law in Canada*, 2d Edition (Toronto: Irwin Law, 2013) Chapters 9 and 10.

Background Reading: M.H. Ogilvie, *Bank and Customer Law in Canada*, 2d Edition (Toronto: Irwin Law, 2013) Chapter 8, pages 267–304.

(a)   *Marzetti v. Williams*†

At the trial before Parke J., at the London sittings after Michaelmas Term, 1829, it appeared that the amount of the balance due from the defendants to the plaintiff, on the evening of Dec. 17, 1828, was £69 19s. 6d. A few minutes before eleven o'clock on the morning of the 19th, a further sum of £40, being a Bank of England note, was paid in to his account. On the same day, about ten minutes before three o'clock, a cheque drawn by the plaintiff in favour of Messrs. Sampson and Hooper, for £87 7s. 6d., was presented at the banking-house of the defendants for payment. The clerk, to whom it was presented, after having referred to a book, said there were not sufficient assets, but that the cheque might probably go through the clearing house. The cheque was paid on the following day.

Upon this evidence it was contended by counsel for the defendants, first, that the plaintiff, having declared in tort as for a breach of duty, must be nonsuited, inasmuch as he had not proved any damage. Secondly, that a banker was not bound to know that a particular sum had been paid in an hour or half an hour before the cheque of his customer was drawn. He must be allowed a reasonable time to ascertain the state of the account between him and them, and it was not to be supposed he could know without special notice that a sum paid in by a cus-

tomer, was to be drawn out an hour or two afterwards, the state of the account, in point of practice, being generally ascertained at the close of each day when the books were made up, it could only be expected that the clerk should look at the book at the time when the cheque was presented, and give an answer according to the state of the account as it then appeared.

The learned judge was of opinion, that a banker who received a sum of money belonging to his customer, became his debtor the moment he received it, and was bound to pay a cheque drawn by such customer after the lapse of such a reasonable time as would afford an opportunity to the different persons in his establishment of knowing the fact of the receipt of such money, and that the refusal to pay a cheque under such circumstances was a breach of duty for which an action would lie; and he directed the jury to find for the plaintiff, if they were of opinion that such a reasonable time had intervened between the receipt of the money at eleven o'clock and the presentment of the cheque at three, observing also, that it could not be expected if a sum of money was paid to a clerk in a large banking office, and immediately afterwards a cheque presented to another clerk in a different part of the office, that the clerk to whom the cheque was presented, should

---

† [1824–1834] All E.R. Rep. 150 (K.B.).

be immediately acquainted with the fact of the cash having been paid in, but a reasonable time must be allowed for that purpose, and he told the jury that in forming their judgment whether such a reasonable time had elapsed, they must consider whether the defendants ought or ought not, between eleven and three o'clock, to have had in some book, an entry of the £40 having been paid in, which would have informed all their clerks of the state of the account. The jury having found for the plaintiff on the first three counts, counsel for the defendants asked whether they found that the defendants acted maliciously. The learned judge said there was no evidence of malice in fact; and if malice was a question for the jury, they must be taken to have negatived malice. The defendants obtained a rule nisi for a new trial.

Brougham and *Thesiger* for the plaintiff, showed cause against the rule.

Sir James Scarlett, Campbell, Justice and *Williams* for the defendants, supported the rule.

[LORD TENTERDEN C.J.:]

I think that the plaintiff is entitled to have a verdict for nominal damages, although he did not prove any actual damage at the trial. I cannot think there can be any difference as to the consequences resulting from a breach of contract by reason of that contract being either express or implied. The only difference between an express and an implied contract is in the mode of substantiating it. An express contract is proved by an actual agreement; an implied contract by circumstances, and the general course of dealing between the parties; but whenever a contract is once proved, the consequences resulting from the breach of it must be the same, whether it be proved by direct or circumstantial evidence. Counsel for the defendants was compelled to admit in this case that if the action were founded on an express contract, the plaintiff would have been entitled to recover nominal damages, although no actual damages were proved. This action is, in fact, founded on a contract, for the banker does contract with his customer that he will pay cheques drawn by him, provided he, the banker, has money in his hands belonging to that customer. Here that contract was broken, for the defendants would not pay the cheque of the plaintiff, although they had in their hands money belonging to him, and had had a reasonable time to know that such was the fact. In this case a plaintiff might, for the breach of that contract, have declared in assumpsit. So in *Burnett v. Lynch*, the plaintiff might have declared as for breach of a contract. It is immaterial in such a case whether the action in form be in tort or in assumpsit. It is substantially founded on a contract; and the plaintiff, though he may not have sustained a damage in fact, is entitled to recover nominal damages. At the same time I cannot forbear to observe, that it is a discredit to a person, and, therefore, injurious in fact, to have a draft refused payment for so small a sum, for it shows that the banker had very little confidence in the customer. It is an act particularly calculated to be injurious to a person in trade. My judgment in this case, however, proceeds on the ground that the action is founded on a contract between the plaintiff and the bankers, that the latter, whenever they should have money in their hands belonging to the plaintiff, or within a reasonable time after they should have received such money, would pay his cheques; and there having been a breach of such contract, the plaintiff is entitled to recover nominal damages.

[PARKE J.:]

I am of the same opinion. This action being substantially founded on a contract, I think it can make no difference whether it is in form tort or assumpsit. There is no authority for any such distinction. This case, therefore, must be considered as if the action were founded on a contract by the bankers, to pay all drafts presented within a reasonable time after they receive such money, so as to allow them to pass it to their customer's account. It is admitted that, where there is a breach of an express contract, nominal damages may be recovered. The only difference, however, between an express and an implied contract, is as to the mode of proof. An express contract is proved by direct evidence; an implied contract by circumstantial evidence. Whether the contract be proved by evidence direct or circumstantial, the legal consequences resulting from the breach of it must be the same; one is, that wherever there is a breach of contract or any injury to the right arising out of that contract, nominal damages are recoverable. An extreme case may be put where a party who had sustained no inconvenience, might bring an action; but the remedy in that case would be to deprive such party of costs.

[TAUNTON J.:]

The defendants were guilty of a breach of duty, which duty the plaintiff at the time had a right to have performed. The jury have found that when the cheque was presented for payment, a reasonable time had elapsed to have enabled the defendants to enter the £40 to the credit of the plaintiff, and, therefore, that they must or ought to have known that they had funds belonging to him. That was sufficient to entitle the plaintiff to recover nominal damages, for he had a right to have his cheque paid at the time when it was presented, and the defendants were guilty of a wrong by refusing to pay it. The form of the declaration, whether it be in tort or assumpsit, makes no substantial difference, nor can it be any real ground of distinction whether the foundation of the action be an express or an implied assumpsit.

There are many instances where a wrong, by which the right of a party may be injured, is a good cause of action although no actual damage be sustained. Trespass, *quare clausum fregit*, is maintainable for an entry on the land of another, though there be no real damage, because repeated acts of going over the land might be used as evidence of a title to do so, and thereby the right of the plaintiff might be injured. So an action may be maintained by a commoner for an injury done to his common, without proving actual damage. In *Wells v. Watling*, which was an action by a commoner for surcharging the common, the evidence was that the defendant, in 1777, turned on a greater number of sheep than he ought. There was no evidence that the plaintiff had turned on any sheep in that year. It was objected that the action was not maintainable, because the plaintiff, not having used the common during the period of the defendant's misfeasance, could not by possibility have sustained any damage. But it was held that the action was maintainable; De Grey C.J., said that it was sufficient if the right be injured, whether it be exercised or not; and Nares J., observed, that in the case of the dippers at Tunbridge Wells (*Weller v. Baker*), it was held that a probable damage was a sufficient injury on which to ground an action.

Here, independently of other considerations, the credit of the plaintiff was likely to be injured by the refusal of the defendants to pay the cheque; and as it was the duty of the defendants to pay the cheque when it was presented, and that duty was not performed, I think the plaintiff, who had a right to its being performed, is entitled to recover nominal damages. The case put in argument, of the holder of a cheque being refused payment, and called back within a few minutes and paid, is an extreme case, and a jury probably would consider that as equivalent to instant payment. That, however, is not the present case. Here the refusal to pay was not countermanded till the following day.

[PATTESON J.:]

I think the verdict was right. The action is in form founded in tort, but is in substance founded on a contract. The relation in which the parties stood to each other, viz., that of banker and customer, was created by their own contract, not by the general operation of law. *Green v. Greenbank*, shows that the circumstances of the action being in form for a tort is immaterial, if the substantial ground of it be a contract. This action, therefore, lies, if the plaintiff could have brought assumpsit, and as it is quite clear that he could have maintained assumpsit for the breach of contract, he may on the same ground maintain this action of tort, unless there be some distinction in this respect between an express and an implied contract. But the only distinction between the two species of contracts is as to the mode of proof. The one is proved by the express words used by the parties, the other by circumstances showing that the parties intended to contract. As soon as it is made out, either by direct or circumstantial evidence, that there was such a contract, either of the parties may maintain an action against the other without showing any actual damage. The rule for entering a nonsuit must, therefore, be discharged.

Rule discharged.
Judgment for plaintiff for nominal damages.

(b) Carew v. Duckworth†

The cause was tried before Pigott B., at the Middlesex sittings in Trinity Term. It was proved that the cheque was given after banking hours on the 25th of February, and it was then agreed that it

---

† (1869), L.R. 4 Exch. 313.

should not be presented for several days. The defendant then had £106 in the bank. The cheque was presented on the 10th of March, and dishonoured.

On the morning of March 2, the balance in the defendant's favour was £18 17s. 2d. ; in the course of the day £48 6s. 8d. was paid in, and £58 5s. 2d. was drawn out, leaving a balance of £8 18s. 8d.; and from that day to the 10th of March, the largest sum in the bank to the defendant's credit was £9 8s. 4d. On the 10th £107 was paid in, and £99 drawn out, which left to the defendant's credit a balance of £1 15s. 11d.

It was also proved that the defendant had on a former occasion overdrawn his account, and that the bank had thereupon given him notice they would not honour overdrafts.

The jury found all the averments of the declaration in favour of the plaintiff. A verdict was entered for the plaintiff, with leave to the defendant to move to enter a verdict for him. A rule having been obtained accordingly, and for a new trial, on the ground that the verdict was against evidence,

[BRAMWELL B.:]

I cannot think that the law on this point is in a very satisfactory condition. The true rule should be, that no notice of dishonour is required where it would convey no information, that is, when the party sued knew beforehand that the bill would not be paid; but that where he did not know, it is right that he should be informed of the nonpayment. If this rule should be adopted, the question would be, did he, practically speaking, know beforehand that the bill would not be honoured? This may depend on a variety of circumstances; he might think that the cheque would be honoured by favour, though, in fact, there were no assets to meet it. But though this ought to be the rule, at all events in the case of cheques (and I am not sure that it is not the rule in fact), yet it is not always to be found laid down in these terms, and perhaps it could not be established without doing violence to some of the cases.

The first question then is, had the defendant funds in the hands of the bank to meet this cheque? which here becomes the question, whether there was evidence from which the jury could find this fact in the negative? The defendant had the sum of £106 in the bank at the time when he drew the cheque, but the question of his right to notice of dishonour must be considered in connection with his request that the cheque should not be presented for several days. Now the important question is, whether the drawer thinks that there will be funds to meet the draft,

whether bill or cheque, when it is presented for payment? If I, in London, draw on a bank in York, where I have £1,000, which I know will be drawn out to-day, while the cheque cannot be presented till to-morrow, it is idle to say that, knowing there will be no funds there at any time when the cheque can be presented, I am entitled to notice of dishonour. The question therefore is, what was the state of the funds at the time when the bill ought in regular course to have been presented? Then the question arises, what is the meaning of several days or a few days? The jury may well have thought that it at least postponed the presentment till the 2nd of March. Now from March the 2nd till the 10th, when the cheque was actually presented, there was not at any time a greater sum than £9 8s. 4d. available for its payment. There was evidence in the accounts to show that the defendant paid in money to his account, but he at once drew out as much as he paid in, or the money was so paid in and dealt with that it was not applicable to the payment of this cheque. This was evidence on which the jury might find that the defendant had not, in fact, funds in the bank at the time when the bill was presented.

But Mr. Sharpe says, that if there were any funds, the defendant was entitled to notice of dishonour. This cannot be so; the question must be whether, practically, there were funds to such an amount as that at the time of drawing he could reasonably expect payment? For though the expression "any funds" is used in some cases, it is preposterous to suppose that because there was an old balance of 5s. to the credit of a customer, he would therefore be entitled to notice of dishonour of a cheque for £5,000. The question then must be, whether there were any such funds as the drawer might reasonably and properly draw against, with an expectation that the draft would be honoured. We may read the allegation in the declaration that the defendant had not sufficient, nor any, funds for the payment of the cheque, as meaning that he had no funds adequate for its payment, no funds against which he was entitled to draw the cheque in question. Therefore, as to this first question, I think there was evidence for the jury that there were no such funds in hand, from the time when the defendant would expect the cheque to be presented up to the time when it was presented in fact, as to give him ground to suppose that the cheque would be honoured, and I think that this fact was rightly so found. Secondly, it is quite plain that there was evidence for the jury that the defendant had no reason to expect that the cheque would be honoured; and I also think that they were right in so finding. There were eight entire days after the time when the defendant might first expect the cheque to be presented, on none of which had he any reason to expect that it would be paid, for he had no right to expect that any cheque would be paid which he had not sufficient effects to meet.

[CHANNELL B.:]

I am of the same opinion. There is no ground for saying either that the verdict was against evidence, or that there was no evidence to go to the jury in support of the declaration. The evidence was that the cheque was not to be presented for a few days; the jury have found that when it was presented a reasonable time had elapsed, and I think they were warranted in so finding. There had been then eight days during which there were no funds in the hands of the bank to meet the cheque. There is, therefore, no ground to contend that the defendant had a reasonable expectation of the cheque being paid; and the case bears no resemblance to cases where funds might be expected to come in — as, for instance, in the case of a landlord whose tenants were accustomed to pay their rents into the bank, and who had therefore a right to expect there would be assets to meet his draft, and might perhaps, for want of notice, lose his opportunity of recovering rent by distress.

[CLEASBY B.:]

I am also of the same opinion. The issue is distinct, and involves the question whether the defendant had reasonable ground for expecting that the cheque would be paid. That this is a material question, appears from *Kemble v. Mills*, where the declaration being objected to, Tindal C.J., says: "I suppose the objection is, that it is not stated that the defendant had no reason to expect that the bill would be paid;" this shows (though the declaration was in that case held sufficient) that the allegation of want of reasonable ground for the expectation of payment is an important and a necessary averment, and is, therefore, an essential matter for consideration. The existence of such reasonable ground must obviously be a question for the jury. Now, here the cheque was given with a request that it should not be presented for a few days, but it is nevertheless said that if at the time of drawing it there were funds, the drawer is entitled to notice of dishonour. But can it be said that after a cheque has been given with such a request, and its drawer next day draws out the whole of his funds, and never afterwards pays in a farthing, nor has any reasonable expectation of funds coming in, so that he must well know that there never can be any funds to meet the cheque, he is not completely aware that the cheque will not be paid in fact? Then put the case of a small sum being paid in, quite insufficient to satisfy the cheque, the question will still be, was there any reasonable expectation that there would be funds to meet the cheque? The jury have found that the defendant had no reasonable expectation that the cheque would be paid, and I think there was sufficient ground for that finding.

[BRAMWELL B.:]

I wish to add, that if there were funds in the hands of the bank sufficient to meet the cheque, the drawer would be entitled to notice though he knew that the bank would not honour the cheque, for he would be entitled to say they were bound to honour it, even though they had told him they would not.

Rule discharged.

(c) *Thermo King Corp. v. Provincial Bank of Canada*†

[WILSON J.A.:]

The defendant, Hamilton Transport Refrigeration Limited ("Hamilton"), is a franchised dealer of the plaintiff, Thermo King Corporation ("Thermo King"), and was at all material times a customer of the defendant bank. The shareholders of Hamilton were the sole shareholders of a company called

---

† (1981), 34 O.R. (2d) 369 (C.A.).

Southern Ontario Truck Sales and Services Inc. ("Southern") which was also a customer of the bank and very heavily indebted to it. H.B. Morris was the president of both Hamilton and Southern and, when he and the other shareholders of Southern acquired the shares of Hamilton, they borrowed the purchase money from the bank. As security for the loan they gave the bank their personal guarantees of the debts of both companies. In addition each company gave the bank an assignment of its book debts and a debenture in the amount of $100,000. The companies also guaranteed each other's debts.

In the summer of 1973 it was decided, with the concurrence of the bank, that Southern would be wound down and Hamilton would take over its operations which included its franchise from Thermo King. Southern ceased to do business in late 1974 or early 1975 leaving the bank to look henceforth to Hamilton and the personal guarantors for the payment of the debts of both companies. The indebtedness of Southern in June of 1976 when the events giving rise to this litigation took place amounted to $304,869 plus accumulated interest of $73,975.

From the end of 1973 on the bank permitted Hamilton to operate with an overdraft in its current account varying from a few hundred dollars to as high as $30,086 in May, 1976. In cross-examination Mr. Morris admitted that at the end of April, 1976, the bank threatened not to honour Hamilton's cheque that was to be used to purchase a draft for Thermo King but he was able to persuade the bank manager to change his mind. There is also evidence that at the end of May, 1976, the bank refused to pay some $18,000 to Thermo King. However, the evidence also discloses that after these incidents the bank continued to permit Hamilton to operate on an overdraft. The bank was aware of the course of dealing between Hamilton and Thermo King. It knew that refrigeration units were ordered by Hamilton on a pre-sold basis. When Hamilton received orders from its customers, Thermo King sold and delivered the required units to Hamilton on the basis that payment for the units would be made by Hamilton on the 25th of the month next following the month in which delivery of the units was made. Payment was always made by Hamilton to Thermo King by means of a draft from the bank payable to Thermo King in U.S. funds.

The evidence disclosed that in the early part of 1976 Hamilton's business was showing signs of improvement. In the first four months of that year sales equalled the combined sales of the previous two years.

In March, 1976, Hamilton received orders from three customers and ordered the requisite units from Thermo King. These orders were worth $68,762 U.S., $10,988 U.S. and $14,540 U.S. respectively. Mr. Morris testified that he told Mr. Gibson, the bank manager, about these orders and indeed gave him copies of them. Mr. Gibson acknowledged that he received a copy of the largest order but could not recall being told about the other two. However, he did acknowledge that it was Mr. Morris's practice to discuss all orders with him.

In any event, on June 25, 1976, Mr. Morris attended at the bank to deposit a number of cheques totalling $102,211, including the cheques from three customers for whom he had ordered the units from Thermo King. He asked Mr. Gibson to issue a draft for $100,000 U.S. payable to Thermo King and suggested that the bank might wire the funds to Thermo King. This suggestion was prompted by the fact that payment had to be made to Thermo King by June 25th if Hamilton was to get its dealer discount on the orders. Mr. Gibson checked into the cost of wiring the money and advised Mr. Morris that it would be cheaper for him to fly to Thermo King's offices in Minneapolis. He also said that he would require the largest cheque to be certified before he could issue the draft. Mr. Morris got the cheque certified but was told by Mr. Walker, the assistant bank manager, that there had been a delay in issuing the draft but that it would be available to be picked up on June 28th. On June 28th and June 29th Mr. Gibson advised Mr. Morris he was awaiting head office approval to issue the draft. At approximately 4:30 p.m. on June 29th Mr. Gibson arrived at Hamilton's premises along with Mr. Manton, the receiver manager appointed by the bank under the Hamilton and Southern debentures. Mr. Manton took immediate possession of the premises. Mr. Gibson testified that the prime reason for the bank's action on June 29th was the large deposits made to Hamilton's account on June 25th.

Thermo King sued Hamilton for the price of the units. It joined the bank as a co-defendant, claiming against it damages for breach of contract (as third party beneficiary), a declaration that the bank held the Canadian equivalent of the $100,000 U.S. draft in trust for it, damages for deceit, and damages for the bank's interference with Thermo King's contractual relations with Hamilton. The first three causes of action foundered on the trial judge's finding that Mr. Gibson gave no undertaking to Mr. Morris at any time that he would issue the $100,000 U.S. draft. The learned trial judge rejected Mr. Morris's evidence that Mr. Gibson promised to issued the draft if he, Mr. Morris, had the largest cheque certified. This left Thermo King with its action in tort for the bank's alleged interference with the contractual relations between Thermo King and Hamilton.

Addressing this aspect of the case, the learned trial judge said:

> The plaintiff pleads that the bank wrongfully induced Hamilton to breach its contract with the plaintiff and relied on the principle which is set out in *Clerk and Tindsell on Torts*, 14th ed. (1975), at para. 792 as follows:
>
> > Knowingly to procure or, as it is sometimes put, to induce a third party to break his contract to the damage of the other contracting party without reasonable justification or excuse is a tort.
>
> On the facts in this case the action of the bank was justified and not wrongful. Hamilton's account was overdrawn, it had assigned its receivables to the bank and had given a guarantee for the indebtedness of Southern. The cheques included in the deposit were apparently covered by the assignment. Even if the assignment did not cover the cheques, the bank acted *bona fide* and in the honest belief that the cheques fell within its terms. The bank acted not with any intention of inflicting harm on the plaintiff but to protect its legitimate interests. The plaintiff cannot succeed on this ground.

Thermo King appeals on the basis that the learned trial judge erred in holding that the bank was "justified" in refusing to follow its customer's instructions to issue the draft to the plaintiff. It points out that it is implicit in the passage from the learned trial judge's reasons quoted above that, but for his finding of "reasonable justification", he would have found the bank liable for the tort. Counsel on the appeal accordingly focused in on the finding of "reasonable justification".

He broke his submissions down into the following:

1. A bank must honour its customer's drafts without delay to the extent of the balance standing to the customer's credit;
2. Where a bank has followed a course of conduct in permitting a customer to operate on a modest overdraft, it must give notice to its customer that it no longer intends to follow this course;
3. A bank cannot "lawfully" appropriate its customer's funds to itself pursuant to a guarantee of its customer until it has first made a demand under the guarantee;
4. A guarantor must be given a reasonable opportunity to meet the demand once it has been made;
5. A bank can only resort to a general assignment of book debts if there is a debt due and owing to the bank at the time of such resort because an assignment of book debts is essentially a security document. The debt in this case would have to be either (a) the overdraft or (b) the guarantee and no notice had been given on either.

For his first proposition counsel for the appellant relied on Foley v. Hill (1848), 2 H.L. Cas. 28, 9 E.R. 1002, and *N. Joachimson v. Swiss Bank Corp.*, [1921] 3 K.B. 110. As Lord Justice Bankes pointed out in the *Joachimson* case the principle of *Foley v. Hill* is correctly set forth in the headnote as follows [at p. 118 K.B.]:

> The relation between a banker and customer who pays money into the bank, is the ordinary relation of debtor and creditor, with a super-added obligation arising out of the custom of bankers to honour the customer's drafts; and that relation is not altered by an agreement by the banker to allow the interest on the balances in the bank.

Lord Justice Bankes then went on to point out, however that an obligation was implied in the relation of banker and customer to which no reference was made in *Foley v. Hill*. Reference was made to it by Lord Haldane in *London Joint Stock Bank, Ltd. v. Macmillan et al.*, [1918] A.C. 777, where he said at p. 814:

> Ever since this House in 1848 decided *Foley v. Hill* it has been quite clear that the relation between a banker and the customer whose balance he keeps is under ordinary circumstances one simply of debtor and creditor. But in other judgments and notably by a later decision of this House, *Scholfield v. Earl of Londesborough*, [1896] A.C. 514, it was made equally clear that along with this relation and consistently with it there may subsist a second one.... But the customer of a bank is under a yet more specific duty. *The banker contracts to act as his mandatory and is bound to honour his cheques without any delay to the extent of the balance standing to his credit.* The customer contracts reciprocally that in drawing his cheques on the banker he will draw them in such a form as will enable the banker to fulfil his obligation, and therefore in a form that is clear and free from ambiguity. [Emphasis added.]

303

Counsel submits therefore that when Hamilton instructed the bank to issue the draft for $100,000 U.S. in favour of Thermo King, the bank should have done so. Hamilton had delivered over to the bank cheques from three of its customers totalling $102,211. At that time it therefore had no overdraft. It had a credit balance of $89,949. The overdraft prior to the deposit of the cheques was $11,236. The overdraft which would have been created by the issue of the draft in the amount of $100,000 U.S. *i.e.* $13,447, would have been well within the limits permitted to Hamilton over the prior three years.

In aid of its submission that the bank was obliged to issue the draft, counsel made its second submission, namely that the bank was obliged to give Hamilton notice that it was no longer prepared to carry it in an overdraft position. For this proposition counsel relied on *Cumming v. Shand* (1860), 5 H.&N. 95, 157 E.R. 1114, and *Johnston v. Commercial Bank of Scotland* (1858), 20 Dunl. (Ct. of Session) 790.

. . . .

The appellant in the instant appeal relies upon the *Johnston* case for the *obiter dicta* of the Lord Ordinary and the Lord Justices of Appeal to the effect that, if there has been a history of advances which the customer has come to rely on, a bank may have to give prior notice to a trader of an intention to cut off his credit. In the *Johnston* case such prior notice was found to have been given and the plaintiff had therefore no cause for complaint.

In *Paget's Law of Banking*, 8th ed. (1972), at p. 82 the editors discuss when the limitation period starts to run against a bank in a proposed action against its customer on an overdraft. They point out that on the authority of *Parr's Banking Co. Ltd. v. Yates*, [1898] 2 Q.B. 460, the statute starts to run from the date of each advance even if the advances are guaranteed. The reason for this is that no demand is necessary as against the principal debtor. But *Parr's* case was overruled insofar as a guarantor is concerned by *Bradford Old Bank, Ltd. v. Sutcliffe*, [1918] 2 K.B. 833, which made it clear that a guarantor only becomes liable once a demand has been made. The reason for the distinction is that a guarantee is a "collateral" security. The editors of *Paget* then go on to point out, however, that in the case of the principal debtor:

A course of business might be established by which a banker who was acquiesced for a period in overdrafts to a certain amount would be precluded from withdrawing such accommodation and dishonouring cheques without notice: see

Cumming v. Shand (1860), 5 H.&N. 95, but this does not necessarily preclude the operation of the statute.

And at p. 132 of *Paget* the editors, in discussing the nature of an overdraft, state:

An overdraft is money lent: "A payment by a bank under an arrangement by which the customer has an overdraft is a lending by the bank to the customer of the money". *Per* Harman J., in *Re Hone (a bankrupt), Ex parte Trustee v. Kensington Borough Council*, [1951] Ch. 85, at p. 89; [1950] 2 All E.R. 716, at p. 719. *A banker is not obliged to let his customer overdraw unless he has agreed to do so or such agreement can be inferred from course of business ... Cumming v. Shand* (1860), 5 H.&N. 95...; borrowing and lending are a matter of contract not necessarily premeditated but, possibly, spontaneous, as where a customer, without previous arrangement, draws a cheque, payment of which overdraws his account. It is generally assumed that temporary advances are repayable on demand and forms of charge over security invariably provide that the advance is so payable, *i.e.* without notice. How far this militates against the right of the customer not to have his account closed except after a reasonable notice, where the advance is by way of overdraft, is not clear. In any event the bank could insist that the advance should be repaid within a reasonable time and that it should not rise in the meantime; *but they could probably not insist on immediate repayment to the extent of ignoring outstanding cheques, for instance, unless the limit of overdraft had already been reached ... Johnston v. Commercial Bank* (1858), 20 D. 790.... *There are clearly conflicting interests but, providing the banker is in possession of a document by which the customer agreed to repay on demand, the banker would be entitled to take any action necessary to safeguard his interests, even if it prejudiced those of his borrower.* [Emphasis added.]

In effect, counsel for the appellant submits on the basis of his first two propositions that, having given no notice to Hamilton of its intention to stop permitting Hamilton to operate on an overdraft, the bank was obliged to issue the draft on its customer's instructions without delay. By virtue of the course of dealing between the parties, he submits, Hamilton was entitled to be credited by the bank with the modest amount of overdraft that would have resulted from the issuance of the $100,000 U.S. draft against its then existing credit balance.

It seems to me that there may be merit in this position unless the bank was entitled on June 25, 1976, to appropriate to itself the cheques delivered to it by Hamilton with instructions that they be deposited in its account. Counsel for the appellant's last three propositions are designed to persuade us that the bank was not entitled to do this either under the general assignment of book debts it held from Hamilton or under Hamilton's guarantee of the indebtedness of Southern.

Dealing with the guarantee first, counsel directed our attention to the following language in the first paragraph:

> ... and the liability of the undersigned is to arise first when notice in writing is given to the undersigned requiring payment.

He directed us also to the fourth paragraph of the guarantee which reads:

> Upon default in payment of any sum owing by the Customer to the Bank at any time, the Bank may treat the whole of the indebtedness hereby secured as due and payable and may forthwith collect from the undersigned the total amount hereby guaranteed and may apply the sum so collected upon the Customer's debt or may place it to the credit of a special account. [Emphasis added.]

Counsel points out that no demand had been made by the bank in writing when it refused to issue the draft and that, indeed, no demand in writing was made until Mr. Gibson attended with the receiver manager at Hamilton's premises on June 29, 1976. Accordingly, Hamilton's liability under the guarantee did not arise until that time at the earliest. Counsel relies, however, on the decision of Griffiths J. in *Pullman Trailmobile Canada Ltd. v. Hamilton Transport Refrigeration Ltd. et al.* (1979), 23 O.R. (2d) 553, 96 D.L.R. (3d) 322, and the decision of this Court in *Ronald Elwyn Lister Ltd. et al. v. Dunlop Canada Ltd.* (1979), 27 O.R. (2d) 168, 104 D.L.R. (3d) 702, 32 C.B.R. (N.S.) 4, for the proposition that the debtor must be given a reasonable time in which to attempt to meet the demand. Counsel submits, moreover, that even if Hamilton's liability arose "forthwith" upon his receipt of the demand in writing under the guarantee, there was no liability under the guarantee when the bank refused to issue the draft on June 25, 1976. Can the bank, he asks, refuse to honour its customer's drafts in anticipation of a liability to itself which has not yet matured? Counsel relies on *Bank of British North America v. Standard Bank of Canada* (1915), 34 O.L.R. 648, 26 D.L.R. 777; affirmed 38 O.L.R. 570, 35 D.L.R. 761, for the answer that it can not.

In that case a customer of the defendant bank had drawn certain cheques upon it which were endorsed by the payees of the cheques to the plaintiff bank. The cheques went through the Toronto clearing house and on presentation to the defendant bank were dishonoured. The plaintiff bank, being admittedly the lawful holder of the cheques, sued the defendant bank to recover the aggregate amount of them less payments made thereon and was held entitled to recover on the basis that there was money standing to the credit of the drawer of the cheques at the time they were presented or that there would have been such money but for the improper acts of the defendant bank. Mr. Justice Middleton affirmed the general principle that a bank must honour its customer's drafts if there are funds available in its account to meet them and went on to say at pp. 653–54 O.L.R.:

> The case is of importance as indicating the possibilities of a situation that must frequently arise, and it is open to question whether legislation is not needed to remedy the evil. When a customer draws a cheque upon his bank, and there are funds to answer it when presented, why should the bank be at liberty to refuse to honour it, retaining the money to meet some demand of its own which has not yet matured, or to pay some other cheque drawn by the customer?
>
> ...
>
> If the contention of the defendant bank in this action is right, a bank, on learning that its customer is in trouble, may refuse to pay any cheques, retaining the balance to the customer's credit to meet all liabilities, direct or indirect, which may thereafter accrue due to it by the customer.

Counsel turned next to the general assignment of book debts and his preliminary submission with respect to it was that it was a security document only. He submitted, in other words, that in order to resort to it the bank would first have to establish a debt presently owing to the bank for which the assignment was security. The debt in the circumstances of this case would have to be either the overdraft or the liability on the guarantee. Counsel submitted that neither could be relied on as constituting a debt presently due and owing to the bank at the time it purported to act on the assignment because no notice had been given to Hamilton on either the overdraft or the guarantee as is, he submitted, required by law.

Counsel is undoubtedly correct that the general assignment of book debts is a security document. It is stated to be such on its face. Paragraph (2) read:

> (2) This assignment and transfer shall be a continuing collateral security to the Bank without

impairment or novation of any other existing or future security and shall operate as a general security for all present and future indebtedness and other liability of the assignor to the Bank so long as the assignor shall remain indebted or otherwise liable to the Bank or shall continue to be receiving advances from the Bank: but the assignor shall be entitled upon the discharge of all indebtedness and other liability of the assignor to the Bank to the cancellation hereof.

However, in paras. (8) and (9) of the assignment it is provided:

(8) It is hereby agreed *that all monies received by the assignor* in payment of any debts, demands and choses in action which are now due, owing or accruing due, or which may hereafter become due, owing or accruing due to the assignor or in payment of any claims of whatsoever nature or kind which the assignor now has or may hereafter have including claims against the Crown and claims under insurance policies, *shall be received and held by the assignor in trust for the Bank.*

(9) The Bank shall have the right at any time to appropriate any payment made to any portion of the said indebtedness whether the same be represented by open account, overdraft, or by any bill, note, or other instrument *and whether then due or to become due* and may from time to time revoke or alter such appropriation and appropriate payments to any other portion of the said indebtedness as in its sole and uncontrolled discretion it may see fit. [Emphasis added.]

Do these provisions in the assignment present an insurmountable obstacle for the appellant on this aspect of its argument? The question they seem to pose is whether, regardless of any notice having been given of an intention to terminate the course of dealing on an overdraft or any demand having been made under the guarantee, the bank is nevertheless entitled to appropriate the cheques to the discharge of Hamilton's liability to itself. Do paras. (8) and (9) expressly negate the application of the principles contained in the case law already referred to? Are they a blanket dispensation with the need for prior notice, prior demand, or even for an existing debt which has already matured?

I do not think this can be so. While these provisions appear on their face to constitute the assignor a trustee for the bank of any payments it receives from its customers and to permit the bank to appropriate them at will, *whether or not any debt is then due to the bank by the assignor*, this seems to be quite incompatible with the nature of the instrument as a collateral security. I have no doubt that in circumstances where no notice or demand with respect

to the primary debt is required, immediate recourse may be had to the collateral security. But where as in this case such notice or demand is required, then I believe it follows that the assignment of book debts cannot be resorted to until that has been done. While para. (9) expressly confers to the bank the right to appropriate payments made to the customer "to any part of the said indebtedness ... and whether then due or to become due" I do not think this is intended to permit the bank at any time, whether or not there is any existing indebtedness, to start appropriating payments made to the customer to prospective future debts. I think the prospective language in the assignment is there because it is a "continuing collateral security". In other words, I think the intent of the document is that the security attaches not only to presently existing debts but to debts which may arise in the future *i.e.* subsequent to the giving of the security.

Assuming then for the moment that counsel's submissions on the law thus far are sound, was the factual basis for their application established at trial? Did Thermo King prove a course of dealing between the bank and Hamilton which would trigger a requirement of notice before the bank could terminate the overdraft? The learned trial judge made no finding on this aspect of the case but I believe that the evidence and the exhibits amply support that Hamilton operated with a continuous, fluctuating overdraft from the time it started business in 1973 up until June 25, 1976. Indeed, its overdraft on June 25, 1976, was lower than it had been in several months. The testimony had exhibits also disclose, however, that the bank as an internal matter was concerned about Hamilton's "unauthorized overdraft" and that Mr. Gibson, the bank manager, had been instructed by his superiors in March and again in May of 1976 that "loans to this company are to be placed on a strictly reducing basis unless you have our prior approval". Mr. Gibson was asked at trial whether his bank in March and April of 1976 were reluctant to honour Hamilton's cheques until further deposits were made to its account and he said he thought that this was true. On being asked the reason he stated (transcript p. 277):

Q. And what was the reason for the bank's reluctance?
A. The bank was concerned as to the ultimate recovery of those loans. The account at that time was in overdraft. *We didn't want to see the overdraft become too high.*
Q. Did Hamilton Transport ever have an authorized line of credit?
A. No.

Q. *It operated simply on an overdraft basis?*
A. *Yes.* [Emphasis added.]

I do not believe that this evidence, assuming it was accepted by the trial judge, can be viewed as notice to Hamilton that it was no longer going to be permitted to function on an overdraft basis. On the contrary, if anything, it suggests that at that time the bank was quite prepared to continue the overdraft provided it was kept within reasonable limits.

I have concluded that the bank, having decided after Southern was wound down to look to Hamilton for repayment of Southern's debt, embarked on a course of dealing to accommodate Hamilton in it (the bank's) own long term interests. However, as Mr. Gibson acknowledged, the substantial deposits made to Hamilton's account on June 25, 1976, presented too good an opportunity to be missed and the bank decided at that point to "lower the boom" on Hamilton. I do not believe the bank had the right to do this in the circumstances without any prior notice to Hamilton. Nor do I think it can rely on the guarantee in support of its refusal to issue the draft since no demand was made on it until Mr. Gibson attended with the receiver manager at Hamilton's premises three days later. I think the bank had no basis for refusing to follow its customer's instructions once its requirements of certification of the largest of the deposited cheques was met.

It is submitted by counsel for the appellant that the bank's wrongful act in refusing to issue the draft in its favour when instructed to do so by Hamilton constituted the tort of inducing breach of contract: see *Lumley v. Gye* (1853), 2 E.&B. 216, 118 E.R. 749; *Quinn v. Leathem*, [1901] A.C. 495. He submits that the bank not only knew of the contract between Thermo King and Hamilton but knew its precise terms. It knew that by refusing to issue the draft it was making it impossible for Hamilton to perform its obligation under the contract. Counsel submits therefore that it intended to bring about the breach or, at the very least, should be presumed to have so intended from the fact that the breach was to its knowledge the inevitable result of its refusal to issue the draft. Counsel further submitted, given that the essential elements of the tort were established, that the bank's wrongful act cannot constitute "reasonable justification" in law.

In his factum counsel states:

It is implicit in the reasons of the trial judge that he found that the requisite elements of the tort had been proved, but that he held that, "On the facts of this case, the action of the bank was justified and not wrongful."

It is perhaps unfortunate that the learned trial judge did not address himself to the element of intent as an ingredient of the tort but dealt with it rather in the context of "reasonable justification". In that context he found that:

The bank acted not with any intention of inflicting harm on the plaintiff, but to protect its legitimate interests.

Although this is an express finding of intention by the learned trial judge, it seems to me that he put in apposition the intention to inflict harm on the plaintiff and the intention to protect its own interests because he was directing his mind to whether the bank's conduct should be excused in law. The trial judge, it seems to me, was really asking the question: What motivated the bank? What caused it to do what it did? Did it have a legitimate and defensible reason? He found that it did. It was seeking to protect its own legitimate interests. And hence he found it did nothing wrongful.

Having concluded that the learned trial judge erred in finding that the bank did nothing wrongful, the Court must now ask itself: Did the plaintiff succeed in establishing the essential elements of the tort? The bank's wrongful act cannot constitute "reasonable justification", but the plaintiff still has to prove its cause of action. Did the bank intend to cause Hamilton to breach its contract with the plaintiff? It seems to me that it clearly did. That was the only way in which it could retain the funds in Hamilton's account for its own use. I do not think this is a case of presumed intent. In other words, I do not think that the bank's act in refusing to issue the draft should be approached on the basis that, because the breach was the inevitable consequence of the bank's conduct, an intention to cause the breach must be presumed against it. Presumed intent may not be enough: see *D.C. Thomson & Co. Ltd. v. Deakin et al.*, [1952] Ch. 646, *per* Upjohn J. at p. 663. I approach the matter rather on the basis that the bank's objective of applying the funds towards Hamilton's indebtedness to it could only be attained by disabling Hamilton from performing its contract with Thermo King: see *Torquay Hotel Co. Ltd. v. Cousins et al.*, [1969] 2 Ch. 106; *Celona v. Kamloops Centennial (Pacific No. 269) Branch Royal Canadian Legion et al.*, [1974] 2 W.W.R. 144. The bank knew the relationship between Hamilton and Thermo King. It also knew that if the draft was not issued, the contract between Hamilton and Thermo King would be breached. It intended to cause that breach. It may have intended it in order to further its own purposes, but it intended it nonetheless. On the facts of this case I have no difficulty in finding that the bank knowingly induced the breach of contract.

If the bank's action had been lawful as the learned trial judge found, then it would have constituted reasonable justification for its conduct. As is pointed out by the editors of *Paget, supra*, a banker is entitled to put his own interests ahead of the conflicting interests of his customer or those dealing with his customer but only if he does so in exercise of a legal right. A banker has this right absent any course of dealing giving rise to a requirement of notice. I have concluded, however, that there was such a course of dealing in this case.

I would allow the appeal, set aside paras. (2) and (3) of the judgment and award the plaintiff damages against the bank in the amount fixed by the learned trial judge. I would give the plaintiff its costs both here and in the court below.

Appeal allowed.

(d) *Chambers v. Miller*†

[ERLE C.J.:]

I am of opinion that this rule should be discharged. This is an action for a trespass committed by the defendants, in assaulting and imprisoning the plaintiff under a plea that certain money which was in the pocket of the plaintiff was the property of the defendants, and that the latter had a right to detain him and take it from him. The question reserved for our consideration — and upon which we are called upon to decide both as judge and jury — is, whether, under the circumstances proved at the trial, the money had passed to the plaintiff or still remained the property of the defendants. The ordinary rule of law is, that the property in a chattel passes according to the intention of the parties. In an ordinary transaction of sale, where the proposed seller says to the proposed buyer, "I will sell you such and such goods at such a price," the assent of the buyer signified by the word "done" is enough to fix the right of property. In the case of a gift, the property passes by delivery. And so with all the ordinary transactions of life. With regard to cheques, the well-known course of business is this: When a cheque is presented at the counter of a banker, the banker has authority on the part of his customer to pay the amount therein specified on his account. The money in the banker's hands is his own money. On presentment of the cheque, it is for the banker to consider whether the state of the account between him and his customer will justify him in passing the property in the money to the holder of the cheque. In this case, the banker's clerk had gone through that process, and so far as in him lay did that which would pass the property in the money to the plaintiff. He counted out the notes and gold and placed them on the counter for the plaintiff to take up. It no longer remained a matter of choice or discretion with him whether he would pay the cheque or not. The plaintiff had taken possession of the money, counted it once, and was in the act of counting it again, when the clerk, who had gone from the counter, finding that there was a mistake, not as between him and the bearer of the cheque, but as between him and the customer, returned and claimed to revoke the act of payment which on his part was already complete, and claimed to have the money back. Now, the bankers had parted with the money, and the plaintiff had accepted it. It is true he had not finished counting it, and that, if he had found a note too much or a note short, there was still time to rectify the mistake. But, according to the intention of the parties, and the course of business, the money had ceased to be the money of the bankers, and had become that of the party presenting the cheque. It was the clear opinion of the jury that the property passed: and equally clear am I, if it was a question of law for me, that the bankers did by that which took place pass the property in the money to the holder of the cheque. On that ground I am of opinion that the plaintiff is entitled to retain his verdict. That which passed amounted to payment of the

---

† (1862), C.B. (N.S.) 125; 143 E.R. 50 at 52–55.

cheque; and the plaintiff was entitled to retain the money. Some of the cases which were cited might be applicable, if the customer had obtained by mistake from the banker money to which he was not entitled. In *Kelly v. Solari*, 9 M.&W. 54, the administratrix was not entitled to receive the money. The policy under which the payment had been made to her was a lapsed policy, and the money was paid under a mistake of fact. That being so, and it being against all equity and good conscience that she should retain it, the money was held to be recoverable back. But, as between the parties here, there was no manner of mistake. The banker's clerk chose to pay the cheque; and the moment the person presenting the cheque put his hand upon the money it became irrevocably his.

[WILLIAMS J.:]

I am entirely of the same opinion. Drawing the inference which is fairly deducible from the facts proved, it seems to me that the person who acted as cashier of the bank upon the occasion in question meant to part with the money, and that the person who presented the cheque meant to receive it and did receive it. There was a complete and absolute transfer of the money under the authority of the drawer of the cheque. It is said that the transaction was not complete, because the plaintiff had not finished counting the money, and therefore that he did not consider that the matter had come to an end. I cannot by any means assent to that. The recipient had a right to count the money, or he might if he pleased have taken it off the counter without counting it. I see no ground whatever for saying that the transaction was incomplete. There was no evidence that anything further remained to be done to complete it. The act of counting was no indication on the part of the plaintiff that he had not accepted the money. That argument was founded upon a mistaken view of the mode in which the question arises. Where money is paid, not in performance of a promise, at the precise day on which it ought to have been paid, but in satisfaction of a breach of promise, there must be not only payment but acceptance in satisfaction. That, however, is not so where the payment is made in performance of an agreement on the precise day, or where the creation of the right to receive the money and the act of payment are simultaneous. In these cases, where the money finds its way into the hands of the person to whom the payment is to be made, the transaction is complete. If, in this case, after the money had been placed by the cashier upon the counter, and drawn towards him by the plaintiff, a thief had come in and stolen it whilst he was in the act of counting it, the loss would clearly have fallen upon the plaintiff, and the bankers would not have been under any obligation to pay the amount over again. Then it is said, that, the money having been paid under a mistake of fact, money had and received would lie to recover it back, and therefore that the defendants were justified in seizing the plaintiff and forcibly regaining possession of it. It is quite unnecessary to consider that. There was no mistake of fact within the meaning of the rule on the subject. One acting as the cashier of the bank, with the authority of the bankers, transfers the possession of the money to the plaintiff under an impression that he is the bearer of a genuine cheque, and takes the cheque from him in the ordinary way. All the facts are precisely as the cashier apprehended them. There is no mistake. It may be that, if the cashier had at the time been aware of the state of customer's account, he would not have paid the cheque. But, if we were to go into all the remote considerations by which parties may be influenced, it would be opening a very wide field of conjecture, and would lead to infinite confusion and annoyance.

[BYLES J.:]

I am of the same opinion. The property in the money passed to the recipient, and the cheque was paid. It is true that the money remained upon the banker's counter. But a banker's counter is no more than a table which is provided by the banker for the more convenient carrying on cash transactions between him and his customers and those who come to pay and receive money there: and the same rule must be applied whether the payment is made from one side of the counter or the other. Here, the cheque was received by the cashier, and the money handed over to the person presenting it. The latter had counted the money once, and was in the act of counting it again when the cashier claimed a right to recall it. I must confess that I should be inclined to hold, as matter of law that, so soon as the money was laid upon the counter for the holder of the cheque to take it, it became the money of the latter. It has been suggested that it was still competent to the party to object to one of the notes, for instance, that it was forged. What then? The only consequence would be that he would have a right to demand another note in place of it. His right to rescind the transaction so far would not prevent the property in the rest from vesting in him. The only point upon which I have felt any hesitation, is whether there could be any retraction of the payment. I think, however, it would be extremely dangerous, and would create a great sensation in the city of London, if it were to be held in Westminster Hall that, after a cheque had been regularly handed over the banker's counter and the money received for it, and in the act of being counted, the banker might treat the cheque as unpaid, because he has subsequently to his taking the cheque and handing over the amount ascertained that the state of the customer's account was unfavorable. If it were so held, it certainly would be so for the first time. This was not a payment made under any mistake of facts. The bankers (or their agent, the cashier), had full notice in writing of all the facts. And, even if this had been a payment made under such a mistake of facts as would have entitled the bankers to recover back the money from the holder of the cheque, by an action for money had and received, I must entirely withhold my assent from the proposition that they could justify the act of seizing the person to whom they had voluntarily paid the money, and picking his pocket. I am quite aware that a question has lately arisen, as to whether or not a party (or his servants) whose property is wrongfully in another's possession may by retaking it administer summary redress to himself.[1] But, be that as it may, when the subject-matter in question is money, the possession and the property in which are inseparable, I entertain no doubt whatever that he could do nothing of the sort. For these reasons, it appears to me that there has been no failure of justice here, and that the plaintiff is entitled to retain his verdict.

[KEATING J.:]

I also am of opinion, upon the facts proved in this case, that the verdict should stand. I cannot for a moment doubt that the delivery of the money by the cashier to the holder of the cheque was complete,

and that the property in it vested in the latter. The cashier counted out the money, and placed it on the counter for the purpose and with the clear intention of putting it under the control of the person who presented the cheque. This was no conditional payment — as if the cashier had said to the party, "I hand you this money in payment of the cheque, on condition of your counting it, and assenting to its correctness." Suppose the plaintiff had been content to take up the money without stopping to count it — could anybody doubt that the property would have passed? It does not the less pass because the recipient chooses to count it before he puts it into his pocket. If, then, the property passed, the other question does not arise. No case has ever yet held that a party has a right to re-take by force property which has already passed and vested in another. Mr. Manisty has suggested that, even if the property passed by the act of payment, it only passed in a qualified and limited manner, leaving the banker at liberty to revoke the payment on discovering that the customer had not sufficient effects in his hands. I cannot assent to that proposition. Having once parted with the money animo solvendi, it was out of his power to recall it. The plaintiff is clearly entitled to retain his verdict.

Rule discharged.

Note

1. *Blades v. Higgs*, ante, vol. x., p. 713, and vol. xii., p. 501. The question there was whether the things seized (rabbits) *were* the *property* of the master. This court upon the first occasion decided that, assuming that they were, the seizure was justifiable. On the second occasion, they held that the rabbits were under the circumstances the subject of property. The propriety of the first decision was not questioned: and the decision of the court upon the second occasion has since been affirmed on appeal: vide post.

(e)   *Gibbons v. Westminster Bank Ltd.*[†]

[LAWRENCE J.:]

In this case, the plaintiff brought an action against the defendant bank for dishonouring a cheque of

hers when her account was in funds. The cheque was dishonoured owing to a mistake. The plaintiff had paid in previously a sum of money, and this had been credited, by a slip, to a wrong account, and the

---

† [1939] 3 All E.R. 577 (K.B.D.).

bank was therefore under the impression that the plaintiff had no funds to meet her cheque. She gave a cheque to her landlords for her rent, and this cheque was dishonoured. She went and saw the bank manager when she heard of this, and she was paid £1 1s. by the bank manger, and the question which was fought out before the jury was whether she accepted that £1 1s. which was so paid to her by the bank manager in full satisfaction of any claim she might have in respect of the dishonour of her cheque. The jury found that she did not so accept it.

The question was raised at an early stage of the case, on behalf of the defendants, whether the plaintiff was entitled to nominal damages only, as she had not pleaded any special or actual damage, and it was agreed between counsel that the question of damages should be left to the jury and that this question as to whether the plaintiff was entitled to recover anything more than nominal damages should be considered after the jury had given their verdict on the basis that she was entitled to recover substantial damages. The jury accordingly gave their verdict for the amount of substantial damages to which they thought she was entitled — namely, the sum of £50. It has now been argued before me as to whether the plaintiff is entitled to anything more than nominal damages for the dishonour of her cheque by the defendant bank. It has also been argued before me that the plaintiff ought to have leave to amend the pleading so as to allege as special damage the damage which it is said she suffered from the dishonour of this cheque, in that on Aug. 18, Messrs. Ainslie, her landlords, wrote to her as follows:

> In view, however, of the unsatisfactory way in which your rent has been paid in the past, and the incident of your cheque being returned on the last occasion, we think it is easier for all concerned if your were to remit your rent in future in cash.

Since that date, the plaintiff says that she has had to remit her rent in cash. I do not think that it would be right for me to allow an amendment in respect of this alleged damage. The letter in question was not pleaded, and nothing was pleaded in regard to any actual damage of that sort suffered by the plaintiff. The letter was not disclosed until after a payment in had been made, the amount of which I do not know, and it would, therefore, be an obvious injustice to the defendant to allow the plaintiff to raise the other matter of special damage at this stage. Therefore, I refuse the application for an amendment of the pleading, and I have to consider the question whether or not the plaintiff, who, it is argued, is a trader, is entitled to recover more than nominal damages for the dishonour of her cheque without pleading or proving special damage.

The authorities which have been cited to me all lay down that a trader is entitled to recover substantial damages without pleading and proving actual damage for the dishonour of his cheque, but it has never been held that that exception to the general rule as to the measure of damages for breach of contract extends to anyone who is not a trader. The cases in which this view has been taken, and which have been cited to me, are *Marzetti v. Williams*, *Rolin v. Steward*, *Bank of New South Wales v. Milvain* and *Kinlan v. Ulster Bank, Ltd.* The rule is so expressed in *Grant On Banking*, 7th Edn., pp. 88, 89, and in *Smith's Leading Cases*, 13th Edn., Vol. 2, p. 574, where it is also stated that the exception to the general rule is an exception which ought not to be extended, and reference there is made to the opinion of Lord Atkinson in the House of Lords in *Addis v. Gramophone Co., Ltd.*, at p. 495. In my opinion, I ought to treat this matter as covered by these authorities, and I must hold that the corollary of the proposition which is laid down by these cases is the law — namely, that a person who is not a trader is not entitled to recover substantial damages unless the damages are alleged and proved as special damages. I am therefore of opinion that the plaintiff, whom I hold not to be a trader, is entitled to recover only nominal damages, and she will have judgment for 40s.

Judgment for the plaintiff for 40s.

(f) *Kpohraror v. Woolwich Building Society†*

[EVANS L.J.:]

On 9 September 1991 the plaintiff drew a cheque for £4,550 on his current bank account with the defendants at their branch at 136 Clapham High Street. London SW4. He is a Nigerian and he had described himself as a self-employed 'exporter/importer' as well as a part-time employee of two south London businesses when he converted his six-month-old savings account to a current account in June 1991. He stated that his income was below £5,000 pa.

The cheque was drawn in favour of Phils (Wholesalers) Ltd in the sum of £4,550. The current balance at the time was about £4,800 including a cheque for £3,000 which was credited to the account on 3 September.

The cheque was presented for payment on 10 September at the payee's bankers with a request for special clearance. Sometime during that day the defendants refused payment on the ground 'Cheque reported lost' and this was reported by the payee to the plaintiff. He went to the defendants' branch where he had his account before 5 p.m. The error, for it was an error, was acknowledged and the manageress told the payee by telephone at the plaintiff's request that there were sufficient funds in the account. She persuaded the payee to accept the defendants' own corporate cheque and gave this to the plaintiff at about 5.15 p.m. He took it to the payee, Phils (Wholesalers) Ltd, next morning, who accepted it as payment then and agreed to release goods which the plaintiff required for shipment to Nigeria. The goods were cosmetic products which the plaintiff had bought for re-sale there.

The plaintiff claims damages for wrongful dishonour of the cheque in breach of his current account contract with the defendants, and liability is admitted. The assessment of damages came before Master Tennant in chambers on 16 February 1994. He awarded £5,550 with interest as general damages for the injury to the plaintiff's credit by reason of the dishonour of the cheque and the apparently discreditable reason given for it, which was of course unfounded. He rejected the defendants' submission that the damages award should be nominal only, and

he likewise rejected the plaintiff's claim for a much greater sum, pleaded as £57,185.68.

The plaintiff and the defendants appeal and cross-appeal respectively. We have had the benefit, as did the master, of detailed and helpful submissions from Miss Loebl for the plaintiff and Miss McQuail for the defendants.

The claim is for general damages for loss of business reputation and credit and for special damages of which particulars are given in the amended statement of claim. These can be set out verbatim:

PARTICULARS OF SPECIAL DAMAGE

The said cheque was drawn to pay for goods which were due to be collected from the said Phils (Wholesale) on 12th September 1992 for shipment for McTeri Ltd in Nigeria which shipment could not take place by reason whereof the Plaintiff's contract with the said McTeri Ltd was terminated and the said goods had to be sold elsewhere.

(1)	Claim from McTeri Ltd in Nigeria for N300,000.00 (Niras) [sic] conversion as at October 18th 1991 Nairas to the pound	15,949.49
(2)	Losses due to selling below sale price	4,996.81
(3)	Profit loss for December caused by cancellation of Contract	3,294.60
(4)	Profit loss for four shipments 1992 caused by cancellation of Contract assessed on the basis of £3,298.49 per shipment	13,178.40
(5)	Profit loss for four shipments for 1993 based on profit per shipment of £3,298.49	13,178.40
(6)	Profit loss for two shipments/consignments for 1994 assessed on the basis of £3,298.49 per shipment	6,596.98
	Total	57,185.68

(Strangely, a pleaded claim for general damages in para 6 of the original statement of claim was deleted by amendment, but it is not suggested that no such award should be made for this reason.)

---

† [1996] 4 All ER 119 at 121–28 (C.A.).

The claim is for damages for breach of contract, rather than in tort, although the award of substantial damages for loss of business reputation appears to have an obvious affinity with tortious claims.

In Ellinger and Lomnicka *Modern Banking Law* (2nd edn, 1994) p 387, in their chapter dealing with "The customer's remedies for wrongful dishonour of his cheques', the authors write: 'A re-examination of the basic principle is timely.' Counsel submit that the present case provides the opportunity for doing so. The basic principle referred to has the authority of the House of Lords in *Wilson v. United Counties Bank Ltd.* [1920] AC 102, [1918–19] ALL ER Rep 1035 and of this court (O'Connor and Park LJJ) as recently as 1987, in *Rae v. Yorkshire Bank plc* [1988] BTLC 35. It is open to us, however, to consider what the principle is and what its limits are.

Both parties accept that the claim is governed by the general law, that is to say the plaintiff may recover general damages under the first head of the rule in *Hadley v. Baxendale* (1854) 9 Exch 341, [1843–60] All ER Rep 461 and special damages under the second head of the rule when the necessary facts are proved. This is not the only sense in which the terms 'general' and 'special' damages are used nor the only context in which a distinction is made between them. One such distinction is that special damages must be expressly claimed and pleaded, whereas general damages need not (see generally *McGregor on Damages* (15th edn, 1988) para. 19).

The claim for general damages rests upon the first part of the rule in *Hadley v. Bexandale*, namely, they are claimed as damages 'arising naturally (which means in the normal course of things)' from the defendant's breach (see *Monarch Steamship Co Ltd v. Karlshamns (AB) Oljefabriker* [1949] 1 All ER 1 at 12, [1949] AC 196 at 221 per Lord Wright). It is not disputed that a claim does arise for loss of credit or business reputation, but the defendants say that the amount should be nominal unless special facts are proved which were made known to them when the contract was made; in other words, that this should properly be regarded under the second, not the first part of the *Hadley v. Baxendale* rule. They rely upon a number of reported cases where nominal damages only were awarded: by a jury in *Evans v. London and Provincial Bank* (1917) 3 LDAB 152, by Lawrence J in *Gibbons v. Westminster Bank Ltd* [1939] 3 All ER 577, [1939] 2 KB 882 and by this court in *Rae v. Yorkshire Bank plc*, where a claim for substantial damages for 'inconvenience and humiliation' was dismissed.

However, the plaintiff relies upon the line of authority which holds that actual damage need not be alleged or proved by 'a trader', which he claims that he was. The defendants say that they were unaware of this, and that the rule does not apply, for that reason alone.

As will appear below, the issue in my view is whether a person who is not 'a trader' for the purposes of the common law rule — and it is not at all clear what the limits of that category are — can recover substantial rather than nominal damages for loss of business reputation when his cheque is wrongly dishonoured by the bank. A subsidiary question is how much the measure of damages is affected by the extent of the bank's knowledge of its customer and of the purposes for which he uses his account.

I will start with the authorities which establish that a 'trader' is entitled to recover substantial, rather than nominal, damages for loss of business reputation without proof of actual damage. This was recognised and applied, although in a different context, by the House of Lords in *Wilson v. United Counties Bank Ltd* [1920] AC 102, [1918–19] All ER Rep 1035. Lord Birkenhead LC said:

> The objection was taken by the defendants that this finding of the jury cannot be supported without proof of special damage. In deciding this point, I do not lay down a rule of general law, but I deal with the exceptional language of an exceptional contract. The defendants undertook for consideration to sustain the credit of the trading customer. On principle the case seems to me to belong to that very special class of cases in which a banker, though his customer's account is in funds, nevertheless dishonours his cheque. The ratio decidendi in such cases is that the refusal to meet the cheque, under such circumstances, is so obviously injurious to the credit of a trader that the latter can recover, without allegation of special damage, reasonable compensation for the injury done to his credit. The leading case upon this point is that of *Rolin v. Steward* ((1854) 14 CB 595, 139 ER 245). The direction of Lord Campbell to the jury has been generally accepted and treated as an accurate statement of the law. If it be held that there is an irrebuttable presumption that the dishonour of a trader customer's cheque in the events supposed is injurious to him and may be compensated by other than nominal damages, the conclusion would appear to follow almost a fortiori that such damages may be given where the defendant has expressly contracted to sustain the financial credit of a trading customer and has committed a breach of his agreement. (See

[1920] AC 102 at 112, [1918–19] All ER Rep 1035 at 1037.)

(See also [1920] AC 102 at 120, 132–133, [1918–19] All ER Rep 1035 at 1038, 1041 per Viscount Finlay and Lord Atkinson.)

Two passages should be quoted from *Rolin v. Steward* (1854) 14 CB 595, 139 ER 245. Lord Campbell CJ directed the jury to give 'not nominal, nor excessive, but reasonable and temperate damages' (see 14 CB 595 at 605, 139 ER 245 at 249). In the Court of Common Pleas, Williams J said that —

> when ... the [customer] is a trader ... the jury, in estimating the damages, may take into their consideration the natural and necessary consequences which must result to the [customer] from the [bank's] breach of contract: just as in the case of an action for a slander of a person in the way of his trade, or in the case of an imputation of insolvency on a trader, the action lies without proof of special damage.' [See (1854) 14 CB 595 at 607, 139 ER 245 at 250.)

The rule so stated made it necessary to consider in every case whether or not the plaintiff was a trader. In Australia in 1884 a farmer was not (see *Bank of New South Wales v. Milvain* 10 VLR 3). In England, in 1940, a bookmaker was (see *Davidson v. Barclays Bank Ltd* [1940] 1 All ERR 316), but it is an open question whether professionals such as solicitors and accountants who are 'akin to businessmen' are within the rule (see *Ellinger and Lomnicka* p 387).

It is abundantly clear, in my judgment, that history has changed the social factors which moulded the rule in the nineteenth century. It is not only a tradesman of whom it can be said that the refusal to meet his cheque is 'so obviously injurious to [his] credit' that he should 'recover, without allegation of special damage, reasonable compensation for the injury done to his credit' (see [1920] AC 102 at 112, [1918–19] All ER Rep 1035 at 1037 per Load Birkenhead LC). The credit rating of individuals is as important for their personal transactions, including mortgages and hire-purchase as well as banking facilities, as it is for those who are engaged in trade, and it is notorious that central registers are now kept. I would have no hesitation in holding that what is in effect a presumption of some damage arises in every case, in so far as this is a presumption of fact.

So the question becomes, whether the authorities compel the conclusion as a matter of law that the presumption cannot extend the category of trader. In my judgment, they do not. The most directly relevant are *Gibbons v. Westminster Bank Ltd* [1939] 3 All ER 577, [1939] 2 KB 882 and *Rae v.*

Yorkshire Bank plc [1988] BTLC 35. In the former case, Lawrence J regarded the presumption in favour of a trader as one of four exceptions to the general rule that the plaintiff in a claim for damages for breach of contract cannot recover substantial damages in the absence of proof that same actual damage has been suffered, and he felt unable to extend the exception to non-traders (see *Addis v. Gramophone Co Ltd* [1909] AC 488 at 495, [1908–10] All ER Rep 1 at 5 per Lord Atkinson). He said:

> The authorities which have been cited to me all lay down that a trade is entitled to recover substantial damages without pleading and proving actual damage for the dishonour of his cheque, but it has never been held that that exception to the general rule as to the measure of damages for breach of contract extends to any one who is not a trader. (See [1939] 3 All ER 577 at 579, [1939] 2 KB 882 at 888.)

In *Rae v. Yorkshire Bank plc* the plaintiff's claim was for damages for 'inconvenience and humiliation' (see [1988] BTLC 35 at 37). Parker LJ, with whom O'Connor LJ agreed, cited *Bliss v. South East Thames Regional Health Authority* [1987] ICR 700, where Dillon LJ held that the general rule laid down in *Addis v. Gramophone Co Ltd* is that —

> where damages fall to be assessed for breach of contract rather than in tort it is not permissible to award general damages for frustration, mental distress, injured feelings or annoyance occasioned by the breach. (See [1987] ICR 700 at 717–718.)

Dillon LJ also noted a further exception to the general rule which is now permitted 'where the contract which has been broken was itself a contract to provide peace of mind or freedom from distress' (see [1987] ICR 700 at 718). Parker LJ continued ([1988] BTLC 35 at 37): 'That authority, and *Gibbons*, are two of many which in my view make Mr Rae's an appeal which must inevitably fail.' Clearly, the judgment in *Rae v. Yorkshire Bank plc* was based primarily in the application of the law as stated by Dillon LJ to the facts of that case, where the claim was for 'inconvenience and humiliation' (only). That is a different kind of damage from loss of reputation or credit, unless 'humiliation' is intended to include such injury in the eyes of third parties, but that point was not taken in *Rae's* case because the kinds of damage referred to by Dillon LJ all refer to the injured feelings of the plaintiff himself.

The trial judge in *Rae* had referred to *Gibbons* and said (see [1988] BTLC 35 at 36): 'It is clear that Mr Rae was not a trader and that in those circumstances, damages are purely nominal'. Apart from the passing reference to *Gibbons* in the passage already quoted, the 'trader' rule, or exception, was not considered in the judgments in the Court of Appeal.

In these circumstances, neither *Rae* nor *Gibbons* itself is binding authority which precludes this court from considering whether a bank's customer who is not a trader is precluded from recovering substantial damages for injury to his reputation or credit, unless special damage is alleged and proved. The trader exception itself recognises, as does the general rule regarding the recovery of damages for tort, that this is a kind of injury recognised by law. If the trader is an exception to the general rules regarding damages for breach of contract, then the explanation may lie in the tortious analogy with damages for injury to business credit. In *Addis v. Gramophone Co Ltd* Lord Atkinson did not refer to any 'trader' rule, but generally to 'actions against a banker for refusing to pay a customer's cheque when he has in his hands funds of the customer's to meet it' (see [1909] AC 488 at 495, [1908–10] All ER Rep 1 at 5). *McGregor* deals with the rule as applying only to traders but also states generally that 'loss by injury to credit and reputation caused by the defendants' failure to honour the plaintiff's drafts may be presumed' (see paras 1222, 1785). (Damages for loss of reputation simpliciter are excluded, whether in contract or for torts other than defamation (see *Joyce v. Sengupta* [1993] 1 All ER 897, [1993] 1 WLR 337).)

Moreover, if the exception is a presumption of fact then it is open to the court, in my judgment, to hold that changing social circumstances should cause the presumption to be reviewed and if necessary expanded in order to take those changes into account.

For these reasons, I will reject the defendants' allegation by way of cross-appeal that the master was wrong to award more than a nominal sum by way of general damages. I should, however, also refer to their contention that the master was wrong to do so when the defendants denied that they had knowledge of the fact that he was a trader. In none of the reported cases where a trader has succeeded in recovering substantial damages has the bank's knowledge been in issue. The master decided this effectively as a preliminary issue. The defendants wished to call as a witness their employee who dealt with the plaintiff when he converted his savings account into a current account in June 1991. She would have denied, as her affidavit evidence indicated, that he told her that the account would be used for trading purposes. So the master gave 'part 1' of his judgment holding that substantial damages could

be awarded even where the bank had no knowledge 'actual or implied of the plaintiff's status as a trader and the use of his account'. If the trader 'exception' is good law then I doubt whether this can be correct, if only because it offends against the basic requirement of both parts of the rule in *Hadley v. Baxendale* which is that the test of remoteness and therefore of the right to recover a particular head of damage depends upon the state of the defendant's knowledge of the likely, or 'not unlikely' (see *The Heron II, Koufos v. C Czarnikow Ltd* [1967] 3 All ER 686, [1969] 1 AC 350), consequences of his breach, whether 'in the usual course of things' because of what the defendant is taken to have known or by reason of his actual knowledge of special facts. But it is unnecessary to express a concluded view, because the evidence is that the plaintiff described himself in the application form as a part-time self-employed 'exporter/importer' although clearly on a modest scale. This evidence is not and cannot be disputed and it is sufficient in my judgment to fix the defendants with knowledge that that was the self-styled description of the plaintiff for the purposes of the contract between them with regard to the current account. To this extent, it was a question of 'status' and the defendants knew what that status was. If it is objected that they should also have knowledge that the account was to be used for trading purposes, then this is a further refinement of the trader exception — the dishonour of a personal cheque could be no less harmful to the trader's credit than of one drawn on a trading account, perhaps even more so — and an additional reason why in my judgment, the exception or rule should not be confined as the defendants say that it should.

SPECIAL DAMAGES

I come therefore to the plaintiff's main ground of appeal. He asserts, in the 'particulars of special damage' already quoted, there he is entitled to recover damages for his loss of profit on the transaction in question and on ten further shipments which, he says, would have followed from it if the first shipment had not been delayed. He claims, moreover, that his losses in respect of the goods which were delayed included a very large sum ('Claim from McTeri Ltd in Nigeria for N300,000 (converted as) £15,949.49') which he was compelled to pay to his Nigerian customer both by reason of his legal liabilities, as he asserts, owed to that customer and because considerable pressures, both commercial and social, were brought to bear upon him and his father and family by that customer in Nigeria. So, Miss

315

Loebl submits on his behalf, these were all heads of damage which could reasonably be contemplated by the defendants when the banking contract was made, not because they had any knowledge of the circumstances of the particular transaction or of any intended transaction, but because they knew, as the plaintiff asserts, that he was an 'exporter/importer' and that he intended to use the account for his business activities. To these might be added the fact which is undisputed that the defendants knew that the plaintiff is Nigerian and so, it might be submitted, were also aware that exports of goods might be delivered there.

The master dealt with this part of the claim on the assumption that the plaintiff was correct as to the extent of the defendants' knowledge. He held that nevertheless these damages could not be recovered, either under the first limb of *Hadley v. Baxendale* ('this was such an extraordinary outcome it could not possibly be regarded as a natural consequence of a banker's breach of contract') or under the second limb, because even on the basis of the defendants' assumed knowledge 'this claim ... raises a narrative of events which though not unimaginable is certainly not foreseeable in the ordinary course'.

Miss Loebl submits that it is not necessary for the plaintiff to prove either that the precise sequence of events was foreseeable or that the losses might be as extensive as they were. She relies in particular upon *H Parsons (Livestock) Ltd v. Uttley Ingham & Co Ltd* [1978] 1 All ER 525, [1978] QB 791 and the recent judgments in *Brown v. KMR Services Ltd* [1995] 4 All ER 598. Given the facts which were known, or are asserted to have been known by the defendants, they could reasonably contemplate, it is submitted, that a breach of contract such as occurred might cause him losses of the kind which he alleges that he has suffered.

For my part, I cannot regard this as a claim falling within the second limb of *Hadley v. Baxendale*. It is not a case where the defendant is said to have had knowledge of 'special circumstances' so that this part of the rule applies. Rather, the question is, in my judgment, whether, given the plaintiff's general description of himself and of the purposes for which he intended to use the account, it can be said that damages arising from the loss or late performance of his contract to sell and deliver the goods to Nigeria can reasonably be supposed to have been in the contemplation of both parties when the contract was made, or as the 'not likely consequence' of the defendants' breach, if it should occur (*The Heron II*). This is the first rather than the second limb of the rule, although as I shall say below I am doubtful

whether it assists to make a rigid distinction of this sort.

In my judgment, and in agreement with the master, these damages were too remote to be claimed under this head. Even if the defendants were told that the account was to be used for the plaintiff's business, even trading activities, there was nothing to indicate that a cheque, even one drawn in favour of a goods wholesaler, was required for the purposes of international trade and in circumstances where even one day's delay in payment would or might cause the loss of a transaction or a substantial trading loss for the plaintiff. What might would give the defendants special notice of the need for immediate clearance so that, if they were willing to do so, a special arrangement could be made.

There is also the pragmatic reason given by the master, which is that there is no reported case where a bank's customer has recovered damages such as these for the wrongful dishonour of a cheque, where no special circumstances were alleged to exist.

GENERALLY

The above conclusions mean that I would dismiss both the appeal and the cross-appeal, and would uphold the master's award of general damages of £5,550. He said that it was 'somewhat coincidental' that this was £1,000 more than the amount of the cheque, although I think he meant by this that the appropriate sum by way of general damages could be calculated in that way in the circumstances of this case. This amount, as he explained, contained some allowance, though not very great, for injury to the plaintiff's credit and reputation in Nigeria such as was alleged to have occurred. This is consistent with a correct approach to the award of general damages in a case where the plaintiff claim that he was an exporter/importer and therefore the defendants could reasonably contemplate that he might suffer some injury to his credit in a country overseas.

The contentions for both parties were presented as if in a straitjacket imposed by the strict application of the rule in *Hadley v. Baxendale* so as to require the separate consideration of each of the two limbs. Miss Loebl submitted that there should be an award of general damages for injury to credit and of special damages for the trading losses allegedly sustained by reason of the delay to the particular shipment. Miss McQuail for the defendants submitted that general damages should be confined to 'loss flowing naturally being the unavailability to the customer of his money' — a difficult submission, in the light of the House of Lords decision in *President of*

India v. La Pintada Cia Navegacion SA [1984] 2 All ER 773 esp at 778, 789, [1985] AC 104 esp at 115, 129 — and 'other loss depending upon the matters known to the parties at the time of the contract', which might include damages for loss of reputation or credit and for trading losses, in appropriate circumstances. The master held that the bank's knowledge of whether the customer was 'a trader' or whether the account was to be used for trading purposes was irrelevant as a matter of law to the loss of credit claim. I would prefer to hold that the starting point for any application of *Hadley v. Baxendale* is the extent of the shared knowledge of both parties when the contract was made (see generally *Chitty on Contracts* (27th edn, 1994) vol 1, para 26–023, including the possibility that knowledge

of the defendant alone is enough). When that is established, it may often be the case that the first and the second parts of the rule overlap, or at least that it is unnecessary to draw a clear line of demarcation between them. This seems to me to be consistent with the commonsense approach suggested by Scarman LJ in *H Parsons (Livestock) Ltd v. Uttley Ingham & Co Ltd* [1978] 1 All ER 525 at 541, [1978] QB 791 at 813, and to be applicable here.

As stated above, I would dismiss both the appeal and the cross-appeal and uphold the master's award.

Appeal and cross-appeal dismissed.
Leave to appeal to the House of Lords refused.

(g) *Villiers v. Bank of Montreal*†

Wright J. in an oral judgment delivered at the conclusion of the trial said that the evidence established that on May 5th, 1933, the plaintiff issued two cheques, drawn on the defendant bank, one payable to the Bell Telephone Company for $2.50, and the other to the Lincoln Electric Light and Power Company for the sum of $3.00. These two cheques were cleared to the Bank of Montreal on the morning of May 8th before the hour of 10 o'clock. At that date the books of the Bank of Montreal showed a balance to the credit of the plaintiff of $1.29, but owing to an error in the computation of discount on a note the real balance was $3.74; thus there was only $3.74 available to pay two cheques totalling $5.50. It was argued on behalf of the plaintiff that, having proved that there were sums in the bank of more than $2.50 on May 8th when the cheque payable to the Bell Telephone Co., was presented and that the bank refused to pay and returned the cheque, he has established a breach of contract on the part of the bank and that the burden of proof was upon the defendant bank to establish a good reason for not paying the cheque when presented. That position may be correct but these two cheques were presented simultaneously, as near as can be determined

from the evidence, on the morning of May 8th before the hour of 10 o'clock when the bank opened for business; when they were brought to the attention of the ledgerkeeper she noticed that there were not sufficient funds to pay both of these cheques, and after consultation with the manager they were both marked "N.S.F." and payment refused.

The learned Justice said that he was of the opinion that the bank was not called upon to keep an exact note of which of these two cheques came to the attention of the ledgerkeeper first when they were in point of fact presented practically simultaneously; it would be imposing an intolerable burden on the bank if they were compelled to keep a record of presentment in the matter of seconds; there was practically simultaneous presentment of the two cheques. The bank officials were justified in refusing payment of both. It would have been a breach of duty on the part of the officials if they had paid one cheque and refused payment of the other. Both had to be treated alike. There were not sufficient funds to pay both of them, and, therefore, both should be refused. The defence has been clearly established and the plaintiff's action must fail.

---

† [1933] O.W.N. 649 (H.C.J.).

Perusal of the record shows that the defence on which the bank now succeeds was not raised in the pleadings. It ought to have been. It is stated that the first intimation that the plaintiff had of it was upon the examination of an officer of the bank for discovery. That being so the proper disposition to make of the cost would be to dismiss the action with costs limited to the costs subsequent to the examination of the manager of the bank for discovery.

Action dismissed with special order as to costs.

(h) *Advance Bank v. Toronto Dominion Bank*†

[G. SPEIGEL J.:]

Two banks dispute which should bear the loss from a forged cheque. The forged cheque was drawn on the defendant, Toronto Dominion Bank ("TD"), and was deposited to an account at the plaintiff, Advance Bank ("Advance"), in Illinois. A former customer of Advance has been named as a third party to these proceedings, but has made no reply and has been noted in default. The forged cheque was fraudulent and the money is now in the hands of a rogue.

Each bank moves for summary judgment against the other, relying on Rules 20 and 21 of the *Rules of Civil Procedure*. Both banks agree that the facts are not in dispute in these motions for summary judgment. The Court is being asked to determine the legal effect of the evidence as to whether the cheque was "accepted" or "paid" by TD; if it was, TD is liable and, if not, TD is not liable.

THE FACTS

Advance is a community retail bank with sixteen branches in the greater Chicago area. Dorothy Hutson, the third party, opened a chequing account at one of Advance's branches in 1998. Hutson carried on business as D&J Import and Export ("D&J").

On April 4, 2001, Hutson deposited a cheque (the "Cheque") for $285,000 CDN made out to D&J. The Cheque appeared to be signed by the officers of Blue Mountain Resorts Limited ("BMR") and appeared to be drawn on BMR's account at the TD branch in Collingwood, Ontario.

Advance advised Hutson, when she deposited the Cheque, that Advance would hold the funds for seven days. After that time had elapsed, Advance paid out the amount of the Cheque either to Hutson or on her order.

Accordingly, TD is the purported "drawee" of the Cheque, BMR is the purported "drawer", Advance is the "collecting bank", and Hutson (i.e. D&J) is the purported "payee".

In order to process the Cheque, a number of steps were taken. On April 4, 2001, Advance deposited the Cheque to its account at American National Bank of Chicago ("ANBC"), which acts as Advance's clearing agent for all domestic and foreign cheques. On April 5, 2001, ANBC telephoned TD in Collingwood to verify that there were sufficient funds in BMR's account to cover the Cheque, and that there was no stop-payment in effect. Once this was done, ANBC advised Advance on April 6, 2001 that its account would be credited for $179,407.50 in American dollars, which was the value of the Cheque according to the exchange rate at that time.

The following business day, the Cheque was deposited to ANBC's account at the Bank of Nova Scotia ("BNS") in Toronto. An American bank normally processes a Canadian cheque by this method. American national and regional banks typically maintain accounts at Canadian banks for clearing cross-border items.

BNS received the Cheque at its Toronto Data Centre on April 9, 2001. That day, the Cheque was delivered to TD's Toronto Data Centre through the Canadian cheque clearing system (the "Clearing"). The Clearing processes cheques payable in Canadian funds through Regional Settlement Points, one of which is Toronto. At each settlement point, cheques are exchanged by deliveries several times each day among the banks involved in the Clearing. The

---

† (2003), 227 D.L.R. (4th) 755 at 758–68 (Ont. S.C.J.).

Canadian Payment Association Rules ("the Rules") govern the Clearing.

An independent service provider, Symcor Services Incorporated ("Symcor"), operates TD's Toronto Data Centre. The Data Centre carries out automated processing of cheques drawn from TD branches. This process culminates in an automatic date stamp being imprinted on the back of each cheque. When this happens, the TD customer's account is debited automatically. Accordingly, the Data Centre received the Cheque, processed it, and stamped the back of it with the date April 9, 2001.

Through this process, TD debited BMR's account on April 9, 2001 by the amount of the Cheque. That day, the officers of BMR contacted the Collingwood TD branch to question the debit of $285,000 from their account. They had noticed the debit as an item on their daily electronic statement. The Collingwood TD branch requested a copy of the Cheque, and received the copy on April 16, 2001. Also on April 16, 2001, the BMR officers made a declaration that they had not signed the Cheque and that the Cheque was a forgery.

In the meantime, however, on April 11, 2001, Advance's seven-day hold on the Cheque ended. Over the following week, Hutson withdrew the Cheque's funds from her account in Illinois.

There is some dispute in the evidence with respect to when Advance first received notification that the Cheque was a forgery. TD gave this notification either on April 17, 2001 (according to TD's evidence) or April 25, 2001 (according to Advance's evidence). On or about April 20, 2001, BMR's account at TD was credited the amount of the Cheque. Counsel submit, and I agree, that this discrepancy does not affect the result in this matter.

On or about April 26, 2001, TD obtained the original Cheque and returned it to Advance directly by courier. It arrived by overnight courier at Advance's branch in Illinois.

On May 15, 2001, TD returned a certified true copy of the Cheque to Advance through the Federal Reserve Bank of Chicago ("FRC") and the FRC deducted the funds paid on the Cheque from Advance's account at the FRC. Advance protested the return of the Cheque because it was returned after the period permitted for returns under the US cheque clearing rules. However, the FRC did not allow Advance's protest because the Cheque was a Canadian item and therefore could not be processed under the US cheque clearing system. Accordingly, TD returned the Cheque and was compensated outside of the Clearing; Advance protested this return at the FRC and lost.

I note that it appears something happened in the US Federal Reserve clearing system when the Cheque was returned, the result of which was that Advance was debited $285,000 in American dollars, not in Canadian dollars. The Federal Reserve System has resolved this error and the error is now irrelevant to these proceedings.

A summary is therefore as follows: TD had provisionally settled the Cheque through its automated settlement point in Toronto; TD first debited and then credited BMR's account; TD notified Advance and returned the Cheque by courier; Advance had already distributed the funds to its customer.

As the matter currently stands, Advance is bearing the loss of this Cheque. Advance argues that TD is liable on the Cheque and that therefore TD ought to bear the loss.

ANALYSIS

Advance frames its position in the law of unjust enrichment. This claim requires that Advance demonstrate the following three elements: TD has enjoyed a benefit; Advance has suffered a corresponding deprivation; and there is no juristic reason for the benefit or corresponding deprivation: *Peel (Regional Municipality) v. Canada*, [1992] S.C.R. 762.

Advance's position is that TD has benefited insofar as it was spared the expense of bearing the loss of the Cheque, and that Advance has suffered a deprivation by bearing the loss. It is true that a "benefit" need not mean that TD has gained any money in the transaction. For the purposes of the unjust enrichment analysis, a benefit can consist in being "spared an expense which [the party] would have been required to undertake": *Peel (Regional Municipality) v. Canada, supra*, at para. 46. The argument therefore is that when TD was spared this expense, and when Advance bore it, this constituted the benefit and corresponding deprivation in the unjust enrichment claim.

Regarding the third condition for unjust enrichment, Advance argues that there is no juristic reason for the loss to fall in this way. Advance submits that TD is liable on the Cheque either because the Cheque was deemed to have been paid by the operation of the Rules governing the Clearing, or because TD paid the cheque by accepting it or upon presentment.

Advance takes the following three alternative positions with respect to payment:

(a) The negotiation of the Cheque is governed by the Rules, such that Advance was not permitted to return it when it did.

(b) TD accepted the Cheque and was therefore not entitled to return it.

(c) TD paid the Cheque upon presentment and was therefore not entitled to return it.

In contrast, TD's position is that it did not accept or pay the Cheque, either under the Rules or under the legal understanding of acceptance or presentment. TD argues that if this is the case, TD is not liable on the instrument and therefore no unjust enrichment has taken place.

The question for this Court, therefore, is whether TD accepted or paid the Cheque and is therefore liable on it.

1. The Clearing Rules

The Canadian Payments Association ("CPA") was established under the *Canadian Payments Act*, R.S.C. 1985, c. C-21. Evans J.A. in *National Bank of Greece (Canada) v. Bank of Montreal*, [2001] 2 F.C. 288 (F.C.A.) noted that Canadian banks are statutorily required to be CPA members. Evans J.A. then described the CPA as follows at para. 17:

> ... the CPA is also a self-regulatory body of a vital sector of Canada's financial services industry, namely the clearance of cheques and similar items among member institutions. ... In addition, membership in the CPA is voluntary for financial institutions other than banks, as is the members' use of the CPA's clearance system. However, as a practical matter, it is necessary for those offering their customers the benefit of a chequing account to avail themselves of the clearance system.

For the following reasons, Advance is not entitled to rely on the CPA Rules regarding the clearing of cheques.

First, Advance did not plead the Rules in its statement of claim. Indeed, in its initial communication with TD on the matter, Advance indicated it was not intending to rely on the Rules to support its position.

Second, and more importantly, Advance is not a member institution of the CPA. The CPA membership consists of the Bank of Canada and all banks operating in Canada. Certain other financial institutions operating in Canada, as well as authorized foreign banks, are eligible to become members: *Canadian Payments Act*, s. 4.

It is true that the Cheque was introduced into the Clearing by BNS (after it had travelled from Advance to ANBC in Chicago and subsequently to BNS in Toronto). It is also true that BNS is a member of the CPA. However, BNS is not a party to the case at bar. Moreover, counsel for Advance stated in oral argument that Advance is not asserting rights of membership in the CPA through BNS. Counsel for TD also argued that there was no harm or wrong *vis-à-vis* BNS, and that BNS's presence is therefore not required here. For these reasons, the involvement of BNS as a member of the CPA is not a factor in this decision.

Section 29 of the *Canadian Payments Act* provides that members of the CPA, of which TD Bank is one, shall accept and arrange for settlement of cheques in accordance with the by-laws and Rules. The Rules provide for the mechanisms by which cheques and similar items are processed. As part of the arrangement, members of the CPA effectively agree to abide by time restrictions that limit their rights of recourse through these CPA mechanisms. Specifically, there is a two-day limit to return dishonoured cheques through the Clearing: Rule A4, s. 5.

The result of this mutual agreement is that the benefits and risks of the CPA are allocated among members, who consent to having their rights and obligations governed by the Rules. This includes their rights and obligations regarding the risk of forgery. As counsel for TD puts it, "a hard and fast two-day limit to return forgeries through the Clearing may be hard luck for a member one day and good fortune the next."

Since Advance is not a member of the CPA, the Rules do not bind it. It does not assume any of the risks of the Rules and, therefore, cannot claim the benefit of the Rules. Advance cannot assert the Rules to create obligations upon TD or anyone else. Indeed, Bradley Crawford notes that it "seems to be clear in principle that the time limit [for return of a dishonoured item] is binding only between members of the CPA": "Late Return of Dishonoured Cheque" (2001) 36 C.B.L.J 1 at 10.

Indeed, in *National Bank of Greece (Canada) v. Bank of Montreal*, *supra*, Evans J.A. noted that the Rules are not "general law". Rather, they apply "only to the banks, and to other financial institutions that have voluntarily become members of the CPA, when they use the CPA's clearing system": at para. 13. Evans J.A. also noted that whatever private law rights and remedies the parties may enjoy outside the Rules are not superseded by those Rules.

2. Acceptance

The second of Advance's arguments is that TD accepted the Cheque for payment within the meaning of the *Bills of Exchange Act*, R.S.C., 1985 c. B-4 (as amended) (the "*BEA*") at its Toronto Data Centre, through Symcor as its agent. If TD accepted the Cheque, it would be precluded from setting up a forgery under s. 48(1) of the *BEA*. Acceptance is similar to certification, by which a bank irrevocably lends its own credit to an instrument: see *AE LePage Real Estate Services v. Rattray Publications Ltd.* (1994) 21 O.R. (3d) 164 (C.A.). However, the formal requirements of acceptance are different from those of certification: *Bank of Nova Scotia v. Canada Trust Co.* (1998), 39 O.R. (3d) 84 (Gen. Div.).

"Payment" is not defined in the *BEA* and is not a technical term: Bradley Crawford, *Payment, Clearing and Settlement in Canada* (Vol. 1) looseleaf (Aurora, Ont.: Canada Law Book Inc., 2002) at §26.02.1(a). Nor is there anything in the *BEA* describing what is known under the Rules as "provisional settlement", namely a settlement subject to a period of time to set aside that settlement.

Section 126 of the *BEA* gives immunity to a drawee bank on a particular item unless the drawee bank accepts it:

> **126.** ... the drawee of a bill who does not accept as required by this Act is not liable on the instrument.

Moreover, there is no time limit in the *BEA* within which a bank must act to advise anyone of its non-payment: see Crawford, "Late Return of Dishonoured Cheque", *supra* at 6; *Caisse Populaire D'Alfred Ltée v. Lapensée*, [1985] O.J. No. 1287 (H.C.J.) at paras. 15–16, Saunders J.

Acceptance is governed by a series of provisions in the *BEA*. The *BEA* requires that the drawee sign for acceptance of a cheque. Section 35(1)(a) of the *BEA* states that an acceptance is invalid unless it is both written on the bill and signed by the drawee.

The *BEA* also provides in s. 35(2) as follows: "The mere signature of the drawee written on the bill without additional words is a sufficient acceptance". In *Bank of Nova Scotia v. Canada Trust Co.*, *supra*, E.M. Macdonald J. noted that it was conceded in that case that "the drawee's signature is required for acceptance of the cheque."

Section 4 of the *BEA* provides that a signature may be placed on a cheque by an agent:

> **4.** Where, by this Act, any instrument or writing is required to be signed by any person, it is not necessary that he should sign it with his own hand, but it is sufficient if his signature is written thereon by some other person by or under his authority.

Advance argues that if Symcor was an agent of TD, the stamp placed on the Cheque at the Toronto Data Centre was a valid signature and, therefore, a valid acceptance under the BEA. Advance submits that TD's conduct would lead a third party to conclude that Symcor was the agent of TD for receiving and accepting cheques and that this is sufficient for acceptance under the BEA.

TD submits that acceptance requires a signature and that there was never a signature from TD placed on the Cheque. The Toronto Data Centre placed a date stamp on the back of the Cheque, and automatic electronic debits and credits appeared in BMR's and BNS's accounts respectively. TD argues that these are insufficient to constitute acceptance for payment. I agree. Even assuming that Symcor is TD's agent, affixing a stamp, which is done automatically on every cheque that arrives at the Data Centre, can hardly be said to be acceptance.

The automatic debit and credit, which are meant to be provisional under the Rules, also do not create acceptance. There must be something more; the drawee must put its mind to final payment. Until the date when TD communicated its decision not to honour the Cheque, Advance had only the fallout of a provisional electronic settlement, upon which it relied. Advance was not entitled to rely as it did because, as discussed above, it is not a member of the CPA. The electronic set-off, and the relevant timelines under the Rules to decide to dishonour, apply only to dealings between members.

My conclusion on this aspect of the matter is bolstered by the *National Slag* case that dealt with payment but applies equally well to acceptance. In *National Slag v. Canadian Imperial Bank of Commerce* (1982), 140 D.L.R. (3d) 473 (Ont. H.C.J.), affirmed at [1985] O.J. No. 149 (C.A.), Labrosse J. dealt with a case in which a bank attempted to return a cheque after the permissible time limit under the Rules in place at the time. On the question of whether "payment" had been made upon the deposit of the cheque, Labrosse J. commented: "On the facts of this case I cannot accept the argument that the cheque was 'paid' by the debits and credits made through the clearing procedure established for banking convenience any more than the cheque was paid when C.I.B.C. credited the plaintiff on deposit of the cheque": at p. 476.

Labrosse J.'s statement is quoted in Bradley Crawford's text, *Payment, Clearing and Settlement in Canada, supra*. Crawford states that "the initial settlement given for items exchanged in a bulk clearing such as occurs daily at all regional settlement points in Canada is not an irrevocable payment of any item exchanged:" §9.01(5)(c). The automatic debits and credits that occur each night in the Clearing cannot constitute payment in law. Provisional settlement is not payment, because even under the Rules an item may be returned and the provisional settlement reversed, as of right, if the drawee decides to return it. Section 5 of Rule A4 provides that members of the CPA lose the right to return a cheque through the clearing after a specific time:

> **5.** Subject to section 6 [which sets out exceptions that do not apply in this case],[1] each Item being returned through the Clearing shall be returned by the Drawee, to the Negotiating Institution, as set out in section 11, no later than the business day following receipt by the first organizational unit of the Drawee that is able to make or act upon a decision to dishonour an Item.

The evidence from TD is that Symcor operates the Toronto Data Centre by processing cheques that come through the Regional Settlement Point. The contract between Symcor and TD expressly states that each party is an independent contractor and cannot bind the other, nor create any obligation on behalf of the other. Symcor does not have the authority to accept the Cheque on behalf of TD.

The relevant organizational unit referred to in s. 5 of Rule A4 is the Collingwood TD branch, not Symcor. Bradley Crawford, in his text *Payment, Clearing and Settlement in Canada supra* at §9.01(5)(c), writes that "the effective decision of a bank whether to pay or to dishonour is made at the branch of account, not at the clearing house or data centre." The one business day deadline for return through the Clearing therefore ran from the date of receipt at the Collingwood TD branch.

In summary, the requirements for acceptance under the *BEA* were not met in this case. The automatic date stamp placed by Symcor on the cheque did not constitute acceptance, nor did the automatic debits and credits to BMR's and BNS's accounts.

3. Presentment for Payment

Advance's third argument is that TD paid the Cheque upon presentment and therefore was not entitled to return it when it did. In s. 84(1) of the *BEA*, presentment is a requirement for payment to be made. To have presented the Cheque for payment, Advance would have been required to exhibit it at the proper place (as defined in s. 87 of the *BEA*), and "either to the person designated by the bill as payer or to his representative or a person authorized to pay or to refuse payment on his behalf" (s. 86(1)). The manner of presentment is also provided for in s. 84(3) of the *BEA*, namely that the holder of a bill must exhibit it to the person from whom he demands payment in order to effect presentment.

Advance argues that the Clearing is a modern method of presentment and that in reality most cheques never make it to the branches of the banks on which they are drawn. Accordingly, Advance argues that the cheque was presented when it was delivered through the Clearing to the TD and was paid when TD debited the funds from BMR's account.

TD argues that Advance sending the Cheque to the Toronto Data Centre did not constitute "presentment" under the *BEA* because it was not to the proper place and Symcor was not a person authorized to pay or to refuse payment on TD's behalf. In this vein, TD argues, and I accept, that when members of the CPA exchange cheques through the Clearing, the *BEA* prerequisites for presentment for payment are, in effect, mutually waived by members of the CPA for their common benefit and detriment in the operation of the Clearing.

The Toronto Data Centre was not the proper place for Advance to effect presentment, nor was Symcor authorized to pay or refuse payment on TD's behalf. TD did not waive the *BEA*'s requirements with respect to its dealings with Advance and the prerequisite of presentment for payment was not fulfilled.

Although it might be argued that modern commercial reality requires that introduction of a cheque into the Clearing constitutes sufficient presentment, this argument would lead to the conclusion that the Clearing trumps the *BEA* and the common law. This is precisely the argument that was rejected in *Bank of Nova Scotia v. Toronto-Dominion Bank*, [2001] O.J. No. 1717, in which the Ontario Court of Appeal held that the *BEA* prevails over the internal rules of the CPA. Advance could have avoided this dispute by presenting the Cheque at the TD location that was authorized to make a decision on it. While this may seem cumbersome, it is a necessary part of the risk assessment that banks, and indeed all participants in the commercial world, must make on an ongoing basis.

CONCLUSION

There was no acceptance of the Cheque, nor was there payment on the Cheque either through the Clearing or upon presentment. Absent acceptance or payment, TD is not liable on the Cheque. Since TD was only spared an expense that it was not required to incur, it cannot have been unjustly enriched.

In the result, TD's motion for summary judgment is granted and Advance's motion is dismissed.

If counsel are unable to agree upon costs, they may make written submissions to me within 15 days of the release of these reasons.

Action dismissed.

Note

1. Section 6(a) does provide that there is no time limit for the return of an Item with a Forged Endorsement (i.e. on the back of the cheque). It also provides that an Item with both a Forged Endorsement *and* a Forged or Unauthorized Signature shall be returned in accordance with Section 5. Section 6 does not provide any exceptions for cheques with only a Forged or Unauthorized signature (i.e. on the front of the cheque).

(i)   *National Bank of Greece (Canada) v. Bank of Montreal*†

[EVANS J.A.:]

The issue in this case is whether a compliance panel set up by the National Clearings Committee of the respondent, the Canadian Payments Association (the CPA), erred in law when it ordered the appellant, the National Bank of Greece (Canada) (the NBG), to pay to the respondent, the Bank of Montreal (the BMO) the amount of a cheque (and interest) that a customer had drawn on the appellant, but which the appellant dishonoured for insufficient funds.

The panel found that the NBG had breached section 5 of Rule A4 (Returned and Redirected Items) of the Association's Rules, in that it had returned into the clearing system a dishonoured cheque more than a day after it was in a position to decide whether to honour it. The panel's conclusion that the appellant was in breach of this provision is not challenged in this proceeding.

The question in dispute is whether the panel erred in law when it remedied the breach by making the impugned order pursuant to its power under paragraph 8(2)(d) of Rule A11 (Compliance) to issue

> An order requiring the making of restitution to any Member that has suffered <u>a loss</u> as a result of the acts or omissions of a Member under the jurisdiction of the CPA. [Emphasis added.]

The appellant argued that the BMO had suffered no loss because its customer, the payee of the cheque, had funds in its account that enabled the BMO to charge back the credit and thus to recoup from its customer any loss that it would have sustained as a result of initially crediting its customer with the proceeds of the subsequently dishonoured cheque.

The Motions Judge [(1999), 175 F.T.R. 232] dismissed the application for judicial review on the ground that, for the purpose of determining whether the BMO had sustained a "loss" under paragraph 8(2)(d) of Rule A11, it was irrelevant whether the BMO was able effectively to reverse the credit in its customer's account. The CPA administers the system for the clearing of cheques and the settlement of transactions among member institutions pursuant to the *Canadian Payments Association Act*, R.S.C., 1985, c. C-21 (the CPAA), and the by-laws and rules enacted by the Association under sections 18 and 19. Any order made by a compliance panel to remedy a breach of the by-laws or rules does not derogate from whatever rights and remedies may be available to the banks, or their customers, under the private law relating to negotiable instruments or to the contractual relationship of banker and customer.

The Motions Judge accepted the CPA's argument that the BMO had suffered a loss because, as a result of the NBG's returning the dishonoured

---

† [2001] 2 F.C. 288 at 291–96 (F.C.C.A.).

cheque through the clearing system, the BMO effectively lost the credit with the Bank of Canada that it had obtained when it credited its customer's account with the amount of the cheque and put the cheque into the clearance system. Further, he relied on the fact that, by returning the cheque in breach of the Rules, the NBG had gained a credit in its settlement account with its clearing agent, the Royal Bank of Canada. Although named as a respondent, the BMO took no part in the application for judicial review or in the appeal.

A preliminary issue addressed neither by the parties in their memoranda, nor by the learned Judge, is the standard of review to be applied to the panel's interpretation of paragraph 8(2)(d) of Rule A11. It appears to have been assumed that, if the NBG established that the panel's interpretation was not correct, then the panel erred in law. When the standard of review issue was raised from the Bench, counsel for the appellant took the position that correctness was the appropriate standard because whether the BMO had suffered a "loss" was a jurisdictional question that the panel had to decide correctly. When counsel for the respondent was invited to address this issue, she argued that the Court should only intervene if it concluded that the panel's interpretation of the word "loss" was unreasonable.

In our opinion, the standard of review should always be considered by a reviewing court before embarking on an examination of an administrative tribunal's decision. Otherwise, if the court were later to conclude that, on the basis of a pragmatic and functional analysis, a deferential standard is appropriate, it would have strayed beyond its proper role, and asked itself the wrong question, namely whether the tribunal's decision was right.

By not determining the standard of review first, a court may unwittingly encumber the administration of a statutory scheme by a tribunal whose decisions are not subject to review for correctness. Thus, if the reviewing court concludes that the tribunal's interpretation of its enabling legislation was correct, this interpretation will be binding on other panels, and thereby deprive the tribunal of the power subsequently to take a different view. On the other hand, if the court concludes that the tribunal was wrong, but not unreasonable, it makes it extremely difficult for the tribunal to follow its earlier interpretation that has been pronounced by a court on an application for judicial review to be "wrong", even though not requiring judicial intervention. Moreover, for a reviewing court to start by assuming that its task is to determine the correct meaning of the legislation

puts it into the wrong mind set for playing a limited role in the interpretative process.

Accordingly, the proper starting point of the analysis in this case is a consideration of the standard of review applicable to the panel's interpretation of paragraph 8(2)(d) of Rule A11, under which the panel could make a "restitution" order when a member's breach of the by-law occasioned a loss to another member. We should add that there was no challenge to the legal authority of the Association under sections 18 and 19 of the CPAA to enact a rule or by-law authorising the panel to order restitution.

For the following reasons, a pragmatic and functional analysis clearly indicates that the Motions Judge should have confined himself to asking whether the compliance panel's determination that the BMO had suffered a "loss" for the purpose of paragraph 8(2)(d) was unreasonable, even though its decisions are not protected by a privative clause.

First, the panel was composed of three employees of members of the CPA, other than those involved in the dispute. The understanding of the operation of the clearance and settlement systems that the panel members have by virtue of their employment in member financial institutions is relevant to the interpretation of the Association's Rules, even though the panel seems to exercise an essentially adjudicative function on an *ad hoc* basis. Moreover, before rendering its decision, the panel held a hearing at which the appellant was represented by counsel.

Second, the issues in dispute concern the interpretation of a provision of the enabling statutory framework under which the panel operates. It is not "general law", but applies only to the banks, and to other financial institutions that have voluntarily become members of the CPA, when they use the CPA's clearing system. The statutory rules governing the technical operation of the clearance and settlement systems are peculiar to this specialized regulatory regime, and do not draw upon general legal concepts or values.

Third, while the remedial order in question adversely affected the NBG's financial interests, it did not supersede whatever private law rights that the appellant may have against either the BMO, or the payer or payee of the cheque. Indeed, as part of his argument for why the appeal should be allowed, counsel for the NBG claimed that the panel's decision was "sterile" or "absurd" because the appellant could offset whatever it owed by virtue of the panel's order against what it was entitled to recover from the BMO under the *Bills of Exchange Act*, R.S.C., 1985, c. B-4.

Fourth, the reasons for the creation of the regulatory scheme governing the clearance of cheques and the settlement of transactions among member banks indicate that judicial surveillance should be restrained. The expeditious and final decision making required for the prompt clearance of cheques, and similar items, within Canada's banking system, and the settlement of transactions, might be undermined if a party aggrieved by a compliance panel's decision could bring an application for judicial review to ask the Court to determine *de novo* the issue in dispute before the panel.

Fifth, the CPA is a statutory body that derives its regulatory powers and duties from federal legislation. In addition, banks are statutorily required to belong to the CPA: CPAA, section 4 [as am. by S.C. 1999, c. 28, s. 111]. Hence, decisions of the compliance panel of the Association are subject to public law.

On the other hand, the CPA is also a self-regulatory body of a vital sector of Canada's financial services industry, namely the clearance of cheques and similar items among member institutions. Thus, members of the CPA elect the board of directors of the Association, except for one who is nominated by the Bank of Canada: CPAA, sections 8 and 9 [as am. *idem*, s. 112]. In addition, membership in the CPA is voluntary for financial institutions other than banks, as is the members' use of the CPA's clearance system. However, as a practical matter, it is necessary for those offering their customers the benefit of a chequing account to avail themselves of the clearance system.

Accordingly, the "domestic" or "private" aspect of this regulatory scheme, under which, after holding a hearing, panels set up by a committee of the Association interpret and apply rules promulgated by the Association, indicates that the Court should be more reluctant to intervene than might be appropriate in

respect of decisions by a statutory regulatory body of a more obviously external, governmental nature. Similarly, the consensual aspects of grievance arbitration in labour disputes, as well as the need for expeditious and final decision making, have led courts to limit the intensity of their review of arbitrators' interpretations of collective agreements, even though legislation also regulates important dimensions of the process.

In our opinion, the Motions Judge did not err when he dismissed the application for judicial review. However, the basis of our decision is that the panel's conclusion that the BMO had suffered a "loss" for the purpose of paragraph 8(2)(d) of Rule A11 was not unreasonable. We have reached this conclusion by having regard to section 5 of the CPAA which provides that the objects of the CPA are to establish and administer a national clearing and settlement system. This system operates only at the level of banking and similar institutions, and, as counsel for the appellant conceded, decisions of the compliance panel have no impact on either the private law rights and duties of banks, their customers, and the payers and payees of cheques, or the remedies available to enforce them.

Accordingly, in determining whether a loss had been sustained and restitution should be ordered, the panel was not unreasonable in regarding as irrelevant the relationship, or the state of accounts, between the negotiating bank and its customer, and in focussing only on the BMO's settlement account with the Bank of Canada and on the NBG's settlement account with its clearing agent, the Royal Bank. Looked at in that way, it is incontrovertible that, as a result of sending back a cheque through the clearing system in breach of the Rules, the NBG gained a credit, and the BMO incurred a corresponding debit.

For these reasons, the appeal will be dismissed with costs.

(j)   *Bills of Exchange Act*†

Definitions

163.1 The following definitions apply in this section and sections 163.2 to 163.6.

"bank" has the same meaning as in section 164.

"eligible bill" means a bill that is of a class specified by a by-law, a rule or a standard made under the *Canadian Payments Act*.

"official image", in respect of an eligible bill, means an image of that eligible bill created by or on

† R.S.C. 1985, C. B-4, as am. by S.C. 2007, c. 6, ss. 164–167.

behalf of a bank in accordance with by-laws, rules or standards made under the *Canadian Payments Act*, together with any data in relation to the eligible bill prepared in accordance with those by-laws, rules and standards, and includes a display, a printout, a copy or any other output of that image and that data created by or on behalf of a bank in accordance with those by-laws, rules and standards.

Status of official image

163.2 An official image of an eligible bill may be dealt with and used for all purposes as though it were the eligible bill.

Electronic presentment

163.3(1) Despite anything in this Act, a bank may present for payment an official image of an eligible bill electronically in accordance with by-laws, rules or standards made under the *Canadian Payments Act* and, if it does so, the requirements of this Act respecting the presentment for payment of the eligible bill are deemed to have been complied with.

Discharge by payment

(2) The eligible bill and its official image are discharged if payment in due course is made by or on behalf of the drawee after the electronic presentment for payment of the official image of the eligible bill.

Presumption

163.4(1) In the absence of evidence to the contrary, a document purporting to be an official image of an eligible bill is presumed to be an official image of the eligible bill.

Admissibility

(2) An official image of an eligible bill is admissible in evidence for all purposes for which the eligible bill would be admitted as evidence without proof that the official image was created by or on behalf of a bank in accordance with the by-laws, rules or standards made under the *Canadian Payments Act*.

True copy of contents

(3) In the absence of evidence to the contrary, an official image of an eligible bill is presumed to be a true and exact copy of the contents of the eligible bill.

Effect of destruction

163.5 If an eligible bill is destroyed in accordance with by-laws, rules or standards made under the *Canadian Payments Act* and there is an official image of the bill,

(a) a person's rights and powers in relation to the eligible bill are not affected by reason only that the person does not possess it;

(b) the destruction does not affect any person's rights, powers, duties and liabilities in relation to the eligible bill; and

(c) the eligible bill is not considered to be lost or to have been materially altered or intentionally cancelled.

Warranty

163.6(1) A bank that creates or purports to create an official image of an eligible bill, or on whose behalf an official image of an eligible bill is created or purported to be created, warrants that the official image or the purported official image, as the case may be, was created in accordance with by-laws, rules or standards made under the *Canadian Payments Act* and that it accurately represents the eligible bill.

Damages

(2) Any person who has suffered damages as a result of a breach of the warranty has a cause of action for damages against the bank.

Definition of "bank"

164. In this Part, "bank" includes every member of the Canadian Payments Association established under the *Canadian Payments Association Act* and every local cooperative credit society, as defined in that Act, that is a member of a central, as defined in that Act, that is a member of the Canadian Payments Association.

Cheque

165.(1) A cheque is a bill drawn on a bank, payable on demand.

(2) Except as otherwise provided in this Part, the provisions of this Act applicable to a bill payable on demand apply to a cheque.

(3) Where a cheque is delivered to a bank for deposit to the credit of a person and the bank credits him with the amount of the cheque, the bank

acquires all the rights and powers of a holder in due course of the cheque.

Presentment for payment

166.(1) Subject to this Act,

(a) where a cheque is not presented for payment within a reasonable time of its issue and the drawer or the person on whose account it is drawn had the right at the time of presentment, as between him and the bank, to have the cheque paid, and suffers actual damage through the delay, he is discharged to the extent of the damage, that is to say, to the extent to which the drawer or person is a creditor of the bank to a larger amount than he would have been had the cheque been paid; and

(b) the holder of the cheque, with respect to which the drawer or person is discharged, shall be a creditor, in lieu of the drawer or person, of the bank to the extent of the discharge, and entitled to recover the amount from it.

(2) In determining what is a reasonable time, within this section, regard shall be had to the nature of the instrument, the usage of trade and of banks and facts of the particular case.

Authority to pay

167. The duty and authority of a bank to pay a cheque drawn on it by its customer are determined by

(a) countermand of payment; or
(b) notice of the customer's death.

(k) *Shapera v. Toronto-Dominion Bank*†

[TRITSCHLER C.J.Q.B.:]

Plaintiff's action is to recover $2,000 debited to his account upon a cheque in respect of which plaintiff alleges he stopped payment.

At the conclusion of the trial I gave my findings of fact and reserved to consider points of law submitted by counsel. I said that defendant's witnesses — Pollock, Calof and Buschau — were credible and persuasive witnesses and that I accepted their evidence without question; that plaintiff was not a credible witness; that his story about conditions being attached to the giving of the cheque and the offer to purchase property was not true. I did not accept plaintiff's evidence when it was in conflict with that of defendant's witnesses, particularly Calof.

The facts may, therefore, be stated in bare outline, leaving out details which very often told strongly against plaintiff.

Plaintiff has an account at defendant's Portage Avenue and Ainslie Street branch. I shall refer to it as the "defendant".

On 26th January 1968 plaintiff, through Calof's firm, Morgan Real Estate, made an offer in writing to purchase an apartment block for $62,000, payable $2,000 by a deposit, $8,000 in cash on or before possession or adjustment date, which was 1st May 1968, and the balance by mortgage. The deposit was plaintiff's cheque, the subject matter of this action. It is dated 26th January 1968, drawn on defendant for $2,000 and payable to Morgan Real Estate, who were the vendor's agents. There were several vendors. It is not necessary to give their names. For brevity I shall refer to them as the "vendor".

The offer provided that after acceptance by the vendor the deposit should become part of the purchase price and that if plaintiff failed to comply with the terms of the offer the vendor might cancel the agreement and retain the deposit.

On 27th January 1968 the vendor accepted the offer and plaintiff received notice of the acceptance and a completed copy of the accepted offer.

Plaintiff asked Calof to hold the cheque, saying that he had certain banking arrangements to make. He gave Calof the impression that he was arranging at a bank, other than defendant, for the full $10,000 cash required. Calof, who was plaintiff's close friend, delayed sending the cheque to the vendor's solicitors but several times reminded plaintiff of

† [1971] 1 W.W.R. 442 (Man. Q.B.).

his obligation to do so. On 27th March 1968 the vendor's solicitors became insistent and required the cheque to be turned over to them. On 9th April 1968 Calof caused the cheque to be endorsed by Morgan Real Estate and sent it by letter to the vendor's solicitors. In the letter Calof asked the solicitors to hold the cheque as plaintiff "has made his arrangements for the total down payment at another bank. Kindly check with Mr. Pollock, the purchaser's solicitor when the total amount of $10,000.00 will be paid over to you." In doing this Calof acted in perfectly good faith. He had told plaintiff that he was being pressed to turn over the deposit and would have to do so. Plaintiff did not object and did not mention anything about stopping payment of the cheque.

On 18th April 1968 the cheque was presented, presumably by vendor's solicitors, to defendant and upon request was accepted or "certified" and debited to plaintiff's account.

On *20th February 1968* plaintiff, without notice to anyone other than defendant, attended on defendant and signed a "stop payment" form, reading, in part:

> PLEASE STOP PAYMENT of cheque No. S/A 2622 (this was the number of plaintiff's account, not of the cheque, which was unnumbered) Dated the *27* day of January, 1968 for $2,000.00 issued by the undersigned and payable to Morgan Real Estate. (The italics are mine).

In accordance with custom and practice a "stop payment" sticker was affixed to the ledger card of plaintiff's account, which read:

ACC. No. 2622	STOP PAYMENT	
DATE	PAYEE	AMOUNT
Jan. 27/68	Morgan Real Estate	$2,000

When one side of a ledger card is filled with entries and the opposite side is to be used the usual practice of defendant is to carry forward "stop payment" information by placing a "stop payment" sticker at the top of the new side. This was not done in the case of plaintiff's ledger card and when, on 18th April 1968, plaintiff's cheque dated 26th January 1968 was presented for acceptance, the "stop payment" sticker relating to a cheque dated 27th January 1968 was not on the side of plaintiff's ledger card then in use but on the other side of that card. It was not noticed by defendant's officer who certified the cheque.

Plaintiff, having learned that his account had been debited with $2,000, raised objection and defendant communicated with Morgan Real Estate and the vendor's solicitors and sent them a letter, as follows:

Morgan Real Estate Agency
859 Portage Ave.,
Winnipeg, Man.

April 25th, 1968.

Attention: Mr. Calof

Dear Sir:

> **Re**: Cheque of Dr. Monty G. Shapera issued January 27th 1968 in the amount of $2,000.

With reference to our telephone conversation of todays date, we wish to advise that a Stop Payment was placed on the above cheque on February 20th, 1968.

The above cheque was therefore certified in error through a clerical error made at this office.

Yours truly,

G.C. Buschau
pro Manager

c.c. Sokolov Wolinsky & Co.
(The solicitors for the vendor).

It must be noted that when this letter was written defendant's officer did not have before him the cheque in question which is dated 26th January 1968, and that the letter refers to a cheque issued 27th January 1968, which was the date of the cheque covered by the "stop payment". This and a verbal admission of error was made on the assumption that the cheque certified was one dated 27th January 1968. Defendant is not estopped by these statements.

On 30th April 1968 the certified cheque dated 26th January 1968 was presented for payment by the Royal Bank of Canada. It is agreed that this bank was a holder in due course and that defendant was obliged to pay and did so.

Defendant's first answer to plaintiff's claim is one which it might not have raised had plaintiff sustained any loss as a result of the certification of the cheque. It is my opinion that in the circumstances defendant is fully justified in submitting that it did not act in breach of plaintiff's instructions in dealing as it did with the cheque. Plaintiff's "stop payment" related to a cheque dated 27th January 1968, and defendant did not certify or pay a cheque so dated. The "stop payment" did not cover the cheque in question.

In Canadian custom and theory certification of a cheque at the request of the holder is equivalent to payment: see Baxter, The Law of Banking, 2nd ed., pp. 17, 18, and Maclaren's Bills, Notes and Cheques, 6th ed., pp. 444 et seq.; Falconbridge, The Law of Negotiable Instruments in Canada, pp. 44 et seq., and Falconbridge, Banking and Bills of Exchange, 7th ed., p. 860. Whether or not a bank is under obligation to certify a cheque, the practice is well established and a bank has the right to certify and, having done so, becomes liable to the holder. A refusal without cause to certify a cheque could result in the same kind of damage to the reputation of a customer as a refusal to pay.

Plaintiff could have issued two cheques for the same amount to Morgan Real Estate — that is not fanciful, for he still had $8,000 of the cash payment to make up. Had this been the case and defendant wrongly refused to certify the cheque dated 26th January on the strength of the "stop payment" relating to a cheque dated 27th January, plaintiff's reputation might have suffered and he would have had a cause of complaint — if not of action.

Of course, had defendant's officer who certified the cheque noticed the "stop payment" sticker relating to the cheque of another date, he would have attempted to get in touch with plaintiff. This raises as many questions as it answers — suppose plaintiff had not been immediately available by telephone, would defendant have been compelled to take the risk of assuming that the "stop payment" signed by plaintiff contained an error and of damaging plaintiff's reputation by refusing to certify?

Westminster Bank Ltd. v. Hilton (1926), 136 L.T. 315, illustrates the dilemma of a banker who has received a countermand of payment in which only the number of the cheque is wrongly specified. In that case the bank was requested to stop payment of a cheque No. 117283 for £8 1s. 6. in favour of one Poate. A cheque bearing No. 117285 for the same amount in favour of Poate was presented and cashed. The facts in *Hilton* differ from those in the case before me because in *Hilton* the banker did not overlook the "stop payment" but reasoned incorrectly that the cheque presented was a duplicate cheque and the bank was bound to cash it. Lord Wrenbury indulged in another speculation at p. 321:

> It might well be that owing to differences between the drawer and drawee the drawer might have stopped a first cheque and then by reason of those differences being settled he might have given a second cheque for the same sum. Had those been the facts and had the bank dishonoured the second cheque they would have

been liable to an action. Their conduct was I think completely justified.

Does it follow that if, in the case before me, the defendant had noticed the "stop payment" and speculated that it did not relate to the cheque in question, it would have been completely justified in certification but that as it did not notice the "stop payment" or speculate it cannot take advantage of the fact that the "stop payment" did not in terms relate to the cheque in question? In my opinion this is not the result and I would apply or extend to defendant here the words of Lord Shaw in the *Hilton* case at p. 320:

> The case has reference to the stoppage of a cheque of a particular number, name, date, and amount. When a banker is in possession of sufficient funds to meet such a cheque from a customer, the duty of the bank is to honour that cheque by payment, and failure in this duty may involve the bank in serious liability to its customer.
>
> This duty is ended, and on the contrary when the cheque is stopped another duty arises, namely, to refuse payment. In a case of that character it rests upon the customer to prove that the order to stop reached the bank in time and was unequivocally referable to a cheque then in existence and signed and issued by the customer prior to the notice to stop.
>
> It would, of course, be intolerable in business to permit the form of stoppage to be applied to a non-existent and non-issued cheque.

In Byles on Bills of Exchange, 22nd ed., the *Hilton* case is used by the editor to support the statement at p. 261:

> The countermand must not be expressed in ambiguous terms; it must unequivocally refer to the particular cheque which is stopped.

Defendant is entitled to succeed on this plea.

Defendant also pleads that it is entitled to equitable relief. It is submitted that as plaintiff was obliged to pay the $2,000, represented by the cheque, to the vendor he has suffered no damage as the result of defendant's certifying or paying the cheque. On the evidence it was clear that plaintiff was absolutely bound by the accepted offer and that the vendor was entitled to enforce the agreement or to forfeit the deposit, which he has done. Had the vendor brought action against plaintiff on the cheque he would have been obliged to pay. Plaintiff said that the offer to purchase and the cheque were "provisional" and he was not to be bound until he had received the advice of his accountant on the proposed transaction; that the cheque ought not to have been cashed by the vendor. If plaintiff's story had been true he could have recovered the cheque or the amount of it from Morgan Real Estate and Calof and their principals, the vendor, all of whom appear to be responsible people — one of the vendors is a well-known chartered accountant. Of course, plaintiff's story is not true and I have rejected it but it is significant that plaintiff admitted that he did not make any attempt to get back the money from any of the persons mentioned nor even ask them to return it. It is clear that plaintiff had decided, without excuse, to default on the agreement to purchase and realized that so far as the vendor was concerned he had lost his deposit and guessed, correctly, that the vendor would not ask for specific performance but would be content to rest on the forfeiture of the deposit.

In the circumstances it is inequitable that plaintiff should succeed in this action.

There are equitable doctrines under which a person who pays the debt of another without author-ity may be allowed the advantage of the payment. This equity may be extended, if the circumstances justify, to a banker who pays a cheque without authority if it is shown that the payment discharged a legal liability of the customer. The reasoning which supports the equity is put by Wright J. in *B. Liggett (Liverpool) Ltd. v. Barclays Bank Ltd.*, [1928] 1 K.B. 48 at p. 64:

> The customer in such a case is really no worse off, because the legal liability which has to be discharged is discharged, though it is discharged under circumstances which at common law would not entitle the bank to debit the customer.

In my view the circumstances fully justify the extension of the equity to defendant in this case. Payment of the cheque discharged a clear legal liability of plaintiff. To allow plaintiff's claim would be in substance to make defendant pay plaintiff's debt.

The action is dismissed, with costs.

(l) *Remfor Industries Ltd. v. Bank of Montreal*[†]

[DUBIN J.A.:]

The issue on this appeal is whether the defendant bank was liable for certifying a cheque of the plaintiff company, a customer of the said bank, following a direction given to it to stop payment on the cheque. The learned trial Judge held that the direction was not an effective countermand, but nevertheless the bank was negligent under the circumstances. It is from that judgment that the bank appeals on the issue of liability; no question being raised as to the amount of damages assessed against it.

On or about July 12, 1972 the plaintiff company drew a postdated cheque in the amount of $10,853, dated September 12, 1972 against a line of credit which it had with the defendant. On September 6, 1972 the president of the plaintiff company called the account manager of the branch of the defendant with which the plaintiff company had its account advising the bank to stop payment on the cheque since the plaintiff company was no longer indebted to the payee. The account manager was advised of the date of the cheque, the cheque number, and the name of the payee. He was advised that the cheque was in the amount of $10,800, and in this respect the president of the plaintiff company was in error.

In accordance with the standard practice of the bank a stop payment order on a cheque for $10,800 was programmed into a central computer. The information processed was limited to the amount of the cheque and the account number only. Because of the manner in which the computer was programmed, the clerks of the bank would only be alerted to stop payment if the amount of the cheque presented for payment was exactly the same as was programmed into the computer.

The cheque was presented for certification on September 25, 1972, and since the amount of the

---

† (1978), 5 B.L.R. 22 (Ont. C.A.).

cheque was not the exact amount as was recorded, the clerk was unaware of the direction given by the customer and the cheque was certified without any further inquiry.

As I have already observed, the learned trial Judge held that the instructions given to the bank did not constitute an effective countermand. In arriving at that conclusion, he felt the issue was resolved by what was stated by this Court in the case of *Giordano v. Royal Bank*, [1973] 3 O.R. 771, 38 D.L.R. (3d) 191 [reversed at p. 191n (S.C.C.)]. On that issue Kelly J.A., speaking for the Court, stated at p. 774:

> When a customer issues a cheque he has given a formal order to the bank to pay to the payee the face amount of the cheque out of funds held by the bank for the account of the customer. This order, by the very nature of the cheque, is an unconditional one and one which the bank may not disregard without subjecting itself to liability to its customer.
>
> In order that a bank may with impunity refuse to follow the prior instructions of its customer contained in a cheque, s. 167 [of the *Bills of Exchange Act*, R.S.C. 1970, c. B-5] lays down conditions under which a bank may disregard the order conveyed to it by the cheque and act upon the subsequent direction to stay payment.
>
> Section 167 reads as follows:
>
> **167.** The duty and authority of a bank to pay a cheque drawn on it by its customer, are determined by
>   (a) countermand of payment;
>   (b) notice of the customer's death.
>
> If the bank is to be able to rely on the countermand as a termination of its duty to pay a cheque, the cheque countermanded must be identified by particulars furnished in the countermand. Date of issue, payee and amount, as well as the number when there be one, are well known features identifying the cheque to be countermanded. *Since the bank may incur liability by refusing to pay, it is entitled to have an unambiguous description of the cheque set out in the countermand*, for if the customer has given instructions which are ambiguous, the customer cannot hold the bank liable for proceeding on the basis of an interpretation which the bank fairly and honestly assumes it to bear: *Westminster Bank Ltd. v. Hilton* (1927), 43 T.L.R. 124 at p. 126. [The italics are mine.]

And at p. 775 he concluded as follows:

> In the instant case, due to the discrepancy in the name of the payee and in the amount of the cheque sought to be countermanded, the notice of countermand did not carry to the bank notification of the change of purpose of the customer as to the exact order he had given in issuing the cheque in question. On this account, I am of the opinion that the customer did not countermand the cheque within the meaning of that term as used in s. 167 and that the bank was therefore not required to treat his instructions as a countermand.

It is to be observed that in the *Giordano* case, supra, there was a discrepancy in the name of the payee as well as in the amount of the cheque.

In the case of *Westminster Bank Ltd. v. Hilton*, supra, the customer had telegraphed the bank to stop payment on a cheque, the number of which he had misdescribed. It was also, however, of significance that the bank was not alerted to the fact that the cheque was postdated. When the cheque was tendered for payment, it was paid. In exonerating the bank, Viscount Dunedin concluded as follows at p. 126:

> It must always be remembered that a bank can be sued just as much for failing to honour a cheque as for cashing a cheque that had been stopped. Under the regulations the bank had to inform the clearing house by 3.30 p.m. whether they honoured the cheque or not. They did not know the plaintiff's address, and *when it comes to a question of identification it must always be remembered that the number of a cheque is the one certain item of identification. There can be only one cheque bearing a printed number; there may be many cheques in favour of the same drawee and for the same amount.* I was at one time inclined to think that, inasmuch as both the cashier and the manager knew that there was a stop on a cheque they ought, on August 6, to have made certain investigations, but I find that they did do so. They followed the ordinary practice. They looked at the ledger, and the ledger showed that no cheque in favour of Poate had come in. *I think, therefore, that the view of the officials was correct that the cheque presented being subsequent to the date of the stop instructions might be a duplicate cheque, and that they were bound to cash it.* [The italics are mine.]

Lord Shaw of Dunfermline, in the same case, made the additional following observations at pp. 129–30:

> My Lords: I concur. The case has reference to the stoppage of a cheque of a particular number, name, date, and amount. When a banker is in possession of sufficient funds to meet such a cheque from a customer, the duty of the bank is to honour that cheque by payment, and failure

in this duty may involve the bank in serious liability to its customer.

This duty is ended, and on the contrary when the cheque is stopped another duty arises — namely, to refuse payment. In a case of that character *it rests upon the customer to prove that the order to stop reached the bank in time and was unequivocally referable to a cheque then in existence, and signed and issued by the customer before the notice to stop.*

It would, of course, be intolerable in business to permit the form of stoppage to be applied to a non-existent and non-issued cheque. *Further, in the ordinary course of trade a cheque is signed on the date it bears. This being so the notice of stoppage on reaching the bank will properly be treated as only applying to a cheque bearing a date the same as, or anterior to, the date of stoppage.*

To carry the scope of stoppage further and to make it apply to the case (exceptional and out of the ordinary course of business transactions) *— the case of cheques which though subsequent to stoppage in date were yet anterior to stoppage at the time of signature and issue, namely, post-dated cheques* — it is, in my view, necessary for the customer to prove and explain the post-dating, but further to prove that this fact was brought clearly home to the mind of the banker so as to bring the post-dated cheque within the order of stoppage. [The italics are mine.]

And further at p. 130:

The perplexity arose from the fact that the cheque as presented was for the same sum and to the same payee. But this perplexity arose not from any act of the bank but was actually caused by the acts of the customer, and *Ireland v. Livingston* (L.R. 5 H.L. 395) clearly applies. In the circumstances stated, was the banker to enter into a conjecture that the stopped cheque was the same cheque as one bearing a different number and appearing to have come into existence after the date of stoppage? And did he fail in his duty by not coming to a conclusion of identity? I do not see my way so to affirm, and for myself, I should have thought it highly dangerous in business to act upon any conjecture of the kind, or to dishonour such a cheque except upon clear and unmistakable instructions.

In the instant case, the bank was aware that the cheque referred to by the customer was postdated. It was also aware of the number of the cheque itself, the account number, and the payee. The case is, therefore, distinguishable from the Giordano and *Westminster Bank* cases.

In the case of *Shude v. Amer. State Bank*, 248 N.W. 886 at 889 the following statement appears:

The law does not require a perfectly detailed description but instead the notice is sufficient if the check is described with reasonable accuracy.

In my opinion, notwithstanding the minor discrepancy with respect to the amount of the cheque, the detailed information provided by the customer so clearly identified the cheque which was presented for certification that the customer's instructions constituted an effective countermand, and, with respect, the learned trial Judge erred in holding to the contrary. The bank was, therefore, unauthorized to certify the cheque.

In any event, even if there were no effective countermand in this case, I am of the opinion that the learned trial Judge was correct in holding that having regard to the information given to it by the plaintiff, the bank was under a duty to inquire from its customer as to whether the cheque presented for certification was the cheque with respect to which the direction to stop payment had been given. The bank's failure to do so constituted negligence. The information given to the bank was correct in every respect other than the amount. The instructions clearly related to the cheque, the number of which had been given to the bank. The bank's internal procedure in limiting the information supplied to its computer, by reference to account number and the amount of the cheque only, cannot relieve the bank of its duty where the customer has supplied such precise additional information. In that respect what was said by Kelly J.A. in *Giordano v. Royal Bank*, supra, at p. 776, is on point:

It is my opinion that the bank's duty to its customer under the foregoing circumstances required it to use ordinary diligence to enlist the assistance of the customer before making the decision to pay the cheque: *Marsh v. Keating* (1834), 1 Bing. (N.C.) 198 at p. 220, 131 E.R. 1094. It is not necessary to consider what might have been the result if steps had been taken by the bank to speak to the customer and they had proven abortive, since no efforts at all were made to get into communication with the customer. Admittedly the bank did not attempt to reach the customer. In this respect the bank failed in the duty it owed the customer and its breach of that duty resulted in the payment of the cheque.

For these reasons therefore, I would dismiss the appeal with costs.

Appeal dismissed.

(m) *Capital Associates Ltd. v. Royal Bank*†

[RIVARD J.A. (translation):]

The judgment appealed from given by the Superior Court of the District of Montreal on April 30, 1970, dismissed with costs the action of the appellant for a sum of $109,990.92.

The record reveals the following facts.

On June 30, 1965, the appellant, Capital Associates Ltd., hereinafter called Capital, deposited to its account, at the Royal Bank, Montreal branch, a cheque for $109,990.92, dated June 30, 1965, made payable to the order of Capital and signed by All-Canadian Group Distributors Ltd. hereinafter called All-Canadian.

All-Canadian had its account at the same branch of the Royal Bank.

The deposit of this cheque at the branch of the defendant bank was dealt with by the teller of the branch and credited to the account of Capital. Neither then nor subsequently was it debited to the account of All-Canadian.

After the deposit of this cheque, the record reveals certain particular circumstances as follows.

The cheque in question was signed by one Van Vogt who, on the morning of June 30th, was president of All-Canadian and also president of Capital, and by one Préfontaine, an officer of All-Canadian.

As to the motives which do not appear on the record, it is clear that difficulties arose that morning between the management of the two companies, and one Harold Anthony Hampson, also a director of All-Canadian, communicated with the authorities of the defendant bank to tell them that instructions would be addressed to the bank shortly for stopping payment of the cheques signed by Van Vogt and Préfontaine.

The deposit of this cheque was made by the teller of the defendant bank about noon of June 30th. About 12:30 on the same day a meeting of directors of All-Canadian took place and Van Vogt and Préfontaine, the signatories of the cheque filed as ex. P-1, in the amount of $109,990.92, were dismissed from their offices, and Hampson, mentioned above, was elected president of the company.

A letter was then addressed to the defendant bank ordering it to stop the payment of certain cheques, one of which was this ex. P-1, in the amount of $109,990.92, to the order of Capital Associates.

This letter dated June 30, 1965, ex. D-1, D.C. vol. 1, p. 50, read as follows:

All-Canadian Group
Distributors Limited
Executive Offices — 1310 Greene Avenue
Montreal 6, Que. Te. 935–1171

June 30, 1965

The Manager
Royal Bank of Canada
Montreal Branch
1 Place Ville Marie
Montreal 2, Quebec

Dear Sir,

Pursuant to and in accordance with the Resolution of the Directors regarding Banking and Security passed by the Board of Directors of All-Canadian Group Distributors Limited on November 11, 1964, enclosed please find List of Officers and Directors on the form provided by the Royal Bank of Canada with specimens of their respective signatures thereto attached. All previous Lists of Officers and Directors are hereby cancelled.

The said List of Officers and Directors avails as well for the Resolution of the Board of Directors for facsimile signatures passed by the Board of Directors on October 25, 1962, and as amended by the Board of Directors on January 29, 1963.

Would you please stop payment on any cheque drawn by All-Canadian Group Distributors Limited payable to any one of the following:

Capital Associates Ltd.
Ira van Vogt
Edmund van Vogt
Michel L. deMartigny

Would you please acknowledge receipt of this letter and contents.

Yours very truly
(Signed) H.A. HAMPSON
H.A. Hampson
President

---

† (1975), 36 D.L.R. (3d) 579 (Ont. C.A.).

This order to stop payment was communicated on the same day, June 30th, to the officers of the defendant bank, and at the same time Hampson gave to them a new list of officers and directors of All-Canadian.

This communication was received with the relevant documents by the bank which acknowledged receipt the same day, June 30th, 1965, by letters signed by the assistant manager of the bank, ex. D-3, D.C. vol. 1, p. 52, which read as follows:

Dear Mr. Hampson:

As requested, we acknowledge receipt of your letter of June 30th providing us with details of the changes effected in the executive of All-Canadian Group Distributors Ltd. Your instructions included therein with respect to cheques of the company payable to anyone of the following will be carried out: —

> Capital Associates Ltd.,
> Ira Van Vogt
> Edmund Van Vogt
> Michel L. deMartigny

Your concurrent letters to our branches at Ste. Catherine & Greene, Westmount and Robson & Granville, Vancouver, will be forwarded together with copies of the revised list of officers and the signature cards provided by Mr. Lannaman.

> Yours truly,
> Original signed by
> J.M. WALKER
> J.M. WALKER
> Assistant Manager

This letter stopping payment of the cheque in the amount of $109,990.92 was communicated to the assistant manager of the current accounts department, Charles Dunseath, with instructions to see that the stop-payment order was carried out. Dunseath prepared a memorandum dated June 30, 1965, ex. D-6, D.C. vol. 1, p. 55, which read as follows:

June 30, 1965

ALL CANADIAN GROUP DISTRIBUTORS

Please read carefully the attached letter and ensure that all staff dealing with the public are warned not to negotiate cheques of our customer payable to the within named parties. Any questions arising should be referred to the undersigned or J.M. Walker, Assistant Manager.

(Signed) G.J.E. DUNSEATH
G.J.E. DUNSEATH

At the same time an order was given to stop payment of this cheque, on the instructions of the drawer, to the computer at the proof centre of the defendant Royal Bank.

The evidence revealed the following system which the bank operated, in relation to cheques deposited by its customers. A proof centre of the Royal Bank, called the regional proof centre, which operated by means of a computer, received at the main office of the bank all the cheques that had been deposited at its branches during the day. In the course of the night, this computer to which the cheques were remitted with, in appropriate circumstances, special instructions, for example, for cancellation or remission, made a report which ordinarily was communicated to the various branches of the bank on the next day.

The next day after the June 30th happened to be a legal holiday, and consequently this report was sent to the branch where the cheque had been deposited on July 2nd, and since the stop-payment order had been sent to the computer along with the cheque, the payment was stopped and the account of Capital was debited with the amount of this cheque, which had on June 30th been accredited to that account.

I repeat that the evidence does not show the account of All-Canadian was ever debited with this cheque.

The banking system that I have just described is revealed very clearly by lengthy evidence in the record.

The result was then that on the day of the deposit of this cheque, June 30th, on the instructions of the drawer, All-Canadian, an order was received to stop payment of the cheque in question.

The sole question arising on the present appeal is whether the defendant bank committed a wrong in deducting from the account of Capital the amount of this cheque which the drawer refused to pay.

One must make a distinction between a cheque deposited at a bank and one paid in cash. If the bank pays the amount of the cheque without making necessary inquiries, in view of the importance and amount, then a demand may be made on the drawee for the amount which it has so paid, perhaps without making necessary inquiries. The case would be the same where certification of a cheque is requested.

It seems clear to me that in these two cases, the bank having paid the amount or having certified, would make inquiry to see if the cheque were good, if the account of the drawer were sufficiently in funds to meet the cheque, and that if it paid or certified without assuring itself at least of these two conditions, it might be said to commit a wrong for which it ought to suffer the consequences.

But this is not the present case. I do not accept the proposition submitted by the appellant that in depositing the cheque with the Royal Bank, it was presenting it for payment.

Capital, in depositing the cheque, did not demand payment, but gave authority to the bank to present the cheque for payment to All-Canadian. All-Canadian refused to pay, and the bank cannot be responsible to Capital.

Falconbridge, in his book, *Banking and Bills of Exchange*, 7th ed. (1969), pp. 276–7, writes:

> If, for example, the customer endorses a cheque, even a certified cheque, to his bank for collection, the mere fact that the collecting bank credits the customer with the amount of the cheque does not prove that the bank has discounted or bought the cheque so as to make the bank the debtor of its customer in respect of the amount of the cheque. Again, if there is deposited in one bank, for collection, a cheque on another bank, or if one bank is instructed to obtain a transfer of a deposit account from another bank, the exact time when the cheque is actually cleared, or the transfer of the account is actually completed, may be decisive of the question whether the collecting bank has become the debtor of its customer in respect of the amount of the cheque or the account, as the case may be. A collecting bank which employs an agent for collection becomes the debtor of its customer so soon as payment of the item in question is actually received by its agent.

The fact that the account of Capital and that of All-Canadian were at the same branch makes no difference, and I see nothing in the law of bills of exchange nor in the Canadian cases, such as they are, that could modify the conclusion of the trial Judge on the facts mentioned above.

The bank accepted the deposit of this cheque but it seems to me useful to mention the terms of the agreement entered into between the bank and Capital, on October 12, 1961, ex. D-2, D.C. vol. 1, p. 51, of which contract I reproduce the following parts:

> (2) That the Bank is authorized to present for payment or acceptance or collect the instruments through such banks or other agents as the Bank may deem best, at the sole risk and expense of the undersigned, and, save to the extent that definite instructions have been received by the Bank from the undersigned, to give to such banks or other agents such instructions as to collection as the Bank may deem best, and that the Bank may accept either cash or bank drafts, cheques, settlement vouchers, clearing house slips or any other evidence of payment, in payment of the instruments or in remittance therefor.

> ...

> (4) That the Bank is authorized to debit the account of the undersigned with any of the instruments, or any of the evidence of payment referred to in Section (2) hereof, which are not paid on presentation or which if paid the Bank may be called upon to refund, or which may be dishonoured by non-acceptance or non-payment or any party to which is bankrupt or insolvent, or which, or the proceeds of which, through no fault of the Bank have been lost, stolen or destroyed or which, or the proceeds of which, for any reason the Bank is unable to collect or withdraw, together with all costs, charges and expenses incurred by the Bank in connection therewith and/or to debit the account of the undersigned with any cheques drawn on the branch of the Bank at which the account of the undersigned is being carried and which have been cashed, negotiated or credited to the account of the undersigned but which have not been found good.

> (5) That the Bank is authorized to pay as in the case of an ordinary cheque and debit the account of the undersigned in the customary manner with every promissory note or acceptance of the undersigned presented for payment at the branch of the Bank at which the account of the undersigned is being carried.

> (6) That the undersigned will repay to the Bank all amounts debited to the account of the undersigned in accordance with the provisions of this agreement.

> (7) That should the undersigned conduct an account or accounts at more than one branch of the Bank, the provisions of this agreement shall apply to each of such accounts unless the undersigned gives the Bank special written instructions to the contrary designating the particular account or accounts to which the provisions of this agreement shall not apply.

> (8) That this is to be a continuing consent and agreement and shall bind the undersigned and the heirs, executors, administrators, successors and assigns of the undersigned.

The clauses mentioned above authorize the bank to debit its customers' accounts for certain amounts in certain circumstances.

The appellant submits that the stop-payment order of All-Canadian did not make the cheque deposited "not good".

I agree entirely with the trial Judge when he said on this matter [15 D.L.R. (3d) 234 at p. 241]:

> The plaintiff submitted the argument that a cheque the payment of which has been stopped by the drawer prior to its payment from the drawer's account is not a cheque "which has not been found good" and that therefore the agree-

ment cannot apply in the present case. It was contended that these words can only include a cheque drawn on accounts which are without sufficient funds to pay them, or cheques which are stale dated or which bear irregular signatures. In the opinion of the undersigned, the words include any cheque which has not been paid regardless of the reason. For no matter what rule of construction be applied to them, they must mean any cheque which upon presentation for payment has not been honoured and paid. The contrary would be a bad cheque and a bad cheque must mean any cheque which upon presentation for payment has been dishonoured. It may have been dishonoured for any number of reasons including the drawee's refusal to pay it upon instructions from the drawer (s. 95). It would distort the meaning of the words to hold that a cheque which is dishonoured and unpaid by reason of an order from the drawer countermanding payment is a "good" cheque.

Together with the learned trial Judge, I must come to the conclusion that the defendant committed no fault of imprudence or negligence which could make it responsible for the amount that has been deducted from the appellant's account.

In the circumstances, the trial Judge was right to dismiss the action of the appellant against the defendant, and consequently the appeal is dismissed with costs.

Appeal dismissed.

(n) *Toronto-Dominion Bank v. Pella/Hunt Corp.*[†]

[CHADWICK J.:]

In October 1990, the defendant Pella sold windows and doors to Timbercraft Post & Beam Limited. Timbercraft issued a cheque dated March 20, 1991 for $9,148.30. The cheque was drawn on its account with the plaintiff bank, the Toronto-Dominion Bank. The cheque was forwarded by Timbercraft to Pella by ordinary post. On March 22, 1991, Timbercraft instructed its bank, the Toronto-Dominion Bank to stop payment on the cheque. On March 28, 1991 the cheque was presented for payment by the defendant Pella. By mistake the bank's employee overlooked the stop-payment order and honoured the cheque. There were sufficient funds in Timbercraft's account.

Timbercraft objected to the bank debiting its account in view of the stop-payment order. The bank reinstated the funds in the Timbercraft account. The bank now demands that Pella return to them the moneys they had advanced to Timbercraft. Other than the moneys received from the bank Pella has not paid for its shipment to Timbercraft.

In support of his position Mr. Reil, on behalf of the Toronto-Dominion Bank, relies upon the principles as established in *Barclays Bank Ltd. v. W.J. Simms Son & Cooke (Southern) Ltd.*, [1979] 3 All E.R. 522 (Q.B.).

Ms. Eagleson on behalf of the defendant distinguishes the Barclays Bank decision and argues that I must consider the equities between all of the parties including Timbercraft who is not a party.

The facts in the *Barclays Bank* decision are somewhat similar to the facts in this particular case. Goff J. In his judgment carefully reviews the law of England leading to restitution and moneys paid by way of mistake of fact. At p. 535 he concludes as follows:

> From this formidable line of authority certain simple principles can, in my judgment, be deduced.
> 1. If a person pays money to another under a mistake of fact which causes him to make the payment, he is prima facie entitled to recover it as money paid under a mistake of fact.
> 2. His claim may however fail if: (a) the payer intends that the payee shall have the money at all events, whether the fact be true or false, or is deemed in law so to intend; (b) the payment is made for good consideration, in particular if the money is paid to discharge, and does discharge, a debt owed to the payee (or a principal on whose behalf he is authorised to receive the payment) by the payer or by a third party by whom he is

---

[†] (1992), 10 O.R. (3d) 634 at 635–37 (Gen. Div.).

authorised to discharge the debt; (c) the payee has changed his position in good faith, or is deemed in law to have done so.

In formulating these principles Goff J. acknowledges that he has not considered defences of general application in the law of restitution.

Both counsel have referred me to a number of cases where the Barclays Bank decision has been reviewed and also where the courts have considered the equity between the parties: *Toronto-Dominion Bank v. Anker Electric & Motor Equipment Co.* (1978), 22 O.R. (2d) 369, 93 D.L.R. (3d) 510 (Co. Ct.); *Royal Bank v. LVG Auctions Ltd.* (1983), 43 O.R. (2d) 582, 2 D.L.R. (4th) 95 (H.C.J) [affirmed (1984), 47 O.R. (2d) 800, 12 D.L.R. (4th) 768 (C.A.)]; *Toronto-Dominion Bank v. Crown Real Estate & Insurance Ltd.* (1980), 7 Sask. R. 58 (Dist. Ct.); *Shapera v. Toronto-Dominion Bank* (1970), 17 D.L.R. (3d) 122, [1971] 1 W.W.R. 442 (Man. Q.B.); *B. Liggett (Liverpool) Ltd. v. Barclays Bank Ltd.*, [1928] 1 K.B. 48, [1927] All E.R. Rep. 451; *Bank of Nova Scotia v. Organ Fisheries* (1984), 51 Nfld. & P.E.I.R. 322 (Nfld. Dist. Ct.); *Bank of Nova Scotia v. Cheng* (1981), 33 Nfld. & P.E.I.R. 89 (Nfld. T.D.); *Royal Bank v. Huber* (1971), 23 D.L.R. (3d) 209, [1972] 2 W.W.R. 338 (Sask. C.A.).

The authors, Peter Maddaugh and John McCamus, in *The Law of Restitution* (Aurora: Canada Law Book Inc., 1990), commented upon the decision of Goff J. in *Barclays Bank Ltd., supra.* At p. 239 they state:

> When reduced to its essentials, Goff J.'s restatement of the law of mistaken payments underscores the importance of the distinction between restitutionary recovery, on the one hand, and the setting aside of transactions on the basis of contractual mistake doctrines, on the other. It then states as a general principle that moneys paid under a mistake of fact shall be recoverable, provided, first, that the mistake has caused the payment, second, that the payor did not intend the payee to have the money at all events and, third, that the defendant cannot raise a defence of change of position. Having carefully cleared away the debris left by the dicta in the leading authorities, Goff J. has provided a restatement of the general principles permitting relief which provides a sensible rationalization of the conflicting interests of the payor and the payee. The new rule grants relief where the payee can have no conscientious objection to doing so and provides the payee with a defence in cases where the payee would be injured as a result of the plaintiff's error.

The authors also acknowledge that the equitable relationship between the parties must be considered.

In this case Pella has its right of action against Timbercraft for the price of goods sold and delivered to them. If there is an issue between Timbercraft and Pella as to the quality or the manufacturing of the goods then that is something that must be determined between these parties. The bank on the other hand has no contractual relationship with either Timbercraft or Pella other than the banking agreement. As such the bank is not in a position to enforce Pella's account against Timbercraft.

Under the circumstances, it would appear to me that the equities favour the bank. This falls squarely within the principles as enunciated by Goff J. in *Barclays Bank Ltd. v. W.J. Simms.*

As such I find that the defendant Pella is responsible to the bank for the amount advanced by them.

In view of the novelty of this issue there will be no order as to costs.

Judgment for plaintiff without costs.

(o) *Keyes v. The Royal Bank of Canada†*

[KERWIN J. (for himself and Rinfret C.J.):]

The appellant, A. M. Keyes, had a sum of money on deposit in a savings account in the main office, in Calgary, of the respondent, the Royal Bank of Canada. On January 8, 1945, he issued a cheque dated January 9, 1945, to a Mrs. J. I. Mundy on this account for two thousand dollars. At the opening of

---

† 1947 SCC 26. [Notes omitted]

business on the 9th, he attended at the main office to stop payment of the cheque but found that it had been marked "certified" the previous day. Later, on the 9th, the amount of the cheque was paid through the clearing house to the Canadian Bank of Commerce which had been instrumental on the 8th in having it so marked. If that were all, there would be no difficulty, as the law is clear that, a cheque being merely an order of a customer on his banker to pay a sum of money, such order may be countermanded before the time of its payment as designated by its ostensible date. The respondent, however, relies upon the circumstances of the case to void this result and the Appellate Division of the Supreme Court of Alberta agreed with it and, reversing the judgment at the trial, dismissed Keyes' action to recover the two thousand dollars.

The tale commences with the friendship between Keyes and Mrs. Mundy. He had previously given or loaned her several small sums, when she requested a loan of two thousand dollars to help finance the purchase of a tea room in Calgary. The transaction was to be closed on January 8th, and, while Keyes stated at one stage in his evidence that he told Mrs. Mundy he would think over the matter, at another he testified that he said he would deposit the required sum to her credit in the Bank of Commerce where she had a savings account and where he also had an account. Accordingly, on the afternoon of the 8th he attended the proper branch of the latter institution in Calgary and made out and signed the cheque on his account with the main office of the respondent in Calgary for two thousand dollars payable to J. I. Mundy or order, but dated the cheque January 9th. He did this, he explained, because he intended, if the proposed purchase did not materialize, to stop payment of the cheque. He made out an undated deposit slip in Mrs. Mundy's name and endorsed the cheque since, again according to his evidence, that was his custom. He presented the cheque and deposit slip to the teller, who filled in the date, January 8th, on the latter. Keyes asked the teller the present total to the credit of Mrs. Mundy's account including the $2,000, which information the teller declined to give. The teller did not notice that the cheque was postdated but, in accordance with the Bank of Commerce's custom when dealing with cheques of $1,000 and over, sent this cheque, by messenger, to the Royal Bank's main office, where the latter's proper officers, not noticing the date, marked the cheque "certified" and returned it to the messenger. Later the same afternoon Mrs. Mundy withdrew by a cheque on her account with the Bank of Commerce the sum of $2,000.

That evening Mrs. Mundy telephoned Keyes and asked if he had deposited the two thousand dollars to her account and was told he had. Despite the efforts of the respondent, it was impossible to secure the attendance of Mrs. Mundy at the trial, but it is evident that she must have known that Keyes had deposited the two thousand dollars to her account, as otherwise she had not a sufficient sum to her credit to permit the withdrawal of that amount. During the course of the telephone conversation just mentioned, Keyes asked her if the purchase of the tea room had been completed and was told that it had not. He then decided to stop payment of the cheque and the next morning presented himself at the respondent's main office before the doors were open and gave the necessary instructions. He was told that the cheque had been marked "accepted" the previous day and that nothing could be done about the matter.

Nothing of what transpired was, of course, known to the respondent except that on January 8th the Bank of Commerce presented a cheque dated January 9th drawn by Keyes on his account with the former and that the cheque bore his endorsement as well as his signature as drawer. The cheque was never endorsed by Mrs. Mundy, as it was explained by various witnesses that when a cheque is deposited to the credit of the account of a payee, it is not considered necessary by the banks to insist upon the latter's endorsement. The respondent did not know that the cheque had been deposited by Keyes to Mrs. Mundy's account in the Bank of Commerce.

By section 165 of the *Bills of Exchange Act*, R.S.C. 1927, chapter 16, a cheque is a bill of exchange drawn on a bank, payable on demand, and except as otherwise provided, the provisions of the Act applicable to a bill of exchange payable on demand apply to a cheque. By section 167, the duty and authority of a bank to pay a cheque drawn on it by its customer are determined by countermand of payment. While some criticism[s] of postdated cheques appear in English textbooks, the practice in this country is well established, and by section 27 of the Act (which applies to cheques) a bill is not invalid by reason only that it is antedated or postdated. The respondent, however, relied upon section 29 of the Act:

29. Where a bill or an acceptance, or any endorsement on a bill, is dated, the date shall, unless the contrary is proved, be deemed to be the true date of the drawing, acceptance or endorsement, as the case may be and argued that it has been shown that the true date of the cheque was January 8th and not January 9th. It is contended that by presenting the cheque on the earlier date to the Bank of Commerce with the request that the two thousand dollars be deposited to Mrs. Mundy's credit, and by inquiring the present total to her credit, the plaintiff must be taken to have meant that the true date of the cheque was the 8th.

It is unnecessary to consider the effect of the actions of the plaintiff as between him and the Bank of Commerce, except to note that it would apparently be held in some jurisdictions that the Bank of Commerce, by obtaining the respondent's certification of the cheque, must be taken to have accepted the latter as its debtor, — since the certification took place, not at the instance of the drawer, but of the holder after the issue of the cheque. Whatever the position might be as between the Bank of Commerce and Keyes, his evidence makes it clear that the 9th was the true date.

As pointed out in Paget on Banking, 4th edition, page III: — "his [the banker's] business is not to pay it [a cheque] before the ostensible date, that being his customer's intention and direction." On the following page the same author draws attention to the fact that efforts had been made to get out of the difficulty by representing the banker as having purchased the cheque during its currency, and so being holder in due course entitled to sue the drawer. In effect that was another of the arguments advanced by the respondent, but the case of *Da Silva v. Fuller*[3] has been accepted for many [years] as correctly stating the law. In that case a postdated cheque was lost and was paid by the banker on the day before its date and it was held that the banker was not protected and must repay the loser. The case is unreported but it is mentioned in the 6th edition of Bayley on Bills at page 319 and in the 11th edition of Chitty on Bills of Exchange at pages 188 and 279. It was also referred to by Baron Parke during the course of the argument in *Morley v. Culverwell*[4] at the end of the following statement:

> The condition of an indorser of a bill payable after date is this, that he is a surety for the payment of it by the acceptor at a particular time and place, on presentment for payment. If the acceptor pays the bill before it is due to a wrong party, he is not discharged. It has been so held in the case of a banker's cheque payable to bearer; if the banker pays it before it is due, he is not protected.

See also Hart's Law of Banking, 4th edition, p. 366, and Halsbury, 2nd edition, vol. 1, pp. 820–821. I agree with the statement in Grant on Banking, 7th edition, p. 67, that the decision of the Supreme Court of Queensland in *Magill v. Bank of North Queensland*[5] is in direct conflict with the cases in England. The decision to the contrary, of the Court of Appeal of New Zealand, in *Pollock v. Bank of New Zealand*[6] is to be preferred.

It is contended that by signing his name on the back of the cheque, Keyes became an endorser, and reliance is placed upon sections 131 and 133 of the Act. By the former, when a person signs a bill otherwise than as a drawer or acceptor, he thereby incurs the liability of an endorser to a holder in due course and is subject to all the provisions of the Act respecting endorsers. By the latter, an endorser engages, on due presentment, that the bill shall be accepted and paid according to the tenor and that, if it is dishonoured, he will compensate the holder who is compelled to pay it. The argument fails *in limine* because under the rule mentioned the respondent did not become a holder in due course.

At the suggestion and with the leave of the Appellate Division and notwithstanding the appellant's objection, the respondent amended its defence by pleading estoppel. Accepting the leave of the Appellate Division, the plea fails because the two employees of the respondent who participated in the certification of the cheque did not rely upon the appellant's endorsement. This is clear from the evidence and in fact is admitted in the respondent's factum, although it is argued that that fact could not alter the express provisions of the statute, which, however, for the reasons already given, are not applicable.

The appeal should be allowed and the judgment at the trial restored with costs throughout.

[ESTEY J. (for himself and Taschereau J.):]

The appellant at Calgary on January 8, 1945, drew a cheque for $2,000 upon the Royal Bank of Canada where he had a savings account, postdating the cheque January 9th and making it payable to J. I. Mundy or order. Mrs. Mundy was negotiating the purchase of a restaurant and appellant had agreed to assist her in the purchase thereof to the extent of $2,000. She had asked that he deposit this to her account in the Canadian Bank of Commerce at Calgary on January 8th. The appellant had an account at the same branch of the Canadian Bank of Commerce and some time in the afternoon of January

8th tendered to the teller of that bank the cheque in question for $2,000 for deposit to the account of Mrs. J. I. Mundy. He did not draw the teller's attention to the fact that the cheque was postdated, nor did the teller notice that fact, but rather accepted it for deposit, and at once the amount thereof was credited to Mrs. Mundy's account. The teller in the course of receiving the cheque endorsed Mrs. Mundy's name thereon, and deposed that this was the usual banking practice. In so doing the bank was acting as agent for its customer, Mrs. J. I. Mundy.

> A banker undertakes to do what is in the proper course of a banker's business, and so far differs from an agent who is not a banker.

Bank of England v. Vagliano Brothers[7].

Subsequently on the same afternoon Mrs. Mundy drew from her account $2,000. There is no allegation of fraud on the part of the appellant or of collusion between the appellant and Mrs. Mundy.

Immediately the cheque was deposited on January 8th in the Canadian Bank of Commerce it was sent by messenger to the Royal Bank of Canada for certification, where again the postdating was overlooked by the clerks of that bank and the cheque certified.

On the evening of January 8th Mrs. Mundy informed the appellant that negotiations were concluded, at least for the time being, and she was not purchasing the restaurant. As a consequence, immediately the bank opened on January 9th and before the cheque reached the Royal Bank of Canada in the ordinary course of banking, appellant called at that bank and asked that payment of the cheque be stopped, when he was informed that, because it had been certified on the previous day, payment could not be stopped.

The appellant brought this action to recover from the Royal Bank of Canada the sum of $2,000, which he alleges was improperly charged to his account following the certification of the aforementioned cheque.

The Appellate Court in Alberta reversed the judgment of the learned trial judge in favour of the appellant and directed that judgment be entered for the respondent.

The appellant contends that he had a right to stop payment of the cheque on the morning of January 9th, and the respondent that if he had, he was by his own conduct estopped from doing so. The respondent asks judgment on its counterclaim on the basis that the appellant is either an endorser or that it is a holder in due course of the cheque.

The appellant in connection with his savings account received from the Royal Bank of Canada a pass or bank book setting forth "Savings Regulations" paragraph 2 of which reads:

> Funds deposited will be paid only to the depositor in person or upon presentation of his written order.

A cheque is a written order and the law imposes an obligation upon the bank to pay the depositor's cheque according to its tenor if the depositor has funds to the amount thereof at his credit. Halsbury, 2nd Ed., Vol. 1, p. 820:

> A banker is bound to pay cheques drawn on him by a customer in legal form provided he has in his hands at the time sufficient and available funds for the purpose.

A postdated cheque since 1776 has been accepted as a negotiable instrument. *Da Silva v. Fuller*[8]; *Emanuel v. Robarts*[9].

In Falconbridge on Banking and Bills of Exchange, 5th Ed., p. 553:

> A cheque which is "postdated is none the less a cheque, and is therefore payable, without grace, on demand on or after its date; but for some purpose it may be treated as if it were a bill of exchange payable at a future date.

Halsbury, 2nd Ed., Vol. 1, p. 820:

> Postdated cheques are not invalid, but the banker should not pay such a cheque if presented before its ostensible date.

Paget's *Law of Banking*, 4th Ed., p. 111:

> The real trouble is where a banker inadvertently pays a postdated cheque before the ostensible date. He cannot debit it then, and he must not dishonour cheques presented in the interval up to the ostensible date, which, but for paying the postdated one, he would otherwise have paid.

See also *Pollock v. Bank of New Zealand*[10]:
The *Bills of Exchange Act*, R.S.C. 1927, chapter 16, section 165:

> A cheque is a bill of exchange drawn on a bank, payable on demand.

Section 27:

> A bill is not invalid by reason only that it
> * * *
> (d) is antedated or postdated, * * *

Bank of Baroda, Ld. v. Punjab National Bank Ld.[11]. On June 13, 1939, Mitter took to the respondents, Punjab National Bank, Ld., a cheque dated June 20th drawn upon appellant, Bank of Baroda Ld., marked or certified "Marked good for payment on 20.6.39. For the Bank of Baroda, Limited, M. P. Amin, Manager." On June 19th the appellant bank suspended Amin and on the 20th sent notice to the respondent and other banks that his power of attorney was cancelled. Appellant bank refused to pay the cheque on June 20th notwithstanding its having been previously marked. The Appellate Division of the High Court of Calcutta affirmed the judgment at trial in favour of the respondent on the basis that the appellant had, by marking or certifying the cheque, accepted it. The Privy Council reversed this decision on the ground that the ostensible authority of the manager did not extend to cover the certification of postdated cheques and that in the present case the manager had no authority in fact to do so. Lord Wright in delivering the judgment of the Privy Council, stated at p. 187:

> Their Lordships have referred to these matters as tending to support the view that certification is different both in its history and its effects from acceptance, even in jurisdictions in which either by statute or by custom it is declared to be "equivalent" to an acceptance.

Then, after pointing out that a postdated bill is under the English Act, section 13, subsection 2, as in the Canadian *Bills of Exchange Act*, section 27, not invalid by reason only that it is postdated, he continued at p. 193:

> But the material invalidity is that of the certification, taken in connection with the fact that the cheque was postdated. The true anomaly or invalidity consists in the attempt to apply certification to a cheque before it is due. Certification of a cheque when it is due may have operative effect and be valid as being directed to a cheque due in praesenti, such certification being presumably followed by debiting the drawer's account with the amount. This is particularly apparent when regard is had to the American or Canadian theory, that certification is equivalent to payment. It is impossible to treat the cheque as paid before it is due. The position might be different in jurisdictions where by law or custom certification is equivalent to acceptance, but nothing of the sort is applicable here. Even in such cases the difficulty of saying that there was constructive payment would remain. It is not easy to see why novel and anomalous theories should be invented to justify an unusual and unnecessary proceeding. This case can, however, be decided simply and sufficiently

on the ground that the ostensible authority of the manager did not extend to cover the certifying of postdated cheques, and that in the present case the manager had no actual authority to do so. The bank accordingly was not bound. This in itself would be a sufficient ground for rejecting the respondent's claim.

It would appear from the foregoing that the Royal Bank of Canada had no ostensible authority to certify the appellant's cheque before its date, nor does the evidence suggest that it had any actual authority from the appellant to do it and, therefore, the certification as against the appellant was invalid.

The *Bills of Exchange Act* does not specifically deal with postdated cheques. A postdated cheque, however, has been accepted as a negotiable instrument and usually as a bill of exchange payable on the date thereof. Even an ordinary cheque has been described by Parke B. as "a peculiar sort of instrument, in many respects resembling a bill of exchange, but in some entirely different." *Ramchurn Mullick v. Luchmeechund Radakissen*[12]. It is a bill of exchange that is also a cheque and possesses the differences which distinguish a bill of exchange from a cheque as enumerated by Lord Wright at p. 184 in *Bank of Baroda, Ld. v. Punjab National Bank, Ld.*,[13] and in particular the basic difference that the liability of the drawee of a cheque does not depend upon acceptance by the drawee as in a bill of exchange, but rather upon the contractual relationship between the drawer-depositor and the drawee-bank, under which the obligation of the drawee-bank is to pay the cheque if funds of the drawer are available when it is presented on the date thereof or a reasonable time thereafter.

In *Ex parte Richdale. In re Palmer*[14], it was contended that when the drawer of a postdated cheque received notice that a declaration of bankruptcy had been made with respect to the payee it was his duty to stop payment of the cheque. There the cheque was drawn by the purchasers of a business in favour of the vendor for the balance of the purchase price. It was postdated and, because of the reason given by the appellant in the case at bar, it is interesting to note the reason in that case. The report indicates at p. 410:

> The cheque was postdated the 28th of April, the reason for this being that the licences could not be transferred without a written authority signed by Palmer, and Richdale & Tomlinson wished to be able to stop payment of the cheque in case this authority should not be given.

Palmer was declared a bankrupt on April 27th. It was held that the giving of the cheque was a dealing within the meaning of the *Bankruptcy Act* and that there was no obligation upon the drawers, when they heard of the payee's bankruptcy, to stop payment of the cheque.

In the foregoing case it was contended that the right to countermand should have been exercised. In many cases the countermanding of postdated cheques has taken place and without any suggestion that such a right did not exist in the drawer. See *Union Bank of Canada v. Tattersall*[15]; *Carpenter v. Street*[16]; *The Royal Bank of Scotland v. Tottenham*[17]; *Westminster Bank Ld. v. Hilton*[18]. In the latter case the drawer brought an action against the drawee-bank for payment of a postdated cheque after he as drawer had instructed the bank to countermand payment thereof. His instructions to countermand were contained in a telegram in which he gave an incorrect number of the cheque. The plaintiff failed in his action, not because he had not the right to countermand, but because his instructions giving the incorrect number did not cover the cheque in question.

It has been suggested that a postdated cheque is so far a bill of exchange that the provisions relevant to cheques contained in Part 3 of the *Bills of Exchange Act* are not applicable thereto. In referring to a document in the form of a postdated cheque, Mr. Justice Duff (later Chief Justice) stated (in *Leduc v. La Banque d'Hochelaga*[19].

> A "cheque" is defined by the *Bills of Exchange Act* (s. 165) as "a bill of exchange drawn on a bank, payable on demand." The order in question, as accepted, is obviously not payable on demand, and consequently is not a cheque within this definition.

These remarks are restricted to section 165. The essential differences between a cheque and a bill of exchange, as already indicated, make it plain that, while it is a bill of exchange for some purposes, it cannot be so regarded for all purposes; in particular the drawee's liability under a cheque is not that of the drawee-acceptor under the *Bills of Exchange Act*. Moreover, because countermanding with respect to postdated cheques has been so long recognized in the courts, it would appear that the provision of section 167 of the *Bills of Exchange Act* in providing for countermanding is merely setting forth the common law with regard thereto.

Section 167:

> The duty and authority of a bank to pay a cheque drawn on it by its customer, are determined by
> (*a*) countermand of payment;

It follows that the appellant on January 9th, before the Royal Bank of Canada made payment of the cheque, was within his rights in asking that the bank stop payment of his cheque in favour of Mrs. Mundy.

It was further contended that the appellant was estopped from denying that in reality the cheque was dated January 8th, because by his conduct he detracted the attention or in some way prevented the teller from noticing the postdating. It is true that he did not draw to the attention of the teller of the Canadian Bank of Commerce the fact that his cheque was postdated. It is important to note that the positions of the Royal Bank of Canada and that of the Canadian Bank of Commerce are in their respective relations to the appellant entirely different and that in this action we are concerned only with the relationship which exists between the appellant and the Royal Bank of Canada. Apart from the question raised in the counterclaim as to the drawer being an endorser and the Royal Bank of Canada becoming a holder in due course, which will be dealt with later, the position as between the appellant and the respondent bank is as stated by Lord Atkinson in *Westminster Bank Ltd. v. Hilton*[20]:

> It is well established that the normal relation between a banker and his customer is that of debtor and creditor, but it is equally well established that *quoad* the drawing and payment of the customer's cheques as against money of the customer's in the banker's hands the relation is that of principal and agent. The cheque is an order of the principal's addressed to the agent to pay out of the principal's money in the agent's hands the amount of the cheque to the payee thereof.

The foregoing indicates the relationship between the appellant and the Royal Bank of Canada, while the Canadian Bank of Commerce, in receiving the cheque for deposit, derives its rights through the negotiating of the cheque. *The Royal Bank of Scotland v. Tottenham*[21]. It would seem that the positions of the two banks with respect to the appellant are entirely different.

The appellant in tendering for deposit to Mrs. Mundy's account his cheque to the Canadian Bank of Commerce was negotiating a postdated cheque. While certain dangers incident to the practice of issuing postdated cheques have been from time to time emphasized, these cheques are nevertheless recognized in law as valid negotiable instruments, and the Canadian Bank of Commerce became at least a holder for value in receiving the cheque as it did. *The Royal Bank of Scotland v. Tottenham*(2). There is no allegation of fraud on the part of the appellant or of collusion between the appellant and Mrs. Mundy, and no evidence that he had any intention to deceive or mislead the Canadian Bank of Commerce, nor circumstances deposed to which would justify such an inference. If Mrs. Mundy had purchased the restaurant, the cheque was to be used to assist her. The record does not suggest that the appellant had any intimation that Mrs. Mundy would use the funds for any other purpose. Without that act on her part it is probable that, in spite of the fact that the postdating was overlooked by employees of both banks, this litigation would never have developed.

Whatever took place between the Canadian Bank of Commerce and the appellant, it is clear upon the evidence that the only reason, the Royal Bank of Canada certified this cheque was because its employees overlooked the fact that the cheque was postdated. The appellant was no party to this, and, with great deference for the opinion of the learned judges in the Appellate Court, it would appear that the essentials to found an estoppel as set forth in *Greenwood v. Martins Bank*[22], are not present in this case.

The respondent by its counterclaim asks judgment against the appellant either because he is an endorser or, alternatively, that it is a holder in due course of the cheque from the Canadian Bank of Commerce. When asked why he had put his name on the back of the cheque, appellant replied: "Well, just, there are lots of cheques that I put my signature on the back of them, just as a matter of form." Even if the signature of the appellant so placed on the back of the cheque be deemed an endorsement under section 131 of the *Bills of Exchange Act*, his liability therefor is determined by section 133. That section provides that "the endorser of a bill * * * engages that on due presentment it shall be accepted and paid according to its tenor." This being a cheque, the respondent's duty was to honour it by payment according to its tenor. Before it was ever received by the bank on January 9th, the appellant had instructed the bank to countermand payment. The bank at that time was under a duty to carry out his instructions. Even if, therefore, the appellant be regarded as an endorser, the respondent under these circumstances cannot succeed.

The respondent received the cheque, as already stated, upon the terms of its contractual relationship with its depositor and its relationship is determined on that basis, and it cannot under the circumstances claim as a holder in due course as against its principal-drawer.

The appeal should be allowed with costs throughout and the judgment of the learned trial judge restored.

(p) A.E. LePage Real Estate Services v. Rattray Publications Ltd.†

[FINLAYSON J.A.:]

This is an appeal from the judgment of the Honourable Mr. Justice Montgomery, dated October 2, 1991 [reported 5 O.R. (3d) 216, 84 D.L.R. (4th) 766 (Gen. Div.)] in which he ordered the Canadian Imperial Bank of Commerce ("C.I.B.C.") to pay the respondent A.E. LePage Real Estate Services Ltd. ("LePage") $20,825.89 on a certified cheque in that amount, plus prejudgment interest, for a total of $35,577.31. The cheque was made payable to LePage and drawn on C.I.B.C. by Rattray Publications Ltd. ("Rattray"). It was certified at the request of LePage.

ISSUE

The issue in this case is whether a drawee bank can withdraw certification of a cheque, granted erroneously after a stop payment order by the drawer, where that certification has been granted pursuant to a request by the payee.

† (1994), 21 O.R. (3d) 164 at 166–76 (C.A.).

In finding that the drawee bank, C.I.B.C., was obligated to honour its certification, the trial judge rejected the concept that there was a difference in law between cheques certified at the request of the drawer and those certified at the request of the payee. In doing so, he relied upon the prevailing mercantile perception of the irrevocability of bank's obligations to facilitate the acceptability of bankers' instruments as cash substitutes. I agree with the trial judge and would dismiss the appeal.

FACTS

The trial judge decided the case on an agreed statement of facts submitted by the parties. The statement stipulated that LePage and London Life Insurance Company ("London Life") were at all material times the landlords of 33 Yonge Street, Toronto. On or about March 15, 1985, Rattray approached LePage and London Life to discuss the possibility of leasing space at 33 Yonge Street. On April 12, 1985, Rattray executed an offer to lease referable to portions of the premises. The offer was accompanied by Rattray's cheque in the amount of $20,825.89 as a deposit, which was to apply to the first rent to become due under the lease contemplated by the offer. The cheque was payable to LePage and was drawn on Rattray's account at the Mississauga branch of C.I.B.C.

The offer was, by its terms, conditional on approval by Rattray's solicitor no later than April 18, 1985. On that day, this condition was deleted and the offer became firm and binding. By April 24, 1985, the offer had been accepted by LePage. There had been a suggestion by Rattray to LePage of a change of heart about the terms of the lease to be entered into pursuant to the offer, but on that day, LePage delivered the offer to London Life for signature and on April 25, 1985, London Life accepted the offer.

On April 25, 1985, Rattray's controller telephoned the Mississauga branch and instructed C.I.B.C. to stop payment of the cheque. In the result, a stop payment request was entered into the bank's computer at that branch. On April 26, 1985, because of Rattray's suggestion of a change of heart, a representative of LePage presented Rattray's cheque for certification at C.I.B.C.'s Queensway branch.

In response to the request to certify the cheque, a teller at the Queensway branch telephoned a Ms. Standing at the Mississauga branch of C.I.B.C. to obtain certification approval. Ms. Standing was not aware of Rattray's prior countermand instructions. She entered information about the cheque into the Mississauga branch's computer terminal. The terminal showed a stop payment match and a warning which stated "supervisor override required". Ms. Standing missed the stop payment instruction but acted on the supervisor override by referring the cheque to a supervisor for approval of the overdraft which would be created by the cheque. The cheque was certified and funds in the amount specified on the cheque were authorized for credit to Rattray's account and then transferred to a segregated "outstanding items" account pending clearance.

The cheque, as certified, was deposited into LePage's trust account at the Toronto-Dominion Bank branch at 123 Eglinton Avenue on April 30, 1985. It was not endorsed over to any third party. The Mississauga branch of C.I.B.C. received the cheque on May 1, 1985 in the usual course through the clearing system, but returned it to the Toronto-Dominion Bank on May 2, 1985 without honouring it, on the basis that it had been certified in error. C.I.B.C. reversed the transfer of funds to the segregated account and credited Rattray's overdraft. Other than its feeling of security in having Rattray's security deposit in the form of a certified cheque, LePage did not change its position or give fresh value to any third party as a result of having certified the cheque.

On April 25, 1986, LePage and London Life obtained default judgment against Rattray in the amount of $1,305,255 in respect of the rent that would have been payable under the lease contemplated by the offer. That judgment remains unsatisfied.

In addition to the above, we were advised by counsel on appeal that LePage was charged a fee by C.I.B.C. for the certification. We do not know on what basis the amount of the fee was determined. We were also advised that in the normal course of business, when a cheque is presented for certification and the drawer's account has a sufficient balance, the drawer's account is debited on certification and the bank pays no interest on the funds transferred to the segregated account. This is so regardless of who presents the cheque for certification.

ANALYSIS

The practice of cheque certification is well established in Canada even though it is not expressly provided for in the *Bills of Exchange Act*, R.S.C. 1985, c. B-4. It has been described by Benjamin Geva, "Irrevocability of Bank Drafts, Certified Cheques and Money Orders" (1986) 65 *Can. B. Rev.* 107 at p. 123 as follows:

"Certification" is the name given to the marking of a cheque by the drawee bank to show that it is drawn by the person purporting to draw it, that it is drawn upon an existing account with the drawee, and that there are sufficient funds to meet it. Certification is demonstrated by some physical marking on the cheque, normally stamping on its face the word "certified". (Footnotes omitted.)

The practice of certification is not accepted in the United Kingdom and consequently English cases dealing with the liability of a drawee bank must be approached with some caution. The practice is well established in the United States, but authorities from there are of little assistance because the consequences of certification have been codified in para. 3–411 of the *Uniform Commercial Code*. The lack of precise statutory authority in Canada has resulted in the concept of certification developing without a clear theory underlying the obligations which it imposes. As a consequence, some anomalies have arisen in the law governing the subject. Chief among these is the differing effects certification has, depending on whether it is undertaken at the request of the drawer of the cheque or at the request of the payee: See Geva, *supra*, at pp. 123–25.

The distinction is pivotal to the case on appeal, because counsel for C.I.B.C. concedes that had it certified the cheque in question at the request of Rattray, the drawer of the cheque, it would have been obligated to honour the cheque on presentation by the payee, LePage. However, it submits, since it certified the cheque at the request of the payee, LePage, the consequences are different.

The rationale for this submission is that the bank's primary obligation is to its customer (the drawer), with whom it has a contractual relationship. Its mandate is to pay funds from its customer's account at the direction of the customer. That authority or duty to pay is terminated by the drawer's countermand (ss. 165 and 167 of the *Bills of Exchange Act*). In these circumstances, its duty is to refuse payment on presentation by the payee of the cheque.

Counsel for C.I.B.C. relies upon *Barclay's Bank Ltd. v. W.J. Simms, Son & Cooke (Southern) Ltd.*, [1979] 3 All E.R. 522 at p. 539, [1980] 2 W.L.R. 218 (Q.B), and upon the judgment of this court in *Maubach v. Bank of Nova Scotia* (1987), 62 O.R. (2d) 220n, 44 D.L.R. (4th) 575n. I do not think that *Maubach* assists the appellant C.I.B.C. It is certainly authority for the first part of the bank's proposition that if the cheque had been certified at the request of the drawer Rattray, Rattray could not counter-

mand it. In my view, however, it is not authority for the balance of the proposition, that the fact that it was the payee who requested certification mandates a different result. The court expressly declined to comment as to what would follow if the cheque had been certified at the request of the payee.

The facts in *Maubach* were set out by the trial judge ((1987), 60 O.R. (2d) 189 at p. 191, 40 D.L.R. (4th) 134 (H.C.J.)). The bank had certified a cheque at the request of the drawer and the cheque was lost. The drawer countermanded payment and asked the bank to issue a replacement cheque, but the bank refused to do so without a bond of indemnity. In holding that once the cheque was certified, the bank could not honour the drawer's countermand, Gray J. stated at p. 197:

> The conclusion I have reached is that although certification by the drawee bank is not "acceptance" of the cheque by the drawee bank within the meaning of s. 35 of the *Bills of Exchange Act, certification is equivalent to an acceptance* with the result that the drawee bank is liable on a certified cheque to the payee and any holder thereof. This follows from the authorities I have quoted. By certification, the respondent [bank] upon presentation undertakes to pay the cheque: *Campbell v. Raynor* (1926), 59 O.L.R. 466 at p. 470; *Commercial Automation Ltd. v. Banque Provinciale du Canada* (1962), 39 D.L.R. (2d) 316 at p. 321; *Boyd et al. v. Nasmith* (1888), 17 O.R. 40 at p. 46. [Emphasis added.]

The decision of Gray J. was affirmed on appeal to this court, *supra*. While specifically declining to express an opinion as to the legal consequences of the relationship that exists between a drawer and a payee, the court said this about the facts in *Maubach* at p. 221:

> We are in agreement with the reasons of the weekly court judge and his conclusion, with one variation. *In our view the certification of a cheque by a bank is equivalent to acceptance.* Further, on the facts of this case the certification of the cheque constituted an acceptance. The cheque was marked "accepted" and signed by an employee of the bank. The manner of the endorsement of the acceptance of the cheque complied with the requirements of ss. 35 and 36 of the *Bills of Exchange Act*, R.S.C. 1970, c. B-5, so as to duly constitute acceptance. The bank thus became liable to pay the cheque when it was presented. [Emphasis added.]

Counsel for C.I.B.C. stressed that the sentence I have emphasized is restricted to the facts of *Maubach* where the cheque was certified at the request of the drawer. Since the court also held that "on the facts of this case the certification of the cheque constituted an acceptance", the statement I rely upon about certification being the equivalent of acceptance must relate to a situation not covered by the facts of the case. Although the statement is clearly *obiter dicta*, it is a very strong assertion that certification creates a status in the cheque which is the equivalent of acceptance regardless of who is responsible for the certification.

The great advantage of treating certification as acceptance, whether at the instance of the payee or the drawer, is that it brings a certified cheque squarely within the framework of the *Bills of Exchange Act* and codifies the consequences of certification. The relevant provisions of the *Bills of Exchange Act* are as follows:

> **2.** "acceptance" means an acceptance completed by delivery or notification.
>
> ...
>
> **38.** Every contract on a bill, whether it is the drawer's, the acceptor's or an endorser's, is incomplete and revocable until delivery of the instrument in order to give effect thereto, but where an acceptance is written on a bill and the drawee gives notice to, or according to the directions of, the person entitled to the bill that he has accepted it, the acceptance then becomes complete and irrevocable.
>
> ...
>
> **127.** The acceptor of a bill by accepting it engages that he will pay it according to the tenor of his acceptance.

Professor Geva argues persuasively that acceptance is the proper theoretical basis underlying certification. After undertaking a detailed examination of certified cheques in his article, *supra*, he identifies three premises for this theory in his examination at pp. 110–11:

> First of all, the irrevocability of the banker's obligation facilitates the acceptability of banker's instruments as cash substitutes. Secondly, prevailing mercantile perceptions as to irrevocability attached to any type of instrument should be reflected in existing law. Thirdly, it is preferable to explain the irrevocability of the banker's obligation in the framework of the law of negotiable instruments rather than under general principles of law. Indeed, fitting irrevocability into a known category of statutory engagement under the Act is bound to produce a greater certainty than the application of broad and often open-ended general principles.

The above was relied upon by the trial judge in the case on appeal.

Counsel for C.I.B.C. raised a number of problems banks would encounter if LePage were to succeed in maintaining the irrevocability of the certification. However, on analysis, they appear to me to lack substance. I have great difficulty in understanding how, as a practical matter, the bank is more affected by mistakenly certifying a cheque at the request of its customer than it is if it certifies it at the request of the payee. The bank's remedies in either case would appear to be the same. The problem on appeal, is not that the bank does not have a remedy, but that its customer, the party against whom it has the remedy, is insolvent.

If counsel for C.I.B.C. is correct, the significance of certification at the hands of the payee would be minimized to the point of having almost no value. He submits that when a cheque is certified at the request of the payee, the only assurance the payee receives is that the cheque will not be countermanded from that time forward. However, as this case illustrates, the bank is not prepared to acknowledge that certification amounts to a representation that the cheque has not already been countermanded, or that the customer's account has sufficient funds to pay the cheque on presentation. In other words, the customer's cheque is subject to all the frailties which the payee hoped to avoid by having the instrument certified. There would be very little commercial utility in a payee obtaining certification. It would not have a promise to pay from the bank, independent from the drawer's obligation to pay.

Counsel says that before the bank can be held liable in this case, the payee LePage must have negotiated the cheque in good faith and for value to a third party or have taken some step in relation to the cheque which would have the legal effect of creating an estoppel between the bank and itself. But it is apparent on the facts of this case that neither negotiation nor estoppel was ever a live issue. The cheque in question was intended as security for the first month's rent under the lease. It could not be cashed or negotiated otherwise than in accordance with the conditions under which it was delivered. The number of certified cheques which are held under these or similar conditions must be legion. To state, as appears in the agreed statement of facts, that all LePage received was a feeling of security that the cheque was good is to disregard the reality that security was all that LePage sought in certifying the cheque.

Counsel for C.I.B.C. takes the position that the bank made an innocent mistake and that it is for the court to determine who, other than C.I.B.C., is to take the loss. He submits that for the court to take any other position would be to grant LePage a windfall. Counsel treats the bank as a mere conduit between the drawer and the payee and submits that it can only be held responsible for its own mistake in limited circumstances. Even if that is so, I think that the facts of this case create one of those limited circumstances.

The analysis begins with *Barclay's Bank v. Simms, supra*, a case on all fours with the one on appeal, save that there was no issue about certification. Goff J. of the English Court of Queen's Bench stated at p. 542:

> In the light of the above principles, it is plain that in the present case Barclays are entitled to succeed in their claim. First, it is clear that the mistake of the bank, in overlooking the drawer's instruction to stop payment of the cheque, caused the bank to pay the cheque. Second, since the drawer had in fact countermanded payment, the bank was acting without mandate and so the payment was not effective to discharge the drawer's obligation on the cheque; *from this it follows that the payee gave no consideration for the payment*, and the claim cannot be defeated on that ground. Third, there is no evidence of any actual change of position on the part of either of the defendants or on the part of National Westminster; and since notice of dishonour is not required in a case such as this, the payee is not deemed to have changed his position by reason of lapse of time in notifying them of Barclays' error and claiming repayment. [Emphasis added.]

Then, Goff J. embarked upon a review of authority dealing with the right of recovery of a bank that has mistakenly paid out on a cheque. He said at p. 535:

> From this formidable line of authority certain simple principles can, in my judgment, be deduced.
>
> 1. If a person pays money to another under a mistake of fact which causes him to make the payment, he is prima facie entitled to recover it as money paid under a mistake of fact.
> 2. His claim may however fail if: (a) the payer intends that the payee shall have the money at all events, whether the fact be true or false, or is deemed in law so to intend; (b) the payment is made for good consideration, in particular if the money is paid to discharge, and does discharge, a debt owed to the payee (or a principal on whose behalf he is authorised to receive the payment) by the payer or by a third party by whom he is

authorised to discharge the debt; (c) the payee has changed his position in good faith, or is deemed in law to have done so.

Barclay's Bank v. Simms is the accepted authority explaining the obligations of a bank to its customer and its redress against the payee of a cheque who appears to be taking advantage of an innocent mistake on the part of the bank employee. However, it seems to me that it is the result in *Barclay's Bank v. Simms* that a payee in Canada seeks to avoid by having the cheque certified.

In the portion of the quotation from p. 542, Goff J. relies upon the lack of consideration on the part of the payee. It is well established that a drawee bank is not under a general duty to certify a cheque for anyone (Bradley Crawford, *Crawford and Falconbridge Banking and Bills of Exchange*, 8th ed. (Toronto: Canada Law Book, 1986), vol. 2, at p. 1799) and, accordingly, when it undertakes to do so for a fee, a mistake on the part of a bank employee loses some of its innocence. Certainly, LePage regarded the certified cheque of Rattray as irrevocable; otherwise there would have been no purpose in having it certified. It was its concern that Rattray would countermand the cheque that caused LePage to take the action that it did. It wanted to turn a revocable instrument into an irrevocable one. It wanted to have the equivalent of cash in its hands, with which it could deal, subject only to its agreement with Rattray under the lease.

Barclay's Bank v. Simms contemplates that a bank that has paid money under mistake of fact can recover it from the payee in an action for unjust enrichment. One defence to such an action is that the payee acted on the certification to his detriment. This would estop the bank from denying its representation, made through certification, that the cheque was valid. The position of C.I.B.C., that it can only be liable to a mere holder of a certified cheque if that holder can demonstrate that the bank is estopped from denying its representation that the cheque is valid is explained in *Crawford and Falconbridge, supra*, at p. 1794:

> A third theory [of the bank's liability] is that in certifying at the request of the holder [payee], the drawee bank makes a representation to the holder and to any subsequent endorsee from the holder that the cheque is valid and will be paid. But, of course, in order to qualify as an estoppel of the bank, that representation must be acted upon by the holder to his detriment.

Unfortunately, the author gives no explanation as to why estoppel should apply to a negotiable instrument, where the payee has paid consideration to the bank for the certification. I do not understand the rationale for the proposition that a bank can charge a fee to a payee for representing that the drawer's cheque is valid and not be held to that representation *simpliciter*. Why is a bank entitled to insist that it can only be held accountable to innocent third parties or in circumstances where the payee has acted to its detriment?

Estoppel is a rule of evidence. It is defined by *Jowitt's Dictionary of English Law*, 2nd ed., John Burke ed., follows at vol. 1, p. 726:

> The general rule is that where a man by his words or conduct wilfully or by negligence causes another to believe in the existence of a certain state of things, and induces him to act on that belief, so as to alter his own previous position, the former is concluded from denying the existence of that state of facts.

Since estoppel is a rule of evidence, not of law, it cannot be the foundation of a claim, nor is it substantive defence. However, it can be an evidentiary defence to a large number of civil claims. It is usually invoked by the person who acted to his detriment where no consideration flowed to the person who caused him to so act. With this concept in mind, pleading that the bank is estopped from denying the validity of the cheque may be an available option over and above substantive defences which a payee may use to resist an action by the bank for repayment. In the case on appeal, I can think of no reason why LePage, as payee, cannot rely upon the consideration it gave to the bank for the representation as justification for relying upon it. If estoppel is also available, then so much the better for LePage.

Given the fact that LePage did not change its position or give fresh value to any third party as a result of the certification, I have grave doubts that LePage could establish the legal basis for estoppel in the case under appeal: the feeling of insecurity it obtained would be insufficient. However, I do not see why estoppel is necessary when dealing with a negotiable instrument. LePage thought that Rattray's cheque, once certified, was the equivalent of cash. In my opinion that is reliance enough upon the representation by C.I.B.C. that the cheque would be honoured upon presentation. While LePage did not act to its detriment in reliance upon the certification in any legal sense, had certification been refused, one can only speculate as to what action LePage might have taken to minimize its losses on the rental agreement.

Counsel for C.I.B.C. stresses the vulnerability of the bank in this situation. He submits that it cannot recoup the amount of the cheque from its customer because it acted contrary to the express instructions of its customer who had ordered a stop payment. In addition, it had no authority to provide the funds to the customer's account to cover the cheque.

I think the answer to this concern is that there is case law, in addition to *Barclay's Bank v. Simms, supra*, that establishes that where a drawee bank honours a cheque notwithstanding a valid countermand and the effect is to satisfy a just debt, the bank may successfully defend an action by its customer/drawer for reimbursement: see J. Reynolds, "Countermand of Cheques" (1981), 15:2 *U.B.C.L. Rev.* 341 at pp. 363–65; *Liggett (Liverpool) Ltd. v. Barclays Bank Ltd.*, [1928] K.B. 48; *Shapera v. Toronto-Dominion Bank*, [1971] 1 W.W.R. 442, 13 D.L.R. (3d) 122 (Man. Q.B.). This is so even where the drawee bank made an independent decision to create an overdraft to allow a cheque to be certified: see *Bank of Nova Scotia v. Organ Fisheries* (1984), 51 Nfld. & P.E.I.R. 322, 150 A.P.R. 322 (Nfld. Dist. Ct.). Further in certain circumstances, the bank may have an action in restitution against the holder of a certified cheque, where payment does not satisfy a just debt: see Reynolds, *supra*, at pp. 359–63; *Toronto-Dominion Bank v. Anker Electric Motor & Equipment Co.* (1978), 22 O.R. (2d) 369, 93 D.L.R. (3d) 510 (Co. Ct.); and *Royal Bank of Canada v. LVG Auctions Ltd.* (1983), 43 O.R. (2d) 582, 2 D.L.R. (4th) 95 (H.C.J.). The authors of Maddaugh and McCamus, *The Law of Restitution* (1990), review the above authorities and others and conclude at p. 243:

> The combined effect of these lines of authority is that the bank should, in the normal case, be able to indemnify itself either by recovering the moneys paid under a mistake from the payee or, where such relief is unavailable, by debiting the customer's account.

The bank, however, does not want to find itself in a position where it is obliged to prove that its customer's cheque was in payment of a just debt. It says that it should not be subject to all the issues that could arise between its customer and its payee relating to the consideration for the cheque. I have little sympathy with this argument. The only reason that the bank on appeal finds itself in this situation is that (1) its clerk made a mistake in missing the customer's stop payment instruction and (2) a supervisor authorized an advance of the bank's funds by way of loan to an otherwise overdrawn account.

If my position is correct, the bank is exposed to the same liability whether it certified the cheque in error at the instance of its customer or of the payee. I do not know why this should trouble the bank so much. Certainly, it can be in no worse position *vis-à-vis* the payee than if it had cashed the cheque in error. More than that, absent error on its part, the bank takes the same precautions to protect itself from liability when a payee asks for certification as when its customer does. It appears that, notwithstanding that the bank throughout stressed its primary obligation was to its customer, the court was told that it is not the practice for a bank to contact its customer when the payee presents its customer's cheque for certification. It simply debits its account. The customer will not know that the cheque has been certified and that funds to cover it have been transferred from its account until it receives its bank statement.

In the case on appeal, both as pleaded and agreed upon in the statement of facts, the bank has restricted its defences to estoppel and third party intervention. In this case, it was paying a just debt of its customer and was entitled to debit its customer's account with the amount of its overdraft. The fact that its customer appears to be in financial difficul-

ties does not justify resort against the payee, LePage. The irrevocability of certification is not the problem here, much less who was responsible for the certification. If the C.I.B.C. had actually paid the cheque in error, it would not have been able to recover from LePage on the authority of *Barclay's Bank v. Simms, supra*, because it had paid a just debt.

In conclusion, I am of the opinion that the distinction between a certification obtained at the request of the payee, and certification obtained at the request of the drawer, is artificial and unsupportable on any theory relating to negotiable instruments. I endorse the following statement of the trial judge [at p. 219] on what is the only issue in this appeal.

> I see no reason why there should be any different conclusion in the case of a holder who has the cheque certified. There should be consistency in the law. I conclude that in certification procured by the holder, the bank cannot refuse to honour the cheque.

For the reasons given above, I would dismiss the appeal with costs.

Appeal dismissed.

(q) *RCL Operators Ltd. v. National Bank of Canada*†

[HOYT C.J.N.B. (Rice J.A. concurring):]

This appeal is about a bank's payment of a countermanded cheque.

RCL Operators Ltd., RGL Realty Inc. and RCL Contractors Inc. are or were all part of the Rocca Group of companies, companies that are or were owned or controlled by Pat Rocca or members of his family. For the purposes of this decision, it is sufficient to identify RCL Contractors as a contracting company that performed worked for Westray Mines Ltd. in Nova Scotia in 1991. RCL Contractors, because it had no staff or equipment, subcontracted the work to various trades. The management of the contract was subcontracted

to RCL Operators, whose fee was to be the difference between the amount of the contract and the amount paid to the various other subcontractors who performed the work. Towards the end of the Westray contract, the Rocca group of companies was experiencing cash flow problems. As a result, one of the subcontractors for the Westray contract, Dawcolectric Inc., was not fully paid. After negotiations, Dawcolectric accepted a post-dated cheque from RCL Contractors for $318,180.36 dated March 30, 1992, for the balance of the moneys owing to it.

The National Bank was the banker for the Rocca group of companies. RCL Operators maintained a line of credit with the bank. The moneys

† (1995) 131 D.L.R. (4th) 86 at 87–91 (N.B.C.A.).

of the Rocca companies were controlled using the RCL Operators line of credit. Lawrence Hanlon, the vice-president of finance and administration for the Rocca Group, and David Henry, the bank's account officer for the Rocca account, testified about the banking arrangements between the Rocca group of companies and the bank. The trial judge described the arrangements as follows [150 N.B.R. (2d) 180 at p. 183, 48 A.C.W.S. (3d) 1210]:

> Although Operators held the only line of credit extended by the bank an invariable and honoured practice developed whereby the bank was called each day by [Mr.] Hanlon to check for overdrafts incurred by operators' associated companies and, without fail, honoured overdrafts within 24 hours. This daily practice became known and accepted as the 24 hour overdraft privilege. In the event Operators had not so honoured these cheques within the 24 hour period it was open to the bank to return the cheques N.S.F.

On March 27, 1992, RCL Contractors stopped payment of the March 30th cheque to Dawcolectric. The bank debited $7.50 from RCL Contractors account for, according to Mr. Henry, "the service of placing a stop payment on the account". The stop-payment order executed by RCL Contractors contained no errors in that the amount of the cheque, the date of the cheque, cheque number and the payee were all accurately described. The stop-payment order contained the following waiver or exculpatory clause above the signatures of RCL Contractors signing officers:

> I, the undersigned, hereby undertake to hold the Bank harmless from any and all liabilities concerning said amount together with disbursements and charges which the Bank could incur following refusal of payment; furthermore, I undertake not to hold the Bank responsible for payment made contrary to the present request, should payment be effected inadvertently.

On April 16, 1992, following a meeting with Mr. Hanlon and Jack McQuinn, the president of RCL Operators and RCL Contractors, two officers of Dawcolectric went to the Saint John branch of the National Bank and requested certification of the cheque. The bank teller, when viewing the computer screen showing RCL Contractors' account, apparently overlooked the March 29th countermand. I say apparently because the teller, although present during the trial, did not testify. The teller then, following a discussion with Mr. Henry, and upon payment of a $7.50 fee by Dawcolectric, certified the cheque.

The cheque was then deposited by Dawcolectric in its bank.

When the error was discovered on the next business day, April 20th, Mr. Henry called Mr. Hanlon and obtained a cheque from RCL Operators payable to the order of RCL Contractors Inc. for $317,721.85 to cover the overdraft caused by the cheque's certification. Mr. Henry testified that he obtained the cheque so that the earlier cheque could be covered and that when he discussed the matter with Mr. Hanlon it was agreed that the new cheque was furnished without prejudice to RCL Contractors right to question the bank's payment of the countermanded cheque. Mr. Henry testified:

> I attended his [Mr. Hanlon's] office at the Rocca Construction building, and was given this cheque after some discussion between he, Mr. John Rocca and myself, pertaining to the rights of RCL Contractors to dispute payment of the cheque.
>
> ...
>
> I returned to the branch with that cheque in the morning of April 20th, gave it to the branch accountant, who deposited to the account of RCL Contractors.
>
> ...
>
> I agreed that RCL Contractors would have the right to dispute payment of the cheque, and whatever other related company acquired those rights from RCL Contractors.

On April 22, 1992, Mr. Henry wrote the following letter to RCL Contractors respecting the April 20th cheque:

> We acknowledge that your confirmation of today's date of your indebtedness to National Bank of Canada (the "Bank") is without prejudice (subject to the Bank's rights which are hereby specifically reserved and subject to the terms of the stop payment) to your right to claim as a setoff or request a refund of, whichever may be applicable, the amount of $318,180.36 representing a cheque from RCL Contractors Inc. to Dawcolectric Inc. on which a stop payment instruction was given by you to the Bank of March 27th, 1992, which instruction we hereby acknowledge was received by us prior to the time the Bank honoured the cheque to Dawcolectric Inc.

After various attempts to resolve the dispute failed, this action was commenced. The trial judge concluded that RCL Operators decided to pay RCL Contractors' lawful debt to Dawcolectric with the issuance and delivery of the April 20, 1992 cheque. The evidence, however, such as that cited above, discloses that the April 20th cheque was delivered to the bank by RCL Operators specifically reserving its right to question the failure of the bank to honour the March 27th countermand of the March 30th RCL Contractors cheque to Dawcolectric for $318,180.36. The question for us then is the effect of the bank's payment over countermand. For that reason, the evidence of the banking accommodation extended to the Rocca companies by the bank becomes important. As the judge described, the bank offered 24-hour overdraft privileges to the Rocca companies so that they could move money from one account to another and to permit them to determine which, if any, cheques they did not wish to honour. He said [at p. 193]:

> Rocca Construction/Operators consistently honoured all obligations of its associate companies without exception during all times relevant to this matter.
>
> The bank's Henry consistently acted on this assumption and practice and Operators/Rocca knew this.

The bank submits, correctly in my view, that the appellants somewhat overstate their case by saying that payment over countermand prevents a bank from recovering from its customer. As the bank's counsel put it in his written submission, "payment over countermand leads to an examination of the circumstances to examine whether recovery by the Bank is justified".

In my view, there are two such circumstances in this case, namely, whether the waiver or exculpatory clause in the stop-payment order is effective and whether the countermanded cheque satisfied a just debt of the drawer thus resulting in an unjust enrichment. The trial judge, because of his view of the evidence, did not have to deal with the waiver issue. He did, however, consider unjust enrichment. Because I propose to dispose of the appeal on the second point, I will not comment on the effect of the waiver in the stop-payment order. If a different result had been reached on the unjust enrichment issue, it would have been necessary to consider the waiver or exculpatory clause in the countermand.

The issue then is whether, as the judge found, an unjust enrichment will result if the bank is unable to recover its payment of the RCL Contractors cheque, which was to satisfy an undisputed debt of RCL Contractors. This proposition was recently referred to in *A.E. LePage Real Estate Services Ltd. v. Rattray Publications* (1994), 120 D.L.R. (4th) 499, 21 O.R. (3d) 164, 77 O.A.C. 280 *sub nom. LePage*

(A.E.) Investments Ltd. v. Canadian Imperial Bank of Commerce (C.A.), where Finlayson J.A. reviewed the authorities outlining this proposition.

The statutory effect of a stop payment or countermand is found in s. 167 of the *Bills of Exchange Act*, R.S.C. 1985, c. B-4. which provides:

> **167.** The duty and authority of a bank to pay a cheque drawn on it by its customer are determined by
> (a) countermand of payment; or
> (b) notice of the customer's death.

A bank's entitlement to reimbursement from the drawer of a countermanded cheque where the drawer would otherwise be unjustly enriched was considered in *B. Liggett (Liverpool), Ltd. v. Barclays Bank, Ltd.*, [1928] 1 K.B. 48 at p. 64, where Wright J. said: "[T]he banker will be entitled to the benefit of that payment if he can show that that payment went to discharge a legal liability of the customer." In *Barclays Bank Ltd. v. W.J. Simms Son & Cooke (Southern) Ltd.*, [1979] 3 All E.R. 522 (Q.B.), Goff J. held that when a party pays money to another under a mistake of fact that actually causes the payment, the payment is *prima facie* recoverable, unless the payment discharges a debt owed by the drawer. In 3(1) Hals., 4th ed., p. 153, para. 175, reissue (London: Butterworth's, 1989), the rule is stated as follows:

> Subject to questions of statutory protection, estoppel or adoption, a banker who has paid a cheque drawn without authority or who has paid one in contravention of his customer's order, or, probably, negligently, cannot debit the customer's account with the amount. However, if such a cheque is paid in discharge of the customer's debts, the banker is entitled to take credit for it.

This rule was followed in *Meier Medical Supplies Ltd. v. Canadian Imperial Bank of Commerce*, [1994] B.C.J. No. 1409 (QL) (B.C.S.C.) [summarized 48 A.C.W.S.(3d) 997]. In *Clansmen Resources Ltd. v. Toronto-Dominion Bank* (1990), 47 B.L.R. 54 at p. 67, [1990] W.W.R. 73, 43 B.C.L.R. (2d) 273 (C.A.), Southin J.A. said:

> [I]t is, I think, a general principle of equity that a man shall not be *unjustly* enriched at the expense of another. He shall not by the operation of a principle of law receive a windfall.

See also *Shapera v. Toronto-Dominion Bank* (1970), 17 D.L.R. (3d) 122, [1971] 1 W.W.R. 442 (Man. Q.B.).

In *LePage*, Finlayson J.A. said at p. 509:

> [T]here is case law ... that establishes that where a drawee bank honours a cheque notwithstanding

a valid countermand and the effect is to satisfy a just debt, the bank may successfully defend an action by its customer/drawer for reimbursement.

In my opinion, the principle that a person should not be unjustly enriched by such a mistake of fact has application here. Dawcolectric has been paid and thus has no reason to pursue RCL Contractors for payment. Because the cheque was certified, the bank cannot recover from Dawcolectric. Thus, as the bank cannot recover its payment from Dawcolectric, RCL Contractors benefits by successfully avoiding paying its legal obligation. The cheque was in satisfaction of a legal debt owing by RCL Contractors to Dawcolectric and, as the trial judge found, mistakenly paid by the bank. I am not attracted to the suggestion that because RCL Operators, who paid the bank, was not Dawcolectric's debtor, the above authorities have no application. RCL Operators paid the bank on the express agreement that the issue

for determination was the bank's payment over countermand of RCL Contractors' undisputed debt to Dawcolectric. RCL Operators placed the bank in funds and, by agreement, put itself in the place of RCL Contractors. It cannot now resile from its agreement.

In my view, the three elements enumerated by McLachlin J. in *Peter v. Beblow* (1993), 101 D.L.R. (4th) 621 at p. 643, [1993] 1 S.C.R. 980, 48 E.T.R. 1, namely, an enrichment, a corresponding deprivation and the absence of a juristic reason for the deprivation have all been met. RCL Contractors was enriched, the bank was correspondingly deprived and there was no juristic reason for the enrichment. For that reason, it is my view that RCL Contractors is not entitled to recover the amount of the cheque that the bank paid to Dawcolectric.

I would dismiss the appeal with costs of $1,250 payable by the appellants to the respondent.

(r)   *B.M.P. Global Distribution Inc. v. Bank of Nova Scotia*†

[DESCHAMPS J. (for the Court):]

1.   FACTS

[1] The issue in this case is whether a bank must pay damages to customers for debits made from their accounts when reversing credits that had been entered in relation to a forged cheque. The trial judge, although acknowledging that his conclusion was absurd, found for the holders of the accounts. With respect, I agree with the Court of Appeal, albeit for different reasons, that the law does not dictate such a result. I also conclude that where money has been transferred in circumstances in which it can still be identified, tracing is permitted.

[2] As Saunders J.A. wrote for the Court of Appeal, the tale in this case is a strange one. It started when Audie Hashka and Paul Backman met Sunn Newman in the United States. Newman was said to be associated with a concern called Sunrise Marketing. Hashka and Backman owned interests in the appellant, B.M.P. Global Distribution Inc. ("BMP"), a

company operating in British Columbia that distributed non-stick bakeware without any formal licence or written agreement with its supplier. As the trial judge found, neither party was known to the other and neither had any business information concerning the other. According to Hashka and Backman, upon their return to Canada, an oral agreement was reached by telephone that Newman or Sunrise Marketing would purchase the right to distribute the bakeware in the United States. In the trial judge's words, "Backman agreed that Hashka arrived at the price of US $1.2 million by pulling the number out of the air", (2005 BCSC 1091, 8 B.L.R. (4th) 247, at para. 13). No projected cash flow statements, business plans or marketing plans were used as a basis for the negotiations, and BMP had conducted no research into Newman or Sunrise Marketing. The trial judge added: "Further, Newman did not request copies of BMP Global's financial statements or sales records (indicating a net loss of approximately $3,500), nor did BMP Global offer to provide this kind of information to Newman" (para. 13). Accord-

† 2009 SCC 15.

ing to Backman, he and Hashka decided to do business with Newman because he "was a sharp-looking guy that seemed like he had a lot of potential". Hashka testified that Newman "seemed like a businessman" because he "dressed well".

[3] On October 22, 2001, Hashka went to a Burnaby branch of the Bank of Nova Scotia ("BNS") where BMP held an account. He said that he wanted to deposit an unendorsed cheque for C$904,563 that was payable to BMP. He informed the branch manager that the cheque was a down payment for distributorship rights for BMP's products in the eastern United States (trial judgment, at para. 20). The cheque was drawn on an account of a corporation called First National Financial Corporation ("First National") at a Toronto branch of the Royal Bank of Canada ("RBC"). The cheque had been received the same day, without a cover letter, in an envelope on which the sender's name and address appeared as E. Smith of 6-6855 Airport Road, Mississauga, Ontario, L4V 1Y9, (416) 312-7205. Neither the drawer of the cheque nor the sender was known to Hashka or Backman or was apparently linked to Newman. No attempts were made to contact either First National or E. Smith before the cheque was taken to the bank.

[4] On receiving the cheque, BNS recorded it as a deposit to BMP's account. The cheque was not endorsed. BNS did not provide immediate access to the $904,563, because the funds already credited to the account were not sufficient to cover the amount of the cheque: the balance prior to the deposit was $59.67. The circumstances were so unusual that the branch manager informed Hashka and Backman that the funds would be held until the bank was satisfied that the instrument was authentic (trial judgment, at para. 282). BNS contacted RBC to ensure that there were sufficient funds in First National's account and that a hold had not been placed on the cheque. BNS eventually received the funds in the ordinary course of business and released them on October 30, 2001. On that date and over the next ten days, BMP made numerous transactions, including a transfer of US$20,000 to a Citibank account in New York City whose holder Hashka and Backman said they did not know. The largest transfers were to accounts of Hashka and Backman and to an account opened on November 2, 2001 in the name of a holding company, 636651 B.C. Ltd., that was wholly controlled by Hashka. The Court of Appeal described this flurry of transactions as a dispersion of funds, (2007 BCCA 52, 24 B.L.R. (4th) 201, at para. 11).

[5] The movements of funds involving BMP's account and the accounts of Hashka, Backman and 636651 B.C. Ltd. can be summarized as follows:

1. On November 5, two cheques drawn on BMP's account were deposited in the account of 636651 B.C. Ltd., one, certified by BNS, in the amount of $100,000 and the other in the amount of $300,000. Prior to these deposits totalling $400,000, the balance of the account was zero. After the deposits, $7,000 was used to pay travelling expenses and personal expenses incurred by Hashka.

2. A total of $70,000 was transferred from BMP's account to Backman's chequing account by way of deposits of $50,000 on October 29 and $20,000 on November 1. Prior to these deposits, the balance in the account was $45.87. A total of $52,351.81 was used to make purchases and retire outstanding debts incurred before the forged cheque was deposited in BMP's account. A deposit of $17.11 was made on November 3 as a result of a point of sale refund from a Future Shop store.

3. An amount of $3,000 was transferred from Backman's chequing account to his savings account. The prior balance of the savings account was $74.35. No other deposits were made into this account. From the savings account, $428.56 was used to pay outstanding debts incurred prior to the receipt of the forged cheque.

4. A total of $20,000 was transferred from BMP's account to Hashka's account. The prior balance in Hashka's account was $236.29. In addition, a payroll cheque for $3,022.49 was deposited on October 30. A total of $10,153.91 was used to pay personal debts, day-to-day expenses and entertainment expenses.

5. A certified cheque in the amount of $300,000 dated November 2, drawn by BMP and made to the order of BMP, was taken to the Bank of Montreal. On November 7, a bank draft issued by the Bank of Montreal for $300,100 was deposited by BMP in its account at BNS. No explanation has been provided for the disbursement or the subsequent deposit.

[6] On November 9, 2001, RBC notified BNS that the cheque for $904,563 deposited in BMP's account on October 22, 2001 was counterfeit, as the drawer's signatures were forged and asked for BNS's assistance. BNS interrupted all transactions in BMP's account and in all related accounts and asked BMP

for assistance in recovering the proceeds of the forged cheque. BMP insisted on retaining the amount it still held. BNS then restrained the following amounts in accounts under its control that it had linked to the forged cheque:

BMP's account	$350,188.65
636651's account	$393,000.00
Backman's chequing account	$ 17,711.17
Hashka's account	$ 13,104.87
Backman's savings account	$ 2,645.79
Total	$776,650.48

In addition, BNS recovered $685.56 by reversing bill payments made from BMP's account. (When referring globally to the accounts other than that of BMP, I will call them the "related accounts".)

[7] On December 6, 2001, RBC and BNS entered into an agreement in which RBC represented and warranted that the "cheque dated October 12, 2001, in the amount of nine hundred and four thousand five hundred and sixty-three dollars ($904,563.00) payable to BMP Global Distribution Inc. was counterfeit ... [and] was deposited into Scotiabank account number 30460 00178-17 ... [and] that the proceeds of the Counterfeit Cheque are proceeds of fraud". Under this agreement, BNS was, at RBC's request, to transfer the restrained funds to RBC and RBC was to indemnify BNS for any losses related to the restraint and transfer. On December 7, 2001, BNS transferred $777,336.04 to RBC.

[8] BMP's account was governed by a standard-form financial services agreement ("service agreement"). The relevant clauses are discussed below.

[9] BMP, Hashka, Backman and 636651 B.C. Ltd. claimed damages equivalent to the restrained amounts, non-pecuniary damages for stress, wrongful disclosure of information and defamation, aggravated and punitive damages. Backman also claimed damages regarding BNS's failure to honour certain payment instructions while his account was restrained. The issue of damages for stress, wrongful disclosure of information and defamation is not before this Court.

2. DECISIONS OF THE COURTS BELOW

2.1 *British Columbia Supreme Court, 2005 BCSC 1091, 8 B.L.R. (4th) 247*

[10] Cohen J. found that since BMP was not suing to enforce payment of the cheque, whether or not the cheque was a nullity or whether or not accepting BMP's position would allow a windfall to accrue to

BMP had no bearing on the outcome of the litigation (paras. 284–85). In his view, BNS had violated the service agreement as well as the law applicable to banker/customer relations by charging back amounts credited to the accounts of BMP and the other plaintiffs. Cohen J. interpreted the service agreement as incorporating the clearing rules of the Canadian Payments Association ("clearing rules") and precluding BNS from charging back against its customer's account. He reasoned that once "final settlement on the deposit of the Counterfeit Cheque had been reached between the BNS and the RBC", the funds in BMP's account "went from being a 'provisional' credit to being a 'final' credit. At that stage the relationship between the BNS and the plaintiffs was that of debtor/creditor" (para. 306). Regarding the related accounts, Cohen J. found that the law prevented a bank charging back against a customer's account without the customer's permission. He awarded the plaintiffs pecuniary damages because they had "suffered a loss of their right to demand repayment from the BNS of the BNS' debt to them by reason of the BNS' wrongful charge backs against their respective bank accounts" (para. 423). He assessed the total pecuniary damages at $777,336.04, the sum of all the charge backs and the reversed payments. He also awarded Backman $13.50 for a late charge due to BNS's failure to honour certain payment instructions while his account was restrained. Cohen J. also awarded damages for wrongful disclosure of information and defamation.

2.2 *British Columbia Court of Appeal, 2007 BCCA 52, 24 B.L.R. (4th) 201*

[11] The unanimous judgment of the Court of Appeal was rendered by Saunders J.A. She framed the issue as a fraud designed to place a credit in BMP's account for which BMP gave nothing. In her view, the courts were being asked to indirectly complete the fraud. She accepted the trial judge's finding that BNS had breached its banking agreement when it reversed the credit in BMP's account over BMP's opposition. However, she found that two characteristics of the case made it unusual. The first was that

the fact of two banks, and the consequent issues arising of clearing rules and the *Bills of Exchange Act*, confuse what would be otherwise a simple conclusion in these circumstances. The interposition in the fraudster's scheme of the Royal Bank of Canada created the screen of the clearing system. In this sense, the fraud may be described as extra-layered. The issue is whether that extra layering, in the circumstances I have just described, entitles BMP to recover from the Bank of Nova Scotia, as ordered by the trial judge. [para. 26]

Indeed, Saunders J.A. said that if only one bank had been involved in the payment, it would have been entitled to debit BMP's account, because the money was paid under a mistake of fact. The second unusual characteristic was the fact that

> BMP is an innocent in the fraud. Thus we know that BMP did not overtly assist the author of the scheme in its iniquitous aspects, whether or not the author has already been paid, unknowingly, by the cheque to Citibank, or was a gratuitous fraudster, or was a fraudster who has not yet presented his bill. For that reason, the many cases concerning recovery of monies from persons implicated in a fraud have no bearing on this case. [para. 27]

[12] Saunders J.A. did not delve further into what she called "the screen of the clearing system". She went on to find that

> on a plain reading of s. 48, the counterfeit cheque, because of the forged signatures on it, was wholly inoperative, setting the stage for a claim for return of monies advanced in reliance upon it.

> Section 48 demonstrates the *prima facie* empty asset that BMP builds its claim around.

> In equity, then, would this cheque have provided a basis upon which BMP could hope to retain the funds credited to its account? In my view the answer is no. [paras. 33–35]

[13] Saunders J.A. then found that it would be against good conscience to give a monetary judgment that would accomplish the substance of the fraud. She added that BMP could not claim the windfall — it had lost nothing: it did not change its position as a result of the charge back. She found that the arguments about the alleged rights of BMP, 636651 B.C. Ltd., Hashka and Backman under the clearing system rules were inconsistent with the principles of equity. She also found that, except for the $100 added to the original amount of $300,000, the funds linked to the bank draft issued by the Bank of Montreal bore the same character as the credit obtained from the deposit of the forged cheque. Thus, BMP could not retain any proceeds essentially derived from fraud. Saunders J.A. awarded BMP nominal damages of $1 for BNS's reversal of the credit over BMP's opposition (paras. 30 and 51) plus the remaining $100 from the bank draft, and dismissed the cross-appeal on punitive damages.

[14] As to the funds traced in the related accounts, Saunders J.A. found that the transfers were proper and that the cheques were actual bills of exchange, unlike the forged cheque. Absent a finding that the cheques in question were improper, BNS was entitled only to "a remedy of tracing, or an enquiry into the true ownership of the accounts" (para. 56). The appeals against 636651 B.C. Ltd., Hashka and Backman were thus dismissed.

[15] BMP appeals the Court of Appeal's reversal of the trial judge's conclusion on damages and also asks for punitive damages. BNS cross-appeals on the issue of tracing in the related accounts. It seeks the reversal of the Court of Appeal's decision and of the trial judge's damages award in favour of the holders of the related accounts.

3. POSITIONS OF THE PARTIES

[16] BMP asks that the award of damages be restored. It argues that, whether the claim is viewed as one for debt or for damages for breach of contract, BNS's liability is the same: "It is not necessary for BMP to prove that it suffered a loss, other than the loss of its right to demand repayment of [the amount credited to] its account [at] BNS" (A.F., at para. 82). BMP also asks for punitive damages to sanction BNS for its conduct.

[17] BNS takes the position that BMP never had any interest in the proceeds of the forged cheque and that it is not entitled to damages, whether general or punitive, resulting from BNS's decision to return the funds to the victim of the fraud. BNS asserts what is essentially a defence *in rem*, relying on the inherent nullity of an instrument bearing the forged signatures of the drawer. It argues that this defence suffices for it to resist BMP's claim. In addition, BNS appeals the decision on the tracing of the funds in the related accounts on the basis that those funds were clearly identified as proceeds of the forged cheque and that none of the parties involved gave any consideration or suffered any detriment. BNS does not contest the $13.50 awarded as damages by the trial judge in relation to a late-payment charge Backman had to pay to a third party.

[18] As the Court of Appeal mentioned, the case would have been simpler had only one bank been involved. However, in my view, BNS was not precluded from acknowledging that RBC could rely on the well-established doctrine of mistake of fact. Moreover, the conditions for tracing the funds in the related accounts are, in my view, met.

[19] In sum, this case is about the restitution of amounts paid by RBC by mistake and the right to trace the proceeds. Since the case can be resolved by applying the common law rules on mistake of fact, I will begin by reviewing those rules. I will then apply the rules to the facts, and in doing so I will explain how the rules apply in the context of the relationship between the drawee and the collecting bank and between the customer and the bank; this will require a further discussion of the common law inasmuch as it has not been changed by the *Bills of Exchange Act*, R.S.C. 1985, c. B-4 ("*BEA*"). Finally, I will explain why, in my view, BNS could resist the claims of BMP and the holders of the related accounts.

4. ANALYSIS

[20] In *Bank and Customer Law in Canada* (2007), M.H. Ogilvie writes (at p. 284):

> [B]anks make payments by mistake for a variety of reasons, including simple error, either personal or by computer, in making a payment more than once, payment over an effective countermand, payment where there are insufficient funds, or payment of a forged or unauthorized cheque. *Prima facie*, in these situations, with the exception of insufficient funds which is treated as an overdraft, the bank is liable to reimburse the customer's account because it is in breach of contract with the customer. But the bank is also permitted to look to the recipient of the mistaken payment for restitution of the sum paid under a mistake of fact.

[21] That a bank has a right to recover from a recipient a payment made under a mistake of fact was made clear in a restatement of the law by Goff J. (as he then was) in *Barclays Bank Ltd. v. W. J. Simms Son & Cooke (Southern) Ltd.*, [1979] 3 All E.R. 522 (Q.B.), at p. 541. Canadian courts have long recognized that right on the basis of the analytical framework adopted in *Royal Bank v. The King*, [1931] 2 D.L.R. 685 (Man. K.B.). Since *Simms*, however, and I agree with this approach, many Canadian courts have relied on the English case as setting the conditions for recovery in restitution by a bank, subject to Canadian law with respect to change of position, an issue that will be discussed below: *Royal Bank of Canada v. LVG Auctions Ltd.* (1983), 43 O.R. (2d) 582 (H.C.J.), aff'd (1984), 12 D.L.R. (4th) 768 (Ont. C.A.); *Toronto-Dominion Bank v. Pella/Hunt Corp.* (1992), 10 O.R. (3d) 634 (Gen. Div.); *A.E. LePage Real Estate Services Ltd. v. Rattray Publications* (1994), 120 D.L.R. (4th) 499 (Ont. C.A.), at p. 507: "*Barclays Bank v. Simms* is the accepted authority explaining the obligations of a bank to its customer and its redress against the payee of a cheque who appears to be taking advantage of an innocent mistake on the part of a bank employee"; *Central Guaranty Trust Co. v. Dixdale Mortgage Investment Corp.* (1994), 24 O.R. (3d) 506 (C.A.), at p. 512, fn. 1; Ogilvie, at p. 285; P. D. Maddaugh and J. D. McCamus, *The Law of Restitution* (loose-leaf), at p. 10-32.

4.1 Simms Test for Recovering Money Paid Under a Mistake of Fact

[22] The test laid down in *Simms* for recovering money paid under a mistake of fact (at p. 535) is straightforward:

1. If a person pays money to another under a mistake of fact which causes him to make the payment, he is prima facie entitled to recover it as money paid under a mistake of fact.
2. His claim may however fail if: (a) the payer intends that the payee shall have the money at all events, whether the fact be true or false, or is deemed in law so to intend; (b) the payment is made for good consideration, in particular if the money is paid to discharge, and does discharge, a debt owed to the payee (or a principal on whose behalf he is authorised to receive the payment) by the payer or by a third party by whom he is authorised to discharge the debt; (c) the payee has changed his position in good faith, or is deemed in law to have done so.

[23] The right of BNS to resist the claims of the appellant and the cross-respondents cannot be examined without regard to RBC's right to ask BNS to transfer the funds. Consequently, RBC's position is the starting point for the analysis.

4.2 Application of the Test

4.2.1 *Prima Facie Right to Recover*

[24] On the first step of the *Simms* test, RBC has a *prima facie* right to recover. It is common ground that payment was made on the basis of a forged instrument. According to s. 48(1) *BEA*, a forged signature is wholly inoperative. It does not create a right to give a discharge for the bill or to enforce payment. RBC made the payment before discovering that the drawer's signatures were forged. BMP no longer disputes the fact that the instrument is a forgery, but it contends that RBC must bear the loss and that BNS was not entitled to restrain the funds

and transfer them to RBC. This argument goes to the second step of the test. At the first step, there is no basis for denying that RBC has a *prima facie* right to recover the funds.

4.2.2 Right of the Payee to Keep the Proceeds, Consideration and Change of Position

[25] I reiterate that the second step of the test involves three enquiries: (1) Did the payor intend that the payee keep the money in any event or is the payor precluded by law from raising the mistake? (2) Did the payee give consideration? (3) Did the payee change its position?

4.2.2.1 RIGHT TO KEEP THE PROCEEDS

[26] In the first enquiry, the question is whether the payor intends or is deemed in law to intend the payee to receive the funds. In the case at bar, the drawee provided the funds under the mistaken assumption that the drawer's signatures were genuine. It is not in dispute — and is well settled in law — that RBC, as the drawee, had no right to pay the cheque out of the funds it held to the credit of First National, the purported drawer, and that RBC would be liable to reimburse its customer if it used the customer's funds to make the payment. Nor is the relationship between BNS and RBC in dispute. It is that of a collecting bank receiving funds from the drawee in order to remit them to the payee. The issue before the Court in this case is whether, as BMP argues, the loss must fall on the drawee bank.

[27] Where a drawee provides funds to a collecting bank on presentation of an instrument bearing a forged signature of the drawer, the drawee will usually — unless a specific factual context dictates otherwise — be in a position to assert that it did not intend the payee to keep the funds. As I mentioned above, the drawee in this situation pays without the authority to do so and is liable to its customer, who has not signed as the drawer. Without such an instruction from the drawer, the payor cannot be said to have intended the payee to keep the money in any event. This is not a case where a party pays a debt it owes or where other similar circumstances preclude the payor from denying that it intended the payee to keep the funds.

[28] However, whether the payor is deemed in law to intend that the payee keep the money requires further elaboration. BMP put forward three arguments in support of its claim. The first is that the principle of finality of payment forms part of the common law and that it prevents the drawee bank from recovering the paid proceeds of a forged cheque from anyone other than the forger. The second is that the scheme of the *BEA* does not allow RBC to recover from BNS or BMP. The third is that the service agreement between BNS and BMP precludes BNS from recovering such proceeds from BMP.

4.2.2.1.1 Principle of Finality of Payment

[29] In Canadian law, the argument that the drawee should bear the loss is sometimes said to have originated in *Bank of Montreal v. The King* (1907), 38 S.C.R. 258. I will turn to that case in a moment, but since the two judges (Girouard J., with whom Maclennan J. concurred) who supported the principle of finality relied heavily on the older case of *Price v. Neal* (1762), 3 Burr. 1354, 97 E.R. 871, I will begin by discussing the latter.

[30] In *Price v. Neal*, a drawee paid a first bill of exchange bearing a forged signature of the drawer. He then accepted a second, also bearing a forged signature of the drawer. After that acceptance, the bearer discounted the second bill, which the drawee eventually paid. A considerable amount of time elapsed before the drawee found out that the signatures on both bills were forged. Lord Mansfield held that the drawee was not entitled to recover in such a case.

[31] *Price v. Neal* has been interpreted in various ways over the centuries. One of the interpretations serves as a basis for a broad statement that the principle of finality of payment requires the drawee to bear the loss where the drawer's signature is forged, irrespective of detrimental reliance (see S. A. Scott, "Comment on Benjamin Geva's Paper: 'Reflections on the Need to Revise the Bills of Exchange Act — Some Doctrinal Aspects'" (1981–82), 6 *Can. Bus. L.J.* 331 ("Comment on Reflections"), at p. 342). A second interpretation of *Price v. Neal* is that the drawee cannot rely on the forgery after acceptance (or payment) of a bill bearing a signature he should know to be forged or is deemed to have negligently omitted to verify. Yet a third interpretation put forward for *Price v. Neal* limits its scope to instances where two innocent parties have equal equities but the holder of the bill has legal title to the money (see *Lipkin Gorman v. Karpnale Ltd.*, [1991] 2 A.C. 548 (H.L.); B. Geva, "Reflections on the Need to Revise the Bills of Exchange Act — Some Doctrinal Aspects: Panel Discussion" (1981–82), 6 *Can. Bus. L.J.* 269 ("Reflections"), at pp. 308–9; J. S. Ziegel, B. Geva and R. C. C. Cuming, *Commercial and Consumer*

Transactions: Cases, Text and Materials (3rd ed. 1995), vol. II, at p. 396, citing J. B. Ames, "The Doctrine of Price *v.* Neal" (1891), 4 *Harv. L. Rev.* 297, at pp. 297–99). In view of the various interpretations of *Price v. Neal*, I do not accept that it provides a basis for an unqualified rule that a drawee will never have any recourse against either the collecting bank or the payee where payment has been made on the forged signature of the drawer.

[32] In Canada, *Bank of Montreal v. The King* is sometimes relied on in support of the principle of finality of payment. Upon closer examination, however, it cannot be said to stand for a hard and fast rule that the drawee is in all circumstances precluded from recovering from the collecting bank. First, the judges in *Bank of Montreal v. The King* who invoked *Price v. Neal* as having endorsed the principle of finality of payment did not discuss the third interpretation of that case. Second, the other judges who wrote in *Bank of Montreal v. The King* took a far more nuanced approach to the problem of the forged signature of the drawer.

[33] In *Bank of Montreal v. The King*, the bank had honoured cheques bearing the forged signatures of officers of the Government of Canada. As the Government of Canada had not authorized the payments, it sought to recover the amounts of the forged cheques from the Bank of Montreal. The Bank of Montreal in turn took action against the collecting banks to recover the amounts they had received as a result of the forged cheques. Four different judges wrote reasons. All of them concluded that the drawee, the Bank of Montreal, had to return the funds to the drawer, the Government of Canada. All of them also rejected the claim against the collecting banks, although the reasons they gave cannot easily be categorized.

[34] Three of the five judges in *Bank of Montreal v. The King* (Davies, Idington and Duff JJ.) were of the view that if the position of a collecting bank is altered, that bank can resist a claim by the drawee. Two of the judges (Davies and Idington JJ.) explicitly rejected Girouard J.'s adoption of the argument, based on *Price v. Neal*, of presumed or actual negligence on the drawee's part and the third (Duff J.) did not pronounce on it. Therefore, to argue that there is a clear rule that the drawee must suffer the loss is not supported by what is labeled as the *fons et origo* of the Canadian precedents on forged instruments. In addition, the fact that the Canadian courts subsequently embraced *Simms* also weakens the finality of payment argument significantly in a case involving payment of an instrument bearing a forged signature.

[35] The assessment of the drawee's rights requires a more nuanced enquiry. The principle of finality of payment underlies both the common law rules and the *BEA*'s provisions and serves as a general goal, but as laudable as it is, it does not negate rights that may otherwise accrue to a party. It cannot be raised by a payee as an indiscriminate bar to the recovery of a mistaken payment. I agree with Scott, "Comment on Reflections", at p. 342, that:

> [N]o very convincing reason can be offered for refusing the drawee relief in the single instance where the mistake involves acceptance or payment on a forged drawer's signature, whilst relief is freely given to the drawee on all *other* acceptances or payments by mistake (including indeed various other kinds of forgeries; even the case where the drawer's own endorsement is forged on a bill payable to his order (s. 129(*b*)) [now s. 128(*b*)].

4.2.2.1.2 Provisions of the BEA

[36] On the issue of whether the payor is deemed in law to intend that the payee keep the money, two provisions of the *BEA* warrant comment: ss. 128(*a*) and 165(3). These provisions are relevant in view both of BNS's role as BMP's agent for the purposes of collection on the instrument, and of the special status granted to a bank that receives an unendorsed cheque.

[37] Section 128(*a*) *BEA* reads as follows:

> **128.** [Estoppel] The acceptor of a bill by accepting it is precluded from denying to a holder in due course
> (*a*) the existence of the drawer, the genuineness of his signature and his capacity and authority to draw the bill;

[38] In the instant case, the drawee (RBC), in requesting restitution from the collecting bank (BNS), was in fact denying to both the collecting bank and the payee the genuineness of the drawer's signatures. Consequently, the question is whether the payee and the collecting bank were holders in due course and therefore entitled to rely on s. 128(*a*) *BEA*. I will discuss the payee's situation first, because the collecting bank has a special status which, in this case, is governed by s. 165(3), to which I will turn below.

[39] The most common view is that a payee is not, as a general rule, a holder in due course because he or she has not acquired the instrument by way of

negotiation (s. 55(1)(*b*) *BEA*). Yet in some factual circumstances, dealings may take place before the payee becomes the holder of the instrument, and some commentators consider that the negotiation requirement needs to be revisited: Geva, "Reflections", at pp. 289 ff.; see also *St. Martin Supplies Inc. v. Boucley*, [1969] C.S. 324. This question need not be resolved for the purposes of the present case, however. It is another requirement for qualifying as a holder in due course under s. 55(1)(*b*) *BEA* that is lacking here: BMP did not take the instrument for value, so it was not a holder in due course. Since only a holder in due course can benefit from s. 128(*a*) *BEA*, even if RBC were deemed — by payment — to have accepted the forged cheque, it would not be precluded from denying to BMP the genuineness of the drawer's signatures.

[40] The other provision that is relevant to RBC's right to recover the money it paid by mistake from BNS is s. 165(3) *BEA*. This provision reads as follows:

> **165.** ...
>
> (3) Where a cheque is delivered to a bank for deposit to the credit of a person and the bank credits him with the amount of the cheque, the bank acquires all the rights and powers of a holder in due course of the cheque.

[41] According to this provision, BNS acquired the status of a holder in due course by receiving the cheque from the payee and crediting the amount to the payee's account. Section 165(3) *BEA* deems the collecting bank to be in the same position as a party who has taken the bill free from any defect of title of prior parties. It has the same right as a party who has given consideration. Consequently, it can be argued that if BNS had chosen to do so, it could have refused to transfer to RBC the money it held on account of the fraudulent instrument. However, the question is not whether it could rely on the protection of s. 165(3) *BEA*, but whether it could restore the funds to RBC.

[42] Section 165(3) *BEA* has been commented on many times. Parliament was initially criticized for acting at the request of the banking industry without understanding the potentially wide scope of the amendment (see S. A. Scott, "The Bank is Always Right: Section 165(3) of the Bills of Exchange Act and its Curious Parliamentary History" (1973), 19 *McGill L.J.* 78). Then, following *Boma Manufacturing Ltd. v. Canadian Imperial Bank of Commerce*, [1996] 3 S.C.R. 727, Ogilvie expressed the view in *Bank and Customer Law in Canada*, at p. 295, that the effect of the Court's narrow interpretation of s. 165(3) has been to make the collecting bank the drawer's insurer. The least that can be said is that the interpretation of the scope of s. 165(3) *BEA* is taking shape.

[43] No prior case has concerned the effect s. 165(3) *BEA* will have where the deposited instrument bears a forged signature of the drawer. In *Boma*, at para. 43, Iacobucci J. explicitly refrained from discussing the applicability of the defence available to the collecting bank in circumstances where the instrument might be found not to be a bill of exchange. Although I have serious doubts about the soundness of an argument which would deprive the collecting bank of all protection on the basis that the instrument is a sham, not a cheque, I need not discuss it here in view of my position that the collecting bank is not required to rely on the protection potentially afforded by s. 165(3) *BEA*.

[44] As Ogilvie clearly points out:

> Section 165(3) is drafted in broad terms, with the obvious policy of protecting a bank from liability in relation to cheques deposited in a customer's account by permitting a bank to presume that it was the drawer's intention that the payee receive the proceeds of the cheque, in complete contrast to the earlier law, where a bank enjoyed no such presumption. [pp. 292–93]

[45] Section 165(3) *BEA* affords protection to a bank. The bank is not obligated to rely on this protection when restitution is claimed from it. The payee stands as a third party with respect to the protection. He or she cannot use the bank's shield as a sword against it. The purpose of granting the bank the status of a holder in due course is not to create an entitlement for the payee of a forged instrument. The payee may benefit from defences that are inherent in the rules on mistake of fact, but not from the protection afforded to a bank by s. 165(3) *BEA*. In other words, if the forged instrument were held to be a bill of exchange, BMP could not argue, for the purposes of the *Simms* test, that BNS was deemed in law to be entitled to receive the funds irrespective of the validity of the drawer's signatures.

4.2.2.1.3 *The Service Agreement*

[46] BMP also argued, and the trial judge agreed, that BNS was not entitled to restrain the funds and transfer them to RBC because the service agreement governing the contractual relationship did not authorize this.

[47] Historically, a contract governing a bank account consisted mainly of implied terms: *Bank of Montreal v. Attorney General of Quebec*, [1979] 1 S.C.R. 565, at p. 569 (*per* Pratte J.), citing *Joachimson v. Swiss Bank Corp.*, [1921] 3 K.B. 110 (C.A.), at p. 117 (*per* Bankes L.J.). Those terms were developed by the common law courts, and some of them were later codified in what is now the *BEA*.

[48] Today, most bank account agreements, including the service agreement between BMP and BNS, are standard form contracts. However, terms may still be implied: *Canadian Pacific Hotels Ltd. v. Bank of Montreal*, [1987] 1 S.C.R. 711, at pp. 776–77; G. R. Hall, *Canadian Contractual Interpretation Law* (2007), at p. 125. In the instant case, BMP argues that under the service agreement, BNS could charge back only the credits for which it had not received settlement. According to BNS, nothing in the service agreement precluded it from returning the funds to RBC and resisting the claim for damages.

4.2.2.1.3.1 The Provisional Payment Clause

[49] The service agreement contains provisions under which amounts may be charged back in certain circumstances. Clause 4.7 reads as follows:

> **4.7** You authorize us to charge the following to any of your accounts, even if they are not specifically designated for the instruction or service:
> - the amount you ask us to pay in any instruction
> - the amount of any instruction we have paid to you or credited to your account and for which we do not receive settlement for any reason (including fraud, loss or endorsement error) together with all related costs
> - payment of any amount you owe us, including fees, charges, costs and expenses.

[50] The right to charge back provisional credits when a customer's instruction to collect on a bill cannot be carried out has long been recognized at common law. Clause 4.7 clarifies that right but does not rule out other reversals of credit that are available at common law. Clause 4.7 gives the bank an explicit right to charge back amounts credited to the customer's account if an instrument is not settled. In the context of the service agreement, it is clear that the settlement referred to in this clause is the receipt of the funds through the banking system, and more particularly through the clearing mechanism available to members of the Canadian Payments Association.

[51] The trial judge seems to have understood the doctrine of mistake of fact to be limited to provisional credits or, in other words, to situations where the collecting bank has not received the funds. This is not so. As a matter of fact, both the seminal cases of *Bank of Montreal v. The King* and *Royal Bank v. The King*, to which I referred above, concerned forgeries discovered long after the forged cheques had been paid. In *Royal Bank v. The King*, the drawee bank was held to be entitled to claim the amounts of the cheques from the payee, who was also its customer. *Royal Bank v. The King* shows that a bank is not necessarily precluded from claiming funds from the payee long after the instrument has been cleared.

[52] The doctrine of mistake of fact is so ingrained in our law that it can be seen as an implied term of the contract. This is even more true in the case at bar, as a clause of the service agreement explicitly provides that BNS retains its rights under "any law". Clause 17.3 reads as follows:

> **17.3** This agreement takes precedence over any other agreement, service request or service materials relating to any instruction or services. However, we retain all our rights under any law respecting loans, set-off, deposits and banking matters even if they are not described in this agreement.

[53] Although the restraint of the funds by BNS could not be based on clause 4.7, since BNS had received settlement from RBC, the contract does not preclude the application of the common law where a payment has been made under a mistake of fact. Rather, the common law is implicitly incorporated, since it does not conflict with the explicit terms of the contract. Thus, clause 4.7 is not a bar to applying the common law to the relationship between BNS and BMP where BNS's role is no longer that of a collecting bank.

4.2.2.1.3.2 The Clearing Rules

[54] In concluding that BNS did not have the right to restrain the funds and transfer them to RBC, the trial judge interpreted the service agreement as incorporating the clearing rules of the Canadian Payments Association. Cohen J. held that "the Agreement specifically refers to, and incorporates the time limit set out in the [clearing] [r]ules" (para. 292). With respect, I do not agree that the clearing rules are an obstacle to recovery.

[55] The clearing rules themselves provide for the survival of the members' common law rights. Clause 1(b) of Rule A4 allows a negotiating bank to seek recourse outside the clearing system:

Nothing in this Rule precludes a Drawee or a Negotiating Institution from exercising its rights and seeking recourse outside of the Clearing.

Moreover, the preamble to the rules contains an express disclaimer of application to third parties:

> Nothing in the Rules shall affect or be interpreted to affect the rights or liabilities of any party to any Payment Item, except as expressly provided in the Rules.

[56] It is also recognized in the authorities that the clearing rules apply only to relations between members of the Canadian Payments Association and that they do not create entitlements for third parties. As B. Crawford states in *Payment, Clearing and Settlement in Canada* (2002), vol. 1, at p. 168:

> ... it must be abundantly clear in principle that the ACSS Rules, being internal documents of a corporation, may legitimately govern the relations of the members of the corporation but cannot place burdens on members of the public or bestow benefits on them in connection with their use of the CPA's clearing and settlement system.

[57] I agree with the following statement by Evans J.A. in *National Bank of Greece (Canada) v. Bank of Montreal*, [2001] 2 F.C. 288 (C.A.), at para. 19:

> This system operates only at the level of banking and similar institutions, and ... decisions of the compliance panel have no impact on either the private law rights and duties of banks, their customers, and the payers and payees of cheques, or the remedies available to enforce them.

(See also *Bank of Nova Scotia v. Regent Enterprises Ltd.* (1997), 157 Nfld. & P.E.I.R. 102 (C.A.), at para. 38; *Toronto-Dominion Bank v. Dauphin Plains Credit Union Ltd.* (1992), 90 D.L.R. (4th) 117 (Man. Q.B.), at p. 121, rev'd on other grounds (1992), 98 D.L.R. (4th) 736 (Man. C.A.), leave to appeal to SCC refused, [1993] 2 S.C.R. vii.)

[58] Finally, I disagree with the trial judge that the service agreement governing the relationship between BNS and BMP incorporated the clearing rules for BMP's benefit. The trial judge based this conclusion on his analysis of clauses 4.1, 4.3, 4.4 (para. 296) and 4.7 (para. 297), as well as on the testimony of the branch manager, who stated: "[The service agreement] uses — That's correct. It used the clearing settlement system" (para. 291). This statement supports the fact that BNS "used" the clearing system. However, it does not mean that the rules were incorporated into the service agreement. Clauses 4.1, 4.3

and 4.4, to which the trial judge referred, read as follows:

> **4.1** You are responsible for settling payment of your instructions. Unless you have made specific arrangements with us, you will ensure that your accounts have sufficient cleared funds to settle any instructions at the time that you give us an instruction. We are not required to settle an instruction if sufficient cleared funds are not available in your account. The reported balances for your account may include amounts which are not cleared funds. Cleared funds means cash or any funds from any deposit which have been finally settled through the clearing system.
>
> **4.3** You acknowledge that we must clear instructions using a clearing system and are bound by the rules of any clearing system we use, including rules for endorsement of instructions, identity of payee and the time for final settlement. These rules affect our ability to honour your request to cancel instructions and the procedures we must follow to settle your instructions and clear funds for you.
>
> **4.4** We reserve the right to clear and transfer instructions by whatever method we choose, whether they are drawn on your account or negotiated by you. You grant us sufficient time to settle all instructions. You acknowledge that we may delay crediting your account until we receive the cleared funds for the instruction.

[59] Clause 4.1 is a restatement of the bank's common law obligation to honour its customer's cheques and instructions when the customer has sufficient credit. Under clause 4.3, BMP acknowledged that BNS was bound by the clearing rules. The only consequence of this acknowledgment was that BMP would be precluded from claiming a breach of the agreement if a failure by BNS to honour its instructions was justified by the clearing rules BNS must abide by in dealing with other banks. Clause 4.4 essentially gave BNS three types of rights: (1) to clear instructions in whatever way it chose; (2) to take sufficient time to settle instructions; and (3) to take sufficient time to credit the account. Clause 4.4 was silent as to whether the "credit" ever became a final and irreversible credit to BMP's account. It may be that the restraint of the funds by BNS was based on no express provision, but it is clear that the clearing rules were neither expressly nor implicitly incorporated for BMP's benefit.

[60] In summary, the trial judge could not rely on the clearing rules to arrive at the conclusion that BMP had a right to the proceeds of the forged cheque. Consequently, I find that the first answer at

the second step of the *Simms* test is that RBC did not intend and is not deemed in law to have intended that BMP receive the funds. Two other enquiries remain: whether consideration was given and whether a change of position occurred.

4.2.2.2 CONSIDERATION

[61] The question whether BMP has given consideration is easily answered in light of the trial judge's finding of fact that BMP gave no value for the instrument. At the same time, BMP's position that RBC should bear the loss entails an implicit acknowledgment that neither itself nor BNS has given consideration for the instrument.

4.2.2.3 CHANGE OF POSITION

[62] The question in the third enquiry is whether the payee has changed its position. In *Simms*, the condition that money cannot be recovered in the event of a change of position was seen to be linked to the defendant's being deprived of an opportunity to give a notice of dishonour. This prompted comments that the defence of change of position is more specific than the label would suggest: Geva, "Reflections", at pp. 308 ff. However, leading English commentators on the subject now observe that the law has evolved and may now include defences of change of position that are not related to the *BEA*'s notice requirements: Lord Goff and G. Jones, *The Law of Restitution* (6th ed. 2002), at p. 852; see *Lipkin Gorman v. Karpnale Ltd*. Similarly, leading Canadian commentators consider that since *Rural Municipality of Storthoaks v. Mobil Oil Canada, Ltd.*, [1976] 2 S.C.R. 147, the defence of change of position has been "an established feature of the Canadian law of mistaken payments": Maddaugh and McCamus, at p. 10-35, §10:500.10; see also G. H. L. Fridman, *Restitution* (2nd ed. 1992), at p. 458. I see no reason why the general defence of change of position should not apply to mistaken payments made on forged cheques.

[63] To conduct the change of position enquiry, it is necessary to determine whether the payee parted with the funds. In this case, BNS, as the collecting bank, received the funds from RBC for the benefit of the payee, BMP, and credited BMP's account. Once the collecting bank receives the funds from the drawee and credits the payee, its role as a collecting bank is terminated. It then becomes the holder of the funds under its contract with its customer. It is settled law that a customer is a creditor of the bank when he or she deposits funds into an account and that the bank holds these funds as its own until the customer asks for repayment. This principle has gone

unquestioned since *Foley v. Hill* (1848), 2 H.L.C. 28, 9 E.R. 1002. See *Crawford and Falconbridge: Banking and Bills of Exchange* (8th ed. 1986), vol. 1, at pp. 742–43; Ogilvie, at p. 179.

[64] Thus, although BNS's role was changed from that of a collecting bank to that of a borrower, for the purposes of the change of position analysis, it must be concluded that BNS remained the holder of the funds. Moreover, at the time they were restrained, the funds now claimed by BMP were still credited to its account. Therefore neither BNS as the holder of the funds nor the payee had changed its position.

[65] In conclusion, BMP had not changed its position and the defence was available neither to it nor to BNS. It is worth noting that cases in which a person who is not a party to the fraud has neither given consideration nor changed its position will be rare. However, that is what has happened here according to the facts found by the trial judge. In these circumstances, all the conditions for recovery of the payment made by mistake are met. Other objections have been made, though, and I will discuss them now.

4.3 Jus Tertii Defence, Self-Help Arguments and Policy Considerations

[66] The trial judge found that it was wrong for BNS to transfer the funds to RBC. He was of the view that BNS had favoured a bank to its customer's detriment. In his opinion, BNS was not entitled to exercise any of the rights that could have been exercised by RBC.

[67] The *jus tertii* argument the trial judge relied on could be accepted only if RBC had no right to recover the funds from BNS. Only then could BNS be said to have acted in RBC's stead. Since I have concluded that BNS was entitled to give effect to RBC's claim for restitution of the moneys paid under mistake of fact, the *jus tertii* argument fails. This is the result of the application of the law to the highly singular facts of this case.

[68] It is worth recalling some of the extremely unusual circumstances of this case: the sale price of the unlicensed distributorship was arrived at by "pulling the number out of the air", the cheque was received without a cover letter, the names of the sender and the drawer of the cheque were unknown, Newman, the purchaser, could not be reached and the payee had given no consideration. The fraud could not be clearer, nor could the origin of the

funds. In my view, since the rightful owner had a legitimate claim against the recipient, BNS had no duty to give preference to BMP.

[69] The funds received by BNS were RBC's own funds and RBC had no right to be repaid out of First National's account. BNS acted in a way that could have enabled the parties to avoid going through a series of judicial proceedings. This Court's reasoning in *Bank Canadian National v. Gingras*, [1977] 2 S.C.R. 554, at p. 564, applies with equal force here. BNS asked BMP for support in recovering the proceeds of the forged cheque. BMP insisted on retaining the funds even though it had given no consideration for them and even though the fraud was beyond dispute. In this case, BNS's actions entailed no risk of curtailing the protection from which a holder in due course is entitled to benefit.

[70] Furthermore, BMP objected to the joinder of the action RBC had eventually instituted against BMP, which was pending at the time this case was heard. It might have been easier for the trial judge to assess the parties' rights had the two proceedings been joined. In these circumstances, the argument that BNS had exercised a third party right or resorted to a self-help remedy not only sounds hollow and opportunistic, but is procedurally unfounded.

[71] I can conceive of no policy consideration that would preclude BNS from responding to RBC's common law right in this case. As I mentioned above, neither *Price v. Neal* nor *Bank of Montreal v. The King* stands for a strict rule that the drawee must in all circumstances bear a loss resulting from a cheque bearing a forged signature of the drawer. There is no rule preventing RBC or BNS from arguing that the payment to BMP was made by mistake. The commentators find no convincing reason to establish an absolute rule against relief in the case of payment on the drawer's forged signature (B. Geva, "Conversion of Unissued Cheques and the Fictitious or Non-Existing Payee — *Boma v. CIBC*" (1997), 28 *Can. Bus. L.J.* 177, at p. 189; Scott, "Comment on Reflections", at p. 342).

[72] At common law, the principle of finality of payment must be balanced against the right of the owner of the funds to recover money paid under a mistake of fact. The common law affords a defence to an innocent party who has given consideration or changed his or her position. However, the person who is still in possession of the funds is in the best position to stop the fraud. To preclude means to prevent the continuation of a fraud in order to allow a fraudulent payment to be finalized would be a

strange policy. Thus, there is no overarching policy consideration that would bar the payee's bank from resisting a claim based on a signature that has been proven to be forged where the payee has not used the funds and has neither given consideration for them nor changed his or her position.

[73] The trial judge was of the view that BMP and the holders of the related accounts had "suffered a loss of their right to demand repayment from the BNS of the BNS' debt to them by reason of the BNS' wrongful charge backs against their respective bank accounts" (para. 423). In my view, BNS was entitled to object that since the cheque was forged, the funds could be and were returned to their rightful owner. The deposit of the forged instrument could not result in a debt to BMP in this case. Therefore, BMP did not lose anything because the funds had to be returned to RBC. The trial judge's conclusion that BMP had lost the right to demand payment of a debt owed by BNS is erroneous, because the credit entry in the account had been made by mistake.

[74] I have found that RBC made a mistaken payment, that nothing precluded it from recovering the funds and that BMP had no defence to the claim. More particularly, BNS was entitled not to raise a defence based on s. 165(3) *BEA*. RBC, in trying to trace the sums it had mistakenly paid, was informed that a portion amounting to over $776,000 was being held by BNS at the time the fraud was discovered. An amount of $350,188.65 was still in BMP's account. BNS also restrained funds in the related accounts. The question the Court must now answer is whether the rules of evidence are a bar to restitution. I will now discuss this issue.

4.4 Right to Claim the Amounts in BMP's Account and to Trace Funds in the Related Accounts

[75] Tracing is an identification process. The common law rule is that the claimant must demonstrate that the assets being sought in the hands of the recipient are either the very assets in which the claimant asserts a proprietary right or a substitute for them.

[76] In the instant case, RBC's funds were first transferred through the clearing system to BNS in its capacity as collecting bank — and thus as agent — for BMP. BNS then made the entry in BMP's account to reflect the receipt of the funds from RBC. Finally, BMP made withdrawals from its account by

way of transfers or cheques for deposit in the related accounts and, in the case of the transactions involving the $300,000 cheque, back to its own account. What is at issue here is a non-specific fund.

[77] Under ordinary circumstances, an agent cannot be sued in the principal's stead. However, as stated by Lord Goff and Jones in *The Law of Restitution*, at p. 847, citing *British American Continental Bank v. British Bank for Foreign Trade*, [1926] 1 K.B. 328 (C.A.),

> where the agent has paid the money over to his principal but has received it back again so that his position is as it was before he paid it over, he must make restitution.

Save for the $100 added to the bank draft, there is no issue of identification of the money in BMP's account. The unchallenged evidence is that it comes from the funds received from RBC. BNS, as agent, received the funds from RBC and, after crediting them to its principal, BMP, received them back under the banking contract. Having received the funds back, BNS had to make restitution to RBC. Therefore, BNS has a valid defence against BMP (see *Bavins, Junr. & Sims v. London and South Western Bank, Ltd.*, [1900] 1 Q.B. 270 (C.A.)). BNS's status with respect to the funds in the related accounts is different. BNS was not acting as agent of the holders of the related accounts. A review of the rules on tracing will therefore be helpful.

[78] It has been accepted that the English case of *Agip (Africa) Ltd. v. Jackson*, [1992] 4 All E.R. 451 (C.A.) (aff'g [1992] 4 All E.R. 385 (Ch.)), has been accepted as setting out rules with respect to tracing of money: *Citadel General Assurance Co. v. Lloyds Bank Canada*, [1997] 3 S.C.R. 805.

[79] According to the Court of Appeal in *Agip*, tracing at law is permitted where a person has received money rightfully claimed by the claimant. Liability is based on mere receipt, and the extent of liability will depend on the amount received (*Agip* (C.A.), at pp. 463–64; *Agip* (Ch.), at p. 399; *Banque Belge pour l'Étranger v. Hambrouck*, [1921] 1 K.B. 321 (C.A.)). It is sometimes said that funds cannot be traced to bank accounts at common law. This view overstates the rule and fails to take into account the fact that, as an evidentiary process, tracing is possible if identification is possible (see D. R. Klinck, "'Two Distincts, Division None': Tracing Money into (and out of) Mixed Accounts" (1988), 2 *B.F.L.R.* 147, at p. 148, and L. D. Smith, *The Law of Tracing* (1997), at pp. 183 ff.). Indeed, no statement that tracing is

impossible can be found in the case that is most often cited in support of the theory that funds cannot be traced to bank accounts at common law. If Lord Ellenborough C.J.'s comment in *Taylor v. Plumer* (1815), 3 M. & S. 562, 34 E.R. 721, is read in its entirety, it is clear that tracing is impossible only when the means of ascertainment fail:

> It makes no difference in reason or law into what other form, different from the original, the change may have been made, whether it be into that of promissory notes for the security of the money which was produced by the sale of the goods of the principal, as in *Scott v. Surman*, Willes, 400, or into other merchandize, as in *Whitecomb v. Jacob*, Salk. 160, for the product of or substitute for the original thing still follows the nature of the thing itself, as long as it can be ascertained to be such, and the right only ceases when the means of ascertainment fail, which is the case when the subject is turned into money, and mixed and confounded in a general mass of the same description. The difficulty which arises in such a case is a difficulty of fact and not of law, and the dictum that money has no ear-mark must be understood in the same way; i.e. as predicated only of an undivided and undistinguishable mass of current money. [Emphasis added; p. 726.]

[80] That it is possible at common law to trace money to bank accounts is illustrated by the cases of *Hambrouck* and *Agip*. In *Hambrouck*, a man named Hambrouck had fraudulently procured cheques drawn on the Banque Belge pour l'Étranger. He endorsed the cheques and deposited them in his account at Farrow's Bank. The cheques were cleared through the banking system and credited to Hambrouck's account. "In substance no other funds were paid into the account than the proceeds of these forged cheques" (Atkin L.J., at p. 331 (emphasis added)). Hambrouck then paid money out of that bank account to a Ms. Spanoghe, with whom he was living. A deposit was made in Ms. Spanoghe's account at the London Joint City and Midland Bank and, according to Atkin L.J., "[n]o other sums were at any time placed to that deposit account" (p. 332). On the basis of those facts, Bankes and Atkin L.JJ. were both of the opinion that the funds could be traced at common law to Ms. Spanoghe's account (pp. 328 and 335–36). Two points drawn from that case are important for our purposes: neither the fact that a cheque is cleared through the banking system before being deposited in the payee's account nor the fact that the payee has mixed the funds with other funds is sufficient to bar recovery at common law.

[81] To fully understand the parallel between *Hambrouck* and *Agip*, it is important to follow the sequence of events in the latter case. In *Agip*, the Banque du Sud ("BdS") in Tunis received a payment order of $518,822.92 in favour of Baker Oil. BdS instructed Citibank to debit its account and credit an account at Lloyds Bank. Lloyds Bank credited Baker Oil's account before receiving the funds from Citibank, thereby assuming the delivery risk. The next day, pursuant to instructions from accountants Jackson & Co., who controlled Baker Oil on behalf of their clients, Lloyds Bank transferred the funds to Jackson & Co.'s account. At the time the credit was entered in Baker Oil's account, there was no other money in the account; however, the balance of Jackson & Co.'s account was US$7,911.80 before the transfer. The Court of Appeal agreed with the trial judge that the mixing of the funds with the amount already in Jackson & Co.'s account was of no consequence and did not preclude tracing (pp. 465–66). In first instance, Millett J., as he then was, had stated in *Agip*, at p. 399:

> A fortiori it can be no defence for [Jackson, a partner of Jackson & Co.] to show that he has so mixed it with his own money that he cannot tell whether he still has it or not. <u>Mixing by the defendant</u> himself must, therefore, be distinguished from mixing by a prior recipient. The former <u>is irrelevant</u>, but the latter will destroy the claim for it will prevent proof that the money received by the defendant was the money paid by the plaintiff. [Emphasis added.]

[82] In *Agip*, the time when the funds the plaintiff sought to trace ceased to be identifiable was when Lloyds Bank made the transfer to Jackson & Co.'s account before receiving the funds from Citibank: even though Lloyds Bank later recouped them, the funds used to make the payment belonged to Lloyds, and BdS's funds had to be traced through the clearing system. On that issue, the Court of Appeal also agreed with Millett J. and quoted him (at p. 466):

> Unless Lloyds Bank's correspondent bank in New York was also Citibank, this involves tracing the money [BdS's funds] through the accounts of Citibank and Lloyd's Bank's correspondent bank with the Federal Reserve Bank, where it must have been mixed with other money. The money with which Lloyds Bank was reimbursed cannot therefore, without recourse to equity, be identified as being that of the Banque du Sud.

[83] What distinguishes *Agip* from *Hambrouck* is that Lloyds Bank, having assumed the delivery risk, paid with its own money. This broke the link between the funds it paid and the funds it received from Citibank. If passage through the clearing system could on its own eliminate any possibility of identifying the money, tracing at common law would long ago have become totally obsolete and the dictum of the Court of Appeal in *Agip* that mixing in Jackson & Co.'s account was of no consequence would be of little use. I cannot accept that the result in *Hambrouck* can be explained by an oversight that occurred because the interruption caused by passage through the clearing system was not argued: P. J. Millett, "Tracing the Proceeds of Fraud" (1991), 107 *L.Q. Rev.* 71, at p. 74, fn. 7. When, as in *Agip*, the chain is broken by one of the intervening parties paying from its own funds, identification of the claimant's funds is no longer possible. However, the clearing system should be a neutral factor: P. Birks, "Overview: Tracing, Claiming and Defences", in P. Birks, ed., *Laundering and Tracing* (2003), 289, at pp. 302–5. Indeed, I prefer to assess the traceability of the asset after the clearing process and not see that process as a systematic break in the chain of possession of the funds. Just as the collecting bank receives the funds as the payee's agent, the clearing system is only a payment process. Paying through the clearing system amounts to no more than channelling the funds.

[84] In *Hambrouck*, the funds received through the clearing system by Farrow's Bank, acting as the collecting bank, from the Banque Belge pour l'Étranger had not lost their "identity". In the same way, the funds in the case at bar have not lost theirs. BNS, acting as the collecting bank, received the funds from RBC through the clearing system and credited them to BMP. The asset traced by RBC is simply its own. It is not the chose in action or the account [holders'] personal claim against BNS: R. M. Goode, "The Right to Trace and its Impact in Commercial Transactions — I" (1976), 92 *L.Q. Rev.* 360, at p. 380. The transactions that followed were all conducted by the recipient and persons related to it who received the money from BMP. Moreover, the fact that some of the accounts had prior balances is not a bar to recovery. Not only were the balances not substantial — only one of the accounts contained over $100 — but the withdrawals by the holders significantly exceeded the balances. It is also worth noting that BNS was both the drawee and the payees' banker in all the transactions at issue, namely the transfers and payments from BMP's account and to the related accounts. There was no hiatus like the one in *Agip*, and the holders of the related accounts

were not third parties who had given consideration or changed their positions.

[85] In my view, *Taylor*, *Agip* and *Hambrouck* show that it is possible at common law to trace funds into bank accounts if it is possible to identify the funds. (See also Goode, at pp. 378, 390–91 and 395.) According to *Agip* and *Hambrouck*, mixing by the recipient is not a bar to recovery. I do not see those cases as exceptions to a common law rule against tracing in mixed funds. Rather, I accept the view advanced by Lord Millett in *Foskett v. McKeown*,[2001] 1 A.C. 102 (H.L.), at p. 132, that the rules for tracing money are the same as those for tracing into physical mixtures. This view is also supported by Professor L. D. Smith in his treatise *The Law of Tracing*, at pp. 74 and 194 ff. For our purposes, there is no need to review all the rules applicable to physical mixtures (*Lawrie v. Rathbun* (1876), 38 U.C.Q.B. 255; *Carter v. Long & Bisby* (1896), 26 S.C.R. 430, at pp. 434–35; J. Ulph, "Retaining Proprietary Rights at Common Law Through Mixtures and Changes", [2001] *L.M.C.L.Q.* 449). Suffice it to say that, as between innocent contributors, contributions are followed first to amounts they have withdrawn. In the case at bar, since the withdrawals of all those who received funds far exceeded their contributions, RBC can trace its own contribution to the balances remaining in the accounts.

[86] As Atkin L.J. mentioned in *Hambrouck*, the question to be asked is whether the money deposited in those accounts was "the product of, or substitute for, the original thing" (p. 335). In the instant case, the identification process is quite simple. I will not go back over the issue of the funds in BMP's account: there was no relevant movement of funds. Regarding the funds in the related accounts when BNS acted on BMP's instructions and transferred money to the accounts of 636651 B.C. Ltd., Backman (chequing and savings accounts) and Hashka, the transferred funds were clearly related to the forged cheque BNS had mistakenly credited to BMP's account. The moneys used for the transfers came from BMP's account. The link is made with the funds RBC had used to pay the forged cheque.

[87] One issue that was raised is whether certification of the cheques would be a bar to tracing. When a cheque is certified, the certification does not affect the nature of the funds. In discussing the effect of certification in *Rattray Publications*, at p. 505, Finlayson J.A. stated that certification of a cheque, like acceptance, is irrevocable; see also *Centrac Inc.*

v. Canadian Imperial Bank of Commerce (1994), 21 O.R. (3d) 161 (C.A.). As a matter of law, to hold that certification is irrevocable would contribute to the acceptability of certified cheques as substitutes for cash and would also reflect the prevailing perception in the business world that it is irrevocable. However, BNS's intention in the instant case was not to revoke the certification. In fact, the certified cheques had already been honoured. As Maddaugh and McCamus point out:

> The fact that the drawee bank cannot resist payment on a cheque it has certified does not necessarily insulate the payee, however, from a subsequent restitutionary claim by the paying bank. [p. 10-57]

[88] In *Rattray Publications*, Finlayson J.A. stated that "where a drawee bank honours a cheque notwithstanding a valid countermand and the effect is to satisfy a just debt, the bank may [debit the customer's account and] successfully defend an action by [the] customer/drawer for reimbursement" (p. 509). Further, where a payment does not satisfy a just debt, the bank "may have an action in restitution against the holder of a certified cheque" (*ibid.*). Indeed, if a bank has certified a cheque, it cannot deny the authenticity of the drawer's signature and the sufficiency of the funds. However, certification does not affect the traceability of the underlying funds.

[89] What remains to be discussed is the claim by way of cross-appeal concerning punitive damages.

4.5 Damages

[90] The Court of Appeal found that BNS had breached the service agreement by reversing the credit in BMP's account without having been instructed to do so by BMP. However, it also found that BMP had suffered no real injury and accordingly awarded nominal damages of $1. In addition, it ordered BNS to pay BMP the difference of $100 between the bank draft of November 7, 2001, and the certified cheque of November 2, 2001. BNS does not contest this conclusion. BMP seeks an increase in the damages and Hashka, Backman and 636651 B.C. Ltd. seek an order for damages.

[91] In light of my conclusion that BNS could resist BMP's claim on the basis of the doctrine of mistake of fact, it is my view that no additional damages can be awarded. Since RBC could trace the funds with the assistance of BNS, the same reasoning applies to the restraint of funds and the reversal of credits.

Therefore, the claim to have the trial judge's award restored fails.

[92] BMP also seeks an award of punitive damages. The trial judge rejected this claim, finding that BNS's conduct did not warrant such an award. In view of my conclusions on BNS's right, this claim, too, can only fail.

5.   CONCLUSION

[93] Beyond the strangeness of its factual substratum, this case involves an application of the well-established doctrine of mistake of fact to very unusual facts. The business of collecting banks will rarely lend itself to the application of this doctrine because most of the time, the bank will have changed its position, or its customer will have drawn on the credited amount, or the funds will have been mixed in a way that precludes tracing. In this case, however, the application of common law principles leads to a logical conclusion. The Court of Appeal found support for that conclusion in equity and it may be that support can be found there, but the same result can be obtained at common law.

[94] The appeal should be dismissed with costs and the Court of Appeal order affirmed. The cross-appeal should be allowed with costs and the awards of damages in favour of 636651 B.C. Ltd., Hashka and Backman set aside, save for the amount of $13.50 payable to Backman, which BNS does not contest.

Appeal dismissed with costs and cross-appeal allowed with costs.

The Collecting Bank

Background Reading: M.H. Ogilvie, *Bank and Customer Law in Canada*, 2d Edition (Toronto: Irwin Law, 2013) Chapter 8, pages 304–315.

(a) *Stanley Works of Canada Ltd. v. Banque Canadienne Nationale*†

[MONTGOMERY J.:]

This is an appeal from a judgment of the Superior Court for the District of Montreal dated November 15, 1976, dismissing the action whereby appellant sought to recover $44,000, being the amount of two cheques drawn upon the respondent Banque Canadienne Nationale and deposited by appellant in its account with the respondent Royal Bank of Canada.

There is little dispute as to the facts. Appellant was at all material times carrying on a manufacturing business in the City of Hamilton, Ontario, where it maintained an account with the Royal Bank of Canada (to which I shall hereinafter refer to "the RBC"). In 1974 it was given a series of postdated cheques by a customer that owed it money, Daly & Morin Limited, of Lachine, Quebec. These cheques were drawn upon the Montreal branch of Banque Canadienne Nationale (to which I shall hereinafter refer as "the BCN"), with which Daly & Morin did its banking business. As the due date of each cheque approached, appellant deposited it in its account with the RBC.

A number of the Daly & Morin cheques were duly paid by the BCN when presented, and difficul-

ties did not arise until the cheque dated July 25 (Ex. P-1) was presented by the RBC to the BCN in accordance with normal banking practice. While the cheque was immediately debited to the account of Daly & Morin, it remained in the hands of the BCN, which had apparently conceived doubts as to its customer's solvency. Then, another cheque for $22,000 was presented by the RBC, this one dated August 1 (Ex. P-2). The BCN finally took action. It returned the two cheques to the RBC, marked "not sufficient funds", reversed the charges that it had made to its customer in respect of them, and took steps to realize its security, thereby forcing Daly & Morin into bankruptcy.

The RBC accepted the return of the two cheques from the BCN and debited appellant's account accordingly. However, at the instigation of appellant, which was clearly dissatisfied, the RBC on August 12, wrote to the BCN asking for an explanation of the delay. No satisfactory reply was received, and on August 28, the RBC sent copies of this correspondence to appellant. (These letters were filed en bloc by the RBC as EX. DW-1.)

In April 1975 appellant took action against the BCN, claiming the amount of the two cheques, i.e., $44,000. It invoked the delay of the BCN in return-

---

† (1981), 20 B.L.R. 282 (Que. C.A.).

ing the said cheques, saying in respect of the first of these:

4. THAT the Defendant further contravened the normal rules of the banking trade, which states that if a cheque passes through the national clearing house, remains in the possession of the drawer's bank longer than 48 hours, the said cheque is declared to be paid, however, the Defendant retained the cheque for 11 days following presentation of the said cheque through the national clearing house and Plaintiff had rightfully assumed that the said cheque had been paid.

There was a similar allegation in respect of the second cheque (para. 6), but the delay was stated to be four days, not eleven. The BCN pleaded in May, saying (in para. 10):

...les règlements de la Chambre de Compensation, qui ne sont pas des règlements publics, ne s'appliquent qu'entre les banques.

In June, appellant made a motion to implead the RBC, which was apparently granted. In July it served upon the RBC a "declaration of plaintiff-in-warranty", asking that the RBC carry on the proceedings against the BCN and, in the event of these being unsuccessful, that it be condemned to pay to appellant the said sum of $44,000 together with all costs. In para. 11 of this declaration, it alleged as follows:

The rules and by-laws of the Clearing House, and more particularly, article 27 provides that the return of unpaid cheques must be returned within forty-eight (48) hours, by the drawee Bank to the Bank that endorsed it, and in default so to do, the said cheques are deemed to have been accepted for payment.

The RBC did not take up the action on behalf of appellant. It filed a general denial, followed by a detailed plea in March 1976. In answer to para. 11 of the declaration in warranty, it said:

That as regards paragraph 11 of the Plaintiff in Warranty/Plaintiff's Declaration the Defendant in Warranty states that the rules and regulations respecting clearing houses speak for themselves but that the said rules and regulations are irrelevant to the present case, as such are irregularly and illegally pleaded and refers to its further Plea.

In para. 21 of its plea, it further said:

That the rules and regulations respecting clearing houses (being Article 24 of the By-laws of the

Canadian Bankers Association) are rules and regulations relating to the conduct of the business of banking between the chartered banks of Canada who have adhered thereto, are res inter alios acta, contain no stipulation and are not intended to contain any stipulation for the benefit of a third party who is not a party thereto, without prejudice to the foregoing do not provide the Plaintiff in Warranty/Plaintiff with any recourse against the Defendant in Warranty and are completely irrelevant to the present dispute and as such illegally and irregularly pleaded by the Plaintiff in Warranty/Plaintiff.

I agree with the trial Judge that appellant could not base its action upon any provision of the Bills of Exchange Act, R.S.C. 1970, c. B-5. In my mind, the principal question is the extent to which appellant can invoke the Rules and regulations respecting clearing houses. I note that neither bank appears to deny that these Rules and regulations existed substantially as alleged by appellant; they rather take the position that these Rules and regulations were, as regards appellant, res inter alios acta; see the RBC's factum (at pp. 4–8).

I agree with the trial Judge that there is no lien de droit between appellant and the BCN. There was no contractual relationship or any direct contact whatsoever, and I do not consider that appellant can invoke the clearing house regulations against this bank. I therefore agree with the trial Judge that the action against the BCN was properly dismissed. Being, however, of the opinion that the BCN provoked the action by its tergiversations and disregard of normal banking practice, I would award it no costs, either here or in the Court below, and would amend the judgment a quo accordingly.

The situation is more complex as regards the RBC, because there was a contractual relationship between it and appellant, the usual relationship between bank and customer: see the "Agreement re Operation of Account" and "Verification of Account Agreement", filed together by the RBC as Ex. DW-2. Appellant had, in my opinion, the right to expect that the services of the RBC would include the exercise of reasonable diligence for the protection of its interests. I recognize that there is some doubt whether the clearing house Rules invoked by appellant do more than regulate the conduct of banks as between themselves, but no one appears to deny their existence and binding force, at least as between the banks, and they provide an indication of what a bank can do and may reasonably be expected to do to protect its customers' interests. No one appears to contest that, as between the two banks, the RBC could have refused to accept the return of the two cheques and insisted that the BCN honour them because of its failure to return them within the period of 48 hours. Why did the RBC not do this? It may well have been out of courtesy to a fellow bank. Professional courtesy (like professional licence) may be carried too far, and it is, in my opinion, carrying it too far to exercise it at the expense of a customer. One may wonder whether the RBC would have exhibited the same courtesy had its customer become insolvent before the return of the cheques.

The RBC invokes the two banking documents filed by it. While the "Agreement re Operation of Account" gives the bank wide discretion, I find nothing in it to relieve it of liability under the present circumstances. We have here more than a simple error of judgment. We have the neglect of the bank to exercise what appear to have been its clear legal rights, thereby prejudicing its customer. Any such document limiting liability should, in my opinion, be restrictively construed and any doubt resolved against him who seeks to avoid liability. Regarding the "Verification of Account Agreement", the RBC particularly invokes the following cl. C:

> The undersigned will, within the 30 days following the time when a statement of account and relative vouchers should be received, notify the Bank in writing at the branch or agency where the account is kept of any alleged omissions

from or debits wrongly made to or inaccurate entries in the account as so stated.

It is true that notice in writing was not given within the delay of 30 days, but the exchange of correspondence filed by the bank (Ex. DW-1) shows that within that delay the bank was well aware of its customer's dissatisfaction but was making efforts to direct this dissatisfaction against the BCN. Under the special circumstances of the case, I consider that the requirement to give notice in writing was waived.

The loss suffered by appellant as the result of the RBC's failure to take the required action to protect its customer was the total amount of the two cheques, i.e., $44,000, there being no question of the BCN's solvency. I do not find it necessary to speculate whether, had it been notified more promptly of the insolvency of Daly & Morin, appellant might have been able to take any effective action against that company.

I would dismiss the appeal without costs, as against the BCN, but would modify the judgment a quo to the extent of relieving appellant of its condemnation to pay costs in the Superior Court. I would maintain the appeal against the RBC and condemn it to pay to appellant the sum of $44,000, with interests and costs throughout. It may be that the RBC my still have a recourse against the BCN, but this we are not required to decide.

(b) *National Slag v. Canadian Imperial Bank of Commerce*†

[LABROSSE J. (orally):]

This is an action on a cheque in the amount of $21,888.83. The facts are fully stated in the statement of agreed facts filed as ex. 46. At the outset, on consent, the action was dismissed as against the Clarkson Company Limited without costs.

It comes out of the agreed facts that General Concrete Limited made a cheque in favour of the plaintiff as payment of a debt. The cheque was drawn on the Bank of Montreal, James St. branch in Hamilton, the banker of General Concrete. Upon

receiving the cheque on January 17, 1980, the plaintiff presented it and endorsed it for deposit in its account at the Canadian Imperial Bank of Commerce, Brant St. branch in Hamilton.

In the course of the clearing process, the cheque went from the C.I.B.C. branch to the C.I.B.C. Data Centre in Toronto, to the Bank of Montreal Data Centre in Toronto, to the Bank of Montreal Regional Data Centre in Burlington and to the Bank of Montreal, James St. branch. The cheque reached the Bank of Montreal Data Centre in Toronto on Thursday the 17th or early Friday

---

† (1982), 140 D.L.R. (3d) 473 at 474–77 (Ont. H.C.J.).

the 18th. It was then forwarded to the Bank of Montreal Regional Centre in Burlington and then to the James St. branch. In the ordinary course of business, the cheque should have arrived at the branch on Friday the 18th. For some unexplained reason, the cheque arrived at the branch on Monday the 21st, as agreed by the parties.

It was the practice of the account manager of the branch to accept or refuse payment of the cheque when it was received. If the decision was to refuse payment, the cheque was returned through the clearing system. In this case the decision was postponed.

General Concrete Limited was indebted to the branch for an amount in excess of three-and-a half million dollars. The branch had securities which included debentures, an assignment of book debts and a security pursuant to s. 88 of the *Bank Act*, R.S.C. 1970, c. B-1 [now s. 178, Part V of the *Bank Act* as re-enacted by the *Banks and Banking Law Revision Act*, 1980 (Can.), c. 40, s. 2]. The securities covered everything General Concrete had.

On Friday the 18th, the branch had received instructions to call its loan. The loan was called on Monday morning at 8:50 a.m. The bank wished to continue the business of General Concrete Limited and it also wished to appoint a receiver-manager. This was done on Tuesday the 22nd.

The decision to dishonour the cheque was made on the 22nd after consultation with the receiver-manager. On the 23rd the cheque was placed in the clearing system for return. It went from the branch to the Bank of Montreal Regional Data Centre in Burlington, to the Bank of Montreal Data Centre in Toronto, to the C.I.B.C. Data Centre where it was received on the 23rd or early the 24th and from there, it went to the C.I.B.C. branch where it was received on Friday the 25th. On that same date the plaintiff was advised by telephone that the cheque had been dishonoured and it had the cheque picked up.

In the meantime, any automatic credit or debit between the two banks made as the cheque went through the clearing houses were reversed and on the 25th the plaintiff's account was debited by the amount of the cheque. General Concrete Limited had been taken over by the Bank of Montreal and the plaintiff was left with an NSF cheque.

The plaintiff brings this action against C.I.B.C. on the basis of moneys had and received and for breach of duty in failing to make inquiry before debiting the plaintiff's account in order to ascertain if the cheque could be properly returned. As against the Bank of Montreal, the claim is based on negligence for breach of duty to pay or refuse to pay without delay. All claims are closely related to the issue of delay on the part of the Bank of Montreal and the failure of the C.I.B.C. to inquire into that delay.

The Manual of Inter-Bank Procedures and Standards of the Canadian Bankers' Association is developed, approved and published with the consent of all chartered banks. It represents the agreement of all chartered banks. The manual sets out the procedures for the handling and/or returning of cheques between banks. Item 5 or rule 5 of section A4 of the manual specifies as follows:

> 5. If an item is held by the drawee bank branch ... beyond the business day following the date of receipt, it may not be returned through the clearing, unless certified.

The evidence confirmed that the rule applies to cheques being returned as NSF.

The Bank of Montreal distributed to its employees a "Policies and Procedures" manual. On the topic of "Return of Dishonoured and Other Items by Drawee Branch" it provided:

> It is the bank's policy to pay or dishonour on day of receipt items received in the clearing or presented over the counter, otherwise recourse against the presenting bank may be lost.

It also provided as follows:

> If clearings are received unduly late, dishonoured items must be returned no later than the next business day.

Both items underline the importance of quickly returning dishonoured cheques.

The branch had the cheque from January 21st to the 23rd. Mr. Leishman has had considerable experience with the clearing rules of the Manual of Inter-Bank Procedures and Standards of the Canadian Bankers' Association. I accept his evidence that the Bank of Montreal contravened rule 5 by returning the cheque on the 23rd. It broke the standards accepted by all chartered banks and it broke its own standards as set out in its policies and procedures manual. It may also have contravened s. 97 of the *Bills Exchange Act*, R.S.C. 1970, c. B-5.

The delay of the Bank of Montreal and the failure of the C.I.B.C. to do anything about it before debiting the plaintiff's account are the basis of the plaintiff's claim against the defendants, whether based on contract or negligence.

In my opinion, this case, which involves numerous legal issues, raises a practical one. A breach of contract or negligence does not automatically result in damages. On the facts of this case I cannot accept the argument that the cheque was "paid" by the debits and credits made through the clearing procedure established for banking convenience any more than the cheque was paid when C.I.B.C. credited the plaintiff on deposit of the cheque. In my view, the plaintiff must prove that it suffered real damages because of the conduct of the defendants.

On Monday, January 21st, the Bank of Montreal branch had two accounts with General Concrete Limited: a current account and a loan account with a debit of three-and-a-half million dollars, an amount far in excess of any credit in the current account. The two accounts cannot be considered as if they had no connection. At 9:50 a.m. the branch called its loan. In my opinion, on that date the branch was entitled to dishonour the plaintiff's cheque. Had it done so, the cheque would have entered the return process to go back to the C.I.B.C. branch where it would have arrived, possibly, on the 22nd and probably on the 23rd.

Assuming that the cheque had arrived at the C.I.B.C. branch on the 22nd, what could the plaintiff have done to recover its money from General Concrete Limited? Whether one speaks of probability or practical possibility of recovering against General Concrete, the result is the same. The plaintiff had no chance of recovery. On the basis of its securities, the bank had taken over as of Monday morning and the receiver-manager was appointed in the afternoon of the 22nd. There is no doubt that the bank had the right to take over.

In my opinion, the plaintiff has not suffered a prejudice as a result of the conduct of the defendants. Had the Bank of Montreal acted within the time-limits, the plaintiff could not have recovered its money. I fail to see how, by breaching inter-bank rules, the plaintiff became entitled to damages. The plaintiff cannot say to the defendants: "Had you done what you were supposed to do, I would have suffered no loss."

As stated earlier, the action raised numerous legal issues which will have to deal with when the facts require them to be dealt with. In view of my conclusion, my opinions on those issues would not be of any benefit. I would point out that the additional part of the claim has not been proved. By the time the plaintiff would have found out about the cheque, the last delivery would probably have been made.

The action is, therefore, dismissed. Unless counsel for the defendants wish to make submissions, I propose to dismiss the action without costs.

[After counsel indicated they had no submissions, His Lordship continued:]

I have endorsed the record: "For reasons given, the action is dismissed without costs."

Action dismissed.

(c)   *Re*Collections Inc. v. Toronto-Dominion Bank*†

[STRATHY J.:]

[1] The plaintiffs move to certify these actions as class actions under the *Class Proceedings Act, 1992*, S.O. 1992, c. 6 (the "*C.P.A.*"). They allege that a bank profits at its customer's expense when it places a "hold" on a cheque deposited in the customer's account. They assert that there is a delay between the time the cheque is "paid" by the drawee bank and the time the funds are made available to the customer at the branch of deposit. During this delay, the bank makes use of its customer's money. The plaintiffs claim that this is a breach of the bank's contractual and common law obligations to its customer.

I.   BACKGROUND

(a)   Overview

[2] The banking system in Canada is dominated by six major chartered banks, including the three defen-

---

† 2010 ONSC 6560. [Notes omitted.]

dants, Toronto-Dominion Bank ("TD"), Bank of Montreal ("BMO") and Bank of Nova Scotia ("BNS"). There are over 8,000 bank branches and 18,000 automatic teller machines ("ATMs") in Canada. Approximately four million cheques pass through the Canadian clearing system every business day.[2]

[3] A cheque drawn on a Canadian bank and deposited in Canada is a bill of exchange under the *Bills of Exchange Act*, R.S.C. 1985, c. B-4. Some simple definitions will assist the discussion that follows. As Perell J. explained in *Benjamin v. The Toronto Dominion Bank* (2006), 80 O.R. (3d) 424, [2006] O.J. No. 1253 (S.C.J.) at para. 29:

> The person who writes a bill of exchange, including a cheque, is known as the "drawer". In writing a bill of exchange, the drawer requests a person known as the "drawee" to pay a sum of money to a third person, who is known as the "payee". Translated into everyday affairs, a customer of a bank (the drawer) writes a cheque to withdraw money from his or her bank account (the drawee) to pay a creditor (the payee).

[4] The payee's bank, into which the cheque is deposited, is referred to as the "collecting bank" because it is responsible for collecting the funds from the drawee. It will sometimes be referred to in these reasons as the "bank of deposit".

[5] When the payee of a domestic cheque[3] deposits the cheque to his or her account, either by going to the bank in person or by using an ATM, the practice of all Canadian banks is that the amount of that cheque is immediately, but provisionally, credited to the payee's account. The credit is described as provisional because it can be reversed if the cheque is ultimately returned dishonoured — for example, because there are insufficient funds, or the drawee's account has a "stop payment" or "hold" on it, or the cheque is forged, or for any of a number of other reasons. In Bradley Crawford, *The Law of Banking and Payment in Canada*, loose leaf (Aurora, Ont.: Canada Law Book, 2008) ("*The Law of Banking and Payment*"), the author notes at para. 10.30.30(4) that this practice facilitates the clearing of cheques between banks and benefits the customer, who is generally able to access the amount of the deposit (unless there is a hold) pending collection:

> The proceeds of deposited items are therefore technically used by the collecting bank to reimburse itself for the advance it has previously made to the credit of the customer's account. This ownership of the float during collection enables the netting of positions on which the clearing depends. If the funds were still the

property of the millions of different owners of the items being collected, the clearing, to the extent that it might still be based on mutuality of set-off, rather than statutory enablement, would not be possible. The customer has generally had the use of the funds since the moment of deposit. Only a credit judgment by the collecting bank is involved. Obviously, a bank cannot be obliged to extend credit to a customer in the absence of a specific agreement. Failure by a bank to extend the usual credit in any particular case would not give rise to any claim by the depositing customer unless the practice were held to have created an implied term in the banking relationship on the particular facts of the case. This is a matter that may be affected by express or implied agreement or by special circumstances.

[6] If the account is interest-bearing, the deposited funds immediately begin to earn interest according to the terms of the account agreement. This is the case even though the bank of deposit has not yet received unconditional payment of the cheque from the drawee bank. Effectively, as Crawford notes, except in cases where the bank exercises a credit judgment by placing a hold on the funds to restrict access to them, the bank of deposit extends credit to its customer for the amount of the cheque while it works its way through the clearing system.

[7] The terms of each defendant's contracts with its customers permit a "hold" to be placed on cheque deposits, restricting the customer's ability to access the funds for specific periods of time. This is consistent with Crawford's observation that a bank has no obligation to extend credit to a customer. At any given time, on an industry-wide basis, less than one percent of bank accounts are subject to holds.[4] Holds are always imposed on ATM deposits, because the bank has no way of knowing that there really is a cheque in the deposit envelope or whether the customer has accurately keyed in the amount of the cheque. When a deposit is made in person, at the branch, the bank's service representative decides whether to place a hold on the funds, based on a host of considerations applicable to the customer or the transaction, as set out in the particular bank's policies.

[8] The plaintiffs' basic complaint is that the "hold" periods imposed by the banks are excessive and have the result of giving the banks the ability to use money that belongs to the depositor between the time it is allegedly "paid" by the drawee bank and the time the hold is released and the funds are available to the customer. They say that this is a

breach of their contracts with the banks. They also say that it gives rise to other causes of action and is an unjust enrichment of the banks at their expense.

[9] The banks say that [a] hold is a legitimate risk-management practice that is authorized by their contracts with their customers and sanctioned by the federal regulator, the Department of Finance. They say that the hold provides some protection for the bank and its customer against the subsequent dishonour of the cheque, something that can happen long after the initial deposit of the cheque.

[10] To put the issues on this motion in perspective, I will begin with a description of the clearing system operated by the Canadian Payments Association (the "Payments Association"). I will then describe in more detail the practice of placing holds on cheques and the policies of the banks in that regard. I will then describe the individual transactions at issue in these three actions. Finally, I will consider and apply the five-part test in s. 5 of the *C.P.A.* for the certification of a class action.

(b) The Clearing System

[11] The modern clearing system traces its origin to the City of London in the early 1700s.[5] After cheques made an appearance in British commerce in the latter part of the 17th century, the banks began to employ "walk clerks" whose job it was to call at other banks and to physically present cheques for payment in exchange for cash. As the use of cheques increased, the work became more strenuous and fast-paced and the clerks decided to conserve their energy by meeting at a central location to exchange cheques and settle the differences in the total. Initially, the practice was informal, but in due course in 1773 a room was rented — conveniently located in the "Five Bells Tavern" on Lombard Street. Ultimately, under the auspices of the banks, a clearing house building was built on Lombard Street in 1833.[6]

[12] In Canada, the clearing system was established in 1900 when amendments to the *Bank Act* enabled the Canadian Bankers' Association to establish clearing houses and to make rules for their operation. The system is run by the Payments Association, an entity owned and operated by the banks and established by the *Canadian Payments Act*, R.S.C. 1985, c. C-21. The system is called the Automated Clearing Settlement System or "ACSS". All Canadian banks are required to be members of the Payments Association. Financial institutions other than banks can be members on a [voluntary] basis, but as a practical matter any Canadian institution that offers chequing

services to its customers will have to clear through the Payments Association. If it is not a direct clearer, it will have to have a relationship with a direct clearer to clear its items.

[13] Pelletier J. of the Federal Court of Canada gave a helpful overview of the clearing system in *National Bank of Greece (Canada) v. Bank of Montreal* (1999), 175 F.T.R. 232, [1999] F.C.J. No. 1694 at paras. 1 and 2, aff'd, [2001] 2 F.C. 288, [2000] F.C.J. No. 2105 (C.A.):

> Because of the enormous amount of money which changes hands every day through cheques (and other forms of funds transfer which are not relevant to this case), an efficient system of settling accounts between institutions which deal in cheques is necessary. Every day a bank will take in millions of dollars in cheques drawn on a variety of other banks at the same time as all the other banks are accepting cheques drawn on the first bank. It is necessary for these transactions to be processed (cleared) and for the funds to be transferred to the parties entitled to them (settlement). The institution responsible for seeing that this happens is the Canadian Payments Association (the "CPA"), a creation of the Canadian Payments Association Act, R.S., 1985, c. C-21 [*sic*] ... All banks are required to be members of the CPA.
>
> The CPA operates clearinghouses through which cheques are routed for clearing and settlement. Clearing occurs when the transactions are accounted for as between the member banks of the CPA. At the end of a clearing day, all cheques drawn on a particular bank (the drawee) and presented for payment that day will have been posted as amounts owed by the drawee to the banks who accepted the cheques ("the negotiating banks"). But at the same time, the drawee bank will itself have accepted millions of dollars worth of cheques drawn on other banks. So at the end of the day, a particular bank will owe a series of other banks millions of dollars and will itself be owed millions of dollars by a series of banks. These accounts are settled daily by the settlement system, which operates through the Bank of Canada. The settlement system is intended to move the necessary funds from those who owe money to those who are owed money. Some banks have a clearing account with the Bank of Canada through which their accounts are settled daily. If they are a net creditor, their account is credited and if they are a net debtor, funds are withdrawn from their account. The role of the Bank of Canada is to act as croupier, taking from those who owe for distribution to those who are owed. The end result should be that at the end of each banking day, all transactions are current, both from the point of view of

accounting for the transactions (clearing) and from the point of view of settlement of accounts between all parties to the system (settlement).

[14] In simple overview, the clearing system facilitates the adjustment of the financial positions of Canadian banks based on what each "owes" to the other on a daily basis. Domestic cheques and other items, such as electronic payments, are cleared through the system, which sorts out, provisionally and on a gross basis, what each institution owes to every other institution.

[15] Near the end of each banking day, or during the evening, the domestic cheques deposited in each branch of every bank and in ATMs are bundled, totaled, and sent by air or ground courier to the regional clearing center for that bank. There are six regional centres in Canada, each operated by the Payments Association. At these locations, the cheques are exchanged between up to twelve major financial institutions (including the three defendants), known as "direct clearers", who clear on their own behalf and as agents for other financial institutions, known as "indirect clearers". This exchange, or clearing, results in provisional credits being posted to each bank of deposit and provisional debits being charged to each drawee bank. The cumulative totals of these debits and credits results in net balances being owed, or payable, by each bank to every other bank.

[16] Direct clearers are required to maintain settlement accounts with the Bank of Canada. During the morning of each business day, the Bank of Canada adjusts the financial positions of the individual direct clearers by transferring funds among their accounts to reflect the net balances of the previous day's clearing, which will also include items that were initially credited and debited, but which were subsequently returned dishonoured. The indirect clearers settle with their own direct clearers through special accounts they maintain with them.

[17] After the initial clearing has taken place, the cheques proceed to the data centre for the drawee bank, which is located in the same facility, for processing. The cheques are sorted based on the drawee branch and the amount of each cheque is posted to the account of the drawer. If there are not sufficient funds in that account, if the account is closed, subject to a hold or payment of the cheque has been stopped, or if for some other reason payment of the cheque is blocked, the cheque will be physically sent to the branch of the drawee (or to a unit acting on its behalf) for the "pay/no pay" decision — that is, a

decision whether or not to honour the cheque. In the language of the *Bills of Exchange Act*, this is the "presentment" of the cheque. This usually occurs the day following the initial clearing, unless the drawee is an indirect clearer or the drawee branch and the branch of deposit are not in the same region of the country, in which case it may take two or three days for the cheque to reach the drawee branch or its agent.

[18] Under the rules of the Payments Association, following receipt of the cheque, the branch of the drawee has until the next business day to dishonour the cheque by initiating its return through the clearing system to the collecting bank. The cheque then retraces its journey back through the clearing process where the totals of returned items are settled as part of the day's clearing, and is forwarded to the branch of deposit or to some central location designated by it. This entire process may involve the cheque being processed through reading and sorting machines at the clearing centre up to eight times and transported up to four times. The end result is that the provisional credit posted to the payee's account and the provisional debit charged to the drawee are reversed.

[19] The amount of time the cheque spends in transit between moving to the unit making the "pay/no pay" decision and its return to the bank of deposit depends on a number of factors, including the number of institutions involved, whether they are direct or indirect clearers, the geographic distance between the branch of deposit and the drawee branch, and the physical state of the cheque — i.e., whether it can be read by machine readers or must be processed manually. The evidence establishes that, under normal circumstances, it can take as long as five or six days between the deposit of a cheque at the collecting bank and its physical return, dishonoured, to that same bank.

[20] Depending on the unique factual circumstances, a domestic cheque can be returned dishonoured, and the initial settlement of provisional credits and debits can be reversed, days, weeks, months or even years after the cheque was first deposited. The permissible time within which the drawee may return the cheque can be extended for a number of reasons, including the cheque being materially altered, post-dated or forged. If, however, the drawee is dishonouring the cheque for insufficient funds, for example, it must commence the return process within the time prescribed by the Payments Association, failing which its only remedy is to collect the funds from its customer. The collecting bank is entitled to treat the

cheque as having been honoured if the drawee has failed to initiate the return of the cheque within the allowed time.

[21] It is important to note that no mechanism exists in the clearing process, which operates in totals between financial institutions, to inform the collecting bank that a specific cheque has been dishonoured by a particular drawee branch. The outcome of the "pay/no pay" decision is not communicated by the drawee to the collecting bank, except by physically returning the dishonoured cheque to the collecting bank through the clearing. The fact that a particular cheque has <u>not</u> been dishonoured is not communicated by the drawee bank to the collecting bank.

[22] The evidence, and the authorities, support the conclusion that dishonour of a cheque cannot occur until it has been received by the collecting bank after being returned through the clearing. As a practical matter, as Crawford notes, Canadian banks are prepared to operate on the premise that if the cheque has not been returned dishonoured within a reasonable time (determined in their contracts with their customers) it can be paid. He puts it as follows in Bradley Crawford, "Late Return of a Dishonoured Cheque" (2001) 36 Can. Bus. L.J. 1 at 4:

> The collection of a cheque through the CAD Clearing is a process of uncertain duration. It is virtually impossible to deduce that a cheque has been paid merely by the passage of any particular amount of time. The banks appear to operate on the principle that no news is good news. If greater certainty and more secure reliance are important to the payee or holder, they may be achieved with modest effort by requesting the certification of the instrument.

[23] In referring to the principle of "no news is good news", Crawford echoes the words of Harding L.J.S.C. in *Garon Realty & Insurance Ltd. v. James* to the effect that, if the cheque has not been returned dishonoured within what is considered to be a reasonable time, the bank is prepared to assume that it has cleared.[7]

[24] Since the collecting bank has no way of knowing whether a cheque has been dishonoured until it is returned through the clearing, it has no duties in relation to the cheque until it has been returned.

[25] If the collecting bank has given its customer access to the funds represented by a deposited cheque before it is returned dishonoured through the clearing, it risks financial loss if the provisional credit posted to its customer's account is reversed and the funds have been withdrawn in the meantime. The drawee bank, having initiated the dishonour process within the time provided by the Payments Association rules, is entitled to demand reimbursement from the collecting bank. The collecting bank must make the reimbursement regardless of whether it is able to collect the funds from its customer.

(c) Clearing of U.S. and Foreign Cheques

[26] The process described above refers to the clearing of domestic cheques. United States and foreign cheques are not processed through the Payments Association clearing.

[27] The hold policies of the defendants with respect to foreign cheques are not entirely uniform, but in general they give the banks authority to hold cheques drawn on U.S. banks for periods that range from 15 to 30 days and to hold other foreign cheques for 22 to 40 days.

[28] The evidence adduced by the banks establishes that there is no body in the United States similar to the Payments Association and therefore no nationwide and industry-wide coordination of the clearing and settlement process. The "system" in the United States is a patchwork of bilateral agreements made between individual U.S. financial institutions and, in the case of Canada–U.S. clearings, bilateral agreements between individual Canadian and U.S. institutions. While some larger U.S. financial institutions clear electronically, a large proportion of cheques drawn on United States banks are cleared by physical transfer from bank to bank. The process of dishonour takes place in a similar fashion. The evidence establishes that a U.S. cheque can be dishonoured weeks or months after the initial deposit. Mr. Robin Harper, an officer of BMO who swore an affidavit applicable to all three proceedings, deposed that Canadian banks may, in some circumstances, have to wait for as long as 10 days for a U.S. drawee bank to return a dishonoured cheque in the ordinary course. In less common instances, the dishonour and return process can take more than 30 days from the date of deposit. Where the cheque is believed to be counterfeit or to bear a forged signature, the time line can be substantially extended.

[29] The evidence establishes that cheques drawn on foreign banks outside the U.S. are not cleared through the clearing system but rather are cleared by "collection". In some cases, the branch of deposit may post a provisional credit in the customer's account and in other cases it will not credit the

account until collection is complete. In the former case, the bank may nevertheless place a hold on the cheque. The manner of collection varies from bank to bank and sometimes involves direct collection from the foreign financial institution. At other times it involves the use of a correspondent bank to facilitate the collection. Again, the evidence establishes that it may take as long as 60 to 90 days to collect an international cheque.

(d) Legal Effect of the Clearing Process

[30] Before leaving the clearing process, it is appropriate to note several principles that are established in the case law. First, it is well-settled that the clearing process is an administrative procedure that was instituted as a convenience to the banks to enable clearing of cheques and other instruments to take place on a timely and efficient basis. The clearing rules apply only to relations between members of the Payments Association and do not create rights for third parties: *B.M.P. Global Distribution Inc. v. Bank of Nova Scotia*, [2009] 1 S.C.R. 504, [2009] S.C.J. No. 15 at para. 56. See also: *National Bank of Greece (Canada) v. Bank of Montreal*, above, at para. 14:

> It is clear that clearing and settlement rules and bylaws do not create rights and obligations on the part of banks to their customers. Any rights and remedies created by the rules are between banks and the Payments Association.

[31] Second, as previously noted, the clearing is done on a net basis between financial institutions and it is provisional only, subject to later reversal. It has nothing to do with the payment of a particular item. This point is made in *The Law of Banking and Payment* at para. 10:10.50(3):

> The initial settlement given for items exchanged in bulk clearing such as occurs daily at all regional settlement points in Canada is not an irrevocable payment on any item exchanged except, of course, for the settlement vouchers given by the banks for their net debit balance in the clearing. The effective decision of a bank whether to pay or to dishonour is made at the branch of account [i.e., the branch of the drawee bank], not at the clearing house or data centre.

[32] The learned author also refers to the observation of Labrosse J., as he then was, in *National Slag v. Canadian Imperial Bank of Commerce* (1982), 140 D.L.R. (3d) 473 at 476, [1982] O.J. No. 3686 (H.C.J.), aff'd 19 D.L.R. (4th) 383, [1985] O.J. No. 14 (C.A.): "I cannot accept the argument that the cheque was 'paid' by the debits and credits made

through the clearing procedure established for banking convenience". Similarly, Spiegel J., referring to *Payment, Clearing and Settlement in Canada*, above, at para. 9.01(5)(c), stated in *Advance Bank v. Toronto Dominion Bank* (2003), 65 O.R. (3d) 46, [2003] O.J. No. 2027 (S.C.J.) at para. 45:

> The automatic debits and credits that occur each night in the Clearing cannot constitute payment in law. Provisional settlement is not payment, because even under the [Clearing] Rules an item may be returned and the provisional settlement reversed, as of right, if the drawee decides to return it.

[33] The quoted statement in *Payment, Clearing and Settlement in Canada* at 9:01.5(c) is as follows:

> The initial settlement given for items exchanged in a bulk clearing such as occurs daily at all regional settlement points in Canada is not an irrevocable payment of any item exchanged.

[34] A similar observation is made by Professor R.M. Goode, in an interesting article "When is a cheque paid?" [1983] J. Bus. L. 164. Although banking practices in England [differ] in some ways from those in Canada, the differences are not material in this respect. Professor Goode makes the point that the cheque is not being paid in the clearing and that it cannot, at that time, be placed unconditionally at the disposal of the customer. The paying bank (drawee) only becomes irrevocably committed to paying the cheque when it informs the collecting bank that the cheque will be honoured or if it fails to return the cheque within the time allowed by the clearing rules:

> Under the present system all cheques delivered to the clearing are for accounting convenience and speed credited to the collecting bank and debited to the paying bank, in the clearing before being transmitted to the paying branches by way of presentation for payment. Hence whilst the amount of the cheque is included in the computation of the net balance transferred from one bank to the other through the Bank of England, that transfer is no more than an advance payment by the paying bank to the collecting bank in anticipation that the cheque will be met when presented. Thus the paying bank is not at that stage paying the cheque; rather, it is paying *for* the cheque under reserve, so that, if the cheque is not honoured, it is entitled to recourse against the collecting bank, effected through a debit to the collecting bank in the ensuing day's settlement. Prior to presentation and honouring of the cheque the collecting bank holds the amount of the cheque, in a balance of

account, without at that stage being able to place it unconditionally at the disposal of its customer. The 'pay date' at which the funds become available to the Creditor is when the paying bank becomes irrevocably committed to paying the cheque, either because it has informed the collecting bank that the cheque will be met or because it fails to return the cheque within the limited time allowed by the Clearing House Rules. [At pp. 166–7; emphasis in original; footnotes omitted.]

[35] Third, there is no mechanism in place, in the clearing system or elsewhere, to determine on an absolute basis, that a cheque has "cleared" in the sense of having been honoured. The drawee bank, which has no way of knowing that the branch of deposit has placed a hold on a particular cheque, has no reason or obligation to inform that branch that the cheque has been honoured or has "cleared" to use the plaintiff's term. The system operates by exception, through return of dishonoured items. The branch of deposit will likely know, within a number of days, whether the cheque has been returned dishonoured according to the Payments Association rules, but even then there may be extenuating circumstances or the cheque may be dishonoured at a later time for various reasons, not the least of which is forgery. The point is made in *The Law of Banking and Payment* at para. 10:10.60(2) as follows:

Banks and other deposit-taking members of the CPA have elaborate and detailed schedules in accordance with which items are delivered to, and collected from, the various branches and offices in their organizations. The typical branch would receive incoming items sometime in the mid-morning. The CAD Clearing Rules delegate to the regional clearing associations the deadline for the physical exchange of returned items each day. A branch account manager would therefore normally have something like 30 hours in which to decide whether to honour an instrument or not. However, it cannot be deduced that the collecting bank or the payee will necessarily know the fate of any particular instrument within a day or two after depositing it for collection. The CAD Clearing process reaches every branch of every deposit-taking financial institution in the country. The time required to present an item physically to the branch of account varies from a day or two for branches in major centres, to six or eight days for those in more remote towns and villages. Accidents, weather and human error may add to the time elapsed in getting an item to the appropriate place. It is the same for the return of an item and, in the case of USD denominated instruments, the delays may be even longer. However, the rule is the same for all and, so long as the branch with the power to make the pay/no pay decision begins the return process by putting the item back into the correct channel of the clearing for return to the collecting member, it complies with the time limit and is entitled to obtain reimbursement of its provisional settlement in the clearing. [Emphasis added.]

[36] Thus, while the accounts as between banks may be adjusted within the hold period such that Bank A receives a provisional credit from Bank B that may or may not be reversed, there is no mechanism available, other than physical return of a dishonoured cheque, to inform the collecting bank, Bank A, that the cheque itself has been dishonoured. Again, Crawford anticipates the issue in *The Law of Banking and Payment* at para. 10:10.30(2):

The problem of whether or not funds standing to the credit of a customer's account are in fact cleared and irrevocably available is quite common in Canada at present. This is due to the fact that current Canadian banking practice is for the bank to show in the customer's account immediate credit for the full face amount of all cheques deposited for collection and to receive immediate settlement for them in the clearing from the bank on which they are drawn. However, that settlement is provisional only and may be reversed upon return of an item. Since there is no reliable limit on the time during which an item may be dishonoured and returned to a collecting bank, the bank often does not know with any degree of certainty what the true available balance of "good funds" in an account may be. Banks may protect themselves by reserving, in their contracts with customers, the right to refuse cheques and other requests for withdrawal against "uncleared effects", that is, against items with respect to which the bank may not be confident of successful collection.

[37] A hold on funds is precisely the kind of protection to which Crawford refers.

[38] Fourth, and finally, the evidence on this motion, and the authorities, are clear that the credits and debits posted during the clearing posting are provisional only and are subject to being reversed if a cheque is dishonoured. While the provisional settlement of accounts between banks generally (but not always) occurs within two or three days of deposit, it may take five or six days or sometimes even more for a domestic cheque to work its way back to the branch of deposit. The process can take considerably

longer if the cheque is drawn on a U.S. or foreign institution.

[39] Crawford makes the point in "Late Return of A Dishonoured Cheque", above, at p. 3:

> The CPA has promulgated rules to govern the operation of the CAD Clearing, which is the process by which cheques are exchanged between deposit-taking financial institutions that are members of the CPA and collected for the accounts of depositing customers. Those rules create a legal duty upon drawee members of the CPA and collected for the accounts of depositing customers. Those rules create a legal duty upon drawee member financial institutions to accept delivery of every cheque that is presented to them by another member and to pay its full face amount without examination. <u>But that payment is provisional only, not final.</u>
>
> The CAD Clearing Rules also provide for the automatic reimbursement of that <u>provisional</u> settlement upon the timely return of dishonoured cheques through the CAD Clearing. In doing so, the rules limit the time that a bank may delay before becoming precluded from returning a dishonoured item through the CAD Clearing. [Emphasis added.]

[40] The evidence regarding the clearing process in Canada, considered in light of the foregoing well-settled principles, discloses the underlying fault line in the foundation of the plaintiff's case. The theory that a cheque is "paid" when it passes through the clearing, or when a debit is charged to the drawer's account, has no basis in fact or law. If a bank was required to release "held" funds when a cheque went through the initial clearing, or even within a few days thereafter, it would be at risk that the cheque would be dishonoured by the drawee within the time permitted by the Payments Association rules and it would have to chase its customer for recovery of the funds. This fundamental flaw runs through the plaintiffs' claim for breach of contract on which these proposed class actions are based, and makes the claim unsuitable for certification.

(e) Holds on cheques

[41] The contracts between the defendants and their customers authorize the banks to place holds on cheques. A hold is an exception to the general practice, referred to earlier, of giving the customer full credit for a cheque and access to the funds at the time of deposit. A bank has no obligation to extend such credit to its customer. When the circumstances take the account or the cheque outside the comfort zone permitted by the bank's policies, the bank is entirely within its rights to inform that customer that it will not give credit until the cheque has been collected. Even then, operating under the "no news is good news" principle referred to above, the banks have agreed to maximum periods within which they will hold cheques, even though there is a possibility that a cheque will be dishonoured outside the period.

[42] When a customer deposits a cheque through an ATM, a screen will display indicating that a hold will be placed on the funds for a stated period and asking whether the customer wishes to proceed with the deposit. If the customer does not signify his or her consent, the transaction will not proceed. On an in-person deposit, if the teller determines that a hold is required, the customer will be informed of the hold and its duration and will generally acknowledge the hold on the deposit slip. In either case, if immediate access to the funds is required by the bank's policy, the customer has the option of not proceeding with the deposit and can, for example, have the cheque certified, obtain cash or a bank draft from the drawer/payor, or make arrangements for a wire transfer.

[43] Crawford indicates that there is no case law concerning the time within which a bank is required to deposit collected funds in its customer's account and suggests that it is explained by the practice of Canadian banks of giving immediate credit for deposits. In *The Law of Banking and Payment* at para. 10:30.30(4), he states:

> In a previous edition of this treatise I expressed an opinion on the issue of a bank's duty to post credits promptly, which I regarded as one of first impression at that time. I thought that a Canadian court would allow a bank a reasonable time in all the circumstances. That is, the time limit would not start until after the bank had received final settlement for the incoming item, and would not end until the expiration of a reasonable time in all the circumstances of the case. There is now some support for that view in the fairly recent decision of Lane J. [in *Independent Multi-Funds Inc. v. Bank of Nova Scotia*].

[44] I will return to a discussion of *Independent Multi-Funds Inc. v. Bank of Nova Scotia*, [2004] O.J. No. 340 (S.C.J.) later in these reasons.

[45] I will review the specific terms of the plaintiffs' contracts with the banks shortly, but in overview they permit the banks to hold cheques for various lengths of time depending on whether the cheque is drawn

on a domestic bank, a United States bank or a foreign bank. As I have noted, holds invariably occur on ATM deposits, but they take place with considerably less frequency on deposits made in person. There is no doubt that a hold can be inconvenient, because the customer cannot get access to the funds during the hold period. It cannot be said that a hold is unfair, however, because the customer is paid interest on held funds in accordance with the account terms.[8] As well, as I have noted, the customer does have other options, such as getting the cheque certified. The customer can also negotiate the length of the hold period, or a partial "lifting" of the hold imposed by the bank, depending on the circumstances. The evidence indicates that the hold period applied by banks is not inflexible. It may be wholly or partially lifted prior to the maximum time, as in fact occurred in some of the plaintiffs' transactions, discussed below.

[46] As might be expected, the banks have policies and procedures governing when a hold should be placed on a cheque. The evidence establishes that holds are made on an individual basis, depending on a variety of circumstances peculiar to the customer and the transaction, many of which are set out in the bank's hold policy. Some of the circumstances unique to the customer include:

- the customer's credit history and the status of his or her accounts with the bank;
- the customer's relationship with the branch, including the length of time he or she has been a customer and, in particular, whether the account is a new one;
- the customer's average account balance (whether there are usually sufficient funds in the account to cover a charge-back of the item);
- whether there are consistent loan or mortgage payments on the account(s) of the customer, indicating credit-worthiness;
- the value of the customer's portfolio with the bank;
- whether there has been recent regular activity in the account;
- the time of deposit (is this a weekend deposit? an after-hours deposit? a statutory long weekend?); and
- whether the customer has a history of items being returned as unpayable for insufficient funds or other reasons.

[47] The banks' policies also require that the person responsible for the hold decision must consider circumstances that are unique to the transaction, including whether:

- the transaction is unusual in the account history;
- the cheque is negotiable;
- the cheque appears to have been altered;
- the amounts in words and figures do not agree;
- the cheque is payable to a company, partnership, or person in an official capacity, but is sought to be deposited to another account;
- the cheque is post-dated or stale-dated;
- there is a drawer signature;
- the cheque appears to be a photocopy or otherwise a forgery;
- the cheque is double endorsed;
- the cheque bears any prior bank endorsements;
- the cheque is damaged or mutilated;
- the cheque is drawn by an unknown drawer or by a known, reliable drawer; or
- the cheque is drawn on a foreign bank.

[48] When a bank decides to place a hold on funds, it is telling the customer that it is not prepared to run the risk of treating the cheque as "good" until it has a reasonable measure of certainty that the cheque will be honoured by the drawee. That measure of certainty is provided by the fact that the cheque has not been returned dishonoured within a reasonable time after it was placed in the clearing system. That reasonable time is defined by the agreement between the bank and its customer. It is not a complete protection, because cheques can be returned for a variety of reasons long after the deposit.

[49] The practice of placing holds on cheque deposits has been sanctioned by the Department of Finance. It published a White Paper in 2006[9] discussing a number of issues in the financial services sector. The review process involved regulators, representatives of financial institutions, and consumer representatives. The paper acknowledged that hold periods have an important risk management function, but noted a concern by consumer groups and smaller businesses about the length of holds which, at the time, was a maximum of ten days for domestic cheques. It observed that the Payments Association was proposing to make changes to its system to facilitate electronic cheque imaging, which would expedite the cheque settlement process. As a result of discussions between the regulator and the banking community, the banks undertook to immediately reduce the hold period for domestic cheques to seven days. They also undertook to reduce it further to four days, once electronic imaging of cheques was

fully implemented. The White Paper, at p. 11, noted that "[t]his would be a significant improvement over the current maximum hold period of 10 days or more and a major step forward for consumers". Thus, the banks' current policy of a maximum seven day hold period for domestic cheques has been accepted by the Department of Finance as a reasonable upper limit, for the time being.

[50] The White Paper indicated that the government intended to amend the *Bank Act*, S.C. 1991, c. 46, to provide authority to make regulations to limit hold periods, but that in light of the anticipated agreement with the banks, no regulations would be introduced at that time.

[51] Hold periods are the result of a compromise between the banks and their customers. Customers would prefer to have access to the funds immediately; banks would like to have longer hold periods to further reduce the risk of the cheque being dishonoured after the funds have been made available to the customer. The evidence establishes that placing holds on cheques is a legitimate risk management tool for banks and that it reflects the realities of the modern clearing process.

II. THE CLAIMS OF THE PLAINTIFFS

[52] In this section I will summarize the claim of each plaintiff, including the terms of the account agreement, the transactions at issue, and the pleading. The relevant terms of the account agreements of each plaintiff are set out in Appendix A.

(a) Re*Collections and TD

(i) Account terms

[53] Re*Collections Inc. ("Re*Collections") signed an account agreement with TD on April 29, 2004 which set out TD's right to hold funds. The relevant terms were:

> When you deposit a cheque to your business account, either at a branch or through the Green Machine, you may not be able to access the full amount of the funds from that deposit immediately, if that deposit is subject to a "hold". Your access to those funds, or a portion of them, will be restricted. You will not be able withdraw money from those funds being held, and we will not pay any of your cheques or preauthorized debits from those funds until the end of the hold period. Hold funds decisions will be different for each customer. We will take into account factors such as the length or [*sic*] time you have

dealt with TD Canada Trust and the amount of funds already in your account. The decision will also vary depending on the institution on which the cheque has been drawn, as well as the amount and the issuer of the cheque.

[54] The agreement then indicated that deposits subject to a hold would be held for different lengths of time depending on whether the cheque was drawn on a domestic, US or foreign bank, and whether the cheque was drawn on a TD branch or another Canadian bank. The hold period for the latter was a minimum of five days and a maximum of ten.

[55] The agreement continued:

> These hold periods are estimates and apply where we have credited the funds to your account. We may extend such hold periods if payment for the cheque has not been received by us from the US or foreign financial institution within the initial maximum hold period. Some cheques may be sent on "collection" — this means that the funds will be credited to your account only if and when the cheque clears.

[56] A new form of agreement was issued by TD to all small business customers, such as Re*Collections, in November 2006. It provided, in part:

> You agree that we may place a "hold" on funds in any of your account(s):
> (i) restricting your right to make a withdrawal based on any Instrument until we receive actual and irrevocable payment from the drawee. Any credit to any of your account(s) for any Instrument before we receive actual and irrevocable payment is provisional and subject to reversal ...

[57] In February 2007, TD sent out an additional notice to its customers, including Re*Collections, as part of its compliance with the banks' new agreement with the Department of Finance, described in the White Paper. It provided:

> **Our Hold Funds Policy**
>
> When you deposit a cheque to your personal deposit account, either at a branch or through the Green Machine, you may not be able to access the full amount of the funds from the deposit immediately, if that deposit is subject to a "hold". Your access to those funds, or a portion of them, will be restricted. You will not be able to withdraw money from those funds being held, and we will not pay any of your cheques or pre-authorized debits from those funds until the end of the hold period.

Hold funds decisions will be different for each customer. We will take into account factors such as the length of time you have dealt with TD Canada Trust and the amount of funds already in your account. The decision will also vary depending on the institution on which the cheque has been drawn, as well as the amount and the issuer of the cheque.

Deposits subject to a hold will be held for the following number of business days:

	Minimum	Maximum
Cheques drawn on TD Canada Trust	3	6
Cheques drawn on another Canadian financial institution	5	7
— unknown or unencoded	7	14
Cheques drawn on U.S. institution*	15	30
Cheques drawn on other foreign financial institutions*	22	40

When you enrol in a direct deposit program, no hold is placed on the money deposited because it is credited directly to your account.

* These hold periods are estimates and apply where we have credited the funds to your account. We may extend such hold periods if payment for the cheque has not been received by us from the U.S. or foreign financial institution within that initial maximum hold period. Some cheques may be sent on "collection" — this means that the funds will be credited to your account only if and when the cheque clears.

[58] The evidence establishes that, at the time of deposit, TD customers were advised whether a hold would be placed, the amount that would be held, and the duration of the hold. Customers were required to confirm their agreement to the hold terms. If the deposit was made in person, the customer was required to execute a deposit slip recording the hold terms. If the deposit was made through an ATM, the customer was required to select the "OK to continue" option after seeing a computer screen displaying the hold terms for the proposed deposit transaction. If the customer did not agree to the terms of the hold, the deposit transaction would not proceed and the item would be returned to the customer.

[59] Under TD policies and procedures, holds could be applied only to personal and small business accounts. Holds were not placed on cheque deposits to commercial accounts — that is, those that require credit facilities of at least $500,000 to $1 million and require sophisticated cash management services.

[60] Although any interest payable on a TD account is earned and paid regardless of a hold or subsequent dishonour, the Re*Collections' account to which the cheque in issue was deposited was not interest-bearing.

(ii) The representative transaction

[61] On February 28, 2007, Re*Collections deposited a cheque for US$10,000, drawn on a U.S. bank in New Jersey, to the credit of its TD account in Toronto. At the time of deposit, Re*Collections was informed that a hold would be placed on the funds until March 22, 2007. This was confirmed on the deposit slip signed by the company's treasurer.

[62] The 22 day hold period was authorized by TD's account agreement with Re*Collections, which permitted TD to hold cheques drawn against a U.S. institution for a minimum of 15 days and a maximum of 30 days. TD's evidence is that a cheque drawn on a U.S. institution can take as long as several months to clear.

[63] The funds were in fact released and Re*Collections was given access to them on March 22, 2007, the hold date stated at the time of deposit. There is no evidence that anyone on behalf of Re*Collections requested access to the funds at any earlier date or objected to the hold being placed.

[64] In the five months before Re*Collections deposited the cheque with TD, it had deposited five cheques, totaling $22,670.00, which had been returned dishonoured. This history of returned items was sufficient grounds under TD's policies for a hold to be placed on the funds, in light of its financial exposure if the cheque was dishonoured.

[65] Re*Collections produced evidence that the payor's account was debited the sum of US$10,000.00 on March 2, 2007 and says that this is evidence that the cheque "cleared" on that date.

(iii) The pleading

[66] Re*Collections pleads the terms of a Financial Services Agreement with TD that allegedly[10] provided, in part:

> The reason that we have a Hold Funds Policy is that a cheque is not the same as cash, it is a promise to pay by one party to another party ... A hold period allows us sufficient time to verify

that the promise to pay will be carried out, i.e. that funds will be available from the other financial institution to pay the item.

[67] It also pleads the term of the November 2006 agreement, referred to above, which I reproduce for the sake of convenience:

> You agree that we may place a "hold" on funds in any of your account(s):
>
> (i) restricting your right to make a withdrawal based on any Instrument until we receive actual and irrevocable payment from the drawee. Any credit to any of your account(s) for any Instrument before we receive actual and irrevocable payment is provisional and subject to reversal ...

[68] Based on these provisions, the plaintiff pleads:

> Accordingly, pursuant to the relevant terms and conditions of Plaintiff's account and the accounts of all applicable Class Members, with regard to personal accounts held with Defendant, Defendant is contractually obligated to release the funds to its Personal account-holders upon Defendant having the ability to *verify* that the cheque will be paid, and *a fortiori* upon Defendant *receiving* payment for such Deposit, and with regard to Business account-holders governed by the Business Banking and Services Agreement, such as Plaintiff's account with Defendant, defendant is contractually obligated to release the funds to the relevant account-holder upon Defendant <u>receiving final payment</u> for a financial instrument deposited into the relevant depositor's account. [Italics in original; underlining added.]

[69] The statement of claim goes on to plead that if the drawee bank does not dishonour a cheque, it will be "settled" or "finally paid" by that institution within 12–18 hours of the clearing of that cheque: "Thus, a cheque deposited in a Canadian financial institution that is drawn on a Canadian financial institution will generally be settled within two business days of its deposit in the Collecting Bank".

[70] Re*Collections pleads that TD had a common law duty to release the funds "within a reasonable time period" of the date the bank received payment of the cheque. Similar pleadings are made in the other two actions.

(b) Herskovits and BMO

(i) *Account terms*

[71] The relationship between BMO and Yeshya Herskovits ("Herskovits") was governed by an account agreement, which provided in part as follows:

Holding of Funds

On new accounts, we may apply a "hold" to non-cash deposits. This is to make sure that the deposits are [*sic*] clear. During this period, we will hold each non-cash deposit (excluding direct deposits) to your account for six days before you are able to withdraw it. This hold period will last for 30 days after the first transaction on your new account. (Your branch may decide on a longer or shorter hold period.)

The following applies to all accounts (including new accounts as described above):

- When you deposit a fully encoded cheque drawn on a financial institution's branch located in Canada, we may apply a "hold" for a maximum of 10 calendar days, before you are able to withdraw the funds. This is to make sure that the deposit clears.
- When you deposit an unencoded or partially encoded cheque drawn on a financial institution's branch located in Canada, we may apply a "hold" for a maximum of 15 calendar days, before you are able to withdraw the funds. This is to make sure that the deposit clears.
- When you deposit a cheque drawn on a financial institution's branch located outside of Canada, we may apply a "hold" for a maximum of 30 calendar days, before you are able to withdraw the funds. This is to make sure that the deposit clears.

[72] In February 2007, the agreement was amended as follows:

Holding of Funds

There may be a period of 30 days (your branch may decide on a different length of time) after the first transaction on your new account where each non-cash deposit (excluding direct deposits) to your account will be subject to a hold. During this period, we will place a hold on cheques as set out below and place a hold on all other non-cash deposits for a maximum of 7 business days.

The following applies to all accounts (including new accounts as described above):

- When you deposit a fully encoded Canadian dollar or US dollar cheque drawn on a financial institution's branch located in Canada, we may apply a "hold" for a maximum of 7 business day, before you are able to access the funds.
- When you deposit an unencoded or partially encoded Canadian dollar or US dollar cheque drawn on a financial institution's branch located in Canada, we may apply a "hold" for a maximum of 15 calendar days, before you are able to access the funds.

- When you deposit a cheque drawn on a financial institution's branch located outside of Canada, or a fully encoded cheque in a currency other than Canadian dollars or US dollars drawn on a financial institution's branch located in Canada we may apply a "hold" for a maximum of 30 calendar days, before you are able to access the funds.
- A hold provides no guarantee that a cheque or other non-cash deposit will not be returned unpaid after the hold period has expired. If a cheque or other non-cash deposit is returned to us unpaid for any reason at any time, either during or after the expiry of the applicable hold period, we have the right to charge the amount of the cheque or non-cash deposit to your account.

(ii) The representative transaction

[73] On February 14, 2007 Herskovits deposited a cheque for US$2,500, drawn on a U.S. bank, to the credit of his U.S. dollar account with BMO in Toronto. As it was drawn on a U.S. bank, the cheque was cleared through the United States clearing system.

[74] At the time of the deposit, BMO released US$600.00 of the funds immediately, which was used to pay Herskovits' MasterCard bill. BMO placed an initial hold on the remaining US$1,900 for a period of 15 days. That was within the 30 day hold period allowed for US cheques as specified in the account agreement. Herskovits was advised of the 15-day hold when he made the deposit.

[75] After payment of his MasterCard bill, Herskovits had an account balance of US$1,935.05. On February 16, 2007, he made two further cash deposits in the amounts of US$400 and US$100, resulting in a new balance of US$2,435.05, of which US$1,900 was subject to the hold.

[76] On February 20 and 21, 2007, Herskovits wrote three cheques against his account, in the aggregate amount of US$2,105. These cheques were honoured by BMO, notwithstanding the 15-day temporary hold on the US$1,900. The result is that, within the hold period, Herskovits had the use of the funds that were subject to the hold. Throughout the hold period, Herskovits earned interest at the contractual rate. The interest was credited to his bank account throughout the hold period in accordance with his account agreement.

[77] Herskovits has produced evidence that the sum of US$2,500.00 was deducted from the payor's account on February 15, 2007 and claims that BMO received "payment" of the cheque on February 16, 2007.

(iii) The pleading

[78] Herskovits pleads that his accounts with BMO were governed by standard form contracts that were updated from time to time. He says that the applicable BMO hold funds policy was stated to be as follows:

> When you deposit a fully encoded cheque drawn on a financial institution's branch located in Canada, we may hold your cheque for a maximum of ten (10) calendar days. This is to make sure the deposit clears.

> When you deposit a fully encoded cheque drawn on a financial [institution's] branch located outside of Canada, we may hold your cheque for a maximum of thirty (30) calendar days. This is to make sure the deposit clears.

[79] Herskovits pleads that:

> ... pursuant to the relevant terms and conditions of Plaintiff's account and the accounts of the applicable Class Members, upon the clearing of cheques deposited with Defendant, Defendant is contractually obligated to release such funds to its depositors.

[80] He goes on to plead that a cheque generally "clears" by 11:00 a.m. or even earlier on the first business day after it is deposited by the customer. The pleading continues:

> It is important to note that although the cheque may undergo additional processing after the *clearing*, such as presentation for verification at the branch of the Drawee Bank, the *clearing* process is completed upon the debiting of the payor's account by the particular processing centre of the Drawee Bank.

> Accordingly, under the relevant terms and conditions governing account held with Defendant, Defendant has a contractual duty to release the funds in respect of cheques deposited with Defendant to the applicable depositor upon *clearing*. Stated another way, pursuant to the relevant terms and conditions of accounts held with Defendant, Defendant is obligated to release the funds to its depositor upon the receipt and processing by the data centre of the Drawee Bank of the particular cheque. [Emphasis in original.]

[81] Herskovits pleads that he deposited the cheque for US$2,500 on February 14, 2007 into his US dollar account with BMO and that, although US$500 was released immediately, BMO held the remaining US$2,000 for 15 days and that the funds were only

released on March 2, 2007. He pleads that the cheque "cleared" within three business days of the deposit. The pleading continues:

> Plaintiff pleads that he was legally entitled to have access to the Held Deposit on the Clear date immediately on the *clearing* of the Cheque, or in the alternative, plaintiff pleads that he was legally entitled to receive access to the Held Deposit on the first business day following the Clear Date, in respect of the Cheque, pursuant to the Account Agreement and the terms and conditions therein governing Defendant's 'hold funds policy'.
>
> Plaintiff pleads that Defendant wrongfully retained the Held Deposit, in respect of the Cheque, after the Clear Date, in breach of its contractual obligations to the Plaintiff, and that as a result of such breach, Plaintiff suffered damages.

[82] Herskovits pleads that BMO:

> .. systematically and intentionally implements standard arbitrary hold periods on depositors' cheques without consideration as to when such cheques clear, and, without consideration as to when Defendant actually receives payment on such cheques.

[83] Essentially, Herskovits asserts that the words "[t]his is to make sure the deposit clears", contained in the account agreement, mean that BMO is contractually required to release the funds when the cheque "clears".

(c) Fleising and BNS

(i) Account terms

[84] The account agreement between Sol Fleising ("Fleising") and BNS provided in part as follows:

A few notes about processing your transactions

We may put a hold on your funds

Cheques presented for cash or deposit to your account may not always be cashed right away. A hold may be placed on the funds because we need to know that the cheque will not be returned by the institution on which the cheque is drawn.

...

the maximum hold that may be placed on deposits made to your account are:

- Cheques drawn on a branch of a financial institution located in Canada — maximum hold of 10 business days
- Cheques drawn on a branch of a financial institution located in the United States — maximum hold of 20 business days
- Cheques drawn on any other financial institution located outside of Canada or the United States — maximum hold of 30 business days

The length of time you have dealt with the branch, the amount of funds already in your account, and the amount and characteristics of the cheque being deposited may all influence whether the funds will be held.

For immediate access to deposited funds (up to a pre-authorized limit), please contact your branch about our CashBack feature, which can be set up on your ScotiaCard banking card. [Emphasis in original; footnotes omitted.]

(ii) The representative transaction

[85] On June 26, 2006, Fleising deposited two cheques totaling C$21,689.91 to the credit of his BNS account in Vaughan. The particulars of the cheques were as follows:

(a) a cheque for $20,000, which was "double endorsed." It was dated June 5, 2006, drawn in Canadian dollars on an account maintained at BMO Nesbitt Burns, and was payable to "Lola Pila" and had purportedly been endorsed by Lola Pila;

(b) a cheque for $1,689.91, which was dated June 19, 2006 payable to Fleising, and was drawn on an account in the name of "Toby and Henry Battle Developmental Centre" at a Royal Bank branch in Toronto. The account into which Fleising deposited these cheques did not pay interest, although he had an interest-bearing savings account with BNS.

[86] The deposits were made at an ATM and were subject to an automatic hold on funds. In the course of making the deposits, Fleising was required to consent to the terms of the hold in order to complete the transaction.

[87] In addition, the BNS hold policies stipulate that BNS employees are to consider whether a cheque is double-endorsed as a factor in making the discretionary decision to place a hold, and that this factor is particularly important with respect to cheques deposited through ATMs.

[88] As of June 26, 2006, Fleising's account had a "CashBack" feature and limit of $2,000.00. Prior to deposit of the two cheques, the account also had a credit balance of $4,354.31. Accordingly, after making the deposits, Fleising had immediate unrestricted access to draw up to $6,354.31 from the account, while the remaining $19,690.00 was subject to a hold.

[89] However, on the same date that the above deposits were made, the account was debited a total of $10,604.00 to pay cheques that Fleising wrote in the amounts of $10,000.00 (payable to Lola Pila), $160.00, $300.00, and $144.00. When these cheques were initially presented for payment against the account, the holds on the account meant that there would normally have been insufficient funds available to pay the $10,000.00 cheque.

[90] Despite this, the Manager at Fleising's BNS branch made the discretionary decision to lift the automatic holds on funds (on the same day that the hold was placed) to permit payment of the $10,000.00 cheque to Lola Pila. Had the hold been kept in place, that cheque would have been returned for the reason "funds not clear".

[91] The hold on the remaining deposited funds was lifted on July 10, 2006, which is nine business days after the date of deposit (the account agreement at the time permitted BNS to hold for a maximum of 10 business days). As a result, on Fleising's own evidence: (a) he was given immediate access to over half the amount he deposited, without even having to request that the hold be lifted; (b) he was given access to the balance of the amount of the cheque (when demand for payment was made) within the hold period permitted by his contract with BNS; and (c) he agreed to the hold, both when he signed the account agreement and when he navigated through the various ATM screens notifying him of the hold.

(iii) The pleading

[92] Fleising pleads certain provisions of a booklet issued by BNS setting out the terms and conditions of its hold funds policy. The specific clause relied upon provides as follows:

> Cheques presented for cash or deposit to your account may not be cashed right away. A hold may be placed on the funds because we need to know that the cheque will not be returned by the institution on which the cheque is drawn ...

[93] The pleading then continues:

> Accordingly, pursuant to the relevant terms and conditions of Plaintiff's account and the accounts of all applicable Class Members, Defendant is contractually obligated to release the funds to its Personal account-holders upon Defendant having the ability to *verify* that the cheque will be paid, and *a fortiori* upon Defendant *receiving* payment for such deposit. [Emphasis in original.]

[94] The plaintiff then pleads:

> Generally, in the event that the payor institution [i.e., the drawee] does not choose to dishonor a particular cheque, such cheque will be *settled*, or "finally paid" by the payor institution within 12–18 hours of the clearing of a particular cheque or even earlier in some cases. Thus a cheque deposited in a Canadian financial institution that is drawn on a Canadian financial institution will generally be settled within two business days of its deposit in the Collecting Bank[.]

(d) Summary of the Representative Transactions

[95] The foregoing summary of the claims of the three plaintiffs demonstrates some important facts:

- while the account agreements are different, the decision to hold funds in each case was authorized by the bank's agreement with the customer, and was consistent with the particular bank's policies;
- the decision to impose a hold is made individually and focuses on the customer's history and the nature of the transaction;
- the holds were not always for the maximum permitted period — in the Re*Collections case it was for 22 days and not for the full 30 permitted; in the Herskovits case it was for 15 days and not the maximum 30;
- the customers were aware of the hold policies of the banks and, in the case of ATM deposits, were made aware that a hold would be placed and agreed to it at the time of deposit — in the Re*Collections case, the deposit slip signed by the depositor acknowledged and accepted the terms of the hold; and
- holds were not absolute — Herskovits was given immediate access to $600 from the held funds and every subsequent draw he made on the funds was honoured; Fleising was as well.

[96] The pleadings in the three actions are substantially the same. At their core, they assert that the banks were obliged to release held funds on the funds "clearing", or the bank having "received payment" or being "finally paid" or being able to "verify payment" or on the cheque having been "settled".

[97] Against this background, I will now turn to the application of the test for certification.

III. THE TEST FOR CERTIFICATION

[98] The test for certification is set out at section 5(1) of the *C.P.A.*:

> The Court shall certify a class proceeding if:
> (a) the pleading or the notice of application discloses a cause of action;
> (b) there is an identifiable class of two or more persons that would be represented by the representative plaintiff or defendant;
> (c) the claims or defences of the class members raise common issues;
> (d) a class proceeding would be the preferable procedure for the resolution of the common issues; and,
> (e) there is a representative plaintiff or defendant who,
>> (i) would fairly and adequately represent the interests of the class,
>> (ii) has produced a plan for the proceeding that set out a workable method of advancing the proceeding on behalf of the class and of notifying class members of the proceeding, and
>> (iii) does not have, on the common issues for the class, an interest in conflict with the interests of other class members.

[99] Section 5(1) should be generously construed so as to promote access to justice, judicial economy and behaviour modification, as envisioned by the *C.P.A.*: *Cloud v. Canada (Attorney General)* (2004), 73 O.R. (3d) 401, [2004] O.J. No. 4924 (C.A.) at paras. 37–39, leave to appeal to S.C.C. refused, [2005] S.C.C.A. No. 50; *Hollick v. Toronto (City)*, [2001] 3 S.C.R. 158, [2001] S.C.J. No. 67 ("*Hollick*") at paras. 14–16; *Pearson v. Inco Ltd.* (2006), 78 O.R. (3d) 641, [2006] O.J. No. 4918 (C.A.) at paras. 3 and 44, leave to appeal to S.C.C. refused, [2006] S.C.C.A. No. 1.

[100] The purpose of a certification motion is to determine how the litigation is to proceed and not to test the merits of the plaintiffs' claim. It is a procedural motion that focuses on the form of the action, not whether or not the action is likely to succeed on the merits: *Hollick* at para. 16. It is not part of my responsibility to conduct a summary judgment motion or to subject the plaintiffs' claims to scrutiny on the merits.

[101] The evidentiary requirement for certification is low — the plaintiffs need only show "some basis in fact" for each of the certification requirements in s. 5(1), other than the requirement in s. 5(1)(a) that the pleading discloses a cause of action: *Hollick* at paras. 16 and 25; *Boulanger v. Johnson & Johnson Corp.* (2007), 40 C.P.C. (6th) 170, [2007] O.J. No. 179 (S.C.J.) at para. 20, leave to appeal to Div. Ct.

refused, [2007] O.J. No. 1991 (S.C.J.), supplemental reasons at [2007] O.J. No. 2043 and [2007] O.J. No. 2766 (S.C.J.). I will discuss this in more detail below.

(a) Cause of Action

[102] Section 5(1)(a) of the *C.P.A.* requires that the pleading disclose a cause of action. The test is identical to that applied on a motion under rule 21.01(1)(b) of the *Rules of Civil Procedure*, R.R.O. 1990, Reg. 194 to strike a statement of claim on the ground that it discloses no cause of action. The court must consider whether it is "plain and obvious" that the pleading does not disclose a cause of action. The test is a low one and the court errs on the side of giving access to justice. The applicable principles were summarized by Lax J. in *Fresco v. Canadian Imperial Bank of Commerce* (2009), 71 C.P.C. (6th) 97, [2009] O.J. No. 2531 (S.C.J.) at para. 22:

> * no evidence is admissible for the purposes of determining the s. 5(1)(a) criterion: *Hollick v. Toronto (City)*, 2001 SCC 68, [2001] 3 S.C.R. 158 at para. 25;
>
> * all allegations of fact pleaded, unless patently ridiculous or incapable of proof, must be accepted as proven and thus assumed to be true;
>
> * the pleading will be struck out only if it is plain, obvious and beyond doubt that the plaintiff cannot succeed and only if the action is certain to fail because it contains a radical defect: *Cloud v. Canada (Attorney General)* (2004), 73 O.R. (3d) 401 (C.A.) at para. 41, leave to appeal to S.C.C. refused, [2005] S.C.C.A. No. 50;
>
> * matters of law not fully settled in the jurisprudence must be permitted to proceed: *Ford v. F. Hoffmann-LaRoche Ltd.* (2005), 74 O.R. (3d) 758 (S.C.J.) at para. 17(e); and
>
> * the pleading must be read generously to allow for inadequacies due to drafting frailties and the plaintiffs' lack of access to key documents and discovery information: *Hunt v. Carey Canada Inc.*, [1990] 2 S.C.R. 959 at 980; *Anderson v. Wilson* (1999), 44 O.R. (3d) 673 (C.A.) at 679.

[103] In this case, a variety of causes of action have been pleaded, and I will discuss each in turn. As the claim has been presented, and argued, squarely on the basis of contract, I will deal with that cause of action first.

(i) Breach of contract

[104] It is settled law that a customer is a creditor of the bank when he or she deposits funds into an account and that the bank holds the funds as its own

until the customer asks for repayment: *B.M.P. Global Distribution Inc. v. Bank of Nova Scotia*, above, at para. 63, referring to *Foley v. Hill* (1848), 2 H.L.C. 28, 9 E.R. 1002; Bradley Crawford, *Crawford and Falconbridge: Banking and Bills of Exchange*, 8th ed. (Toronto: Canada Law Book, 1986) vol. 1 at 742–3; and *Baldwin v. Daubney* (2006), 83 O.R. (3d) 308, [2006] O.J. No. 3824 (C.A.) leave to appeal to S.C.C. refused, [2006] S.C.C.A. 475. Thus, when a cheque is deposited in a customer's account, title to the funds is transferred to the bank and the relationship between the customer and the bank is one of creditor and debtor. That relationship is contractual and the terms are set out in the account agreement.

[105] The plaintiffs base their claims on the breach of an express term of their account agreements with their respective banks. Counsel for the plaintiffs distilled this case, in his factum, to the following central question:

> What are the legal ramifications of the Defendants intentionally holding Deposits for longer than the applicable hold period allowed under common law, and for longer than the Defendants' own respective terms allow? This is a centralized, Defendant-based question, focused on the terms of a standardized contract.

[106] As we have seen, the plaintiffs' account agreements are not identical, but their hold terms are similar.

[107] In assessing whether the pleading discloses a cause of action for breach of contract, a motion judge is entitled to consider contractual documents that are referred to in the pleadings and that form an integral part of the plaintiff's claim. These are not "evidence", but rather are incorporated into the pleading: *Web Offset Publications Ltd. v. Vickery* (1999), 43 O.R. (3d) 802, [1999] O.J. No. 2760 (C.A.), leave to appeal to S.C.C. refused, [1999] S.C.C.A. No. 460, referring to *Montreal Trust Co. of Canada v. Toronto Dominion Bank* (1992), 40 C.P.C. (3d) 389 at 395–96, [1992] O.J. No. 1274 (Gen. Div.); *Lubarevich v. Nurgitz*, [1996] O.J. No. 1457 (Gen. Div.); *Vaughan v. Ontario (Minister of Health)* (1996), 49 C.P.C. (3d) 119 at p. 123, [1996] O.J. No. 1618 (Gen. Div.). The court is entitled to review the documents in order to test the adequacy of the pleaded claim. In this case, the terms of the plaintiffs' account agreements can therefore be considered as if they were incorporated into the pleading.

[108] A proper pleading of breach of contract requires sufficient particulars to identify the nature of the contract, the parties to the contract, the facts supporting privity of contract between the plaintiff and defendant, the relevant terms of the contract, which term was breached, the conduct giving rise to the breach, and the damages that flow from that breach: *McCarthy Corporation PLC v. KPMG LLP*, [2007] O.J. No. 32 (S.C.J.).

[109] The plaintiffs submit that the express terms of their account agreements can reasonably be construed as meaning that funds will be released to the customer when the funds are "paid" to the bank, or, in the case of BMO at an earlier time, when the funds "clear". The submission can be understood by returning to and re-examining the pleading in *Herskovits v. BMO*. It pleads an account agreement as follows:

> When you deposit a fully encoded cheque drawn on a financial institutions branch located in Canada, we may hold your cheque for a maximum of ten (10) calendar days. This is to make sure the deposit clears. [Emphasis added.]

[110] Relying on this clause, Herskovits pleads:

> Accordingly, pursuant to the relevant terms and conditions of Plaintiff's account and the accounts of the applicable Class Members, upon the *clearing* of cheques deposited with Defendant, Defendant is contractually obligated to release such funds to its depositors. [Emphasis in original.]

[111] Later the plaintiff pleads:

> Under the relevant terms and conditions governing accounts held with Defendant, Defendant has a contractual duty to release the funds in respect of cheques deposited with Defendant to the applicable depositor upon *clearing*. Stated another way, pursuant to the relevant terms and conditions of accounts held with Defendant, Defendant is obligated to release the funds to its depositor upon the receipt and processing by the data centre of the Drawee Bank of the particular cheque. [Emphasis in original.]

[112] The plaintiff pleads that holding the cheques after the applicable "clear date" was a breach of the bank's contractual obligations under the account agreement.

[113] A similar pleading is made in the case of *Fleising v. BNS*, in which the plaintiff relies on the following term in the account agreement:

> A hold may be placed on the funds because we need to know that the cheque will not be returned by the institution on which the cheque is drawn.

[114] The account agreement at the time permitted a hold period of up to ten days for domestic cheques.

[115] Fleising then pleads that:

> Defendant is contractually obligated to release the funds to its Personal account-holders upon defendant having the ability to *verify* that the cheques will be paid, and *a fortiori* upon Defendant *receiving* payment for such Deposit. [Emphasis in original.]

[116] The pleading in the case of *Re*Collections v. TD* is similar.

[117] As I have noted earlier, each of the plaintiffs' agreements contains provisions authorizing holds of various durations, depending on the nature of the cheque. There are no allegations that the maximum hold periods set out in the account agreements were exceeded.

[118] The plaintiffs argue, however, that there is an inconsistency between the terms of the account agreements that allow maximum hold periods and the language that suggests that the purpose of a hold period is to enable the bank to verify whether the cheque will be "paid" or the deposit has "cleared". They submit that it is not my responsibility to resolve this alleged inconsistency by interpreting the contract or to choose between two possible constructions and that this should be left for trial or for a motion for summary judgment.

[119] There is a difference between interpreting a contract and determining whether the plaintiff has properly pleaded the breach of an express contractual term that is capable of supporting a cause of action for breach of contract. I am required to discharge the latter function on this motion. I am also required to determine whether the term is express or implied as this will determine whether issues exist that are capable of resolution on a common basis. This was precisely the analysis that was undertaken by E. M. Macdonald J. in *Arabi v. Toronto Dominion Bank*, [2006] O.J. No. 2072 at para. 45 (S.C.J.), aff'd *sub nom. McLaine v. London Life Insurance Co.*, [2007] O.J. No. 5075 (Div. Ct.).

[120] The plaintiffs have failed to identify and plead any express term that has been breached. There is no promise made by the banks, or obligation undertaken by them, that is alleged to have been breached. The words relied upon ("we need to know that the cheque will not be returned" and "this is to make sure the deposit clears") are simply explanations for the hold periods that are expressly permitted by the contracts. They cannot reasonably be regarded as express contractual promises or obligations.

[121] There is, moreover, no pleading that any plaintiff made a demand for payment of, or access to the held funds. As noted above, it is well-settled that the bank holds deposited funds as its own until the customer asks for repayment: see *B.M.P. Global Distribution Inc. v. Bank of Nova Scotia*, above. In the absence of a demand for funds, the bank has no contractual obligation to pay them to the customer.

[122] Although the plaintiffs disavow any reliance on an implied term, they are really alleging an implied term that, notwithstanding the express maximum hold period, the bank must release the funds once the cheque "clears" or is "settled" or is "finally paid", to mention only a few of the expressions used in the pleadings. The best illustration of this implied term, as advanced by the plaintiffs, is the pleading in *Fleising v. BNS* (which is similar to the pleading in *Re*Collections v. TD*) that the words "we need to know that the cheque will not be returned" mean that:

> Defendant is contractually obligated to release the funds to its Personal account-holders upon Defendant having the ability to *verify* that the cheque will be paid, and *a fortiori* upon Defendant *receiving* payment for such deposit. [Emphasis in original.]

[123] Put another way, the plaintiffs are really relying on an implied term to the following effect:

> Although we can hold funds for up to seven days in the case of a domestic cheque, since the purpose of the hold is to determine that the cheque will be paid and will not be returned, we will release the funds within a reasonable time after we have been paid.

[124] The assertion is not very different from the "common law" claim, which I will discuss shortly, that the hold must be released within a "reasonable time" of "payment".

[125] There are insurmountable difficulties with the implication of an implied term of this nature. First, a term will not readily be implied in a contract. As Perell J. noted in *McCracken v. Canadian National Railway Co.*, 2010 ONSC 4520, [2010] O.J. No. 3466 (S.C.J.), at para. 217:

> Terms may be implied in a contract: (1) based on custom or usage; (2) as the legal incidents of a particular class or kind of contract; or (3) based on the presumed intention of the parties where the implied term must be necessary to give business efficacy to a contract or as otherwise meeting the "officious bystander" test as a term that the parties would say, if questioned,

that they had obviously assumed: *M.J.B. Enterprises Ltd. v. Defence Construction (1951) Ltd.*, [1999] 1 S.C.R. 619; *Canadian Pacific Hotels Ltd. v. Bank of Montreal*, [1987] 1 S.C.R. 711; *Wallace v. United Grain Growers Ltd.*, [1997] 3 S.C.R. 701, at para. 137.

[126] There is no basis in the evidence that would suggest that an implied term, of the kind asserted by the plaintiffs, could be established by custom or usage. Indeed, the evidence is quite to the contrary. Nor could an implied term be found under the second category, as one of the legal incidents of an agreement between a bank and its customer. If an implied term can exist at all in this case, it must be under the third category — based on the presumed intention of the parties, to give their contract business efficacy.

[127] No facts have been pleaded to establish the circumstances that give rise to an implied term or to establish that the implication of a term is necessary to give the contract business efficacy. On the contrary, the uncontroverted evidence establishes that the bank of deposit cannot know when a particular cheque has been "paid" or "cleared" and that to release the funds when the plaintiffs say they should be released would not be conducive to business efficacy, because it would expose the bank to the unreasonable risk that a particular cheque will be returned, dishonoured, within the time permitted by the Payments Association Rules. It would not promote business efficacy to require banks to release held funds before they can safely assume that the cheque will not be dishonoured.

[128] In *McCracken v. Canadian National Railway Co.*, above, Perell J. also referred, at para. 218, to the cautionary words of Cory J., as he then was, in *G. Ford Homes Ltd. v. Draft Masonry (York) Co. Ltd.* (1983), 43 O.R. (2d) 401, 1 D.L.R. (4th) 262 (C.A.) at para. 9, concerning the need for restraint in the implication of terms, so as to avoid re-writing the contract the parties have made:

> When may a term be implied in a contract? A court faced with that question must first take cognizance of some important and time-honoured cautions. For example, the courts will be cautious in their approach to implying terms to contracts. Certainly a court will not rewrite a contract for the parties. As well, no term will be implied that is inconsistent with the contract. Implied terms are as a rule based upon the presumed intention of the parties and should be founded upon reason. The circumstances and background of the contract, together with its precise terms, should all be carefully regarded

before a term is implied. As a result, it is clear that every case must be determined on its own particular facts.

[129] In this case, the implied term is, on its face, inconsistent with the express terms of the account agreements authorizing hold periods. There can be no room for the implication of a term "where the parties have made an express contract covering the very facts in litigation": *Peter Kiewit Sons' Co. v. Eikins Construction Ltd.*, [1960] S.C.R. 361 at 369; see also *Arabi v. Toronto Dominion Bank*, above, and *Marinangeli v. Marinangeli* (2003), 66 O.R. (3d) 40, [2003] O.J. No. 2819 (C.A.) at para. 65.

[130] For these reasons, the plaintiffs have failed to plead a cause of action for breach of either an express or implied term of their contracts.

(ii) Breach of Common Law Duty and Negligence

[131] The plaintiffs plead that each bank had a "common law duty" to release their funds within a "reasonable time period" of the date on which the bank was "paid" in respect of the particular cheque. They plead that the next business day after the payment date is a reasonable time and that by retaining deposits for more than one business day after "payment" the bank breaches its duty. The plaintiffs also claim that, by implementing standard hold periods of 7, 10, 15, or 30 days, without investigating the true "payment date", banks breach an alleged common law duty to allow the plaintiffs access to their deposits within a reasonable time.

[132] The plaintiffs also plead a cause of action, in negligence, for breach of a duty of care by the defendants by not releasing the customer's funds and by instituting a "hold funds policy" that was greater than the "permissible" time for the holding of deposits.

[133] In arguing for the existence of a common law duty, the plaintiffs rely on an extract from *The Law of Banking and Payment*, to which I referred earlier, to the effect that a Canadian court would allow a bank a "reasonable time" to post credits to a customer's account. In support of that observation, Crawford refers to the decision of Lane J. in *Independent Multi-Funds Inc. v. Bank of Nova Scotia*, above. In that case, the plaintiff's bank had received an electronic transfer of $20 million, but did not post it to the customer's account immediately. The bank continued to hold the funds due to a concern that money-laundering might have been involved. When the plaintiff failed to answer the bank's inquiries, the funds were returned to the sender at the

plaintiff's request. Lane J. held that the bank had acted reasonably, in the circumstances, in declining to release the funds.

[134] An observation similar to Crawford's is made by Ogilvie in *Canadian Banking Law*, above, at 627:

> Although there is no case law on the point, it would appear in the light of the foregoing that the collecting bank's duty once it has received the funds as cleared funds from the drawee bank is to deposit the proceeds in the customer's account within a reasonable time of final settlement, as determined on the facts of the case. At that time the provisional credit in the customer's account would become final, and the customer can draw freely on those funds. The legal right enjoyed by American banks to hold funds after final settlement by the drawee bank does not exist in Canada or in the United Kingdom. Once the customer's account has been credited finally, the bank's duty of collection in respect to that cheque is completed.

[135] Both Crawford and Ogilvie are speaking of a situation in which there has been "final settlement, as determined by the facts of the case", to use Ogilvie's expression. Crawford uses similar language. Both writers are speaking of a situation in which the bank actually collects and receives the funds and both are referring to circumstances in which there are no relevant contractual terms. The cases before me do not involve the receipt of collected funds by the banks.

[136] In these cases, the plaintiffs' complaints about the conduct of the banks falls squarely within their contractual agreements. The contractual provisions are an agreement by the parties to arrange their respective rights and duties in a particular way and must prevail over any duty in tort: see *B.G. Checo International Ltd. v. British Columbia Hydro and Power Authority*, [1993] 1 S.C.R. 12, [1993] S.C.J. No. 1 at paras. 15–16:

> In our view, the general rule emerging from this Court's decision in *Central Trust Co. v. Rafuse*, [1986] 2 S.C.R. 147, is that where a given wrong *prima facie* supports an action in contract and in tort, the party may sue in either or both, except where the contract indicates that the parties intended to limit or negative the right to sue in tort. This limitation on the general rule of concurrency arises because it is always open to parties to limit or waive the duties which the common law would impose on them for negligence. This principle is of great importance in preserving a sphere of individual liberty and commercial flexibility. Thus if a person wishes to

engage in a dangerous sport, the person may stipulate in advance that he or she waives any right of action against the person who operates the sport facility: *Dyck v. Manitoba Snowmobile Association Inc.*, [1985] 1 S.C.R. 589. Similarly, if two business firms agree that a particular risk should lie on a party who would not ordinarily bear that risk at common law, they may do so. So a plaintiff may sue either in contract or in tort, subject to any limit the parties themselves have placed on that right by their contract. The mere fact that the parties have dealt with a matter expressly in their contract does not mean that they intended to exclude the right to sue in tort. It all depends on how they have dealt with it.

> Viewed thus, the only limit on the right to choose one's action is the principle of primacy of private ordering — the right of individuals to arrange their affairs and assume risks in a different way than would be done by the law of tort. It is only to the extent that this private ordering contradicts the tort duty that the tort duty is diminished. The rule is not that one cannot sue concurrently in contract and tort where the contract limits or contradicts the tort duty. It is rather that the tort duty, a general duty imputed by the law in all the relevant circumstances, must yield to the parties' superior right to arrange their rights and duties in a different way. In so far as the tort duty is not contradicted by the contract, it remains intact and may be sued upon. For example, where the contractual limitation on the tort duty is partial, a tort action founded on the modified duty might lie. The tort duty as modified by the contractual agreement between the parties might be raised in a case where the limitation period for an action for breach of contract has expired but the limitation period for a tort action has not. If one says categorically, as we understand Iacobucci J. to say, that where the contract deals with a matter expressly, the right to sue in tort vanishes altogether, then the latter two possibilities vanish.

[137] In this case, even if the bank is subject to a common law duty to credit the customer's account within a reasonable time of being aware that a cheque has not been dishonoured, it is open to the parties to define the limits of that reasonable time. The selection of a defined time period, as opposed to a vague notion of "reasonable time" is a fair protection of the bank that preserves its commercial flexibility.

(iii) Conversion

[138] The plaintiffs plead the tort of conversion. They claim that the defendants':

... systematic refusal to release the Held Deposits to the Plaintiff and to the Class, after the applicable Payment Date, amounts to conversion of Plaintiff's Deposit and the Deposits of the class by Defendant, and further is a breach of Defendant's common law and other duties owed to the Plaintiff and to the Class.

[139] The tort of conversion is the intentional and wrongful interference with specific personal property that the plaintiff either owns or in which he/she has a possessory interest. It has been defined by the Supreme Court of Canada in *Boma Manufacturing Ltd. v. Canadian Imperial Bank of Commerce*, [1996] 3 S.C.R. 727, [1996] S.C.J. No. 111 at para. 31 as:

A wrongful interference with the goods of another, such as taking, using or destroying these goods in a manner inconsistent with the owner's right of possession. The tort is one of strict liability, and accordingly, it is no defence that the wrongful act was committed in all innocence.

[140] There can be no conversion in these cases for several reasons: (a) through the account agreement, the customer consents to the banks holding funds; (b) the customer retains no possessory or proprietary interest in the funds — when funds are deposited in the bank, they become the money of the banker, not the customer: *Vukovich v. Royal Bank* (1998), 158 D.L.R. (4th) 37, [1998] O.J. No. 1483 (C.A.) at para. 19; *Foley v. Hill* (1848), 2 H.L.C. 28 at 36, 9 E.R. 1002 at 1005; *B.M.P. Global Distribution Inc. v. Bank of Nova Scotia*, above; and (c) the funds on deposit are not personal property — they are simply a chose in action.

(iv) Breach of Fiduciary Duty and Agency Relationship

[141] The plaintiffs plead that each bank acted as an agent on behalf of its customers to receive payment on deposits made with the bank and to deposit the funds "collected" into the accounts of its customers. They plead that it was a breach of that duty to retain those funds and to make "secret profits" from them, while wrongfully holding the deposits from the customers.

[142] The relationship between a bank and its customer is a commercial and contractual one and does not give rise to a fiduciary duty in the absence of exceptional circumstances: *Pierce v. Canada Trustco Mortgage Co.* (2005), 254 D.L.R. (4th) 79, [2005] O.J. No. 1886 (C.A.) at para. 27; *Baldwin v. Daubney*, above, at paras. 12, 15; *Bank of Montreal v. Witkin* (2005), 9 B.L.R. (4th) 256, [2005] O.J. No.

3221 (S.C.J.) at para. 54; *The Law of Banking and Payment* at para. 9:50.10; Mark Vincent Ellis, *Fiduciary Duties in Canada*, loose leaf (Toronto: Carswell, 2004) at 7-2.1 to 2.2. There is no pleading of facts or circumstances that could reasonably give rise to a fiduciary duty. The actions of the banks in holding funds are expressly authorized by the account agreements and are a reasonable measure of protection for both the bank and the customer.

(v) Unjust enrichment

[143] The plaintiffs claim that by holding cheques beyond the time permitted by their account agreements, the banks have been enriched at their expense. One of the essential elements of a claim for unjust enrichment is the absence of a "juristic reason" for the enrichment: *Garland v. Consumers' Gas Co.*, [2004] 1 S.C.R. 629, [2004] S.C.J. No. 21 at para. 44. In this case, the existence of a lawful contract is a juristic reason for the enrichment: *CIBC v. Melnitzer* (1993), 23 C.B.R. (3d) 161, [1993] O.J. No. 3021 (S.C.J.) at paras. 103–105, aff'd (1997) 50 C.B.R. (3d) 79, [1997] O.J. No. 4634 (C.A.); *Brouilette Building Supplies v. 1662877 Ontario Inc.*, [2009] O.J. No. 92 (S.C.J.) at para. 22; *Windisman v. Toronto College Park Ltd.* (1996), 28 O.R. (3d) 29, [1996] O.J. No. 552 (Gen. Div.) at paras. 68–70; *Georgian (St. Lawrence) Lofts Inc. v. Market Lofts Inc.*, [2007] O.J. No. 81 (S.C.J.) at para. 44.

[144] In the absence of a pleading that the plaintiffs' contracts are invalid, the claim for unjust enrichment is untenable.

(vi) Waiver of Tort

[145] Waiver of tort has not been pleaded. The plaintiffs' factum asserts that the defendants are liable to disgorge the benefits they have obtained, based on waiver of tort:

... if the defendant bank is found to have committed a tort such as conversion, breached a contract or breached a common law or other duty, they may be found liable to disgorge the profits derived from their unlawful activity under the doctrine of waiver of tort.

[146] The plaintiffs rely on *Serhan Estate v. Johnson & Johnson*, [2006] O.J. No. 2421 (Div. Ct.) at paras. 50–52. As the Court of Appeal noted in *Aronowicz v. Emtwo Properties Inc.* (2010), 258 O.A.C. 222, [2010] O.J. No. 474, the precise scope of the waiver of tort remedy is controversial. Doubts exist as to whether it is an independent cause of action or requires the operation of an independent tort and proof of harm

to the plaintiff. It is clearly established, however, that waiver of tort requires some form of wrongdoing on the part of the defendant. The fact of a "gain" by the defendant, without a wrong being perpetrated on the plaintiff, does not give rise to a remedy in waiver of tort.

Summary of Cause of Action

[147] As I noted earlier, the plaintiffs put their claims squarely on breach of contract. No other cause of action was referred to in argument, although the other causes of action were not abandoned. Although the claims are pleaded, and argued, based on breach of an express term, I have concluded that the express language of the contracts is not capable of the interpretation advanced. The claims are fundamentally for breach of implied terms, and there is no pleading, and no basis, for the implication of any such terms.

[148] I also find that there is no other tenable cause of action pleaded.

[149] These conclusions are sufficient to dispose of this motion. Nevertheless, I will consider the other requirements of s. 5(1) of the *C.P.A.*

(b) Identifiable Class

[150] Section 5(1)(b) of the *C.P.A.* requires that there be an "identifiable class of two or more persons that would be represented by the representative plaintiff". The plaintiffs propose the following class definition:

> All current and former clients of the [defendant bank] resident in Canada, who, between 2001 and the date of judgment in this action ("the Class Period"):
> (i) held one or more accounts at [bank's] branches; and
> (ii) made deposits into such accounts either by wire transfer, cheque, or any other means ("Deposit(s)"), during the Class Period; and
> (iii) had their funds held by the [bank].

[151] The defendants acknowledge that, if all other requirements of s. 5 of the *C.P.A.* are met, the plaintiffs have identified a class capable of certification. I accept the plaintiffs' submission that, with some modifications, the class is appropriate for certification. It is objectively defined, not dependant on the merits of the claim and class members will be able to self-identify.

[152] The class definition would, however, require adjustment. The commencement of the class period in 2001 is based on the fact that the three actions were commenced in 2007 and the six-year limitation period would permit claims back to 2001. The start date for the class period in each case would be the date six years prior to the commencement of each action. The class period should end on the date of certification rather than the date of judgment. There cannot be a constantly changing class composition as there would be no mechanism for newly-added members to opt out. There is no evidence that holds are placed on wire transfers or on transactions other than cheques and the words "wire transfer" and "or any other means" should be deleted from the definition.

[153] No party has provided an estimate of the size of the class in its affidavit materials. It is probable that it consists of millions of customers of each bank.

(c) Common Issues

[154] Section 5(1)(c) of the *C.P.A.* requires that "the claims or defences of the class members raise common issues". These are defined in s. 1 as "(a) common but not necessarily identical issues of fact, or (b) common but not necessarily identical issues of law that arise from common but not necessarily identical facts".

[155] Common issues are at the very heart of what a class action is intended to accomplish. It is through the resolution of the common issues that a class action achieves the goals of access to justice, judicial efficiency, and behavior modification. The analysis of the common issues should take a purposive approach, keeping those goals in mind.

[156] The underlying foundation of a common issue is whether its resolution will avoid duplication of fact-finding or legal analysis: *Western Canadian Shopping Centres Inc. v. Dutton*, [2001] 2 S.C.R. 534, [2000] S.C.J. No. 63, at para. 39.

[157] As Perell J. observed in *McCracken v. Canadian National Railway*, above, at para. 315:

> The focus of the analysis of whether there is a common issue is not on how many individual issues there might be but whether there are issues the resolution of which would be necessary to resolve each class member's claim and which could be said to be a substantial ingredient of those claims: *Cloud v. Canada (Attorney General)* (2004), 73 O.R. (3d) 401 (C.A.) at para. 55,

leave to appeal to the S.C.C. ref'd, [2005] S.C.C.A. No. 50, rev'g, (2003), 65 O.R. (3d) 492 (Div. Ct.).

[158] The principles applicable to the common issues analysis have been set out in many of the authorities. I summarized some of them in *Singer v. Schering-Plough Canada Inc.*, 2010 ONSC 42, [2010] O.J. No. 113 (S.C.J.) at para. 140; see also Perell J. in *McCracken v. Canadian National Railway*, above, at paras. 312–320.

[159] It has been repeatedly stated that the common issues criterion is a "low bar" and not a "high legal hurdle": see *Cloud v. Canada (Attorney General)*, above, at para. 52. That said, the plaintiff must adduce evidence to show "some basis in fact" for the existence of the common issues: *Dumoulin v. Ontario* (2005), 19 C.P.C. (6th) 234, [2005] O.J. No. 3961 (S.C.J.) at para. 25; *Fresco v. CIBC*, above, at para. 21; *Hollick* at paras. 16–26; *Lambert v. Guidant Corporation* (2009), 72 C.P.C. (6th) 120, [2009] O.J. No. 1910 (S.C.J.) at paras. 56–74; *Cloud v. Canada (Attorney General)*, above, at paras. 49 to 52; *Grant v. Canada (Attorney General)* (2009), 81 C.P.C. (6th) 68, [2009] O.J. No. 5232 (S.C.J.) at para. 21; *LeFrancois v. Guidant Corp.*, [2009] O.J. No. 2481 (S.C.J.) at paras. 13–14, leave to appeal to Div. Ct. refused [2009] O.J. No. 4129 (Div. Ct.); *Ring v. Canada (Attorney General)*, 2010 NLCA 20, [2010] N.J. No. 107 (Nfld. C.A.) at paras. 12–14.]

[160] The "some basis in fact" requirement is not an inquiry into the merits or a requirement that the plaintiff establish a *prima facie* case or a genuine issue for trial: *Glover v. Toronto (City)* (2009), 70 C.P.C. (6th) 303, [2009] O.J. No. 1523 (S.C.J.) at para. 15. It does require that there be some factual basis for the claims made by the plaintiff and to which the common issues relate. As Cullity J. noted in *Grant v. Canada (Attorney General)*, above, at para. 21:

> If that were the test, certification motions would indeed involve some assessment of the merits of the plaintiff's claims and they would be considerably more protracted. At least for the purposes of the inquiry into commonality, it appears that the evidence must show merely that there is some basis in reality for the assertion that the Class members have claims raising issues in common with the claims of the plaintiff.

[161] The evidence before the court must be examined to determine whether there is a basis for the existence of common issues in the claim asserted by the plaintiff. Some basis in fact must be found to

show that a common issue exists and that its resolution will move the claims of the class forward.

[162] These actions are theories in search of a basis in fact. There is no basis in reality for the existence of common issues. As I have noted earlier, the common issues proposed by the plaintiffs, set out in full in Appendix B, flow from a premise that is flawed and that has no basis in fact or law — namely, that the funds subject to the hold are "paid" to the collecting bank, in a final and unqualified sense, at some point before the end of the hold period (usually when the cheque "clears" within a day or two after deposit) and that the collecting bank wrongfully makes use of that "payment" for an unreasonable time before making the funds available to the customer. The premise is set out in the plaintiffs' factum, in which it is asserted that each of the defendants hold[s] funds "even after it has received the funds from the paying institution, thus enabling the Defendant to continue using the held funds for profit making activity".

[163] At the risk of repetition, the evidence establishes that this theory has no factual foundation. Although the accounts between banks are reconciled through the clearing, and the account of the drawer is generally debited (assuming funds are available and there is not some other impediment) within a short time after the clearing, the debiting of the drawer's account has nothing to do with "payment" to the bank of deposit. The "payment" to the collecting bank through the clearing is provisional only, because the cheque may be dishonoured. Until the cheque is physically returned to it by the drawee, the collecting bank has no way of knowing whether a particular cheque has been dishonoured. The hold is established to protect the collecting bank and its customer against this possibility — a possibility the banks are prepared to accept after the passage of the time provided for in their contracts.

[164] The uncontradicted evidence is that the interbank clearing and settlement process does not mean finality of the settlement or payment of any particular cheque. If a dishonoured cheque is returned through the clearing on a timely basis, the drawee bank will recover the amount of the cheque from the collecting bank as part of the settlement process, but the collecting bank will not know that has occurred until the cheque has been physically returned to it.

[165] The evidence is also clear that under normal circumstances, such as a domestic cheque being dishonoured and returned for insufficient funds, it may

take the cheque five or six days to return to the bank of deposit, depending on a variety of factors. It can take much longer in more unusual circumstances, such as fraud. In the meantime, the bank of deposit has no means of knowing whether a particular cheque has been "paid" and will be exposed to risk if the funds are released to its customer.

[166] Finally, the evidence is clear that a collecting bank cannot know whether a cheque will be dishonoured until it is in fact dishonoured, and that this can occur long after the settlement and clearing between banks.

[167] If one accepts the proposition that a bank has an obligation to credit funds to its customer's account within a reasonable time of "collection", the banks' hold terms represent a pre-defined bargain about what is reasonable: the banks agree to honour a domestic cheque subject to a hold within seven days, even though they have not received unconditional payment of the cheque in the meantime. The bargain is a reasonable one in light of (a) the banks' practice of giving credit for most cheques immediately on deposit; (b) the banks' payment of interest on held cheques; (c) the discretion exercised by the banks to depart from the hold periods in appropriate cases; (d) the options available to the customer; and (e) the protection afforded to banks by the clearing rules. There is no evidence whatsoever that the practice has been abused by the banks and, as I have noted, the hold periods are sanctioned by the federal regulator.

[168] The common issues are entirely predicated on a theory that has no foundation in fact. As such, their resolution could do nothing to advance the claims of the class.

[169] The common issues can be divided into two categories, issues dealing with liability and issues dealing with damages. Since the latter flow from the answers to the former, I will deal with the liability issues first.

[170] The first liability common issue is:

1. If the Defendant holds its depositor's funds past the point at which the funds have been paid, is that:
   (a) a breach of contract?
   (b) a breach of common law duty?
   (c) the tort of conversion?
   (d) a breach of fiduciary duty?

[171] There is no basis in the evidence for the assertion that the defendants hold their customers' funds past the point at which they have been "paid" because the "payment" through the clearing is provisional and subject to reversal if the cheque is returned dishonoured. There is no evidence that the hold periods ever exceeded the duration set out in the plaintiffs' account agreements or that the banks ever denied a request for access to funds within the hold periods. In fact, there is some evidence that access was given. I have found that the plaintiffs have no causes of action under the headings set forth above.

[172] The second common issue asks:

2. Under the terms of the Defendant's contract what is the time that the Defendant is required to release the funds to its depositors?

[173] This common issue would only advance the claims of class members if there were some basis to conclude that the relevant time could be something other than the maximum time set out in the plaintiffs' account agreements. As I have said, this could only be established through an implied term of "reasonable time" or, as the plaintiffs assert, "once the funds have been cleared" or "once the funds have been paid". Even if the plaintiffs could overcome the difficulty of establishing these implied terms, the existence of such a term would depend, in each case, on all the circumstances, including the nature of the relationship between the bank and its customer and the circumstances of the particular transaction: see *Nadolny v. Peel (Region)*, 78 C.P.C. (6th) 252, [2009] O.J. No. 4006, (S.C.J.) at para. 70; *Macleod v. Viacom Entertainment Canada Inc.* (2003), 28 C.P.C. (5th) 160, [2003] O.J. No. 331 (S.C.J.) at para. 24. This question could not be resolved on a common basis.

[174] The third common issue asks:

3. Is settlement on the books of the bank of Canada payment for purposes of the contract for cheques that clear in Canada?
   a. If not, what is the time of payment?
   b. What is the time of payment for cheques that do not use the Canadian clearing system such as:
      i. U.S. cheques?
      ii. "on Us" cheques?

[175] The plaintiffs say that the evidence of Mr. Harper on behalf of the banks discloses "that the Defendants hold cheques past the time that the funds settle on the books of the Bank of Canada and past the time that they receive the funds from the drawee institution". This is not an accurate state-

ment of the evidence. Mr. Harper's evidence is clear that settlement between banks is on a gross basis and is provisional. Settlement through the clearing is not "payment" of any particular cheque.

[176] This common issue is based on the same flawed premise as the first issue, namely that settlement between banks through the clearing is "payment". It is clear that it is not and that the clearing process has nothing to do with the contract between the bank and its customer. There is no reasonable basis on which reference to a cheque "clearing" in the contract between the bank and its customer could possibly refer to the clearing process.

[177] The alternative common issues set out in sub (a) and sub (b) of the third common issue asks "what is the time of payment"? Again, the hold period is necessary because there is no unconditional "payment" to the bank and the collecting bank will be liable to the drawee bank if the cheque is returned dishonoured.

[178] These common issues, therefore, are not capable of a meaningful answer that would advance the resolution of the claims of the class members.

[179] Proposed common issue 3(b)(ii) asks "what is the time of payment for 'on us' cheques["?] An "on us" cheque is one where the collecting bank and the drawee bank are the same — from the perspective of the collecting bank, the check is therefore "written on us". The evidence is that such cheques do not go through the clearing because the amount of the credit and debit will be the same for the institution — thus the Payments Association rules do not apply to such cheques. Nevertheless, "on us" cheques are covered by the *Bills of Exchange Act* and are subject to being dishonoured for any number of reasons. There is no specific pleading with respect to "on us" cheques, none of the representative transactions involved "on us" cheques and there is no evidentiary basis on which I could conclude that the claims of the class raise common issues with respect to "on us" cheques.

[180] The fifth common issue is whether the defendant was "unjustly enriched by its practices with regard to cheque holding". As I have found that there is no cause of action for unjust enrichment, the answer to this question would not advance the claims of the class.

[181] Similarly, common issues 4, 5(a) and 6(a), which ask how damages should be calculated, do not derive from any tenable cause of action and do not advance class claims.

The Issue of Aggregate Assessment of Damages

[182] Proposed common issues 7 and 8 ask:

7. Can the amount of damages be determined using statistics pursuant to section 23 of the *C.P.A.*?
8. Can the aggregate amounts of the Defendants['] liability be determined for purposes of section 24 of the *C.P.A.*?

[183] Section 23(1) of the *C.P.A.* provides:

> For the purposes of determining issues relating to the amount or distribution of a monetary award under this Act, the court may admit as evidence statistical information that would not otherwise be admissible as evidence, including information derived from sampling, if the information was compiled in accordance with principles that are generally accepted by experts in the field of statistics.

[184] Section 24 provides, in part:

> (1) The court may determine the aggregate or a part of a defendant's liability to class members and give judgment accordingly where,
> (a) monetary relief is claimed on behalf of some or all class members;
> (b) no questions of fact or law other than those relating to the assessment of monetary relief remain to be determined in order to establish the amount of the defendant's monetary liability; and
> (c) the aggregate or a part of the defendant's liability to some or all class members can reasonably be determined without proof by individual class members.
>
> (2) The court may order that all or a part of an award under subsection (1) be applied so that some or all individual class members share in the award on an average or proportional basis.
>
> (3) In deciding whether to make an order under subsection (2), the court shall consider whether it would be impractical or inefficient to identify the class members entitled to share in the award or to determine the exact shares that should be allocated to individual class members.

[185] These common issues are also relevant to the "preferable procedure" criterion for certification, which will be discussed under the next heading. The ability to determine damages on an aggregate basis, and to distribute them to the class without individual proof of damages, will invariably have a bearing on

the preferability of a class action to other types of relief.

[186] The plaintiffs have filed a report of Wise Blackman LLP in support of their assertion that sections 23 and 24 of the *C.P.A.* could be used to determine the aggregate amount of the defendants' liability.

[187] Wise Blackman was asked to give an opinion as to whether each class member suffered damages during the class period as a result of the banks holding deposits beyond the "clearing time" for the deposits, "during which time the defendants could earn profits on said funds ... such retention causing the Plaintiffs delays in access their funds and resulting in their incurring opportunity costs and/or lost opportunity."[11] They were also asked whether damages could be assessed on an aggregate basis and could be divided among class members applying statistical methods.

[188] Wise Blackman was asked to make certain assumptions, namely:

- the banks regularly held deposits belonging to class members;
- the hold period extended for a period of time beyond the point at which the banks "settled" the deposits;
- the retention of the deposits caused delays to the class members in accessing their funds, resulting in losses; and
- the "overhold" (referred to as a "period of time beyond the point at which the banks 'settled' deposits belonging to class members") was unlawful or was a breach of the contract with their customers.

[189] Based on these assumptions, it is hardly surprising that Wise Blackman came to the conclusion that:

> ... each of the Class Members suffered Damages during the Class Period as a result of the Challenged Conduct ... [defined as the alleged wrongful and unlawful holding of deposited funds beyond the clearing time during which the defendants earned profits on the funds].

and that:

> ... the Defendants have been unjustly enriched as a result of the Challenged Conduct.

[190] Although it claims to have made a "review and analysis" of information provided to it, nowhere in the report does Wise Blackman test the validity of its assumptions and nowhere does it bring its alleged expertise to bear on the subject of this opinion. It simply re-states, as a conclusion, the assumption it was asked to make. As such, its conclusion on this issue is meaningless.

[191] In coming to this conclusion, Wise Blackman applied, without question, the assumption that it is possible to identify a time at which the banks "settled" the deposits, whatever that term means. The term seems to be used as synonymous with other confusing and undefined terms in the report such as "the clearing time", "the date on which cash settlement was received", "the date on which the funds were obtained ... [by the bank] ... from the drawee's financial institution", the "date that the cheque cleared or was settled", and the "point in time at which the Defendants received payment". Nowhere in the report does Wise Blackman define what these terms mean. Nowhere does it express an opinion, as a professed expert, that these terms have any technical meaning in banking practice or, most important to its conclusions, that they are capable of being ascertained with any precision.

[192] Wise Blackman also concluded that the amount of damages could be assessed on an aggregate basis and that the damages could be allocated among class members on a statistical basis.

[193] The methodology proposed by Wise Blackman was to determine:

  (i) the aggregate amount of "held deposits" held by each bank for each month during the class period;
  (ii) the average number of days that deposits are held beyond the time when the court finds that the bank should have released the funds;
  (iii) by sampling a representative deposits, the date on which "cash settlement" was received from the drawee bank and the date on which the funds became accessible to the depositor; and
  (iv) interest earned by the plaintiffs on their deposits during the hold period as compared to money made by the banks from the held funds.

[194] This simple process would basically identify an average number of days of alleged "overholding" and would identify the difference between what the customers were paid in interest and what the banks earned from the use of the customers' money.

[195] Wise Blackman stated that in order to apply this methodology, it would need to have, among other data, information concerning the date on which

"cash settlement" was received from the drawee bank. This would be necessary to calculate the length of the overholding under the equation:

[length of hold] minus [days for cash settlement + court allowed time] = length of overhold

[196] As I noted above, nowhere does Wise Blackman state what the date of "cash settlement" is, whether it can be determined or how it can be determined. Nowhere in the report is there any evidence that Wise Blackman has expertise concerning the cheque clearing process or otherwise that would make it capable of making that determination. Since this is fundamental to its opinion that damages can be determined on an aggregate basis, this omission is startling.

[197] Wise Blackman's conclusion that each member of the class suffered damages as a result of the bank's hold practices was self-fulfilling because it also assumed that "the retention of deposits caused delays to the [class members] in accessing their funds, resulting in opportunity costs and/or economic losses". It came to this conclusion in spite of the following:

- there was no evidence that any of the representative plaintiffs was denied access to their funds or made a request for access that was not fulfilled;
- there was no evidence that any of the representative plaintiffs suffered damages as a result of the hold on their funds; and
- it is obvious that not every class member would want to use the held funds for more profitable endeavours — some might wish to leave them to earn interest, others might wish to withdraw them for consumption or entertainment.

[198] The Wise Blackman report is based on the same erroneous premise upon which this action is framed — that the banks receive unconditional payment of held funds at some ill-defined time before the funds are released to the customer. This shortcoming, and the failure of the expert to consider the validity of the premise, makes the report of no value.

(d) Preferable Procedure

[199] Section 5(1)(d) of the *C.P.A.* requires the court to determine whether a class proceeding would be the preferable procedure for the resolution of the common issues. Both parties rely on *Markson v. MBNA Canada Bank*, 2007 ONCA 334, 85 O.R. (3d) 321 at para. 69, leave to appeal to S.C.C. refused, [2007] S.C.C.A. No. 346, in which the Court of Appeal summarized the approach to the preferable procedure analysis:

> The preferability inquiry should be conducted through the lens of the three principal advantages of a class proceeding: judicial economy, access to justice and behaviour modification;
>
> "Preferable" is to be construed broadly and is meant to capture the two ideas of whether the class proceeding would be a fair, efficient and manageable method of advancing the claim and whether a class proceeding would be preferable to other procedures such as joinder, test cases, consolidation and any other means of resolving the dispute; and,
>
> The preferability determination must be made by looking at the common issues in context, meaning, the importance of the common issues must be taken into account in relation to the claims as a whole.

[200] The banks' submissions on this issue are largely based on propositions that I have accepted, to the effect that the hold provisions of their contracts are reasonable contractual stipulations for risk-management purposes. The banks say that there is no need for behaviour modification, since the banks have already voluntarily agreed to reduce their hold periods and will do so again once the technology has been advanced. They also say that judicial economy will not be advanced because the resolution of the common issues will not obviate the need for individual inquiries into the circumstances of each cheque, each account and each class member.

[201] In this case, if I had found tenable causes of action and an evidentiary basis for common issues of fact or law that would advance the claims of the class, then access to justice and judicial economy considerations would speak in favour of a class action being the preferable procedure, in view of the very large number of relatively small claims and the absence of any other realistic procedure for redress. In light of my conclusions, the issue is academic.

(e) Representative Plaintiffs

[202] Section 5(1)(e) of the *C.P.A.* requires that there be a representative plaintiff who would fairly and adequately represent the interest of the class, has produced a workable litigation plan and does not have a conflict with the interests of other class members.

[203] The defendants allege that the proposed plaintiffs would not fairly and adequately represent the class. Their main complaints are that:

(a) the plaintiffs' own evidence shows that they have no cause of action because they were given access to their funds within the hold periods set out in the account agreements;

(b) none of the plaintiffs ever made an unsatisfied demand for funds during the hold period;

(c) none of the plaintiffs has presented credible evidence that they actually sustained damages as a result of holds;

(d) the plaintiffs have failed to demonstrate that they can vigorously and capably prosecute the action and will bring informed and independent judgment to bear when instructing counsel; and

(e) the plaintiffs have close personal connections to class counsel and have made little effort to inform themselves of the issues.

[204] In connection with the last complaint, it would be naïve to think that representative plaintiffs are not frequently enlisted through the efforts of counsel. Few individuals are likely to contemplate commencing a class action without counsel taking the initiative to identify a large-scale wrong and to assess the prospect of providing access to justice to a large number of victims. "Recruitment" of the representative plaintiff, as such, should not be a disqualifier. What must be avoided, however, is the representative plaintiff simply being a "stickman", a "benchwarmer" or a "puppet", who relinquishes all responsibility to counsel. This is not "fair and adequate representation", which, in my view, requires some familiarity with the issues and active participation in the proceeding. The reasons for requiring an involved class representative have been identified in other decisions and I will not elaborate: see *Singer v. Schering-Plough Canada Inc.*, above, at para. 216 quoting Perell J. in *Fantl v. Transamerica Life Canada* (2008), 60 C.P.C. (6th) 326, [2008] O.J. No. 1536 (S.C.J.) at para. 63, aff'd (2008) 66 C.P.C. (6th) 203, [2008] O.J. No. 4928, aff'd (2009) 95 O.R. (3d) 767, [2009] O.J. No. 1826 (C.A.).

[205] There is certainly no reason, or evidence, to think that the plaintiffs have undertaken these proceedings as a result of a personal sense of dissatisfaction with the actions of the defendant banks. There is no evidence that they complained about the holds placed on their funds and, as the evidence discloses, they were all able to access as least part of their funds during the hold periods. There is no evidence that they suffered any damages as a result of the defendants' actions. Although there is no obligation on the plaintiffs to attend the certification motion, it is unfortunate that none of them, each of whom seeks to represent a class of millions of bank customers, had a sufficient sense of obligation, or even curiosity, to attend even a short part of the hearing.

[206] I am not aware of any case that has not been certified only for lack of an adequate representative plaintiff. Had I found that these proceedings were otherwise suitable for certification I would have considered whether further inquiries into the plaintiffs' suitability was required. In the circumstances, I do not propose to do so.

IV. CONCLUSION

[207] I have concluded that these actions cannot be certified. The plaintiffs have built a theory that has no basis in fact or law and have attempted to construct a class action around it. The theory is that:

(a) a cheque is "paid" at some point in the clearing system, either in the clearing between the banks or when the drawee bank debits its customer's account;

(b) the time of "payment" can be identified;

(c) a hold cannot be justified for more than a "reasonable time" after the cheque has been paid; and

(d) the judge at a common issues trial can determine what that time should be.

[208] Although expressed in more neutral terms, the common issues are premised on the validity of this theory.

[209] The problem with this theory is that it focuses on the clearing, and on the actions of the drawee bank, which have nothing to do with the relationship between the collecting bank and its customer.

[210] We do not live in the 18th century when cheques were physically presented by the collecting bank to the drawee bank in exchange for cash. Holds on cheques were not required in those days because payment or dishonour occurred on the same day. The modern hold process is necessary because the collecting bank only knows that it can safely assume that the cheque will be honoured when it has not been returned dishonoured through the clearing within the time permitted by the clearing rules. Even then, those rules only define the time within which the return must be initiated by the drawee — they do not define the time within which the collecting bank must be actually notified that the cheque will not be honoured. The evidence is clear that there is no specific date on which a bank can know definitively that a cheque will not be hon-

oured. As a practical matter, however, the banks are prepared to accept the risk, subject to their rights of indemnity, after the passage of the times set out in their account agreements. The plaintiffs agreed to those terms. The actions of the defendants, as pleaded, were consistent with those terms.

[211] For these reasons, the motion for certification is dismissed. Costs, if not resolved, may be addressed by written submissions.

(d) *Canada Trustco Mortgage Co. v. Canada*†

[DESCHAMPS J. (for herself, Binnie, Rothstein and Cromwell JJ.):]

[1] Few jurists thrive on exploring the mechanisms rooted in the *Bills of Exchange Act*, R.S.C. 1985, c. B-4 ("*BEA*"); most find them technical and tedious. Important as electronic transactions have become in an increasingly paperless world, cheques are still popular bills of exchange that are processed daily in a multitude of transactions across Canada based on recognized mechanisms. The arguments accepted by the courts below disregard those mechanisms. If accepted, their interpretation would require a bank to which a third party has made a demand for payment to determine not only whether its customer is liable to pay the third party, but also whether the payee is liable to do so. No reason was advanced for imposing such an obligation. For the following reasons, I am of the view that the bank in this case was at no point liable to pay the tax debtor the proceeds of the cheques. I would allow the appeal with costs throughout.

[2] Section 224 of the *Income Tax Act*, R.S.C. 1985, c. 1 (5th Supp.) ("*ITA*"), provides that the Minister of National Revenue may require a person who is, or will be within one year, liable to make a payment to a tax debtor to instead pay the money the person owes the tax debtor to the Receiver General ("requirement to pay"). The Minister's authority to issue a requirement to pay in appropriate circumstances is not in dispute. The issue in this appeal is whether a bank that receives a cheque payable to the tax debtor for deposit in an account held jointly by that debtor and a third party becomes liable to make a payment to the tax debtor.

[3] The facts are uncontested. At the relevant time, the appellant, Canada Trustco Mortgage Company ("Trustco"), was authorized to offer financial services in Canada. The parties have described Trustco as a bank, as has the Tax Court of Canada, and for the sake of convenience, I will also refer to it as a bank.

[4] Cameron Clyde McLeod was a practising member of the Law Society of British Columbia. For the purposes of his law practice, he maintained a trust account with Trustco at the latter's King George Highway branch in Surrey, B.C. In addition, he and another lawyer, Herbert Maier, held a joint account at the same branch. Each of the accounts was governed by an agreement.

[5] Mr. McLeod owed tax to the federal government. The Minister became aware that cheques payable to Mr. McLeod were being drawn on the trust account and deposited in the joint account. The Minister issued three requirements to pay to Trustco. According to these requirements, Trustco was to pay to the Receiver General moneys otherwise payable to Mr. McLeod. In response to the requirements to pay, Trustco disputed its liability on the ground that it was "not indebted to the [taxpayer] alone".

[6] Each of the cheques on which the claim is based was issued during the period of effectiveness of the requirements to pay, was drawn on the trust account, was payable to Mr. McLeod and was delivered to Trustco with an instruction to deposit the funds in the joint account. This instruction was given by writing "Dep to" and the account number on the back of the cheque. Although the evidence is silent as to the identity of the person or persons who delivered the cheques and gave the instructions to deposit

† 2011 SCC 36.

them, neither the authority to do so of the person or persons in question nor the legitimacy of Trustco's receipt of the cheques for deposit is at issue. Trustco credited the joint account, sent the cheques to a third party for collection, processing and settlement — the third party's stamp appears on the back of the cheque filed as a sample — and, on the following day, debited the trust account.

[7] The Minister assessed Trustco for the amounts of the cheques for failing to comply with the three requirements to pay. Trustco filed notices of objection. After they were rejected, it appealed to the Tax Court of Canada.

[8] I will pause here to underscore the various capacities in which the parties in this appeal interacted, capacities that must not be conflated. A bank's relationship with a customer is based on a contract made up of both implied and express terms; I will elaborate on this below. Where a cheque is involved, the parties' rights and obligations are also governed by the *BEA*. In most transactions involving cheques, a bank acts in only one capacity, that is, as either the drawee, the negotiating bank or the collecting bank, and the bank's customer acts as either the drawer or the holder of a cheque. In this case, Trustco acted at times as the collecting bank and at other times as the drawee. Mr. McLeod acted variously as the drawer (he was the holder of the trust account), as the payee of the cheques (the cheques were made out to him) and as one of the two holders of the joint account.

[9] It is also important to point out that the respondent, Her Majesty The Queen (hereinafter referred to as "Canada") made two significant concessions at trial (2008 TCC 482, [2009] 1 C.T.C. 2264, at para. 11):

(a) the requirements to pay do not apply to funds on deposit in the trust account, and Trustco accordingly had no obligation to remit funds on deposit in the trust account; and

(b) the requirements to pay do not apply to funds in the joint account, and Trustco accordingly had no obligation to remit funds on deposit in the joint account.

[10] Since Canada's position does not rest on funds being held in the trust account or in the joint account, the question becomes whether Trustco was liable to make payments to the tax debtor, Mr. McLeod, because of the fact that he was named as the payee of the cheques. To answer this question, Trustco's obligations must be examined in the two

capacities in which it acted, as mentioned above: (1) as the collecting bank and (2) as the drawee of the cheque.

[11] Little J. dismissed Trustco's appeal. He applied the test from *National Trust Co. v. Canada* (1998), 162 D.L.R. (4th) 704 (F.C.A.), to determine whether s. 224(1) of the *ITA* had been triggered. He asked whether Trustco was "liable" to make a payment and whether the amount would be "payable" to a tax debtor within a year. The need to "stop [the analysis] before considering that it was cheques that were presented to the bank" was pivotal to his reasoning (para. 20). He focussed on the "repayment" of the funds in the trust account (para. 12 (emphasis in original)).

[12] Little J. considered that the proceeds of the cheques were "payable" to Mr. McLeod because the debtor–creditor relationship between Trustco and Mr. McLeod required the former to repay the funds deposited in the trust account to the account holder on demand (para. 22). In his view, Trustco's liability arose when Mr. McLeod "presented the bank with the cheques" (para. 28). This led Little J. to conclude that he did not need to examine the fact that the moneys had actually been transferred from the trust account to the joint account (para. 30).

[13] In addition, although he acknowledged that the "writing [of] a cheque is not by itself a withdrawal", Little J. found that the situation was different once "the cheque is presented to the bank" (para. 31). He took into consideration the fact that Mr. McLeod was not only the payee but also the drawer and that as the drawer he was in a position to enforce the payment because of the debtor–creditor relationship that existed between Trustco and himself (*ibid.*). Little J. recognized — and he noted that Canada had conceded the point — that a bank is not liable to the payee of a cheque (para. 39). However, in his view, Trustco remained liable to pay the cheques to Mr. McLeod in his capacity as holder of the trust account. He accepted Canada's submission that Mr. McLeod was the bearer of the cheque (para. 41).

[14] The Federal Court of Appeal found that no "palpable or overriding error" had been made and unanimously upheld Little J.'s decision (2009 FCA 267, 2009 DTC 5171 (p. 6205), at para. 1).

[15] Trustco argues that the trial judge failed to differentiate between a demand for repayment of funds deposited in an account and the delivery of a cheque for deposit. In its view, it was liable only — as drawee — to pay funds out of the trust account upon

proper presentment for payment by the holder of the cheque. At no point was it liable to make a payment to Mr. McLeod, the tax debtor.

[16] Canada contends that there is no distinction between presentment of a cheque to the drawee for the payment of cash to Mr. McLeod and presentment of a cheque for deposit to the joint account. Its position is that when Mr. McLeod delivered the cheques to Trustco and instructed it to pay the amounts into the joint account, he acted as payee, creditor, drawer and depositor, but that his role as depositor is irrelevant.

[17] Canada's contention implies that Trustco became liable to make a payment to Mr. McLeod when it accepted the cheque for deposit. To determine whether Trustco is liable to make a payment to the Receiver General, it will be necessary to review the relevant legal relationships.

I.   ANALYSIS

[18] The analysis of a bank's relationship with its customers must begin with the seminal case of *Foley v. Hill* (1848), 2 H.L.C. 28, 9 E.R. 1002:

> The relation between a Banker and Customer, who pays money into the Bank, is the ordinary relation of debtor and creditor....
>
> ...
>
> ... I am now speaking of the common position of a banker, which consists of the common case of receiving money from his customer on condition of paying it back when asked for, or when drawn upon, or of receiving money from other parties, to the credit of the customer, upon like conditions to be drawn out by the customer, or, in common parlance, the money being repaid when asked for, because the party who receives the money has the use of it as his own, and in the using of which his trade consists, and but for which no banker could exist, especially a banker who pays interest. [pp. 1002 and 1008]

[19] Implicit in the debtor–creditor relationship is the bank's obligation to repay the funds deposited in the account when its customer demands payment. In the case at bar, Trustco is a party in two separate contractual relationships: the first is in connection with the trust account and the second with the joint account. Having conceded that it cannot attach funds in either of these accounts, Canada cannot rely merely on the debtor–creditor relationships that arose from the fact that funds were at some point in time held in them. Canada accordingly focusses on the fact that cheques were made to the order of Mr.

McLeod, the tax debtor, which narrows the issues and makes it necessary to review the obligations a bank must meet upon receipt of a cheque for deposit and upon presentment of a cheque drawn on it.

A.   Obligation of the Collecting Bank

[20] Counsel for Canada argues that the best way to view the receipt of the cheques for deposit is to break the transactions down into two steps: at the first, Mr. McLeod demanded to be paid as payee of the cheques and also demanded, as drawer, that the amounts be repaid out of funds owed to him in relation to the trust account; at the second, he instructed Trustco to deposit the funds into the joint account. In other words, notional payments were made to Mr. McLeod before the funds were deposited into the joint account.

[21] This approach disregards the instructions to deposit the funds into the joint account. The evidence shows that the cheques were initially received at the branch with instructions to deposit the funds into the joint account, not that Mr. McLeod, as drawer, demanded that payments be made to him as payee. The evidence is also clear that the cheques were credited to the joint account before being sent for clearing and before the funds were debited from the trust account. At no point did Trustco actually make a payment to Mr. McLeod.

[22] The argument of counsel for Canada also disregards the nature of the instrument used by the parties: a cheque. A cheque is an instrument that embodies both common law and statutory concepts. This means that both the statute governing the instrument — the *BEA* — and the common law must be taken into consideration.

[23] The argument accepted by the Tax Court judge that Mr. McLeod was the bearer of the cheque (para. 41) is inconsistent with the definition of the term "bearer" in the *BEA*, according to which a bearer is a specific type of holder, namely "the person in possession of a bill or note that is payable to bearer" (s. 2 *BEA*). To be payable to bearer, a cheque must be expressed to be so payable, or the only or last endorsement on it must be an endorsement in blank (s. 20(3) *BEA*). In this case, the cheques were neither expressed to be payable to bearer nor endorsed in blank. After the cheques had been delivered for deposit into the joint account, Mr. McLeod was no longer in possession of them, was not entitled to them and was therefore not their holder.

[24] More importantly, Canada's approach and the Tax Court judge's interpretation disregard the capacity in which Trustco acted. The receipt by a bank of a cheque for deposit carries with it obligations grounded both in the common law and in the banking agreement. Professor Ogilvie describes the bank's legal position in such a situation as follows:

> When a customer, the payee of a cheque, deposits a cheque or other instrument in an account with the customer's bank, that bank takes on the role of collecting bank, which involves presenting the cheque for payment through the clearing system to the paying bank, that is, the bank of the drawer of the cheque from whose account at the paying bank it is expected that the cheque will be paid.
>
> (M. H. Ogilvie, *Bank and Customer Law in Canada* (2007), at p. 288)

Whereas it was in *Foley v. Hill* that the House of Lords made clear that the bank is under an implied contractual duty to honour cheques drawn by its customers, it was in *Joachimson v. Swiss Bank Corp.*, [1921] 3 K.B. 110, that the duty to collect the proceeds of a cheque was characterized as one of the common law incidents of the banking contract: "The bank undertakes to receive money and to collect bills for its customer's account" (p. 127). (See also Ogilvie, at p. 288.) Professor Goode adds that when the customer is silent about what is expected from the bank, the bank may be presumed to act as a collecting bank: R. M. Goode, "When is a cheque paid?", [1983] *J. Bus. L.* 164, at p. 164.

[25] For the collecting bank's duty to its customer to be triggered, there must be a properly payable cheque and no suspicious circumstances. In undertaking to collect a deposited cheque, the collecting bank must select the collection method with reasonable care, promptly present the deposited cheque for collection, receive payment for it and credit the customer's account or, if applicable, give notice of dishonour (B. Crawford, *The Law of Banking and Payment in Canada* (loose-leaf), vol. 2, at pp. 10-43, 10-46 and 10-51; E. P. Ellinger, E. Lomnicka and R. Hooley, *Modern Banking Law* (3rd ed. 2002), at p. 598).

[26] The situation of a bank that credits its customer's account before actually receiving the proceeds of collection raises, in Crawford's words (p. 24-6), an "interesting conceptual problem". However, as he correctly points out, this interesting question is of no practical importance in Canada. Section 165(3) of the *BEA* provides that a bank which receives a cheque for deposit acquires all the rights and powers of a holder in due course (Crawford, at p. 10-78; J. S. Ziegel, B. Geva and R. C. C. Cuming, *Commercial and Consumer Transactions: Cases, Text and Materials* (3rd ed. 1995), vol. II, at pp. 362–63).

[27] In the case at bar, Trustco was put in possession of the cheques by the payee, Mr. McLeod, or by someone acting on his behalf, with instructions to deposit them. Not only was Mr. McLeod one of the holders of the joint account, but Trustco's contract with the account's holders authorized it to accept cheques from persons who provided the account number. It has not been suggested that the instructions to deposit the cheques were not actually given or that there was any doubt that the payee or his agent had the authority to give them. Since Trustco was in lawful possession of the cheques, it can safely be concluded that, once it had received the cheques for deposit and credited them to the joint account, it acquired the rights of a holder in due course pursuant to s. 165(3) of the *BEA* and was under a contractual obligation to the holders of the joint account to present the cheques for payment.

[28] With some exceptions that do not apply in this case, presentment is a precondition for payment (s. 84(1) *BEA*). Presentment must be made by a holder (s. 84(3) *BEA*), and payment must be made to a holder (s. 138(2) *BEA*). This mechanism rests not on formalism, but on the internal logic of the *BEA* and on the contractual relationship of a bank with its account holders. The manner in which cheques deposited into bank accounts are processed is grounded in the premise that banks deal primarily with persons who hold accounts with them and in the implicit contractual undertaking of banks to collect the proceeds of cheques deposited in their customers' accounts. In this case, Trustco collected the cheques on behalf of Mr. McLeod and Mr. Maier jointly, not of Mr. McLeod alone. As the Chief Justice acknowledges, there are good reasons not to confound the holders of a joint account with a single one of its holders: M. H. Ogilvie, "Why Joint Accounts Should Not Be Garnished — *Westcoast Commodities Inc. v. Jose Chow Chen*" (1986–1987), 1 *B.F.L.R.* 267. This means that in the instant case, the payee, Mr. McLeod, cannot be confused with the holders of the joint account even though he is one of them.

[29] In addition to the contract clause authorizing Trustco to accept deposits to the joint account from any person who could provide the account number, there was a clause to the effect that the amount of any instrument previously cashed, negotiated or cred-

ited by Trustco and returned unpaid or unsettled could be debited from the joint account. These clauses are relevant to a situation in which a bank receives a cheque, credits an account and then presents the cheque for payment. If the cheque is returned unpaid, the collecting bank may debit its customer's account. The clauses in question do not support an inference that the receipt of a cheque for deposit in the joint account would on its own suffice for Trustco to become liable to make a payment to Mr. McLeod.

[30] In discharging its duties as the collecting bank, Trustco had to be alert to suspicious circumstances. However, the fact that cheques are drawn on a trust account is not material to the collecting bank's duties. As Garon T.C.C.J. pointed out in *Bank of Montreal v. M.N.R.*, [1992] 1 C.T.C. 2292, it is generally not incumbent on a bank to police a trust account (p. 2295). In crediting the joint account, sending the cheques to a third party for clearing, and receiving the proceeds, Trustco was acting on the basis of its contractual relationship with the holders of the joint account and not on behalf of Mr. McLeod personally. When Trustco debited the trust account the next day, it was not making a payment to Mr. McLeod or to an agent acting for him alone.

[31] The Chief Justice expresses the opinion that Trustco never became the holder of the cheques. With respect, the fact that the cheques were not endorsed does not mean that Trustco did not acquire the rights of a holder in due course which results from having received valid cheques in good faith. Section 165(3) of the *BEA* was in fact adopted to avoid the argument that a bank that receives for deposit a cheque bearing a restrictive endorsement or no endorsement at all is not a holder — its purpose was not to protect against fraudulent endorsements (see s. 67(2) *BEA*; *Boma Manufacturing Ltd. v. Canadian Imperial Bank of Commerce*, [1996] 3 S.C.R. 727, at paras. 76–81; *J.C. Creations Ltd. v. Vancouver City Savings Credit Union*, 2004 BCCA 107, 236 D.L.R. (4th) 602; *Westboro Flooring & Décor Inc. v. Bank of Nova Scotia* (2004), 241 D.L.R. (4th) 257 (Ont. C.A.)). However, the fact that Trustco had acquired the rights and powers of a holder in due course of the cheques — as uncontroversial as it may be — is not the reason why Trustco was not liable to pay moneys to the tax debtor, Mr. McLeod. The reason Trustco owed no money to Mr. McLeod is that it was acting as the collecting bank for its customers, the holders of the joint account. It

did not collect the proceeds of the cheques as agent for the payee, Mr. McLeod.

[32] The Chief Justice relies on *B.M.P. Global Distribution Inc. v. Bank of Nova Scotia*, 2009 SCC 15, [2009] 1 S.C.R. 504, in support of the proposition that, in the case at bar, Trustco, as the collecting bank, acted as agent for the payee. *B.M.P.* concerned a payment made under a mistake of fact. In it I wrote, in discussing the equitable defence of change of position (para. 63) and the consequences on tracing of the passage of a cheque through the clearing system (paras. 76 and 83), that the Bank of Nova Scotia, as the collecting bank, had received the funds as agent for the payee, B.M.P. In that case, because the payee had instructed its bank to deposit the cheque into its own account, the distinction in the instant case between the payee and the account holder on whose behalf the cheque is collected did not arise. The payee and the account holder were the same person, B.M.P. Since the contractual duty to collect the proceeds of a cheque is owed to the customer in whose account the cheque is deposited, it would have been more precise to say that the collecting bank acts as agent for the person in whose account the cheque has been deposited. This choice of words in a case dealing with mistake of fact and tracing cannot serve as a basis for holding that a collecting bank has a contractual relationship with someone other than the holder of the account to which the cheque is credited.

[33] In the case at bar, the only instructions received were to deposit the cheques to the credit of the joint account, and it is these instructions that triggered the duty to collect the proceeds of the cheques. The contract that incorporates the implied term imposing on the bank the duty to proceed to collect on the cheque is the one between Trustco and the holders of the joint account. There is no contract between a bank and a payee in his or her capacity as payee.

[34] This approach is not formalistic. No significance is attached to the fact that the cheques were processed through the clearing system. Trustco's acceptance of the cheques for deposit in the joint account could not have resulted in a liability to pay the Receiver General: the obligation resulting from that acceptance was to the holders of the joint account, and Canada concedes that the funds in the joint account could not be attached.

[35] Canada nonetheless contends that the focus should be on the fact that Mr. McLeod was acting in this case in his capacity as payee and as a creditor

of Trustco by virtue of his status as holder of the trust account, and that he was demanding payment from Trustco in its capacity as drawee. Since the Chief Justice accepts this argument, I will now explain why it must fail.

B. Obligation of a Drawee

[36] *Schroeder v. Central Bank of London* (1876), 34 L.T. 735 (C.P. Div.), is important to an understanding of the nature of the obligations of a drawee bank to the payee. In it, the payee contended that the cheque constituted an absolute assignment of the funds in his hands and that he was therefore entitled to receive payment from the drawee bank. The drawee bank countered that a bank on which a cheque is drawn is under no liability to pay the holder of the cheque. The court agreed with the bank (at p. 737):

> A cheque is a request to pay and nothing more; it does not purport to be an assignment, and it is impossible, therefore, to regard it as an assignment of so much money. The bankers hold their customer's money on an implied contract to pay his cheques up to the amount of his balance in their hands, for breach of which they would be liable in damages to the drawer. But there is no contract by the bankers with the payees of the cheque, and they can have no remedy against the bank unless by the statute.

[37] This approach is consistent with the reasoning in *Foley v. Hill*. A banker's obligation arises out of the debtor–creditor relationship created when a bank account is opened. The payee is not a party to this contractual relationship, and the mere fact of being a payee does not entail such a relationship with the drawee.

[38] For the purpose of determining whether, absent any contractual relationship with the payee of a cheque, a drawee bank owes the payee any duty, the definition of a cheque in the *BEA* is relevant: "A cheque is a bill drawn on a bank, payable on demand" (s. 165(1)). A bill is defined as follows (s. 16(1) *BEA*):

> **16.**(1) A bill of exchange is an unconditional order in writing, addressed by one person to another, signed by the person giving it, requiring the person to whom it is addressed to pay, on demand or at a fixed or determinable future time, a sum certain in money to or to the order of a specified person or to bearer.

[39] In addition, the *BEA* explicitly states that the mere issuance of a cheque does not operate as an assignment of funds in the hands of the drawee (s. 126 *BEA*):

> **126.** A bill, of itself, does not operate as an assignment of funds in the hands of the drawee available for the payment thereof, and the drawee of a bill who does not accept as required by this Act is not liable on the instrument.

[40] These provisions, read together, mirror the principles stated in *Schroeder* and incorporate them into the statute. A cheque operates neither as an assignment of funds in the hands of the payee nor as an assignment of funds in the hands of the drawee. It is a document by means of which a customer orders his or her banker to pay funds the banker owes the customer to a person or to the order of that person out of the account specified on it. In and of itself, a cheque imposes no obligation on a drawee bank to the payee. This interpretation is well entrenched in our law and was accepted by Canada at trial: *Schroeder*; *Thomson v. Merchants Bank of Canada* (1919), 58 S.C.R. 287, at p. 298; *Schimnowski Estate, Re*, [1996] 6 W.W.R. 194 (Man. C.A.), at para. 19.

[41] The statutory duty of a bank to pay a cheque is governed by the rules applicable to presentment. With some exceptions, as I mentioned above, presentment is mandatory (s. 84(1) *BEA*). The general rule for presentment of a cheque is as follows (s. 86(1) *BEA*):

> **86.**(1) Presentment of a bill must be made by the holder or by a person authorized to receive payment on his behalf, at the proper place as defined in section 87, and either to the person designated by the bill as payer or to his representative or a person authorized to pay or to refuse payment on his behalf, if with the exercise of reasonable diligence such person can there be found.

A bank may incur other liabilities in circumstances which do not arise in the case at bar, upon acceptance within the meaning of s. 34 of the *BEA*, for example. That is not the case here. At the time of presentment, Mr. McLeod was no longer a holder. Only Trustco had the rights and powers of a holder in due course.

[42] *Bank of Montreal* illustrates clearly that the duty to honour the customer's cheque is triggered only at the time the holder presents the cheque to the drawee for payment. In that case, requirements to pay had been issued to the Bank of Montreal in relation to tax owed by a customer of the bank who held a trust account there. The tax debtor drew

cheques payable to himself on the trust account and endorsed them in blank. The cheques were subsequently endorsed by his wife and presented to the Bank of Montreal for payment. Garon T.C.C.J. found, correctly in my view, that

> [i]n the present case the moneys payable by virtue of the two cheques in issue were not payable to the tax debtor, since at the time of presentment of the cheques to the bank, after the endorsement by Mrs. Lynn Morgan, Mr. Morgan was no longer the bearer of these cheques. He was not at that point in time entitled to receive the proceeds of the cheques. [p. 2294]

[43] This Court applied the same rule in *Capital Associates Ltd. v. Royal Bank of Canada* (1976), 65 D.L.R. (3d) 384, aff'g (1973), 36 D.L.R. (3d) 579 (Que. C.A.). In that case, Capital Associates Ltd. deposited a cheque in its account at the Royal Bank. The cheque was drawn by All-Canadian Group Distributors Ltd. on an account at the same branch of the Royal Bank. After the cheque had been deposited, All-Canadian ordered the bank to stop payment on it. All-Canadian's account had not yet been debited at the time of the stop payment order. The Royal Bank refused payment. In the Court of Appeal, Rivard J.A., with whose reasons this Court agreed, adopted the view that the facts in that case should be distinguished from those of a case in which the bank pays in cash or certifies a cheque. He explained the process as follows (at pp. 583–84):

> [TRANSLATION] I do not accept the proposition submitted by the appellant that in depositing the cheque with the Royal Bank, it was presenting it for payment.
>
> Capital, in depositing the cheque, did not demand payment, but gave authority to the bank to present the cheque for payment to All-Canadian. All-Canadian refused to pay, and the bank cannot be responsible to Capital.

[44] *Capital Associates* illustrates not only the distinction between delivery of a cheque for deposit and presentment for payment, but also the rationale for the rules that a bank to which a payee delivers a cheque owes no duty to that person as payee and that it is only when the cheque is presented to the bank in its capacity as drawee that it is requested to disburse the funds. Between the time the cheque is issued and the time it is presented for payment, many intervening circumstances are possible: for example, payment could be stopped as in *Capital Associates*, the cheque could be negotiated to a third party, an excessive delay could occur, or the drawer could become insolvent or incapacitated. In general,

a bank does not assume any risks that may be incurred between the time it receives the cheque for deposit and the time it presents the cheque to the drawee for payment. The funds used by the drawee bank to pay the cheque are funds of the drawer. It is the drawer who transfers funds using the cheque mechanism. As is stated in the *BEA*, it is the drawer who promises that upon presentment, payment will be made (s. 129 *BEA*):

> **129.** The drawer of a bill by drawing it
> (*a*) engages that on <u>due presentment</u> it shall be accepted and paid according to its tenor, and that if it is dishonoured he will compensate the holder or any endorser who is compelled to pay it, if the requisite proceedings on dishonour are duly taken; ...

[45] It is clear from the rules applicable to presentment that the drawee bank's obligation — to make payment to the holder of the cheque — is to the drawer only and that this obligation is triggered only when the cheque is presented to it. It is also clear that, except as provided in the *BEA*, the drawee is obliged, as between itself and the drawer, to disburse the funds only upon presentment of the bill by the holder — the person who is entitled to receive them — or by the holder's agent.

[46] In addition, it is clear from the above discussion that, viewed either from the angle of Mr. McLeod being the payee or from that of Trustco being the drawee, the mere fact that cheques payable to Mr. McLeod were delivered to Trustco for deposit did not make the latter liable to make a payment to the former within the meaning of s. 224(1) of the *ITA*.

[47] In her reasons in this case, the Chief Justice relies on a comment by Prof. Ogilvie in support of the proposition that there may be a contract between the payee and the drawee bank (*Bank and Customer Law in Canada*, at pp. 288–91). With respect, I do not read Prof. Ogilvie's comment as supporting this broad proposition. Rather, it is in explaining the different recourses available to a bank's customer in respect of a delayed payment in a scenario in which a cheque has been deposited in the payee's account and the accounts of both the payee and the drawer are at the same bank that she states that the payee can bring an action in breach of contract against the bank — in her example, the bank would have breached its duty to its client to present the cheque within a reasonable time. It should be noted that, in such circumstances, the bank that causes the delay happens to be the collecting bank — a party to the contract with the holder of the account in which the

cheque is deposited. It cannot, in my view, be inferred from Prof. Ogilvie's comment that there is a contractual obligation to pay the amount of a cheque to the payee merely because the payee and the drawer are customers of the same bank. If a bank has a contractual duty to a customer, it flows from the fact that the customer has either given the bank instructions as the drawer of the cheque and holder of the account from which the cheque is to be paid, or instructed the bank to collect the cheque as the holder of the account in which the cheque is deposited. I would add that the situation is different where, as in the case at bar, the payee is not the sole holder of the account in which the cheque is deposited.

[48] In this case, Mr. McLeod's rights as the holder of an account with the bank do not inform or affect his rights as payee of the cheques. If we assume for the sake of argument that the requirements to pay did not exist and that Canada did not make the concessions it has made, Trustco would, had Mr. McLeod presented the cheques at his branch for immediate payment to himself (i.e. cashed them), have been in breach of its contractual obligations to Mr. McLeod as the holder of the trust account had it failed to pay. In any event, this is not what happened. Not only were the cheques deposited, anonymously, to the credit of a joint account, but they had to go through the clearance system first before being presented for payment. *Capital Associates* makes it clear that presentment for payment and deposit are not synonymous. This distinction is critical to the disposition of this case.

[49] The fact that Trustco received the cheques both for deposit and for payment as drawee — although not simultaneously — has complicated the resolution of the dispute. The English case of *Boyd v. Emmerson* (1834), 2 Ad. & E. 184, 111 E.R. 71, is one that involved facts similar to those of the instant case. In *Boyd*, the plaintiff had told the cashier of a bank to place a cheque to his credit. The same bank was the drawee. It refused to honour the cheque, because the drawer did not have sufficient funds. Lord Denman C.J. held that the bank was within its right to refuse the payment, because it had taken the cheque for collection. The bank had followed its customer's instruction to credit the cheque to his account. As a result, the credit was subject to the contingency of there being sufficient funds in the drawer's account.

[50] *Boyd*, *Bank of Montreal* and *Capital Associates* are relevant to the case at bar. The fact that the

cheques were drawn on and deposited with Trustco did not alter Trustco's legal position. It did not receive the cheques as drawee, and the instructions to deposit the funds made it a collecting bank. In that capacity, it was not liable to pay any funds to Mr. McLeod.

II. CONCLUSION

[51] The fact that a person is designated as payee on the face of a cheque does not on its own mean that the bank is liable to make a payment to the person. First, a drawee is answerable to the drawer. Second, the question is to whom the drawee may make the payment. What is on the back of the cheque — the instructions or the endorsement — is crucial to this question. In this case, the instructions were to deposit the cheques into the joint account. There were no instructions that made the moneys payable to Mr. McLeod, the tax debtor.

[52] Canada cannot say that the joint account is out of reach while at the same time treating the holders of that account as one and the same person, namely Mr. McLeod. As Canada takes the position that it could attach neither of the accounts, Trustco's liability to pay moneys to Mr. McLeod personally cannot be confused with its liability to pay moneys to the holders of the joint account. Canada had to show either that Trustco was liable to pay Mr. McLeod as payee, which, as I have demonstrated above, it cannot do, or that it had the right to attach the funds deposited into the joint account, which Canada has conceded it cannot do.

[53] A bank's liability to pay can arise only under a statute, at common law or under a contract. In this case, Canada can rely on none of these sources. This outcome is perfectly consistent with Canada's concessions that it cannot attach funds in either the trust account or the joint account, and with the fact that the funds were credited by Trustco to the joint account, not paid to Mr. McLeod.

[54] To accept Canada's position would mean that the presentment for payment was made by the payee to the drawee before the cheques were deposited. That is not what happened in this case. To accept that Trustco became liable to pay Mr. McLeod would also mean that a drawee bank which honours a cheque makes payment to the payee without determining who the holder of the cheque is. Canada's position is inconsistent with the fact that a bank that accepts a cheque for deposit does not in so doing act in the capacity of a drawee even if it also hap-

pens to be the drawee. Canada's interpretation would also mean that whenever demands are made by third parties, banks would have to determine whether payees — who, when cheques are negotiated, are often not even their customers — are liable to make payments. No such requirement exists at common law or is provided for in the *BEA*.

[55] For these reasons, I would allow the appeal, set aside the decisions of the Federal Court of Appeal and the Tax Court of Canada and vacate the assessments with costs throughout.

[McLachlin C.J. (for herself and Fish and Abella JJ., dissenting):]

[56] Having read the reasons of Deschamps J., I am respectfully of the view that the appeal should be dismissed.

[57] While I agree with much of Deschamps J.'s analysis, there are two narrow points that divide us, and that lead us to a different result in this case. First, according to Deschamps J., when a customer delivers a cheque to his or her bank with instructions to deposit the funds into his or her account, the bank becomes the holder of the cheque, and therefore any funds collected from the cheque are paid to the bank itself. In my view, the bank does not become the holder of a cheque, but rather collects the funds as agent for its principal: *B.M.P. Global Distribution Inc. v. Bank of Nova Scotia*, 2009 SCC 15, [2009] 1 S.C.R. 504, at para. 83.

[58] Second, Deschamps J. relies on the alternative argument that where funds are deposited into a joint account, as they were here, the funds are payable to both account holders, rather than just payable to the payee of the cheque. I do not agree. In my view, a "bank receives the funds as the payee's agent" (*B.M.P.*, at para. 83 (emphasis added)), and while they are in transit the funds are only payable to the payee. I develop these points below.

[59] In this appeal, Canada Trustco Mortgage Company (the "Bank") concedes that the only live question is whether it was liable to make a payment to the tax debtor ("Mr. McLeod") as a result of the cheques he wrote to himself. If it was, the Bank's obligation to pay the Receiver General was triggered, and the Bank would be liable for failure to remit the funds pursuant to the requirement to pay.

[60] It is central to the analysis that follows that we are dealing exclusively with the circumstances in which a tax debtor draws a cheque in favour of himself or herself, and not a third party. It is also important to bear in mind that, in this case, the drawee bank is the same as the collecting bank.

[61] I will first briefly review the applicable legal principles. I will then go on to explain the application of s. 224(1) of the *Income Tax Act*, R.S.C. 1985, c. 1 (5th Supp.) ("*ITA*"), to the facts before us.

I.   THE LAW

A.   The Operation of Section 224(1) of the *Income Tax Act*

[62] The operation of s. 224(1) of the *ITA* informs the subsequent analysis, and it is necessary to understand how it works before proceeding. The requirement to pay provision may be restated for present purposes as follows:

> **224.**(1) Where ... a person is ... liable to make a payment to another person ... (... the "tax debtor"), the Minister may ... require the person to pay ... the moneys otherwise payable to the tax debtor ... to the Receiver General on account of the tax debtor's liability ....

[63] There is no special, technical definition ascribed to the precondition that the person served with the requirement to pay be "liable" to the tax debtor. As stated in *National Trust Co. v. Canada* (1998), 162 D.L.R. (4th) 704 (F.C.A.), at paras. 46–47:

> The ordinary meaning of the word "liable" in a legal context is to denote the fact that a person is responsible at law. Hence, I am in respectful agreement with McLachlin J. (as she then was) when she stated in *Discovery Trust Company v. Abbott*, a case in which a section 224(1) requirement was served upon a trustee, that:
>
> > ... the demand on third parties [a subsection 224(1) requirement] by which the Crown's claim is made in this case is not confined to a debtor–creditor relationship, as is a garnishee order; it is stated to extend to *any case* where the trustee is "liable to make a payment to the taxpayer". [Emphasis added.]
>
> It is my respectful view, therefore, that the Tax Court Judge was wrong in law to limit the phrase "liable to make a payment" only to situations where a debtor–creditor relationship exists. In so doing, he precluded himself from asking the only relevant question when one is confronted with construction of the subsection. It is this: did the respondent have a responsibility at law to make a payment to the tax debtor on 1 February 1994? [Text in brackets in original.]

[64] Nor is there a particular construction for the prerequisite that the funds be "payable" to the tax debtor. Again, *National Trust Co.* holds, at paras. 61–62:

> I turn now to consider the issue whether the proceeds were "payable" within the meaning of subsection 224(1). In my view this issue is governed by *DeConinck*, *supra*, and the decision of this Court in *Canada v. Yannelis* where Stone J.A., for the Court, said at 636:
>
> > The word "payable" is not a term of art. Nor is it defined in the regulations. I do not see that it was used in any special sense. In my view, therefore, it should be interpreted in the light of ordinary dictionary definitions ...
>
> And 638:
>
> > I have come to the conclusion that the word "payable" in s. 58(8)(*b*)(i) [of the *Unemployment Insurance Act*] refers to the point in time when vacation pay is due to a claimant in the sense that he is entitled by his contract of employment or by the general law to have it paid to him and his employer is under an obligation to pay it. In other words, it is payable when a claimant is in a position at law to enforce payment. [Text in brackets in original.]

[65] I take from the authorities that the person or institution served by the Minister with a requirement to pay must have a responsibility at law to make a payment to the tax debtor. The scope of the operation of s. 224(1) is not narrowly confined, but exists wherever the tax debtor is in a position at law to enforce payment from the party served with the requirement to pay. To adopt a more restrictive view of its content would be to undermine the proper functioning of the power the provision grants the Minister.

[66] With this understanding of the governing provision in mind, I turn now to the nature of the legal relationship between the bank and its customer and how it plays out within the parameters of s. 224(1).

B. The Nature of the Legal Relationship Between Bank and Customer

[67] The relationship between a bank and its customer is one of creditor and debtor, where the bank is the debtor: *Foley v. Hill* (1848), 2 H.L.C. 28, 9 E.R. 1002. The duty of repayment is triggered when the customer makes a demand for payment from the bank. A demand for repayment may be made for payment in cash or by cheque.

[68] Ordinarily, the bank on which a cheque is drawn (the drawee bank) is under no liability to pay the payee of a cheque; its legal obligations are owed exclusively to its customer (the drawer): *Schroeder v. Central Bank of London* (1876), 34 L.T. 735 (C.P. Div.); *Thomson v. Merchants Bank of Canada* (1919), 58 S.C.R. 287, at p. 298; *Schimnowski Estate, Re*, [1996] 6 W.W.R. 194 (Man. C.A.), at para. 19. This principle is confirmed by ss. 16(1) and 126 of the *Bills of Exchange Act*, R.S.C. 1985, c. B-4 ("*BEA*"). The legal relationship between the drawer and the drawee bank arises from the banking contract between them; if the payee is not a party to this contract, it is not in privity with the bank.

[69] However, where the payee and the drawer are the same person, i.e. when an individual writes a cheque to him- or herself, the bank is liable to the payee once the cheque is presented. This is so because the bank has a duty to repay its customer the funds on deposit when the customer makes a demand: *Foley*. When a customer writes a cheque to him- or herself, seeking to draw on the funds on deposit at the bank, the bank is under a contractual duty to pay the cheque once it is presented and once it has ensured that it is properly payable.

[70] The authorities also suggest that the drawee bank is liable to the payee if the payee is also a customer at the same bank. In such cases, there is a contract between the payee and the drawee bank. As stated by M. H. Ogilvie, "[w]here the drawer and payee are customers of the same bank, the payee can sue directly in breach of contract, as well for a delay in collection" (*Bank and Customer Law in Canada* (2007), at p. 291).

C. Is a Deposited Cheque Payable to the Payee/Customer or to the Bank?

[71] According to the Bank, once the cheques were deposited, they were no longer "payable" to Mr. McLeod, but "were now payable to the Bank pursuant to subsection 165(3) of the *Bills of Exchange Act*" (Factum, at para. 51). The Bank argues that once a cheque is delivered to a bank for collection, the bank becomes the holder of the cheque, and any payment made on the cheque is made to the bank alone. Consequently, s. 224(1) of the *ITA* cannot be triggered, because the Bank is never liable to make a payment to the payee (Mr. McLeod), but only to

itself as intermediary. The reasons of Deschamps J. accept this proposition. With respect, I cannot.

[72] In my view, the appellant misstates the relationship between a bank and its customer who deposits a cheque. First, a bank that collects the funds from a deposited cheque receives the funds as agent for the customer (the payee): *B.M.P.*; see also *Westminster Bank Ltd. v. Hilton* (1926), 43 T.L.R. 124 (H.L.), at p. 126. This involves two transactions. The funds are initially "credit[ed] ... to its principal", the payee/customer: *B.M.P.*, at para. 77, *per* Deschamps J. The bank then "receive[s] them back under the banking contract" (*ibid.*). The fact that these transactions follow one on the other does not change the conclusion that, legally, they are two distinct episodes. As such, a deposited cheque is payable to the customer when it is deposited; at no time is the cheque payable to the bank.

[73] In *B.M.P.* (at para. 83), this Court argued against employing a formalistic analysis to describe transactions through the clearing system, stating that

> the clearing system should be a neutral factor .... I prefer to assess the traceability of the asset after the clearing process and not see that process as a systematic break in the chain of possession of the funds. Just as the collecting bank receives the funds as the payee's agent, the clearing system is only a payment process. [Emphasis added.]

Where a customer draws a cheque in favour of him- or herself and deposits that cheque into another account, we should attach no significance to the fact that the moneys pass through a clearing process and the fact that a bank handles the funds as agent for its customer.

[74] Second, s. 165(3) of the *BEA* does not establish that the bank *becomes* a holder of the cheque. Rather, that provision establishes:

> **165.** ...
>
> (3) Where a cheque is delivered to a bank for deposit to the credit of a person and the bank credits him with the amount of the cheque, the bank acquires all the rights and powers of a holder in due course of the cheque.

[75] There is an important distinction between an actual holder of a cheque to whom the cheque is payable, and merely acquiring "all the rights and powers of a holder in due course". This distinction was underlined by the majority in *Boma Manufacturing Ltd. v. Canadian Imperial Bank of Commerce*, [1996] 3 S.C.R. 727, at paras. 69–70, *per* Iacobucci

J., and by B. Crawford, *The Law of Banking and Payment in Canada* (loose-leaf), at p. 10-83. The narrow object of s. 165(3) was described by Iacobucci J. in *Boma* as follows:

> When a collecting bank is presented with a cheque for deposit to the credit of the payee, the bank is entitled, essentially, to assume that it was truly the intention of the drawer that the payee receive the proceeds of the cheque. [para. 78]

[76] Subsection 165(3) sought to clear the collecting bank from liability when it deposits fraudulent cheques. This limited objective is achieved by granting the collecting bank "all the rights and powers of a holder in due course", and does not require the bank to be actually designated a holder in due course: Crawford, at p. 10-83. Accordingly, I agree with the respondent that the Bank's use of this provision bears no relation to its purpose and should be rejected.

[77] On this basis, I conclude that a deposited cheque is payable to the payee, and at no time is it payable to the bank other than as agent for the payee.

D. Is There Legal Significance to the Fact That the Cheques Were Deposited Into a Joint Account?

[78] The reasons of Justice Deschamps further argue that if the Bank was not itself the holder of the cheque, then the Bank was only ever liable to the two account holders jointly. With respect, it seems to me that the result of the majority is wrong in law and unfortunate in its impact.

[79] I agree that the Minister could not garnish moneys once they were in the joint account. However, it does not follow that the Minister could not intercept funds in transit before they arrived in the joint account. A requirement to pay in s. 224(1) of the *ITA* intercepts funds while they are in transit.

[80] Once funds are irrevocably deposited in a joint account, they become the property of joint account holders jointly under the terms of their banking contract. At this point, the funds cannot be garnished by the Minister because they are no longer the sole property of the tax debtor: *Macdonald v. Tacquah Gold Mines Co.* (1884), 13 Q.B.D. 535 (C.A.); *Hirschorn v. Evans*, [1938] 2 K.B. 801 (C.A.); *Westcoast Commodities Inc. v. Chen* (1986), 55 O.R. (2d) 264 (H.C.J.); M. H. Ogilvie, "Why Joint Accounts Should Not Be Garnished — *Westcoast*

Commodities Inc. v. Jose Chow Chen" (1986–1987), 1 B.F.L.R. 267. Professor Ogilvie identified the following rationale for the rule against garnishment of joint accounts:

> Since all monies deposited in a joint account are deemed to be joint property, neither joint account holder individually may sue the bank for recovery of funds in the account. Such an action is one in debt ... and the joint creditors of the bank, the joint account holders, must sue jointly. [Emphasis added; pp. 270–71.]

Since neither joint account holder could sue the bank on his or her own for recovery of the funds, it follows that the account cannot be garnished when only one of the two account holders owes a debt to a third party.

[81] However, before the funds arrive in the joint account and while the funds are being transferred, the drawee bank is only liable to make a payment to the payee of the cheque. The other joint account holder had no right to the funds before they arrived in the account. Mr. McLeod could have sued the Bank *on his own* if the Bank failed to honour his cheque. Therefore, it is only the tax debtor's status as *payee* that matters for the purpose of triggering s. 224(1), in the presence of a joint account.

[82] I would add that when a requirement to pay is issued, the Minister must indicate the identity of the tax debtor involved. Banks issued with a requirement to pay are thus never put in the position of having to monitor the liabilities of unknown third parties: they are only required to redirect payments that they are liable to make to tax debtors specifically named by the Minister.

[83] I am also concerned that Deschamps J.'s view of the legal significance of the joint account in this case may negatively impact other areas of the law. There are potentially dangerous repercussions of a restrictive interpretation of garnishment powers when applied, for example, to family maintenance. Child and spousal support ought not be defeated by the mere existence of a joint account.

II. APPLICATION TO THE FACTS

[84] Applying this analysis to the case at bar, once the Bank received Mr. McLeod's cheques to himself, its liability to its customer was triggered. The Bank was therefore contractually bound to honour its customer's demand to pay him. As such, all of the requirements of s. 224(1) were met, and the requirement to pay attached to the money in transit between Mr. McLeod's accounts.

III. CONCLUSION

[85] For these reasons, I would dismiss the appeal with costs.

Appeal allowed with costs, MCLACHLIN C.J. and FISH and ABELLA JJ. dissenting.

Background Reading: M.H. Ogilvie, *Bank and Customer Law in Canada*, 2d Edition (Toronto: Irwin Law, 2013) Chapter 8, pages 315–323.

(a) *C.P. Hotels Ltd. v. Bank of Montreal*†

[Le DAIN J.:]

The general question raised by this appeal is the extent of the duty of care owed by a customer to a bank in respect of the prevention and detection of forgery in the drawing of the customer's cheques. The particular issue is whether, in the absence of an express agreement (generally referred to as a "verification agreement"), the customer owes a duty to examine bank statements and vouchers with reasonable care and to report any discrepancies within a reasonable time. There is also the question whether a "sophisticated commercial customer" owes a duty to its bank to maintain an acceptable system of internal controls, reflecting proper accounting practices and procedures, for the prevention and minimization of loss through forgery.

The appeal is by leave of this court from the judgment of the Ontario Court of Appeal on June 25, 1982, (1982), 139 D.L.R. (3d) 575n, dismissing an appeal from the judgment of Montgomery J. in the Supreme Court of Ontario on May 11, 1981, 122 D.L.R. (3d) 519, 32 O.R. (2d) 560, 14 B.L.R. 1, which dismissed the appellant's action against the respondent bank for $219,644.92, being the total amount debited to the appellant's account for the payment of 23 cheques bearing the forged signatures of signing officers, on the ground that the appellant

was precluded by negligence from setting up the forgeries against the bank.

I

The cheques in issue were drawn during the period April, 1976 to July, 1977, inclusive on the chequing account, at the respondent Bank of Montreal ("the Bank"), of the operating unit or division of the appellant Canadian Pacific Hotels Limited ("CP Hotels"), at the Toronto International Airport, known as the Chateau Flight Kitchen (sometimes referred to as the "Malton Flight Kitchen" and hereinafter referred to as the "Flight Kitchen"). The banking operations of CP Hotels, including those of the Flight Kitchen, were part of the overall banking arrangements made with the Bank by Canadian Pacific Limited ("CP") for itself and its subsidiary and associated companies. CP operated a centralized banking arrangement known as "treasury" under which the Flight Kitchen maintained separate deposit and disbursement accounts with the Bank and a treasury account with CP. Deposits were transferred on a daily basis to the treasury account, and an amount was transferred daily from the treasury account to the disbursement account to restore the balance in that account to zero. Disbursements by the Flight Kitchen to other participants under the

---

† (1987), 40 D.L.R. (4th) 385 at 388–96, 414–34 (S.C.C.).

treasury banking arrangements were made by inter-company payment orders (ICPO's), which were non-negotiable cheques drawn on the treasury account. The Bank submitted a daily bank statement with vouchers to the Flight Kitchen. The CP Hotels procedure manual required the accountant of the Flight Kitchen to prepare monthly bank reconciliations with a list of outstanding cheques and to forward them to the assistant accountant of the head office of CP Hotels.

During the relevant period the staff of the Flight Kitchen concerned with banking and accounting matters consisted of the manager, Donald Saunders; the accountant, Robert Hird, who left in January, 1977; the assistant accountant, Morris Sands (also known and referred to by the trial judge as "Morris Sigulim"), who assumed the position of accountant some two months after the departure of Hird; the disbursement clerk, W. Uddin; and the purchasing agent, the payroll clerk and the general clerk, whose functions and responsibilities, unlike those of the others, were not the subject of comment by the trial judge. During the relevant period the cheques of the Flight Kitchen required the signature of two signing officers: that of the manager, Saunders, and that of the accountant, Hird, and later that of Sands. As the accountant, Hird was responsible for the bank reconciliations based on the daily bank statements and the disbursement records, including the cancelled cheques, but he delegated that function to the assistant accountant, Sands. Uddin was responsible for keeping the disbursement records, including the cancelled cheques. Hird received a summary statement of the monthly bank reconciliation from Sands, generally without a list of the outstanding cheques. He did not otherwise check the work of Sands in the preparation of the bank reconciliation. He did not examine the daily bank statements or the cancelled cheques, nor did he check the work of Uddin.

During the relevant period the defendant Sands forged the signature of Saunders on all 23, and the signature of Hird on 19, of the cheques for which the claim is made. He made the cheques payable to the defendant companies, Dundas Discounts Limited and Sig-Mor Sales Limited, which were controlled by him. The forgeries were not discovered until August, 1977. CP Hotels gave the Bank notice of them on August 25, 1977.

The daily bank statement sent to the Flight Kitchen contained the following statement: "Please check this statement promptly. Any errors, irregularities, or omissions found therein should be reported within 30 days of delivery or mailing, otherwise it will be considered correct." CP was not required by the Bank to sign a verification agreement obliging it and its subsidiary and associated companies to verify bank statements and report discrepancies within a specified period of time. Neither the general agreement between CP and the Bank respecting the Bank's renumeration nor the "Operation of Account Agreement" contained any reference to the verification of bank statements.

The action of CP Hotels against the Bank for recovery of the amount of $219,644.92 is framed as one for conversion and alternatively for money had and received and alleges breach of contract and negligence by the Bank in honouring the forged cheques. In its defence the Bank alleges that CP Hotels is "estopped or otherwise denied" from recovering the amounts debited in respect of the forged cheques by the breach of a duty, arising out of the banker and customer relationship, to check its bank statements and vouchers on at least a monthly basis, with a bank reconciliation for such purpose, and to notify the Bank immediately of any errors. The Bank also sets up in relation to this alleged duty the defence of a stated or settled account. The Bank further alleges the breach of CP Hotels of a duty to take reasonable precautions to prevent fraud by its employees in relation to dealings with the Bank by the maintenance of adequate supervision and internal accounting controls and also invokes the responsibility of a principal for the fraud of an agent acting within the scope of his actual or apparent authority.

Both CP Hotels and the Bank rely on s. 49(1) of the *Bills of Exchange Act*, R.S.C. 1970, c. B-5, which provides:

> **49.**(1) Subject to this Act, where a signature on a bill is forged, or placed thereon without the authority of the person whose signature it purports to be, the forged or unauthorized signature is wholly inoperative, and no right to retain the bill or to give a discharge therefor or to enforce payment thereof against any party thereto can be acquired through or under that signature, unless the party against whom it is sought to retain or enforce payment of the bill is precluded from setting up the forgery or want of authority.

CP Hotels relies on s. 49(1) for the rule that a forged signature is wholly inoperative and thus the Bank had no authority to pay the cheque and debit CP Hotels for the amount of them. Both the Bank and CP Hotels rely on s. 49(1) for the extent to which the general rule respecting the effect of a forged signature has been qualified by the words "unless the party against whom it is sought to retain or enforce payment of the bill is precluded from setting up the forgery or want of authority". Thus the issue in the case is whether CP Hotels is precluded, within the meaning of s. 49(1), from setting up the forgeries against the Bank.

Despite the absence of a verification agreement, Montgomery J. in the Supreme Court of Ontario held that CP Hotels owed a duty to the Bank to examine its bank statements with reasonable care and to report any discrepancies within a reasonable time. He also held that a "sophisticated commercial customer", such as CP Hotels, owed a duty to its bank to maintain an acceptable system of internal controls for the prevention and minimization of loss through forgery. Such controls included a division or segregation of duties and supervision and verification of the work of those responsible for the bank reconciliation and the records on which it must be based. The trial judge found that CP Hotels was in breach of both duties and that its negligence was the cause of the loss resulting from the forgeries. In particular, he found that the accountant, Robert Hird, had been negligent in delegating the bank reconciliation to Sands and not supervising or checking his work and that of the disbursement clerk, Uddin. He also found a lack of supervision by the manager of the Flight Kitchen and by the head office of CP Hotels, particularly after Sands had assumed the duties of accountant. The trial judge found that it was the lack of supervision and other internal controls that permitted Sands to conceal the forgeries for as long as he did by manipulation of the bank reconciliation and the accounting records on which it was based, and that but for the negligence of CP Hotels the irregularities would have been discovered as early as April 1976. The trial judge also found that the Bank, which employed verification clerks to verify the signatures of customers, had not been negligent. He held that CP Hotels was precluded by its negligence from setting up the forgeries against the Bank, and he accordingly dismissed its action.

A majority of the Ontario Court of Appeal (Jessup and Houlden JJ.A.) dismissed the appeal from this judgment for the reasons of Montgomery J. Lacourcière J.A., dissenting, was of the view that it was not open to the trial judge, on the existing authorities and in the absence of a verification agreement, to base a dismissal of the action of CP Hotels on the breach of a duty to examine bank statements with reasonable care and to report discrepancies within a reasonable time. While intimating that the imposition of such a duty might be desirable, he held that it could only be properly imposed by an amendment to s. 49(1) of the *Bills of Exchange Act* or by a judgment of this court, depart-

ing from "its traditional interpretation of s. 49". I quote his brief dissenting reasons in full because they serve to indicate the general focus of the issue in the appeal:

> In my opinion the learned trial judge was not free to dismiss the appellant's action on the basis of its failure to examine the bank statements with reasonable care and to report discrepancies within a reasonable time. In the absence of a verification agreement, no such duty has ever been fastened upon bank customers in Canada. If this is to be done, as I think perhaps it should, it is for Parliament to modify s. 49 of the *Bills of Exchange Act*, R.S.C. 1970, c. B-5, along the lines of the *United States Uniform Commercial Code*, the relevant provisions of which are quoted in *Arrow Transfer Co. Ltd. v. Royal Bank of Canada et al.* [1972] S.C.R. 845, 27 D.L.R. (3d) 81, [1972] 4 W.W.R. 70. Alternatively, it is open to the Supreme Court of Canada to depart from its traditional interpretation of s. 49. Only in that way will the desirable uniformity be achieved. Unless that is done, a bank which debits a customer's account in respect of forged cheques as the respondent bank did in the present case is liable to the customer in the absence of a suitable verification agreement or other circumstances creating a true estoppel: see *Arrow Transfer, supra*, at p. 851 S.C.R., p. 84 D.L.R. In my view, the doctrine of *stare decisis* was departed from by the learned trial judge, albeit in a progressive and well-reasoned judgment.

II

As suggested by the reasons of Montgomery J. and the dissenting reasons of Lacourcière J.A., the issue in the appeal turns initially on the view which one takes of the judgment of the majority of this court, delivered by Martland J., and the separate reasons, concurring in the result, of Laskin J. (as he then was) in *Arrow Transfer Co. Ltd. v. Royal Bank of Canada et al.* [1972] S.C.R. 845, 27 D.L.R. (3d) 81, [1972] 4 W.W.R. 70. In that case the majority of the court held that the customer was precluded by a verification agreement from recovering the amount debited to its account by the bank pursuant to the payment of cheques on which the customer's signature had been forged. In the course of his judgment for the majority, Martland J. said at p. 84 D.L.R., p. 851 S.C.R. (the statement to which Lacourcière J.A. was presumably referring): "In the absence of the verification agreement, a bank which debited a customer's account in respect of a forged cheque would be liable to him." Laskin J. was of the view that the verification agreement did not apply to the forged drawing of a cheque, but he found that the customer was precluded by negligence from recovering against the bank. After concluding that the verification agreement did not provide the bank with a defence, Laskin J. said at p. 99 D.L.R., p. 870 S.C.R.: "Is then the Royal Bank's only defence to the claim of the appellant that the latter is (to refer to what is stated in s. 49(1) of the *Bills of Exchange Act*) precluded from setting up any or all of the forgeries?" After referring to the American law, as reflected in the judgment of the United States Supreme Court in *Leather Manufacturer's Bank v. Morgan*, (1885), 117 U.S. 96, and in s. 4-406 of the *Uniform Commercial Code* (to which Lacourcière J.A. referred), Laskin J. said at p. 101 D.L.R., p. 873 S.C.R.: "I do not think it is too late to fasten upon bank customers in this country a duty to examine bank statements with reasonable care and to report account discrepancies within a reasonable time." In the result, Laskin J. held that the customer was precluded by the breach of a wider duty of care, comparable to the wider duty found by Montgomery J., from recovering against the Bank. It was contended by counsel for CP Hotels, as was apparently assumed by Lacourcière J.A., on the basis of the statement quoted above from the judgment of Martland J., that the majority judgment of this court in *Arrow Transfer* decided, in effect, that a customer could not, in the absence of a verification agreement, be precluded from recovering against a bank by the breach of a duty to examine bank statements with reasonable care and to report any discrepancies within a reasonable time. For the reasons indicated more fully in the later discussion of *Arrow Transfer*, I am of the respectful opinion that this was not the case, and that having based its conclusion on the verification agreement the majority did not purport to address the question raised by Laskin J., which is the issue in the present appeal.

While we are not, in my opinion, prevented by the opinion of the majority in *Arrow Transfer* from adopting the view expressed by Laskin J. in that case, as Montgomery J. did, that result would undoubtedly represent a departure in the law respecting the duties owed by a customer to a bank in respect of the prevention and detection of forgery in the drawing of his cheques, in the absence of a verification agreement. It would involve the recognition of a duty of care extending beyond those that have been recognized by judicial authority in England, as reflected in *London Joint Stock Bank v. Macmillan*, [1918] A.C. 777 (H.L.); *Greenwood v. Martin Bank Ltd.*, [1933] A.C. 51 (H.L.), and most recently, *Tai Hing Cotton Mill Ltd. v. Liu Chong*

Hing Bank Ltd., [1986] A.C. 80 (P.C.). These are the duty of a customer to use reasonable care to draw his cheques in such a manner as not to facilitate forgery or material alteration of them, and the duty, upon learning of forgery, to give the bank prompt notification of it. At least until the opinion of Laskin J. in *Arrow Transfer*, these duties were accepted in Canadian law as indicating the limits, in the absence of a verification agreement, of the customer's duties in respect of the prevention and detection of forgery in the drawing of his cheques: see *Columbia Graphophone Co. v. Union Bank of Canada* (1916), 34 D.L.R. 743n, 38 O.L.R. 326 (H.C.). Montgomery J. acknowledged that he was breaking new ground. Referring to the decisions of this court in *Ewing v. Dominion Bank* (1904), 35 S.C.R. 133; *Bank of Montreal v. The King* (1907), 38 S.C.R. 258, and *Arrow Transfer*, and the decision of the Ontario High Court in *Columbia Graphophone*, Montgomery J. said at p. 528:

> There is no explicit statement that the customer will be estopped by reason of his own negligence in failing to adequately examine the bank statements or in failing to adequately supervise the fraudulent clerk.
>
> It is to this last point that the counsel for the defence addressed a most reasoned and persuasive argument. Can it be reasonably said that principles of law enunciated at the beginning of the century must remain unchanged in the context of the present-day relationship between an extremely sophisticated commercial customer and his bank?

Counsel for the Bank also conceded in argument that the court was being invited to extend the customer's duty of care. Referring to the two duties of the customer clearly established by the existing authority, which counsel described as a duty "not to draw a cheque in a manner which might facilitate alteration" and a duty "promptly to report the forgery of his signature on a cheque when he becomes aware of it", counsel for the Bank stated in their factum: "Given these duties, it is but a short and logical step to suggest that a customer who receives a periodic statement of his account (daily in the case of the Appellant) and, more importantly, the original vouchers, should be required to look at them and report discrepancies." Counsel also referred to the trial judge's "extension of the customer's duty of care". Counsel for the Bank did argue an estoppel by silence on the basis of what would amount to imputed knowledge of forgery but this also would appear to involve finding a duty to examine bank statement with reasonable care and to report discrepancies within a reasonable time.

The breach of such a contractual duty, if it existed, would, in my opinion, clearly fall within the meaning of "precluded" in s. 49(1), assuming of course that it could be shown to have caused prejudice or detriment, because it could be properly characterized (as it was in *Leather Manufacturer's Bank*) as resulting in that species of estoppel by representation often referred to as estoppel by conduct or estoppel by negligence. I am therefore of the view that it is necessary to determine whether such a duty exists. I do not find it necessary or desirable for purposes of the present appeal to express a view as to the extent to which a party may be precluded by negligence under s. 49(1) from setting up a forgery. I am satisfied that whatever be the proper scope and meaning to be assigned to the word "precluded" in s. 49(1) it cannot be construed as freezing the kinds of duties, the breach of which may be properly characterized by resulting in an estoppel by representation.

The issue, as I see it, is whether, apart from the question of policy, on which opinions obviously differ, there is a sound basis in law for such a duty. Laskin J. did not address this issue in *Arrow Transfer*, nor did Montgomery J. explore it in any depth in the present case. It was, however, fully canvassed in relation to a wider duty of care in the judgments of the Hong Kong Court of Appeal and the Judicial Committee of the Privy Council in *Tai Hing*. The consideration of this issue requires a review of the existing authorities with respect to a customer's duty of care to a bank in respect of the prevention and detection of forgery in the drawing of his cheques.

Before undertaking this review something should perhaps be said about the apparent scope, relationship and basis of the two duties affirmed by Montgomery J.: the duty, in the absence of a verification agreement, to examine bank statements with reasonable care and to report any discrepancies within a reasonable time, and the duty to maintain an acceptable system of internal controls for the prevention and minimization of loss through forgery. It would appear that Montgomery J. regarded both of these duties as applicable to the "sophisticated" customer, and that he found the basis for them in "commercial custom" adopted as an implied term of the contract between banker and customer. He began his reasons for judgment with the following question at p. 520: "What is the duty a sophisticated customer owes to its banker?" After referring to what was said by Pratte J. in *Bank of Montreal v. A.-G. Que.* (1978), 96 D.L.R. (3d) 586 at pp. 589–90, [1979] 1 S.C.R.

565 at pp. 569–70, 25 N.R. 330 *sub nom. Province of Quebec v. Bank of Montreal*, concerning the role of commercial custom in the banker and customer relationship, and quoting at length from the opinion of Laskin J. in *Arrow Transfer*, Montgomery J. said at p. 532:

> In my view the majority judgment in *Bank of Montreal v. A.-G. Que., supra*, by referring to "commercial custom" permits me to imply the type of duty contemplated by Laskin J. in *Arrow Transfer, supra*, to the banking relationship between CP and the bank, quite apart from their express banking agreement. I cannot see that a large sophisticated bank customer who receives daily statements of account from its bank, whose daily bank transactions amount to many thousands of dollars, can be absolved of responsibility for checking the accuracy of those statements in respect of cheques bearing forged signatures. If the bank is to be held liable to its customer for honouring cheques bearing forged signatures surely it must be considered a part of commercial custom that the customer take steps to identify forgeries and prevent their recurrence as part of normal business practice. The Price Waterhouse report indicated unequivocally that had CP Hotels followed proper accounting practices and procedures, Sigulim would not have been able to succeed in his scheme. Such practices and procedures necessarily include proper bank reconciliations.

With reference to the requirement of an acceptable system of internal controls, he said at p. 533:

> In a commercial context an efficient internal control system is designed to prevent frauds against the corporation without regard to specific provisions of the *Bills of Exchange Act*. In my opinion a bank dealing with a sophisticated commercial customer has a right to expect that the customer will have such internal controls in place. The customer owes a duty to the bank to operate an acceptable internal control system so that both the bank and its customer are jointly engaged in prevention and minimization of losses occurring through forgeries.
>
> To impose such a duty on a sophisticated customer does not run counter to the spirit of the *Bills of Exchange Act*....

In this court counsel for the Bank contended chiefly for a duty of general application to examine bank statements with reasonable care and report discrepancies within a reasonable time, as indicated by his opening submission in oral argument that the court should recognize a duty of the kind set out in s. 4-406 of the *Uniform Commercial Code*, although I did not understand him to abandon reliance on a duty to maintain an adequate system of internal accounting controls for the prevention and minimization of loss through forgery.

. . . .

IV

. . . .

The Canadian position with respect to the verification of bank statements, prior to *Arrow Transfer*, was established by the judgment of Middleton J. in *Columbia Graphophone Co. v. Union Bank of Canada* (1916), 34 D.L.R. 743n, 38 O.L.R. 326. It recognized the binding effect of a verification agreement, but held, referring with approval to *Kepitigalla*, that in the absence of knowledge of forgeries a customer was not estopped from setting up forgeries against his bank by his failure to notify the bank of discrepancies following receipt of his bank statement and vouchers. The case involved a series of forgeries and the skilful concealment of them by a confidential clerk over a period of several months. The clerk had been left in control of the bank statements and vouchers. Because of the importance of verification agreements in Canadian banking practice I quote, as an illustration, the form of agreement which was held to be binding on the customer in *Columbia Graphophone* [at pp. 331–32 O.L.R.]:

> The undersigned customer of the Union Bank of Canada hereby acknowledges receipt of his pass-book or statement of current account, shewing a balance to the end of the month, May 30, 1914, of $1,598.50 at credit, together with vouchers for all debit items against the undersigned appearing therein since the date of the last statement of account; and, for valuable consideration, the undersigned agrees with the said bank that he will, within ten days from the date hereof, examine the said vouchers and check the debit and credit entries in the said pass-book or statement of account (and especially all debit entries purporting to be represented by such vouchers), and will in writing point out to the said bank any errors therein, and from and after the expiration of the said period of ten days, except as to improper charges or errors previously pointed out, it shall be conclusively settled as between the bank and the undersigned that the vouchers in respect of all such debit items are genuine and properly chargeable to and charged against the undersigned, and that the undersigned was not entitled to be credited with any sum not credited in the said pass-book or statement of account.

With respect to the binding effect of such acknowledgement or agreement, which has the effect of creating a stated or settled account Middleton J. said at p. 332:

> I can see no reason why these acknowledgements and agreements should not bind the customer. They were intended to be real agreements and to define the relation between the parties, and, I think, relieve the bank from all liability down to the 30th May, 1914.

With respect to the forgeries not covered by the verification agreement, Middleton J. rejected the contention

> that the rendering of the accounts, and the handing over of the vouchers, with the request for an immediate examination, and the request for the signature of such an acknowledgement each month, and the failure of the customer to make any complaints, preclude it from now objecting to the items charged.

He said that "it is a matter of no importance that the customer has so conducted his business as to render forgery by a clerk easy", and emphasized that the duty, the breach of which may result in an estoppel by representation, will only arise upon acquiring knowledge of a forgery or alteration. On this point he said at pp. 333–34:

> Any conduct on the part of the customer after he has knowledge that a forged cheque has been issued or that a genuine cheque has been altered, which is calculated to mislead or deceive the banker, or which will facilitate the commission of a fraud upon the banker, will preclude the customer from asserting that his signature is not genuine; but all these cases rest upon the existence of a duty or obligation which it is assumed arises from the knowledge of the existence of the forged document. This duty or obligation arises generally from the contractual relationship of the parties, but the Supreme Court of Canada found that it may also arise, when there is no contractual relation, from moral and commercial obligation: *Ewing v. Dominion Bank* (1904), 35 S.C.R. 133, [1904] A.C. 806.

With respect to the issue of policy, Middleton J. said at p. 334:

> Here the case is in one aspect a hard one on the bank, but the bank could have protected itself in any one of three ways. It might have, in the first place, insisted upon a contract with the customer imposing upon him the duty to state accounts monthly and to accept as genuine all items not objected to in a reasonable time — or

it might have insisted upon the regular signature of the monthly acknowledgements — or it might have delivered the statements and vouchers into the hands of the manager, instead of to the fraudulent clerk.

The binding effect of verification agreements was recognized in several cases after *Columbia Graphophone*, indicating that they had become a well established part of Canadian banking practice: see *Rutherford v. Royal Bank of Canada*, [1932] 2 D.L.R. 332, [1932] S.C.R. 131; *Mackenzie v. Imperial Bank of Canada*, [1938] 2 D.L.R. 764n, [1938] O.W.N. 166; *B.&G. Construction Co. Ltd. v. Bank of Montreal*, [1954] 2 D.L.R. 753, 10 W.W.R. (N.S.) 553; *Syndicat des Camionneurs Artisans v. Banque Provinciale du Canada* (1969), 11 D.L.R. (3d) 610, [1970] Que. C.A. 425; and *Bad Boy Appliances & Furniture Ltd. v. Toronto-Dominion Bank* (1972), 25 D.L.R. (3d) 257, [1972] 2 O.R. 221. These cases were cited in the judgment of this court in *Arrow Transfer Co. Ltd. v. Royal Bank of Canada* (1972), 27 D.L.R. (3d) 81, [1972] S.C.R. 845, [1972] 4 W.W.R. 70, to which I referred earlier in these reasons and to which I now turn for a more detailed consideration.

V

In *Arrow Transfer*, the chief accountant of the customer forged the signature of signing officers on 73 cheques of the company over a period of five years and managed to conceal the forgeries for that length of time. The customer had signed a verification agreement undertaking to verify the correctness of each bank statement and to notify the bank within a specified period of "any alleged omissions from or debit wrongly made to or inaccurate entries in the account as so stated" and agreeing that at the end of the specified period "the account as kept by the Bank shall be conclusive evidence without any further proof that except as to any alleged errors so notified and any payments made or forged or unauthorized endorsements the account contains all credits that should be contained therein and no debits that should not be contained there and all the entries therein are correct and subject to the above exception the Bank shall be free from all claims in respect of the account". The customer failed to give the bank notice of all but the last of the forgeries within the specified period. The issue on which there was a difference of opinion in the court between the majority (Abbott, Martland, Ritchie and Spence JJ.) and Laskin J. (as he then was), who concurred in

the result but for different reasons, was whether the words "debits wrongly made" in the verification agreement contemplated entries for the payment of cheques on which the drawer's signature had been forged. The majority held that they did. They drew support for this conclusion from the express exception for forged endorsements. Laskin J. was of the view that the verification agreement was not sufficiently clear or explicit to cover cheques on which the signature of the customer had been forged. Since the majority were of the view that the verification agreement was a complete answer to the customer's claim against the drawee bank for the amount of the 72 forged cheques of which it had failed to give the bank the required notice, they did not have to deal with the question addressed by Laskin J. — whether the customer was also precluded by negligence from setting up the forgeries against the bank. In the course, however, of the judgment which he delivered for the majority, Martland J. said at p. 84 D.L.R., p. 851 S.C.R.: "In the absence of the verification agreement, a bank which debited a customer's account in respect of a forged cheque would be liable to him." It was argued in this court whether this statement necessarily implied a rejection of the view adopted by Laskin J., that even in the absence of an applicable verification agreement the customer owes a duty to his bank to examine his bank statements with reasonable care and to report any discrepancies within a reasonable time. As I indicated earlier in these reasons, I do not think that this brief statement by Martland J., which was not necessary to the disposition of the appeal and makes no allusion to other possible bases for the preclusion, such as an estoppel, can have been intended to be the expression of a considered opinion on the issue raised by Laskin J. We are not, therefore, as I said earlier, prevented by the judgment of the majority in *Arrow Transfer* from considering whether, as suggested by Laskin J., a customer owes a duty to his bank, in the absence of a verification agreement, to examine bank statements with reasonable care and to report discrepancies within a reasonable time.

After his reference to the American law on this question, and his statement, "I do not think it is too late to fasten upon bank customers in this country a duty to examine bank statements with reasonable care and to report account discrepancies within a reasonable time", Laskin J. disposed of the issue of negligence on what appears to have been the basis of a broader duty of care, comparable to that affirmed by Montgomery J. in the present case. He said at pp. 102–3 D.L.R., pp. 874–75 S.C.R.:

The facts found in the present case go, however, beyond any failure to meet the duty that I have suggested, and hence make it unnecessary for me to determine how many of the forgeries would have to be borne by the bank by reason of a breach of duty which arose only in relation to the submission of statements of account to the appellant. The trial Judge absolved the bank of any negligence in relation to the forgeries, which were skilfully executed, and dealing with the appellant's conduct of its business, he made the following finding [9 D.L.R. (3d) 693 at pp. 705–6, 72 W.W.R. 19]:

> The plaintiff employed a person they knew had been found to be untrustworthy in the past and placed him in a position of complete trust where no one checked upon his work adequately. The procedures followed by the plaintiff and its auditors were inadequate to discover the fraud and to discover that its books had not balanced for a number of years. Cheques remain today in which the duplicate shows one payee and the original another. The accounts payable had not balanced for years. In each of the months in which there was a forged cheque Mr. Seear was permitted to extract the cheque and complete the balancing. He was a very personable fellow, well trained in accounting. If the plaintiff had employed proper procedures it seems reasonable to expect that it would have discovered some of the forgeries, that its bank's returns did not balance in many months, that its accounts payable did not balance, or that its cheques were not in accordance with the duplicate register. One would have expected that in an organization handling money in the amount that this plaintiff handled, no person would be so wholly entrusted with responsibility that no other person's duties would involve a check upon him. In this case the plaintiff knew that the person in that position had been discharged from his former employment because it was found that he could not be trusted.

On these findings, relating as they do to the particular facts of this case, I am of the opinion that the appellant is precluded from claiming against the Royal Bank on any of the seventy-two cheques which are the subject of its action.

The implication of this passage, as I read it, is that Laskin J. was of the view that not only did the customer have a duty to examine its bank statements and vouchers with reasonable care and to report any discrepancies within a reasonable time, but that it also had a wider duty to carry on it business in such a way as to maintain proper supervision, verification and other internal controls for the prevention and detection of forgery in the drawing of its cheques. The opinion did not, however, explore the issues concerning the legal basis for either duty. The basis for a wider duty of care in respect of the prevention and detection of forgery in the drawing of a customer's cheques was very fully canvassed in the judgments of the Hong Kong Court of Appeal and the Privy Council in *Tai Hing Cotton Mill Ltd. v. Liu Chong Hing Bank Ltd.*, [1986] 1 A.C. 80 (P.C.), reversing [1984] 1 Lloyd's Rep. 555 (C.A.), to which I now turn.

VI

Tai Hing involved a pattern of forgery and concealment of it by an employee of a corporate customer comparable to that in *Arrow Transfer* and in the present case, although it extended over a longer period and resulted in greater loss. An accounts clerk of the textile company forged the signature of the managing director of the company on some three hundred cheques totalling approximately HK$5.5 million. The forgeries extended over the period November, 1974 to May, 1978, and were not discovered until the end of that period because of inadequate internal controls. The company instituted an action for a declaration that the three banks involved were not entitled to debit its accounts for the payment of the forged cheques. The banks contended that the company was precluded from setting up the forgeries by the breach of a duty of care owing to the banks. The banks relied on what was referred to as the "wider duty" — "to take such precautions as a reasonable customer in his position would take to prevent forged cheques being presented to his bank for payment" — and also on what was referred to as the "narrower duty" — "to take such steps to check his monthly bank statements as a reasonable customer in his position would take to enable him to notify the bank of any items debited therefrom which were not or may not have been authorized by him": [1984] 1 Lloyd's Rep. 555 at p. 556. Reliance was also placed on the customer's agreement at the time of opening the accounts to comply with the banks' rules and procedures governing the conduct of the accounts. In each case there was a rule to the general effect that upon failure to notify the bank within a specified period of any error in the bank statement, which was sent to the customer without return of the cancelled cheques, the statement would be deemed to be approved or confirmed. These provisions were referred to by the Court of Appeal as the "express terms of business" and by the Privy Council as the "express conditions". I shall refer to them as the "express agreements".

Both duties were rejected by the trial judge as unsupported by the authority that was binding on him, but he found as a fact that, if such duties existed, the customer was in breach of them, and that finding of fact was not challenged. The trial judge also held that the express agreements did not have the effect by themselves of precluding the customer from setting up the forgeries. Despite, however, the absence of either of the duties contended for by the banks, and the lack of conclusive effect in the express agreements, the trial judge held that the customer was estopped by its conduct, following the receipt of its bank statements, from setting up the forgeries against two of the banks. He held that the failure of the customer to object to debits following receipt of its bank statements amounted to a representation that the debits were correct on which two of the banks relied to their detriment. The judgment of the trial judge, which is apparently not reported, is more fully referred to on this point by the Privy Council than by the Court of Appeal: [1986] 1 A.C. 80 at p. 100.

On the appeal from this judgment, the Hong Kong Court of Appeal (Cons and Fuad JJ.A., and Hunter J.) [1984] 1 Lloyd's Rep. 555, held that apart from any express agreement a customer owed a duty to his bank to take reasonable care to see that in the operation of his account the bank was not injured. The court held that the duty arose both as an implied term of the contract between the banker and the customer and as a duty of care in tort because of the relationship of proximity between them. It further held that the duty was a general one, applicable to all customers regardless of their nature or size. Referring to the judgment of Montgomery J. in the present case, which he quoted in support of his general conclusion, Cons J.A. said at p. 564: "A factor that seems to have carried great weight with the learned Judge is that the customer was a large and 'sophisticated commercial customer'. With every respect, it seems to me that the existence or otherwise of a general duty of this kind ought not to depend upon the nature of the customer's business." The Court held that, whether on the basis of breach of duty or on the basis of estoppel, the customer was precluded from setting up the forgeries against the banks. Cons J.A. was of the view that the customer was also precluded from setting up the forgeries by the express agreements. Hunter J., with

whom Fuad J.A. concurred on this point, took at different view of the effect of these agreements.

The Privy Council (Lord Scarman, Lord Roskill, Lord Brandon of Oakbrook, Lord Brightman and Lord Templeman), [1986] A.C. 80, allowed the appeal from the judgment of the Court of Appeal on the ground that there was no basis for the "wider duty" or the "Narrower duty" as either an implied term of the contract between banker and customer or as a duty of care in tort, and that in the absence of any duty there could not be an estoppel. The Privy Council was also of the view that the customer was not precluded by the express agreements from setting up the forgeries against the banks. On this point it agreed with the view of the trial judge and Hunter J. whose approach to the interpretation of the express agreements had been similar to that of Laskin J., with respect to the verification agreement in *Arrow Transfer*. It is necessary to consider the reasoning of the Court of Appeal and the Privy Council concerning the possible basis for a duty of care extending beyond the duties recognized by the House of Lords in the *Macmillan* and *Greenwood* cases.

In the Court of Appeal, Cons J.A. approached the question whether the duty contended for should be recognized as an implied term of the contract between banker and customer on the basis of what was said in *Lister v. Romford Ice & Cold Storage Co. Ltd.,* [1957] A.C. 555, and *Liverpool City Council v. Irwin,* [1977] A.C. 239, concerning the implication of a term as a legal incident of a particular class or kind of contract, without regard to the presumed intention of the parties, as distinguished from the implication of a term to fill a gap in a particular contract on the basis of presumed intention, in accordance with the business efficacy and "officious bystander" tests laid down in the *The "Moorcock"* (1889), 14 P.D. 64; *Reigate v. Union Manufacturing Co. (Ramsbottom) Ltd.* [1918] 1 K.B. 592; and *Shirlaw v. Southern Foundries (1926), Ltd.,* [1939] 2 K.B. 206.

In *Lister*, one of the issues was whether it should be an implied term of the contractual relationship between master and servant, where the servant had certain duties respecting the driving of a motor vehicle, that the master would indemnify the servant against liability arising out of the use of the vehicle in the course of his employment. In a passage which was quoted by Cons J.A. in *Tai Hing*, Viscount Simonds distinguished the implication of a term as a legal incident of a particular class or kind of contract from the implication of a term in a particular contract on the basis of presumed intention as follows at p. 576:

For the real question becomes, not what terms can be implied in a contract between two individuals who are assumed to be making a bargain in regard to a particular transaction or course of business; we have to take a wider view, for we are concerned with a general question, which, if not correctly described as a question of status, yet can only be answered by considering the relation in which the drivers of motor-vehicles and their employers generally stand to each other. Just as the duty of care, rightly regarded as a contractual obligation, is imposed on the servant, or the duty not to disclose confidential information (see *Robb v. Green* [1895] 2 Q.B. 315, 11 T.L.R. 517), or the duty not to betray secret processes (see *Amber Size and Chemical Co. Ltd. v. Menzel* [1913] 2 Ch. 239), just as the duty is imposed on the master not to require his servant to do any illegal act, just so the question must be asked and answered whether in the world in which we live today it is a necessary condition of the relation of master and man that the master should, to use a broad colloquialism, look after the whole matter of insurance. If I were to try to apply the familiar tests where the question is whether a term should be implied in a particular contract in order to give it what is called business efficacy, I should lose myself in the attempt to formulate it with the necessary precision. The necessarily vague evidence given by the parties and the fact that the action is brought without the assent of the employers shows at least *ex post facto* how they regarded the position. But this is not conclusive; for, as I have said, the solution of the problem does not rest on the implication of a term in a particular contract of service but upon more general considerations.

The same distinction was drawn by Lord Tucker as follows at p. 594:

Some contractual terms may be implied by general rules of law. These general rules, some of which are now statutory, for example, Sale of Goods Act, Bills of Exchange Act, etc., derive in the main from the common law by which the have become attached in the course of time to certain classes of contractual relationships, for example, landlord and tenant, innkeeper and guest, contracts of guarantee and contracts of personal service. Contrasted with such cases as these there are those in which from their particular circumstances it is necessary to imply a term to give efficacy to the contract and make it a workable agreement in such a manner as the parties would clearly have done if they had applied their minds to the contingency which has arisen. These are the "officious bystander" type of case, to use Mackinnon L.J.'s well known

words. I do not think the present case really comes in that category, it seem to me to fall rather within the first class referred to above.

In *Liverpool City Council*, the relevant issue was whether there should be implied in the relationship between landlords and tenants in multi-storey dwellings an obligation on the part of the landlords to keep the common parts of the building over which they retained control in repair. In the Court of Appeal, [1976] 1 Q.B. 319, the question of implication was approached with reference to the business efficacy and "officious bystander" tests as one of implication of a term in a particular contractual relationship on the basis of presumed intention. Lord Denning M.R. expressed the view that despite these expressions of the test for implication the cases showed that the test was really what was reasonable. He had a few months earlier expressed the same opinion in *Greaves & Co. (Contractors) Ltd. v. Bynham Meikle & Partners*, [1975] 3 All E.R. 99 (C.A.) at p. 103. Roskill L.J. and Ormrod L.J. disagreed saying that the courts should not imply a term unless it is both reasonable and necessary. The House of Lords, [1977] A.C. 239, agreed with the majority in the Court of Appeal on this point, and that the proposed implied term could not meet the test for implication on the basis of presumed intention. But they held that it could, and should, be implied as a legal incident of that particular kind of contractual relationship, regardless of presumed intention. They held, however, that the test for that kind of implication was also necessity. Lord Wilberforce said at p. 254: "In my opinion such obligation should be read into the contract as the nature of the contract itself implicitly requires, no more, no less: a test, in other words, of necessity." With reference to the necessity of the implied term in respect of the facilities in issue he said on the same page:

All these are not just facilities, or conveniences provided at discretion: they are essentials of the tenancy without which life in the dwellings, as a tenant, is not possible. To leave the landlord free of contractual obligation as regards these matters, and subject only to administrative or political pressure, is, in my opinion, inconsistent totally with the nature of this relationship. The subject matter of the lease (high rise blocks) and the relationship created by the tenancy demand, of their nature, some contractual obligation on the landlord.

Lord Wilberforce said at pp. 524–25: "The necessity to have regard to the inherent nature of a contract and of the relationship thereby established was stated in this House in *Lister v. Romford Ice and Cold Storage Co. Ltd.* [1957] A.C. 555." He referred to the statement by Viscount Simonds in *Lister*, saying that it made "a clear distinction between a search for an implied term such as might be necessary to give 'business efficacy' to the particular contract and a search, based on wider considerations, for such a term as the nature of the contract might call for, or as a legal incident of this kind of contract". The other members of the House of Lords also appear, on the whole, to have regarded the test for this kind of implication as one of necessity. Apart from their express dicta on this point, this view is to be inferred from their reliance on the statement by Viscount Simonds in *Lister*, in which he said the question was whether the proposed implied term was a "necessary condition" of the master and servant relationship. Lord Cross of Chelsea was the only one to suggest that the test for this kind of implication is whether it would be reasonable to imply the term in question. He said at pp. 257–58:

> When it implies a term in a contract the court is sometimes laying down a general rule that in all contracts of a certain type — sale of goods, master and servant, landlord and tenant and so on — some provision is to be implied unless the parties have expressly excluded it. In deciding whether or not to lay down such a prima facie rule the court will naturally ask itself whether in the general run of such cases the term in question would be one which it would be reasonable to insert. Sometimes, however, there is no question of laying down any prima facie rule applicable to all cases of a defined type but what the court is being in effect asked to do is too rectify a particular — often a very detailed — contract by inserting in it a term which the parties have not expressed. Here it is not enough for the court to say that the suggested term is a reasonable one the presence of which would make the contract a better or fairer one; it must be able to say that the insertion of the term is necessary to give — as it is put — "business efficacy" to the contract and that if its absence had been pointed out at the time both parties — assuming them to have been reasonable men — would have agreed without hesitation to its insertion.

Lord Salmon was clearly of the view that the test was one of necessity. Using the words of Bowen L.J. in *Miller v. Hancock*, [1893] 2 Q.B. 177, which was also relied on by Lord Wilberforce, he said at p. 263:

> I find it difficult to think of any term which it could be more necessary to imply than one without which the whole transaction would become futile, inefficacious and absurd as it would do if

in a 15 storey block of flats or maisonettes, such as the present, the landlords were under no legal duty to take reasonable care to keep the lifts in working order and the staircase lit.

It is also an implication of the speech of Lord Edmund-Davies, in which he referred to the "new approach" to implication based on the statement of Viscount Simonds in *Lister* and to the reference by Bowen L.J. in *Miller v. Hancock* to "necessary implication" that he regarded the test for this kind of implication as one of necessity. Lord Fraser of Tullybelton said [at p. 270] that he agreed with Lord Wilberforce that "there is to be implied, as a legal incident of the kind of contract between these landlords and these tenants, an obligation on the landlords to take reasonable care to maintain the common stairs, the lifts and the lighting on the common stairs". The inference is that he also agreed that the test was one of necessity. Statements that in implying a term as a legal incident of a particular class or kind of contract courts will consider whether the proposed term would be reasonable do not necessarily exclude the requirement that it must also be shown to be necessary. Cf. Cheshire and Fifoot's *Law of Contract*, 10th ed. (1981), p. 125, and Treitel, *The Law of Contract*, 5th ed. (1979), p. 148, in which it is said, in the context of a reference to *Liverpool City Council*, that in deciding whether to imply a term as a legal incident of a particular class or kind of contract the courts will consider whether it would be reasonable to do so. This is in effect what was said by Lord Cross of Chelsea in *Liverpool City Council* but even assuming that he meant to limit the test in such a case to one of reasonableness it cannot be doubted for the reasons I have indicated that the view of the majority was that the test was one of necessity. In this regard, it is interesting to compare the opinion if Lord Denning M.R. in *Shell U.K. Ltd. v. Lostock Garage Ltd.*, [1977] 1 All E.R. 481 (C.A.) at p. 487, citing Lord Cross, that the test for the kind of implication made in *Liverpool City Council* is one of reasonableness, and the opinions of Stephenson L.J. in *Mears v. Safecar Security Ltd.*, [1982] 2 All E.R. 865 (C.A.) at p. 879, and of Oliver L.J. in *Harvela Investments Ltd. v. Royal Trust Co. of Canada (C.I.) Ltd.*, [1985] 1 All E.R. 261 (C.A.) at p. 272, that the test applied in *Liverpool City Council*, at least by the majority, was one of necessity.

In the Court of Appeal in *Tai Hing*, Cons J.A., quoting from *Lister* and *Liverpool City Council*, appears to have accepted the contention of counsel that the "new approach" referred to by Lord Edmund-Davies was what a particular contractual relationship required or demanded in the way of reciprocal obligations. He said that *Macmillan* reflected this approach, referring especially to what Viscount Haldane said in that case about the "correlative obligation" of the customer. Cons J.A. also referred to the contention of counsel that the wider duty of care contended for was the reciprocal of the general duty of care in the conduct of the customer's business imposed on banks by the decisions in *Selangor United Rubber Estates Ltd. v. Cradock (No. 3)*, [1968] 1 W.L.R. 1555, and *Karak Rubber Co. Ltd. v. Burden (No. 2)*, [1972] 1 W.L.R. 602. In those cases, which were also relied on by counsel for the Bank in the present case, the courts held that a banker owed a duty of care to a customer, in carrying out the instructions reflected in his cheques, to make sure, when put upon inquiry, that the customer's funds were not being misapplied. In the end, however, Cons J.A. appears to have accepted the test of necessity and to have concluded that the wider duty of care contended for was a "necessary condition" of the modern banker and customer relationship, as it appears from the following passage in his reasons for judgment at p. 560:

> It cannot be said that the imposition of a duty of care on the customer is absolutely essential to the relationship. The banks could I think manage to service current accounts without that assistance. So could, I think, the tenant of the high rise flats have managed to live there without the benefit of lifts, lights on the staircase or garbage chutes. But that did not deter their Lordships. They took a more practical view of necessity. They inquired if the transaction would become "futile, inefficacious or absurd" if these amenities were not maintained. For my part I can think of little more futile than for the operator of an active bank account to throw his monthly statements in the waste paper basket without ever bothering to looking [sic] at them; little more inefficacious than to leave the operation of that account to a clerk whose work is never checked; and little more absurd than to expect the bank to insure the honesty of the customer's clerk when the customer deliberately puts into the clerk's hands the weapons with which he can plunder and rob the bank. It cannot be economically feasible nowadays for a bank to subject the signature on each and every cheque presented to a thorough examination or comparison with the specimen signature card. Banks must look to other protection. Thus, after a great deal of hesitation, I find myself finally led to the conclusion that, in the world in which we live today, it *is* a necessary condition of the relation of banker and customer that the customer should take reasonable care to see that in the operation of the account the bank is not injured.

In the Privy Council, Lord Scarman said that Cons J.A. had adopted the right test for implication but had reached the wrong conclusion. With reference to the applicable test he said at pp. 104–5:

> Their Lordships agree with Cons J.A. that the test of implication is necessity. As Lord Wilberforce put it in *Liverpool City Council v. Irwin* [1977] A.C. 239, 254:
>
>> such obligation should be read into the contract as the nature of the contract itself implicitly requires, no more, no less: a test, in other words, of necessity.
>
> Cons J.A. went on to quote an observation by Lord Salmon in the *Liverpool* case to the effect that the term sought to be implied must be one without which the whole transaction would become "inefficacious, futile and absurd" (p. 262).
> Their Lordships accept as correct the approach adopted by Cons J.A. Their Lordships prefer it to that suggested by Hunter J. which was to ask the question: does the law impose the term? Implication is the way in which necessary incidents come to be recognized in the absence of express agreement in a contractual relationship. Imposition is apt to describe a duty arising in tort, but inept to describe the necessary incident arising from a contractual relationship.

With reference to the proper conclusion on the application of this test, Lord Scarman said at pp. 105–6:

> The argument for the banks is, when analyzed, no more than that the obligations of care placed upon banks in the management of a customer's account which the courts have recognized have become with the development of banking business so burdensome that they should be met by a reciprocal increase of responsibility imposed upon the customer: and they cite *Selangor United Rubber Estates Ltd. v. Cradock (No. 3)*, [1968] 1 W.L.R. 1555 (Ungoed-Thomas J.) and *Karak Rubber Co. Ltd. v. Burden (No. 2)*, [1972] 1 W.L.R. 602 (Brightman J.). One can fully understand the comment of Cons J.A. that the banks must today look for protection. So be it. They can increase the severity of their terms of business, and they can use their influence, as they have in the past, to seek to persuade the legislature that they should be granted by statute further protection. But it does not follow that because they may need protection as their business expands the necessary incidents of their relationship with the customer must also change. The business of banking is the business not of the customer but of the bank. They offer a service, which is to honour their customer's cheques when drawn upon an account in credit or within

an agreed overdraft limit. If they pay out upon cheques which are not his, they are acting outside their mandate and cannot plead his authority in justification of their debit to his account. This is a risk of the service which it is their business to offer. The limits set to the risk in the *Macmillan* [1918] A.C. 777 and *Greenwood* [1933] A.C. 51 cases can be seen plainly necessary incidents of the relationship. Offered such a service, a customer must obviously take care in the way he draws his cheque, and must obviously warn his bank as soon as he knows that a forger is operating the account. Counsel for the banks asked rhetorically why, once a duty of care was recognized, should it stop at the *Macmillan* and *Greenwood* limits. They submitted that there was no rational stopping place short of the wider duty for which they contended. With very great respect to the ingenious argument addressed to the Board their Lordships find in certain observations of Bray J. in *Kepitigalla's* case [1909] 2 K.B. 1010 a convincing statement of the formidable difficulties in the way of this submission....

Lord Scarman then quoted the passage from the judgment of Bray J., which I have quoted above, beginning with the sentence, "I think Mr. Scrutton's contention equally fails when it is considered apart from authority".

The Court of Appeal also held, as I have indicated, that the customer owed a duty of care in tort as well as in contract on the basis of the principles affirmed in Anns v. Merton London Borough Council, [1978] A.C. 728. Reference was made to *Esso Petroleum Co. Ltd. v. Mardon*, [1976] Q.B. 801, and *Midland Bank Trust Co. v. Hett, Stubbs & Kemp*, [1979] Ch. 384, for recognition that a duty of care may arise from a relationship of proximity or neighbourhood that would not have existed but for a contract. The Privy Council expressed disagreement with the characterization of obligations or duties as at the same time both contractual and tortious, particularly in the case of the banker and customer relationship, but held that in any event there could not be a wider duty in tort than that which existed as an implied term of the contract. On this point Lord Scarman expressed himself as follows at p. 107:

Their Lordships do not, therefore, embark on an investigation as to whether in the relationship of banker and customer, it is possible to identify tort as well as contract as a source of the obligations owed by the one to the other. Their Lordships do not, however, accept that the parties' mutual obligations in tort can be any greater than those to be found expressly or by necessary implication in their contract. If, therefore, as their Lordships have concluded, no duty wider

than that recognized in *Macmillan* [1918] A.C. 777 and *Greenwood* [1933] A.C. 51 can be implied into the banking contract in the absence of express terms to that effect, the banks cannot rely on the law of tort to provide them with greater protection than that for which they have contracted.

Finally, the Privy Council held that since the customer did not owe the duty of care contended for by the banks there could not be an estoppel resulting from its conduct following receipt of its bank statements. This was a clear rejection of estoppel on the basis of imputed knowledge, apart from the breach of a duty to examine bank statements. Lord Scarman said at p. 110:

Their Lordships having held that the company was not in breach of any duty owed by it to the banks, it is not possible to establish in this case an estoppel arising from mere silence, omission, or failure to act.

Mere silence or inaction cannot amount to a representation unless there be a duty to disclose or act: *Greenwood*'s case [1933] A.C. 51, 57. And their Lordships would reiterate that unless conduct can be interpreted as amounting to an implied representation, it cannot constitute an estoppel: for the essence of estoppel is a representation (express or implied) intended to induce the person to whom it is made to adopt a course of conduct which results in detriment or loss: *Greenwood*'s case, *per* Lord Tomlin, at p. 57.

VII

With this background of authority with reference to the policy issue and the legal basis for a wider duty of care owing by a customer to a bank in respect of the prevention and detection of forgery in the drawing of his cheques, I come at last to my own conclusions on the issues in the appeal.

First, I would question the attempt in the present case to limit the application of the duties affirmed, as a matter of general principle, to a particular class or category of customers characterized somewhat vaguely as the "sophisticated commercial customer". With great respect, I do not think there is a sound basis in law for implying a duty in the banker and customer relationship with such a limitation. I agree with Cons J.A. in *Tai Hing* that such a duty, if it exists, must apply in every case of the banker and customer relationship and to all customers, whether sophisticated or not. Such a limitation or qualification, even if it were sound legally, would lead to great uncertainty. It does, however, serve to indicate that the trial judge was not so convinced as to where the balance lay on the policy issue with respect to the ordinary or unsophisticated customer. The duty to examine bank statements and vouchers with reasonable care and to report any discrepancies within a reasonable time, which was the duty principally contended for by the Bank, would, in my view, have to be a duty that applied to all customers.

As I have indicated, the trial judge based the implication of the duties affirmed by him on "commercial custom", attaching particular importance to the following statement by Pratte J. in *Bank of Montreal v. A.-G. Que.* (1978), 96 D.L.R. (3d) 586 at p. 590, [1979] S.C.R. 565 at p. 570, 25 N.R. 330 *sub nom. Province of Quebec v. Bank of Montreal*:

> However, bank contracts, such as the one between the Government and the bank, are somewhat special in that they are usually silent as to their contents; the parties rely on commercial custom and the law. It is therefore appropriate to apply art. 1017 *C.C.*, which reads as follows:
>
> > **1017.** The customary clauses must be supplied in contracts, although they be not expressed.

There is no doubt that the implication of terms in a contract on the basis of custom or usage is a well recognized category of implication that has been particularly important with respect to commercial contracts. It was noted in *Hutton v. Warren* (1836), 1 M.&W. 446 at p. 475, 150 E.R. 517 at p. 521, where Parke B. said:

> It has long been settled, that, in commercial transactions, extrinsic evidence of custom and usage is admissible to annex incidents to written contracts, in matters with respect to which they are silent. The same rule has also been applied to contracts in other transactions of life, in which known usages have been established and prevailed; and this has been done upon the principle of presumption that, in such transactions, the parties did not mean to express in writing the whole of the contract by which they intended to be bound, but a contract with reference to those known usages.

Implication on the basis of custom or usage was referred to by Lord Wilberforce in *Liverpool City Council*, where in his discussion of the various kinds of implications, he said at p. 253:

> Where there is, on the face of it, a complete, bilateral contract, the courts are sometimes willing to add terms to it, as implied terms: this is very common in mercantile contracts where there is an established usage: in that case the courts are spelling out what both parties know and would, if asked unhesitatingly agree to be part of the bargain.

As the statements of Parke B. and Lord Wilberforce indicate, however, implication on the basis of custom or usage is implication on the basis of presumed intention. (Of course custom is being used here as more or less synonymous with usage and not in the sense of custom that has become a rule of law. Cf. *The "Freiya" v. The "R.S."* (1922), 65 D.L.R. 218, 21 Ex. C.R. 232, [1922] 1 W.W.R. 409, for a discussion of the distinction between custom and usage). It is not too clear to me what the trial judge found in the present case to be the commercial custom on which he based the duties of care affirmed by him, but it would appear to have been the practice of a sophisticated commercial customer such as CP Hotels, which he found to be known to and relied upon by the Bank, to operate a system of internal accounting controls which included a monthly bank reconciliation. With great respect, I would question whether this was sufficient to constitute a custom or usage on which a duty of care could be grounded as an implied term of the contract. It would seem to me that the evidence of the practice constituting such a custom or usage would have to be such as to support an inference of an understanding between the bank and the customer that the customer would examine his bank statements with reasonable care and report any discrepancies within a reasonable time, failing which he would be precluded from setting up the discrepancies against the bank. I question whether the evidence in the present case supports such an inference. In any event, there could be no such custom or usage with respect to the ordinary customer. Moreover, it is difficult to see how custom or usage could be found in the face of an established rule of law to the effect that in the absence of a verification agreement a customer does not owe a duty to his bank to examine bank statements with reasonable care and to report discrepancies within an reasonable time.

For similar reasons I am of the opinion that the duty contended for cannot be implied as a term of the banker and customer relationship in a particular case under the other category of implication based on presumed intention — the implication of a term as necessary to give business efficacy to a contract or as otherwise meeting the "officious bystander" test as a term which the parties would say, if questioned, that they had obviously assumed. It is clear from the established law and practice, including the recognition and use of verification agreements, that the duty contended for is not necessary to the business efficacy of the banker and customer relationship and cannot otherwise be presumed to have been intended by the customer. Banks in this country have managed to get along without it for a very long time.

There remains the question whether the duty contended for can and should be implied under the third category of implication which does not depend on presumed intention — the implication of terms as legal incidents of a particular class or kind of contract, the nature and content of which have to be largely determined by implication. Such is clearly the ordinary relationship of banker and customer with respect to the operation of an account. The issue here, as I see it, is whether the test for such implication is to be reasonableness or necessity. This is an important issue of judicial policy respecting the limits of judicial power to impose obligations or duties on the parties to a contract by implication. It is reflected in the differing opinions of the Court of Appeal in *Liverpool City Council*. Although what was said there was said with reference to implication on the basis of presumed intention under the business efficacy or "officious bystander" tests, I think it applies equally to implication under what I have referred to as the third category. I am, therefore, with great respect, in agreement with the view expressed by the majority in the House of Lords in *Liverpool City Council* that the test in such a case of implication should also be one of necessity. It is said that not all the terms that have been implied in the banker and customer relationship reflect a test of necessity. That may well be arguable, although it is my impression from a consideration of the cases that most, if not all, of the terms that have been implied could be regarded as being required by the nature of that particular contractual relationship, to use the approach adopted by Viscount Simonds in *Lister* and Lord Wilberforce in *Liverpool City Council*. I think that is reflected in *Macmillan* and in other cases which have considered the implication of terms in the banker and customer relationship, such as *Joachimson v. Swiss Bank Corp.*, [1921] 3 K.B. 110, and *Tournier v. National Provincial & Union Bank of England*, [1924] 1 K.B. 461. I think it also affords a rationale for the duty of care that was held to be owing by banks to their customers in *Selangor* and *Karak Rubber*. In my opinion, a duty, in the absence of a verification agreement, to examine bank statements with reasonable care and report discrepancies within a reasonable time is not necessary or required by the contractual relationship in this sense. It should not, therefore, be imposed by judicial decision. If banks consider it to be necessary they may

insist on verification agreements or obtain appropriate legislation if they can. What I have said about a duty to examine bank statements and report discrepancies applies, of course, *a fortiori*, to a duty to maintain an adequate system of internal controls for the prevention and minimization of loss through forgery.

In conclusion, then, I am of the opinion that a customer of a bank does not, in the absence of a verification agreement, owe a duty to the bank to examine his bank statements and vouchers with reasonable care and to report any discrepancies within a reasonable time, nor does a customer, "sophisticated" or otherwise, owe a duty to its bank to maintain an adequate system of internal accounting controls for the prevention and minimization of loss through forgery.

It was not argued in this court that if either of the duties of care contended for by the Bank did not exist in contract, they could arise in tort. Although some reliance was placed in argument on the judgment of the Hong Kong Court of Appeal in *Tai Hing*, which found a basis in tort as well as in contract for a wider duty of care with respect to the forgery of a customer's cheques, a possible basis in tort for either the wider or narrower duty of care contended for in the present case was not seriously explored in this court. Nor was any consideration given as to whether, as a matter of principle, a duty of care in tort could be held to arise in a contractual relationship from which the same duty had been excluded by the courts as an implied term of the contract. The appeal was argued before the judgment of this court in *Central Trust Co. v. Rafuse* (1986), 31 D.L.R. (4th), [1986] 2 S.C.R. 147, 75 N.S.R. (2d) 109. In order, however, that there should not remain uncertainty, in view of the manner in which this case was argued, as to whether the customer of a bank could owe a duty in tort, in the absence of a verification agreement, to examine bank statements with reasonable care and to report any discrepancies within a reasonable time, I am of the opinion, assuming it to be arguable that such a duty could arise in tort, that the principle of concurrent or alternate liability in contract and in tort affirmed in *Rafuse* cannot extend to the recognition of a duty of care in tort when that same duty of care has been rejected or excluded by the courts as an implied term of a particular class of contract.

For these reasons I am of the opinion that the appellant was not in breach of any duty owing to the respondent and is therefore not precluded from setting up the forgeries against the respondent. I would accordingly allow the appeal, set aside the judgments of the Court of Appeal and the trial court and enter judgment in favour of the appellant for the amount of its claim against the respondent, with interest and costs.

[La FOREST J.:]

I have had the advantage of reading the judgment of my colleague, Le Dain J. I am in general agreement with him but have some concerns about his comments in the latter part of his judgment regarding concurrent liability in contract and tort.

My colleague puts the matter on the ground that the principle of concurrent or alternate liability in contract and in tort cannot extend to the recognition of a duty of care in tort where that same duty of care has been rejected or excluded by the courts as an implied term of a particular class of contract. I would not approach it in this way. One should not, I think, focus discretely on the banker-customer contract without reference to its informing context. In interpreting this contract, the courts were dealing with only one aspect of a larger enterprise, namely, the elaboration of a general system or code governing bills of exchange which had been part of the law merchant and had its own policy and structural requirements. Not the least of the needs of this system was the necessity for clear rules of general application. In the case of forged cheques, the rule was clear. The banker was supposed to know his customer's signature and the liability was his if he honoured a cheque on which his customer's signature had been forged. There were exceptions based on estoppel, but these were narrow. Attempts to impose on the customer a wider duty were, as Le Dain J. notes, firmly rejected.

A major reason for the rejection of a wider duty is that already mentioned: the need for a rule that was clear in most circumstances, cutting within a narrow compass the cases where the loss was directly attributable to the customer because of negligence or otherwise. Parke B. clearly expressed the policy militating against a wider duty in *Bank of Ireland v. Evans' Trustees* (1855), 5 H.L.C. 389 at pp. 410–11, 10 E.R. 950 at p. 959:

> If such negligence could disentitle the Plaintiffs, to what extent is it to go? If a man should lose his cheque-book, or neglect to lock up the desk in which it is kept, and a servant or stranger should take it up, it is impossible in our opinion to contend that a banker paying his forged cheque would be entitled to charge his customer with that payment.

Such broad uncertainty is out of place in the governance of negotiable instruments.

A further justification for restricting the duty within narrow bounds was later advanced, namely, that this effected a better distribution of loss. As Bray J. put it in *Kepitigalla Rubber Estates Ltd. v. Bank of India Ltd.*, [1909] 2 K.B. 1010 at p. 1026: "To the individual customer the loss would often be serious; to the banker, it is negligible." Whether that ground existed earlier I have not attempted to determine.

The fact is, however, that a choice was made in favour of a narrow duty at a time before and during which notions of tort and contract were emerging. That policy choice was based on considerations having nothing to do with distinctions between tort and contract. It was felt to be appropriate to the governance of negotiable instruments. To introduce a wider duty today under the rubric of the tort of negligence would effect the same uncertainties as those referred to by Parke B. in the *Bank of Ireland* case. The line between carelessness and negligence in many everyday situations can be extremely hard to draw, and as I mentioned before there is need for more precise boundaries in this area.

It was against the background above described that the *Bills of Exchange Act*, now R.S.C. 1970, c. B-5, and in particular s. 49(1), was enacted. Generally, what Parliament sought to do by the *Bills of Exchange Act* was to codify the pre-existing law. It must, as in other cases, be presumed to have known the law in enacting the provision that now governs the situation. I cannot believe Parliament by the word "precluded" (which embodies the only exceptions to the general rule), would have meant to authorize at this late date a wide divergence from the rules for loss allocation that it sought to codify. This does not mean that the law is completely frozen, but it does mean that it cannot be expanded in such a way as to give rise under a new label to a wider duty that is inconsistent with the basic policy choice it sought to codify.

I would, therefore, dispose of the appeal in the manner proposed by Le Dain J.

Appeal allowed

(b) *Le Cercle Universitaire D'Ottawa v. National Bank of Canada†*

[STEELE J.:]

The applicant (the customer) seeks a declaration that the terms of an operation of account agreement (the agreement), signed by it with the respondent (the bank), does not provide a complete defence to the customer's claim for loss caused by the bank's admitted negligence. The application is brought in the customer's name by its insurer who has paid the loss and claims subrogation of the customer's rights.

The bookkeeper of the customer normally attended at the bank to make deposits of cheques payable to its commercial account. On four separate occasions between February 11 and August 23, 1982, in fraud of her employer, she made deposits of cheques payable to the customer to her own personal account. These cheques were clearly marked for deposit to the customer's account only and the bank has admitted its negligence in not detecting the incorrect deposits. At the end of each of the applicable months, the bank, pursuant to the agreement, delivered account statements to the customer. These statements omitted the amounts that had been wrongly deposited to the employee's personal account and which had not been paid into the customer's account. The customer gave no notice to the bank of any error, irregularity or omission in the statements, or that there were any irregularities with the cheques within the time period contained in the agreement. The customer now claims the amounts of its loss caused by the bank's negligence, and the bank relies on the terms of the agreement as a defence.

The applicable portion of the agreement is as follows:

> IN CONSIDERATION of the Bank dealing with or continuing to deal with the undersigned (herein called the "Customer") in the way of its business as a bank, the Customer agrees with the Bank as follows:
>
> ...
>
> 8. The Bank may from time to time deliver to the Customer or to his duly authorized representative a statement of his account with relative cheques and other vouchers, or may

forward the same by ordinary mail to the said Customer. The Customer will examine the said cheques and vouchers and all the credit and debit entries in each of the statements and will within thirty (30) days from the date of each of such deliveries or from the date of each of such mailings, as the case may be, point out to the Bank in writing any errors, irregularities or omissions therein. The Customer agrees implicitly that the producing by the Bank of the mailing and delivery record of the said items and statements duly initialled by the persons appointed to such duties, will constitute a positive proof of such delivery, mailing and receipt to and by the Customer of the said items and statements. After the expiration of the said 30 days (except as to any errors, irregularities or omissions previously pointed out to the Bank as aforesaid and except as to payments made on forged or unauthorized endorsements) it shall be conclusively settled as between the Bank and the Customer that the amount of the balance shown in such statement is correct, that the said cheques and other vouchers are genuine and properly chargeable to and charged against the Customer and that the Customer was not entitled to be credited with any sum not credited in such statement.

If there had been no negligence on the part of the bank the agreement would preclude the claim by the customer: see *Arrow Transfer Company Ltd. v. Royal Bank of Canada* (1972), 27 D.L.R. (3d) 81, [1972] S.C.R. 845, [1972] 4 W.W.R. 70. It is clear that absent an agreement to the contrary a customer owes no duty to its bank to examine bank statements with reasonable care and report any discrepancies within a reasonable time: see *Canadian Pacific Hotels Ltd. v. Bank of Montreal et al.*, June 4, 1987, unreported [since reported 40 D.L.R. (4th) 385, [1987] 1 S.C.R. 711, 77 N.R. 161].

The customer relies on the *obiter* in the single judgment of Laskin J. In the *Arrow Transfer* case, and the finding of the Privy Council in *Tai Hing Cotton Mill Ltd. v. Liu Chong Hing Bank Ltd.*, [1986] 1 A.C. 80 at p. 110. It submits that the agreement is

† (1987), 43 D.L.R. (4th) 147 at 147–50 (Ont. H.C.J.).

not clear and unambiguous and does not "bring home to the customer" the express obligation that it must challenge the statement even when the dispute relates to the bank's own negligence. In this case, the admitted negligence was depositing the cheques to the wrong account, but the argument would also cover innocent but incorrect bookkeeping or computer records. For reasons stated later I think the agreement is clear and unambiguous and brings home the customer's obligation.

The customer also submits that there was a fundamental breach of contract when the bank deposited the cheques to the wrong account. It relies on the statement in *Cathcart Inspection Services Ltd. v. Purolator Courier Ltd.* (1982), 39 O.R. (2d) 656 at pp. 658–59, 139 D.L.R. (3d) 371 at p. 374, as follows:

> The question must now be considered and determined according to the true construction of the contract. In the *Beaufort* case in the Court of Appeal (*Chomedy Aluminum Co. Ltd. v. Belcourt Construction (Ottawa) Ltd. et al.* (1979), 24 O.R. (2d) 1, 97 D.L.R. (3d) 170), Wilson J.A. concluded that the proper test was whether it was fair and reasonable to attribute to the parties the intention that the exclusionary clause should survive notwithstanding a fundamental breach by the party in whose favour it was drawn....

In the *Cathcart* case the contract related to the delivery of goods. There was an exclusionary clause as to the liability for damages "for any reason whatever including delay in delivery". The court held that it was not fair and reasonable to conclude that these words included the fundamental breach of non-delivery. The *Cathcart* case does not help the customer. Its primary point is that the matter must be determined in accordance with a true construction of the contract.

In my opinion, the negligent depositing of the cheques in the wrong account was not a fundamental breach of the agreement on its true construction. It was a failure of the duty owed by the bank to the customer. The agreement contemplates that there could be failures of duty and sets out the rights of the parties if such happens. The agreement clearly covered all credit and debit entries and cast a positive obligation on the customer to notify the bank within 30 days of any omissions therein. The cheques in question not having been shown therein, were clearly omissions. If the customer had advised the bank within the 30 days, its rights would have been preserved. By failing to do so, its rights were lost pursuant to the contract terms.

The decision in *Stewart v. Royal Bank of Canada*, [1930] 4 D.L.R. 694, [1930] S.C.R. 544, is distinguishable and does not help the customer. In that case the agreement related to vouchers and was found to be ambiguous. It did not clearly relate to credit and debit entries as in the present case. The applicant also submits that it would be unreasonable to assume that the agreement would cover the bank's own negligence. The agreement does not specifically use the word negligence, but it does specifically provide that the customer is not entitled to any sums not credited to the statement. The agreement is wide and, by expressly excluding forgeries or unauthorized endorsements, can only have any substantial meaning by interpreting it to cover all aspects of negligence by the bank. It is hard to visualize what else it could apply to.

For these reasons I am of the opinion that the agreement provides a complete defence on the facts of this case and a declaration will issue to that effect. Costs to the respondent bank.

Declaration accordingly.

(c) *Kelly Funeral Homes Ltd. v. C.I.B.C.*†

[WALSH J.:]

This action raises several interesting questions as to the relationship, duties and obligations between a bank and its customers.

Lorne Kelly, the founder and major shareholder of the plaintiff, commenced his relationship with the defendant bank shortly after he opened his first funeral home in 1954. Although the plaintiff's business has greatly prospered and expanded since then,

† (1990), 72 D.L.R. (4th) 276 at 277–85 (Ont. H.C.).

to its now five locations in the Ottawa area, the defendant sill continues to be its banker.

Up until 1976, Kelly personally directed, managed and oversaw almost all of his company's operations. However, as by then he had also become deeply involved in the operation of both the Canadian and the International Funeral Associations, he appointed one Patrick Larkin to be his manager of funeral homes and delegated to him most of the administrative duties and authority he, himself, had previously exercised, particularly with regard to all banking and financial matters.

Patrick Larkin started with Kelly Funeral Homes in 1964, having been introduced by one Father Ferraro, of St. Patrick's Parish, as a young man with lots of personality and promise, but also as one who had been in some mischief. This mischief Kelly understood to have been his stealing from others while he was a seminary student but, in fact, Larkin had been jailed for taking money from a bank. When he began, Larkin lived with and was treated almost like another son of Kelly. Over the next 20 years, Larkin quickly learned each and every aspect of the funeral home business and, in doing so, became not only Kelly's best friend, but also his most trusted employee and confidant.

Sadly, as events later proved, Kelly's trust in Larkin was misplaced. For in the late summer of 1984, it was discovered that Larkin had been stealing from Kelly Funeral Homes since early 1976 and had, over the course of those eight years, stolen, in total, some $240,095. This he had accomplished in several ways, by paying his wife an exorbitant salary, himself unearned bonuses, as well as purchasing an automobile with company funds. However, he obtained the vast majority of these stolen funds by fraudulently negotiating cheques written on the Kelly Funeral Homes' account at the defendant's Bank and Cooper Sts. branch in Ottawa.

To understand this fraudulent "scheme by Larkin to defraud the plaintiff through the defendant bank", being the allegation pleaded in the statement of claim herein, it is necessary to review the plaintiff's internal arrangements as to the paying of its accounts and the authority of its officers to write cheques on the company's behalf. Curiously, the plaintiff, it would seem, at least for the eight years in question, did not keep a corporate minute book nor, indeed, did it keep or retain any copies of its banking documents. In 1977 its banking resolution provided that any one of Lorne Kelly, Patrick Larkin and John Laframboise (the company's assistant general manager) was authorized to sign cheques on

behalf of the company. In 1981 Peter Vallee was added as an additional signing officer.

Laframboise, by letter dated August 9, 1978, and delivered personally by him to the defendant's Bank and Cooper Sts. branch on that date, advised that, thereafter, all cheques of Kelly Funeral Homes that exceeded $1,000 must be signed by two of the company's then three signing officers. This particular letter, it would appear, was either lost or misplaced by the Bank and Cooper Sts. branch and did not surface again within the defendant bank until after the transfer in 1984 of the plaintiff's account from the Bank and Cooper Sts. branch to the defendant's Ottawa Commercial Banking Centre, 119 Sparks St.

Kelly Funeral Homes use the One Write Cheque and Accounting System with Ward Mallette, its chartered accountants, supplying monthly computer printouts, as well as preparing its financial statements. It books were not audited nor did it have in place any supervision over its signing financial officers. Kelly testified that he, himself, did not go over the monthly statements but just reviewed the year-end financial statement. Most of the Kelly Funeral Homes' cheques were written by their bookkeeper, Judy Sully, under Laframboise's supervision and required an invoice to back up their issue. It was, however, not unusual for cheques to be written by Larkin or at his direction and, if any of these did not have a back-up invoice, it appeared he was always able to supply a plausible explanation for the issue of the cheque.

During the eight years in question, Larkin was responsible for most of the plaintiff's dealings with the bank and almost every day either he or Laframboise would attend at the Bank and Cooper Sts. branch to make deposits. As general manager of Kelly Funeral Homes, one of that branch's largest accounts, he was well known and on a first-name basis with the entire staff who enjoyed his presence there, as it would seem he always took the time to exchange pleasantries with them and to tell a joke or story.

The plaintiff produced some 189 cheques drawn on its account which it alleged the defendant bank had wrongly paid. Each of these cheques was negotiated in some manner by Larkin.

Larkin was subpoenaed by the defendant and questioned on the various methods he used to steal money from his employer through the medium of these cheques. Larkin explained that when he personally received a bill from a company, he would issue a cheque on the Kelly Funeral Homes' account at the defendant bank payable to the company from which he received the bill and forward the cheque to that company in payment of his own personal bill. It would appear he did this for the cheques payable to Valley Aluminum, McIntosh & Watts, Simpson-Sears, P&M. Construction and some nine other companies or organizations.

He explained he would also issue cheques drawn on Kelly Funeral Homes' account payable to named individuals, some of whom were real persons, others, names he had made up, and would present these cheques for payment when he attended at the bank to make the Kelly Funeral Home deposits. He would forge an endorsement of the name of the payee he had used on the cheque and advise the teller that the payee would prefer cash or, in other instances, would request payment by way of a personal money order. He is said to have negotiated some 78 cheques in this manner. Larkin indicated at the time he wrote these cheques there was never any intention on his part that anyone other than himself would receive the benefit of them. He also explained he had no difficulty writing these cheques due to the position he held at Kelly Funeral Homes and had no difficulty negotiating them as all the employees at the Bank and Cooper Sts. branch liked and trusted him.

As part of its banking documents, the plaintiff also executed on the defendant bank's printed form 70-75 two identical agreements, one in 1977, the other in 1981, styled, "Agreement Re Operation of Account".

The relevant portions of this agreement provided, as follows:

4. Within thirty days of the date of each delivery from time to time to or to the order of the Customer of a statement of the Customer's account together with the relative cheques and vouchers, or, if the Customer has instructed the Bank to forward such statements and cheques and vouchers by mail to the Customer, within thirty days of the date of each such mailing as shown by the records of the Bank, the Customer will examine such cheques and vouchers and all entries appearing in such statement and will notify the Bank in writing of any errors, irregularities or omissions therein or therefrom; and upon the expiration of said period of thirty days (save as to any errors, irregularities or omissions previously notified to the Bank as aforesaid and save as to payments made on forged or unauthorized endorsements) it shall be finally and conclusively settled and agreed as between the Bank and the Customer that the amount of the balance shown in such statement is true and correct, that the said cheques and vouchers are genuine, that all amounts charged in the said account are properly chargeable to the Customer, that the Customer is not entitled to be credited with any amount not shown on the said statement and that Bank is released from all claims by the Customer in respect of any and every item in the said statement. If the Customer has not taken delivery of any statement together with the relative cheques and vouchers by collecting the same on or before the thirtieth day following the date on which they became available (as to which the Bank's records shall be conclusive evidence), the same shall be deemed to have been delivered to the Customer on such thirtieth day.

No notice with respect to any one of the 189 cheques which form the subject-matter of this action was ever given to the defendant bank by the plaintiff within the prescribed period required by this agreement.

As this fact is not in dispute, the defendant bank therefore submits this agreement provides it with a complete defence to this action.

The plaintiff, however, contends that all of the cheques in question are excluded from this agreement, as they were payments made by the bank on forged or unauthorized endorsements.

It was also the plaintiff's contention that only the second agreement executed in 1981 could be operative, as the 1977 agreement produced by the defendant had a diagonal line drawn across it and the word "Obsolete" written above this line. However, as the agreement also contained a stamp WHL 79, which the evidence disclosed would have been placed thereon by a bank inspector, I find that this agreement remained in full force and effect until replaced by the 1981 agreement.

It is the plaintiff's principal submission that there was a fundamental breach of contract by the defendant bank with regard to the 189 cheques in question because the bank in its handling of them did not comply with the standard rules of banking practice nor with the provisions of the *Bills of Exchange Act*, R.S.C. 1985, c. B-4.

During the eight-year period in question, the number of cheques issued by the plaintiff corporation numbered well in excess of 30,000. At issue in this case are approximately 189 cheques. Based on the numbers alone, I find it difficult to characterize the bank's dealing with these cheques as a fundamental breach of contract. In *Cercle Universitaire Ottawa v. National Bank of Canada* (1987), 43 D.L.R. (4th) 147, 61 O.R. (2d) 456, 6 A.C.W.S. (3d) 377 (H.C.J.), where a similar argument was raised, Steele J. found that the actions of the bank in that case, in depositing a number of cheques into a wrong bank account, did not amount to a fundamental breach, but were instead a failure of the bank's duty to its customer, a failure, moreover, which was covered by the terms of the verification agreement. I am, likewise, not persuaded on the evidence before me that there was a fundamental breach in this case.

For the purpose of clarity, I have divided the cheques in issue into three groups: those of which Larkin never intended anyone but himself to receive the benefit; those payable to companies or organizations in satisfaction of Larkin's personal debts; and those cheques requiring two signatures but which were cashed with only one.

THE "FICTITIOUS PAYEE"

It is clearly settled that, where a person with signing authority writes a cheque to a named payee, but who is never intended to receive the amount drawn, the payee is treated as "fictitious" within the meaning of s. 20(5) of the *Bills of Exchange Act*, which states:

> **20.**(5) Where the payee is a fictitious or non-existing person, the bill may be treated as payable to the bearer.

Since the decision of the House of Lords in *Bank of England v. Vagiano Bros.*, [1891] A.C. 107, and subsequent decisions, it is clear that it is the intention of the *drawer* of the cheque that is determinative of whether or not the payee is "fictitious". If the drawer never intended to pay the payee, the payee may be treated as fictitious and, therefore, any endorsement on the bank of the cheque, whether forged or otherwise, is irrelevant. Such a cheque is, instead, negotiated by delivery and no endorsement is required.

On the other hand, where a person is duped into signing a cheque, believing that it is intended for the payee named thereon, the cases have held that this is not a fictitious payee situation since the drawer believes, in this instance, that the cheque is a debt owed to the person named.

A question may be raised, therefore, when there are two signatories to the cheque. One of these, for argument's sake, is the unscrupulous employee who intends to pocket the proceeds of the cheque; the other is the employee who is tricked into signing the cheque by his colleague in the belief that it will be paid to the person named. In this instance, there are two intentions at work. The courts have resolved this issue by determining which is the controlling intention. For example, in *Bromont v. Banque Canadienne Nationale*, [1973] C.S. 959, the evidence showed that

the co-signee seldom questioned his unscrupulous colleague about the cheques, never asked to see any supporting documentation and, in short, relied on him completely that the cheques presented were genuine. The court found, therefore, that the latter's intention was controlling and that the payees on the cheques were indeed fictitious within the meaning of the *Bills of Exchange Act*.

Similarly, in this instance, on his own evidence, Patrick Larkin admitted that he never had any intention that the cheques would be paid to those named on them. I am also satisfied on the evidence that Larkin was given a more or less free hand in the running of the company. Few, if any, questions were asked when the cheques were issued. The evidence showed that, with regard to those cheques requiring two signatures, the co-signee merely signed as Larkin requested. I find that, with regard to these cheques, it was the intention of Larkin that was controlling and also hold the payees of these cheques to be "fictitious" within the meaning of the *Bills of Exchange Act*.

The plaintiff laid emphasis on the fact that the manner in which some of the cheques were handled, namely, in exchanging a cheque over the counter for cash or a money order, should have alerted the suspicions of the bank. The bank counters this argument by pointing out that, since Larkin had authority to write the cheque, there was no difference between his exchanging the cheque for cash and his deleting the name of the payee on the cheque and writing the words "payable to cash" on it instead.

A somewhat similar fact situation came before the Supreme Court of Canada in *Fok Cheong Shing Investments Ltd. v. Bank of Nova Scotia* (1983), 146 D.L.R. (3d) 617, [1982] 2 S.C.R. 488, 46 N.R. 181. In that case, Peter Chan wrote a cheque in favour of Loong Wai, his business partner, as he had authority to do. He then took the cheque to the bank and exchanged it for a bank draft in Hong Kong dollars, taking the balance in cash. The bank draft was payable to a name other than Loong Wai. Hughes J., at trial, held that the cheque was payable to a fictitious payee. His decision was upheld by both the Ontario Court of Appeal and the Supreme Court of Canada. In that court, the plaintiff/appellant raised the question of negligence on the part of the bank in failing to question the act of Peter Chan in exchanging the cheque for the bank draft. Unfortunately, this was an issue that had not been pleaded, nor had it been raised at trial. Nevertheless, Ritchie J., who delivered the unanimous judgment in the Supreme Court of Canada, would have been prepared to find that the "plaintiff's fraud was such a controlling factor in causing the cheque to be created, presented and cashed that no action can lie at the suit of the plaintiff based on any actions of the respondent" (p. 619).

THE EFFECT OF THE VERIFICATION AGREEMENT

The verification agreement reproduced earlier in these reasons places a very specific onus on the customer to check its account statement, including the returned cheques, and to notify the bank within 30 days of any errors, omissions, or discrepancies. After the 30-day period, the statement is deemed to be correct, except as to those matters for which notice was given. The agreement also operates as a release of all claims by the customer against the bank as to any item contained in the bank statement.

Aside from the fictitious payee situation, which, if it were necessary, I would find was also covered by the terms of the verification agreement, the effect of the agreement must be considered in the light of the two remaining groups of cheques.

Cheques Payable to Companies for Larkin's Personal Expenses

I am unable to see how liability can be attributed to the bank for the payment of cheques for Larkin's personal expenses. There is no question but that the cheques written by Larkin were genuine. He was an authorized signing officer of the company. That the fraud went undiscovered for so long seems to me to indicate that the fault lies with the plaintiff's bookkeeping procedures. In these circumstances, I do not feel it inequitable that the plaintiff bear the burden of this loss. Larkin was its employee. It would be inappropriate for the plaintiff to recover when it was the fraudulent acts of its own officer that caused the loss. A close examination of the cancelled cheques might have uncovered the deception and prevented further acts. The plaintiff's failure to notify the bank of the problem meant that the fraud continued for an extended period. I find, therefore, that the plaintiff did not carry out its obligations under the terms of the verification agreement and, accordingly, find that the plaintiff is bound by the statement of account and the bank is not liable for the money debited for these cheques.

Cheques Requiring Two Signatures

With regard to those cheques in excess of $1,000 and which were required by company policy to bear two signatures, it is clear on the evidence that the bank was unaware of this change in the company practice, as a result of its misplacing the letter of August 9, 1978. If the bank was unaware of the change, however, the same cannot be said for the plaintiff who instigated the practice. It would have been a relatively simple matter for the plaintiff company to discover the problem if there had been a proper examination of the cancelled cheques, as it was required to do under the terms of the verification agreement. I apply the agreement equally to this situation and hold the plaintiff bound by it.

I am supported in my view by the Supreme Court of Canada in *Rutherford v. Royal Bank of Canada*, [1932] 2 D.L.R. 332, [1932] S.C.R. 131, 13 C.B.R. 372. In this instance, an employee of the plaintiff signed a "verification slip", acknowledging that the bank's statement was correct, as he was authorized to do. Subsequently, a cheque bearing only one signature was discovered and the plaintiff brought an action against the bank for cashing the cheque without proper authority. The Supreme Court of Canada denied recovery, holding that the plaintiff was bound by the verification slip.

In conclusion, given the volume of transactions which pass through a bank daily and present-day computerized cheque-processing systems which do not read signatures, it is not economically feasible to expect a bank to scrutinize every transaction that passes through a customer's account. It surely makes sense, therefore, to shift the burden of monitoring its cheques to the customer who generally has far better opportunities of uncovering irregularities on the part of its employees. Any potential losses to the customer can be offset somewhat by the use of surety bonds and proper accounting procedures. Although it has been made clear that no such obligation to monitor its accounts can be imposed on the customer at common law (*Canadian Pacific Hotels Ltd. v. Bank of Montreal* (1987), 40 D.L.R. (4th) 385 [1987] 1 S.C.R. 711, 41 C.C.L.T. 1), the duty may be imposed in the context of a verification agreement. In my view, this is not an unreasonable onus on a bank customer.

While I find that the verification agreement affords the bank a complete defence to this action such that I must dismiss the plaintiff's claim in its entirety, however, as the bank is not without fault, such dismissal is without costs.

Action dismissed.

(d) *Don Bodkin Leasing Ltd v. Toronto-Dominion Bank*†

[THE COURT:]

Don Bodkin Leasing Limited (the "appellant" or "Don Bodkin") appeals the judgment of Ewaschuk J. [reported (1993), 14 O.R. (3d) 571, 10 B.L.R. (2d) 94] which awarded the appellant the sum of $25,428.45 but denied it a further claim in excess of $800,000.

During a period of approximately four years, the appellant's accountant ("Williams") forged 78 company cheques (the "forged cheques", totalling $569,916.90) and gave fraudulent directions in connection with 23 bank cheques (the "bank cheques", totalling $264,959.22) payable to the respondent (the "Bank"). The appellant sued the Bank under numerous causes of action and the Bank relied upon the verification clause in its operation of account agreement with the appellant. That clause required the appellant to notify the Bank of errors in the monthly bank statements within 30 days from the time that the monthly bank statements should have been received by the appellant, failing which the appellant was deemed to accept the entries as correct.

The trial judge held that the appellant was only entitled to recover the proceeds of three forged cheques in the amount of $25,428.45, for which the appellant gave the Bank timely notice of the forgeries in accordance with the verification clause. The Bank had conceded its liability with respect to these three cheques.

Although the appeal raises questions of general principle relating to the law governing the relationship of banker and customer, it is essentially dependent on the facts as found by the trial judge.

THE FORGED CHEQUES

Section 48 of the Bills of Exchange Act

The appellant's principal submission in relation to the forged cheques was that absent the verification clause the Bank was strictly liable pursuant to s. 48 of the *Bills of Exchange Act*, R.S.C. 1985, c. B-4 for paying out on the forged cheques. The appellant submits that the verification clause has no appli-

cation because the monthly bank statements together with the cancelled cheques were delivered to Williams. The appellant argues that the Bank had no authority to give the statements and cheques to Williams as he was not one of the authorized officers named in the banking resolution. The trial judge did not deal directly with Williams' authority because he found that the material that was received by Don Bodkin was sufficient for the appellant to have detected the fraud, had Don Bodkin carried out the duty imposed on the customer by the clause. On that basis, he held that the verification clause applied and barred any recovery by the appellant.

The evidence accepted by the trial judge indicates that Don Bodkin never instructed any of the officers named in the banking resolution to pick up the statements and cheques. Don Bodkin himself did not pick them up. None of the authorized signing officers considered it to be his or her job to pick up the statements. At least one of the signing officers, Beryl Youlton, was aware that Williams was picking up the package from the Bank. The trial judge found that she gave him a written direction to give to the Bank to permit him to do so. In our view, in the circumstances of this case, nothing turns on whether this officer had the express authority to permit Williams to pick up the statement package. Over a period of four years, Williams or his delegates picked up the banking package on a monthly basis. Williams was held out by the appellant as the person responsible for the banking. In our view, on these facts, the only reasonable conclusion is that Williams had actual or apparent authority to pick up the monthly banking package and that accordingly the appellant received the statement and cheques within the meaning of the verification clause.

There is another basis upon which, in our view, the verification clause applied. Don Bodkin, the directing mind of the appellant, expressly delegated to Williams the task of the bank reconciliation. That could only be done by providing to Williams the cheques and the statements. Williams admittedly received all of the cheques and the statements. Don Bodkin, having delegated the duties under the verification clause to Williams, cannot now claim that the appellant did not receive the statements and cheques

† (1998), 40 O.R. (3d) 262 at 263–70 (C.A.).

or that Williams did not have authority to receive them on behalf of the company.

Finally, even assuming that Williams had no authority to receive the cheques and that his actual receipt cannot be imputed to the appellant, we agree with the trial judge that since Don Bodkin did receive the bank statements and the cheques (save for the forged cheques) the verification clause applied. As found by the trial judge, the material that Don Bodkin did receive was more than sufficient to have permitted him to detect the fraud. He was therefore required to notify the Bank of any error or objections within 30 days. Except for the last three cheques, he failed to do so. The verification agreement applied and barred the appellant's claim based on s. 48 of the *Bills of Exchange Act.*

Breach of Contract

On the issue of breach of contract, the argument is essentially the same as on the first issue. It was argued that the Bank improperly permitted Williams, who was not an authorized signing officer for the appellant, to pick up the monthly bank statements. As a result, Williams removed the forged cheques from the monthly statements before they were delivered to the appellant and thereby prevented the appellant from detecting the forgeries. On the facts, as found by the trial judge, the appellant never instructed any authorized signing officer to pick up the monthly statements and the statements were never picked up by a signing officer. They were picked up half the time by Williams and the rest of the time by other office personnel.

Although he was not an authorized signing officer, Williams had extensive authority and responsibilities with respect to accounting and banking matters of the appellant and there is ample evidence to support a conclusion that he had the authority or apparent authority to pick up the monthly bank statements. There is also ample evidence that the appellant knew or ought to have known that Williams was picking up the monthly bank statements. For the reasons set out above, in our view, Williams had actual or apparent authority to pick up the banking package and accordingly there was no breach of contract based on the failure to comply with the banking resolution. However, assuming there was a breach of contract, in our view it was not the cause of the loss. The evidence is clear that sufficient material was delivered one way or another to Don Bodkin from which he could have detected the fraud if he had acted prudently.

In any event, the express words of the verification clause released the Bank from "all claims" in respect of any item in the statement and this would include a claim based on breach of contract. In our view, it does not matter whether the conduct of the Bank in turning over the statements and cheques to Williams could be characterized as "negligent". There is no ambiguity in the verification clause. It releases the Bank from all claims by the customer in respect of any and every item in the statement.

Negligence

The appellant relied upon the decision of the British Columbia Court of Appeal in *Cavell Developments Ltd. v. Royal Bank of Canada* (1991), 78 D.L.R. (4th) 512, 54 B.C.L.R. (2d) 1, as authority for the proposition that a broadly worded verification clause cannot release the bank from claims based on the bank's negligence. In that case, the trial judge found that the bank was negligent in the way that it obtained a certification of a new directors' resolution that led to the loss. The proper resolution had required two signatures on any cheque. The president of the company as a prelude to a fraud upon the company went to the bank and executed a new resolution specifying that his signature alone was sufficient. The new resolution was not valid as it did not contain the signature of the company secretary and had not been approved by the company's board of directors. Nevertheless, the bank accepted cheques signed only by the president. It can be seen that the loss was directly attributable to the negligence of the bank. In those circumstances, the Court of Appeal held that the verification clause did not apply. In this case, however, there was no finding of negligence by the trial judge with respect to the forged cheques or that the loss was occasioned by the Bank's negligence. On the contrary, the trial judge found that the Bank had provided the necessary material to the appellant from which the fraud could have been detected had the customer complied with its contractual obligation. As a result of the trial judge's findings of fact with respect to the forged cheques, *Cavell* can have no application to the facts of this case in respect of the forged cheques claim. The impact of *Cavell* on the bank cheques is discussed below.

The Forged Endorsement Exception

The appellant also submitted that the verification clause had no application to the forged cheques by reason of para. 5(b) of the verification clause. That paragraph provides that the customer is not precluded from later objecting to any "unauthorized or forged endorsement of the payee". The short answer is that the appellant adduced no evidence that the endorsements by the various payees of the forged cheques were in any way forged or unauthorized. We agree with the trial judge that it is not reasonable to interpret para. 5(b) as applying in any case where, as here, the name of the *payer* has been forged. In our view, *Arrow Transfer Co. v. Royal Bank of Canada*, [1972] S.C.R. 845 at pp. 850–51, 27 D.L.R. (3d) 81 at p. 84 is an answer to this argument.

THE BANK CHEQUES

Breach of Contract and Money Had and Received

It was also argued that the Bank improperly accepted directions from Williams with respect to the bank cheques. As pointed out by the trial judge, the charges from the bank cheques were reflected in the monthly bank statements and the cancelled cheques received by Don Bodkin. The verification clause applied and released the Bank from any claim based on the bank cheques, subject to application of the *Cavell* case discussed below. In our view, the verification clause applied whether the appellant's claim is founded in breach of contract or money had and received.

Unlike the circumstances with respect to the forged cheques, the appellant has a finding in its favour that the Bank was negligent in accepting the directions from Williams with respect to the bank cheques. The appellant therefore argued that the holding in *Cavell* applies. *Cavell* itself relies in part upon the decision of the Alberta Court of Appeal in *Royal Bank of Canada v. Larry Creighton Professional Corp.* (1989), 45 B.L.R. 217, 65 Alta. L.R. (2d) 178. In the latter case Stratton J.A. quoted with approval from the reasons of Laskin J. in *Arrow Co. v. Royal Bank, supra*, at p. 869 S.C.R., p. 98 D.L.R. as follows:

> The construction that I would put on the verification agreement is consistent with the approach to contractual limitations of liability in other kinds of relationships, such as bailee and bailor, carrier and consignor, retailer and purchaser. Risks that are by contract to be passed by a party, upon whom they would otherwise rest, to the other party to the relationship must be brought home expressly if they are to be effec-

tive; at least this is so when the limitation would still have subject-matter if unexpressed risks be found to be outside its general language.

Laskin J. therefore held that the verification clause in that case did not apply to errors in the account based on forged cheques. Laskin J. went on, however, to dismiss the customer's appeal because he would have imposed a common law duty upon the customer similar to the duty expressed in the verification clause.

Stratton J.A. in the *Larry Creighton* case applied the passage quoted above from the reasons of Laskin J. to errors caused by the bank's negligence. In other words, just as Laskin J. held that the clause did not apply to losses resulting from forgery, so Stratton J.A. held that the applicable clause could not apply to losses caused by the bank's negligence. The decision of Laskin J. on this issue was not the judgment of the majority of the court. As a result, the decisions relying on Laskin J.'s minority judgment are of limited application. Martland J., speaking for the other four members of the court, held that the verification agreement did apply to forgeries. He stated as follows at p. 853 S.C.R., p. 86 D.L.R.:

> The verification agreement in question in the present case is not ambiguous. It is a contract under which the customer undertakes a duty to the bank to disclose within a limited period, among other things, debits wrongly made. *In the present case, the appellant received the statements and the relevant vouchers. Having failed to perform his contractual duty, the agreement made the statements conclusive evidence against him.* (Emphasis added)

In our view, the majority holding in *Arrow Transfer* applies in this case. The appellant, through Don Bodkin, received the statements and the relevant vouchers (the bank cheques). He failed to perform his contractual duty and thus the agreement made the statements conclusive evidence against it. Moreover, in its terms the agreement in this case released the Bank from "all claims". We note as well that in *Arrow Transfer* an argument was made by the customer based on money had and received (see reasons of Laskin J. at p. 876 S.C.R., p. 103 D.L.R.). There is nothing to indicate that the holding of the majority as to the conclusive effect of the verification agreement was not intended to apply to that claim as well.

The reasons of Laskin J. in *Arrow Transfer*, as they relate to the customer's duty, cannot, we think, be reconciled with the subsequent decision of the Supreme Court in *Canadian Pacific Hotels Ltd. v.*

Bank of Montreal, [1987] 1 S.C.R. 711, 40 D.L.R. (4th) 385. In that case, Le Dain J. for the court held that there was no common law duty upon the customer as suggested by Laskin J. to examine the monthly statements and report any errors to the bank. In the result, since the customer had not been required to sign an agreement containing a verification clause, the bank was strictly liable under (now) s. 48 of the *Bills of Exchange Act* for having paid out on the forged cheques, notwithstanding the customer's negligence.

The appellant also relies upon the decision of the Alberta Court of Appeal in 239199 *Alberta Ltd. v. Patel* (1993), 10 B.L.R. (2d) 40, 105 D.L.R. (4th) 739. However, the Court of Appeal merely followed the decision in *Cavell* and its own decision in *Larry Creighton*. Harradence J.A. wrote as follows at p. 45 after referring to the excerpt from the decision of Laskin J. in *Arrow Transfer* quoted above:

> I reiterate that in *Arrow Transfer* the Agreement operated as a complete defence, but no negligence on the part of the bank was found. Had the bank been found to have been negligent, the comments and reasoning of Laskin J. lead one to conclude that he may have found differently in the result.

However, as we noted above, Laskin J. was not writing for the majority on that issue and Harradence J.A. did not explain how his decision could be reconciled with the reasons of Martland J. for the majority. In any event, the wording of the clause in the *Patel* case is different from that of the clause in this appeal and in particular does not purport to release the bank from "all claims".

Constructive Trust

The appellant argues that the Bank was a constructive trustee for a breach of trust by Williams. As conceded by the appellant, the degree of knowledge required to impose liability on a stranger includes a reckless disregard by the stranger of circumstances indicating the breach of trust. The trial judge found that the 78 forgeries were "good" signatures and that the bank was not negligent in failing to detect the forgeries. The 23 bank cheques had been properly executed by a signing officer and

made payable to the Bank. The Bank had no reason to suspect that the directions given by Williams were fraudulent. Williams gave legitimate directions to the Bank for bank cheques on many occasions and he had the authority or the apparent authority to give these directions. There were no unusual or suspicious circumstances to alert the Bank to the fact that Williams was acting dishonestly or without authorization. Mr. Leslie argued, however, that the Bank showed the requisite degree of recklessness with respect to the bank cheques that were used to purchase travellers cheques. We do not agree. The claim based upon trust principles was properly dismissed. Accordingly, the appeal must be dismissed.

THE SETTLEMENT WITH THE AUDITORS

A further issue was raised on this appeal by the Bank. Subsequent to the judgment, the appellant, in a separate action, recovered $1.3 million from its auditors. The Bank argued that this payment raised an issue of double recovery and was a complete defence to the main action. In light of our disposition of the appeal, it is not necessary to deal with this issue.

THE CROSS-APPEAL

In a companion action, the Bank sought contribution and indemnity from Don Bodkin, personally, for any amount which might be awarded to the appellant on this appeal. That action was dismissed by the trial judge and the Bank appealed in the event that this court set aside the trial judgment and granted relief to the appellant. Again, in light of our disposition of the main appeal, it is not necessary to deal with the companion appeal.

DISPOSITION

Accordingly, the appeal is dismissed with costs and the appeal of the Bank in the companion action is dismissed without costs.

Appeal dismissed with costs.

(e) *S.N.S. Industrial Products Limited v. Bank of Montreal*†

[MacPHERSON, CRONK and KARAKATSANIS JJ.A.:]

[1] The appellant, Bank of Montreal (the "Bank"), appeals from the trial judge's decision awarding the respondent, S.N.S. Industrial Products Limited ("SNS"), the sum of $186,488 for losses arising from forged cheques drawn on its account with the Bank, together with prejudgment interest and costs. SNS cross-appeals from the trial judgment, seeking further compensatory damages in the amount of $66,000 on account of additional forged cheques drawn on its account and an award of punitive damages against the Bank in the amount of $132,000.

[2] In our view, both the appeal and cross-appeal must be dismissed.

I.   THE APPEAL

[3] The sole issue on appeal concerns the interpretation of a verification of account clause (the "Verification Clause") in a banking agreement between the parties that was in force when various cheques were improperly drawn on SNS' account with the Bank by an SNS employee who forged the signature of SNS' authorized signing officer on the cheques.

[4] The Verification Clause read as follows:

> 6.5 The Bank shall render each month (unless otherwise instructed in writing) to the Corporation a statement of its account together with cheques and other vouchers where applicable for amounts charged to the said account. The Corporation will advise the Bank promptly if the monthly statement has not been received within ten days of the date upon which it is normally received.

> 6.6 Upon receipt of the aforesaid statement of account, the Corporation will check the debit and credit entries, examine the cheques and vouchers and notify the Bank in writing of any errors, irregularities or omissions. This notice will be provided to the Bank within 30 days of the mailing to the Corporation or if not mailed, within 30 days of the delivery to the Corporation. At the expiration of the 30 day period (except as to any alleged errors, irregularities or omissions outlined on the said notice) it shall be

conclusively settled between the Bank and the Corporation, subject to the right of the Bank either during or after the 30 day period to charge back items for which payment has not been received, that the statement and the balance shown thereon are correct, the said cheques and vouchers are properly charged to the Corporation's account and the Corporation is not entitled to be credited with any sum not credited in the statement. It shall be conclusively settled as between the Bank and the Corporation that the Bank is not liable for any loss or claim arising from the breach by the Corporation or any third party of any fiduciary duty or trust in respect of the sums or dealings noted in the said statements.

[5] SNS sued the Bank for recovery of the amount of the forged cheques that were debited to its account by the Bank, relying on s. 48(1) of the *Bills of Exchange Act*, R.S.C. 1985, c. B. 4. Under that provision, "where a signature on a bill of exchange is forged, or placed thereon without the authority of the person whose signature it purports to be, the forged or unauthorized signature is wholly inoperative ...".

[6] The Bank defended the action, arguing that the Verification Clause provided a complete defence to SNS' claim. The trial judge disagreed. He held, in effect, that the Verification Clause did not apply to forged cheques because the honouring of a forged cheque did not constitute an "error, irregularity or omission" within the meaning of those terms as used in the Verification Clause.

[7] We agree that the Verification Clause does not afford a valid defence to the Bank in this case, although for reasons that differ somewhat from those of the trial judge.

[8] The applicable principles of contractual interpretation are well-established. As this court recently stated in *Dunn v. Chubb Insurance Company of Canada* (2009), 97 O.R. (3d) 701 (C.A.), at para. 32, "The primary goal of contractual interpretation is to give effect to the intentions of the parties." See also *Bell Canada v. The Plan Group* (2009), 96 O.R. (3d) 81 (C.A.), at para. 37. In accordance with the nor-

---

† 2010 ONCA 500.

mal rules of construction, the court searches for an interpretation of a disputed contract which, from the whole of the document, "would appear to promote or advance the true intent of the parties at the time of entry into the contract": *Consolidated-Bathurst Export Ltd. v. Mutual Boiler and Machinery Insurance*, [1980] 1 S.C.R. 888, at p. 901. In this interpretive inquiry, the context or factual matrix surrounding the contract is relevant. As this court has indicated, commercial contracts are to be interpreted, "with regard to objective evidence of the factual matrix underlying the negotiation of the contract, but without reference to the subjective intention of the parties": *Dunn*, at para. 34, note 4 (citations omitted).

[9] The Verification Clause does not refer expressly to forged cheques or otherwise to cheques debited to a customer's account for improper purposes or by illegal means. Further, the terms "error", "irregularity" and "omission" are not defined in the Verification Clause. Nor is their meaning clear on a plain reading of the Verification Clause as a whole. Thus, the meaning of these terms is not apparent on the face of the Verification Clause. Certainly, the scope of these terms would not be self-evident to many, if any, customers of the Bank without clarification or explanation. It is difficult to conceive, therefore, absent evidence to the contrary that does not exist in this case, that both parties intended, when the banking agreement was entered into, that the Verification Clause would extend to forged cheques honoured by the Bank.

[10] Obviously, the Bank was free to include a specific definition or other clarification of these terms in the Verification Clause if it wished to do so. Indeed, the evidence at trial, and the Bank's own pleading, established that the Bank included specific reference to forgery — albeit in the context of cheque endorsements — in a subsequent version of a verification of account clause in a later banking agreement with this same customer — SNS.

[11] It is true that the Verification Clause imposed certain obligations on SNS in relation to monthly account statements furnished by the Bank. It is also true that the Verification Clause afforded certain protections to the Bank, which were designed to limit its liability, if SNS did not fulfil its obligations under the Verification Clause.

[12] But in this case, when SNS sought specific information from the Bank regarding the timelines for verification of its account entries, it was informed in a memorandum by its contact at the Bank as follows:

Message: Hi Don,

As requested by Choui and Tara here is the information you requested:

1. Forged Endorsement — there is no time line if there is a forged endorsement on cheques, there is a declaration form that needs to be filled out and signed for the file.
2. Altered Cheques — if a cheque is altered you have 90 days following receipt of the cheque, there is a declaration form that needs to be filled out and signed for the file as well.
3. Counterfeit Items — if a cheque is counterfeit you have 24 hours following receipt of the cheque to have it returned.
4. Stolen — if a cheque is stolen, you notify the bank immediately and we put a stop payment on it. After 6 months the cheque becomes stale dated and will not be processed for this reason.

[13] This memorandum can only have left SNS with the impression that no verification timeline applied and, therefore, that the Verification Clause did not apply, to forged cheques. We note that the subject heading to the memorandum read: "Timeline for Forged/Altered/Counterfeit/Stolen Cheques". No distinction was drawn in the memorandum between forged "endorsements" and other types of cheque forgeries. Moreover, the memorandum set out applicable timelines for the recovery of funds from the Bank in relation to altered, counterfeit and stolen cheques. There was no indication that forged cheques not involving forged "endorsements" fell into a separate and more exacting verification category. There is no suggestion that the information contained in the memorandum was withdrawn or corrected at any time by the Bank.

[14] Verification of account clauses of the type at issue here form part of the Bank's standard form account documents prepared by the Bank to govern its relations with its customers. We agree with SNS that clauses of this kind are to be construed strictly and, in the event of any ambiguity, against the Bank, as the author of the clause, in accordance with the doctrine of *contra preferentem*: see *Dunn*, at para. 36.

[15] A forged cheque is not simply a bill of exchange that does not conform with requisite formalities. As properly acknowledged by the Bank before this court, it is an invalid cheque for want of proper authorization. By operation of s. 48(1) of the *Bills of Exchange Act*, except for specific circumstances that are inapplicable here, a forged signature on a cheque is "wholly inoperative". It might reasonably be expected, therefore, that any intention by the parties to include forged cheques in the ambit of the

Verification Clause would have been stated in clear and unambiguous language. That did not occur in this case.

[16] In all these circumstances, we are not persuaded that the Verification Clause operates in this case to afford the Bank a defence to SNS' claim. The trial judge was therefore correct to hold that the Verification Clause did not exempt the Bank from liability under s. 48(1) of the *Bills of Exchange Act*. We endorse the trial judge's observation that, on this record, it appears that "[no one] on either side gave the verification agreement a thought".

II.   CROSS-APPEAL

[17] There are two aspects to SNS' cross-appeal. First, SNS argues that the trial judge erred by failing to award additional compensatory damages in the amount of $66,000 for other cheques allegedly forged by SNS' employee and honoured by the Bank.

[18] We reject this claim. The focus of SNS' pleading was on compensation for forged cheques totalling $186,488. This is the amount eventually awarded to SNS by the trial judge. SNS led no properly admissible evidence at trial to prove forged cheques in any additional amount. As the Bank points out, various means were available to SNS to do so, including: the calling of evidence from the police officers involved in the forgery investigation; moving prior to or at trial to compel production by the Bank of copies of the additional cheques that the police regarded as forged; or, cross-examining the Bank's witnesses at trial concerning these additional cheques. SNS, however, failed to take any of these steps. In these circumstances, the trial judge was fully justified in concluding that SNS had failed to meet its evidential burden to prove the honouring by the Bank of forged cheques in excess of those reflected in the compensatory damages awarded by the trial judge.

[19] The second aspect of SNS' cross-appeal concerns its renewed claim that it is entitled to punitive damages. The trial judge fully considered and rejected this claim. On the factual findings of the trial judge, he was right to do so. We note, in particular, the trial judge's findings that SNS' employee "did a good job at forging the signature of her principals"; that the Bank was not negligent for cashing the cheques in question; and that while the Bank's conduct, including its treatment of SNS after the fraud was discovered, was "inefficient and unimpressive", it was not "such as to give rise to aggravated or punitive damages". We see no basis on which to interfere with these findings or with the trial judge's ruling that punitive damages were not warranted.

III.   DISPOSITION

[20] For the reasons given, the appeal and cross-appeal are dismissed. As success has been divided, we make no order as to the costs of this proceeding.

(f)   *United Overseas Bank v. Jiwani*[†]

[MacKENNA J.:]

The plaintiffs, a Swiss bank in Geneva, sue the defendant, their customer, for $9,892.10 and interest. As my statement of the facts will make clear, the claim is in substance one for money paid under a mistake of fact and the defence one of estoppel by representation.

The facts relating to the payment and to the mistake were proved by the oral evidence of the plaintiffs' sub-manager, M. Cottet, and by the documents in the case. They can be briefly narrated.

The defendant opened the account on 13th October 1969. He was then resident in Uganda, being one of the Asian subjects of that state. His object in opening the account was to build up a reserve of assets outside Uganda in case of trouble in the future. There were a few payments into the account in 1969 and 1970. The first was made shortly after the opening of the account. This was a

---

† [1977] 1 All E.R. 733 (Q.B.D.).

payment of $3,000 described in the credit advice sent by the plaintiffs to the defendant on 20th October 1969, as remittance received in his favour from Mr. and Mrs. Ghelani. There was another in September 1970 of $13,343.30 which, again according to the plaintiffs' credit advice, had been provided by a Mr. Alibhai. The third in December 1970, also provided by Mr. Alibhai, was $29,985. On 31st December 1971 the balance was $34,323. Drawings on the account were made by the defendant during the summer of 1972 and these drawings reduced the balance to $10,108.50 by the end of August. Some of the money had been drawn to cover the defendant's living expenses in Europe where he had come from Uganda some time in May 1972. There was a drawing on 18th August of $12,212 in favour of a Mr. Pirani, a London businessman with whom the defendant had some complicated business dealings during that summer culminating in November 1972 in the purchase by the defendant of an hotel owned by Mr. Pirani's private company. It is doubtful whether this particular drawing had anything to do with that purchase. Its effect, at all events, was to reduce the balance to the figure I have given of $10,108.50.

On 6th October 1972 a telex message from a bank in Zurich informed the plaintiffs in Geneva that they were crediting them as from that date with the sum of $11,000 in favour of the defendant on the instructions of an unnamed client. The plaintiffs were told in the message that the transfer would be made through the Union of Swiss Banks in Geneva, which I take to be some sort of clearing house. On the same day, 6th October, the plaintiffs sent the defendant in London a credit advice informing him that the Zurich bank had made this transfer of $11,000 in his favour available for him to draw against from 9th October. It is apparently the practice of Swiss banks when they receive a sum of money for a client on one day to credit it to his account not on that day but on the next working day which in this case, as 6th October was a Friday, was Monday, 9th October. The statement of the defendant's current account contains a credit entry against the date 9th October of $11,000. The balance was then $21,108.50. On the same day as they had sent the telex message the Zurich bank posted to the plaintiffs a written advice of payment stating as follows: 'Through Union de Banques Suisses we transferred to you $11,000 as from October 6, which please utilise by order of one of our clients for account of [the defendant].' The document bears stamped words in German and in French stating that it is sent in confirmation of a telex message. These words would have been put on in Zurich. It was

probably received by the plaintiffs on 9th October. The clerk who dealt with it, he or she, apparently overlooked the stamped words, treated the document as if it were a new transfer of a second sum of $11,000, caused another credit entry to be made in the defendant's statement of account which brought the apparent balance to $32,108.50, and caused him to be sent a second credit advice informing him that the Zurich bank had made a transfer of $11,000 in his favour available for him to draw against from 10th October.

The defendant says that he enquired from the plaintiffs by telephone from London on or before 16th October about the state of his account and was given this figure of $32,108.50, and that he visited the bank at Geneva on 17th October when he was again given the figure of $32,108.50. I see no reason for disbelieving this part of the defendant's evidence. The plaintiffs had not yet discovered their error. The defendant had already on, 2nd October, drawn a cheque in favour of Mr. Pirani for the sum $20,000. He now gave instructions to the plaintiffs to transfer to Ontario another $11,000.60 for Mr. Pirani's credit, which the plaintiffs did. The statement of account shows, if I read it correctly, that the $20,000 was paid on 17th October and that the transfer of $11,000.60 was made on 19th October. These payments reduced the apparent credit balance to $1,107.90. As the account had been over-credited with $11,000, the account, if it had been correctly stated, was not now in credit but was overdrawn by $9,892.10.

On 20th October 1972, a M. Losi, an employee of the plaintiffs, when making a routine check, discovered their mistake. He informed the lady dealing with the defendant's account. She caused a debit advice to be prepared debiting the defendant with $11,000 and sent it to him under cover of an explanatory letter dated 25th October asking the defendant to cover the overdraft. I am satisfied that the defendant received this letter in the month of October within a few days of its being posted on 25th October, and, at all events, before the purchase of the hotel was completed, to which I have already briefly referred. The defendant did not answer this or a number of other letters. In May 1973 one of the plaintiffs' representatives visited the defendant in England and took from him a promissory note for the amount of the overdraft and interest which had accrued in the meantime. The note was eventually dishonoured and this action begun.

I have no doubt whatever that the bank transferred the $11,000 to Mr. Pirani on the defendant's instructions under a mistake of fact, believing that the Zurich bank had transferred for his credit two sums of $11,000, whereas they had transferred only one. In my opinion, it can make no difference to the right of the plaintiff, to recover this money from the defendant that they made the payments to Mr. Pirani at the defendant's request and not to the defendant himself. In the circumstances of this case it is exactly the same as it they had paid money to the defendant and that he had transferred it by some means to Mr. Pirani in Ontario.

The defendant has given me some sort of explanation of his dealings with Mr. Pirani and of the value he received in exchange for the transfer of $11,000. It was a confused explanation. All things considered, including the want of documents passing between the gentlemen in question, I think it likely that the value given by Mr. Pirani for the $11,000 must have been one or more of the large sums of money paid into the defendant's account with Lloyds Bank Ltd. at Ealing in October 1972, probably the sum of £4,969 credited to that account on 19th October.

I have already mentioned that the defendant bought an hotel from Mr. Pirani's private company in November 1972. To be more accurate, he acquired the sub-lease of that hotel, the completion date being 3rd November. I think it is probable that the transfer to Mr. Pirani of the $11,000, which was the use to which the defendant put the overpayment, made it easier for the defendant to complete this purchase which he effected by drawing on his account with Lloyds Bank Ltd. and with the help of a loan from that bank.

I am reasonably sure that if the $11,000 had not been forthcoming in the way it was (that is through the plaintiffs' error) the defendant would have found the extra money for his purchase in some other way, either by a larger borrowing from Lloyds Bank Ltd. or, if they were unwilling to lend, by Mr. Pirani giving him more time to pay. I am equally certain that the purchase of the hotel was for the defendant and his family a good investment. If it be a relevant consideration, I find that the defendant knew of the plaintiffs' mistake before the date when he completed his contract to buy the hotel. Lastly, and again if it be a relevant consideration, I believe that if he is now required to repay the plaintiffs he will be able to do so by borrowing if he has not the cash available. He is a man of property. He owns, in addition to the hotel, a dwelling-house which he acquired at about the same time as the hotel for some £18,000.

The question remains whether the defendant is liable to repay the plaintiffs the sum with which they credited him in error. In my opinion, which I base on the statement of the law in Goff and Jones's The Law of Restitution,[1] he is liable unless he can show that the plaintiffs are estopped from claiming restitution, and there are three conditions to be satisfied by him if he is to make good this estoppel. First, he must show that either the plaintiffs were under a duty to give him accurate information about the state of this account and that in breach of this duty they gave him inaccurate information, or that in some other way there was a misrepresentation made to him about the state of the account for which the plaintiffs are responsible. Secondly, he must show that this inaccurate information in fact misled him about the state of the account and caused him to believe the plaintiffs were his debtors for a larger sum than was the case and to make the transfer to Mr. Pirani in that mistaken belief. Thirdly, he must show that because of his mistaken belief he changed his position in a way which would make it inequitable to require him now to repay the money. I have no doubt that the first of these requirements is satisfied. I shall assume for the moment that he has satisfied the second, returning to that mater a little later in this judgment. He has, I think, completely failed to establish the essential third condition.

Counsel for the defendant contended that if a bank's customer has spent the money with which he has been mistakenly credited, he cannot, in any case whatever, be required to repay it. If he has to show a detriment making it inequitable to require him to repay, he shows that detriment, it is argued, by proving that he has spent the money, irrespective of the purpose for which it was spent or of the effects of the expenditure, and that he will have to make it good, if at all, out of other moneys. To test counsel for the defendant's proposition I put the case to him of a customer who uses the overpayment to buy a gilt-edged security which can be immediately re-sold and which rises in value between the date of the purchase and the date when the mistake is discovered and he is called on to repay. Counsel for the defendant did not shrink from accepting the logical consequence of his argument. He said that in such a case the customer would be under no obligation to repay; he could treat his acquisition of the security as a windfall and let the bank whistle for its money. I do not believe that is the law.

Undoubtedly there are cases in which the customer who has spent the money in ignorance that he was being overpaid will not be required to repay. *Holt v. Markham*[2] was such a case. *Skyring v. Greenwood and Cox*,[3] which *Holt's case*[2] followed, was another. A third was *Lloyds Bank Ltd. v. Brooks*.[4]

There was reason for believing in each of these cases that the defendant would have acted differently if he had not mistakenly believed that he was richer than he was, that because of his mistake, he had, to use Goff and Jones's words,[5] altered his mode of living. There was the further fact in *Holt's case*[2] that the defendant had invested part of the overpayment in a company which had since gone into liquidation. There is in the present case, as I have already said, no reason for thinking that the defendant would have acted differently in the matter of the purchase or in any other way if the extra dollars had not been mistakenly made available to him. He would still have completed the purchase of the hotel by a further borrowing from Lloyds Bank Ltd. or in some other way. The completion of the purchase, wherever he got the money to do it with, was in itself a benefit and is a continuing benefit, unlike the investment in *Holt's case*.[2]

Other cases cited by counsel for the defendant are distinguishable in the same way. There was the case of the customer who had paid the money over to a third party which he was not bound to do if the money were not truly his own and who was unable to recover it from the third party on the discovery of the mistake. The decision in *Deutsche Bank (London Agency) v. Beriro & Co. Ltd.*[6] that the customer in that case was not liable to repay the bank does not help counsel for the defendant.

What I have said already is enough to show that there must be judgment in the plaintiffs' favour, but I have something to add, before I finish, on the second of the three requirements, namely that the bank's mis-statement caused the defendant to believe that there had in fact been two transfers of $11,000 to the credit of his account. He told me a story which I did not believe about the reason why he thought that there had been two transfers. He said that after he had left Uganda in May 1972 he had spoken on the telephone to his brother, who was still living there, and had asked him to arrange with Mr. Alibhai, whom I have already mentioned, for the transfer to the plaintiffs for the defendant's credit of a sum in dollars equivalent to 245,000 Ugandan shillings to be paid in Uganda to Mr. Alibhai along with his commission. The defendant told me that it was his understanding and his brother's that the equivalent of this amount of Ugandan currency would be about $24,000. He said that on some date which he could not now remember he had received a telephone call in London from Mr. Alibhai speaking from Uganda who told him that he had transferred, or was going to transfer, $11,000 that day and that either that evening or the next day or after two days

he would transfer the balance. After this conversation with Mr. Alibhai the defendant expected, so he said, that there would be two transfers made by Mr. Alibhai and that, therefore, when he received the information from the plaintiffs about the supposed second transfer, he believed that it represented the amount of the second expected transfer. Mr. Alibhai, it seems, did not in fact transfer any other money to the defendant who had not heard from him since. He does not know where he is.

The defendant's brother gave evidence supporting him to some extent. He said that he had spoken to the defendant on the telephone, that the defendant had told him to arrange with Mr. Alibhai for the transfer of $23,000, of which he said the Ugandan equivalent was then 175,000 shillings, and that he had made the arrangement.

My reasons for not accepting the defendant's story about the two expected transfers can be stated very shortly. There is, it seems to me, an improbability in the substance of the supposed telephone conversation with Mr. Alibhai — why the two transfers? Why not a single transfer made when Mr. Alibhai had the whole amount available which would be, at the latest, in a day or two and might even be the day on which he was speaking? That is one reason. Another is the strange coincidence that the defendant should have been expecting two transfers at about the same time and of about the same amount from Mr. Alibhai and that the plaintiffs should, as they undoubtedly did, wrongly mistake the confirmation of the telex for a second transfer. The improbability of this coincidence is, it seems to me, the greater when it is realized that Mr. Alibhai never in fact made any second transfer. This goes against the view that there was an arrangement with him that he should send any larger sum than the $11,000 which he sent in fact, or that he had told the defendant on the telephone that he would be making a second transfer. A third reason, I think, can be found in the fact already mentioned that on 2nd October the defendant had drawn a cheque on his account with the plaintiffs for $20,000 in favour of Mr. Pirani which Mr. Pirani apparently did not present until 16th October. On 2nd October the credit balance was, as I said earlier, $10,108.50. It is not unreasonable to infer that at the time when he drew the cheque, only a few days before the plaintiffs received the transfer of $11,000, the defendant was expecting the transfer of a sum which would put him in credit to an amount sufficient to meet the cheque. If on 2nd October he was (1) expecting a much larger transfer than $11,000 and (2) intending to give Mr. Pirani not $20,000 but $31,000 namely the amount of the cheque and of the subsequent transfer to Ontario, why did he not give Mr. Pirani in the first instance a cheque for the larger amount? If, as I believe, the burden is on the defendant of satisfying me that on 17th October or thereabouts he honestly believed that there had been a second transfer made by Mr. Alibhai, he has not discharged that burden. It seems to me equally possible that he knew or strongly suspected that the plaintiffs were making a mistake.

In saying this I do not exclude the possibility that the defendant, though not expecting a second transfer from Mr. Alibhai, on hearing from the plaintiffs that there had been two transfers, may have thought that some arrangement, of which he had not previously been told, had been made by his brother either with Mr. Alibhai or with somebody else for the transfer of this further sum. But that is not the story told by the defendant in the witness box and I see no reason why I should speculate about this possibility.

For these two reasons (1) that the defendant has not satisfied me that he honestly believed that the two transfers had been made, and (2) that in any event, he has not proved that, if he was misled by the plaintiffs, he changed his position in such a way as would make it inequitable to require him to repay the money, I hold that this action succeeds.

I have been told that it is agreed between the parties that the correct amount for which judgment should be given is $13,302.50 and there will be judgment for that amount.

Judgment for the plaintiffs for $13,302.50

(g) *Holland v. Manchester and Liverpool District Banking Co.*†

Entries by a banker in his customer's passbook, although subject to adjustment, are *prima facie* evidence against the banker of the amount standing to the credit of the customer, and the customer, in the absence of negligence or fraud on his part, is entitled to rely upon such entries.

The plaintiff, a customer of the defendant bank, finding on examining his pass-book that it showed a balance of £70 17s. 9d. in his favour, drew a cheque for £67 11s. in favour of a firm to whom he owed that amount. On the cheque being presented by that firm it was dishonoured by the defendants, whereby the plaintiff suffered damage in respect of which he sued the defendants. It appeared in evidence that at the time the plaintiff drew the cheque for £67 11s. he had a balance at the bank of £60 5s. 9d. only, but that in his pass-book one of the bank clerks had, in error, entered to the plaintiff's credit a sum of £10 12s, twice, with the result that from the pass-book the plaintiff appeared to be in credit to the amount of £70 17s. 9d.

Held, that although the defendants were entitled to have the wrong entry ultimately corrected, the plaintiff (who had not been guilty of any negligence or fraud in connexion with the matter) was entitled until that correction had been made to act upon the defendants' statements in the pass-book; and that, having acted upon those statements and suffered damage thereby, he was entitled to recover against the defendants the amount of such damage.

––––––––––

This case was tried at Manchester Assizes, before the Lord Chief Justice and a special jury.

The plaintiff, Joseph Lees Holland, leather merchant and tanner, of Lowick-green, Greenodd, near Ulverston, claimed damages for breach of contract by the defendant bank to honour one of his cheques. The bank pleaded by their defence that at the time the cheque was presented the amounts standing to the credit of the plaintiffs account was not sufficient to meet it, and further that as soon as the plaintiff had subsequently paid the sufficient money they did in fact honour the cheque.

––––––––––

† (1909), 25 T.L.R. 386 (Manchester Assizes).

Mr. Tobin, K.C., and Mr. Openshaw appeared for the plaintiff: Mr. Langdon, K.C., and Mr. Acton for the defendant bank.

The plaintiff in the summer of 1907 opened an account with the Lancaster Banking Company at their Ulverston branch. Very soon afterwards this company was amalgamated with the defendant bank. On September 21, 1907, the plaintiff, after examining his pass-book and finding a balance of £70 17s. 9d. in his favour there, drew a cheque for £67 11s. in favour of a firm named Reynolds and Co. to whom he owed a trade debt. Reynolds and Co. presented the cheque, which was dishonoured without any communication being made to the plaintiff. It transpired that in fact at the time when he drew the cheque the plaintiff had a balance at the bank of £60 5s. 9d. only, but in his pass book one of the bank clerks had in error entered to his credit a sum of £10 12s. twice, with the result that from that book he appeared to be in credit to the amount of £70 17s. 9d. Although the bank wrote to Messrs. Reynolds and Co. explaining their mistake and apologizing, Messrs. Reynolds refused to do any further business with the plaintiff except upon cash terms, and the matter having leaked out other creditors began to press the plaintiff. By consent, the only question left to the jury was as to the amount of damages; and all other questions of fact and inferences to be drawn from the evidence were left to the Lord Chief Justice.

The jury assessed the damages at £100 subject to the Court's decision upon the point of law as to whether a customer of a bank was entitled to draw the cheque in the circumstances set out.

Mr. Tobin, K.C., for the plaintiff, argued that a bank was not entitled, without any communication with a perfectly solvent customer, to dishonour the cheque when that cheque had been drawn on the faith of entries made by the bank itself in his own pass-book. The customer had a perfect right to assume that the entries in his pass-book were correct, and if without negligence on his part and upon the faith of such entries the customer acted to his prejudice, the bank must be liable. It might be wise for the customer to check his pass-book at intervals, but there was no obligation upon him to do so at all, most certainly not before each particular cheque was drawn. He referred to the remarks of Mr. Justice Bigham in the case of *Akrokerri Mines, Limited v. Economic Bank* (20 *The Times L.R.*, 564: [1904] 2 K.B., 465), where he said (at page 470) that the pass-book "belongs to the customer, and the entries made in it by the bank are statements on which the customer is entitled to act". He cited also *Capital and Countries Bank v. Gordon* ([1903], A.C., 240) and referred to a passage in Lord Lindley's judgment (p. 249) where he said, "It must never be forgotten that the moment a bank places money to his customer's credit, the customer is entitled to draw upon it, unless something occurs to deprive him of that right.

Mr. Langdon, K.C., for the defendant bank, submitted that the remarks of Mr. Justice Bigham and of Lord Lindley were *obiter* and were not necessary for the decision of the case. The entries in a pass-book were not conclusive against the bank and did not debar the bank from showing the real nature of the transactions which they were intended to record, see *Garden v. Newfoundland Savings Bank* ([1899] A.C. 231; 15 *The Times L.R.* 228). It was the customer's duty to see that he did not draw a cheque for an amount greater than that he had in the bank, and the bank's only duty was to honour a customer's cheques so long as they had money of that customer with which to do so.

The Lord Chief Justice, in giving judgment, said that the case was of the greatest importance, and but for the pressure of business at the assizes he should have taken time to consider his decision. Owing to that pressure, however, and to the fact that in any event the case might go to the Court of Appeal, he would deal with the matter at once to the best of his ability. He considered that the plaintiff had told the truth in his evidence and he did not think that the plaintiff was negligent in the discharge of any duty he owed to the bank, or that he was guilty of any fraud. The effect of a pass-book entry did not seem to have been clearly decided in the Courts, but he considered that, whilst the bank in this case were entitled to have any wrong entry ultimately corrected, until the correction was made the customer had the right to act upon the bank's statements in the pass-book, and to receive them as statements by the bank that there was so much money to his credit. The pass-book in all cases although subject to adjustment was *prima facie* evidence against the bank of the amount standing to the credit of a customer, upon which that customer, in the absence of negligence or fraud on his part, was entitled to rely. He was supported in this view by the judgment of Lord Campbell, L.C., in *Commercial Bank of Scotland v. Rhind* (3 Macq. H.L., 643). He therefore held that the plaintiff in this case was entitled to recover and judgment must be entered in his favour of £100 and costs.

A stay of execution for 14 days was granted.

Keeping Secrets

Background Reading: M.H. Ogilvie, *Bank and Customer Law in Canada*, 2d Edition (Toronto: Irwin Law, 2013) Chapter 8, pages 324–338.

(a) *Tournier v. National Provincial and Union Bank of England*†

[ATKIN L.J.:]

This is an action brought by the plaintiff against the defendant bank in respect of words spoken by the manager of a branch of the bank. The plaintiff alleges as causes of action: (A) slander; (B) breach of an implied contract not to divulge information concerning the plaintiff's transactions with the bank. The second point involves a question of considerable public importance, and I propose to consider it first.

In *Joachimson v. Swiss Bank Corporation*[1] this Court had to consider what were the terms of the contract made between banker and customer in the ordinary course of business when a current account is opened by the bank. All the members of the Court were of opinion that the contract included several implied terms, some of which were then stated, so far as was necessary for the determination of that case, which turned upon the necessity of a demand before the customer could sue the bank for the account of his credits balance. It is now necessary to consider whether there is any, and if so what, implied term as to an obligation of secrecy on the part of the bank. The question of what terms are to be implied in a contract is a question of law: *In re Comptoir Commercial Anversois and Power*;[2] and the rules by which the Court should be guided are contained in passages from the judgments of Lord Esher

in *Hamlyn v. Wood*,[3] and of Lord Watson in *Dahl v. Nelson, Donkin & Co.*,[4] cited by Bankes L.J.[5] The principle is stated by Scrutton L.J. in words substantially to the same effect:[6] "The Court", he says, "and not the jury, are the tribunal to find such a term; they ought not to imply a term merely because it would be a reasonable term to include if the parties had thought about the matter, or because one party, if he had thought about the matter, would not have made the contract unless the term was included; it must be such a necessary term that both parties must have intended that it should be a term of the contract, and have only not expressed it because its necessity was so obvious that it was taken for granted." Is there any term as to secrecy to be implied from the relation of banker and customer? I have myself no doubt that there is. Assuming that the test is rather stricter than Lord Watson would require, and is not merely what the parties, as fair and reasonable men, would presumably have agreed upon, but what the Court considers they must necessarily have agreed upon, it appears to me that some term as to secrecy must be implied. The bank find it necessary to bind their servants to secrecy; they communicate this fact to all their customers in their pass-book, and I am satisfied that if they had been asked whether they were under an obligation as to

---

† [1924] 1 K.B. 461 (C.A.). [Notes omitted.]

secrecy by a prospective customer, without hesitation they would say yes. The facts in this case as to the course of business of this bank do not appear to be in any degree unusual in general banking business. I come to the conclusion that one of the implied terms of the contract is that the bank enter into a qualified obligation with their customer to abstain from disclosing information as to his affairs without his consent. I am confirmed in this conclusion by the admission of counsel for the bank that they do, in fact, consider themselves under a legal obligation to maintain secrecy. Such an obligation could only arise under a contractual term.

The important point, and one which presents difficulties, is as to the extent of the obligation. The plaintiff's pleading alleged the obligation in wide terms as absolute and unconditional. The learned judge, as I think quite rightly, ruled that there was no such absolute duty, and the trial then proceeded without further amendment of the pleadings on the footing that the plaintiff relied on a breach of the true contract, whatever it was. The learned judge directed the jury:

> If the banker has made the disclosure justifiably, that is to say, if, under the circumstances of the particular case, it was reasonable and proper that he should make the communication, then there is no breach of contract on his part.

Without any further direction he left to the jury the question:

> Was the communication with regard to the plaintiff's account at the bank made on a reasonable and proper occasion?

The direction and question appear to follow the direction to the jury given by Byles J. in *Hardy v. Veasey*,[7] affirmed by the Court of Exchequer. I think that the decision in that case was based on the fact that the formula approved was that adopted by the plaintiff's counsel in his pleading, and accepted by him as representing the true issue to be left to the jury. In fact, however, to leave to the jury what is "justifiable" or "proper" is merely to tell them that the bank may not divulge information except on occasions when they may divulge it, and that of what those occasions are the jury are the judges. This appears to me to treat as fact what is matter of law, and to afford no guidance to the jury, leaving the rights and duties as between customer and banker to vary with the individual views of juries in each case.

The first question is: To what information does the obligation of secrecy extend? It clearly goes beyond the state of the account, that is, whether there

is a debit or a credit balance, and the amount of the balance. It must extend at least to all the transactions that go through the account, and to the securities, if any, given in respect of the account; and in respect of such matters it must, I think, extend beyond the period when the account is closed, or ceases to be an active account. It seems to me inconceivable that either party would contemplate that once the customer had closed his account the bank was to be at liberty to divulge as it pleased the particular transactions which it had conducted for the customer while he was such. I further think that the obligation extends to information obtained from other sources than the customer's actual account, if the occasion upon which the information was obtained arose out of the banking relations of the bank and its customers — for example, with a view to assisting the bank in conducting the customer's business, or in coming to decisions as to its treatment of its customers. Here, again, counsel for the bank admitted that the bank treated themselves as under such an obligation, and this, I think, would be in accordance with ordinary banking practice. In this case, however, I should not extend the obligation to information as to the customer obtained after he had ceased to be customer. Speaking for myself, I find little assistance from considering the implications that have been found by the Courts to arise from contracts in other occupations and protections, such as those of solicitors or doctors. The limitation of the implied term must vary with the special circumstances peculiar to each class of occupation. On the other hand, it seems to me clear that there must be important limitations upon the obligation of their bank not to divulge such information as I have mentioned. It is plain that there is no privilege from disclosures enforced in the course of legal proceedings. But the bank is entitled to secure itself in respect of liabilities it incurs to the customer, or the customer to it, and in respect of liabilities to third parties in respect of the transactions it conducts for or with the customer. It is difficult to hit upon a formula which will define the maximum of the obligations which must necessarily be implied. But I think it safe to say that the obligation not to disclose information such as I have mentioned is subject to the qualification that the bank have the right to disclose such information when, and to the extent to which it is reasonably necessary for the protection of the bank's interests, either as against their customer or as against third parties in respect of transactions of the bank for or with their customer, or for protecting the bank, or persons interested, or the public, against fraud or crime. I have already stated the obligation as an obligation not to disclose without the customer's consent.

It is an implied term, and may, therefore, be varied by express agreement. In any case the consent may be express or implied, and to the extent to which it is given the bank will be justified in acting. A common example of such consent would be where a customer gives a banker's reference. The extent to which he authorizes information to be given on such a reference must be a question to be determined on the facts of each case. I do not desire to express any final opinion on the practice of bankers to give one another information as to the affairs of their respective customers, except to say it appears to me that it is justified it must be upon the basis of an implied consent of the customer.

As to the rest of the case based on slander, I think that this issue must also be submitted for a new trial. I do not think that it is a sufficient direction to a jury on what is meant by "defamatory" to say, without more, that it means: Were the words calculated to expose the plaintiff to hatred, ridicule, or contempt, in the mind of a reasonable man? The formula is well known to lawyers, but it is obvious that suggestions might be made very injurious to a man's character in business which would not, in the ordinary sense, excite either hate, ridicule, or contempt — for example, an imputation of a clever fraud which, however much to be condemned morally and legally, might yet not excite what a member of a jury might understand as hatred, or contempt. Speaking for myself, I also think that it is undesirable where an issue of privilege is raised to leave a question of express malice to be decided by the jury before the judge has ruled whether the occasion is privileged. The judge has to determine, not only whether the occasion is privileged, but whether the defendant has gone beyond the privilege which the occasion creates: *Adam v. Ward*.[8] In the words of Lord Loreburn:

All this is for the judge alone, and the question of malice, which is for the jury, cannot arise till the judge has ruled on the whole question of privilege.

In many cases, and I think this is one, the jury cannot form a correct opinion as to what is express malice until the judge has ruled whether the circumstances exist, as to legal or social duty and so forth, on which the legal privilege depends; and if the occasion is not privileged, or has been, in fact, exceeded, the question of express malice is irrelevant; and I think it is a disadvantage to the administration of justice that questions should be asked of the jury unnecessarily when the final decision may appear to conflict with their answers. It is also, I think, clear that the plaintiff was entitled to put before the jury his case that the words proved, though not the very words pleaded, were words substantially to the same effect. Whether this be done by amending the pleading, by framing the question to the jury so as to raise the point, or by directing the jury that the words pleaded would be proved by proof of words substantially to the same effect, seems to me immaterial. No slander of any complexity could ever be proved if the *ipsissima verba* of the pleading had to be established. There appears to me to be ample authority in well established every day practice, and in the decisions upon the form of interrogatories in such cases, to support the view that I am expressing.

For the above reasons, without expressing an opinion the points raised between the parties at the trial, I come to the opinion that this appeal must be allowed, and a new trial ordered.

Appeal allowed.

(b) *Canadian Imperial Bank of Commerce v. Sayani*†

[TAYLOR J.A.:]

This case has to do with the duty imposed on a bank to keep in confidence information gained in the course of its dealings with or for its customer concerning its customer's affairs.

Mr. Justice Callaghan gave judgment at trial [[1991] B.C.W.L.D. 2684] in favour of the Canadian

---

† [1994] 2 W.W.R. 260 at 261–69 (B.C.C.A.).

Imperial Bank of Commerce against the Sayani brothers for $518,064, being the balance owing on loans advanced to them and accrued interest, and dismissed their counterclaim for damages for breach by the bank of its contractual duty of confidentiality with respect to the existence and history of this debt.

The Sayani brothers do not dispute the judgment against them but appeal the dismissal of their counterclaim.

They say the trial judge ought to have found that the bank, through its solicitor and a loan officer, breached the term as to confidentiality implied by law in the contract between bank and customer by disclosing to a mortgage lender which was about to refinance a housing project for them that they had defaulted on a settlement with the bank in respect to their indebtedness to it, and that they then owed the bank more than $300,000, information which was not disclosed in the financial statements supplied to the proposed lender on their behalf.

The appellants say that as a result of the bank's disclosures the lender thereafter declined to make the advance on terms previously agreed between them, and was in the end willing to advance funds only on unacceptable terms.

THE BACKGROUND

The Sayani brothers entered into negotiations for the financing for their housing project with the mortgage lender, Confederation Trust, in the fall of 1988 through City Fund, a brokerage firm retained as their agent.

The judge summarizes the state of these negotiations in September, 1988, as follows [pp. 15–16]:

> As a result, City Fund prepared a mortgage presentation package which contained, amongst other things, personal financial statements for Sayani brothers dated December 31, 1987, a credit report, developers' financing requirement and a copy of the construction cost estimate for servicing the development. The Sayanis were seeking a loan of $10,500,000 at prime + 1-1/2% for a period of twelve months. The personal financial statements, for the Sayani brothers, did not include a reference to the amount outstanding to the Canadian Imperial Bank of Commerce.
>
> Further correspondence ensued between City Fund and Confederation Trust. By letter dated September 19th, 1988, on the basis of information provided and representations made by City Fund on behalf of Badru, Sadru and Nazir Sayani, Confederation Trust authorized financing

in the amount of $6 million for a 90-unit townhouse project located at 2900 block Guildford Way, Coquitlam, and authorized a further $4,500,000 to provide interim mortgage financing on unimproved land at 2900 block Guildford Way, Coquitlam.

Confederation Trust referred completion of the proposed financing to its Vancouver lawyers. By coincidence, this same firm was already acting for the bank in connection with the default by the appellants in repayment of their indebtedness to it.

For the history of dealings between the appellants and the bank it is necessary to go back to July, 1985. As a result of default on repayment of loans totalling $515,926 the bank then commenced foreclosure proceedings against properties in North Vancouver on which the loans were partially secured.

The appellants as a result made a settlement offer. The bank agreed to take $310,000 in full payment, $200,000 to be paid in November, 1985, and the balance by September 11, 1986. The settlement was agreed to by the bank on the advice of its loan inspector who felt that the appellants' assets were effectively "sheltered", and that there would be little hope of collecting on a judgment. The appellants defaulted on the November, 1985 payment, with the result that the balance of the original indebtedness again became due. The matter stood thus until August, 1987, when they made a new settlement with the bank. Under the new agreement they would be discharged in return for payment of $(U.S.)92,500, of which $(U.S.)40,000 was paid forthwith and the balance of $(U.S.)52,000 was to be paid by a series of post-dated cheques, the first due September 30, 1987. It was again provided that default in any payment would result in the full balance of the original indebtedness becoming due.

The Sayanis again defaulted. In late 1987 the bank put the account into the hands of its solicitors for collection, the amount owing then being in excess of $(Can.) 300,000. It was a year after this that Confederation Trust put its refinancing for the Sayanis into the hands of the same solicitors.

THE DISCLOSURES

Roger Howay, a solicitor in the law firm, then telephoned Robert MacFarlane, regional manager of the trust company, to say that the law firm would be unable to act for his company because of a conflicting prior retainer.

The judge describes the conversation between Mr. Howay and Mr. MacFarlane as follows [p. 16]:

Mr. Howay informed him that the firm was acting for a financial institution which had a dispute with the Sayanis involving loan arrangements and there was a possibility that the dispute could lead to litigation. At that point, Mr. MacFarlane asked Mr. Howay if he could disclose the name of his client but he was told he could not. Howay indicated to MacFarlane that if he wished further information regarding the dispute, he should ask the right questions of the Sayanis regarding the matter. He offered the observation that the Sayanis had not conducted themselves in a reliable manner and that it may be in the interest of Confederation Trust to obtain a credit analysis.

While the judge says that this conversation occurred on October 14, 1990, it is apparent that the conversation must have taken place on October 14, 1988.

Five days later Mr. MacFarlane telephoned the bank's loan superintendent, Don Ellwood. The judge says [pp. 16–17]:

> Mr. Ellwood gave Mr. MacFarlane the usual disclaimer with respect to providing confidential information. MacFarlane then asked whether the loans of the Sayanis were nonperforming. This was confirmed. He wanted to know whether the bank had commenced litigation. He was advised that was not the case. Mr. Ellwood was then asked, specifically, what debts were outstanding and he indicated the bank was in the process of making interest calculations and had not determined the exact amount, but that the balance due and owing to the Granville & Dunsmuir branch would be in the area of $300–400,000. Mr. MacFarlane then advised Mr. Ellwood that if Confederation Trust proceeded with the loan, it would only be on the basis that the Sayanis had a settlement agreement with the bank.

Apparently as a result of his initial conversation with Mr. Howay, Mr. MacFarlane had by then made inquiries of other companies which had done business with the appellants, and had learned of some financial and construction problems encountered by the appellants in connection with previous ventures.

It is conceded that neither Mr. Ellwood nor Mr. Howay had authority from the appellants to make the disclosures which they did concerning the appellant's dealings with the bank. As a result of the enquiries undertaken by Mr. MacFarlane, the trust company, at his suggestion, cancelled the intended mortgage loan to the appellants. The Sayanis were unable to accept the new terms on which the company later made a different offer of financing, and the project as a consequence did not proceed as planned. By their counterclaim the Sayanis claim substantial damages for the losses which they said they suffered.

The judge found that Mr. Howay was not in a "direct fiduciary relationship" with the appellants, but "nonetheless owed the Sayanis a duty, by his agency relationship with the plaintiff bank, to respect the confidences of the Sayanis". He concluded that the fiduciary relationship had its basis in contract. He found that Mr. Howay's disclosure was made for the protection of the bank's interests and for this reason permissible under the implied covenant described in the leading case of *Tournier v. National Provincial & Union Bank of England*, [1924] 1 K.B. 461 (C.A.).

The judge describes the nature of the financial statements supplied to the trust company by the Sayanis [pp. 26–27]:

> But it was the conduct of the Sayanis that placed the bank and Mr. Howay in a difficult and delicate situation.
>
> The financial statements that were forwarded by City Fund to Confederation Trust in July of 1988 were prepared by the Sayanis' accountant pursuant to instructions received. The accountant was not advised of the amount due and owing to the Bank of Commerce by the Sayanis and, consequently, the financial statements were incomplete and inaccurate. If Confederation Trust had been aware of the Sayanis' true financial picture, it is doubtful whether it would have committed itself to the project, at least without further investigation.

The judge concludes [p. 27]:

> Mr. Howay, in keeping within the exceptions to the contract of confidentiality, enunciated in *Tournier*, was entitled to reveal the existence of the dispute between the plaintiff bank and the Sayanis in order to protect the interests of the bank in collecting on its debt when the Sayanis were attempting to incur additional debt obligations, and to protect the interests of Confederation Trust, who had not been informed of the dispute between the bank and the Sayanis.

The judge did not deal with the disclosure subsequently made by Mr. Ellwood, the bank's loan officer.

The judge went on to find that the collapse of the financing did not, in any event, result from these disclosures.

THE CASE ON APPEAL

The appellants argue that the judge ought to have found the disclosures to be a breach of the bank's duty of confidentiality, that they could not be justified on the basis that they were made to serve the interests either of the bank or of the trust company, and that they caused the collapse of the loan arrangement with Confederation Trust, while the bank contends that Confederation Trust was "a victim of misrepresentation" and the bank was entitled to alert it to this fact.

I regard the last point as decisive of this appeal.

It has now long been recognized in the common law world that the contract between customer and bank includes an implied term imposing on the bank an obligation subject to exceptions not to disclose information concerning the customer's dealings with it; but the scope of the exceptions to this obligation have rarely been discussed in the cases, and never clearly defined.

Of the very few decisions in this area of banking law that most frequently cited is the decision of the Court of Appeal in *Tournier v. National Provincial & Union Bank* (above). It is to the judgment of Bankes L.J. that reference is most often made, because it includes (at p. 473) four enumerated classifications within which the exceptions are sometimes said to be encompassed:

(a) Where disclosure is under compulsion by law;

(b) where there is a duty to the public to disclose;

(c) where the interests of the bank require disclosure;

(d) where the disclosure is made by the express or implied consent of the customer.

It must be observed at once that these are broadly defined categories. It must also be noted that two other eminent commercial-law judges sat on the appeal, and each expressed his own view on the implied duty of confidence.

Scrutton L.J. restricted his remarks to "the exceptions material to the present case". He said (at p. 481):

> I think it is clear that the bank may disclose the customer's account and affairs to an extent reasonable and proper for its own protection, as in collecting or suing for an overdraft; or to an extent reasonable and proper for carrying on the business of the account, as in giving a reason for declining to honour cheques drawn or bills accepted by the customer, when there are insufficient assets; or when ordered to answer questions in the law Courts; *or to prevent frauds* or crimes. I doubt whether it is sufficient excuse for disclosure, in the absence of the customer's consent, that it was in the interests of the customer, where the customer can be consulted in reasonable time and his consent or dissent obtained. [Emphasis added.]

The third member of the court, Atkin L.J., while equally reluctant to provide any exhaustive definition of the exceptions to the duty of confidence, said (at p. 486):

> But I think it safe to say that the obligation not to disclose information such as I have mentioned is subject to the qualification that the bank have the right to disclose such information when, and to the extent to which it is reasonably necessary for the protection of the bank's interests, either as against their customer or as against third parties in respect of transactions of the bank for or with their customer, or *for protecting* the bank, or *persons interested*, or the public, *against fraud* or crime. [Emphasis added].

Thus both Scrutton L.J. and Atkin L.J. specifically include protection against fraud among the purposes for which a bank may disclose a customer's confidential information to a third party. It seems that this exception — that is to say *prevention* of fraud as opposed to its prosecution — probably falls also within the second category enunciated by Bankes, L.J, that is to say: "where there is a duty to the public disclose".

It seems to me that such an exception would have to be part of the implied term of the contract between bank and customer defining the bank's duty of confidentiality. It seems to me inconceivable that an honest banker would ever be willing to do business on terms obliging the bank to remain silent in order to facilitate its customer in deceiving a third party. I think it equally unreasonable that any would-be customer could expect a bank to be willing to be silent in such circumstances,. Implied terms must, of course, be such as reasonable people making such a contract would expect and accept.

The financial statements prepared by the Sayanis' accountant and forwarded to Confederation Trust were plainly incomplete and materially misleading.

They are said in the accountant's accompanying comments to have been compiled from information supplied by the appellants. The accountant who prepared them confirmed in evidence that he spoke to the appellants for that purpose and that they at no time mentioned to him the fact that they were in any way indebted to the Canadian Imperial Bank of Commerce.

THE "FRAUD" EXCEPTION

The two judges in *Tournier* who spoke of the prevention of "fraud or crime" as a basis for exception from the duty of confidentiality chose language intended to show that the exception is not limited to fraud in the criminal sense, and all of the judges make it clear that the exceptions could not be exhaustively defined and would develop through the cases.

I have concluded that there must be an exception which meets the case of misrepresentation such as that involved here, whether or not it constitutes fraud or deceit in law.

But for the bank's disclosure of the truth, the trust company would have acted in reliance on financial statements which were materially misleading. They contained no reference to any obligation to the bank, yet the appellants owed the bank several hundred thousand dollars at the date as at which the statements were prepared, and that amount had increased by the date when the statements were forwarded to the trust company. Such an outstanding debt would obviously be an important consideration for a prospective lender assessing a debtor's ability to repay a further substantial borrowing, and particularly be so where, as here, the loan was in substantial default, no payment whatever by then having been made for more than a year.

If the misrepresentation was due to some misunderstanding or oversight, one would not expect the customer to object to the representee learning from a third party that which had been omitted. But the position of the appellants in these proceedings seems to be that they had a right to mislead the trust company, and that the bank was contractually obligated to facilitate this by maintaining silence in the present circumstances.

The only explanation suggested to us for the appellant's failure to disclose their indebtedness to the bank is that contained in a letter to their broker dated October 25, 1988. It was written by one of the appellants after settlement negotiations with the bank had been re-opened. It says:

> Finally, we realize that Mr. MacFarlane was concerned with the fact that this portion of the liability was not explicitly mentioned in our Financial Statements. We assure you that the U.S. dollar debt was calculated as a part of the accounts payable to Qualico Homes Inc. In so far as Dawson account is concerned, we have never executed any personal guarantees; the Bank has never sent any demand notices to commence legal action; and after five years, cannot say for certain what the actual amount should be. We further assure you that the final settlement amount due Canadian Imperial Bank of Commerce in total would be less than $100,000. We shall endeavour to clear off the U.S. dollar

> amount within the allotted period of 30 days; and the Dawson account within a year, or less.

Yet it is known to the appellants that their personal indebtedness to the bank at that time well exceeded $300,000, and that a prospective lender would, of course, be concerned to know the amount for which their creditors could take judgment and execute against available assets after the proposed financing was in place, not the amount for which they hoped to be able to settle the debt as a condition of the money being loaned. The letter does not seem to me to explain the misleading omission of their debt to the bank from the financial statements.

The dilemma which faced the bank at the time of its disclosures is described by its loan officer, Mr. Ellwood, in a memorandum of October 19, 1988:

> We advised our solicitor of our concern that we were in double jeopardy by divulging information which might result in the loss of a mortgage commitment and, on the other hand, possibly been accused of concealing information which resulted in the Trust Company making a loan which proved to be undesirable.

It would, in my view, be unreasonable for the law to imply a covenant on the part of the bank that it would resolve such a dilemma in such circumstances by remaining silent.

I am for these reasons satisfied that the case falls within an exception from the banker's duty of confidentiality.

CONCLUSION

The disclosures made by Mr. Howay and Mr. Ellwood did not reveal more than that which the trust company would have learned had the appellants' dealing with the bank been disclosed by them in the financial statements, as they should have been.

At the time he first spoke to Mr. MacFarlane, Mr. Howay had not, of course, seen the misleading financial statements. But the circumstances were such as to show that the trust company had not been informed of important facts concerning the appellants' affairs of which a proposed lender would expect to be informed. Counsel for the appellants could suggest no rational basis on which a distinction might for the present purpose be drawn between, on the one hand, situations in which a bank makes a disclosure which prevents someone from being misled by its customer when the bank is unaware of the customer's actual misleading representation, and, on the other hand, cases in which the bank is aware of the customer's misleading representation before it makes such a disclosure. I can think of no good reason why liability should be imposed in the former cases and not in the latter.

In making such a disclosure a bank may, of course, be "taking a chance" if it does not know with certainty that the party to whom it is made has been misled by its customer. But if purpose and effect of the disclosure is to prevent that party from being misled by the customer, it seems to me, for the reasons which I have given, that the case cannot come within the scope of the bank's implied covenant of confidentiality.

I agree, therefore, with the conclusion reached by the trial judge, but for somewhat different reasons.

I would not wish to seem to support the view that the bank's representatives acted in the bank's own interests, or that the disclosures if made in the bank's own interests would in this case fall within the "third exception" suggested by Bankes L.J. in *Tournier*. The scope of that exception must, of course, be a limited one, for if the bank could make disclosure of its customer's confidential information whenever this served its interests, the duty of confidentiality would have little meaning, but I need not deal with this. I find it also unnecessary to deal with the principles discussed in *International Corona Resources Ltd. v. LAC Minerals Ltd.* (1989), 61 D.L.R. (4th) 14 (S.C.C.), since the appellants sought to rest their case solely on the contractual duty described in *Tournier*, and in this they have failed.

At the conclusion of argument for the appellants I was for these reasons of the view that the appeal must be dismissed, without hearing counsel for the bank.

Appeal dismissed.

(c) *R. v. Lillico*†

[McCOMBS J. (orally):]

OVERVIEW

This trial began with a *voir dire* to determine the admissibility of bank records sought to be relied upon by the Crown in support of its position that Mr. Lillico had committed theft. It was contended that the records had been obtained in violation of his s. 8 Charter rights and that the evidence should be excluded under s. 24(2). At the conclusion of the *voir dire*, I ruled that the evidence was admissible. The following are the reasons for my ruling.

THE INVESTIGATION

The police first became aware of Mr. Lillico's possible criminal conduct in August or September, 1991, when Mr. Patrick Kelly, a retired veteran police officer, spoke to a former colleague, who referred him to Detective Patrick Nealon. Mr. Kelly told Detective Nealon that he and his son Steven, also a police officer, may have been defrauded by Mr. Lillico, a former police officer as well. He told Detective Nealon that on August 3, 1989, he had given Mr. Lillico a cheque for $100,000 payable to "James Lillico in Trust" for shares in a bar in Newmarket to be franchised by Don Cherry's Grapevine Franchise Inc. The bar was to open in the fall of 1989. Mr. Kelly told Detective Nealon that the project had failed, and that despite repeated requests that he do so, Mr. Lillico had failed to account for the money which the Kellys had paid him.

Detective Nealon and his partner interviewed Mr. Lillico at his lawyer's office several months later on December 6, 1991. I accept Mr. Nealon's testimony, supported in part by his partner's notes (ex. A on the *voir dire*) that Mr. Lillico acknowledged receiving the funds and depositing them in his account. He also told the officers that the $100,000 had gone to the development of the franchise, but the Don Cherry organization had arbitrarily withdrawn its support, and that the matter had become bogged down in civil litigation. Detective Nealon

---

† (1994), 92 C.C.C. (3d) 90 (Ont. Gen. Div.).

asked Mr. Lillico about his bank accounts, and told him that the police would be checking the bank records. Neither Mr. Lillico nor his lawyer raised an objection.

Detective Nealon, I find, also spoke by telephone to Mr. Richard Scully, president of the Don Cherry organization, who told him that except for an initial $10,000 deposit which Mr. Lillico submitted along with an application for a franchise, the organization had received no further moneys from him, and had not heard from him for months.

As well, Detective Nealon was aware that Mr. Lillico had recently bought a new motor vehicle, and believed that he was living rather well for someone who was unemployed.

On the strength of the information which Detective Nealon then had, he contacted an investigator in the corporate security branch of the Royal Bank, former police officer Steve Schwets. He asked Mr. Schwets to confirm that the $100,000 cheque had been deposited to Mr. Lillico's account at the Newmarket branch of the Royal Bank, and whether there had been disbursements after the deposit.

Mr. Schwets confirmed to Detective Nealon that there had been significant activity in the account soon after the $100,000 deposit was made. Mr. Schwets testified that the request "was a normal call that we get from time to time from police departments", and that the practice is to check the records and either confirm or deny the fact of the deposit and whether there has been subsequent activity, but never to provide the police with more specific information without a search warrant. I accept the testimony of Detective Nealon and Mr. Schwets that further details as to the amount of money disbursed, or where it went, were neither requested nor provided.

THE ALLEGED BREACH OF CONFIDENTIALITY

(a) The Argument

The information obtained from the bank investigator was included in the affidavit prepared for the justice of the peace in support of the application for a search warrant.

The defence has argued that disclosure by bank officials of information concerning a private bank account, however general that disclosure may be, constitutes a serious breach of the customer's right to privacy, and if the information is conveyed to a law enforcement officer, it constitutes a breach of s. 8 of the Charter. The defence position is that the confidential information concerning the $100,000 deposit and subsequent activity in Mr. Lillico's account was obtained in a manner that violated the Charter, and without that information, a justice could not, acting judicially, have issued the search warrant. The defence submits that the search warrant must therefore be quashed.

(b) The Issue

The submission raises the question of the extent to which, if at all, a financial institution may disclose to the police, without judicial authorization, any information concerning the financial affairs of one of its customers.

(c) The Law

The Supreme Court of Canada has recognized that there is an inherent privacy interest in information, which may attract the protection of s. 8 of the *Canadian Charter of Rights and Freedoms*. In *R. v. Dyment* (1988), 45 C.C.C. (3d) 244 at pp. 255–6, 55 D.L.R. (4th) 503, [1988] 2 S.C.R. 417, La Forest J. stated:

> ... there is privacy in relation to information. This too is based on the notion of the [privacy and] dignity and integrity of the individual ... "[it] ... derives from the assumption that all information about a person is in a fundamental way his own, for him to communicate or retain for himself as he sees fit." In modern society, especially, retention of information about oneself is extremely important.

Not all commercial information is protected by s. 8 however. The information must be of a "confidential or personal" nature before it is protected. In holding that a warrantless search of computerized hydro consumption records was not an unreasonable search contrary to s. 8 of the Charter, Sopinka J., in *R. v. Plant* (1993), 84 C.C.C. (3d) 203, [1993] 3 S.C.R. 281, 24 C.R. (4th) 47, noted that there were several factors to be considered in determining whether a particular piece of information attracts the protection of s. 8. He said [at p. 212]:

> Consideration of such factors as the nature of the information itself, the nature of the relationship between the party releasing the information and the party claiming its confidentiality, the place where the information was obtained ... and the seriousness of the crime being investigated, allow for a balancing of the societal interest in protecting individual dignity, integrity and autonomy with effective law enforcement.

Although Sopinka J. left open the question of whether commercial records such as cancelled cheques are subject to s. 8 protection, he affirmed the American rule, enunciated in *United States v. Miller*, 425 U.S. 435 (1976), that in order for constitutional protection to be extended, the information seized must be of a "personal and confidential" nature. In considering the meaning of that phrase, he stated, at p. 213:

> In fostering the underlying values of dignity, integrity and autonomy, it is fitting that s. 8 of the Charter should seek to protect a *biographical core of personal information* which individuals in a free and democratic society would wish to maintain and control from dissemination to the state. This would include information which tends to reveal intimate details of the lifestyle and personal choices of the individual. (Emphasis added.)

Although Canadian law does not recognize any privilege in relation to banking information (see, for example, *R. v. Spencer* (1983), 2 C.C.C. (3d) 526 at p. 535, 145 D.L.R. (3d) 344, 31 C.P.C. 162, *per* MacKinnon A.C.J.O.), the bank nevertheless has an obligation to keep the information confidential. It is an implied term of the contract between a bank and its customer that the bank will not divulge information about the state of the customer's account or any of the transactions, or any information relating to the customer acquired through the keeping of the account, unless the bank is either compelled by a court order to do it, or the circumstances give rise to a public duty of disclosure: see *Tournier v. National Provincial and Union Bank of England*, [1924] 1 K.B. 461 (C.A.).

(d) Conclusion

I conclude that financial institutions have a general duty to protect the confidentiality of banking records. On the other hand, a balance must be struck between the customer's right to confidentiality and the public's right to effective law enforcement. In my opinion, disclosure of only the most general information by confirming only that a particular cheque was deposited into the customer's account, and that there was subsequent activity in the account, does not threaten the "biographical core of personal information" which is inherent in the meaning of the phrase "Private and confidential". Therefore, it does not constitute an infringement of the privacy of the individual so as to attract the protection of s. 8 of the Charter.

I therefore conclude that in this case, the police obtained the information lawfully, and the disclosure made by the bank employee did not constitute a breach of s. 8.

THE "BELIEF" OF THE INVESTIGATING OFFICER

The findings of fact which I have already made, lead me to conclude that at the time the affidavit in support of the application for a search warrant was prepared, Detective Nealon believed, on reasonable grounds, that:

1. The Kellys had given James Lillico $100,000 in August, 1989, "in trust" for the development of a Don Cherry Franchise in Newmarket.
2. The franchise project had failed and Mr. Lillico had not provided the Kellys with an accounting for the funds despite repeated requests that he do so.
3. Mr. Lillico had informed the police that the $100,000 had gone for development of the franchise.
4. The president of Don Cherry Franchise Inc. had confirmed that the organization had received only $10,000.
5. There had been significant activity in the form of disbursements from Mr. Lillico's account soon after the $100,000 had been deposited.
6. Mr. Lillico had purchased a new motor vehicle and had some source of income despite being unemployed.

THE AFFIDAVIT, OR "INFORMATION" IN SUPPORT OF THE APPLICATION FOR A SEARCH WARRANT

(a) The Content of the Affidavit

Exhibit B on the *voir dire* is an unsworn copy of the affidavit which was prepared in support of the search warrant application pursuant to s. 487 of the *Code*. It sets out in 11 paragraphs, the information then known to the police. In my opinion, the information contained in the affidavit was not misleading, but rather sets out fairly and accurately the information in the possession of the police at the time.

There was no false, misleading, or unlawfully obtained information put before the authorizing justice.

(b) The Scope of Review — Sufficiency

The scope of review on an application to quash a search warrant based on sufficiency of the information before the authorizing justice, is limited to jurisdictional error. The test at the review stage is whether evidence existed upon which the justice of the peace could determine that a warrant should be issued. I do not have the right to interfere with the decision of the authorizing justice unless I am satisfied that he could not, acting judicially, have authorized the issuance of the search warrant: see *R. v. Church of Scientology* (1987), 31 C.C.C. (3d) 449, 30 C.R.R. 238, 1 W.C.B. (2d) 327 (Ont. C.A.); leave to appeal refused, 33 C.R.R. 384*n*, 23 O.A.C. 320*n*, 82 N.R. 392*n* (S.C.C.). In my opinion, the justice of the peace was entitled to make the order which he made based on the information before him.

CONCLUSION

In the result, the application to quash the search warrant is dismissed.

Application dismissed.

(d) *Personal Information Protection and Electronic Documents Act*†

An Act to support and promote electronic commerce by protecting personal information that is collected, used or disclosed in certain circumstances, by providing for the use of electronic means to communicate or record information or transactions and by amending the Canada Evidence Act, the Statutory Instruments Act and the Statute Revision Act

Her Majesty, by and with the advice and consent of the Senate and House of Commons of Canada, enacts as follows:

SHORT TITLE

Short title

1. This Act may be cited as the *Personal Information Protection and Electronic Documents Act*.

PART 1
PROTECTION OF PERSONAL INFORMATION IN THE PRIVATE SECTOR

INTERPRETATION

Definitions

2.(1) The definitions in this subsection apply in this Part.

"alternative format", with respect to personal information, means a format that allows a person with a sensory disability to read or listen to the personal information.

"commercial activity" means any particular transaction, act or conduct or any regular course of conduct that is of a commercial character, including the selling, bartering or leasing of donor, membership or other fundraising lists.

"Commissioner" means the Privacy Commissioner appointed under section 53 of the *Privacy Act*.

"Court" means the Federal Court.

"federal work, undertaking or business" means any work, undertaking or business that is within the legislative authority of Parliament. It includes
  (a) a work, undertaking or business that is operated or carried on for or in connection with navigation and shipping, whether inland or maritime, including the operation of ships and transportation by ship anywhere in Canada;
  (b) a railway, canal, telegraph or other work or undertaking that connects a province with another province, or that extends beyond the limits of a province;
  (c) a line of ships that connects a province with another province, or that extends beyond the limits of a province;

---

† S.C. 2000, c. 5, P-8.6, as am. by S.C. 2010, c. 23, ss. 1–29, Schedule 1.

(d) a ferry between a province and another province or between a province and a country other than Canada;

(e) aerodromes, aircraft or a line of air transportation;

(f) a radio broadcasting station;

(g) a bank;

(h) a work that, although wholly situated within a province, is before or after its execution declared by Parliament to be for the general advantage of Canada or for the advantage of two or more provinces;

(i) a work, undertaking or business outside the exclusive legislative authority of the legislatures of the provinces; and

(j) a work, undertaking or business to which federal laws, within the meaning of section 2 of the *Oceans Act*, apply under section 20 of that Act and any regulations made under paragraph 26(1)(k) of that Act.

"organization" includes an association, a partnership, a person and a trade union.

"personal health information", with respect to an individual, whether living or deceased, means

(a) information concerning the physical or mental health of the individual;

(b) information concerning any health service provided to the individual;

(c) information concerning the donation by the individual of any body part or any bodily substance of the individual or information derived from the testing or examination of a body part or bodily substance of the individual;

(d) information that is collected in the course of providing health services to the individual; or

(e) information that is collected incidentally to the provision of health services to the individual.

"personal information" means information about an identifiable individual, but does not include the name, title or business address or telephone number of an employee of an organization.

"record" includes any correspondence, memorandum, book, plan, map, drawing, diagram, pictorial or graphic work, photograph, film, microform, sound recording, videotape, machine-readable record and any other documentary material, regardless of physical form or characteristics, and any copy of any of those things.

Notes in Schedule 1

(2) In this Part, a reference to clause 4.3 or 4.9 of Schedule 1 does not include a reference to the note that accompanies that clause.

PURPOSE

Purpose

3. The purpose of this Part is to establish, in an era in which technology increasingly facilitates the circulation and exchange of information, rules to govern the collection, use and disclosure of personal information in a manner that recognizes the right of privacy of individuals with respect to their personal information and the need of organizations to collect, use or disclose personal information for purposes that a reasonable person would consider appropriate in the circumstances.

APPLICATION

Application

4.(1) This Part applies to every organization in respect of personal information that

(a) the organization collects, uses or discloses in the course of commercial activities; or

(b) is about an employee of the organization and that the organization collects, uses or discloses in connection with the operation of a federal work, undertaking or business.

Limit

(2) This Part does not apply to

(a) any government institution to which the *Privacy Act* applies;

(b) any individual in respect of personal information that the individual collects, uses or discloses for personal or domestic purposes and does not collect, use or disclose for any other purpose; or

(c) any organization in respect of personal information that the organization collects, uses or discloses for journalistic, artistic or literary purposes and does not collect, use or disclose for any other purpose.

Other Acts

(3) Every provision of this Part applies despite any provision, enacted after this subsection comes into force, of any other Act of Parliament, unless the other Act expressly declares that that provision operates despite the provision of this Part.

Certificate under Canada Evidence Act

4.1(1) Where a certificate under section 38.13 of the *Canada Evidence Act* prohibiting the disclosure of personal information of a specific individual is issued

457

before a complaint is filed by that individual under this Part in respect of a request for access to that information, the provisions of this Part respecting that individual's right of access to his or her personal information do not apply to the information that is subject to the certificate.

Certificate following filing of complaint

(2) Notwithstanding any other provision of this Part, where a certificate under section 38.13 of the *Canada Evidence Act* prohibiting the disclosure of personal information of a specific individual is issued after the filing of a complaint under this Part in relation to a request for access to that information:

(a) all proceedings under this Part in respect of that information, including an investigation, audit, appeal or judicial review, are discontinued;

(b) the Commissioner shall not disclose the information and shall take all necessary precautions to prevent its disclosure; and

(c) the Commissioner shall, within 10 days after the certificate is published in the *Canada Gazette*, return the information to the organization that provided the information.

Information not to be disclosed

(3) The Commissioner and every person acting on behalf or under the direction of the Commissioner, in carrying out their functions under this Part, shall not disclose information subject to a certificate issued under section 38.13 of the *Canada Evidence Act*, and shall take every reasonable precaution to avoid the disclosure of that information.

Power to delegate

(4) The Commissioner may not delegate the investigation of any complaint relating to information subject to a certificate issued under section 38.13 of the *Canada Evidence Act* except to one of a maximum of four officers or employees of the Commissioner specifically designated by the Commissioner for the purpose of conducting that investigation.

DIVISION 1
PROTECTION OF PERSONAL INFORMATION

Compliance with obligations

5.(1) Subject to sections 6 to 9, every organization shall comply with the obligations set out in Schedule 1.

Meaning of "should"

(2) The word "should", when used in Schedule 1, indicates a recommendation and does not impose an obligation.

Appropriate purposes

(3) An organization may collect, use or disclose personal information only for purposes that a reasonable person would consider are appropriate in the circumstances.

Effect of designation of individual

6. The designation of an individual under clause 4.1 of Schedule 1 does not relieve the organization of the obligation to comply with the obligations set out in that Schedule.

Collection without knowledge or consent

7.(1) For the purpose of clause 4.3 of Schedule 1, and despite the note that accompanies that clause, an organization may collect personal information without the knowledge or consent of the individual only if

(a) the collection is clearly in the interests of the individual and consent cannot be obtained in a timely way;

(b) it is reasonable to expect that the collection with the knowledge or consent of the individual would compromise the availability or the accuracy of the information and the collection is reasonable for purposes related to investigating a breach of an agreement or a contravention of the laws of Canada or a province;

(c) the collection is solely for journalistic, artistic or literary purposes;

(d) the information is publicly available and is specified by the regulations; or

(e) the collection is made for the purpose of making a disclosure

(i) under subparagraph (3)(c.1)(i) or (d)(ii), or

(ii) that is required by law.

Use without knowledge or consent

(2) For the purpose of clause 4.3 of Schedule 1, and despite the note that accompanies that clause, an organization may, without the knowledge or consent of the individual, use personal information only if

(a) in the course of its activities, the organization becomes aware of information that it has reasonable grounds to believe could be useful in the investigation of a contravention of the laws of Canada, a province or a foreign jurisdiction that has been, is being or is about to be committed, and the information is used for the purpose of investigating that contravention;

(b) it is used for the purpose of acting in respect of an emergency that threatens the life, health or security of an individual;

(c) it is used for statistical, or scholarly study or research, purposes that cannot be achieved without using the information, the information is used in a manner that will ensure its confidentiality, it is impracticable to obtain consent and the organization informs the Commissioner of the use before the information is used;

(c.1) it is publicly available and is specified by the regulations; or

(d) it was collected under paragraph (1)(a), (b) or (e).

Disclosure without knowledge or consent

(3) For the purpose of clause 4.3 of Schedule 1, and despite the note that accompanies that clause, an organization may disclose personal information without the knowledge or consent of the individual only if the disclosure is

(a) made to, in the Province of Quebec, an advocate or notary or, in any other province, a barrister or solicitor who is representing the organization;

(b) for the purpose of collecting a debt owed by the individual to the organization;

(c) required to comply with a subpoena or warrant issued or an order made by a court, person or body with jurisdiction to compel the production of information, or to comply with rules of court relating to the production of records;

(c.1) made to a government institution or part of a government institution that has made a request for the information, identified its lawful authority to obtain the information and indicated that

    (i) it suspects that the information relates to national security, the defence of Canada or the conduct of international affairs,

    (ii) the disclosure is requested for the purpose of enforcing any law of Canada, a province or a foreign jurisdiction, carrying out an investigation relating to the enforcement of any such law or gathering intelligence for the purpose of enforcing any such law, or

    (iii) the disclosure is requested for the purpose of administering any law of Canada or a province;

(c.2) made to the government institution mentioned in section 7 of the *Proceeds of Crime (Money Laundering) and Terrorist Financing Act* as required by that section;

(c.2) made to the government institution mentioned in section 7 of the *Proceeds of Crime (Money Laundering) Act* as required by that section;

(d) made on the initiative of the organization to an investigative body, a government institution or a part of a government institution and the organization

    (i) has reasonable grounds to believe that the information relates to a breach of an agreement or a contravention of the laws of Canada, a province or a foreign jurisdiction that has been, is being or is about to be committed, or

    (ii) suspects that the information relates to national security, the defence of Canada or the conduct of international affairs;

(e) made to a person who needs the information because of an emergency that threatens the life, health or security of an individual and, if the individual whom the information is about is alive, the organization informs that individual in writing without delay of the disclosure;

(f) for statistical, or scholarly study or research, purposes that cannot be achieved without disclosing the information, it is impracticable to obtain consent and the organization informs the Commissioner of the disclosure before the information is disclosed;

(g) made to an institution whose functions include the conservation of records of historic or archival importance, and the disclosure is made for the purpose of such conservation;

(h) made after the earlier of

    (i) one hundred years after the record containing the information was created, and

    (ii) twenty years after the death of the individual whom the information is about;

(h.1) of information that is publicly available and is specified by the regulations;

(h.2) made by an investigative body and the disclosure is reasonable for purposes related to investigating a breach of an agreement or a contravention of the laws of Canada or a province; or

(i) required by law.

Use without consent

(4) Despite clause 4.5 of Schedule 1, an organization may use personal information for purposes

other than those for which it was collected in any of the circumstances set out in subsection (2).

Disclosure without consent

(5) Despite clause 4.5 of Schedule 1, an organization may disclose personal information for purposes other than those for which it was collected in any of the circumstances set out in paragraphs (3)(a) to (h.2).

Definitions

7.1(1) The following definitions apply in this section.

"access" means to program, to execute programs on, to communicate with, to store data in, to retrieve data from, or to otherwise make use of any resources, including data or programs on a computer system or a computer network.

"computer program" has the same meaning as in subsection 342.1(2) of the *Criminal Code*.

"computer system" has the same meaning as in subsection 342.1(2) of the *Criminal Code*.

"electronic address" means an address used in connection with

(a) an electronic mail account;

(b) an instant messaging account; or

(c) any similar account.

Collection of electronic addresses, etc.

(2) Paragraphs 7(1)(a), (c) and (d) and (2)(a) to (c.1) and the exception set out in clause 4.3 of Schedule 1 do not apply in respect of

(a) the collection of an individual's electronic address, if the address is collected by the use of a computer program that is designed or marketed primarily for use in generating or searching for, and collecting, electronic addresses; or

(b) the use of an individual's electronic address, if the address is collected by the use of a computer program described in paragraph (a).

Accessing a computer system to collect personal information, etc.

(3) Paragraphs 7(1)(a) to (d) and (2)(a) to (c.1) and the exception set out in clause 4.3 of Schedule 1 do not apply in respect of

(a) the collection of personal information, through any means of telecommunication, if the collection is made by accessing a computer system or causing a computer system to be accessed in contravention of an Act of Parliament; or

(b) the use of personal information that is collected in a manner described in paragraph (a).

Written request

8.(1) A request under clause 4.9 of Schedule 1 must be made in writing.

Assistance

(2) An organization shall assist any individual who informs the organization that they need assistance in preparing a request to the organization.

Time limit

(3) An organization shall respond to a request with due diligence and in any case not later than thirty days after receipt of the request.

Extension of time limit

(4) An organization may extend the time limit
(a) for a maximum of thirty days if
  (i) meeting the time limit would unreasonably interfere with the activities of the organization, or
  (ii) the time required to undertake any consultations necessary to respond to the request would make the time limit impracticable to meet; or
(b) for the period that is necessary in order to be able to convert the personal information into an alternative format.

In either case, the organization shall, no later than thirty days after the date of the request, send a notice of extension to the individual, advising them of the new time limit, the reasons for extending the time limit and of their right to make a complaint to the Commissioner in respect of the extension.

Deemed refusal

(5) If the organization fails to respond within the time limit, the organization is deemed to have refused the request.

Costs for responding

(6) An organization may respond to an individual's request at a cost to the individual only if
(a) the organization has informed the individual of the approximate cost; and
(b) the individual has advised the organization that the request is not being withdrawn.

Reasons

(7) An organization that responds within the time limit and refuses a request shall inform the individual in writing of the refusal, setting out the reasons and any recourse that they may have under this Part.

Retention of information

(8) Despite clause 4.5 of Schedule 1, an organization that has personal information that is the subject of a request shall retain the information for as long as is necessary to allow the individual to exhaust any recourse under this Part that they may have.

When access prohibited

9.(1) Despite clause 4.9 of Schedule 1, an organization shall not give an individual access to personal information if doing so would likely reveal personal information about a third party. However, if the information about the third party is severable from the record containing the information about the individual, the organization shall sever the information about the third party before giving the individual access.

Limit

(2) Subsection (1) does not apply if the third party consents to the access or the individual needs the information because an individual's life, health or security is threatened.

Information related to paragraphs 7(3)(c), (c.1) or (d)

(2.1) An organization shall comply with subsection (2.2) if an individual requests that the organization

(a) inform the individual about

  (i) any disclosure of information to a government institution or a part of a government institution under paragraph 7(3)(c), subparagraph 7(3)(c.1)(i) or (ii) or paragraph 7(3)(c.2) or (d), or

  (ii) the existence of any information that the organization has relating to a disclosure referred to in subparagraph (i), to a subpoena, warrant or order referred to in paragraph 7(3)(c) or to a request made by a government institution or a part of a government institution under subparagraph 7(3)(c.1)(i) or (ii); or

(b) give the individual access to the information referred to in subparagraph (a)(ii).

Notification and response

(2.2) An organization to which subsection (2.1) applies

(a) shall, in writing and without delay, notify the institution or part concerned of the request made by the individual; and

(b) shall not respond to the request before the earlier of

  (i) the day on which it is notified under subsection (2.3), and

  (ii) thirty days after the day on which the institution or part was notified.

Objection

(2.3) Within thirty days after the day on which it is notified under subsection (2.2), the institution or part shall notify the organization whether or not the institution or part objects to the organization complying with the request. The institution or part may object only if the institution or part is of the opinion that compliance with the request could reasonably be expected to be injurious to

(a) national security, the defence of Canada or the conduct of international affairs;

(a.1) the detection, prevention or deterrence of money laundering or the financing of terrorist activities; or

(a.1) the detection, prevention or deterrence of money laundering; or

(b) the enforcement of any law of Canada, a province or a foreign jurisdiction, an investigation relating to the enforcement of any such law or the gathering of intelligence for the purpose of enforcing any such law.

Prohibition

(2.4) Despite clause 4.9 of Schedule 1, if an organization is notified under subsection (2.3) that the institution or part objects to the organization complying with the request, the organization

(a) shall refuse the request to the extent that it relates to paragraph (2.1)(a) or to information referred to in subparagraph (2.1)(a)(ii);

(b) shall notify the Commissioner, in writing and without delay, of the refusal; and

(c) shall not disclose to the individual

  (i) any information that the organization has relating to a disclosure to a government institution or a part of a government

461

institution under paragraph 7(3)(c), sub-paragraph 7(3)(c.1)(i) or (ii) or paragraph 7(3)(c.2) or (d) or to a request made by a government institution under either of those subparagraphs,

    (ii) that the organization notified an institution or part under paragraph (2.2)(a) or the Commissioner under paragraph (b), or

    (iii) that the institution or part objects.

When access may be refused

(3) Despite the note that accompanies clause 4.9 of Schedule 1, an organization is not required to give access to personal information only if

    (a) the information is protected by solicitor-client privilege;

    (b) to do so would reveal confidential commercial information;

    (c) to do so could reasonably be expected to threaten the life or security of another individual;

(c.1) the information was collected under paragraph 7(1)(b); or

    (d) the information was generated in the course of a formal dispute resolution process; or

    (e) the information was created for the purpose of making a disclosure under the *Public Servants Disclosure Protection Act* or in the course of an investigation into a disclosure under that Act.

However, in the circumstances described in paragraph (b) or (c), if giving access to the information would reveal confidential commercial information or could reasonably be expected to threaten the life or security of another individual, as the case may be, and that information is severable from the record containing any other information for which access is requested, the organization shall give the individual access after severing.

Limit

(4) Subsection (3) does not apply if the individual needs the information because an individual's life, health or security is threatened.

Notice

(5) If an organization decides not to give access to personal information in the circumstances set out in paragraph (3)(c.1), the organization shall, in writing, so notify the Commissioner, and shall include in the notification any information that the Commissioner may specify.

Sensory disability

10. An organization shall give access to personal information in an alternative format to an individual with a sensory disability who has a right of access to personal information under this Part and who requests that it be transmitted in the alternative format if

    (a) a version of the information already exists in that format; or

    (b) its conversion into that format is reasonable and necessary in order for the individual to be able to exercise rights under this Part.

DIVISION 2
REMEDIES

FILING OF COMPLAINTS

Contravention

11.(1) An individual may file with the Commissioner a written complaint against an organization for contravening a provision of Division 1 or for not following a recommendation set out in Schedule 1.

Commissioner may initiate complaint

(2) If the Commissioner is satisfied that there are reasonable grounds to investigate a matter under this Part, the Commissioner may initiate a complaint in respect of the matter.

Time limit

(3) A complaint that results from the refusal to grant a request under section 8 must be filed within six months, or any longer period that the Commissioner allows, after the refusal or after the expiry of the time limit for responding to the request, as the case may be.

Notice

(4) The Commissioner shall give notice of a complaint to the organization against which the complaint was made.

INVESTIGATIONS OF COMPLAINTS

Examination of complaint by Commissioner

12.(1) The Commissioner shall conduct an investigation in respect of a complaint, unless the Commissioner is of the opinion that

(a) the complainant ought first to exhaust grievance or review procedures otherwise reasonably available;

(b) the complaint could more appropriately be dealt with, initially or completely, by means of a procedure provided for under the laws of Canada, other than this Part, or the laws of a province; or

(c) the complaint was not filed within a reasonable period after the day on which the subject matter of the complaint arose.

Exception

(2) Despite subsection (1), the Commissioner is not required to conduct an investigation in respect of an act alleged in a complaint if the Commissioner is of the opinion that the act, if proved, would constitute a contravention of any of sections 6 to 9 of *An Act to promote the efficiency and adaptability of the Canadian economy by regulating certain activities that discourage reliance on electronic means of carrying out commercial activities, and to amend the Canadian Radio-television and Telecommunications Commission Act, the Competition Act, the Personal Information Protection and Electronic Documents Act and the Telecommunications Act* or section 52.01 of the Competition Act or would constitute conduct that is reviewable under section 74.011 of that Act.

Notification

(3) The Commissioner shall notify the complainant and the organization that the Commissioner will not investigate the complaint or any act alleged in the complaint and give reasons.

Compelling reasons

(4) The Commissioner may reconsider a decision not to investigate under subsection (1), if the Commissioner is satisfied that the complainant has established that there are compelling reasons to investigate.

Powers of Commissioner

12.1(1) In the conduct of an investigation of a complaint, the Commissioner may

(a) summon and enforce the appearance of persons before the Commissioner and compel them to give oral or written evidence on oath and to produce any records and things that the Commissioner considers necessary to investigate the complaint, in the same manner and to the same extent as a superior court of record;

(b) administer oaths;

(c) receive and accept any evidence and other information, whether on oath, by affidavit or otherwise, that the Commissioner sees fit, whether or not it is or would be admissible in a court of law;

(d) at any reasonable time, enter any premises, other than a dwelling-house, occupied by an organization on satisfying any security requirements of the organization relating to the premises;

(e) converse in private with any person in any premises entered under paragraph (d) and otherwise carry out in those premises any inquiries that the Commissioner sees fit; and

(f) examine or obtain copies of or extracts from records found in any premises entered under paragraph (d) that contain any matter relevant to the investigation.

Dispute resolution mechanisms

(2) The Commissioner may attempt to resolve complaints by means of dispute resolution mechanisms such as mediation and conciliation.

Delegation

(3) The Commissioner may delegate any of the powers set out in subsection (1) or (2).

Return of records

(4) The Commissioner or the delegate shall return to a person or an organization any record or thing that they produced under this section within 10 days after they make a request to the Commissioner or the delegate, but nothing precludes the Commissioner or the delegate from again requiring that the record or thing be produced.

Certificate of delegation

(5) Any person to whom powers set out in subsection (1) are delegated shall be given a certificate of the delegation and the delegate shall produce the certificate, on request, to the person in charge of any premises to be entered under paragraph (1)(d).

DISCONTINUANCE OF INVESTIGATION

Reasons

12.2(1) The Commissioner may discontinue the investigation of a complaint if the Commissioner is of the opinion that

(a) there is insufficient evidence to pursue the investigation;

(b) the complaint is trivial, frivolous or vexatious or is made in bad faith;

(c) the organization has provided a fair and reasonable response to the complaint;

(d) the matter is already the object of an ongoing investigation under this Part;

(e) the matter has already been the subject of a report by the Commissioner;

(f) any of the circumstances mentioned in paragraph 12(1)(a), (b) or (c) apply; or

(g) the matter is being or has already been addressed under a procedure referred to in paragraph 12(1)(a) or (b).

Other reason

(2) The Commissioner may discontinue an investigation in respect of an act alleged in a complaint if the Commissioner is of the opinion that the act, if proved, would constitute a contravention of any of sections 6 to 9 of *An Act to promote the efficiency and adaptability of the Canadian economy by regulating certain activities that discourage reliance on electronic means of carrying out commercial activities, and to amend the Canadian Radio-television and Telecommunications Commission Act, the Competition Act, the Personal Information Protection and Electronic Documents Act and the Telecommunications Act* or section 52.01 of the *Competition Act* or would constitute conduct that is reviewable under section 74.011 of that Act.

Notification

(3) The Commissioner shall notify the complainant and the organization that the investigation has been discontinued and give reasons.

COMMISSIONER'S REPORT

Contents

13.(1) The Commissioner shall, within one year after the day on which a complaint is filed or is initiated by the Commissioner, prepare a report that contains

(a) the Commissioner's findings and recommendations;

(b) any settlement that was reached by the parties;

(c) if appropriate, a request that the organization give the Commissioner, within a specified time, notice of any action taken or proposed to be taken to implement the recommendations contained in the report or reasons why no such action has been or is proposed to be taken; and

(d) the recourse, if any, that is available under section 14.

(2) [Repealed, 2010, c. 23, s. 84]

Report to parties

(3) The report shall be sent to the complainant and the organization without delay.

HEARING BY COURT

Application

14.(1) A complainant may, after receiving the Commissioner's report or being notified under subsection 12.2(3) that the investigation of the complaint has been discontinued, apply to the Court for a hearing in respect of any matter in respect of which the complaint was made, or that is referred to in the Commissioner's report, and that is referred to in clause 4.1.3, 4.2, 4.3.3, 4.4, 4.6, 4.7 or 4.8 of Schedule 1, in clause 4.3, 4.5 or 4.9 of that Schedule as modified or clarified by Division 1, in subsection 5(3) or 8(6) or (7) or in section 10.

Time of application

(2) A complainant must make an application within 45 days after the report or notification is sent or within any further time that the Court may, either before or after the expiry of those 45 days, allow.

For greater certainty

(3) For greater certainty, subsections (1) and (2) apply in the same manner to complaints referred to in subsection 11(2) as to complaints referred to in subsection 11(1).

Commissioner may apply or appear

15. The Commissioner may, in respect of a complaint that the Commissioner did not initiate,

(a) apply to the Court, within the time limited by section 14, for a hearing in respect of any matter described in that section, if the Commissioner has the consent of the complainant;

(b) appear before the Court on behalf of any complainant who has applied for a hearing under section 14; or

(c) with leave of the Court, appear as a party to any hearing applied for under section 14.

Remedies

16. The Court may, in addition to any other remedies it may give,

(a) order an organization to correct its practices in order to comply with sections 5 to 10;

(b) order an organization to publish a notice of any action taken or proposed to be taken to correct its practices, whether or not ordered to correct them under paragraph (a); and

(c) award damages to the complainant, including damages for any humiliation that the complainant has suffered.

Summary hearings

17.(1) An application made under section 14 or 15 shall be heard and determined without delay and in a summary way unless the Court considers it inappropriate to do so.

Precautions

(2) In any proceedings arising from an application made under section 14 or 15, the Court shall take every reasonable precaution, including, when appropriate, receiving representations ex parte and conducting hearings in camera, to avoid the disclosure by the Court or any person of any information or other material that the organization would be authorized to refuse to disclose if it were requested under clause 4.9 of Schedule 1.

DIVISION 3
AUDITS

To ensure compliance

18.(1) The Commissioner may, on reasonable notice and at any reasonable time, audit the personal information management practices of an organization if the Commissioner has reasonable grounds to believe that the organization is contravening a provision of Division 1 or is not following a recommendation set out in Schedule 1, and for that purpose may

(a) summon and enforce the appearance of persons before the Commissioner and compel them to give oral or written evidence on oath and to produce any records and things that the Commissioner considers necessary for the audit, in the same manner and to the same extent as a superior court of record;

(b) administer oaths;

(c) receive and accept any evidence and other information, whether on oath, by affidavit or otherwise, that the Commissioner sees fit, whether or not it is or would be admissible in a court of law;

(d) at any reasonable time, enter any premises, other than a dwelling-house, occupied by the organization on satisfying any security requirements of the organization relating to the premises;

(e) converse in private with any person in any premises entered under paragraph (d) and otherwise carry out in those premises any inquiries that the Commissioner sees fit; and

(f) examine or obtain copies of or extracts from records found in any premises entered under paragraph (d) that contain any matter relevant to the audit.

Delegation

(2) The Commissioner may delegate any of the powers set out in subsection (1).

Return of records

(3) The Commissioner or the delegate shall return to a person or an organization any record or thing they produced under this section within ten days after they make a request to the Commissioner or the delegate, but nothing precludes the Commissioner or the delegate from again requiring that the record or thing be produced.

Certificate of delegation

(4) Any person to whom powers set out in subsection (1) are delegated shall be given a certificate of the delegation and the delegate shall produce the certificate, on request, to the person in charge of any premises to be entered under paragraph (1)(d).

Report of findings and recommendations

19.(1) After an audit, the Commissioner shall provide the audited organization with a report that contains the findings of the audit and any recommendations that the Commissioner considers appropriate.

Reports may be included in annual reports

(2) The report may be included in a report made under section 25.

DIVISION 4
GENERAL

Confidentiality

20.(1) Subject to subsections (2) to (6), 12(3), 12.2(3), 13(3), 19(1), 23(3) and 23.1(1) and section 25, the Commissioner or any person acting on behalf or under the direction of the Commissioner shall not disclose any information that comes to their knowledge as a result of the performance or exercise of any of the Commissioner's duties or powers under this Part.

Public interest

(2) The Commissioner may make public any information relating to the personal information management practices of an organization if the Commissioner considers that it is in the public interest to do so.

Disclosure of necessary information

(3) The Commissioner may disclose, or may authorize any person acting on behalf or under the direction of the Commissioner to disclose, information that in the Commissioner's opinion is necessary to

(a) conduct an investigation or audit under this Part; or

(b) establish the grounds for findings and recommendations contained in any report under this Part.

Disclosure in the course of proceedings

(4) The Commissioner may disclose, or may authorize any person acting on behalf or under the direction of the Commissioner to disclose, information in the course of

(a) a prosecution for an offence under section 28;

(b) a prosecution for an offence under section 132 of the *Criminal Code* (perjury) in respect of a statement made under this Part;

(c) a hearing before the Court under this Part; or

(d) an appeal from a decision of the Court.

Disclosure of offence authorized

(5) The Commissioner may disclose to the Attorney General of Canada or of a province, as the case may be, information relating to the commission of an offence against any law of Canada or a province on the part of an officer or employee of an organization if, in the Commissioner's opinion, there is evidence of an offence.

Disclosure

(6) The Commissioner may disclose information, or may authorize any person acting on behalf or under the direction of the Commissioner to disclose information, in the course of proceedings in which the Commissioner has intervened under paragraph

50(c) of *An Act to promote the efficiency and adaptability of the Canadian economy by regulating certain activities that discourage reliance on electronic means of carrying out commercial activities, and to amend the Canadian Radio-television and Telecommunications Commission Act, the Competition Act, the Personal Information Protection and Electronic Documents Act and the Telecommunications Act* or in accordance with subsection 58(3) or 60(1) of that Act.

Not competent witness

21. The Commissioner or person acting on behalf or under the direction of the Commissioner is not a competent witness in respect of any matter that comes to their knowledge as a result of the performance or exercise of any of the Commissioner's duties or powers under this Part in any proceeding other than

(a) a prosecution for an offence under section 28;

(b) a prosecution for an offence under section 132 of the *Criminal Code* (perjury) in respect of a statement made under this Part;

(c) a hearing before the Court under this Part; or

(d) an appeal from a decision of the Court.

Protection of Commissioner

22.(1) No criminal or civil proceedings lie against the Commissioner, or against any person acting on behalf or under the direction of the Commissioner, for anything done, reported or said in good faith as a result of the performance or exercise or purported performance or exercise of any duty or power of the Commissioner under this Part.

Libel or slander

(2) For the purposes of any law relating to libel or slander,

(a) anything said, any information supplied or any record or thing produced in good faith in the course of an investigation or audit carried out by or on behalf of the Commissioner under this Part is privileged; and

(b) any report made in good faith by the Commissioner under this Part and any fair and accurate account of the report made in good faith for the purpose of news reporting is privileged.

Consultations with provinces

23.(1) If the Commissioner considers it appropriate to do so, or on the request of an interested person, the Commissioner may, in order to ensure that personal information is protected in as consistent a manner as possible, consult with any person who, under provincial legislation, has functions and duties similar to those of the Commissioner with respect to the protection of such information.

Agreements or arrangements with provinces

(2) The Commissioner may enter into agreements or arrangements with any person referred to in subsection (1) in order to

(a) coordinate the activities of their offices and the office of the Commissioner, including to provide for mechanisms for the handling of any complaint in which they are mutually interested;

(b) undertake and publish research or develop and publish guidelines or other instruments related to the protection of personal information;

(c) develop model contracts or other instruments for the protection of personal information that is collected, used or disclosed interprovincially or internationally; and

(d) develop procedures for sharing information referred to in subsection (3).

Sharing of information with provinces

(3) The Commissioner may, in accordance with any procedure established under paragraph (2)(d), share information with any person referred to in subsection (1), if the information

(a) could be relevant to an ongoing or potential investigation of a complaint or audit under this Part or provincial legislation that has objectives that are similar to this Part; or

(b) could assist the Commissioner or that person in the exercise of their functions and duties with respect to the protection of personal information.

Purpose and confidentiality

(4) The procedures referred to in paragraph (2)(d) shall

(a) restrict the use of the information to the purpose for which it was originally shared; and

(b) stipulate that the information be treated in a confidential manner and not be further disclosed without the express consent of the Commissioner.

Disclosure of information to foreign state

23.1(1) Subject to subsection (3), the Commissioner may, in accordance with any procedure established under paragraph (4)(b), disclose information referred to in subsection (2) that has come to the Commis-

sioner's knowledge as a result of the performance or exercise of any of the Commissioner's duties or powers under this Part to any person or body who, under the legislation of a foreign state, has

(a) functions and duties similar to those of the Commissioner with respect to the protection of personal information; or

(b) responsibilities that relate to conduct that is substantially similar to conduct that would be in contravention of this Part.

Information that can be shared

(2) The information that the Commissioner is authorized to disclose under subsection (1) is information that the Commissioner believes

(a) would be relevant to an ongoing or potential investigation or proceeding in respect of a contravention of the laws of a foreign state that address conduct that is substantially similar to conduct that would be in contravention of this Part; or

(b) is necessary to disclose in order to obtain from the person or body information that may be useful to an ongoing or potential investigation or audit under this Part.

Written arrangements

(3) The Commissioner may only disclose information to the person or body referred to in subsection (1) if the Commissioner has entered into a written arrangement with that person or body that

(a) limits the information to be disclosed to that which is necessary for the purpose set out in paragraph (2)(a) or (b);

(b) restricts the use of the information to the purpose for which it was originally shared; and

(c) stipulates that the information be treated in a confidential manner and not be further disclosed without the express consent of the Commissioner.

Arrangements

(4) The Commissioner may enter into arrangements with one or more persons or bodies referred to in subsection (1) in order to

(a) provide for cooperation with respect to the enforcement of laws protecting personal information, including the sharing of information referred to in subsection (2) and the provision of mechanisms for the handling of any complaint in which they are mutually interested;

(b) establish procedures for sharing information referred to in subsection (2);

(c) develop recommendations, resolutions, rules, standards or other instruments with respect to the protection of personal information;

(d) undertake and publish research related to the protection of personal information;

(e) share knowledge and expertise by different means, including through staff exchanges; or

(f) identify issues of mutual interest and determine priorities pertaining to the protection of personal information.

Promoting the purposes of the Part

24. The Commissioner shall

(a) develop and conduct information programs to foster public understanding, and recognition of the purposes, of this Part;

(b) undertake and publish research that is related to the protection of personal information, including any such research that is requested by the Minister of Industry;

(c) encourage organizations to develop detailed policies and practices, including organizational codes of practice, to comply with sections 5 to 10; and

(d) promote, by any means that the Commissioner considers appropriate, the purposes of this Part.

Annual report

25.(1) The Commissioner shall, as soon as practicable after the end of each calendar year, submit to Parliament a report concerning the application of this Part, the extent to which the provinces have enacted legislation that is substantially similar to this Part and the application of any such legislation.

Consultation

(2) Before preparing the report, the Commissioner shall consult with those persons in the provinces who, in the Commissioner's opinion, are in a position to assist the Commissioner in reporting respecting personal information that is collected, used or disclosed interprovincially or internationally.

Regulations

26.(1) The Governor in Council may make regulations

(a) specifying, by name or by class, what is a government institution or part of a government institution for the purposes of any provision of this Part;

(a.01) specifying, by name or by class, what is an investigative body for the purposes of paragraph 7(3)(d) or (h.2);

(a.1) specifying information or classes of information for the purpose of paragraph 7(1)(d), (2)(c.1) or (3)(h.1); and

(b) for carrying out the purposes and provisions of this Part.

Orders

(2) The Governor in Council may, by order,

(a) provide that this Part is binding on any agent of Her Majesty in right of Canada to which the *Privacy Act* does not apply; and

(b) if satisfied that legislation of a province that is substantially similar to this Part applies to an organization, a class of organizations, an activity or a class of activities, exempt the organization, activity or class from the application of this Part in respect of the collection, use or disclosure of personal information that occurs within that province.

Whistleblowing

27.(1) Any person who has reasonable grounds to believe that a person has contravened or intends to contravene a provision of Division 1, may notify the Commissioner of the particulars of the matter and may request that their identity be kept confidential with respect to the notification.

Confidentiality

(2) The Commissioner shall keep confidential the identity of a person who has notified the Commissioner under subsection (1) and to whom an assurance of confidentiality has been provided by the Commissioner.

Prohibition

27.1(1) No employer shall dismiss, suspend, demote, discipline, harass or otherwise disadvantage an employee, or deny an employee a benefit of employment, by reason that

(a) the employee, acting in good faith and on the basis of reasonable belief, has disclosed to the Commissioner that the employer or any other person has contravened or intends to contravene a provision of Division 1;

(b) the employee, acting in good faith and on the basis of reasonable belief, has refused or stated an intention of refusing to do anything that is a contravention of a provision of Division 1;

(c) the employee, acting in good faith and on the basis of reasonable belief, has done or stated an intention of doing anything that is required to be done in order that a provision of Division 1 not be contravened; or

(d) the employer believes that the employee will do anything referred to in paragraph (a), (b) or (c).

Saving

(2) Nothing in this section impairs any right of an employee either at law or under an employment contract or collective agreement.

Definitions

(3) In this section, "employee" includes an independent contractor and "employer" has a corresponding meaning.

Offence and punishment

28. Every person who knowingly contravenes subsection 8(8) or 27.1(1) or who obstructs the Commissioner or the Commissioner's delegate in the investigation of a complaint or in conducting an audit is guilty of

(a) an offence punishable on summary conviction and liable to a fine not exceeding $10,000; or

(b) an indictable offence and liable to a fine not exceeding $100,000.

Review of Part by parliamentary committee

29.(1) The administration of this Part shall, every five years after this Part comes into force, be reviewed by the committee of the House of Commons, or of both Houses of Parliament, that may be designated or established by Parliament for that purpose.

Review and report

(2) The committee shall undertake a review of the provisions and operation of this Part and shall, within a year after the review is undertaken or within any further period that the House of Commons may authorize, submit a report to Parliament that includes a statement of any changes to this Part or its administration that the committee recommends.

. . . .

SCHEDULE 1
(SECTION 5)

PRINCIPLES SET OUT IN THE NATIONAL STANDARD OF CANADA ENTITLED MODEL CODE FOR THE PROTECTION OF PERSONAL INFORMATION, CAN/CSA-Q830-96

4.1 Principle 1 — Accountability

An organization is responsible for personal information under its control and shall designate an individual or individuals who are accountable for the organization's compliance with the following principles.

4.1.1 Accountability for the organization's compliance with the principles rests with the designated individual(s), even though other individuals within the organization may be responsible for the day-to-day collection and processing of personal information. In addition, other individuals within the organization may be delegated to act on behalf of the designated individual(s).

4.1.2 The identity of the individual(s) designated by the organization to oversee the organization's compliance with the principles shall be made known upon request.

4.1.3 An organization is responsible for personal information in its possession or custody, including information that has been transferred to a third party for processing. The organization shall use contractual or other means to provide a comparable level of protection while the information is being processed by a third party.

4.1.4 Organizations shall implement policies and practices to give effect to the principles, including

(a) implementing procedures to protect personal information;

(b) establishing procedures to receive and respond to complaints and inquiries;

(c) training staff and communicating to staff information about the organization's policies and practices; and

(d) developing information to explain the organization's policies and procedures.

4.2 Principle 2 — Identifying Purposes

The purposes for which personal information is collected shall be identified by the organization at or before the time the information is collected.

4.2.1 The organization shall document the purposes for which personal information is collected in order to comply with the Openness principle (Clause 4.8) and the Individual Access principle (Clause 4.9).

4.2.2 Identifying the purposes for which personal information is collected at or before the time of collection allows organizations to determine the information they need to collect to fulfil these purposes. The Limiting Collection principle (Clause 4.4) requires an organization to collect only that information necessary for the purposes that have been identified.

4.2.3 The identified purposes should be specified at or before the time of collection to the individual from whom the personal information is collected. Depending upon the way in which the information is collected, this can be done orally or in writing. An application form, for example, may give notice of the purposes.

4.2.4 When personal information that has been collected is to be used for a purpose not previously identified, the new purpose shall be identified prior to use. Unless the new purpose is required by law, the consent of the individual is required before information can be used for that purpose. For an elaboration on consent, please refer to the Consent principle (Clause 4.3).

4.2.5 Persons collecting personal information should be able to explain to individuals the purposes for which the information is being collected.

4.2.6 This principle is linked closely to the Limiting Collection principle (Clause 4.4) and the Limiting Use, Disclosure, and Retention principle (Clause 4.5).

4.3 Principle 3 — Consent

The knowledge and consent of the individual are required for the collection, use, or disclosure of personal information, except where inappropriate.

> Note: In certain circumstances personal information can be collected, used, or disclosed without the knowledge and consent of the individual. For example, legal, medical, or security reasons may make it impossible or impractical to seek consent. When information is being collected for the detection and prevention of fraud or for law enforcement, seeking the consent of the individual might defeat the purpose of collecting the information. Seeking consent may be impossible or inappropriate when the individual is a minor, seriously ill, or mentally incapacitated. In addition, organizations that do not have a direct relationship with the individual may not always be able to seek consent. For example, seeking consent may be impractical for a charity or a direct-marketing firm that wishes to acquire a mailing list from another organization. In such cases, the organization providing the list would be expected to obtain consent before disclosing personal information.

4.3.1 Consent is required for the collection of personal information and the subsequent use or disclosure of this information. Typically, an organization will seek consent for the use or disclosure of the information at the time of collection. In certain circumstances, consent with respect to use or disclosure may be sought after the information has been collected but before use (for example, when an organization wants to use information for a purpose not previously identified).

4.3.2 The principle requires "knowledge and consent". Organizations shall make a reasonable effort to ensure that the individual is advised of the purposes for which the information will be used. To make the consent meaningful, the purposes must be stated in such a manner that the individual can reasonably understand how the information will be used or disclosed.

4.3.3 An organization shall not, as a condition of the supply of a product or service, require an individual to consent to the collection, use, or disclosure of information beyond that required to fulfil the explicitly specified, and legitimate purposes.

4.3.4 The form of the consent sought by the organization may vary, depending upon the circumstances and the type of information. In determining the form of consent to use, organizations shall take into account the sensitivity of the information. Although some information (for example, medical records and income records) is almost always considered to be sensitive, any information can be sensitive, depending on the context. For example, the names and addresses of subscribers to a newsmagazine would generally not be considered sensitive information. However, the names and addresses of subscribers to some special-interest magazines might be considered sensitive.

4.3.5 In obtaining consent, the reasonable expectations of the individual are also relevant. For example, an individual buying a subscription to a magazine should reasonably expect that the organization, in addition to using the individual's name and address for mailing and billing purposes, would also contact the person to solicit the renewal of the subscription. In this case, the organization can assume that the individual's request constitutes consent for specific purposes. On the other hand, an individual would not reasonably expect that personal information given to a health-care professional would be given to a company selling health-care products, unless consent were obtained. Consent shall not be obtained through deception.

4.3.6 The way in which an organization seeks consent may vary, depending on the circumstances and the type of information collected. An organization should generally seek express consent when the information is likely to be considered sensitive. Implied consent would generally be appropriate when the information is less sensitive. Consent can also be given by an authorized representative (such as a legal guardian or a person having power of attorney).

4.3.7 Individuals can give consent in many ways. For example:

(a) an application form may be used to seek consent, collect information, and inform the individual of the use that will be made of the information. By completing and signing the form, the individual is giving consent to the collection and the specified uses;

(b) a checkoff box may be used to allow individuals to request that their names and addresses not be given to other organizations. Individuals who do not check the box are assumed to consent to the transfer of this information to third parties;

(c) consent may be given orally when information is collected over the telephone; or

(d) consent may be given at the time that individuals use a product or service.

4.3.8 An individual may withdraw consent at any time, subject to legal or contractual restrictions and reasonable notice. The organization shall inform the individual of the implications of such withdrawal.

4.4 Principle 4 — Limiting Collection

The collection of personal information shall be limited to that which is necessary for the purposes identified by the organization. Information shall be collected by fair and lawful means.

4.4.1 Organizations shall not collect personal information indiscriminately. Both the amount and the type of information collected shall be limited to that which is necessary to fulfil the purposes identified. Organizations shall specify the type of information collected as part of their information-handling policies and practices, in accordance with the Openness principle (Clause 4.8).

4.4.2 The requirement that personal information be collected by fair and lawful means is intended to prevent organizations from collecting information by misleading or deceiving individuals about the purpose for which information is being collected. This requirement implies that consent with respect to collection must not be obtained through deception.

4.4.3 This principle is linked closely to the Identifying Purposes principle (Clause 4.2) and the Consent principle (Clause 4.3).

4.5 Principle 5 — Limiting Use, Disclosure, and Retention

Personal information shall not be used or disclosed for purposes other than those for which it was collected, except with the consent of the individual or as required by law. Personal information shall be retained only as long as necessary for the fulfilment of those purposes.

4.5.1 Organizations using personal information for a new purpose shall document this purpose (see Clause 4.2.1).

4.5.2 Organizations should develop guidelines and implement procedures with respect to the retention of personal information. These guidelines should include minimum and maximum retention periods. Personal information that has been used to make a decision about an individual shall be retained long enough to allow the individual access to the information after the decision has been made. An organization may be subject to legislative requirements with respect to retention periods.

4.5.3 Personal information that is no longer required to fulfil the identified purposes should be destroyed, erased, or made anonymous. Organizations shall develop guidelines and implement procedures to govern the destruction of personal information.

4.5.4 This principle is closely linked to the Consent principle (Clause 4.3), the Identifying Purposes principle (Clause 4.2), and the Individual Access principle (Clause 4.9).

4.6 Principle 6 — Accuracy
Personal information shall be as accurate, complete, and up-to-date as is necessary for the purposes for which it is to be used.

4.6.1 The extent to which personal information shall be accurate, complete, and up-to-date will depend upon the use of the information, taking into account the interests of the individual. Information shall be sufficiently accurate, complete, and up-to-date to minimize the possibility that inappropriate information may be used to make a decision about the individual.

4.6.2 An organization shall not routinely update personal information, unless such a process is necessary to fulfil the purposes for which the information was collected.

4.6.3 Personal information that is used on an ongoing basis, including information that is disclosed to third parties, should generally be accurate and up-to-date, unless limits to the requirement for accuracy are clearly set out.

4.7 Principle 7 — Safeguards
Personal information shall be protected by security safeguards appropriate to the sensitivity of the information.

4.7.1 The security safeguards shall protect personal information against loss or theft, as well as unauthorized access, disclosure, copying, use, or modification. Organizations shall protect personal information regardless of the format in which it is held.

4.7.2 The nature of the safeguards will vary depending on the sensitivity of the information that has been collected, the amount, distribution, and format of the information, and the method of storage. More sensitive information should be safeguarded by a higher level of protection. The concept of sensitivity is discussed in Clause 4.3.4.

4.7.3 The methods of protection should include
  (a) physical measures, for example, locked filing cabinets and restricted access to offices;
  (b) organizational measures, for example, security clearances and limiting access on a "need-to-know" basis; and
  (c) technological measures, for example, the use of passwords and encryption.

4.7.4 Organizations shall make their employees aware of the importance of maintaining the confidentiality of personal information.

4.7.5 Care shall be used in the disposal or destruction of personal information, to prevent unauthorized parties from gaining access to the information (see Clause 4.5.3).

4.8 Principle 8 — Openness
An organization shall make readily available to individuals specific information about its policies and practices relating to the management of personal information.

4.8.1 Organizations shall be open about their policies and practices with respect to the management of personal information. Individuals shall be able to acquire information about an organization's policies and practices without unreasonable effort. This information shall be made available in a form that is generally understandable.

4.8.2 The information made available shall include
  (a) the name or title, and the address, of the person who is accountable for the organization's policies and practices and to whom complaints or inquiries can be forwarded;
  (b) the means of gaining access to personal information held by the organization;
  (c) a description of the type of personal information held by the organization, including a general account of its use;
  (d) a copy of any brochures or other information that explain the organization's policies, standards, or codes; and
  (e) what personal information is made available to related organizations (e.g., subsidiaries).

4.8.3 An organization may make information on its policies and practices available in a variety of ways. The method chosen depends on the nature of its business and other considerations. For example, an organization may choose to make brochures available in its place of business, mail information to its customers, provide online access, or establish a toll-free telephone number.

4.9 Principle 9 — Individual Access

Upon request, an individual shall be informed of the existence, use, and disclosure of his or her personal information and shall be given access to that information. An individual shall be able to challenge the accuracy and completeness of the information and have it amended as appropriate.

> Note: In certain situations, an organization may not be able to provide access to all the personal information it holds about an individual. Exceptions to the access requirement should be limited and specific. The reasons for denying access should be provided to the individual upon request. Exceptions may include information that is prohibitively costly to provide, information that contains references to other individuals, information that cannot be disclosed for legal, security, or commercial proprietary reasons, and information that is subject to solicitor-client or litigation privilege.

4.9.1 Upon request, an organization shall inform an individual whether or not the organization holds personal information about the individual. Organizations are encouraged to indicate the source of this information. The organization shall allow the individual access to this information. However, the organization may choose to make sensitive medical information available through a medical practitioner. In addition, the organization shall provide an account of the use that has been made or is being made of this information and an account of the third parties to which it has been disclosed.

4.9.2 An individual may be required to provide sufficient information to permit an organization to provide an account of the existence, use, and disclosure of personal information. The information provided shall only be used for this purpose.

4.9.3 In providing an account of third parties to which it has disclosed personal information about an individual, an organization should attempt to be as specific as possible. When it is not possible to provide a list of the organizations to which it has actually disclosed information about an individual, the organization shall provide a list of organizations to which it may have disclosed information about the individual.

4.9.4 An organization shall respond to an individual's request within a reasonable time and at minimal or no cost to the individual. The requested information shall be provided or made available in a form that is generally understandable. For example, if the organization uses abbreviations or codes to record information, an explanation shall be provided.

4.9.5 When an individual successfully demonstrates the inaccuracy or incompleteness of personal information, the organization shall amend the information as required. Depending upon the nature of the information challenged, amendment involves the correction, deletion, or addition of information. Where appropriate, the amended information shall be transmitted to third parties having access to the information in question.

4.9.6 When a challenge is not resolved to the satisfaction of the individual, the substance of the unresolved challenge shall be recorded by the organization. When appropriate, the existence of the unresolved challenge shall be transmitted to third parties having access to the information in question.

4.10 Principle 10 — Challenging Compliance

An individual shall be able to address a challenge concerning compliance with the above principles to the designated individual or individuals accountable for the organization's compliance.

4.10.1 The individual accountable for an organization's compliance is discussed in Clause 4.1.1.

4.10.2 Organizations shall put procedures in place to receive and respond to complaints or inquiries about their policies and practices relating to the handling of personal information. The complaint procedures should be easily accessible and simple to use.

4.10.3 Organizations shall inform individuals who make inquiries or lodge complaints of the existence of relevant complaint procedures. A range of these procedures may exist. For example, some regulatory bodies accept complaints about the personal-information handling practices of the companies they regulate.

4.10.4 An organization shall investigate all complaints. If a complaint is found to be justified, the organization shall take appropriate measures, including, if necessary, amending its policies and practices.

(e)   *Guertin v. Royal Bank of Canada*†

[CROMARTY J.]

The plaintiffs were customers of the Royal Bank of Canada Branch in the Timmins Square Shopping Centre (the Bank) of which the defendant, Arcand, was manager. All the outstanding shares in the numbered company are in the name of Arcand's wife. The plaintiffs claim damages for the breach of an alleged fiduciary duty owing to them in connection with their proposed purchase of a snack bar in the shopping centre, a declaration that they own the snack bar, a mandatory order that it be conveyed to them, an accounting of its profits and punitive damages.

The snack bar was a relatively modest business operated by Mantas Brothers Limited for which Mrs. Guertin worked from December, 1978, to August 17, 1979, latterly as manager. Mantas also owned the Versailles restaurant, a full service, licensed, sit-down establishment in the same complex. In late March or early April, 1979, one Lise Labonte, the manager of the Versailles to whom Mrs. Guertin reported daily on business matters, told her that the snack bar was for sale because the person buying the Versailles did not want to buy the snack bar. She discussed it with her husband and then went to see Mr. Mantas who told her that indeed it was for sale at $30,000. He also told her: "There are two other guys and I'm asking them $45,000, but I'd rather see you have it." He asked about financing and she told him they had a vacant lot and some money and that her husband would go to the bank for a loan. This was her only meeting with Mantas and at no time did she ask for or receive any financial statements, a copy of the lease or any other information with respect to the expenses of operating the restaurant. In her employment she had learned of some of the expenses and of the income. She regarded the reference to "two other guys" as mere puffery and thought they did not exist.

The plaintiffs did their ordinary banking at the Bank and had borrowed money from it to purchase at least two cars and $15,000 in connection with remedial work on a house. Mr. Guertin went to see Arcand on April 6th, a week after he had borrowed $5,000 from the Bank in connection with a car pur-chase. They had a short talk about Guertin and his wife buying the snack bar, an operation in which he said: "They could make a good buck." He showed Arcand a sketchy memorandum made by his wife of some figures dealing with the snack bar and told him that the asking price was $30,000 but they hoped to get it for $20,000 to $23,000 because they felt Mr. Mantas, who lived in Orilla, would not want to be looking after such a small operation in Timmins after he got rid of the Versailles. He also told Arcand they hoped to put on an extra shift and broaden the menu in order to increase the income. According to Guertin he asked Arcand what to do and was told: "Get the figures and we will work it out, I don't foresee too many problems." At a casual meeting in the Bank about one and a half weeks later, after the Versailles was "almost" sold, he says Arcand asked him if he had made up his mind to which he replied: "No, I am going to wait till the Versailles is sold and then I'll make him an offer." Guertin knew Arcand would have to get head office approval for this loan because of his earlier loans.

At this time the Guertins owned an unencumbered vacant lot recently appraised for the Bank at $15,500, he had $3,000 in his bank account, an almost new car and a newly purchased house of a value of about $43,000 which was substantially encumbered and he owed the Bank $5,000. He and his wife had a combined annual income of about $24,000. Mr. Guertin's repayment record was very good. On a loan application in June of 1978, Arcand had noted: "Customer has been dealing here since branch opened — all dealings satisfactory" and on one of March, 1979: "(1) good job (2) good credit (3) good savings (4) no other debts (5) we recommend — good people".

On April 6th after Guertin saw Arcand, he and his wife went to see their friends, the Wallingfords. Mrs. Wallingford described Mrs. Guertin as being very excited on her arrival. Guertin told them of his talk with Arcand. They asked the Wallingfords if they would be willing to put up some money if the Bank would not provide all they needed. Wallingfords, who seemed to be financially secure, agreed to lend up to half of the excess needed and if more than that was required to come in as part-

---

† (1983), 1 D.L.R. (4th) 68 (Ont. H.C.J.).

ners and advance their share of the amount needed. There was no "business" discussion such as sales, expenses, cash flow, rent or improvements required, or about any security arrangements. A good deal of self-serving evidence was given in connection with this meeting which I have excluded from my consideration.

Arcand agrees that Guertin came to see him in April, he thought about mid-month, with respect to a loan in connection with the proposed purchase of the snack bar. He confirms Guertin's evidence about his prior dealings with the Bank, of his having a piece of paper showing some of the snack bar's affairs, about his wife being told by Mantas the asking price of $30,000, of their hopes of getting it for about $20,000, and his saying that he could do well with the place. Arcand says he told Guertin that it was highly improbable that he could get him a $30,000 loan. He did not take a written application and said that he himself could not make such a loan until it was approved by his superiors. Guertin never again came to see him about the proposed loan. He did not recall seeing Guertin about a week or so later and asking if he had made up his mind.

Arcand's branch of the Bank was in the centre and was the banker for the centre's owners. In June of 1978 he was given a copy of an offer to purchase both the Versailles and the snack bar and was asked to verify the credit of the proposed purchaser. He knew then that the snack bar was for sale but only as part of a package with the larger restaurant. This deal progressed no further.

In November or December, 1979, Mr. Nick Mantas, one of the operators of the restaurants, asked him if he knew of any possible buyers for both the restaurants. Shortly afterwards Arcand spoke to a Mr. Conrad Deschamps, an old friend of his, and arranged a meeting with Mantas in January or February, 1979. Neither place was then listed for sale with any real estate agent. At this meeting, an offer was discussed but not formally made. A somewhat different offer was made in writing on March 17, 1979, and accepted on March 19th for the Versailles restaurant only. This was prepared after a meeting at the Bank at which Arcand, Deschamps, Ted Mantas and Mr. Sullivan, his solicitor, were present. It contains several conditions but makes no reference at all to the disposition of the snack bar. Deschamps said he had a "gentlemen's agreement" with Mantas that the snack bar went along with the Versailles and that "if Mantas wanted to dump the snack bar on someone else I would not have met the conditions in the offer and it would be null and void — if he tried to sell to anyone else I would not

have raised the $150,000 or tried to get a liquor licence". No mention was made of a price or terms for the snack bar at this time.

According to Arcand, Deschamps had discussed Mrs. Arcand's buying the snack bar some time in February and said that when the funds for the purchase of the Versailles were confirmed he would advise Mantas that a verbal option would be granted to Mrs. Arcand. Deschamps, however, swore that when he signed the offer (March 17th) he was interested in selling the snack bar to Arcand, but he knew that a bank manager could not be interested in a private enterprise, but he wanted Arcand to have it "more than her". Deschamps also said when he was negotiating for the Versailles before March 17th he told Mrs. Arcand that the snack bar would be a great chance for her to get out of the house and that he suggested to her that she buy it. He also said that at the meeting of March 17th the snack bar may have been mentioned.

On April 4th, Mantas gave a birthday party for Deschamps which was also a celebration of the authorization of the funds for the purchase of the Versailles. Arcand says that the snack bar was discussed at this meeting and that it was "confirmed by all that it would be appropriate for my wife to buy it, the price of $20,000 was discussed", and that before meeting Guertin "everything was pretty well settled". However, the following questions from his examination for discovery were put to him:

171. Q. Was there any discussion that you recall about filing a loan application for credit at that time? (at the time of the meeting with Guertin).

A. None was requested and none was submitted or none was taken. It was just an inquiry.

172. Q. At that time had you and Mr. Mantas already decided on a price of the snack bar or what was the stage at that time of your negotiations with Mr. Mantas?

A. They were still verbal.

173. Q. I realize that but what had you or had you not agreed to at that time, with Mr. Mantas?

A. I think we were strictly in the talking stage.

Arcand's explanation for these answers was that the discovery is incorrect, there was no writing and no closing but that $20,000 cash had been agreed to. As another example of Arcand's confusion his fresh as amended statement of defence (para. 8) contradicts that by saying that before March 19th he had agreed with Mantas and Deschamps to purchase the snack bar.

On May 3rd an offer in Mrs. Arcand's name was made to Ted Mantas Ltd. to purchase the snack bar for $20,000, payable $5,000 on closing, $5,000 in 90 days and $10,000 one year after closing, the deal to close on May 15, 1979. It was accepted also on May 3rd. It contains no clause requiring or showing the approval of the sale by Deschamps nor any reference to the sale of the Versailles. It is his evidence that the sale of the snack bar separately was governed by a verbal agreement between Mantas and Deschamps and that Mantas was obliged to hold the snack bar for him or for Deschamps as he recalled.

Some time later Arcand came to the snack bar and asked Mrs. Guertin if he might come in behind the counter. She refused him entry—which seems strange since she and her husband were seeking a loan in connection with the purchase of this very establishment. He replied, "It's okay. I have just bought it" so she let him in. Later he told her he would keep her on as an employee. She said she was upset at the time but she made no complaint to him or to the Bank until late August. She continued to work there for Mantas, apparently until August 17th when she went on holidays. Shortly after this and after speaking to a solicitor in Toronto, she spoke to some senior bank officials to complain of Arcand's behaviour. As a result of the complaint and after a number of meetings with his superior, he resigned in October.

Some time after Guertin's visit to the Bank and before Arcand put in his offer on May 3rd, Mantas told him that Mrs. Guertin had asked him about the sale of the snack bar. Arcand does not recall what answer he made to Mantas, but this question and answer from his discovery was put to him:

> 228.   Q. Did Mr. Mantas indicate to you what stage his negotiations were at with Mrs. Guertin? Or Mr. Guertin?
>
> A. He told me that they just inquired and he told them the price and that was it.

He agrees that he made that answer and said he then just shrugged his shoulders. When asked if price was discussed he answered: "Maybe he told me the price was $30,000." However, he agreed that since the discoveries were held two years ago his memory was then better than it was at trial. He made no comment to Mantas when told this because his negotiations with him were complete and as he had made an agreement on May 4th, there was nothing to say. He did not know why Mantas would quote her a price when he had a deal with him, and he did not ask: "I have a deal with you, why would you be quoting a price to her?"

On June 19th the numbered company was incorporated with Mrs. Arcand as the sole shareholder, and on July 10th, at the insistence of Mantas, the terms of the offer were changed so that the purchase price became $23,000, the cash payment was increased from $5,000 to $20,000 and the $3,000 balance was payable without interest on December 15, 1979. Possession and closing were to be within five days after Campeau (the owner of the centre) consented to the assignment of the lease. The statement of adjustments on this basis was dated August 15, 1979, and Arcand commenced operations at the snack bar on either August 14th or 16th. He borrowed all of the money due on closing, $13,000 from Deschamps, $5,000 from one Davis, a customer of the Bank, and $5,000 by loan from Banque Canadienne Nationale. In Arcand's opinion it was a bargain at $23,000.

On cross-examination Arcand was asked why he did not tell Mr. Guertin that he or his wife were interested in the snack bar. He answered that it was his personal affair, there was no reason for Guertin to know about it, the discussions had been going on for about eight months. He said he did not tell his wife about the Guertins' involvement in the snack bar until August when he had a call from his superiors about the complaint by Guertin.

It was a strict rule of the Bank that employees might not be engaged in any outside business and indeed employees were required to sign a document in this regard. Arcand frequently refers to his wife buying the snack bar but in some places he refers to it being bought either by "us" or by himself. He told Mr. Thalheimer (his solicitor) to draw the offer from his wife because as a bank manager he could not have an outside business. She said she had no contact with the solicitor about the offer to purchase except to sign it, nor had she had any negotiations with Mantas or Deschamps, but that her husband did all of the financing and all of the dealing and the offer was made in her name because of the Bank guide-lines and it was put into the company for tax reasons. She also said that her husband decided to put it in her name to protect his position at the Bank. She had nothing to do with the deal but left it to her husband as he did not want problems with the Bank. Much of this effectively contradicts Deschamps' evidence. She confirms the birthday party on April

4th and that Mantas said she could have the restaurant and that Deschamps was in favour.

Much of the difficulty in determining what went on between Arcand and Deschamps and what information Arcand had might have been avoided by calling Mantas as a witness. The failure of Arcand to call him leads me to believe that his evidence would not have been helpful to them at all and that it would have failed to confirm much that it is suggested Mantas said. Mr. Wise made this point early in argument when he said that he understood Mr. Mantas was in Ottawa. He later said that he had learned that Mantas was in Greece and that he would withdraw his comments. I am not sure what this meant but neither Arcand nor the numbered company sought an adjournment either before or during trial to permit them to call Mantas. I found the evidence given by Arcand and Deschamps confusing and contradictory and I accept it only where it is independently confirmed by other evidence or by very strong inference.

The plaintiffs were unsophisticated people, neither of whom is particularly well-educated but their story was consistent within itself and consistent with any reasonable analysis of all the evidence. While they have an obvious interest in the outcome of the action they were not seriously challenged on cross-examination nor were they shown to have over-reached or contradicted themselves. I accept their evidence in preference to that given by Arcand and Deschamps wherever there is any difference between them.

I find as facts that Guertin and his wife were established customers of the Bank and that on April 6th Mr. Guertin told Arcand that they were interested in buying the snack bar, that his wife had spoken to Mantas who quoted a $30,000 purchase price, but that they hoped, for the reasons already set out, to be able to buy it for about $20,000 to $23,000 when the Versailles was sold, that he asked Arcand what he would have to do to get a loan for the purchase of the snack bar, that he showed him a memorandum of some sketchy figures provided by his wife which were not at that time known to Arcand. I find that Arcand did not then have the single sheet of paper proved later by Mantas which, according to the reply to demand for particulars, he only received in the week of April 8th to 14th, nor did he have the figures worked up by Deschamps. I further find that Guertin told Arcand of his plans to add an extra shift and to expand the menu in the snack bar to increase revenues and that Arcand told him: "When you get the figures come back and we'll work it out. I don't foresee too many problems." I also

find that about one to one and a half weeks later Guertin saw Arcand in the Bank casually and that Arcand then asked him if they had made an offer yet, to which Guertin replied: "No, I'm trying to get them down."

As a result, on April 6th, Arcand was armed with all of his "competitors" information. The figures in Arcand's offer to purchase and in the July amendment are so close to the figures discussed with Guertin as to confirm that Arcand made use of them as he did of all the other information he was given by Guertin.

What information did Arcand have on that date not obtained from Guertin? He understood only that the snack bar was for sale independently of the Versailles with the consent of Deschamps; however, there is no acceptable evidence of any impediment to Mantas' right to sell the snack bar separately and on May 3rd he certainly accepted an offer with no written approval by or reference to Deschamps. Deschamps' evidence that he had a right to control its sale to protect his competitive position is hardly believable since it was sold, it is said with his agreement, to someone whose right of immediate resale was unfettered. Arcand had no agreement with Mantas as to its selling price on April 6th, since this question was being discussed "all through April". He had not seen the snack bar lease. As to financial details he said that during the week following the week of April 4th (*i.e.*, the week of April 11th), or during that week, Mantas produced a statement of profit and loss disclosing his revenues, expenses and what was left for profit. He was shown the Versailles lease and was told that the snack bar lease was the same (the Versailles lease was not produced in evidence). He was then asked if he had this statement of operations at the first meeting with Guertin to which he replied: "To the best of my recollection I did. I brought it to Deschamps to look at and for his opinion, he gave me some figures showing what future sales could be." His memory on this is not very good since it was his evidence that he first saw Guertin in mid-April, while I have found, based on other believable evidence, that it was on April 6th. Deschamps had no recollection of when he got the sheet. It cannot have been of much significance since Deschamps tore it up and threw it away. He prepared a projection which showed substantial future revenues.

On May 3rd when Arcand made his offer in his wife's name, he knew, because of the advice he had given Guertin to get a figure and come back, that he was safe from a return visit and from an approach by Guertin to another financial institution to seek a loan. In my view, after Guertin's hand had been disclosed, Arcand owed him a positive duty to disclose his interest in becoming the purchase of the snack bar so that Guertin might seek financial assistance elsewhere and if necessary make a better offer to Mantas.

Arcand was most explicit that Guertin's only request was about a loan of $30,000 and that he did not ask to fill out an application form. He said if Guertin had asked him for an application to be filled in he would have sent him to another bank to avoid a conflict. In my opinion, there is no difference between a verbal inquiry and a request that it be reduced to writing in this regard. Given Guertin's assets, earnings and record with the Bank, it does not seem entirely unlikely that the Bank would agree to lend enough to cover the difference between what the Guertins had and the $23,000 final price.

THE LAW

What is the relationship between a bank and its customer and what are the duties which flow from that relationship?

Mr. Wise quoted and relied upon *The Law and Practice of Banking*, J.M. Holden, 2nd ed. (1974), vol. 1, p. 32, para. 2-2:

> 2-2. The contractual relationship which exists between banker and customer is a complex one founded originally upon the customs and usages of bankers. Many of those customs and usages have been recognized by the courts, and, to the extent that they have been so recognized, they must be regarded as implied terms of the contract between banker and customer. It follows, therefore, that this is a branch of the law where implied terms are of vital importance.

Perhaps the following statement is of more help — *The Law of Banking*, Ian F.G. Baxter, 3rd ed. (1981), p. 10:

> *The Confidential Character of the Banker-Customer Relationship*
>
> The relationship between a banker and customer is of a confidential character and there is implied in the contract a duty of secrecy as regards the customer's affairs. The *locus classicus* for the nature of the duty is the case of *Tournier v. National Provincial Bank*, [1924] 1 K.B. 461. A drew a cheque in favour of B, both A and B being customers of the same bank. B's account was overdrawn and he had signed an agreement to repay the advance by weekly installments.

When B defaulted the bank manager discovered that he had dealings with a bookmaker and disclosed this to his prospective employers.

> It was held that the disclosure of information was a breach of the bank's contractual duty to B. Bankes L.J. considered that the banker has a contractual duty to his customer not to disclose his affairs.

In *Tournier v. National Provincial & Union Bank of England*, [1924] 1 K.B. 461 at pp. 483–84, Atkin L.J. said:

> It is now necessary to consider whether there is any, and if so what, implied term as to an obligation of secrecy on the part of the bank. The question of what terms are to be implied in a contract is a question of law.... Is there any term as to secrecy to be implied from the relation of banker and customers? I have myself no doubt that there is. Assuming that the test is rather stricter than Lord Watson [in *Dahl v. Nelson, Donkin & Co.* (1881), 6 App. Cas. 38] would require, and is not merely what the parties, as fair and reasonable men, would presumably have agreed upon, but what the Court considers they must necessarily have agreed upon, it appears to me that some term as to secrecy must be implied. The bank find it necessary to bind their servants to secrecy; they communicate this fact to all their customers in their pass-book, and I am satisfied that if they had been asked whether they were under an obligation as to secrecy by a prospective customer, without hesitation they would say yes. The facts in this case as to the course of business of this bank do not appear to be in any degree unusual in general banking business. I come to the conclusion that one of the implied terms of the contract is that the bank enter into a qualified obligation with their customer to abstain from disclosing information as to his affairs without his consent. I am confirmed in this conclusion by the admission of counsel for the bank that they do, in fact, consider themselves under a legal obligation to maintain secrecy. Such an obligation could only arise under a contractual term.

Holden at p. 67, discusses *Tournier* as follows:

> 2-100. The leading case on the duty of secrecy is *Tournier v. National Provincial and Union Bank of England*, which is important not only because of the particular point that arose but also because of the general principles laid down in the judgments in the Court of Appeal.... The trial took place before Avory J., and a jury, and judgment was entered for the bank. The plaintiff appealed.

2-101. The Court of Appeal allowed the appeal and ordered a new trial. There is nothing in the law reports to indicate whether or not a new trial ever took place: possibly the action was settled. All three members of the Court of Appeal, Bankes, Scrutton and Atkin L.JJ., held that a bank does owe a duty of secrecy to its customers.... Thus Atkin L.J. said:

> The first question is: To what information does the obligation of secrecy extend? ... I further think that the obligation extends to information obtained from other sources than the customer's actual account, if the occasion upon which the information was obtained arose out of the banking relations of the bank and its customers — for example, with a view to assisting the bank in conducting the customer's business, or in coming to decisions as to its treatment of its customers.

I think I need not pursue the question further since Mr. Ballard in argument conceded that a duty of confidence flowed from the bank-customer relationship and that a bank manager may not disclose confidential information to others nor may he use information received by him from a customer for his own advantage, and counsel for the Bank adopted his argument.

The defendants argue strongly that no confidence was breached by Arcand because he already had a deal arranged before Guertin came in to see him and that his failure to disclose his interest in the snack bar was only an error of judgment. They rely on *Midwestern News Agency Ltd. v. Vanpinxteren* (1975), 62 D.L.R. (3d) 555, 24, C.P.R. (2d) 47, [1976] 1 W.W.R. 299. The factual situation there was not what I have found it to be here. The defendant was the manager of the plaintiff company; one of his duties was to look for a retail outlet in Saskatoon. It was generally known in the industry that the Saskatoon News Agency would be for sale. When the defendant told his manager early on that Saskatoon News was for sale he treated it as old news and said in effect: "Everyone knows that." The defendant inquired if the plaintiff was interested and was told to obtain financial information. He did not do so for some months but made arrangements to buy it himself. At p. 566:

> There was nothing confidential about the Saskatoon News Agency being for sale. I have already found that Mr. Fichel described that "news" to the male defendant when the latter acquainted Fichel with what he had heard in this regard as something akin to it being old hat. In

any event, the plaintiff had not acquainted the male defendant with the possibility of the sale of this business. It was the exact opposite — the male defendant told the plaintiff of the possibility over four months before the business was purchased.

and at p. 569 [quoting from Goff and Jones, *Law of Restitution*, 1st ed. (1966), p. 456]:

> "The recipient's duty not to use confidential information for his own benefit terminates, subject to a contrary agreement between the parties, when the information becomes public knowledge, for the 'secret, as a secret, has ceased to exist'."
> I am satisfied that there never was any secret about the Saskatoon News Agency being for sale....

They also relied on *Tombill Gold Mines, Ltd. v. Hamilton et al.*, [1956] S.C.R. 858, 5 D.L.R. (2d) 561, which does not support their position. The majority judgment of the Supreme Court of Canada is summarized in the headnote:

> ... *held*, on appeal, by a majority, the action could not succeed. The retainer and agreement for consulting and engineering services could not support an allegation that the engineering company was bound to work exclusively for the mining company in the search for new mining properties. In so far as plaintiffs relied on a conversation between its president and official of the engineering company who informed the former that he was going to inspect some valuable properties (those now in dispute) and if possible try and get some claims staked in the same area for plaintiffs, there was no ground for saying that this was anything but gratuitous and it created no fiduciary obligation.

At the opening of trial the Bank withdrew its pleading that:

> 5. This defendant denies that it is in law responsible for the actions of its then Manager, Robert [*sic*] Arcand, as alleged in paragraph 13 of the statement of claim, and pleads that such actions, if they were taken, which is not admitted but denied, were taken by the said defendant in a purely personal capacity and not within the scope, course or authority of his employment with this defendant.

There is no dispute that Arcand was employed by the Bank as the manager of its branch at the centre at all relevant times and the Bank is clearly liable for his acts as manager. One case is sufficient authority for that: *Lloyd v. Grace, Smith & Co.*, [1912] A.C. 716 at p. 725, where Lord Loreburn said:

> I have only to say, as to the authority of *Barwick v. English Joint Stock Bank*. L.R. 2 Ex. 259, that I entirely agree in the opinion about to be delivered by Lord Macnaghten. If the agent commits the fraud purporting to act in the course of business such as he was authorized, or held out as authorized, to transact on account of his principal, then the latter may be held liable for it.

The prayer for relief is as follows:

> **18.** The Plaintiffs therefore claim damages against the Defendants:
> (a) Damages against the Defendants, the Royal Bank of Canada and Hubert Arcand for breach of fiduciary duty in the sum of $100,000.00;
> (b) A declaration that Mantas' Snack Bar is the property of the Plaintiffs and a mandatory injunction requiring the Defendant, 418397 Ontario Limited, to convey its interest in the same to the Plaintiffs for $23,000.00;
> (c) An accounting of profits from Mantas' Snack Bar from the date of closing of the purchase to the date of conveyance to the Plaintiffs and judgment to the Plaintiffs in a sum equal to such profits;
> (d) Punitive damages in the sum of $100,000.00;
> (e) Costs of this action;
> (f) Such further and other relief as this Honourable Court may seem just.

With respect to para. (b) I do not think that in mid-1983 a court should either in equity or good conscience make a declaration or give a mandatory injunction to reverse a deal which was closed on about August 15, 1979, and has been undisturbed since, and especially so as no injunction was asked for in the original or amended writ of summons. In addition, even if an injunction were granted as asked, the court cannot compel the landlord to accept the Guertins as tenants and an order should not go which cannot be enforced. This has the effect of making the claim in para. (c), as now amended, meaningless, but the plaintiffs should not be so deprived of their right to an accounting. There is no doubt that an amendment allowing an accounting up to the date of judgment can go without any unfairness to the defendants since if granted that would be the date of an injunction so the defendants knew of that possible claim. The occasions on which a judge may make an amendment *ex mero motu* are few indeed. It was done by Riddell J. who had earlier said a judge should not so grant amendments in

Leftley v. Moffat (1925), 57 O.L.R. 260, [1925] 3 D.L.R. 825, an action for specific performance by the purchaser in which damages were not asked as an alternative and the property had been told before the *lis pendens* was registered. The trial judge said at p. 264 O.R., pp. 828–29 D.L.R.:

> There has been some difficulty as regards the power and policy of the Court in respect of damages where specific performance cannot be awarded; the case of *McIntyre v. Stockdale* (1912), 27 O.L.R. 460, lays it down that damages may be awarded where the defendant by his own act disables himself from giving specific performance, and I follow that case, agreeing with it as I do.
>
> But, if there were otherwise any difficulty, it may and should be got over on ordinary principles of amendment. The plaintiff may amend his record by claiming damages directly as in a common law action without claiming specific performance or he may claim damages as in a common law action in the alternative.
>
> I think judgment should go for the plaintiff for damages and costs on the Supreme Court scale....

Damages for breach of fiduciary duty which the law now seems to regard as an alternative to an accounting are claimed under para. (a) against Arcand and the Bank so the only defendant affected by an amendment would be the numbered company and only for such moneys as are to be accounted for after the date of the formal judgment. In my opinion, an amendment should go deleting the words "to the date of conveyance to the Plaintiffs" and such an amendment will be made to the record.

As some support for doing this see *McGregor on Damages*, 14th ed. (1980), pp. 975–76:

> Infringements of rights in such immaterial property as trade marks, patents and copyrights are today made tortious by statute ... so that if the statutory action should fall because, for instance, the plaintiff has failed to register the trade mark, he may fall back upon injurious falsehood.
>
> In relation to remedies all these cases have much in common, and several common factors may usefully be consolidated at this point. (1) The heads of pecuniary damage for which recovery is given are similar throughout: the principle damage is the loss of profits caused by the diversion of the plaintiff's customers, existing or potential, to the defendant. (2) Non-pecuniary loss does not feature in the awards.... (3) An action for damages is only one method whereby a plaintiff may seek redress. He will frequently apply for an injunction and, if granted, this can affect the amount of recoverable damages since

prospective loss may have been thereby largely eliminated. More important in relation to damage is the plaintiff's equitable remedy by way of an account of profits. This remedy is alternative to the action for damages, whether the infringement is of a trade mark, a patent or a copyright, and is to be preferred by a plaintiff where the defendant has made more profit out of the infringement than the plaintiff has lost....

In addition to actions for infringements of rights in statutorily protected property, it has now become recognized that "if a defendant is proved to have used confidential information, directly or indirectly obtained from the plaintiff, he will be guilty of an infringement of the plaintiff's rights."

It may well be that this relief comes under para. 18(f):

> (f) Such further and other relief as this Honourable Court may seem just.

An accounting before a master would be time-consuming and expensive and no more satisfactory than if done by me now on the evidence already given.

Punitive damages as claimed in para. (d) do not appear appropriate in the circumstances here. In *Pretu et al. v. Donald Tidey Co. Ltd.*, [1966] 1 O.R. 191, 53 D.L.R. (2d) 504, Brooke J. said at p. 196 O.R., p. 508 D.L.R.:

> When may exemplary or punitive damages be awarded? In actions for damages for tort, the Court may take into account matter of aggravation and may award exemplary damages where the conduct of the defendant has been malicious or high-handed. See *Jenks' Digest of English Civil Law*. 2nd ed., p. 370.

Such damages were also discussed in *Fern Brand Waxes Ltd. v. Pearl et al.*, [1972] 3 O.R. 829, 29 D.L.R. (3d) 662. The defendant was a director, secretary-treasurer, auditor and accountant of the plaintiff company and made use of his fiduciary position to transfer funds without authority to companies which he controlled. The plaintiff sued successfully for the return of those amounts with interest. McGillivray J.A. (with whom Brooke J.A. agreed) said at p. 837 O.R. p. 670 D.L.R.:

> In the matter of the punitive damage awarded the appeal must also be allowed. The claim in this action is for an accounting. No claim is made in tort. No precedent exists to justify an award of punitive damages in this type of action. While the trial Judge had ample reason for castigating the defendant Pearl for his nefarious conduct his judgment awarding punitive damages

cannot be supported and the appeal in this respect must be allowed.

They were also considered in *Bendix Homes Systems Ltd. v. Clayton et al.* (1977), 33 C.P.R. (2d) 230 at p. 252, [1977] 5 W.W.R. 10, by MacFarlane J. of the British Columbia Supreme Court:

> They were not entitled to conduct themselves as they did, and were disloyal to their employers but their conduct, in my opinion, was not, in all the circumstances, of the reprehensible character which ought to be marked by an award of punitive or exemplary damages.

Shabby as it was, I do not think Arcand's conduct comes within the description in those cases nor that punitive damages should be awarded.

The leading case on fiduciary obligations and damages for their breach is *Canadian Aero Service Ltd. v. O'Malley et al.*, [1974] S.C.R. 592, 40 D.L.R. (3d) 371, 11 C.P.R. (2d) 206. Two passages from the judgment of the Chief Justice of Canada are of importance in the present case. For several years Canaero had been seeking a contract to conduct an aerial survey project in Guyana for its government. The defendants, as senior officers of the company, had been engaged in making a tender on the project. Shortly before its tender was made they left Canaero and formed their own company which successfully tendered on and obtained the contract for the work thus breaching their fiduciary responsibility to Canaero. At pp. 606–7 S.C.R., pp. 381–82 D.L.R.:

> It follows that O'Malley and Zarzycki stood in a fiduciary relationship to Canaero, which in its generality betokens loyalty, good faith and avoidance of a conflict of duty and self-interest. Descending from the generality, the fiduciary relationship goes at least this far: a director or a senior office like O'Malley or Zarzycki is precluded from obtaining for himself, either secretly or without the approval of the company (which would have to be properly manifested upon full disclosure of the facts), any property or business advantage either belonging to the company or for which it has been negotiating; and especially is this so where the director or officer is a participant in the negotiations on behalf of the company.
>
> An examination of the case law in this Court and in the Courts of other like jurisdictions on the fiduciary duties of directors and senior officers shows the pervasiveness of a strict ethic in this area of the law. In my opinion, this ethic disqualifies a director or senior officer from usurping for himself or diverting to another per-

son or company with whom or with which he is associated a maturing business opportunity which his company is actively pursuing....

and at pp. 621–22 S.C.R., p. 392 D.L.R.:

> Liability of O'Malley and Zarzycki for breach of fiduciary duty does not depend upon proof by Canaero that, but for their intervention, it would have obtained the Guyana contract; nor is it a condition of recovery of damages that Canaero establish what its profit would have been or what it has lost by failing to realize the corporate opportunity in question. It is entitled to compel the faithless fiduciaries to answer for their default according to their gain. Whether the damages awarded here be viewed as an accounting of profits or, what amounts to the same thing, as based on unjust enrichment, I would not interfere with the quantum.

The evidence for an accounting or an assessment of general damages is sparse but in my opinion adequate to comply with the rule set out by Gale J. in *T.T.C. v. Aqua Taxi Ltd. et al.*, [1957] O.W.N. 65 at pp. 65–66, 6 D.L.R. (2d) 721 at pp. 743–44, 75 C.R.T.C. 42, and frequently referred to since:

> It is a well-established principle that where the damages are by their inherit [*sic*] nature difficult to assess, the court must do the best it can in the circumstances. Such is the case where the court estimates the damages for loss of expectation of life or for pain and suffering, it being impossible to measure the loss with mathematical accuracy. That is not to say, however, that a litigant is relieved of his duty to prove the facts upon which the damages are estimated: *Williams v. Stephenson* (1903), 33 S.C.R. 323.
>
> Mayne on Damages, 11th edition, points out at p. 5:
>
> > A distinction must be drawn between cases where absence of evidence makes it impossible to assess damages, and cases where the assessment is difficult because of the nature of the damage proved. In the former case only nominal damages can be recovered. In the latter case, however, the difficulty of assessment is no ground for refusing substantial damages, as, for instance, in an action against a banker for not paying his customer's cheque, or on a covenant to pay off incumbrances....

In *Canaero* the contract was tendered for at 2.3 million dollars on which the profit would have been about $300,000; however, Canaero would have shared the work equally with another company so that its profit would have been about $150,000 subject to some reductions. Grant J. said in his judgment at trial, 61 C.P.R. 1 at p. 48:

> While evidence as to general damages is meager, I would have fixed the same at $125,000 if the plaintiff had been successful in this action.

Arcand bought the snack bar for $23,000, a price which both he and Guertin described as a bargain. Its lease ran until March 31, 1995, at a rent of $7,200 per annum to March 31, 1980, and $8,000 per annum thereafter, both plus 7% of gross sales above the minimum rent and plus a share of the landlord's expenses for water, taxes, cleaning common areas and insurance. The total rent shown in the statements for the year ending January 31, 1981, is $9,158 and for the next year $12,146.

Statements prepared by chartered accountants were filed for the five-and-a-half-month period from August 18, 1979 to January 31, 1980, and the two subsequent 12-month periods. At the time of trial the statement for the year ending January 31, 1983, was not available. The first one contains accountant's comments which show that:

> In order to prepare these financial statements we made a review, consisting primarily of enquiry, comparison and discussion of such information. However, in accordance with the terms of our engagement, we have not performed an audit and consequently do not express an opinion on these financial statements.

The other two statements each contain this very significant disclaimer:

> The statements of earnings, deficit and changes in financial position of 418397 Ontario Limited (operating as B.J.'s Burger) for the year ended January 31, 1981 and the balance sheet as at that date *have been compiled solely for income tax purposes*. We have not audited, reviewed or otherwise attempted to verify their accuracy or completeness. [My emphasis.]

The persons who prepared these statements were not called as witnesses. In the first the sales for five and a half months are shown as $33,848 which mathematically gives annual sales of $73,850. The statement at January 31, 1981, shows the sales for that year to be $91,062, and the third statement shows them to be $111,704 or a 23% increase in each year. The first statement shows a deficit for the period of $78, the second shows net earnings of $72, and the third one net earnings of only $15. These figures bear no relationship to the increasing sales. In para. 2 of his reply to demand for particulars which forms part of the record however, Arcand says that a profit-and-loss statement given to him by Mantas in April 1979, showed gross sales of $42,000 and net profit of approximately $12,000 for a one-year period but he does not know what the period was. This leads me to doubt the honesty of the three statements.

Some time after the one of January 31, 1982, was prepared, Arcand approached a real estate agent, apparently to sell the snack bar and provided him with a plain sheet of paper headed "Earnings and Expenses, Year Ended January 31, 1982". It sets out comparative figures for 1981 and 1982. The figures generally follow the headings in the unaudited statements subject to some omissions and rearrangement. The same gross sales figures are used but the cost of sales is reduced by $5,000 in 1981 and $6,000 in 1982. Salaries and social benefits shown in the 1981 statement at $24,340 are divided in Arcand's statement into salaries and benefits $10,000, and management salaries $14,340. In the January 31, 1982 statement salaries and benefits are $33,097 but in Arcand's statement they are shown as $10,000 and management salaries of $23,097. The general and administrative expenses are reduced in the first statement from $46,612 to $39,876 and in the second statement from $59,456 to $50,386. In the result a profit of $14,393 is shown for 1981 and $17,360 in 1982. Arcand could not say where these figures came from.

I find that the changes were produced by Arcand with the obvious intention of making the business look more attractive to a prospective buyer since management salaries are introduced and the deductions result in substantial profits. The evidence suggests that the $10,000 represents the wages of an employee and the two Arcand teen-aged children and that the management salaries are the amounts paid to Arcand and his wife. I find that these statements are much closer to the truth than those made by the chartered accountants "solely for income tax purposes" and that they are supported by Mantas' earlier statement.

The matter of a figure for the gain in the future was not discussed by counsel. While this is not a contract case I have looked at some such cases for assistance with respect to a basis on which future gain might be calculated, while noting that damages for breach of contract and loss resulting from breach of fiduciary duty are not entirely the same. I have found a surprising paucity of cases on the point.

In coming to assess the damages or in making an accounting, I follow what was said by the Chief Justice of Canada. I am not concerned with whether or not the plaintiffs might have obtained the lease nor what profit they might have made, but I must attempt to establish Arcand's "gain" and, in my opinion, I should look no further into the future than March 31, 1995, the date of the termination of the lease. There is also a general proposition from *Fern Brand Waxes Ltd. v. Pearl et al., supra.* It was found that Mr. Pearl stood in a fiduciary relationship to the plaintiff, his employer, from whom he improperly transferred money to companies of his own which may be more or less equated to the numbered company defendant here. McGillivray J.A. said at p. 836 O.R., p. 669 D.L.R.:

> The defendant Albert Pearl should not be allowed to profit from this breach of trust and in these circumstances, the corporate character of his two companies, the defendants ... is no shield to such conduct as each was his instrument and used to divert funds for his own purposes from his principal.

Haack et al. v. Martin, [1927] S.C.R. 413, [1927] 3 D.L.R. 19, also considers a related question of damages. It arose out of a breach by Martin of a covenant for quiet enjoyment in a lease of farm property. At the time of the wrongful eviction there were more than five years remaining in the six-year term. The only issue before the Supreme Court was the quantum of damages to be awarded. At trial [[1926] 1 D.L.R. 76, [1925] 3 W.W.R. 769] the damages for the loss of the unexpired term were assessed at $22,500 which was reduced by the Saskatchewan Court of Appeal to $2,500 [[1926] 4 D.L.R. 527, 3 W.W.R. 11, 21 Sask. L.R. 19]. Rinfret J. said at pp. 416–19 S.C.R., pp. 21–24 D.L.R.:

> In the case of a lease, the compensation will not be confined to the value of the term, but will include all loss naturally resulting from the eviction.
>
> ...
>
> The difficulty, however, lies in ascertaining the true extent of the pecuniary loss naturally flowing from the breach.
>
> With regard to the first year after the eviction, there are in the record, as will appear presently, sufficient elements to estimate the loss with a reasonable degree of certainty. It is not so for the subsequent years, as to which the exact data are of course lacking and the evidence is somewhat conjectural. The average yield since 1910 of the lands rented, and the normal cost of production and of marketing are known. It is established that the land "is always better," and would ordinarily produce per acre five bushels more, than the "average land". Experience has shown that failures are unusual in that district and that none have occurred for the last

fifteen years. Such evidence — which is uncontradicted — goes towards extenuating some of the possibilities and of the contingencies dreaded by the Court of Appeal. It is not unreasonable to assume that the same land, year in and year out, will produce the same results. Estimates must be based on the assumption, not of unusual, but of normal, conditions as they have existed in the past. Otherwise the ordinary conduct of business would be a practical impossibility.

...

The learned trial judge did take into consideration the average crop for the last ten years, the total absence of failures during a still longer period of years, the cost of operating the farm and of marketing the grain, and he estimated thereby the yearly profit which that would represent for the five years to run of the unexpired lease. He did not however allow any offset for the uncertainty of the price of wheat, a very material element in the computation of damages of this character. Neither did he consider the possibility of the appellants earning on another farm. Although, during the interval between the eviction and the trial, they were "unable to get a similar lease of as good land in the Milestone district", it cannot be expected that such a condition would be likely to persist during the remaining four years. They had been set free and they could work elsewhere. They may possibly have secured a lease yielding benefits equal to — if not higher than — those which they could have derived from the cancelled lease. In either case, their loss after the first year would be negligible, if not wholly eliminated.

It must not be forgotten also that any amount awarded to the appellants is to be paid at once and can be put to profitable use immediately, while the money earned on the farm would be available only by fractions and from year to year.

We agree therefore with the Court of Appeal that the award made by the trial judge was excessive and could not be maintained. But the appellants have also satisfied us that the allowance of $2,500 made by the Court of Appeal for the whole of the unexpired term is utterly insufficient.

...

It is obviously impossible to assess the damages "with mathematical accuracy", but that is not necessary, and such impossibility "does not relieve the wrongdoer of the necessity of paying for his breach of contract" (*Chaplin v. Hicks*, [1911] 2 K.B. 786).

Any amount awarded must be to some extent speculative. We must proceed "largely as a jury". We have, however, the benefit of the calculations made by the learned trial judge and by the Court of Appeal. If we apply to their figures the corrections which, in our view, are made necessary for the reasons which we have given, we think that an amount of $15,000, covering both the summer-fallowing and the loss of the unexpired term is justified upon the evidence in the record.

Turning now to assessing damages in the case at bar, I propose to ignore the figures for the broken period ending on January 31, 1980. When Arcand took over there was, of course, not only a change of ownership but a change of personnel and a rehabilitation of the premises. Had the plaintiffs become the owners, Mrs. Guertin, who had had some experience in that snack bar plus a little managerial experience might have done better, but I accept the fact that the upset caused by the change would reduce the profit for that period to some extent.

In the next two years a very conservative figure for Arcand's gain is the profit of $14,393 in the year ending January 31, 1981, and of $17,360 for the year ending January 31, 1982, as shown in his own statement, and, as would likely be the case, the same for the year ending January 31, 1983, a total of $49,113. Sales in the future may increase somewhat but probably not at the same rate as in those two years. The increase between 1981 and 1982 can be attributed to the reopening of at least two good-size stores which had been closed for quite some time. The rent expenses would have increased by 7% of sales as they went up. Other expenses would inevitably have risen as well, however, other stores might close, economic conditions might have worsened and for various reasons traffic in the centre might have been reduced. I do not think I am required to consider the plaintiffs' earnings from other sources, as they have had other earnings all along and the damages are measured by Arcand's gain and not by the plaintiffs' losses. The value of the future earnings of the snack bar must be discounted because the plaintiffs are entitled only to a present sum as they need not wait for the profits to come in year by year. Arcand may sell the snack bar for more than the $23,000 cost price and the several thousand dollars over and above that for the improvements which he made. If he makes a profit on the sale above those figures, the plaintiffs are entitled to it. When he sells, and there was evidence that he was interested in selling, his annual gain would come to an end and the plaintiffs would be entitled to nothing further.

From the evidence it seems that leases on the food outlets in the centre changed hands for various reasons fairly frequently and Arcand was not averse to selling. If he retains the snack bar until the end of the lease, 12 years from last March, and if the profits remain at the 1982 level, his apparent gain would be ($17,360 x 12) $208,320. The gain on the sale might be as great as 50% of his investment of say $38,000 or $19,000 bringing the total gross gain to $227,320.

In my opinion, it is likely that he will sell after about two more years of operation and for perhaps a 25% net gain over his purchase price and cost of additions, an amount of perhaps $9,500. At that time he will have had an annual future gain of $17,360 for two years or $34,720, in all $44,220 from which I think it reasonable to deduct for all contingencies the sum of $8,220 and to assess the plaintiffs' total damages or profits under either para. 18(a) or (c) at $85,113. The plaintiffs shall also have interest under s. 36 of the *Judicature Act*, R.S.O. 1980, c. 223, on $14,373 from January 31, 1981, on $17,360 from January 31, 1982, and on $17,360 from January 31, 1983, together with their costs of the action.

Judgment for plaintiffs.

VI

Accounts

Background Reading: M.H. Ogilvie, *Bank and Customer Law in Canada*, 2d Edition (Toronto: Irwin Law, 2013) Chapter 7, pages 256–266.

(a) *Devaynes v. Noble; Clayton's Case*†

[SIR WM. GRANT:]

Though the Report, following (I presume) the words of the inquiry directed by the Decree, states the Master's opinion to be that Mr. *Clayton* has, by his dealings and transactions with the surviving partners, subsequent to the death of Mr. *Devaynes*, released his estate from the payment of the cash balance of £1,713, yet the ground of that opinion is, not that the acts done amount constructively to an exoneration of Mr. *Devaynes's* estate, but that the balance due at his death has been actually paid off — and, consequently, that the claim now made is an attempt to revive a debt that has once been completely extinguished.

To a certain extent, it has been admitted at the bar, that such would be the effect of the claim made before the Master, and insisted upon by the exception. To that extent it is, therefore, very properly abandoned; and all that is claimed is the sum to which the debt had at one time been reduced.

It would, indeed, be impossible to contend that, after the balance, for which alone Mr. *Devaynes* was liable, had once been diminished to any given amount, it could, as against his estate, be again augmented, by subsequent payments made, or subsequent credit given, to the surviving partners. On the part of Mr. *Devaynes's* representatives, however, it is denied that any portion of the debt due at his death now

remains unsatisfied. That depends on the manner in which the payments made by the house are to be considered as having been applied. In all, they have paid much more than would be sufficient to discharge the balance due at *Devaynes's* death — and it is only by applying the payments to subsequent debts, that any part of that balance will remain unpaid.

This state of the case has given rise to much discussion, as to the rules by which the application of indefinite payments is to be governed. Those rules we, probably, borrowed in the first instance, from the civil law. The leading rule, with regard to the option given, in the first place to the debtor, and to the creditor in the second, we have taken literally from thence. But, according to that law, the election was to be made at the time of payment, as well in the case of the creditor, as in that of the debtor, "in re praesenti; hoc est statim atque solutum est: — caeterum, postea non permittitur." (Dig. Lib. 46, tit. 3, Qu. 1, 3.) If neither applied the payment, the law made the appropriation according to certain rules of presumption, depending on the nature of the debts, or the priority in which they were incurred. And, as it was the actual intention of the debtor that would, in the first instance, have governed; so it was his presumable intention that was first resorted to as the rule by which the application was to be determined. In the absence, therefore, of any express declaration

---

† (1816), 1 Mer. 572 at 603–11; 35 E.R. 791.

by either, the inquiry was, what application would be most beneficial to the debtor. The payment was, consequently, applied to the most burthensome debt — to one that carried interest, rather than to that which carried none — to one secured by a penalty, rather than to that which rested on a simple stipulation — and, if the debts were equal, then to that which had been first contracted. "in his quae praesenti die debentur, constat, quotiens indistincte quid solvitur, in graviorem causam videri solutum. Si autem nulla praegravet — id est, si omnia nomina similia fuerint — in antiquiorem." (Dig. L. 46, t. 3, Qu. 5.)

But it has been contended that, in this respect, our Courts have entirely reversed the principle of decision, and that, in the absence of express appropriation by either party, it is the presumed intention of the creditor that is to govern; or, at least, that the creditor may, at any time, elect how the payments made to him shall retrospectively receive their application. There is, certainly, a great deal of authority for this doctrine. With some shades of distinction, it is sanctioned by the case of *Goddard v. Cox* (2 Stra. 1194); by *Wilkinson v. Sterne* (9 Mod. 427); by the ruling of the Lord Chief Baron in *Newmarch v. Clay* (14 East, 239); and by *Peters v. Anderson* (5 Taunt. 596), in the Common Pleas. From these cases, I should collect, that a proposition which, in one sense of it, is indisputably true — namely, that, if the debtor does not apply the payment, the creditor may make the application to what debt he pleases — has been extended much beyond its original meaning, so as, in general, to authorise the creditor to make his election when he thinks fit, instead of confining it to the period of payment, and allowing the rules of law to operate where no express declaration is then made.

There are, however, other cases which are irreconcilable with this indefinite right of election in the creditor, and which seem, on the contrary, to imply a recognition of the civil law principle of decision. Such are, in particular, the cases of *Megott v. Mills* (Ld. Raym. 287), and *Dowe v. Holdsworth Peake*, (N.P. 64). The creditor, in each of these cases, elected, *ex post facto*, to apply the payment to the last debt. It was, in each case, held incompetent for him so to do. There are but two grounds on which these decisions could proceed — either that the application was to be made to the oldest debt, or that it was to be made to the debt which it was most for the interest of the debtor to discharge. Either way, the decision would agree with the rule of the civil law, which is, that if the debts are equal, the payment is to be applied to the first point in time — if one be more burthensome, or more penal, than another, it is to it that the payment shall be first

imputed. A debt on which a man could be made a bankrupt, would undoubtedly fall within this rule.

The Lord Chief Justice of the Common Pleas explains the ground and reason of the case of *Dowe v. Holdsworth* in precise conformity to the principle of the civil law.

The cases then set up two conflicting rules — the presumed intention of the debtor, which, in some instances at least, is to govern — and the *ex post facto* election of the creditor, which, in other instances, is to prevail. I should, therefore, feel myself a good deal embarrassed, if the general question, of the creditor's right to make the application of indefinite payments, were now necessarily to be determined. But I think the present case is distinguishable from any of those in which that point has been decided in the creditor's favour. They were all cases of distinct insulated debts, between which a plain line of separation could be drawn. But this is the case of a banking account, where all the sums paid in form one blended fund, the parts of which have no longer any distinct existence. Neither banker nor customer ever thinks of saying, this draft is to be placed to the account of the £500 paid in on *Monday*, and this other to the account of the £500 paid in one *Tuesday*. There is a fund of £1,000 to draw upon, and that is enough. In such a case, there is no room for any other appropriation than that which arises from the order in which the receipts and payments take place, and are carried into the account. Presumably, it is the sum first paid in, that is first drawn out. It is the first item on the debit side of the account, that is discharged, or reduced, by the first item on the credit side. The appropriation is made by the very act of setting the two items against each other. Upon that principle, all accounts current are settled, and particularly cash accounts. When there has been a continuation of dealings, in what way can it be ascertained whether the specific balance due on a given day has, or has not, been discharged, but by examining whether payments to the amount of that balance appear by the account to have been made? You are not to take the account backwards, and strike the balance at the head, instead of the foot, of it. A man's banker breaks, owing him, on the whole account, a balance of £1,000. It would surprise one to hear the customer say, "I have been fortunate enough to draw out all that I paid in during the last four years; but there is £1,000, which I paid in five years ago, that I hold myself never to have drawn out; and therefore, if I can find any body who was answerable for the debts of the banking-house, such as they stood five years ago, I have a right to say that it is that specific sum which is still due to me, and not the £1,000 that I paid in last week." This is exactly the nature of the present claim. Mr. *Clayton* travels back into the account, till he finds a balance, for which Mr. *Devaynes* was responsible; and then he says — "That is a sum which I have never drawn for. Though standing in the centre of the account, it is to be considered as set apart, and left untouched. Sums above it, and below it, have been drawn out; but none of my drafts ever reached or affected this remnant of the balance due to me at Mr. *Devaynes's* death." What boundary would there be to this method of re-moulding an account? If the interest of the creditor required it, he might just as well go still further back, and arbitrarily single out any balance, as it stood at any time, and say, it is the identical balance of that day which still remains due to him. Suppose there had been a former partner, who had died three years before Mr. *Devaynes* — What would hinder Mr. *Clayton* from saying, "Let us see what the balance was at his death? — I have a right to say, it still remains due to me, and his representatives are answerable for it; for, if you examine the accounts, you will find I have always had cash enough lying in the house to answer my subsequent drafts; and, therefore, all the payments made to me in *Devaynes's* lifetime, and since his death, I will now impute to the sums I paid in during that period — the effect of which will be, to leave the balance due at the death of the former partners still undischarged." — I cannot think, that any of the cases sanction such an extravagant claim on the part of a creditor.

If appropriation be required, here is appropriation in the only way that the nature of things admits. Here are payments, so placed on opposition to debts, that, on the ordinary principles on which accounts are settled, this debt is extinguished.

If the usual course of dealing was, for any reason, to be inverted, it was surely incumbent on the creditor to signify that such was his intention. He should either have said to the bankers — "Leave this balance altogether out of the running account between us," — or — "Always enter your payments as made on the credit of your latest receipts, so as that the oldest balance may be the last paid." Instead of this, he receives the account drawn out, as one unbroken running account. He makes no objection to it — and the report states that the silence of the customer after the receipt of his banking account is regarded as an admission of its being correct. Both debtor and creditor must, therefore, be considered as having concurred in the appropriation.

But there is this peculiarity in the case — that it is, not only by inference from the nature of the dealings and the mode of keeping the account, that we are entitled to ascribe the drafts or payments to this balance, but there is distinct and positive evidence that Mr. *Clayton* considered, and treated, the balance as a fund, out of which, notwithstanding *Devaynes's* death, his drafts were to continue to be paid. For he drew, and that to a considerable extent, when there was no fund, except this balance, out of which his drafts could be answered. What was there, in the next draft he drew, which could indicate that it was not to be paid out of the residue of the same fund, but was to be considered as drawn exclusively on the credit of money more recently paid in? No such distinction was made; nor was there anything from which it could be inferred. I should, therefore, say, that, on Mr. *Clayton's* express authority, the fund was applied in payment of his drafts in the order in which they were presented.

But, even independently of this circumstance, I am of opinion, on the grounds I have before stated, that the Master has rightly found that the payments were to be imputed to the balance due at Mr. *Devaynes's* death, and that such balance has, by those payments, been fully discharged.

The Exception must, therefore, be over-ruled.

(b)   *Re Ontario Securities Commission and Greymac Credit Corp.*†

[MORDEN J.A.:]

In this case a trustee deposited in an account in its name funds entrusted to it by two separate beneficiaries. Following this mingling of the funds the trustee made unauthorized disbursements from the account, with the result that there were insufficient funds remaining in the name of the trustee to reimburse

---

† (1986), 30 D.L.R. (4th) 1 (Ont. C.A.).

each beneficiary in full. This proceeding is concerned with the resolution of the beneficiaries' competing proprietary claims to the remaining funds.

Against the background of the comprehensive and detailed reasons of Parker A.C.J.H.C., the judge of first instance, which are reported at 51 O.R. (2d) 212, 19 D.L.R. (4th) 470, 19 E.T.R. 157, I can state the facts which are material to this appeal in relatively brief compass. The trustee is Greymac Credit Corporation. For the purpose of this proceeding three trust companies, Greymac Trust Company, Crown Trust Company and Seaway Trust Company ("the companies") can be regarded, collectively, as one of the two beneficiaries. The other beneficiary, again collectively, is the Chorny Mortgage Investor Participants ("the participants").

On December 14, 1982, the trustee held $4,683,00 in trust for the companies in its account at the Greymac Trust Company. On December 15, 1982, the trustee deposited into this account the sum of $1,013,600. Of this amount, $841,285.26 belonged to the participants and the balance of $172,314.74 belonged to the trustee itself. The balance in the account at that time, then, was $5,696,600.

In the light of the ultimate findings of the trial judge respecting other transactions, which are accepted by the parties to this appeal, the next material transaction was the trustee's withdrawal of $4,000,000 from the Greymac Trust account on December 17, 1982, and its deposit, in the trustee's name, in an account at the Crown Trust Company. Following this the balance in the Greymac Trust account was $1,696,600.

Further withdrawals by the trustee which, unlike the $4,000,000 withdrawal deposited in the Crown Trust account, were dissipated, brought the balance in the Greymac Trust account down to $353,408.66 as of January 7, 1983.

In summary, when the funds were originally mingled in the Greymac Trust account, the trustee, the companies, and the participants had deposited, or had deposited on their behalves the amounts of $172,314.74, $4,683,000 and $841,285.26, respectively, for a total of $5,696,600. The amount remaining, after dissipated withdrawals of $1,343,191.34, was $4,353,408.66 — $4,000,000 in the Crown Trust account and $353,408.66 in the Greymac Trust account.

The companies and the participants each asserted proprietary claims against the remaining funds of $4,353,408.66. The general issue, then, is: in the light of the shortfall of $1,343,191.34 what principle should be applied to govern how these funds are divided between the claimants?

PARKER A.C.J.H.C.'S DISPOSITION AND THE PARTIES' BASIC CONTENTIONS

Parker A.C.J.H.C. held that the total loss of $1,343,191.34 must be allocated first against the trustee's interest. There is no appeal from this decision. He then decided that the funds should be divided in proportion to the respective contributions of the claimants. This resulted in the finding that the companies were entitled to a total amount of $3,690,434.47 ($299,588.58 from the Greymac Trust account and $3,390,845.89 from the Crown Trust account) on their total claim of $4,683,000 and that the participants were entitled to $662,974.19 ($53,820.08 from the Greymac Trust account and $609,154.11 from the Crown Trust account) on their total claim of $841,285.26.

The companies appeal from this decision. Their basic submission is that the trial judge erred in distributing the funds on a *pro rata* basis rather than on the basis of the rule in *Clayton's Case* (*Devaynes v. Noble; Clayton's Case* (1816), 1 Mer. 572, 35 E.R. 781). This well-known case was concerned with the resolution of the state of accounts between a bank and its customer. Parker A.C.J.H.C. considered it in some detail (at pp. 231–33 O.R., pp. 489–91 D.L.R.) and I will not repeat what he said beyond also quoting from a portion of the reasons of Sir William Grant M.R. in *Clayton's Case* at pp. 608–9:

> But this is the case of a banking account, where all the sums paid in form one blended fund, the parts of which have no longer any distinct existence. Neither banker nor customer ever thinks of saying, this draft is to be placed to the account of the £500 paid in on *Monday*, and this other to the account of the £500 paid in on *Tuesday*. There is a fund of £1,000 to draw upon, and that is enough. *In such a case, there is no room for any other appropriation than that which arises from the order in which the receipts and payments take place, and are carried into the account. Presumably, it is the sum first paid in, that is first drawn out.* It is the first item on the debit side of the account, that is discharged, or reduced, by the first item on the credit side. The appropriation is made by the very act of setting the two items against each other. Upon that principle, all accounts current are settled, and particularly cash accounts. When there has been a continuation of dealings, in what way can it be ascertained whether the specific balance due on a given day has, or has not, been discharged, but by examining whether payments to the amount of that balance appear by the account to have been made? You are not to take the account

backwards, and strike the balance at the head, instead of the foot, of it. [Emphasis added.]

The short form statement of the rule in *Clayton's Case* is "first in, first out". The result of its application in the present case, which the appellants seek, is as follows. The first moneys paid into the trustee's account (the Greymac Trust account) were those of the companies in the amount of $4,683,000 and the second moneys paid in were those of the participants in the amount of $841,285.26. Accordingly, the $4,000,000 which was taken out and deposited into the Crown Trust account must be regarded as the money of the companies. On this approach, the companies would still, at that point, have $683,000 in the Greymac Trust account. However, this amount must be taken to have been dissipated as the first part of the subsequent withdrawals of $1,343,191.34. The remainder in the account must then be regarded as the money of the participants. The result is that the participants are entitled, and only entitled, to the balance of $353,408.66 in this account.

The participants submit that if the rule in *Clayton's Case* is to be applied it should apply only to the transactions following the deposit of the $4,000,000 into the Crown Trust account, with the result that the participants would be entitled to $590,727.99 from the Crown Trust account (as found by Parker A.C.J.H.C.) and the balance in the Greymac Trust account of $353,408.66, minus the amount of the overpayment of their total claim that would result from applying this approach. I should mention that Mr. Lax, on behalf of the participants, did not press this approach. The main burden of his submission was that Parker A.C.J.H.C.'s approach is the correct one.

Parker A.C.J.H.C. (at pp. 221–26 O.R., pp. 479–84 D.L.R.) dealt first with the $4,000,000 deposit in the Crown Trust account. He held that at the time the $4,000,000 was deposited in the Crown Trust account the companies and the participants could have traced their funds into both the Crown Trust and the Greymac Trust accounts. In reference to the judgment of the English Court of Appeal in *Re Diplock; Diplock v. Wintle (and Associated Actions)*, [1948] 1 Ch. 465, where the effect of the application of the rule in *Clayton's Case* was to enable a beneficiary to trace its funds into an investment made from a mixed account, he said at p. 224 O.R., p. 482 D.L.R.:

> With the greatest respect, in my view, the error in the argument is that the court perceived the rule in *Clayton's Case* as being a rule developed to create interests in funds, whereas in fact it is a rule designed to allocate losses. Had no disbursements from the account occurred, it would seem from the general principles outlined at pp. 533 and 539 [of *Re Diplock*] that the volunteer and beneficiaries would have ranked equally and shared *pro rata*. Why should the priorities change if the only disbursement is not a loss but the purchase of an asset?

Then returning to the facts of the case before him he said at pp. 225–26 O.R., pp. 483–84 D.L.R.:

> It seems to me that the trustees and beneficiaries therefore had an interest in the separate account proportionate to their respective traceable interests in the mingled fund at the date the $4,000,000 was disbursed from that fund and put into the separate account.
>
> As between the trustee and the beneficiaries, it is my view that, at that time, both beneficiaries ranked ahead of the trustee in their claims to the separate account and the mingled fund to the extent of their respective traceable contributions to the mingled funds.
>
> As between the two innocent beneficiaries, it is my view that, at that time, they ranked equally in their claims to the separate account and the mingled fund to the extent of their respective traceable contributions to the mingled fund.
>
> If the rule in *Clayton's Case* does apply to allocate subsequent losses to the mingled fund, I do not see how a rule triggered by subsequent disbursements in an account can retroactively transform interests in a separate account from interests which ranked equally into interests which ranked in an order of priority.
>
> Therefore, it is my view that whether or not the rule in *Clayton's Case* applies to allocate the losses sustained in the Greymac Trust General Account, nevertheless, the $4,000,000 in the Crown Trust Savings Account ought to be allocated in proportion to the trustee's, the companies' and the Participants' respective traceable interests in the Greymac Trust General Account at the date the $4,000,000 was disbursed. As between themselves, the beneficiaries of course rank equally. However, since the beneficiaries rank ahead of the trustee, the trustee's interest in the separate account, unlike the interests of the beneficiaries in that account, can be affected by disbursements out of the mingled fund which occurred subsequent to the opening of the separate account. It is also my view that that part of the trustee's interest which is required to satisfy the beneficiaries' outstanding claims must be shared rateably between the beneficiaries in proportion to each beneficiary's share of the losses.

Parker A.C.J.H.C. (at pp. 226–41 O.R., pp. 484–99 D.L.R.) then dealt with whether the rule in *Clayton's Case* should be applied in determining the allocation of the losses in the Greymac account and, hence, the entitlement of the two competing beneficiaries to the $353,408.66 balance available for distribution. For reasons which he gave immediately following he said at p. 226 O.R., p. 484 D.L.R.:

> Such an allocation of losses and distribution of trust funds between innocent beneficiaries [resulting from the application of the rule in *Clayton's Case*] is, in my view, neither logical nor fair. Nor am I alone in my expression of consternation over such a result.

He then (at pp. 226–30 O.R., pp. 484–88 D.L.R.) set forth several published criticisms of the application of the rule in *Clayton's Case* to the determination of the competing claims of beneficiaries to trust moneys and then (at pp. 230–41 O.R., pp. 488–99 D.L.R.) he examined the origin of the rule in *Clayton's Case* and several authorities, beginning with *Pennell v. Deffell* (1853), 4 De G.M. & G. 372, 43 E.R. 551, concerned with its application to beneficiaries' claims relating to mingled trust funds. He concluded at pp. 239–40 O.R., pp. 497–98 D.L.R.:

> Having reviewed the authorities on the origins and extension of the rule in *Clayton's Case*, and the views of the academic commentators, it is my view that the rule in *Clayton's Case* arose out of the debtor-creditor relationship and should be restricted to that relationship. In my view, the general equitable rules of tracing, as stated in *Re Diplock, supra*, at pp. 533 and 539, are quite capable of dealing with the problem of allocating losses to a mingled fund.
>
> In the present case, the trustee and the beneficiaries originally had an interest in the mingled fund in proportion to their respective traceable contributions to the fund. As between the trustee and the beneficiaries, the beneficiaries ranked ahead of the trustee with respect to their claims to the mingled fund. Hence, losses to that fund must first be allocated against the interest of the trustee in the fund.
>
> As between the two innocent beneficiaries, they each had an interest in the mingled fund in proportion to their respective traceable contributions to the fund. Those interests ranked equally. Therefore, losses to that fund should be allocated against the interests of the beneficiaries in proportion to their respective traceable interests in the fund at the time the loss occurred. Hence, the beneficiaries (and the trustee to the extent of his remaining interest after losses have been

> deducted) would rank equally and share proportionately in the remaining funds. I express no opinion on the power of the court to make a disposition on some other basis where it is not possible to determine what proportion the mixed funds bear each to the other.
>
> ...
>
> The application of the general equitable rules of tracing referred to *supra* is both logical and fair. In this age of computerized banking, it can hardly be argued that in most instances an application of such principles will cause much inconvenience, difficulty or complication. These same principles are often applied to quite complicated dealings which do not involve bank accounts.

He concluded at pp. 240–41 O.R., pp. 498–99 D.L.R., that the requirements of *stare decisis* did not stand in the way of his view of the proper way in which the funds should be distributed.

THE APPELLANTS' CHALLENGE

The appellants challenge the judgment on two bases, principle and authority. This reflects a fair approach to the problem and I shall follow it in addressing the issues that require resolution.

THE RIGHT PRINCIPLE

Under this compendious heading I include matters relating to the most relevant concepts and to logic, justice and convenience.

Before entering the area of contention it is of value to state what is undoubtedly common ground between the parties. Before the $4,000,000 withdrawal on December 17, 1982, there was $5,696,600 in the Greymac Trust account and, at that point, the companies had a $4,683,000 property interest in the account and the participants had a $841,285.26 property interest in it. The mixing of their contributions did not stand in the way of the assertion of these property rights: *Pennell v. Deffell, supra; Frith v. Cartland* (1865), 2 H.&M. 417, 71 E.R. 525; *Re Hallett's Estate* (1879), 13 Ch. D. 696 (C.A.), and *Goodbody et al. v. Bank of Montreal et al.* (1974), 4 O.R. (2d) 147, 47 D.L.R. (3d) 335.

The potential remedies for enforcing these property rights were either those of an equitable lien (also called a charge) or by way of constructive trust. At that point the selection of the particular remedy would have been immaterial. The parties' position is described in Scott, *The Law of Trusts*, vol. 5, 3rd ed. (1967), at pp. 3612–13, as follows:

As long as the mingled fund remains intact it is immaterial whether the owner of the misappropriated money claims a lien upon the mingled fund for the amount of his money which went into it, or claims by way of constructive trust a share of the mingled fund in such proportion as his contribution to the fund bears to the whole of the fund. In either event he is entitled to receive out of the fund the amount of his contribution, no more and no less. The character of his claim, whether to enforce an equitable lien or a constructive trust, becomes important only if other property is acquired with the mingled fund, or withdrawals are made form the fund, or the fund diminishes in value. Such cases are considered in the sections which follow. If the fund remains intact, he is entitled to reimbursement out of the fund on either theory, and although the wrongdoer is insolvent, he is entitled to priority over other creditors with respect to the fund.

In this case, however, the total fund did not remain intact and the shortfall has put an end to the common ground between the parties.

The appellants' basic argument with respect to the division of the $4,000,000 in the Crown Trust account is that the judge of first instance erred in failing to keep separate two issues: (a) the identification of whose property went into the Crown Trust account, and (b) the appropriate rule or remedy to apply in the allocation of the loss between two innocent beneficiaries. They submit, with respect to (a), that mingled funds were not placed in the Crown Trust account. This would have been the case only if the full amount of the Greymac account had been transferred to the Crown Trust account.

The judge of first instance was wrong, the appellants submit, to have relied upon *Sinclair v. Brougham et al.*, [1914] A.C. 398 (at p. 222 O.R., p. 480 D.L.R.), in support of his conclusion that the parties were entitled to share *pari passu* according to their respective contributions in the $4,000,000 deposit because *Sinclair v. Brougham* was concerned with competing entitlements to a total fund and not with entitlement to funds withdrawn form a mingled fund.

The appellant's argument comes down to the assertion that the only concept or rule available to enable to the court to identify "whose" money went into the Crown Trust account is the rule in *Clayton's Case*, which clearly identifies it as the companies' money because it preceded the participants' money into the Greymac Trust account.

The basic rejoinder of the participants is the adoption of the position accepted by Parker A.C.J.H.C. that, whatever application the rule in *Clayton's Case* may have with respect to allocating losses in mingled trust funds, it cannot be used, as the appellants seek to use it, to trace trust funds from one account to another or to an investment or some other purchase.

In a sense the appellants' approach — that only by the application of the rule in *Clayton's Case* can one identify the beneficial ownership of the money deposited into the Crown Trust account — begs the question to be decided. There are, I think, two approaches to the question which are in conflict and the answer should turn on which is the better one.

The other approach, contrary to that asserted by the appellants, may be outlined as follows. Immediately before the transfer of the $4,000,000 each beneficiary had a property right in the total fund of $5,696,600 in proportion to its contribution. This position did not alter after the transfer of the $4,000,000. All that then occurred was that their respective entitlements, in the same proportions, were spread over the two accounts. In this respect I refer to the following passages in Scott, *The Law of Trusts*, vol. 5, 3rd ed. (1967), at p. 3620:

> The claimant has an equitable lien upon the mingled fund, and when a part of the fund is withdrawn *he has an equitable lien on the part withdrawn and on the part which remains*. If the part which is withdrawn is dissipated so that it can no longer be traced, the claimant still has his equitable lien on the part which remains. So also, as we shall seem if the part which is withdrawn is preserved and the part which remains is subsequently dissipated, the claimant has an equitable lien upon the part which is withdrawn. It is impossible and unnecessary to determine whether the claimant's money is included in the part withdrawn or in the part which remains. It is impossible to determine which part is the claimant's money, since his money has been so commingled as to lose its identity. *It is unnecessary to determine which part is the claimant's money, since he is entitled to an equitable lien upon both parts*. [Emphasis added.]

At p. 3623:

> It is true that where the part of the fund which is withdrawn is dissipated and the balance is preserved, the claimant is certainly entitled to payment of his claim out of the balance. The reason is that his lien on the entire fund undoubtedly includes the balance of the fund after a part has been withdrawn.

At p. 3624:

> The only tenable principle is that the claimant can enforce a lien upon any part of the product of any part of the mingled fund.

It is true that these passages appear in the context of situations where the mingled funds are those of only one beneficiary and of the trustee, but this does not, in my view, affect their applicability to the situation where the money of more than one beneficiary is mingled. Certainly this is the view of Scott as appears later on in his treatise where he deals with the mingling of the money of several beneficiaries (pp. 3639–41). While acknowledging that there is a conflict of authority on the question he says, with respect to the situation where the money of several claimants is mingled and subsequently withdrawals are made by the wrongdoer from the mingled fund (at p. 3639):

> It seems clear on principle that they should be entitled to share pro rata both in the money withdrawn or its product and in that remaining. If the amount withdrawn is dissipated or cannot be traced, the claimants should share the balance remaining in proportion to their contributions.

This is an appropriate place to deal briefly with the appellants' argument that Parker A.C.J.H.C. misapplied the decision of the House of Lords in *Sinclair v. Brougham, supra,* to support his conclusion that the parties were entitled to share *pari passu* in the $4,000,000 deposit. In my view, the learned judge did not misapply this rather difficult and complex decision: see *Re Diplock; Diplock v. Wintle, supra,* at pp. 516 and 518.

First, I do not think that Parker A.C.J.H.C. relied upon *Sinclair v. Brougham* for anything more than the proposition that where a trustee mixes the money of each of two innocent beneficiaries "the relationship of the innocent beneficiaries one to the other" (p. 222 O.R., p. 480 D.L.R.) is that of equality, *i.e.,* neither can claim priority over the other. No exception can be taken to this.

Secondly, even if *Sinclair v. Brougham* were relied upon in support of the view that following the transfer of the $4,000,000 the respective interests of the innocent beneficiaries were then spread, *pro rata,* over each of the two accounts, this would, in my view, be a reasonable application of one of the basic principles implicit in the reasoning in that decision — that the beneficiaries had equitable liens over the whole and each part of the mingled fund: see *Sinclair v. Brougham,* pp. 422 (Viscount Haldane), 438 (Lord Dunedin) and 442 (Lord Parker). This point is made by P.F.P. Higgins in "Re Diplock — A Reappraisal" (1963–64), 6 *U.W. Aust. L. Rev.* 428 at pp. 434–35. Indeed Higgins forcefully expresses the view that *Re Diplock,* which was criticized by Parker

A.C.J.H.C., "was contrary to the express decision" in *Sinclair v. Brougham.* At pp. 438–39 he says:

> In *Re Diplock* a large part of the judgment in rem was devoted to a careful analysis of what was said in *Sinclair v. Brougham* but in its conclusions the Court of Appeal completely ignored what the House of Lords had eventually decided. In that case the House of Lords having laid down the equitable principles upon which the equal equities of the rival claimants to the mixed funds were based, proceeded to make an order that they should have a charge *pari passu* on the mixed fund. Now, as we have already observed the balance of the fund was not sufficient to meet the claims in full and, therefore, there must have been some withdrawals from the fund after the depositors and shareholders had made their respective contributions. However, it was at no time suggested that the rule in *Clayton's Case* should be applied to determine the respective rights of the rival claimants to the balance of the mixed fund. On the contrary, it was decided that they should share the balance rateably.
>
> It is true that it was said in *Re Diplock* that where the equities of the contributors to a mixed fund are equal, they will have a charge upon it *pari passu* but, if this charge is confined, as it was in that case, to cases where there have been no withdrawals from the mixed fund after the trust funds were deposited in it, it involves giving a different interpretation to the expression *pari passu* from the one placed upon it in *Sinclair v. Brougham.* If there have been no withdrawals there can be no question of a rateable disposition of the mixed fund because each of the claimants will be fully reimbursed. Exceptionally, if there were an overdraft at a time when the account owners' money and the trust money were deposited *simultaneously* in the account there would be a proportionate disposition of the balance even though the principles in *Re Diplock* were to be applied. It would only be in such an unlikely combination of events that the principles laid down in *Re Diplock* can possibly produce the same result as the decision in *Sinclair v. Brougham.*
>
> It is submitted that in so far as *Re Diplock* decided that the rule in *Clayton's Case* is to be applied to the determination of the respective rights of claimants to the balance of a mixed fund, when the equitable rights of the claimants are equal, it was contrary to the express decision of the House of Lords in *Sinclair v. Brougham* that in such circumstances the balance is to be shared rateably.

The decision of Joyce J. in *Re Oatway,* [1903] 2 Ch. 356, also supports the proposition that a beneficiary can assert his equitable title on any part of the mixed fund even after it has been divided into more than one part. If this be so with respect to the claim of a beneficiary against a trustee it should also be the case with respect to the claims of more than one beneficiary against the trustee and, also, as between or among themselves.

With respect, I do not think that it is a direct approach to the problem to say that the rule in *Clayton's Case* is to be used only for the purpose of allocating losses when there is a shortfall in a mingled account and not for enabling an owner to trace funds withdrawn form it. It appears to me that *if* it is a proper approach to determining "whose" money remains in an account to ascertain "whose" money was taken out, it would be inconsistent not to allow a claimant whose money is deemed to be taken out to claim the product in which this money was invested and, at the same time, to reduce his claim to the remaining balance by the amount of "his" money which was earlier disbursed.

As I have already indicated, however, the real question is which is the better approach.

Before there is a shortfall in the total amount of the mingled funds, there is no need to decide upon the theory underlying the respective claims of the beneficiaries. In the present case, immediately following the transfer of the $4,000,000 to the Crown Trust account there were sufficient total funds in both accounts to satisfy the claims of both beneficiaries on the approach of either the rule in *Clayton's Case* or *pro rata* sharing. At that point, however, before there was a loss, I do not think that it would have made much sense to say that the trust companies owned the $4,000,000 in the Crown Trust account and the "top" $683,000 in the Greymac Trust account — and that the participants' claim lay against the "next" $841,285.26 in the Greymac account. If a theory had to be adopted the most obvious and natural one is that each beneficiary had an equitable lien on both accounts to secure the amount of its total contribution.

When the Greymac account, following this, went into a shortfall position, thus requiring resort to some kind of theory to justify a resolution of the competing proprietary claims of the two beneficiaries, it appears to me to be the more natural and reasonable of the two alternative ones to say that the beneficiaries continued to share *pro rata* in the two accounts rather than to say that it was the companies money that was first taken from the Greymac account and then that of the participants. This latter approach does involve, as Parker A.C.J.H.C. noted, the retroactive application of a rule upon a loss subsequently occurring, which has the effect of altering

existing property entitlements — specifically, in this case, expanding the entitlement of the companies and reducing that of the participants to the same extent.

The foregoing indicates to me that the fundamental question is not whether the rule in *Clayton's Case* can properly be used for tracing purposes, as well as for loss allocation, but, rather, whether the rule should have any application at all to the resolution of problems connected with competing beneficial entitlements to a mingled trust fund where there have been withdrawals from the fund. From the perspective of basic concepts I do not think that it should. The better approach is that which recognizes the continuation, on a *pro rata* basis, of the respective property interests in the total amount of trust moneys or property available.

There is another aspect of the underlying concepts at work which should be examined. Parker A.C.J.H.C. rightly, in my view, questioned "why a court could not apply the rule in *Clayton's Case* to determine which debts owed by the bank to its customer were paid off, and still apply tracing rules to allocate losses to the account among the customer as trustee and his innocent beneficiaries" (p. 234 O.R., p. 493 D.L.R.). That is, he would confine the rule in *Clayton's Case* strictly to the bank-customer relationship and would not extend it to the relationship between two innocent beneficiaries.

Pennell v. Deffell (1853), 4 De G.M.&G. 372, 43 E.R. 551, was the first case to apply the rule in *Clayton's Case* to determine the rights of beneficiaries whose funds were deposited by the trustee in a bank account. In that case the funds were mixed with the personal funds of the trustee. It may be noted that the court's holding that the rule in *Clayton's Case* should be applied to resolve the conflicting claims of the beneficiaries, on the one hand, and of the trustee on the other, was overruled by the Court of Appeal in *Re Hallett's Estate* (1879), 13 Ch. D. 696. *Pennell v. Deffell* was not concerned with a competition between beneficiaries. I refer to this case, however, for its underlying reasoning relating to the suggested connection between the rule in *Clayton's Case* and the distribution of trust funds in bank accounts. With respect to this, Turner L.J. said at pp. 393–94:

> Now Green [the trustee] opened and kept these banking accounts upon the usual footing, and the Plaintiff [who represented the beneficiaries], taking the benefit of the accounts, cannot, as I think, be entitled to alter their character. Adopting them for the purpose of establishing his demand against Green's estate he must, I think

adopt them with all their incidents, one of which is that the monies drawn out are to be applied to the monies first paid in. Upon any other footing this consequence would follow, that a debt which had been extinguished at law by the course of payment would be revived in equity by an alteration in that course.

Since this reasoning apparently goes to the root of a beneficiary's claim it is appropriate to quote at length the following criticism of it, which I accept, of D.A. McConville in "Tracing and the Rule in Clayton's Case" (1963), 79 Law Q. Rev. 388 at p. 401:

> But is it true that the beneficiary takes the "benefit of the accounts" between the banker and the trustee or seeks to alter them in any way to make good his claim? The reasoning of Turner L.J. would be appropriate where the beneficiary was claiming to be subrogated to the rights of the trustee against the banker, for there he might be interested in how accounts stood between them. But in *Pennell v. Deffell* (and in all the tracing situations reviewed), the claim was not against the banker at all but against the trustee. Also it was not in any sense a "personal claim" depending on the enforcing of debts, but "proprietary" in that it sought to take out of a particular asset, property which belonged to the trust. As the claim is made against the trustee, it pre-supposes that it is he who has the asset and not the banker. As between the trustee and the beneficiary the bank account is a piece of property or an asset in the trustee's hands. This is something quite distinct and independent of its position as between the banker and the trustee, where it is a series of debts or personal liabilities *inter se*.
>
> A bank account should therefore be considered as two different things and consequently two different sets of rules apply to decide problems arising in respect of it. When it is necessary to consider it as a debt, rules as to appropriation of debts, including *Clayton's Case* apply, but when it has to be considered as a piece of property, rules as to competing titles and confusion of identical property are appropriate.

At p. 403:

> Nor should it make any difference that instead of a mixing taking place between one trust fund an the trustee's private money, the mixing is that of two or more trust funds either with each other or with private money as well. Here, instead of there being one charge on the mixed fund, there are two or more. If there is not enough money to pay all claims, the charges should abate proportionately.

In the light of the foregoing it can be seen that the application of the rule in *Clayton's Case* to the problem under consideration is arbitrary and unfair. It is based on a fiction. As Learned Hand J. said in *Re Walter J. Schmidt & Co.* (1923), 298 Fed. 314 at p. 316, in a passage quoted by Parker A.C.J.H.C. (at pp. 227–28 O.R., pp. 485–86 D.L.R.):

> The rule in *Clayton's Case* is to allocate the payments upon an account. Some rule had to be adopted, and though any presumption of intent was a fiction, priority in time was the most natural basis of allocation. It has no relevancy, whatever to a case like this. Here two people are jointly interested in a fund held for them by a common trustee. There is no reason in law or justice why his depredations upon the fund should not be borne equally between them. To throw all the loss upon one, through the mere chance of his being earlier in time, is irrational and arbitrary, and is equally a fiction as the rule in *Clayton's Case, supra.* When the law adopts a fiction, it is, or at least it should be, for some purpose of justice. To adopt it here is apportion a common misfortune through a test which has no relation whatever to the justice of the case.... Such a result, I submit with the utmost respect, can only come from a mechanical adherence to a rule which has no intelligible relation to the situation.

In this case, however, Hand J. was obliged by authority, *Re A. Bolognesi & Co.* (1918), 254 Fed. 770, to apply the rule in *Clayton's Case*. He said of *Bolognesi*, a judgment of the Circuit Court of Appeals, Second Circuit, that "it constitutes authority absolutely binding upon me" (p. 320).

I am not aware of any argument of logic (apart from that in *Pennell v. Deffell* which, for the reasons I have set out, I do not accept) or fairness which would support the application of the rule to the problem. The only argument advanced in its favour is that of convenience: see, *e.g., Pennell v. Deffell* at pp. 393–94, and *Re Diplock; Diplock v. Wintle* at pp. 553–54. It is said to be more convenient to apply than that of *pro rata* sharing.

Before considering the convenience argument in favour of the rule, I should, however, deal with one of the appellants' criticisms of the judgment under appeal related to *its* logic and fairness. The matter covered by this criticism also has some bearing on the question of convenience. The appellants submit that if the equality, that is, *pro rata* sharing, approach is to be followed, then to do justice more money furnished by the companies to the trustee than the $4,683,000 balance of December 15, 1982, should be taken into account. The ledger of the trustee's account with Greymac Trust shows that the companies were the source of $9,698,000 placed into the account between November 30 and December 15, 1982, and not just the $4,683,000 balance. If the proper approach is equality, then, it is submitted, this fact should be taken into account. On this point reference is made to the comment of Professor Donovan Waters in his *Law of Trusts in Canada* (1974), p. 895, quoted by Pennell J. in *Re Law Society of Upper Canada and Riviera Motel (Kitchener) Ltd. et al.* (1981), 33 O.R. (2d) 65 at pp. 70–71, 123 D.L.R. (3d) 409 at p. 415, 9 E.T.R. 188 *sub nom. Re Delaney*:

> ... it would have been preferable, if, instead of juggling with the accidental time sequence of events [this was said of the judgment in *Bailey v. Jellett et al.* (1882), 9 O.A.R. 187], the court had proportioned the loss between the clients *according to the amounts due them respectively.* [Emphasis added. The same passage appears in Waters, *Law of Trusts in Canada*, 2nd ed. (1984), at pp. 1050–51.]

Quite apart from the fact that the question of whether any part of the original $9,698,000, down to the $4,683,000, was returned to the companies in some form was not inquired into, I do not think that this particular argument of the appellants is of assistance to them. We are concerned with the resolution of competing proprietary, not personal, claims. At the time of the mingling of the trust funds the companies had $4,683,000 in the account. Regardless of how much they had earlier in the account, they cannot say that they had a proprietary interest in any more than the amount in the account to their credit on and after December 15, 1982: see *James Roscoe (Bolton), Ltd. v. Winder*, [1915] 1 Ch. 62, and *Re Norman Estate*, [1951] O.R. 752, [1952] 1 D.L.R. 174.

While it might, possibly, be appropriate in some circumstances to recognize claims on the basis of a claimant's original contribution (but see Scott *The Law of Trusts*, vol. 5, 3rd ed. (1967), at pp. 3647–52), I do not think that it is appropriate where the contributions to the mixed fund can be simply traced, as in the present case. See also the very useful report of the Law Reform Commission of British Columbia — *Report on Competing Rights to Mingled Property: Tracing and the Rule in Clayton's Case* (1983), at pp. 48–49 and 53–57.

Returning to the matter of convenience, it must be noted that the rule in *Clayton's Case*, if it is to be applied, applies only to trustee's current bank accounts. It does not apply where the trust property of more than one beneficiary is mingled otherwise than in a current bank account. This indeed was the result with respect to one of the claims in *Re Diplock* itself (at pp. 554–56), one concerned with the shortfall in a mixture of corporate shares. At p. 555 Lord Greene M.R. said with respect to this claim: "We see no justification for extending that rule [the rule in *Clayton's Case*] beyond the case of a banking account."

While acknowledging the basic truth of Lord Atkin's observation that "[c]onvenience and justice are often not on speaking terms" (*General Medical Council v. Spackman*, [1943] A.C. 627 at p. 638), I accept that convenience, perhaps more accurately workability, can be an important consideration in the determination of legal rules. A rule that is in accord with abstract justice but which, for one or more reasons, is not capable of practical application, may not, when larger considerations of judicial administration are taken into account, be a suitable rule to adopt. However, I am not persuaded that considerations of possible inconvenience or unworkability should stand in the way of the acceptance, as a general rule, of *pro rata* sharing on the basis of tracing. That it is sufficiently workable to be the general rule is indicated by the fact that it appears to be the majority rule in the United States (see Scott, *The Law of Trusts*, vol. 5, 3rd ed. (1967), pp. 3639–41; J.F. Ghent, *Distribution of Funds Where Funds of More Than One Trust Have Been Commingled by Trustee and Balance is Insufficient to Satisfy Act Trust Claims* (Annotation) (1968), 17 A.L.R. (3d) 937) and has been adopted in the *Restatement of the Law: Trusts (2nd)* (s. 202) and the *Restatement of Restitution* (s. 213). D.A. McConville, in the article from which I have earlier quoted ("Tracing and the Rule in Clayton's Case" (1963), 79 Law Q. Rev. 388 at p. 405), after citing examples firmly expressed the following view:

> Applying strictly proprietary rules ... and by always going back to the amounts originally mixed and treating the claimants on the footing of equality, it is submitted there will be found no situations, "incapable of solution" as the Court of Appeal thought was the fatal objection to any rule other than the rule in *Clayton's Case* to decide the problem in *Re Diplock* noted earlier.

He went on to say at p. 405:

> Naturally the number of accounts, investments and transactions can be multiplied to a point where calculations become too complicated and expensive to undertake.

One of the examples he gave of a solution to this kind of problem was *Sinclair v. Brougham* itself where the "House of Lords split the assets in the proportion indicated by the respective total amounts of deposits [by the depositors] and investments [by the shareholders] one to another. There being a deficiency of assets, each bore the loss rateably" (p. 407).

Ford and Lee's *Principles of the Law of Trusts* (1983), deals with the matter of convenience as follows at p. 744:

> It is submitted that whether moneys in a bank account should be shared between claimants following the rule in *Clayton's Case* or on a proportionate basis depends on whether it is feasible to ascertain the proportion attributable to all possible claimants. It is unlikely that it will be feasible where there have been many deposits and withdrawals of funds belonging to many claimants. The difficulties of ascertainment, including the difficulties of evidence, are conveniently resolved by resort to the rule in *Clayton's Case*, following the practice of bankers in similar cases. But where the convenience of that rule is not needed because the account is of short duration and the position of claimants is clear, it is submitted that a proportionate shareout is preferable.

I refer to this passage simply to indicate the authors' point that where the convenience of the rule in *Clayton's Case* is not needed, because it is feasible to ascertain the proportion attributable to all claimants, proportionate sharing is preferable. I might add that it may well be that proportionate sharing on the basis of the claimants' original contributions (that is, not on the basis of tracing) may be just as convenient or, possibly, more convenient than the application of the rule in *Clayton's Case* and, also, fairer.

With respect to this point Parker A.C.J.H.C. said (at p. 240 O.R., p. 498 D.L.R.) in a part of his reasons which have already been quoted:

> I express no opinion on the power of the court to make a disposition on some other basis where it is not possible to determine what proportion the mixed funds bear each to the other.

I accept this qualification and would add the modifier "practically" before "possible" to introduce an element of flexibility to the approach and to avoid the situation where the nature of the substantive justice to be achieved would not justify the tracing exercise.

Another exception, an obvious and necessary one, which might often overlap with the kind of case just referred to, would be the case where the court finds that the claimants have, either expressly or by implication, agreed among themselves to a distribution based otherwise than on a *pro rata* division following equitable tracing contributions.

ARE WE BOUND TO APPLY THE RULE IN CLAYTON'S CASE?

Apart from examining the case-law in Ontario, I do not intend to review the state of the law on this point in detail. In England, in view of the decision of the Court of Appeal in *Re Diplock; Diplock v. Wintle, supra*, one might reasonably think that the Court of Appeal in that country and all lower courts would apply the rule in *Clayton's Case* to the competing claims of beneficiaries (or of a beneficiary and an innocent volunteer) where the trust moneys have been mingled in a current bank account. Although there are several judicial *dicta* to this effect, the only other English decision of which I am aware which actually applied the rule in these circumstances is that of Fry J. at first instance in *Re Hallett's Estate* (1879), 13 Ch. D. 696. (On the appeal there was, ultimately, no issue of priorities between beneficiaries and so the Court of Appeal did not decide the question.)

English texts on the subject, while not generally questioning that the point has been decided or the clarity of the Judicial *dicta*, have not hesitated to criticize or question the application of the rule in *Clayton's Case* to the competing claims of beneficiaries. I refer to: *Hanbury & Maudsley Modern Equity*, 12th ed. (1985), p. 643 — "[the rule should not] appear in any aspect of the present subject, but it has unfortunately been applied as a means of determining entitlement in a mixed banking account between rival persons with a right to trace..."; Sheridan & Keeton, *The Law of Trusts*, 11th ed. (1983), p. 419: "The rule in *Clayton's Case* probably applies to the account of a trustee as between beneficiaries under two separate trusts ... though it is open to argument that such beneficiaries rank on the account *pari passu*;" Underhill, *Law of Trusts and Trustees*, 13th ed. (1979), at p. 719: "A rateable burden would seem fairer...;" Nathan & Marshall, *A Casebook on Trusts*, 5th ed. (1967), p. 324 in footnote 7: "The contrary view is persuasively argued ... that *Clayton's case* has no application" (referring to the McConville article in 79 *Law Q. Rev.* 388 and to Higgins, "Re Diplock — A Reappraisal" (1963–64), 6

U.W. Aust. L. Rev. 428), and Goff & Jones, *The Law of Restitution*, 2nd ed. (1978), p. 58: "The result is capricious and arbitrary."

McConville, in the concluding part of his article "Tracing and the Rule in Clayton's Case" (1963), 79 Law Q. Rev. 388 at p. 408, says:

> ... it is submitted the introduction of [*Clayton's Case*] into the law of tracing arose from a confusion of two unconnected branches of law, deceptively similar in that they both relate to bank accounts. In view of the fact that the underlying principles have only once been examined [by Turner L.J. in *Pennell v. Deffell, supra*, at pp. 393–94] and the authorities are conflicting [here, I believe, he refers to *Re Oatway*, [1903] 2 Ch. 356 and *Re British Red Cross Balkan Fund, British Red Cross Society v. Johnson*, [1914] 2 Ch. 419 — see pp. 399–400], it is hoped a modern court might feel at liberty to remodel the law of tracing on more rational lines in this respect by holding *Clayton's Case* to be irrelevant.

I have earlier quoted the view of P.F.P Higgins that *Re Diplock* is contrary to the decision of the House of Lords in *Sinclair v. Brougham et al.*, [1914] A.C. 398: "Re Diplock — A Reappraisal" (1963–64), 6 *U.W. Aust. L. Rev.* 428 at pp. 438–39.

With respect to Canada, Professor Waters has expressed the opinion that "a similar view [to that of Fry J. in *Re Hallett's Estate* that the rule in *Clayton's Case* applies] has been reiterated on sufficient occasions that it must be considered as finally settled in this country": *The Law of Trusts in Canada*, 2nd ed. (1984), at p. 1050. He cites, by way of example, three decisions: *Bailey v. Jellett* (1882), 9 O.A.R. 187 (C.A.); *British Canadian Securities Ltd. v. Martin et al.*, [1917] 1 W.W.R. 1313, 27 Man. R. 423 (Man. Q.B.), and *Re C.A. Macdonald & Co. Ltd.* (1958), 17 D.L.R. (2d) 416, 26 W.W.R. 116, 37 C.B.R. 119 (Alta. S.C.). With respect, I do not read the *British Canadian Securities* judgment as applying the rule in *Clayton's Case* to an issue between beneficiaries. In any event, reference may also be made to the following additional decisions which have applied the rule in *Clayton's Case* to issues between beneficiaries: *Re Coville Transport Co. Ltd.* (1947), 28 C.B.R. 262 (Ont. S.C. in Bankruptcy); *Re Law Society of Upper Canada and Riviera Motel (Kitchener) Ltd. et al.*, *supra*, and *Corbett et al. v. McKee, Calabrese & Whitehead et al.* (1984), 54 N.B.R. (2d) 107, 16 E.T.R. 200 (N.B.Q.B.).

Professor Waters also observed, after the quoted sentence: "As one might suppose, the operation of the rule is sufficiently formulaic that it works some odd and hardly justifiable results" (p. 1050).

The report of the Law Reform Commission of British Columbia, to which I have already referred, although it leaves no doubt as the unsuitability of the rule in *Clayton's Case* in this context, says "... given the preponderance of case authority in favour of the rule in *Clayton's Case*, we doubt whether courts will depart from it. There is a need for legislative action." (*Report on Competing Rights to Mingled Property: Tracing and the Rule in Clayton's Case* (1983), at p. 44.) This appears to be a less firm view than that of Waters. It is, possibly, more one of pessimism respecting judicial action, accompanied by a corresponding exhortation for a legislative solution.

Although I appreciate that the value of uniformity among the provinces is an important one to be weighed in the balance, I am not persuaded that the decisions from Alberta, Manitoba (if, indeed, it bears on the point in issue) and New Brunswick, to which I have referred, necessarily represent the law of those provinces. None of these, decisions are of appellant courts and, even if this were the case, we would not be obliged to follow them, even if a point of federal law were at issue, unless we were persuaded to do so on their merits or for other independent reasons: *Wolf v. The Queen*, [1975] 2 S.C.R. 107 at p. 109, 47 D.L.R. (3d) 741 at p. 742, 17 C.C.C. (2d) 425. As far as the dictates of precedent are concerned our main attention must be employed in examining the 1982 decision of this court in *Bailey v. Jellett, supra*.

I shall take the facts of this case as set forth in the reasons for judgment of Spragge C.J.O. and refer only to those essential to the point under consideration. In that case a trustee, Jellett, had on deposit in his personal bank account the funds of two beneficiaries: first in time, those of the plaintiffs, in the amount of $4,901 and, second in time, those of the defendant Mrs. Suzor, in the amount of $1,182.95. The balance at that time was, then, $6,083,95. From this balance he paid $3,000 into another account for the plaintiff and dissipated $93. The final balance was $2,991. Accordingly, there was a shortfall of $93 having regard to the contributions of the plaintiff and the defendant Mrs. Suzor as of the date these were mixed in the account. Spragge C.J.O.'s reasons on the point are set forth in pp. 201–2:

> It is not, as it appears to me, necessary to determine whether the rule in *Clayton's Case* should apply as between *cestuis que trust* of the same fund (except, perhaps, as to a small sum which I will notice presently), because we can in this case trace and follow the moneys of Mrs. Suzor at the bank, as well as what may have remained of the moneys of the plaintiff. Before the pay-

ment in Mrs. Suzor's money there stood to Jellett's credit $4,901 that being $1,599 (not counting cents) less than the moneys of the plaintiff, the difference it is to be assumed having been used by Jellett himself. If Jellett had died at that time, and Mrs. Suzor's money had not been paid in, the plaintiff would have been entitled to that sum, $4,901. What occurred after the date that I have named was this: Mrs. Suzor's money, $1,182.95, was paid in, and no other sum; and there were paid out four cheques, amounting together to $93; and $3,000 was drawn out and placed to the plaintiffs's credit, leaving at Jellett's credit, at the date of his death, $2,991. That sum was composed of the $1,182, belonging to Mrs. Suzor, which is as distinctly traceable as it would have been if it had been the only entry on the face of the account after the paying in of that money. It is fact the only entry on that side of the account.

The only possible question could be as to the cheques amounting to $93, and as to them it may be necessary to resort to the rule in *Clayton's Case* as a convenient rule, where some rule is necessary.

There is indeed room for the presumption that Jellett drew those cheques intending not to touch Mrs. Suzor's money, for he had drawn against the plaintiff's money before her money was paid in; and when he did make a payment to the plaintiff he left unpaid a considerable sum which he might have paid, still leaving Mrs. Suzor's money intact.

Upon that branch of the case my conclusion, therefore, is that Mrs. Suzor's claim is to be preferred.

With respect, it may be thought that it is not quite accurate to begin with the assumption that the moneys of each of the plaintiff and Mrs. Suzor could be traced and followed and, later, that Mrs. Suzor's money was "distinctly traceable." If this was meant to defer to all of her money it does not take into account that there was a shortfall of $93 and that this shortfall had to be allocated in some manner. This may have been conceded in the statement that the "only possible question could be as to the cheques amounting to $93...."

It is not clear to me, however, from the passage that I have quoted, that Spragge C.J.O. clearly endorsed the application of the rule in *Clayton's Case* ("[i]t is not ... necessary to determine whether the rule in *Clayton's Case* should apply as between *cestuis que trust* of the same fund (except, perhaps, as to a small sum which I will notice presently)...") or, indeed, that he applied it rather than making a finding of fact on the evidence that the trustee had

expended the plaintiff's money in withdrawing the $93.

I shall return to these reasons but before doing so I shall indicate the reasons of the other three members of the court.

Burton J.A. made no mention of *Clayton's Case*, or any other decision, in concluding that Mrs. Suzor's money remained in the account throughout (p. 204) and that the money improperly withdrawn, a large part of which must have preceded the deposit of Mrs. Suzor's money, was the plaintiff's (p. 205).

Patterson J.A. is reported merely as having concurred (p. 206).

Osler J.A. had no hesitation in holding that on the basis of the rule in *Clayton's Case* Mrs. Suzor should be reimbursed in full and that the plaintiff should absorb the shortfall of $93. He said at pp. 209–10:

> ... the case of *Re Hallett-Knatchbull v. Hallett*, 13 Ch. D. 696, appears to be a sufficient authority for the contention that the plaintiff and Mrs. Suzor are respectively entitled to a charge on the balance at Jellett's credit in the bank; and also, as Mr. Scott argued, that as between them the rule in *Clayton's Case* applies in dealing with the question of the appropriation of payments, so that the earliest drawings are to be appropriated to the earliest deposits.

If the judgment of Osler J.A. were that of the Court it could not be denied that the decision was based on the rule in *Clayton's Case*. However, as I have indicated, the judgment of Spragge C.J.O. on this point is, I think, ambiguous, possibly intentionally so. Burton and Patterson JJ.A. gave no indication at all of the basis of their decisions.

I will not dwell much longer on the judgment of the court in *Bailey v. Jellett*. With respect, I do not agree with *Re Coville Transport Co. Ltd., supra*, and *Re Law Society of Upper Canada and Riviera Motel (Kitchener) Ltd. et al., supra*, which treated it as a decision in favour of the application of the rule in *Clayton's Case*. No doubt, the result was to place the total loss, as small as it was, on one of the beneficiaries rather than dividing it *pro rata* and so it clearly cannot be regarded as a decision which supports *pro rata* sharing of losses. Also, if Spragge C.J.O. relied on the trustee's factual intent rather than the *Clayton's Case* fiction, it was obviously still in an approach closer to that of the rule in *Clayton's Case* than to that of *pro rata* sharing.

Notwithstanding these considerations I do not interpret the decision in *Bailey v. Jellett* as resting on the "first in, first out" approach of *Clayton's Case*. In this regard contrast the clear statement of the rule of the Second Circuit Court of Appeals in *Re A. Bolognesi & Co.* (1918), 254 Fed. 770 at p. 773, which Learned Hand J. Held to be binding on him in *Re Walter J. Schmidt & Co.* (1923), 298 Fed. 314.

In summary, for the following reasons I think that, as a matter of authority, Parker A.C.J.H.C. was right in not applying the rule in *Clayton's Case.*

1. *Bailey v. Jellett* does not squarely decide the point.

2. If the rule in *Clayton's Case* is not to be applied, it is not necessary to fashion a new rule or set of rules to replace it. There are already in place basic concepts and principles upon which to base the *pro rata* sharing approach. Indeed, the application of the rule in *Clayton's Case* to trust money in active bank accounts is itself the exception to these general principles: see *Re Diplock; Diplock v. Wintle, supra*, at p. 555.

3. The *pro rata* approach is more logical and just.

4. Assuming that the rule in *Clayton's Case* is part of the law of Ontario on the point in question, its function in this context is not such that it would be relied upon by affected persons in drawing documents or arranging their affairs. It is, more or less, a remedial rule, which is applied after all of the relevant events have taken place without regard to the future application of any particular rule. Contrast, for example, the function of the rule in *Howe v. Earl of Dartmouth* (1802), 7 Ves. Jun. 137, 32 E.R. 56, the authoritative nature of which was dealt with in the Supreme Court of Canada in

Lottman et al. v. Stanford et al., [1980] 1 S.C.R. 1065, 107 D.L.R. (3d) 28, 6 E.T.R. 34.

In the absence of binding authority clearly on point it may reasonably be said that the law *is* what it ought to be. "Do not the questions 'Is it law?' and 'Is it good law?' generally overlap?": Laskin, *Book Review* (1940), 18 Can. Bar Rev. 660 at p. 660. In *Re Hallett's Estate* (1879), 13 Ch. D. 696 at p. 710, Jessel M.R. said:

> ... the moment you establish the fiduciary relation, the modern rules of Equity, as regards following trust money, apply. I intentionally say modern rules, because it must not be forgotten that the rules of Courts of Equity are not, like the rules of the Common Law, supposed to have been established from time immemorial. *It is perfectly well known that they have been established from time to time-altered, improved, and refined from time to time.* [Emphasis added.]

Clearly, if the application of the *pro rata* approach is seen as an alteration in the rule to be applied, it is one that involves improvement and refinement. In this respect see, for example, the development treatment of the constructive trust from *Murdoch v. Murdoch*, [1975] 1 S.C.R. 423, 41 D.L.R. (3d) 367, 13 R.F.L. 185, through *Rathwell v. Rathwell*, [1978] 2 S.C.R. 436, 83 D.L.R. (3d) 289, 1 R.F.L. (2d) 1, to *Pettkus v. Becker*, [1980] 2 S.C.R. 834, 117 D.L.R. (3d) 257, 19 R.F.L. (2d) 165.

For the reasons given I would dismiss this appeal with costs.

Appeal dismissed.

(c) *Law Society of Upper Canada v. Toronto Dominion Bank*†

[BLAIR J. (*ad hoc*):]

PART I — BACKGROUND AND FACTS

Between December 16, 1990 and September 24, 1991, Philip Upshall, a solicitor, misappropriated

over $900,000 from his clients' trust account at the Toronto Dominion Bank. This appeal involves the claims of competing beneficiaries to the shortfall of funds remaining in that trust account when it was frozen on October 2, 1991, and the manner in which their respective shares are to be determined. It

---

† (1998), 42 O.R. (3d) 257 at 259–76 (C.A.); leave to appeal to S.C.C. dismissed November 4, 1999, (1999) 45 O.R. (3d) i.

raises issues concerning what is known as "the rule in *Clayton's Case*" and a descendant concept called "the lowest intermediate balance rule" (frequently referred to by the acronym "LIBR").

The account was frozen after the Bank was advised that Mr. Upshall had been hospitalized in a psychiatric ward and that the Law Society would be managing the operation of his trust account from that point on. Mr. Upshall was subsequently found guilty of misappropriating client moneys by the Law Society of Upper Canada, and disbarred. He made an assignment into bankruptcy on December 21, 1993.

As is customary in the case of lawyers' trust accounts, the funds deposited for the account of Mr. Upshall's clients were co-mingled. Clients' claims to the trust funds in the account as at October 2, 1991 total $656,703.06, and there is a significant shortfall in what remains for distribution to the claimants. The evidence is that both the list of clients and the amounts credited to each client as deposits are known and not in dispute.

The last misappropriation from the trust fund occurred on September 24, 1991. At the time, the balance in the account was $66,242.68. On September 25, the TD Bank deposited the sum of $173,000 into the trust account. It did so to enable Mr. Upshall to advance mortgage funds to its client, Douglas Crump. Mr. Upshall was acting as solicitor for the Bank and for Mr. Crump in connection with this mortgage transaction. The funds were deposited on condition that they be released by Mr. Upshall to the borrower, or as the borrower may direct, once the solicitor was satisfied that the Bank would have a good and valid first charge on title. The account was frozen before this transaction was completed.

On October 2 — immediately following notification that Mr. Upshall had been hospitalized and that the Law Society would thereafter be managing the account — the Bank withdrew the $173,000 from the trust account, without authorization, and transferred it to another solicitor to complete the mortgage transaction. On the application by the Law Society before Mr. Justice Farley the appropriateness of the Bank's conduct in doing this was very much in issue (he held it was inappropriate). Before this court, the Bank took the position that the appeal should be decided on the basis that the moneys which had been removed by it from the account were still in the account and available for distribution. It is therefore unnecessary to deal with the grounds of appeal initially raised which relate to the issue of the Bank's removal of the funds from the trust account.

The question on this appeal is whether all clients of Mr. Upshall with funds deposited in the trust account have a claim against the whole of the funds standing to the credit of the account as at the date of its being frozen (including the Bank's deposit of $173,000 made *after* the misappropriations had ceased), or whether the claims of those clients other than the Bank are confined to a smaller sum no larger than the $66,242.68 balance which existed at the time the last funds were wrongly removed. The appellant Bank argues for the latter position, on the basis of the lowest intermediate balance rule. The Law Society submits that the appropriate approach is that of a *pro rata* distribution based upon the entirety of the fund as at the date the account was frozen.

Farley J. held that the lowest intermediate balance rule did not apply in the circumstances of this case, and ordered that the co-mingled funds should be distributed on *a pro rata* basis. In summary, his reasoning was:

(a) that once trust funds are co-mingled in an account they lose their "earmarked" identity to particular clients and become a single mixed trust fund;

(b) that each client — although possessed of an individual trust claim against the trustee for the funds advanced to the trustee — then has an equal claim against the mixed account;

(c) that the timing of the misappropriations is irrelevant and the appropriate point in time for determining the claimants' entitlement is the date on which the trust account was frozen (or more technically, perhaps, the time when the last injection of funds was made), because it is the money in the mixed trust account which has been stolen and not that of any particular client — "the mixed trust account cannot be segregated into a 'tainted' pot (of X$) and an 'untainted' pot (of $173,000)"; and,

(d) that a trust account which involves co-mingled funds should be distributed on a *pro rata* basis in circumstances where the account is in a shortfall position and the clients, along with the deposits attributable to them are known: see *Ontario (Securities Commission) v. Greymac Corp.* (1985), 51 O.R. (2d) 212, 19 D.L.R. (4th) 470 (H.C.J.); affirmed (1986), 55 O.R. (2d) 673, 30 D.L.R. (4th) 1 (C.A.); affirmed [1988] 2 S.C.R. 172, 65 O.R. (2d) 479*n* (S.C.C.), and cases following that decision.

I agree with the conclusion of Farley J., for the reasons which follow.

PART II — LAW AND ANALYSIS

A. A Consideration of "The Rule in Clayton's Case" and "The Lowest Intermediate Balance Rule"

Overview

The Bank's attempt to invoke the lowest intermediate balance rule in the circumstances of this case amounts to nothing more, in my opinion, than an attempt to re-invoke the rule in *Clayton's Case*, which was rejected by this court and by the Supreme Court of Canada in *Ontario (Securities Commission) v. Greymac Credit Corp., supra*. The effect of applying the "lowest intermediate balance rule" to the competing claims of the trust fund beneficiaries is to permit the Bank — the last contributor — to recover what for practical purposes is all of its deposit,[1] exactly the result which would transpire upon the application of the rule in *Clayton's Case*. I do not think that result is called for in the circumstances of this case.

The Rule in Clayton's Case

What is known as the rule in *Clayton's Case* derives from the decision of the English Court of Appeal in *Devaynes v. Noble, Baring v. Noble (Clayton's Case)* (1816), 1 Mer. 572, 35 E.R. 781. The so-called rule — which is really a statement of evidentiary principle — presumes that in the state of accounts as between a bank and its customer the sums first paid in are the sums first drawn out, absent evidence of an agreement or any presumed intent to the contrary: see *Clayton's Case, per* Sir William Grant, at pp. 608–9. As Morden J.A. remarked in *Greymac*, at p. 677 "the short form statement of the rule ... is 'first out'". In the result, where there are competing claims against a shortfall, the shortfall is applied first to the first deposits made, and later contributors to the fund take the benefit of what remains.

The role of the rule in *Clayton's Case* in competing beneficiary cases, and its history, were examined thoroughly by this court in *Greymac*. The application of the rule was rejected as being "unfair and arbitrary" and "based on a fiction" (p. 686). The court concluded that it was not bound to apply the rule in *Clayton's Case*, and it did not do so. Nor, for that matter, did it apply the lowest intermediate balance rule.

Speaking for a unanimous court in *Greymac*, Morden J.A. resolved that as a general rule the mechanism of *pro rata* sharing on the basis of tracing was the preferable approach to be followed, although he left room for other possibilities such as those circumstances where it is not practically possible to determine what proportion the mixed funds bear to each other, or where the claimants have either expressly or by implication agreed among themselves to a distribution based otherwise than on a *pro rata* division following equitable tracing of contributions (pp. 685–90). Whatever approach was chosen, Morden J.A. was concerned that it should be one which met the test of convenience — or "workability", as he termed it (p. 688). The core of the court's conclusions is to be found in the following passage from his judgement, at p. 685:

> The foregoing indicates to me that *the fundamental question is* not whether the rule in *Clayton's Case* can properly be used for tracing purposes, as well as for loss allocation, but, rather, *whether the rule should have any application at all to the resolution of problems connected with competing beneficial entitlements to a mingled trust fund where there have been withdrawals from the fund. From the perspective of basic concepts I do not think that it should.* The better approach is that which recognizes the continuation, on a *pro rata* basis, of the respective property interests *in the total amount of trust moneys or property available.* (Emphasis added)

Having determined that the rule in *Clayton's Case* ought not to be applied in cases involving the claims of competing trust beneficiaries, Morden J.A. concluded in *Greymac* that *pro rata* sharing based on the respective property interests of the claimants in the total amount of trust money or property available, should be applied. He accepted such *pro rata* sharing as the general method of determining such competing claims. Whether, as some have suggested,[2] he also recognized and incorporated into the *pro rata* sharing exercise the concept of the lowest intermediate balance rule, and if so to what extent, is an issue that will be dealt with momentarily. First, however, I propose to turn to an analysis of the history and application of the LIBR notion.

The Lowest Intermediate Balance Rule: An Outline

The "lowest intermediate balance rule" states that a claimant to a mixed fund cannot assert a proprietary interest in that fund in excess of the smallest balance in the fund during the interval between the original contribution and the time when a claim with respect to that contribution is being made against the fund: see Maddaugh and McCamus, The Law of Restitution, at pp. 153–54.

The LIBR concept is a descendant of the rule in *Clayton's Case*. It was originally articulated by Sargant J. in *James Roscoe (Bolton) Ltd. v. Winder*, [1915] 1 Ch. 62. In that case the purchaser of a business, Mr. Winder, who had contracted to collect the outstanding book debts of the business and to pay them to the company, did the former but not the latter. Over time he collected £455 and deposited the funds into his own general account, but he subsequently drew out all but £25, before eventually putting in more moneys of his own and, again, drawing on the account for his own purposes. There was a credit balance in the account of £358 at the time of his death. The court held that he was a trustee of the £455 for the benefit of the company, but that the company's claim against the fund was limited to the lowest intermediate balance in the account of £25.

Sargant J. erected the LIBR foundation upon two principle footings. The first of these was the premise that the rules of proprietary tracing preclude a beneficiary, after a mixed fund has been depleted, from reaching any subsequent contributions made by others to that fund (in the absence of some actual or presumed intention to replenish the fund). The second was a rejection of the notion that the account may be treated as a whole and the balance from time to time standing to the credit of that account viewed as being subject to one continual charge or trust. In outlining the rationale for his conclusion, Sargant J. said (at pp. 68–69):

> [Counsel] did say "No. I am only asking you to treat the account as a whole, and to consider the balance from time to time standing to the credit of that account as subject to one continual charge or trust." But I think that really is using words which are not appropriate to the facts. You must, for the purpose of tracing, which was the process adopted in *In re Hallett's Estate* [(1880), 13 Ch. D. 696], put your finger on some definite fund which either remains in its original state or can be found in another shape. That is tracing, and tracing, by the very facts of this case, seems to be absolutely excluded except as to the 25*l* 18*s*.
>
> ...
>
> Certainly, after having heard *In re Hallett's Estate* stated over and over again, I should have thought that the general view of that decision was that it only applied to such an amount of the balance ultimately standing to the credit of the trustee as did not exceed the lowest balance of the account during the intervening period.

The LIBR principle has never been analyzed by Ontario or other Canadian courts. However, it has been applied several times at the trial level — in bankruptcy situations — in this province: see *Re Thompson, ex parte Galloway* (1930), 11 C.B.R. 263 (Ont. S.C. in Bankruptcy); *Re Wineberg* (1969), 14 C.B.R. (N.S.) 182 (Ont. S.C. in Bankruptcy, Registrar); *Re 389179 Ontario Ltd.* (1980), 29 O.R. (2d) 304, 113 D.L.R. (3d) 207 (Ont. S.C. in Bankruptcy, Saunders J.). Its existence has been accepted (with very little comment) on two occasions in this court in decisions preceding *Greymac*: see *Re Norman Estate*, [1951] O.R. 752 (C.A.): and *General Motors Acceptance Corp. of Canada Ltd. v. Bank of Nova Scotia* (1986), 55 O.R. (2d) 438 (C.A.) at p. 443. The LIBR concept has also been accepted by the British Columbia Court of Appeal in *British Columbia v. National Bank of Canada* (1994), 119 D.L.R. (4th) 669 at pp. 687–89, 99 B.C.L.R. (2d) 358, leave to appeal to S.C.C. refused September 28, 1995; and by the British Columbia Supreme Court in *Re 1653 Investments Ltd.* (1981), 129 D.L.R. (3d) 582 at p. 597.

No Canadian authority has attempted to describe how the LIBR principle is to be employed. Nonetheless, from a review of the foregoing authorities, I take the rationale underlying the LIBR theory in relation to co-mingled trust funds to encompass at least the following concepts:

1. that beneficiaries are entitled, through the equitable and proprietary notion of tracing, to follow their contribution into the mixed fund;

2. that beneficiaries of such a fund have a lien or charge over the totality of the trust fund to the extent of their interest in it;

3. but that once a wrongful withdrawal has been made from the fund, the claims of beneficiaries with moneys in the fund at the time of the withdrawal are thereafter limited to the reduced balance, and that depositors to the trust fund are not entitled to claim further against any subsequent amounts contributed to the fund either by the trustee (unless made with the intent to replenish the withdrawn amount) or other by other beneficiaries; and

4. that this inability to claim against anything in excess of the smallest balance in the fund during the interval between the original contribution and the time of the claim flows from the inability to claim a *proprietary right* to subsequent amounts deposited, since it is not possible to trace the original claimant's contribution to property contributed by others.

505

This latter concept is grounded, ultimately, on the premise that tracing rights are predicated upon the model of property rights. LIBR seeks to recognize that at some point in time, because of earlier misappropriations, an earlier beneficiary's money has unquestionably left the fund and therefore cannot physically still be in the fund. Accordingly, it cannot be "traced" to any subsequent versions of the fund that have been swollen by the contributions of others, beyond the lowest intermediate balance in the fund. Such is the theory, at any rate.

The Decision in Greymac and the Parameters and Practical Application of LIBR

GREYMAC

In *Greymac*, this court did *not* apply the lowest intermediate balance rule. Indeed, it was not necessary for the court to consider LIBR. Once it had been decided that the claimants had a right to trace their contributions to both the account into which the deposits had originally been made and the second account at Crown Trust into which the $4 million withdrawal had been placed, there was only one balance to be concerned about. While *Greymac* clearly rejects the rule in *Clayton's Case* as a means of determining how the moneys in a mixed trust account are to be allocated in the event of a shortfall, and adopts the notion *of pro rata* sharing based upon tracing as the general rule, it *does not* apply the lowest intermediate balance rule in the context of such *pro rata* sharing.

The view that Morden J.A. affirmed the lowest intermediate balance rule[3] — or at least acknowledged it with approval[4] in the *Greymac* case has its source in the following passage from his reasons, at p. 688:

> We are concerned with the resolution of competing proprietary, not personal, claims. At the time of the mingling of the trust funds the companies [*i.e.*, one group of claimants] had $4,683,000 in the account. Regardless of how much they had earlier in the account, they cannot say that they had a proprietary interest in any more than the amount in the account to their credit on and after December 15, 1982: see *James Roscoe (Bolton), Ltd. v. Winder*, [1915] 1 Ch. 62, and *Re Norman Estate*, [1951] O.R. 752, [1952] 1 D.L.R. 174.

It is important to note that Morden J.A. made these remarks in the context of dealing with an argument that more moneys than those to the credit of the claimants *at the time the fund had become a* *mixed fund* should have been taken into account if the funds were to be divided on a *pro rata* basis. The date referred to — December 15, 1982 — was the date on which the funds had become a co-mingled trust account. I therefore regard the foregoing comments of Morden J.A. as referring as much to *timing* as to anything else. He was concerned with determining when the parties' respective proportionate interests should begin to be assessed — *i.e.*, to the timing as of when the *pro rata* calculations should be triggered (namely when the fund first took on its character as a "mixed fund"). I note in particular in this regard, that in the passage for which the *Roscoe* case is cited as authority, Morden J.A. states that the claimants "cannot say that they had a proprietary interest in any more than the amount in the account *to their credit*" at the time the funds were intermingled. This is the language of deposits made by the claimants. It is not the language of the *lowest balance* in the account, which is what LIBR deals with. I do not interpret Morden J.A.'s comments as indicating an intention to adopt the concept of LIBR for purposes of calculating *pro rata* sharing in *Greymac*.

PARAMETERS AND PRACTICAL APPLICATION OF LIBR

The British Columbia Law Reform Commission seemed to endorse a LIBR approach in its *Report on Competing Rights to Mingled Property: Tracing and the Rule in Clayton's Case* (1983). In a rare attempt to define both the problem which LIBR seeks to address *and* the mechanics of its proposed solution, the Commission stated (see pp. 53–54):

> Terms like "pari passu", "pro rata", "rateably", and "proportionately" are inherently ambiguous. Do they mean that shortfalls or accretions to a fund are shared in proportion to the original interests claimants to that fund possessed? Or do they mean that shortfalls or accretions to a fund are shared *in proportion to those interests claimants to that fund possess after each transaction made with respect to that fund is taken into account?* In the Working Paper we tentatively concluded that the latter meaning was fairest.
>
> For example, A, a trustee, deposits $1,000 of B's money in his account, mixing it with $1,000 of his own money. A removes $1,500. A then deposits $1,000 of C's money. B and C should not share the fund of $1,500 equally, notwithstanding that B's original interest in the fund was $1,000 and that C's current interest is $1,000. B's interest in the fund has been reduced by $500. B's lien should be reduced from securing $1,000 to now securing $500, the minimum balance of the fund following the deposit of his

money and preceding the deposit of C's money. C would be entitled to a lien of $1,000. No transactions have occurred yet to reduce his interest in the fund. To avoid confusion, legislation enacting these recommendations should define exactly how "pari passu" sharing takes place. One possible formulation is as follows:

If there are two or more persons with interests in a fund, the amount of any shortfall from or accretion to the fund which would have affected their respective interests, and which is not appropriated to a specific interest or interests, is divided and attributed to their respective interests in such proportion as their respective interests bore to the sum of those interests before the shortfall or accretion occurred. (Additional emphasis added)

As far as I am aware, no such legislation has ever been enacted. In my view, however, this approach is too complex and impractical to be accepted as a general rule for dealing with cases such as this.

It was precisely for this reason that a version of LIBR — referred to as the "rolling charge" or "North American" approach, because it was considered to be derived from various North American authorities, including *Greymac* — was rejected by the English Court of Appeal in *Barlow Clowes International Ltd. (in liq.) v. Vaughan*, [1992] 4 All E.R. 22. *Barlow Clowes International* involved a very large and complex insolvency. Saying that the North American approach was "not a live contender" because of the costs involved and the complexity of its application, Lord Justice Woolf instead adopted what he labelled "the *pari passu ex post facto*" solution. This solution involved a simple rateable sharing of the remaining funds based upon "establishing the total quantum of the assets available and sharing them on a proportionate basis among all the investors who could be said to have contributed to the acquisition of those assets, ignoring the dates on which they made their investments" (p. 36). It is a solution which, in my opinion, makes sense in most situations.

None of the authorities to which we have been referred has applied LIBR in the context of a relationship between innocent beneficiaries; and whether the same set of assumptions as those governing LIBR and outlined in the earlier portions of these reasons, should operate to resolve situations where the competition is not between trust claimants and the wrongdoer, but between the trust claimants themselves in relation to a shortfall of funds in the trust account, is to my mind a different question.

In the latter type of situation, everyone is a victim of the wrongdoer. Presumptions about what the wrongdoer may or may not have intended — in terms

of replenishing the fund with subsequent contributions, or in terms of being honest and using his or her own funds first — are of little assistance. Moreover, competing trust claimants are not in the same position as ordinary creditors of the wrongdoer. They are wronged *trust* beneficiaries, and as a result of that relationship they are entitled not only to a personal remedy for breach of trust against the wrongdoer, but also to a proprietary remedy against the fund in respect of which the trust relationship exists. It is always open to a trust contributor to gain protection from having to share a shortfall with others by insisting upon the funds being placed in a separate trust account.

In determining how a *pro rata* distribution is to be effected in circumstances of co-mingled trust funds, the issue whether this *proprietary remedy* must be inflexibly tied to a pre-existing *proprietary right* — *i.e.*, the purely logical application of tracing rules — is an important question. In my view, in circumstances such as this, they need not be inflexibly tied together, and the concept of the mixed trust fund as a "whole fund", the balance of which from time to time is subject to a continual charge or trust — rejected by Sargant J. in *James Roscoe (Bolton) Limited v. Winder, supra* — should be reconsidered.

Sargant J.'s rejection of the "whole-fund continual-charge-or-trust" notion was founded upon an interpretation of the earlier decision in *Re Hallett's Estate* (1880), 13 Ch. D. 696. To the extent that there is any support for this view in that case, however, it is limited to an *obiter dicta* comment made by Thesiger L.J. in dissent (see pp. 745–46); and in my reading of *Re Hallett's Estate* I can find nothing which otherwise suggests or mandates any such conclusion. I shall return to this issue later.

B.   A Choice of Governing Principles

Where, then, does all of this lead?

In the end, there remain two general approaches which may be taken to the resolution of how *pro rata* distributions are to be made in circumstances such as this case — the rule in *Clayton's Case* having now been discarded for such purposes. The first is that of applying the lowest intermediate balance rule. The second is that of applying what Woolf L.J. called the "*pari passu ex post facto*" approach, in *Barlow Clowes International*. There seems to be no binding authority compelling the application of one approach or the other to circumstances such as those in this case. The court should therefore seek to apply the method which is the more just, convenient and equitable in the circumstances.

No authority has ever applied the lowest intermediate balance rule in circumstances involving the rival claims of trust beneficiaries, as I have already noted. The mechanics of how the lowest intermediate balance rule actually works have never been fully explained. Indeed, even in situations concerning defaulting trustees and beneficiaries, where the rule has been invoked, it does not appear to have been implemented in any case involving more than a small number of competing beneficiaries and a correspondingly small number of transactions. This, I suspect, is because although LIBR may be "manifestly fairer"[5] in the pure sense of a tracing analysis, it is manifestly more complicated and more difficult to apply than other solutions.

What LIBR involves — as best I can ascertain it from the authorities and the literature bearing on the subject — is a transaction by transaction examination of the mixed fund, in terms of deposits made by the beneficiaries and withdrawals taken by the wrongdoer, and the application of a proportionality formula in respect of each such transaction. This approach has not found favour in cases where the problem has been faced, and acknowledged, directly: see, for example, *Barlow Clowes International*; and *Winsor v. Bajaj* (1990), 1 O.R. (3d) 714, 75 D.L.R. (4th) 198 (Gen. Div.).

The Governing Principle

In my view, the method which should generally be followed in cases of *pro rata* sharing as between beneficiaries is not the LIBR approach but the *pari passu ex post facto* approach, which has the advantage of relative simplicity. This approach involves taking the claim or contribution of the individual beneficiary to the mixed fund as a percentage of the total contributions of all those with claims against the fund at the time of distribution, and multiplying that factor against the total assets available for distribution, in order to determine the claimant's *pro rata* share of those remaining funds.

This solution is the type of resolution which has been adopted, on a practical basis, in most cases involving more than two or three competing beneficiaries. It is the solution applied by this court in *Greymac*, and by the English Court of Appeal in *Barlow Clowes International*. It is the solution applied in a number of other recent decisions at the superior court level in this Province involving mixed trust funds,[6] and it is the solution applied by Farley J. in the case under appeal. But it is not LIBR.

It is, however, the approach which I favour.

My conclusion in this regard is based both upon the "convenience" aspect (or the "workability"

aspect, as Morden J.A. characterized it in *Greymac*) pertaining to the application of the LIBR principle, and upon my analysis of the concept of a mixed trust account and of its nature and purpose.

The "Convenience" Rationale

First, with regard to "convenience", I note the following comment of Morden J.A. in *Greymac*, at pp. 688–89:

> While acknowledging the basic truth of Lord Atkin's observation that "[c]onvenience and justice are often not on speaking terms" (*General Medical Council v. Spackman*, [1943] A.C. 627 at p. 638), I accept that convenience, perhaps more accurately workability, can be an important consideration in the determination of legal rules. A rule that is in accord with abstract justice but which for one or more reasons, is not capable of practical application, may not, when larger considerations of judicial administration are taken into account, be a suitable rule to adopt.

LIBR is difficult to apply in cases involving any significant number of beneficiaries and transactions. Even in this age of computer technology, I am not convinced that trustees of mixed funds — who might be in a position of having to sort out misappropriation transactions on such an account and the distribution of what remains — should be assumed or required to possess the software to enable a LIBR type of calculation to be done in the myriad of situations that might arise. Indeed, there is no evidence that such software programs exist, although it may well be that they do — at what cost and difficulty we do not know.

In this case it is not practicable to conduct the LIBR exercise. There are over 100 claimants. There were misappropriations in the area of $900,000 in bits and pieces. It is not even clear that each deposit and debit can be looked at individually, on the state of the record, although the total amounts deposited by each of the claimants are apparently known. Notwithstanding this, if the LIBR principle is to be applied to a *pro rata* distribution in the circumstances of this case, it would be necessary to consider not only the deposits of each individual claimant and the timing of such deposits, but also what was the lowest balance in the Upshall account between each deposit and the imposition of the freeze. This would involve analyzing the pattern and timing of each misappropriation and applying the results to each individual depositor's circumstances. It is not at all clear on the evidence that this exercise can be done.

The Rationale Based upon the Nature and Purpose of a "Mixed" Trust Fund

On broader principles as well, in my opinion, the preferred approach in cases involving competing beneficiaries is that of *pro rata* sharing based upon the proportion of a claimant's contributions to the total contributions of all claimants, multiplied by the amount to be shared — i.e., the *"pari passu ex post facto"* approach. This method spreads the misappropriations rateably amongst the contributors who remain, but at the same time does not arbitrarily affect earlier contributors adversely by limiting their charge or constructive trust in relation to the fund to the lowest balance in the account. It preserves what Morden J.A. referred to in *Greymac* at p. 684) as the participant's claim to "an equitable lien ... *to secure the amount of its total contribution*", and it is consistent with his statement (at p. 685) that:

> The better approach is that which recognizes the continuation, on a *pro rata* basis, of the respective property interests *in the total amount of trust moneys or property available.* (Emphasis in both citations added)

In regard to this conclusion, it is useful to consider both the practical considerations pertaining to a mixed trust fund and the nature of such a fund itself.

A mixed trust fund is a device whereby a trustee — typically, but by no means exclusively, a lawyer — holds funds in trust for different persons or entities. It is in many ways a mechanism of convenience, *i.e.*, it avoids the necessity, and the cost, and the cumbersome administrative aspects of having to set up individual trust accounts, and the records relating to such accounts, for the transactions relating to every beneficiary. This practical characteristic of mixed trust funds should be recognized in considering the nature of such funds. It provides an economic and organizational benefit to the public. As Farley J. noted, in the context of this case, "Upshall was effectively acting as a banker in a safekeeping capacity".

What follows from this, it seems to me, is that a mixed fund of this nature should be considered as a whole fund, at any given point in time, and that the particular moment when a particular beneficiary's contribution was made and the particular moment when the defalcation occurred, should make no difference. The happenstance of timing is irrelevant. The fund itself — although an asset in the hands of the trustee to which the contributors have recourse — is an indistinguishable blend of debits and credits reflected in an account held by the trustee in a bank or other financial institution. It is a *blended* fund. Once the contribution is made and deposited it is no longer possible to identify the claimant's funds, as the claimant's funds. All that can be identified, in terms of an asset to which recourse may be had, is the trust account itself, and its balance.

The theme of a co-mingled trust account as a blended fund is reflected in the reasons of Woolf L.J. and Dillon L.J. in *Barlow Clowes International* (at pp. 27 and 35) and in those of Morden J.A. in *Greymac* (at p. 682[7]). In *Clayton's Case* itself, Sir William Grant, in introducing his "first in, first out" concept, stated (at p. 608 Mer):

> But this is the case of *a banking account, where all the sums paid in form one blended fund,* the parts of which have no longer any distinct existence. Neither the banker nor customer ever thinks of saying, this draft is to be placed to the account of the £500 paid in on Monday, and this other to the account of the £500 paid in on Tuesday. There is a fund of £1000 to draw upon, and that is enough. (Emphasis added)

This notion of co-mingled sums as being "in form one blended fund, the parts of which have no longer any distinct existence" continues to describe correctly the nature of a mixed trust fund, in my view.

In contrast to the blended fund concept is that of the mixed fund as an amalgam of the contributions which have been placed in it, identifiable for some purposes. This approach is reflected in such decisions as *Re Diplock's Estate*, [1948] 2 All E.R. 318 (C.A.). In that case, Lord Greene M.R. attributed to equity the adoption of "a more metaphysical approach" to the nature of a mixed fund. "[Equity] found no difficulty", he said (at p. 346):

> ... in regarding a composite fund as an amalgam constituting the mixture of two or more funds each of which could be regarded as having, for certain purposes, a continued separate existence. Putting it in another way, equity regarded the amalgam as capable, in proper circumstances, of being resolved into its component parts.

It is noteworthy that both the "fund as amalgam" and the "fund as a blend" approaches enable equity to offer the remedy of a charge, lien or constructive trust *vis à vis* the remaining balance in the fund. The former has the [effect], however, of limiting the reach of these proprietary remedies. To my mind such a restriction is not necessary. While "proprietary tracing" may serve as the equitable vehicle which enables a claimant to have recourse to a mixed trust fund in the first place, equity can move beyond the strictures of that doctrine to provide a remedy to the claimant once the connection to the fund has been made. The nexus is to be found in the concepts need not, in my view, be confined to any part of the fund because, by their very nature, they have always been applied against *the whole* of the fund.

This idea is well expressed in a critique of the analysis in *Re Diplock's Estate*, in an article by Dennis R. Klinck entitled "'Two Distincts, Divisions None': Tracing Money into (and out of) Mixed Accounts" (1987–1988), 2 *Banking & Finance Law Rev*. 147. Having dealt with Lord Greene M.R.'s "amalgam" concept, the author states, at p. 179:

> The alternative conceptualization of equitable tracing in this context is implied in the notion of a charge on the mixed fund. Rather than purporting to distinguish parts of the funds and attribute them to particular claimants, this approach sees the claimants as having a proportional claim on the whole fund. If the whole diminishes in extent or value, the proportional claims remain the same, albeit that what the claimants get will be less because the fund is reduced. Arguably, this does not, strictly speaking, involve "tracing" because there is no pretence that that fund is being divided and a particular claimant's property identified.

I accept, and adopt, the blended fund approach. At the end of the day, when the trust account has been frozen and there is a shortfall, that shortfall must be divided amongst the beneficiaries who continue to have claims against the fund. I do not think that an analysis which is based on the premise that *some* beneficiaries' interests in the fund have been reduced by earlier misappropriations and therefore that their respective claims have been reduced accordingly, should be preferable to one which simply says that *each* beneficiary has suffered a loss relating to the same misappropriations from the same mixed fund by the same wrongdoer, and accordingly their charge or constructive trust should continue to apply against the whole fund to the proportionate extent of their contributions, *i.e.*, the shortfall should be divided in such proportions as their respective interests bear to what is to be divided up at the particular time.

The fund is still the fund, and as Farley J. noted in this case, it is not the Bank's money or the money of any particular contributor that has been stolen; it is *the fund* which has been wrongfully depleted. I agree with his comments in the following passages from his first reasons released on October 26, 1995 (at pp. 3–4):

> If the Bank had insisted upon a separate trust bank account being set up, then it need not be worried about the claims of other clients. However all funds advanced by those concerned were deposited by Upshall in a mixed trust bank account at the Bank. As a result each client (including the Bank) had a claim concerning that mixed account. When the Bank's funds went into that account they went the same way as other fungible funds attributable to the other clients. The funds in that account were not individually earmarked dollar by dollar for any particular client. Rather all clients as beneficiaries would have a claim against all the funds ...

And at pp. 5–6:

> Let me observe that a bank account involves a debtor (bank)-creditor (depositor) relationship.... When funds are deposited to a mixed trust account they lose their earmarked identity. Thus *each client* through the trust relationship with Upshall/Society *has a claim upon the loan granted to the Bank through the operation of this mixed trust account.... It is the money in the mixed trust account which has been stolen; not that of any particular client.* (Emphasis added)

PART III — CONCLUSION

The significant problem with LIBR is that its application, in a form true to its tracing origins and rationale, is too complicated. It may be "manifestly fairer" than the rule in *Clayton's Case* in the sense that it attributes debits from the account equally and proportionately amongst the contributors. "Fairness" may be relative, however. Is the rule necessarily "fairer" when it limits contributors to the lowest intermediate balance in the account between the times of contribution and distribution? The rule in *Clayton's Case* works "unfairly" against the first contributors to the fund, because it attributes the first wrongful withdrawals to those contributions, eliminating some claims but allowing others to be compensated in full. The application of LIBR can have similar effect, as the circumstances of this case indicate, because its "last in, first out" regime favours later contributors. At the same time, a *pro rata* sharing based simply on the claimants' contributions measured proportionately to the assets available for distribution can work *against* late depositors, as the circumstances of this case also illustrate.

What is at play here, in reality, is a choice of fictions. The rule in *Clayton's Case* and LIBR are both fictions. Any other rationale which endeavours to establish a rule or principle on which equity will divide a shortfall amongst those entitled to claim against it is a fiction. Farley J. recognized the role of fictions, or "artificial rules" when he said, in his second reasons, at pp. 6–7:

> I do not see it as fair, equitable or practicable in the circumstances (and more especially since the Bank effected an inappropriate and unauthorized self help remedy to the detriment of the other claimants) to invoke LIBR. It seems to me somewhat artificial (recognizing that all the rules involved in this area are artificial rules which must be applied with caution so as to maintain the closest approximation of fairness, equity and reasonability, while recognizing practicality) to invoke LIBR which by its very nature "rewards" those innocents who are later on the scene as compared with those innocents who have been taken advantage of earlier when it is fairly clear that the wrongdoer would continue to fleece all the innocents if given the chance. Recovery should not be so dependent on a fortuitous accident of timing.

I agree. Earlier in these reasons I alluded to this court's rejection, in *Greymac*, of the rule in *Clayton's Case* as "unfair and arbitrary" and "based on a fiction". In this latter regard, Morden J.A. cited (at pp. 686–87) the following oft-quoted passage from the decision of learned Hand J. in *Re Walter J. Schmidt & Co.*, 298 Fed. 314 (1923) at p. 316:

> The rule in Clayton's Case is to allocate the payments upon an account. Some rule had to be adopted, and though any presumption of intent was a fiction, priority in time was the most natural basis of allocation. It has no relevancy whatever to a case like this. Here two people are jointly interested in a fund held for them by a common trustee. There is no reason in law or justice why his depredations upon the fund should not be borne equally between them. To throw all the loss upon one, through the mere chance of his being earlier in time, is irrational and arbitrary, and is equally a fiction as the rule in Clayton's Case, *supra*. *When the law adopts a fiction, it is, or at least it should be, for some purpose of justice. To adopt it here is to apportion a common misfortune through a test which has no relation whatever to the justice of the case... Such a result, I submit with the utmost respect, can only come from a mechanical adherence to a rule which has no intelligible relation to the situation.* (Emphasis added)

Such is the case here, in my view. To apply the LIBR principle in the circumstances of this case

would be "to throw all the loss upon [some], through the mere chance of [their] being earlier in time". It would be "irrational and arbitrary". It would be "to apportion a *common misfortune* through a test which has no relation whatever to the justice of the case". I do not favour it.

In *Greymac*, Morden J.A. observed that "if the application of the *pro rata* approach is seen as an alteration in the rule to be applied [*i.e.*, the rule in *Clayton's Case*], it is one that involves improvement and refinement". Here, I am satisfied that the application of the mechanics of such a *pro rata* approach in the form I have advocated — the *pari passu ex post facto* approach — as opposed to the application of the LIBR principle in such circumstances, also involves what Jessel M.R. characterized in *Re Hallett's Estate, supra*, at p. 720, as "the gradual refinement of the doctrine of equity".

For the foregoing reasons, I would dismiss the appeal with costs.

Appeal dismissed with costs.

Notes

1. The Bank concedes that the amount of its deposit into the trust account, $173,000, must be reduced by a small amount of approximately $2,500 to accommodate some minor transactions which occurred following its deposit and before the freezing of the account. The application of LIBR would result in the Bank retaining $170,448.45 of the $173,000 deposited.
2. See, Maddaugh, Peter D. and McCamus, John D., *The Law of Restitution*, Canada Law Book, pp. 153–54; *British Columbia v. National Bank of Canada* (1994), 119 D.L.R. (4th) 669 at pp. 688–89, 99 B.C.L.R. (2d) 358 (C.A.).
3. See Maddaugh and McCamus, *The Law of Restitution, supra*, at pp. 153–54.
4. See *British Columbia v. National Bank of Canada, supra*, at pp. 688–89.
5. *Per* Woolf L.J. in *Barlow Clowes International Ltd.*, at p. 35. LIBR is said to be fairer because it approaches the allocation problem from the perspective of the "proportions [that] the different interests in the account...bear to each other at the moment before the withdrawal is made" (p. 35).
6. See *Winsor v. Bajaj, supra*; *Chering Metals Club Inc. (Trustee of) v. Non-Discretionary Cash Account Trust Claimants* (1991), 7 C.B.R. (3d) 105 at p. 111 (Ont. Gen. Div.); *Law Society of Upper Canada v. Squires* (Ont. Gen. Div., unreported decision of Farley J. released October 17, 1994); *Law Society of Upper Canada v. Sproule Estate* (unreported decision of Pitt J., released April 7, 1995 (Ont. Gen. Div.) [reported 8 E.T.R. (2d) 156]; *Holden Financial Corp. v. 411454 Ontario Ltd.* (unreported decision of Rosenberg J. released August 28, 1992, at p. 33); *Ontario (Securities Commission) v. Consortium Construction Inc.* (unreported decision of Rosenberg J. released June 21, 1993, at paras. 76–77).
7. Citing from Scott, *The Law of Trusts*, Vol. 5, 3rd ed. (1967), at pp. 3620 and 3624.

(d) *Deeley v. Lloyds Bank Ltd.*†

[LORD SHAW OF DUNFERMLINE:]

My Lords, Mr. John Glaze was the owner of the Brockmoor Steel and Iron Works, in the county of Stafford, and of certain messuages or dwelling-houses there. He carried on a steel and iron business and was in the position of requiring advances of capital. He was a customer of Lloyds Bank Limited, the respondents in this appeal. He executed three mortgages over his property. The first of these need not be referred to. The second was dated September 21, 1893. By it it was stipulated "that the mortgagor hereby covenants with the company that he, the mortgagor, will, on demand, or if no demand is made in his lifetime, then his heirs, executors, or administrators will, on his death, pay to the company the balance then owing from the mortgagor on his account current with the company for cheques, notes, or bills drawn, accepted, or endorsed by him, or for advances made to him or for his accommodation or benefit." The indenture contained other clauses usual in similar circumstances, and it was "provided always that the amount to be secured by these presents shall not exceed the sum of £2,500." It is an ordinary bank mortgage to secure to the extent of £2,500 a current account.

About two years thereafter, namely, on December 2, 1895, Mr. Glaze granted a further mortgage over the same property in favour of the appellant. Notice thereof was duly given on behalf of the appellant to the bank. The proceedings in this case have been protracted, and much of the delay and elaboration has been due to a denial by the bank that this notice was received. In the witness-box their agent maintained that it had not; and indeed he explained his conduct with regard to his method of keeping the account and of treating subsequent payments by the circumstance that he had not been apprised of the second mortgage. This defence had been held to unfounded in fact, and it was not maintained at your Lordships' Bar. I incline to the view that the bank agent was of opinion — an opinion entirely justified by the value of the Brockmoor property while there was a going business therein — that the subsequent mortgage was a matter of no moment, looking to the enormous margin of security which still remained for the bank. In these circumstances I think it not unlikely that he took no special account at the time of the notice of the subsequent mortgage, and has forgotten all about it ever since.

Mr. Glaze's circumstances, however, became more and more embarrassed. The bank, after the usual procedure, realized the property by private sale at a price just sufficient to cover the amount of its security together with a prior mortgage which the bank had acquired. In these circumstances the bank maintains that no surplus is available for payment of anything to the appellant. The appellant, however, maintains that payments were made at times and of sufficient amount to extinguish the bank's security, and that consequently her mortgage ranks prior in date to that of the bank, and the debt due thereon should be satisfied accordingly. It is agreed that if this be so the bank mortgage would be effective for any balance due from the property after satisfaction of the appellant's mortgage.

The position of the accounts may be stated in a word. The important date is December 2, 1895, being the date of the appellant's mortgage. According to the bank pass-books of Mr. John Glaze, there was at that date a debit balance of £3,379 on his current account. This to the extent of £2,500 was secured by the bank mortgage. When, however, notice was given of the execution in the appellant's favour by Mr. Glaze of the second mortgage on December 2, 1895, that notice was ignored. Mr. Glaze's account with the bank was continued as before. No fresh account was opened nor fresh security asked. Not even the course, alluded to in argument, of drawing in a line across the bank account to distinguish fresh from former payments or advances was taken. Mr. John Glaze continued to pay in money to his credit, and within three weeks, namely, by December 21, 1895, these payments more than extinguished the total amount of the £2,500 secured by the bank mortgage. In about another fortnight, namely, by January 7, 1896, further payments were made by Mr. Glaze to the credit of his account which more than extinguished the entire balance due by him secured and unsecured to the bank on December 2 previous.

---

† [1912] A.C. 756 (H.L.). [Notes omitted.]

The case, my Lords, is very similar indeed to that which was expressed many years ago in the compendious phraseology of Lord Chelmsford, which is quoted in the opinion of the Lord Chancellor (Lord Campbell) in *Hopkinson v. Rolt*:[1]

> A prior mortgage for present and future advances; a subsequent mortgage of the same description; each mortgagee has notice of the other's deeds; advances are made by the prior mortgagee after the date of the subsequent mortgage, and with full knowledge of it; is the prior mortgagee entitled to priority for these advances over the antecedent advance made by the subsequent mortgagee?

My Lords, there are dicta of the learned judges in this case, and in particular of Fletcher Moulton L.J., to which I shall afterwards refer, which make it appear almost necessary to recapitulate the general rules applicable to this subject. These general rules do not appear to have been left unsettled, but, in the view which I take of the judgment of Fletcher Moulton L.J., and with the high respect which I have for that learned judge, it humbly appears to me that these rules would be subjected to considerable change if his judgment were affirmed by your Lordships' House.

Upon the topic of the rights arising between a bank which has obtained a first mortgage over the property of a customer, and a second mortgagee who has obtained a second mortgage over the same property and has given notice thereof to the bank as first mortgagee, it may be necessary to state the law of the transaction from its commencement. I think that the rules simply stated are these:

1. In the case of a grant of a mortgage to a bank by a customer in security of advances made and to be made, there, of course, still remains in the customer an estate capable of being disposed of by sale or affected by subsequent mortgage, and if a second mortgage is granted and notice given to the first mortgagee, it is contrary to good faith upon the part of the bank as first mortgagee to make in its own favour encroachments upon that remanent estate which would in effect enlarge the scope of the first mortgage and make it stands as cover for fresh advances. I have been anxious to place this proposition in the forefront of the case because it appears to me to be well founded in principle, to be amply warranted by authority, and to dispose of not a few of the arguments in reference to the equities as between the bank and its customers which have been freely used in this case. On the matter of authority I am humbly of opinion that the judgment of Lord Lindley (then Master of the Rolls) in *West v. Williams*[2] is of the highest value. That learned Lord says,[3] summing up what in his opinion was the effect of *Hopkinson v. Rolt*,[4] *Bradford Banking v. Briggs*,[5] and *Union Bank of Scotland v. National Bank of Scotland*:[6]

> These three cases shew very clearly that the principle which underlies the rule established in *Hopkinson v. Rolt*[4] is simply this, that an owner of property, dealing honestly with it, cannot confer on another a greater interest in that property than he himself has. The rule rests on no technicality of English law; it is based on the plainest good sense, and it is as much the law of Scotland as the law of England. When a man mortgages his property he is still free to deal with his equity of redemption in it, or, in other words, with the property itself subject to the mortgage. If he creates a second mortgage he cannot afterwards honestly suppress it, and create another mortgage subject only to the first. Nor can any one who knows of the second mortgage obtain from the mortgagor a greater right to override it than the mortgagor himself has.

2. It is also contrary to good faith upon the part of the mortgagor himself, who has granted two successive mortgages, to do anything which would facilitate the enlargement of the scope of the first mortgage to the detriment of the second, or would minimize the value of that remanent estate which as mortgagor he had assigned by the second mortgage subject to the first. This rule stands in the same position as the former in principle. It is covered also by the authority of Lord Lindley, just referred to, and in the *Union Bank Case*[7] Lord Halsbury made it particularly clear. "The question is," said his Lordship, "whether Mrs. McArthur" (the mortgagor) "having bargained away and made an assignation of her reversionary right to the knowledge of the National Bank could obtain further advances upon the security of an interest which she had for valuable consideration already assigned to a third person. My Lords, it seems to me that such a proceeding is contrary to good faith, and the decision of your Lordships' House in *Hopkinson v. Rolt*[8] establishes the principle, and establishes it upon the broadest grounds of natural justice."

Language to the same effect, and put in principle upon the same basis, is used by Chitty L.J. in *West v. Williams*.[9]

3. This being the basis upon which the doctrine under discussion rests, the third general rule springs therefrom, and is applicable in the case of a bank holding a first mortgage in security of advances

made and to be made on current account as follows: After notice to the bank of a second mortgage by the customer, the debit is struck at the date of notice, and in the ordinary case, that is to say, where an account is merely continued without alteration, or where no specific appropriation of fresh payments is made, such payments are credited to the earliest items on the debit side of the account, and continue so to be credited until the balance secured under the first mortgage is extinguished.

My Lords, the judgment of Eve J. in this case, although in my view it is erroneous in holding that the general rule was by the conduct of the parties departed from, humbly appears to me to state that general rule, and also the effect of the series of authorities under which it has been canvassed, clearly and luminously, and I respectfully adopt that part of the learned judge's judgment. After referring to *Sherry's Case*,[10] he says:

> In giving judgment the Lord Chancellor (Lord Selborne) says this:
>
> > The principle of *Clayton's Case*[11] and of the other cases which deal with the same subject, is this, that where a creditor having a right to appropriate moneys paid to him generally, and not specifically appropriated by the person paying them, carries them into a particular account kept in his books, he *prima facie* appropriates them to the account, and the effect of that is, that the payments are *de facto* appropriated according to the priority in order of the entries on the one side and on the other of that account.
>
> I understand that to mean this: According to the law of England, the person paying the money has the primary right to say to what account it shall be appropriated; the creditor, if the debtor makes no appropriation, has the right to appropriate; and if neither of them exercises the right, then one can look on the matter as a matter of account and see how the creditor has dealt with the payment, in order to ascertain how he did in fact appropriate it. And if there is nothing more than this, that there is a current account kept by the creditor, or a particular account kept by the creditor, and he carries the money to that particular account, then the Court concludes that the appropriation has been made; and having been made, it is made once for all, and it does not lie in the mouth of the creditor afterwards to seek to vary that appropriation.

This is substantially the view taken by the learned Master of the Rolls in his clear opinion in this case, and I respectfully agree with that opinion.

There are two passages, however, my Lords, in the judgment of Fletcher Moulton L.J. which appear to me to deserve grave consideration. In that learned judge's view, the law applicable to the ordinary case of a mortgage to a banker to secure a current account is this:

> When the bank receives notice of a second mortgage by the customer to a third person it does not in my opinion affect the nature of the security. It remains a security for the balance of the account from moment to moment. But it puts a limit to the amount of that security. It cannot be increased beyond the balance at the date of the notice, but it may be diminished. If the debit balance is at any moment brought lower than this by the subsequent payments in and out, the secured amount is correspondingly reduced, and once reduced cannot again be raised.

In a subsequent passage the same learned judge says:

> In the simple case, therefore, of a secured account with subsequent payments in and payments out I am of opinion that the presumed intention should be to apply the payments in to the unsecured items in order of date in priority to the secured items.

My Lords, I am humbly of opinion that these passages, which express a principle for an perhaps against which much could be said upon general grounds, are not and have not for many years been any part of the law of England or of Scotland. They appear to me to be in direct contradiction to authority, from *Clayton's Case*[12] downwards to the judgments of Eve J. and the Master of the Rolls in the present case. Lord Blackburn, commenting upon the series of decisions, and in particular on *Hopkins v. Rolt*,[13] puts the matter thus:[14]

> A mortgage to secure future advances not exceeding a certain amount, though perfectly good as against the mortgagor, gave the mortgagee no equity to postpone advances made by the second mortgagee with notice to the first to advances made by the first mortgagee after notice of the second mortgage.

In short, I do not see my way to hold that the passages to which I have referred can stand alongside of the high authorities in the other direction.

4. Of course, upon the extinction of the first mortgage by the credit payments, the latter mortgage, its predecessor being thus satisfied, attains priority, and, subject to the priority of the second mortgage,

the mortgagor still remains answerable as debtor, and his property, or any remanent value thereof covered by the mortgage, remains the security to the bank.

My Lords, once these rules have been established, it seems late in the day to put forward considerations, such as appear in this case, as to either their inherent impropriety or their harshness in operation as against bankers. For, in the first place, the rules are, it may be affirmed, universally known and accepted in the banking world; and, secondly, the mode of protection open to bankers is as familiar and as simple as could be imagined. This case itself is an excellent illustration of the familiarity of the subject, and of the mode in which a bank quite easily and naturally secures its own protection. The respondents in this appeal had a printed rule upon the subject. That rule was in the following terms:

Wherever notice is received of a second mortgage or second charge on any security on which the bank holds a proper charge, the account must at once be ruled off and a separate account opened for subsequent transactions.

Accordingly, in the present case, when the notice of the second mortgage, which it is now admitted was duly received, as given, the bank's procedure was laid down by the rules which it itself had set up. As I have already indicated, my view is that its agent, who swore in the witness-box that the notice had not been given, and who I think had not remembered the circumstance, treated the whole matter as of little consequence on account of what he considered the ample margin of security. As it was, what occurred was that the account was continued in the ordinary way, no change whatever being made in the direction either of stopping the existing account or of appropriating fresh payments, until after the time when, on the principle of *Clayton's Case*,[15] the debt due to the bank had been extinguished. In the language of Lord Blackburn in *Ratcliffe's Case*,[16]

"The bank might, if they pleased, have taken the payments on such terms as to prevent the application of that rule" (*Clayton's Case*[17]), "but, not having done so, it seems to me that the old bal-

ance was, before the end of the year, 1873, paid off."

The whole question of possible hardship upon bankers was discussed fully by Lord Chancellor Campbell fifty years ago in *Hopkinson v. Rolt*:[18]

"The hardship upon bankers," said the Lord Chancellor, "from this view of the subject at once vanishes when we consider that the security of the first mortgage is not impaired without notice of a second, and that when this notice comes, the bankers have only to consider (as they do as often as they discount a bill of exchange), what is the credit of their customer, and whether the proposed transaction is likely to lead to profit or to loss."

And in another passage he says:[19]

How is the first mortgagee injured by the second mortgage being executed, although the first mortgagee having notice of the mortgage, the second mortgagee should be preferred to him as to subsequent advances? The first mortgagee is secure as to past advances, and he is not under any obligation to make further advances. He has only to hold his hand when asked for a further loan. Knowing the extent of the second mortgage, he may calculate that the hereditaments mortgaged are an ample security to the mortgagees; and if he doubts this, he closes his account with the mortgagor, and looks out for a better security.

In the present case what the bankers did was to ignore the notice of the second mortgage and to ignore their own rule, and, in fact, to make no specific appropriation whatever; and their dealings with the account were exactly the same as if there never had been a second mortgage or the rights of a second mortgagee. Speaking for myself, I cannot, in such circumstances, understand how the conduct spoken to in evidence can be held to amount to a recognition of a second mortgage, which throughout was maintained not to have been known. Nor does it seem possible to me that such conduct instituted or implied transactions so arranged as to avoid the incidence of the *Clayton* principle, the bank's own rule for the latter being plain and having been ignored.

I am humbly of opinion that the judgment of the Courts below should be reversed.

(e) *City Discount Co. v. McLean*†

Error from the judgment of the Court of Common Pleas in favour of the plaintiffs upon a special case stated by order of *nisi prius*, of which the facts were in substance as follows:

The plaintiffs were a company whose chief business was discounting bills. The action was brought to recover £750, being the sixth part of the sum of £5,000, after deducting from that sum the moneys realised from the sale of certain leasehold premises, which sum of £750 was alleged to be due from the defendant under a guarantee given by him and five other persons to the plaintiffs under the following circumstances:

Between November, 1865, and May, 1867, the plaintiffs had discounted in the way of their business certain bills for a Mr. Henry Southgate, who carried on business as Southgate & Co., and at the time when the guarantee was entered into he was indebted to the plaintiffs in discount transactions about £208. He was also indebted to plaintiffs to the extent of £1,660 on discount transactions previous to November, 1865, and both these two amounts were afterwards added to his debt to the plaintiffs of £27,704 after-mentioned. Southgate carried on business as an auctioneer of pictures, &c., and the bills discounted by him up to the 3rd of May, 1867, the date of the guarantee, were all connected with his business. In May, 1867, he was desirous of obtaining an advance of £5,000 for reasons which then pressed him, one of the principal being a debt by him of £2,914 to Messrs. Ward, Lock, & Tylar, and he at first offered by way of security to the plaintiffs to deposit with them the lease of his premises. Further security was required, and the following guarantee was given and signed by six persons, one of them being the defendant:

> To the City Discount Company, Limited,
>
> Gentlemen — You having agreed to advance Messrs. H. Southgate & Co. a sum not exceeding £5,000 on the deposit of their lease of the premises, No. 143, Strand, in the county of Middlesex, and certain life policies not included in this undertaking, we hereby undertake and agree to guarantee and indemnify you to the extent of £800 each, or to the extent of a sixth part of any deficiency of the said advance that may remain due to you after sale of the said lease; this undertaking being given on the understanding that the said lease shall be sold and the purchase-money realised before we are severally called upon for the deficiency (if any), and that this guarantee shall last for a period not exceeding two years from this date. Dated the 3rd of May, 1867.

A mortgage of the lease was also given by Southgate as a security for the advance.

After the 3rd of May, 1867, and between that date and December, 1868, when Southgate stopped payment, and was indebted to the plaintiffs on the balance of accounts in a sum of £27,704 the company, in various sums at different times, advanced to Southgate money amounting in the whole to the sum of £44,784, Southgate being on several occasions during that period indebted to the plaintiffs in respect of advances made by them to him in a sum exceeding £5,000; a large portion of this debt of £27,041 was made up of returned and renewed bills, and discounts, and commissions. During the same period, from the 3rd of May, 1867, to December, 1868, Southgate discounted with the plaintiffs trade bills amounting in the whole to the sum of £40,326 5s., he being at the date of such discount credited in the books of the plaintiffs with the amount of such bills, less interest and commission, and if such bills were paid at maturity to the plaintiffs by the acceptors such credit remained, but if they were dishonoured he was debited with the full amount of such bills.

After the 3rd of May, 1867, another class of bills were also discounted by Southgate with the plaintiffs. These were bills which he drew, and which were accepted for his accommodation, and were then discounted by him with the plaintiffs, who guaranteed the acceptors against all liabilities in respect of the same, and who credited Southgate at the time of the discount with the amount of the said bills, less interest and commission; and when the same became due, and as a matter of course were unpaid either by Southgate or the acceptors, debited Southgate with the full amount of the same. When the trade bills before mentioned, and the last-mentioned class of bills, arrived or were about to arrive at maturity, Southgate took to the plaintiffs other bills to

---

† (1874), L.R. 9 C.P. 692. [Notes omitted.]

something like the same amount, either trade bills or bills of the last-mentioned class, and discounted them with the plaintiffs, and the same mode of crediting and debiting him was pursued as before mentioned in respect of the two classes of bills respectively; and this mode of dealing continued till the time of Southgate's bankruptcy. Southgate took the accommodation bills to plaintiffs at the request of their manager to keep the company out of cash advances, they re-discounting the bills Southgate had discounted with them, and the gross amount of such bills was about £14,000. Both classes of bills were brought as above by Southgate to the plaintiffs in order to keep the company out of cash advances, and were brought from time to time, having regard to the amount of such advances, though not exactly corresponding with such amounts, or with the times when the said advances were made.

The advances made were made from time to time, and extended over the whole period from the 3rd of May, 1867, to December, 1868. The case then set out the dates and amounts of various advances made on the 8th of May, 1867, and immediately subsequent days, which were contended by the plaintiffs be advances made under the guarantee.[1]

About the time of these advances accommodation bills of the character before adverted to were discounted by Southgate with the company in order to cover these advances, which said wills were from time to time renewed according to the mode before mentioned with respect to this class of bills, and have never been paid, and on all advances made to Southgate by plaintiffs bills of one sort or another were brought by Southgate to plaintiffs to be discounted by them, with the object of keeping them out of cash advances. Between the 3rd of May, 1867, and December, 1868, considerably more than £5,000 of the trade bills had been paid. More than £5,000 was advanced by the plaintiffs to Southgate between the 3rd of May, 1867, and the 4th of September, 1867, and more than £5,000 between the 24th of September, 1867, and December, 1868. It appeared from the books of the plaintiffs that from May, 1867, to December, 1868, the accounts were made up and shewed only a small balance against Southgate, e.g. at the end of 1867 one of £273, and at the end of June, 1868, one of £1,060 odd, but at the time of his bankruptcy in December, 1868, the accounts shewed a balance against him of £27,740. The plaintiffs in June, 1869, exercised the power of sale in the mortgage, and the premises were sold on the 25th of February, 1869. The action was brought to recover £750, being the sixth part of £4,500, the deficiency out of £5,000 after the sale.

The case contained the following statements as to the course of business between the plaintiffs and Southgate. The plaintiffs mode of keeping accounts was this, not only with regard to Southgate & Co., but all their customers. The amount of discount and commission was arranged and deducted from the nominal amount of the bills. The transaction was entered in the day-book. If the total amount of the balance was then and there received and taken away by the customer, the transaction was frequently not entered in the ledger at all. If part only was taken then the amount left and not then received was entered to his credit in the ledger, and when that amount was afterwards taken up by the customer and was paid to him, the amount was then debited to him in the books. If the balance, after deducting discount and commission, was not then taken up, the whole amount of the balance was credited to the customer in the ledger, and when the customer received the advance, which was usually within a day or two, the amounts so paid and received were entered in the ledger. If the discounted bills were not paid on maturity by the acceptor or the customer, and were paid by the plaintiffs, the amount was debited to the customer as before described. Sometimes the customer came to the manager and told him that he intended to bring bills for discount and requested an advance by anticipation. This advance was then debited to him in the ledger, and when the bills were brought he was credited with their nominal amount, less the interest and commission, as above-mentioned.

The balances before mentioned as appearing against Southgate from the books of the plaintiffs when the accounts were made up, were arrived at by taking into account the sums on the credit side, which represented the amount of the bills, less interest and commission for discount, which were current at the date of the balance being struck, and of promissory notes of Southgate, some of which bills and notes were not paid at maturity, and were included in the ultimate balance of £27,704 against Southgate. The plaintiffs from time to time sent to Southgate accounts which were copies of their ledger, which thus shewed the above balances.[2]

The Court was to draw inferences of fact.

The question for the Court was, whether the defendant was liable to pay the sum of £750, or any part thereof.

[BLACKBURN J. (Mellor J. concurring):]

I agree that the judgment of the Court below should be affirmed, subject to its being reduced by the amount given up by the plaintiffs' counsel. We must assume that the construction of the guarantee is that it was not a continuing guarantee for the balance that might be due, during the two years, up to £5,000, but of advances to the amount of £5,000. I understand the fact to be that £5,000 was advanced, and if that amount has not been paid off the plaintiffs are entitled to recover the sixth part of so much of the amount as has not been actually satisfied, which amounts to about £550. It is contended, however, on the part of the defendant, that the whole £5,000 has been paid off in this way, *viz.* that in the account it appears that, after the advance was made, payments were made by Southgate greatly exceeding £5,000, and half-yearly accounts were rendered from time to time shewing this to be so; and it is urged that by operation of law, or as an inference of fact which we are bound to draw, the £5,000 has been satisfied. I cannot come to that conclusion. It has been considered a general rule since *Clayton's Case*,[3] that when a debtor makes a payment he may appropriate it to any debt he pleases, and the creditor must apply it accordingly. If the debtor does not appropriate it, the creditor has a right to do so to any debt he pleases, and that not only at the instant of payment, but up to the very last moment, as was decided on *Mills v. Fowkes*,[4] following a previous case of *Simson v. Ingham*.[5] We have, therefore to consider whether this right of the creditor has in the present case been so exercised or barred. It may be, as a general rule in ordinary cases, and if there is nothing to show a contrary intention, the terms of credit must be appropriated to the items of debit in order of date, and that the half-yearly account rendered would constitute a fresh point of departure. *Clayton's Case*[6] and other similar cases shew that when a partner dies and there is change of the partnership, and the transactions with the new and old firms are all mixed up together in one account, the law treats the whole as one entire account, and applies the items of credit to those of debit according to date, in favour of the estate of the deceased partner. But when the parties remain the same, the question is whether the rendering of the account amounts to an appropriation of the items to one another in order of date. In such a case as this, where the earlier items constituting the £5,000 were secured by a mortgage and a guarantee, it never could have been the intention that they should be so appropriated. But it is contended that as a matter of law, though there is no authority so deciding, or as an inference of facts, though it is contrary to all probability, we are bound to hold that the £5,000 is to be considered as paid off; and if so paid off, it follows that it must be treated as paid off in six months, though by the terms of the guarantee a period of two years was contemplated. I cannot draw such an inference, either as matter of law or of fact. The true rule is that laid down in *Henniker v. Wigg*,[7] which is that accounts rendered are evidence of the appropriation of payments to the earlier items, but that may be rebutted by evidence to the contrary. Lord Denman C.J., referring to the rule in *Clayton's Case*,[8] there says,

> It is equally certain that a particular mode of dealing, and more especially and stipulation between the parties, may entirely vary the case.

That judgment seems to me to be sound sense.

Here the surety had nothing to do with the accounts. Southgate executed a mortgage and procured a guarantee to last for two years. Is it not obvious that it was meant that the £5,000 was not to be considered as paid off out of the first amounts credited to Southgate in the course of the subsequent discount transactions, but was to stand over and be treated independently of such transactions? If so, this rebuts any presumption arising from the state of the accounts. It does not appear that in point of fact the balance due was less than £5,000 after the advance.

(f) *Cory Brothers and Co. Ltd. v. The "Mecca"*†

[LORD MACNAGHTEN (Lord Morris concurring):]

In April, 1894, the appellants were the holders of four dishonoured bills of exchange accepted by, or on behalf of, a Turkish company called the Hamidieh Steamship Company. The bills had been given in payment for necessaries supplied in Egypt by the appellants, or their agents, to the steamships

---

† [1897] A.C. 286 (H.L.). [Notes omitted.]

Mecca and *Medina*. The first bill, due April 7, was for £267 14s. on account of the *Medina*; the second, due April 26, for £176 5s. on account of the *Mecca*. The other two both fell due on the 27th of the same month. One was for £194, 8s. on account of the *Mecca*, and one for £630 on account of the *Medina*.

Money was coming to the Hamidieh Company, as owners of the *Mecca*, from underwriters in England for salvage services to the *Medina*, and it was arranged that Messrs. H.E. Moss & Co., who were acting for the company in London, should pay a share of the amount, when collected, to the appellants, on an undertaking by them not to enforce their claim against the two vessels for three months. The undertaking was given by letter of June 22.

On August 15, 1894, the sum of £900 was accordingly paid to the appellants by H.E. Moss & Co. The appellants gave a receipt for that sum expressed to be on account of moneys owing them by the Hamidieh Company, adding, "the drafts embodying this amount being in Egypt, we cannot now return them, but herewith agree to take no further action in connection therewith during the period agreed upon between us."

On August 22, 1894, a letter was written on behalf of the appellants to the manager of the company acknowledging the receipt of the £900. The writer expressed a hope that it was the company's intention to remit at once the balance due, "namely," he says, "£401 2s. 9d., as per statement herewith ... and thus obviate the necessity of our taking further steps to secure it."

The statement which accompanied the letter of August 22, was headed: —

August 22nd 1894.
Messrs. The Hamidieh Company, Constantinople, in a/c with Messrs. Cory Brothers & Co., Limited.

Then followed particulars of the four bills with notarial expenses added. The bills were entered in order of date, but the *Medina* bill for £630 came after the *Mecca* bill of the same date. A charge of £7 2s. 5d. for telegrams on August 22, and an item "to interest date at 5 per cent, £20 6s. 4d.," which was the last item in the account, brought the total up to £1,301 2s. 9d., thus shewing the balance of £401 2s. 9d.

The period of grace having expired, the present action *in rem* was brought against the *Mecca*, which was found at Cardiff in the beginning of October, 1894. The action was brought to recover the moneys due in respect of the necessaries supplied to the *Mecca*, and an account was delivered appropriating the £900 to the *Medina* bills and legal expenses in connection with that vessel.

In addition to other defences which failed, the respondents pleaded that part of the money paid to the plaintiffs by H.E. Moss & Co. "was in respect of the whole amount sought to be recovered by the plaintiffs" in the action.

At the trial the defendants' counsel relied on the statement of account of August 22, 1894, as an appropriation by the plaintiffs of the £900 towards the payment of the four bills in the order in which they were entered in the account, and contended that by such appropriation the *Mecca* bills had been paid.

Bruce J. held that the payment was, by law, appropriated to the earlier items in the account, and gave judgment for the defendants. The judgment was affirmed by the Court of Appeal (Lord Esher M.R., Kay and A.L. Smith L.JJ.)

The plaintiffs brought the present appeal.

[LORD MACNAGHTEN (after stating the facts given above):]

My Lords, I have some difficulty in following the reasoning of the learned judges in the Court of Appeal. There seems to be an error in the short-hand notes, because the Master of the Rolls is made to say that the account came in the first instance from the company. But, if I understand his meaning aright, he does say that the account passing between the parties did not of itself operate as an appropriation, or afford any indication of an intention to appropriate it: it was as if each party in turn had said, "Here is the account. I do not appropriate." Kay L.J. treats the case as governed by *Clayton's Case*[1] to which the Master of the Rolls also refers. "I cannot see any reason," Kay L.J. says, "Why *Clayton's Case*[1] does not apply to the facts before us." Later on, after stating the facts as they appeared to him, "That is," he observes, "the very case to which *Clayton's Case*[1] would apply." A.L. Smith L.J. seems to take the same view as the Master of the Rolls. "Neither party," he says, "appropriated the payments to anything." Then he adds: "the £900 by the law goes to the earlier items." If what occurred in August did not amount to an appropriation, it is difficult to see why the appellants were not at liberty to make their election in October, when they found the *Mecca* at Cardiff. And certainly I am at a loss to understand that bearing the doctrine of *Clayton's Case*[1] can have upon the question.

Now, my Lords, there can be no doubt what the law of England is on this subject. When a debtor is making a payment to his creditor he may appropriate the money as he pleases, and the creditor must apply it accordingly. If the debtor does not make any appropriation at the time when he makes the payment the right of application devolves on the creditor. In 1816, when *Clayton's Case*[1] was decided, there seems to have been authority for saying that the creditor was bound to make his election at once according to the rule of the civil law, or at any rate, within a reasonable time, whatever that expression in such a connection may be taken to mean. But it has long been held and it is now quite settled that the creditor has the right of election "up to the very last moment," and his is not bound to declare his election in express terms. He may declare it by bringing an action or in any other way that makes his meaning and intention plain. Where the election is with the creditor, it is always his intention expressed or implied or presumed, and not any rigid rule of law that governs the application of the money. The presumed intention of the creditor may no doubt be gathered from a statement of account, or anything else which indicates an intention one way or the other and is communicated to the debtor, provided there are no circumstances pointing in an opposite direction. But so long as the election rests with the creditor, and he has not determined his choice, there is no room, as it seems to me, for the application of rules of law such as the rule of the civil law, reasonable as it is, that if the debts are equal the payment received is to be attributed to the debt first contracted. Now, *Clayton's Case*[1] was this. Clayton had a current account with a firm of bankers. One of the firm died. Some time afterwards the bank failed. The customer's account was kept from first to last as one unbroken account. At the date of the death of the deceased partner the customer had a large balance to his credit. Afterwards he drew out sums which in the aggregate exceeded that balance. On the other hand, moneys were paid in form time to time to his credit, and at the date of the failure the balance in his favour was rather larger than it was at the date of the death. He claimed to attribute his drawings after the death to subsequent payments in. But Sir W. Grant said, No. He distinguished the case from authorities which had been cited in favour of the claimant by saying:

> They were all cases of distinct insulated debts between which a plain line of separation could be drawn; but this is the case of a banking account where all the sums paid in form one blended fund, parts of which have no longer any

distinct existence; neither banker nor customer ever thinks of saying this draft is to be place to the account of the £500 paid in on Monday, and this other to the account of the £500 paid in on Tuesday. There is a fund of £1,000 to draw upon, and that is enough. In such a case there is no room for any other appropriation than that which arises from the order in which the receipts and payments take place and are carried into the account. Presumably it is the sum first paid in that is first drawn out. It is the first item on the debit side of the account that is discharged or reduced by the first item on the credit side. The appropriation is made by the very act of setting the two items against each other. Upon that principle all accounts current are settled, and particularly cash accounts.

The facts of the present case are very different. There is no current account between the parties here. There was no account between them at all until the bills were dishonoured. The debts were distinct. But it is, I think, important to observe that even in cases *prima facie* falling within the doctrine of *Clayton's Case*[1] the account between the parties, however it may be kept and rendered, is not conclusive on the question of appropriation. In a case in the Exchequer Chamber in 1874 (*City Discount Co. v. McLean*[2]), where there was a current and unbroken account between the parties, *Clayton's Case*[1] was pressed upon the Court. "I quite agree," said Bramwell B., "with the principle of the cases cited such as *Clayton's Case*[1] and *Bodenham v. Purchas*,[3] and I think we ought to follow them when applicable.... But we must decide every case according to its own circumstances." "The true rule," added Blackburn J., "is that laid down in *Henniker v. Wigg*,[4] which is that accounts rendered are evidence of the appropriation of payments to the earlier items, but that may be rebutted by evidence to the contrary." The rule in *Clayton's Case*[1] was very much considered in *Hallett's Case* in 1880[5] by the Court of Appeal, consisting of Sir George Jessel M.R. and Baggallay and Thesiger L.JJ. "It is a very convenient rule," said the Master of the Rolls, "and I have nothing to say against it unless there is evidence either of agreement to the contrary or of circumstances from which a contrary intention must be presumed, and then of course that which is a mere presumption of law gives way to those other considerations." "*Clayton's Case*",[1] observed Baggallay L.J., "was decided upon the principle that in the absence of any expressed intention to the contrary or special circumstances from which such an intention could be implied, the appropriation of drawings out to the payments in, as adopted in that case, represented what must be presumed to have been the intention of the parties concerned; and so viewed the decision is quite consistent with the like presumption being rebutted or modified in another case in which the circumstances were such as to negative any intention to make such an appropriation of the drawings out to the payments in."

Now, if the rule in *Clayton's Case*,[1] which certainly at one time was considered to be a rule of such force and stringency as to interfere even with the equity of following trust moneys into the bank account of a fraudulent trustee, is to be accepted with this qualification, and if an account stated between the parties is only evidence of appropriation of payments, it seems to me that, in order to determine the question at issue on this appeal, it is necessary to consider the circumstances of the case more closely than they were considered in the Courts below. If you look at the position of the parties when the payment of the £900 was made, and the purpose for which the statement of account of August 22, 1894, was sent, and examine the terms of the account itself, and the letter which accompanied it, it is, I think, impossible to suppose that the appellants could have intended to appropriate the £900 in a manner inconsistent with the rights which they asserted when they arrested the *Mecca*. It is, I think, equally impossible to suppose that they could have intended to renounce or waive their privilege of election.

It is quite clear that when the bills were dishonoured the appellants were alive to their rights. They intimated very distinctly that they were prepared to seize both the vessels which were then lying at Suez. It was this threat that brought the company to terms. For some time the appellants could not obtain any satisfactory assurance from H.E. Moss & Co. The Hamidieh Company put them off with empty promises. But at last the company got frightened, and on June 15, 1894, they wrote to H.E. Moss & Co., referring to the steamers and saying,

> As Messrs. Cory Brothers & Co., threaten to take proceedings against both the above-mentioned steamers if they will not promptly receive from us a satisfactory assurance that they will soon be paid, we beg you will not delay to give them such an assurance, otherwise the results will be very detrimental to the Hamidieh Company and to our Mr. Constantine A. Theodoridi.

So on June 22 H.E. Moss & Co. gave the required assurance, on an undertaking by the appellants that they would not, for three months from that date, arrest any of the property of the Hamidieh Company, either in this country or abroad, unless meantime the amounts to be received from the salvage claims on underwriters should fall short of the amounts of the bills held by them. Now, after that I rather doubt whether it would have been right for the company to try and steal a march upon their creditors by attempting to appropriate the money so as to release any part of their property. However that may be, the receipt which was given on August 15 seems to shew that the intention of the parties was that at the expiration of the period of grace the appellants should be remitted to their original rights, giving credit on general account for any sums received. Again, it seems to me that the letter of August 22 conveyed a distinct intimation that the appellants would exercise their rights unless the balance were paid. It was for the purpose of shewing what the balance was, and for no other purpose whatever, that the account was made up. It is impossible to suppose that the appellants, while looking forward to exercising their rights in case of default, would have made up an account with the intention of releasing one of the two vessels when they could not tell upon which of the two they might be able to lay their hands. Then it seems to me that the very frame of the account affords some indication that it was not intended to apply the payment in discharge of the first three bills, for the interest on those bills is the very last item in the account. If the intention had been to discharge bills which carried interest, it surely would have been intended at the same time to discharge the accrued interest on which no interest would be payable. If the company thought that the appellants intended to discharge the *Mecca* bills, why did they not, when they received the account, ask for their return? I cannot help thinking that if they had made such a request they would have received a very indignant reply. The result might have been the return of the cheque and immediate seizure of the two vessels, which would hardly have answered the company's purpose.

In the result I am of opinion that it was competent for the appellants to arrest the *Mecca* in October, 1894, and at that time to appropriate the money which they had received from H.E. Moss & Co. to the *Medina* bills.

I think that the appeal ought to be allowed.

Order of the Court of Appeal reversed with costs here and below; judgment to be entered for the appellants for £401 2s. 9d.; cause remitted to the Admiralty Division.

(g) *Re European Bank*†

In the year 1866 the *Oriental Commercial Bank* had three accounts with *Agra and Masterman's Bank*, namely, a loan account, a discount account, and a general account. The *Oriental Commercial Bank* were in the habit of applying to *Agra and Masterman's Bank* for accommodation loans to a considerable amount, which were entered in the loan account, and they from time to time deposited securities to meet these loans. On the 4th of May, 1866, the general manager of the *Oriental Commercial Bank* sent to the general manager of *Agra Masterman's Bank* a letter in the following terms: —

> 4 May, 1866.
>
> Dear Sir, — I am advised by our correspondents, Messrs. *Felli A. Carava, of Patras*, that they have valued upon your bank for our account, pursuant to an antecedent order of ours, for £10,500, by the drafts specified at foot; but since by this time our credit with you will no longer afford a margin to that extent, I hasten to hand to you, to hold by way of collateral security, the following bills, &c.: —
>
> > £1250 on *European Bank*, due 5 August;
> > £1500 on *European Bank*, due 5 August;
> > £1750 on *European Bank*, due 5 August.

[Then followed some bills, with other acceptors; and the letter continued: —]

> I request, therefore, that you will be pleased to honour the drafts of Messrs. *Paiba* as usual; I of course engaging to provide you with funds to meet such drafts before maturity.
>
> > Yours faithfully,
> > *Demetrio Pappa,*
> > General Manager

The *Agra and Masterman's Bank* accordingly accepted the drafts of the correspondents of the *Oriental Commercial Bank* to the amount of £10,500, and paid the acceptances when due, and carried the amount to the loan account.

The *Oriental Commercial, the European,* and the *Agra and Masterman's Banks* were all now being wound up voluntarily under the supervision of the Court.

After the commencement of the winding-up the assets of *Agra and Masterman's Bank* were transferred to the *Agra Bank*, the present claimants.

The *Oriental Commercial Bank* was largely indebted to *Agra and Masterman's Bank* on all their three accounts, and the *Agra Bank* had received dividends on the joint balance. By means of these dividends and the securities which they held, all the balance due on the loan account was covered, but a balance still remained due on the general account.

They now claimed a lien on the bills for £4500, so far as they were not required to cover the balance of the loan account, for the deficiency on the general account, and took out a summons in the winding-up of the *European Bank* to enforce their claim.

It appeared from the books of the *Agra and Masterman's Bank* that the securities deposited from time to time by the *Oriental Commercial Bank* were applied to cover the balance due on the loan account, without regard to the particular transaction in respect of which they were deposited, but there was no evidence that they were ever treated as applicable to the balance due on the other two accounts.

It also appeared that the bills had been accepted by the *European Bank* for the accommodation of the *Oriental Commercial Bank*.

The Vice-Chancellor held that the *Agra Bank* were entitled to retain the bills to answer the general balance, and allowed the claim; and from this decision the liquidator of the *European Bank* appealed.

[SIR W.M. JAMES L.J. (Sir G. Mellish L.J. concurring):]

I am of opinion that the order of the Vice-Chancellor is correct. If the matter depended simply upon the letter of the 4th of May, 1866, possibly there might have been some ambiguity which would have entitled the *European Bank* to say to the *Agra Bank*, "These are accommodation bills. You never gave any value for them, except by means of that particular transaction, and that value has been repaid." But when we look at the books, it is clear that there was no particular reason for treating these three accounts

---

† (1872), L.R. 8 Ch. 41.

as distinct matters. It was only for convenience that the loan account was kept separately. It was admitted by the Appellant that the bills in question might have been applied to discharge the balance of the loan account, without regard to the particular transaction in respect of which they were deposited. In truth, as between banker and customer, whatever number of accounts are kept in the books, the whole is really but one account, and it is not open to the customer, in the absence of some special contract, to say that the securities which he deposits are only applicable to one account.

I am of opinion that the *Agra Bank* have a right to hold these bills as security for the general account. The appeal must be dismissed with costs.

(h) *National Westminster Bank Ltd. v. Halesowen Presswork & Assemblies Ltd.*†

[VISCOUNT DILHORNE:]

My Lords, the respondent company's account with the Halesowen branch of the appellants was in February 1968 overdrawn to the extent of £11,339. Mr. F.I. Lewis was at all material times a director of the respondent company. He was also interested in two other associated companies, Lewis Distributors Ltd. and Jack Lewis Properties (Halesowen) Ltd., both of which had accounts with the appellants which were in debit in February 1968, the bank being owed £143,289 by Lewis Distributors Ltd. and £8,943 by Jack Lewis Properties (Halesowen) Ltd.

The bank being concerned about the position, their assistant manager in Birmingham saw Mr. Lewis on February 23 and, after their meeting, wrote him a letter dated February 23. In the letter he recorded that he had stated at the meeting that the accounts of the respondent company and Lewis Distributors Ltd. were "unacceptable to the bank, which itself needs to reserve all its rights of action." The assistant manager said that additional security was required in the absence of cash as an initial measure and enclosed debentures and guarantees to be issued and given by Lewis Distributors Ltd. and the respondent company which, he said, had been prepared "in accordance with what you agreed".

Mr. Lewis then consulted a Mr. Bernard Phillips, an accountant and member of the firm of Bernard Phillips & Co., who wrote to the assistant manager on Mr. Lewis's behalf in reply to the letter of February 23. In his letter Mr. Phillips said that from a draft statement of affairs which had been prepared it was "clear that a proper realisation of the company's assets would enable the company to discharge all its debts and obligations in full" but that "a forced realisation would ... show a position of insolvency." Consequently, he said, if the directors were to comply with the bank's request they might be accused of attempting a fraudulent preference, or, if the company were to be wound up within 12 months, the debenture would prove invalid. He went on to say that active steps had been taken to dispose of the business as a going concern and that the figures involved in such a transaction would "certainly" enable all the creditors of the respondent company to be paid in full and he asked that a reasonable opportunity should be given to the directors "to effect a transaction which will enable all the company's liabilities to be dealt with equally."

On March 15, 1968, Mr. Phillips wrote to the bank saying that no one had shown any interest in making an offer for the respondent company's factory and that the bank were right in assuming that the respondent company's banking business was being passed through the company's account at Lloyds Bank, Halesowen. The account at Lloyds had been opened, as Mr. Lewis admitted at a meeting on April 4, as he was afraid to pay in receipt to the bank's branch at Halesowen lest the bank should freeze on to them. The account at Lloyds was conducted on a credit basis.

A memorandum of that meeting on April 4, presented by a district manager of the bank, records that Mr. Lewis:

---

† [1972] A.C. 785 (H.L.).

mindful in particular of the incidence of interest on the large debts, said that in no circumstances would he persist in his endeavour to sell [the respondent company] as a going concern for more than six months. In fact, he might in four months' time come to this decision so as to sell on a break-up basis in the two-month remaining period.

Later the memorandum stated:

> If we (the bank) are able to arrange for Mr. Lewis to have the time which he seeks it was agreed that an active credit account would be reopened at Birmingham branch with the existing indebtedness there ... entirely frozen.

On April 17, 1968, the assistant general manager of the bank wrote to Mr. Lewis, saying *inter alia*:

> In an endeavour to resolve the present somewhat disastrous situation of your two companies we have now obtained approval to proceed on the lines we discussed with you on April 4.... So far as the existing account at our Birmingham branch of Halesowen Presswork & Assemblies Ltd. is concerned, this is to be frozen at its present figure and no further transactions save for permanent reduction are to take place thereon.... As part of the arrangements it was agreed that all the company's current business should be passed through Westminster Bank, and I look to you, therefore, to arrange for the account with Lloyds Bank to be closed so that all transactions henceforward may be passed through a new account to be opened at Birmingham branch. This new account is, of course, to be maintained strictly on a credit basis and you should bear in mind that the bank charges, including interest on the indebtedness at Birmingham, will, in the usual way, be debited to this new account.... There is, I feel, no need for me to underline the bank's concern regarding the overall indebtedness, and in acknowledgement of this you undertook to come to a decision regarding a sale of Halesowen Presswork & Assemblies Ltd., or failing this the disposal of its assets, within the next four months, and in the absence of materially changed circumstances in the meantime we for our part will adhere to the present scheme of arrangements for this period of time.

Mr. Lewis replied to this letter on April 22 saying that he accepted the conditions and arrangements that had been laid out.

A new account, called No. 2 account, in the name of the respondent company was opened at the Halesowen branch of the appellants.

Then, on May 20, 1968, just a month later, the respondent company gave notice (received by the appellants on May 24) that on June 12 a meeting of creditors would be held for the purposes mentioned in sections 294 and 295 of the *Companies Act* 1948. This notice was acknowledged by the bank by letter dated May 28, 1968, in which they said:

> Needless to say, in the light of these events the bank wishes the company's No. 2 account to be maintained in credit at all times and I am sure that we can rely on your cooperation to provide cleared funds in the account to meet cheques which may be presented.

It was common ground that the giving of the notice of the meeting of creditors was a material change of circumstance which would have entitled the bank to treat the arrangement made in the letters of April 17 and 22 as at an end. The letter of May 28 shows that they did not do so. They were, despite that material change of circumstance, prepared to allow the respondent company to continue to operate the No. 2 account provided that it was kept in credit.

On June 12 a cheque drawn by Girling Ltd. in favour of the respondent company for £8,611 5s. 10d. was paid into the No. 2 account of the appellants' Halesowen branch before the creditors' meeting was held that afternoon. At that meeting a resolution was passed for the voluntary winding up of the company and Mr. Bernard Phillips was appointed liquidator.

The amount of £8,611 5s. 10d. was credited to the No. 2 account on June 13 and the cheque was cleared on June 14.

By letter dated June 19 the bank told the liquidator that they considered their claim in the liquidation would be "for the net balance between all accounts, plus outstanding interest and commission." On this basis they said that the net amount due to the bank was £3,219 17s. 10d.

Mr. Phillips did not agree. He maintained that the bank were in no better position than any other creditor and claimed to be entitled to the £8,611 5s. 10d. and asserted that that could not be set off against the company's indebtedness to the bank.

On January 7, 1969, a writ was issued by the respondent company against the appellants. The company alleged that the bank had wrongfully and in breach of their agreement refused to pay over the £8,611 5s. 10d. and claimed that, as the proceeds of the cheque for that amount were collected after the commencement of the winding up, the bank were accountable therefor to the liquidator. In the statement of claim it was also alleged that it was agreed at the meeting on April 4, 1968, that "at no time should the ... bank have the right to consolidate the two ... accounts."

The bank strenuously denied ever having agreed to that. The action was tried by Roskill J. who accepted the evidence given on behalf of the bank and rejected that given on behalf of the company on this issue. He said that they had failed to satisfy him that any such agreement had been made.

The learned judge's finding on this has not been challenged either in the Court of Appeal or in this House but the company have throughout contended that the bank were not entitled to consolidate the two accounts. If they are right, then the agreement they alleged would have been superfluous.

If I read his judgment correctly, Roskill J. held that the banker's right of lien, though abrogated as long as the banker-customer relationship continued between the company and the bank:

> became enforceable as soon as that relationship determined as it did on June 12 by reason of the resolution to wind up. At that moment the Girling cheque had already passed into the possession of the bank and upon the resolution to wind up the bank's right of lien extended to that cheque and subsequently to its proceeds as well as to the whole balance on the No. 2 account [1971] 1 Q.B. 1, 25.

The bank did not at the trial seek to rely on section 31 of the *Bankruptcy Act* 1914, as applied to companies by section 317 of the *Companies Act* 1948, so the effect of that section was not considered by Roskill J. who gave judgment for the bank.

On appeal his decision was reversed by a majority (Lord Denning M.R. and Winn L.J., Buckley L.J. dissenting). Lord Denning M.R. thought that the use of the word "lien" in this context was misleading and that one should speak simply of a banker's "right to combine accounts" or a right to "set off" one account against the other [1971] 1 Q.B. 1, 33–34. Buckley L.J. said, at p. 46:

> When that cheque was cleared, as it was on June 14, 1968, it ceased to be a negotiable instrument and also ceased to be in the possession of the bank. Any lien of the bank on the cheque must thereupon have come to an end.... The money or credit which the bank obtained as the result of clearing the cheque became the property of the bank, not the property of the company. No man can have a lien on his own property and consequently no lien can have arisen affecting that money or that credit.

I agree with Buckley L.J. It was not contended in this House that the bank was entitled to set off one account against the other in the exercise of any

lien, and, if the bank were credited to do so, that must depend on other grounds.

In the Court of Appeal and in this House the bank relied on the provisions of section 31 of the *Bankruptcy Act* 1914, which so far as material is in the following terms:

> Where there have been mutual credits, mutual debts or other mutual dealings, between a debtor against whom a receiving order shall be made under this Act and any other person proving or claiming to prove a debt under the receiving order, an account shall be taken of what is due from the one party to the other in respect of such mutual dealings, and the sum due from the one party shall be set off against any sum due from the other party, and the balance of the account, and no more, shall be claimed or paid on either side respectively....

The *Companies Act* 1948, section 317, provides as follows:

> In the winding up of an insolvent company ... the same rules shall prevail and be observed with regard to the respective rights of secured and unsecured creditors and to debts provable ... as are in force for the time being under the law of bankruptcy in England with respect to the estates of persons adjudged bankrupt....

The respondent company in the Court of Appeal and in this House contended that section 31 did not apply. They did so on two grounds: first, that the dealings were not mutual; secondly, that by the agreement made in April the bank had contracted out of their rights under the section. This second ground involves consideration of two separate questions: (1) could the bank contract out of section 31 and (2) had the bank by entering into the agreement purported to do so?

There is a conflict of judicial opinion on whether it is possible to contract out of section 31. In *Ex parte Fletcher, In re Vaughan* (1877) 6 Ch. D. 350, where the debtors alleged an agreement "by the creditors to keep them upon their legs, if possible; and, in order to enable them to do so, to suspend their rights, and that all goods supplied on either side should be paid for in cash" (p. 335), Bacon C.J. held that the agreement could not put an end to the pre-existing rights of creditors if the time came

> when those suspended rights must be enforced.... But the Act of Parliament is plain, and it provides that when a man becomes bankrupt the accounts are to be taken in the manner stated by Lord Selborne L.C. in *Ex parte Barnett, In re*

Deveze (1874) 9 Ch. App. 293, where he says, at p. 295:

> ... when there have been mutual credits, debts, or mutual dealings ... and a proof is to be made in bankruptcy, there is to be a rule of set off, not, as I understand it, at the option of either party, but an absolute statutory rule — 'The balance of such account, and no more, shall be claimed or paid on either side respectively.'

> The law of mutual credit, therefore, is an especial [*sic*] statutory law, and if there were such an agreement as alleged by the debtors, that law put an end to it. [6 Ch. D. 350, 356].

In *Mersey Steel and Iron Co. Ltd. v. Naylor, Benzon & Co.* (1884) 9 App. Cas. 434 Lord Selborne L.C. said, at p. 438:

> Your Lordships observe that it is not that it *may be* — it is not a thing which is optional, but is a positive, absolute rule for the purpose of proof in bankruptcy, and nothing can be proved according to that rule in such cases except the balance of the account; that only is regarded as the claim which it is competent for the creditor to make when he comes in to prove under the bankruptcy.

In both *Ex parte Barnett*, 9 Ch. App. 293 and the *Mersey Steel* case the statutory provisions under consideration were similar in all material respects to section 31 of the *Bankruptcy Act* 1914. In both cases Lord Selborne L.C. said there was an absolute statutory rule. By that I understand him to have said that it was a rule the operation of which could not be avoided. In *Ex parte Barnett* he said that the rule was "not ... at the option of either party"; in the *Mersey Steel* case that it was "not a thing which is optional". He did not seek to distinguish between an option exercised by one party and an agreement between debtor and creditor or an option sought to be exercised consequent upon an agreement between the parties. I take him to have meant that the absolute statutory rule could not be waived either at the option of one party or at the option of both.

Ex parte Fletcher, 6 Ch. D. 350 went to the Court of Appeal. The report of the proceedings in that court is very brief. It shows that the point was taken that it was competent to exclude by special agreement the right of set off given by section 39 of the *Bankruptcy Act* 1869, but it does not indicate what arguments were advanced or whether any authorities were cited in support of that proposition. The judgments, if given as reported, were very brief. All three members of the court held that the agree-

ment was not one to exclude the right to set off but James L.J. and Baggallay L.J. also indicated that such an agreement, if made, would have been effective. James L.J. said, at p. 357: "The respondents are entitled to the set off which they claim unless there is some agreement binding at law or in equity which excludes their right," and Baggallay L.J. said at p. 357: "The right to the set off is clear unless the respondents have precluded themselves from enforcing it by some special agreement."

One cannot reconcile their statements with the observations of Bacon C.J. and Lord Selborne L.C. Neither James L.J. nor Baggallay L.J. are reported as having referred to the observations of Bacon C.J., or to those of Lord Selborne L.C. which he cited. I think that it is very odd that, if they intended to disagree with him, they should not have said so and stated their reasons for doing so. The headnote of the report is clearly inaccurate and I think that the accuracy of the reports of the judgments in the Court of Appeal is open to question. In any event, the remarks of James L.J. and Baggallay L.J., if correctly reported, were clearly *obiter*.

In *Deering v. Hyndman* (1886) 18 L.R. Ir. 323 May C.J. and Johnson J. followed the observations of James L.J. and Baggallay L.J. and held that the statutory right of set off of mutual debts and credits under section 251 of the *Irish Bankrupt and Insolvent Act* 1857 was excluded. Their decision was affirmed on appeal, 18 L.R. Ir. 467. And in *Watkins v. Lindsay & Co.* (1898) 5 Mans. 25 Wright J. said, at p. 29:

> in order to prevent the set off (which in bankruptcy is automatic and not dependent on the option of the party) there must be something equivalent to a binding agreement that there shall be no set off.

He thus appears to distinguish between the exercise of an option by one party to waive his rights under the section from its exercise pursuant to an agreement. I cannot think that this is a valid distinction. Why should a creditor be unable to waive the right to set off of his own volition but able to do so if and only if he has made an agreement to do so.

The exclusion of the set off was sought to be justified in *Deering v. Hyndman*, 18 L.R. Ir. 323: 18 L.R. Ir. 467 by the application of the principle "*quilibet potest renunciare juri pro se introducto,*" but, if this principle is to be applied, it would equally apply in relation to the exercise of an option by a claimant to waive the set off.

In *Victoria Products Ltd. v. Tosh & Co. Ltd.* (1940) 165 L.T. 78 Hallett J. considered the effect of

Ex parte Fletcher, 6 Ch. D. 350. He expressed the view that it was impossible to find in the judgments of the Court of Appeal in that case "any really clear indication whether the Lords Justices would or would not have upheld the decision of the Chief Judge in Bankruptcy on the other point" (i.e. whether it is possible to contract out of the right to set off.) He thought that the true view was that expressed of Bacon C.J. and Lord Selborne L.C., and said, at p. 80:

> The object and effect of section 31 is ... that all the mutual claims of the character there contemplated should be dealt with by the process there laid down in the course of the bankruptcy or the winding up; and an attempt to leave outside that process some particular item is one which should be regarded as against the policy of the insolvency laws and, therefore, defeated.

In *In re City Life Assurance Co. Ltd.* [1926] Ch. 191 Pollock M.R. in relation to section 31 of the Act of 1914 said, at p. 203: "It is not merely permissive, but it is a direct statutory enactment that the balance only is to be claimed in bankruptcy."

In *In re Fenton, Ex parte Fenton Textile Association Ltd.* [1931] 1 Ch. 85 Lord Hanworth made similar observations.

In *Rolls Razor Ltd. v. Cox* [1967] 1 Q.B. 552 Lord Denning M.R. at p. 570 and Danckwerts L.J. at p. 573 said that parties cannot contract out of section 31, a view repeated in this case by Lord Denning M.R. and accepted by Buckley L.J.

The weight of opinion expressed in the cases to which I have referred appears to me to be in favour of the conclusion that it is not possible to contract out of section 31. The word used in that section is "shall", not "may" (the word used in section 34 in relation to a trustee's power to make a payment out of the bankrupt's property for the use of an apprentice). Looking at the Act by itself, while recognizing that it is sometimes right to interpret the word "shall" in an Act as meaning "may", I think that the terms of section 31 and of the sections that follow it show that "shall" was used in all those sections in its directory and mandatory sense, prescribing the course to be followed in the administration of the bankrupt's property.

If, contrary to my view, it is possible to contract out of section 31, the agreement made in this case did not, in my opinion, purport to do so. It was an agreement similar in some respects to that in *Ex parte Fletcher*, 6 Ch. D. 350. It was to enable the company to carry on so that they might, if they

could, sell the business as a going concern; an agreement whereby the bank agreed not to seek to secure payment of the amount owed to them for four months unless there was a material change of circumstance. It was not an agreement to provide what should happen in the event of liquidation.

In *British Guiana Bank Ltd. v. Official Receiver* (1911) 27 T.L.R. 454 the bank agreed with its customer that another current account, to be called the No. 2 account, should be opened and that the bank would not appropriate any sum in credit on that account in reduction of the overdraft on the No. 1 account without the customer's knowledge and consent. Lord Macnaghten, delivering the judgment of the board, said, at p. 454, that

> the whole question turned upon the meaning of the agreement.... In their Lordships' opinion it was an ordinary business agreement intended to be operative as long as the accounts were alive, but no longer. There was nothing in it to exclude the operation of the right of set off.

The Supreme Court of British Guiana has held that it was possible to contract out of the statutory obligation to set off in a liquidation. I do not think that the fact that Lord Macnaghten did not refer to this justifies the conclusion that he accepted their view. As he held that there was nothing in the agreement to exclude the right to set off, it was unnecessary for him to consider whether, if there had been, it would have been effective.

The agreement in the *British Guiana* case is indistinguishable from that in this case where in my view there was nothing in the agreement to exclude the right to set off. It follows that, if the debit on the No. 1 account and the credit on the No. 2 account amounted to "mutual credits, mutual debts or other mutual dealings," within the meaning to be given to those words in section 31, that section applies.

Lord Denning M.R. and Winn L.J. thought that there were not mutual dealings. Lord Denning M.R. thought [1971] 1 Q.B. 1, 36 that the arrangements were so special as to deprive them of mutuality and Winn L.J. thought, at p. 44, that the agreement provided that the balance on the frozen No. 1 account should be treated as separated out from the future mutual dealings of the bank and customer "all of which were expressly to be effected and recorded upon the No. 2 account."

I do not myself think that the arrangements made by the agreement made in April 1968 were so special as to deprive them of mutuality. They do not seem to me more special than the arrangements made in the *British Guiana Bank* case, 27 T.L.R. 454 which were said to constitute "an ordinary business agreement." The bank and the company could have achieved the same result by agreeing that the over-draft should remain at its then level for four months unless there was a material change of circumstances but that the bank would honour cheques drawn on that account if and only if amounts sufficient to cover the cheques had been credited to the account. It was, we were told, only because it was easier to secure that the overdraft did not increase that the No. 2 account was opened and the existing debit frozen.

The account which became the No. 1 account had been the company's current account. It did not change its character when the company ceased to use it; nor do I think that its character was changed when the bank and the company agreed that it should be frozen, i.e., that the company would continue not to use it, and when they agreed that no further transactions would take place on it for a limited period "save for permanent reduction" of the overdraft.

While it is true that after the agreement all future dealings save for the reduction of the debit were to take place on the No. 2 account, I do not think that that fact and the agreement itself lead to the conclusion that the debit balance was to be separated out from mutual dealings and to be regarded as not having arisen therefrom.

In my view Buckley L.J. put the matter correctly when he said [1971] 1 Q.B. 1, 49:

> The effect of the agreement was to postpone the right of the bank to require payment of the amount due on the No. 1 account during the currency of the agreement. The debit on the No. 1 account remained a debit owing by the company to the bank, although it ceased to be presently payable. Each of the obligations on either side upon the two banking accounts arose from the relationship between the parties as banker and customer.... The agreement was intended to have a temporary effect only, at the end of which the parties contemplated that both accounts would become part of their general relationship as bank and customer. In my judg-ment, notwithstanding the fact that the agree-ment had the temporary effect of precluding the bank from appropriating any credit on the No. 2 account towards discharging the debit on the No. 1 account, the dealings giving rise to the obligations were 'mutual' dealings within the meaning of section 31 and the credits were 'mu-tual credits'.

I agree with Buckley L.J. in thinking that section 31 applies and consequently that on this ground the appeal should be allowed.

The appellants also contended that, quite apart from section 31, they were entitled to set off one account against the other. That they would have been entitled, had they chosen to do so, to regard the receipt of the notice of the creditors' meetings as a material change of circumstances was not dis-puted, but in my opinion their letter of May 28, 1968, shows clearly that they did not wish to treat the agreement as terminated on that account.

Considerable argument was directed to the question [of] whether the agreement was only termi-nable by the bank by notice. It may be that, if the bank had decided to treat the agreement as brought to an end by the receipt of that notice, they would have been under an obligation to inform the com-pany of that but I do not think it necessary to express an opinion on the matter as the bank did not so decide.

The agreement was, to use the words of Lord Macnaghten in *British Guiana Bank Ltd. v. Official Receiver*, 27 T.L.R. 454, only "intended to be opera-tive as long as the accounts were alive", that is to say, while the relationship of banker and customer existed and the company was a going concern. In my opinion the agreement came to an end when the winding up resolution was passed.

Could the bank then, the agreement being at an end, combine the two accounts? For the reasons very clearly stated by Roskill J. [1971] 1 Q.B. 1, 23–25 in my opinion the answer is, Yes.

I would therefore allow the appeal on this ground also.

15 Joint Accounts

Background Reading: M.H. Ogilvie, *Bank and Customer Law in Canada*, 2d Edition (Toronto: Irwin Law, 2013) Chapter 7, pages 248–255.

(a) *Southby v. Southby*†

[RIDDELL J.:]

The plaintiff claims a declaration that half the money in an account in the Molsons Bank, West Toronto, is hers.

The account was opened by the defendant, her husband, and herself, in May, 1915, under a direction signed by both in the following terms: —

> *The Molsons Bank.*
> To the Manager West Toronto, Ont., Branch.
>
> Dear Sir: — We, the undersigned, request you to open a joint account in our names. All moneys which may be deposited by us or either of us to *the said account* are our joint property, but such moneys may be withdrawn by either one of us, or the survivor of us.
>
> Yours truly,
> Minnie Southby.
> A.H. Southby.
>
> Dated at West Toronto, Ont.,
> May 4, 1915.
>
> Memo. for Branch.
> Account opened as No. 2760.

The defendant, who had been living with the plaintiff, his wife, in Toronto, was going to Montreal in May, 1915, his wife to remain in Toronto. He had some property in Toronto, mortgages outstanding, rents to be collected, etc., and the wife was to attend to all his business in this city. As the wife says:

> He said that he would take me over to the bank and put the money in a joint account.... I had to stay here to look after (my son at school) and also look after our property here ... he told me there were certain payments ... he told me to draw any money out that I would meet at any time and told me to pay any small bills and such like.

There is no pretence that any of the money originally placed in the "joint account" was in the name of the plaintiff. She had, indeed, before May, 1915, let her husband have money from time to time; but this was money she had been able to save out of the housekeeping money which he allowed her in varying amounts for household expenses while they were living together.

The moneys she thus let him have were merged in his general account, which ultimately had by May, 1915, come to $215.62, placed to "joint account".

All subsequent deposits in the joint account were from rents collected from the defendant's property, from a mortgage belonging to the defendant, but put in his wife's name for convenience, etc. — none of the money was from the wife's earnings.

---

† (1917) 38 D.L.R. 700 (Ont. C.A.).

529

The grounds upon which the wife claims are apparently two in number: —

1. That the money she saved from money given her by her husband for housekeeping, "or to buy clothes or such like," became hers to do with as she pleased, and what she did not spend remained hers, her "housekeeping savings" were hers absolutely.
2. And in any case the placing of money in a joint account was a gift to her of half the money placed at any time in the account.

I do not think either of these contentions can be sustained. The law is quite clear — the Court will not prevent a husband from giving his wife what profits she can make out of his cows, poultry, etc., as "but a reasonable encouragement to the wife's frugality," especially where there is "no creditor of the husband to contend with:" *Slanning v. Style* (1734), 3 P.Wms. 334, especially at pp. 338, 339; but savings by her out of moneys allowed for household expenses, etc., do not become hers without his consent (unless they are living apart): *Eversley on Domestic Relations*, 2nd ed., p. 294; *Barrack v. McCulloch* (1856), 3 K.&J. 110: "Any money given to her by her husband for household purposes, or for dress, or the like ... would belong to her husband:" p. 114, *per* Page Wood V.-C. — and the same fate would attach to investments made of such moneys: *ib.*

There can be no pretence, therefore, that the plaintiff had any claim to any part of this money in law: and she must rely upon the "joint property" document.

It is of importance to understand precisely why this document was made. As has been said, the defendant was going to Montreal, leaving his wife behind in Toronto — he had made certain mortgages, upon which payments was falling due in Toronto, and the reason of making the joint account was, that the wife might draw out any money needed to make the accruing payments on the mortgages and "pay all small bills and such like." It is impossible to deduce from this any intention on the part of the husband to make a present to his wife of any part of this money. It is unnecessary to go through the cases — the result is fairly stated in *Lush on Husband and Wife*, 3rd ed., p. 211: "All the surrounding circumstances of the case should be taken into consideration to determine whether a gift or a resulting trust was intended:" and, if the conclusion is that "it was not intended to be a provision for the wife, but simply a mode of conveniently managing the husband's affairs ... it leaves the money ... still his property:" *Marshal v. Crutwell* (1875), L.R. 20 Eq. 328, at p. 331, *per* Jessel M.R.

For the strictness with which a gift of this kind must be proved, see *Mews v. Mews* (1852), 15 Beav. 529.

The case of *Everly v. Dunkley* (1912), 27 O.L.R. 414, 8 D.L.R. 839, may also be consulted: there a very similar matter was under consideration, and the like conclusion reached.

I would allow the appeal with costs here and below.

Lennox, J. agreed with Riddell, J.

Rose, J., agreed in the result.

Appeal allowed.

(b) *Marshal v. Crutwell*†

On the 12th of November, 1874, *Henry Marshal* (who had for some time previously been in failing health, and frequently unable to attend to business) called at the *London and County Bank*, where he kept his banking account. The balance standing to his credit on that day was £980 2s. 4d., and he drew a cheque for that amount, and requested the manager to open an account in the joint names of himself and his wife, and to honour any cheques drawn upon the bank either by himself or his wife. He at the same time remarked to the manager (as the manager deposed) that the balance of the account would belong to the survivor of himself and his wife.

---

† (1875), **L.R.** 20 Eq. 328. [Notes omitted.]

An account was accordingly opened by the bank in the joint names of *Marshal* and his wife. The sum of £980 2s. 4d. was placed to the credit of the account so opened, and considerable sums were afterwards paid in by *Marshal* to the credit thereof. *Marshal* never himself drew any cheques, but his wife by his direction drew cheques, which were duly honoured. The proceeds of the cheques were applied in payment of household and other expenses.

Henry Marshal died in April, 1875, having by his will appointed his wife and the Defendant *Crutwell* executrix and executor.

At his death the sum of £1225 0s. 2d. was standing to the credit of the account. His widow claimed to be entitled to this sum for his own use, and instituted this suit against *Crutwell* and the persons beneficially interested under the will to establish her right.

It did not appear that *Marshal* ever made any statement to the Plaintiff as to his intention in opening the joint account.

Mr. *Bush*, for the Plaintiff, submitted that the Plaintiff was entitled to the fund, citing *Dummer v. Pitcher*;[1] *Gosling v. Gesling*.[2]

The Master of the Rolls referred to *Fowkes v. Pascoe*.[3]

Mr. *Marcy*, for the Defendants, was not called upon.

[SIR G. JESSEL M.R.:]

The question I have to decide is one of some importance, because it involves the consideration of what is the rule of law to be followed in cases of this description. The law on the subject has been recently laid down in *Fowkes v. Pascoe*, by which I am bound, and from which I must not be understood as dissenting in any way, nor do I suggest that it does not present a rational view of the law, though I am not quite sure whether it agrees with previous decisions. As I understand it, the law is this: The mere circumstance that the name of a child or a wife is inserted on the occasion of a purchase of stock is not sufficient to rebut a resulting trust in favour of the purchaser if the surrounding circumstances lead to the conclusion that a trust was intended. Although a purchase in the name of a wife or a child, if altogether unexplained, will be deemed a gift, yet you may take surrounding circumstances into consideration, so as to say that it is a trust, not a gift. So in the case of a stranger, you may take surrounding circumstances into consideration, so as to say that a purchase in his name is a gift, not a trust.

Now in the present case the husband, being in failing health, goes to the bank and says, "Change the account from my own name into the name of myself and my wife, and I authorize you to honour the cheques of either of us." The bank manager says (but I cannot rely on loose conversations, of which he has evidently no specific recollection), that he said also, "the balance of the account will belong to the survivor." Whether he said so or not, I think is not very material, because the word "belong" is an ambiguous word, and no real conclusion can be drawn from that.

What afterwards occurred was this: — The man's health not improving he never drew a cheque. His wife drew all cheques against the account, and she applied the proceeds to household purposes, and I suppose small sums to her own use. All the sums afterward paid in by the husband were carried to the credit of the account in the joint names. Of course the theory is, that not only the sum transferred, but all the sums paid in from time to time, would go to the wife. Now, in all the cases in which a gift to the wife has been held to have been intended, the husband has retained the dominion over the fund in this sense, that the wife during the lifetime of the husband has had no power independently of him, and the husband has retained the power of revoking the gift. In transferring a sum of stock there is no obvious motive why a man should put a sum of stock into the name of himself and his wife. She cannot receive the dividends; he can and must, and it is difficult to see any motive of convenience or otherwise which should induce a man to buy a sum of shock, or transfer a sum of stock (if there is any difference between the two) in or into the names of himself and his wife, except the motive of benefitting her in case she survives. But here we have the actual fact, that the man was in such a state of health that he could not draw cheques, and the wife drew them. Looking at the fact that subsequent sums are paid in from time to time, and taking into view all the circumstances (as I understand I am bound to do), as a juryman, I think the circumstances shew that this was a mere arrangement for convenience, and that it was not intended to be a provision for the wife in the event which might happen, that at the husband's death there might be a fund standing to the credit of the banking account. I take into account the circumstance that the wife could draw upon the fund in the husband's lifetime, so that it would not necessarily be a provision for her after his death; and also the circumstances that the amount of the fund at his death must be altogether uncertain; and, having regard to the rule which is now binding on me, that I must infer from the surrounding circumstances what the nature of the transaction was, I come to the conclusion that it was not intended to be a provision for the wife, but simply a mode of conveniently managing the testator's affairs, and that it leaves the money therefore still his property.

There will be a declaration that the widow is not entitled to the fund, and the costs will come out of the estate.

(c) *Hill v. Bank of Hochelaga*†

[HARVEY C.J. (oral):]

The view I take is that where a deposit is made as this was in the name of either of two persons it is a notification that either one may deal with the funds and that the account will be subject to the control of either of them in the absence of any special directions that may be given.

In this case right at the start it was made quite clear that the amount that was deposited was on the face of it something which apparently was the property of William Hill. The statement made to the manager was that he wanted his wife's name put on the account so that she could draw out such amounts as she might require for her household needs. The conduct of the business of the account all the way through simply was such as to confirm the manager in the view of the correctness of that representation. Mr. Hill did treat the account as his. He used it for his own affairs, dealing with the company and otherwise, and Mrs. Hill checked out small amounts from time to time. If Mr. Hill had checked out the whole amount to the company, if he had transferred it before October 11 to the Kelly Coal account, I do not think there could have been any question or any fault found with the bank. When October 11 came the situation changed. Then the bank received notice the statement made in the beginning was not strictly accurate, and that Mrs. Hill claimed the whole amount of what was left. I think her memory is not to be relied on when she says that she told the bank manager anything about the half section of land in the beginning. I think she has forgotten. That did not take place. She perhaps has satisfied herself now that she did, but I do not think there is sufficient to warrant me to come to the conclusion that she is right about that, so that

the manager had no notice I think of her having any special interest in the money until October 11, but on October 11 she told him she claimed it all. I think then the bank was taking its own risks in dealing with the money thereafter in any way that might affect that claim of hers. I think there are one or two small cheques that the husband must have issued. I have forgotten just what explanation was given about that. I think the manager said he allowed Mr. Hill to issue one cheque. The cheque of $50 on October 2 must have been one of his because it does not appear to be one of those of Mrs. Hill, but beyond that Mr. Hill exercised no authority over the account itself. Then we have to consider the indebtedness of the Kelly Coal Company which was a concern that Mr. Hill was largely personally interested in and was managing, and the bank manager I have no doubt from his evidence and from what appears did place reliance on the fact that Mr. Hill had this personal account to meet obligations of the Kelly Coal Company in case they were not made by the Kelly Coal Company and to meet his own obligation under his guarantee that he gave. It appears to me in that aspect, if it happened that on October 11 Mr. Hill himself had demanded this money instead of Mrs. Hill, if no question had come between them but he had demanded the money instead of Mrs. Hill, the bank would have said that on the faith of your representations and relying on this money in this account we have advanced money to the Kelly Coal Company which is due to us and we are entitled therefore to claim from you the making good of the obligation which has been incurred by the Kelly Coal Company under your personal obligation. If that view is correct it seems to me that Mrs. Hill's position at that stage cannot be any better than his would be, and that the amount that

---

† [1921] 3 W.W.R. 430 (Alta. S.C.).

was at that time due from the Kelly Coal Company is an amount which the bank would be entitled to have set off against the moneys that are in this account now. I think that any advances after that to the Kelly Coal Company were not such advances as the bank is entitled to claim to have set off. I do not agree with the suggestion made by Mr. Ewing that they were under any obligation to make these further advances. If they had been then perhaps they might be entitled to set them off, but I do not think there is anything on the evidence disclosed which would justify the inference that the bank could not have stopped making advances if it saw fit. It did make several advances. The account shows there were several hundred dollars more advanced, and that is part of the claim they are now making; but I think they cannot succeed as to that.

As to the argument of Mr. McCaul that the plaintiff has not made out she is entitled to these moneys — she has sworn why she is entitled to them, which is evidence which would perhaps be sufficient under some circumstances, but at any rate as between her and her husband, who were the only persons who could have any interest in the money, the matter has been adjudicated as is shown by the copy of judgment put in wherein it has been held that she is entitled to the money as against her husband. Of course, one can see that an arrangement of that sort might be come to [sic] and a certain judgment might be given for the purpose of defeating the bank in its claim, but there is nothing here to warrant any suspicion of that sort. Her own evidence

I think is quite clear. I have no hesitation in accepting her evidence on that score, that the money was hers and that therefore there is not any reason for concluding that there is anything not perfectly straight-forward in the transaction.

In the result therefore I think the plaintiff ought to succeed to the extent of judgment for the amount of the moneys in the account with the accrued interest up to date less the amount of the indebtedness of the Kelly Coal Company on October 11, which appears to be from the ledger account $502.99. There will be judgment accordingly.

Mr. McCaul: I presume as we have practically succeeded in our defence of set off as at that date at any rate, if we do not get the costs, at least that no costs be given against us.

Mr. Ewing: The defendant was wrong in defending the action except as to $500. Why should they not pay the costs?

The Court: I think the costs will be in the usual way. The plaintiff succeeds, who will get costs of the action. That has been roaming through my mind, but there is no reason why costs should not go.

Mr. McCaul: The amount of costs warranted by the amount recovered under the judgment, which is under $1,000.

The Court: Yes. If you find in working it out there has been any mistake in regard to the figures, those can be checked up.

(d) *Mathews v. National Trust Co. Ltd.*†

[ROSE J.:]

The accounts with the banks were opened in September, 1921, pursuant to requests addressed to the banks respectively, signed by Mr. and Mrs. Mathews. The request addressed to the Bank of Montreal purports to express an agreement between the two depositors and the bank and an agreement by each depositor with the other that all monies deposited

may be withdrawn by either depositor and that the death of one shall not affect the right of the survivor to withdraw all the money. The request addressed to the Bank of Hamilton does not profess to witness an agreement between the two depositors; but the two join in authorizing the bank to honour the cheque of either or of the survivor. There is no statement in either document to the effect that the depositors are joint owners of the monies deposited.

---

† [1925] 4 D.L.R. 774 (Ont. S.C.).

The money deposited belonged to Mathews at the time of the deposit; there is to say, Mathews had earned it, and legally it was his, although Mrs. Mathews seems to think that she had some interest in it, inasmuch as she had helped to save it. There is no evidence of any statement made by Mathews at or before the time of the opening of the accounts as to his reason for opening them in the names of himself and his wife; but Mrs. Mathews says that at a later time he said that the money would be hers "when he was through" — "when he had passed out."

The accounts were opened some 19 months before Mathews' death. Some 5 months after they had been opened, Mathews became incapacitated through illness to sign cheques. Thereafter such cheques as were drawn against the accounts were signed by Mrs. Mathews — she does not think that she had signed any before. Most of the cheques signed by Mrs. Mathews were for small amounts for housekeeping necessities, and some of them were drawn after Mathews' death but before the defendant had obtained letters of administration. There was, however, one cheque for $1,000 in favour of Mathews' sister, which cheque Mrs. Mathews thinks she signed at her husband's request — the money being a gift to the sister.

When application was being made for letters of administration Mrs. Mathews made an affidavit in which the money on deposit was stated to be part of the estate; and after the defendants had become administrators cheques in their favour for the amounts standing at the credit of the accounts were signed by them and Mrs. Mathews. But the making of the affidavit and the signing of the cheques are of no great weight as evidence that Mathews was the sole owner of the money; Mrs. Mathews was without any advice as to her rights or as to the effect of what she was doing; she signed what was put before her; and unless it can be assumed that her mind was much more active then than it is now — and there is nothing to justify such an assumption — her acts, which in the case of a well-informed person, mentally alert, would have been important as admissions, are really no evidence at all that she believed that the money was not hers. Having regard to her appearance in the witness-box and to the fact that she was not advised as to her rights, or even, so far as appears, as to the nature or purpose of the documents that she was signing, the documents, in my opinion, can have no such effect as was given to the affidavit in *Daly v. Brown* (1907), 39 S.C.R. 122.

The law applicable to cases such as this has been discussed so fully and so recently — notably in *Re Hodgson* (1921), 67 D.L.R. 252, 50 O.L.R. 531, and *Re Reid* (1921), 64 D.L.R. 598, 50 O.L.R. 595 — that no review of the cases is desirable. It suffices to state that the rule as it is to be applied in the circumstances of this case seems to be this: — the transaction itself — the deposit by a husband in the name of himself and his wife raises a presumption of an intention to create a joint tenancy with all its incidents, including the incident of beneficial ownership by the survivor; so that the question is whether in the parol evidence as to declarations made by the person who owned the money before it was deposited or as to the circumstances or conduct of the parties or as to admissions made by the claimant or as to other relevant facts, there is sufficient to rebut the presumption, as, for instance, by leading to a finding that the deposit in the two names was merely for the convenience of the owner of the fund — a means of enabling the other person named to withdraw the money for the purposes of the true owner, much as much other person would have done if he had been given a power of attorney.

In such an inquiry as to whether there is anything to rebut the presumption raised by the deposit, a consideration of the form of the document, if any, signed at the time of the deposit may or may not be important. In the present case its importance is not very great, seeing that the requests to open accounts were on printed forms presented by the banks and were not identical, and that the plaintiff's knowledge of the effect of written instruments, is apparently slight. However, it may be repeated for what the observation is worth that in each of the documents the right of the survivor of the depositors to withdraw the fund is stated expressly; so that any evidence introduced in support of a contention that the real intent of Mathews was that the fund should continue to be his alone is in reality evidence to contradict a written document, as was pointed out by Middleton J., in *Re Hodgson*, 67 D.L.R., at p. 225. It may be remarked also that, inasmuch as the documents in this case do evidence the right of the survivor to draw cheques against the account, they are more strongly in favour of the plaintiff's contention than a document such as that used in *Re Hodgson, supra*, would have been; but, on the other hand, that the absence of a declaration, such as was contained in the document in *Re Reid*, 64 D.L.R. 598, that the monies are the joint property of the persons to whose credit they stand, deprives the plaintiff of one argument that might have been open to her if the *Reid* case form of document had been used. But, as has been stated already, my opinion is that the case is not to be decided upon any minute examination of the documents, but rather upon the effect of a transaction (in any form) by which the owner of money transfers it to the joint credit of himself and his wife, and upon the evidence, if any, which points to the conclusion that his act was not intended to produce its natural result. In the present case, such evidence seems to me to be very weak.

The affidavit and the concurrence in the withdrawal of the money by the trust company have been dealt with, and my opinion that they are to be disregarded has been stated. The signing of the cheque in favour of Mathews' sister is an equivocal act; it seems to have been at the request of Mathews, but no one says that the gift was not really decided upon by Mr. and Mrs. Mathews. The most that can be said of the signing of the cheque is that it was a recognition by the plaintiff of her husband's right [which was undeniable] to draw upon the fund. It is not equivalent to an admission that the plaintiff had not an equal right. Another bit of evidence is the evidence that, as far as is known, Mrs. Mathews did not sign any cheques while Mathews was in good health; but this is of no value; there is no suggestion but that such money as Mathews drew was applied to the purposes to which both of the spouses desired it to be applied, and no suggestion that Mrs. Mathews wanted money which Mathews did not get for her. In all this evidence there seems to me to be nothing to justify a finding that the transaction was not intended to have its natural effect; nor is there anything in the fact not hereinbefore mentioned, that Mathews gave $1,000 to his wife by his will. The testator in *Re Hodgson*, 67 D.L.R., at p. 253, gave "all moneys in the bank" to his wife subject to the payment of his debt and funeral and testamentary expenses; but this was not enough to show that he intended to charge his wife's property — her right as the surviving joint tenant — with his debts so as to put her to her election. In the present case the gift is: — "I bequeath the sum of one thousand dollars to my wife Charlotte Mathews absolutely," and

there is nothing to indicate that the testator intended that the money should come from the funds in the banks or thought that it would come from such funds.

My conclusion is that there is no rebuttal of the presumption that the plaintiff became a joint owner with her husband of all monies deposited in the banks, and, as the survivor, is entitled to the monies which came to the hands of the defendants. There will be judgment in her favour for $6,504.60. Under Mathews' will the plaintiff is entitled to the income derived from the residue of the estate. As I understand it, the money in question has been treated as part of that residue, and the plaintiff has had the interest earned by it, so that the judgment ought to be only for the amount withdrawn from the banks by the defendants.

The case does not seem to be one in which there should be an order as to costs. It is unfortunate for the plaintiff that she did not take advice as to her rights and withdraw the money from the banks instead of concurring in its payment to the administrators; but she did concur in what was done, and thereafter the administrators could not very well admit her claim; and it would hardly be right that her costs of establishing her title should be thrown upon the testator's estate. On the other hand, there would be no justification for charging the plaintiff's money with the administrators' costs of the defence of the action. Those costs, probably, will be allowed to them as part of their costs of the administration when they come to pass their accounts; but that is a matter to be determined by the Judge of the Surrogate Court when the administrators and all the beneficiaries are before him.

Perhaps it will not be deemed officious if I express a hope that Mrs. Mathews will be advised to make some settlement of her money which, while leaving the trustees free to make inroads upon the capital for her maintenance if such inroads seem to them to be necessary in her interest, will safeguard her from the consequences of injudicious disbursement — and that she will act upon the advice tendered.

Judgment for plaintiff.

(e) *Hill v. Hill*[†]

[ANGLIN J.:]

William Hill, deceased, owned $400 on deposit in the Bank of Ottawa to his credit. He procured from the bank a deposit receipt for this amount, "payable to William Hill Sr. and John R. Hill, his son, or either, or the survivor". The understanding between William Hill and his son was, that the money should remain subject to the father's control and disposition while living, and that whatever should be left at his death should then belong to the son. The father's request to the bank manager, upon which the deposit receipt issued was "to fix the money so that his son John would get it when he was done with." He told John himself that he wanted him to get the money when he (the father) was gone. He retained the deposit receipt intact in his own possession, and it was found amongst his papers at the time of his death. These facts are deposed to by the son John, who is now suing his father's personal representative for a declaration that the deposit receipt and the moneys represented by it are his property, and do not form part of the estate of his deceased father.

If the deposit receipt stood unexplained, so that I might treat its form as truly evidencing the substance of the transaction to which it owes its existence, the plaintiff's contention might be sustained upon the authority of such cases as *Payne v. Marshall* (1889), 18 O.R. 488, and *Re Ryan* (1900), 32 O.R. 224, though in both cases the circumstantial evidence that the survivor prior to the decease of his co-depositor was in fact a joint owner was much stronger than the deposit receipt taken by itself would have afford.

But, upon the plaintiff's own evidence, I find myself driven to the conclusion that the purpose of William Hill, deceased, was by this means to make a gift to his son, the plaintiff, in its nature testamentary. As such it could only be made effectually by an instrument duly executed as a will. The father retaining exclusive control and disposing power over the $400 during his lifetime, the rights of the son were intended to arise only upon and after his father's death. This is, in substance and in fact, a testamentary disposition of the money, and, as such, ineffectual.

Neither can I regard the receipt as equivalent to a voluntary settlement, reserving to the settlor a life interest with a power of revocation. See *Tompson v. Browne* (1835), 3 My.&K. 32.

I am, therefore, obliged to discuss this action.

But, inasmuch as the deceased William Hill, by what I find to be his ineffectual attempt to make a testamentary gift, created the difficulties which the present litigation removes, it will not be unfair to deal with the costs of this action as if incurred in an unsuccessful attempt to establish a testamentary document as such in similar circumstances. The costs of both parties will, therefore, be paid out of the fund in question, those of the defendant to be taxed between solicitor and client.

(f) *Re Reid*[‡]

[MEREDITH C.J.O. (MacLaren and Magee JJ.A. concurring):]

The question that has arisen is as to the obligation of the respondent Andrew Reid, who is one of the executors to account for two sums $600 and $2,690, which the appellant claims to form part of the assets of the estate and which the respondent Andrew Reid claims to be his own, and the solution of the question depends on whether or not there was a gift of

---

[†] (1904), 8 O.L.R. 710 (S.C.).
[‡] (1921), 64 D.L.R. 598 (Ont. S.C. — A.D.).

these sums by the testator, who was his son, to the respondent.

The facts as to the $2,690 are not in dispute. The son, having made up his mind to give to his father that sum, to come into his possession after the son's death, drew a cheque for it on the bank in which he had money on deposit, payable to his father at his (the son's) death. He went to his solicitors, shewed him the cheque, and asked if it was all right. The solicitor told him that that would not answer his purpose; that, if the banker learned of his death, the cheque would not be honoured, and that his best course would be to give the money to his father outright; the son then went to the bank and drew from it $2,690, which he placed on deposit to the credit of a joint account in his own name and that of his father. It was understood between them that the father was not to draw the money during the son's lifetime, and that the son, if he needed the money for himself, should be at liberty to draw what he required. The son was then ill of the disease of which he died about three weeks after, and there was little probability that the son would need to use any of the money.

It is settled law that if a man deposits money to the joint credit of himself and another who is neither his child, adopted child, nor wife, there is *prima facie* no gift, but a resulting trust for the person making the deposit; but this presumption may be rebutted, and it is clearly rebutted in the case at bar.

It is argued, however, that because of the understanding between the son and his father which I have mentioned, the gift was not complete; but I am not of that opinion.

The principle of the decision of the Court of Appeal in *Standing v. Bowring*, (1885), 31 Ch. D. 282, is, in my opinion, applicable. In that case, the plaintiff, a widow, caused $6,000 consols to be transferred into the joint names of herself and the defendant, who was her godson. She did this with the express intention that the defendant in the event of his surviving her should have the consols for his own benefit, but that she should have the dividends during her life. The plaintiff afterwards changed her mind and sought to have the stock retransferred to her, and brought a suit to compel the defendant to retransfer it. It was held that the legal title of the defendant was as a joint tenant of the stock, and that the plaintiff could not claim a retransfer on equitable grounds, the evidence clearly shewing that she did not when she made the transfer intend to make the defendant a mere trustee for her except as to the dividends. Stating his opinion, Cotton L.J., said, (p. 287): —

The rule is well settled that where there is a transfer by a person into his own name jointly with that of a person who is not his child, or his adopted child, then there is *prima facie* a resulting trust for the transfer. But that is a presumption capable of being rebutted by shewing that at the time the transferor intended a benefit to the transferee, and in the present case there is ample evidence that at the time of the transfer, and for some time previously, the plaintiff intended to confer a benefit by this transfer on her late husband's godson.... That being so, the presumption that there would be a resulting trust for her is entirely rebutted, and it must be taken here, that although she did not intend Bowring to have any right to the dividends during her lifetime, she intended to give him a beneficial interest in the stock, and that on her death, as he survived her, the legal right must prevail, and he must take the property for his own benefit.

I refer also, without quoting it, to what was said by Lindley L.J., in the same case. See also *Toronto General Trusts Corporation v. Keyes* (1907), 15 O.L.R. 30, 35, 36.

I see no difference in principle between the retention by the donor of the dividends on the consols and the retention by the son of the right to draw from the fund what, if anything, he might require to use.

The *raison d'etre* of the rule of law applied in *Standing v. Bowring* is that the right which was asserted was an equitable right, and that it could be set up against the legal right of the defendant, because the evidence established that the intention of the plaintiff was that the fund should be the godson's at her death.

In *Central Trust and Safe Deposit Co. v. Snider*, [1916] 1 A.C. 266, 35 O.L.R. 246, 25 D.L.R. 410, a somewhat similar principle was applied.

The short ground upon which I rest my judgment is that upon the death of the son the legal right to the fund became vested in the father, and that there is no ground for enforcing the equitable right which the appellant sets up, it being clear that the son's intention was that at his death the fund, or what remained of it, should belong to his father.

As to the $600 there is no question as to the right to it of the father. There was a complete gift of it.

The widow having died, there is no reason why the infants represented by Mr. Ramsey should not be substituted for her as appellants.

I would affirm the judgment of my brother Latchford and dismiss the appeal with costs.

(g) *Stefaniuk v. Toronto-Dominion Bank*†

[HAMILTON J.:]

This motion involves the question of whether the surviving owner of a joint bank account is entitled to all the moneys in the account.

The applicant and Russel Deslauriers were not married. They became engaged and started living together in the summer of 1977. On 26th May 1978 they opened a savings account. They directed that any withdrawal require both signatures. The applicant says the funds were "monies which we were saving for our wedding." Unfortunately the marriage never took place as Mr. Deslauriers was killed in a motor vehicle accident on 24th July 1978.

The bank has declined to release the money in the account until it receives a death certificate and letters probate. Although it was not represented on this motion and is satisfied to follow the court's direction, it pointed out to counsel for the applicant that in its opinion this particular account contains no right of survivorship. I have examined the documents signed on the opening of the account. The only descriptive phrase that appears is "savings account". The term "joint account" does not appear on the banking documents, but it is one chosen by the applicant and may or may not be the appropriate description in law.

In *Daly v. Brown* (1907), 39 S.C.R. 122, Davies J. stated the applicable principle at p. 131:

> In every case it is a question of intention to be gathered from the special facts and circumstances and the family relations or otherwise of the parties.

In that case a father had opened a joint account in his name and in the name of a daughter. Either could make withdrawals on the presentation of the pass book. As the father kept exclusive control of the pass book, the court found no intention to gift any of the moneys to the daughter.

In *Re Hodgson* (1921), 50 O.L.R. 531, 67 D.L.R. 252, a husband and wife opened an account in their names and directed the bank to honour cheques drawn by either of them. Although the term "survivor" was not used, it was held that there was nothing to rebut the presumption of gift. Middleton J. stated the principle at p. 254:

> Where real or personal property is voluntarily placed in the name of the owner and another there will be a resulting trust in favour of the transferor if the other is a stranger, but this presumption is changed where the other is the wife or a child. It is then presumed that the intention was to create a joint tenancy and that the survivor would take beneficially, this being the ordinary incident of the joint interest created.

In the present case there are two factors which prevent me from drawing an inference of gift, but lead me to conclude there was a resulting trust in the deceased with respect to the money deposited by him. First, each party maintained control over the account by requiring both signatures to effect a withdrawal. Secondly, the deposits were made for a specific purpose, a wedding. The purpose was frustrated by the death. Even if death had not intervened, what would have become of the money in the bank if the marriage plans had been terminated by agreement? The presumption is they would have been turned to the depositors. That inference is, in my opinion, the logical one to be drawn from the facts. There are insufficient facts to warrant a presumption of gift.

The applicant is entitled to the return of moneys deposited by her, and to her share of accumulated interest. The moneys deposited by the deceased belong to his estate.

---

† [1979] 3 W.W.R. 382 (Man. Q.B.).

(h) *McIntosh's Estate v. Kenny*†

[RIORDON J.:]

The present action brought by the Executor of the Estate of the late Helen McIntosh is one in which a claim is made for a declaration that money that was on deposit in the joint names of the defendant, Rose Kenny and her mother, the late Helen McIntosh, is an asset of the Estate. An Order is also requested that Rose Kenny pay to the plaintiff as Executor of the Estate of Helen McIntosh the monies that were on deposit in the joint bank account plus interest.

Helen McIntosh was the widow of Edward McIntosh. They were the parents of nine children. Mr. McIntosh died on October 14, 1985. On October 22, 1985, Helen McIntosh signed her last Will and Testament naming her son, Kenneth McIntosh, as her Executor. She left all her property, both real and personal, to her daughter, Rita McIntosh-Crawford.

Shortly after the death of Edward McIntosh, several members of the family advised Helen McIntosh that she should have a joint bank account with one of the members of the family. Kenneth McIntosh testified that he suggested to his mother that this should be done "in case she would be sick and bills had to be paid".

On November 4, 1985 a bank account at the Bank of Montreal, Newcastle, was opened by Helen McIntosh in the joint names of Helen McIntosh and her daughter, Rose Kenny. This account was closed and a new account also in the joint names of Helen McIntosh and Rose Kenny was opened on May 31, 1988. This transaction was completed so as to earn a higher rate of interest.

All money deposited to the joint account was that of Helen McIntosh. She declared all interest income on her tax returns and during her lifetime she alone withdrew money from the joint account.

Helen McIntosh died while on a trip with family members in the State of Maine, United States of America, on October 26, 1988. At the time she was 78 years of age. At the date of her death Helen McIntosh was the owner of a home located on Radio Street in Newcastle and also had $40,400.61 on deposit with the Bank of Montreal, Newcastle, in the joint names of herself and Rose Kenny. The only other assets included furniture, clothing and three cheques payable to Helen McIntosh that were received after her death for somewhere in the range of $850.00.

On October 27, 1988, four days prior to the funeral of Helen McIntosh and the day after her death, Rose Kenny withdrew the entire balance of the monies on joint deposit comprising $40,400.61 and deposited the money in an account in the joint names of herself and her husband.

On November 30, 1988 Kenneth McIntosh was formally appointed the Executor of the Estate of his mother by Letters Probate of that date issued by the Probate Court of New Brunswick. He had administered the Estate and paid some expenses but some accounts are outstanding and unpaid and there is insufficient cash available to pay outstanding real property taxes and for the administration of the Estate. Funeral expenses of $4,922.75 were paid by Rose Kenny with monies that she had held on joint deposit with her mother.

The present action was instituted by Kenneth McIntosh in his capacity as Executor of the Estate of his mother on December the 6, 1988 for proper administration of the Estate. He claims from Rose Kenny the balance of the monies that were on joint deposit in the names of Helen McIntosh and Rose Kenny as of October 26, 1988 and interest. He alleges that on the death of Helen McIntosh there was a resulting trust in favour of her estate.

Rose Kenny alleges that it was the intention of Helen McIntosh that the monies on joint deposit in the names of herself and her mother would become her property upon the death of Helen McIntosh and was a gift to her by her mother. She denies that there was a resulting trust in favour of the Estate.

Although Kenneth McIntosh had taken his mother to a lawyer to have her Will prepared, he was not aware that she had named him as Executor until October 27, 1988, the day after his mother's death. On that day he received a telephone call from his sister, Rita, the beneficiary named in the Will at around 3 p.m. informing him that he was the Executor of the Estate. Approximately one hour later he was called by Rose Kenny who told him

---

† (1989), 101 N.B.R. (2d) 100 at 102–15 (Q.B. T.D.).

that their mother had left her the money on deposit in the bank account and it comprised some $10,000.00. Earlier that same day, shortly after the bank had opened for business, Rose Kenny had closed the account that had been opened by her mother in their joint names and which at the time had a balance on deposit of $40,400.61.

The family members met the night before and the night after the funeral of their mother. At the time of the first meeting Kenneth McIntosh did not have a copy of his mother's Will nor was he aware of the withdrawal of funds by Rose Kenny from the joint bank account. At the second meeting he did have a copy of the Will and by that time had learned that funds had been withdrawn from the bank account by his sister, Rose. After the second meeting, which was not attended by Rose Kenny, Kenneth McIntosh called her and asked her to remit the monies that had been in the joint bank account to him as the Executor of the Estate. She refused to remit the funds and he subsequently called her on several occasions for the return of the money and she refused and actually did act in a rude manner, hanging up the telephone.

Helen McIntosh was a quiet person who did not discuss her business matters with anyone. When her husband was living, he looked after her and helped her around the house. After his death all the children helped her in the various household chores.

Compared to the other children of the family Rita McIntosh-Crawford, the beneficiary named in the Will was disadvantaged. Rita has a physical handicap which has persisted since birth. She is unable to lift her left arm. She has had marital problems, is separated from her husband and divorced. She has the custody of her five children and has not benefitted from any child support payments from her former husband. Even while she lived with her husband, he did not provide adequate support for her and her five young children and family members, especially her parents, assisted her regularly. Rita has had to rely on social assistance benefits for herself and her children and of course family members have always helped to provide for her and the children. It was necessary for her and her children to live with her parents from time to time and her oldest daughter lived with her grandparents for long periods of time.

Other than the special attention given to Rita and her children because of their particular circumstances, Helen and Edward McIntosh wanted to and tried to treat each of their children equally. Rita's sister, Winifred McIvor, testified that all of

her brothers and sisters were financially independent except Rita.

The only issue is to determine whether the monies that were on deposit in the joint names of Helen McIntosh and Rose Kenny at the date of her death of Mrs. McIntosh are an asset of the Estate of Helen McIntosh or are the property of Rose Kenny.

In the determination of the answer to this question I do not think it is necessary to give weight to the joint account form signed by Helen McIntosh and Rose Kenny with the Bank of Montreal to determine the relationship between Mrs. McIntosh and Mrs. Kenny. The form contract that was completed at the time of the opening of the joint bank account sets out obligations and rights between the Bank and its customers. The agreement provides in part as follows:

Joint Account Agreement

We having opened a deposit account with the Bank in our joint names, hereby jointly and severally agree with the Bank and with each other that all monies from time to time deposited to the said account, and interest, may be withdrawn by any one of us or his or her attorney or agent and each of us hereby irrevocably authorizes the said Bank to from time to time accept as a sufficient acquittance for any amounts withdrawn from said account, any receipt, cheque or other instrument signed by any one or more of us, his, her or their agents, without any further signature or consent of the other or others of us thereto.

*It is further agreed that the Bank is hereby authorized to credit the said account with all monies paid to the Bank (i) at the branch of account or (ii) at any branch other than the branch of account for the credit of any one or more of us, the proceeds of any orders or promises for the payment of money, of bonds, debentures, coupons or other securities signed by or drawn by or payable to or the property of, or received by the said Bank (i) at the branch of account or (ii) at any branch other than the branch of account for the credit of us or any one or more of us, and to endorse any of such instruments on behalf of us or any one or more of them. It is agreed that the Bank is relieved from all liability for so doing.

**The death of one or more of us shall in no way affect the right of the survivors, or any one of them, to withdraw all monies deposited in the said account as aforesaid.

A similar conclusion was reached by the Supreme Court of Canada in the case of *Re Mail-*

man, [1941] S.C.R. 368; [1941] 3 D.L.R. 449. At pages 455 and 456 of the latter report the following appears:

> As to the agreement itself, it is to be observed in the first place that it is in the form of a letter addressed to the bank on a closely printed form, which apparently was intended for general use without alteration in the various branches of the bank on the opening of any and every joint deposit account, whether in the names of two or three or more persons and regardless of any private agreement which may have taken place between the parties named in any particular deposit account. It contains no reference, express or implied, to the ownership of the money when deposited or to any previous agreement having been entered into between the parties concerning the opening of the account. It begins merely with the statement that 'The undersigned, having opened a deposit account with you in their joint names, *hereby agree with you and with each other that*,' etc. For my part I cannot see how these words can be taken as necessarily implying that there was or had been any other agreement with the bank or between the signatories than that which is embodied in the document itself. It does not even indicate the relationship of the parties to the account. Its sole purpose and effect, as I read it, is to authorize the bank to accept from time to time as a sufficient acquittance for any amounts withdrawn from the deposit account any receipt, cheque or document signed by either. That it was intended to have no particular reference to any private arrangement or understanding between the two signatories seems to me to be conclusively shown by the last paragraph, *viz.*: 'That the death of one or more of the undersigned shall in no way affect the right of the *survivors*, or any one of them to withdraw all moneys deposited in said account as aforesaid.' It is this particular paragraph upon which the appellant's counsel chiefly relied to support his claim that Mrs. Mailman intended to create a joint tenancy in favour of her husband. It will be noticed, however, that the paragraph merely provides that the death of one of the signatories shall not *affect the right* of the survivors or any one of them to *withdraw* the moneys deposited in the account, and that it in no way purports to provide that if any when the surviving signatory does withdraw such moneys he or she shall be deemed to do so as sole owner thereof. It merely preserves the right of either party, in the event of the death of the other, to withdraw all moneys deposited in the account in the same way as he or she might have done during the lifetime of both.
>
> No doubt had the letter of instructions to the bank not contained this provision, the appel-lant's right to withdraw any money from the deposit account would have ended with his wife's death. In that event the bank could not safely have accepted any cheque or order made by the appellant against the deposit moneys in its hands without proof that he was entitled to receive the outstanding balance, either as administrator of his intestate wife's estate or in his own right. That seems to me to be the only consistent explanation of the inclusion in the bank's general printed form of joint deposit account agreements of the particular provision relied on by the appellant, i.e., that it is a provision inserted in all its joint deposit agreements for the bank's own protection and convenience, and having no reference to the rights of the parties named as between themselves other than the right of each to draw upon the deposit account in the manner stated.

There are many decided cases with similar factual situations as the present. In the case of *Re Mailman (supra)* it was decided that there is a legal presumption in such cases that there was no intention on the part of the owner to divest herself of exclusive ownership and control of the joint deposit and to make her husband a joint tenant. Such a presumption is rebuttable evidence.

Another Supreme Court of Canada case that considered the matter of joint accounts is that of *Niles v. Lake*, [1947] S.C.R. 291; [1947] 2 D.L.R. 248. The headnote of the latter report is as follows:

> Where A, without any previous discussion of the matter, decided to open a joint account with a sister B, and they both executed the standard bank form for joint accounts under seal and A advanced all the money that went into the account and operated it alone, *held*, although B, as survivor, became legal owner of the account, she held it on resulting trust for A's estate since there was no evidence to show that B was to get any beneficial interest. The bank form, although it may have indicated a joint tenancy by way of beneficial interest, merely defined the relationship between the holders of the account and the bank and, even though it was under seal, it could not be deemed decisive as to the relationship between A and B *inter se*.

At page 254 and 255 of that report Taschereau J., said:

> The law is well settled, I think, that when a person transfers his own money into his own name jointly with that of another person, except in cases with which we are not concerned, then there is *prima facie* a resulting trust for the transferor. This presumption, of course, is a pre-

sumption of law which is rebuttable by oral or written evidence or other circumstances tending to show there was in fact an intention of giving beneficially to the transferee.

At page 262 Rand J., said:

> To hold otherwise would, as the result of the bank's requirement, deny to a depositor the privilege of opening a joint account for the purpose of convenience: that, in other words, the bank would dictate the terms of beneficial ownership, irrelevant to its protection, as a condition of that form of accommodation. The common sense of the situation is confirmed by the language of the agreement in negativing such a construction.
>
> In *Re Mailman*, [1941] 3 D.L.R. 449 at p. 456, S.C.R. 368 at p. 378, Crocket J., says: 'Even if one were disposed to regard it as an agreement between the parties themselves as to their respective rights concerning the deposit fund, those rights as already appears, are definitely restricted to the authority of each to withdraw money from the account in the manner stated in the first paragraph. This does not itself necessarily imply the right of the appellant to take the money as his own.' There was no clause declaring the property to be joint, but what is significant is the evident hesitation to treat the terms as defining the interests of the depositors *inter se*, as intended to do more than specify the basis of deposit from the standpoint of the bank.

At page 264 Kellock J., said:

> So far as the evidence in the case at bar goes there is no evidence that the deceased intended the beneficial interest to go to the respondent. As to the language in the document, which it is contended has that effect, the deceased was ignorant of this as she had never read it. In my opinion the document is to be construed as not intended to affect the beneficial title as between the sisters at all but merely to facilitate the bank in its dealing with the account.

A third Supreme Court of Canada decision that is similar to the facts before me in this case is that of *Edwards v. Bradley* (1957), 9 D.L.R. (2d) 673. In that case an elderly widowed mother transferred her bank account into the joint names of her and a married daughter. It was held that no presumption of advancement arose and that there was the ordinary presumption of a resulting trust. At pages 677 and 678 Cartwright J., said:

> Assuming that on the death of the late Alice Maud Edwards the respondent had the legal right to withdraw the money on deposit in the joint bank account and on making the with-

drawal would have the legal title to the money withdrawn, the question is whether she is beneficially entitled to that money or holds it in trust for her mother's personal representative.

As all the moneys deposited in the account were the sole property of the mother the daughter would *prima facie* hold the fund to which she had the legal title on a resulting trust for the mother's estate. In *Dyer v. Dyer*, 2 *White & Tudor's Leading Cases in Equity*, 9th ed. 749 at pp. 750–51, Eyre C.B., says:

> It is the established doctrine of a Court of equity, that this resulting trust *may be rebutted* by circumstances in evidence.
>
> The cases go one step further and prove that the *circumstance of one or more of the nominees being a child or children of the purchaser, is to operate by rebutting the resulting trust*; and it has been determined in so many cases that the nominee being a child shall have such operation as a circumstance of evidence, that we should be distributing land-marks if we suffered either of these propositions to be called in question, namely, that such circumstance shall rebut the resulting trust, and that it shall do so as a circumstance of evidence.... Considering it as a circumstance of evidence, there must be, of course, evidence admitted on the other side.

Dyer v. Dyer was a case of father and son. In my opinion the result of the decisions in cases of mother and child is correctly summarized in the following passage in *Halsbury's Laws of England*, 3rd ed., vol. 18, p. 387: 'There is no presumption of a gift where the purchase of investment is made by a mother, even though living apart from her husband, or a widow, in the name of her child or in the joint names of herself and her child, though in the case of a widowed mother very little evidence to prove the intention of a gift is required.'

Giving full effect to the existence of the relationship of mother and daughter, as a circumstance of evidence, I agree with the Chief Justice and my brother Rand that the proper inference to be drawn from all the evidence in the case at bar is that it has not been shown that the mother intended to pass the beneficial interest to the respondent either in her lifetime or on her death. It necessarily results from this finding of fact that the appeal succeeds.

The law dealing with joint accounts is also dealt with in detail in the cases of *Bourque v. Landry* (1936), 10 M.P.R. 108; *Re Dolan Estate* (1947), 21 M.P.R. 213; *Re Sourour Estate* (1987), 72 N.B.R. (2d) 168; 183 A.P.R. 168; *Slater Estate v. Bartlett et al.* (1987), 73 N.B.R. (2d) 119; 184 A.P.R. 119, and *Estate of Albert W. Alldritt v. Everett* (1970), 2 N.B.R. (2d) 256.

In my opinion the facts in the present case are distinguishable from the facts in the cases of *Estate of Albert W. Alldritt v. Everett* (*supra*) and *Bourque v. Landry* (*supra*).

The funds on deposit belonged to Helen McIntosh, no control of her funds was ever exercised by Rose Kenny prior to the death of her mother. The joint account was opened shortly after the death of the husband of Helen McIntosh. The account was opened on suggestion from family members that it should be done for her benefit in the event that she would become incapacitated. The joint account, in my opinion, was one of convenience for Mrs. Helen McIntosh. The Will of Helen McIntosh was made at about the same time as the joint account was opened. The Will, which is dated October 22, 1985, could have clearly specified a bequest of money to Rose Kenny if that was the intention of Mrs. Helen McIntosh. The evidence, in my view, does not show an intention to make a gift to Rose Kenny and does not rebut the presumption of a resulting trust in favour of the Estate of Helen McIntosh. The evidence does not satisfy me that Helen McIntosh intended the beneficial interest of the joint bank account to go to Rose Kenny.

I therefore conclude that the money withdrawn from the joint account by Rose Kenny on October 27, 1988, comprising $40,400.61, belongs to the Estate of Helen McIntosh. The defendant must account for these funds and also for interest on the money at the rate paid by the Bank of Montreal on the account from which they were withdrawn. The amount of $40,400.61 together with accumulated interest less the funeral expenses paid by Rose Kenny are to be forthwith paid to Kenneth McIntosh, the Executor of the Estate of Helen McIntosh.

I direct that the costs of each party be payable by the Estate of Helen McIntosh. I fix the costs of the plaintiff at $4,125.00 plus disbursements and those of the defendant at $1,500.00 plus disbursements.

Judgment for plaintiff.

(i) *Shaw v. MacKenzie Estate*†

[MacDONNELL J.:]

This proceeding was commenced by originating notice (Action) issued on the 7th day of November, 1991. The plaintiff sought a declaration that she was the beneficial owner of funds originally in the name of Mary Jane MacKenzie alone, and later transferred to a joint bank account in the name of Mary Jane MacKenzie, and the plaintiff. The funds were later transferred into an account in the name of the plaintiff alone. At the time the action commenced, Central Guaranty Trust Company had been appointed guardian of the estate of Mary Jane MacKenzie, an incompetent person. Central Guaranty Trust Company claimed the funds in the joint account on behalf of the incompetent, Mary Jane MacKenzie.

A defence was filed by Central Guaranty Trust Company, as guardian in the estate of Mary Jane MacKenzie, on December 3rd, 1991.

Mary Jane MacKenzie died on June 6th, 1993. Probate of her Last Will and Testament was granted to Central Guaranty Trust Company as sole executor and trustee, by the Court of Probate, at Pictou, N.S., on June 30th, 1993.

By virtue of s. 4(1) of the *TD Trust Company Act*, 1993, being c. 13 of the Statutes of Nova Scotia, 1993, TD Trust Company was substituted in the place and stead of Central Guaranty Trust Company in respect of every trust, deed, will, codicil or other testamentary document.

By Consent Order, the heading of this action was amended to show the Estate of Mary Jane MacKenzie as a deceased person, defended by TD Trust Company, executor and trustee of the estate of the late Mary Jane MacKenzie.

An order of this court directed that the solicitor for the estate of Mary Jane MacKenzie be appointed to represent the interests of the estate, and of the

---

† (1994), 131 N.S.R. (2d) and 371 A.P.R. 118 at 119–29 (N.S.S.C.).

residuary legatee under the Last Will and Testament of Mary Jane MacKenzie. As the residuary legatee in the estate of Mary Jane MacKenzie was named as "The Cancer Fund of Nova Scotia", and upon the court being satisfied that no such entity as "The Cancer Fund of Nova Scotia" existed, it was ordered that notice of the proceeding be given to both the Canadian Cancer Society, Nova Scotia Division, and to the Nova Scotia Cancer Centre, and to all the next-of-kin of the deceased, Mary Jane MacKenzie.

The issues before the court are:

- Did Mary Jane MacKenzie make a valid gift to Marion Shaw when her bank account at the Bank of Nova Scotia, New Glasgow, was made joint with Marion Shaw?
- If Mary Jane MacKenzie made a valid gift of the joint bank account to Marion Shaw, what is the nature of the gift, i.e., was it an inter vivos gift or was it a *donatio mortis causa* gift?
- Does s. 45 of the *Evidence Act*, R.S.N.S. 1989, c. 154, have any application to this action?

Marion Shaw, the plaintiff, is a 73-year-old widow, who resides at Scotsburn, Pictou County, N.S. She had been married for some 46 years, and is the mother of five children.

Mrs. Shaw gave evidence to the effect that she was a second cousin of Mary Jane MacKenzie, commonly known and hereinafter referred to as "Janie". There are about 31 other second cousins of Janie in the province; there were no closer relatives living at the relevant times. Janie was born in 1900, at Dalhousie Mountain, Pictou County, and had a brother, Alexander, and a sister, Margaret, both predeceased her. There was approximately one and a half years difference in age between Margaret and Janie. Both sisters taught school in Westville, N.S. from the time they were 18 years of age to age 65, during which period they resided in Westville. After their retirement, they resided in an apartment in New Glasgow for seven or eight years. In February 1985, the MacKenzie sisters moved to the Edward Mortimer Place, a home for special care, in the Town of Pictou, N.S. Approximately a month later, Margaret died.

After Mrs. Shaw's parents died in 1976 and 1977, the MacKenzie sisters relied on her to do a great many things for them. In 1984, Janie became quite ill, and Margaret asked Mrs. Shaw to take care of the sisters. She moved in with them, and looked after their needs, prepared their food, both were incontinent, looked after their laundry, changed their bedding, and all the other chores required to take care of two old ladies. She was paid $35 a day for these services. It is to be noted that this was a 24 hour day she was required to be on duty.

Also during the period that Mrs. Shaw looked after Margaret and Janie's personal need prior to their moving to the Edward Mortimer Home, she, at their request, attended to their banking, investments, and all other financial matters. On September 27th, 1984, Janie gave Mrs. Shaw a power of attorney, drafted by a local barrister. As well, on the same date she was given a power of attorney, on the usual bank form, also executed by Janie. Following Margaret's death, in March of 1985, Janie was very upset and unable to walk. As Mrs. Shaw was going to British Columbia for a trip, she arranged with Central Trust Company to look after Janie's financial affairs. She delivered all of Janie's securities to Central Trust Company, and received a receipt for same.

Mrs. Shaw returned home from her visit to British Columbia in August, 1985, to find Janie in much improved health. She was not completely happy with the manner in which Central Trust Company was looking after her affairs, however, after discussion with Mrs. Shaw she agreed that they would continue to attend to her financial matters.

In the month of February 1986, Janie indicated that she wished to make some changes to her will, and arranged for James Bailey, of Central Trust Company, to attend at the Edward Mortimer Home. She also wished Mrs. Shaw to be present at this meeting. She directed that a codicil to her will be drafted, included in the changes in her will was a bequest of $20,000 to Mrs. Shaw, to replace a bequest of $10,000 in the original will. One or two other small changes were made to the will, and the residuary legatee was changed to "The Cancer Fund of Nova Scotia", deleting the Oddfellows Home, which in the original will was entitled to two thirds of the residue.

On the same afternoon, after Mr. Bailey had left, Janie discussed the changes with Mrs. Shaw. She indicated that she was afraid she had not provided sufficiently for Mrs. Shaw in the new codicil, and told her that she wished to make a gift to Mrs. Shaw of her bank account in the Bank of Nova Scotia, at New Glasgow. Mrs. Shaw stated that although no stipulations were made by Janie, she promised that she would not use the bank account while Janie was alive. Included in the exhibits presented to the court was a copy of a joint deposit agreement dated February 14th, 1986, signed by both Janie and Mrs. Shaw. Bank records produced in evidence showed that the balance in the account on February 11th, 1986, and transferred to the joint account was $10,227.85. This account had originally been opened by Janie on September 25th, 1974. All parties agree that all the funds in this account were deposited by or on the behalf of Janie.

At or about this time an account was opened at the Royal Bank of Canada, in Pictou, in the joint names of Janie and Mrs. Shaw. All Janie's pension cheques were deposited at the Royal Bank of Canada account, and her expenses paid from this account.

On the advice of Mrs. Shaw, the Bank of Nova Scotia in New Glasgow account was changed on April 10, 1989, to a high interest bearing account. At this time a new signature card and joint deposit agreement were signed both by Janie and Mrs. Shaw. The reason for this change being a much better interest rate was paid on this type of account by the bank. The new joint account No. 9021523 opening balance of $19,650.46.

In October 1990, Central Guaranty Trust Company commenced proceedings to have a guardian appointed for the person and the estate of Mary Jane MacKenzie, pursuant to the *Incompetent Persons Act*. An order was issued by the court on July, 18, 1991, appointing Central Guaranty Trust Company as guardian of the financial estate, and the plaintiff, Marion Shaw, as guardian of the person of Mary Jane MacKenzie.

On the 26th day of November, 1990, Mrs. Shaw transferred $25,610.78 from the joint account at the Bank of Nova Scotia, in New Glasgow, leaving $100 in the account, and opened a new account in her name alone, being account number 9029826. This account was frozen by court order issued on November 29th, 1991, and the amount together with accrued interest, remains in the name of the plaintiff.

After Central Guaranty Trust was appointed guardian of the estate of Mary Jane MacKenzie, an incompetent person, the joint account at the Royal Bank, in Pictou, in the amount of $29,788.76 was transferred to the Trust Company, as guardian of the estate. It was at this time the Trust Company demanded the funds in the joint account in the Bank of Nova Scotia, thus causing this action.

Janie died on June 7th, 1993. Probate of her Last Will and Testament with codicils attached, was granted to Central Guaranty Trust Company, and letters testamentary issued on June 30th, 1993, by the Registrar of Probate for the County of Pictou. The inventory and valuation of the property of the estate of Mary Jane MacKenzie, dated September 21st, 1993, filed with the Probate Court, indicates a value of $579,347.84, not including the bank account at issue in this action. The inventory indicates that all of the assets of Janie's estate were stocks, bonds, and bank accounts.

Mrs. Shaw gave evidence that she had discussed the bequests in Janie's will, and the gift of the bank account with close friend Alice Moffatt. This was shortly after being advised by Janie that she wished the joint account to be hers as a gift.

Mrs. Shaw also discussed the contents of Janie's will and the gift of the joint account with her daughter, Cheryl Dyack, during the period of June to October 1986, when her daughter was visiting with her.

Her evidence was to the effect that Central Guaranty Trust Company had been made aware that the joint account in the Bank of Nova Scotia, New Glasgow, had been a gift to her from Janie. She was requested by the Halifax solicitor for the Trust Company to turn both the New Glasgow and Pictou accounts over to Central Guaranty Trust Company, as guardian of Mary Jane MacKenzie, an incompetent person, however she was not prepared to turn over the bank account at the Bank of Nova Scotia, as she considered this had been a gift to her, and was not part of Janie's assets. She had no problem in transferring the Pictou account to the Trust Company.

Alice Moffatt died during 1994, and with consent of both Counsel, her evidence given at an examination for discovery on September 1st, 1993, was admitted into evidence.

Cheryl Dyack is a registered nurse, married to a doctor, who has practiced since 1979 in the United Arab Emirates, or Saudi Arabia, except for two years in Nova Scotia. At the time of the trial, Mrs. Dyack was residing in the United Arab Emirates, and with consent of counsel, her evidence given at an examination for discovery on September 1st, 1993, was admitted as part of the record.

Alice Anderson Moffatt, hereinafter called "Moffatt", had lived in Scotsburn, Pictou County, for some 27 years, and was 60 years old at the time of the discovery evidence.

Her evidence was to the effect that she had known Mrs. Shaw for over 25 years, and they were close neighbours and friends. She saw Mrs. Shaw almost on a daily basis, and weather permitting, they would take long walks. She also had met Janie MacKenzie on several occasions. She stated that Mrs. Shaw looked after Janie, attending to all of her business, including the banking. Mrs. Moffatt gave evidence as to a conversation she had with Mrs. Shaw some time after Margaret MacKenzie died, but some years before Janie died, the transcript of this evidence reads:

Q. Alright, and now I want to.... I want to ask you about a conversation that you say you had with Marion Shaw one day, when you were out walking, about Janie and about the joint bank account and about her will.

A. Oh yes.

Q. Okay, now that we've got you located on the subject matter, I want you to tell, in your own words, to Mr. MacDonald, what was said by Marion Shaw to you on those subjects?

A. I don't think ... it didn't sort of ... Marion didn't specifically start to tell me about this thing. We were talking about the Oddfellows Home, since my husband is an Oddfellow and she had mentioned that Janie had planned to leave a substantial amount of her funds or her money to the Oddfellows Home but then had recently changed her will because it was now a government-run organization or something and so the conversation sort of just went from there about....

Q. Okay, now I just want to ask you about whether ... whether she mentioned any other changes that were made in the will at that time?

A. Well she had mentioned about ... as I say, we talked about everything so she had mentioned about bequests and all the different bequests that Janie was going to leave, obviously, she was an old lady, to ... to all these cousins.... Marion's cousins.... Marion and her cousins and she felt that she would like to do something ... that Janie had said she wanted to do something extra for Marion.

Q. And what was the something extra?

A. And she had mentioned about a joint bank account that had been formed....

Q. Alright, and....

A. And it was, you know, in the way of a gift for Marion, as an extra because she was ... you know, she ... well she did so much for her. It was just a thank you ... in the form of a thank you.

Q. Alright, and you don't have any problem recollecting that conversation?

A. Oh no. No.

Mrs. Moffatt confirmed that at the time of the conversation with Mrs. Shaw regarding the bank account, that Janie was completely competent in every regard.

Carol Ann Dyack, hereinafter called Dyack, is the daughter of Marion Shaw. She is married to a medical doctor, who worked almost exclusively in the Middle East from 1979. Dyack is a registered nurse,

who has since 1979 worked in various countries in the Middle East, including Saudi Arabia and the United Arab Emirates. She knew both MacKenzie sisters quite well, and had visited them with her mother when they lived in New Glasgow, and also when she was home she would visit with her mother at the Edward Mortimer guest home in Pictou. Her mother visited Janie on a daily basis. She gave evidence of returning to Canada in June of 1986, and remaining in Canada until November of the same year. A transcript of Dyack's evidence as to conversations with her mother during that period reads:

Q. Alright, and did you, during the period of time you were home, ever have occasion to discuss with your mother anything that had taken place between your mother and Janie?

A. Yes.

Q. I want you to tell us about that.

A. She had told me that she had signed ... she had....

Q. First of all, let's determine who she is?

A. She ... my mother had told me that she and Janie had a joint bank account in the bank of.... I believe it was the Bank of Nova Scotia.

Q. Alright, and did she tell you anything about how that joint bank account came to be set up?

A. Yeah, she said that Janie wanted to give her a gift. She said she had ... also had given money ... a bequest to my mother in her will but my mother had been so kind to her that she wanted to thank her and she gave this as a gift to her.

Q. Okay, and when was it that you mother was to obtain this gift?

A. My understanding that she was to obtain this gift upon Janie's death.

Q. Okay, and I want you to ... I want you to tell me about whether you ever had any idea of the amount of money that was in the joint bank account?

A. It was in the thousands.

Dyack also gave evidence as to residing in Nova Scotia from October 1987, to October 1989, whilst her husband was employed at the Aberdeen Hospital. There were further discussions with her mother, Mrs. Shaw, during that period about the bequest under Janie's will, and the gift of the joint bank account. Dyack was present when the bank account was transferred to a higher interest account in the month of April 1989. Dyack signed as a witness to Janie's signature.

Counsel for both parties have referred me to a great many authorities governing the situation before the court, including *Keddy v. McGill* (1991), 106 N.S.R. (2d) 306; 288 A.P.R. 306 (T.D.); *Levy v. Levy Estate* (1981), 50 N.S.R. (2d) 14; 98 A.P.R. 14 (T.D.); *Adshade v. Adshade* (1984), 67 N.S.R. (2d) 83; 155 A.P.R. 83 (T.D.); *Johnson v. Nova Scotia Trust Co. et al.* (1973), 6 N.S.R. (2d) 88 (C.A.); *Samson Estate v. Tanner* (1984), 66 N.S.R. (2d) 119; 152 A.P.R. 119 (C.A.); *Niles v. Lake*, [1947] S.C.R. 291; *MacCarthy, Re* (1970), 16 D.L.R. (3d) 72 (N.S. Prob Ct.); *Central Trust Co. v. West* (1985), unreported, S.H. No. 511115 and *Fenton Estate, Re* (1977), 26 N.S.R.(2d) 662; 40 A.P.R. 662 (T.D.). I have reviewed all these cases, some of which are relevant to the issues before the court.

Counsel for both parties are in general agreement as to the relevant law governing joint bank accounts. There is no question raised by either counsel as to the competency of Janie at the time the bank account was made joint, in 1986, or to the fact that the sole source of the funds in the joint account was from Janie.

Counsel differ as to the corroborative value of the evidence, and to the application of s. 45 of the *Evidence Act* to the facts before the court.

The Ontario Court of Appeal considered a set of facts very similar to those before this court in *Edwards v. Bradley* (1956), 2 D.L.R. (2d) 382, where MacKay J.A., at 386, stated:

> With respect to the question whether the gift fails as being an attempted testamentary disposition, and therefore invalid because it does not comply with the provisions of the *Wills Act*, I think the legal effect of establishing a joint bank account, in the circumstances that exist in this case, is as follows: Where A deposits money in a joint account in the names of himself and B the legal title to the money vests in the bank and the relationship between the bank and the depositor is that of debtor and creditor. The right of the depositor is the right to withdraw or demand payment of the money from the bank. It is a chose in action that may be assigned and by the terms of the joint deposit agreement with the bank, signed by both A and B, A assigns the legal right to withdraw the money to himself and B jointly, with the right to the survivor to withdraw the balance in the event of the death of A or B. The right of survivorship exists independently of any agreement in the case of joint ownership of personal property. Choses in action not yet in existence may be assigned: *Tailby v. The Official Receiver* (1888), 13 App. Cas. 523, so

> that the agreement operates as an immediate assignment of the legal right to withdraw any subsequent deposits that may be made in the joint account. The title to the chose in action being vested in A and B jointly on the execution of the agreement with the bank, each, under the terms of the agreement, has a legal right to withdraw the money during their joint lives and the survivor has the legal right to withdraw on the death of the other. B's legal title cannot be divested except with his consent or by his dying before A, although A may defeat B's title or interest by drawing all the money out of the account. *Because of the application of the equitable doctrine of resulting trusts, the beneficial interest in the money does not necessarily follow the legal title to the right to withdraw or demand payment. Whether B takes the beneficial interest as well as the legal title, either during their joint lives or on the death of A, or both, depends on A's intention. His intention is to be determined from all the circumstances of the case, after applying the appropriate presumptions and considering the evidence.* The legal right to take the balance in the account if A predeceases him being vested in B on the opening of the account, it cannot be the subject of a testamentary disposition. If A's intention was that B should also have the beneficial interest, B already has the legal title and there is nothing further to be done to complete the gift of the beneficial interest. If A's intention was that B should not take the beneficial interest, it belongs to A or his estate and he in not attempting to dispose of it by means of the joint account. In either event B has the legal title and the only question that can arise on A's death is whether B is entitled to keep any money that may be in the account on A's death or whether he holds it as trustee under a resulting trust for A's estate. [Emphasis added.]

The Supreme Court of Canada dealt with the question of a joint account in *Lillian Niles et al. v. Blanche V. Lake, supra*, where Taschereau J., at p. 300 stated:

> The law is well settled, I think, that when a person transfers his own money into his own name jointly with that of another person, except in cases with which we are not concerned, then there is prima facie a resulting trust for the transferor. This presumption, of course, is a presumption of law which is rebuttable by oral or written evidence or other circumstances tending to show there was in fact an intention of giving beneficially to the transferee.

Section 45 of the *Evidence Act*, R.S.N.S. 1989, c. 154 reads:

45. On the trial of any action, matter or proceeding in any court, the parties thereto, and the persons in whose behalf any such action, matter or proceeding is brought or instituted, or opposed, or defended, and the husbands and wives of such parties and persons, shall, except as hereinafter provided, be competent and compellable to give evidence, according to the practice of the court, on behalf of either or any of the parties to the action, matter or proceeding, provided that in any action or proceeding in any court, by or against the heirs, executors, administrators or assigns of a deceased person, an opposite or interested party to the action shall not obtain a verdict, judgment, award or decision therein on his own testimony, or that of his wife, or of both of them, with respect to any dealing, transaction or agreement with the deceased, or with respect to any act, statement, acknowledgement or admission of the deceased, unless such testimony is corroborated by other material evidence. R.S., c. 94, s. 42.

On behalf of Mrs. Shaw, counsel submits that s. 45 of the *Evidence Act* has no relevance to the present action, as the triggering condition for the application of the said section is the commencement of a proceeding "against the heirs, executors, administrators or assigns of a deceased person." As the present proceeding was commenced against the estate of Mary Jane MacKenzie, an incompetent person, by the plaintiff, and as Mary Jane MacKenzie was still alive at that time, then the section does not apply.

On behalf of the defendant, it is submitted that the relevant date to be looked at is the trial of the action, rather than when the proceeding was commenced, and as at the trial of the action of Mary Jane MacKenzie was deceased, the section must be applied.

I find that s. 45 of the *Evidence Act* becomes relevant if at the time of trial the party against whom the action is taken is dead, thus in the present case, it is necessary that Mrs. Shaw's evidence be corroborated.

The common law in dealing with gifts to a deceased person is set out in *Halsbury's Laws of England* (3rd ed., 1955), vol. 18, at p. 371, where it states:

A gift alleged to have been made by a deceased person cannot, as a general rule, be established without some corroboration. In some cases the judges have definitely stated that the court cannot act on the unsupported testimony of a person in his own favour, but there is now no hard and fast rule that the evidence of the alleged donee must be disbelieved if uncorroborated. It must be examined with scrupulous care, even with suspicion, but if it brings conviction to the tribunal which has to try the case that conviction will be acted on.

In *Johnson v. Nova Scotia Trust Co. et al.*, Coffin J.A., in delivering the judgment of the Nova Scotia Supreme Court, Appeal Division, and reviewing the question of corroboration required by s. 42 (now s. 45) of the *Evidence Act*, stated at p. 105:

In *Ryan v. Whitton*, [1963] 1 O.R. p. 97, Gale J., was considering s. 14 of the Ontario *Evidence Act*, which reads as follows:

14. In an action by or against the heirs, next of kin, executors, administrators or assigns of a deceased person, an opposite or interested party shall not obtain a verdict, judgment or decision on his own evidence, in respect of any matter occurring before the death of the deceased person, unless such evidence is corroborated by some other material evidence.

He made the comment that it was apparent the purpose of the section was to discourage dishonest or ill-founded claims against estates and quoted Mr. Justice Anglin, as he then was, in *McKean v. Black* (1921), 68 D.L.R. 34, 62 S.C.R. 290, and referred with approval to *Radford v. Macdonald* (1891), 18 O.A.R. 167, with the words at p. 46 D.L.R., p. 308 S.C.R.

... all that the statute requires is that the evidence to be corroborated shall be "strengthened by some evidence which appreciably helps the judicial mind to believe one or more of the material statements or facts deposed to", and, as was said in *Green v. McLeod* (1896), 23 A.R. (Ont.) 676, "the 'material evidence' in corroboration may consist of inferences or probabilities arising from other facts and circumstances".

After mentioning certain other authorities, including *Smallman v. Moore*, [1948] 3 D.L.R. 657, [1948] S.C.R. 295, Gale J., now C.J.O., said at p. 101:

On those authorities, therefore, it would be my conclusion that if there is evidence corroborating or tending to corroborate evidence of the plaintiff in an action of this kind on some of the material issues which have been raised by the pleadings the purpose of the Act has been satisfied, although, I repeat, the court may thereby be given little or no assistance in its endeavour to decide the veracity of the plaintiff on the matters that are in dispute.

The trial judge pretty well accepted this view, and he said,

> As to what constitutes corroboration, it is clear from the authorities that it is not necessary that the whole of the evidence should be corroborated, but it should at least be so far corroborated as to justify the court in treating the whole of it as credible. To corroborate, said one learned judge, means to strengthen, to give additional strength to, to make more certain.

In *Central Guaranty Trust Co. v. West*, Kelly J., in considering the question of corroboration, stated at p. 14:

> In determining the proper manner to consider such evidence I refer to the decision of O'Hearn J., in *Re McCarthy* (1970), 16 D.L.R. (3d) 72 where he applied his usually scholarly approach in discussing the nature of corroborating evidence. He referred to various texts and cases as authorities in this area — and provided us with a summary of the manner in which corroborating evidence should be treated. Some of his points on pp. 86–89 are as follows:
> (a) Corroboration is of no avail if the claimant's story is not believed.
> (b) A mere scintilla of corroborating evidence is not sufficient.
> (c) Evidence that is consistent with two views or two opposing views is not corroboration of either.
> (d) The corroborating evidence need not be sufficient in itself to establish the case.
> (e) The direct testimony of the second witness is unnecessary for sufficient corroboration.
> (f) The corroboration may be afforded by circumstances alone.

In *Samson Estate v. Tanner* (1984), 66 N.S.R. (2d) 119; 152 A.P.R. 119, Morrison J.A., reviewed the corroboration requirements in s. 42 (now s. 45) of the *Evidence Act*, and quoted with approval the decision of Coffin J.A., in *Johnson v. Nova Scotia Trust Co.*

The evidence of Mrs. Shaw, who I found to be a very credible witness, was that Janie wished to show her appreciation for the many extra kindnesses performed on her behalf by Mrs. Shaw, and told her that the account at the Bank of Nova Scotia was to be a gift to Mrs. Shaw. To ensure that this transaction was completed, arrangements were made to have the account transferred to a joint account in the name of Janie and Mrs. Shaw. At the time that

this was completed Mrs. Shaw advised Janie that she would not touch the account until after Janie's death. This account was at a later date transferred into another joint account bearing higher rates of interest at the same bank.

At or about the same time a new joint account was opened at the Royal Bank in Pictou. It was to this Royal Bank joint account which all Janie's pension cheques were deposited, and it was from this account that her living expenses were paid.

As to why Janie would wish to gift the Bank of Nova Scotia account to her second cousin, Mrs. Shaw, it is interesting to note while there were some 31 second cousins of Janie's in the province, the only one to provide the care, assistance and attention for a substantial period of time to Janie was Mrs. Shaw.

Mrs. Shaw very shortly after the transferring of Janie's account into a joint account at the Bank of Nova Scotia, told Mrs. Moffatt about the gift of the joint account, and the circumstances surrounding it. Also, Mrs. Shaw told her daughter, Mrs. Dyack, about the gift of the joint account from Janie. And, in fact, Mrs. Dyack was present when the original joint account was changed into another joint account bearing higher interest, also at the Bank of Nova Scotia, in New Glasgow.

Although the evidence of Mrs. Moffatt and Mrs. Dyack cannot be taken to verify the truth of the transaction between Janie and Mrs. Shaw, nevertheless their evidence is very strongly corroborative of the evidence as to what happened, as testified by Mrs. Shaw.

I find, taking into consideration all of the evidence, that the corroboration required by s. 45 of the *Evidence Act* has been met, and the presumption of a resulting trust of the joint account in favour of Janie has been rebutted. Mary Jane MacKenzie, on February 14th, 1986, made a good and valid inter vivos gift of the funds in joint bank account number 2600420, at the Bank of Nova Scotia, in New Glasgow, to Marion Shaw. Although Mrs. Shaw indicated to Mary Jane MacKenzie at that time that she would not use the funds whilst Mary Jane was still alive, this does not affect the validity of the gift, or the fact that it becomes effective as of that date.

The question has been raised by counsel that the gift of the joint bank account was a *donatio mortis causa* gift.

In *Re Fenton Estate*, 26 N.S.R. (2d) at 687, Cowan C.J.T.D., at para. 61 stated:

> The three essentials for a *donatio mortis causa* are, first, that the gift must be made in contemplation of the death of the donor, although not necessarily in expectation of death; second, that

there must be a delivery of the subject matter of the gift to the donee or his agent, or a transfer of the means of, or part of the means of, getting at the property, and, third, that the circumstances must be such as to establish that the gift is to take complete effect upon, but only upon, the death of the donor.

If I had found that the joint account at the Bank of Nova Scotia, in New Glasgow, was a valid inter vivos gift from Janie to Mrs. Shaw, I would have had no difficulty in finding that the requirements set out in *Re Fenton Estate* had been met. It is clear from the evidence that Mary Jane MacKenzie, having just completed and executed a codicil to her will, was contemplating death, though not necessarily expecting death, and by making her account in the Bank of Nova Scotia, in New Glasgow, joint with Mrs. Shaw, was in effect delivering the subject matter of that account as a gift to Mrs. Shaw, and the fact that Mrs. Shaw assured Janie that she would not

use the funds in the joint account while Janie was still alive, is sufficient to establish that the gift was to be complete upon the death of the donor.

I find that the plaintiff, Mary Shaw, is the beneficial owner, and entitled to the funds in the bank account No. 9029826 opened on November 26th, 1990, at the Bank of Nova Scotia, Provost St., New Glasgow, in the amount of $25,610.78, together with accrued interest thereon, as well as the sum of $100 remaining in the joint account No. 9021523 at the Bank of Nova Scotia, Provost Street, New Glasgow, together with accrued interest thereon. An order to this effect shall issue.

At the request of counsel, the question of costs is reserved, and if counsel cannot agree on costs, then I shall hear further representations from them in writing at their earliest convenience.

Order accordingly.

(j)　*Vokey v. Vokey Estate*†

[SOPER J.:]

This action was taken to determine whether funds which were in a joint account in the names of the applicant and the late Stafford Vokey legally belong to the applicant or to the estate of the late Mr. Vokey.

Stafford Vokey was a bachelor who lived in his own home in the community of Burlington. He had three brothers and one sister. His brother Alec, who was the applicant's father, is dead; his brother Walter lives in Baie Verte; his brother Ernest lives in Stephenville and his sister, May Bartlett, lives in Grand Falls.

Evidence at trial was given by the applicant, by Alvin Vokey, one of the applicant's sons, by Joy Vokey, the wife of another of the applicant's sons and by Pearl Dawson, who is Ernest Vokey's daughter. Ernest Vokey is ill, Walter Vokey is in a home for seniors and Mrs. Bartlett has a severe arthritic condition which restricts her movement, so those

members of the family were not called as witnesses. They may not have been able to give any helpful evidence, but I note their absence because they are among the beneficiaries of Stafford Vokey's estate.

Stafford Vokey had lived all of his life in Burlington. He lived in his own house until 16 or 17 months before he died. He was financially independent and looked after his own affairs. The applicant on occasion helped him do some repairs on his house and Alvin Vokey, the applicant's son, used to help him get wood. Over a period of 14 or 15 years the applicant's wife baked bread for him and took a "scattered meal" to him. He did not pay Mrs. Vokey for the meals that she took to him but he paid her $3.00 a loaf for his bread.

Stafford had a bank account in the Baie Verte branch of the Bank of Nova Scotia. In December 1980 he opened a joint account in his own name and in Mrs. Bartlett's name. There was supposed to be a signature card with Stafford's and Mrs. Bartlett's signatures on it but it was never filed with the

---

† (1994), 123 Nfld. and P.E.I.R. 59 (Nlfd. S.C. — T.D.).

Bank. There was no evidence as to the reason for the card's not being returned to the bank but the account was in the names of Stafford and Mrs. Bartlett. The only defect was that Mrs. Bartlett did not have signing authority.

In July 1991 youths attempted to break into Stafford's house. Next day Stafford went to the applicant's house, which was about one-quarter mile away from his own house. He ended up remaining with the applicant and his wife and did not return to live in his own house again. In August 1991 at Stafford's suggestion the applicant made an addition to his house for Stafford to live in. It measured about 20 feet by 11 feet and contained a bedroom, sitting room and washroom which had in it a toilet and sink. Stafford bought the materials and the applicant helped him with labour. Stafford lived in that apartment but took his meals with the applicant and his wife, who also looked after Stafford's laundry. Stafford paid Mrs. Vokey $400 a month for his meals and laundry. I must note at this point that the applicant admitted in evidence that the addition of Stafford's apartment increased the value of the house.

Stafford closed out the joint account with May Bartlett on November 18, 1992. He then transferred the balance in the account to a new joint account which he opened in his own name and in the applicant's name. A perusal of the statement for his account from November 15th, 1991 to the time of his death in January 1993 shows that there were regular deposits, usually for the same amount, and only debit entry, on March 13th, 1992. There was no evidence that anybody other than Stafford dealt with his account and there was no suggestion by either party to this action that anybody other than Stafford dealt with it. Indeed, it is safe to conclude that his only reason for having a joint account was so that if he became incapacitated there would be somebody who might attend to his financial affairs. I must now look at the evidence, albeit scant, which touches on any intentions that he may have had about the disposal of his estate.

The Applicant said that a couple of times after moving in with the applicant and his wife Stafford said that he was going to get the applicant's name on the joint account. It was Stafford who brought up the subject. Stafford went to Baie Verte and met the applicant at his place of employment. They went together to the Bank of Nova Scotia. A new account was opened with the deposit of the balance that had been in the joint account with Mrs. Bartlett. The applicant said that Stafford told him that when he died he wanted "a good funeral", that the applicant was to pay all funeral and burial expenses and that

after he had done that the remainder of the money in the joint account would be for the applicant and his wife. The applicant said that he "told us that on a couple of occasions". He said that he suggested that Stafford should have a will, that Stafford said that he was thinking about it but he did nothing about it.

Alvin Vokey said that one night in the autumn of 1992 he was chatting with Stafford in the latter's apartment. He said that Stafford "told me what he wanted done when he died", that "he wanted a good funeral and a good gift for father and mother when he died". Alvin said there was nobody else present when Stafford made those statements.

Joy Vokey used to see Stafford when she visited her in-laws. She stayed in their house during Christmas 1992 while the applicant's wife was in Toronto. She looked after Stafford during that time. She said that he told her that there would be a "good gift" for the applicant and his wife after he died. On another occasion Stafford told the applicant's wife that "when I'm gone there's a great gift for you and Roy".

Pearl Dawson lives in Seal Cove, about 35 miles from Burlington. She said that he often came to her to get things done. She used to take Sunday dinner and Christmas dinner to him when he lived alone. She did not take meals to him after he began to live with the applicant and his wife.

Mrs. Dawson took Stafford to Grand Falls for medical examinations and treatment four times in June, July, August and November 1992. He paid her for those trips.

She said that Stafford often told her that there was money for a "decent burial" and headstone for him, that she would not be forgotten, that his car was to be for her, that there would be money for her and the applicant and Alvin was to get his house. She said that he would name some who, he felt, did not need anything, that some had done nothing for him, that some should be rewarded. She also said that he always said that the applicant would not get it all. She said that she understood that he intended that his bank account was to be for her and the applicant. She said that she told him he should put his wishes in writing, that he told her he was going to make a will. He did not speak to her about particular amounts but he did speak to her in general terms about the disposal of his estate. She said that he thought a lot about the applicant and his wife, especially after the youths tried to enter his house. She wanted him to come and live with her but he did not want to leave Burlington.

Stafford died on January 17th, 1993. The applicant withdrew $47,233.16 from the joint bank account January 25th, 1993 and the account was closed. On

July 9th, 1993 the Registrar of the Supreme Court was appointed administrator of Stafford's estate. This brings me to the question of whether Stafford intended the applicant should receive the money that was in the joint account or whether it should be part of his estate to be divided by the administrator according to the *Intestate Succession Act*. The parties agree that I need not be concerned with any question of whether any of them should be paid for any service they rendered to Stafford. He paid them for any services which they performed and for which he might be expected to pay.

Before considering the law applicable to this case I must look at the joint deposit agreement between the Bank of Nova Scotia and its customers, the applicant and Stafford Vokey. Only two paragraphs of that agreement are relevant to this application. Paragraph 9 reads:

> All money in your account and any interest earned on it shall be held as joint property with the last survivor being entitled to payment of all money in your account (right of survivorship). Subject to any law or regulation now or afterwards in force, the death of any one or more of you does not affect the right of any survivor or the last survivor to withdraw or order the payment of any credit balance in your account.

Paragraph 10 reads:

> All money credited to your account and all interest earned on it, if any, shall be held by you as your joint property. In consideration of each of you having entered into this agreement with us and with each other, then in the event of the death of one of you, he or she shall be deemed never to have had any right to the funds in your account, which funds shall be deemed to have belonged to the surviving joint account holder(s) as of the date of this agreement.

Those paragraphs are part of the agreement between the Bank of Nova Scotia and its customers, not an agreement between the customers, that is, in this case, between Stafford and the applicant. To determine what Stafford intended we must look at the evidence surrounding his dealings with the applicant and with the joint account and at any other evidence which may bear on his intentions.

First of all, I must consider s. 16 of the *Evidence Act*, R.S.N. 1990, c. E-16:

> In an action or proceeding by or against the representatives of a deceased person, an opposite or interested party to the action shall not obtain a verdict, judgment or decree in the action on his or her own evidence in respect of a matter unless that evidence is corroborated by some other material evidence.

That section of the *Evidence Act* is substantively the same as s. 11 of the *Evidence Act* of Prince Edward Island. It was considered by Mullally J., of the Supreme Court of Prince Edward Island, General Division, in *McKenna Estate v. McKenna* (1986), 61 Nfld. & P.E.I.R. 51; 185 A.P.R. 51 at pages 56–57, where he considered several authorities cited there. I shall not review all of them but I shall quote from a portion of the decision of the Supreme Court of Canada in *Smallman v. Moore*, [1948] S.C.R. 295 where Kellock J., said at page 301:

> ... the section here does not say that every fact necessary to be proved to establish a cause of action must be corroborated by evidence other than that of the interested party but that the evidence of the interested party itself is to be corroborated by some other material evidence....

In the same decision Kellock J., referred to a decision of the Supreme Court of Canada in *Thompson v. Coulter* (1903), 34 S.C.R. 261 in which Killam J., approved this statement of Jessel M.R., in *In re Finch*:

> As I understand corroboration is some testimony proving a material point in the testimony which is to be corroborated. It must not be testimony corroborating something else — something not material.

The applicant's claim is supported by the following evidence:

(a) The account itself
(b) The applicant's statement that on a number of occasions Stafford had told him and his wife that after all funeral and burial expenses had been paid the remainder of the money in the joint account would be for them.
(c) Alvin Vokey's statement that Stafford had told him that he wanted "a good gift for father and mother when he died".
(d) Joy Vokey's statement that Stafford had told her that there would be "a good gift" for the applicant and his wife after he died and that on another occasion he told the applicant's wife that when he was "gone ... there's a great gift for you and Roy".

As against that evidence, I must consider the following:

(a) It may be a splitting of hairs, but the applicant did not say that Stafford told him that the money in the joint account would be his but that it would be for him and his wife.

(b) Alvin Vokey's statement did not refer specifically to the joint account but only to Stafford's statement that he wanted "a good gift" for the applicant and his wife. Considering the fact that Stafford had a substantial bank balance, his house and a 1991 model car, he had an estate out of which he might give a "good gift" without giving the entire bank balance to any one person. The same observation must be made about Joy Vokey's statements.

(c) In her evidence Pearl Dawson made significant statements that related to Stafford's estate generally and to his money in particular. Those statements were:

(i) that his car was to be for her;

(ii) that Alvin was to get his house

(iii) that there would be money for the applicant and her; and

(iv) that the applicant "would not get it all".

None of the evidence can be regarded as corroborative of evidence that Stafford intended that the applicant should have the right of survivorship to the joint account. Both the applicant and Mrs. Dawson said that they had suggested to Stafford that he should have a will and that he had indicated that he intended to make one. The evidence suggests that he was thinking about how he was going to dispose of his estate and that he was thinking about the possible division of his bank account. It does not support the applicant's claim to the bank account. That brings me to the law respecting joint bank accounts.

The leading case on which we can rely is the decision of the Supreme Court of Canada in *Niles v.*

Lake, [1947] 2 D.L.R. 248. In that case Taschereau J., said at pages 254–55:

> The law is well settled, I think that when a person transfers his own money into his own name jointly with that of another person, except in cases with which we are not concerned, then there is prima facie a resulting trust for the transferor. This presumption, of course, is a presumption of law which is rebuttable by oral or written evidence or other circumstances tending to show there was in fact an intention of giving beneficially to the transferee.

There is no doubt about the origin of the funds which Stafford Vokey deposited in the Bank of Nova Scotia. They were his and his alone. There is no dispute about the management of that account. Stafford Vokey alone dealt with it. He was independent and paid his way, so that he did not place himself under any financial obligation to anybody else. He was concerned that he should have a "good funeral" and, as I have already said, it is safe to conclude that his only reason for having a joint account was so that if he became incapacitated there would be somebody who might attend to his financial affairs. The evidence suggests that he was mentally disposing of his estate, possibly in anticipation of making his will. In any case, the evidence does not show that in fact he had an intention of giving his bank account "beneficially to the transferee", that is, to the applicant. The applicant's application is, therefore, dismissed.

Since this application was really made for directions, party and party costs will be borne by the Estate.

Order accordingly.

(k) *Bank of Montreal v. Hancock*†

[O'BRIEN J.:]

This is a claim against two defendants for amounts outstanding arising from an overdraft on a joint account in the names of the defendants, husband and wife, and for an amount owing on a promissory note signed by both. The amount of the claim in connection with the overdraft is $8,941.86. The amount claimed in connection with the promissory note is $63,974.79.

† (1982), 137 D.L.R. (3d) 648 (Ont. H.C.J.).

The case raises the issues of the liability of one of two persons opening a joint account for an overdraft created without knowledge that overdraft privileges are being extended to the other, and the obligation of a bank to advise a wife to seek independent advice when signing a promissory note in connection with an outstanding loan owed by her husband.

In this case the defendant husband has not defended. Default judgment has gone against him in connection with both claims.

The background of the matter is of some significance. The marriage between the two defendants was an unhappy one for a number of years prior to the events in question; the husband had a serious drinking problem for which he had received treatment and the parties had separated on a number of occasions, the final separation occurring in June of 1977; they were divorced in 1979.

The background of the relevant banking arrangements are that the defendant husband commenced dealing with the plaintiff bank prior to 1973. At that time he was an officer and part-owner of a business known as Trader Hancock Limited which at that time was quite a successful appliance company. The husband dealt with a branch of the plaintiff bank in Scarborough on Brimley Rd., managed by a Mr. Catchpole. His personal account and the account of the business were both at that branch. The husband arranged with Catchpole that he would have overdraft privileges in connection with his personal account and the overdraft would be covered periodically by draws which he received from the company.

In October of 1974, arrangements were made to turn the husband's personal account into a joint account with his wife. I accept the evidence of the wife that this was done for convenience and for her use as a household account. When the account was opened it was in an overdraft in the amount of $6,789. This was unknown to the wife. I further accept the evidence of the wife that only the husband made deposits to that account and, while statements of the account were kept in the name of both defendants, the statements were mailed in a letter addressed to the husband only: she did not open that letter nor look at the statements. The wife further testified she had a personal account in another bank which she used for her personal use. I accept her evidence on that point also.

The wife further testified that she did not know that the husband had borrowed substantial amounts from the bank; in particular, she testified she was unaware that her husband had signed a promissory note in favour of the plaintiff bank on July 29, 1975, for $27,000. She was also unaware of the fact that the joint account was almost constantly in an overdraft position. I accept that evidence.

I also accept her evidence that she did not ask for overdraft privileges and assumed that deposits made by the husband were sufficient to cover cheques which they were both writing on the account.

The statement of claim alleges that, when the defendants arranged for the joint chequing account, there was a written agreement whereby the defendants agreed to repay to the plaintiff all sums advanced or loaned by the plaintiff to the defendants by way of overdraft or otherwise on cheques drawn by the defendants on the chequing account operated jointly by them. The deposit account agreement which was filed as an exhibit in this action contains no reference whatever to an overdraft situation, nor any guarantee by either party in connection therewith. I am satisfied on the evidence that the only arrangement made in connection with an overdraft was that made between the husband and Mr. Catchpole which was an oral arrangement and which was unknown to the wife.

The manager, Mr. Catchpole, testified that the bank, as a practice, frequently allowed overdraft privileges to customers who did not ask for that privilege, and frequently no security was obtained for such overdraft.

Throughout the year 1976, the wife encountered a variety of personal problems. These included the death of her father, the fact that her children were giving her a great deal of difficulty, the oldest boy was charged with car theft, two of the girls were truant from school, one was charged with vandalism, the defendant husband's drinking problems were severe, and in March of 1976 he entered into the out-patient programme at the Donwood Foundation in Toronto. These problems culminated in the wife's nervous breakdown which occurred in January of 1976, at which time she was confined to hospital for two weeks.

The wife testified that throughout 1976 she had been taking Valium by prescription and, in addition, was obtaining Valium from her husband and other persons, and was taking much more Valium than had been prescribed for her. The significance of this is that the wife testified she has no recollection whatsoever of signing the promissory note which is the subject of this litigation and which was signed on September 24, 1976. She frankly admits that the signature on the note is hers but indicates she has a complete blank as to the events which led to the signing of that note. I accept that evidence.

The evidence in connection with the execution of the promissory note, which I accept, is that the account manager of the bank, Mr. Irwin, obtained a loan application from the husband in the month of September, 1976, and that the stated purpose of the loan was to refinance the $27,000 demand loan which the husband had previously signed, to cover the overdraft which then exited in the joint account, and that the balance was for "further renovations" (on a house which the defendants had recently purchased). Irwin had the husband sign a new promissory note for $63,974.79 and asked the husband to have his wife sign the note.

I accept the evidence of the wife that the renovations to the house in question were covered completely by profit made on the sale of another house owned by the defendants and that none of the cheques written on the account with the plaintiff bank were for that purpose.

Irwin testified that the husband first signed the note and a few days thereafter the defendant wife came to the bank and also signed it. The only explanation he gave her as to the note was that it included 13% interest on $60,000. He gave her no other advice concerning signing the note. At that time an undertaking was obtained from the defendants that they would agree not to further encumber their residential property known as 420 Rosemary Rd. in Toronto.

When the wife came to the bank to execute the note she also had some conversation with Mr. Catchpole. As he described it, that conversation was more in the nature of a public relations exercise than it was about the note or the husband's finances. He was very vague about the details of the conversation and indicated that the loan application had really been handled by Irwin, although, in view of the amount, it was necessary for him to authorize it.

Catchpole testified he did not tell the defendant wife she did not have to sign the note. He had no recollection of giving her any advice as to the nature or effect of signing the note, said nothing to her about what would happen if she refused to sign it, did not recommend she get any independent legal advice, and did not tell her that part of the loan proceeds were to pay off the husband's prior loan or to cover the overdraft which existed on the joint account. I am satisfied that nothing was said to her about the nature or effect of the promissory note which she was asked to sign. I am also satisfied on the evidence that when the promissory note was signed, Mr. Catchpole or Mr. Irwin, or both of them,

realized the bank had no security for the account overdraft or for the promissory note which had been signed in July, 1975, by the husband, and that the house in which the defendant then lived was registered in the name of the wife.

The next event which occurred in connection with this matter was that the defendant wife was asked by her husband to sign a renewal note in March of 1977. At that time she was unaware of the extent of her obligation under the promissory note signed in September, 1976. She made some inquiries and, as a result, refused to sign the renewal note. Her husband then told her he would be financially ruined if she would not sign. There was some contact with Mr. Catchpole and the wife was given a copy of the promissory note which she had signed in September. The wife subsequently discovered her husband was in very serious financial trouble and, shortly thereafter, the business of which he was a joint owner, went bankrupt.

The wife had a further conversation with Mr. Catchpole about the promissory note in which he told her that he was in a bad position; she said she appreciated that but she was in a similar position herself.

Mr. Catchpole testified that he did not know the husband's business was in financial trouble in 1976 when he obtained the wife's signature to the promissory note. Given the fact that the business account was in the branch which Mr. Catchpole managed and that that business went bankrupt in early 1977, I do not accept his evidence and conclude he must have had some indication that the husband's business was in financial trouble when the promissory note was signed by the wife. At that point there was some $53,000 outstanding against the husband for which there was no security, and when Catchpole discovered the only security to which the bank might look was the house which was registered in the wife's name. I believe Mr. Catchpole was attempting to make the best of a bad situation for his employer, the bank. I do not think it is an unfounded conjecture to consider the fact Mr. Catchpole might have been in some difficulty with his employer because he had made an unsecured loan of that size. The comment he made to the wife about being in trouble reinforced that thought. I will now deal with the wife's liability in connection with the amount claimed on the overdraft on the joint account.

Surprisingly, there is very little Canadian authority on this point. The only case in Ontario to which I have been referred and I have been able to find is the case of *Bank of Montreal v. Vaillancourt and*

Watson (unreported), which is a decision of District Court Judge Bernstein.

In that case the two defendants opened a joint account with the plaintiff bank. One of those, Watson, eventually was sent to jail for a fraud committed against a number of investors who believed their money was going into the American commodities market. Vaillancourt acted as Watson's agent and no allegation of fraud was made against him. The problem eventually arose when Watson cashed cheques for some $59,000 which were of no value; that amount was charged to the joint account as an overdraft. A default judgment was obtained against Watson and the action proceeded to trial and against Vaillancourt.

The decision indicates it was important in that case that only Vaillancourt was known to the bank and that he was a valued customer before the joint account was opened. Following the opening of the joint account, before the final fraudulent act occurred, on a number of occasions when n.s.f. cheques were presented by Watson, Vaillancourt had asked the bank to charge them against the account as an overdraft because he believed the problem was caused by reason of a slow transfer of funds. The decision indicates that while the court found Vaillancourt had no beneficial interest in the account, it relied on the fact that he had asked the bank to charge n.s.f. cheques as overdrafts and that Vaillancourt had received and reviewed monthly statements indicating the joint account was in an overdraft position.

On the basis of those findings of fact, Vaillancourt was held liable to the bank for the overdraft created by the fraudulent cheque cashing. The decision reviews two California authorities, one a decision of the Supreme Court of California, *Popp v. Exchange Bank* (1922), 208 P. 113, 189 Cal. 296, and a decision of the California Court of Appeal, *Faulkner et al. v. Bank of Italy* (1924), 231 P. 380, Cal. App. 370. Those two cases are in substantial conflict. In *Popp v. Exchange Bank, supra*, a wife who held a joint chequing account with her husband was held liable for an overdraft in the account created by cheques issued by the husband, which were returned n.s.f. In the *Faulkner v. Bank of Italy* case, it was held in the absence of conduct by the innocent joint owner which would imply consent to overdrafts or to the actions of a fraudulent party and where the innocent party derived no benefit from the funds, there was no liability on him for any amount greater than that contained in the joint account.

The California Court of Appeal, in *Faulkner*, refused to follow the decision in *Popp v. Exchange Bank*, noting that no authority was cited in support of the statement relied upon by that court and pointing out that, while it was not an uncommon thing for a bank to permit a customer to overdraw, it was in fact nothing but a very dangerous and irregular loan where the bank had no security beyond the right of action against the drawer of the cheque.

In my view, the conclusion of the California Court of Appeal in *Faulkner v. Bank of Italy* is preferable, and I rely upon it. I further note there was nothing in the agreement between the plaintiff and the defendants in this case which authorized either party to overdraw, nor was there anything by which one party guaranteed to pay any overdraft created. I rely on the fact that the wife had no knowledge of the overdraft privileges which had been extended to her husband and was totally unaware of the fact that the account was frequently in an overdraft position. I find it difficult to accept that the wife would have been indebted to the bank in the amount of the overdraft when the husband's account became a joint account in October, 1974, on the basis of the agreement signed at that time.

I therefore dismiss the action of the plaintiff as against the defendant wife in connection with the overdraft.

I now deal with the question of the bank's obligation to advise the defendant wife or to suggest that she obtain independent advice before signing the promissory note in September, 1976.

The wife relies on the following authorities: *Lloyds Bank Ltd. v. Bundy*, [1974] 3 All E.R. 757; *McKenzie v. Bank of Montreal et al.* (1975), 7 O.R. (2d) 521, 55 D.L.R. (3d) 641 [affirmed] 12 O.R. (2d) 719, 70 D.L.R. (3d) 113]; *Royal Bank of Canada v. Hinds* (1978), 20 O.R. (2d) 613, 88 D.L.R. (3d) 428, 4 B.L.R. 241, and *Bank of Nova Scotia v. MacLellan* (1980), 28 N.B.R. (2d) 709 [reversed 30 N.B.R. (2d) 596 and 31 N.B.R. (2d) 141].

In *Bank of Nova Scotia v. MacLellan, supra*, the New Brunswick Court of Queen's Bench found that a wife was forced to sign a promissory note by her husband; there was a finding that she was completely dominated by her husband, lived in fear of him and was under his undue influence throughout their marriage, and was frequently abused by him. There was also a finding that the bank was unaware of the husband's undue influence. The court held that where the wife was not the primary debtor, the bank owed a duty to the wife to ensure that she signed the note in complete awareness of the responsibilities and liabilities which she undertook, and should have advised her to seek independent advice.

In the case of *Royal Bank of Canada v. Hinds*, it was held that where a widow, shortly following her husband's death, was asked to sign documents by the bank which amounted to her taking over the husband's debts to the bank, and signed the documents without appreciating the nature and effect of the documents, nor her own legal position, the documents were not enforceable. Stark J. held that the bank had an obligation to ensure the widow, who was a customer, was fully apprised of the hazardous course she was taking and the free choice that was open to her. He pointed out that at the very least this was a case where it was incumbent on the bank to satisfy itself that the customer was independently advised and pointed out that any lawyer or unprejudiced banker would have advised the defendant widow against assuming her husband's loan. He found the bank permitted its own interests to prevail and the widow never received the information or advice to which she was entitled. In my view, that statement is particularly applicable to the present case. I find the plaintiff bank did not discharge the obligation which it owed to the wife, its customer. For these results the second part of this action will also be dismissed.

In the result the action is dismissed with costs.

Action dismissed.

(l)   *Bank of Montreal v. Vaillancourt*†

[WEATHERSTON J.A.:]

The issue in this appeal is as to the liability of the defendant Vaillancourt for an overdraft in a joint account which he and the other defendant, Watson, had with the plaintiff bank.

Vaillancourt and Watson are brothers-in-law, and were good friends. Watson persuaded Vaillancourt that he had devised a foolproof scheme for making money by investing in the commodities market. Vaillancourt was enlisted to find other investors from amongst his friends in North Bay. He invested a sizeable amount of money himself.

In May, 1980, Vaillancourt and Watson attended at a branch of the bank in North Bay, and opened a joint account. To avoid the usual delay in clearing funds from California, where Watson lived, the bank officials were persuaded to immediately credit the joint account with the amount of cheques to be sent by Watson for deposit. The plan was that Vaillancourt would then draw cheques on the account to distribute the profits of the enterprise.

The bank accepted this arrangement, relying on the undoubted integrity of Vaillancourt, who was a long-time customer of the bank.

I fear that Watson was not an honest man. All but one of the cheques he sent to the bank for deposit were returned N.S.F. Before they were returned, Vaillancourt drew cheques on the account in favour of local investors, including his wife. Watson also drew cheques in favour of himself for considerable sums. These cheques were all paid by the bank. When all the deposited cheques had been returned, it was found that the account had been overdrawn by $59,211.05.

The relations between a bank and its customer depend on the contract between them: see *Bank of Montreal v. A.-G. Que.*, [1979] 1 S.C.R. 565, 96 D.L.R. (3d) 586, 25 N.R. 330.

There is no general rule of law that both parties to a joint bank account are jointly liable to the bank for any overdraft in the account. Liability depends on the express or implied terms of the contract with the bank, but may also be founded on agency, representation or estoppel. The trial judge referred to two California cases, *Popp v. Exchange Bank*, (1922), 189 Cal. 296, and *Faulkner et al. v. Bank of Italy* (1924), 69 Cal. App. 370.

In the first case, the court was considering an overdraft occasioned by cheques drawn by the husband on a joint account of a man and his wife. The court said at p. 300:

> The account was in the names of the plaintiff, Lenora S. Popp and J. Popp, and was opened with money belonging to plaintiff, by the deposit of checks payable to her. She thinks she never drew any checks against the account, and in any event, not more than one or two; nevertheless

† (1983), 42 O.R. (2d) 545 (C.A.).

the overdraft was in law as much her indebtedness as that of her husband.

In the later case, the Court of Appeal said as to this passage [at p. 375]:

> No authorities are cited in support of this statement, and no reasons are given or circumstances pertaining to the deposit upon which the conclusion is based. Whether there was any course of dealing from which the bank was authorized to allow overdrafts on the part of the husband or whether there were any directions which amounted to an authorization on the part of the wife to the husband to create an overdraft, or whether the above language is intended as an abstract statement of the law irrespective of its application to the particular case, we cannot ascertain from the language of the opinion.

In *Bank of Montreal v. Hancock et al.* (1982), 39 O.R. (2d) 82, 137 D.L.R. (3d) 648, O'Brien J. relied on the conclusion of the court in *Faulkner et al. v. Bank of Italy, supra*. In the present case, the trial judge said:

> I am of the view that the most satisfactory statement of the law was set out in the judgment of the Court of Appeals in California in *Faulkner et al. v. Bank of Italy, supra*. In the absence of conduct by the innocent joint owner which would imply consent to overdrafts or to the actions of the fraudulent party, and if the innocent party derived no benefit from the funds, I do not believe it equitable to hold him liable for any amount greater than that contained in the joint account.

I agree. The fact that a person is a party to a joint account does not, without more, make him liable to the bank for an overdraft created by the other party.

The express terms of the contract between the bank and the defendants are set out in a joint deposit account agreement, a bank form, as follows:

To the Bank of Montreal
2012 Cassells Street
1 — 2445 North Bay, Ont.

The undersigned, having opened a deposit account with you in their joint names, hereby jointly and severally agree with you and with each other that all moneys from time to time deposited to the said account, and interest, may be withdrawn by any one of the undersigned or his or her attorney or agent, and each of the undersigned hereby irrevocably authorizes the said Bank to from time to time accept as a sufficient acquittance for any amounts withdrawn from said account, any receipt, cheque or other instrument signed by any one or more of the undersigned, his, her or their agents, without any further signature or consent of the other or others of the undersigned thereto.

It is further agreed that the Bank is hereby authorized to credit the said account with all moneys paid to the Bank (i) at the branch of account or (ii) at any branch other than the branch of account for the credit or any one or more of the undersigned, the proceeds of any orders or promises for the payment of money, of bonds, debentures, coupons or other securities, signed by or drawn by or payable to or the property of, or received by the said Bank (i) at the branch of account or (ii) at any branch other than the branch of account for the credit of the undersigned or any one or more of the undersigned, and to endorse any of such instruments on behalf of the undersigned or any one or more of them. It is agreed that the Bank is relieved from all liability for so doing.

The question was raised during argument whether by this agreement Vaillancourt and Watson did not in express terms authorize the bank to credit Watson's cheques to the account and, while the account showed a credit balance, to honour the cheques of either defendant. The point was not pursued by either counsel, and I say no more about it. In any event, the trial judge made the following finding of fact:

> I am also satisfied that the bank did not abrogate its duty of care to Vaillancourt by crediting the joint account the uncertified and unclear deposit cheques submitted by Watson. Vaillancourt clearly knew that this was the procedure being followed; indeed Vaillancourt had indicated to the plaintiff that the problem to be solved was one of slow transfer of his funds from Watson and the joint account was created to overcome this difficulty. It was prepared to deal with Watson's cheques in this manner only because of Vaillancourt's participation in the account and to assist a good client.

and later in his reasons for judgment:

> In the present case however, Vaillancourt did know of the overdraft position created in the account from time to time. He received the monthly bank statement showing this to be the case. He was also aware that Watson was withdrawing funds from the account before his deposit cheques were cleared. The evidence indicates that Watson's actions worried him even before the fraud was discovered, but he took no steps to warn the bank or clarify his position with respect to liability for the account. The

bank was providing the service to this account because of its high regard for Vaillancourt.

I think this finding is conclusive of the matter. For if, by the arrangements between the bank and the defendants, the bank was to credit the account with the amount of cheques sent by Watson for deposit, it became obligated to honour cheques drawn on the account by either Watson or Vaillancourt up to the amount of the credit so created. Neither Watson or Vaillancourt can be heard to say that the credit was not good, nor to dispute their liability to make good the cheques of either of them.

The trial judge was right in finding Vaillancourt liable to the bank for the amount by which the account was overdrawn, even though he was a victim of Watson's fraud. The appeal must be dismissed with costs.

Appeal dismissed.

(m) *Pecore v. Pecore*†

[ROTHSTEIN J. (McLachlin C.J. and Bastarache, Binnie, LeBel, Deschamps, Fish, Charron JJ. concurring):]

I. INTRODUCTION

This appeal involves questions about joint bank and investment accounts where only one of the account holders deposits funds into the account. These types of joint accounts are used by many Canadians for a variety of purposes, including estate planning and financial management. Given their widespread use, the law relating to how these accounts are to be treated by courts after the death of one of the account holders is a matter appropriate for this court to address.

Depending on the terms of the agreement between the bank and the two joint account holders, each may have the legal right to withdraw any or all funds from the accounts at any time and each may have a right of survivorship. If only one of the joint account holders is paying into the account and he or she dies first, it raises questions about whether he or she intended to have the funds in the joint account go to the other joint account holder alone or to have those funds distributed according to his or her will. How to answer this question is the subject of this appeal.

In the present case, an ageing father gratuitously placed his mutual funds, bank account and income trusts in joint accounts with his daughter, who was one of his adult children. The father alone deposited funds into the accounts. Upon his death, a balance remained in the accounts.

It is not disputed that the daughter took legal ownership of the balance in the accounts through the right of survivorship. Equity, however, recognizes a distinction between legal and beneficial ownership. The beneficial owner of property has been described as "[t]he real owner of property even though it is in someone else's name": *Csak v. Aumon* (1990), 69 D.L.R. (4th) 567 (Ont. H.C.J.), at p. 570. The question is whether the father intended to make a gift of the beneficial interest in the accounts upon his death to his daughter alone or whether he intended that his daughter hold the assets in the accounts in trust for the benefit of his estate to be distributed according to his will.

While the focus in any dispute over a gratuitous transfer is the actual intention of the transferor at the time of the transfer, intention is often difficult to ascertain, especially where the transferor is deceased. Common law rules have developed to guide a court's inquiry. This appeal raises the following issues:

1. Do the presumptions of resulting trust and advancement continue to apply in modern times?
2. If so, on what standard will the presumptions be rebutted?
3. How should courts treat survivorship in the context of a joint account?
4. What evidence may courts consider in determining the intent of a transferor?

† 2007 SCC 17.

In this case, the trial judge found that the father actually intended a gift and held that his daughter may retain the assets in the accounts. The Court of Appeal dismissed the appeal of the daughter's ex-husband.

I conclude that there is no basis to overturn this result. The appeal should be dismissed.

II. FACTS

The dispute is between Paula Pecore and her ex-husband Michael Pecore regarding who is entitled to the assets held in joint accounts between Paula and her father upon her father's death. The assets in the joint accounts in dispute totalled almost $1,000,000 at the time Paula's father died in 1998.

Paula has two siblings but of the three, she was the closest to their father. In fact, her father was estranged from one of her sisters until shortly before his death in 1998. Unlike her siblings who were financially secure, Paula worked at various low-paying jobs and took care of her quadriplegic husband Michael. Her father helped her and her family financially by, for example, buying them a van, making improvements to their home, and assisting her son while he was attending university.

In 1993, Paula's father was told by a financial advisor that by placing his assets in joint ownership, he could avoid "the payment of probate fees and taxes and generally make after-death dispositions less expensive and less cumbersome" ((2004), 7 E.T.R. (3d) 113, at para. 7). In February of 1994, he began transferring some of his assets which were mainly either in bank accounts or in mutual funds to himself and to Paula jointly, with a right of survivorship (*ibid.*, at para. 6). In 1996, Paula's father was advised by his accountant that for tax purposes, transfers to his daughter (as opposed to a spouse) could trigger a capital gain, with the result that tax on the gain would be due as of the year of disposition. As a result, Paula's father wrote letters to the financial institutions purporting to deal with the tax implications. In these letters he stated that he was "the 100% owner of the assets and the funds are not being gifted to Paula" (*ibid.*, at para. 10).

Paula's father continued to use and control the accounts after they were transferred into joint names. He declared and paid all the taxes on the income made from the assets in the accounts. Paula made some withdrawals but was required to notify her father before doing so. According to her, this was because her father wanted to ensure there were sufficient funds available for her to withdraw.

In early 1998, Paula's father drafted what was to be his last will. By this time, he had already transferred the bulk of his assets into the joint accounts with Paula. For the first time, he named Michael in his will. The will left specific bequests to Paula, Michael and her children (whom Michael had adopted), but did not mention the accounts. The residue of the estate was to be divided equally between Paula and Michael.

The lawyer who drafted the will testified that he asked Paula's father "about such things as registered retirement savings plans, R.R.I.F.s, registered pension plans, life insurance, and in each case satisfied [him]self that they were not items which would pass as the result of a will and so that they needn't be included in the will" (*ibid.*, at para. 37). There was no discussion about the joint investment and bank accounts.

In 1998, Paula's father moved into Paula and Michael's house. In 1997 and 1998, the father had expressed to others, including one of Paula's sisters, that he was going to take care of Paula after his death, but said the "system" would take care of Michael.

Paula's father died in December 1998. His estate paid tax on the basis of a deemed disposition of the accounts to Paula immediately before his death.

Paula and Michael later divorced. The dispute over the accounts arose during their matrimonial property proceedings.

III. JUDICIAL HISTORY

A. *Ontario Superior Court of Justice (2004), 7 E.T.R. (3d) 113*

The trial judge looked at the operation of the presumption of a resulting trust and the presumption of advancement and found that the latter applied given Paula's relationship with her father. Karam J. concluded that the evidence failed to rebut the presumption of advancement and held that the money in the joint accounts therefore belonged to Paula. He found that the evidence clearly indicated that Paula's father intended to gift the beneficial ownership of those assets held in joint ownership to her while he continued to manage and control them on a day-to-day basis before his death.

B. *Ontario Court of Appeal (2005), 19 E.T.R. (3d) 162*

The Court of Appeal agreed with the trial judge that there was ample evidence to show that Paula's father intended to give Paula beneficial interest in his investments when he placed them in joint ownership. As a result, Lang J.A. found that it was not necessary to rely on the presumption of advancement, saying that a presumption is only relevant when evidence of actual intention is evenly balanced or when there is no evidence of actual intention.

IV. ANALYSIS

A. Do the Presumptions of Resulting Trust and Advancement Continue to Apply in Modern Times?

A discussion of the treatment of joint accounts after the death of the transferor must begin with a consideration of the common law approach to ascertaining the intent of the deceased person.

A resulting trust arises when title to property is in one party's name, but that party, because he or she is a fiduciary or gave no value for the property, is under an obligation to return it to the original title owner: see D.W.M. Waters, M.R. Gillen and L.D. Smith, eds., *Waters' Law of Trusts in Canada* (3rd ed. 2005), at p. 362. While the trustee almost always has the legal title, in exceptional circumstances it is also possible that the trustee has equitable title: see *Waters' Law of Trusts*, at p. 365, noting the case of *Carter v. Carter* (1969), 70 W.W.R. 237 (B.C.S.C.).

Advancement is a gift during the transferor's lifetime to a transferee who, by marriage or parent–child relationship, is financially dependent on the transferor: see *Waters' Law of Trusts*, at p. 378. In the context of the parent–child relationship, the term has also been used because "the father was under a moral duty to <u>advance</u> his children in the world": A.H. Oosterhoff et al., *Oosterhoff on Trusts: Text, Commentary and Materials* (6th ed. 2004), at p. 573 (emphasis added).

In certain circumstances which are discussed below, there will be a presumption of resulting trust or presumption of advancement. Each are rebuttable presumptions of law: see e.g. *Re Mailman Estate*, [1941] S.C.R. 368, at p. 374; *Niles v. Lake*, [1947] S.C.R. 291; *Rathwell v. Rathwell*, [1978] 2 S.C.R. 436, at p. 451; J. Sopinka, S.N. Lederman and A.W. Bryant, *The Law of Evidence in Canada* (2nd ed. 1999), at p. 115. A rebuttable presumption of law is a legal assumption that a court will make if insufficient evidence is adduced to displace the presumption. The presumption shifts the burden of persuasion to the opposing party who must rebut the presumption: see Sopinka et al., at pp. 105–6.

For the reasons discussed below, I think the long-standing common law presumptions continue to have a role to play in disputes over gratuitous transfers. The presumptions provide a guide for courts in resolving disputes over transfers where evidence as to the transferor's intent in making the transfer is unavailable or unpersuasive. This may be especially true when the transferor is deceased and thus is unable to tell the court his or her intention in effecting the transfer. In addition, as noted by Feldman J.A. in the Ontario Court of Appeal in *Saylor v. Madsen Estate* (2005), 261 D.L.R. (4th) 597, the advantage of maintaining the presumption of advancement and the presumption of a resulting trust is that they provide a measure of certainty and predictability for individuals who put property in joint accounts or make other gratuitous transfers.

1. The Presumption of Resulting Trust

The presumption of resulting trust is a rebuttable presumption of law and general rule that applies to gratuitous transfers. When a transfer is challenged, the presumption allocates the legal burden of proof. Thus, where a transfer is made for no consideration, the onus is placed on the transferee to demonstrate that a gift was intended: see *Waters' Law of Trusts*, at p. 375, and E. E. Gillese and M. Milczynski, *The Law of Trusts* (2nd ed. 2005), at p. 110. This is so because equity presumes bargains, not gifts.

The presumption of resulting trust therefore alters the general practice that a plaintiff (who would be the party challenging the transfer in these cases) bears the legal burden in a civil case. Rather, the onus is on the transferee to rebut the presumption of a resulting trust.

In cases where the transferor is deceased and the dispute is between the transferee and a third party, the presumption of resulting trust has an additional justification. In such cases, it is the transferee who is better placed to bring evidence about the circumstances of the transfer.

2. The Presumption of Advancement

The presumption of resulting trust is the general rule for gratuitous transfers. However, depending on the nature of the relationship between the transferor and transferee, the presumption of a resulting trust will not arise and there will be a presumption of advancement instead: see *Waters' Law of Trusts*, at p. 378. If the presumption of advancement applies, it will fall on the party challenging the transfer to rebut the presumption of a gift.

Historically, the presumption of advancement has been applied in two situations. The first is where the transferor is a husband and the transferee is his wife: *Hyman v. Hyman*, [1934] 4 D.L.R. 532 (S.C.C.), at p. 538. The second is where the transferor is a father and the transferee is his child, which is at issue in this appeal.

One of the earliest documented cases where a judge applied the presumption of advancement is the 17th century decision in *Grey (Lord) v. Grey (Lady)* (1677), Rep. Temp. Finch 338, 23 E.R. 185 (H.C. Ch.):

> ... the Law will never imply a *Trust*, because the natural Consideration of Blood, and the <u>Obligation which lies on the Father in Conscience</u> to provide for his Son, are predominant, and must over-rule all manner of Implications. [Underlining added; p. 187.]

As stated in *Grey*, the traditional rationale behind the presumption of advancement between father and child is that a father has an obligation to provide for his sons. See also *Oosterhoff on Trusts*, at p. 575. The presumption also rests on the assumption that parents so commonly intend to make gifts to their children that the law should presume as much: *ibid.*, at pp. 581 and 598.

While historically the relationship between father and child gave rise to the presumption of advancement, courts in Canada have been divided as to whether the relationship between mother and child does as well. Some have concluded that it does not: see e.g. *Lattimer v. Lattimer* (1978), 18 O.R. (2d) 375 (H.C.J.), relying on Cartwright J.'s concurring judgment in *Edwards v. Bradley*, [1957] S.C.R. 599. Others have found that it does: see e.g. *Rupar v. Rupar* (1964), 49 W.W.R. 226 (B.C.S.C.); *Dagle v. Dagle Estate* (1990), 38 E.T.R. 164 (P.E.I.S.C, App. Div.); *Re Wilson* (1999), 27 E.T.R. (2d) 97 (Ont. Ct. (Gen. Div.)). In concluding that the presumption applies to mothers and children in *Re Wilson*, Fedak J., at para. 50, took into consideration "the natural affection between a mother and child, legislative changes requiring mothers to support their children, the economic independence of women and the equality provisions of the Charter".

The question of whether the presumption applies between mother and child is not raised in these appeals, as the transfers in question occurred between a father and daughter, but I shall deal with it briefly. Unlike when the presumption of advancement was first developed, women today have their own financial resources. They also have a statutory obligation to financially support their children in the

same way that fathers do. Section 26.1(2) of the *Divorce Act*, R.S.C. 1985 c. 3 (2nd Supp.), for instance, refers to the "principle" that spouses have a "joint financial obligation to maintain the children", and s. 31(1) of the *Family Law Act*, R.S.O. 1990, c. F.3, provides that "[e]very parent has an obligation to provide support for his or her unmarried child who is a minor or is enrolled in a full time program of education, to the extent that the parent is capable of doing so." Oosterhoff et al. have also commented on this issue in *Oosterhoff on Trusts*, saying at p. 575, "Mothers and fathers are now under equal duties to care for their children and are equally likely to intend to make gifts to them.... In Canada, it is now accepted that mothers and fathers should be treated equally."

I agree. As women now have both the means as well as obligations to support their children, they are no less likely to intend to make gifts to their children than fathers. The presumption of advancement should thus apply equally to fathers and mothers.

Next, does the presumption of advancement apply between parents and adult independent children? A number of courts have concluded that it should not. In reaching that conclusion, Heeney J. in *McLear v. McLear Estate* (2000), 33 E.T.R. (2d) 272 (Ont. S.C.J.), at paras. 40–41, focussed largely on the modern practice of elderly parents adding their adult children as joint account holders so that the children can provide assistance with the management of their parents' financial affairs:

> Just as Dickson J. considered "present social conditions" in concluding that the presumption of advancement between husbands and wives had lost all relevance, a consideration of the present social conditions of an elderly parent presents an equally compelling case for doing away with the presumption of advancement between parent and adult child. We are living in an increasingly complex world. People are living longer, and it is commonplace that an ageing parent requires assistance in managing his or her daily affairs. This is particularly so given the complexities involved in managing investments to provide retirement income, paying income tax on those investments, and so on. Almost invariably, the duty of assisting the ageing parent falls to the child who is closest in geographic proximity. In such cases, Powers of Attorney are routinely given. Names are "put on" bank accounts and other assets, so that the child can freely manage the assets of the parent.
>
> Given these social conditions, it seems to me that it is dangerous to presume that the elderly parent is making a gift each time he or

she puts the name of the assisting child on an asset. The presumption that accords with this social reality is that the child is holding the property in trust for the ageing parent, to facilitate the free and efficient management of that parent's affairs. The presumption that accords with this social reality is, in other words, the presumption of resulting trust.

Heeney J. also noted that the fact that the child was independent and living away from home featured very strongly in Kerwin C.J.'s reasons for finding that no presumption of advancement arose in *Edwards v. Bradley*. A similar conclusion was reached by Klebuc J., as he was then, in *Cooper v. Cooper Estate* (1999), 27 E.T.R. (2d) 170 (Sask. Q.B.), at para. 19: "I have serious doubts as to whether presumption of advancement continues to apply with any degree of persuasiveness in Saskatchewan in circumstances where an older parent has transferred property to an independent adult child who is married and lives apart from his parent." Waters et al., too in *Waters' Law of Trusts*, at p. 395, said: "It may well be that, reflecting the financial dependency that it probably does, contemporary opinion would accord [the presumption of advancement] little weight as between a father and an independent, adult child."

I am inclined to agree. First, given that a principal justification for the presumption of advancement is parental obligation to support their dependent children, it seems to me that the presumption should not apply in respect of independent adult children. As Heeney J. noted in *McLear*, at para. 36, parental support obligations under provincial and federal statutes normally end when the child is no longer considered by law to be a minor: see e.g. *Family Law Act*, s. 31. Indeed, not only do child support obligations end when a child is no longer dependent, but often the reverse is true: an obligation may be imposed on independent adult children to support their parents in accordance with need and ability to pay: see e.g. *Family Law Act*, s. 32. Second, I agree with Heeney J. that it is common nowadays for ageing parents to transfer their assets into joint accounts with their adult children in order to have that child assist them in managing their financial affairs. There should therefore be a rebuttable presumption that the adult child is holding the property in trust for the ageing parent to facilitate the free and efficient management of that parent's affairs.

Some commentators and courts have argued that while an adult, independent child is no longer financially dependent, the presumption of advancement should apply on the basis of parental affection for their children: see e.g., *Madsen Estate*, at para. 21;

Dagle; *Christmas Estate v. Tuck* (1995), 10 E.T.R. (2d) 47 (Ont. Ct. (Gen. Div.)); and *Cho Ki Yau Trust (Trustees of) v. Yau Estate* (1999), 29 E.T.R. (2d) 204 (Ont. S.C.J.).

I do not agree that affection is a basis upon which to apply the presumption of advancement to the transfer. Indeed, the factor of affection applies in other relationships as well, such as between siblings, yet the presumption of advancement would not apply in those circumstances. However, I see no reason why courts cannot consider evidence relating to the quality of the relationship between the transferor and transferee in order to determine whether the presumption of a resulting trust has been rebutted.

The remaining question is whether the presumption of advancement should apply in the case of adult dependent children. In the present case the trial judge, at paras. 26–28, found that Paula, despite being a married adult with her own family, was nevertheless dependent on her father and justified applying the presumption of advancement on that basis.

The question of whether the presumption applies to adult dependent children begs the question of what constitutes dependency for the purpose of applying the presumption. Dependency is a term susceptible to an enormous variety of circumstances. The extent or degree of dependency can be very wide ranging. While it may be rational to presume advancement as a result of dependency in some cases, in others it will not. For example, it is not difficult to accept that in some cases a parent would feel a moral, if not legal, obligation to provide for the quality of life for an adult disabled child. This might especially be the case where the disabled adult child is under the charge and care of the parent.

As compelling as some cases might be, I am reluctant to apply the presumption of advancement to gratuitous transfers to "dependent" adult children because it would be impossible to list the wide variety of the circumstances that make someone "dependent" for the purpose of applying the presumption. Courts would have to determine on a case-by-case basis whether or not a particular individual is "dependent", creating uncertainty and unpredictability in almost every instance. I am therefore of the opinion that the rebuttable presumption of advancement with regards to gratuitous transfers from parent to child should be preserved but be limited in application to transfers by mothers and fathers to minor children.

There will of course be situations where a transfer between a parent and an adult child was intended to be a gift. It is open to the party claiming that the transfer is a gift to rebut the presumption of resulting trust by bringing evidence to support his or her claim. In addition, while dependency will not be a basis on which to apply the presumption of advancement, evidence as to the degree of dependency of an adult transferee child on the transferor parent may provide strong evidence to rebut the presumption of a resulting trust.

B. On What Standard Will the Presumptions Be Rebutted?

There has been some debate amongst courts and commentators over what amount of evidence is required to rebut a presumption. With regard to the presumption of resulting trust, some cases appear to suggest that the criminal standard, or at least a standard higher than the civil standard, is applicable: see e.g. *Bayley v. Trusts and Guarantee Co.*, [1931] 1 D.L.R. 500 (Ont. C.A.), at p. 505; *Johnstone v. Johnstone* (1913), 12 D.L.R. 537 (Ont. C.A.), at p. 539. As for the presumption of advancement, some cases seem to suggest that only slight evidence will be required to rebut the presumptions: see e.g. *Pettitt v. Pettitt*, [1970] A.C. 777 (H.L.), at p. 814; *McGrath v. Wallis*, [1995] 2 F.L.R. 114 (Eng. C.A.), at pp. 115 and 122; *Dreger (Litigation Guardian of) v. Dreger* (1994), 5 E.T.R. (2d) 250 (Man. C.A.), at para. 31.

The weight of recent authority, however, suggests that the civil standard, the balance of probabilities, is applicable to rebut the presumptions: *Burns Estate v. Mellon* (2000), 48 O.R. (3d) 641 (C.A.), at paras. 5–21; *Lohia v. Lohia*, [2001] EWCA Civ 1691, at paras. 19–21; *Dagle*, at p. 210; *Re Wilson*, at para. 52. See also Sopinka et al., at p. 116. This is also my view. I see no reason to depart from the normal civil standard of proof. The evidence required to rebut both presumptions, therefore, is evidence of the transferor's contrary intention on the balance of probabilities.

As in other civil cases, regardless of the legal burden, both sides to the dispute will normally bring evidence to support their position. The trial judge will commence his or her inquiry with the applicable presumption and will weigh all of the evidence in an attempt to ascertain, on a balance of probabilities, the transferor's actual intention. Thus, as discussed by Sopinka et al. in *The Law of Evidence in Canada*, at p. 116, the presumption will only determine the result where there is insufficient evidence to rebut it on a balance of probabilities.

C. How Should Courts Treat Survivorship in the Context of a Joint Account?

In cases where the transferor's proven intention in opening the joint account was to gift withdrawal rights to the transferee during his or her lifetime (regardless of whether or not the transferee chose to exercise that right) and also to gift the balance of the account to the transferee alone on his or her death through survivorship, courts have had no difficulty finding that the presumption of a resulting trust has been rebutted and the transferee alone is entitled to the balance of the account on the transferor's death.

In certain cases, however, courts have found that the transferor gratuitously placed his or her assets into a joint account with the transferee with the intention of retaining exclusive control of the account until his or her death, at which time the transferee alone would take the balance through survivorship: see e.g. *Standing v. Bowring* (1885), 31 Ch. D. 282, at p. 287; *Edwards v. Bradley*, [1956] O.R. 225 (C.A.), at p. 234; *Yau Estate*, at para. 25.

There may be a number of reasons why an individual would gratuitously transfer assets into a joint account having this intention. A typical reason is that the transferor wishes to have the assistance of the transferee with the management of his or her financial affairs, often because the transferor is ageing or disabled. At the same time, the transferor may wish to avoid probate fees and/or make after-death disposition to the transferee less cumbersome and time consuming.

Courts have understandably struggled with whether they are permitted to give effect to the transferor's intention in this situation. One of the difficulties in these circumstances is that the beneficial interest of the transferee appears to arise only on the death of the transferor. This has led some judges to conclude that the gift of survivorship is testamentary in nature and must fail as a result of not being in proper testamentary form: see e.g. *Hill v. Hill* (1904), 8 O.L.R. 710 (H.C.), at p. 711; *Larondeau v. Laurendeau*, [1954] O.W.N. 722 (H.C.); Hodgins J.A.'s dissent in *Re Reid* (1921), 64 D.L.R. 598 (Ont. S.C., App. Div.). For the reasons that follow, however, I am of the view that the rights of survivorship, both legal and equitable, vest when the joint account is opened and the gift of those rights is therefore *inter vivos* in nature. This has also been the conclusion of the weight of judicial opinion in recent times: see e.g. *Mordo v. Nitting*, [2006] B.C.J. No. 3081 (QL), 2006 BCSC 1761, at paras. 233–38;

Shaw v. MacKenzie Estate (1994), 4 E.T.R. (2d) 306 (N.S.S.C.), at para. 49; and *Reber v. Reber* (1988), 48 D.L.R. (4th) 376 (B.C.S.C.); see also *Waters' Law of Trusts*, at p. 406.

An early case that addressed the issue of the nature of survivorship is *Re Reid* in which Ferguson J.A. of the Ontario Court of Appeal found that the gift of a joint interest was a "complete and perfect *inter vivos* gift" from the moment that the joint account was opened even though the transferor in that case retained exclusive control over the account during his lifetime. I agree with this interpretation. I also find MacKay J.A.'s reasons in *Edwards v. Bradley* (C.A.), at p. 234, to be persuasive:

> The legal right to take the balance in the account if A predeceases him being vested in B on the opening of the account, it cannot be the subject of a testamentary disposition. If A's intention was that B should also have the beneficial interest, B already has the legal title and there is nothing further to be done to complete the gift of the beneficial interest. If A's intention was that B should not take the beneficial interest, it belongs to A or his estate and he is not attempting to dispose of it by means of the joint account. In either event B has the legal title and the only question that can arise on A's death is whether B is entitled to keep any money that may be in the account on A's death or whether he holds it as a trustee under a resulting trust for A's estate. [Emphasis added.]

Edwards v. Bradley was appealed to the Supreme Court of Canada but the issue of survivorship was not addressed.

Some judges have found that a gift of survivorship cannot be a complete and perfect *inter vivos* gift because of the ability of the transferor to drain a joint account prior to his or her death: see e.g. Hodgins J.A.'s dissent in *Re Reid*. Like the Ontario Court of Appeal in *Re Reid*, at p. 608, and *Edwards v. Bradley*, at p. 234, I would reject this view. The nature of a joint account is that the balance will fluctuate over time. The gift in these circumstances is the transferee's survivorship interest in the account balance — whatever it may be — at the time of the transferor's death, not to any particular amount.

Treating survivorship in these circumstances as an *inter vivos* gift of a joint interest has found favour in other jurisdictions, including the United Kingdom and Australia: see *Russell v. Scott* (1936), 55 C.L.R. 440, at p. 455; *Young v. Sealey*, [1949] 1 All E.R. 92 (Ch. Div.), at pp. 107–8; (in *obiter*) *Aroso v. Coutts*,

[2002] 1 All E.R. (Comm) 241, [2001] EWHC Ch 443, at paras. 29 and 36.

While not entirely analogous, the American notion of the "Totten trust" (sometimes referred to as the "Bank account trust") is now recognized as valid in most states in the United States; an individual places money in a bank account with the instruction that upon his or her death, whatever is in that bank account will pass to a named beneficiary: see *Restatement (Third) of Trusts* (2003), at para. 26 of Part 2, Chapter 5. The Totten trust is so named for the leading case establishing its validity: see *Matter of Totten*, 179 N.Y. 112 (1904). While a Totten trust does not deal with joint accounts as such, it recognizes the practicality of the depositor having control of an account during his or her lifetime but allowing the depositor's named beneficiary of that account to claim the funds remaining in the account upon the death of the depositor without the disposition being treated as testamentary: see e.g. *Matter of Berson*, 566 N.Y.S.2d 74 (1991); *Matter of Halpern*, 303 N.Y. 33 (1951).

Of course, the presumption of a resulting trust means that it will fall to the surviving joint account holder to prove that the transferor intended to gift the right of survivorship to whatever assets are left in the account to the survivor. Otherwise, the assets will be treated as part of the transferor's estate to be distributed according to the transferor's will.

Should the avoidance of probate fees be of concern to the legislature, it is open to it to enact legislation to deal with the matter.

D. What Evidence May a Court Consider in Determining Intent of the Transferor?

Where a gratuitous transfer is being challenged, the trial judge must begin his or her inquiry by determining the proper presumption to apply and then weigh all the evidence relating to the actual intention of the transferor to determine whether the presumption has been rebutted. It is not my intention to list all of the types of evidence that a trial judge can or should consider in ascertaining intent. This will depend on the facts of each case. However, I will discuss particular types of evidence at issue in this appeal and its companion case that have been the subject of divergent approaches by courts.

1. Evidence Subsequent to the Transfer

The traditional rule is that evidence adduced to show the intention of the transferor at the time of the transfer "ought to be contemporaneous, or nearly so," to the transaction: see *Clemens v. Clemens Estate*, [1956] S.C.R. 286, at p. 294, citing *Jeans v. Cooke* (1857), 24 Beav. 513, 53 E.R. 456 (Rolls Ct.). Whether evidence subsequent to a transfer is admissible has often been a question of whether it complies with the Viscount Simonds' rule in *Shephard v. Cartwright*, [1955] A.C. 431 (H.L.), at p. 445, citing *Snell's Principles of Equity* (24th ed. 1954), at p. 153:

> The acts and declarations of the parties before or at the time of the purchase, [or of the transfer] or so immediately after it as to constitute a part of the transaction, are admissible in evidence either for or against the party who did the act or made the declaration.... But subsequent declarations are admissible as evidence only against the party who made them....

The reason that subsequent acts and declarations have been viewed with mistrust by courts is because a transferor could have changed his or her mind subsequent to the transfer and because donors are not allowed to retract gifts. As noted by Huband J.A. in *Dreger*, at para. 33: "Self-serving statements after the event are too easily fabricated in order to bring about a desired result."

Some courts, however, have departed from the restrictive — and somewhat abstruse — rule in *Shephard v. Cartwright*. In *Neazor v. Hoyle* (1962), 32 D.L.R. (2d) 131 (Alta. S.C., App. Div.), for example, a brother transferred land to his sister 8 years before he died and the trial judge considered the conduct of the parties during the years after the transfer to see whether they treated the land as belonging beneficially to the brother or the sister.

The rule has also lost much of its force in England. In *Lavelle v. Lavelle*, [2004] EWCA Civ 223, at para. 19, Lord Phillips, M.R., had this to say about *Shephard v. Cartwright* and certain other authorities relied on by the appellant in that case:

> It seems to me that it is not satisfactory to apply rigid rules of law to the evidence that is admissible to rebut the presumption of advancement. Plainly, self-serving statements or conduct of a transferor, who may long after the transaction be regretting earlier generosity, carry little or no weight. [Emphasis added.]

Similarly, I am of the view that the evidence of intention that arises subsequent to a transfer should not automatically be excluded if it does not comply with the *Shephard v. Cartright* rule. Such evidence, however, must be relevant to the intention of the transferor at the time of the transfer: *Taylor v. Wallbridge* (1879), 2 S.C.R. 616. The trial judge must assess the reliability of this evidence and determine what weight it should be given, guarding against evidence that is self-serving or that tends to reflect a change in intention.

2. *Bank Documents*

60 In the past, this Court has held that bank documents that set up a joint account are an agreement between the account holders and the bank about legal title; they are not evidence of an agreement between the account holders as to beneficial title: see *Niles* and *Re Mailman*.

While I agree that bank documents do not necessarily set out equitable interests in joint accounts, banking documents in modern times may be detailed enough that they provide strong evidence of the intentions of the transferor regarding how the balance in the account should be treated on his or her death: see B. Ziff, *Principles of Property Law* (4th ed. 2006), at p. 332. Therefore, if there is anything in the bank documents that specifically suggests the transferor's intent regarding the beneficial interest in the account, I do not think that courts should be barred from considering it. Indeed, the clearer the evidence in the bank documents in question, the more weight that evidence should carry.

3. *Control and Use of the Funds in the Account*

There is some inconsistency in the caselaw as to whether a court should consider evidence as to the control of joint accounts following the transfer in ascertaining the intent of the transferor with respect to the beneficial interest in the joint account. In the present case, for example, Paula's father continued to manage the investments and to pay the taxes after establishing the joint accounts. The Court of Appeal, at para. 40, held that this factor was not determinative of Paula's father's intentions: "[w]hile control can be consistent with an intention to retain ownership, it is also not inconsistent in this case with an intention to gift the assets." In contrast, in *Madsen Estate*, at para. 34, one of the main factors the Court of Appeal relied on to show that the father did not intend to create a beneficial joint tenancy was that he remained in control of the accounts, and that he paid the taxes on the interest earned on the funds in the accounts.

I am of the view that control and use of the funds, like the wording of the bank documents, should not be ruled out in the ascertainment of the transferor's intention. For example, the transferor's retention of his or her exclusive beneficial interest in the account in his or her lifetime may support the finding of a resulting trust, unless other evidence proves that he or she intended to gift the right of survivorship to the transferee. However, evidence of use and control may be of marginal assistance only and, without more, will not be determinative for three reasons.

First, it may be that the dynamics of the relationship are such that the transferor makes the management decisions. He or she may be more experienced with the accounts. This does not negate the beneficial interest of the other account holder. Conversely, evidence that a transferee controlled the funds does not necessarily mean that the transferee took a beneficial interest. Ageing parents may set up accounts for the sole purpose of having their adult child manage their funds for their benefit.

Second, in cases involving an ageing parent and an adult child, it may be that the transferee, although entitled both legally and beneficially to withdraw funds, will refrain from accessing them in order to ensure there are sufficient funds to care for the parent for the remainder of the parent's life.

Finally, as previously discussed, the fact that a transferor controlled and used the funds during his or her life is not necessarily inconsistent with an intention at the time of the transfer that the transferee would acquire the balance of the account on the transferor's death through the gift of the right of survivorship.

4. *Granting of Power of Attorney*

Courts have also relied to varying degrees on the transferor's granting of a power of attorney to the transferee in determining intent. The Court of Appeal in *Madsen Estate*, at para. 72, noted that the transferor had granted the transferee power of attorney but did not view it "as a factor that suggested that the joint account was not set up merely as a tool of convenience for mutual access to funds". The Court of Appeal in the present case, on the other hand, placed substantial weight on Paula's father having given her both joint ownership of the accounts and power of attorney in finding that he intended to gift the assets to her. Lang J.A. reasoned, at para. 34, that had Paula's father intended only for Paula to assist in the managing of the accounts, this could have been accomplished solely by giving her power of attorney: "With that power of attorney, joint ownership of the investments was unnecessary unless [Paula's father] intended something more: to ensure the investments were given to Paula and to avoid probate fees, both entirely legitimate purposes." Lang J.A. also found, at para. 35,

that the weight to be afforded a particular piece of evidence is a matter within a trial judge's discretion.

I share Lang J.A.'s view that the trier of fact has the discretion to consider the granting of power of attorney when deciding the transferor's intention. This will be especially true when other evidence suggests that the transferor appreciated the distinction between granting that power and gifting the right of survivorship. Again however, this evidence will not be determinative and courts should use caution in relying upon it, because it is entirely plausible that the transferor granted power of attorney and placed his or her assets in a joint account but nevertheless intended that the balance of the account be distributed according to his or her will. For example, the transferor may have granted power of attorney in order to have assistance with other affairs beyond the account and may have made the transferee a joint account holder solely for added convenience.

5. *Tax Treatment of Joint Accounts*

Courts have relied to varying degrees on the transferor's tax treatment of the account in determining intent. In *Madsen Estate*, the trial judge relied in part on the fact that the transferor was the one who declared and paid income tax on the money in the joint accounts in finding that the transferor intended a resulting trust ((2004), 13 E.T.R. (3d) 44, at para. 29). In the present case, at para. 44, the trial judge noted that Paula's father continued to pay taxes on the income in joint accounts but nevertheless found that he intended to gift the joint accounts to her. I do not find either of these approaches inappropriate. The weight to be placed on tax-related evidence in determining a transferor's intent should be left to the discretion of the trial judge. However, whether or not a transferor continues to pay taxes on the income earned in the joint accounts during his or her lifetime should not be determinative of his or her intention in the absence of other evidence. For example, it may be that the transferor made the transfer for the sole purpose of obtaining assistance in the management of his or her finances and wished to have the assets form a part of his or her estate upon his or her death. Or, as discussed above, it is open to a transferor to gift the right of survivorship to the transferee when the joint accounts are opened, but to retain control over the use of the funds in the accounts (and therefore to continue to pay taxes on them) during his or her lifetime.

As for the matter of taxes on capital gains, it was submitted to this Court that for public policy reasons, transferors should not be permitted to transfer beneficial title while asserting to the tax authorities that such title has not been passed in order to defer or avoid the payment of taxes: appellant's factum, at p. 24. In principle, I agree. Where, in setting up a joint account, the transferor intends to transfer full legal and equitable title to the assets in the account immediately and the value of the assets reflects a capital gain, taxes on capital gains may become payable in the year the joint account is set up. However, where the transferor's intention is to gift the right of survivorship to the transferee but retain beneficial ownership of the assets during his or her lifetime, there would appear to be no disposition at the moment of the setting up of the joint account: see s. 73 of the *Income Tax Act*, R.S.C. 1985, c. 1 (5th Supp.). That said, the issue of the proper treatment of capital gains in the setting up of joint accounts was not argued in this appeal. I can say no more than these are matters for determination between the Canada Revenue Agency and taxpayers in specific cases.

E. Should the Decision of the Trial Judge Be Overturned?

71 The trial judge in the present case found that, at the time of the transfers, Paula and her father had a very close relationship and that Paula "clearly was the person, other than his wife, that he was closest to and most concerned about" (para. 32). Given this relationship and her financial hardships, her father preferred her over her siblings. Indeed, he was estranged from one of his daughters at the time the accounts were set up (para. 25). While he may have grown close to his son-in-law, the trial judge concluded they were simply "good friends" (para. 38). Moreover, his wife was seriously ill and not expected to outlive him.

Paula and her family relied on her father for financial assistance. While he maintained control of the accounts and used the funds for his benefit during his life, the trial judge found his concern lay with providing for Paula after his death. This is consistent with an intention to gift a right of survivorship when the accounts were set up.

The statements of Paula's father while drafting his last will are also an important indicator of intention. Although the statements were made in years subsequent to the transfer, the trial judge considered the lawyer's testimony about them reliable. The lawyer had nothing to gain from his testimony. This evidence indicates that Paula's father was of the view that the accounts had already been dealt with and understood these assets would not form part of the estate. I agree with the trial judge that

"if [the father's] intention was to have his jointly held assets devolve through the estate, they were of such magnitude that he would have at least discussed that matter with his solicitor, since they constituted a substantial proportion of what he owned" (para. 43), particularly after the lawyer asked him about life insurance policies, RRIFs and other assets. All of this evidence is consistent with Paula's father having gifted away the right of survivorship when the joint accounts were opened, and thus is relevant to his intention at the time of the transfer.

There is of course the issue of Paula's father writing to financial institutions saying that the transfers were not gifts to Paula. Consistent with these letters, Paula's father continued to control the funds in the accounts and paid income tax on the earnings of the investments before his death. The trial judge found that Paula's father's intention when he wrote the letters was "simply to avoid triggering an immediate deemed disposition of the assets in question, and therefore avoid capital gains taxes" (para. 39). I agree with the trial judge that this is not inconsistent with an intention that the balance remaining in the accounts would belong to Paula on his death.

The trial judge erred in applying the presumption of advancement. Paula, although financially insecure, was not a minor child. Karam J. should therefore have applied the presumption of a resulting trust. Nonetheless, this error does not affect the ultimate disposition of the appeal because the trial judge found that the evidence "clearly demonstrate[d] the intention" on the part of the father that the balance left in the joint accounts he had with Paula were to go to Paula alone on his death through survivorship (para. 44). I am satisfied that this strong finding regarding the father's actual intention shows that the trial judge's conclusion would have been the same even if he had applied the presumption of a resulting trust.

V.   DISPOSITION

For the reasons above, I would dismiss this appeal, with costs. Michael Pecore asked this Court for costs throughout from Paula or the estate. As noted in the judgment of the Ontario Court of Appeal, at para. 48, the trial judge denied Michael costs out of the estate or from Paula. He did so because he found that on the issues raised in the divorce proceeding, success was divided, Paula made an offer to settle that exceeded the result, and Michael's conduct was "less than candid". I see no reason to interfere with that disposition, or that costs should not follow the event in this Court.

[ABELLA J. (concurring):]

Tolstoy wrote at the beginning of *Anna Karenina* that "Happy families are all alike, every unhappy family is unhappy in its own way". That unhappiness often finds its painful way into a courtroom.

This appeal involves a father who opened joint bank accounts with his daughter, signing documents that specifically confirmed that the daughter was to have a survivorship interest. The daughter's entitlement to the remaining funds in the accounts was challenged by her ex-husband. The trial judge, who was upheld in the Court of Appeal ((2005), 19 E.T.R. (3d) 162), applied the presumption of advancement and concluded that the father's intention was to make a gift of the money to his daughter ((2004), 7 E.T.R. (3d) 113). In the companion appeal, *Madsen Estate v. Saylor*, 2007 SCC 18, the daughter's entitlement to the funds was challenged by her siblings. The trial judge applied the presumption of resulting trust rather than the presumption of advancement, and concluded that the father had *not* intended to make a gift to his daughter ((2004), 13 E.T.R. (3d) 44). The issue in both appeals is which presumption applies and what the consequences of its application are.

ANALYSIS

Historically, the presumption of advancement has been applied to gratuitous transfers to children, regardless of the child's age. If we are to continue to retain the presumption of advancement for parent–child transfers, I see no reason, unlike Rothstein J., to limit its application to non-adult children. I agree with him, however, that the scope of the presumption should be expanded to include transfers from mothers as well as from fathers.

The presumptions of advancement and resulting trust are legal tools which assist in determining the transferor's intention at the time a gratuitous transfer is made. The tools are of particular significance when the transferor has died.

If the presumption of advancement applies, an individual who transfers property into another person's name is presumed to have intended to make a gift to that person. The burden of proving that the transfer was not intended to be a gift, is on the challenger to the transfer. If the presumption of resulting trust applies, the transferor is presumed to have intended to retain the beneficial ownership. The burden of proving that a gift *was* intended, is on the recipient of the transfer.

There is an ongoing academic and judicial debate about whether the presumptions, and particularly the presumption of resulting trust, ought to be removed entirely from the judicial tool box in assessing intention. E. E. Gillese and M. Milczynski offer the following criticism, echoed by others, in *The Law of Trusts* (2nd ed. 2005):

> ... modern life has caused many to question the utility of the presumptions. When I voluntarily transfer title to property to another, is it more sensible to assume that I have made a gift or that I transferred title under the assumption that the transferee would hold title for me? Surely, it is more likely that, had I intended to create a trust, I would have taken steps to expressly create the trust and document it. It is more plausible to presume the opposite to that which equity presumed. If someone today gives away property, it is at least as likely that he intended a gift as that they intended to create some type of trust. And, if they did intend to create a trust, they should be held to the requirements that exist for express trusts and not be favoured by the presumption of a resulting trust. The fact that the presumption is out of step with modern thought explains the courts' new approach to such cases, which is to look at all the evidence with an open mind and attempt to determine intention on that basis. If that were the end of the matter, we could say that the presumption of resulting trust had been eradicated. Unfortunately, the courts have not gone that far, and the presumption will operate where the evidence is unclear. [pp. 109–10]

Similarly, in *Nelson v. Nelson* (1995), 184 C.L.R. 538, the High Court of Australia dealt with a case involving a mother's purchase of a house which she then transferred into the names of her children. In his concurring reasons, McHugh J. made the following comments about the presumption of resulting trust:

> No doubt in earlier centuries, the practices and modes of thought of the property owning classes made it more probable than not that, when a person transferred property in such circumstances, the transferor did not intend the transferee to have the beneficial as well as the legal interest in the property. But times change. To my mind — and, I think, to the minds of most people — it seems much more likely that, in the absence of an express declaration or special circumstances, the transfer of property without consideration was intended as a gift to the transferee. ...
>
> A presumption is a useful aid to decision making only when it accurately reflects the prob-

ability that a fact or state of affairs existed or has occurred. ... If the presumptions do not reflect common experience today, they may defeat the expectations of those who are unaware of them. [Emphasis added; p. 602]

McHugh J.'s allusion to "earlier centuries" reflects the origins of the presumption of resulting trust. In the 15th century, it was not uncommon for landowners in England to have title to their property held by other individuals on the understanding that it was being held for the "use" of the landowner and subject to his direction. This had the effect of separating legal and beneficial ownership. The purpose of the scheme was to avoid having to pay feudal taxes when land passed from a landowner to his heir.

It became so common for owners to transfer land to be held for their own use, that the courts began to *presume* that a transfer made without consideration, or gratuitously, was intended to be for the transferor's own use, giving rise to the presumption of resulting use. Because these nominal transfers caused a significant loss of revenue to the Crown, the *Statute of Uses, 1535* was enacted, which "executed the use", reuniting legal and equitable title (R. Chambers, "Resulting Trusts in Canada" (2000), 38 *Alta. L. Rev.* 378; *Cho Ki Yau Trust (Trustees of) v. Yau Estate* (1999), 29 E.T.R. (2d) 204 (Ont. S.C.J.)).

The presumption of resulting trust is the vestigial doctrine that emerged from the evolutionary remains of the executed use. The presumption of advancement, on the other hand, evolved as a limited exception to the presumption of resulting trust, generally arising in two situations: when a gratuitous transfer was made by a father to his child; and when a gratuitous transfer was made by a husband to his wife.

The traditional presumption of advancement as between husband and wife has been largely abandoned, both judicially (*Pettitt v. Pettitt*, [1970] A.C. 777 (H.L.), and *Rathwell v. Rathwell*, [1978] 2 S.C.R. 436) and legislatively (New Brunswick, *Marital Property Act*, S.N.B. 1980, c. M-1.1, s. 15(1); Prince Edward Island, *Family Law Act*, R.S.P.E.I. 1988, c. F-2.1, s. 14(1); Nova Scotia, *Matrimonial Property Act*, R.S.N.S. 1989, c. 275, s. 21(1); Newfoundland and Labrador, *Family Law Act*, R.S.N.L. 1990, c. F-2, s. 31(1); Ontario, *Family Law Act*, R.S.O. 1990, c. F.3, s. 14; Northwest Territories and Nunavut, *Family Law Act*, S.N.W.T. 1997, c. 18, s. 46(1); Saskatchewan, *The Family Property Act*, S.S. 1997, c. F-6.3, s. 50(1); Yukon, *Family Property and Support Act*, R.S.Y. 2002, c. 83, s. 7(2)).

But in the case of gratuitous transfers to children, the presumption "appears to retain much of its original vigour" (D.W.M. Waters, M.R. Gillen and L.D. Smith, eds., *Waters' Law of Trusts in Canada* (3rd ed. 2005), at p. 381). As noted by Cullity J. in *Yau Estate*, at para. 35:

> [I]t would be a mistake to extrapolate the treatment of the equitable presumptions in *Rathwell* out of their matrimonial property context to other situations including those involving the acquisition, or transfer, of property between strangers and between parents and their children.

Rothstein J. rejects parental affection as being a basis for the presumption, stating that "a principal justification for the presumption of advancement" in the case of gratuitous transfers to children was the "parental obligation to support their dependent children" (para. 36). With respect, this narrows and somewhat contradicts the historical rationale for the presumption. Parental affection, no less than parental obligation, has always grounded the presumption of advancement.

It is in fact the rationale of parental affection that was cited in *Waters' Law of Trusts in Canada* as an explanation for the longevity of the presumption of advancement in transfers to children:

> The presumption of advancement between father and child has not been subjected to the same re-evaluation which in recent years has overtaken the presumption between husband and wife. ... The factor of affection continues to exist, something which cannot be presumed in the relationship between strangers, and possibly for this reason the courts have seen no reason to challenge its modern significance. [Emphasis added; p. 395.]

In his article, "Reassessing Gratuitous Transfers by Parents to Adult Children" ((2006), 25 *E.T.P.J.* 174), Prof. Freedman acknowledges that while the "original rationale of the advancement rule is somewhat difficult to pin down" (p. 190), it did not arise only from the parental obligation to provide support for dependent children:

> Would that satisfaction of legal obligations was the explicit rationale of the presumption of advancement in the older cases; unfortunately, the authorities are inconsistent in approach and lead to little certainty in justifying doctrine. Indeed, this was decidedly an inquiry into gifting, not compelling support payments, and gratuitous transfers were recognized as advancements in a number of situations that are problematic for this elegant explanation of the

equitable doctrine — for example, where the donee was of legal age and even independent of his father, or was already provided for, or was illegitimate, or where the *loco parentis* principle was liberally applied to a wider class of people that would not be the object of any enforceable legal obligation. While later cases have gone on to demonstrate the highly refined skills of both counsel and judges in distinguishing one case from another based on factual considerations in determining whether the presumption ought to apply in any given circumstance, I would suggest that no uniform principle can be found in the cases. The simple fact is that the extent of the obligation between the transferor and transferee was never the focus of the inquiry, only the probable intent of the transferor in seeking to retain the beneficial interest for himself in the context of a given relationship that on its face gave rise to reasonable expectations that such gifts might be forthcoming. [Emphasis added; pp. 190–91.]

Even at the elemental stage in the development of the doctrine, the court in *Grey (Lord) v. Grey (Lady)* (1677), 2 Swans. 594, 36 E.R. 742 (H.C. Ch.), identified natural affection as a rationale for the application of the presumption of advancement:

... For the natural consideration of blood and affection is so apparently predominant, that those acts which would imply a trust in a stranger, will not do so in a son; and, *ergo,* the father who would check and control the appearance of nature, ought to provide for himself by some instrument, or some clear proof of a declaration of trust, and not depend upon any implication of law. ... [Emphasis added; p. 743.]

In *Yau Estate*, Cullity J. also observed that parental affection is a rationale for the presumption, leading Prof. Freedman in his article to conclude:

In other words, parental affection grounds the presumption and is the greatest indicator of the probable intent of the transferor. This is an attractive argument which I suggest most would agree accords with common experience. [p. 196]

Because parental affection has historically been seen as a basis for the presumption of advancement, it was routinely applied to adult as well as to minor children. In *Sidmouth v. Sidmouth* (1840), 2 Beav. 447, 48 E.R. 1254 (Rolls Ct.), for example, the court applied it in the case of a gratuitous transfer to an adult son, explaining:

As far as acts strictly contemporaneous appear, there does not appear to be anything to manifest an intention to make the son a trustee for the father. The circumstance that the son was adult does not appear to me to be material. It is said that no establishment was in contemplation, and that no necessity or occasion for advancing the son had occurred, but in the relation between parent and child, it does not appear to me that an observation of this kind can have any weight. The parent may judge for himself when it suits his own convenience, or when it will be best for his son, to secure him any benefit which he voluntarily thinks fit to bestow upon him, and it does not follow that because the reason for doing it is not known, there was no intention to advance at all. [Emphasis added; p. 1258.]

(See also *Scawin v. Scawin* (1841), 1 Y. & C.C.C. 65, 62 E.R. 792 (Ch. Ct.), and *Hepworth v. Hepworth* (1870), L.R. 11 Eq. 10.)

It is true, as was noted in *Oosterhoff on Trusts: Text, Commentary and Materials* (6th ed. 2004), at pp. 581–86, that some courts in the mid-90s began questioning whether the presumption of advancement should apply to transfers between parents and their adult children (see *Dreger (Litigation Guardian of) v. Dreger*, ((1994), 5 E.T.R. (2d) 250 (Man. C.A.), *Cooper v. Cooper Estate* (1999), 27 E.T.R. (2d) 170 (Sask. Q.B.), and *McLear v. McLear Estate* (2000), 33 E.T.R. (2d) 272 (Ont. S.C.J.)).

But in most cases, the presumption of advancement continues to be applied to gratuitous transfers from parents to their children, regardless of age. In *Madsen Estate v. Saylor*, for example, the companion appeal, the Ontario Court of Appeal found that the trial judge erred in applying the presumption of resulting trust, concluding that "the presumption of advancement can still apply to transfers of property from a father to a child, including an independent adult child" ((2005), 261 D.L.R. (4th) 597, at para. 21).

And in this appeal, the Ontario Court of Appeal took no issue with the trial judge's application of the presumption of advancement to the transfer by the father, notwithstanding that the beneficiary of the transfer, his daughter, was an adult at the time. (See also *Young v. Young* (1958), 15 D.L.R. (2d) 138 (B.C.C.A.); *Oliver Estate v. Walker*, [1984] B.C.J. No. 460 (QL) (S.C.); *Dagle v. Dagle Estate* (1990), 38 E.T.R. 164 (P.E.I.S.C., App. Div.); *Christmas Estate v. Tuck* (1995), 10 E.T.R. (2d) 47 (Ont. Ct. (Gen. Div.)); *Reain v. Reain* (1995), 20 R.F.L. (4th) 30 (Ont. Ct. (Gen. Div.)); *Sodhi v. Sodhi*, [1998] 10 W.W.R. 673 (B.C.S.C.); *Re Wilson* (1999), 27 E.T.R. (2d) 97 (Ont. Ct. (Gen. Div.)); *Yau Estate*; *Kappler v. Beaudoin*, [2000] O.J. No. 3439 (QL) (S.C.J.); *Clarke v. Hambly* (2002), 46 E.T.R. (2d) 166, 2002 BCSC 1074; and *Plamondon v. Czaban* (2004), 8 E.T.R. (3d) 135, 2004 ABCA 161.

The origin and persistence of the presumption of advancement in gratuitous transfers to children cannot, therefore, be attributed only to the financial dependency of children on their father or on the father's obligation to support his children. Natural affection also underlay the presumption that a parent who made a gratuitous transfer to a child of any age, intended to make a gift.

Rothstein J. relied too on the argument made in *McLear*, at paras. 40–41, against applying the presumption of advancement to adult children, namely, that since people are "living longer" and there are more aging parents who will require assistance in the managing of their daily financial affairs, it is "dangerous to presume that the elderly parent is making a gift each time he or she puts the name of the assisting child on an asset".

This, with respect, seems to me to be a flawed syllogism. The intention to have an adult child manage a parent's financial affairs during one's lifetime is hardly inconsistent with the intention to make a gift of money in a joint account to that child. Parents generally want to benefit their children out of love and affection. If children assist them with their affairs, this cannot logically be a reason for assuming that the desire to benefit them has been displaced. It is equally plausible that an elderly parent who gratuitously enters into a joint bank account with an adult child on whom he or she depends for assistance, intends to make a gift in gratitude for this assistance. In any event, if the intention is merely to have assistance in financial management, a power of attorney would suffice, as would a bank account without survivorship rights.

The fact that some parents may enter into joint bank accounts because of the undue influence of an adult child, is no reason to attribute the same impropriety to the majority of parent–child transfers. The operative paradigm should be based on the norm of mutual affection, rather than on the exceptional exploitation of that affection by an adult child.

I see no reason to claw back the common law in a way that disregards the lifetime tenacity of parental affection by now introducing a limitation on the presumption of advancement by restricting its application to minor children. Since the presumption of advancement emerged no less from affection than from dependency, and since parental affection flows from the inherent nature of the relationship, not of the dependency, the presumption of advancement should logically apply to all gratuitous transfers from parents to any of their children, regardless of the age or dependency of the child or the parent. The natural affection parents are presumed to have for their adult children when both were younger, should not be deemed to atrophy with age.

While, as Rothstein J. observes, affection arises in many relationships, familial or otherwise, it is not affection alone that had earned the presumption of advancement for transfers between father and child. It was the uniqueness of the parental relationship, not only in the legal obligations involved, but, more significantly, in the protective emotional ties flowing from the relationship. These ties are not attached only to the financial dependence of the child. Affection between siblings, other relatives, or even friends, can undoubtedly be used as an evidentiary basis for assessing a transferor's intentions, but the reason none of these other relationships has ever inspired a legal presumption is because, as a matter of common sense, none is as predictable of intention.

It seems to me that bank account documents which specifically confirm a survivorship interest, should be deemed to reflect an intention that what has been signed, is sincerely meant. I appreciate that in *Re Mailman Estate*, [1941] S.C.R. 368, *Niles v. Lake*, [1947] S.C.R. 291, and *Edwards v. Bradley*, [1957] S.C.R. 599, this Court said that the wording of bank documents was irrelevant in determining the intention behind joint bank accounts with respect to beneficial title. Fifty years later, however, I have difficulty seeing any continuing justification for ignoring the presumptive, albeit rebuttable, relevance of unambiguous language in banking documents in determining intention. I think it would come as a surprise to most Canadian parents to learn that in the creation of joint bank accounts with rights of survivorship, there is little evidentiary value in the clear language of what they have voluntarily signed.

It is significant to me that even though the presumption of advancement has generally been replaced in the spousal context by the presumption of resulting trust, it has nonetheless been conceptually retained in the case of spousal property which is jointly owned, such as joint bank accounts. Section 14(a) of the Ontario *Family Law Act*, for example, provides that "the fact that property is held in the name of spouses as joint tenants is proof, in the absence of evidence to the contrary, that the spouses are intended to own the property as joint tenants". Section 14(b) further specifies that "money on deposit in the name of both spouses shall be deemed to be in the name of the spouses as joint tenants for the purposes of clause (a)".

Equally, a presumed intention of joint ownership in the case of jointly held property should apply to parent–child relationships, and the appropriate mechanism for achieving this objective, absent legislative intervention, is the application of the presumption of advancement.

The trial judge, whose conclusion was upheld by the Court of Appeal, properly applied the correct legal presumption to the facts of the case. Like Rothstein J., therefore, I would dismiss the appeal.

Appeal dismissed with costs.

(n) *Madsen Estate v. Saylor*†

[ROTHSTEIN J. (for himself, McLachlin C.J. and Bastarache, Binnie, LeBel, Deschamps, Fish, and Charron JJ.):]

I. INTRODUCTION

This appeal, like its companion case, *Pecore v. Pecore*, 2007 SCC 17 (released concurrently), involves questions about joint bank and investment accounts. As discussed more fully in *Pecore*, joint accounts are used by many Canadians for a variety of purposes, including estate planning and financial management.

While the focus in any dispute over a gratuitous transfer is the actual intention of the transferor at the time of the transfer, intention is often difficult to ascertain, especially in cases where the transferor is deceased. The common law has developed certain rebuttable presumptions of law over many years to guide a court's inquiry.

In this case, the trial judge found that there was no evidence to support Patricia's position that her father intended to gift the joint accounts to her and held that the joint bank account and joint investments be included in the transferor's estate. The Court of Appeal dismissed the appeal.

I conclude that there is no basis to overturn this result. The appeal should be dismissed.

II. FACTS

The dispute in this appeal is between Patricia Brooks, who was made a joint account holder by her father, and her two siblings. The trial judge found that the joint accounts in dispute totalled $185,000.

The father and mother prepared their wills in 1982. In the event there was no surviving spouse, the estate was to be divided into two halves. One half was to be divided equally between Patricia and her two siblings. The other half was to be divided equally between their eight grandchildren. This will was never changed.

At that time, Patricia was named alternate executor and was also named an alternate power of attorney. She claimed that her mother had told her she had passed various "tests" that showed she was the most responsible child; it was for this reason that her parents gave her these powers.

Patricia's mother died in 1986. In 1991, the father made Patricia a joint signatory on his bank accounts, which provided for a right of survivorship. He also executed a new power of attorney in her favour. In September of 1997, the joint accounts were closed and the funds deposited into another bank account and an investment account, which again was a joint account with Patricia and had a right of survivorship.

The father retained control of the bank accounts and the funds were used solely for his benefit during his life. He also declared and paid all taxes on income made from the accounts.

In 1994, Patricia's brother (and later his wife) moved in with the father. In 1997, the father moved in with Patricia due to his declining health and Patricia provided him care. In 1998, he moved into a nursing home.

There was conflicting evidence from Patricia and her siblings as to their relationships with their father. Patricia claimed to be the preferred child and that her father's relationship with her siblings was strained. Her siblings claimed to have a good relationship with their father.

† 2007 SCC 18.

In late 1998, Patricia's father died. The litigation was commenced by her siblings against her as executor because she did not include the accounts in the distribution of the estate.

III. JUDICIAL HISTORY

A. *Ontario Superior Court of Justice* (2004), 13 E.T.R. (3d) 44

Van Melle J. found that there was no evidence to support Brooks' position that her father intended to gift the contents of the joint accounts to her. As a result, she ordered that the joint bank account and joint investments be included in the estate and ordered Patricia to pay to the estate a sum of $185,000. With respect to the general issue of the status of the law of the presumptions of advancement and resulting trust, Van Melle J. stated at paras. 24–25 she thought that it was time for the presumption of advancement from father to child to be abandoned in favour of the presumption of resulting trust in all but the most limited cases.

B. *Ontario Court of Appeal* (2005), 261 D.L.R. (4th) 597

LaForme J.A., in writing for the majority, reviewed the relevant presumptions of resulting trust and advancement. He determined that the trial judge was incorrect in applying the law of resulting trust and should have applied a presumption of advancement; however, he added that the trial judge was not required to consider either presumption because here the intention of the father at the time of transfer was demonstrated on the evidence. He found that regardless of whether the trial judge applied a presumption of advancement or resulting trust, it was evident from her detailed reasons that she carefully weighed all of the evidence before arriving at the conclusion that at the time of transfer the joint bank account and joint investments were not intended as gifts but rather were intended to be included as part of the estate. He concluded that there was no basis upon which the court should interfere with the trial judge's factual findings and conclusions.

Feldman J.A., in dissent, disagreed with the approach and conclusion reached by LaForme J.A. She held that the trial judge had erred in law by concluding that (1) the presumption of advancement from father to child must be abandoned in favour of the presumption of resulting trust in all but limited cases; (2) that the presumption of resulting trust applied in this case; and (3) that the onus was on Patricia to prove that her father intended to gift the joint investments to her. She therefore held that the appeal should be allowed, the order of the trial judge set aside and a new trial ordered.

IV. ANALYSIS

How the rebuttable presumptions of a resulting trust and advancement operate and guide a court's analysis is discussed in the *Pecore* decision.

In the present case, a presumption of a resulting trust applies to the gratuitous transfer of assets by Patricia's father into the joint accounts with Patricia. The presumption of advancement has no application because Patricia was not a minor child of her father. Patricia therefore had the burden of rebutting the presumption of a resulting trust by showing that her father intended to gift the assets in the accounts to her on the balance of probabilities.

Van Melle J. found that there was no evidence to support Patricia's position that her father intended to gift the contents of his joint accounts to her — there was no documentation to that effect, there was no clear statement to anyone and the father's conduct *vis-à-vis* the joint accounts while he was alive did not support this contention. Indeed, she also did not believe much of Patricia's evidence, finding that she was "evasive and gave conflicting evidence" and that she purposely misrepresented events (para. 51). Van Melle J. found that the father had sole control of the assets in the accounts during his lifetime and he declared and paid all income tax on the income generated from the joint accounts and investments. She concluded that the joint account agreement was not determinative of the father's intention. She could not find evidence of an intention to benefit Patricia financially over the other children.

As discussed in *Pecore*, at paras. 62–66, the fact that a transferor maintains sole control over or use of funds in a joint account will not be determinative of whether a transferee is entitled to the balance in the account upon the transferor's death. Whether or not a transferor continues to pay tax on the income of the joint accounts is also not determinative.

However, I am unable to agree with the trial judge that there was no evidence to suggest that Patricia's father intended for her alone to have the assets in the joint accounts. On the relevant financial institution documents, the father elected to have the joint accounts carry a right of survivorship. Patricia testified that both she and her father acknowledged that they understood at the time that this meant that on the death of one of the joint account holders, the other would become the sole owner.

As discussed in *Pecore*, at para. 61, banking documents may, in modern times, be detailed enough that they provide strong evidence of the intention of the transferor regarding how the balance in the accounts should be treated on his or her death. The clearer the evidence in the documents, the more weight that evidence should carry.

Therefore, the financial institution documents and Patricia's evidence about them did constitute some evidence that was relevant to the father's intention. The question now is whether this matter should be remitted to the trial judge to redetermine the result taking account of the evidence that she ignored in her initial decision or whether it is appropriate for this court to substitute its decision for that of the trial judge.

Patricia's father died in 1998. This matter has been outstanding for over eight years. The amount in dispute is some $185,000. To remit the matter to the trial judge in these circumstances would involve more costs, more time and potentially further appeals. Having regard to the fact that this case has been to trial — a trial which lasted approximately 15 days — has been to appeal and now has been further appealed to this Court, it is difficult to see how any of the litigants will benefit if the matter is remitted for yet another trial.

It is well established that where the circumstances warrant, appellate courts have the jurisdiction to make a fresh assessment of the evidence on the record: *Hollis v. Dow Corning Corp.*, [1995] 4 S.C.R. 634, at para. 33; *Prudential Trust Co. v. Forseth*, [1960] S.C.R. 210, at pp. 216–17. Having regard to the circumstances of the present appeal, I think it is both feasible on a practical level and within the interests of justice for this Court to consider the evidence not considered by the trial judge and make a final determination rather than sending the case back to trial.

Beyond the fact that both accounts were designated as carrying the right of survivorship, the banking documents do not contain any express reference to beneficial entitlement to the assets in the accounts. The Toronto-Dominion Account Agreement provided:

> If the account *has a right of survivorship* then if any one or more of us dies any moneys standing to the credit of the account are to be subject to withdrawal by the survivor or, if more than one, by any one or more of the survivors.... [Emphasis in original.]

The CIBC Wood Gundy Account Agreement provided:

> The following provisions shall apply upon the death of any Applicant: (i) the survivor(s) will promptly notify you of such death; (ii) the survivor(s) will provide you with a certified copy of the death certificate...; (iii) the estate of the deceased shall continue to be liable for any amounts owing...; and (iv) the survivor(s) shall continue to have the same rights as described in paragraph 12(c) [providing for the operation of the accounts by the survivor].

Having regard to the lack of clarity in the documents on this critical point, I would accord them little weight insofar as the issue of beneficial entitlement to the assets in the accounts is concerned.

As to Patricia's testimony, the trial judge found that she "was evasive and gave conflicting evidence" and that "she purposely misrepresented events" (para. 51). The trial judge observed that contrary to instructions given to her not to discuss her testimony while under cross-examination, she contravened that admonition. The trial judge also noted that Patricia removed estate files from the estate's solicitor without authorization and failed to return them despite requests to do so. For these reasons, little weight can be accorded to Patricia's evidence as to what her father understood at the time the joint accounts were opened about beneficial title to the assets in the accounts on his death.

Thus, even having regard to the financial institution documents and Patricia's testimony in relation to them, such evidence is insufficient to rebut the presumption of resulting trust. This conclusion is consistent with the trial judge's conclusion based on the evidence she did consider.

Patricia also argued that the closing balances of the joint accounts at the death of the father was $167,675.09. The respondents maintained that the factual finding by the trial judge that the amount was $185,000 should be upheld. The trial judge heard evidence on the matter and in her judgment ordered Patricia to pay $185,000. I see no reason to disturb that result.

Patricia also argued that this Court should find that the respondents are indebted to the estate in the sum of $35,900 and $26,360 respectively. According to Patricia, her father insisted that she have the respondents sign promissory notes to evidence their indebtedness to him. The trial judge considered the matter and found that collection of the notes is statute barred and that even if it were not, she was not satisfied that Patricia had successfully established that the promissory notes were outstanding and were meant to be repaid to the estate. Again, I see no palpable and overriding error in the trial judge's finding of fact which would merit disturbing the result.

V.   DISPOSITION

I would dismiss this appeal, with costs to the respondents payable by Ms. Brooks and not out of the estate.

[ABELLA J. (dissenting):]

My views on the scope of the presumption of advancement are discussed in the *Pecore* decision (2007 SCC 17), released concurrently. Like the majority, I would apply the presumption of advancement to all gratuitous transfers from parents to their children regardless of the parent's gender. Unlike the majority, I would not restrict its application to transfers to non-adult children. In *Pecore*, the difference in our legal approaches did not lead me to a different result. In this appeal, it does. I would allow the appeal and order a new trial.

Both the majority and dissent in the Court of Appeal agreed that in applying the presumption of resulting trust, the trial judge erred, improperly placing the onus on the daughter, Patricia Ann Brooks, to prove that her father, Niels Madsen, intended to make a gift to her of the funds held jointly in her and her father's name: (2005), 261 D.L.R. (4th) 597.

When Mr. Madsen's wife died, all funds in their joint bank accounts accrued to him by virtue of his right of survivorship. On May 3, 1991, he transferred the funds in these accounts to a joint account in his and his daughter's name. The bank documents, as in the case of those with his wife, provided for a right of survivorship. These were the accounts that were transferred into the joint account with Ms. Brooks on September 9, 1997.

There was conflicting evidence at trial about the relationship between the father and his three children. Ms. Brooks' evidence was that the reason her father decided to make a gift of the joint accounts to her was that by the spring of 1991, she had been widowed and was ill with complications from cancer. According to her, her father wanted to provide her and her children with financial security.

Her evidence was vigorously disputed by her brother and sister. Their evidence was that they had a very good relationship with their father and that

Mr. Madsen treated all of his children equally. They pointed out, by way of example, that at Christmas in 1996, two years before he died, their father gave each of his children a gift of $1,000.

Feldman J.A., in dissent in the Ontario Court of Appeal, observed at para. 86 that, like *Pecore*, this case is a situation where there is "no issue of undue influence or overbearance, but strictly a voluntary and intentional transfer into a joint account". Yet, as she noted, several factors relied on by the trial judge and the Court of Appeal in *Pecore* ((2004), 7 E.T.R. (3d) 113 and (2005), 19 E.T.R. (3d) 162) to *confirm* the father's intention to make a gift of funds in joint bank accounts to his adult daughter were either disregarded by the trial judge in this case or used as evidence of a contrary intention.

In *Pecore*, the trial judge, applying the presumption of advancement, used the following factors as confirmation of an intention to make a gift:

- the father had personal knowledge that the consequence of having a joint account was that the daughter would have a right of survivorship in the funds; and
- the joint bank accounts were not needed as a tool of convenience to assist the father since the daughter already had a power of attorney.

In addition, the father's control of the bank accounts during his lifetime was found by the Court of Appeal in *Pecore* not to be inconsistent with his intention to make a gift of the funds. In this case, Mr. Madsen's control was held to be evidence of an intention *not* to make a gift of the funds.

These inconsistencies were cogently amplified by Feldman J.A. as follows:

> In *Pecore*, the father put significant funds into joint accounts with one of his three adult children, Paula, because she was the most financially in need. In his will, the father named Paula and her dependant husband as residuary beneficiaries. After the father's death, the husband separated from Paula, learned that he was a residuary beneficiary under his ex-father-in-law's will, and, in the course of his divorce proceedings against Paula, challenged her right of survivorship to the jointly-held funds, because the effect of the right of survivorship was that those funds did not form part of the estate.
>
> In the context of examining the facts that might speak to the father's intention at the time he transferred his investments into joint ownership, the court first noted that the father was familiar with joint ownership as an estate planning tool because he and his wife had held their investments jointly and they had devolved to

him as the survivor. The court concluded that the father therefore knew that on his death, his joint investments would devolve to Paula as his survivor.

In this case, there was evidence that the father had also held his investments in joint tenancy with his wife, and they devolved to him on her death. Following his wife's death, he opened a joint account with his daughter, [Ms. Brooks]. A court could therefore conclude that he knew that when he died, his joint investments would devolve to [Ms. Brooks] as his survivor. However, neither the trial judge nor my colleague chose to take this factor into account.

A second factor considered by the court in *Pecore* was that the father gave Paula his power of attorney. The court took that as evidence that he was not using the joint account with Paula as a tool of convenience to give her signing access on the account. She would have that with the power of attorney. Rather, it showed that the father intended something more.

Similarly, in this case, the father also gave [Ms. Brooks] his power of attorney. [Ms. Brooks] was also the executrix of his estate and looked after him physically at the end of his life. Again, neither the trial judge nor my colleague viewed the giving of the power of attorney as a factor that suggested that the joint account was not set up merely as a tool of convenience for mutual access to funds.

A third factor considered by the court in *Pecore* involved the significance of the father maintaining control over the investments during his life. In *Pecore*, Paula and her father had agreed that he would manage the investments and pay the taxes on them. This court held that "[w]hile control can be consistent with intention to retain ownership, it is also not inconsistent in this case with an intention to gift the assets. Hence, this factor was not determinative of [the father's] actual intention" (para. 40). In contrast, in this case, one of the main factors my colleague relies on to show that the father did not intend to create a beneficial joint tenancy is that he remained in control of his finances and that he paid the taxes on the interest on the funds. [paras. 68–73]

The fact that the trial judge ignored or drew contrary inferences from certain factors considered by the Court of Appeal in *Pecore* to be reflective of an intention to make a gift, illustrates how her error in applying the presumption of resulting trust may have influenced her findings of fact and credibility. The key finding made by the trial judge in this case, a finding which reflects the erroneous assignment of the burden of proof to Ms. Brooks, was that there is "no evidence to support Patricia Brooks' position that [her father] intended to gift the contents of his joint account to her", emphasizing the lack of "documentation to this effect" and the lack of a "clear and unequivocal statement in this regard to anyone" ((2004), 13 E.T.R. (3d) 44, at para. 58).

In the final analysis, I share the views of Feldman J.A. who observed:

> As demonstrated, the factors a court may take into account in its attempt to determine the transferor's intention at the time of transfer will be given different weight. This will depend on how the trial judge views the whole of the evidence, including the credibility of the witnesses, and the trial judge's view of the evidence may be affected by the onus of proof he or she applies. Since the trial judge in this case applied the incorrect onus of proof and relied on evidence that occurred years after the joint account was established, I am of the view that this court ought not to rely on her assessment of the evidence in order to determine the actual intention of the father when he put his funds into joint accounts with the appellant, nor should it determine the weight to be given to the factors that speak to the father's intent at the time he established the joint account. Instead, in order to fairly decide this case, it seems to me that a new trial must be ordered. [para. 74]

I would therefore allow the appeal and order a new trial.

Appeal dismissed with costs, ABELLA J. dissenting.

Trust Accounts and Trust Obligations

Background Reading: M.H. Ogilvie, *Bank and Customer Law in Canada*, 2d Edition (Toronto: Irwin Law, 2013) Chapter 6, pages 227–234; Chapter 7, pages 255–256.

(a) *Banque Belge pour L'Etranger v. Hambrouck*†

[ATKIN L.J.:]

The facts in this case appear to be as follows. A.M. Pelabon, trading as the Pelabon Works, in 1917 and onwards employed as a clerk in the cashier's department a man named Hambrouck. During his employment between June 5, 1917, and August 31, 1919, Hambrouck obtained from the plaintiff Bank, the bankers of the Pelabon Works, the sum of £6,680 13s. 6d. by means of cheques purporting to be drawn *per pro.* the Pelabon Works, but in fact without the authority of that firm. The cheques material to this action were drawn in favour of Hambrouck himself to his order, and as Hambrouck used the firm's form of cheque which had a printed crossing on them, the cheques were crossed. They therefore had to pass through a bank. Hambrouck accordingly opened an account with Farrow's Bank, Richmond Branch, and having indorsed the cheques paid them into his account. Farrow's Bank cleared through the then London and South Western Bank now merged in Barclays Bank, through whom the account of these cheques was collected from the plaintiff Bank and the proceeds were placed to Hambrouck's credit. In substance no other funds were paid into the account than the proceeds of these forged cheques. I call them forged because Hambrouck being indicted for forging them pleaded guilty and has been sentenced

for forgery. As between M. Pelabon and the plaintiff Bank there has been a dispute whether Hambrouck had ostensible authority, which has been resolved since action brought by M. Pelabon withdrawing his claim as against the Bank. This seems to me not to affect the right of the parties, as will hereafter appear. Hambrouck during this time was living with the defendant Spanoghe as his mistress. He made her a monthly allowance for housekeeping, and in addition gave her sums of money. In particular the defendant during the time she lived with Hambrouck received from him in notes at various dates the sum of £465. It seems immaterial whether part of that sum was or was not her savings from the housekeeping money. If it were, presumably Hambrouck acquiesced in her keeping it, and the learned judge has found, and it is impossible to dispute his finding, that all these sums were given to the defendant as the consideration for the continuance of illicit cohabitation. The sums in question all came from Hambrouck's banking account; they were paid by the defendant into a deposit account which she opened at the Twickenham Branch of the defendant Bank, the London Joint City and Midland Bank. No other sums were at any time placed to that deposit account. £150 was drawn out by the defendant for the purpose of Hambrouck's defence. The balance,

---

† [1921] 1 K.B. 321 (C.A.). [Notes omitted.]

£315, is the subject of the present action. It is claimed by the plaintiffs; the defendant Bank under an order of the Court dated October 7, 1919, have paid the amount into Court; and the action has been discontinued against them, and proceeded against the other defendant.

The money was obtained from the plaintiff Bank by the fraud of Hambrouck. It does not appear to be necessary for this case to determine whether Hambrouck stole the money or obtained it by false pretences. At present it appears to me that the plaintiff Bank intended to pass the property in and the possession of the cash which under the operations of the clearing house they must be taken to have paid to the collecting bank. I will assume therefore that this is a case not of a void but of a voidable transaction by which Hambrouck obtained a title to the money until the plaintiffs elected to avoid his title, which they did when they made their claim in this action. The title would then revest in the plaintiffs subject to any title acquired in the meantime by any transferee for value without notice of the fraud.

The appellant however contends that the plaintiffs cannot assert their title to the sum of money which was on a deposit account: 1. because it has passed through one if not two bank accounts and therefore cannot be identified as the plaintiffs' money; 2. because in any case a transfer to an innocent donee defeats the original owner's claim. The course of the proceedings in this case is not quite clear. The statement of claim alleges specifically that the money is the property of the plaintiffs which they are entitled to follow, and the relief asked is not for a money judgment against the defendants, but an order that the sum paid into Court by the defendant Bank should be paid out to the plaintiffs. In giving judgment however, the learned judge has treated the claim as one for money had and received, and the judgment entered is an ordinary judgment against the appellant on a money claim for £315 together with an order that the sum in Court should be paid out to the plaintiffs in part satisfaction. The two forms of relief are different, and though in this case there is no substantial difference in the result, the grounds upon which relief is based might have been material.

First, does it make any difference to the plaintiffs' right that their money was paid into Farrow's Bank, and that the money representing it drawn out by Hambrouck was paid to the defendant Bank on deposit? If the question be the right of the plaintiffs in equity to follow their property, I apprehend that no difficulty arises. The case of *In re Hallett's Estate*[1]

makes it plain that the Court will investigate a banking account into which another person's money has been wrongfully paid, and will impute all drawings out of the account in the first instance to the wrongdoer's own moneys, leaving the plaintiffs' money intact so far as it remains in the account at all. There can be no difficulty in this case in following every change of form of the money in question, whether in the hands of Hambrouck or of the appellant, and it appears to me that the plaintiffs were, on the grounds alleged in the statement of claim, entitled to a specific order for the return of the money in question, and, as it is now represented by the sum in Court, to payment out of Court of that sum.

The question whether they are entitled to a common law judgment for money had and received may involve other considerations. I am not without further consideration prepared to say that every person who can in equity establish a right to have his money or the proceeds of his property restored to him, can, as an alternative, bring an action against the person who has been in possession of such money or proceeds for money had and received; still less that he can always bring trover or detinue. But the common law rights are large and are admirably stated in *Taylor v. Plumer*,[2] which was a case stated for the opinion of the Court of King's Bench after trial before Lord Ellenborough at the London Sittings. The facts are significant. Sir Thomas Plumer wishing to invest in exchequer bills gave his broker, Walsh, a draft on his bankers for £22,200 to be invested accordingly. Walsh cased the draft, receiving bank notes. He bought £6,500 exchequer bills. With the balance he bought certain American securities, paying for them with the actual notes received from the bank. But he gave one of the notes to his brother-in-law, from whom he received a draft on the brother-in-law's bankers for £500. With this draft he bought bullion — namely 71-1/2 doubloons — intending to abscond to North America via Lisbon. Sir Thomas Plumer's attorney overtook Walsh at Falmouth, and secured from him a return of the American securities and the bullion. Walsh, who was afterwards indicted, tried, found guilty subject to the opinion of the judges and pardoned without judgment having been passed, was made bankrupt on an act of bankruptcy alleged to have been committed before he returned the property. His assignees in bankruptcy brought trover against Sir Thomas Plumer. It was held by Lord Ellenborough delivering the judgment of the Court that the defendant was entitled to succeed, for he had repossessed himself of that of which he never ceased to be the lawful

579

proprietor. "The plaintiff", he says, "...is not entitled to recover if the defendant has succeeded in maintaining these propositions in point of law — *viz.*, that the property of a principal entrusted by him to his factor for any special purpose belongs to the principal, notwithstanding any change which that property may have undergone in point of form, so long as such property is capable of being identified, and distinguished from all other property.... It makes no difference in reason or law into what other form, different from the original, the change may have been made, whether it be into that of promissory notes for the security of the money which was produced by the sale of the goods of the principal, as in *Scott v. Surman*,[3] or into other merchandise, as in *Whitecomb v. Jacob*,[4] for the product of or substitute for the original thing still follows the nature of the thing itself, as long as it can be ascertained to be such, and the right only ceases when the means of ascertainment fail, which is the case when the subject is turned into money, and mixed and confounded in a general mass of the same description." I notice that in *Sinclair v. Brougham*[5] Lord Haldane L.C. in dealing with this decision says: "Lord Ellenborough laid down, as a limit to this proposition, that if the money had become incapable of being traced, as, for instance, when it had been paid into the broker's general account with his banker, the principal had no remedy excepting to prove as a creditor for money had and received," and proceeds to say "you can, even at law, follow, but only so long as the relation of debtor and creditor has not superseded the right *in rem*." The words above "as for instance" *et seq.* do not represent and doubtless do not purport to represent Lord Ellenborough's actual words; and I venture to doubt whether the common law ever so restricted the right as to hold that the

money became incapable of being traced, merely because paid into the broker's general account with his banker. The question always was: Had the means of ascertainment failed? But if in 1815 the common law halted outside the bankers' door, by 1879 equity had had the courage to life the latch, walk in and examine the books: *In re Hallett's Estate*.[1] I see no reason why the means of ascertainment so provided should not now be available both for common law and equity proceedings. If, following the principles laid down in *In re Hallett's Estate*,[1] it can be ascertained either that the money in the bank, or the commodity which it has bought is "the product of, or substitute for, the original thing," then it still follows "the nature of the thing itself." On these principles it would follow that as the money paid into the bank can be identified as the product of the original money, the plaintiffs have the common law right to claim it, and can sue for money had and received. In the present case less difficulty than usual is experienced in tracing the descent of the money, for substantially no other money has ever been mixed with the proceeds of the fraud. Under the order of the Court in this case I think the money paid into Court must be treated as paid in on behalf of the defendant Spanoghe, and the money judgment, together with the order for payment out to the plaintiffs, effectually secures their rights.

Secondly, so far as it is contended that the bankers are entitled to retain possession where they have not given value, I think that has been concluded by what I have already said as to valuable consideration.

I agree that the appeal should be dismissed.

Appeal dismissed.

(b)   *Arthur Andersen Inc. v. Toronto-Dominion Bank*†

[GRANGE and McKINLAY JJ.A.:]

These appeals are taken from the judgment of O'Brien J. after a 14-day trial wherein he ordered the defendant, The Toronto-Dominion Bank (the

"Bank"), to pay into court sums of money totalling approximately $10,500,000 together with interest, all on account of its dealings with the Penta Stolp Corporation ("Stolp"), a real estate company, its subsidiaries and associated companies. The Bank's liability

† (1994), 17 O.R. (3d) 363 at 366–88 (C.A.).

arose in part because of the trial judge's interpretation of a contract between the Bank and the companies and in part from his conclusion that the conduct of the Bank amounted to a breach of trust.

There was nothing remarkable in the early relations between the Bank and the companies. Stolp involved itself, starting in 1982, in many real estate projects, each conducted under a separate corporate name (the "Stolp companies"). Each company had a separate bank account with the Bank at its Mississauga branch. By March 1986, there were at least 19 separate projects, each with its own corporate name and each with its separate account. There was no particular financial difficulty with any of them, but from time to time they incurred overdrafts which necessitated communication and paper work between the Bank and the company concerned. It became an administrative headache, and in March of 1986 the Bank suggested a solution in the form of a "mirror system" of accounting. An agreement (attached as Sch. "A" [see pp. 396–406 *post*]) was entered into between the Bank and each of the Stolp companies, whereby there would be created a mirror or offset account corresponding to each working of "designated" account for each project.

Clause 5(a) of the agreement required that, at the end of each day, there would be deposited in or withdrawn from each mirror account an amount equal to the debit or credit balance in its corresponding designated account. Thus, each mirror account would exactly offset the balance in its designated account, resulting in a combined balance of zero at the end of each day. The agreement also required the creation of an account, which was in the name of Stolp Homes (Toronto) Inc., referred to in the agreement as the "concentration account". Clause 5(b) of the agreement required that any balance deposited to or withdrawn from a mirror account would be offset by a withdrawal from or deposit in the concentration account of a similar amount.

It is obvious that the result of the agreement was to permit an informal transfer of debits and credits between all of the operating companies. As long as the companies as a group were in a credit balance with the Bank (as reflected in the concentration account), there was no problem in funding the day-to-day operations of all companies in the group. Deposits went into the designated accounts, and cheques issued against those accounts were paid. Only if the concentration account went into overdraft was there a problem, and in such an event the Bank would require Stolp to provide funds to remedy the situation. As a result, the Bank and the officers of Stolp were freed from constant discussion about temporary overdrafts in individual accounts. Additional benefits to Stolp were that banking administration costs were decreased, and interest was paid to Stolp on credit balances in the concentration account. Previously the Bank had charged interest on overdrafts in the individual accounts, but no interest had been paid on credit balances.

The total agreement is relevant to the relationship that followed, but paras. 5 and 6 are crucial and they are set out below.

> 5. As of the end of each banking day:
>   (a) the Bank shall make deposits to and withdrawals from the offset accounts of each Participant so that, at the end of each banking day, the balance (whether a debit or credit) in each designated account or, in the case where a group of designated accounts is carried in the name of any one Participant, the net balance thereof, is exactly offset by a contra balance (an amount which when added to the balance in the designated account or the net balance in the group of designated accounts with total zero) in a related offset account and,
>   (b) each and all amounts deposited to and withdrawn from the offset accounts under sub-paragraph (a) above, shall be offset by withdrawing a similar amount from or depositing a similar amount to the concentration account.
>
> 6. The concentration account shall be held for and in the name of Concentrator. The amount of any credit balance on deposit in the concentration account is the property of Concentrator and the amount of any overdraft which the Bank may permit in the concentration account, and interest thereon, is an obligation owed by Concentrator to the Bank. The Bank may permit Concentrator temporarily to overdraw the concentration account; it is a condition of this Agreement that Concentrator have at all times an authorized line of credit, with the Bank, sufficient to support the transactions in the concentration account.
>
> The Concentrator will ensure that at all times any overdraft in the Concentration Account will be kept within credit limit authorized by the Bank. The Bank may refuse to honour any drawing upon a designated account which in the opinion of the Bank would result in a transfer from the Concentration Account being made that would cause liability in the Concentration Account to exceed such credit limit.

The designated accounts were maintained to show the financial state of each separate project, but they no longer (at least in the view of the Bank) represented the state of financial affairs between the Bank and the particular company. And therein lies the problem. The trial judge held that on the termination of the relationship by the Bank on February 11, 1991, each separate company was entitled to the balance in its designated account regardless of the existence of the mirror account or of the state of the concentration account.

The Bank took the position on termination that none of the credit balances in the designated accounts existed, having been transferred through the mirror accounts to the concentration account where the Concentrator, Stolp Toronto, had a credit balance of $244,969.38. The Bank, making no claim to that money for itself, eventually paid that amount together with interest pursuant to a court order to the plaintiff, Arthur Andersen Inc. ("A.A.I."), which had been appointed trustee of the Stolp companies pursuant to the provisions of the *Construction Lien Act*, R.S.O. 1990, c. C. 30 (the "*Lien Act*"). The Bank maintained that credit balances in the designated accounts did not represent true credit balances because those balances were offset by debit balances in the mirror accounts. The designated accounts merely showed the state of the particular project for internal accounting purposes.

INTERPRETATION OF THE AGREEMENT

The trial judge found that the agreement was ambiguous, and was capable of two interpretations. After admitting and examining extrinsic evidence, including understandings of various officers of the participating companies (the "participants") and the Bank, he held that all transfers out of the designated accounts were notional, not real, and that every credit balance remained in the particular designated account for the credit of each individual participant. As he put it, that conclusion was "probably sufficient to dispose of the litigation" but he went on, in any event, to dispose of the "trust fund issue" as will we also, in due course.

To resolve the issue relating to the "mirror system", we cannot agree with the conclusion of the trial judge that pursuant to the agreement the credit balances in the designated accounts truly represented the moneys owing by the Bank to each participant. We quite frankly can see no ambiguity in the agreement and can see no ground for admitting the view of the parties or their officers as to its meaning. There may be some ground for considering the

details of its operation, but we find nothing in its operation contrary to its plain meaning.

The agreement, by cl. 5(a), provides for the Bank to make deposits to or withdrawals from each mirror or offset account equal to the balance in the designated account of each participant so that the designated account balance is exactly offset. Clause 5(b) provides that the offset account will be reflected in the concentration account. Paragraph 6 provides that the credit balance in the concentration account is the property of the Concentrator (Stolp Homes (Toronto) Inc.), and that any debit balance is a debt of the Concentrator to the Bank. The Bank governed its affairs, including honouring cheques drawn on all designated accounts, on the basis of the balance in the concentration account. The agreement simply cannot be taken to mean that, despite the use of funds for the benefit of all Stolp companies, the balance in each designated account remained the property of each particular participant. Such an interpretation would result (as indeed this judgment has resulted) in large sums being in the Bank to the credit of some participants, and large debit balances of some participants being ignored, or regarded merely as a bad debt of the Bank. If the agreement had so provided, the parties might have been bound by it, but it did not so provide, and to insert such a term makes no commercial sense whatever. The Stolp companies, as a group, took advantage of the agreement for many years, and it is hard to believe that they would question its interpretation at such a late stage. However, they do, and their arguments as to its interpretation, and those of the other respondents, must be addressed.

All respondents express the view that the use of the mirror system is inappropriate in a construction context, where moneys which could constitute trust funds under the *Lien Act* are deposited into operating accounts. At least one bank officer agreed with that view. However, although the fact that the system was used in such a context could well result in the Bank being liable to construction trust fund claimants, this issue is irrelevant to the interpretation of the agreement.

Before dealing with his interpretation of the agreement, the trial judge considered the right of a bank to combine or set off debts and accounts. With respect, although the law on that point is clear and undisputed, it is not relevant in this case, since we are dealing here with a specific contract which provides for set-off. The only general law which could apply in such a situation is law *precluding* set-off specifically agreed to by contract.

The trial judge also referred to a passage in Crawford and Falconbridge, *Banking and Bills of Exchange*, 8th ed., at pp. 784–85, commenting on the operation of mirror accounting systems. It appears that it is this comment which raises the question of whether or not transfers within such a system are "notional" or "real". As mentioned above, the trial judge came to the conclusion in this case that the transfers between the mirror and concentration accounts were "notional". Without either agreeing or disagreeing with the validity of that distinction when dealing with accounts created by agreement, we are of the view that, in this case, the transfers had to be real. They resulted in the automatic availability to all Stolp companies of funds transferred to the concentration account via the mirror system, at times when those accounts otherwise would have been overdrawn.

As stated earlier, we see no ambiguity in the agreement, but the trial judge certainly did. He stated at p. 12 of his reasons: "On the basis of the agreement in this case, I am satisfied there are two reasonable alternative interpretations and have therefore considered evidence given at trial on that matter." Given his findings, it is appropriate to comment on the factors he considered relevant to his conclusion that the agreement provided only for notional transfers, and that the "real" funds were in the designated accounts at all times.

Contra Proferentem

The trial judge considered it appropriate in this case to apply the *contra proferentem* rule to the agreement. For statements of the rule, he quotes *Anson's Law of Contract*, 25th ed. (1979), at p. 151:

> The words of written documents are construed more forcibly against the party using them. The rule is based on the principle that a man is responsible for ambiguities in his own expressions and has no right to induce another to contract with him on the supposition that his words mean one thing, which he hopes the court will adopt a construction by which they would mean another thing, more to his advantage.

And he quotes *McClelland & Stewart Ltd. v. Mutual Life Assurance Co. of Canada*, [1981] 2 S.C.R. 6 at p. 15, 125 D.L.R. (3d) 257:

> That principle of interpretation applies to contracts and other documents on the simple theory that any ambiguity in a term of a contract must be resolved against the author if the choice is between him and the other party to the contract who did not participate in its drafting.

He also quotes *Hillis Oil & Sales v. Wynn's Canada Ltd.*, [1986] 1 S.C.R. 57 at p. 68, 25 D.L.R. (4th) 649:

> The rule is, however, one of general application whenever, as in the case at bar, there is ambiguity in the meaning of a contract which one of the parties as the author of the document offers to the other with no opportunity to modify its wording.

The trial judge assumes that Le Dain J. in the *Hillis* case did not intend to modify the general nature of the *contra proferentem* rule by requiring that before the rule can apply there must be evidence that there was no opportunity to modify the wording of the contract before its execution. Whether or not that assumption is correct, in this case there was no indication in the evidence that the Stolp companies did not have an opportunity to modify the wording of the agreement. They did not even consider doing so.

The approach taken by the trial judge, as stated at p. 23 of his reasons, is the general approach quoted above from Anson and from the *McClelland & Stewart* case. The problem with applying these principles is, first, that one must find an ambiguity in the contract before applying the rule, rather than after, as done by the trial judge; and second, there is no indication in the evidence that the Bank induced the Stolp companies to contract on the supposition that the agreement meant one thing, while hoping that the court would adopt a construction more favourable to it. In our view, the *contra proferentem* rule has no application in the case.

Factual Context of the Agreement

On p. 23 of his reasons, the trial judge refers to, and purports to apply, the words of Ryan J. in *Delisle v. Bulman Group Inc.* (1991), 54 B.C.L.R. (2d) 343 at pp. 345–46, [1991] 4 W.W.R. 637 (S.C.):

> 3. If, after examining the agreement itself in its factual matrix, including the particular words used in their immediate context and in the context of the agreement as a whole, there remain two reasonable alternative interpretations, then additional evidence may be admitted. This evidence includes evidence of the facts that led up to the making of the agreement, evidence of the circumstances as they existed at the time the agreement was made, and evidence of subsequent conduct of the parties to the agreement. The two existing reasonable interpretations may be the result of ambiguity aris-

ing from doubt, uncertainty or difficulty of construction.

The trial judge states: "On the basis of the agreement in this case, I am satisfied there are two reasonable alternative interpretations and have therefore considered evidence given at trial on that matter." No analysis is given of how, in applying the first portion of the above quotation from the *Delisle* case, the trial judge arrived at his conclusion that there are two possible interpretations of the contract. First, the words of the contract must be analyzed "in its factual matrix", and a conclusion arrived at that there are two possible interpretations of the contract. Then, and only then, may the trial judge look at other facts, including facts leading up to the making of the agreement, circumstances existing at the time the agreement was made, and evidence of subsequent conduct of the parties to the agreement.

The factual matrix in this case has been referred to earlier in these reasons. The purpose of the agreement was to provide for decreased administrative complexity in the operation of all accounts of Stolp companies, to decrease administrative costs, to allow for transfer of funds between companies, and to provide for payment of interest on credit balances. All of these objectives were accomplished by the agreement, but they could not have been accomplished unless the agreement operated in one way only — by a real transfer of funds into and out of the concentration account. That being the case, viewing the contract in the context of its execution points to only one possible meaning — that the transfers were real.

Operation of the Mirror Agreement

Given his view that the contract was capable of two possible interpretations, the trial judge considered evidence of the actual operation of the agreement, which he considered supported his conclusion that the transfer of funds within the mirror system was merely notional. Much of his analysis of evidence confused the two major issues in these proceedings — the meaning and operation of the agreement between the immediate parties, and the effect of its operation on third parties. The nature of the funds deposited into the designated accounts, and the appropriateness of the use of a mirror accounting system by bankers of clients in the construction industry, are clearly relevant to possible liability of banks to construction trust fund claimants and to other third parties, but they do not assist in determining the rights of the parties to the written agreement.

There were two principal witnesses for the Bank — Ross Hamilton, who became involved significantly only when the system was terminated in February of 1991; and Tim Herbison, who had been one of the six account managers at the Mississauga branch dealing with the Stolp accounts between 1984 and 1989, and who took primary responsibility for these accounts from the fall of 1989. The trial judge was unimpressed with them as witnesses, because he viewed them as "advocates for the T.D.B. position".

Two principal witnesses for the respondents, both chartered accountants, were Jack Wrobel who, as comptroller, was the main Stolp contact with the Bank from 1984 to 1989, and Malcolm West, who, as corporate treasurer for the group, was the main contact with the Bank from June of 1989. The trial judge found both of these men to be credible witnesses, who "seemed prepared to admit mistakes they had made".

The trial judge accepted the evidence of Mr. Wrobel that a Mr. Stannard, an account manager in the Mississauga branch of the Bank, suggested early in 1986 that a mirror system be used to alleviate the administrative and interest concerns which have been described earlier in these reasons. He found that "there was no discussion about a change of ownership of funds deposited in the designated accounts, that there was no discussion of inter-company lending, no warning about the type of funds that could be deposited and, specifically, no suggestion that trust funds should not be deposited in the system". The questions of ownership of funds deposited in the designated accounts, the type of funds that could be deposited, and the deposit of trust funds are relevant only to the rights of third parties, and particularly of construction trust claimants. This question will be dealt with later in these reasons. It suffices to say, at this point, that there is no suggestion in the agreement itself that only funds beneficially owned by a designated account-holder could be deposited in such an account.

With respect to the question of inter-company lending, whether or not this was specifically discussed, any person with a minimum of business experience would have known, by a careful reading of the agreement, that the use by participants in the system of funds from accounts of other participants was the whole basis of the operation of the system. There is no indication that any Bank officer represented otherwise before the various executions of the agreement.

The trial judge accepted the argument of the respondents that failure of the Bank to call Mr. Stannard as a witness justified drawing an adverse inference against the Bank that his evidence would have been helpful to the respondents. He relied on the decision of this court in *Clairborne Industries Ltd. v. National Bank of Canada* (1989), 69 O.R. (2d) 65 at pp. 77, 59 D.L.R. (4th) 533. The *Clairborne* case was one involving allegations against a bank of breach of trust and conspiracy to defraud, resulting from the complex transfer of funds from the accounts of a corporation to accounts of other corporations in which the president of the first corporation had a personal interest. The allegations were that the bank was a party to the conspiracy, or at least to a breach of trust. The bank failed to call four bank officers and one bank employee, who could have shed light on the dealings of various corporate officers with the bank. This court considered it appropriate in the circumstances to draw an adverse inference from that failure. This case is a significantly different one, in which there are no allegations of dishonesty on the part of the Bank. The findings of the trial judge as to discussions before the adoption of the system are set out on p. 35 of his reasons:

> I believe it significant that Mr. Stannard was not called as a witness at trial and no explanation was given for the failure to do so. It is well established that such failure relating to a witness who can give relevant evidence leaves open the natural inference that that evidence would be helpful to the opposite party: see *Claiborne Industries v. National Bank of Canada*, 69 O.R. (2d) 65 (C.A.) at p. 77.
>
> I accept Wrobel's evidence that there was no discussion about a change of ownership of funds deposited in the designated accounts, that there was no suggestion of inter-company lending, no warning about the type of funds that could be deposited and, specifically, no suggestion that trust funds should not be deposited in the system.

Those findings are based on uncontradicted evidence adduced by the respondents. There was no reason for the Bank to call Mr. Stannard, other than to give evidence of a contrary position, which could only have been of benefit to the Bank. The failure to call Mr. Stannard was of no significance in this case.

The respondents take comfort from the fact that there is no clear and consistent articulation by Bank officers of their interpretation of the agreement. Mr. Hamilton admitted that he was aware of the operation of the system by "hands on" experience with it in this and other situations. While he disagreed with the view that the only transfer of funds was between the mirror accounts and the concentration account,

his view is irrelevant if the agreement states otherwise — and it does.

In cross-examination by counsel for Municipal Financial Corporation ("M.F.C."), he was referred to a Domestic Commercial Credit Review, dated March 21, 1986, sent from the branch to the head office credit department, and to the response of the senior vice-president dated March 31, 1986. The last paragraph of that credit review, headed "Recommendation", states in part:

> While overdrafts in the various accounts within the group will not be eliminated with the Mirror Accounting System, we have confirmed that the Bank has right of offset to credit balances within the system which funds may be available to fluctuate the requested operating line and/or provide repayments to the term if required. Overall we feel our funds are well placed.

Mr. Hamilton had earlier stated his view that there were transfers daily from the designated accounts to the concentration account. Counsel attempted to get an acknowledgement from Mr. Hamilton that this paragraph was a direct contradiction of that evidence. The two positions are in fact contradictory; however, Mr. Hamilton was not giving evidence as a legal expert, but as a banking administrator. There is no evidence that he had ever read the agreement, but even if he had he could have no expert opinion as to its legal effect. He gave evidence that when any new account was put on the system there would be a designated account and an offset or mirror account opened. From that time on the system was completely automated. The fact that Mr. Hamilton thought that funds were transferred daily from designated accounts to the concentration account was irrelevant. What actually happened was what the agreement said happened — the entries in the designated accounts were mirrored in the offset accounts, and the debit and credit balances in those offset accounts were transferred to the concentration account. The balances in the designated accounts were always as shown in the statements of those accounts, but each entry was offset by a mirror entry in the offset accounts.

As stated earlier, the trial judge unfortunately confused the interpretation of the mirror system, and its effect between the immediate parties, with his view of the inappropriateness of its use in the construction industry. At p. 44 of his reasons he stated:

> I conclude the use of a mirror accounting system like this one was not appropriate for companies involved in the construction industry or with the receipt and use of trust funds. This conclusion is probably sufficient to dispose of this litigation.

However, in the event this matter is considered by another court I will deal with the issue involving the trust funds.

As far as the Bank officers dealing with the system were concerned, once the agreement was executed by each participant, the accounts for that participant were placed on the computer and the system operated automatically. Various Bank officers in addition to Mr. Hamilton expressed opinions as to what might be termed the legal effect of the agreement. They did so in internal bank correspondence and by way of *viva voce* evidence at trial. None of them professed legal expertise, and none was dealing with the provisions of the agreement itself, but rather with what they considered to be the effect of its operation. Any evidence of theirs as to the interpretation of the agreement is really of no value to the court. The only assistance they could give the court is a description of the way the system operated, and there was no evidence of its operation which was contrary to the clear meaning of the words of the agreement.

Account Agreement and Confirmation of Balances

The respondents and the trial judge relied substantially on a confirmation of account balances provision in the standard agreement which is generally executed by customers on opening new accounts with the bank. Such an agreement was executed in this case as each new designated account was opened. Clause 5(a) of that agreement states that account statements delivered by the Bank are accepted by the customer as correct in the absence of notification of errors or objections within 30 days following delivery of the statement to the customer. Since the statements received by the Stolp companies showed no transfer of funds into or out of designated accounts, it was argued by the respondents that receipt of the statements constituted the Bank's confirmation that no funds had been so transferred.

The fact is that the agreement does not contemplate that funds will be transferred in and out of the designated accounts by virtue of the operation of the system. Clause 5(a) of the mirror system agreement merely provides that *the Bank* shall make deposits into and withdrawals from *the offset (mirror) accounts*, so that at the end of each day each designated account is completely offset by its corresponding mirror account. Balances are then transferred from *the offset accounts* to the concentration account. The monthly statement received by each designated account holder was completely accurate. Each designated account was in fact in debit or credit as shown in the statement. However, as between the participants and the Bank, those balances were offset by countervailing balances in the mirror accounts.

Some problems could have arisen from the fact that the designated account balances were confirmed by the Bank to the Stolp auditors, and included in the financial statements of the individual Stolp companies without notice from the Bank to the auditors of those companies that there was an offsetting account in existence. Any detrimental effect that this might have had was not a detrimental effect to the Stolp companies, whose officers knew, or should have known, of the existence of the mirror accounts. Indeed, as they are primarily responsible for the production of information on which the auditors base their audit of the financial condition of the companies, it was incumbent on the Stolp officers to inform their auditors of the existence of the mirror accounts.

The evidence indicates that, although regular statements of the designated accounts were sent by the Bank to its customers, it did not send statements of the mirror accounts. It would have been prudent for the Bank to do so in its own interest. However, for the information of the Stolp companies it should have been completely unnecessary, since the mirror accounts were just that — a mirror image of the designated accounts. Regular information of balances in the concentration account was given to the Stolp group, and there is no evidence that those balances were disputed.

If any third parties were misled by lack of information of the existence of the mirror accounts, it was partially because of the lack of information supplied by Stolp to its auditors. The Stolp witnesses excused themselves by stating that they had not read the agreement, or that they did not understand it, or that the Bank had failed to explain it to them. As stated earlier, the agreement, if carefully read, is quite clear as to the agreed operation of the system. The fact that Bank officers did not explain the system to Stolp officers from time to time means nothing. Stolp officers were signatories to the mirror agreement. Had they had any questions as to its operation, they could have inquired. There was no evidence that Stolp officers inquired of the Bank as to the operation of the system over the years and, obviously, they were content to accept the benefits the system provided. It is our view that the agreement in this case is clear, and that the debits and credits in the mirror accounts, and transfers from those accounts to the concentration account were real.

TERMINATION OF AGREEMENT

That is, of course, not the end of the matter. Claims are made in both actions under the *Lien Act* or for general breach of trust, and they must be dealt with. There is, however, a claim over by certain of the Stolp companies against the Bank for breach of the agreement of March 17, 1986, in the manner of termination on February 11, 1991, which we should now deal with. The trial judge found that the Bank had indeed breached the contract, and he ordered a reference to the Master in Toronto to determine the damage arising from that breach. We now proceed to determine the correctness of that finding.

The provision of the agreement for termination was para. 14, set out here for convenience:

> 14. This Agreement shall terminate thirty days from the date on which the Bank gives notice in writing to any of the Participants or Concentrator, or on which any of the Participants or Concentrator gives a notice in writing to the Bank, of its intention to terminate. Such notice shall be hand delivered or sent by prepaid registered post during any period of normal mail delivery and shall be addressed to the Bank at 5100 Dixie Road at Eglinton Ave., Mississauga, Ontario L4W 1C9 and in the case of the Participants and Concentrator at the addresses set out opposite the name of each in Schedule "A" attached hereto and shall be deemed to have been given upon receipt by the addressee, or if posted, on the second postal delivery day following the date of posting. Notwithstanding the foregoing this Agreement shall automatically terminate forthwith in the event of any default in the payment of the present or future indebtedness or liability of any one or more of the Participants or Concentrator to the Bank, or in the event that Concentrator fails to maintain a sufficient line of credit.

The agreement worked well for many years after its inception until at least July of 1990 with the concentration account generally in a credit position. From July 1990 to January 1991, no doubt because of the depressed real estate market, there were nine instances of overdrafts in the concentration account. However, on each occasion the overdraft was corrected by deposits made by one or more of the participants to one or more of the designated accounts. In November 1990, the officers of the Bank met with officers of Stolp to discuss the operation of the system, the latter conceding some cash management problems. The Bank at that meeting requested Stolp to take steps to wind down the system. On January 30, 1991, the Bank wrote to Stolp giving notice of termination in 30 days. In that letter the Bank also stated that if an overdraft occurred in the concentration account the agreement would be terminated immediately. On February 7, 1991, Stolp wrote cheques on its designated accounts totalling $6,500,000 which to the Bank seemed out of the ordinary course of business and it refused to process them. On February 8, 1991 certain participant companies wrote cheques to third parties outside the system which if honoured would have created a deficit in the concentration account of $650,000. The Bank did not honour those cheques but instead terminated the agreement, and the system was wound up on February 11, 1991.

The trial judge, as noted above, found that the Bank in so doing was in breach of the agreement. It is not clear what he deemed to constitute the breach, but he makes reference on several occasions to the "improper" seizure by the Bank of the credit balances in the designated accounts. In our opinion there was no seizure. There was nothing in the designated accounts to seize. All of the Stolp credits were consolidated in the concentration account and that credit was eventually turned over by the Bank to the trustee of the trade creditors of Stolp. The Bank was entitled to terminate the agreement in accordance with its terms. The only complaint can be that it did not wait out the full 30 days after giving notice on January 30, 1991, but in our opinion the events of February 7 and 8 automatically terminated the agreement and fully justified the Bank's action in winding up the system.

BREACH OF TRUST

As stated earlier, the trial judge unfortunately confused the interpretation of the mirror system, and its effect between the immediate parties, with his view of the inappropriateness of its use in the construction industry. At p. 44 of his reasons he stated:

> I conclude the use of a mirror accounting system like this one was not appropriate for companies involved in the construction industry or with the receipt and use of trust funds. This conclusion is probably sufficient to dispose of this litigation. However, in the event this matter is considered by another court I will deal with the issue involving the trust funds.

He proceeded to find the Bank in breach of the trust under the provisions of the *Lien Act*, and with respect to funds claimed by M.F.C. Sections 7 to 13 of the *Lien Act* contain the trust provisions. It is important to note that the only named trustees under the *Lien Act* are owners of land (as defined), contractors, and subcontractors. Therefore, a bank can only be liable for breaches of trust where there has first been a breach by one of the named trustees who is a customer of that bank. There was no evidence that any Stolp officer warned the Bank that Stolp companies were in breach of the trust provisions as a result of non-payment of trades. Nor was there evidence that the Bank was made aware from any other source, before the very end of the relationship, that any of the Stolp companies were in breach of their trust obligations under the *Lien Act*. Therefore, the Bank could only be liable if it had a duty to inquire as to the state of the accounts between the individual Stolp companies and their trades. No one would suggest that a bank has a duty to monitor, on a daily basis, the operation of its clients (even construction clients) merely because it knows that those clients have funds on deposit which may be impressed with a trust — statutory or otherwise. Indeed, s. 206(1) and (2) of the *Bank Act*, R.S.C. 1985, c. B-1, specifically states that a bank is not bound to see to the execution of any trust, whether express, implied, or constructive, to which any deposit is subject, and that, where a bank has notice of a trust, a receipt or cheque signed by the person in whose name the account stands is a sufficient discharge to all concerned.

It is not contended in this action that s. 206 represents protection to banks in all circumstances. The real question is: at what stage in its dealings with a customer with trust funds on deposit does a bank's knowledge of its customer's affairs impose a duty on the bank to inquire as to the possible misapplication of trust funds?

The law is replete with cases dealing with the obligation of banks in their dealings with construction companies and the effect of the trust provisions of the *Lien Act* and its predecessors, including the *Mechanics' Lien Act*, R.S.O. 1980, c. 261. An early clear statement of the appropriate test is stated in *John M.M. Troup Ltd. v. Royal Bank of Canada*, [1962] S.C.R. 487 at p. 501, 34 D.L.R. (2d) 556, *per* Cartwright J.:

> I agree with the view which Porter C.J.O. summarized in the following passage:
>
>> The test to be applied is whether the Bank manager knew that the customer was committing a breach of trust and he knowingly participated therein.
>>
>> ...
>>
>> The law applicable to this branch of the matter is, in my opinion, accurately stated in the

following passages in *Underhill on Trusts*, 11th ed., 1959 at pp. 565 and 566:

> Where, however, a trustee has overdrawn his banking account, his bankers have a first and paramount lien on all moneys paid in if they have no notice that they are trust moneys; for where the equities are equal the law prevails, and, in the case supposed, the bankers have in point of law received the money in payment of their debt.

and at p. 606:

> So, as has been already stated, where a trustee has overdrawn his banking account, his bankers have a first and paramount legal lien on all moneys paid in by him, unless they have notice, not only that they are trust moneys, but also that the payment to them constitutes a breach of trust.

The learned trial judge made many findings against the Bank on the issue and we summarize them as follows:

1. The Bank knew that the customer was in the construction business and the source of its funds was capital investments, mortgage funds, deposits and sales.

2. The Bank knew that many of the Stolp company enterprises were joint ventures, partnership or co-tenancies with other companies.

3. The Bank (at least by 1990) knew the mirror system was inappropriate for construction companies as those companies invariably deal in trust moneys.

4. From January 1990 on, the Bank had or should have had misgivings about the financial stability of the Stolp companies exemplified by the following:
   (a) In January 1990, a Bank official authorized an internal memo to the effect that it was an "uncertain" climate for builders.
   (b) In August 1990, there was an overdraft (later eliminated) of $1,300,000.
   (c) The Bank knew in the summer of 1990 that construction draws from one project were being used to retire overdrafts caused by deficiencies of other accounts.
   (d) By December 1990, there had been an overdraft eight times in the concentration account.
   (e) The official Herbison of the Bank, who was in charge of the account and gave

evidence, was not a credible witness and indeed was "wilfully blind" to the true state of the Stolp accounts.

It is interesting that the trial judge did not find (apart from the "wilful blindness" of Herbison) that the Bank knew of any breach of trust on the part of Stolp prior to January of 1991. The basis of the breach of trust by the Bank is its failure to pursue an inquiry into the affairs of Stolp. We consider that the law on this point can be summarized thus: in the absence of sufficient facts or circumstances indicating that there is a good possibility of trust beneficiaries being unpaid there is no duty of inquiry on a bank to determine whether the trades have been paid or will be able to be paid. Accordingly, we must examine the findings of the trial judge to see if they meet that test prior to February 11, 1991. We take that date as determinative because at that time the Bank "wound up not only the mirror account but all the Stolp accounts and in due course turned over the credit balance to the lien trustee, Arthur Andersen Inc. ('A.A.I.')".

The trial judge's conclusions on the trust issue, found at p. 50 of his reasons are as follows:

> I conclude that from August, 1990, the T.D.B. knew or would have discovered on reasonable inquiry that breaches of trust were occurring. In the circumstances, on the basis of the authorities outlined above, I conclude there was a duty on the T.D.B. to make such reasonable inquiries. Not only did it fail to do so but at least one of its account managers deliberately ignored that duty.
>
> On the basis of these conclusions the T.D.B. seizure of the accounts now under the control of A.A.I. was improper.

As is indicated in the above summary of the trial judge's findings of fact, in concluding that the Bank had a duty to inquire from August 1990 the trial judge relied on the fact that the Bank was aware that the Stolp companies were in the development and construction business and, consequently, that trust moneys were being deposited into participant's accounts; that an internal Bank memorandum in January 1990 had indicated an uncertain business climate for builders and developers; and that there was an overdraft in the concentration account in early August 1990 which was satisfied by a deposit of funds which were impressed with a trust.

The fact that the Stolp companies were in the contracting business is only relevant to the extent that the Bank must be deemed to have been aware at all times that trust funds were being depos-

ited regularly into all participants' accounts. The respondents argue that the daily transfers through the mirror system make it inevitable that there would be daily breaches of trust by the Stolp companies of which the Bank would be aware, since accounts could not have been settled with the trades on a daily basis. That argument is surely untenable. The result of its acceptance would be that in a case where a contractor had only one project and only one account with a bank, an overdraft accommodation by a bank could never be satisfied by future deposits without the bank being deemed to have notice of a breach of trust by its customer, because there would inevitably be some trade creditors who were unpaid. Placing such a high duty on a bank would be to require it to be aware of the status of each and every trade debt of its construction customer on a daily basis — an impossible task. Only if a bank is aware of facts which would indicate that trades would not be paid in the normal course of business should it be charged with a duty of special inquiry.

Was there, as the trial judge found in this case, such a duty to inquire as a result of facts known to the Bank in August of 1990? In the early part of 1990 the Bank had acknowledged internally that the business climate for the construction industry was uncertain, and the trial judge, therefore, was of the view that in early August, when there was a substantial overdraft in the concentration account the Bank was put on its inquiry. He also found that Mr. Herbison, the account manager for the Bank, was wilfully blind as to the status of the trades at that time. What the trial judge ignored was the fact that the Stolp officers until the end of 1990 were representing not only to the Bank, but also to M.F.C., Barclays Bank and the Canadian Imperial Bank of Commerce, who were financing some of the projects, that the trades were being paid. An assessment of how far a lender must go to make reasonable inquiries cannot be made in a vacuum; reasonableness must depend on the knowledge that the lender has and on the length and nature of the relationship between the lender and its customer. In this case there had been an ongoing and mutually satisfactory banking relationship between the Bank and the Stolp group for eight years. Occasional overdrafts were always satisfied from one source or another, and the overall viability of the group was not of concern to the Bank. A number of projects had been satisfactorily completed, and the Bank had no reason to think that the trades would not be paid.

There was no specific finding by the trial judge, and indeed such a finding would have been difficult on the evidence presented, that there were breaches of trust resulting from non-payment of trades in the summer of 1990. To the extent that such a finding is implied by the words in the paragraph quoted above, we are of the view that a clearer and more specific finding would be necessary to result in liability of one of the trustees named in the *Lien Act*, let alone liability of a party which is not a named trustee, but which must be deemed to be liable for breach of trust as a result of a duty to inquire.

Of all the findings of the trial judge, the most important, and perhaps the dispositive one is that relating to Herbison and his "wilful blindness". There is no question the trial judge did not find Herbison a credible or impressive witness. He described him as a "biased, argumentative and evasive witness" and "very protective of his own position". The trial judge's conclusions as to the "wilful blindness", indeed as to the whole duty of inquiry, were expressed thus:

> I conclude it was, or should have been obvious, that trust funds from one construction project were being used to pay overdrafts. It should also have been obvious that that use of trust funds could well mean there would be insufficient money to pay trades on the projects from which money was diverted.
>
> It is an obvious intention of the *Construction Lien Act* that a trust is imposed on funds to prevent their use, other than to pay trades. Herbison was aware of the purpose of the Act, and the improper use of those funds. He chose to ignore it.
>
> During one part of his cross-examination he admitted that he "compartmentalized" his thinking. In my view he used this to avoid seeing what should have been obvious, or to ignore it completely. I had the impression he was functioning almost in the role of a salesman in dealing with the Stolp account. Whenever he was cross-examined on his actions which might have been questionable, he took refuge in the answer "Stolp was a valued customer".
>
> I was not impressed with his credibility or his approach to this matter.
>
> I conclude that from August, 1990, the T.D.B. knew or would have discovered on reasonable inquiry that breaches of trust were occurring. In the circumstances, on the basis of the authorities outlined above, I conclude there was a duty on the T.D.B. to make such reasonable inquiries. Not only did it fail to do so but at least one of its account managers deliberately ignored that duty.

There is no question that "wilful blindness", when established, can result in liability upon a stranger to a trust who applies trust funds for his own purposes — see *Air Canada v. M. & L. Travel Ltd.*, S.C.C., October 21, 1993 [now reported [1993] 3 S.C.R. 787, 108 D.L.R. (4th) 592], p. 24. But wilful blindness can only be of relevance from the time when a duty to inquire arises. The evidence indicates that during the fall of 1990 there were a series of substantial overdrafts in the concentration account. Bank officers met with Stolp officers on November 29, 1990, and stated their concern about the situation. They were informed that the overdrafts resulted from cash flow problems and that they would be corrected, which they were. We are of the view that at this point in time the Bank should have known, or at least suspected, that as a result of these cash flow problems the trade accounts were not being satisfied. It was incumbent on the Bank to make further inquiries at that time. What inquiries should have been made it is not necessary to say, since none was made. Although it would undoubtedly have taken some time to obtain the necessary information to make an appropriate assessment of the situation, we are of the view that the Bank should have ceased to transfer funds to the concentration account through the mirror system after November 29, 1990.

The final disposition of the trial judge resulted in liability of the Bank for credit balances in all of the designated accounts as of the date of the termination of the system. We do not consider this solution appropriate. The Bank can only be liable for a breach of trust, and that breach would have to involve making use for its own benefit of money held on a trust for trade creditors after November 29, 1990. Consequently, there must be evidence of the debts owing to trade creditors, the amount of trust moneys received by the Bank and the amount recovered for the trade creditors by A.A.I. after that date.

It may be that the trial judge, having already determined that the Stolp companies were entitled to all credit balances in the designated accounts, and that through them the trade creditors would be paid, considered there was no need for further inquiry. In any event, it is our view that such an inquiry must now be made. The provisions of ss. 10, 11 and 12 of the *Lien Act* must be applied in determining the amount, if any, of the Bank's liability. Those sections read:

> **10.** Subject to Part IV (holdbacks), every payment by a trustee to a person the trustee is liable to pay for services or materials supplied to the improvement discharges the trust of the trustee making the payment and the trustee's obligations and liability as trustee to all beneficiaries of the trust to the extent of the payment made by the trustee.

11.(1) Subject to Part IV, a trustee who pays in whole or in part for the supply of services or materials to an improvement out of money that is not subject to a trust under this Part may retain from trust funds an amount equal to that paid by the trustee without being in breach of the trust.

(2) Subject to Part IV, where a trustee pays in whole or in part for the supply of services or materials to an improvement out of money that is loaned to the trustee, trust funds may be applied to discharge the loan to the extent that the lender's money was so used by the trustee, and the application of trust money does not constitute a breach of the trust.

12. Subject to Part IV, a trustee may, without being in breach of trust, retain from trust funds an amount that, as between the trustee and the person the trustee is liable to pay under a contract or subcontract related to the improvement, is equal to the balance in the trustee's favour of all outstanding debts, claims or damages, whether or not related to the improvement.

There is evidence to support the finding of the trial judge that Herbison knew that the business of Stolp involved the deposit of trust funds, and that through the mirror system unorthodox use of construction draws was being made to retire overdrafts and was wilfully blind to the possible results. However, Herbison was wilfully blind to these facts from the commencement of his involvement with the Stolp group. His wilful blindness only became important when the Bank knew, or should have known, that it was likely that trade accounts of Stolp would not be paid. As stated earlier in these reasons, that could not have been before November 29, 1990.

We accept the trial judge's conclusion that the Bank was a constructive trustee and may have participated in a breach of trust, but only after November 29, 1990.

That does not mean, however, that the remedy chosen was the correct one. As we have noted above, no consideration appears to have been given to the extent of the breach, the amounts owing to unpaid creditors and the amounts recovered for the trade creditors by the plaintiff A.A.I.

We must deal with the two other findings of the trial judge which resulted in judgments against the Bank.

Claims of Municipal Finance Corporation

The first is that relating to the plaintiff M.F.C. M.F.C. and Stolp were partners in the development

of property in Barrie under a co-tenancy agreement. The property was managed by Stolp Homes (Barrie) Limited (Developers), M.F.C. providing financing. In March 1989, Developers asked to become part of the mirror system, and agreed to be bound by the terms of the mirror agreement. M.F.C. also had a similar co-tenancy agreement with Stolp on a property adjacent to Developers called Stolp Homes (Veterans Drive) Inc. — hereafter referred to as "Veterans Drive". Again Stolp managed the affairs of the project. There is no doubt that money received by Developers and Veterans Drive could constitute trust moneys under the *Lien Act*, but there is no evidence that the Bank was aware of the trust interest claimed by M.F.C. The balances in the designated accounts on February 11, 1991 were:

Developers	$1,002,228.08
Veterans Drive	462,156.66

These amounts were not claimed by A.A.I. for trade creditors, but the judgment ordered a reference to determine if trade debts existed on the projects and, subject to any such debts, the balance was to be paid to M.F.C.

We do not understand the basis for M.F.C.'s claim or the judgment in response to it. The moneys claimed may have turned out to be trust moneys as between Stolp and M.F.C., but the Bank knew nothing of that. Stolp had authority from M.F.C. to manage the projects, and Stolp placed the projects on the mirror system with the Bank. As stated earlier in these reasons, banks are not normally required by law to see to the proper application of trust funds on deposit in customers' accounts, even if those accounts are named as trust accounts — see the *Bank Act*, s. 206. Only in special circumstances, such as those involved in *Air Canada v. M. & L. Travel Ltd., supra*, would a bank be liable. There was no evidence of wilful blindness respecting the agreements between Stolp and M.F.C. on the Developers or Veterans Drive projects or respecting any trust that may have been established between the parties to those agreements. The Bank dealt with Developers and Veterans Drive as customers and, as we have said, may be liable to trade creditors for the money in the designated accounts, but we can see no liability for moneys not protected by the *Lien Act*.

Vogue II

Finally, there is a third party counterclaim by Vogue Developers (Phase II) Inc. ("Vogue II") against the Bank in the M.F.C. action. Vogue II was a company controlled by Stolp, engaged in the development of a high-rise condominium project in North York. The project was commenced in the fall of 1988, but there were delays and the project was never completed. The trial judge found that two Stolp accounts were opened at the request of Stolp employees as trust accounts — one at the Mississauga branch and one at a branch on Yonge Street in North York. Stolp requested that the accounts be placed on the mirror system. Before funds were deposited in the accounts the Bank informed Stolp that internal Bank rules would not permit trust accounts to be placed on the system. They were then informed by Stolp that the accounts were not trust accounts but, rather, were deposit accounts. This was confirmed in writing to the Bank. The accounts were placed on the system but due to a clerical error the name of the account at the Yonge Street branch was not changed and that account was placed on the system names as a trust account. The trial judge found on the evidence that nothing turned on this error. He stated in his reasons, at p. 55: "I do not accept argument of Stolp's counsel that the indication of trust account on the statements establishes anything." None the less, he ordered the amount to the credit of the Vogue II accounts at the time of the termination of the system ($2,795,000) be "repaid by T.D.B. and is to be paid into court pending further court order".

At a meeting with West, representing Stolp, on November 29, 1990, West informed Herbison and Stevenson that the funds which were deposited in the Vogue II accounts were purchaser deposits. Mr. Stevenson then stated that they were trust funds and should not have been in the mirror system. Section 53(1) of the *Condominium Act*, R.S.O. 1990, c. C.26, requires all such deposits to be held by the declarant (Vogue II in this case) in a separate account designated as a trust account in a bank listed in Sch. I or II of the *Bank Act* until its disposition to the person entitled to the moneys, or until delivery to the purchaser of security for repayment. The trust is imposed on Vogue II in this case, and if any party was in breach of trust it was Vogue II. The Bank had no way of knowing whether or not Vogue II had fulfilled the conditions for release of the trust funds. It had been informed in 1988 that the account was not a trust account, and it would have had no reason to disbelieve its customer, or to consider that the requirements of the *Condominium Act* were not being met. Before the November 29, 1990 meeting

all funds in the accounts had been offset by the operation of the mirror system, and there was no further activity in those accounts after that date.

The only stated basis for the trial judge's decision is on p. 56 of the reasons:

> I conclude T.D.B. knew the amounts in that account were trust funds at least by November 29, 1990, and when the seizure was made in February 1991, was fixed with that knowledge.

That part of his decision results from confusion of the rights of the immediate parties to the mirror agreement with possible rights of third parties to claim a breach of trust in which the Bank has participated to its benefit. In the case of Vogue II there are no trust claimants who are parties to the action involved. Only Vogue II, which was the party which may have been in breach of the trust provisions of the *Condominium Act* made a claim against the Bank. Its claim is that the moneys in the Vogue II accounts were trust moneys, and that the moneys, which it claims were seized by the Bank, should be returned to it. However, as decided earlier in these reasons, there was no seizure of funds in the designated accounts on February 11, 1991, because the Bank had a right, as between it and Vogue II, to set off debit balances in the relevant offset accounts against any credit balances in Vogue II-designated accounts and that had been done prior to November 29, 1990.

DISPOSITION

Considering all of these issues, we would allow the appeal, set aside the judgment below and order a reference to determine amount, if any, owing to the plaintiff A.A.I. bearing in mind the trust provisions of the *Lien Act* as they affect transaction after November 29, 1990. The costs of the reference and the interest rate allowable will be in the discretion of the referee. A.A.I will be entitled to its costs of the trial and one-half its costs of this appeal against the Bank. We would dismiss the M.F.C. claim against the Bank and allow the Bank its costs of the trial and this appeal against M.F.C. We would also dismiss the cross-claim of the Stolp defendants against the Bank and Vogue II's claim against the Bank both with costs here and at trial.

(c) *Citadel General Assurance Co. v. Lloyds Bank Canada†*

[La FOREST J. (Gonthier, Cory, McLachlin, Iacobucci and Major JJ. concurring):]

This appeal concerns the liability of a bank for its customer's breach of trust. The appellants, as beneficiaries of the trust, seek recovery for unpaid insurance premiums collected by the trustee and deposited with the respondent banks. The principal question in this appeal is this: Are the respondent banks liable as constructive trustees for the breach of trust committed by one of their clients? This question deals with the liability of strangers who participate in a breach of trust and, in particular, the degree of knowledge required for the imposition of liability as a constructive trustee.

I.   FACTUAL BACKGROUND

The Citadel General Assurance Company and The Citadel Life Assurance Company ("Citadel") are insurance companies which carried on business in Alberta. Beginning in 1979, Citadel's business operations involved another Alberta corporation, Drive On Guaranteed Vehicle Payment Plan (1982) Limited ("Drive On"). As a wholly owned subsidiary of International Warranty Company Limited ("International Warranty"), Drive On sold consumer life, casualty and unemployment insurance to auto dealers. The insurance premiums were collected by auto dealers at the time vehicles were sold and then remitted to Drive On. After collecting the premiums, Drive On paid commissions and settled any current claims under the policies. The balance of the premiums was remitted on a monthly basis to Citadel, the underwriter of the insurance policies. In early 1987, the premiums received during a calendar month were normally forwarded to Citadel at the end of the following month. This arrangement continued satisfactorily until August 1987 when Drive On defaulted on its payments to Citadel. As well, from 1979 until late August 1987, there was no written agreement between Citadel and Drive On.

In December 1986, the International Warranty Group of Companies, including Drive On and International Warranty, started banking with the now-amalgamated Lloyds Bank Canada and Hong Kong Bank of Canada (hereinafter collectively called "the Bank"). During 1987, the only banker of Drive On was the Bank. Drive On used one bank account for all its transactions. The only deposits to that account were either insurance premiums collected from auto dealers or transfers of funds from International Warranty. Through its senior officers, the Bank was aware that insurance premiums were being deposited into Drive On's account. During the period after April 1, 1987, Drive On's account was usually in an overdraft position. On April 8, the Bank received instructions from International Warranty's signing officers (who were identical to Drive On's signing officers) to transfer funds between the International Warranty and Drive On accounts to cover overdrafts on either account.

Also in April 1987, the Presidents of Drive On and Citadel met to discuss their business relationship. As a result of the meeting, Citadel and Drive On agreed that a written agreement would be prepared to formalize their business relationship. It was also agreed that Drive On would no longer settle claims under the insurance policies. From June 1, 1987, Citadel assumed the adjudication and payment of all claims. As a result, the monthly premiums payable to Citadel were increased significantly. Also as a result of the presidents' meeting, Citadel ordered a detailed examination of Drive On's current procedures. A "trip report" was delivered by one of Citadel's employees on May 14. The report found that Drive On was depositing insurance premiums in a general bank account which was not set up as a trust account. The report also indicated that Drive On was somewhat reluctant to establish a trust account but would do so if necessary.

On June 5, 1987, the Bank received instructions from International Warranty's signing officers to transfer all funds in the Drive On account to the International Warranty account at the end of each business day. In July and August, the transfer of funds between the International Warranty and Drive On accounts resulted in an overall reduction in International Warranty's overdraft.

---

† (1997) 152 D.L.R. (4th) 411 at 413–38 (S.C.C.).

On August 7, 1987, Drive On forwarded the June premiums to Citadel. In late August, Citadel first learned of Drive On's financial difficulties. The President of Drive On advised Citadel that the July and August premiums could not be remitted. A new arrangement, effective September 1, was set in place whereby all premium monies would be forwarded directly to Citadel. With regard to the outstanding July and August receipts, Drive On agreed to pay Citadel by way of promissory note dated September 21, 1987. The note provided for monthly payments of $100,000.00. Drive On made a number of payments until it, and the other members of the International Warranty Group of Companies, ceased carrying on business in December. Citadel sued Drive On and the guarantor on the promissory note but has been unsuccessful in collecting anything. The parties agree that the outstanding amount payable to Citadel is $633,622.84.

Citadel brought an action against the Bank for the outstanding insurance premiums. At trial, Citadel was successful and judgment was entered against the Bank for $633,622.84: [1993] A.J. No. 680 (QL) [reported 19 C.C.L.I. (2d) 282]. The Court of Appeal allowed the Bank's appeal and dismissed Citadel's claim: (1996), 181 A.R. 76, 116 W.A.C. 76, 37 Alta. L.R. (3d) 293, [1996] 5 W.W.R. 9, 33 C.C.L.I. (2d) 241, [1996] A.J. No. 59 (QL).

II.   DECISIONS BELOW

A.   Court of Queen's Bench of Alberta

The trial judge, Marshall J., found that a relationship of trust existed between Citadel and Drive On. This finding was based in part on s. 124(1) of the *Insurance Act*, R.S.A. 1980, c. 1–5, which provides that an agent or broker who negotiates a contract of insurance with an insurer and receives insurance premiums for that contract is deemed to hold the premiums in trust for the insurer. As well, the trial judge found that the arrangement between Citadel and Drive On had the three certainties of a trust, namely, certainty of subject-matter, certainty of intent, and certainty of object. Further, the trial judge held that a breach of trust occurred when Drive On failed to remit the insurance premiums collected on Citadel's behalf.

The trial judge stated that in order for the Bank to be liable as a stranger to the trust, the Bank must have had knowledge that the funds were trust monies or the circumstances must have required it to inquire before dealing with the money. In scrutinizing the evidence, the trial judge found that Drive On's instructions to empty its account daily were "very suspicious" (para. 26), given the Bank's knowledge that insurance premiums were being deposited in the account. As well, the trial judge concluded that the Bank, having received a benefit from Drive On's breach of trust, was under a greater duty to explain its actions. Liability was imposed on the following basis (at para. 33):

> The Bank had actual knowledge of the nature of the funds in the Drive On account and had an obligation to inquire about their position in the circumstances. The Bank shut its eyes in circumstances which should have caused it to inquire of its customer at least. It did not do so. The Bank had constructive knowledge and is a constructive trustee within the cases....

The plaintiffs received judgment for $633,622.84.

B.   Alberta Court of Appeal (1996), 181 A.R. 76

On appeal to the Alberta Court of Appeal, Kerans J.A. speaking for the court, began by noting, at p. 77, that there was "no serious difficulty with the finding of creation of the trust made by the trial judge". As such, Kerans J.A. was willing to assume that a trust existed between Citadel and Drive On and that a breach of trust occurred.

In Kerans J.A.'s view, the real difficulty with the case was the imposition of liability on the Bank. More specifically, he disagreed with the trial judge's conclusion that constructive knowledge was sufficient to render the Bank liable as a constructive trustee. Relying on this Court's decision in *Air Canada v. M & L Travel Ltd.*, [1993] 3 S.C.R. 787, 108 D.L.R. (4th) 592, Kerans J.A. concluded that only actual knowledge, recklessness, or wilful blindness could render the Bank liable for a breach of trust from which it received a benefit. This test was not met in the present case because, although the Bank had "shut its eyes" in the circumstances, the trial judge refused to find that the Bank was actually aware it was taking money in breach of trust. However, since *Air Canada v. M & L Travel Ltd.* was decided after the trial judge rendered judgment in the present case, the parties were invited to re-argue the facts before the Court of Appeal. Nonetheless, even after reconsidering the facts, Kerans J.A. concluded for the court at p. 78:

> ... we have come to the conclusion that we cannot say on the balance of probabilities that this bank, when it honoured the direction to pay, was aware that it was moving out money in breach

of any trust between the defaulting company and the insurance company. We do not have any difficulty with the trial finding that the bank had some warning that this was the case. But that is not enough. Nor do we think this is an appropriate case in which to rely on wilful blindness.

The Court of Appeal accordingly allowed the Bank's appeal and dismissed the claim.

III. ISSUES

As mentioned, one main question is raised on this appeal: Under what circumstances can the respondent banks be held liable as constructive trustees for the breach of trust committed by one of their customers?

IV. ANALYSIS

A. The Nature of the Relationship between Citadel and Drive On

Before beginning my analysis regarding the liability of the Bank as a constructive trustee, I note that I have read the reasons of Iacobucci J. in *Gold v. Rosenberg*, No. 25064, judgment issued concurrently, a case also dealing with the liability of a bank for a breach of trust committed by one of its customers [now reported *ante*, p. 385]. I generally agree with Iacobucci J.'s approach in *Gold* and, indeed, consider it similar to my own in the present appeal.

There can be no doubt that the relationship between Citadel and Drive On was one of trust. In this Court, the parties did not dispute the existence of a trust relationship. Relevant to the arrangement between Citadel and Drive On is s. 124(1) of the *Insurance Act*, which provides:

> 124(1) An agent or broker who acts in negotiating, renewing or continuing a contract of insurance with an insurer licensed under this Act, and who receives any money or substitute for money as premium for such a contract from the insured, shall be deemed to hold the premium in trust for the insurer.

From 1979 to 1987, Drive On, the insurance agent, was in the business of selling insurance policies underwritten by Citadel, the insurer. In negotiating insurance policies on Citadel's behalf, Drive On collected insurance premiums from auto dealers, paid commissions, and settled current claims under the policies. However, on June 1, 1987, the arrangement was changed and the premiums collected by Drive On were to be forwarded without deductions for pol-

icy claims. However, even when Citadel assumed the adjudication of all claims, Drive On still acted as agent or trustee and Citadel remained the principal or beneficiary of the insurance premiums. Moreover, I agree with the trial judge that the repayment arrangements between Citadel and Drive On did not amount to a revocation of the trust. The promissory note dated September 21, 1987, was merely confirmation of the amount owed by Drive On to Citadel. By agreeing to have the promissory note prepared in its favour, Citadel did not revoke its beneficial interest in the insurance premiums.

As well, the arrangement between Citadel and Drive On meets the three characteristics of a trust, namely certainty of intent, certainty of subject-matter, and certainty of object; see *Air Canada v. M & L Travel Ltd.*, *supra*, at pp. 803–4; *Canadian Pacific Air Lines Ltd. v. Canadian Imperial Bank of Commerce* (1987), 61 O.R. (2d) 233, at p. 237, 42 D.L.R. (4th) 375 (H.C.J.). The arrangement in the present case was based on the collection of insurance premiums by the insurance agent, Drive On, and the remittance of these premiums, subject to adjustments, to the insurer, Citadel. The intent to create a trust clearly follows from this principal-agent relationship. The object of the trust is the insurer, Citadel. Finally, the insurance premiums constitute the subject-matter of the trust.

The fact that the trust funds in Drive On's account were commingled with other funds does not undermine the relationship of trust between the parties. As Iacobucci J. wrote for the majority of this Court in *Air Canada v. M & L Travel Ltd.*, *supra*, at p. 804, "[w]hile the presence or absence of a prohibition on the commingling of funds is a factor to be considered in favour of a debt relationship, it is not necessarily determinative"; see also *R. v. Lowden* (1981), 27 A.R. 91 (C.A.), at pp. 101–2; *Bank of Nova Scotia v. Société Générale (Canada)*, [1988] 4 W.W.R. 232 (Alta. C.A.), at p. 238.

The intention of the parties in the present case was to create a trust relationship. That Drive On deposited the funds in a general bank account, as opposed to a special trust account, does not alter this intention. In May 1987, Citadel prepared a report of Drive On's procedures. This report found that a trust account had not been set up by Drive On. However, the report also noted that Drive On would establish a trust account if required by Citadel. The report indicates, therefore, that the parties had turned their minds to the possibility of setting up a trust account to prohibit the commingling of funds. Even though the trust account was never established, the fact that the parties considered this possibility confirms that the relationship was viewed by Citadel and Drive On as one of trust.

B. The Liability of the Bank as a Stranger to the Trust

1. General Principles

Having found that the relationship between Citadel and Drive On was one of trust, it is clear that Drive On's actions were in breach of trust. Quite simply, Drive On failed to remit to Citadel the insurance premiums collected on Citadel's behalf in July and August 1987. Moreover, I agree with the trial judge that Citadel did not acquiesce in the breach of trust by asking for and receiving the promissory note from Drive On. By accepting the note, Citadel did not represent that it was acquiescing in the use of the funds by the Bank. Consequently, Citadel is not barred from bringing an action against the bank for breach of trust; see *Fletcher v. Collis*, [1905] 2 Ch. 24 (C.A.); P.H. Pettit, *Equity and the Law of Trusts*, 7th ed. (London: Butterworths, 1993), at p. 491. The question remains whether the Bank, as a stranger to the trust between Citadel and Drive On, can be liable as a constructive trustee.

There are three ways in which a stranger to a trust can be held liable as a constructive trustee for breach of trust. First, a stranger to the trust can be liable as a trustee *de son tort*. Secondly, a stranger to the trust can be liable for breach of trust by knowingly assisting in a fraudulent and dishonest design on the part of the trustees ("knowing assistance"). Thirdly, liability may be imposed on a stranger to the trust who is in receipt and chargeable with trust property ("knowing receipt"; see *Air Canada v. M & L Travel Ltd., supra*, at pp. 809–11).

To be liable as trustees *de son tort*, strangers to the trust must commit a breach of trust while acting as trustees. Such persons are not appointed trustees but "take on themselves to act as such and to possess and administer trust property"; see *Selangor United Rubber Estates, Ltd. v. Cradock (No. 3)*, [1968] 2 All E.R. 1073 (Ch. D.), at p. 1095. This type of liability is inapplicable to the present case. The Bank never assumed the office or function of trustee; nor did it administer the trust funds on behalf of the beneficiary Citadel.

The two remaining categories of liability, namely "knowing assistance" and "knowing receipt", relate to strangers to the trust who knowingly participate in a breach of trust. In *Air Canada v. M & L Travel Ltd., supra*, this Court considered the requirements for bringing a case within the "knowing assistance" category. In that case, the defendant travel agency collected funds from the sale of Air Canada tickets and held them in trust to be remitted to Air Canada. The funds were kept in the agency's general bank account. The individual directors of the travel agency, who had personally guaranteed a demand loan, authorized the bank to withdraw funds from the general account to cover monies owing on the loan. A dispute arose between the directors with regard to misappropriation of funds. The bank sent demand notices to the directors and withdrew the full amount owing under the loan from the agency's general account. As a result, Air Canada did not receive monies owed to it for ticket sales. The issue arose whether the appellant director, as stranger to the trust, was liable to Air Canada for the travel agency's breach of trust.

This Court found the director liable for knowingly assisting in a breach of trust. The liability of the director was based on his knowledge of, and assistance in, a fraudulent and dishonest breach of trust on the part of the trustees. With regard to the knowledge requirement, Iacobucci J. wrote for the majority, at p. 811: "The knowledge requirement for this type of liability is actual knowledge; recklessness or wilful blindness will also suffice." He expressly excluded constructive knowledge from this test. Iacobucci J. defined constructive knowledge, at p. 812, as "knowledge of circumstances which would indicate the facts to an honest person, or knowledge of facts which would put an honest person on inquiry".

The Court of Appeal in the present case relied on the knowledge requirement set out in *Air Canada v. M & L Travel Ltd., supra*. Assuming the present case falls under the "knowing assistance" category, it is clear that only actual knowledge, recklessness, or wilful blindness will render the Bank liable for participating in the breach of trust. Constructive knowledge will not suffice. The trial judge's conclusions regarding the knowledge of the Bank were as follows (at para. 33):

> The Bank had actual knowledge of the nature of the funds in the Drive On account and had an obligation to inquire about their position in the circumstances. The Bank shut its eyes in circumstances which should have caused it to inquire of its customer at least. It did not do so. The Bank had constructive knowledge and is a constructive trustee.

Kerans J.A. considered this passage from the trial judge's reasons and concluded, at p. 77:

> It is true that the judge used the words "shut its eyes", but reading the passage in its entirety, it

seems clear that the judge is refusing to say that the bank was actually aware that it was taking money in breach of trust, as opposed to what it should have known or what its duty was.

I agree with Kerans J.A. that the trial judge refused to make a finding of actual knowledge by the Bank. Rather, the trial judge restricted his findings to constructive knowledge, based on the Bank's duty to inquire of its customer in the circumstances. Moreover, there was no finding of recklessness or wilful blindness as such. It follows from the trial judge's findings that the Bank does not meet the knowledge requirement set out in *Air Canada v. M & L Travel Ltd., supra*. Since the Bank had only constructive knowledge, it cannot be liable under the "knowing assistance" category of constructive trusteeship.

The only basis upon which the Bank may be held liable as a constructive trustee is under the "knowing receipt" or "knowing receipt and dealing" head of liability. Under this category of constructive trusteeship it is generally recognized that there are two types of cases. First, although inapplicable to the present case, there are strangers to the trust, usually agents of the trustees, who receive trust property lawfully and not for their own benefit but then deal with the property in a manner inconsistent with the trust. These cases may be grouped under the heading "knowing dealing". Secondly, there are strangers to the trust who receive trust property for their own benefit and with knowledge that the property was transferred to them in breach of trust. In all cases it is immaterial whether the breach of trust was fraudulent; see *Halsbury's Laws of England*, 4th ed. (London: Butterworths, 1995), vol. 48, at para. 595; Pettit, *supra*, at p. 168; Underhill and Hayton, *Law Relating to Trusts and Trustees*, 14th ed. (London: Butterworths, 1987), at p. 357. The second type of case, which is relevant to the present appeal, raises two main issues: the nature of the receipt of trust property and the degree of knowledge required of the stranger to the trust.

2. *Liability for Knowing Receipt*

(A) THE RECEIPT REQUIREMENT

Liability on the basis of "knowing receipt" requires that strangers to the trust receive or apply trust property for their own use and benefit; see *Agip (Africa) Ltd. v. Jackson*, [1990] 1 Ch. 265, affirmed [1992] 4 All E.R. 451 (C.A.); *Halsbury's Laws of England, supra*, at paras. 595–96; Pettit, *supra*, at p. 168. As Iacobucci J. wrote in *Air Canada v. M & L Travel Ltd., supra*, at pp. 810–11, the "knowing receipt" category of liability "requires the

stranger to the trust to have received trust property in his or her personal capacity, rather than as an agent of the trustees". In the banking context, which is directly applicable to the present case, the definition of receipt has been applied as follows:

> The essential characteristic of a recipient ... is that he should have received the property for his own use and benefit. That is why neither the paying nor the collecting bank can normally be made liable as recipient. In paying or collecting money for a customer the bank acts only as his agent. It sets up no title of its own. It is otherwise, however, if the collecting bank uses the money to reduce or discharge the customer's overdraft. In doing so it receives the money for its own benefit. ... [Footnotes omitted.]

P.J. Millett, "Tracing the Proceeds of Fraud" (1991), 107 L.Q.R. 71, at pp. 82–83.

Thus, a distinction is traditionally made between a bank receiving trust funds for its own benefit, in order to pay off a bank overdraft ("knowing receipt"), and a bank receiving and paying out trust funds merely as agent of the trustee ("knowing assistance"); see Underhill, *supra*, at p. 361.

In the present case, we saw, Drive On deposited trust funds, namely insurance premiums collected on Citadel's behalf, in an operating account at the Bank. Drive On's parent company, International Warranty, also had an account at the Bank. In April 1987, the Bank transferred funds between the Drive On and International Warranty accounts to cover overdrafts in either account. As well, in June, the Bank transferred the balance of any funds in the Drive On account to the International Warranty account on a regular basis. As a result of the transfers between the accounts in July and August, a net amount was transferred to the International Warranty account. This amount, which was in excess of the July and August premiums deposited by Drive On, was used to reduce International Warranty's overdraft. Although the Bank was instructed by Drive On's signing officers to make the transfers, the Bank did not act as mere agent in the circumstances. The Bank's actions went beyond the mere collection of funds and payment of bills on Drive On's behalf. The Bank, by applying the deposit of insurance premiums as a set-off against International Warranty's overdraft, received a benefit. This benefit, of course, was the reduction in the amount owed to the Bank by one of its customers. It follows that the Bank received the trust funds for its own use and benefit.

In this Court, the respondents argued that they could not be liable on the basis of "knowing receipt" because they had not received the trust property. The respondents took the position, accepted by the authorities, that a bank deposit is simply a loan to the bank; see *Foley v. Hill*, [1843–60] All E.R. Rep. 16 (H.L.); *Fonthill Lumber Ltd. v. Bank of Montreal* (1959), 19 D.L.R. (2d) 618 (Ont. C.A.), at 628. Accordingly, the deposit of money in Drive On's account was characterized as a debt obligation owed by the Bank to Drive On. This debt obligation gave rise to a credit in Drive On's favour. On instruction from its customer, the Bank simply transferred "credits" from Drive On's account to International Warranty's account. The transfer of credits had the incidental effect of reducing an overdraft in the International Warranty account. In other words, the transfers between the accounts in July and August simply amounted to an off-setting of debt obligations. In the respondents' view, the Bank was not receiving trust property but simply transferring credits from one account to another.

The respondents' arguments are not convincing. A debt obligation is a chose in action and, therefore, property over which one can impose a trust. This conclusion is supported by the House of Lords' decision in *Lipkin Gorman v. Karpnale Ltd.*, [1991] 3 W.L.R. 10. In that case, a firm of solicitors was authorized to operate a client's bank account. One of the firm's partners subsequently stole funds from the account and used them for casino gambling. Considering whether the solicitors could trace their client's funds at common law, Lord Goff of Chieveley wrote, at pp. 28–29:

> The relationship of the bank with the solicitors was essentially that of debtor and creditor; and since the client account was at all material times in credit, the bank was the debtor and the solicitors were its creditors. Such a debt constitutes a chose in action, which is a species of property; and since the debt was enforceable at common law, the chose in action was legal property belonging to the solicitors at common law.

The respondents cannot avoid the "property" issue by characterizing the deposit of trust monies in Drive On's account as a debt obligation. The chose in action, constituted by the indebtedness of the Bank to Drive On, was subject to a statutory trust in Citadel's favour. That same chose in action can also be the subject of a constructive trust in Citadel's favour.

Nonetheless, the respondents' arguments reflect a difficulty with the traditional conception of "receipt" in "knowing receipt" cases. In my view, the receipt requirement for this type of liability is best characterized in restitutionary terms. In *Lac Minerals Ltd. v. International Corona Resources Ltd.*, [1989] 2 S.C.R. 574, at p. 669, 61 D.L.R. (4th) 14, I stated that a restitutionary claim, or a claim for unjust enrichment, is concerned with giving back to someone something that has been taken from them (a restitutionary proprietary award) or its equivalent value (a personal restitutionary award). As well, in *Air Canada v. British Columbia*, [1989] 1 S.C.R. 1161, at pp. 1202–3, 59 D.L.R. (4th) 161, I stated that the function of the law of restitution "is to ensure that where a plaintiff has been deprived of wealth that is either in his possession or would have accrued for his benefit, it is restored to him. The measure of restitutionary recovery is the gain the [defendant] made at the [plaintiff's] expense." In the present case, the Bank was clearly enriched by the off-setting of debt obligations, or transferring of credits between the Drive On and International Warranty accounts. That is, the amount due to the Bank was reduced. As well, the Bank's enrichment deprived Citadel of the insurance premiums collected on its behalf. Moreover, the fact that the insurance premiums were never in Citadel's possession does not preclude Citadel from pursuing a restitutionary claim. After all, the insurance premiums would have accrued to Citadel's benefit. The Bank has been enriched at Citadel's expense. Thus, in restitutionary terms, there can be no doubt that the Bank received trust property for its own use and benefit.

(B) THE KNOWLEDGE REQUIREMENT

The first requirement for establishing liability on the basis of "knowing receipt" has been satisfied. The Bank received the trust property for its own benefit and, in doing so, was enriched at the beneficiary's expense. The second requirement relates to the degree of knowledge required of the Bank in relation to the breach of trust. With regard to this knowledge requirement, there are two lines of authorities. According to one line of jurisprudence, the knowledge requirement for both "knowing assistance" and "knowing receipt" cases should be the same. More specifically, constructive knowledge should not be the basis for liability in either type of case. A second line of authority suggests that a different standard should apply in "knowing assistance" and "knowing receipt" cases. More specifically, the authorities favour a lower threshold of knowledge in "knowing receipt" cases.

A leading case in relation to the first line of authority is *Re Montagu's Settlement Trusts*, [1987] 1 Ch. 264. That case involved a dispute arising out of a 1923 settlement in which the future tenth Duke of

Manchester had made an assignment of certain chattels to a number of trustees. The trustees were under a fiduciary duty to select and make an inventory of the chattels after the ninth Duke of Manchester died. The selection and inventory did not occur and the tenth Duke took absolutely whatever chattels he wanted. Megarry V.-C. held that the Duke was not liable as a constructive trustee because he did not know that the chattels were subject to a trust. In discussing the degree of knowledge required of the Duke, Megarry V.-C. emphasized that liability in "knowing receipt" cases is personal in nature and arises only if the stranger's conscience is sufficiently affected to justify imposing a constructive trust. Although cases involving actual knowledge, recklessness, and wilful blindness justify imposing a constructive trust, Megarry V.-C. doubted, at p. 285, whether the carelessness associated with constructive knowledge cases could sufficiently bind the stranger's conscience.

Re Montagu's Settlement Trusts was followed in *Polly Peck International plc v. Nadir (No. 2)*, [1992] 4 All E.R. 769 (C.A.). There, the plaintiff company sought to impose liability on a bank for assisting in the misapplication of trust funds and for receiving and dealing in some way with trust property. The bank had been instructed by the trustee to transfer substantial trust funds into offshore accounts. Scott L.J. dealt with the case on the basis of both "knowing assistance" and "knowing receipt" because some of the transfers were made by the banker as agent while others were received for the bank's own benefit. With regard to the "knowing receipt" claim, the plaintiff beneficiary argued that, in the circumstances, the bank should have been put on inquiry as to whether there were improprieties in the transfers. Addressing the "knowing receipt" claim, Scott L.J. commented, at p. 777:

> Liability as constructive trustee in a "knowing receipt" case does not require that the misapplication of the trust funds should be fraudulent. It does require that the defendant should have knowledge that the funds were trust funds and that they were being misapplied. Actual knowledge obviously will suffice. Mr. Potts [lawyer for the plaintiff] has submitted that it will suffice if the defendant can be shown to have had knowledge of facts which would have put an honest and reasonable man on inquiry, or, at least, if the defendant can be shown to have wilfully and recklessly failed to make such inquiries as an honest and reasonable man would have made.... I do not think there is any doubt that, if the latter of the two criteria can be established against the Central Bank, that will suffice. I have some

doubts about the sufficiency of the former criterion but do not think that the present appeal is the right occasion for settling the issue.

It should be noted that Scott L.J. went on to apply the test for constructive knowledge, but found that the bank was not liable because it did not have cause to suspect improprieties and was not put on inquiry.

The English approach favouring exclusion of constructive knowledge received the approval of the Manitoba Court of Appeal in *Canadian Imperial Bank of Commerce v. Valley Credit Union Ltd.*, [1990] 1 W.W.R. 736, 63 D.L.R. (4th) 632. In that case, a business obtained a line of credit from the plaintiff bank. Under the bank's general security agreement, the customer became trustee of monies paid to it with respect to accounts receivable or sales of inventory. The customer subsequently opened an account with the defendant credit union and used this account to deposit trust monies. The bank became aware of the other account, eventually called the customer's loans, and brought an action against the credit union to recover the funds in the customer's account. Philp J.A. refused to find the credit union liable as constructive trustee. Without distinguishing between the categories of "knowing assistance" and "knowing receipt", Philp J.A. doubted whether the carelessness associated with constructive knowledge was sufficient to impose liability on the bank as a constructive trustee. Relying in part on *Re Montagu's Settlement Trusts, supra*, he stated, at p. 747:

> I do not think that it can be said that it has been authoritatively decided in Canada that carelessness or negligence is sufficient to impute constructive knowledge to a stranger, and to impose upon him liability as a constructive trustee. I think that it is a doubtful test, particularly in the case of a bank. The relationship between a bank and its customer is contractual and a principal obligation of the bank is to pay out as directed the moneys its customer has deposited. It seems to me that that obligation should be a paramount one, save in special factual circumstances sufficient to hold the bank privy to its customer's breach.

It should be noted, however, that later in his reasons Philp J.A. applied the test for constructive knowledge, but found that it had not been met in the circumstances.

That constructive knowledge should be excluded as a basis for liability in "knowing receipt" cases is also supported by the Ontario Court of Appeal's decision in *Bullock v. Key Property Management Inc.*

(1997), 33 O.R. (3d) 1. There, a trustee had deposited trust funds in a bank account. The funds were then used to service the trustee's own interests, including the reduction of the trustee's indebtedness to the bank. The court dismissed the action against the bank on the grounds that it did not have the requisite degree of knowledge of the breach of trust. The court did not deal with the categories of "knowing assistance" and "knowing receipt" and apparently found it unnecessary to distinguish between the various heads of liability. Apparently assuming that there was only one category of liability, the court concluded, at p. 4:

> As the law presently stands, a stranger to a trust will be held liable for a breach of that trust by the trustee only where the stranger has actual knowledge or is reckless or wilfully blind as to both the existence of the trust and the dishonest conduct of the trustee in connection with the trust. The inquiry must be directed to what the stranger to the trust actually knew or suspected and not to what the stranger would have known had reasonable inquiries been made. Failure to make reasonable inquiries may have evidentiary value in determining what the stranger to the trust in fact knew or suspected, but it is not a basis for the imposition of liability as a constructive trustee.

As well, the Court of Appeal in the present case concluded, without restricting its comments to any particular head of liability, that constructive knowledge should be excluded as a basis for imposing liability on a stranger to the trust. Relying on Iacobucci J.'s reasons in *Air Canada v. M & L Travel Ltd., supra*, Kerans J.A. wrote, at p. 77, that "[a] stranger to a trust is not liable for a breach of trust from which it received a benefit unless it had both actual knowledge of the trust and participated in the breach."

According to a second line of authority, however, constructive knowledge is sufficient to find a stranger to the trust liable on the basis of "knowing receipt". A leading English authority, in terms of formulating the test for constructive knowledge in breach of trust cases, is *Selangor, supra*. There, a company director carried out a fraudulent takeover bid by using the company's funds to purchase its own shares. Two banks were involved in the takeover. One bank acted on behalf of the director by paying, for a fee, those shareholders who had agreed to sell. The bank's fee was paid for by way of an advance from a second bank, where the company's account had been transferred. The second bank was repaid with trust funds drawn from the company's

account. In addressing the banks' liability, Ungoed-Thomas J. did not distinguish between receipt and assistance cases. He presumed, at p. 1095, that there was only one category of liability for strangers to the trust who, unlike trustees *de son tort*, "act in their own right and not for beneficiaries". Relying on this single category of liability, Ungoed-Thomas J. held, at p. 1104:

> The knowledge required to hold a stranger liable as constructive trustee in a dishonest and fraudulent design, is knowledge of circumstances which would indicate to an honest, reasonable man that such a design was being committed or would put him on enquiry, which the stranger failed to make, whether it was being committed.

Ungoed-Thomas J. found both banks liable as constructive trustees.

The Selangor decision was followed by the British Columbia Court of Appeal in *Groves-Raffin Construction Ltd. v. Bank of Nova Scotia* (1975), 64 D.L.R. (3d) 78. There, a construction company deposited trust funds collected from building contracts with the defendant bank. These trust funds were then used to repay the company's indebtedness to the bank and to reduce personal overdrafts belonging to a director of the company. As well, the director stole trust monies from the company's account and transferred them to a personal account at a second bank. Addressing the liability of the second bank as a constructive trustee, Robertson J.A. wrote, at p. 136, that he was dealing with a "collecting bank" and not a "paying bank", thereby suggesting that the case fell under the "knowing receipt" category. Relying in part on *Selangor, supra*, Robertson J.A. found, at p. 138:

> Under what I think is the proper test no necessity to take care arises until either it is clear that a breach of trust is being, or is intended to be, committed, or until there has come to the attention of the person something that should arouse suspicion in an honest, reasonable man and put him on inquiry. The person, for his own protection, in the first event should have nothing to do with the improper transaction, and in the second event should not continue to be involved in the suspected transaction until his inquiry shows him or, more correctly, would show a reasonable man that the suspicion is unfounded.

The *Selangor* decision was also applied by this Court in *Carl B. Potter Ltd. v. Mercantile Bank of Canada*, [1980] 2 S.C.R. 343, 112 D.L.R. (3d) 88. In that case, the plaintiff bid for the construction of a waste treatment plant. The bid was accompanied by a tender deposit cheque, to be held in trust by the owner of the project. The proceeds of the tender cheque eventually found their way into the owner's collateral account where they were drawn upon to meet the owner's obligations to the defendant bank. In these circumstances, it appears that the trust funds were received by the bank for its own use and benefit, thereby meeting the first requirement under the "knowing receipt" head of liability. Ritchie J., at p. 347, approved of the following test regarding the bank's knowledge of the breach of trust:

> The position of a banker who has been placed "on inquiry" in the manner aforesaid is summarized in the following brief paragraph from *Halsbury's Laws of England* (4th ed.) vol. III, para. 60:
>
> > "A banker may be a constructive trustee of money in his customer's account and in breach of that trust if he pays the money away, even on the customer's mandate, in circumstances which put him upon inquiry."

The footnote references for this passage, although not referred to by Ritchie J., included *Selangor, supra.* Ritchie J. went on to apply this test to the facts and found the bank liable for breach of trust.

A similar test of constructive knowledge was applied by the Ontario Court of Appeal in *Arthur Andersen Inc. v. Toronto-Dominion Bank* (1994), 17 O.R. (3d) 363, leave to appeal refused, [1994] 3 S.C.R. v. In that case, the defendant bank was sued by a trustee appointed under the *Construction Lien Act.*, R.S.O. 1990, c. C.30. The bank had agreed to administer the accounts of a number of associated construction companies, in accordance with a "mirror accounting system". Among other things, this system eliminated the need to monitor overdrafts in individual accounts and permitted the informal transfer of debits and credits between all of the operating companies' accounts. The trial judge's findings implied that the funds in the accounts were transferred in breach of the trust requirements under the *Construction Lien Act.* Considering the liability of the bank as a constructive trustee, Grange and McKinlay JJ.A. thus wrote in their joint reasons, at pp. 381–82:

> We consider that the law on this point can be summarized thus: in the absence of sufficient facts or circumstances indicating that there is a good possibility of trust beneficiaries being unpaid there is no duty of inquiry on a bank to determine whether the trades have been paid or will be able to be paid.
>
> ...

> Only if a bank is aware of facts which would indicate that trades would not be paid in the normal course of business should it be charged with a duty of special inquiry.

It should be noted that Grange and McKinlay JJ.A. formulated this test without distinguishing between receipt and assistance cases. However, their comment, at p. 385, that the "Bank can only be liable for a breach of trust, and that breach would have to involve making use for its own benefit of money held on a trust for trade creditors", suggests that the case fell under the "knowing receipt" head of liability.

This analysis was endorsed by the Manitoba Court of Appeal in *Glenko Enterprises Ltd. v. Ernie Keller Contractors Ltd.* (1996), 134 D.L.R. (4th) 161. On facts similar to *Arthur Anderson, supra*, the court, at pp. 164–65, considered "whether a bank which has applied trust funds received from a building contractor to reduce an account overdraft has participated in a breach of trust and must therefore account to the beneficiaries of that trust for those funds". The funds in question, which were misappropriated by the defendant contractor, were subject to trust requirements under the *Builders' Liens Act*, R.S.M. 1987, c. B91. Considering whether the bank was a party to a breach of trust by its customer, Scott C.J.M. held, at p. 167:

> ... the Bank is not liable for the builder's breach of trust if the Bank, in the ordinary course of business, accepted deposits and allowed cheques to be written thereon — or for that matter if it applied the funds on the overdraft — unless it had or clearly should have had knowledge of the breach of trust by the contractor or of facts to put it on notice.

The court went on to agree with the trial judge, at p. 176, that the bank, although it apparently received the trust funds for its own benefit, was not liable because "the inquiries and arrangements for further information which were made by the bank ... were reasonable in all the circumstances".

There are also a number of recent English authorities supporting the view that constructive knowledge is sufficient to impose liability on the basis of "knowing receipt". In *Agip (Africa) Ltd.* (Ch.), *supra*, Millett J. made a number of comments regarding "knowing receipt" cases, even though the case before him was of the "knowing assistance" category. With regard to the degree of knowledge required in "knowing receipt" cases, he wrote, at p. 291:

> The first [category of "knowing receipt" cases] is concerned with the person who receives for his

own benefit trust property transferred to him in breach of trust. He is liable as a constructive trustee if he received it with notice, actual or constructive, that it was trust property and that the transfer to him was a breach of trust; or if he received it without such notice but subsequently discovered the facts.

However, Millett J.'s comments must be read in light of a later passage, at p. 293, where he refused to express an opinion as to whether constructive knowledge sufficed in "knowing receipt" cases.

Millett J.'s comments were subsequently referred to by Knox J. in *Cowan de Groot Properties Ltd. v. Eagle Trust plc*, [1992] 4 All E.R. 700 (Ch.). In this "knowing receipt" case the issue arose whether a purchaser company had knowledge of a breach of duty arising out of the sale of another company's property. The purchaser's liability as a constructive trustee turned on whether or not it had knowledge that the directors of the vendor company were deliberately selling at a gross undervalue. Knox, J. noted, at p. 758, that there was a "substantial body of authority in favour of the proposition that constructive notice based on what a reasonable man would have concluded though falling short of want of probity on the part of the person charged as a constructive trustee may suffice in a knowing receipt case". Despite this body of authority, Knox J. preferred a test based on actual knowledge, wilful blindness, or recklessness. However, he added that if, contrary to his view, constructive knowledge was sufficient, there would still have been no liability on the facts before him. As well, at p. 761, he suggested "that the underlying broad principle which runs through the authorities regarding commercial transactions is that the court will impute knowledge, on the basis of what a reasonable person would have learnt, to a person who is guilty of commercially unacceptable conduct in the particular context involved".

Millett J. reiterated the views he expressed in *Agip (Africa) Ltd., supra*, in *El Ajou v. Dollar Land Holdings plc*, [1993] 3 All E.R. 717 (Ch.). That case involved a massive share fraud carried out by three Canadians in Amsterdam between 1984 and 1985. The plaintiff, the largest single victim of the fraud, claimed to be able to trace some of the proceeds of the fraud from Amsterdam through locations in Geneva, Gibraltar, Panama, back to Geneva, and then to London, where they were invested in a joint venture to carry out a property development project. In this "knowing receipt" case, Millett J. was prepared to assume that constructive knowledge was a sufficient basis for liability. At p. 739, he stated:

In the absence of full argument I am content to assume, without deciding, that dishonesty or want of probity involving actual knowledge (whether proved or inferred) is not a precondition of liability; but that a recipient is not expected to be unduly suspicious and is not to be held liable unless he went ahead without further inquiry in circumstances in which an honest and reasonable man would have realized that the money was probably trust money and was being misapplied.

According to the second line of authority, then, the degree of knowledge required of strangers to the trust should be different in assistance and receipt cases. Generally, there are good reasons for requiring different thresholds of knowledge under the two heads of liability. As Millett J. wrote in *Agip (Africa) Ltd., supra*, at pp. 292–93:

The basis of liability in the two types of cases is quite different; there is no reason why the degree of knowledge required should be the same, and good reason why it should not. Tracing claims and cases of "knowing receipt" are both concerned with rights of priority in relation to property taken by a legal owner for his own benefit; cases of "knowing assistance" are concerned with the furtherance of fraud.

In other words, the distinction between the two categories of liability is fundamental: whereas the accessory's liability is "fault-based", the recipient's liability is "receipt-based". In an extrajudicial opinion, Millett J. described the distinction as follows:

... the liability of the accessory is limited to the case where the breach of trust in question was fraudulent and dishonest; the liability of the recipient is not so limited. In truth, however, the distinction is fundamental; there is no similarity between the two categories. The accessory is a person who either never received the property at all, or who received it in circumstances where his receipt was irrelevant. His liability cannot be receipt-based. It is necessarily fault-based, and is imposed on him not in the context of the law of competing priorities to property, but in the application of the law which is concerned with the furtherance of fraud. [Footnotes omitted; "Tracing the Proceeds of Fraud", *supra*, at p. 83.]

S. Gardner makes a similar point in "Knowing Assistance and Knowing Receipt: Taking Stock" (1996), 112 L.Q.R. 56, at p. 85:

... it is questionable whether knowing receipt is about wrongfully causing loss at all. There may be more than one other thing that it could be about, but most modern opinion takes it to be a restitutionary liability, based on the fact that the defendant has acquired the plaintiff's property.

The same view was expressed by the Privy Council in *Royal Brunei Airlines Sdn. Bhd. v. Tan*, [1995] 3 W.L.R. 64, at p. 70: "Different considerations apply to the two heads of liability. Recipient liability is restitution-based; accessory liability is not." These comments are also cited with approval by Iacobucci J. in *Gold, supra*, at para. 41.

Given the fundamental distinction between the nature of liability in assistance and receipt cases, it makes sense to require a different threshold of knowledge for each category of liability. In "knowing assistance" cases, which are concerned with the furtherance of fraud, there is a higher threshold of knowledge required of the stranger to the trust. Constructive knowledge is excluded as the basis for liability in "knowing assistance" cases; see *Air Canada v. M & L Travel Ltd., supra*, at pp. 811–13. However, in "knowing receipt" cases, which are concerned with the receipt of trust property for one's own benefit, there should be a lower threshold of knowledge required of the stranger to the trust. More is expected of the recipient, who, unlike the accessory, is necessarily enriched at the plaintiff's expense. Because the recipient is held to this higher standard, constructive knowledge (that is, knowledge of facts sufficient to put a reasonable person on notice or inquiry) will suffice as the basis for restitutionary liability. Iacobucci J. reaches the same conclusion in *Gold, supra*, where he finds, at para. 46, that a stranger in receipt of trust property "need not have actual knowledge of the equity [in favour of the plaintiff]; notice will suffice".

This lower threshold of knowledge is sufficient to establish the "unjust" or "unjustified" nature of the recipient's enrichment, thereby entitling the plaintiff to a restitutionary remedy. As I wrote in *Lac Minerals, supra*, at p. 670, "the determination that the enrichment is 'unjust' does not refer to abstract notions of morality and justice, but flows directly from the finding that there was a breach of a legally recognized duty for which the courts will grant relief". In "knowing receipt" cases, relief flows from the breach of a legally recognized duty of inquiry. More specifically, relief will be granted where a stranger to the trust, having received trust property for his or her own benefit and having knowledge of facts which would put a reasonable person on inquiry, actually fails to inquire as to the possible misapplication of trust property. It is this lack of inquiry that renders the recipient's enrichment unjust.

Some commentators go further and argue that a recipient may be unjustly enriched regardless of either a duty of inquiry or constructive knowledge of a breach of trust. According to Professor Birks, a recipient of misdirected funds should be liable on a strict, restitutionary basis. In his article "Misdirected funds: restitution from the recipient", [1989] L.M.C.L.Q. 296, he argues that a recipient's enrichment is unjust because the plaintiff did not consent to it, not because the defendant knew that the funds were being misdirected. In particular, he writes, at p. 341, that "[t]he 'unjust' factor can be named 'ignorance', signifying that the plaintiff, at the time of the enrichment, was absolutely unaware of the transfer from himself to the defendant." Birks, however, lessens the strictness of his approach by allowing a defendant to take advantage of special defences, including a defence arising out of a bona fide purchase for value. (See also P. Birks, "Overview: Tracing, Claiming and Defences", in P. Birks, ed., *Laundering and Tracing* (Oxford: Clarendon Press, 1995), 289, at pp. 322 *et seq.*)

In my view, the test formulated by Professor Birks, while not entirely incompatible with my own, may establish an unjust deprivation, but not an unjust enrichment. It is recalled that a plaintiff is entitled to a restitutionary remedy not because he or she has been unjustly *deprived* but, rather, because the defendant has been unjustly *enriched*, at the plaintiff's expense. To show that the defendant's enrichment is unjustified, one must necessarily focus on the defendant's state of mind not the plaintiff's knowledge, or lack thereof. Indeed, without constructive or actual knowledge of the breach of trust, the recipient may very well have a lawful claim to the trust property. It would be unfair to require a recipient to disgorge a benefit that has been lawfully received. In those circumstances, the recipient will not be unjustly enriched and the plaintiff will not be entitled to a restitutionary remedy.

In the banking context of the present case, it is true that s. 206(1) of the *Bank Act*, R.S.C. 1985, c. B-1, negates any duty on the part of a bank to see to the execution of any trust, whether express, implied or constructive, to which a deposit is subject. In accordance with this provision, a bank is not under a duty to regularly monitor the activities of its clients simply because the funds deposited by those clients are impressed with a statutory trust. Nonetheless, this provision does not render a bank immune from liability as a constructive trustee or prevent the recognition of a duty of inquiry on the part of a bank. Indeed, in certain circumstances, a bank's knowledge of its customer's affairs will require the bank to make inquiries as to possible misapplication of trust funds. As discussed earlier, the degree of knowledge required is constructive knowledge of a possible breach of trust. It follows that a bank which is enriched by the receipt of trust property and has knowledge of facts that would put a reasonable person on inquiry is under a duty to make inquiries of its customer regarding a possible breach of trust. If the bank fails to make the appropriate inquiries, it will have constructive knowledge of the breach of trust. In these circumstances, the bank will be unjustly enriched and, therefore, required to disgorge the benefit it received at the plaintiff's expense.

The respondents argued that imposing liability on a banker who merely has constructive notice of a breach of trust will place too great a burden on banks, thereby interfering with the proper functioning of the banking system. While this may be true in assistance cases where a banker merely pays out and transfers funds as the trustee's agent, the same argument does not apply to receipt cases where a banker receives the trust funds for his or her own benefit. Professor Harpum addresses this point in "The Stranger as Constructive Trustee" (1986), 102 L.Q.R. 114, at p. 138:

> Although there should be a reluctance to allow the unnecessary intrusion of "the intricacies and doctrines connected with trusts" into ordinary commercial transactions, considerations of speed and the importance of possession which normally justify the exclusion of these doctrines, are less applicable to a banker who chooses to exercise his right of set-off than they are to other commercial dealings. Where a banker combines accounts, he alone stands to gain from the transaction. Because of that benefit, more should be expected of him than if he gained nothing. [Footnotes omitted.]

In "knowing receipt" cases, therefore, it is justifiable to impose liability on a banker who only has constructive knowledge of a breach of trust.

In the present case, it has already been established that the Bank was enriched at Citadel's expense by the receipt of insurance premiums collected by Drive On and subject to a statutory trust in favour of Citadel. The only remaining question is whether the Bank had the requisite degree of knowledge to render the enrichment unjust, thereby entitling the plaintiff insurer to a remedy.

On this issue, it is clear from the trial judge's findings that the Bank was aware of the nature of the funds being deposited into, and transferred out of, Drive On's account. On discovery, two of the Bank's employees stated that they knew Drive On's

sole source of revenue was the sale of insurance policies. The Bank also knew that premiums collected by Drive On were payable to the plaintiff insurer. The Bank's knowledge of the nature of Drive On's deposits must also be considered in conjunction with the activities in Drive On's account. It is recalled that in April 1987 the Bank began transferring funds between the Drive On and International Warranty accounts to cover overdrafts in either account. As well, in June 1987, the Bank was directed to empty the Drive On account on a daily basis, again to facilitate the transfer of funds to the International Warranty account.

In light of the Bank's knowledge of the nature of the funds, the daily emptying of the account was in the trial judge's view "very suspicious". In these circumstances, a reasonable person would have been put on inquiry as to the possible misapplication of the trust funds. Notwithstanding the fact that the exact terms of the trust relationship between Citadel and Drive On may have been unknown to the Bank, the Bank should have taken steps, in the form of reasonable inquiries, to determine whether the insurance premiums were being misapplied. More specifically, the Bank should have inquired whether the use of the premiums to reduce the account overdrafts constituted a breach of trust. By failing to make the appropriate inquiries, the Bank had constructive knowledge of Drive On's breach of trust. In these circumstances, the Bank's enrichment was clearly unjust, thereby rendering it liable to Citadel as a constructive trustee.

I make one additional point regarding the nature of the Bank's liability in the present case. As already established, recipient liability is restitution-based. The imposition of liability as a constructive trustee on the basis of "knowing receipt" is a restitutionary remedy and should not be confused with the right to trace assets at common law or in equity. The principles relating to tracing at law and in equity were thus set out by the English Court of Appeal in *Agip (Africa) Ltd., supra*, at pp. 463–64 and 466:

> Tracing at law does not depend upon the establishment of an initial fiduciary relationship. Liability depends upon receipt by the defendant of the plaintiff's money and the extent of the liability depends on the amount received. Since liability depends upon receipt the fact that a recipient has not retained the asset is irrelevant. For the same reason dishonesty or lack of inquiry on the part of the recipient are irrelevant. Identification in the defendant's hands of the plaintiff's asset is, however, necessary. It must be shown that the

money received by the defendant was the money of the plaintiff. Further, the very limited common law remedies make it difficult to follow at law into mixed funds.

...

Both common law and equity accepted the right of the true owner to trace his property into the hands of others while it was in an identifiable form. The common law treated property as identified if it had not been mixed with other property. Equity, on the other hand, will follow money into a mixed fund and charge the fund.

In my view, a distinction should be made between the imposition of liability in "knowing receipt" cases and the availability of tracing orders at common law and in equity. Liability at common law is strict, flowing from the fact of receipt. Liability in "knowing receipt" cases is not strict; it depends not only on the fact of enrichment (i.e. receipt of trust property) but also on the unjust nature of that enrichment (i.e. the stranger's knowledge of the breach of trust). A tracing order at common law, unlike a restitutionary remedy, is only available in respect of funds which have not lost their identity by becoming part of a mixed fund. Further, the imposition of liability as a constructive trustee is wider than a tracing order in equity. The former is not limited to the defence of purchaser without notice and "does not depend upon the recipient still having the property or its traceable proceeds"; see *Re Montagu's Settlement Trusts, supra*, at p. 276.

Despite these distinctions, there appears to be common thread running through both "knowing receipt" and tracing cases. That is, constructive knowledge will suffice as the basis for imposing liability on the recipient of misdirected trust funds. Notwithstanding this, it is neither necessary nor desirable to confuse the traditional rules of tracing with the restitutionary principles now applicable to "knowing receipt" cases. This does not mean, however, that a restitutionary remedy and a tracing order are mutually exclusive. Where more than one remedy is available on the facts, the plaintiff should be able to choose the one that is most advantageous. In the present case, the plaintiff did not seek a tracing order. It is therefore unnecessary for me to decide whether such a remedy would have been available on the facts of the present appeal, and I have not explored the issue.

V.   DISPOSITION

For these reasons, I would allow Citadel's appeal with costs and restore the judgment rendered at trial.

[SOPINKA J.:]

Subject to my reasons in *Gold v. Rosenberg*, S.C.C., No. 25064, issued concurrently [now reported *ante*, p. 385], I agree with Justice La Forest.

Appeal allowed.